EDUCATION

Culture, Economy, and Society

EDITED BY

**A. H. Halsey, Hugh Lauder,
Phillip Brown, and Amy Stuart Wells**

OXFORD
UNIVERSITY PRESS

OXFORD
UNIVERSITY PRESS

Great Clarendon Street, Oxford OX2 6DP

Oxford University Press is a department of the University of Oxford.
It furthers the University's objective of excellence in research, scholarship,
and education by publishing worldwide in

Oxford New York

Athens Auckland Bangkok Bogotá Buenos Aires Calcutta
Cape Town Chennai Dar es Salaam Delhi Florence Hong Kong Istanbul
Karachi Kuala Lumpur Madrid Melbourne Mexico City Mumbai
Nairobi Paris São Paulo Singapore Taipei Tokyo Toronto Warsaw

with associated companies in Berlin Ibadan

Oxford is a registered trade mark of Oxford University Press
in the UK and in certain other countries

Published in the United States
by Oxford University Press Inc., New York

British Library Cataloguing in Publication Data

Data available

Library of Congress Cataloging in Publication Data

Data available

ISBN 0-19-878187-3 (Pbk.)
ISBN 0-19-878188-1

Printed in Great Britain
on acid-free paper by
Biddles Ltd,
Guildford and King's Lynn

EDUCATION

Preface

This is, in effect, a third attempt to review the scope and the trends of sociological writing on education. The first version, published in 1960, was introduced as an illustrative version of the issue of *Current Sociology* (7/3, 1958) where an appraisal of European and American work was offered in the light of the postwar flowering of sociology on these two continents. The old thesis of correlation with industrialism was our interpretation of education in those early days of enthusiastic new professionalism. Much talent was attracted to the exciting new possibilities of a new sub-discipline. Many subsequently famous names appeared in Europe and America.

On a second round, in 1976, the subject reflected the eruption of new student radicalisms. A 'new sociology of education' was announced in the early 1970s. It made its mark on the 'old' sociology as a criticism of the 'black box' of the school class and the teaching revolution, but was associated with ethnomethodology and other forms of phenomenology, and yielded meagre results. The main impulse was Marxist, a concern with education as an apparatus of social selection and control over proletarians and peasants which was uneasily adapted to feminism and largely indifferent to class or race. Above all, however, there was a concern to connect the micro-analysis of teaching to the macro-analysis of cultural reproduction. We looked, then, for a new synthesis based on the thought of Bernstein and Bourdieu. Unhappily, a new inheriting generation did not appear. Instead, there was a sturdy resurgence of older methods, for example at Edinburgh, where Andrew MacPherson and David Raffe developed a flourishing centre of educational sociology; in Chicago, where James Coleman and his students also pursued sophisticated multivariate methods; and in Mannheim, where Walter Müller did pioneering comparative work on advanced industrial societies. In general the advances were more statistical than theoretical. Harvey Goldstein, Peter Mortimore, Robert Eriksson, Jan Jonsson, Sewell, *et al.* were conspicuous contributors.

The most remarkable transformation of education has taken place since the second version was written in the mid-1970s. Student radicalism was already in rapid decline—a phenomenon now seldom remarked. In its place there has been a reappraisal of the significance of education for economic development, replacing the pessimism of the 1970s concerning the achievement of the liberal programme of reform towards popular equality of opportunity. The outcome in most advanced countries has been paradoxical. Expansion at all levels has been truly remarkable, effectively offering wider opportunities to women and minorities. But this is a by-product: the main thrust has been to enhance the quality of the workforce while, at the same time, economizing as much as possible on state expenditure. So virtually everywhere educational budgets are in crisis and old issues of selection, class size, choice, and diversity are again in serious contention. We thus republish against a lively background of chaos and conflict.

Our own view in the light of all the evidence is that the prospects for a sociology of education as political arithmetic in the service of the great values of a truly modern democracy are, as always, difficult but also extraordinarily bright. Difficult, because class structures are shifting, feminist claims are insistent, and ethnic demands are a challenge to the liberal campus. Bright because liberty and equality are more nearly within our reach than they were for our grandparents, and belief in a community which is chosen rather than ascribed, will be the next great ambition of 21st-century schooling. The main obstacles in our collective path are no longer what our grandparents called 'the curse of Adam'. We have unprecedented command over the physical world; but, paradoxically, we lack social science, political will, and moral courage. We are tempted by a galaxy of essentially irrational beliefs to accept the wilder flights of postmodernism. That amalgam of bewilderment and scepticism, which held back the progress of enlightenment in earlier centuries, still menaces the college and the school. The sociology of education is a major instrument for further rational enlightenment.

We would urge those readers interested in the history of the sociology of education to see this new reader in the context of its predecessors and to regard it as a summary contribution to the macroscopic study of educational sociology. The three readers together are, in effect, a record of professional continuity and discontinuity since the early, brave days of postwar excitement. Since that time there has been a succession of dominant ideas, people, and events. We anticipate still further transformation in the processes of learning for workers and citizens; meanwhile, we note with regret the death of such outstanding scholars as James Coleman and Barry Troyna, to whom our discipline will always owe a great debt.

Finally, we wish to thank Nicola Kerry, Sarah McGuigan, and Shelly Robbey for their secretarial and administrative support in preparing this third edition. Our gratitude also extends to Tim Barton and Jenni Scott at Oxford University Press. They gave encouraging advice at every stage, were firm but patient, and were impressively efficient.

A. H. Halsey

Oxford
July 1996

ABOUT THE EDITORS

A. H. HALSEY is Emeritus Professor and Fellow of Nuffield College, Oxford. He is a senior fellow of the British Academy and a foreign member of the American Academy of Arts and Sciences. He has been associated with the sociology of education since 1950 and, apart from the three readers, his main works in the sub-discipline are *The British Academics* (1971) with Martin Trow; *The Decline of Donnish Dominion* (1992; 2nd edition, 1995); *Origins and Destinations* (1980) with Anthony Heath and John Ridge; and an autobiography, *No Discouragement* (1996).

PHILLIP BROWN is Professor of Social and Educational Research at the University of Wales, Cardiff. His interest in sociology stems from the four years he worked as a craft apprentice in the car industry in Cowley, Oxford in the early 1970s. He subsequently trained as a teacher and youth worker before going to University College, Swansea, South Wales to study for a Ph.D. This was later published as *Schooling Ordinary Kids: Inequality, Unemployment and the New Vocationalism* (1987). After working as a researcher at the Institute of Criminology, University of Cambridge, he took a lectureship in sociology at the University of Kent in 1987. He has written, co-authored, and co-edited several books, including *Education for Economic Survival: From Fordism to Post-Fordism?* (edited with H. Lauder); and *Higher Education and Corporate Realities* (with R. Scase). He is currently completing a book with Hugh Lauder on capitalism, globalization, and social progress.

HUGH LAUDER is Professor of Education at the University of Bath. He taught in London schools between 1970 and 1976 and was Lecturer and Senior Lecturer at the University of Canterbury, New Zealand, between 1979 and 1990. From 1990 to 1995 he was Professor of Education at the Victoria University of Wellington. Some of his recent publications are (edited with P. Brown), *Education in Search of a Future* (1988); (edited with C. Wylie), *Towards Successful Schooling* (1990); (edited with P. Brown), *Education for Economic Survival* (1992); (edited with David Hughes and others), *The Creation of Market Competition for Education in New Zealand* (1994); (edited with P. Brown), 'Education, Globalization and Economic Development', *Journal of Education Policy* (Spring, 1996).

AMY STUART WELLS is Associate Professor of Educational Policy in the Graduate School of Education and Information Studies at the University of California in Los Angeles. Her research and writing has focused on the role of race in educational policy-making and implementation. More specifically, she studies school desegregation; school-choice policy, including charter schools; and detracking in racially mixed schools. She received her Ph.D. from Columbia University in the Sociology of Education, in a joint programme between the Teachers' College and the Graduate School of Arts and Sciences in 1991. She is author of several journal articles and books, including *Time to Choose: America at the Crossroads of School Choice Policy* (1993); first author, with Irene Serna, of 'The Politics of Culture: Understanding Local Political Resistance in Detracking in Racially Mixed Schools',

Harvard Educational Review (Spring, 1996); and first author, with Robert L. Crain, of *Stepping over the Color Line: African American Students in White Suburban Schools* (Yale University Press, forthcoming).

Acknowledgements

'The Forms of Capital' by Pierre Bourdieu, translated by Richard Nice, is taken from J. G. Richardson (ed.), *Handbook of Theory and Research for the Sociology of Education* (Greenwood Press, 1986) 241–58, and is reprinted with permission. It was originally published as 'Ökonomisches Kapital, kulturelles Kapital, soziales Kapital', in *Soziale Ungleichheiten* (Soziale Welt, Sonerheft 2), ed. by Reinhard Kreckel (1983), 183–98.

'Class and Pedagogies: Visible and Invisible', by Basil Bernstein, is taken from *Class, Codes and Control*, Vol.3 (Routledge and Kegan Paul, 1975), 116–56. Reprinted with permission.

'Social Capital in the Creation of Human Capital', by James S. Coleman, is taken from *American Journal of Sociology*, 94 (Supplement, 1988), S95–S120. Reprinted with permission. © 1988 by The University of Chicago.

Extracts from 'The Post-Modern Condition', by Krishan Kumar, are taken from *From Industrial to Post-Modern Society: New Theories of the Contemporary World* (Blackwell, 1995) 1–4, 121–37, 172–8, and 201. Reprinted with permission.

Extracts from 'Crossing the Boundaries of Educational Discourse: Modernism, Post-modernism, and Feminism', by Henry Giroux, is taken from *Border Crossings: Cultural Workers and the Politics of Education* (Routledge, 1992) 39–88. Reprinted with permission.

'Having a Postmodernist Turn or Postmodernist *Angst*: A Disorder Experienced by an Author Who is Not Yet Dead or Even Close to It', by Jane Kenway, is taken from R. Smith and P. Wexler (eds.) *After Postmodernism: Education, Politics and Identity* (Falmer, 1995) 36–55. Reprinted with permission.

'Feminisms and Education', by Gaby Weiner, is taken from her *Feminisms in Education: An Introduction* (Open University Press, 1994) 51–67. Reprinted with permission.

'Why the Rich are Getting Richer and the Poor, Poorer', by Robert B. Reich, is taken from *The Work of Nations: A Blueprint for the Future* (Simon and Schuster, 1991) 208–24. Reprinted with permission.

'Education, Globalization, and Economic Development', by Phillip Brown and Hugh Lauder, is taken from *Journal of Education Policy*, 11 (1996), 1–24. Reprinted with permission.

Extracts from 'The New Knowledge Work', by Stanley Aronowitz and William De Fazio, are taken from *The Jobless Future: Sci-Tech and the Dogma of Work* (University of Minnesota Press, 1994) 13–23, 46–56. Reprinted with permission.

'Education, Skill Formation, and Economic Development: The Singaporean Approach', by David N. Ashton and Johnny Sung, was commissioned for this volume.

Extract from 'Human Capital Concepts', by Maureen Woodhall, is taken from G. Psacharopoulos (ed.), *Economics of Education: Research and Studies* (Pergamon Press, 1987) 21–4. These extracts have also been published in G. Esland (ed.), *Education, Training, and Employment, Vol. 2: The Educational Response* (1991), 27–34.

Extracts from 'The Gendering of Skill and Vocationalism in Twentieth-Century Australian Education', by Jill Blackmore, are taken from *Journal of Education Policy*, 7 (1992), 351–8 and 367–77. Reprinted with permission.

'Can Education Do It Alone?', by Henry M. Levin and Carolyn Kelley, is taken from *Economics of Education Review* 13 (1994) 97–108. Reprinted with permission of Elsevier Science Ltd., Oxford, England.

Extracts from 'Education and the Role of the State: Devolution and Control Post-Picot', by John Codd, Liz Gordon, and Richard Harker, are taken from H. Lauder and C. Wylie (eds.), *Towards Successful Schooling* (Falmer Press, 1990) 15–32. Reprinted with permission.

'The State and the Governance of Education: An Analysis of the Restructuring of the State–Education Relationship', by Roger Dale, was commissioned for this volume.

'Educational Achievement in Centralized and Decentralized Systems', by Andy Green, was commissioned for this volume.

'Marketization, the State, and the Re-Formation of the Teaching Profession', by Geoffrey Whitty, was commissioned for this volume.

'Politics, Markets, and Democratic Schools: On the Transformation of School Leadership', by Gerald Grace, was commissioned for this volume.

'Assessment, Accountability, and Standards Using Assessment to Control the Reform of Schooling', by Harry Torrance, was commissioned for this volume.

'Restructuring Schools for Student Success', by Linda Darling-Hammond, is taken from *Daedalus*, 124 (1995), 153–62. Reprinted with permission.

'Restructuring Restructuring: Postmodernity and the Prospects for Educational Change', by Andy Hargreaves, is taken from *Journal of Education Policy*, 9 (1994), 47–65. Reprinted with permission.

'Politics, Markets, and the Organization of Schools', by John E. Chubb and Terry M. Moe, is taken from *American Political Science Review*, 82 (1988), 1065–87. Reprinted with permission.

'Education, Democracy, and the Economy', by Hugh Lauder, is taken from *British Journal of Sociology of Education*, 12 (1991), 417–31. Reprinted with permission.

'The "Third Wave": Education and the Ideology of Parentocracy', by Phillip Brown, is taken from *The British Journal of Sociology of Education*, 11 (1990), 65–85. Reprinted with permission.

'Circuits of Schooling: A Sociological Exploration of Parental Choice of School in Social Class Contexts', by Stephen J. Ball, Richard Bowe, and Sharon Gewirtz, is taken from *The Sociological Review*, 43 (1995), 52–78. Reprinted with permission of Blackwell Publishers. © The Editorial Board of *The Sociological Review* 1995.

'African-American Students' View of School Choice', by Amy Stuart Wells, is taken from B. Fuller, R. Elmore, and G. Orfield (eds.), *Who Chooses? Who Loses? Culture, Institutions, and the Unequal Effects of School Choice* (Teachers College Press, 1996). Reprinted with permission.

'Choice, Competition, and Segregation: An Empirical Analysis of A New Zealand Secondary School Market, 1990–93', by Sietske Waslander and Martin Thrupp, is taken from *Journal of Education Policy*, 10 (1995), 1–26. Reprinted with permission.

'[Ap]parent Involvement: Reflections on Parents, Power, and Urban Public Schools', by Michelle Fine, is taken from *Teachers College Record*, 94 (1993), 682–710. Reprinted with permission. © Teachers College, Columbia University.

'Can Effective Schools Compensate for Society?', by Peter Mortimore, was commissioned for this volume.

'Introduction: Our Virtue', by Allan Bloom, is taken from *The Closing of the American Mind: How Higher Education Has Failed Democracy and Impoverished the Souls of Today's Students* (Simon and Schuster, 1987), 25–43. Reprinted with permission.

'The New Cultural Politics of Difference', by Cornel West, is taken from *October*, 53 (Summer 1990), 93–109. Reprinted with permission.

'Multiculturalism and the Post-Modern Critique: Towards a Pedagogy of Resistance and Transformation', by Peter McLaren, is taken from H. A. Giroux and P. McLaren (eds.), *Between Borders: Pedagogy and the Politics of Cultural Studies* (Routledge, 1994).

'Nonsynchrony and Social Difference: An Alternative to Current Radical Accounts of Race and Schooling', by Cameron McCarthy, is taken from *Race and Curriculum: Social Inequality and the Theories and Politics of Difference in Contemporary Research and Schooling* (Falmer Press, 1990). Reprinted with permission.

'On Race and Voice: Challenges for Liberal Education in the 1990s', by Chandra Talpade Mohanty, is taken from *Cultural Critique* (1990). Reprinted with permission.

'Feminist Scholarship as a Vocation', by Patricia J. Gumport, is taken from *Higher Education*, 20 (1990), 231–43. Reprinted with permission of Kluwer Academic Publishers.

'The Silenced Dialogue: Power and Pedagogy in Educating Other People's Children', by Lisa D. Delpit, is taken from L. Weiss and M. Fine (eds.), *Beyond Silenced Voices: Class, Race and Gender in United States Schools* (1993) 119–39. Originally published in Harvard Educational Review, 58 (1988), 280–98. © 1988 by the President and Fellows of Harvard College. Reprinted with permission.

'What Postmodernists Forget: Cultural Capital and Official Knowledge', by Michael W. Apple, is taken from *Curriculum Studies*, 1 (1993), 301–16. Reprinted with permission.

'The Big Picture: Masculinities in Recent World History', by R. W. Connell, is taken from *Theory and Society*, 22 (1993), 597–623. Reprinted with permission of Kluwer Academic Publishers.

'Is the Future Female? Female Success, Male Disadvantage, and Changing Gender Patterns in Education', by Gaby Weiner, Madeleine Arnot, and Miriam David, was commissioned for this volume.

'Trends in Access and Equity in Higher Education: Britain in International Perspective', by A. H. Halsey, is taken from *Oxford Review of Education*, 19 (1993), 129–40. Reprinted with permission of Carfax Publishing Company.

'Education and Occupational Attainments: The Impact of Ethnic Origins', by Anthony Heath and Dorren McMahon, is taken from V. Karn (ed.) *Education, Employment and Housing Among Ethnic Minorities in Britain* (HMSO, 1997). Reprinted with permission.

'Problems of "Meritocracy"', by John H. Goldthorpe, is taken from R. Erikson and J. O. Jonsson (eds.), *Can Education be Equalized? The Swedish Case in Comparative Perspective* (Westview Press, 1996), 255–87. Reprinted with permission.

'Equalization and Improvement: Some Effects of Comprehensive Reorganization in Scotland', by Andrew McPherson and J. Douglas Willms, is taken from *Sociology*, 21 (1987), 509–39. Reprinted with permission. © American Sociological Association.

'Social-Class Differences in Family-School Relationships: The Importance of Cultural Capital', by Annette Lareau, is taken from *Sociology of Education*, 60 (1987), 73–85. Reprinted with permission.

'The Politics of Culture: Understanding Local Political Resistance to Detracking in Racially Mixed Schools', by Amy Stuart Wells and Irene Serna, is taken from *Harvard Educational Review*, 66 (1996), 93–118. © 1996 by the President and Fellows of Harvard College. Reprinted with permission.

'Cultural Capital and Social Exclusion: Some Observations on Recent Trends in Education, Employment, and the Labour Market', by Phillip Brown, is taken from *Work, Employment and Society*, 9 (1995), 29–51. Reprinted with permission.

'Studying Inner-City Social Dislocations: The Challenge of Public Agenda Research', by William Julius Wilson, is taken from *American Sociological Review*, 56 (1991), 1–14. Reprinted with permission. © American Sociological Association.

'Extracts from 'Racial Stratification and Education in the United States: Why Inequality Persists' by John U. Ogbu are taken from *Teachers' College Record*, 96 (1994), 264–71 and 283–98. Reprinted with permission. © Teachers College, Columbia University.

'Introduction to *The Bell Curve Wars*', by Steven Fraser, is taken from his *The Bell Curve Wars* (Basic Books, 1995), 1–10. Reprinted with permission.

'The Family and Social Justice', by A. H. Halsey and Michael Young, was commissioned for this volume.

Contents

xiv   **Contents**

List of Contributors

PROFESSOR MICHAEL W. APPLE, University of Wisconsin, Madison, USA
DR MADELEINE ARNOT, Cambridge University, UK
PROFESSOR STANLEY ARONOWITZ, Graduate Centre, City University of New York, USA
PROFESSOR DAVID ASHTON, University of Leicester, UK
PROFESSOR STEPHEN J. BALL, King's College, University of London, UK
PROFESSOR BASIL BERNSTEIN, Institute of Education, University of London, UK
PROFESSOR JILL BLACKMORE, Deakin University, Australia
PROFESSOR ALLAN BLOOM, University of Chicago, USA
PROFESSOR PIERRE BOURDIEU, College de France, Paris, France
DR RICHARD BOWE, King's College, University of London, UK
DR PHILLIP BROWN, Reader in Sociology, University of Kent, UK
PROFESSOR JOHN E. CHUBB, Senior Fellow, The Brookings Institution, Washington DC, USA
PROFESSOR JOHN CODD, Massey University, NZ
PROFESSOR JAMES COLEMAN, Department of Sociology, University of Chicago, USA
PROFESSOR R. W. CONNELL, University of Sydney, Australia
PROFESSOR ROGER DALE, University of Auckland, NZ
PROFESSOR LINDA DARLING-HAMMOND, WILLIAM F. RUSSELL PROFESSOR, Foundation of Education, Columbia University, USA
PROFESSOR MIRIAM DAVID, South Bank University, UK
PROFESSOR WILLIAM DE FAZIO, St John's University, New York, USA
DR LISA D. DELPIT, Baltimore City Schools, USA
PROFESSOR MICHELLE FINE, Graduate Centre, City University of New York, USA
DR STEVEN FRASER, Vice-President and Executive Editor, Basic Books, USA
DR SHARON GEWIRTZ, King's College, University of London, UK
PROFESSOR HENRY GIROUX, Pennsylvania State University, USA
JOHN GOLDTHORPE, Nuffield College, Oxford, UK
DR LIZ GORDON, Senior Lecturer, University of Canterbury, NZ
PROFESSOR GERALD GRACE, University of Durham, UK
DR ANDY GREEN, Institute of Education, University of London, UK
PROFESSOR PATRICIA J. GUMPORT, Stanford University, California, USA
PROFESSOR A. H. HALSEY, Nuffield College, Oxford, UK
PROFESSOR ANDY HARGREAVES, Ontario Institute for Student Education, Toronto, Canada
ASSOCIATE PROFESSOR RICHARD HARKER, Massey University, NZ
PROFESSOR ANTHONY HEATH, Nuffield College, Oxford, UK
PROFESSOR CAROLYN KELLY, Stanford University, California, USA
PROFESSOR JANE KENWAY, Deakin University, Australia
PROFESSOR KRISHAN KUMAR, University of Virginia, USA
PROFESSOR ANNETTE LAREAU, Southern Illinois University, USA
PROFESSOR HUGH LAUDER, University of Bath, UK
PROFESSOR HENRY M. LEVIN, Stanford University, California, USA
ASSOCIATE PROFESSOR CAMERON MCCARTHY, Louisiana State University, USA

PROFESSOR PETER MCLAREN, UCLA, USA

DR DARREN MCMAHON, University College, Dublin, Eire

PROFESSOR ANDREW MCPHERSON, Edinburgh University, UK

PROFESSOR TERRY M. MOE, Stanford University, California, USA

PROFESSOR CHANDRA TALPADE MOHANTY, Hamilton College, USA

PROFESSOR PETER MORTIMORE, Director, Institute of Education, University of London, UK

PROFESSOR JOHN U. OGBU, University of California, Berkeley, USA

PROFESSOR ROBERT B. REICH, John F. Kennedy School of Government, Harvard University, USA

ASSOCIATE PROFESSOR I. SERNA, Graduate School of Education and Information Studies, UCLA, USA

JOHNNY SUNG, University of Leicester, UK

DR MARTIN THRUPP, Waikato University, NZ

DR HARRY TORRANCE, University of Sussex, UK

SIETSKE WASLANDER, University of Groningen, Netherlands

PROFESSOR AMY STUART WELLS, UCLA, USA

PROFESSOR GABY WEINER, South Bank University, UK

PROFESSOR CORNEL WEST, Harvard University, USA

PROFESSOR GEOFF WHITTY, Institute of Education, University of London, UK

PROFESSOR J. DOUGLAS WILLMS, University of British Columbia, Canada

PROFESSOR WILLIAM JULIUS WILSON, Harvard University, USA

DR MAUREEN WOODHALL, University of Wales, Aberystwyth, UK

MICHAEL YOUNG, Institute of Community Studies, London, UK

List of Figures

List of Tables

The Transformation of Education and Society: An Introduction

Phillip Brown, A. H. Halsey, Hugh Lauder, and Amy Stuart Wells

Introduction

Commonly held assumptions about the role of education are now in question due to the economic, cultural, and social transformation of post-industrial societies. The power of the nation state is threatened by the development of a global economy which has removed some of the key instruments used to control the economic destiny of nations. Bureaucracy, the form of organization which delivered mass education and industrial efficiency, is now considered outmoded and inefficient; while the notion of a common culture as the basis for social solidarity is being challenged by various groups asserting the right to educate their children according to their specific religious and cultural values.[1]

These changes in society have been variously described as a shift from industrial to post-industrial, modern to post-modern, and Fordist to post-Fordist. These descriptions are more or less inelegant attempts to grasp the fundamental nature of current social change. If we are to sketch the background to the debates in this book we must, therefore, try to analyze the fundamental continuities and discontinuities of our age in relation to education. To do this we can begin by looking at the history of the relationships between education, culture, economy, and society in the postwar period. If we were to take a longer view we would be retracing the ground covered by the founders of sociology, especially Weber and Durkheim. Thus, for example, Weber understood that China built a nation state by using the highly educated literati as political governors across a huge territory. Or to take a more famous and familiar example,

Durkheim's (1977) analysis of 'pedagogical evolution' in France was, in effect, a sustained attempt to explain how a new shared national morality could be founded on a secular base and adapted to an industrial technology. This was first published in 1938. Seven years later, at the close of the second world war, the era of western economic nationalism began providing one example of the kind of integrated industrial society Durkheim might have envisaged. Between 1945 and 1973 Western societies experienced a period of rapid economic growth and educational expansion against what appeared to be a background of social harmony.

The Foundations of Economic Nationalism, 1945–73

In the postwar period education came to assume a key role in the political economy of nations, contributing to the unprecedented sense of economic and social progress that was a hallmark of the era. Underlying the sense of progress was a spectacular period of sustained economic growth. Output in the advanced capitalist economies was 180 per cent higher in 1973 than it had been in 1950. Of equal importance to the rate of growth was the fact that its dividends were spread evenly across the income range. For workers this meant a rise in real wages of some 3.5 per cent a year. Assuming that the population grew at one per cent a year, each generation could assume to be twice as well off as its parents and four times as well off as its grandparents (Armstrong, Glyn, and Harrison 1991: 117). The key to postwar economic success lay in the development of the doctrine of *economic nationalism*, in which social progress for workers and their families was advanced through the pursuit of national economic growth.

It combined, uniquely, three principles which would underwrite life in the third quarter of the twentieth century: *prosperity*, *security*, and *opportunity*. These principles were threaded through the fabric of everyday life in a tightly woven design which linked government policy, business organizations, families, and education (Brown and Lauder, forthcoming). What tied the three elements of economic nationalism together was the view that the nation state not only had the power to deliver prosperity, security, and opportunity, but that it had a responsibility to do so. Underpinning this sense of state responsibility was an awareness on the part of the state and big business that the most effective way of achieving economic growth and profits was by also delivering economic security through full employment, and opportunity through education, social welfare, and occupational mobility. During the postwar period the pursuit of economic nationalism by western governments was viable, given that a great deal of economic activity took place within the confines of national 'walled' economies, with national 'border' controls over the movement of capital and tradable goods and services (Panic, 1995). The large national corporations needed full employment to achieve the potential for profits by creating mass consumer markets for the first time. But full employment also brought the threat of greater union power to bid up wages and to disrupt production. However, for over two decades economic nationalism based on the triad of prosperity, security, and opportunity succeeded in reconciling the interests of capital and labour.

Economic nationalism was also reinforced by the forging of a common culture through an assimilationist ethic based on what Habermas (1976) has called technical rationality. This touches on two of the great questions of modern capitalism. The first concerns that of social solidarity and social control. How, in a capitalist society based on inequalities of reward and status, are social cohesion and order to be maintained? One answer that has been given consistently is that the free-market society will eventually erode the foundations on which it has been created (Hirschman

1992). The market, it is argued, leads to the break up of non-rational bonds or links between human beings as it promotes a culture of self-interest in the accumulation of wealth. This leads progressively to the individualization and, ultimately, the atomization of society. Arguably, what arrested this process in the postwar years was an emphasis on technical rationality based on a hierarchical ordering of roles at work and in the home, reinforced by attitudes bred during military service in the Second World War.

In the era of economic nationalism the bureaucratic paradigm of work dominated understanding of organizational efficiency and proved a central organizing principle of society. Max Weber described the characteristics of bureaucracy in terms of a form of organization which demanded 'precision, speed, clarity, regularity, reliability and efficiency achieved through the creation of a fixed division of tasks, hierarchical supervision, and detailed rules and regulations' (Morgan 1986: 24–5). In bureaucratic organizations power was concentrated in the hands of a few close to the apex of the organizational hierarchy who, through the control of knowledge and resources, were able to control the whole enterprise. Hence, bureaucratic efficiency depended on the educational system standardizing the pattern of socialization and social control to encourage both blue-collar and white-collar workers to follow clearly prescribed rules, procedures, and practices in order to fulfil routine tasks in a predictable fashion. To get ahead, the individual had to fit into large organizations and 'an ability to play the expected role is one of his or [her] main assets' (Fromm 1949: 82).

In the home, the roles of male as breadwinner and woman as homemaker served to reproduce the patriarchal family which created the cornerstone of the gendered division of labour and welfare-state provision. Patriarchy is, of course, a much older state of human affairs. Certainly Victorian factory production, combined with reforms to keep women out of the mines and children out of chimneys, sharpened the sexual and age division of labour as compared with agrarian economies. The two twentieth-century world wars disrupted the Victorian orders of work and home. In the late 1940s only one in five married women were in paid employment in the United States. In Britain, the figure was slightly higher. Nevertheless, despite some renegotiation of roles in child-rearing both at home and in school, the gender roles within the family continued to be based on the idea that the family wage was earned by the father as head of the family, while the process of child-raising was assigned to the mother.

The security of stable family life was reinforced by the development of the welfare state and the related idea of the social wage. In the postwar period the notion of the social wage came into its own. While there were national differences in the methods of delivery and the levels at which the social wage was struck, welfare-state expenditure increased significantly in all the advanced economies, growing from 15 to 24 per cent in the years between 1952 and 1973 (Armstrong, Glyn, and Harrison 1991: 195). Progressive tax rates were raised, with the result that welfare-state expenditure was heavily redistributed in favour of the poor: an expenditure which did not obviate poverty, but which did reduce its impact. In the United States the share of the bottom 20 per cent of income-earners rose between 1959 and 1968 from 4.9 to 5.6 per cent of total income, and this was enough to reduce the number living in poverty from 22.4 to 12.1 per cent (Levy 1987: 56). This brought the incidence of poverty to about the same level as that of France, but still well above the 7.5 per cent recorded in Britain and the 3 per cent in Germany (Armstrong, Glyn, and Harrison 1991: 197–8). Welfare-state support for the family was therefore linked to the trend of narrowing income differentials.

Built on a consensus between employers and unions, the social wage thus proved to be the linchpin between the labour market and the foundation of the social structure: the typically male-headed nuclear family. The family was, by contemporary trends, a stable institution which encompassed the vast majority of people. In the United States in the immediate postwar period 94 per cent of the population lived in families. Of those, 80 per cent had a husband or wife who were under 65 (Levy 1987: 34). The stability of the family at this time is emphasized by the number of petitions filed for divorce. Just before the war, 1.9 out of every hundred marriages in Britain were dissolved. By 1950 the figure had increased to 7.9, and there it remained constant until 1968, when it began to rise again (Rollett and Parker 1972: 49).

The second problem of 'modern' capitalist societies concerns the alienation caused by the homogenization of culture and the resultant loss of personal identity through a process of assimilation into a common culture. The idea of a common culture clearly has its modern roots in the development of the nation state. Green (1990) has concluded that 'the major impetus for the creation of national educational systems lay in the need to provide the state with trained administrators, engineers and military personnel; to spread dominant national cultures and inculcate popular ideologies of nationhood; and so to forge the political and cultural unity of burgeoning nation states and cement the ideological hegemony of their dominant classes' (p. 309). The Marxist phrasing of Green should, of course, be noted. Marxist failure to offer a persuasive explanation of national solidarity is conspicuous. Most people in most countries have refused to accept the doctrine that 'the working person has no country'. The importance of religious belief and ethnic custom are basic forces, and typically more powerful than schools in forming the outlook of children (Gellner 1983; Smith 1995).

Once more bureaucracy, and especially the bureaucratic schooling characteristic of Fordist industrial development (Brown and Lauder 1992; Darling-Hammond Ch. 22), had a pivotal role to play in drawing the links between nationalism, a common culture, and language into the modern world. Equally, Gellner (1983; 1996) has noted that the technical rationality that has underpinned scientific and social technologies including bureaucracy related to the ability to think consistently, to treat cases and individuals in the same way, and to think from given ends to the most efficient means to attain those ends without reference to superstition or religion. The connection between these constituents of technical rationality and bureaucracy can clearly be traced in many countries.

Bureaucracy and schooling are antidotes to the family, relying on universalism and non-affectivity in Parsonian terms, as distinct from particularism and affectability (Parsons 1949; 1959). Families favour nepotism, schools promote merit. There is a presumption that individuals should be treated equally according to a codified set of rules. Moreover, bureaucracy is intimately tied to the idea of meritocracy because it treats individuals according to 'objective' criteria of individual achievement. In education this has meant that individuals are, in principle, treated according to ability rather than on the basis of ascribed characteristics such as social class, gender, or race. This principle has given rise to the notion of equality of opportunity which, in the context of the development of the nation state, has three functions. It acts as an efficiency principle by (in theory) selecting and allocating individuals for the labour market on the basis of ability; it acts as a moral principle by selecting students on the basis of a theory of justice; and it also acts as a tool of assimilation. It provides the means by which the heterogeneous peoples of a nation, in terms of class and ethnicity, could aspire to and achieve common prizes offered in industrial society. In doing so, it helps to create a single measure of personal success in individualistic industrial societies: the attainment of wealth and status by promotion to professional and senior management positions within corporate and public bureaucracies. It is against the background of these economic, cultural, and social conditions that the role of education in the postwar period can be understood.

Education and Economic Nationalism

For the first time in the postwar period education took a central position in the functioning of the advanced industrial societies, because it was seen as a key investment in the promotion of economic growth as well as a means of promoting social justice. This was premised on two widely held assumptions about the nature of education in advanced industrial societies which have both been confounded by empirical evidence. Firstly, economic efficiency in advanced industrial societies depends on getting the most talented people into the most important and technically demanding jobs, regardless of their social circumstances. Hence, if individuals had the ability to succeed, the old barriers of social class were no more than gossamer threads to be brushed aside in the ascent up the social ladder. The key to this ascent lay in the notion of intelligence. It was assumed that in society there was a limited pool of individuals with high intelligence who were required to run the engines of industrial growth. This pool of talent needed

to be selected and promoted through the education system because, as Halsey and Floud (1961) noted, 'education is a crucial type of investment for the exploitation of modern technology. This fact underlies recent educational development in all the major industrial societies . . . education attains unprecedented economic importance as a source of technological innovation' (p. l).

Secondly, educational opportunities needed to be extended, given that the vast majority of jobs were predicted to become increasingly skilled, requiring extensive periods of formal education. Hence everyone would eventually become middle-class, as semi-skilled and unskilled jobs were replaced by machines and workers became technicians, managers, or were appointed to positions in the expanding professions (Clark 1962; Kerr et al. 1973).

During this period, education was also seen as contributing to the foundations of democracy. The link between education and democracy has long been established in Western thought, and was given particular impetus in the twentieth century by the work of John Dewey in the United States and in Britain by R. H. Tawney, as well as during the 1950s and 1960s through the writings of Anthony Crosland, A. H. Halsey, and others. The focus of the link between education and democracy turned on a fundamental insight of Dewey's that 'a democracy is more than a form of government; it is primarily a mode of associated living, a conjoint communicated experience' (Dewey 1916: 101). The type of school which, it was argued, best contributed to this form of 'associated living' was the common or comprehensive school. Here students from all types of social background, ethnicity, gender, and ability could mix and develop tolerance and mutual respect for each others' point of view, dispositions considered essential in democracy.

The common school ideal embodied much of the spirit of the age. It was designed to provide greater equality of opportunity by deferring the selection of students into 'academic' and 'vocational' streams until later in a student's career, giving them the chance to manifest their academic potential. It also assumed that students of different genders and cultural backgrounds all learnt in much the same way: that they would all benefit from greater equality of treatment. And it assumed that from this common treatment and experience the essential foundations of democratic life could be taught. From the democratic-socialist perspective of the time it could be seen and still can be defended as a major advance in breaking down the barriers of class, gender, and ethnicity. From a post-modernist perspective it could be seen as a continuation of the assimilationist spirit of the age, as we will go on to show.

The optimism attached to education in the age of economic nationalism is reflected in government support for its expansion in the 1950s and 1960s. Indeed, it was common to hear politicians, journalists, and policy-makers extol the virtue of 'keeping politics out of education', given all-party support for the expansion of education and its reorganization along 'comprehensive' lines as a way of achieving the dual objectives of economic efficiency and social justice.

Consequently, the education systems of the western world expanded to perform their new role of providing the human capital, as it came to be called in the mid-1950s, for the expanding middle-class occupations in industry. In 1938 only 8.4 per cent of children in Britain attended state secondary schools between the ages of 11 and 18. By 1951 the figure had risen to 30 per cent, and by 1968 still further to 37 per cent. Higher education also expanded. In 1938 there were 69,000 students in full-time higher education. By 1963 the number had risen to 215,000, and by 1970 that figure had doubled. Despite this expansion it should be noted that Britain, along with its European counterparts, started from a low base in terms of participation, especially in higher education. However, a start had been made, and expenditure on education rose substantially during this period, reflecting the increased participation in education and its newly found importance in advanced capitalist society. In 1940 2.1 per cent of national income in England and Wales was spent on education; by 1965 it had risen to 4.1 per cent. A similar story of expansion is also true of the United States, although historically far higher numbers of American students completed secondary school and attended higher education than in Europe. In 1930 approximately 7 per cent of American students completed four years of college; by 1960 it had risen to 18 per cent.[2]

However, despite the expansion in middle-class jobs and an increasingly educated workforce, the guiding idea that everyone would eventually get a middle-class job and that occupation and status would be determined according to merit were myths. The myths were understandable, given the accelerated expansion in middle-class jobs and educational opportunities; but working-class jobs did not disappear, and the privilege of the already-privileged remained. Universities were still dominated by those from professional and managerial backgrounds; and even when intelligence was taken into account, social background remained a significant factor in individuals' life chances. In effect, the expanding occupational structure had created more room at the top and in the middle of the occupation hierarchy for those originally from working-class backgrounds, but the reproduction of privilege remained.

The Breakdown of Economic Nationalism

The first 'oil shock' in the early 1970s marked the breakdown of economic nationalism as prosperity, security, and opportunity were all called into question in what Schumpeter (1976) would have described as a 'gale of creative destruction'. The world recession which followed the escalation in fuel prices was accompanied by an increasing awareness that in a global economy the mass production of standardized goods and services which characterized Fordism was no longer able to support the economic livelihood of workers and their families (Piore and Sable 1984). The revolution in new technologies coupled with cheaper transportation costs have made it economically viable, if not essential, for multinational corporations to move production to whatever country has comparative advantage (Cowling and Sugden 1994). If the work to be done is relatively low-skilled, such as in the mass production of standardized goods and services, a key factor will be labour costs, and multinational corporations are likely to move standardized mass production to the newly industrializing countries (NICs) where these are significantly cheaper than in North America or Western Europe (Wood 1994). In the Philippines or in Vietnam, for instance, forty-seven workers can be employed for the cost of a single worker in France (Goldsmith 1995: 125). As a consequence it is argued that Western nations must either reduce wage costs to compete with those in Asian or African economies, which will be extremely difficult to achieve, or try to win a competitive advantage at the 'quality' end of the market. Here it is assumed that healthy profits and incomes can still be made by companies and workers who are able to exploit the full potential of new technologies in the creation of niche markets for goods and services (Thurow 1993).

The growing power of transnational corporations to determine where in the world significant investments are to be made has therefore created a *global auction* in investment, jobs, and new technology (Brown and Lauder Ch. 10). In such circumstances transnationals will invest in those nations where tax regimes and labour costs are low, while providing an infrastructure of a highly skilled workforce, sophisticated transport, and financial communications. In effect, the state has to provide or create the conditions where a sophisticated infrastructure is delivered, while controlling tax demands and the costs of social protection.

Consequently, there is a standard view in the literature that the changes in the nature of the global economy since the early 1970s has led to a weakening of the powers of the nation state (Held 1995). The removal of border controls in relation to capital, the rise in power of transnational corporations, and the enhanced communications afforded by the electronic revolution have set new challenges as to how the economy can best be managed. Under these new conditions the policy instruments relating to Keynesian demand-management no longer work. In effect the nation state has one arm tied behind its back while having to confront the 'problems' created by the new economic conditions. However, there remains considerable debate about how far the influence of transnational business extends over national life and economic policy (Hirst and Thompson 1996). Nevertheless, in the Anglophone nations which have embraced the ideology of competitive individualism and market competition since the late 1970s, the breakdown of national barriers to trade have been positively encouraged. Indeed, the development of the welfare state, the social wage, and the powers of the trade unions are all seen to undermine the culture of enterprise

which the New Right believe to be central to the ability of western nations to compete in the global economy.

This has led the New Right to reassert the principles of market competition in every nook and cranny of contemporary life, resulting in cuts in the welfare benefits on which the idea of a social wage depended. They have also introduced anti-union legislation to curtail the power of the trade unions who were seen to bid-up the price of labour 'artificially'. Whether these policies are a symptom of changes in the global labour market as Reich's (Ch. 9) position implies or an ideological response to the global auction, as Brown and Lauder (Ch. 10) suggest is a matter of debate. However, as a consequence of such policies the link between economic growth and prosperity for all has been broken (Krugman 1993). There has been a polarization of wealth and income in Anglophone societies, with a significant decline in income for non-college graduates (Murnane and Levy 1988) and a sharp increase in the level of unemployment. Coupled with the decline in welfare benefits, this has resulted in a sharp rise in the incidence of poverty, which has had a profound effect on children (Halsey and Young Ch. 49).

Global competition, technological innovation, and the shift away from the mass production of standardized goods and services (Piore and Sable 1984) has also led to a sustained attack on the bureaucratic paradigm of organizational efficiency. The bureaucratic paradigm has been identified as a competitive liability in rapidly changing markets for 'value added' products and services. Management gurus such as Rosabeth Moss Kanter have spoken of the need for managers to apply 'entrepreneurial principles to the traditional corporation, creating a marriage between entrepreneurial creativity and corporate discipline, co-operation, and teamwork' (Kanter 1989: 9–10). The convergence of information technologies and their integration in the workplace, the need to free up and speed up the flow of information and decision-making, the increasing emphasis on teamwork and project work, and the need for flexible work practices, along with a new vocabulary of networks, empowerment, leadership, teamwork, downsizing, rightsizing, re-engineering, and contracting out, have all become part of the rhetoric of the flexible or adaptive paradigm (Brown and Scase 1994). This, it is argued, has not only led enlightened organizations to invest heavily in new technology, but has also made them rethink and restructure their systems of recruitment, communications, rewards, and promotion as well as their structure of ranks and grades. Kanter (1989), for instance, argues that this is leading to a shift from position to performance and from status to contribution, where people are paid for what they do rather than for their ability to climb the corporate hierarchy, and for their 'value added' contribution rather than their location in the organizational command structure.

This change in organizational paradigm has resulted in a massive process of corporate restructuring in both private- and public-sector organizations. Enormous variations exist in the way organizations have responded to greater competitive pressures, volatile markets, technological change, and cutting costs. In most cases the progressive features of the flexible paradigm in terms of greater workplace democracy, job satisfaction, and social justice remain a promise rather than a reality. One of the most striking features of corporate restructuring in both the private and public sectors is an increase in occupational insecurity, redundancy, and the demise of the bureaucratic career, as American and British companies have energetically pursued 'downsizing' policies. These include cutting labour costs through layoffs, 'voluntary' redundancy, hiring freezes, and contracting out various activities to other companies, consultants, contractors, or self-employed workers. In the United States, even during a period of rapid employment growth between 1985 and 1989, 4.3 million employees who had been with their employers for at least 3 years were made redundant due to plant closure, business failure, or because they had been designated as 'surplus employees' (Herz 1991). In 1992 American company layoffs amounted to around 1,224,000, whereas a year later they had increased to 1,314,000 employees (Mishra and Mishra 1994). In Britain the largest 1,000 companies shed about 1.5 million workers in the year to March 1993 as they tried to reduce their costs further (Cassell 1993).

The demise of the mass employment organization offering long-term job prospects has forced all categories of workers to 'stay fit' in the market for jobs, as more people find themselves on short-term contracts, self-employed, under-employed, at risk of redundancy, or unemployed. Even the middle classes, who depended on bureaucratic careers in medium- and large-sized organizations, have had to come to terms with uncertain occupational futures (Newman 1993; Butler and Savage 1995). The educational system itself, despite the golden postwar years of expansion, is far from being the safe haven of an 'ivory tower'. On the contrary, short-term employment on 'soft money' in colleges and 'supply teaching' in schools are determining features of academic employment (Halsey 1995). Moreover, this sense of insecurity has been compounded by changes in household composition and structure. Single mothers and divorced women tend to drift towards the bottom of the income array, taking their children with them to new homes and new schools. Schools lose their community characteristics. Even the better-off 'two-earner' families are typically afflicted by anxiety about job tenure.

Finally, the breakdown of economic nationalism has equally undermined postwar ideals about educational opportunity and social mobility. But paradoxically, whereas there has been increased political conflict concerning the funding, control, and organizations of education, there is a new international consensus which recognizes education to be of even greater importance than in the past to the future of individual and national economic prosperity.

Education and the Global Economy: A New Consensus

Although the education system was being blamed for social and economic problems in the 1970s and 1980s, the power of education to deliver the will of its political élites has never been questioned in official circles. Indeed, there is now a new 'consensus' on both the left and right of the political spectrum which has defined education as the key to future economic prosperity (Drucker 1993; Avis 1993; see, however Avis *et al.* 1996). The new consensus is based on the idea that as the 'walled' economies at mid-century have given way to an increasingly global economy, the power of national government to control the outcome of economic competition has been weakened (Reich 1991). Hence, at a time when severe limitations are being imposed on national governments in the sphere of economic policy, education has assumed even greater political significance. Indeed, the competitive advantage of nations is frequently redefined in terms of the quality of national education and training systems judged according to international standards (Carnevale and Porro 1994). The essence of this idea is captured in this extract from a major address on education by Bill Clinton:

The key to our economic strength in America today is productivity growth ... In the 1990s and beyond, the universal spread of education, computers, and high-speed communications means that what we earn will depend on what we can learn and how well we can apply what we learn to the workplaces of America. That's why, as we know, a college graduate this year will earn 70 per cent more than a high school graduate in the first year of work. That's why the earnings of younger workers who dropped out of high school, or who finished but received no further education or training, dropped by more than 20 per cent over the last 10 years alone.[3]

Therefore, if nations are unable to win a competitive advantage through investment in new technology, upgrading the quality of human resources, or reforming industrial relations policies as a way of attracting foreign inward investment to create new employment opportunities, there is little national governments can do to prevent a precipitous drop in living standards, stagnant economic growth, and increasing unemployment (Thurow 1993; ILO 1995). As in the era of economic nationalism, the new education consensus has led to what in many parts of the world amount to dramatic increases in post-compulsory education. In higher education there has been an increase from approximately 8 per cent to 30 per cent in the age cohort attending universities in numerous countries (Halsey Ch. 39). Whatever reasons are given to explain political support for the new education consensus and the expansion of tertiary education, there are a number of issues over the centrality accorded to education in post-industrial societies that require further investigation and analysis. These include the changing relationship between education and the labour market. In particular, we need to ask whether education can lead to improvements in productivity, and to greater scope for individual creativity and fulfilling employment.

Education and Economic Productivity: Questioning the New Consensus

On the question of education and economic productivity there is little doubt that the new consensus maintains a long-standing trend towards a tightening bond between education and the economy in the twentieth century. In their introduction to *Education, Economy and Society*, Floud and Halsey (1961) note:

The striking development of secondary and higher education over the past quarter of a century has been accompanied by a strong trend toward vocationalism. Education increasingly takes on the character of 'training'; specialization takes place earlier, is more thorough-going, and is increasingly of a kind directly related to the requirements of modern trades and professions. (p. 9)

However, whilst there is now widespread agreement that a high-quality general education is more appropriate to conditions of rapid technological change than a narrowly specialized vocational education, the exact relationship between 'vocational' and 'general' education remains unresolved (Pring 1989; Carnevale and Porro 1994). This debate is likely to continue, given the recent argument outlined by Ashton and Sung (see Ch. 12) that in the new economic competition there needs to be a much tighter relationship between education and work than anything that we have yet witnessed in the West. The implication of their argument is that the almost total subordination of the education system to economic utility is becoming a necessary condition for economic prosperity in the twenty-first century. Whether this will become the model relationship between education and the labour market in all post-industrial economies is a moot point, but there is little doubt that in such economies there is an increased demand for more highly educated labour. In the United Kingdom, Gallie and White (1993) show that the introduction of information technologies has increased skill demands in jobs that remain in all but the unskilled manual sectors of the economy. Lidley and Wilson (1995) also estimate that the proportion of managerial, administrative, and professional jobs has risen from 20 per cent in 1981 to 26.4 per cent in 1994 and is projected to reach 28.7 per cent in the year 2001. In the United States, Block (1990) has suggested that on the basis of a variety of evidence about occupational trends since the late 1960s, the majority of American employees were in jobs 'where the skill demands of their jobs are quite substantial', and that technological innovation 'in blue-collar and white-collar settings is generally associated with rising levels of skill' (1990: 86). Moreover, figures published by the Department of Labor predict that between 1990 and 2005 there will be a 76.6 per cent increase in the number of 'managerial' jobs (Silvestri 1993).[4]

Moreover, the increased demand for educated labour is often associated with the shift in employment from manufacturing to service industries. In 1950 in the United States, 33 per cent of jobs were in manufacturing and 53 per cent in service industries. In the UK the figures were 46.5 per cent and 48 per cent. By 1987 the figures for the United States were 27 and 70 per cent respectively, and for the UK 30 and 68 per cent (Maddison 1991). Hence, while manufacturing is no less important to either economy (Cohen and Zysman 1987) the number of workers in factory jobs shrunk dramatically. However, the service sector is heterogeneous, and there are clearly many 'junk' jobs within it. For example, Levy (1987) suggests that blue-collar workers who have entered the service sector receive 60 per cent of their former wage on average in the United States. These figures relate to those who have secured a job; however, as we have indicated, white-collar jobs are increasingly insecure as, for instance, clerical assembly lines are replaced by new technologies through the process known as 're-engineering' (Head 1996; Hammer and Champy 1993). Aronowitz and De Fazio (Ch. 11) take the view that the consequence of the current changes will lead to deskilling and even higher levels of unemployment than witnessed in the past decade. Therefore, this somewhat confused picture of upskilling, reskilling, *and* deskilling (Braverman 1974) is in urgent need of further research. Such research is important because changes in the structure of work will have major implications for the changing nature of the class structure in post-industrial societies (Esping-Andersen 1994). This, in turn, will inevitably have an impact on the distribution of educational success and failure of today's children.

CREDENTIAL INFLATION AND SOCIAL CONFLICT

The problem of understanding current trends

is compounded by the fact that the intellectual history of attempts to chart the link between education and economic productivity have been strewn with good intentions and theoretical and empirical failures (Klees 1986). The main problem is that it is very difficult, if not impossible, to demonstrate a causal relationship between education and economic productivity. There are two related reasons for this. Firstly, the link between education and productivity is mediated by issues of power most clearly seen in the phenomenon of credential inflation. And secondly, changes in the demand for skill are as much a social as a technical issue, subject to vested interests and social conflict.

Credentials are a positional good (Hirsch 1977). A defining characteristic of a positional good is that it is scarce in a socially imposed sense, and that accordingly allocation proceeds through 'the auction of a restricted set of objects to the highest bidder' (pp. 28–9). This then leads to the kinds of effects hypothesized by Collins (1979); for in order to cope with excess demand for educational credentials, the mechanisms of credential inflation and screening emerge. Credential inflation simply increases the hierarchy of scarcity and demands that individuals invest more time in ascending the hierarchy to the scarcest and most valued credential. Screening operates by increasing the resources needed to attain the highest credentials in order to gain selection for a job. However, the resources needed to gain work may be more than intellectual. Several theorists have hypothesized that the purpose of credentials is to screen personalities as much as cognitive achievement (Collins 1979; Bowles and Gintis 1976). This is an important issue, of great relevance to the current situation, and to which we shall return.

Hirsch's analysis of credential inflation clearly undermines the human-capital (Woodhall Ch. 13) assumption, reflected in the quote by President Clinton, that the higher an employee's credentials the higher her or his rate of productivity; and it points to the theory that credential inflation reflects the outcome of a competition within which higher socio-economic groups preserve and reproduce their privilege by raising the educational levels demanded for élite occupations (see Brown Ch. 45). If this is the case then part of the explanation of the expansion of tertiary education should be located in the competition for credentials rather than in any straightforward link between education and economic productivity. Understood in these broad terms, the demand for credentials may well be a function of the pressure of an increasing middle class keen to secure their children's future. If this hypothesis is correct it would explain why even right-wing governments, which in terms of their ideology would reject the expansion of tertiary education on the grounds that there is only an academic élite who can benefit from such an education, have promoted expansionist policies. The alternative would be to lose the middle-class vote.[5] However, a consequence of educational expansion may be an increasing mismatch between the supply of higher-educated workers and the demand for employees with advanced technical and academic qualifications. We can therefore anticipate increasing political fallout from this situation in the future as the 'wastage of talent' is increasingly seen to be one of how to placate a growing army of ambitious and highly educated workers unable to realize their occupational ambitions.

SOCIAL CONFLICT AND THE CHANGING NATURE OF SKILLS

There has also been a significant change in the definition of 'skill' (Block 1990). This is less a reflection of the secular trend towards a more technically skilled workforce than a change in employer definitions of individual competence, with the shift from bureaucratic to flexible paradigms of organizational efficiencies. This has led employers to emphasize the need for employees who have good personal and social skills, together with any technical 'know-how' which may be required. At least among 'core' workers (Atkinson 1985) there is an expectation that they will be able to work in a rapidly changing environment, to engage in 'rule-making' rather than 'rule-following' behaviour, to work in project teams, and to share the same 'personal chemistry' as others in the organization (Brown and Scase 1994).

Hence, the more organizational efficiency is seen to depend on the interpersonal skills of communication, negotiation, and teamwork, the more the bureaucratic legacy in schools, colleges, and universities is seen by employers as a form of 'trained incapacity' (see Merton 1957: 197–8). Moreover, academic qualifica-

tions now tell employers less about what they need to know about potential recruits, given that they convey information about the individual's ability and motivation to jump through the appropriate test and examination hoops, rather than students' potential to work in teams or about their social and personal skills.

Consequently, calls from employers to have a greater say in the affairs of the school are increasingly less concerned about getting the educational system involved with programmes of specific vocational training, and more concerned with enhancing student business awareness, communication skills, and self-management. The use of 'profiling', which incorporates a broader range of student abilities, qualities, and attainment than that which is typically assessed in academic examinations is clearly an attempt to respond to an employer rhetoric of personal and social skills. However, the use of student profiles has as yet had little impact on traditional patterns of education. Nevertheless, increasing external involvement in education does not rule out the possibility of a growing contradiction between the classification and framing of knowledge, interaction, and organizational practices operating in the educational system and in employing organizations (Bernstein Ch. 3). Some of the reasons for this are not difficult to understand, and again they highlight contradictions, unintended consequences, and 'forced' integration between education and the labour market rather than 'correspondence' (Bowles and Gintis 1976). Part of the problem is that group work has tended to be frowned upon because the democratization of education opportunities has depended on the individuation of success and failure. Ability and performance, like the concept of meritocracy, is assumed to be judged on an individual basis. Group assessment which could be introduced as a way of encouraging teamwork in a formal educational context is also rejected, because it is difficult to evaluate when individual grades need to be assigned.

A greater emphasis on the development of personal and social skills in education is also unlikely to gain widespread support, especially from the élite schools, colleges, and universities. This is because the credibility attached to academic credentials remains based on the 'objective' assessment of 'knowledge' epitomized by the 'unseen' examination paper. In such circumstances, the formal teaching of personal and social skills represents the latest version of 'compensatory' education (Halsey 1975) for those who lack the personal qualities which come 'naturally' as part of the informal social education of the middle-class child (Bourdieu and Passeron 1977). However, there seems little doubt that the acquisition of cultural capital based on family background, education, qualification, gender, and ethnicity is increasingly having to be 'repackaged' to incorporate those 'personal qualities' that expose the subjective 'inner world' of the self in the market for jobs (Brown Ch. 45).

GENDER AND SKILL IN A CHANGING LABOUR MARKET
The shift towards service-sector employment has also been associated with a rise in the proportion of women entering the labour market. This represents a considerable challenge to established assumptions about gender divisions in the pattern of socialization and social control. Even in the so-called 'permissive' 1960s it was not difficult to find official statements maintaining the view that boys should be socialized for their future role as 'breadwinners' and girls for that of 'homemakers'. In England, the Newsam Report on the education of average- and below-average-ability students noted that gender divisions in future adult roles would inevitably lead males to show a far greater interest in science. 'A boy is usually excited by the prospect of a science course . . . He experiences a sense of wonder and a sense of power. The growth of wheat, the birth of a lamb, the movement of clouds put him in awe of nature; the locomotive he sees as a man's response; the switch and the throttle are his magic wands. The girl may come to the science lesson with a less eager curiosity than the boy but she too will need to feel at home with the machinery.' (Deem 1978: 60).

However, by the 1980s official statements on science education had changed. In the Department of Education and Science's (1982) consultative document on Science Education in Schools it was noted that: 'Throughout the period of compulsory secondary education every school . . . should adopt the policy of giving all pupils a broad science programme which . . . gives genuinely equal curricular opportunities in science to boys and girls.'

A similar shift in official thinking about what makes an appropriate education for girls and boys can be found in all the advanced Western economies, despite differences in the time in which this shift has taken place. But whereas the socialization of young women has been a focus of educational researchers over the last two decades, it is the socialization of men which has attracted more recent attention. When, for instance, Paul Willis (1977) described working-class resistance of 'the Lads' to school in the mid-1970s, it was based on an assumption that there would be physically tough jobs available at the local steelworks or in other heavy industries for them to fulfil their masculine potential. However, the shift to service-sector employment is making life increasingly difficult for the working-class 'heroic' male. Without formal qualifications his most likely prospect is a life of irregular employment in jobs such as that of security guard, shelf-filler, or cook in a fast-food outlet, if not one among the ranks of the long-term unemployed. The 'problem' of male socialization is not, however, restricted to the working class. There is also evidence to show that middle-class males may in future lose out in the competition for credentials, although feminist researchers continue to demonstrate that there is some distance to travel before men and women leave education with the same academic profiles (Weiner, Arnot, and David Ch. 38). Nevertheless, changes in the occupational structure and the improved performance of young women in the educational system will inevitably sharpen the focus on masculine identities, socialization, and social control (Connell Ch. 37). At the same time, there is very little to suggest that the current 'backlash' against women will reverse current trends. It may be argued that women have benefited from changes in the structure of employment and from the redefinition of skill to include social skills, since women are often considered better 'team players'. However, as Blackmore (Ch. 14) has noted, the changing definition of skill can be considered as a two-edged sword for women. Their social skills are now encouraged purely for their instrumental value and have been thereby co-opted for corporate profit-making rather than as a means of furthering the qualities associated with caring and human development.

EDUCATION AND SOCIAL CONTROL

In the past 20 years the family has become less stable and work more insecure, and hence it can be argued that the hold of these institutions on the processes of socialization and control has weakened. By the same token, the role of education has become more extensive and intensive. Paradoxically, as these institutions have weakened, the demand for greater involvement in schools, colleges, and universities, from employers, entrepreneurs, parents, and community groups points to the increasing diversity and diffusion of education into all corners of people's lives (Chisholm 1996). Equally, the shift from education preparing people for employment to that of enhancing individual employability as a 'life-project' is not restricted to a question of enhancing technical competence. The socio-emotional world of the school child or the adult learner must now be fully and regularly interrogated. The demands made upon people to enhance their employability as well as social and personal skills places paramount importance on inculcating self-discipline, the virtues of self-improvement, and the art of self-management (Rose 1989). The educational system is increasingly expected to encompass much of the 'hidden curriculum' into its remit of explicit activities.

This extension of the scope of education and training at the end of the twentieth century can, of course, be interpreted in significantly different ways. A technicist account of the expansion of education would see it as part of the inexorable move to a 'learning' society (see, however, Ranson 1994; Hughes and Tight 1995). For instance, the spread of certification to increasing spheres of our lives is seen as evidence of increasing social justice. A woman who has taken time out from waged work to bring up young children, which involves the development of a range of skills, including patience, negotiation, time management, compromise, and so on, which are 'transferable' to the labour market, deserves formal recognition from employers and academic institutions for her 'prior learning'. Likewise the high-school student who performs badly at his or her academic studies, but who has shown considerable organizational abilities in organizing a big charity concert, should also have such 'skills' formally recognized by employers. However, this can also be seen as increasing surveillance and disciplin-

ing of the individual (Foucault 1977; Cohen 1985) where every aspect of peoples' lives comes under the formal gaze of 'authority' for certification. In *Imprisoned in the Global Classroom*, Illich and Verne (1976) reject the technicist view. They suggest that 'professional educators, through the institution of permanent education, succeed in convincing men [and women] of their permanent incompetence. The ultimate success of the schooling instrument is the extension of its monopoly, first to all youth, then to every age, and finally to all areas' (p. 14).

Underlying the issues we have raised regarding the enhanced significance of education, two major problems remain. The first is this: how is it possible to promote higher standards in education, when an increasing number of children live in poverty (Brown and Lauder Ch. 10)? One of the clear findings in the sociology of education over the past 20 years has been to establish a link between income and educational performance. The lower the family income, the more educationally disadvantaged students are. The second issue concerns the instability generated by the transformation of Western economies. If knowledge is at the heart of economic survival then the source of future knowledge lies in the education of the present generation of children. But children's education relies heavily on security and stability in the family and at work. However, if working life is highly unstable for many then a crucial question that now needs to be asked, especially in relation to unemployment (Flanagan 1993), is what effect is the instability in the labour market having on the raising and educating of the next generation? Overall, the question raised by Levin and Kelly (Ch. 15), 'Can education do it alone?' is highly pertinent. The key issue is whether a restructured, more effective education system geared to the economy can deliver on the expectations placed upon it, or whether, as Halsey, Heath, and Ridge (1980) noted, education is a 'waste-paper basket' in which difficult problems are simply dumped.

Social Transformation and Education as a Site of Struggle

So far we have described some of the key economic and social factors which have led to the transformation of Western societies in the past 20 years. We have also identified a new policy consensus about the role of education in contemporary society. However, the danger in focusing exclusively on policy formation 'from above' is that it negates the importance of competing interests, values, and power relations. Indeed, on many of the key issues confronting the education system today, including funding, testing, curriculum, school management, educational selection, and teacher training, there is significant conflict rather than consensus. The reason why the educational system is likely to remain a site of struggle stems from what Durkheim observed and Parsons defined as the dual problem of 'socialization' and 'selection' (Parsons 1959). The question of access and selection in education has been inextricably connected to that of social justice and positional competition (Hirsch 1977). We have already noted how meritocratic competition has been a means of legitimating occupational and social inequalities because the doctrine of meritocracy is based on the idea of giving everyone an equal chance to be unequal. At the same time educational selection takes the form of a positional competition between students for access to credentials which can be traded in the labour market to 'purchase' income, status, and employment. It is such sources of conflict which led Michael Young to note that the education system confronts a centuries-old conflict between the principles of selection by family and the principles of selection by merit (Young 1961).

Moreover, since the Enlightenment, education has been seen as necessary to human progress, not only technically and economically but also in terms of emancipation (see Giroux Ch. 7). It is for this reason that education has been intimately linked in Western thought to democracy. In this respect education has always been a focus of struggle between those with the power to define what constitutes legitimate knowledge and those excluded from educational decision-making.

From the inception of public education systems in the latter half of the nineteenth century until the early 1970s the struggle over school knowledge was predominantly characterized in terms of class conflict. More recently, with the re-emergence of feminism (Weiner Ch. 6) and the break-up of colonial rule, that struggle has also related to the eman-

cipation of women and people of colour. Equally, whereas the sociology of education was previously dominated by issues of access, selection, and equality of opportunity, issues of knowledge, pedagogy, and the politics of difference have assumed far greater significance in the study of education as a site of struggle. This reflects broader debates within the social sciences about post-modernism and the cultural politics of difference (see West Ch. 33).

POST-MODERNISM AND THE CULTURAL POLITICS OF DIFFERENCE
Cultural politics (Jordan and Weedon 1995) has brought the struggles of women and people of colour to the fore, in that it seeks to explain their oppression not only in terms of unequal opportunities, but in relation to the culture of their everyday lives, including education. Much of the inspiration for this new cultural politics has come from some of the many strands of post-modernist thought (Docherty 1993; Kumar 1995). Post-modernism as a loosely textured set of theories has its basis in changes in society which are identified as constituting a fundamental break with the modernist society of postwar economic nationalism. The inspiration for this intellectual movement came from France (see Kumar Ch. 5) and placed great emphasis on the significance of images, signs, and language in the constitution of the self and society. From this emerged a cultural politics which sought to criticize the dominant white, male, metropolitan grand theories and images of the social and economic world which had placed women and people of colour in positions of oppression. The basis for this critique is the assumption that there is little or no justification for claiming that one specific theory or view of knowledge is a better representation of reality than another. Hence scientific claims to 'objective truth' are rejected. The work of Foucault (1977; Rainbow 1991) is particularly important in this respect, both for his 'discourse' analysis of thought and practice in which, he suggested, social practices and the self are constructed in such a way as to render social life an interminable conflict between 'dominated' and 'dominating', and that truth and power are inseparable. These ideas enabled him to criticize the grand narratives of the Enlightenment and particularly Marxism, which he understood

not as a praxis for liberation but simply as another rationalization for a practice of domination.

The idea that knowledge is not about truth but is simply a weapon in the struggle between groups, and that individuals are socially constructed and represented in the image of oppressors, has clearly been attractive to some feminists and post-colonial peoples. For them, white, male, metropolitan knowledge could be seen merely as an instrument of domination, and the knowledge of women and post-colonial peoples that has been marginalized could be validated. In so doing it countered the persistent tendency in liberal societies to see the 'disadvantaged' as a problem to be solved and as victims of their own incompetence. Despite the attractions of this position, it has also brought a series of intractable problems. For the educationalists amongst indigenous peoples, the relativism of linking truth and power so tightly conflicted with the claims that there was a past in terms of their own culture, which was authentic and material to the well-being of their people. Similarly, relativism placed the theories of oppression they used to explain their position in jeopardy. After all, if knowledge is just the fiction of the powerful, what status do theories of colonial oppression have? For others there were broader problems in linking a politics of difference to relativism. One of the legacies of the Enlightenment has been that education has been seen as a vehicle for social and personal progress as well as for liberation. A central problem for critical educationalists has therefore been to reconcile the relativism and nihilism of a set of theories denying the possibility of social progress with a politics of difference advancing the liberation of women and people of colour (see, for example, Lather 1989; McLaren 1994; Giroux Ch. 7; and Apple Ch. 36). There is no doubt that postmodern precepts have provided some important insights into the political processes of educational research (e.g. Lather 1991; Bird 1992). But in the case of Lather this has been at the cost of denying the relevance of quantitative analyses to complement qualitative analysis. This is a point to which we shall return in the section on a new political arithmetic.

However, more recently there has been something of a shift away from many of the tenets of post-modernism in educational theory. bel hooks (1991) has argued against the language which many post-modern critical educationalists have adopted. 'Postmodernist discourses are often exclusionary even as they call attention to . . . the experience of difference and Otherness . . . As a discursive practice it is dominated primarily by the voices of white male intellectuals and/or academic élites who speak to and about one another with coded familiarity' (cited in Jordan and Weedon 1995: 540). Kenway (Ch. 8) makes a similar point while noting the irony that at the very moment when post-modernism has denied the significance of grand theories it is one of the oldest of these, that of the 'free market', which has led to the axing of 8,200 teaching positions in her own state of Victoria in Australia. For Kenway, the search is now on for a more adequate basis for a feminist politics of education.

Whatever the difficulties with some of the post-modern and post-structuralist precepts of the new cultural politics, the major strength of this intellectual movement has been to draw attention to the need to make visible and understand the complex relationships between class, gender, and ethnicity in the restructuring of education (Giroux Ch. 7; Davies 1993). If the new directions signalled by Kenway are indicative of a trend, then this particular post-modern turn can perhaps best be understood as one moment in the conflict between what Wallerstein (1995) has called the two modernities, of technology and of liberation, a conflict that has common roots in the Enlightenment. In this context postmodernism can be seen as an aspect of the modern struggle for liberation. In the era of economic nationalism, Wallerstein argues, the two modernities seemed to come together and social progress and liberation were seen as embodied in the progress, security, and opportunity that the period offered. Since the late 1960s, however, the two have been in open conflict.

SOCIAL CLASS AND EDUCATION

If the industrial working class was the driving force behind social change in the nineteenth and early decades of the twentieth century, it is the middle class who are now seen to determine the destiny of post-industrial societies. During the period of economic nationalism the burgeoning middle class benefited most from the expansion of the welfare state, employment security, and the opportunities afforded by comprehensive education and the expansion of post-compulsory provision. Accordingly, within the sociology of education it was the question of working-class access and opportunity which dominated debates about class conflict and inequalities in the postwar period. Now, it is not working-class resistance to education which represents the primary sources of class conflict as predicted by neo-Marxist analysts, but the exclusionary tactics of the middle classes at a time of profound personal and social uncertainty and insecurity. With the breakdown of economic nationalism, the demise of bureaucratic careers and the attendant risks of downward mobility have led the middle classes to reassert their vested interests in an attempt to maximize the reproduction of their class advantage.

Nationally this can be seen in terms of middle-class claims of over-taxation. Since the mid-1960s, tax revenues have risen steadily in all Western nations (Esping-Andersen 1990), initially to provide more adequate social protection while increasing expenditure on education and health, and latterly to fund welfare for the persistent high numbers of unemployed. The problem posed by the global auction of reducing public-expenditure costs while maintaining or increasing efficiencies has been exacerbated in the Anglophone countries by the perceived problem of 'overtaxing'. This had led to a concern by governments that the middle class would no longer pay the costs of welfare. Whether these concerns are well-founded is a matter of debate (Heath 1994). However, it is fair to say that the issue of overtaxing is more likely to have been canvassed by right-wing governments for whom high taxation is anathema, since they assume that it leads to a blunting of incentives to work and is more likely to advantage the middle-class state employees rather than the disadvantaged in whose name welfare taxes have been raised. Galbraith (1992) has coined the phrase 'the culture of contentment' to describe the outlook of the middle classes in these terms. But this notion fails to acknowledge the underlying condition of the middle classes in the late twentieth century. Like their unskilled counterparts, the middle classes have been subject to relatively high unemployment and increasing insecurity as

the social protection afforded by the state has been stripped away.

The cost of health, education, insurance, and pensions have all increased at the same time that far more of these costs have been redefined as a personal rather than a state responsibility. This increasing emphasis on self-reliance has contributed to a climate in which high taxation may appear to be an additional burden to be shouldered by the hard-pressed middle classes, often to support those who are viewed as 'less deserving'.

The increased insecurity confronting middle-class families also has profound implications for the education system, given the importance of gaining credentials in the 'competition for a livelihood'. As Bourdieu (Ch. 2) has argued, cultural capital in the form of academic credentials is essential to the reproduction of middle-class privilege. This, it can be argued, has led to intense class conflict over the question of educational selection, when concerns about ensuring 'equality of opportunity' have been superseded by primarily (although not exclusively) middle-class claims for greater 'choice' over the education of their children. Consequently it has been hypothesized that the middle class will either seek to change the class mechanisms of exclusion and selection in education (see Brown, Wells and Serna, and Lareau in Part 6), or they will secede from state education. However, these hypotheses may be more applicable to one national context than another. For example, the issue of middle-class secession is at the forefront of debate in England, yet in Scotland the consensus concerning the importance of comprehensive (or common-school) state education appears to be holding.

Moreover, it would be a mistake to define this conflict in traditional terms as one involving the working class against the middle class. As the 'new' middle class has grown exponentially in the era of economic nationalism, so aspirations have been raised for its children (Bernstein Ch. 3). This is clearly reflected in the buoyant demand for access to higher education. Therefore at the same time that the 'new' middle class have been demanding increasing access to higher education for their children, the 'old' professional middle class is concerned to preserve its monopoly of access to the élite universities. Hence the changing nature of the 'positional' competition for education at the end of the twentieth century may become increasingly dominated by class conflict within what can be broadly defined as the middle classes.

There is a further intriguing hypothesis concerning the middle class and educational conflict which is worth entertaining. Reich (1991) has argued that what he calls the 'symbolic analysts'—the design engineers, research scientists, bio-technologists, engineers, public relations executives, investment brokers, international lawyers, management consultants—are likely to secede from national commitments to education, health, and social welfare, not because of 'defensive' manoeuvring as a response to middle-class insecurities, but because they operate in a global labour-market, selling their skills, insights, and knowledge to global businesses. Hence, their objections to paying national, state, or neighbourhood taxes are likely to become more vociferous, because they are more likely to use portable private health-care, welfare schemes, and prestigious private schools, colleges, and universities with international reputations. For the moment Reich's argument has the status of a hypothesis with little or no empirical work on it. However, it is indicative of the forces that can potentially be unleashed by a fundamental shift in the global economy over education.

GENDER AND EDUCATION

In the preceding discussion there was little mention of knowledge and pedagogy in the education system. This is because the middle class have a close affinity with the formal system of education, which in many respects is seen to mirror their ways of seeing the world and what they consider really useful knowledge. What this argument ignores, however, is the fact that class conflicts are cross-cut by those of gender. For women, the question of whether the state has enabled them to become full citizens in a democratic society has been long-standing, characterized by the notion of a patriarchal state, dominated by and run in the interests of men (Pateman 1988; Franzway, Court, and Connell 1989; Connell 1990). Recently the structural impediments to women realizing this goal have been added to by women's increased participation in paid work and the feminization of poverty. The issues for women include the question of curriculum and pedagogy: feminist educators

have argued that their interests have been marginalized in a male-dominated curriculum, where the images, messages, and representations conveyed in educational institutions reflect the dominant male culture (Weiner, Arnot, and David Ch. 38). The question, then, is how women's interests and perspectives can be fairly represented through pedagogy, curriculum, and assessment. It is clear from the research that comprehensive education has, by and large, done little to change the dominance of a male perspective in the curriculum and the exclusion of girls in their interactions with teachers in classrooms. One significant consequence has been the increased demand for single-sex schooling. Whether single-sex schooling enables girls to escape the images of a male-dominated society is a matter of debate. However, the criticism of comprehensive education as reproducing the ideologies and practice of patriarchy are really only the tip of the iceberg. Underlying these criticisms are two further challenges to the received liberal view of the links between education and democracy.

The first concerns what is taught in schools as part of the Western heritage of a liberal education. That heritage has been understood as partly comprising the great works of literature and philosophy, written largely by men, though, it could be argued, not exclusively from a male perspective. In the theories of its defenders, a liberal education is intimately linked to the creation of the dispositions needed in a democracy. As Bloom (Ch. 32) has noted, 'Every educational system has a moral goal that it tries to attain and that informs its curriculum. It wants to produce a certain kind of human being . . . Democratic education, whether it admits it or not, wants and needs to produce men and women who have the tastes, knowledge and character supportive of a democratic regime' (p. 26 original). Feminist criticisms of liberal education challenge the assumption that the male-dominated liberal canon of 'great' philosophy and literature constitutes an appropriate curriculum for senior secondary and university students. They argue that rather than initiate students into the forms of knowledge and modes of rationality of Western civilization, a liberal education is an exercise in patriarchal power. Power, in effect, masquerades as truth.

Closely allied to this criticism is that of

the notion of a public sphere in which the issues of a democracy are debated. The public sphere was constituted, in theory, on the idea that 'by recognizing and accepting man's natural rights, men found a fundamental basis of unity and sameness. Class, race, religion, national origin all disappear or become dim when bathed in the light of natural rights, which give men common interests and make them truly brothers' (Bloom p. 27 original). In an important sense this assumption is similar to the universalistic ideals of meritocratic education: in both cases the particular characteristics of individuals in terms of gender, ethnicity, and class are discounted in the wider national interest of democracy and equality.

Bloom's analysis of what is required in order to sustain democracy is clearly open to question. Nancy Fraser (1992*a*; 1992*b*; 1996) has argued that the liberal conception of the public sphere as represented by Bloom, although her work has focused on Habermas, is likely to limit rather than extend democratic participation. In her view, multiple public spheres representing the variety of cultures in a pluralist society are not only desirable but possible. For her, the possibility of a truly multicultural democracy is an empirical question. But Fraser's position is also open to question, since it raises the issue of whether groups from incommensurable communities (Gray 1995) can talk to each other when they differ in their perspectives and values. This is, however, a vital question, since the move to different schools for different ethnic and social groups is likely to increase in strength in many Western societies. Only if the kind of vision articulated by Fraser is possible can a new set of links between education and democracy be forged on the basis of radical cultural diversity.

The debate on single-sex schooling points to further aspects of gender and educational performance: the apparent increasingly superior academic performance of girls over boys. This trend has given a further impetus to the debate by the recent positioning of white working-class boys as anti-education, 'macho', and right-wing (Davis 1995). Clearly, the underlying problem which has led to this 'positioning' has been the process of deindustrialization (Bettis 1996); the decline in unskilled blue-collar work and the consequent rise in working-class youth male unemployment (Weis 1990). The research on the relationship between this relatively recent representation of working-class boys and the desire for single-sex schooling is in its infancy. However, it may be that the motivation for single-sex schooling in terms of providing girls with a more accurate representation of their lives and interests has now been coupled with what is, in effect, a fear of working-class boys. As Connell (Ch. 37) has noted, the nature of masculinity is changing in the new historical conditions, and it is a question of whether the sub-cultures of working-class boys can adapt to the new realities. The mirror image of this representation of working-class boys is that of increasingly educationally successful girls from all classes. In this context, there is much talk of the twenty-first century belonging to women because they are becoming educationally more successful than boys and because the nature of work in the new century is more likely to suit them. Just as the new representation of working-class boys needs research, so this new image of women needs a critical eye. In their paper Weiner, Arnot and David (Ch. 38) challenge the notion that girls are indeed outperforming boys at school, while the idea that the world of work in the twenty-first century belongs to women appears to be difficult to sustain.

We have already noted that throughout Western societies the participation of women in the labour force has increased dramatically, yet much of their work is part-time and low-paid. In the Anglophone societies they have been used to forge a neo-Fordist strategy (see Brown and Lauder Ch. 10) in response to the global economy in which employers use low-paid, casualized employment as a strategy to cut costs and increase profits. But women have also been at the sharp end of another significant trend in Western societies, the feminization of poverty (see Halsey and Young Ch. 49; Wilson Ch. 46). The combination of the polarization of income in Anglophone societies and the increasing number of woman-headed families has meant that the incidence of poverty has fallen unequally on women. This in turn raises general questions about the ability of women in poverty to participate fully as citizens in a democracy (Pateman 1988; 1992) and specific questions about the ability of women with families to have the time and resources to find work or upskill themselves, when the conditions under which they can freely enter the labour force have not been met.

Education has been implicated in these issues because the universal provision of high-quality, early-childhood education is a key factor in enabling women to enter the labour market. Nevertheless, universal provision remains controversial, and a focus of struggle for women (Leira 1992). The reasons for this are not difficult to find. The question of early-childhood education stands at the intersection of several debates concerning the role of women in society and the appropriate education of young children. These include the question of the 'proper' role of mothers in the raising of young children, and whether paid work conflicts with conceptions of the mother's role. These debates often assume, however, that women in general and mothers in particular have a choice as to whether they enter paid employment. Clearly, for many no such choice exists. The post-industrial shift to service-sector work has led to a decline in the traditional 'family wage' paid to men.

EDUCATION IN POST–COLONIAL SOCIETIES

If the state has been seen by women as biased towards the interests of the powerful in society, the same is true of groups whose history is characterized by colonialism. Post-colonialism is the theoretical term that has been broadly adopted in discussions relating people of colour and education.[6] The notion of post-colonialism draws attention to the fact that issues of racism have an historical context and that, for the most part, these are related economically, culturally, and politically to the impact of Western colonization over the past 500 years. At a time of increased global inter-dependency it also highlights once more the relationships between economy and culture and the problems that the new global economy poses for the once colonized (see Mohanty 1991; West Ch. 33).

The re-emergence of a politics of identity, culture, and autonomy among those who have been marked by colonization (West Ch. 33) has been one of the most significant elements in education in the past 20 years. Whether it be the first peoples of North America, Maori in New Zealand, Aborigines in Australia, or the post-colonial peoples who have been drawn to the metropolitan societies like Britain and the United States, the struggle to break out of a Western-dominated mono-

cultural and assimilationist society has been highly significant for education. As Jordan and Weedon (1995) note, the cultural struggle is over the power to name, to represent common sense, to create the 'official' version of history and events, to speak on behalf of or for others (p. 13). In each case the history of post-colonialism has been one of conflict between the perspectives embodied in these powers by the post-colonial state and people of colour, the once-colonized. In this context the drive towards different forms of education and educational institutions for different ethnic and religious groups has constituted a strategy for taking power over these crucial issues of history and culture. Educationally, it has been assumed that there are a series of crucial links between the security of a cultural identity, self-esteem, and educational performance. The educational rationale underlying this theory is that students learning in their own cultural context and, where applicable, their own language are likely to be more successful than if they are educated in ethnically diverse schools (See e.g. Deyhle 1995).

In recent educational debate, this theory is pervasive and has become almost axiomatic. It is, however, a theory which is in some respects testable. McPherson and Willms (Ch. 42), for example, show that the raising of educational achievement in Scotland may largely be attributable to the greater socio-economic mix of students created by the comprehensive system. If so, then one inference to be drawn is that students who attend ethnically homogeneous schools but who are predominantly working-class may not improve their academic performance to the same extent as in ethnically and socially 'mixed' comprehensive schools. The issue, however, is more complex than this potential criticism suggests. It fails to take into account the relationship between issues of power, pedagogy, and knowledge (Delpit Ch. 35; Mohanty Ch. 34). While the projects of culturally autonomous schooling will take years to realize, and hence to evaluate, they need to be judged against the broader aims of the preservation of living cultures and languages and as a way of 'getting out from under': education here is seen as providing a platform for access to power and full democratic participation in society.

The project of culturally autonomous schooling is long-term and in the mean-time the majority of students who may benefit from them remain in state schools. The educational outcomes of these students reinforce the view that they are systematically disadvantaged (see Ogbu Ch. 47). For example, in the United States, Black and Latino students are far less likely to graduate from college (Thomas 1992), while in the UK patterns of mobility over two generations show that, while there are differences between ethnic groups, people of colour in the United Kingdom suffer a penalty, in terms of life chances, as a result of their ethnicity (Heath and McMahon Ch. 40).

The most immediate threat to life chances of some ethnic 'minority' groups concerns poverty. The poverty of the 1980s and 1990s has fallen disproportionately upon people of colour and particularly on the women from these groups, especially in the inner cities (Jencks and Peterson 1991). The state's role in relation to the question of poverty is a matter of debate (see Part 6); however, it is clear that the withdrawal of welfare support has created additional hardship for those in poverty. Most disconcerting of all is that changed policies of taxation and welfare have meant that children have suffered most from the withdrawal of state support (Halsey and Young Ch. 49). In educational terms, children in poverty have begun school disadvantaged and are likely to be further disadvantaged by under-resourced, inner-city, ghetto schools (Kozol 1991). However, Western states have retreated from initiating large-scale programmes to deal with the problem of poverty and education in the inner cities. The questions raised by this response are those of why the state has been reluctant to respond on a large and systematic scale to this problem and, if it did, what kind of response would be most appropriate?

The Restructuring of Education

Over the last decade there has been a fundamental restructuring of education in Western societies. However, to understand the complex causes that have shaped this restructuring involves an attempt to distinguish what is generally applicable to all post-industrial societies from what are specific to particular countries. Throughout the Western world, for instance, there have been similar changes in education, which seems to denote an international 'convergence' irrespective of national ideologies, politics, or power relations. These changes include the development of mass tertiary education with significant increases in age cohorts going to university as part of an overall increase in post-compulsory education; emphasis on life-long education; the attempts to break down the distinction between academic and vocational education; the devolution of educational decision-making; and problems of funding (Halsey Ch. 39). At the same time, it would be difficult to believe that the state-led restructuring of education, particularly in the Anglophone societies, was merely epiphenomenal (Skocpol 1994): that is, merely a reaction to underlying economic and social changes.

The defining element in the restructuring of education in Anglophone societies has been the imposition during the 1980s of economic and cultural renewal guided by what has become known as New Right (Levitas 1986) or Neo-Conservative (Aronowitz and Giroux 1986) ideology. This ideology guided the administrations of Reagan and Thatcher in the United States and Britain, and is equally influential in New Zealand and parts of Australia and Canada. New Right or Neo-Conservative ideology couples a neo-liberal view of the virtues of individual freedom and the free market with a traditional conservative view that a strong state is necessary to keep moral and political order (Gamble 1994). In part this political project attempted to turn deep-seated economic and social change to its own account by interpreting the crisis in Western society and its antecedents according to its own theoretical presuppositions. In post-modernist terms this could be seen as a 'totalizing' modernist project, imposing the grand narrative of the market and competitive individualism as an instrument of cultural renewal. In this specific sense, the advent of the New Right in the 1980s was similar to the kind of political projects advanced by the extreme Left and Right in Europe and the Soviet Union in the 1920s and 1930s. Nevertheless, despite the attempt to reconstruct societies according to their own ideological precepts, New Right theories had to connect with the common experiences of everyday life in a changing society. If they had not, they would have been rejected decisively in democratic elections, yet that was the experience of neither Reagan nor Thatcher. While New Right ideology had to address the way people experienced underlying changes in work, family, and education, it was also the case that it was integral to economic trends in the 1980s. The New Right political project was, for instance, instrumental in the development of the new global competition (Marchak 1991).

The questions concerning an understanding of educational restructuring turn, then, on the way fundamental changes in the economy and society relate to the ideological currents of the New Right which have guided the restructuring of education in Anglophone societies. Distinguishing between these forces of change is more than a purely academic puzzle. There is a practical policy pay-off to such an analysis, for without it, it is difficult to identify the causes of the outcomes of current policy formulations or the foundations on which alternative policies in education can be built.

Clearly one of the major tasks for sociology of education is to attempt to assess the relative consequence of secular changes in the nature of post-industrial or post-modern societies as opposed to the educational and societal changes initiated by the New Right. The difficulty of this task should not be underestimated. Indeed, a failure to grasp the political possibilities of societal changes helps to explain why viable left-of-centre alternatives are currently thin on the ground. However, one way in which research can illuminate the relationship between the New Right project and underlying change in Western Europe is to take seriously Skidelsky's (1995) theoretical view that all Western societies will have to conform to the New Right recipe for economic restructuring if they are to survive in the global economic competition. If this view is borne out it would confirm that there is an underlying and unfolding logic to the political economy of nations conforming to the interpretation of 'reality' advanced by the New Right. In a sense it would validate Mrs Thatcher's claim that 'there is no alternative'. The kind of comparative analysis Skidelsky's hypothesis demands is therefore urgent, and has profound political implications for education.

Before looking at the impact of the New Right on educational restructuring more closely we need to make two cautionary notes. Firstly, the underlying economic and social changes we have described apply unevenly to Western societies, and may have little applica-

tion to other societies such as those of the Pacific Rim, as Ashton and Sung (Ch. 12) and Green (Ch. 18) make clear. The demise of the state socialist societies of Eastern Europe has made social scientists far more sensitive to the differences between capitalisms in contrasting cultures (Clegg et al. 1990). This should alert us to the dangers of assuming that contemporary societies all conform to those of the West, and to the dangers of policy importation without due regard to the social, economic, and cultural context in which they have been 'seen to work' and in which they are to be implanted.

Secondly, as regards the New Right, a similar cautionary note needs to be made with respect to educational restructuring. As a term to describe the ideology behind market reforms in education, we should note that its precise meaning differs between societies (Dale and Ozga 1993). Common to all New Right ideologies are a series of theoretical assumptions derived from neo-classical economics about human nature, society, and social progress which comprise the neo-liberal wing of New Right ideology. In the United States and Britain in particular, these assumptions have been coupled with varieties of conservatism (Whitty 1990), although, as Whitty has noted, there is a question as to whether these two elements of New Right ideology are in tension. Over and above differences in New Right ideology the way its theoretical assumptions are interpreted and implemented also varies in different contexts. For example, in Britain and the United States New Right ideology struck a chord of popular appeal, whereas in New Zealand its policy agenda was largely imposed. However, despite such differences, there is a core of New Right thought that has set the terms for debate in Anglophone societies. We describe this core in what follows, and where appropriate we show its impact in the various societies where it has had a major influence on educational policy.

THE POLITICAL ECONOMY OF THE NEW RIGHT

In the early 1980s, the New Right argued that one of the fundamental causes of the decline of countries like the United States and Britain was cultural and in particular that state involvement in individuals' lives reduced their competitive and enterprising zeal. Economically, it was asserted that there are two pathological effects of state intervention. The first is that every dollar spent by the state was a dollar that would not go into investment in private enterprise. In the jargon of the day, the state 'crowds out' the private sector. Moreover, in so doing it stifles both the entrepreneurial initiative and imagination of rich and poor. It reduces the capacities of the rich because it overtaxes them. Therefore, with less disposable income the rich are not only less likely to invest in productive enterprises, but also the state itself loses out when the incidence of taxation is too high, as the rich will find ways of tax avoidance. For the poor, initiative is impaired because they come to depend upon state welfare 'handouts'. Hence the emergence of the notion of state dependency (Murray 1984; Galbraith 1992). In terms of the wealth and income polarization which has been a feature of Anglophone societies since the 1970s, the New Right take the view that individuals are the authors of their own poverty, and that state action to ameliorate their situation would be counterproductive. At its most extreme, this position is captured by Gilder's (1981) statement, 'In order to succeed, the poor most of all need the spur of their own poverty.' While Gilder's writing represented the extremes of polemic, a similar point is made in a more systematic way by Murray (1984) and Herrnstein and Murray (1994). The idea that the state cannot compensate for individual failure is part and parcel of the New Right view that the state is best out of people's lives. In taking this view the New Right was attempting to reverse the assumption made during the period of economic nationalism that the state had a responsibility to alleviate poverty through policies of full employment, and to create security and opportunity. However, it can be argued that the conservative element of the New Right with its emphasis on a strong state simply changes the configurations of state power in people's lives rather than reducing it, as we shall see when we look at education. The New Right nevertheless assert that economic and social renewal does not depend on state-led initiatives or changes to the underlying structures of society in terms of class, patriarchy, or racism, but on changing the incentives for individuals. It is through the creation of a culture of individual enterprise that economic success can be ensured in the new global economy. Consistent with this view is the assump-

tion that economic reform could not be led by macropolicies, especially of the kind advocated by Keynes and which had guided the full employment policies of the period of economic nationalism. Rather it is microeconomic reform that will lead to world competitiveness, through economic deregulation aimed at releasing market forces. This is seen as essential in order to reform the economy to approximate the neo-classical utopian vision of perfect competition. Given their general catechism—markets good, governments bad (Gamble 1986)—it is not surprising that attempts would also be made to increase market competition within the education system.

MARKET REFORMS IN EDUCATION
The themes of individual motivation, microeconomic change, the virtues of competition, and fiscal restraint all have their parallels in education restructuring. The cornerstone of New Right education policy has been the introduction of market competition into all the education sectors (Lauder Ch. 25; Brown Ch. 26). There are three aspects to this. Firstly, the introduction of market competition involves a devolution of financial, staffing, and policy issues to individual educational institutions. In effect schools, colleges, and universities in the public sector become self-managing on the lines of small- to medium-size businesses. Here there is a parallel between the commitment to microeconomic reform for the private sector and micro-reform in education. For the assumption is that once the market context has been established with the appropriate incentives and market disciplines, competition between educational institutions will serve to raise standards or they will simply go out of business because they cannot attract 'customers'. Educational research primarily, then, focuses on what makes, for example, an effective school (see Mortimore Ch. 31). Secondly, it is assumed that schools could compete successfully irrespective of the nature of the school intake. This argument made in the work of Chubb and Moe (Ch. 24) is particularly attractive to the New Right because it assumes that raising educational standards for all is simply a question of school management and quality teaching. In other words, school success or failure is determined by the management of the school and the quality of the

teachers. In effect, schools could compensate for society, so long, of course, as the appropriate leadership was in place to head the management team (Grace Ch. 20). This then enabled questions about family and child poverty and their impact on educational performance to be regarded as irrelevant. Indeed, the New Right have been quick to criticize any one who raised the link between pupil intake and school performance as evading responsibility. Well-managed schools coupled with pupil self-motivation, it is assumed, will make inroads into the eradication of poverty as individuals bettered themselves through education. Thirdly, the notion of parental choice is treated as unproblematic. As James Coleman (1992: 260) has succinctly noted:

The movement toward choice is the first step in the movement toward getting the incentives right in education—incentives for both the suppliers of educational services, that is, schools and their teachers, and for the consumers of education, that is parents and children. The incentives for schools ... would include an interest in attracting and keeping the best students they could. The incentives for parents and students would include the ability to get into schools they find attractive and to remain in those schools.

However, subsequent research, included in Part 4, has found this view wholly problematic with respect to overall academic achievement, equality of opportunity, democracy, and the impact of restructuring on the teaching profession.

MARKETIZATION, EQUALITY, AND DEMOCRACY

Ball *et al.*'s research (Ch. 27) has found that parents do not come to make choices with equal cultural and material resources. Moreover, the interests of parents and schools are not identical, as Waslander and Thrupp (Ch. 29) show, and for the privileged schools who could choose their intakes there has been little evidence of competition. One of the major flaws in the marketization of education is the assumption that schools can achieve equally, and hence compete successfully, independent of the nature of their intake. As school-effectiveness studies become increasingly sophisticated so Coleman's (1966) original hypothesis that student mix within a school is a key factor in the overall achievement of the school is now a well-confirmed hypothesis (see Willms and McPherson Ch. 42). This being the case, there is an issue

of whether overall standards of education will be raised by competition or whether, as unpopular schools go into a spiral of decline, the educational standards of the students in those schools will also decline: in other words, whether the introduction of competition into schools will lead to a polarization of intakes and educational achievement, thereby eroding the ethos underlying the comprehensive or common school and bringing back covert selection to successful schools. A further issue then emerges with respect to equality of opportunity. If individual schools cannot compensate for society because their student intake's prior achievement is relatively low due to poverty, and if research can show that a socio-economically well-balanced school can best raise their educational achievement, then some organizing principle for the system as a whole needs to be instituted in order to promote equality of opportunity.

However, equality of opportunity has been redefined by the New Right as 'equity', and this seems to mean something more akin to the right of each individual to a sound compulsory education with ever-rising standards, so that individuals can compete in the global labour market. In effect, it turns its back on state intervention to regulate the competition for credentials in order to reduce social disadvantage. This therefore signals a retreat from 'equity' as understood in the strong sense defined by Coleman (1968). In this paper Coleman added, to the standard notions of equality of access to education and equality of treatment, the notion of equality of results. The significance of equality of results was that it applied to identifiable social groups rather than individuals, and implied active intervention by states to create equality of outcomes for different groups.

If the New Right version of equity constitutes a retreat from active state intervention, it is worth noting that equity can also be used in a more radical sense. For groups who have struggled for culturally autonomous schools it can be used to articulate a politics of difference whereby culturally different systems of schooling develop different qualifications. Equity would then be seen as similar to parity of esteem, that is, qualifications from different systems would be seen as commensurate. Such a position is different from Coleman's concept of equality of results, because he envisaged the same outcomes in terms of qual-ifications. In this case, the shift in terminology from equality of results to equity reflects an underlying change from an education system with one relatively linear qualifications struc-ture to a system of parallel structures, reflect-ing a radical pluralist rather than a bureaucratic and assimilationist society. This new terrain of contestation is an example of where fundamental social change has met the New Right head-on.

In relation to democracy, there are two broad criticisms that can be made about the marketization of education. Firstly, the ques-tion of the link between democracy and edu-cation is rejected (see Lauder Ch. 25). The realm of freedom for the New Right is that of private consumption, so that schools are not seen to play any part in the politics of libera-tion. Here there is something of a self-fulfill-ing prediction, for if students are socialized into a competitive market for education then a salient aspect of the hidden curriculum may well be to create the possessive individuals necessary to market behaviour (see Apple 1982). Thus the marketization of education can be seen as a historically decisive moment, in that knowledge is not only structured to be economically productive but itself becomes wholly a commodity under market condi-tions. As Bernstein (1990) has put it, 'Knowl-edge, after nearly a thousand years, is divorced from inwardness and is literally dehuman-ized' (p. 136). This judgement is related to the modernist Marxist view that the inner logic of capitalist society is that of the commodifica-tion of human activity.

THE IMPACT OF RESTRUCTURING ON THE TEACH-ING PROFESSION

The introduction of market reforms in educa-tion can also be viewed as a mechanism for the control of teachers' practice in which rewards are based on individual performance, merit pay, and the threat of unemployment if schools do not perform. However, such rewards and sanctions are both highly prob-lematic in an educational context. Student achievement is the result of a collective effort over many years and cannot be seen as the product of a single teacher, while the reasons for falling school rolls may have little to do with the value they add to a student's learning. There is, therefore, an open question as to whether a market system, in failing to take

account of teacher's sense of collective profes-sional autonomy, can produce the higher stan-dards claimed for it.

Moreover, it has also alienated teachers, since it is assumed that teachers will resist the changes because it is not in their interests to submit themselves to market regimes in edu-cation. This is a central New Right assertion based on what is called 'public choice' theory (see Lauder Ch. 25). According to this theory, teachers who work in the public sector are part of a state monopoly, within which teachers are 'featherbedded'. Through zoning, they were guaranteed students, and hence a job, irre-spective of their performance. This is known by public-choice theorists as 'provider cap-ture' because of their belief that state educa-tion is run in the interests of middle-class providers rather than consumers (students, parents, employers, and taxpayers). This has led New Right governments to implement change rapidly and to attack the sources of teachers' collective strength, their unions and professional organizations. Hargreaves (Ch. 23) calls this 'structural' change because it is imposed 'from above' without the consent of most teachers. What has been offered to teachers in compensation is a variant of what Hargreaves describes as post-modern and Whitty (Ch. 19) post-Fordist organization, which holds out the promise of far greater opportunities in the decision-making of the self-managed school, although comparative research does not tend to support this sense of promise (Whitty Ch. 19). These argu-ments are supported by Darling-Hammond (Ch. 22), who claims that existing educational policies in the United States with respect to funding and teacher education are wholly inadequate for a post-bureaucratic education system. These claims raise serious questions about the nature and strategy of educational restructuring and its impact on teachers and students. As Hargreaves (Ch. 23) notes, there is 'a fundamental choice between restructur-ing as bureaucratic control, where teachers are controlled and regulated to implement the mandate of others, and restructuring as pro-fessional empowerment, where teachers are supported, encouraged, and provided with newly structured opportunities to make improvements of their own'. Hence what Hargreaves calls 'mandates' from the state will not themselves produce more desirable outcomes in education. What may be intended by state policy may be changed or subverted or adapted to teachers' assumptions about their professional role in the classroom (Ball and Bowe 1992).

'FREE' MARKETS IN EDUCATION AND THE STRONG STATE

Markets are always embedded within an institutional context over which the state continues to have a significant influence (Dale Ch. 17). The introduction of market policies in education has been accompanied by increasingly strong powers arrogated by the New Right state. What we have witnessed in countries where a New Right agenda has been close to full implementation is the devolution of certain powers of decision-making in relation to the self-managed school, and greatly increased powers of state regulation. This, then, is another example of the paradox of the strong state and the free market (Gamble 1988).

The increased powers of regulation of education have, in the New Right dominated societies, tended to take three forms. Firstly, in the light of the pressure exerted by the global auction and burgeoning public expenditure, the state has sought to weaken the institutional pressures on increasing state expenditure on education (Codd, Gordon, and Harker Ch. 16). Here the decentralization of educational resourcing involves the attempt to encourage market behaviour, and in doing so seeks to weaken the power of teacher unions, as national or state-wide employment conditions (on which union solidarity is based) are replaced by schools determining their own employment policies. The consequence of these policies of decentralization was a retreat from federal funding in the United States in the 1980s and the capping or reduction of expenditure on education in other New Right dominated countries.

The catchphrase of New Right decentralization policies has been that of greater parental and community choice and control. Choice in relation to educational markets is problematic, but so is the notion of parental or community control. Control in this context can mean the management of schools by parents and communities, rather than bureaucracies (Spring 1993). It is a way of recruiting low-cost educational administrators and removing bureaucracies with expertise to challenge central policies. In effect, parents and communities merely become technical instruments of the state's will under these conditions. However, as Fine (Ch. 30) shows through her case studies of community participation in education, the control and management of education can never be simply a technical question; it always has a political dimension. In Fine's view, unless communities are prepared to mobilize politically, community initiatives in inner-city schools will fail.

A further reason why the promise of devolved control cannot be taken at face value is because at the same time that schools have been given greater 'autonomy' over the allocation of resources and selection policies, the school curriculum has become increasingly centralized (whether it be at state or national levels in the United States, or embodied in national curricula as in Britain or New Zealand). This constitutes the second form of control. The motivations for introducing these centralized curricula are not necessarily linked to economic productivity. Goodson (1990, cited in Hargreaves 1994) has suggested that it is an attempt to reassert a national identity in the face of an increasingly globalized economy and weakened nation states, since subjects like history are particularly prominent while information technology is relegated to a minor role. Ball (1994) sees the introduction of the national curriculum in Britain as a struggle between restorationist and modernizing conservatives. The latter are more concerned to tailor the curriculum to post-Fordist economic possibilities while the former are, as Goodson suggests, more concerned with the shaping of a national identity. Ball suggests that the restorationists have won the day in Britain. It can be argued, however, that these attempts to assert a national identity reflect the interests of the white male élites (Apple Ch. 36; Aronowitz and Giroux 1991). They are therefore a particular, contemporary variant of Green's (1990) view that education has been, historically, integral to the formation of the nation state. In this case, it is not so much the formation of the nation state which is at stake but its re-formation in the light of the restructuring of the state–education relationship (Dale Ch. 17). Such curricula do, therefore, raise the question (addressed in the papers in Part 5) of whose knowledge is to be taught and what kind of national identity such curricula are designed to foster.

There is, however, another side to the introduction of such curricula; it can also be argued that they serve to promote equality of opportunity because all students, irrespective of class, gender, or ethnicity, have to study them. In this sense it removes, in principle, the link between a status hierarchy of subjects and the opportunities such status affords to those fortunate enough to be selected to take them. In the past, research has shown that the higher the status of a subject, the more likely it has been taken by students of a higher social class background. However as Apple (Ch. 36) argues, this is not the case at university, where technical and commercial knowledge is at a premium and is linked to a university's status and the social class and ethnic background of its students.

At the school level, the consequence of the introduction of centralized curricula is that the power of parents and communities over a key aspect of education is removed, leaving them with the technical aspects of management. However, the removal of power is taken a step further by the third form of increased central control. The New Right have also introduced new forms of accountability and performance indicators. These 'reforms' have involved an attempt to link the accountability of educational institutions, and where possible individual teachers, to the assessment of students. There are several reasons for this. The first is related to the programme of educational restructuring: as Torrance shows (Ch. 21), assessment has been used to attempt to change teaching practice. The second is that it has been used to regulate competition between institutions. In Britain this has been most highly developed through various league tables of performance and the flow of resources. In educational systems based on choice and competition, resources follow students on the assumption that students will be attracted to the most successful institutions. Less successful institutions as indicated by league tables will suffer a decline in student numbers while the more successful will attract an increase, and funding will be regulated accordingly. Thirdly, there is clearly a political motivation for introducing modes of accountability which seem to link teaching performance to student success and failure, for it seems as if the state as representative of the people has finally opened the closed shop of professionalism to a set of transparent performance indicators that can be easily understood. However, as Pollitt (1990) has argued, performance indicators in the public sector as a whole are at best proxies for efficiency. Most do not relate to effectiveness or quality: a point forcefully made by Torrance. This then raises the question of whether performance indicators are merely a matter of political expediency. If they are, their effects are none the less real, for educational institutions are being reshaped by them. Indeed, it has been argued by Peters (1990) that the traditional purpose of the university education is undergoing fundamental change from an induction into a Western liberal education to one designed to enhance economically effective knowledge, and that performance indicators are instrumental in initiating this change.

Education, Inequality, and Social Justice

The preceding discussion should serve to remove any lingering remnants of the view popularized by Parsons (1959) and Kerr et al. (1973) that industrial evolution entails education moving inexorably from ascription to merit, dogma to democracy, and inequality to social justice. Indeed, the study of education at the end of the twentieth century compels us to reconsider questions first addressed during the Enlightenment. In these terms it is useful to think of education in the modern, if not post-modern world, as a means of achieving a balance between equality, liberty, and community. We want here to reconsider all three. Though sociologists have contributed heavily to the debate about equality, the problem is much more than a sociological one. In 1651 Hobbes wrote:

Nature hath made man so equal, in the faculties of body, and mind; as that though there be found one man sometimes manifestly stronger in body, or of quicker mind than another; yet when all is reckoned together, the difference between man, and man, is not so considerable, as that one man can thereupon claim to himself any benefit, to which another may not pretend, as well as he. (Thomas Hobbes 1934: 63)

Egalitarian claims and anti-egalitarian rebuttals are probably more strident now, and certainly more often couched in sociological terms, than they were in the seventeenth century. Yet Hobbes's formulation (substituting 'person' for 'man' and a pronoun for both sexes if the English language possessed one) defines the contemporary debate as well as anything written in the intervening 300 years. We would say now that the debate contains empirical propositions from both genetics and sociology, the one referring to natural differences and the other referring to the social psychology of people's perceptions of social rights. But the central assertion is an evaluative one, as it must be. For the debate is fundamentally about the values which ought to be reflected in the actual relations of women and men in society.

Controversy goes on at three relatable but not necessarily related levels. First, there is a clash of priorities between different values presumed to be realizable in society; second, there is the philosophically and logically difficult intellectual task of clarifying the language of the debate; and third, there is the tedious labour of relating theoretical constructions to the changing empirical realities of the social world. The distinctive contribution of sociology must clearly be at the third level. It is well known, of course, that the political persuasion of many western sociologists has leant towards egalitarian politics, by contrast with the typical orientation of biologists and psychologists since Herbert Spencer and Social Darwinism. Perhaps there is a sociology of intellectual culture which might partly explain these persistent political differences in terms of the social consciousness induced by work in the different disciplines and the selective effect of their popular representations on the recruitment of personalities to them. At all events, whatever the provenance of ethical discussion, the premises of argument are set by a moral affirmation about the value of equality in relation to other values such as liberty, efficiency, prosperity, or community sought by people in their dealings with others. In this sense the debate, we suspect, is unresolvable, and for that reason all the better phrased in the blunt banality used by R. H. Tawney to dismiss the inegalitarian— 'if a man likes that sort of dog then that is the sort of dog a man likes'.

Yet to begin with this fundamental simplicity is in no way to detract from the work of those who have contributed to the second level of discussion by seeking greater conceptual clarity as to the meaning of the terms used in the debate. John Rawls's (1971) *A Theory of Justice* is now a classic case in point. He adopts the device of the 'original position'—an 'as if' story of the rational choices that might be expected from an individual contemplating different societies with known different systems of social relationship and distribution but an unknown position within them for the contemplator—to illuminate the problem of value choice. Brian Barry's (1965) *Political Argument* is another example of a book which educates us to avoid terminological confusion and to use words to the fullest extent of their potential for precise distinction (see also Sen 1992). Yet if we only consider Brian Barry's (1973) short book on *The Liberal Theory of Justice* or Rawls's (1971) long one, it becomes clear that no amount of conceptual clarification, however sophisticated and erudite, solves the problem of what we have referred to as the first level. Thus Barry, through an argument of delicate philosophical dissection, clearly demonstrates how a minimal adjustment to Rawls's social and psychological assumptions opens up the possibility of a crucial shift from liberal to egalitarian forms of society. Nevertheless, the problem at the first level remains, and Barry ends with a personal statement of preferences which he does not offer as compelling, only as consonant with his preceding argument. 'I feel a strong attachment to liberalism in relation to ideas while believing that in matters of political, social and economic organization altruistic collaboration is worth giving up a good deal of efficiency for, and fearing that hierarchy is more soundly based in human psychology than I would altogether like' (Barry 1973: 168). At the same time, this passage indicates the existence of a third level of argument which sustains the first and second levels by challenges to test concept against relevant fact, typically under conditions where either the pace of social change or the ingenuity of theorists outpaces the capacity of empirical enquiry.

Of course, politicians can be more or less serious even at the first level. Thus, when a Labour or Democratic politician tells us that she does not like the private sector of education but that the cost of abolition is too great a financial burden to face for the time being, she is offering an honest if debatable ordering of priorities. But when we hear Conservative and Republican politicians suggest that all children should have an equal opportunity of acquiring intelligence, and of developing their talents and abilities to the full, and then go on to tell us that they favour a market system of education, the reader or listener is understandably baffled as to what priorities are being offered. It is only by hearing the first affirmation as amiable rhetoric or the second as assuming the (false) empirical proposition that opportunity to develop intelligence is equal as between children in a market or comprehensive system that the two assertions can be reconciled. In the latter case, given conceptual clarity, empirical enquiry can settle such debate. This we take to be the distinctive business of the social scientist; and we will return to the question in considering a new political arithmetic shortly.

There has been widespread disillusionment and now, again, some renewed optimism concerning the possibilities of reaching a more egalitarian society through educational reform (Mortimore Ch. 31). Much sociological effort is needed to determine what education might contribute to wider participation in the material and cultural abundance potentially available to the members of a rich society. We are, of course, invited on every hand to espouse various utopias, among which Ivan Illich's outline of a convivial society was a previously fashionable one (Illich 1971; 1973). Nevertheless, whether we lean towards Illichian or other nostrums, there is inescapable controversy as to the relation between theory and policy, or what means might appropriately and effectively turn our dreams into realities. Our own view is basically that the society of equals has to be created by economic and political reform, and that the role of education must largely be to maintain such a society once it has been attained.

A good deal may be learned by looking back over the debate on the relation between equality and education, and in this connection Silver's (1991) review of British and American official polity towards poverty from 1960 to 1980 gives a fair picture of this element of intellectual and political history. But, as we shall argue, the origins of the mainstream of theory on which policy has been floated are to be found further back in the nineteenth century.

THE LIBERAL THEORY OF EDUCATIONAL EMBOUR-
GEOISEMENT

Looking back over the history of official policy in Europe and America, one can see through-

out it an unmistakable thread of egalitarianism. No less striking, however, is the fact of failure to realize egalitarian ends by educational means—a failure to which the virulence of current debate is itself a major witness. The basic reason is that the theory which has formed the foundation of Western policy is a false one, consisting of liberal concepts which have not stood the test of historical experience.

This liberal theory came out of the tradition of political economy in which, in Britain at least, the boundaries between economics and sociology were not drawn as sharply as they are now. The classic statement of the theory is to be found in a paper written by Alfred Marshall more than 120 years ago and delivered at the Reform Club in Cambridge, England, on 'The Future of the Working Class'.[7] This famous essay is the *locus classicus* of liberal theories about the relation of education to social class.[8] It is worth reconsidering because he was commenting on social change of a similar magnitude to the social transformation we have described in this chapter. Looking at views of social change can help to throw our own situation into sharper relief. Marshall was, of course, writing at a time and speaking in a place when women's contribution to intellectual life was virtually unrecognized, and when the division of labour between the sexes was such as to place women in the class system derivatively from the occupation of their fathers or husbands. He was in fact a devoted liberal who, in writing his Principles of Economics, was highly appreciative of Mrs Mill's contribution to John Stuart Mill's book on the same subject. The question, as Marshall put it, was:

whether it be true that the resources of the world will not suffice for giving to more than a small proportion of its inhabitants an education in youth and an occupation in after-life, similar to those which we are now wont to consider proper to gentlemen . . . The question is not whether all men will ultimately be equal—that they will certainly not—but whether progress may not go on steadily if slowly till the official distinction between working men and gentlemen has passed away; till, by occupation at least, every man is a gentleman.

Marshall's high-minded Victorian conception of the stratification system was focused on culture and character. These were the defined class attributes to which policy had to be directed. The theory was that culture and character were functions of education (which determine occupation) and occupational experience. The mediating variable was experience in work. The occupations of 'gentlemen' he saw as directly promoting high culture and refinement of character—qualities which require a careful and long–continued education. He further saw the occupational structure of his day as descending (in terms of its propensity to generate admirable personal qualities) through fine gradations from the high professions through the 'intermediate classes' down to 'that darker scene which the lot of unskilled labour presents . . . Vast masses of men who, after long hours of hard and unintellectual toil, are wont to return to their narrow homes with bodies exhausted and minds dull and sluggish.'

Marshall's proposals for liberation from mid-nineteenth-century conditions were contained in a sketch of a 'fancied country', from which the brutalizing effects of long hours of toil had been excluded, and in which no one would have an occupation which tended to make him anything else than a gentleman. This would be assured by technical progress, extensive education, and short hours of work.

He argued that such an education, economy, and society would be practical:

We know, then, pretty clearly what are the conditions under which our fancied country is to start; and we may formulate them as follows. It is to have a fair share of wealth, and not an abnormally large population. Everyone is to have in youth an education which is thorough while it lasts and which lasts long. No one is to do in the day so much manual work as will leave him little time or little aptitude for intellectual and artistic enjoyment in the evening. Since there will be nothing tending to render the individual coarse and unrefined, there will be nothing tending to render society coarse and unrefined.

But then, could such a society be maintained? Marshall went on to rebut the objections which were seriously advanced in Victorian England. First, he argued against the fear that a great diminution of the hours of manual labour would lead to economic ruin. This argument was the stock-in-trade of British employers from the middle of the nineteenth century and survived not only to the slump years of the 1930s, but as far as the Euroscep-tist opposition to the Maastricht Treaty in the 1990s. Thus, when the Bill presenting the Fisher Act of 1918 was before Parliament, we find R. H. Tawney repeating the Marshall argument against a memorandum of the Education Committee of the Federation of British Industries. The proposal was to abolish all exemption from school attendance for children under 14. The Federation of British Industries argued that: 'A period of eight hours a week taken out of working hours would impose a burden upon many industries which they would be quite unable to bear except on a basis of very gradual development.' Gradual indeed: for resistance to the Maastricht social protections remain lively.

Tawney couched the rebuttal in terms of outraged irony:

To suggest that British industry is suspended over an abyss by a slender thread of juvenile labour, which eight hours of continued education will snap, that after a century of scientific discovery and economic progress it is still upon the bent backs of children of fourteen that our industrial organization, and national prosperity, and that rare birth of time, the Federation of British Industries itself, repose—is not all this, after all, a little pitiful? (Hinden 1964)

Marshall's version of the argument is more sober, but otherwise identical. It is based on technological progress and the high return to skilled labour exploiting technologically advanced forms of capital. That knowledge is power was already a well-worn cliché, but that people could possess it with reduced toil was revolutionary thought, contrary to the common sense of all previous experience. None the less, Marshall went so far as to assert that the total work done per head of the population would be greater than it then was. All labour would be skilled and there would be no premium on setting people to tasks that required no skill. Inventions would increase and would be readily applied. His argument at this point reads like the familiar contemporary thesis of official policy throughout the industrialized and industrializing world—that investment in human resources is the cure for all things— but, as was consonant with his elevated view of human nature and society, he stressed the vigorous exercise of increased faculties and saw the direct outcome as an improvement in the level of civility and sensibility and only indirectly as an increase in material wealth. When Tawney developed this theme in the twentieth century the paramountcy of social over economic values became even more sharply emphasized.

In arguing the possibility of maintaining the new society once it had been attained, Marshall also dealt with the objection that a high standard of education could not be kept up because some parents would neglect their duty to their children:

A class of unskilled labourers might again grow up, competing for hard toil, ready to sacrifice the means of their own culture to increased wages and physical indulgences. This class would marry inprovidently: an increased population would press on the means of subsistence, the difficulty of imparting a high education would increase, and society would retrograde until it arrived at a position similar to that which it now occupies—a position in which people, to a great extent, ignore their duty of anticipating, before marriage, the requirements of the bodily and mental nurture of their children; and thereby compels Nature, with her sorrowful but stern hand, to thin out the young lives before they grow up to misery.

We see here the Malthusian spectre which continued to haunt the Victorians into the 1870s. Marshall pinned his faith on the two forces of self-respect (born of education) and external restraint ('Society would be keenly alive to the peril to itself of such failure, and would punish it as a form of treason against the state'). Thus Marshall concluded, 'every single condition would be fulfilled which was requisite for the continued and progressive prosperity of the country which we have pictured. It would grow in wealth—material and mental.'

MARSHALLIAN THEORY IN HINDSIGHT

At the present time, debate over adaptation to the competitive global economy has divided conservatives from socialists along lines of labour protection and social security. The Maastricht Treaty in Europe is the focus, in which Britain and the United States are pitted against the priorities so far followed by Germany, France, and Scandinavia. The ghost of Marshall is ignored in the Anglo-Saxon world, while the French President Chirac insists that job creation must not take precedence over the established worker protections of health, security, and minimum wages. Yet to look at Britain or America now, a century later, is to see that the preconditions postu-

lated in Marshall's 'fancied country' have, if anything, surpassed his youthful expectations in the era of economic nationalism. If unskilled labour is the measure of degradation and brutality, its proportion in the total occupied population of Great Britain had fallen from 14.8 per cent in 1931 to less than 8 per cent in 1971 (Halsey 1971). Indeed, the white-collar occupational groups (what he called the intermediate classes) grew by 176 per cent between 1911 and 1966 and now exceed 50 per cent of the total. Moreover, within their ranks the growing number of skilled scientific and technical workers has proliferated, reflecting a vast investment in human capital and an increasingly scientific and capital-intensive technology.

Meanwhile, from the end of the war until the mid-1970s, hours of work were reduced from 54 to 40 a week, and there was a marked increase, especially since the Second World War, in paid holidays. By 1972 three-quarters of the manual workers in the United Kingdom were enjoying 3 weeks' paid holiday, compared with 1 per cent in 1951 (HMSO 1973: 78). There were rising standards of housing and health. Affluence accumulated: the national product had quadrupled since 1900. In some respects at least, the material conditions of the ordinary person were superior to those of the gentleman in Marshall's day. Moreover, the position of women in society changed fundamentally as women won greater personal, economic, and social independence with the transformation of patriarchal society.

On the other hand, the redistribution of what in Victorian Britain was an almost exclusive concentration of private capital ownership in the hands of the richest 5 per cent of the nation—conditions approximating most closely to a simple Marxist definition of class—proceeded at no more than a snail's pace. In 1911 it was 86 per cent; by the 1950s, 67 per cent; and by 1970, 55 per cent (HMSO 1973). Since the 1970s this trend has been reversed, with the rich increasing their share of national wealth in both Britain and the United States (Commission on Social Justice 1994; Phillips 1991). Moreover, the small minority of the extremely wealthy is matched by another and larger minority of the poor. At the end of 1971 3 million people were receiving supplementary benefit in Britain and these, with their dependants, numbered 4½ million, including about a million children under sixteen. In the early 1990s Field (1995) suggests that half the population live in households drawing one of the principal means-tested benefits; though the middle mass of white-collar and affluent workers have enjoyed a considerable material prosperity, a steep hierarchy of income, power, and advantage remains. However, in the United States many 'middle' Americans have seen a decline in their living standards over the last 20 years (Levy 1987; Peterson 1994).

Universal compulsory education to age 16 has arrived, together with dramatically expanded provision at the secondary and further stages. But educational inequality has also remained. Its documentation is a recurrent theme of the sociology of education. The major burden of recent work is to show that the disparities persist despite educational expansion. Thus, educationally at least, there has been no assimilation of the working class into the middle class, though studies at various points in the century show a rising trend of aspirations for the education of their children among working-class families.

Marshall stood at the Victorian horizon of a century of liberal theories concerning the relations between education, occupation, and class. Halsey has traced the subsequent history of this tradition and theory elsewhere (Halsey 1972) and has argued that it has failed even in its own terms. Its aim—equality of opportunity in education—has eluded the policymakers. It may be, as James Coleman argues, that, as a pure object of policy, whether defined in input or output terms, the concept is useless in a pure form. Of course, if there were universal provision of all stages of education, the aim would be achieved definitionally: but in fact, selection and differential attainment between gender, class, and ethnic groups have remained an integral feature of passage to further stages of education and of entry to the hierarchy of occupational advantage.

Marshall himself, it may be noted, avoided the meritocracy problem which has faced later versions of the liberal theory (Young 1961; Herrnstein 1973), by building in the supply, demand, and price argument with respect to different kinds of labour on the assumption of technological advance. This advance has been realized and, in the post-war period, has resulted in more diverse origins among those in the most elevated occupational destina-

tions. But this pattern of recruitment to 'the top' co-exists with a very large measure of self-recruitment among manual workers.

Education in industrial societies has remained predominantly an avenue for the stable transmission of status from one generation to another, though this has not been incompatible with some inter-generational occupational mobility, not only through the relative expansion of skilled work (because of technical advance) and through the 'replacement' of 'deficient' numbers among the high-born (because of an inverse relation of social class to fertility) but also through successful educational and career competition by a minority of children born in the lower strata. The details of how much social mobility has been experienced in industrial countries in the twentieth century is summarized as 'constant flux' by Erikson and Goldthorpe (1992). The statistics show the steepness of the remaining inequality, with the upper-middle-class children having three times better-than-average chances, and the lower working class having less than half an average chance. Nevertheless, the degree of inequality has lessened with reduction at the top and slight relative improvement at the bottom of the hierarchy of social birth. So much for the progress of educational equality.

Marshall was, in essence, advancing a particular version of the embourgeoisement thesis, the theory that class is inexorably abated by the assimilation of the working class into the middle class as industrial society advances to ever higher levels of wealth and income.[9] For Marshall this assimilation was assured by technological progress leading to an amelioration of economic circumstances in work and social opportunities and attitudes in non-work for the working-classes. Normative assimilation was also crucial to his theory— the spread, that is, of 'gentlemanly' character and culture, partly from occupational experience and reinforced by increased and prolonged education.

However, though Marshall is not specifically mentioned, the theoretical and empirical demolition of the liberal version of the embourgeoisement thesis by Goldthorpe *et al.* (1969) is completely applicable to his essay. As these modern authors have argued,

'increases in earnings, improvements in working conditions, more enlightened and liberal employment policies and so on, do not in themselves basic-ally alter the class situation of the industrial worker in present-day society. Despite these changes, he remains a man who gains his livelihood through placing his labour at the disposal of an employer in return for wages, usually paid by the piece, hour or day.'

Characteristic differences in the work situations of manual and non-manual employees still widely persist. Hence these writers regard with some scepticism the broad evolutionary perspectives of Western industrialism in which 'the emergence of a "middle-class" society is seen as a central process resulting more or less automatically from continuing economic growth'. Rising affluence and advances in the technical organization of industry are not likely in themselves to bring about a radical restructuring of the stratification hierarchy. At best there is a classless inegalitarianism. And the interpretation which Goldthorpe puts on the developments that have occurred is rather one of 'normative convergence between certain manual and non-manual groups'.

Marshall's version of the embourgeoisement prediction has not, therefore, been confirmed by events. Not only has there not been a 'one-way' assimilation of the character and culture of working-class into middle-class life, but it has also not taken the direction of universalizing the life-style of an ideal late-Victorian Cambridge don (Halsey 1992). Marshall did not address himself to the complications of a sophisticated theory of social consciousness. He in effect assumed that the 'gentlemanly' culture of his day would be the common culture for both the women and the men of a rich society. He was only dimly aware of the high cost in cultural terms of the extreme forms of divisions of labour that have been necessitated by technologically-based economic growth.[10] Equally, at the turn of the last century, he could not anticipate the consequences of the breakup of colonialism. Hence he could not foresee the development of socially and ethnically pluralistic societies, within which assimilationist policies and educational programmes would be rejected for failing to recognize the authentic diversity of cultures, lifestyles, and individual preferences, which would characterize post-modern visions of Marshall's 'fancied country'. But what cannot be denied is that, quite apart from its intricate relation to liberty, equality also

presupposes a solid basis in community. It is, of course, for this reason that American scholars, including Coleman (Ch. 4), Bellah *et al.* (1985), and Gans (1988) have examined the relationship between individualism, community, and society. In an educational context, John Dewey's *Democracy and Education* has profound contemporary relevance. Equally, the idea of socialism as fellowship (Terrill 1973) is central to the British native brand of political thought which runs through Tawney to Titmuss. It is this tradition which lends coherent support to the idea of community schooling as an educational means towards both community and equality (Dennis and Halsey 1981).

Determinism and Openness in Social Change

The liberal conceptions underlying official policy have always lacked an adequate theory of learning. For example, the experience of the American Compensatory Education movements or the British Education Priority Areas (EPAs), has had the effect of locating the origins of inequality at earlier and earlier stages in the life-cycle. But in the end the criticism of the liberal approach becomes an attack on the conception of class held by Marshall and later liberal theorists. In its recent history, particularly in the hands of economic liberals, the concept of class is trivialized to the point where differences of parental attitude are conceived of as separate factors rather than as an integral part of the work and community situation of children (see also Mohanty Ch. 34). There are, of course, and always have been variations of ambitiousness and levels of aspirations at any given economic or income level. But it is essential to insist that the effect of class on educational experience is not to be thought of as one factor from which parental attitudes and motivations to succeed in education are independent. A theory which explains educational achievement as the outcome of a set of individual attributes has lost the meaning of those structural forces which we know as class. An adequate theory must also attend to those structural inequalities of resource allocation which are integral to a class society.

Thus, any attempt to free education from its antecedents and consequences in the class system has to include structural forces as well as individual attributes. Both within and outside the formal educational system, there are social forces which weigh systematically against working-class children in respect of those types of learning which make for educational success and subsequently for advantageous occupational placement (Bernstein Ch. 3; Delpit Ch. 35). These include the quality of linguistic and other stimulation in family and neighbourhood, the expectations of teachers, the efficiency of co-operation between teachers and parents, and the occupational horizons which can be seen by children at different social vantage-points. Above all, it is a matter of resources. At every point, again both inside and outside the schools, working-class children have a great deal less spent on their opportunities for learning than have their more fortunate middle-class contemporaries. The association of social class with educational achievement will not therefore be explained by a theory or eliminated by a policy which falls short of including changes in public support for learning in the family and the neighbourhood, the training of teachers, the production of relevant curricula, the fostering of parental participation, the raising of standards of housing and employment prospects and, above all, the allocation of educational resources. The translation of such a theory into action would require political leadership with the will to go beyond the confines of traditional liberal assumptions.

OBSTACLES TO EQUALITY I: AN INELUCTABLE
OCCUPATIONAL HIERARCHY

There are three persistent types of argument against the viability of egalitarian theory which deserve specific consideration. The first concerns the immutability of occupational hierarchy, postulating a *de facto* necessity for some jobs to be more distasteful, unrewarding, and injurious to health than others despite (and possibly because of) the technical advances on which Alfred Marshall pinned so much hope. The global economy and strategies of competition designed by national governments to invest in the skills of the national workforce, are in effect, the globalizing of occupational hierarchy. Given that life-chances in wide measure are determined by the individual's occupation, a hierarchy of social advantage seems to be inescapable and equality as opposed to equality of opportunity

therefore unobtainable. But even accepting this postulate, a more egalitarian society is not thereby rendered sociologically impossible. It is not difficult to imagine a wide range of counteracting social policies (apart from the obvious one of progressive taxation, wealth taxes, etc., against which objections are lodged in the name of liberty and economic efficiency). As Brian Barry has argued:

The first line of attack would be to spread the nastiest jobs around by requiring everyone, before entering higher education or entering a profession to do, say, three years of work wherever he or she was directed. (This would also have educational advantages). To supplement this there could be a call-up of, say, a month every year, as with the Swiss and Israeli armed forces but directed towards peaceful occupations. These steps would, of course, constitute a limited interference with occupational choice but one whose justice would be difficult to deny. (1973: 164)

And there are other such institutional reforms, both inside and outside education, which can be brought into play without making outrageous assumptions about 'human nature' or the price to be paid in terms of other widely held values in society. The development of the social wage into a citizen or participatory income (Parijs 1992), recognizing service to society other than by direct involvement in the labour market, is one such, and a radical step towards worldwide egalitarianism.

Value choice is again the nub of the issue. Hence, with a view to suggesting that equality and liberty need not come immediately and directly into conflict when a more equal society is sought, we may refer to the set of ideas which are labelled recurrent, or life-long, education, and the views of the Swedish economist Gosta Rehn (1972).

The average full-time industrial worker spends something like 100,000 hours of his or her life at work. There is here, therefore, a large arena for the application of both egalitarian and libertarian ideas. Responsible government on behalf of individual liberty has to go beyond the enforcement of contracts voluntarily entered and the natural tendencies of people to conspire against the rigours of the free market. Post-industrial society has to be committed to the efficient production of abundance, the maintenance of full employment, and the abolition of all unnecessary labour. On these assumptions it is possible to arrange deliberately for greater variation and diversity in the life-patterns of education, work, leisure, and retirement, in such a way as to transfer decision as far as possible from the bureaucracy to the individual. The underlying conception is of a modified social contract. The individual has a life-long bargain with society to work in exchange for material rewards and social security. In such a society the individual, within a broad framework of agreed rules, would determine the phasing and placing of the exchange, week by week, year by year, and over the course of the individual's whole lifetime. The sharp divisions of the life-cycle and the established patterns of education, leisure, and work, bequeathed by the harsh necessities of preindustrial society and entrenched in the rigid formulae of statutory school-leaving ages, weekly hours, annual holidays, and compulsory retirement ages would go. Instead, there would be 'flexi-time', study rights at personal discretion, vacation rights not tied to calendar years, sabbaticals, and temporary retirements not tied to old age (Handy 1994).

In order to effect these new freedoms, which are in any case gradually and patchily appearing in the rich countries, it would be desirable, though not absolutely necessary, to systematize the present piecemeal arrangements for providing income to those who are not in paid employment because they are young and in school, or unemployed, or pregnant, or sick, or old and therefore retired. Collectively, it would require decisions on the generalized drawing rights to be allocated to each citizen (see Halsey and Young Ch. 49). Obviously, there would have to be safeguards against improvidence and the absence of 'deferred gratification patterns'. But the general idea is one of institutional movement towards the reduction of bureaucracy and enlargement of personal choice. For example, there would be an age of compulsory schooling, but not as high as that currently set in the richer countries. Then everyone would have a basic study credit, which could go to all age groups, not only to children and the unborn, to cover living and tuition costs for a given number of years. The individual could claim her educational rights according to her own career management, and would not be pressed to extend her childhood as she characteristically now is. People would thus be encouraged to have low-skill jobs in youth,

and occupational status could become more a matter of age than class. And the right to further education could be transferred to leisure or to more affluent retirement if the individual so chose.

The point here is that lifelong education may in principle serve to increase both equality and liberty. The possibility of bringing about greater equality between generations is obvious enough. The danger is, however, that it could so easily be trivialized into gestures towards a more generous provision of adult education classes, sabbaticals, day-release courses, and distance-learning programmes. It would only be if lifelong education were taken seriously as a citizenship right, like social security or pensions, that the transformation of the established system in an egalitarian direction would be possible; and this would require ambitious institutional inventiveness, much more flexible relations between work and education, a move towards 'learning organizations' (Zuboff 1989), more optimistic definitions by teachers of educability and curriculum, a vast development of community schooling, and more bounteous educational budgets.

We have here a problem which is becoming central to educational policy and the correct forecasting of future demand for labour. The traditional theory was simple. Human wishes are limitless, therefore labour supply is essentially a matter of adjusting the flow of trained workers for the demands of an advancing industrial system. By and large, the twentieth century has seen more or less efficient adaptations along these lines. Moreover, the idea of human investment has gained in popularity despite the concurrent rise in determination to reduce public spending.

The other, more contentious theory is that technology is substituting for human labour in every field from manufacturing to surgery. The evidence according to R. Dore (1976) is that unemployment, especially among the unskilled or minimally educated, increases from slump to slump and never fully recovers in subsequent booms. Thus the simplistic expansionism of past policy in education requires more urgent search for paths to full employment, the sharing of scarce work and, above all, new mechanisms for distributing income more equally in an ever-richer society.

OBSTACLES TO EQUALITY 2: THE IMPORTANCE OF SCHOOLING

The second obstacle to be considered may be termed the Jencks pessimism. We are not here concerned with the relation of educational opportunity and educational attainment to social origin, which has always been close and continues to be so, but with the linkage of education to subsequent life-chances, and therefore the possibilities of education as instrument for changing social distributions. This issue lies at the centre of the controversy which was so explosively refuelled by Christopher Jencks (1972; 1977). Jencks argues that the American occupational structure is open in the sense that a relatively loose relation between social origin and occupational destination is largely to be accounted for by factors which, as far as the individual is concerned, might be regarded as luck, even though some of them have a structural basis. Again it needs to be remembered that this argument is based on a study of male workers. Nevertheless, in his formulation, largely derived from the Blau and Duncan (1968) findings, Jencks writes:

While occupational status is more closely related to educational attainment than to any other thing we could measure, there are still enormous status differences among people with the same amount of education. This remains true when we compare people who have not only the same amount of schooling, but the same family background and the same test scores. Anyone who thinks that a man's family background, test scores and educational credentials are the only things that determine the kind of work he can do in America is fooling himself. At most, these characteristics explain about half the variation in men's occupational statuses. This leaves at least half the variation to be explained by factors which have nothing to do with family background, test scores or educational attainment.

Some of this unexplained variation is attributable to intra-generational occupational mobility. But Jencks is concerned to stress a different set of causative factors: 'Much of the variation is probably due to chance (one steel worker gets laid off and takes a temporary job as a painter, while another keeps his job because his plant happens to be busier). Some is due to choice (a businessman decides to give up making underwear and become a clergyman).' And on income equal-

ity, Jencks adds: 'Income also depends on luck: chance acquaintances who steer you to one line of work rather than another, the range of jobs that happens to be available in a particular community when you are job-hunting, the amount of overtime work in your particular plant, whether bad weather destroys your strawberry crop . . . and a hundred other unpredictable accidents.'

Jencks's (1972) argument was a response to the previously orthodox view that education reform was the best mechanism for breaking the inter-generational curse of poverty. In one sense, then, he produced an essay in the demolition of popular explanations of economic inequality, given that we cannot blame economic inequality primarily on genetic differences in individual capacities for abstract reasoning:

since there is nearly as much economic inequality among men with equal test scores as among men in general. We cannot blame economic equality primarily on the fact that parents pass along their disadvantages to their children, since there is nearly as much inequality among men whose parents have the same economic status as among men in general. We cannot blame economic inequality on differences between schools, since differences between schools seem to have very little effect on any measurable attribute on those who attend them.

Academic critics questioned Jencks's statistical analyses (*Harvard Educational Review* 1973). No less an authority than James Coleman was not entirely satisfied with them. He criticizes Jencks essentially for failing to distinguish clearly between two meanings of inequality—inequality of opportunity and inequality of result. He argues, quite correctly, that Jencks's intention is to discuss inequality of result but that in fact he spends his time on inequality of opportunity. What Jencks demonstrates, of course, is that equalizing opportunities through schooling will not change inequality of income between individuals. Schooling explains only about 12 per cent of the variance in income. Coleman complains that the explanation for the inequality of income accruing to jobs cannot explain the people who happen to occupy those jobs. The former problem is not directly tackled by Jencks. By demonstrating the absence of a relation between income distribution and distribution of schooling and family characteristics, on the one hand, however negatively, he points to the direct truth that the basic trouble with the poor is that they have no money. But on the other hand, by the form of analysis adopted, he is left with a large unexplained variance in income which, in various formulations, he attributes to luck and a capriciously if not arbitrarily distributed competence (see Goldthorpe Ch. 41 for a discussion of 'luck' and caprice in a market society).

Then followed, however, a second analysis (Jencks 1977). The $400,000 (Jencks *et al.*'s estimate) spent on this new analysis purchased a restoration of the common picture of the universe we know and do not necessarily love. But sociologists will do well to resist this over-reaction, as they resisted when previously encouraged toward nihilistic despair about the possibility of educational paths to equality. The more sensible judgement is that the Jencks team is to be commended for taking criticisms of *Inequality* seriously, for defining more rigorously the variables of family, personality, and schooling, for using these definitions in a Herculean effort of reanalysis, and for adding to the value of the answers by refining the questions. That way lies the progress in social science to which the profession aspires.

The restoration is, in any case, by no means complete. The old figure for the percentage of variance in occupational status explained by family background was 32; the new figure is 48. The old figure for schooling was 42 per cent; the new is 55 per cent. Combining the variables of family background, test scores, years of schooling, and personality traits, it now appears that the characteristics which people take into the market on first entry explain between 55 and 60 per cent of variance in adult occupational status and between 33 and 41 per cent of variance in male annual earnings.

Thus the general thrust of the *Inequality* argument is not blocked by recalculation. For example, whereas in *Inequality* the expected difference between the occupational status of brothers was 82 per cent of the expected difference between pairs of unrelated men, the new percentage is 72. Clearly the revised figure does not afford dramatically enlarged scope to the social engineers. Yet readers are likely to notice a marked change in tone between the two publications. This is partly because *Who Gets Ahead?* has a lot less to say about public policy. More fundamentally, it is due to a shift in statistical presentation: the earlier book focused on within-group differences (means).

Inequality attacked the utopian hopes of the Great Society for widespread reform through educational engineering. The dramatic effect of that essay in demolition, however, rested largely on its demonstration of the limits of social action. People with similar family backgrounds, test scores, and schooling subsequently scattered themselves over the range of occupational statuses and incomes to about three-quarters the extent of the scatter of people in general. In that sense, American society was an open lottery. But by the same token, the scope for social engineering on behalf of a principled allocation of life chances was woefully small. If schooling explained only 12 per cent of the variance in men's incomes, then complete equalization of schooling would at best reduce income inequality by only 12 per cent. The critics rightly complained that to assume it is possible to change the value of one variable without changing the totality of relations between variables in a system of plural causation is statistically convenient but sociologically invalid. If America gave everyone the same schooling, it would, in the process, completely change the class structure, the labour market, and indeed its whole social self.

In *Who Gets Ahead?* these objections are accepted. Moreover, Jencks *et al.* also accept criticism of the undue importance they previously attributed to luck, narrow their definition of the variables listed above, and discuss the implications for the labour market of a radically equalized distribution of human capital. Paradoxically, however, one of the features of social life in the 1990s is the increased sense (and reality) of economic insecurity experienced by all social groups. Consequently, occupational biographies and careers may be increasingly determined by 'luck' in that corporate organizations are subject to restructuring, rationalization, downsizing, re-engineering, takeovers, and so forth, irrespective of the individual's competence and commitment to his or her employer (Brown Ch. 45).

OBSTACLES TO EQUALITY 3: GENETIC DISTRIBUTIONS
The third obstacle is the alleged structural feature on which Jensen, Hernstein, and Murray in America and Eysenck in Britain lay so much stress—the argument that

differences in educational attainment are rooted in genetic differences between races and classes. A notorious formulation of this argument was published by Arthur Jensen (1969) in the *Harvard Educational Review* ('How Much can we Boost IQ and Scholastic Achievement?'), of which his *Genetics and Education* (1972) is an extended version and of which a popular version was published by Hans Eysenck under the title *Race, Intelligence and Education*. Much of Jensen's extensive marshalling of the evidence is uncontroversial. Whether you take social classes or racial minority groups in America, there are incontrovertible differences in the average scores. On all this it may be said that the scientific mapping of measured performances is necessary to informed discussion; but the explanation for test differences, and even less the question of the relation between test scores and the distribution of whatever we might mean by intelligence (other than that which is measured by IQ tests) remains.

The distributions and correlations of test scores are not at issue. The importance of Jensen is that he advances a theory about causes together with advice about consequences. In both of these realms reasonable people can differ. On the side of causes or explanations, the question he asks is whether the average difference between American blacks and American whites in IQ (a difference of ten to fifteen points) is either genetic, or a combination of genetic and environmental influences, or environmental. Eysenck polemically called the second type of theory hereditarian and the third type environmentalist, whereas obviously the first is hereditarian, the third environmentalist, and the second a combination of the two. Jensen is more careful acknowledging that one cannot formally generalize from within-group heritability to between-group heritability, but concludes that 'a largely genetic explanation of the evidence on racial and social group differences in educational performance is in a stronger position scientifically than those explanations which postulate the absence of any genetic differences in mental traits and ascribe all behavioural variation between groups to cultural differences, social discrimination, and inequalities of opportunity—a view that has long been orthodox in the social sciences and in education'.

Jensen thus places himself behind the second type of explanation, excluding the purely hereditarian view and regarding the purely environmentalist theory as dubious almost to the point of impossibility. Our view of the evidence is that the purely environmentalist theory is much less implausible. For one thing, we take seriously the calculations of heritability produced by Christopher Jencks in his *Inequality*. Curiously enough, Jensen ignores Jencks's calculations, which yield much lower estimates than his own of the variance in IQ attributable to genetic factors.

Still more important is the issue of consequences, for these take us from science to politics. Jensen is last, if not first, an American individualist, and he pleads for diversity of opportunity and treatment in a way which reflects his appreciation, perhaps over-appreciation, of the huge variability in genetic make-up which is such an important fact about the human species. No reasonable person could quarrel with that as such. But, like Eysenck, Jensen has the blinkers of a psychologist and vastly overestimates the importance of IQ. He half-recognizes this when he notices that IQ differences are relevant to differences in levels of performance in traditional school structures. But he assumes, along with many of his environmentalist opponents, that IQ is overwhelmingly important in determining the placing of individuals in the economy. In respect of income distribution in America this is certainly not the case. In addition to Jencks's evidence, Bowles and Gintis (1976) have shown that IQ is of negligible importance by comparison with socioeconomic background and years of schooling in determining economic success as measured by a combination of occupational status and income. But if the Bowles-Gintis argument is taken seriously, the Jensen wrangle becomes largely irrelevant to the underlying questions of political and economic justice for American blacks and the American working class. In this sense, the Jensenist controversy is but a storm in the academic teacup.

However, the hereditarian controversy was fanned into fierce flame again in 1994 by Richard J. Herrnstein and Charles Murray in their *The Bell Curve: Intelligence and Class Structure in American Life*. It is a cunning book. Apparently even-handed and reasonable, it is in fact an explosive intervention from the political right. With respect to the genetics and environment debate no new data are produced, and European contributions e.g. from Bernstein (Ch. 3), Bourdieu (Ch. 2), or Boudon (1974) are ignored. Class is not defined, and the international studies of class mobility are not mentioned. Instead we are presented with a theory of class polarization which argues that the educational selectivity of the system works steadily along lines of IQ segregation to produce a 'cognitive élite' and an unqualified underclass. American blacks are doomed to belong to this underclass because they score a clear standard deviation below whites in IQ tests, and the hereditary component of capacity to show intelligence in tests is, according to Herrnstein and Murray, 60 per cent.

A critical review of their book edited by Steven Fraser (1994), *The Bell Curve Wars*, (see also Ch. 48) goes a long way towards neutralizing Herrnstein and Murray's polemic. Indeed, Stephen Jay Gould (1981) had already anticipated the main argument in his *Mismeasurement of Man* (1981). He deals with the 'four shaky premises' of the Bell Curve authors—that Intelligence is: firstly, a single number; secondly, capable of ranking people in linear order; thirdly, genetically based; and fourthly, effectively immutable. Students of the sociology of education, perhaps especially Americans whose culture specifically enjoins the pursuit of equality, must absorb the evidence on genetic and environmental interactions in education and society.

Arguments for a New Political Arithmetic

The idea of a new *political arithmetic* as a form of 'social accountability' is in our view a powerful one. When we think about all the claims to empirical 'truth' made by politicians and journalists over the last two decades, the need for independent research which subjects such assertions to account is crucial to the future of democracy. Political arithmetic has also represented an important 'methodology' for studying the nature of society and social institutions. This methodology can be traced back to Booth and the Webbs, if not to William Petty in the seventeenth century (Halsey 1994). In more recent times it has been used in many studies of social policy and social stratification, including that conducted by David

Glass in the 1950s and by Halsey *et al.* in the 1970s in order to survey the relationship between family, class, and education in post-war Britain. In their introduction to political arithmetic, Halsey *et al.* note that early proponents were:

concerned to describe accurately and in detail the social conditions of their society, particularly of the more disadvantaged sections, but their interest in these matters was never a disinterested academic one. Description of social conditions was a preliminary to political reform. They exposed the inequalities of society in order to change them. The tradition thus has a double intent; on the one hand it engages in the primary sociological task of describing and documenting the 'state of society'; on the other hand it addresses itself to central social and political issues. It has never, therefore, been a 'value free' academic discipline, if such were in any event possible. Instead, it has been an attempt to marry a value-laden choice of issues with objective methods of data collection. (Halsey, Heath, and Ridge 1980: 1).

At a time of increasing social inequalities and injustice, when the 'self-regulating' market threatens to undermine the foundations of social solidarity; when the advances of post-war welfare reforms have been reversed; and when the dominant ideology of meritocracy in liberal democratic societies has been seriously weakened at the same time that right wing politicians proclaim the 'classless society', a new political arithmetic must be asserted as a vital tool of democracy as well as of sociology. For this to happen, citizens must first have 'access to collective self-knowledge independent of government' (Halsey 1994: 440). Second, there needs to be a sufficient number of trained and motivated researchers to take up the challenge of 'mapping' the changing contours, contradictions, and complexities of advanced post-industrial societies. On both counts there are considerable grounds for concern. It is also clear that the widening inequalities in some of the advanced economies has been mirrored by a drift into post-modernism with its rejection of everything political arithmetic stands for. By rejecting quantitative methods, post-modernist researchers such as Lather (1991) turn their back on the vital task of holding the state to account for its policies. The currency of official justification is statistics, and there needs to be some critical check on the figures used to support policy initiatives and their outcomes.

The social context and understanding of research methodology in which we now work is quite different to that in which political arithmetic was initially developed; but the *aim* of a form of social accountability remains crucial. The work of post-modernists contains important insights into the self-reflexive nature of individuals which corresponds to the wider changes in society referred to by Beck (1992) and Giddens (1991; 1994) as reflexive modernization. Giddens (1994) suggests that:

Social reflexivity is both condition and outcome of a post-traditional society. Decisions have to be taken on the basis of a more or less continuous reflection on the condition's of one's action. 'Reflexivity' here refers to the use of information about the conditions of activity as a means of regularly reordering and redefining what that activity is. It concerns a universe of action where social observers are themselves socially observed; and it is today truly global in scope. (p. 86)

A new political arithmetic would acknowledge the insights relating to these wider changes but deny that they entailed the eschewal of quantitative methods. Quantitative methods are not logically linked to empiricist methodology with its foundationalist assumptions about the theory free nature of observation. There is a distinction to be made between methods such as those used by quantitative researchers and the methodological assumptions in which they are embedded. Proponents of the new political arithmetic would not only take on the role of social accountant, but may view it as part of a committed policy scholarship, and would certainly seek to be aware of the presuppositions that inform their research.

In addition, a new political arithmetic would not only involve counting inputs and outputs, but is also dedicated to an analysis of 'what counts' and why. This is necessary in order to avoid the problem of the 'black box' which was a common criticism of political arithmetic in the 1970s. Studying what counts involves studying 'process' as well as outcomes. In a context of rapid social, economic, and institutional change it has become more important to find ways of linking quantitative and qualitative methods of social research. Actors must be recognized as knowledgeable. Their ideas clearly count in shaping outcomes. Hence, social and educational researchers need to use the knowledge they

generate to engage in a dialogue with people about post-industrial possibilities in relation to the society they live in; and a new political arithmetic must be involved in a process of theory-building as part of a political project dedicated to 'institution building' (Dahrendorf 1985). In this sense, it offers the prospect of addressing enduring questions of political economy as defined above, in a context of changing educational, social, economic, and political conditions at the end of the twentieth century.

For example, the sense of unease about social change in the late twentieth century has been accompanied by a universal crisis of confidence about the aims and purposes of education. In Britain and the United States of America, the New Right have responded to the turmoil of recent decades by arguing that 'we may no longer know what kind of society this is, but we do know that it is a market economy, and the best way to make a market economy work is through a minimum of government interference' (Block 1990: 3). This attitude has characterized educational decision-making in both countries for more than a decade. The education system has frequently been discussed in terms of how it can be organized to conform to the imperatives of the market. Sociologists and educationalists opposed to the moral and political foundations and consequences of the 'free market' have tended to channel their energies into describing and evaluating its consequences for the future of the welfare state. However, this focus has delayed the development of new theoretical and empirical studies of post-industrial possibilities: a task which has become all the more important given, firstly, that the descriptive and analytical powers of theories of industrial society and its social institutions, which have informed sociological insights throughout the twentieth century, have been seriously weakened, and secondly, given recent events in Eastern Europe and the Soviet Union, that the foundation of alternative forms of social arrangements to capitalism have also been subjected to serious re-examination (Giroux Ch. 6; West Ch. 33). As a result it has been difficult to present a coherent programme of reform hinged to a new vision of society. However, as Block (1990) has also noted, 'Those educational reformers who succeeded in linking their proposals to widely shared views of the direction in which the society was moving tended to be more successful than those who were unable to connect their reform proposals to the master concepts of social science' (p. 8).

Notes

1. The nineteenth century was a period of intense modernization which included attempts to homogenize ethnicity through the nation state. The Treaty of Versailles in 1919 was perhaps the culminating moment of redrawing national boundaries to coincide with ethnic divisions. But it was essentially internal to Europe. The creation of African boundaries was a product of colonialism rather than natural separation of potential nations. Bloody civil wars have subsequently erupted. Previously forced amalgamations, e.g. Scotland, Wales, and Northern Ireland with England to form the United Kingdom, are still the object of passionate politics, with the Welsh language and the independent administration of Scottish schools and colleges not least prominent in quarrels about reform. America is the story of genocide and slavery, still struggling to homogenize its child-rearing practices with one language (threatened, of course, by Spanish carried by immigrants into the South-West) and desegregation and militant political correctness on the college campus. The Soviet Union was, before 1989, held up as the political union of a vast array of ethnic communities where educational equality of opportunity demonstrated the superior power of the state over the nation. The Hindu/Muslim conflict after decolonization of India may be held to demonstrate the opposite theories. And the recent educational history of both Germany and France illustrates the never-ending fight over the curriculum and organization of schools attended by poly-glot children. Individualism seems likely to flourish still more in the twenty-first century. Some, like Michael Ignatieff, foresee the possibility of a world in which love and hate are entirely individual. To achieve that end presupposes a radically different culture from that which schools have tried to pass on to past generations. It is a possible but surely implausible dream.

2. These data are taken from the chapters on Schools and Higher Education by Halsey (1972) and from Ringer (1979), 229 and 252.

3. 'They are all our children'; speech delivered at East Los Angeles College, Los Angeles, 14 May 1992.

4. Such predictions are notoriously unreliable and need to be treated with extreme caution.

Mishel and Teixeira (1991), for instance, give an alternative account of the US evidence.

5. See Marginson (1993: 70) for a discussion of the élitist view of universities articulated by leading New Right gurus such as Friedman and Hayek. See also William Rees-Mogg in *The Times* (London, 1 May 1995).

6. The term is being used broadly here to contrast the change from monocultural to pluralist societies which have emerged in large part as a result of the break-up of western colonialism. Not all peoples of colour suffer educational disadvantage, but those who have been in one way or another marked by colonialism and the colonizing mentality tend to. Space does not permit us to discuss the related notions of internal colonialism and institutional racism. There are also differences in the way indigenous peoples are positioned relative to post-colonial immigrants to the metropolitan societies. Any fuller account of racism and education would need to take account of these differences and the various concepts used to analyze them.

7. In 1923 Marshall added a manuscript foot note to this paper that 'it bears marks of the over-sanguine temperament of youth', but he left it unaltered, to be published by Professor A. C. Pigou in *Memorials of Alfred Marshall* (1925).

8. For the most distinguished descendant of the political-economy tradition, see James Meade (1964) *Efficiency, Equality and the Ownership of Property* (London: George Allen and Unwin) 1, and *The Inheritance of Inequalities: Some Biological, Demographic, Social and Economic Factors* (Proceedings of the British Academy 59, London: Oxford Univ. Press, 1973). Meade's work as a modern liberal theorist is not vulnerable to the criticisms offered here against Marshall's essay.

9. Advances in our capacity to agree internationally on the collection of data and in our techniques of measurement promise a clearer view of trends in equality and inequality. One casualty has been the well-known Kuznets curve, an inverted U which was believed in the post-war period to apply to equality of income distribution and national income in advanced countries. In his latest appraisal, A. B. Atkinson comes to the tentative conclusion that European countries are not 'comfortably on the downward part of the Kuznet curve with inequality falling over time' (1995: 63). Indeed, in the 1980s combined progress towards reduced inequality was the exception rather than the rule. In the US, where inequality is high, and in Sweden, where it is low, inequality increased. It also increased in Britain, where inequality was in an intermediate position in the mid-1980s (though accelerated more recently); and it fell in Italy, another

intermediate country. The Scandinavian countries and West Germany have low inequality in disposable equivalent income. Southern Europe and Ireland are high, and France, and Italy are in the intermediate category.

10. The occupational experiences of dons and professional people, which he assumed would spread throughout society, are characterized by high degrees of autonomy and discretion as well as by relations of high trust (Fox 1974). Perhaps he was appreciating the dangers of developing low-discretion and low-trust relationships in and between highly specialized occupational groups in his hope for the development of producer co-operatives as a form of industrial organization. And he was certainly aware of the dilemma which exists between the values of efficiency on the one hand and those of humane work relationships on the other. But the problem has turned out to be much more complicated.

References

Apple, M. (1982), 'Curricular Form and the Logic of Technical Control: Building the Possessive Individual', in Apple, M. (ed.), *Cultural and Economic Reproduction in Education* (London: Routledge).

Armstrong, P., Glyn, A., and Harrison, J. (1991), *Capitalism Since 1945* (Oxford: Basil Blackwell).

Aronowitz, S., and Giroux, H. (1986), *Education Under Siege: The Conservative, Liberal and Radical Debate over Schooling* (London: Routledge).

—— and Giroux, H. (1991), *Postmodern Education: Politics, Culture and Social Criticism* (Minneapolis: Univ. of Minnesota Press).

Ashton, D., and Green, F. (1996), *Education, Training and the Global Economy* (Cheltenham: Edward Elgar).

Atkinson, A. B. (1995), *Incomes and the Welfare State: Essays on Britain and Europe* (Cambridge: Cambridge Univ. Press).

Atkinson, J. (1985), 'The changing corporation', in D. Clutterbuck (ed.), *New Patterns of Work* (Aldershot: Gower).

Avis, J. (1993), 'A New Orthodoxy, Old Problems: Post-16 Reforms', *British Journal of Sociology of Education*, 14: 245–60.

Avis, J., Bloomer, M., Esland, G., Gleeson, D., and Hodkinson, P., (1996) *Knowledge and Nationhood: Education, Politics and Work* (London: Cassell).

Ball, S. (1990), *Education, Inequality and School Reform: Values in Crisis!* (Inaugural Lecture, Centre for Educational Studies, Kings College, London).

—— (1994), *Education Reform: A Critical and Post-Structuralist Approach* (Milton Keynes: Open Univ. Press).

Ball, S., and Bowe, R. (1992), 'Subject Departments and the 'Implementation' of National Curriculum Policy: An Overview of the Issues', *Journal of Curriculum Studies*, 24/2: 97–115.

Barnett, C. (1986), *The Audit of War: The Illusion and Reality of Britain as a Great Nation* (London: Macmillan).

Barry, B. (1973), *The Liberal Theory of Justice* (Oxford: Oxford Univ. Press).

Beck, U. (1992), *Risk Society: Towards a New Modernity* (London: Sage).

Bellah., R., Madsen, R., Sullivan, W., Swidler, A., and Tipton, S. (1985), *Habits of the Heart: Individualism and Commitment in American Life* (Berkeley: Univ. of California Press).

Bernstein, B. (1990), *The Structuring of Pedagogic Discourse*: vol. iv. *Class Codes and Control* (London, Routledge).

Bettis., P. (1996), Urban Students, Liminality and the Postindustrial Context, *Sociology of Education*, 69, April, pp. 105–125.

Bird, L. (1992), 'Girls taking positions of authority at primary school', in S. Middleton and A. Jones (eds.), *Women and Education in Aotearoa* 2 (Wellington, NZ: Bridget Williams).

Blau, P., and Duncan, O. D. (1968), *The American Occupational Structure* (New York: John Wiley).

Block, F. (1990), *Postindustrial Possibilities: A Critique of Economic Discourse* (Berkeley: Univ. of California Press).

Bourdieu, P., and Passeron, J.-C. (1990), *Reproduction* (London: Sage).

Boudon, R. (1974), *Education, Opportunity and Social Inequality* (New York: John Wiley).

Bowles, S., and Gintis, H. (1976), *Schooling in Capitalist America* (London: Routledge).

Braverman, H. (1974), *Labour and Monopoly Capital* (New York: Monthly Review Press).

Brown, P., and Scase, R. (1994), *Higher Education and Corporate Realities: Class Culture and the Decline of Graduate Careers* (London: UCL Press).

—— and Lauder, H. (1992), 'Education, Economy and Society: An Introduction to a New Agenda', in Brown, P., and Lauder, H. (eds.), *Education for Economic Survival* (London: Routledge).

—— and —— (forthcoming), *The Stakeholder Society in a Global Age*.

Butler, T., and Savage, M. (eds.) (1995), *Social Change and the Middle Classes* (London: UCL Press).

Carnevale, A., and Porro, J. (1994), *Quality Education: School Reform for the New American Economy* (Washington: US Department of Education).

Cassell, M. (1993), 'Top 1,000 groups "have cut 1.5 million jobs" ', *The Financial Times*, 1 Nov.

Chisholm, L. (forthcoming), 'From the Knowledgeable Individual to the Learning Society? Schooling and Contemporary Modernisation

Processes', *Pedagogiska Magasiket* (Institute of Future Studies: Stockholm).

Chubb, J., and Moe, T. (1990), *Politics, Markets and America's Schools* (Washington: Brookings Institute).

Clark, B. (1962), *Education and the Expert Society* (San Francisco: Chandler).

Clegg, S., and Redding, S. G. (eds.) (1990), *Capitalism in Contrasting Cultures* (Berlin: de Gruyter).

Cohen, S. (1985), *Visions of Social Control* (Cambridge: Polity Press).

—— and Zysman, J. (1987), *Manufacturing Matters: The Myth of the Post-Industrial Economy* (New York: Basic Books).

Collins, R. (1979), *The Credential Society* (New York: Academic Press).

Coleman, J. (1968), 'The Concept of Equality of Educational Opportunity', *Harvard Educational Review*, 38 (Winter): 7–22.

—— (1990), *Equity and Achievement in Education* (Boulder: Westview Press).

—— (1992), 'Some Points on Choice in Education', *Sociology of Education*, 65: 260–2.

——, Campbell, E., Hobson, C., McPartland, J., Mood, A., Weinfeld, F., and York, R. (1966), *Equality of Educational Opportunity* (Washington: US Government Printing Office).

Commission For Social Justice (1994), *Social Justice: Strategies for National Renewal* (London: Vintage).

Connell, R. (1990), 'The State, Gender and Sexual Politics', *Theory and Society*, 15/5: 507–44.

Cowling, K., and Sugden, R. (1994), *Beyond Capitalism: Towards a New World Economic Order* (London: Pinter).

Dahrendorf, R. (1985), *Law and Order: The Hamlyn Lectures* (London: Stevens and Son).

Dale, R., and Ozga, J. (1993), 'Two Hemispheres, Both New Right? 1980s Education Reforms in New Zealand and Wales', in Lingard, R., Knight, J., and Porter, P. (eds.), *Schooling Reform in Hard Times* (London: Falmer Press).

David, M. (1993a), *Parents, Gender and Education Reform* (Cambridge: Polity Press).

—— Edwards, R., Hughes, M., and Ribbens, J. (1993b), *Mothers and Education: Inside Out? Exploring Family–Education Policy and Experience* (London: Macmillan).

—— West, A., and Ribbens, J. (1994), *Mother's Intuition? Choosing Secondary Schools* (London: Falmer Press).

Davies, B. (1993), *Shards of Glass* (Cresskill, NJ: Hampton Press).

Davis, S. (1995), 'Leaps of Faith: Shifting Currents in Critical Sociology of Education', *American Journal of Sociology*, 100/6: 1448–78.

Deem, R. (1978), *Women and Schooling* (London: Routledge).

Dennis, N., and Halsey, A. H. (1988), *English Eth-*

ical Socialism: Thomas More to R. H. Tawney (Oxford: Clarendon).

Department of Education and Science (1982), *Science Education in Schools* (London: HMSO).

Dewey, J. (1910), *How We Think* (Boston: D. C. Heath and Co).

—— (1916), *Democracy and Education* (New York: Macmillan).

Deyhle, D. (1995), Navajo Youth and Anglo Racism: Cultural Integrity and Resistance, *Harvard Educational Review*, 65, 3, pp. 403–44.

Docherty, T. (1993) (ed.), *Postmodernism: A Reader* (New York: Harvester/Wheatsheaf).

Dore, R. (1976), *The Diploma Disease* (London: George Allen and Unwin).

Drucker, P. E. (1993), *Post-Capitalist Society* (London: Butterworth-Heinemann).

Dunleavy, P. (1991), *Democracy, Bureaucracy and Public Choice* (London: Harvester/Wheatsheaf).

Durkheim, E. (1977), *The Evolution of Educational Thought* (London: Routledge).

Erickson, R., and Goldthorpe, J. (1992), *The Constant Flux: A Study of Class Mobility in Industrial Society* (Oxford: Clarendon).

Esping-Andersen, G. (1990), *The Three Worlds of Welfare Capitalism* (Cambridge: Polity Press).

—— (ed.) (1994), *Changing Classes, Stratification and Mobility in Post-Industrial Societies* (London: Sage).

Eysenck, H. (1971), *Race, Intelligence and Education* (London: Temple Smith).

Field, F. (1995), *Making Welfare Work* (London: Institute of Community Studies).

Flanagan, C. (1993), 'Gender and Social Class: Intersecting Issues in Women's Achievement', *Educational Psychologist*, 28, 4, 357–78.

Fox, A. (1974), *Beyond Contract: Work, Power and Trust Relations* (London: Faber and Faber).

Franzway, S., Court, D., and Connell, R. W. (1989), *Staking a Claim: Feminism, Bureaucracy and the State* (Cambridge: Polity Press).

Fraser, N. (1992a), 'Rethinking the Public Sphere: A Contribution to the Critique of Actually Existing Democracy', in Calhoun, C. (ed.), *Habermas and the Public Sphere* (Cambridge, Mass.: MIT Press).

—— (1992b), 'Sex, Lies and the Public Sphere: Some Reflections on the Confirmation of Clarence Thomas', *Critical Inquiry*, 18 (Spring): 595–612.

Fraser, S. (1995) (ed.), *The Bell Curve Wars* (New York: Basic Books).

Fromm, E. (1949), *Man for Himself* (London: Routledge).

Foucault, M. (1977), *Discipline and Punish* (London: Tavistock).

Galbraith, J. (1992), *The Culture of Contentment* (London: Sinclair-Stevenson).

Gallie, D., and White, M. (1993), *Employee Commitment and the Skills Revolution* (London: Policy Studies Institute).

Gellner, E. (1983), *Nations and Nationalism* (Oxford: Blackwell).

—— (1996), *Conditions of Liberty: Civil Society and its Rivals* (London: Penguin Books).

Gamble, A. (1986), 'The Political Economy of Freedom', in R. Levitas (ed.), *The Ideology of the New Right* (Cambridge: Polity).

—— (1994), *The Free Economy and the Strong State* (2nd edition, London: Macmillan).

Gans, H. (1988), *Middle American Individualism: The Future of Liberal Democracy* (New York: Free Press).

Giddens, A. (1991), *Modernity and Self-Identity: Self and Society in the Late Modern Age* (Cambridge: Polity).

—— (1994), *Beyond Left and Right: The Future of Radical Politics* (Cambridge: Polity).

Gilder, G. (1981), *Wealth and Poverty* (New York: Basic Books).

Goldthorpe, J., Lockwood, D., Bechhofer, F., and Platt, J. (1969), *The Affluent Worker in the Class Structure* (Cambridge: Cambridge Univ. Press).

Goodson, I. (1990), 'Nations at Risk and National Curriculum: Ideology and Identity', in *Politics of Education Association Yearbook* (London: Taylor and Francis).

Gould, S. J. (1981), *The Measure of Man* (New York: W. W. Norton).

Gray, J. (1995), *Enlightenment's Wake* (London: Routledge).

Green, A. (1990), *Education and State Formation* (London: Macmillan).

Habermas, J. (1976), *Legitimation Crisis* (London: Heinemann).

Halsey, A. H. (1971), *Trends in British Society Since 1900* (London: Macmillan).

—— (1972) (ed.), *Educational Priority* 1, 2, 3, and (1974) 4 (London: HMSO).

—— (1975), 'Sociology and the Equality Debate', *Oxford Review of Education*, 1: 9–23.

—— (1994), 'Sociology as Political Arithmetic (The Glass Memorial Lecture)', *British Journal of Sociology*, 45: 427–44.

—— (1995), *Decline of Donnish Dominion: The British Academic Professions in the Twentieth Century* (Oxford: Clarendon).

——, and Floud, J. (1961), 'Introduction', in Halsey, A. H., Floud, J., and Anderson, J. (eds.), *Education, Economy and Society* (New York: Free Press).

—— Heath, A., and Ridge, J. (1980), *Origins and Destinations: Family, Class and Education in Modern Britain* (Oxford: Clarendon).

Hammer, M., and Champy, J. (1993), *Reengineering the Corporation* (New York: Harper Business).

Handy, C. (1994), *The Empty Raincoat: Making Sense of the Future* (London: Hutchinson).

Hargreaves, A. (1994), *Changing Teachers, Changing Times: Teachers' Work and Culture in the Postmodern Age* (London: Cassell).

Harvard Educational Review (1973), Special Issue: Perspectives on Inequality.

Hayek, F. (1976), *Law, Legislation and Liberty* (London: Routledge).

Head, S. (1996), 'The new, ruthless economy', *New York Review of Books*, 29 Feb.: 47–52.

Heath, A., Jowell, R., and Curtice, J. (1994), *Labour's Last Chance? The 1992 Election and Beyond* (Aldershot: Dartmouth).

Held, D. (1995), *Democracy and the Global Order* (Cambridge: Polity Press).

Herrnstein, R. (1973), *IQ in the Meritocracy* (London: Allen Lane).

—— and Murray, C. (1994), *The Bell Curve: Intelligence and Class Structure in American Life* (New York: Free Press).

Herz, D. (1991), 'Worker displacement still common in late 1980s', *Monthly Labor Review*, 114: 3–9.

Hinden, R. (1964) (ed.), *The Radical Tradition* (London: George Allen and Unwin).

Hirsch, F. (1977), *The Social Limits to Growth* (London: Routledge).

Hirschman, A. (1970), *Exit Voice and Loyalty: Responses to Decline in Firms, Organisations and States* (Cambridge, Mass.: Harvard Univ. Press).

—— (1989), *Rival Views of the Market* (Cambridge, Mass.: Harvard Univ. Press).

Hirst, P., and Thompson, G. (1996), *Globalization in Question* (Cambridge: Polity Press).

HMSO (1973), *Social Trends* (London: HMSO).

Hobbes, T. (1934), *Leviathan* (London: Everyman).

Hughes, C., and Tight, M. (1995), 'The Myth of the Learning Society', *British Journal of Educational Studies*, 43/3 (September): 290–304.

Illich, I. (1971), *Deschooling Society* (London: Calder and Boyars).

—— (1973), *Tools for Conviviality* (London: Calder and Boyars).

—— and Verne, E. (1976), *Imprisoned in the Global Classroom* (New York: Writers and Readers).

International Labour Organization (ILO) (1995), *World Employment 1995* (Geneva: ILO).

Jencks, C. (1972), *Inequality: A Reassessment of the Effects of Family and Schooling in America* (New York: Basic Books).

—— (1977), *Who Gets Ahead? The Determinants of Economic Success in America* (New York: Basic Books).

—— and Peterson, P. (eds.) (1991), *The Urban Underclass* (Washington: Brookings Institution).

Jensen, A. (1972), *Genetics and Education* (London: Methuen).

Jordan, G., and Weedon, C. (1995), *Cultural Politics, Class, Gender and Race in the Postmodern World* (Oxford: Blackwell).

Kanter, R. (1989), *When Giants Learn to Dance* (London: Simon and Schuster).

Kerr, C., Dunlop, J., Harbison, F., and Myer, C. (1973), *Industrialism and Industrial Man* (Harmondsworth: Penguin).

Klees, S. (1986), 'Planning and Policy Analysis in Education: What Can Economics Tell Us?', *Comparative Education Review*, 30/4: 574–607.

Kozol, J. (1991), *Savage Inequalities* (New York: Crown Publishers).

Krugman, P. (1993), *Peddling Prosperity: Economic Sense and Nonsense in the Age of Diminishing Expectations* (New York: W. W. Norton).

Kumar, K. (1995), *From Post-Industrial to Post-Modern Society* (Oxford: Blackwell).

Lather, P. (1989), 'Postmodernism and the Politics of the Enlightenment', *Educational Foundations*, 3/3 (Fall): 7–28.

—— (1991), *Getting Smart: Feminist Research and Pedagogy With/in the Postmodern* (New York: Routledge).

Leira, A. (1992), *Welfare States and Working Mothers: The Scandinavian Experience* (Cambridge: Cambridge Univ. Press).

Levitas, R. (1986) (ed.), *The Ideology of the New Right* (Cambridge: Polity).

Levy, F. (1987), *Dollars and Dreams: The Changing American Income Distribution* (New York: Sage).

Lidley, R., and Wilson, R. (1995), *Review of Economy and Employment: An Occupational Assessment* (Institute of Employment Research, Warwick Univ., UK).

McLaren, P. (1994), 'Multiculturalism and the Postmodern Critique: Toward a Pedagogy of Resistance and Transformation', in Giroux, H., and McLaren, P., (eds.), *Between Borders: Pedagogy and the Politics of Cultural Studies* (New York: Routledge).

Maddison, A. (1991), *Dynamic Forces in Capitalist Development: A Long Run Comparative View* (Oxford: Oxford Univ. Press).

Marchak, M. (1991), *The Integrated Circus: The New Right and the Restructuring of Global Markets* (Montreal: McGill-Queen's Univ. Press).

Marginson, S. (1993), *Education and Public Policy in Australia* (Cambridge: Cambridge Univ. Press).

Meade, J. (1964), *Efficiency, Equality and the Ownership of Property* (London: George Allen and Unwin).

—— (1973), 'The Inheritance of Inequalities: Some Biological, Demographic, Social and Economic Factors', *Proceedings of the British Academy*, 59 (London: Oxford Univ. Press).

Merton, R. (1957), *Social Theory and Social Structure* (New York: Free Press).

Mishel, L., and Teixeira, R. (1991), 'The Myth of the Coming Labor Shortage', *The American Prospect* (Fall) 98–103.

Mishra, A., and Mishra, K. (1994), 'The Role of Mutual Trust in Effective Downsizing Strategies', *Human Resource Management*, 33: 261–79.

Mohanty, C. (1991), 'Introduction: Third World Women and the Politics of Feminism', in Mohanty, C., Russo, A., and Torres, L. (eds.), *Third World Women and the Politics of Feminism* (Bloomington: Indiana Univ. Press).

Morgan, G. (1986), *Images of Organizations* (London: Sage).

Murnane, R., and Levy, F. (1993), 'Why Today's High-School-Educated Males Earn Less than their Fathers Did: The Problem and an Assessment of Responses', *Harvard Educational Review*, 63/1: 1–19.

Murray, C. (1984), *Losing Ground: American Social Policy 1950–1980* (New York: Basic Books).

National Commission on Education (1993), *Learning to Succeed* (London: Heinemann).

Newman, K. (1993), *Declining Fortunes: The Withering of the American Dream* (New York: Basic Books).

OECD (1985), *Education in Modern Society* (Paris: OECD).

Parsons, T. (1949), *The Structure of Social Action* (New York: Free Press).

—— (1959), 'The School Class as a Social System: Some of its Functions in American Society', *Harvard Educational Review*, 29: 297–318.

Panic, M. (1995), 'International Economic Integration and the Changing Role of National Governments', in Ha-Joon Chang and Rowthorn, R. (eds.), *The Role of the State in Economic Change* (Oxford: Clarendon Press).

Parijs, P. V. (1992) (ed.), *Arguments for Basic Income* (London: Verso).

Pateman, C. (1989), *The Disorder of Women: Democracy, Feminism and Political Theory* (Cambridge: Polity Press).

Peters, M. (1990), 'Performance and Accountability in "Post-industrial Society": The Crisis of British Universities', *Studies in Higher Education*, 17/2: 123–39.

Peterson, W. (1994), *Silent Depression: The Fate of the American Dream* (New York: W. W. Norton).

Phillips, K. (1991), *The Politics of Rich and Poor* (London: Harper Collins).

Pigou, A. (1925) (ed.), *Memorials of Alfred Marshall* (London: Macmillan).

Piore, M., and Sabel, C. (1984), *The Second Industrial Divide: Possibilities for Prosperity* (New York: Basic Books).

Pollitt, C. (1990), *Managerialism and the Public Services: The Anglo-American Experience* (Oxford: Blackwell).

Pring, R. (1989), 'The Curriculum and the New Vocationalism', *British Journal of Education and Work*, 1: 133–48.

Ranson, S. (1994), *Towards the Learning Society* (London: Cassell).

Rainbow, P. (1991) (ed.), *The Foucault Reader* (London: Penguin).

Rawls, J. (1971), *A Theory of Justice* (Cambridge, Mass.: Harvard Univ. Press).

Reich, R. (1991), *The Work of Nations* (London: Simon and Schuster).

Ringer, F. (1979), *Education and Society in Modern Europe* (Bloomington, Indiana Univ. Press).

Rollett, C. and Parker, J. (1972), 'Population and Family', in A. H. Halsey (ed.), *Trends in British Society since 1900* (London: Macmillan).

Rose, N. (1989), *Governing the Soul: The Shaping of the Private Self* (London: Routledge).

Schumpeter, J. (1976), *Capitalism, Socialism and Democracy* (London: Allen and Unwin).

Sen, A. (1992), *Inequality Reexamined* (Oxford: Clarendon Press).

Silver, H. (1991), *An Educational War on Poverty: American and British Policy-Making 1960–1980* (Cambridge: Cambridge Univ. Press).

Silvestri, G. (1993), 'The American Work Force, 1929–2005. Occupational Employment: Wide Variations in Growth', *Monthly Labor Review* (November): 58–86.

Skidelsky, R. (1995), *The World After Communism: A Polemic for Our Times* (London, Macmillan).

Skocpol, T. (1994), *Social Revolutions in the Modern World* (Cambridge, Cambridge Univ. Press).

Smith, A. (1995), *Nations and Nationalism in a Global Era* (Cambridge: Polity).

Smith, G., and Little, A. (1971), *Strategies of Compensation: A Review of Educational Projects for the Disadvantaged in the United States* (Paris: OECD).

Spring, J. (1980), *Educating the Worker-Citizen* (New York: Longman).

—— (1993), 'A Response to Michelle Fine's *[Ap]parent Involvement: Reflections on Parents, Power and Urban Public Schools*', *Teachers' College Record*, 94/4: 717–19.

Terrill, R. (1973), *R. H. Tawney and His Times: Socialism as Fellowship* (Cambridge, Mass.: Harvard Univ. Press).

Thomas, G. (1992), 'Participation and Degree Attainment of Afro-American and Latino Students in Graduate Education Relative to Other Racial and Ethnic Groups', *Harvard Educational Review*, 62/1: 45–65.

Thurow, L. (1993), *Head to Head: the Coming Economic Battle Among Japan, Europe and America* (London: Nicholas Brealey).

Titmuss, R. M. (1971), *The Gift Relationship: From Human Blood to Social Policy* (London: George Allen and Unwin).

Wallerstein, I. (1995), 'The End of What Modernity?' *Theory and Society*, 24: 471–88.

Warner, L. W., Havighurst, R., and Loeb, M. (1946), *Who Shall Be Educated?* (London: Routledge and Kegan Paul).

Weiner, M. (1981), *English Culture and the Decline of the Industrial Spirit 1850–1980* (Cambridge: Cambridge Univ. Press).

Weis, L. (1990), *Working Class Without Work: High School Students in a De-Industrialising Economy* (New York: Routledge).

Whitty, G. (1990), 'The New Right and the National Curriculum: State Control or Market Forces', in Flude, M., and Hammer, M. (eds.) (1990), *The Education Reform Act, 1988* (London: Falmer Press).

Wilensky, H. (1960), 'Work, Careers and Social Integration', *International Social Science Journal*, 12: 543–60.

Willis, P. (1977), *Learning to Labour* (Farnborough: Saxon House).

Wood, A. (1994), *North–South Trade, Employment and Inequality: Changing Fortunes in a Skill-Driven World* (Oxford: Clarendon).

Young, M. (1961), *The Rise of the Meritocracy* (Harmondsworth: Penguin).

Zuboff, S. (1989), *In the Age of the Smart Machine* (Oxford: Heinemann).

PART ONE

EDUCATION, CULTURE, AND SOCIETY

2

The Forms of Capital

Pierre Bourdieu

The social world is accumulated history, and if it is not to be reduced to a discontinuous series of instantaneous mechanical equilibria between agents who are treated as interchangeable particles, one must reintroduce into it the notion of capital and with it, accumulation and all its effects. Capital is accumulated labor (in its materialized form or its 'incorporated,' embodied form) which, when appropriated on a private, i.e., exclusive, basis by agents or groups of agents, enables them to appropriate social energy in the form of reified or living labor. It is a *vis insita*, a force inscribed in objective or subjective structures, but it is also a *lex insita*, the principle underlying the immanent regularities of the social world. It is what makes the games of society—not least, the economic game—something other than simple games of chance offering at every moment the possibility of a miracle. Roulette, which holds out the opportunity of winning a lot of money in a short space of time, and therefore of changing one's social status quasi-instantaneously, and in which the winning of the previous spin of the wheel can be staked and lost at every new spin, gives a fairly accurate image of this imaginary universe of perfect competition or perfect equality of opportunity, a world without inertia, without accumulation, without heredity or acquired properties, in which every moment is perfectly independent of the previous one, every soldier has a marshal's baton in his knapsack, and every prize can be attained, instantaneously, by everyone, so that at each moment anyone can become anything. Capital, which, in its objectified or embodied forms, takes time to accumulate and which, as a potential capacity to produce profits and to reproduce itself in identical or expanded form, contains a tendency to persist in its being, is a force inscribed in the objectivity of things so that everything is not equally possible or impossible.[1] And the structure of the distribution of the different types and subtypes of capital at a given moment in time represents the immanent structure of the social world, i.e., the set of constraints, inscribed in the very reality of that world, which govern its functioning in a durable way, determining the chances of success for practices.

It is in fact impossible to account for the structure and functioning of the social world unless one reintroduces capital in all its forms and not solely in the one form recognized by economic theory. Economic theory has allowed to be foisted upon it a definition of the economy of practices which is the historical invention of capitalism; and by reducing the universe of exchanges to mercantile exchange, which is objectively and subjectively oriented toward the maximization of profit, i.e., (economically) *self-interested*, it has implicitly defined the other forms of exchange as noneconomic, and therefore *disinterested*. In particular, it defines as disinterested those forms of exchange which ensure the *transubstantiation* whereby the most material types of capital—those which are economic in the restricted sense—can present themselves in the immaterial form of cultural capital or social capital and vice versa. Interest, in the restricted sense it is given in economic theory, cannot be produced without producing its negative counterpart, disinterestedness. The class of practices whose explicit purpose is to

From J. E. Richardson (ed.), *Handbook of Theory of Research for the Sociology of Education* (Greenword Press, 1986); 241–58. Translated by Richard Nice. Reprinted by permission.

maximize monetary profit cannot be defined as such without producing the purposeless finality of cultural or artistic practices and their products; the world of bourgeois man, with his double-entry accounting, cannot be invented without producing the pure, perfect universe of the artist and the intellectual and the gratuitous activities of art-for-art's sake and pure theory. In other words, the constitution of a science of mercantile relationships which, inasmuch as it takes for granted the very foundations of the order it claims to analyze—private property, profit, wage labor, etc.—is not even a science of the field of economic production, has prevented the constitution of a general science of the economy of practices, which would treat mercantile exchange as a particular case of exchange in all its forms.

It is remarkable that the practices and assets thus salvaged from the 'icy water of egotistical calculation' (and from science) are the virtual monopoly of the dominant class—as if economism had been able to reduce everything to economics only because the reduction on which that discipline is based protects from sacrilegious reduction everything which needs to be protected. If economics deals only with practices that have narrowly economic interest as their principle and only with goods that are directly and immediately convertible into money (which makes them quantifiable), then the universe of bourgeois production and exchange becomes an exception and can see itself and present itself as a realm of disinterestedness. As everyone knows, priceless things have their price, and the extreme difficulty of converting certain practices and certain objects into money is only due to the fact that this conversion is refused in the very intention that produces them, which is nothing other than the denial (*Verneinung*) of the economy. A general science of the economy of practices, capable of reappropriating the totality of the practices which, although objectively economic, are not and cannot be socially recognized as economic, and which can be performed only at the cost of a whole labor of dissimulation or, more precisely, *euphemization*, must endeavor to grasp capital and profit in all their forms and to establish the laws whereby the different types of capital (or power, which amounts to the same thing) change into one another.[2]

Depending on the field in which it func-

tions, and at the cost of the more or less expensive transformations which are the precondition for its efficacy in the field in question, capital can present itself in three fundamental guises: as *economic capital*, which is immediately and directly convertible into money and may be institutionalized in the form of property rights; as *cultural capital*, which is convertible, on certain conditions, into economic capital and may be institutionalized in the form of educational qualifications; and as *social capital*, made up of social obligations ('connections'), which is convertible, in certain conditions, into economic capital and may be institutionalized in the form of a title of nobility.[3]

Cultural Capital

Cultural capital can exist in three forms: in the *embodied* state, i.e., in the form of long-lasting dispositions of the mind and body; in the *objectified* state, in the form of cultural goods (pictures, books, dictionaries, instruments, machines, etc.), which are the trace or realization of theories or critiques of these theories, problematics, etc.; and in the *institutionalized* state, a form of objectification which must be set apart because, as will be seen in the case of educational qualifications, it confers entirely original properties on the cultural capital which it is presumed to guarantee.

The reader should not be misled by the somewhat peremptory air which the effort at axiomization may give to my argument.[4] The notion of cultural capital initially presented itself to me, in the course of research, as a theoretical hypothesis which made it possible to explain the unequal scholastic achievement of children originating from the different social classes by relating academic success, i.e., the specific profits which children from the different classes and class fractions can obtain in the academic market, to the distribution of cultural capital between the classes and class fractions. This starting point implies a break with the presuppositions inherent both in the commonsense view, which sees academic success or failure as an effect of natural aptitudes, and in human capital theories. Economists might seem to deserve credit for explicitly raising the question of the relationship between the rates of profit on educational investment and on economic investment (and its evolution). But their measurement of the yield from scholastic investment takes account only of *monetary* investments and profits, or those directly convertible into money, such as the costs of schooling and the cash equivalent of time devoted to study; they are unable to explain the different proportions of their resources which different agents or different social classes allocate to economic investment and cultural investment because they fail to take systematic account of the structure of the differential chances of profit which the various markets offer these agents or classes as a function of the volume and the composition of their assets (see esp. Becker 1964*b*). Furthermore, because they neglect to relate scholastic investment strategies to the whole set of educational strategies and to the system of reproduction strategies, they inevitably, by a necessary paradox, let slip the best hidden and socially most determinant educational investment, namely, the domestic transmission of cultural capital. Their studies of the relationship between academic ability and academic investment show that they are unaware that ability or talent is itself the product of an investment of time and cultural capital (Becker 1964*a*: 63–6). Not surprisingly, when endeavoring to evaluate the profits of scholastic investment, they can only consider the profitability of educational expenditure for society as a whole, the 'social rate of return,' or the 'social gain of education as measured by its effects on national productivity' (Becker 1964*b*: 121, 155). This typically functionalist definition of the functions of education ignores the contribution which the educational system makes to the reproduction of the social structure by sanctioning the hereditary transmission of cultural capital. From the very beginning, a definition of human capital, despite its humanistic connotations, does not move beyond economism and ignores, *inter alia*, the fact that the scholastic yield from educational action depends on the cultural capital previously invested by the family. Moreover, the economic and social yield of the educational qualification depends on the social capital, again inherited, which can be used to back it up.

THE EMBODIED STATE

Most of the properties of cultural capital can be deduced from the fact that, in its funda-

mental state, it is linked to the body and presupposes embodiment. The accumulation of cultural capital in the embodied state, i.e., in the form of what is called culture, cultivation, *Bildung*, presupposes a process of embodiment, incorporation, which, insofar as it implies a labor of inculcation and assimilation, costs time, time which must be invested personally by the investor. Like the acquisition of a muscular physique or a suntan, it cannot be done at second hand (so that all effects of delegation are ruled out).

The work of acquisition is work on oneself (self-improvement), an effort that presupposes a personal cost (*on paie de sa personne*, as we say in French), an investment, above all of time, but also of that socially constituted form of libido, *libido sciendi*, with all the privation, renunciation, and sacrifice that it may entail. It follows that the least inexact of all the measurements of cultural capital are those which take as their standard the length of acquisition—so long, of course, as this is not reduced to length of schooling and allowance is made for early domestic education by giving it a positive value (a gain in time, a head start) or a negative value (wasted time, and doubly so because more time must be spent correcting its effects), according to its distance from the demands of the scholastic market.[5]

This embodied capital, external wealth converted into an integral part of the person, into a habitus, cannot be transmitted instantaneously (unlike money, property rights, or even titles of nobility) by gift or bequest, purchase or exchange. It follows that the use or exploitation of cultural capital presents particular problems for the holders of economic or political capital, whether they be private patrons or, at the other extreme, entrepreneurs employing executives endowed with a specific cultural competence (not to mention the new state patrons). How can this capital, so closely linked to the person, be bought without buying the person and so losing the very effect of legitimation which presupposes the dissimulation of dependence? How can this capital be concentrated—as some undertakings demand—without concentrating the possessors of the capital, which can have all sorts of unwanted consequences?

Cultural capital can be acquired, to a varying extent, depending on the period, the society, and the social class, in the absence of any deliberate inculcation, and therefore quite unconsciously. It always remains marked by its earliest conditions of acquisition which, through the more or less visible marks they leave (such as the pronunciations characteristic of a class or region), help to determine its distinctive value. It cannot be accumulated beyond the appropriating capacities of an individual agent; it declines and dies with its bearer (with his biological capacity, his memory, etc.). Because it is thus linked in numerous ways to the person in his biological singularity and is subject to a hereditary transmission which is always heavily disguised, or even invisible, it defies the old, deep-rooted distinction the Greek jurists made between inherited properties (*ta patroa*) and acquired properties (*epikteta*), i.e., those which an individual adds to his heritage. It thus manages to combine the prestige of innate property with the merits of acquisition. Because the social conditions of its transmission and acquisition are more disguised than those of economic capital, it is predisposed to function as symbolic capital, i.e., to be unrecognized as capital and recognized as legitimate competence, as authority exerting an effect of (mis)recognition, e.g., in the matrimonial market and in all the markets in which economic capital is not fully recognized, whether in matters of culture, with the great art collections or great cultural foundations, or in social welfare, with the economy of generosity and the gift. Furthermore, the specifically symbolic logic of distinction additionally secures material and symbolic profits for the possessors of a large cultural capital: any given cultural competence (e.g., being able to read in a world of illiterates) derives a scarcity value from its position in the distribution of cultural capital and yields profits of distinction for its owner. In other words, the share in profits which scarce cultural capital secures in class-divided societies is based, in the last analysis, on the fact that all agents do not have the economic and cultural means for prolonging their children's education beyond the minimum necessary for the reproduction of the labor-power least valorized at a given moment.[6]

Thus the capital, in the sense of the means of appropriating the product of accumulated labor in the objectified state which is held by a given agent, depends for its real efficacy on the form of the distribution of the means of appropriating the accumulated and objectively available resources; and the relationship of appropriation between an agent and the resources objectively available, and hence the profits they produce, is mediated by the relationship of (objective and/or subjective) competition between himself and the other possessors of capital competing for the same goods, in which scarcity—and through it social value—is generated. The structure of the field, i.e., the unequal distribution of capital, is the source of the specific effects of capital, i.e., the appropriation of profits and the power to impose the laws of functioning of the field most favourable to capital and its reproduction.

But the most powerful principle of the symbolic efficacy of cultural capital no doubt lies in the logic of its transmission. On the one hand, the process of appropriating objectified cultural capital and the time necessary for it to take place mainly depend on the cultural capital embodied in the whole family—through (among other things) the generalized Arrow effect and all forms of implicit transmission.[7] On the other hand, the initial accumulation of cultural capital, the precondition for the fast, easy accumulation of every kind of useful cultural capital, starts at the outset, without delay, without wasted time, only for the offspring of families endowed with strong cultural capital; in this case, the accumulation period covers the whole period of socialization. It follows that the transmission of cultural capital is no doubt the best hidden form of hereditary transmission of capital, and it therefore receives proportionately greater weight in the system of reproduction strategies, as the direct, visible forms of transmission tend to be more strongly censored and controlled.

It can immediately be seen that the link between economic and cultural capital is established through the mediation of the time needed for acquisition. Differences in the cultural capital possessed by the family imply differences first in the age at which the work of transmission and accumulation begins—the limiting case being full use of the time biologically available, with the maximum free time being harnessed to maximum cultural capital—and then in the capacity, thus defined, to satisfy the specifically cultural demands of a prolonged process of acquisition. Furthermore, and in correlation with this, the length of time for which a given individual can prolong his acquisition process depends on the length of time for which his family can provide him with the free time, i.e., time free from economic necessity, which is the precondition for the initial accumulation (time which can be evaluated as a handicap to be made up).

THE OBJECTIFIED STATE

Cultural capital, in the objectified state, has a number of properties which are defined only in the relationship with cultural capital in its embodied form. The cultural capital objectified in material objects and media, such as writings, paintings, monuments, instruments, etc., is transmissible in its materiality. A collection of paintings, for example, can be transmitted as well as economic capital (if not better, because the capital transfer is more disguised). But what is transmissible is legal ownership and not (or not necessarily) what constitutes the precondition for specific appropriation, namely, the possession of the means of 'consuming' a painting or using a machine, which, being nothing other than embodied capital, are subject to the same laws of transmission.[8]

Thus cultural goods can be appropriated both materially—which presupposes economic capital—and symbolically—which presupposes cultural capital. It follows that the owner of the means of production must find a way of appropriating either the embodied capital which is the precondition of specific appropriation or the services of the holders of this capital. To possess the machines, he only needs economic capital; to appropriate them and use them in accordance with their specific purpose (defined by the cultural capital, of scientific or technical type, incorporated in them), he must have access to embodied cultural capital, either in person or by proxy. This is no doubt the basis of the ambiguous status of cadres (executives and engineers). If it is emphasized that they are not the possessors (in the strictly economic sense) of the means of production which they use, and that they derive profit from their own cultural capital only by selling the services and products which it makes possible, then they will be classified among the dominated groups; if it is emphasized that they draw their profits from the use of a particular form of capital, then they will be classified among the dominant groups. Everything suggests that as the cultural capital incorporated in the means of production increases (and with it the period of embodiment needed to acquire the means of appropriating it), so the collective strength of the holders of cultural capital would tend to increase—if the holders of the dominant type of capital (economic capital) were not able to set the holders of cultural capital in competition with one another. (They are, moreover, inclined to competition by the very conditions in which they are selected and trained, in particular by the logic of scholastic and recruitment competitions.)

Cultural capital in its objectified state presents itself with all the appearances of an autonomous, coherent universe which, although the product of historical action, has its own laws, transcending individual wills, and which, as the example of language well illustrates, therefore remains irreducible to that which each agent, or even the aggregate of the agents, can appropriate (i.e., to the cultural capital embodied in each agent or even in the aggregate of the agents). However, it should not be forgotten that it exists as symbolically and materially active, effective capital only insofar as it is appropriated by agents and implemented and invested as a weapon and a stake in the struggles which go on in the fields of cultural production (the artistic field, the scientific field, etc.) and, beyond them, in the field of the social classes—struggles in which the agents wield strengths and obtain profits proportionate to their mastery of this objectified capital, and therefore to the extent of their embodied capital.[9]

THE INSTITUTIONALIZED STATE

The objectification of cultural capital in the form of academic qualifications is one way of neutralizing some of the properties it derives from the fact that, being embodied, it has the same biological limits as its bearer. This objectification is what makes the difference between the capital of the autodidact, which may be called into question at any time, or even the cultural capital of the courtier, which can yield only ill-defined profits, of fluctuating value, in the market of high-society exchanges, and the cultural capital academically sanctioned by legally guaranteed qualifications, formally independent of the person of their bearer. With the academic qualification, a certificate of cultural competence which confers on its holder a conventional, constant, legally guaranteed value with respect to culture, social alchemy produces a form of cultural capital which has a relative autonomy vis-à-vis its bearer and even vis-à-vis the cultural capital he effectively possesses at a given moment in time. It institutes cultural capital by collective magic, just as, according to Merleau-Ponty, the living institute their dead through the ritual of mourning. One has only to think of the *concours* (competitive recruitment examination) which, out of the continuum of infinitesimal differences between performances, produces sharp, absolute, lasting differences, such as that which separates the last successful candidate from the first unsuccessful one, and institutes an essential difference between the officially recognized, guaranteed competence and simple cultural capital, which is constantly required to prove itself. In this case, one sees clearly the performative magic of the power of instituting, the power to show forth and secure belief or, in a word, to impose recognition.

By conferring institutional recognition on the cultural capital possessed by any given agent, the academic qualification also makes it possible to compare qualification holders and even to exchange them (by substituting one for another in succession). Furthermore, it makes it possible to establish conversion rates between cultural capital and economic capital by guaranteeing the monetary value of a given academic capital.[10] This product of the conversion of economic capital into cultural capital establishes the value, in terms of cultural capital, of the holder of a given qualification relative to other qualification holders and, by the same token, the monetary value for which it can be exchanged on the labor market (academic investment has no meaning unless a minimum degree of reversibility of the conversion it implies is objectively guaranteed). Because the material and symbolic profits which the academic qualification guarantees also depend on its scarcity, the investments made (in time and effort) may turn out to be less profitable than was anticipated when they were made (there having been a *de facto* change in the conversion rate between academic capital and economic capital). The strategies for converting economic capital into cultural capital, which are among the short-term factors of the schooling explosion and the inflation of qualifications, are governed by changes in the structure of the chances of profit offered by the different types of capital.

Social Capital

Social capital is the aggregate of the actual or potential resources which are linked to possession of a durable network of more or less institutionalized relationships of mutual acquaintance and recognition—or in other words, to membership in a group[11]—which provides each of its members with the backing of the collectivity-owned capital, a 'credential' which entitles them to credit, in the various senses of the word. These relationships may exist only in the practical state, in material and/or symbolic exchanges which help to maintain them. They may also be socially instituted and guaranteed by the application of a common name (the name of a family, a class, or a tribe or of a school, a party, etc.) and by a whole set of instituting acts designed simultaneously to form and inform those who undergo them; in this case, they are more or less really enacted and so maintained and reinforced, in exchanges. Being based on indissolubly material and symbolic exchanges, the establishment and maintenance of which presuppose reacknowledgment of proximity, they are also partially irreducible to objective relations of proximity in physical (geographical) space or even in economic and social space.[12]

The volume of the social capital possessed by a given agent thus depends on the size of the network of connections he can effectively mobilize and on the volume of the capital (economic, cultural or symbolic) possessed in his own right by each of those to whom he is connected.[13] This means that, although it is relatively irreducible to the economic and cultural capital possessed by a given agent, or even by the whole set of agents to whom he is connected, social capital is never completely independent of it because the exchanges instituting mutual acknowledgment presuppose the reacknowledgment of a minimum of objective homogeneity, and because it exerts a multiplier effect on the capital he possesses in his own right.

The profits which accrue from membership in a group are the basis of the solidarity which makes them possible.[14] This does not mean that they are consciously pursued as such, even in the case of groups like select clubs, which are deliberately organized in order to concentrate social capital and so to derive full benefit from the multiplier effect implied in concentration and to secure the profits of membership—material profits, such as all the types of services accruing from useful relationships, and symbolic profits, such as those derived from association with a rare, prestigious group.

The existence of a network of connections is not a natural given, or even a social given, constituted once and for all by an initial act of institution, represented, in the case of the family group, by the genealogical definition of kinship relations, which is the characteristic of a social formation. It is the product of an endless effort at institution, of which institution rites—often wrongly described as rites of passage—mark the essential moments and which is necessary in order to produce and reproduce lasting, useful relationships that can secure material or symbolic profits (see Bourdieu 1982). In other words, the network of relationships is the product of investment strategies, individual or collective, consciously or unconsciously aimed at establishing or reproducing social relationships that are directly usable in the short or long term, i.e., at transforming contingent relations, such as those of neighborhood, the workplace, or even kinship, into relationships that are at once necessary and elective, implying durable obligations subjectively felt (feelings of gratitude, respect, friendship, etc.) or institutionally guaranteed (rights). This is done through the alchemy of *consecration*, the symbolic constitution produced by social institution (institution as a relative—brother, sister, cousin, etc.—or as a knight, an heir, an elder, etc.) and endlessly reproduced in and through the exchange (of gifts, words, women, etc.) which it encourages and which presupposes and produces mutual knowledge and recognition. Exchange transforms the things exchanged into signs of recognition and, through the mutual recognition and the recognition of group membership which it implies, reproduces the group. By the same token, it reaffirms the limits of the group, i.e., the limits beyond which the constitutive exchange—trade, commensality, or marriage—cannot take place. Each member of the group is thus instituted as a custodian of the limits of the group: because the definition of the criteria of entry is at stake in each new entry, he can modify the group by modifying the limits of legitimate exchange through some form of misalliance. It is quite logical that, in most

societies, the preparation and conclusion of marriages should be the business of the whole group, and not of the agents directly concerned. Through the introduction of new members into a family, a clan, or a club, the whole definition of the group, i.e., its fines, its boundaries, and its identity, is put at stake, exposed to redefinition, alteration, adulteration. When, as in modern societies, families lose the monopoly of the establishment of exchanges which can lead to lasting relationships, whether socially sanctioned (like marriage) or not, they may continue to control these exchanges, while remaining within the logic of laissez-faire, through all the institutions which are designed to favor legitimate exchanges and exclude illegitimate ones by producing occasions (rallies, cruises, hunts, parties, receptions, etc.), places (smart neighborhoods, select schools, clubs, etc.), or practices (smart sports, parlor games, cultural ceremonies, etc.) which bring together, in a seemingly fortuitous way, individuals as homogeneous as possible in all the pertinent respects in terms of the existence and persistence of the group.

The reproduction of social capital presupposes an unceasing effort of sociability, a continuous series of exchanges in which recognition is endlessly affirmed and reaffirmed. This work, which implies expenditure of time and energy and so, directly or indirectly, of economic capital, is not profitable or even conceivable unless one invests in it a specific competence (knowledge of genealogical relationships and of real connections and skill at using them, etc.) and an acquired disposition to acquire and maintain this competence, which are themselves integral parts of this capital.[15] This is one of the factors which explain why the profitability of this labor of accumulating and maintaining social capital rises in proportion to the size of the capital. Because the social capital accruing from a relationship is that much greater to the extent that the person who is the object of it is richly endowed with capital (mainly social, but also cultural and even economic capital), the possessors of an inherited social capital, symbolized by a great name, are able to transform all circumstantial relationships into lasting connections. They are sought after for their social capital and, because they are well known, are worthy of being known ('I know him well'); they do not need to 'make the acquaintance' of all their 'acquaintances'; they are known to more people than they know, and their work of sociability, when it is exerted, is highly productive.

Every group has its more or less institutionalized forms of delegation which enable it to concentrate the totality of the social capital, which is the basis of the existence of the group (a family or a nation, of course, but also an association or a party), in the hands of a single agent or a small group of agents and to mandate this plenipotentiary, charged with *plena potestas agendi et loquendi*,[16] to represent the group, to speak and act in its name and so, with the aid of this collectively owned capital, to exercise a power incommensurate with the agent's personal contribution. Thus, at the most elementary degree of institutionalization, the head of the family, the *pater familias*, the eldest, most senior member, is tacitly recognized as the only person entitled to speak on behalf of the family group in all official circumstances. But whereas in this case, diffuse delegation requires the great to step forward and defend the collective honor when the honor of the weakest members is threatened, the institutionalized delegation, which ensures the concentration of social capital, also has the effect of limiting the consequences of individual lapses by explicitly delimiting responsibilities and authorizing the recognized spokesmen to shield the group as a whole from discredit by expelling or excommunicating the embarrassing individuals.

If the internal competition for the monopoly of legitimate representation of the group is not to threaten the conservation and accumulation of the capital which is the basis of the group, the members of the group must regulate the conditions of access to the right to declare oneself a member of the group and, above all, to set oneself up as a representative (delegate, plenipotentiary, spokesman, etc.) of the whole group, thereby committing the social capital of the whole group. The title of nobility is the form *par excellence* of the institutionalized social capital which guarantees a particular form of social relationship in a lasting way. One of the paradoxes of delegation is that the mandated agent can exert on (and, up to a point, against) the group the power which the group enables him to concentrate. (This is perhaps especially true in the limiting cases in which the mandated agent creates the group which creates him but which only exists through him.) The mechanisms of delegation and representation (in both the theatrical and the legal senses) which fall into place—that much more strongly, no doubt, when the group is large and its members weak—as one of the conditions for the concentration of social capital (among other reasons, because it enables numerous, varied, scattered agents to act as one man and to overcome the limitations of space and time) also contain the seeds of an embezzlement or misappropriation of the capital which they assemble.

This embezzlement is latent in the fact that a group as a whole can be represented, in the various meanings of the word, by a subgroup, clearly delimited and perfectly visible to all, known to all, and recognized by all, that of the *nobiles*, the 'people who are known', the paradigm of whom is the nobility, and who may speak on behalf of the whole group, represent the whole group, and exercise authority in the name of the whole group. The noble is the group personified. He bears the name of the group to which he gives his name (the metonymy which links the noble to his group is clearly seen when Shakespeare calls Cleopatra 'Egypt' or the King of France 'France,' just as Racine calls Pyrrhus 'Epirus'). It is by him, his name, the difference it proclaims, that the members of his group, the liegemen, and also the land and castles, are known and recognized. Similarly, phenomena such as the 'personality cult' or the identification of parties, trade unions, or movements with their leader are latent in the very logic of representation. Everything combines to cause the signifier to take the place of the signified, the spokesmen that of the group he is supposed to express, not least because his distinction, his 'outstandingness,' his visibility constitute the essential part, if not the essence, of this power, which, being entirely set within the logic of knowledge and acknowledgment, is fundamentally a symbolic power; but also because the representative, the sign, the emblem, may be, and create, the whole reality of groups which receive effective social existence only in and through representation.[17]

Conversions

The different types of capital can be derived from *economic capital*, but only at the cost of a more or less great effort of transformation, which is needed to produce the type of power effective in the field in question. For example, there are some goods and services to which economic capital gives immediate access, without secondary costs; others can be obtained only by virtue of a social capital of relationships (or social obligations) which cannot act instantaneously, at the appropriate moment, unless they have been established and maintained for a long time, as if for their own sake, and therefore outside their period of use, i.e., at the cost of an investment in sociability which is necessarily long-term because the time lag is one of the factors of the transmutation of a pure and simple debt into that recognition of nonspecific indebtedness which is called gratitude.[18] In contrast to the cynical but also economical transparency of economic exchange, in which equivalents change hands in the same instant, the essential ambiguity of social exchange, which presupposes misrecognition, in other words, a form of faith and of bad faith (in the sense of self-deception), presupposes a much more subtle economy of time.

So it has to be posited simultaneously that economic capital is at the root of all the other types of capital and that these transformed, disguised forms of economic capital, never entirely reducible to that definition, produce their most specific effects only to the extent that they conceal (not least from their possessors) the fact that economic capital is at their root, in other words—but only in the last analysis—at the root of their effects. The real logic of the functioning of capital, the conversions from one type to another, and the law of conservation which governs them cannot be understood unless two opposing but equally partial views are superseded: on the one hand, economism, which, on the grounds that every type of capital is reducible in the last analysis to economic capital, ignores what makes the specific efficacy of the other types of capital, and on the other hand, semiologism (nowadays represented by structuralism, symbolic interactionism, or ethnomethodology), which reduces social exchanges to phenomena of communication and ignores the brutal fact of universal reducibility to economics.[19]

In accordance with a principle which is the equivalent of the principle of the conservation of energy, profits in one area are necessarily paid for by costs in another (so that a concept like wastage has no meaning in a general science of the economy of practices). The universal equivalent, the measure of all equivalences, is nothing other than labor-time (in the widest sense); and the conservation of social energy through all its conversions is verified if, in each case, one takes into account both the labor-time accumulated in the form of capital and the labor-time needed to transform it from one type into another.

It has been seen, for example, that the transformation of economic capital into social capital presupposes a specific labor, i.e., an apparently gratuitous expenditure of time, attention, care, concern, which, as is seen in the endeavor to personalize a gift, has the effect of transfiguring the purely monetary import of the exchange and, by the same token, the very meaning of the exchange. From a narrowly economic standpoint, this effort is bound to be seen as pure wastage, but in the terms of the logic of social exchanges, it is a solid investment, the profits of which will appear, in the long run, in monetary or other form. Similarly, if the best measure of cultural capital is undoubtedly the amount of time devoted to acquiring it, this is because the transformation of economic capital into cultural capital presupposes an expenditure of time that is made possible by possession of economic capital. More precisely, it is because the cultural capital that is effectively transmitted within the family itself depends not only on the quantity of cultural capital, itself accumulated by spending time, that the domestic group possess, but also on the usable time (particularly in the form of the mother's free time) available to it (by virtue of its economic capital, which enables it to purchase the time of others) to ensure the transmission of this capital and to delay entry into the labor market through prolonged schooling, a credit which pays off, if at all, only in the very long term.[20]

The convertibility of the different types of capital is the basis of the strategies aimed at ensuring the reproduction of capital (and the position occupied in social space) by means of the conversions least costly in terms of conversion work and of the losses inherent in the conversion itself (in a given state of the social power relations). The different types of capital can be distinguished according to their reproducibility or, more precisely, according to how easily they are transmitted, i.e., with more or less loss and with more or less concealment; the rate of loss and the degree of concealment tend to vary in inverse ratio. Everything which helps to disguise the economic aspect also tends to increase the risk of loss (particularly the intergenerational transfers). Thus the (apparent) incommensurability of the different types of capital introduces a high degree of uncertainty into all transactions between holders of different types. Similarly, the declared refusal of calculation and of guarantees which characterizes exchanges tending to produce a social capital in the form of a capital of obligations that are usable in the more or less long term (exchanges of gifts, services, visits, etc.) necessarily entails the risk of ingratitude, the refusal of that recognition of nonguaranteed debts which such exchanges aim to produce. Similarly, too, the high degree of concealment of the transmission of cultural capital has the disadvantage (in addition to its inherent risks of loss) that the academic qualification which is its institutionalized form is neither transmissible (like a title of nobility) nor negotiable (like stocks and shares). More precisely, cultural capital, whose diffuse, continuous transmission within the family escapes observation and control (so that the educational system seems to award its honors solely to natural qualities) and which is increasingly tending to attain full efficacy, at least on the labor market, only when validated by the educational system, i.e., converted into a capital of qualifications, is subject to a more disguised but more risky transmission than economic capital. As the educational qualification, invested with the specific force of the official, becomes the condition for legitimate access to a growing number of positions, particularly the dominant ones, the educational system tends increasingly to dispossess the domestic group of the monopoly of the transmission of power and privileges—and, among other things, of the choice of its legitimate heirs from among children of different sex and birth rank.[21] And economic capital itself poses quite different problems of transmission, depending on the particular form it takes. Thus, according to Grassby (1970), the liquidity of commercial capital, which gives immediate economic power and favors transmission, also makes it more vulnerable than landed property (or even real estate) and does not favor the establishment of long-lasting dynasties.

Because the question of the arbitrariness of appropriation arises most sharply in the process of transmission—particularly at the time of succession, a critical moment for all power—every reproduction strategy is at the same time a legitimation strategy aimed at consecrating both an exclusive appropriation and its reproduction. When the subversive critique which aims to weaken the dominant class through the principle of its perpetuation by bringing to light the arbitrariness of the entitlements transmitted and of their transmission (such as the critique which the Enlightenment *philosophes* directed, in the name of nature, against the arbitrariness of birth) is incorporated in institutionalized mechanisms (for example, laws of inheritance) aimed at controlling the official, direct transmission of power and privileges, the holders of capital have an ever greater interest in resorting to reproduction strategies capable of ensuring better-disguised transmission, but at the cost of greater loss of capital, by exploiting the convertibility of the types of capital. Thus the more the official transmission of capital is prevented or hindered, the more the effects of the clandestine circulation of capital in the form of cultural capital become determinant in the reproduction of the social structure. As an instrument of reproduction capable of disguising its own function, the scope of the educational system tends to increase, and together with this increase is the unification of the market in social qualifications which gives rights to occupy rare positions.

Notes

1. This inertia, entailed by the tendency of the structures of capital to reproduce themselves in institutions or in dispositions adapted to the structures of which they are the product, is, of course, reinforced by a specifically political action of concerted conservation, i.e., of demobilization and depoliticization. The latter tends to keep the dominated agents in the state of a practical group, united only by the orchestration of their dispositions and condemned to function as an aggregate repeatedly performing discrete, individual acts (such as consumer or electoral choices).
2. This is true of all exchanges between members of different fractions of the dominant class, possessing different types of capital. These range from sales of expertise, treatment, or other services which take the form of gift exchange and dignify themselves with the

most decorous names that can be found (honoraria, emoluments, etc.) to matrimonial exchanges, the prime example of a transaction that can only take place insofar as it is not perceived or defined as such by the contracting parties. It is remarkable that the apparent extensions of economic theory beyond the limits constituting the discipline have left intact the asylum of the sacred, apart from a few sacrilegious incursions. Gary S. Becker, for example, who was one of the first to take explicit account of the types of capital that are usually ignored, never considers anything other than monetary costs and profits, forgetting the nonmonetary investments (*inter alia*, the affective ones) and the material and symbolic profits that education provides in a deferred, indirect way, such as the added value which the dispositions produced or reinforced by schooling (bodily or verbal manners, tastes, etc.) or the relationships established with fellow students can yield in the matrimonial market (Becker 1964*a*).

3. *Symbolic capital*, that is to say, capital—in whatever form—insofar as it is represented, i.e., apprehended symbolically, in a relationship of knowledge or, more precisely, of misrecognition and recognition, presupposes the intervention of the habitus, as a socially constituted cognitive capacity.

4. When talking about concepts for their own sake, as I do here, rather than using them in research, one always runs the risk of being both schematic and formal, i.e., theoretical in the most usual and most usually approved sense of the word.

5. This proposition implies no recognition of the value of scholastic verdicts; it merely registers the relationship which exists in reality between a certain cultural capital and the laws of the educational market. Dispositions that are given a negative value in the educational market may receive very high value in other markets—not least, of course, in the relationships internal to the class.

6. In a relatively undifferentiated society, in which access to the means of appropriating the cultural heritage is very equally distributed, embodied culture does not function as cultural capital, i.e., as a means of acquiring exclusive advantages.

7. What I call the generalized Arrow effect, i.e., the fact that all cultural goods—paintings, monuments, machines, and any objects shaped by man, particularly all those which belong to the childhood environment—exert an educative effect by their mere existence, is no doubt one of the structural factors behind the 'schooling explosion,' in the sense that a growth in the quantity of cultural capital accumulated in the objectified state increases the educative effect automatically exerted by the environment. If one adds to this the fact that embodied cultural capital is constantly increasing, it can be seen that, in each generation, the educational system can take more for granted. The fact that the same educational investment is increasingly productive is one of the structural factors of the inflation of qualifications (together with cyclical factors linked to effects of capital conversion).

8. The cultural object, as a living social institution, is, simultaneously, a socially instituted material object and a particular class of habitus, to which it is addressed. The material object—for example, a work of art in its materiality—may be separated by space (e.g., a Dogon statue) or by time (e.g., a Simone Martini painting) from the habitus for which it was intended. This leads to one of the most fundamental biases of art history. Understanding the effect (not to be confused with the function) which the work tended to produce—for example, the form of belief it tended to induce—and which is the true basis of the conscious or unconscious choice of the means used (technique, colors, etc.), and therefore of the form itself, is possible only if one at least raises the question of the habitus on which it 'operated.'

9. The dialectical relationship between objectified cultural capital—of which the form *par excellence* is writing—and embodied cultural capital has generally been reduced to an exalted description of the degradation of the spirit by the letter, the living by the inert, creation by routine, grace by heaviness.

10. This is particularly true in France, where in many occupations (particularly the civil service) there is a very strict relationship between qualification, rank, and remuneration (translator's note).

11. Here, too, the notion of cultural capital did not spring from pure theoretical work, still less from an analogical extension of economic concepts. It arose from the need to identify the principle of social effects which, although they can be seen clearly at the level of singular agents—where statistical inquiry inevitably operates—cannot be reduced to the set of properties individually possessed by a given agent. These effects, in which spontaneous sociology readily perceives the work of 'connections,' are particularly visible in all cases in which different individuals obtain very unequal profits from virtually equivalent (economic or cultural) capital, depending on the extent to which they can mobilize by proxy the capital of a group (a family, the alumni of an elite school, a select club, the aristocracy, etc.) that is more or less constituted as such and more or less rich in capital.

12. Neighborhood relationships may, of course, receive an elementary form of institutionalization, as in the Bearn—or the Basque region—where neighbors, *lous besis* (a word which, in old texts, is applied to the legitimate inhabitants of the village, the rightful members of the assembly), are explicitly designated, in accordance with fairly codified rules, and are assigned functions which are differentiated according to their rank (there is a 'first neighbor,' a 'second neighbor,' and so on), particularly for the major social ceremonies (funerals, marriages, etc.). But even in this case, the relationships actually used by no means always coincide with the relationships socially instituted.

13. Manners (bearing, pronunciation, etc.) may be included in social capital insofar as, through the mode of acquisition they point to, they indicate initial membership of a more or less prestigious group.

14. National liberation movements or nationalist ideologies cannot be accounted for solely by reference to strictly economic profits, i.e., anticipation of the profits which may be derived from redistribution of a proportion of wealth to the advantage of the nationals (nationalization) and the recovery of highly paid jobs (see Breton 1964). To these specifically economic anticipated profits, which would only explain the nationalism of the privileged classes, must be added the very real and very immediate profits derived from membership (social capital) which are proportionately greater for those who are lower down the social hierarchy ('poor whites') or, more precisely, more threatened by economic and social decline.

15. There is every reason to suppose that socializing, or, more generally, relational, dispositions are very unequally distributed among the social classes and, within a given class, among fractions of different origin.

16. A 'full power to act and speak' (translator).

17. It goes without saying that social capital is so totally governed by the logic of knowledge and acknowledgment that it always functions as symbolic capital.

18. It should be made clear, to dispel a likely misunderstanding, that the investment in question here is not necessarily conceived as a calculated pursuit of gain, but that it has every likelihood of being experienced in terms of the logic of emotional investment, i.e., as an involvement which is both necessary and disinterested. This has not always been appreciated by historians, who (even when they are as alert to symbolic effects as E. P. Thompson) tend to conceive symbolic practices—powdered wigs and the whole paraphernalia of office—as explicit strategies of domination, intended to be seen (from below), and to interpret generous or charitable conduct as 'calculated acts of class appeasement.' This naively Machiavellian view forgets that the most sincerely disinterested acts may be those best corresponding to objective interest. A number of fields, particularly those which most tend to deny interest and every sort of calculation, like the fields of cultural production, grant full recognition, and with it the consecration which guarantees success, only to those who distinguish themselves by the immediate conformity of their investments, a token of sincerity and attachment to the essential principles of the field. It would be thoroughly erroneous to describe the choices of the habitus which lead an artist, writer, or researcher toward his natural place (a subject, style, manner, etc.) in terms of rational strategy and cynical calculation. This is despite the fact that, for example, shifts from one genre, school, or speciality to another, quasi-religious conversions that are performed 'in all sincerity,' can be understood as capital conversions, the direction and moment of which (on which their success often depends) are determined by a 'sense of investment' which is the less likely to be seen as such the more skillful it is. Innocence is the privilege of those who move in their field of activity like fish in water.

19. To understand the attractiveness of this pair of antagonistic positions which serve as each other's alibi, one would need to analyze the unconscious profits and the profits of unconsciousness which they procure for intellectuals. While some find in economism a means of exempting themselves by excluding the cultural capital and all the specific profits which place them on the side of the dominant, others can abandon the detestable terrain of the economic, where everything reminds them that they can be evaluated, in the last analysis, in economic terms, for that of the symbolic. (The latter merely reproduce, in the realm of the symbolic, the strategy whereby intellectuals and artists endeavor to impose the recognition of their values, i.e., their value, by inverting the law of the market in which what one has or what one earns completely defines what one is worth and what one is—as is shown by the practice of banks which, with techniques such as the personalization of credit, tend to subordinate the granting of loans and the fixing of interest rates to an exhaustive inquiry into the borrower's present and future resources.)

20. Among the advantages procured by capital in all its types, the most precious is the increased volume of useful time that is made possible through the various methods of appropriating

other people's time (in the form of services). It may take the form either of increased spare time, secured by reducing the time consumed in activities directly channeled toward producing the means of reproducing the existence of the domestic group, or of more intense use of the time so consumed, by recourse to other people's labor or to devices and methods which are available only to those who have spent time learning how to use them and which (like better transport or living close to the place of work) make it possible to save time. (This is in contrast to the cash savings of the poor, which are paid for in time—do-it-yourself, bargain hunting, etc.) None of this is true of mere economic capital; it is possession of cultural capital that makes it possible to derive greater profit not only from labor-time, by securing a higher yield from the same time, but also from spare time, and so to increase both economic and cultural capital.

21. It goes without saying that the dominant fractions, who tend to place ever greater emphasis on educational investment, within an overall strategy of asset diversification and of investments aimed at combining security with high yield, have all sorts of ways of evading scholastic verdicts. The direct transmission of eco-nomic capital remains one of the principal means of reproduction, and the effect of social capital ('a helping hand,' 'string-pulling,' the 'old boy network') tends to correct the effect of academic sanctions. Educational qualifications never function perfectly as currency. They are never entirely separable from their holders: their value rises in proportion to the value of their bearer, especially in the least rigid areas of the social structure.

References

Becker, G. S. (1964a), *A Theoretical and Empirical Analysis with Special Reference to Education* (New York: National Bureau of Economic Research).

—— (1964b), *Human Capital* (New York: Columbia Univ. Press).

Bourdieu, P. (1982), 'Les rites d'institution', *Actes de la recherche en sciences sociales*, 43: 58–63.

Breton, A. (1962), 'The Economics of Nationalism', *Journal of Political Economy*, 72: 376–86.

Grassby, R. (1970), 'English Merchant Capitalism in the Late Seventeenth Century: The Composition of Business Fortunes', *Past and Present*, 46: 87–107.

3

Class and Pedagogies: Visible and Invisible

Basil Bernstein

I shall examine some of the assumptions and the cultural context of a particular form of preschool/infant school pedagogy, a form which has at least the following characteristics:

1. Where the control of the teacher over the child is implicit rather than explicit.
2. Where, ideally, the teacher arranges the *context* which the child is expected to re-arrange and explore.
3. Where within this arranged context, the child apparently has wide powers over what he selects, over how he structures, and over the time scale of his activities.
4. Where the child apparently regulates his own movements and social relationships.
5. Where there is a reduced emphasis upon the transmission and acquisition of specific skills (see Note I).
6. Where the criteria for evaluating the pedagogy are multiple and diffuse and so not easily measured.

Invisible Pedagogy and Infant Education

One can characterise this pedagogy as an invisible pedagogy. In terms of the concepts of classification and frame, the pedagogy is realised through weak classification and weak frames. Visible pedagogies are realised through strong classification and strong frames. The basic difference between visible and invisible pedagogies is in the *manner* in which criteria are transmitted and in the degree of specificity of the criteria. The more implicit the manner of transmission and the more diffuse the criteria the more invisible the pedagogy; the more specific the criteria, the more explicit the manner of their transmission, the more visible the pedagogy. These definitions will be extended later in the paper. If the pedagogy is invisible, what aspects of the child have high visibility for the teacher? I suggest two aspects. The first arises out of an inference the teacher makes from the child's ongoing behaviour about the *developmental* stage of the child. This inference is then referred to a concept of *readiness*. The second aspect of the child refers to his external behaviour and is conceptualised by the teacher as busyness. The child should be busy doing things. These inner (readiness) and outer (busyness) aspects of the child can be transformed into one concept of 'ready to do.' The teacher infers from the 'doing' the state of 'readiness' of the child as it is revealed in his present activity and as this state adumbrates future 'doing.'

We can briefly note in passing a point which will be developed later. In the same way as the child's reading releases the child from the teacher and socialises him into the privatised solitary learning of an explicit anonymous past (i.e. the textbook), so busy children (children doing) release the child from the teacher but socialise him into an ongoing inter-actional present in which the past is invisible and so implicit (i.e. the teachers' pedagogical theory). Thus a non-doing child in the invisible pedagogy is the equivalent of a non-reading child in the visible pedagogy. (However, a non-reading child may be at a greater disadvantage and experience greater difficulty than a 'non-doing' child.)

The concept basic to the invisible pedagogy

From Basil Bernstein, *Class, Codes and Control*, Vol. 3 (Routledge and Kegan Paul, 1975), 116–56. Reprinted with permission.

is that of play. This is not the place to submit this concept to logical analysis, but a few points may be noted.

1. Play is the means by which the child exteriorises himself to the teacher. Thus the more he plays and the greater the range of his activities, the more of the child is made available to the teacher's screening. Thus, play is the fundamental concept with 'readiness' and 'doing' as subordinate concepts. Although not all forms of doing are considered as play (hitting another child, for example) most forms can be so characterised.

2. Play does not merely describe an activity, it also contains an evaluation of that activity. Thus, there is productive and less productive play, obsessional and free-ranging play, solitary and social play. Play is not only an activity, it entails a theory from which interpretation, evaluation and diagnosis are derived and which also indicates a progression. A theory which the child can never know in the way a child can know the criteria which are realised in visible pedagogy. Play implies a potentially all-embracing theory, for it covers nearly all if not all the child's doing and not doing. As a consequence, a very long chain of inference has to be set up to connect the theory with any one exemplar ('a doing' or a 'not doing'). The theory gives rise to a total—but invisible—surveillance of the child, because it relates his inner dispositions to all his external acts. The 'spontaneity' of the child is filtered through this surveillance and then implicitly shaped according to interpretation, evaluation and diagnosis.

3. Both the means and ends of play are multiple and change with time. Because of this, the stimuli must be, on the whole, highly abstract, available to be contextualised by the child, and so the unique doing of each child is facilitated. Indeed, play encourages each child to make his own mark. Sometimes, however, the stimulus may be very palpable when the child is invited to feel a leaf, or piece of velour, but what is *expected* is a *unique* response of the child to his own sensation. What is the code for reading the marks; a code the child can never know, but implicitly acquires. How does he do this?

4. The social basis of this theory of play is not an individualised act, but a personalised act; not strongly framed, but weakly framed encounters. Its social structure may be characterised as one of *overt* personalised organic solidarity, but covert mechanical solidarity. Visible pedagogies create social structures which may be characterised as *covert* individualised organic solidarity and *overt* mechanical solidarity.[1] (See later discussion.)

5. In essence, play is work and work is play. We can begin to see here the class origins of the theory. For the working class, work and play are very strongly classified and framed; for certain sub-groups of the middle class, work and play are weakly classified and weakly framed. For these sub-groups, no strict line may be drawn between work and play. Work carries what is often called 'intrinsic' satisfactions, and therefore is not confined to *one* context. However, from another point of view, work offers the opportunity of symbolic narcissism which combines inner pleasure and outer prestige. Work for certain sub-groups of the middle class is a personalised act in a privatised social structure. These points will be developed later.

Theories of Learning and Invisible Pedagogy

We are now in a position to analyse the principles underlying the selection of theories of learning which invisible pre-school infant school pedagogies will adopt. Such pedagogies will adopt any theory of learning which has the following characteristics.

1. The theories in general will be seeking universals and thus are likely to be developmental and concerned with sequence. A particular context of learning is only of interest in as much as it throws light on a sequence. Such theories are likely to have a strong biological bias.

2. Learning is a tacit, invisible act, its progression is not facilitated by explicit public control.

3. The theories will tend to abstract the child's personal biography and local context from his cultural biography and institutional context.

4. In a sense, the theories see socialisers as potentially, if not actually, dangerous, as they embody an adult focused, therefore reified concept of the socialised. Exemplary models are relatively unimportant and so the various theories in different ways point towards *implicit* rather than explicit hierarchical social relationships. Indeed, the imposing exemplar is transformed into a *facilitator*.
5. Thus the theories can be seen as interrupters of cultural reproduction and therefore have been considered by some as progressive or even revolutionary. Notions of child's time replace notions of adult's time, notions of child's space replace notions of adult's space; facilitation replaces imposition and accommodation replaces domination.

We now give a group of theories, which despite many differences fulfil at a most abstract level all or nearly all of the five conditions given previously:

Table 3.1. Theories exhibiting the five conditions

Piaget	1	2	3	4	5
Freud	1	2	3	4	5
Chomsky	1	2	3	4	5
Ethological theories of critical learning	1	2	3		
Gestalt		2	3	4	5

What is of interest is that these theories form rather a strange, if not contradictory group. They are often selected to justify a specific element of the pedagogy. They form in a way the theology of the infant school. We can see how the crucial concept of play and the subordinate concepts of readiness and doing fit well with the above theories. We can also note how the invisibility of the pedagogy fits with the invisible tacit act of learning. We can also see that the pre-school/infant school movement from one point of view is a progressive, revolutionary, colonising movement in its relationships to parents, and in its relationship to educational levels above itself. It is antagonistic for different reasons to middle class (m.c.) and working class (w.c.) families, for both create a deformation of the child. It is antagonistic to educational levels above itself, because of its fundamental opposition to their concepts of learning and social relationships. We can note here that as a result the child is

abstracted from his family and his future educational contexts.

Of central importance is that this pedagogy brings together two groups of educationists who are at the extremes of the educational hierarchy, infant school teachers, and university teachers and researchers. The consequence has been to professionalise and raise the status of the pre-school/infant school teacher; a status not based upon a specific competence, a status based upon a weak educational identity (no subject). The status of the teachers from this point of view is based upon a diffuse, tacit, symbolic control which is legitimised by a closed explicit ideology, the essence of weak classification and weak frames.

Class and the Invisible Pedagogy

From our previous discussion, we can abstract the following:

1. The invisible pedagogy is an interrupter system, both in relation to the family and in its relation to other levels of the educational heriarchy.
2. It transforms the privatised social structures and cultural contexts of visible pedagogies into a personalised social structure and personalised cultural contexts.
3. Implicit nurture reveals unique nature.

The question is what is it interrupting? The invisible pedagogy was first institutionalised in the private sector for a fraction of the m.c.—the new m.c. If the ideologies of the old m.c. were institutionalised in the public schools and through them into the grammar schools, so the ideology of the new m.c. was first institutionalised in private pre-schools, then private/public secondary schools, and finally into the state system, at the level of the infant school. Thus the conflict between visible and invisible pedagogies, from this point of view, between strong and weak classification and frames, is an ideological conflict within the m.c. The ideologies of education are still the ideologies of class. The old m.c. were domesticated through the strong classification and frames of the family and public schools, which attempted, often very successfully, cultural reproduction. But what social type was reproduced?

We know that every industrialised society produces organic solidarity. Now Durkheim, it seems to me, was concerned with only *one* form of such solidarity—the form which created individualism. Durkheim was interested in the vicissitudes of the types as their classification and framing were no longer, or only weakly, morally integrated, or when the individual's relation to the classification and frames underwent a change. His analysis is based upon the old m.c. He did not foresee, although his conceptual procedures make this possible, a form of organic solidarity based upon weak classification and weak frames; that is, a form of solidarity developed by the new m.c. Durkheim's organic solidarity refers to *individuals* in privatised class relationships; the second form of organic solidarity refers to persons in privatised class relationships. The second form of organic solidarity celebrates the apparent release, not of the individual, but of the persons and *new* forms of social control (see Note II). Thus, we can distinguish *individualised* and *personalised* forms of organic solidarity *within* the m.c., each with their own distinctive and conflicting ideologies and each with their own distinctive and conflicting forms of socialisation and symbolic reality.[2] These two forms arise out of developments of the division of labour within class societies. Durkheim's individualised organic solidarity developed out of the increasing complexity of the economic division of labour; personalised organic solidarity, it is suggested, develops out of increases in the complexity of the division of labour of cultural or symbolic control which the new m.c. have appropriated. The new m.c. is an interrupter system, clearly not of class relationships, but of the *form* of their reproduction. In Bourdieu's terms, there has been a change in habitus, but not in function. This change in habitus has had far-reaching effects on the selective institutionalisation of symbolic codes and codings in the areas of sex, aesthetics, and upon preparing and repairing agencies, such as the family, school, and mental hospitals. In all these areas there has been a shift towards weak classification and frames (see Note III).

This conflict within the m.c. is realised sharply in different patterns of the socialisation of the young. In the old m.c., socialisation is into strong classification and strong framing, where the boundaries convey tacitly critical condensed messages. In the new m.c.,

socialisation is into weak classification and weak frames, which promote, through the explicitness of the communication code, far greater ambiguity and drive this class to make visible the ideology of its socialisation; crucial to this ideology is the concept of the *person* not of the *individual*. Whereas the concept of the *individual* leads to specific, unambiguous role identities and relatively inflexible role performances, the concept of the *person* leads to ambiguous personal identity and flexible role performances. Both the old and the new m.c. draw upon biological theories, but of very different types. The old m.c. held theories which generated biologically fixed types, where variety of the type constituted a threat to cultural reproduction. The new m.c. also hold theories which emphasise a fixed biological type, but they also hold that the type is capable of great variety. This, in essence, is a theory which points towards social mobility—towards a meritocracy. For the old m.c., variety must be severely reduced in order to ensure cultural reproduction; for the new m.c., the variety must be encouraged in order to ensure interruption. Reproduction and interruption are created by variations in the strength of classifications and frames (see Note IV). As these weaken, so the socialisation encourages more of the socialised to become visible, his uniqueness to be made manifest. Such socialisation is deeply penetrating, more total as the surveillance becomes more invisible. This is the basis of control which creates personalised organic solidarity. Thus the forms of socialisation within these two conflicting fractions of the m.c. are the origins of the visible and invisible pedagogies of the school. We have a homologue between the interruption of the new m.c. of the reproduction of the old and the interruption of the new educational pedagogy of the reproduction of the old; between the conflict within the m.c. and the conflict between the two pedagogies: yet it is the conflict between and interruption of *forms* of transmission of class relationships. This point we will now develop. The new m.c. like the proponents of the invisible pedagogy are caught in a contradiction; for their theories are at variance with their objective class relationship. A deep rooted ambivalence is the ambience of this group. On the one hand, they stand for variety against inflexibility, expression against repression, the inter-personal against the inter-positional; on the other hand, there is the grim obduracy of the division of labour and of the narrow pathways to its positions of power and prestige. Under individualised organic solidarity, property has an essentially physical nature, however, with the development of personalised organic solidarity, although property in the physical sense remains crucial, it has been partly psychologised and appears in the form of ownership of valued skills made available in educational institutions. Thus, if the new m.c. is to repeat its position in the class structure, then appropriate secondary socialisation into privileged education becomes crucial. But as the relation between education and occupation becomes more direct and closer in time then the classifications and frames increase in strength. Thus the new m.c. take up some ambivalent enthusiasm for the invisible pedagogy for the early socialisation of the child, but settle for the *visible* pedagogy of the secondary school. And it will continue to do this until the University moves to a weaker classification and a weaker framing of its principles of transmission and selection. On the other hand, they are among the leaders of the movement to institutionalise the invisible pedagogy in State pre-schools and often for its colonisation of the primary school and further extension into the secondary school. And this can be done with confidence for the secondary school is likely to provide both visible and invisible pedagogies,[3] The former for the m.c. and the latter for the w.c.

Symbolic Control[4] and the Identification of the New Middle Class

However a ruling class is defined, it has a relatively direct relationship to the means and forms of production, but a relatively *indirect* relationship to the means and forms of cultural reproduction. It is the various strata of the middle class which have a direct relationship to the means and forms of cultural reproduction, but only an indirect relationship to the means and forms of production. What we call here the old middle class, essentially nineteenth-century, based itself on the ideology of radical individualism (a form of integration referred to as individualised organic solidarity), whether its functions were entrepreneurial or professional. The ideology of radical

individualism presupposes explicit and unambiguous values. It is this clarity in values which is fundamental to the transmission and reproduction of visible pedagogies. The explicit hierarchies of visible pedagogies require legitimation based upon explicit and unambiguous values. The new middle class as a structure is a middle-late twentieth century formation, arising out of the scientific organisation of work. The new middle class is both a product and sponsor of the related expansion of education and fields of symbolic control. It is ambiguously located in the class structure (Bowles and Gintis 1976). The ambiguity of the location is probably related to an ambiguity in its values and purpose. Such ambiguity shifts the modality of social control. Invisible pedagogies rest upon implicit hierarchies, which do not require legitimation by explicit and unambiguous values. The form of integration of this fraction shifts to personalised organic solidarity. This fraction of the middle class can be regarded as the *disseminators* of new forms of social control. The opposition between fractions of the middle class is not an opposition about radical change in class structure, but an opposition based upon conflicting forms of social control. We shall offer a classification of the agencies/agents of symbolic control.

1. Regulators: Members of the legal system, Police, Prison Service, Church.
2. Repairers: Members of the medical/psychiatric services and their derivatives; social services.
3. Diffusers: Teachers at all levels and in all areas. Mass and specialised media.
4. Shapers: Creators of what counts as developments within or change of symbolic forms, in the arts and sciences, including their agents of distribution, e.g. musicians, actors, producers, etc.
5. Executors: Civil Service—Bureaucrats.

Whilst it is true that category (1)—Regulators—might well be classified as *maintainers*, we want to emphasise that they play an important legal role in regulating the flow of people, acts, ideas. In the same way, some repairers may well have more of the function of regulators (in the above sense) than repairers. Further, each category has both its own hierarchy and its own internal ideological conflicts. In the same way, there may well be ideological conflicts *between* the categories which unite agents occupying dissimilar or similar positions in the respective hierarchies. Whilst we can distinguish the structure of integration, social control and processes of transmission which characterise the new middle class, the *agents* will be found in different proportions in different levels of the hierarchy in each category. This is a matter of continuing research. It is a matter of some importance (following Bourdieu) to consider the underlying structure of the cultural field of reproduction constituted by the agents and agencies of symbolic control, the underlying structure of the interrelationships of agents and agencies and the *forms* of symbolic control. Agents may be strongly or weakly classified in terms of the extent of their activity in more than one category and they may employ strong or weak framing procedures. The classification and framing analysis may be applied *within* a category *or* between categories. *The analysis in this paper is focussing upon changes in the form of transmission.*

BRIEF DISCUSSION OF THE CLASSIFICATION

1. Regulators: These are the agencies and agents whose function is to define, monitor and maintain the limits of persons and activities. Why place the official religious agencies with regulators? These agencies at one time both informed and legitimised the features of the legal system. Today the relationship between official religious agencies and the legal system is more complex. The role of official religious agencies as moral regulators has been considerably weakened, although in certain societies, official religious agencies have been active in supporting those who wish to change the system of regulation (e.g. the Roman Catholic Church in Latin America). Official religious agencies have been grouped with the structure of legal agencies because of their *function* as regulating agencies of symbolic control.
2. Repairers: These are the agencies and agents whose function is to prevent, or repair, or isolate what counts as breakdowns in the body, mind, social relationships. As we have mentioned in the text, at different times and in different societies some repairers may well act as regulators, at other times sub-groups may well be in conflict with regulators.
3. Diffusers: These are the agencies and agents whose *function* is to disseminate certain principles, practices, activities, symbolic forms, or to appropriate principles and practices, symbolic forms for the purpose of inducing consumption of symbolic forms, goods, services or activities.
4. Shapers: These are the agencies and agents whose *function* is the developing of what counts as changing, crucial symbolic codes in the arts or sciences. The problem here is that at certain levels there is an overlap with diffusers. We would argue that film producers, gallery owners, theatre owners, publishers, are an *important sub-set* of diffusers on the grounds that they operate specialised media. However, what do we do with performers (actors, musicians, dancers) and specialised critics? I think we would argue that performers should be classified as diffusers and specialised critics should be classified as shapers.
5. Executors: These are the agencies and agents whose function is administrative. The crucial agency here is the Civil Service and Local Government, although it is important to point out that they exist as agents in the above agencies.

We have left out the whole area of sport, which is undoubtedly a crucial agency in its own right, for the following reason. The classification has been set up in order to examine changes in the *form* of symbolic control *crucial* to the problem of the relationship between class and cultural reproduction. From this point of view, and *only* from this point of view, sport is not a crucial agency.

The Class Assumptions of Pedagogies

WOMEN AS CRUCIAL PREPARING AGENTS OF CULTURAL REPRODUCTION WITHIN THE MIDDLE CLASS (SEE NOTE V)
The shift from individualised to personalised organic solidarity in the m.c. changes the structure of family relationships and in particular the role of the woman in socialising the child. Historically, under individualised organic solidarity the mother is not important as a transmitter of physical or symbolic property. She is almost totally abstracted from the means of reproduction of either physical or symbolic property. The caring for and preparation of the children is delegated to others—nanny, governess, tutor. She is essentially a

domestic administrator and it follows she can only be a model for her daughter. The woman was capable of cultural reproduction for often she possessed a more sensitive awareness and understanding of the general literature of the period than her husband. This concept of the abstracted maternal function perhaps reappears in the concept of the pre-school assistant as a baby-minder and the governess as the teacher of elementary competences. Thus individualised organic solidarity might generate two models for the early education by women of the child:

Fig. 3.1. Early education by women of the child

Initially, with individualised organic solidarity, property has a physical basis, existing in forms of capital where ownership and control are combined. Access to, and reproduction of class position here is related to access to and ownership of capital. Although there is clearly a link between class and forms of education, education in itself plays a relatively minor role in creating access to and reproduction of class position. However, with developed forms of capitalism, not only do management functions become divorced from ownership, but there is an expansion of social control positions which have their basis in specialised forms of communication, more and more available from the expanding system of education. With this extension and differentiation of control functions the basis of property becomes partly psychologised, and its basis is located in ownership of specialised forms of communication. These in turn have their origin in specialised *forms of interaction* initiated, developed and focussed very early in the child's life. The role of the mother in the rearing of her children undergoes a qualitative change. The mother is transformed into a crucial preparing agent of cultural reproduction who provides access to symbolic forms and shapes the dispositions of her children so that

they are better able to exploit the possibilities of public education. We can see an integration of maternal functions as the basis of class position becomes psychologised. *Delegated* maternal caring and preparation *becomes* maternal caring and preparation. What is of interest here is the *form* of the caring and the form of the preparation. According to the thesis, the form may be constituted by either a visible or an invisible pedagogy. The old middle class perpetuated itself through a visible pedagogy whereas the new middle class, the bearers of the structures of personalised organic solidarity, developed invisible pedagogies.

With the shift from individualised to personalised organic solidarity within fractions of the middle class, the woman is transformed into a crucial preparing agent of cultural reproduction. There is, however, a contradiction in her structural relationships. Unlike the mother in a context of individualised solidarity (visible pedagogy) she is unable to get away from her child. The weak classification and framing of her child rearing firmly anchor her to her child (see 3 below). For such a mother, interaction and surveillance are totally demanding, whilst at the same time her own socialisation into both a personal and an occupational identity points her away from the family. These tensions may be partly resolved by placing the child early in a pre-school, which faithfully reproduces the ambience of her own child rearing. The infant school, however, may amplify the messages, and wish to extend them into the junior school. Here we can see a second contradiction for such an amplification brings the middle class mother and the school into conflict. The public examination system is based upon a visible pedagogy realised through strong classification and relatively stronger framing. It is this pedagogy which generates symbolic property, the means whereby class position is reproduced. If access to a visible pedagogy is delayed too long, then examination success may be in danger.

The argument here is that an invisible pedagogy is based upon a concept of the woman as a *particular* preparing agent of cultural reproduction. An agent having its origins in a particular fraction of the middle class.

We will now turn to more specific class assumptions of invisible pedagogy.

CONCEPT OF TIME

In the first place, invisible pedagogies are

based upon a middle class concept of time because they pre-suppose a long educational life. If all children left school at fourteen, there would be no invisible pedagogies. Visible pedagogies are regulated by *explicit* sequencing rules; that is the progression of the transmission is ordered in time by explicit rules. In a school the syllabus regulates the progression of a subject and the curriculum regulates the relationships between subjects *and* those selected as appropriate for given ages. The sequencing rules, when they are explicit, define the future expected states of the child's consciousness and behaviours. However, in the case of invisible pedagogies the sequencing rules are not explicit, they are *implicit*. The progression of the transmission is based upon theories of the child's inner development (cognitive, moral, emotional, etc.). The sequencing rules are derived from particular theories of child development. In the case of invisible pedagogies, it is totally impossible for the child to know or be aware of the principles of the progression. He/she cannot know the principles of his/her own development as these are expressed in the regulating theories. Only the transmitter knows the principle, the sequencing rules. The sequencing rules are *implicit* in the transmission rather than explicit. We can generalise and say that the sequencing rules of a transmission define its time dimension. However, they do more than this. In as much as they regulate future expected states of consciousness and behaviours they define what the child is expected *to be* at different points of time. In which case they define the concept of child. It follows that because visible and invisible pedagogies are regulated by different, indeed from one point of view, opposing sequencing rules, then they entail different concepts of time and they also are based upon different concepts of child. Visible and invisible pedagogies are based upon different concepts of childhood and its progressive transformation, which have their origin in different fractions of the middle class.

CONCEPTS OF SPACE
In the first place, invisible pedagogies require for their transmission a different material structure from the material structure upon which a visible pedagogy is based. A visible pedagogy requires only a very small fixed space; essentially a table, a book and a chair. Its material structure is remarkably cheap. However, in order for the material base to be exploited, it still requires a form of acquisition regulated by an elaborated code. However, in the case of an invisible pedagogy, its material basis is a very much larger surface. Consider the large sheets of paper, the space demands of its technology, bricks, kits for doing the creativity thing, an assembly of media whereby the child's consciousness may be uniquely revealed. The technology requires a relatively large space for the child. In this sense the production of an invisible pedagogy in the home cannot be effected in an overcrowded, materially inadequate home. However, invisible pedagogies are based upon a concept of space which is more fundamental. Visible pedagogies are realised through strongly classified space, that is, there are very strong boundaries between one space and another *and* the control of the spaces are equally strongly classified. Rooms in the house have specialised functions, seating arrangements for example at meals are specific to classes of person—mother, father, children, there are explicit, strongly marked boundaries regulating the movement in space of persons at different times. Further, the contents of different spaces are not interchangeable, e.g. dining spaces are dining spaces, children's areas and contents are children's areas and contents, the kitchen is the kitchen, etc. The explicit hierarchy of a visible pedagogy creates spaces and relationships between spaces which carry a specific set of symbolic messages—all illustrating the principle—things must be kept apart.

However, in the case of invisible pedagogies space has a different symbolic significance, for here spaces and their contents are relatively weakly classified. The controls over flow of persons and objects between spaces are much weaker. This means that the *potential space available to the child is very much greater*. The privacy embodied in space regulated by visible pedagogies is considerably reduced. Architects tend to call the spatial organisation of invisible pedagogies 'open-plan living.' *The child learns to understand the possibilities of such weakly classified spaces and the rules upon which such learning is based.* We can point out in passing the irony of, on the one hand, an invisible pedagogy, but on the other the fact of the continuous *visibility* of persons and their behaviour: the possibility of continuous surveillance. Invisible pedagogies are based upon concepts of space derived from a fraction of the middle class.

CONCEPT OF SOCIAL CONTROL

Where the pedagogy is visible the hierarchy is explicit, space and time are regulated by explicit principles, there are strong boundaries between spaces, times, acts, communications. The power realised by the hierarchy maintains the strong boundaries, the apartness of things. As the child learns these rules, he acquires the classification. An infringement of the classification is immediately visible, for any infringement signals *something is out of place*, communication, act, person or object. The task is to get the child to accept (not necessarily to understand) the ordering principles. This can be accomplished (not always necessarily) by linking infringements with an explicit calculus of punishment and relatively simple announcements of proscribing and prescribing rules. Motivation is increased by a gradual widening of privileges through age. The hierarchy is manifest in the classifications, in the strong boundaries, within the insulations. *The language of social control is relatively restricted and the relationships of control, explicitly hierarchical.*[5]

However, where the pedagogy is invisible, the hierarchy is *implicit*, space and time are weakly classified. This social structure does not create in its symbolic arrangements strong boundaries which carry critical messages of control. Because the hierarchy is implicit (*which does not mean it is not there, only that the form of its realisation is different*) there is a relative absence of *strongly marked* regulation of the child's acts, communication, objects, spaces, times and progression. In what lies the control? We will suggest that control inheres in *elaborated inter-personal communication* in a context where maximum surveillance is possible. *In other words, control is vested in the process of inter-personal communication.* A particular function of language is of special significance and its realisation is of an elaborated form in contrast to the more restricted form of communication where the pedagogy is visible. The form of transmission of an invisible pedagogy encourages more of the child to be made public and so more of the child is available for direct and indirect surveillance and control.

Thus invisible pedagogies realise specific modalities of social control which have their origins in a particular fraction of the middle class.

We have attempted to make explicit four class assumptions underlying the transmission of an invisible pedagogy.

1. It presupposes a particular concept of the mother as a crucial preparing agent of cultural reproduction.
2. It presupposes a particular concept of time.
3. It presupposes a particular concept of space.
4. It presupposes a particular form of social control—which inheres in interpersonal communication (elaborated code—person focused).

The educational consequences of an invisible pedagogy will be, according to this thesis, crucially different depending upon the social class position of the child.

We started this section by abstracting the following points from our initial discussion of the invisible pedagogy.

1. The invisible pedagogy is an interrupter system, both in relation to the home and in relation to other levels of the educational hierarchy.
2. It transforms the privatised social structure and cultural contents of visible pedagogies into a personalised social structure and personalised cultural contents.
3. It believes that implicit nurture reveals unique nature.

We have argued that this pedagogy is one of the realisations of the conflict between the old and the new middle class, which in turn has its social basis in the two different forms of organic solidarity, individualised and personalised; that these two forms of solidarity arise out of differences in the relation to and the expansion of the division of labour within the middle class; that the movement from individualised to personalised interrupts the *form* of the reproduction of class relationships; that such an interruption gives rise to different forms of *primary* socialisation within the middle class; that the form of primary socialisation within the middle class is the model for primary socialisation into the school; that there are contradictions within personalised organic solidarity which create deeply felt ambiguities; as a consequence, the outcomes of the form of the socialisation are less certain. The contemporary new middle class are unique, for in the socialisation of their young is a sharp and penetrating contradiction between a subjective personal identity and an objective privatised identity; between the release of the person and the hierarchy of class. The above can be represented diagrammatically:

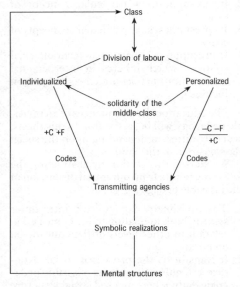

Fig. 3.2. Socialization of the young of the contemporary new middle class

Whereas it is possible for school and University to change the basis of its solidarity from individualistic to personalised, i.e. to relax its classification and frames, it is more difficult for those agencies to change their privatising function, i.e. the creation of knowledge as private property. It by no means follows that a shift to personalised organic solidarity will change the privatising function. Indeed, even the shift in the form of solidarity is more likely to occur in that part of the educational system which creates no private property, as in the case of the education of the lower working class, or in the education of the very young. We are then left with the conclusion that the major effects of this change in solidarity will be in the areas of condensed communication (sex, art, style) and in the form of social control (from explicit to implicit).

CLASS, CULTURE, POWER, AND CONFLICT

This shift from visible to invisible pedagogies at the pre- and primary levels of education changes the relationships between the family and the school. We have already noted the ambiguous attitude of the m.c. to such a shift. In the case of the w.c., the change is more radical. The weak classification and weak framing of the invisible pedagogy potentially make possible the inclusion of the culture of the family and the community. Thus the experience of the child and his everyday world could be psychologically active in the classroom and if this were to be the case, then the school would legitimise rather than reject the class-culture of the family. In as much as the pacing of the knowledge to be transmitted is relaxed and the emphasis upon early attainment of specific competencies is reduced, then the progression is less marked by m.c. assumptions. In the case of visible pedagogies early reading and especially writing are essential. Once the child can read and write such acts free the teacher but of more importance, once the child can read he can be given a book, and once he is given a book he is well on the way to managing the role of the solitary privatised educational relationship. The book is the preparation for receiving the past realised in the text book. And the text book in turn tacitly transmits the ideology of the collection code: for it epitomises strong classification and strong frames. The text book orders knowledge according to an explicit progression, it provides explicit criteria, it removes uncertainties and announces hierarchy. It gives the child an immediate index of where he stands in relation to others in the progression. It is therefore a silent medium for creating competitive relationships. Thus socialisation into the textbook is a critical step towards socialisation into the collection code. The stronger the collection code, that is the stronger classification and frames, the greater the emphasis on early reading and writing. The m.c. child is prepared for this emphasis, but not so in the case of the w.c. child. The weakening of classification and frames reduces the significance of the textbook and transforms the impersonal past into a personalised present. It would appear that the invisible pedagogy carries a beneficial potential for w.c. children. However, because the form we are discussing has its origins in a fraction of the m.c., this potential may not be actualised.

This point we will now develop. From the point of view of w.c. parents, the visible pedagogy of the collection code at the primary level is immediately understandable. The basic competencies which it is transmitting of reading, writing, and counting, in an ordered explicit sequence, make sense. The failures of the children are the children's failures not the school's for the school is apparently carrying out impersonally its function. The school's form of social control does not interfere with the social control of the family. The infant school teacher will not necessarily have high status as the competencies she is transmitting are, in principle, possible also for the mother. In this sense, there is symbolic continuity (or rather extension) between the w.c. home and the school. However, in the case of the invisible pedagogy, there is possibly a sharp discontinuity. The competencies and their progression disappear, the form of social control may well be at variance with the home. The theory of the invisible pedagogy may not be known by the mother or may be imperfectly understood. The lack of stress on competencies may render the child a less effective (useful) member of the family, e.g. running errands, etc. However, there is a more fundamental source of tension. The invisible pedagogy contains a different theory of transmission and a new technology, which views the mother's own informal teaching, where it occurs, or the mother's pedagogical values, as irrelevant if not downright harmful. There are new reading schemes, new mathematics replace arithmetic, an expressive aesthetic style replaces one which aims at facsimile. If the mother is to be helpful, she must be re-socialized or kept out of the way. If it is the former or the latter, then the power relationships have changed between home and school: for the teacher has the power and the mother is as much a pupil as the pupil. This in turn may disturb the authority relationships within the home: this disturbance is further facilitated by the use of implicit forms of social control of the school. Even if the pedagogy draws its contents from the class culture, basic forms of discontinuity still exist. If the mother wishes to understand the theory of the invisible pedagogy, then she may well find herself at the mercy of complex theories of child development. Indeed, whichever way the w.c. mother turns, the teacher has the power:

although the mother may well be deeply suspicious of the whole ambiance.[6]

Where, as in the case of the visible pedagogy there are, for the w.c. relative to the m.c., implicit forms of discontinuity and explicit forms of inequality in the shape of the holding power of the school over its teachers, the size of class and possibly streaming: in the case of the invisible pedagogy, there is also an *explicit* symbolic discontinuity which may well go with inequalities in provision and quality of teaching staff. The teacher also has difficulties, because the invisible pedagogy presupposes a particular form of maternal primary socialisation *and* a small class of pupils *and* a particular architecture. Where these are absent, the teacher may well find great difficulty. Ideally, the invisible pedagogy frees the teacher so that time is available for ameliorating the difficulties of any one child, but if the class is large, the socialisation, from the point of view of the school, inadequate, the architecture inappropriate, then such individual assistance becomes infrequent and problematic. Here again we can see that such a pedagogy, if it is to be successfully implemented in its own terms, necessarily requires minimally the same physical conditions of the middle class school. It is an *expensive* pedagogy because it is derived from an expensive class: the middle class.

From the point of view of the middle class, there is at least an intellectual understanding of the invisible pedagogy, if not always an acceptance of its values and practice. Further, if the middle class child is not obtaining the basic competencies at the rate the mother expects, an educational support system can be organized through private coaching or through the mother's own efforts. The power relationships between the middle class mother and the teacher are less tipped in favour of the teacher. Finally, the middle class mother always has the choice of the private school or of moving near a state school of her choice. However, because of the middle class mother's concept of the function of secondary education, she is likely to be anxious about the acquisition of basic competencies and this will bring her into conflict with the school at some point.

Finally, in as much as age and sex statuses within the family are strongly classified and ritualised, then it is likely that the acquisition, progression and evaluation of competencies obtained within the school will become part of the markers of age and sex status within the family. For example, there is a radical change in the status and concept of the child when he is transformed into a pupil. Now to the extent that the infant/primary school fails to utilise age and sex as allocating categories *either* for the acquisition and progression of competencies *or* for the allocation of pupils to groups and spaces, then the school is weakening the function of these categories in the family and community. Visible pedagogies not only reinforce age and sex classification, they also provide markers for progression within them. Invisible pedagogies are likely to weaken such classifications and in as much as they do this they transform the concept of the child and the concepts of age and sex status.

CLASS, PEDAGOGY, AND EVALUATION
Interesting questions arise over the system of evaluating the pupils. Where the pedagogy is visible an 'objective' grid exists for the evaluation of the pupils in the form of (a) clear criteria and (b) a delicate measurement procedure. The child receives a grade or its equivalent for any valued performance. Further, where the pedagogy is visible, it is likely to be standardized and so schools are directly comparable as to their successes and failures. The profile of the pupil may be obtained by looking across his grades. The pupil knows where he is, the teacher knows where he is and so do the parents. The parents have a yardstick for comparing schools. When children change schools they can be slotted into place according to their academic profile. Further, it is difficult for the parent to argue about the profile for it is 'objective.' Clearly, there are subjective elements in the grading of the children, but these are masked by the apparent objectivity of the grid. In the case of invisible pedagogies, no such grid exists. The evaluation procedures are multiple, diffuse and not easily subject to apparently precise measurement. This makes comparison between pupils complex and also comparisons between schools.[7] Firstly, the invisible pedagogy does not give rise to progression of a *group*, but is based upon progression of a person. Secondly, there is likely to be considerable variation between infant/pre-school groups *within* the general form of the pedagogy. There is less difficulty in slotting a child into a new school because

there is no explicit slot for him. Thus the mother is less able to diagnose the child's progress and as a consequence she cannot *provide specific educational support*. She would be forced into providing a general educational milieu in the home and this she may only be able to do if she had fully internalised the invisible pedagogy's theoretical basis. As we have previously argued, this is less likely to be the case where the parents are working class. Thus these parents are cut off from the evaluation of the child's progress. More, they are forced to accept what the teacher counts as progress.

Because an apparently objective grid exists for the evaluation of the visible pedagogies, then this grid acts selectively on those dispositions of the child which become candidates for labelling by the teacher. Clearly motivation and interest are probably relevant to any pedagogy, but their significance will vary with the pedagogy, and certainly their consequences. In the case of visible pedagogies, the behaviour of the child is focused on the teacher so that, in this case, attentiveness to, co-operation with, the teacher become relevant: persistence and carefulness are also valued by the teacher. Further, it is possible for there to be a conflict between the child's academic profile *and* the teacher's evaluation of his attitudes and motivation. These objective and subjective criteria may have different consequences for different class groups of pupils. Either criteria, irrespective of their validity, are likely to be *understood* by working class parents. In the case of invisible pedagogy, as more of the child is made available, and, because of the theory which guides interpretation, diagnosis and evaluation, a different class of acts and dispositions of the child become relevant. In the case of visible pedagogies we have argued that the attention of the child is focused on the teacher, however, in the case of invisible pedagogies the attention of the teacher is focused on the *whole* child: in its total doing and 'not doing.' This can lead to discrepancies between the teacher's and parents' views of the child unless the parents share the teacher's theory. Indeed it is possible that the dispositions and acts which are subject to evaluation by the teacher may be considered by some parents as irrelevant or intrusive or inaccurate or all three. Where this occurs the child's behaviour is being shaped by conflicting criteria. From the point of view of the teacher, the child becomes an *innovating* message to the home. The invisible pedagogy is not only an interrupter system in the context of educational practice, but it also transforms the child under certain conditions, into an innovating message to the family.

This pedagogy is likely to lead to a change in the school's procedures of evaluation, both objective and subjective. Where the pedagogy is visible, there is a profile which consists of the grading of specific competencies and a profile which consists of the grading of the child's motivation and work attitudes. It is likely that the latter will consist of rather short, somewhat stereotyped unexplicated judgements. In the case of invisible pedagogies, these highly condensed, unexplicated but *public* judgements, are likely to be replaced by something resembling a dossier which will range across a wide variety of the child's internal processes and states *and* his external acts. Further, the connection between inner and outer is likely to be made *explicit*. In other words, there is likely to be an explicit elaborated account of the relationships between the child's internal states and his acts. It is now possible that the school will have a problem of secrecy. How much is to go into the dossier, where is it to be kept, how much of and in what way are its contents to be made available to parents or to others in the school and outside of it? Thus invisible pedagogies may also generate *covert* and *overt* forms and contents of evaluation. Such a system of evaluation increases the power of the teacher to the extent that its underlying theory is not shared by parents *and* even when it is shared.

Finally, the major analysis in this section has been of idealised pedagogies. If, however, the argument is correct, that there may be a disjunction in the forms of socialisation between primary and secondary stages, *or* between secondary and tertiary stages, then behind weak classification and weak frames may well be strong classification and strong frames. Thus we can have a situation where strong Cs and Fs follow weak Cs and Fs, *or* where weak Cs and Fs follow strong Cs and Fs, as, possibly, in the case of the training of infant school teachers in England. It is important not only to understand continuity in the strength of classification and frames, but also *disjunction* and *when* the disjunction occurs. It is more than likely that if we examine empiri-

cally invisible pedagogies we shall find to different degrees a stress on the transmission of *specific* isolated competencies. Thus the 'hidden curriculum' of invisible pedagogies may well be, embryonically, strong classification, albeit with relatively weak frames. It becomes a matter of some importance to find out which children or groups of children are particularly responsive to this 'hidden curriculum.' For some children may come to see or be led to see that there are two transmissions, one overt, the other covert, which stand in a figure-ground relation to each other. We need to know for which teachers, and for which children, what is the figure and what is the ground. Specifically, will middle class children respond to the latent visible pedagogy, or are they more likely to be selected as receivers? Will lower working class children respond more to the invisible pedagogy or receive a weaker form of the transmission of visible pedagogy? The 'hidden curriculum' of invisible pedagogies may well be a visible pedagogy. However, the outcomes of the imbedding of one pedagogy in the other are likely to be different than in the case of the transmission of any *one* pedagogy. From a more theoretical standpoint, the crucial component of visible pedagogy is the strength of its *classification*, for in the last analysis, it is this which creates what counts as valued property, and also in so doing regulates mental structures. Frame strength regulates the modality of the socialisation into the classification. In the microcosm of the nursery or infant class, we can see embryonically the new forms of transmission of class relationships.

Let us take a concrete example to illustrate the above speculation. An infant school teacher in England may experience the following conjunctions or disjunctions in her socialisation:

1. Between socialisation in the family and between primary and secondary school.
2. Between secondary school and teacher training. The higher the qualifications required by the college of education, the more likely that the socialisation in the later years of the secondary school will be through strong classification and frames. On the other hand, the socialisation into the college of education may well be into classification and frames of varying strengths.

Transition Between Stages of Education

We have examined aspects of the transition to school; there is also the question of transition between stages of education, from pre-school to primary, from primary to secondary. These transitions between stages are marked by three inter-related features:

1. An increase in the strength of classification and frames (initiation into the collective code).
2. An increase in the range of different teachers; that is, the pupil is made aware of the insulations within the division of labour. He also learns that the principle of authority transcends the individuals who hold it, for as teachers/subjects change his role remains the same.
3. The weak classification and frames of the invisible pedagogy emphasise the importance of *ways* of knowing, of constructing problems, whereas the strong classification and frames of visible pedagogies emphasise states of knowledge and received problems. Thus there is a crucial change in what counts as having knowledge, in what counts as a legitimate realisation of that knowledge *and* in the social context.

Thus the shift from invisible to visible pedagogies in one phrase is a change in code; a change in the principles of relation and evaluation whether these are principles of knowledge, of social relationships, of practices, of property, of identity.

It is likely that this change of code will be more effectively made (despite the difficulties) by the new middle-class children as their own socialisation within the family contains *both* codes—the code which creates the manifestation of the person and the code which creates private property. Further, as we have argued elsewhere, it is more likely that the working class children will experience continuity in code between stages of education. The class bias of the collection code (which creates a visible pedagogy) may make such a transmission difficult for them to receive and exploit. As a consequence, the continuation of the invisible pedagogy in the form of an integrated code is likely for working class children, and its later institutionalisation for the same children at the secondary level.

We can now begin to see that the condition for continuity of educational code for *all* children, irrespective of class, is the type of code transmitted by the University. Simply expanding the University, increasing differentiation within the tertiary level, equalising opportunity of access and outcome will not fundamentally change the situation at levels below. We will only have expanded the size of the cohort at the tertiary level. From another point of view, although we may have changed the organisational structure we have *not* changed the code controlling transmission; the process of reproduction will not be fundamentally affected. To change the code controlling transmission involves changing the culture and its basis in privatised class relationships. Thus if we accept, for the sake of argument, the greater educational value of invisible pedagogies, of weak classification and frames, the condition for their effective and total institutionalism at the secondary level is a fundamental change of code at the tertiary level. If this does not occur then codes and class will remain firmly linked in schools.

Finally, we can raise a basic question. The movement to invisible pedagogies realised through integrated codes may be seen as a superficial solution to a more obdurate problem. Integraded codes are integrated at the level of ideas, they do *not* involve integration at the level of institutions, i.e. between school and work. Yet the crucial integration is precisely between the principles of education and the principles of work. There can be no such integration in western societies (to mention only one group) because the work epitomises class relationships. Work can only be brought into the school in terms of the function of the school as a selective mechanism or in terms of social/psychological adjustment to work. Indeed, the abstracting of education from work, the hallmark of the liberal tradition, or the linkage of education to leisure, masks the brutal fact that work and education cannot be integrated at the level of social principles in class societies. They can either be separated or they can *fit* with each other. Durkheim wrote that changes in pedagogy were indicators of a moral crisis; they can also disguise it and change its form. However, in as much as the move to weak classification and frames has the *potential* of reducing insulations in mental structures and social structures, has the potential of making explicit the implicit and so creating *greater* ambiguity but less disguise, then such a code has the potential of making visible fundamental social contradictions.

Note I

This raises a number of questions. We cannot consider skills abstracted from the context of their transmission, from their relationships to each other and their function in creating, maintaining, modifying or changing a culture. Skills and their relationship to each other are culturally specific competences. The manner of their transmission and acquisition socialises the child into their contextual usages. Thus, the unit of analysis cannot simply be an abstracted specific competence like reading, writing, counting but the *structure* of social relationships which produces these specialised competences. The formulation 'where there is a reduced emphasis upon transmission and acquisition of specific skills' could be misleading, as it suggests that in the context under discussion there are few specialised repertoires of the culture. It may be better to interpret the formulation as indicating an emphasis upon the inter-relationships between skills which are relatively weakly classified and weakly framed. In this way any skill or sets of skills are referred to the *general features of the socialisation*.

Note II

It is a matter of some interest to consider changes in emphasis of research methodologies over recent decades. There has been a shift from the standardised closed questionnaire or experimental context to more unstructured contexts and relationships. It is argued that the former methodology renders irrelevant the subjective meanings of those who are the object of study. In so doing, the researched offer their experience through the media of the researchers' imposed strong classification and strong frames. Further, it is argued that such a method of studying people is derived from a method for the study of objects and therefore it is an outrage to the subjectivity of man for him to be transformed into an object. These arguments go on to link positivist methods with the political control of man through the use of the technology of social science. The new methodology employs apparently weak classification and weak frames, but it uses techniques (participant observation, tape-recordings, video tapes, etc.) which enable more of the researched to be visible, and its techniques allow a range of others to witness the spontaneous behaviour of the observed. Even if these public records of natural behaviour are treated as a means of dialogue between the recorded and the recorder, this dialogue is, itself, subject to the disjunction between intellectual perspectives which will shape the communication. The self-editing of the researcher's communication is different from that of the researched, and this is the *invisible* control. On the other hand, paradoxically, in the case of a closed questionnaire the privacy of the subject is safeguarded, for all that can be made public is a pencil mark which is transformed into an impersonal score. Further, the methods of this transformation must be made public so that its assumptions may be criticised. In the case of the new methodology, the principles used to restrict the vast amount of information and the number of channels are often implicit. One might say that we could distinguish research methodologies in terms of whether they created invisible or visible pedagogies. Thus the former give rise to a total surveillance of the person who, relative to the latter, makes public more of his inside (e.g. his subjectivity) which is evaluated through the use of diffuse, implicit criteria. We are suggesting that the structural origins of changes in the classification and framing of forms of socialisation may perhaps also influence the selection of research methodologies. The morality of the research relationships transcends the dilemmas of a particular researcher. Research methodologies in social science are themselves elements of culture.

Note III

It is interesting to see, for example, where the invisible pedagogy first entered the secondary school curriculum. In England we would suggest that it first penetrated the *non-verbal* area of *unselective* secondary schools. The area which is considered to be the least relevant (in the sense of not producing symbolic property) and the most strongly classified: the area of the art room. Indeed, it might be said that until very recently, the greatest symbolic continuity of pedagogies between primary and secondary stages lay in the non-verbal areas of the curriculum. The art room is often viewed by the rest of the staff as an area of relaxation or even therapy, rather than a space of crucial production. Because of its strong classification and irrelevance (except at school 'show-off' periods) this space is potentially open to change. Art teachers are trained in institutions (at least in recent times) which are very sensitive to innovation and therefore new styles are likely to be rapidly institutionalised in schools, given the strong classification of art in the secondary school curriculum, and also the belief that the less able child can at least do something with his hands even if he finds difficulty with a pen. We might also anticipate that with the interest in such musical forms as pop on the one hand and Cage and Stockhausen on the other, music departments might move towards the invisible pedagogy. To complete the direction in the non-verbal area, it is possible that the transformation of physical training into physical education might also extend to movement. If this development took place, then the non-verbal areas would be realised through the invisible pedagogy. We might then expect a drive to integrate the three areas of sight, sound and movement; *three* modalities would then be linked through a common code. In summary this movement is from reproduction to production.

Note IV

We can clarify the issues raised in this paper in the following way. Any socialising context must consist of a transmitter and an acquirer. These two form a matrix in the sense that the communication is regulated by a structural principle. We have suggested that the underlying principle of a socialising matrix is realised in classification and frames. The relationship between the two and the strengths show us the structure of the control and the form of communication. We can, of course, analyse this matrix in a number of ways:

1. We can focus upon the transmitter.
2. We can focus upon the acquirer.

3. We can focus upon the principles underlying the matrix.
4. We can focus upon a given matrix and ignore its relationship to other matrices.
5. We can consider the relationships between critical matrices, e.g. family, peer group, school, work.

We can go on to ask questions about the function of a matrix and questions about the change in the form of its realisation, i.e. changes in the strength of its classification and frames. We believe that the unit of analysis must always be the matrix and the matrix will always include the theories and methods of its analysis (see Note II on research methodology). Now any one matrix can be regarded as a reproducer, an interrupter, or a change matrix. A reproduction matrix will attempt to create strong classification and strong frames. An interrupter matrix changes the *form* of transmission, but not the critical relationship *between* matrices. A change matrix leads to a fundamental change in the structural relationship *between* matrices. This will require a major change in the institutional structure. For example, we have argued that within the middle class there is a conflict which has generated two distinct socialising matrices, one a reproducer, the other an interrupter. And these matrices are at work within education for similar groups of children up to possibly the primary stage, and different groups of pupils at the secondary stage. However, in as much as the structural relationship between school and work is unchanged (i.e. there has been no change in the basic principles of their relationship) then we cannot by this argument see current differences in educational pedagogy as representing a change matrix. In other words, the form of the reproduction of class relationships in education has been *interrupted* but not changed. We might speculate that ideological conflict within the middle class takes the form of a conflict between the symbolic outcomes of reproduction and interruption matrices. If one takes the argument one stage further, we have to consider the reproduction of the *change* in the form of class relationships. In this case, the reproduction of an interrupter matrix is through weak classification and weak frames. However, it is possible that such a form of reproduction may at some point evoke its own interrupter i.e. an increase in either classification or frame strength, or both.

Note V

Women played an active role in initiating (Montessori), shaping and disseminating invisible pedagogies. Consider:

1. The application of Freudian theory by Anna Freud to child analysis; the modification of Freudian theory by Melanie Klein and her followers, Hanna Segal, Joan Riviere, Marion Milner; and the development of the interpretation of play as phantasy content in child analysis.
2. The extension of psychoanalytic theory into education and the training of teachers (post 1945) through Susan Isaacs at the University of London Institute of Education, and its further development by Dolly Garner. Parallel work with a Piagetian basis was carried out by Molly Brierley, Principal of the Froebel College of Education.
3. A number of women in a much earlier period were active in the education and training of teachers, e.g. Philippa Fawcett, Rachel McMillan.

It is possible that women were crucial agents in the last quarter of the nineteenth century (and perhaps even before). For in as much as the concept of the child was changed, so was the hierarchy, to which women were subordinate. At the same time, the pedagogy provided the basis of a professional identity. From this point of view, women transformed maternal caring and preparing into a *scientific* activity.

A Note on the Coding of Objects and Modalities of Control

THE CODING OF OBJECTS
The concepts of classification and frame can be used to interpret communication between objects. In other words, objects and their relationships to each other constitute a message system whose code can be stated in terms of the relationship between classification and frames of different strengths.

We can consider:

1. The strength of the rules of exclusion which control the array of objects in a space. Thus the stronger the rules of exclusion the more distinctive the array of objects in the space; that is, the greater the difference between object arrays in different spaces.
2. The extent to which objects in the array can enter into different relationships to each other.

Now the stronger the rules of exclusion the stronger the *classification* of objects in that space and the greater the difference between object arrays in different spaces. In the same way in which we discussed relationships between subjects we can discuss the relationships between object arrays in different spaces. Thus the stronger the classification the more the object arrays resemble a collection code, the weaker the classification the more the object arrays resemble an integrated code. The greater the number of different relationships objects in the array can enter into with each other the weaker their framing. The fewer the number of different relationships objects in the array can enter into with each other the stronger their framing.[8]

We would expect that the social distribution of power and the principles of control to be reflected in the coding of objects. This code may be made more delicate if we take into account:

1. The number of objects in the array.
2. The rate of change of the array.

We can have strong classification with a large *or* a small number of objects. We can have strong classification of large or small arrays where the array is fixed across time *or* where the array varies across time. Consider, for example, two arrays which are strongly classified; a late Victorian middle-class living-room and a middle-twentieth-century, trendy, middle-class 'space' in Hampstead. The Victorian room is likely to contain a very large number of objects whereas the middle-class room is likely to contain a small number of objects. In one case the object array is foreground and the space background, whereas in the second case the space is a vital component of the array. The Victorian room represents both strong classification and strong framing. Further, whilst objects may be added to the array, its fundamental characteristics would remain constant over a relatively long time period. The Hampstead room is likely to contain a small array which would indicate strong classification (strong rules of exclusion), but the objects are likely to enter into a variety of relationships with each other; this would indicate weak framing. Further, it is possible that the array would be changed across time according to fashion.

We can now see that if we are to consider classification (C) we need to know:

1. Whether it is strong or weak.
2. Whether the array is small or large (x).
3. Whether the array is fixed or variable (y).

At the level of frame (F) we need to know: Whether it is strong or weak (p); that is, whether the coding is restricted or elaborated.

It is also important to indicate in the specification of the code the context (c) to which it applies. We should also indicate the nature of the array by adding the concept realisation (r). Thus, the most abstract formulation of the object code would be as follows:

$$f(c, r, C(x,y), F(p))$$

The code is some unspecified function of the variables enclosed in the brackets.

It is important to note that because the classification is weak it does not mean that there is less control. Indeed, from this point of view it is not possible to talk about amount of control only of its modality. This point we will now develop.

CLASSIFICATION, FRAMES, AND MODALITIES OF CONTROL

Imagine four lavatories. The first is stark, bare, pristine, the walls are painted a sharp white; the washbowl is like the apparatus, a gleaming white. A square block of soap sits cleanly in an indentation in the sink. A white towel (or perhaps pink) is folded neatly on a chrome rail or hangs from a chrome ring. The lavatory paper is hidden in a cover and peeps through its slit. In the second lavatory there are books on a shelf and some relaxing of the rigours of the first. In the third there are books on the shelf, pictures on the wall and perhaps a scattering of tiny objects. In the fourth lavatory the rigour is *totally relaxed*. The walls are covered with a motley array of postcards, there is a various assortment of reading matter and curios. The lavatory roll is likely to be uncovered and the holder may well fall apart in use.

We can say that as we move from the first to the fourth lavatory we are moving from a strongly classified to a weakly classified space: from a space regulated by strong rules of exclusion to a space regulated by weak rules of exclusion. Now if the rules of exclusion are strong then the space is strongly marked off from other spaces in the house or flat. The *boundary* between the spaces or rooms is sharp. If the rules of exclusion are strong, the boundaries well marked, then it follows that there must be some strong boundary maintainers (authority). If things are to be kept apart then there must be some strong hierarchy to ensure the apartness of things. Further, the first lavatory constructs a space where pollution is highly visible. In as much as a user leaves a personal mark (a failure to replace the towel in its original position, a messy bar of soap, scum in the washbowl, lavatory paper floating in the bowl, etc.) this constitutes pollution and such pollution is quickly perceived. Thus the criteria for competent usage of the space are both *explicit* and *specific*. So far we have been discussing aspects of classification; we shall now consider framing.

Whereas classification tells us about the structure of relationships in *space*, framing tells us about the structure of relationships in *time*. Framing refers us to interaction, to the power relationships of interaction; that is, framing refers us to communication. Now in the case of our lavatories, framing *here* would refer to the communication between the occupants of the space and those outside of the space. Such communication is normally strongly framed by a door usually equipped with a lock. We suggest that as we move from the strongly classified to the weakly classified lavatory, despite the potential insulation between inside and outside, there will occur a reduction in frame strength. In the case of the first lavatory we suggest that the door will always be closed and after entry will be locked. Ideally no effects on the inside should be heard on the outside. Indeed, a practised user of this lavatory will acquire certain competencies in order to meet this requirement. However, in the case of the most weakly classified lavatory, we suggest that the door will normally be open; it may even be that the lock will not function. It would not be considered untoward for a conversation to develop or even be continued either side of the door. A practised user of this most weakly classified and weakly framed lavatory will acquire certain communicative competencies rather different from those required for correct use of the strongly classified one.

We have already noted that lavatory one creates a space where pollution is highly visible, where criteria for behaviour are explicit and specific, where the social basis of the authority maintaining the strong classification and frames is hierarchical. Yet it is also the case that such classification and frames create a *private* although impersonal space. *For providing that the classification and framing are not violated the user of the space is beyond surveillance.*

However, when we consider lavatory four which has the weakest classification and weakest frames it seems at first sight that such a structure celebrates weak control. There appear to be few rules regulating what goes into a space and few rules regulating communication between spaces. Therefore it is difficult to consider what counts as a violation or pollution. Indeed, it would appear that such a classification and framing relationship facilitates the development of spontaneous behaviour. Let us consider this possibility.

Lavatory one is predicated on the rule 'things must be kept apart' be they persons, acts, objects, communication, and the stronger the classification and frames the greater the insulation, the stronger the boundaries between classes of persons, acts, objects, communications. Lavatory four is predicated on the rule that approximates to 'things must be put together.' As a consequence, we would find objects in the space that could be found in other spaces. Further, there is a more relaxed marking off of the space and communication is possible between inside and outside. We have as yet not discovered the fundamental principles of violation.

Imagine one user, who seeing the motley array and being sensitive to what he or she takes to be a potential of the space decides to add to the array and places an additional postcard on the wall. It is possible that a little later a significant adult might say 'Darling, that's beautiful but it doesn't quite fit' or 'How lovely but wouldn't it be better a little higher up?' In other words, we are suggesting that the array has a principle, that the apparently motley collection is ordered but that the principle is implicit and although it is not easily discoverable it is capable of being violated. Indeed, it might take our user a very long time to infer the *tacit* principle and generate choices in

accordance with it. Without knowledge of the principle our user is unlikely to make appropriate choices and such choices may require a long period of socialisation. In the case of lavatory one no principle is required; all that is needed is the following of the command 'Leave the space as you found it.'[9]

Now let us examine the weak framing in more detail. We suggest that locking the door, avoiding or ignoring communication, would count as violation; indeed anything which would offend the principle of *things must be put together*. However, in as much as the framing between inside and outside is weak then it is also the case that the user is potentially or indirectly under continuous surveillance, in which case there is no privacy. Here we have a social context which at first sight appears to be very relaxed, which promotes and provokes the expression of the person, 'a do your own thing' space where highly personal choices may be offered, where hierarchy is not explicit yet on analysis we find that it is based upon a form of implicit control which carries the potential of total surveillance. Such a form of implicit control encourages more of the person to be made manifest yet such manifestations are subject to continuous screening and general rather than specific criteria. *At the level of classification the pollution is 'keeping things apart'; at the level of framing the violation is 'withholding'; that is, not offering, not making visible the self.*

If things are to be put together which were once set apart, then there must be some principle of the new relationships, but this principle cannot be mechanically applied and therefore cannot be mechanically learned. In the case of the rule 'things must be kept apart,' then the apartness of things is something which is clearly marked and taken for granted in the process of initial socialisation. The social basis of the categories of apartness is implicit but the social basis of the authority is explicit. In the process of such socialisation the insulation between things is a condensed message about the all-pervasiveness of the authority. It may require many years before the social basis of the principles underlying the category system is made fully explicit and by that time the mental structure is well-initiated into the classification and frames. Strong classification and frames celebrate the *reproduction* of the past.

When the rule is 'things must be put

together' we have an *interruption* of a previous order, and what is of issue is the authority (power relationships) which underpin it. Therefore the rule 'things must be put together' celebrates the present over the past, the subjective over the objective, the personal over the positional. Indeed when everything is put together we have a total organic principle which covers all aspects of life *but* which admits of a vast range of combinations and re-combinations. This points to a very abstract or general principle from which a vast range of possibilities may be derived so that individuals can both register personal choices *and* have knowledge when a combination is not in accordance with the principle. What is taken for granted when the rule is 'things must be kept apart' is *relationships* which themselves are made explicit when the rule is 'things must be put together.' They are made explicit by the weak classification and frames. But the latter create a form of implicit but potentially continuous surveillance and at the same time promote the making public of the self in a variety of ways. We arrive finally at the conclusion that the conditions for the release of the person are the absence of explicit hierarchy but the presence of a more intensified form of social interaction which creates continuous but invisible screening. From the point of view of the socialised they would be offering novel, spontaneous combinations.

EMPIRICAL NOTE
It is possible to examine the coding of objects from two perspectives. We can analyse the coding of overt or visible arrays and we can compare the code with the codings of covert or invisible arrays (e.g. drawers, cupboards, refrigerators, basements, closets, handbags, etc.). We can also compare the coding of verbal messages with the coding of non-verbal messages. It would be interesting to carry out an empirical study of standardised spaces, e.g. LEA housing estate, MC suburban 'town' house estate, modern blocks of flats, formal educational spaces which vary in their architecture and in the pedagogy.

I am well aware that the lavatory may not be seen as a space to be *specially contrived* and so subject to *special regulation* in the sense discussed. Some lavatories are not subject to the principles I have outlined. Indeed some may be casually treated spaces where pieces of newspaper may be stuffed behind a convenient pipe, where the door does not close or lock, where apparatus has low efficiency and where sound effects are taken for granted events.

Acknowledgements

This paper was written on the suggestion of Henri Nathan for a Meeting on the effects of scholarisation, itself, a part of the International Learning Sciences Programme, CERI, OECD. I am grateful to Henri Nathan for his insistence on the need to understand the artefacts of learning.

The basis of this paper was written whilst I was a visitor to the École Practique des Hautes Études (Centre de Sociologie Européenne under the direction of Pierre Bourdieu). I am very grateful to Peter Corbishley, graduate student in the Department of the Sociology of Education for his help in the explication of the concept of an 'interrupter system.' The definition used in this paper owes much to his clarification. Finally I would like to thank Gerald Elliot, Professor of Physics (Open University) who whilst in no way ultimately responsible assisted in the formal expression of an 'object code.'

Notes

1. This can be seen if we examine a school class; visible pedagogies create *homogenous* learning contexts, invisible pedagogies create *differentiated* learning contexts.
2. From the production of types of discrete individuals to the production of a type of person.
3. At the secondary level invisible pedagogies are transformed into integrated codes.
4. Symbolic control is the means of cultural reproduction, in the terms of Bourdieu. What is reproduced is a function of the degree of integration within *or* conflict between the transmitting agents *and* the response of those who are subject to the transmission. What must be explored is the complex relationship between changes in the forms of production and changes in the forms of symbolic control.
5. The basic code is elaborated. We are suggesting here that the control of the child is realised through a restricted *variant*.
6. This does *not* mean that *all* teachers wish to have the power or use it.
7. Paradoxically, this situation carries a potential for increasing competitiveness.

8. If the objects in the array can be called lexical items, then the syntax is their relationships to each other. A restricted code is a syntax with few choices: an elaborated code a syntax which generates a large number of choices.
9. The rules of reproduction of lavatory one are explicit and simple but the rules for lavatory four are more implicit and complex. Its apparent casualness is more *difficult* to reproduce.

References

Bernstein, B., Peters, R., and Elvin, L. (1966), Ritual in Education. *Philosophical Transactions of the Royal Society*, Series B, 251, No. 772.

Bernstein, B. (1967), 'Open Schools, Open Society?' *New Society*, 14 Sept.

—— (1971), *Class, Codes and Control*, 1/3 (London: Routledge and Kegan Paul).

—— (1975), *Class, Codes and Control*, 3 (London: Routledge and Kegan Paul).

Boltanski, L. (1969), *Prime Éducation et Morale de Classe* (Paris: The Hague: Mouton).

Blyth, W. A. L. (1965), *English Primary Education*, 1, 2 (London: Routledge and Kegan Paul).

Bourdieu, P., and Passeron, J. C. (1970), *La Reproduction; éléments pour une théorie du système d'enseignement* (Paris: Les Éditions de Minuit).

Brandis, W., and Bernstein, B. (1973), *Selection and Control: a study of teachers' ratings of infant school children* (appendix) (London: Routledge and Kegan Paul).

Cremin, L. (1961), *The Transformation of the School* (New York: Knopf).

Chamboredon, J.-C., and Prevot, J. Y. (1973), 'Le métier d'enfant: définition sociale de la prime enfance et fonctions differentielles de l'école maternelle. Centre de Sociologie Européenne' (Basic paper).

Douglas, M. (1973), *Natural Symbols* (rev. edn., London: Allen Lane).

Durkheim, E. (1933), *The Division of Labour in Society*, transl. George Simpson (New York: Macmillan).

—— (1938), *L'Évolution Pedagogique en France* (Paris: Alcan).

—— (1956), *Education and Sociology*, transl. D. F. Pocock, chs. 2 and 3 (London: Cohen and West).

Gardner, B. (1973), *The Public Schools* (London: Hamish Hamilton).

Goldthorpe, J., and Lockwood, D. (1963), 'Affluence and the Class Structure', *Sociological Review*, 11.

Green, A. G. (1972), *Theory and Practice in Infant Education: A Sociological Approach and Case Study* (M.Sc. diss. Univ. of London Institute of Education Library) (for discussion of 'busyness').

Halliday, M. A. K. (1973), *Exploration in the Function of Language* (London: Edward Arnold).

Houdle, L. (1968), *An Enquiry into the Social Factors affecting the Orientation of English Infant Education since the early Nineteenth Century* (MA dissertation, Univ. of London Institute of Education Library). (Excellent bibliography.)

Plowden Report (1967), *Children and Their Primary Schools: A Report of the Central Advisory Council for Education (England)*, 1 (London: HMSO).

Simon, B. (ed.), (1972), *The Radical Tradition in Education in Britain* (London: Lawrence and Wishart).

Shulman, L. S., and Kreislar, E. R. (eds.), (1966), *Learning by Discovery: A Critical Appraisal* (Chicago: Rand McNally).

Stewart, W. A. C., and McCann (1967), *The Educational Innovators* (London: Macmillan).

Zoldany, M. (1935), *Die Entstehungstheorie des Geistes* (Budapest: Donau).

4

Social Capital in the Creation of Human Capital

James S. Coleman

There are two broad intellectual streams in the description and explanation of social action. One, characteristic of the work of most sociologists, sees the actor as socialized and action as governed by social norms, rules, and obligations. The principal virtues of this intellectual stream lie in its ability to describe action in social context and to explain the way action is shaped, constrained, and redirected by the social context.

The other intellectual stream, characteristic of the work of most economists, sees the actor as having goals independently arrived at, as acting independently, and as wholly self-interested. Its principal virtue lies in having a principle of action, that of maximizing utility. This principle of action, together with a single empirical generalization (declining marginal utility) has generated the extensive growth of neoclassical economic theory, as well as the growth of political philosophy of several varieties: utilitarianism, contractarianism, and natural rights.[1]

In earlier works (Coleman 1986a, 1986b), I have argued for and engaged in the development of a theoretical orientation in sociology that includes components from both these intellectual streams. It accepts the principle of rational or purposive action and attempts to show how that principle, in conjunction with particular social contexts, can account not only for the actions of individuals in particular contexts, but also for the development of social organization. In the present paper, I introduce a conceptual tool for use in this theoretical enterprise: social capital. As background for introducing this concept, it is useful to see some of the criticisms of and attempts to modify the two intellectual streams.

Criticisms and Revisions

Both these intellectual streams have serious defects. The sociological stream has what may be a fatal flaw as a theoretical enterprise: the actor has no 'engine of action'. The actor is shaped by the environment, but there are no internal springs of action that give the actor a purpose or direction. The very conception of action as wholly a product of the environment has led sociologists themselves to criticize this intellectual stream, as in Dennis Wrong's (1961) 'The Oversocialized Conception of Man in Modern Sociology'.

The economic stream, on the other hand, flies in the face of empirical reality: persons' actions are shaped, redirected, constrained by the social context; norms, interpersonal trust, social networks, and social organization are important in the functioning not only of the society but also of the economy.

A number of authors from both traditions have recognized these difficulties and have attempted to impart some of the insights and orientations of the one intellectual stream to the other. In economics, Yoram Ben-Porath (1980) has developed ideas concerning the functioning of what he calls the 'F-connection' in exchange systems. The F-connection is families, friends, and firms, and Ben-Porath, drawing on literature in anthropology and

From *American Journal of Sociology*, 94, Supplement (1988), S95–S120. Reprinted with permission.

sociology as well as economics, shows the way these forms of social organization affect economic exchange. Oliver Williamson has, in a number of publications (e.g. 1975, 1981), examined the conditions under which economic activity is organized in different institutional forms, that is, within firms or in markets. There is a whole body of work in economics, the 'new institutional economics', that attempts to show, within neoclassical economic theory, both the conditions under which particular economic institutions arise and the effects of these institutions (i.e. of social organization) on the functioning of the system.

There have been recent attempts by sociologists to examine the way social organization affects the functioning of economic activity. Baker (1983) has shown how, even in the highly rationalized market of the Chicago Options Exchange, relations among floor traders develop, are maintained, and affect their trades. More generally, Granovetter (1985) has engaged in a broad attack on the 'undersocialized concept of man' that characterizes economists' analysis of economic activity. Granovetter first criticizes much of the new institutional economics as crudely functionalist because the existence of an economic institution is often explained merely by the functions it performs for the economic system. He argues that, even in the new institutional economics, there is a failure to recognize the importance of concrete personal relations and networks of relations—what he calls 'embeddedness'—in generating trust, in establishing expectations, and in creating and enforcing norms.

Granovetter's idea of embeddedness may be seen as an attempt to introduce into the analysis of economic systems social organization and social relations not merely as a structure that springs into place to fulfill an economic function, but as a structure with history and continuity that give it an independent effect on the functioning of economic systems.

All this work, both by economists and by sociologists, has constituted a revisionist analysis of the functioning of economic systems. Broadly, it can be said to maintain the conception of rational action but to superimpose on it social and institutional organization—either endogenously generated, as in the functionalist explanations of some of the

new institutional economists, or as exogenous factors, as in the more proximate-causally oriented work of some sociologists.

My aim is somewhat different. It is to import the economists' principle of rational action for use in the analysis of social systems proper, including but not limited to economic systems, and to do so without discarding social organization in the process. The concept of social capital is a tool to aid in this. In this paper, I introduce the concept in some generality, and then examine its usefulness in a particular context, that of education.

Social Capital

Elements for these two intellectual traditions cannot be brought together in a pastiche. It is necessary to begin with a conceptually coherent framework from one and introduce elements from the other without destroying that coherence.

I see two major deficiencies in earlier work that introduced 'exchange theory' into sociology, despite the pathbreaking character of this work. One was the limitation to microsocial relations, which abandons the principal virtue of economic theory, its ability to make the micro-macro transition from pair relations to system. This was evident both in Homans's (1961) work and in Blau's (1964) work. The other was the attempt to introduce principles in an ad hoc fashion, such as 'distributive justice' (Homans 1964: 241) or the 'norm of reciprocity' (Gouldner 1960). The former deficiency limits the theory's usefulness, and the latter creates a pastiche.

If we begin with a theory of rational action, in which each actor has control over certain resources and interests in certain resources and events, then social capital constitutes a particular kind of resource available to an actor.

Social capital is defined by its function. It is not a single entity but a variety of different entities, with two elements in common: they all consist of some aspect of social structures, and they facilitate certain actions of actors—whether persons or corporate actors—within the structure. Like other forms of capital, social capital is productive, making possible the achievement of certain ends that in its absence would not be possible. Like physical capital and human capital, social capital is not completely fungible but may be specific to certain activities. A given form of social capital that is valuable in facilitating certain actions may be useless or even harmful for others.

Unlike other forms of capital, social capital inheres in the structure of relations between actors and among actors. It is not lodged either in the actors themselves or in physical implements of production. Because purposive organizations can be actors ('corporate actors') just as persons can, relations among corporate actors can constitute social capital for them as well (with perhaps the best-known example being the sharing of information that allows price-fixing in an industry). However, in the present paper, the examples and area of application to which I will direct attention concern social capital as a resource for persons.

Before I state more precisely what social capital consists of, it is useful to give several examples that illustrate some of its different forms.

1. Wholesale diamond markets exhibit a property that to an outsider is remarkable. In the process of negotiating a sale, a merchant will hand over to another merchant a bag of stones for the latter to examine in private at his leisure, with no formal insurance that the latter will not substitute one or more inferior stones or a paste replica. The merchandise may be worth thousands, or hundreds of thousands, of dollars. Such free exchange of stones for inspection is important to the functioning of this market. In its absence, the market would operate in a much more cumbersome, much less efficient fashion.

Inspection shows certain attributes of the social structure. A given merchant community is ordinarily very close, both in the frequency of interaction and in ethnic and family ties. The wholesale diamond market in New York City, for example, is Jewish, with a high degree of intermarriage, living in the same community in Brooklyn, and going to the same synagogues. It is essentially a closed community.

Observation of the wholesale diamond market indicates that these close ties, through family, community, and religious affiliation, provide the insurance that is necessary to facilitate the transactions in the market. If any member of this community defected through substituting other stones or through stealing stones in his temporary possession, he would lose family, religious, and community ties. The strength of these ties makes possible transactions in which trustworthiness is taken for granted and trade can occur with ease. In the absence of these ties, elaborate and expensive bonding and insurance devices would be necessary or else the transactions could not take place.

2. The *International Herald Tribune* of June 21–22, 1986, contained an article on page 1 about South Korean student radical activists. It describes the development of such activism: 'Radical thought is passed on in clandestine "study circles," groups of students who may come from the same high school or hometown or church. These study circles . . . serve as the basic organizational unit for demonstrations and other protests. To avoid detection, members of different groups never meet, but communicate through an appointed representative.'

This description of the basis of organization of this activism illustrates social capital of two kinds. The 'same high school or hometown or church' provides social relations on which the 'study circles' are later built. The study circles themselves constitute a form of social capital—a cellular form of organization that appears especially valuable for facilitating opposition in any political system intolerant of dissent. Even where political dissent is tolerated, certain activities are not, whether the activities are politically motivated terrorism or simple crime. The organization that makes possible these activities is an especially potent form of social capital.

3. A mother of six children, who recently moved with husband and children from suburban Detroit to Jerusalem, described as one reason for doing so the greater freedom her young children had in Jerusalem. She felt safe in letting her eight year old take the six year old across town to school on the city bus and felt her children to be safe in playing without supervision in a city park, neither of which she felt able to do where she lived before.

The reason for this difference can be described as a difference in social capital available in Jerusalem and suburban Detroit. In Jerusalem, the normative structure ensures that unattended children will be 'looked after' by adults in the vicinity, while no such normative structure exists in most metropolitan areas of the United States. One can say that families have available to them in Jerusalem social capital that does not exist in metropolitan areas of the United States.

4. In the Kahn El Khalili market of Cairo, the boundaries between merchants are difficult for an outsider to discover. The owner of a shop that specializes in leather will, when queried about where one can find a certain kind of jewelry, turn out to sell that as well—or, what appears to be nearly the same thing, to have a close associate who sells it, to whom he will immediately take the customer. Or he will instantly become a money changer, although he is not a money changer, merely by turning to his colleague a few shops down. For some activities, such as bringing a customer to a friend's store, there are commissions; for others, such as money changing, merely the creation of obligations. Family relations are important in the market, as is the stability of proprietorship. The whole market is so infused with relations of the sort I have described that it can be seen as an organization, no less so than a department store. Alternatively, one can see the market as consisting of a set of individual merchants, each having an extensive body of social capital on which to draw, through the relationships of the market.

The examples above have shown the value of social capital for a number of outcomes, both economic and noneconomic. There are, however, certain properties of social capital that are important for understanding how it comes into being and how it is employed in the creation of human capital. First, a comparison with human capital, and then an examination of different forms of social capital, will be helpful for seeing these.

Human Capital and Social Capital

Probably the most important and most original development in the economics of education in the past 30 years has been the idea that the concept of physical capital as embodied in tools, machines, and other productive equipment can be extended to include human capital as well (see Schultz 1961; Becker 1964). Just as physical capital is created by changes in materials to form tools that facilitate production, human capital is created by changes in

persons that bring about skills and capabilities that make them able to act in new ways.

Social capital, however, comes about through changes in the relations among persons that facilitate action. If physical capital is wholly tangible, being embodied in observable material form, and human capital is less tangible, being embodied in the skills and knowledge acquired by an individual, *social capital is less tangible yet, for it exists in the relations among persons*. Just as physical capital and human capital facilitate productive activity, social capital does as well. For example, a group within which there is extensive trustworthiness and extensive trust is able to accomplish much more than a comparable group without that trustworthiness and trust.

Forms of Social Capital

The value of the concept of social capital lies first in the fact that it identifies certain aspects of social structure by their functions, just as the concept 'chair' identifies certain physical objects by their function, despite differences in form, appearance, and construction. The function identified by the concept of 'social capital' is the value of these aspects of social structure to actors as resources that they can use to achieve their interests.

By identifying this function of certain aspects of social structure, the concept of social capital constitutes both an aid in accounting for different outcomes at the level of individual actors and an aid toward making the micro-to-macro transitions without elaborating the social structural details through which this occurs. For example, in characterizing the clandestine study circles of South Korean radical students as constituting social capital that these students can use in their revolutionary activities, we assert that the groups constitute a resource that aids in moving from individual protest to organized revolt. If, in a theory of revolt, a resource that accomplishes this task is held to be necessary, then these study circles are grouped together with those organizational structures, having very different origins, that have fulfilled the same function for individuals with revolutionary goals in other contexts, such as the *Comités d'action lycéen* of the French student revolt of 1968 or the workers' cells in tsarist Russia described and advocated by Lenin (1902; 1973).

It is true, of course, that for other purposes one wants to investigate the details of such organizational resources, to understand the elements that are critical to their usefulness as resources for such a purpose, and to examine how they came into being in a particular case. But the concept of social capital allows taking such resources and showing the way they can be combined with other resources to produce different system-level behavior or, in other cases, different outcomes for individuals. Although, for these purposes, social capital constitutes an unanalyzed concept, it signals to the analyst and to the reader that something of value has been produced for those actors who have this resource available and that the value depends on social organization. It then becomes a second stage in the analysis to unpack the concept, to discover what components of social organization contribute to the value produced.

In previous work, Lin (1988) and De Graf and Flap (1988), from a perspective of methodological individualism similar to that used in this paper, have shown how informal social resources are used instrumentally in achieving occupational mobility in the United States and, to a lesser extent, in West Germany and the Netherlands. Lin focused on social ties, especially 'weak' ties, in this role. Here, I want to examine a variety of resources, all of which constitute social capital for actors.

Before examining empirically the value of social capital in the creation of human capital, I will go more deeply into an examination of just what it is about social relations that can constitute useful capital resources for individuals.

OBLIGATIONS, EXPECTATIONS, AND TRUSTWORTHINESS OF STRUCTURES

If A does something for B and trusts B to reciprocate in the future, this establishes an expectation in A and an obligation on the part of B. This obligation can be conceived as a credit slip held by A for performance by B. If A holds a large number of these credit slips, for a number of persons with whom A has relations, then the analogy to financial capital is direct. These credit slips constitute a large body of credit that A can call in if necessary—unless, of course, the placement of trust has been unwise, and these are bad debts that will not be repaid.

In some social structures, it is said that 'people are always doing things for each other.' There are a large number of these credit slips outstanding, often on both sides of a relation (for these credit slips appear often not to be completely fungible across areas of activity, so that credit slips of B held by A and those of A held by B are not fully used to cancel each other out). The El Khalili market in Cairo, described earlier, constitutes an extreme case of such a social structure. In other social structures where individuals are more self-sufficient and depend on each other less, there are fewer of these credit slips outstanding at any time.

This form of social capital depends on two elements: trustworthiness of the social environment, which means that obligations will be repaid, and the actual extent of obligations held. Social structures differ in both these dimensions, and actors within the same structure differ in the second. A case that illustrates the value of the trustworthiness of the environment is that of the rotating-credit associations of Southeast Asia and elsewhere. These associations are groups of friends and neighbors who typically meet monthly, each person contributing to a central fund that is then given to one of the members (through bidding or by lot), until, after a number of months, each of the n persons has made n contributions and received one payout. As Geertz (1962) points out, these associations serve as efficient institutions for amassing savings for small capital expenditures, an important aid to economic development.

But without a high degree of trustworthiness among the members of the group, the institution could not exist—for a person who receives a payout early in the sequence of meetings could abscond and leave the others with a loss. For example, one could not imagine a rotating-credit association operating successfully in urban areas marked by a high degree of social disorganization—or, in other words, by a lack of social capital.

Differences in social structures in both dimensions may arise for a variety of reasons. There are differences in the actual needs that persons have for help, in the existence of other sources of aid (such as government welfare services), in the degree of affluence (which reduces aid needed from others), in cultural differences in the tendency to lend aid and ask for aid (see Banfield 1967) in the closure of social networks, in the logistics of social contacts (see Festinger, Schachter, and Back 1963), and other factors. Whatever the source, however, individuals in social structures with high levels of obligations outstanding at any time have more social capital on which they can draw. The density of outstanding obligations means, in effect, that the overall usefulness of the tangible resources of that social structure is amplified by their availability to others when needed.

Individual actors in a social system also differ in the number of credit slips outstanding on which they can draw at any time. The most extreme examples are in hierarchically structured extended family settings, in which a patriarch (or 'godfather') holds an extraordinarily large set of obligations that he can call in at any time to get what he wants done. Near this extreme are villages in traditional settings that are highly stratified, with certain wealthy families who, because of their wealth, have built up extensive credits that they can call in at any time.

Similarly, in political settings such as a legislature, a legislator in a position with extra resources (such as the Speaker of the House of Representatives or the Majority Leader of the Senate in the US Congress) can, by effective use of resources, build up a set of obligations from other legislators that makes it possible to get legislation passed that would otherwise be stymied. This concentration of obligations constitutes social capital that is useful not only for this powerful legislator but useful also in getting an increased level of action on the part of a legislature. Thus, those members of legislatures among whom such credits are extensive should be more powerful than those without extensive credits and debits because they can use the credits to produce bloc voting on many issues. It is well recognized, for example, that in the US Senate, some senators are members of what is called 'the Senate Club,' while others are not. This in effect means that some senators are embedded in the system of credits and debits, while others, outside the 'Club', are not. It is also well recognized that those in the Club are more powerful than those outside it.

INFORMATION CHANNELS
An important form of social capital is the potential for information that inheres in social relations. Information is important in providing a basis for action. But acquisition of information is costly. At a minimum, it requires attention, which is always in scarce supply. One means by which information can be acquired is by use of social relations that are maintained for other purposes. Katz and Lazarsfeld (1955) showed how this operated for women in several areas of life in a midwestern city around 1950. They showed that a woman with an interest in being in fashion, but no interest in being on the leading edge of fashion, used friends who she knew kept up with fashion as sources of information. Similarly, a person who is not greatly interested in current events but who is interested in being informed about important developments can save the time of reading a newspaper by depending on spouse or friends who pay attention to such matters. A social scientist who is interested in being up-to-date on research in related fields can make use of everyday interactions with colleagues to do so, but only in a university in which most colleagues keep up-to-date.

All these are examples of social relations that constitute a form of social capital that provides information that facilitates action. The relations in this case are not valuable for the 'credit slips' they provide in the form of obligations that one holds for others' performances or for the trustworthiness of the other party but merely for the information they provide.

NORMS AND EFFECTIVE SANCTIONS
When a norm exists and is effective, it constitutes a powerful, though sometimes fragile, form of social capital. Effective norms that inhibit crime make it possible to walk freely outside at night in a city and enable old persons to leave their houses without fear for their safety. Norms in a community that support and provide effective rewards for high achievement in school greatly facilitate the school's task.

A prescriptive norm within a collectivity that constitutes an especially important form of social capital is the norm that one should forgo self-interest and act in the interests of the collectivity. A norm of this sort, reinforced by social support, status, honor, and other rewards, is the social capital that builds young nations (and then dissipates as they grow older), strengthens families by leading family members to act selflessly in 'the family's' interest, facilitates the development of nascent social movements through a small group of dedicated, inward-looking, and mutually rewarding members, and in general leads persons to work for the public good. In some of these cases, the norms are internalized; in others, they are largely supported through external rewards for selfless actions and disapproval for selfish actions. But, whether supported by internal or external sanctions, norms of this sort are important in overcoming the public goods problem that exists in collectivities.

As all these examples suggest, effective norms can constitute a powerful form of social capital. This social capital, however, like the forms described earlier, not only facilitates certain actions; it constrains others. A community with strong and effective norms about young persons' behavior can keep them from 'having a good time.' Norms that make it possible to walk alone at night also constrain the activities of criminals (and in some cases of noncriminals as well). Even prescriptive norms that reward certain actions, like the norm in a community that says that a boy who is a good athlete should go out for football, are in effect directing energy away from other activities. Effective norms in an area can reduce innovativeness in an area, not only deviant actions that harm others but also deviant actions that can benefit everyone. (See Merton (1968: 195–203) for a discussion of how this can come about.)

Social Structure that Facilitates Social Capital

All social relations and social structures facilitate some forms of social capital; actors establish relations purposefully and continue them when they continue to provide benefits. Certain kinds of social structure, however, are especially important in facilitating some forms of social capital.

CLOSURE OF SOCIAL NETWORKS
One property of social relations on which effective norms depend is what I will call closure. In general, one can say that a necessary but not sufficient condition for the emergence of effective norms is action that imposes exter-

nal effects on others (see Ullmann-Margalit 1977; Coleman 1987). Norms arise as attempts to limit negative external effects or encourage positive ones. But, in many social structures where these conditions exist, norms do not come into existence. The reason is what can be described as lack of closure of the social structure. Fig. 4.1 illustrates why. In an open structure like that of Fig. 4.1a, actor A, having relations with actors B and C, can carry out actions that impose negative externalities on B or C or both. Since they have no relations with one another, but with others instead (D and E), then they cannot combine forces to sanction A in order to constrain the actions. Unless either B or C alone is sufficiently harmed and sufficiently powerful vis-à-vis A to sanction alone, A's actions can continue unabated. In a structure with closure, like that of Fig. 4.1b, B and C can combine to provide a collective sanction, or either can reward the other for sanctioning A. (See Merry (1984) for examples of the way gossip, which depends on closure of the social structure, is used as a collective sanction.)

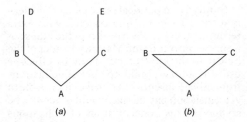

Fig. 4.1. Network without (a) and with (b) closure

In the case of norms imposed by parents on children, closure of the structure requires a slightly more complex structure, which I will call intergenerational closure. Intergenerational closure may be described by a simple diagram that represents relations between parent and child and relations outside the family. Consider the structure of two communities, represented by Fig. 4.2. The vertical lines represent relations across generations, between parent and child, while the horizontal lines represent relations within a generation. The point labeled A in both Fig. 4.2a and Fig. 4.2b represents the parent of child B, and the point labeled D represents the parent of child C. The lines between B and C represent the relations among children that exist within any school. Although the other relations among children within the school are not shown here, there exists a high degree of closure among peers, who see each other daily, have expectations toward each other, and develop norms about each other's behavior.

The two communities differ, however, in the presence or absence of links among the parents of children in the school. For the school represented by Fig. 4.2*b*, there is intergenerational closure; for that represented by Fig. 4.2*a*, there is not. To put it colloquially, in the lower community represented by 4.2*b*, the parents' friends are the parents of their children's friends. In the other, they are not.

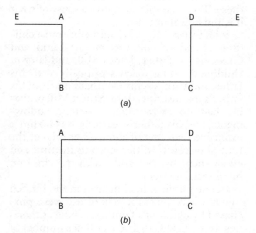

(*a*)

(*b*)

Fig. 4.2. Network involving parents (*A, D*) and children (*B, C*) without (*a*) and with (*b*) intergenerational closure

The consequence of this closure is, as in the case of the wholesale diamond market or in other similar communities, a set of effective sanctions that can monitor and guide behavior. In the community in Fig. 4.2*b*, parents *A* and *D* can discuss their children's activities and come to some consensus about standards and about sanctions. Parent *A* is reinforced by parent *D* in sanctioning his child's actions; beyond that, parent *D* constitutes a monitor not only for his own child, *C*, but also for the other child, *B*. Thus, the existence of intergenerational closure provides a quantity of social capital available to each parent in raising his children—not only in matters related to school but in other matters as well.

Closure of the social structure is important not only for the existence of effective norms but also for another form of social capital: the trustworthiness of social structures that allows the proliferation of obligations and expectations. Defection from an obligation is a form of imposing a negative externality on another. Yet, in a structure without closure, it can be effectively sanctioned, if at all, only by the person to whom the obligation is owed. Reputation cannot arise in an open structure, and collective sanctions that would ensure trustworthiness cannot be applied. Thus, we may say that closure creates trustworthiness in a social structure.

APPROPRIABLE SOCIAL ORGANIZATION

Voluntary organizations are brought into being to aid some purpose of those who initiate them. In a housing project built during World War II in an eastern city of the United States, there were many physical problems caused by poor construction: faulty plumbing, crumbling sidewalks, and other defects (Merton, n.d.). Residents organized to confront the builders and to address these problems in other ways. Later, when the problems were solved, the organization remained as available social capital that improved the quality of life for residents. Residents had resources available that they had seen as unavailable where they had lived before. (For example, despite the fact that the number of teenagers in the community was smaller, residents were *more* likely to express satisfaction with the availability of teenage babysitters.)

Printers in the New York Typographical Union who were monotype operators formed a Monotype Club as a social club (Lipset, Trow, and Coleman 1956). Later, as employers looked for monotype operators and as monotype operators looked for jobs, both found this organization an effective employment referral service and appropriated the organization for this purpose. Still later, when the Progressive Party came into power in the New York Union, the Monotype Club served as an organizational resource for the Independent Party as it left office. The Monotype Club subsequently served as an important source of social capital for the Independents to sustain the party as an organized opposition while it was out of office.

In the example of South Korean student radicals used earlier, the study circles were described as consisting of groups of students from the same high school or hometown or church. Here, as in the earlier examples, an organization that was initiated for one purpose is available for appropriation for other purposes, constituting important social capital for the individual members, who have available to them the organizational resources necessary for effective opposition. These examples illustrate the general point, that organization, once brought into existence for one set of purposes, can also aid others, thus constituting social capital available for use.

It is possible to gain insight into some of the ways in which closure and appropriable social organization provide social capital by use of a distinction made by Max Gluckman (1967) between simplex and multiplex relations.[2] In the latter, persons are linked in more than one context (neighbor, fellow worker, fellow parent, coreligionist, etc.), while in the former, persons are linked through only one of these relations. The central property of a multiplex relation is that it allows the resources of one relationship to be appropriated for use in others. Sometimes, the resource is merely information, as when two parents who see each other as neighbors exchange information about their teenagers' activities; sometimes, it is the obligations that one person owes a second in relationship X, which the second person can use to constrain the actions of the first in relationship Y. Often, it is resources in the form of other persons who have obligations in one context that can be called on to aid when one has problems in another context.

Social Capital in the Creation of Human Capital

The preceding pages have been directed toward defining and illustrating social capital in general. But there is one effect of social capital that is especially important: its effect on the creation of human capital in the next generation. Both social capital in the family and social capital in the community play roles in the creation of human capital in the rising generation. I will examine each of these in turn.

SOCIAL CAPITAL IN THE FAMILY

Ordinarily, in the examination of the effects of various factors on achievement in school,

'family background' is considered a single entity, distinguished from schooling in its effects. But there is not merely a single 'family background'; family background is analytically separable into at least three different components: financial capital, human capital, and social capital. Financial capital is approximately measured by the family's wealth or income. It provides the physical resources that can aid achievement: a fixed place in the home for studying, materials to aid learning, the financial resources that smooth family problems. Human capital is approximately measured by parents' education and provides the potential for a cognitive environment for the child that aids learning. Social capital within the family is different from either of these. Two examples will give a sense of what it is and how it operates.

John Stuart Mill, at an age before most children attend school, was taught Latin and Greek by his father, James Mill, and later in childhood would discuss critically with his father and with Jeremy Bentham drafts of his father's manuscripts. John Stuart Mill probably had no extraordinary genetic endowments, and his father's learning was no more extensive than that of some other men of the time. The central difference was the time and effort spent by the father with the child on intellectual matters.

In one public school district in the United States where texts for school use were purchased by children's families, school authorities were puzzled to discover that a number of Asian immigrant families purchased *two* copies of each textbook needed by the child. Investigation revealed that the family purchased the second copy for the mother to study in order to help her child do well in school. Here is a case in which the human capital of the parents, at least as measured traditionally by years of schooling, is low, but the social capital in the family available for the child's education is extremely high.

These examples illustrate the importance of social capital within the family for a child's intellectual development. It is of course true that children are strongly affected by the human capital possessed by their parents. But this human capital may be irrelevant to outcomes for children if parents are not an important part of their children's lives, if their human capital is employed exclusively at work or elsewhere outside the home. The social capital of the family is the relations between children and parents (and, when families include other members, relationships with them as well). That is, if the human capital possessed by parents is not complemented by social capital embodied in family relations, it is irrelevant to the child's educational growth that the parent has a great deal, or a small amount, of human capital.[3]

I will not differentiate here among the forms of social capital discussed earlier, but will attempt merely to measure the strength of the relations between parents and child as a measure of the social capital available to the child from the parent. Nor will I use the concept in the context of the paradigm of rational action, as, for example, is often done in use of the concept of human capital to examine the investments in education that a rational person would make. A portion of the reason for this lies in a property of much social capital not shown by most forms of capital (to which I will turn in a later section): its public goods character, which leads to underinvestment.

Social capital within the family that gives the child access to the adult's human capital depends both on the physical presence of adults in the family and on the attention given by the adults to the child. The physical absence of adults may be described as a structural deficiency in family social capital. The most prominent element of structural deficiency in modern families is the single-parent family. However, the nuclear family itself, in which one or both parents work outside the home, can be seen as structurally deficient, lacking the social capital that comes with the presence of parents during the day, or with grandparents or aunts and uncles in or near the household.

Even if adults are physically present, there is a lack of social capital in the family if there are not strong relations between children and parents. The lack of strong relations can result from the child's embeddedness in a youth community, from the parents' embeddedness in relationships with other adults that do not cross generations, or from other sources. Whatever the source, it means that whatever *human* capital exists in the parents, the child does not profit from it because the *social* capital is missing.

The effects of a lack of social capital within the family differ for different educational outcomes. One for which it appears to be especially important is dropping out of school. With the *High School and Beyond* sample of students in high schools, Table 4.1 shows the expected dropout rates for students in different types of families when various measures of social and human capital in the family and a measure of social capital in the community are controlled statistically.[4] An explanation is necessary for the use of number of siblings as a measure of lack of social capital. The number of siblings represents, in this interpretation, a

Table 4.1. Dropout rates between Spring, Grade 10, and Spring, Grade 12, for students whose families differ in social capital, controlling for human capital and financial capital in the family[a]

	Percentage Dropping Out	Difference in Percentage Points
1. Parents' presence:		
Two parents	13.1 ⎫	
Single parent	19.1 ⎭	6.0
2. Additional children:		
One sibling	10.8 ⎫	
Four siblings	17.2 ⎭	6.4
3. Parents and children:		
Two parents, one sibling	10.1 ⎫	
One parent, four siblings	22.6 ⎭	12.5
4. Mother's expectation for child's education:		
Expectation of college	11.6 ⎫	
No expectation of college	20.2 ⎭	8.6
5. Three factors together:		
Two parents, one sibling, mother expects college	8.1 ⎫	
One parent, four siblings, no college expectation	30.6 ⎭	22.5

[a] Estimates taken from logistic regression reported more fully in App. Table 4.A1.

dilution of adult attention to the child. This is consistent with research results for measures of achievement and IQ, which show that test scores decline with sib position, even when total family size is controlled, and that scores decline with number of children in the family. Both results are consistent with the view that younger sibs and children in large families have less adult attention, which produces weaker educational outcomes.

Item 1 of Table 4.1 shows that, when other family resources are controlled, the percentage of students who drop out between spring of the sophomore year and spring of the senior year is 6 percentage points higher for children from single-parent families. Item 2 of Table 4.1 shows that the rate is 6.4 percentage points higher for sophomores with four siblings than for those with otherwise equivalent family resources but only one sibling. Or, taking these two together, we can think of the ratio of adults to children as a measure of the social capital in the family available for the education of any one of them. Item 3 of Table 4.1 shows that for a sophomore with four siblings and one parent, and an otherwise average background, the rate is 22.6 per cent; with one sibling and two parents, the rate is 10.1 per cent—a difference of 12.5 percentage points.

Another indicator of adult attention in the family, although not a pure measure of social capital, is the mother's expectation of the child's going to college. Item 4 of the table shows that, for sophomores without this parental expectation, the rate is 8.6 percentage points higher than for those with it. With the three sources of family social capital taken together, item 5 of the table shows that sophomores with one sibling, two parents, and a mother's expectation for college (still controlling on other resources of family) have an 8.1 per cent dropout rate; with four siblings, one parent, and no expectation of the mother for college, the rate is 30.6 per cent.

These results provide a less satisfactory test than if the research had been explicitly designed to examine effects of social capital within the family. In addition, Table 4.A1 in the Appendix shows that another variable that should measure social capital in the family, the frequency of talking with parents about personal experiences, shows essentially no relation to dropping out. Nevertheless, taken all together, the data do indicate that social capital in the family is a resource for education of the family's children, just as is financial and human capital.

SOCIAL CAPITAL OUTSIDE THE FAMILY
The social capital that has value for a young person's development does not reside solely within the family. It can be found outside as well in the community consisting of the social relationships that exist among parents, in the closure exhibited by this structure of relations, and in the parents' relations with the institutions of the community.

The effect of this social capital outside the family on educational outcomes can be seen by examining outcomes for children whose parents differ in the particular source of social capital discussed earlier, intergenerational closure. There is not a direct measure of intergenerational closure in the data, but there is a proximate indicator. This is the number of times the child has changed schools because the family moved. For families that have moved often, the social relations that constitute social capital are broken at each move. Whatever the degree of intergenerational closure available to others in the community, it is not available to parents in mobile families.

The logistic regression carried out earlier and reported in Table 4.A1 shows that the coefficient for number of moves since grade 5 is 10 times its standard error, the variable with the strongest overall effect of any variable in the equation, including the measures of human and financial capital in the family (socioeconomic status) and the crude measures of family social capital introduced in the earlier analysis. Translating this into an effect on dropping out gives 11.8 per cent as the dropout rate if the family has not moved, 16.7 per cent if it has moved once, and 23.1 per cent if it has moved twice.

In the *High School and Beyond* data set, another variation among the schools constitutes a useful indicator of social capital. This is the distinctions among public high schools, religiously based private high schools, and nonreligiously based private high schools. It is the religiously based high schools that are surrounded by a community based on the religious organization. These families have intergenerational closure that is based on a multiplex relation: whatever other relations they have, the adults are members of the same religious body and parents of children in the same school. In contrast, it is the independent private schools that are typically least surrounded by a community, for their student bodies are collections of students, most of whose families have no contact.[5] The choice of private school for most of these parents is an individualistic one, and, although they back their children with extensive human capital, they send their children to these schools denuded of social capital.

In the *High School and Beyond* data set, there are 893 public schools, 84 Catholic schools, and 27 other private schools. Most of the other private schools are independent schools, though a minority have religious foundations. In this analysis, I will at the outset regard the other private schools as independent private schools to examine the effects of social capital outside the family.

The results of these comparisons are shown in Table 4.2. Item 1 of the table shows that the dropout rates between sophomore and senior years are 14.4 per cent in public schools, 3.4 per cent in Catholic schools, and 11.9 per cent in other private schools. What is most striking is the low dropout rate in Catholic schools. The rate is a fourth of that in the public schools and a third of that in the other private schools.

Adjusting the dropout rates for differences in student-body financial, human, and social capital among the three sets of schools by standardizing the population of the Catholic schools and other private schools to the student-body backgrounds of the public schools shows that the differences are affected only slightly. Furthermore, the differences are not due to the religion of the students or to the

degree of religious observance. Catholic students in public school are only slightly less likely to drop out than non-Catholics. Frequency of attendance at religious services, which is itself a measure of social capital through intergenerational closure, is strongly related to dropout rate, with 19.5 per cent of public school students who rarely or never attend dropping out compared with 9.1 per cent of those who attend often. But this effect exists apart from, and in addition to, the effect of the school's religious affiliation. Comparable figures for Catholic school students are 5.9 per cent and 2.6 per cent respectively (Coleman and Hoffer 1987: 138).

The low dropout rates of the Catholic schools, the absence of low dropout rates in the other private schools, and the independent effect of frequency of religious attendance all provide evidence of the importance of social capital outside the school, in the adult community surrounding it, for this outcome of education.

A further test is possible, for there were eight schools in the sample of non-Catholic private schools ('other private' in the analysis above) that have religious foundations and over 50 per cent of the student body of that religion. Three were Baptist schools, two were Jewish, and three from three other denominations. If the inference is correct about the religious community's providing intergenerational closure and thus social capital and about the importance of social capital in depressing the chance of dropping out of high school, these schools also should show a lower dropout rate than the independent

Table 4.2. Dropout rates between Spring, Grade 10, and Spring, Grade 12, for students from schools with differing amounts of social capital in the surrounding community

	Public	Catholic	Other Private Schools
1. Raw dropout rates	14.4	3.4	11.9
2. Dropout rates standardized to average public-school sophomore[a]	14.4	5.2	11.6

	Non-Catholic Religious	Independent
3. Raw dropout rates for students[b] from independent and non-Catholic religious private schools	3.7	10.0

[a] The standardization is based on separate logistic regressions for these two sets of schools, using the same variables listed in n. 5. Coefficients and means for the standardization are in Hoffer (1986, Tables 5 and 24).
[b] This tabulation is based on unweighted data, which is responsible for the fact that both rates are lower than the rate for other private schools in item 1 of the table, which is based on weighted data.

private schools. Item 3 of Table 4.2 shows that their dropout rate is lower, 3.7 per cent, essentially the same as that of the Catholic schools.[6]

The data presented above indicate the importance of social capital for the education of youth, or, as it might be put, the importance of social capital in the creation of human capital. Yet there is a fundamental difference between social capital and most other forms of capital that has strong implications for the development of youth. It is this difference to which I will turn in the next section.

Public-Goods Aspects of Social Capital

Physical capital is ordinarily a private good, and property rights make it possible for the person who invests in physical capital to capture the benefits it produces. Thus, the incentive to invest in physical capital is not depressed; there is not a suboptimal investment in physical capital because those who invest in it are able to capture the benefits of their investments. For human capital also—at least human capital of the sort that is produced in schools—the person who invests the time and resources in building up this capital reaps its benefits in the form of a higher-paying job, more satisfying or higher-status work, or even the pleasure of greater understanding of the surrounding world—in short, all the benefits that schooling brings to a person.

But most forms of social capital are not like this. For example, the kinds of social structures that make possible social norms and the sanctions that enforce them do not benefit primarily the person or persons whose efforts would be necessary to bring them about, but benefit all those who are part of such a structure. For example, in some schools where there exists a dense set of associations among some parents, these are the result of a small number of persons, ordinarily mothers who do not hold full-time jobs outside the home. Yet these mothers themselves experience only a subset of the benefits of this social capital surrounding the school. If one of them decides to abandon these activities—for example, to take a full-time job—this may be an entirely reasonable action from a personal point of view and even from the point of view of that household with its children. The benefits of the new activity may far outweigh the losses

that arise from the decline in associations with other parents whose children are in the school. But the withdrawal of these activities constitutes a loss to all those other parents whose associations and contacts were dependent on them.

Similarly, the decision to move from a community so that the father, for example, can take a better job may be entirely correct from the point of view of that family. But, because social capital consists of relations among persons, other persons may experience extensive losses by the severance of those relations, a severance over which they had no control. A part of those losses is the weakening of norms and sanctions that aid the school in its task. For each family, the total cost it experiences as a consequence of the decisions it and other families make may outweigh the benefits of those few decisions it has control over. Yet the beneficial consequences to the family of those decisions made by the family may far outweigh the minor losses it experiences from them alone.

It is not merely voluntary associations, such as a PTA, in which under investment of this sort occurs. When an individual asks a favor from another, thus incurring an obligation, he does so because it brings him a needed benefit; he does not consider that it does the other a benefit as well by adding to a drawing fund of social capital available in a time of need. If the first individual can satisfy his need through self-sufficiency, or through aid from some official source without incurring an obligation, he will do so—and thus fail to add to the social capital outstanding in the community.

Similar statements can be made with respect to trustworthiness as social capital. An actor choosing to keep trust or not (or choosing whether to devote resources to an attempt to keep trust) is doing so on the basis of costs and benefits he himself will experience. That his trustworthiness will facilitate others' actions or that his lack of trustworthiness will inhibit others' actions does not enter into his decision. A similar but more qualified statement can be made for information as a form of social capital. An individual who serves as a source of information for another because he is well informed ordinarily acquires that information for his own benefit, not for the others who make use of him. (This is not always true. As Katz and Lazarsfeld [1955] show, 'opinion leaders' in an area acquire information in part to maintain their position as opinion leaders.)

For norms also, the statement must be qualified. Norms are intentionally established, indeed as means of reducing externalities, and their benefits are ordinarily captured by those who are responsible for establishing them. But the capability of establishing and maintaining effective norms depends on properties of the social structure (such as closure) over which one actor does not have control yet are affected by one actor's action. These are properties that affect the structure's capacity to sustain effective norms, yet properties that ordinarily do not enter into an individual's decision that affects them.

Some forms of social capital have the property that their benefits can be captured by those who invest in them; consequently, rational actors will not underinvest in this type of social capital. Organizations that produce a private good constitute the outstanding example. The result is that there will be in society an imbalance in the relative investment in organizations that produce private goods for a market and those associations and relationships in which the benefits are not captured—an imbalance in the sense that, if the positive externalities created by the latter form of social capital could be internalized, it would come to exist in greater quantity.

The public goods quality of most social capital means that it is in a fundamentally different position with respect to purposive action than are most other forms of capital. It is an important resource for individuals and may affect greatly their ability to act and their perceived quality of life. They have the capability of bringing it into being. Yet, because the benefits of actions that bring social capital into being are largely experienced by persons other than the actor, it is often not in his interest to bring it into being. The result is that most forms of social capital are created or destroyed as by-products of other activities. This social capital arises or disappears without anyone's willing it into or out of being and is thus even less recognized and taken account of in social action than its already intangible character would warrant.

There are important implications of this public goods aspect of social capital that play a part in the development of children and youth. Because the social structural conditions that overcome the problems of supplying these public goods—that is, strong families and strong communities—are much less often present now than in the past, and promise to be even less present in the future, we can expect that, ceteris paribus, we confront a declining quantity of human capital embodied in each successive generation. The obvious solution appears to be to attempt to find ways of overcoming the problem of supply of these public goods, that is, social capital employed for the benefit of children and youth. This very likely means the substitution of some kind of formal organization for the voluntary and spontaneous social organization that has in the past been the major source of social capital available to the young.

Conclusion

In this paper, I have attempted to introduce into social theory a concept, 'social capital,' paralleling the concepts of financial capital, physical capital, and human capital—but embodied in relations among persons. This is part of a theoretical strategy that involves use of the paradigm of rational action but without the assumption of atomistic elements stripped of social relationships. I have shown the use of this concept through demonstrating the effect of social capital in the family and in the community in aiding the formation of human capital. The single measure of human capital formation used for this was one that appears especially responsive to the supply of social capital, remaining in high school until graduation versus dropping out. Both social capital in the family and social capital outside it, in the adult community surrounding the school, showed evidence of considerable value in reducing the probability of dropping out of high school.

In explicating the concept of social capital, three forms were identified: obligations and expectations, which depend on trustworthiness of the social environment, information-flow capability of the social structure, and norms accompanied by sanctions. A property shared by most forms of social capital that differentiates it from other forms of capital is its public good aspect: the actor or actors who generate social capital ordinarily capture only a small part of its benefits, a fact that leads to underinvestment in social capital.

Appendix

Table 4.A1 Logistic regression coefficients and asymptotic standard errors for effects of student background characteristics on dropping out of high school between sophomore and senior years, 1980–82, public school sample

	b	SE
Intercept	-2.305	.169
Socioeconomic status	-.460	.077
Black	-.161	.162
Hispanic	.104	.138
Number of siblings	.180	.028
Mother worked while child was young	-.012	.103
Both parents in household	-.415	.112
Mother's expectation for college	-.685	.103
Talk with parents	.031	.044
Number of moves since grade 5	.407	.040

Source: Taken from Hoffer (1986).

Notes

1. For a discussion of the importance of the empirical generalization to economics, see Black, Coats, and Goodwin (1973).
2. I am especially grateful to Susan Shapiro for reminding me of Gluckman's distinction and pointing out the relevance of it to my analysis.
3. The complementarity of human capital and social capital in the family for a child's development suggests that the statistical analysis that examines the effects of these quantities should take a particular form. There should be an interaction term between human capital (parents' education) and social capital (some combination of measures such as two parents in the home, number of siblings, and parents' expectations for child's education). In the analysis reported, here, however, a simple additive model without interaction was used.
4. The analysis is carried out by use of a weighted logistic model with a random sample of 4,000 students from the public schools in the sample. The variables included in the model as measures of the family's financial, human, and social capital were socio-economic status (a single variable constructed of parents' education, parents' income, father's occupational status, and household possessions), race, Hispanic ethnicity, number of siblings, number of changes in school due to family residential moves since fifth grade, whether mother worked before the child was in school, mother's expectation of child's educational attainment, frequency of discussions with

parents about personal matters, and presence of both parents in the household. The regression coefficients and asymptotic standard errors are given in the App. Table 4.A1. An analysis with more extensive statistical controls, including such things as grades in school, homework, and number of absences, is reported in Hoffer (1986, Table 25), but the effects reported in Table 4.1 and subsequent text are essentially unchanged except for a reduced effect of mother's expectations. The results reported here and subsequently are taken from Hoffer (1986) and from Coleman and Hoffer (1987).
5. Data from this study have no direct measures of the degree of intergenerational closure among the parents of the school to support this statement. However, the one measure of intergenerational closure that does exist in the data, the number of residential moves requiring school change since grade 5, is consistent with the statement. The average number of moves for public school students is .57; for Catholic school students, .35; and for students in other private schools, .88.
6. It is also true, though not presented here, that the lack of social capital in the family makes little difference in dropout rates in Catholic schools—or, in the terms I have used, social capital in the community compensates in part for its absence in the family. See Coleman and Hoffer (1987: Ch. 5).

References

Baker, W. (1983), 'Floor Trading and Crowd Dynamics', in *Social Dynamics of Financial Markets*, ed. P. Adler and P. Adler (Greenwich, Conn.: JAI), 107–28.

Banfield, E. (1967), *The Moral Basis of a Backward Society* (New York: Free Press).

Becker, G. (1964), *Human Capital* (New York: National Bureau of Economic Research).

Ben-Porath, Y. (1980), 'The F-Connection: Families, Friends, and Firms and the Organization of Exchange', *Population and Development Review*, 6: 1–30.

Black, R. D. C., Coats, A. W., and Goodwin, C. D. W. (eds.) (1973), *The Marginal Revolution in Economics* (Durham, NC: Duke Univ. Press).

Blau, P. (1964), *Exchange and Power in Social Life* (New York: Wiley).

Coleman, J. S. (1986a), 'Social Theory, Social Research, and a Theory of Action', *American Journal of Sociology*, 91: 1309–35.

—— (1986b), *Individual Interests and Collective Action* (Cambridge: Cambridge Univ. Press).

—— (1987), 'Norms as Social Capital', in *Eco-*

nomic Imperalism, ed. G. Radnitzky and P. Bern-holz (New York: Paragon), 133–55.

Coleman, J. S., and Hoffer, T. B. (1987), *Public and Private Schools: The Impact of Communities* (New York: Basic).

DeGraaf, N. D., and Derk Flap, H. (1988), 'With a Little Help from My Friends', *Social Forces*, 67.

Festinger, L., Schachter, S., and Back, K. (1963), *Social Pressures in Informal Groups* (Stanford, Calif.: Stanford Univ. Press).

Geertz, C. (1962), 'The Rotating Credit Association: A "Middle Rung" in Development', *Economic Development and Cultural Change*, 10: 240–63.

Gluckman, M. (1967), *The Judicial Process among the Barotse of Northern Rhodesia* (2nd edn., Manchester: Manchester Univ. Press).

Gouldner, A. (1960), 'The Norm of Reciprocity: A Preliminary Statement' *American Sociological Review*, 25: 161–78.

Granovetter, M. (1985), 'Economic Action, Social Structure, and Embeddedness', *American Journal of Sociology*, 91: 481–510.

Hoffer, T. B. (1986), *Educational Outcomes in Public and Private High Schools* (Ph.D. diss., Univ. of Chicago, Dept. of Sociology).

Homans, G. (1974), *Social Behavior: Its Elementary Forms* (rev. ed., New York: Harcourt, Brace and World).

Katz, E., and Lazarsfeld, P. (1955), *Personal Influence* (New York: Free Press).

Lenin, V. I. (1902; 1973), *What Is To Be Done* (Peking: Foreign Language Press).

Lin, N. (1988), 'Social Resources and Social Mobility: A Structural Theory of Status Attainment' in *Social Mobility and Social Structure*, ed. R. Breiges (Cambridge: Cambridge Univ. Press).

Lipset, S., Trow, M., and Coleman, J. (1956), *Union Democracy* (New York: Free Press).

Merry, S. E. (1984), 'Rethinking Gossip and Scandal', in *Toward a General Theory of Social Control: 1, Fundamentals*, ed. D. Black (New York: Academic), 271–302.

Merton, R. K. (1968), *Social Theory and Social Structure* (2nd edn., New York: Free Press).

—— n.d. 'Study of World War II Housing Projects' (Unpubl. ms., Columbia Univ., Dept. of Sociology).

Schultz, T. (1961), 'Investment in Human Capital', *American Economic Review*, 51 (March): 1–17.

Ullmann-Margalit, E. (1977), *The Emergence of Norms* (Oxford: Clarendon).

Williamson, O. (1975), *Markets and Hierarchies* (New York: Free Press).

—— (1981), 'The Economics of Organization: The Transaction Cost Approach', *American Journal of Sociology*, 87: 548–77.

Wrong, D. (1961), 'The Oversocialized Conception of Man in Modern Sociology', *American Sociological Review*, 26: 183–93.

5

The Post-Modern Condition

Krishan Kumar

Labels, like rumours, can take on a life of their own. The labels of intellectual discourse are no exception. Once sufficiently established, they can govern reality, at least scholarly reality. They inspire conferences, books, television programmes. They can create a whole climate of critical inquiry which, especially in these days of academic entrepreneurship and the multinational scholarly enterprise, feeds on itself. 'The lonely crowd', 'the affluent society', 'the technological society', 'the hidden persuaders', 'the power elite': these are all well-known examples of labels which in recent decades have generated much activity of this sort.

This is not to say that all this intellectual activity is simply self-indulgent. Genuine hypotheses can often be formed out of it; it gives rise to reflections which can be illuminating even and especially in disagreement. But an element of self-regarding publicity inevitably surrounds its utterances. We need to guard ourselves against that in assessing their worth.

During the 1960s and early 1970s, several prominent sociologists elaborated a view of contemporary society that they labelled the theory of post-industrial society. The best-known proponent of this was the Harvard sociologist Daniel Bell, especially as expressed in his book, *The Coming of Post-Industrial Society* (1973). Bell himself, in international conferences and in semi-popular journals such as *The Public Interest*, was an active and able propagator of his views. But the theory of post-industrialism gained even wider currency through some vivid popularizations, notably in such books as Peter Drucker's *The Age of Discontinuity* (1969) and Alvin Toffler's *Future Shock* (1970). In such works the educated public of the west was asked to prepare itself for the possibly uncomfortable transition to a new society, one as different from industrial society as that had been from agrarian society.

The post-industrial idea has been intensively debated. Its shortcomings, as well as the stimulating questions it raises, have been widely noted (see, for example, Gershuny 1978; Kumar 1978). Partly as a result of that, partly as the result of the changed climate of feeling in the western world following the 1973 oil shock, one had the distinct impression that 'post-industrialism' had had its day. The debates of the later 1970s all seemed to be about 'the limits to growth', about containing—not exploiting—the dynamic potential of industrialism. They were about the revival of distributional conflicts as industrial societies ceased to be able to make pay-offs from increased growth (see, for example, Hirsch 1979). A mood of crisis replaced the optimism of the 1960s. Right-wing parties capitalized on this mood, preaching a return to 'Victorian' values and practices of self-help and *laissez-faire*. They called for the abandonment of central planning and state intervention, the most obvious features of the post-1945 settlement and a key premise of the post-industrial idea.

Whatever the future of industrial societies, then, they still seemed to be preoccupied by the same difficulties and dilemmas that had beset them for the past hundred years.[1] In the history of industrialism it was the post-war era of continuous growth that now looked like the

From *Post-Industrial to Post-Modern Society: New Theories of the Contemporary World* 1–4, 121–37, 172–8, and 201. (Blackwell, 1995), reprinted with permission.

exceptional episode, the happy accident. Its ending had restored some of the classic conflicts and debates of industrialism (see, for example, Stretton 1976). The past had reasserted itself. At a time when 'deindustrialization' and economic decline became issues to grapple with, visions of a post-industrial society were bound to appear fanciful, if not irresponsible.

Malcolm Bradbury has called the 1970s 'the decade that never was'. But the 1980s of course came out of the 1970s (just as the 1960s came out of the 1950s). We can now see that during that decade various new forms of post-industrial theory were in the making. On the whole, these forms lack the confident optimism of the 1960s varieties. They do not look forward to the 'super-industrial' society so euphorically anticipated by Alvin Toffler. As the product of left- as much as right-wing thinking, they foresee great stresses and conflicts ahead. But they are as insistent as earlier post-industrial theorists that industrial societies have crossed a divide. Classic industrialism, the kind of society analysed by Marx, Weber, and Durkheim, the kind of society inhabited by most westerners for the past century and a half, is no more.

The greatest continuity with earlier post-industrial theory is shown in the view of contemporary society as 'the information society'. Daniel Bell is here again the most prominent exponent. His post-industrial idea had already singled out 'theoretical knowledge' as the most important feature—the source of value, the source of growth—of the future society. In his later writing he has come to identify this more firmly with the development of the new information technology and its potential application to every sector of society. The new society is now defined, and named, by its novel methods of acquiring, processing and distributing information. Bell is as confident now as in his earlier analysis that this amounts to a revolutionary transformation of modern society.

The concept of the information society fits in well with the liberal, progressivist tradition of western thought. It maintains the Enlightenment faith in rationality and progress. Its current exponents belong generally to the centre of the ideological spectrum. To the extent that knowledge and its growth are equated with greater efficacy and greater freedom, this view, despite its pronouncement of

a radical shift in societal arrangements, continues the line of thought inaugurated by Saint-Simon, Comte and the positivists.

More unexpected is the view of the new society that has emerged from the left side of the ideological spectrum. Marxists had been amongst the most vigorous denouncers of the original post-industrial idea, as the clearest demonstration of late bourgeois ideology (see, for example, Ross 1974). Now some of them have come up with their own version of post-industrial theory. It has most commonly been expressed under the banner of 'post-Fordism'. As mostly Marxists of a kind, they still generally hold to some concept of capitalist development as the engine of change. But so struck are they by the differences between the old and the new forms of capitalism that they feel forced to speak of our times as 'new times', or as the era of 'the second industrial divide'. For many of them Marx, as the supreme theorist of capitalism, remains a relevant thinker. But the changes in society in the latter part of the twentieth century are regarded as so momentous, and constitute so sharp a break with earlier capitalist patterns and practices, that it is clear to these writers that severe revisions will need to be made to Marxist theory if it is to remain serviceable.

A third strand of post-industrial theory has a less familiar provenance. This is the theory of 'post-modern' society. Post-modernism is the most comprehensive of recent theories. It includes in its generous embrace all forms of change, cultural, political and economic. None is seen as the privileged 'carrier' of the movement to post-modernity. What others see as the evidence for 'post-Fordism' or 'the information society' it smoothly subsumes as components of its own ambitious conceptualization of current developments. As eclectic—and elusive—in its ideological make-up as the eclecticism it sees as the principal feature of the contemporary world, post-modernism is the most difficult of contemporary theories to assess. Its terms can lead one into a bewildering circle of self-referentiality. Nevertheless its evident appeal to theorists from all parts of the ideological spectrum gives it a compelling claim on our attention.

Moreover, whether or not the larger claims of the theory carry conviction, it is clear that post-modernism has struck a chord among much of the educated population of the western world. It appears, that is, to speak to their condition—or at least their subjective experience of it.[2] That sociologists have often in the past regarded such feelings as trivial by comparison with the more determining structures of society is only the more reason for attending to such matters of sentiment now. Can post-modernity be a myth if many people believe, or can be persuaded, that they are living in such a condition?

The Post-Modern Condition

In considering the question of how far we may be moving into a post-modern society as well as a post-modern culture, we should start by sketching the broad picture of post-modernity as it has been presented by its leading theorists. We can begin with the more familiar features.

Most theorists claim that contemporary societies show a new or heightened degree of fragmentation, pluralism and individualism. This is partly related to the changes in work organization and technology highlighted by the post-Fordist theorists. It can also be linked to the decline of the nation state and of dominant national cultures. Political, economic and cultural life is now strongly influenced by developments at the global level. This has as one of its effects, unexpectedly, the renewed importance of the local, and a tendency to stimulate sub-national and regional cultures.

The typical institutions and practices of the nation state are correspondingly weakened. Mass political parties give way to the 'new social movements' based on gender, race, locality, sexuality. The 'collective identities' of class and shared work experiences dissolve into more pluralized and privatized forms of identity. The idea of a national culture and national identity is assailed in the name of 'minority' cultures—the cultures of particular ethnic groups, religious faiths, and communities based on age, gender or sexuality. Post-modernism proclaims multi-cultural and multi-ethnic societies. It promotes the 'politics of difference'. Identity is not unitary or essential, it is fluid and shifting, fed by multiple sources and taking multiple forms (there is no such thing as 'woman' or 'black').

Post-modern society typically links the local and the global. Global developments—the internationalization of the economy and of culture—reflect back on national societies, undermining national structures and promoting local ones. Ethnicity receives a renewed impetus. There is an upsurge of regionalism and 'peripheral nationalisms'—the nationalism of small nations which have typically been incorporated in larger units such as the United Kingdom, France, Spain and other historic national groupings. 'Think globally, act locally', the slogan of the 1960s, applies to a good number of the new social movements, most noticeably the feminist and ecological movements. There is a similar link-up in some of the new movements of religious revival, such as Protestant and Islamic fundamentalism.

Post-modernity reverses or qualifies some of the typical spatial movements and arrangements of modernity. The concentration of populations in large cities is countered by a movement of de-concentration, de-centralization and dispersal. Much of this is related to post-Fordist developments. It is also the result of the 'de-industrialization' of many regions of western societies—with much manufacturing being exported to non-western societies—and a post-industrial 're-industrialization' based on high-tech, research-based concerns which have preferred new locations in suburban and ex-urban areas, especially those near university cities. Jobs and people move out of the big cities. Small towns and villages are re-populated. Post-modern architecture reverses the trend to high-rise offices and apartment buildings. The stress now is on small-scale schemes, linking people to neighbourhoods and aiming to cultivate the ethos of particular places and particular local cultures. A new, or renewed, importance attaches to place. There is a re-discovery of territorial identities, local traditions, local histories—even where, as with nationalism, these are imagined or invented.

These features of post-modern society are an amalgam of various elements deriving from some well-known accounts of contemporary western society. Post-modern society is thus far congruent with, if not identical to, post-Fordist society, the information society and 'late' or 'disorganized' capitalism as seen in a number of theories.[3] Even though many of these theorists would have no truck with concepts of post-modernity, they are not likely to find much to demur at in the picture so far sketched. What makes post-modernism so distinctive as an approach is that it goes beyond these familiar features to make wide-ranging and, to many people, outrageous claims about the very nature of society and objective reality. It makes assertions not just about a new society or social reality, but about our understanding of reality itself. It moves from history and sociology to philosophical questions of truth and knowledge.

Once more we can start with the familiar, but given an unfamiliar twist. Most theories of contemporary society attribute an important role to the media of mass communication, especially in the era of telecommunications and the computer. This is most obvious in the theory of the information society, but it is also strong in theories of post-Fordism and in Marxist theories of late capitalism.

For most of these theorists, just as informa-tion really informs—however distorted its uses—so the mass communication media really communicate, however distasteful their products or harmful their effects. Postmod-ernists—following here in the footsteps of Marshall McLuhan—see the effects of the mass media in a quite different way. For them the media today do not so much communicate as construct. In their sheer scale and ubiquity they are building a new environment for us, one which demands a new social epistemology and a new form of response. The media have created a new 'electronic reality', suffused with images and symbols, which has obliter-ated any sense of an objective reality behind the symbols. In the condition of what Jean Baudrillard calls the 'ecstasy of communica-tion', the world, our world, becomes a world purely of 'simulation', 'the generation by models of a real without origin or reality: a hyperreal.' In hyperreality it is no longer pos-sible to distinguish the imaginary from the real, the sign from its referent, the true from the false. The world of simulation is a world of simulacra, of images. But unlike conventional images, simulacra are copies that have no orig-inals, or of which the originals have been lost. They are images which are 'murderers of the real, murderers of their own model'. In such a condition there can be no concept of ideology, no idea of 'the betrayal of reality' by signs or images. There are only signs and images, only the hyperreal. 'History has stopped meaning, referring to anything—whether you call it

social space or the real. We have passed into a kind of hyperreal where things are being replayed ad infinitum' (Baudrillard 1987b: 69; 1988b: 166, 170, 182).

With the growth of an electronically medi-ated reality, the hyperreal is becoming the condition of the whole of the modern world. But postmodernists are particularly drawn to America as the capital, as it were, of hyperre-ality, the model of our future (once again). In such monuments of Americana as the Hearst Castle at San Simeon or the Forest Lawn cemeteries of California, in Disneyland and Disney World, in the desert cities of Las Vegas and Los Angeles, they find the clearest instances of the reign of the hyperreal. Here the copy (or fake) substitutes itself for the real, becomes more real than the real itself. 'The American imagination', says Umberto Eco, 'demands the real thing, and, to attain it, must fabricate the absolute fake.' In the extraordi-nary illusion of realism created in these places, in their extravagant bricolage of styles and objects drawn from all countries and all histo-ries, there is a 'fusion of copy and original'; the copy in fact 'seems more convincing than the model' (Eco 1987: 8, 19).

For Eco, as for many theorists, Disneyland is the apotheosis of the hyperreal, 'at once absolutely realistic and absolutely fantastic', 'a fantasy world more real than reality'. It is the truest art-work of America, its 'Sistine Chapel' (Eco 1987: 43–8). For Baudrillard too 'Disneyland is a perfect model of all the entan-gled orders of simulation.' It allows one to trace the 'objective profile' of the United States, the land par excellence of simulacra. But it is more than a 'digest of the American way of life'.

Disneyland is there to conceal the fact that it is the 'real' country, all of 'real' America, which is Dis-neyland (just as prisons are there to conceal the fact that it is the social in its entirety, in its banal omnipresence, which is carceral).

Disneyland is presented as imaginary in order to make us believe that the rest is real, when in fact all of Los Angeles and the America surrounding it are no longer real, but of the order of the hyperreal and of simulation. (Baudrillard 1988b: 171–2; see also Marin 1984)

This stress on Disneyland not simply as a rep-resentation but as representative of American (hyper)reality is echoed in the observations on what are seen as typically postmodernist American cities. Just as earlier theories of modernity read the whole world through key modernist cities such as Paris and New York, so current theories of post-modernity read the contemporary world through American cities such as Las Vegas and Los Angeles which most clearly seem to embody post-modern patterns. Thus Las Vegas is for Eco (following Robert Venturi) 'a completely new phenomenon in city planning, a "message" city, entirely made up of signs, not a city like the others, which communicate in order to function, but rather a city that functions in order to communicate' (Eco 1987: 40).

The phantasmagoric quality of Las Vegas, its appearance as a desert 'mirage', is paralleled for Baudrillard by Los Angeles, 'a town whose mystery is precisely that it is nothing more than a network of endless, unreal circulation: a town of fabulous proportions, but without space or dimensions' (Baudrillard 1988b: 172; see also 1989: 102–4, 123–8). For Edward Soja, Los Angeles is a 'mesocosm of postmodernity', both the concentrated expression of, and, through its economic and cultural life, the leading contributor to global post-modernity. More than anywhere else in the world Los Angeles shows the urban form of post-modernity. Its 'hyperspace' is made up of a 'dazzling . . . patchwork mosaic' of over four hundred officially designated communities. Many of these—Venice, Naples, Hawaiian Gardens, Ontario—have names and ethnic groups that recall other cultures, other histories. First World (corporate capital) and Third World (migrant labour) mingle promiscuously; history and geography are jumbled up. 'Time and space, the "once" and the "there", are being increasingly played with and packaged to serve the needs of the here and now, making the lived experience of the urban increasingly vicarious, screened through *simulacra* . . .'

Once more, the illusory does not imitate the real, it becomes it. Los Angeles, says Soja, defies conventional descriptions of urban and suburban, community and neighbourhood. 'It has in effect been deconstructing the urban into a confusing collage of signs which advertise what are often little more than imaginary communities and outlandish representations of urban locality.' Underneath the 'semiotic blanket' of Los Angeles there is indeed an economic order—the most advanced in the world—but 'when all that is seen is so fragmented and filled with whimsy and pastiche,

the hard edges of the capitalist, racist and patriarchal landscape seem to disappear, melt into air.'

With exquisite irony, contemporary Los Angeles has come to resemble more than ever before a gigantic agglomeration of theme parks, a lifespace composed of Disneyworlds. It is a realm divided into showcases of global village cultures and mimetic American landscapes, all-embracing shopping malls and crafty Main Streets, corporation-sponsored magic kingdoms, high-technology-based experimental prototype communities of tomorrow, attractively packaged places for rest and recreation. (Soja 1989: 245–6)[4]

The state of hyperreality means not just the dissolution of objective reality, of something 'out there' to which signs and images refer. It also means the dissolution of the human subject, the individual ego that modernity took to be the autonomous thinker and actor in the world. For Baudrillard, as for Foucault, the individual subject—'man'—was a temporary construct lasting for the few centuries of the modern period. He—and it was an almost purely masculine concept—was the Faustian or Promethean hero of Descartes' and Bacon's 'narratives' of modernity (Foucault 1970; Abercrombie *et al.* 1986).

The 'ecstasy of communication' has made such assumptions of an autonomous, sovereign individual impossible. The individual, says Baudrillard, no longer stands in an objective relationship, even an 'alienated' one, to his environment. He is no longer 'an actor or dramaturge but . . . a terminal of multiple networks', like an astronaut in his capsule, through which electronic, computer-controlled messages flow. 'With the television image—the television being the ultimate and perfect object for this new era—our own body and the whole surrounding universe becomes a control screen' (Baudrillard 1983: 127–8).

Baudrillard does not, unlike some celebrants of 'virtual reality' and 'cyberspace', rejoice in this condition. He finds it 'obscene', because it 'puts an end to every representation', obliterates all distinction and distance between the self and the environment. The oppositions subject/object, public/private lose all meaning; they collapse into each other. No secrecy, no interiority, no intimacy remains; everything, including the individual, 'dissolves completely in information and communication'. That is the 'ecstasy of communication', 'all functions abolished in a single dimension, that of communication'. For Baudrillard this is bringing into being 'a new form of schizophrenia'. It induces 'a state of terror proper to the schizophrenic: too great a proximity of everything, the unclean promiscuity of everything which touches, invests and penetrates without resistance, with no halo of private protection, not even his own body, to protect him anymore.'

What characterizes him is less the loss of the real, the light years of estrangement from the real, the pathos of distance and radical separation, as is commonly said: but, very much to the contrary, the absolute proximity, the total instantaneity of things, the feeling of no defence, no retreat. It is the end of interiority and intimacy, the overexposure and transparence of the world which traverses him without obstacle. He can no longer produce the limits of his own being, can no longer play nor stage himself, can no longer produce himself as mirror. He is now only a pure screen, a switching center for all the networks of influence. (Baudrillard 1983: 132–3; see also 1987b: 70–1)

This image of despair—though admittedly not one that Baudrillard consistently presents in his writings—should remind us that many theorists of post-modernity are not celebrators of the condition they diagnose. Their attitude is more generally one of resignation, often tinged with ironic regret at the passing of the more confident modern era. Martin Jay (1993) has likened their feelings to those of clinical melancholia, as analysed by Freud. Certainly there is little of the exuberance exhibited by Marshall McLuhan (1967) in his similar reflections on the effects of the new electronic environment, still less the exhilaration of the new science-fiction explorers of cyberspace (for example, Gibson 1984).

Baudrillard's analysis of the impact of the new communications technology evidently takes him in a quite different direction from theorists of the information society such as Bell, Stonier and Masuda. Where they see an extension of human capacity and power, a Promethean expansiveness on a global scale, he sees the disappearance of the individual in networks of information. But for some theorists of post-modernity this very suppression of the individual contains the seeds of a possible future emancipation. For them it is wrong or impossible to go back to the subject-centred theories of modernity. We must build on the potentialities of the new era to find our freedom in a new way.

Mark Poster, for instance, like Baudrillard rejects Bell's theory of the information society. He finds it 'totalizing', in an old-fashioned modernist mode, and insufficiently attentive to the linguistic dimension of information and communication. He also very much goes along with Baudrillard in his view of the effects of the new electronic media on the traditional conception of the individual. In what he calls the 'mode of information'—paralleling Marx's mode of production—a new stage of 'electronically-mediated exchange' has been reached, accompanying and to good extent displacing orally- and print-mediated exchanges. In this third electronic stage 'the self is decentered, dispersed and multiplied in continuous instability . . . In electronically mediated communications, subjects now float, suspended between points of objectivity, being constituted and reconstituted in different configurations in relation to the discursive arrangements of the occasion.'

In the [new stage of the] mode of information the subject is no longer located in a point in absolute time/space, enjoying a physical, fixed vantage point from which rationally to calculate its options. Instead it is multiplied by databases, dispersed by computer messaging and conferencing, decontextualized and reidentified by TV ads, dissolved and materialized continuously in the electronic transmission of symbols . . . The body is no longer an effective limit of the subject's position. Or perhaps it would be better to say that communications facilities extend the nervous system throughout the Earth to the point that it enwraps the planet in a noosphere, to use Teilhard de Chardin's term, of language. If I can speak directly or by electronic mail to a friend in Paris while sitting in California, if I can witness political and cultural events as they occur across the globe without leaving my home, if a database at a remote location contains my profile and informs government agencies which make decisions that affect my life without any knowledge on my part of these events, if I can shop in my home by using my TV or computer, then where am I and who am I? In these circumstances I cannot consider myself centered in my rational, autonomous subjectivity or bordered by a defined ego, but I am disrupted, subverted and dispersed across social space. (Poster 1990: 6, 11, 15–16)

One would have expected this assessment to lead Poster to a similarly melancholic state to Baudrillard's; and clearly he is by no means complacent. But he attacks Baudrillard for being, like Bell, totalizing. The phenomenon of the hyperreal is illegitimately expanded to incorporate the totality of social life. 'Baudrillard's totalizing position forecloses the possibility of new movements. Sunk in a depressing hyperbole of the hyperreal, he transgresses the line of critical discourse in sweeping, gloomy pronouncements as if he knows the outcome to a story that has not yet been imagined, much less written.' The dissolution of the subject in the new mode of information has for Poster emancipatory potential. In the TV advertisement, for instance, although the subject is partly reconstituted as a spectator/consumer, he or she is also deconstructed as a 'centered, original agent'. Since such an agent in classic modernist theory tends to be 'the rational male bourgeois', this act of deconstruction is liberating. 'As a language/practice the TV ad undermines the type of subject previously associated with the capitalist mode of production and with the associated forms of patriarchy and ethnocentrism.' This is no guarantee of emancipation, of course. But 'in the TV ad a language has been made which leaves/urges viewers to regard their own subjectivity as a constituted structure, to regard themselves as members of a community of self-constituters . . . To the extent that TV ads (and, tendentially, the media in general) constitute subjects as self-constituters, the hegemonic forms of self-constitution are put into question' (Poster 1990: 66–8).

Poster explicitly bases himself on the thinking of the poststructuralists; and his account mirrors the ambivalence towards post-modernity shown by poststructuralist and deconstructionist theorists. This is a group that is generally held to include such French thinkers as Foucault, Derrida, Barthes, Lacan, Kristeva, Lyotard and Baudrillard. It also includes a group of mainly American literary critics—Paul de Man, Stanley Fish, J. Hillis Miller among them—who have been influenced both by these French thinkers and the writings of the Russian theorist Mikhail Bakhtin.

From the very beginning, since the 1960s, the poststructuralists have been linked with theories of post-modernism and post-modernity. But a consideration of them in this context is beset by a number of problems. Firstly they have tended to restrict themselves to questions of literature and philosophy. The implications for society and politics are left for others to draw. Secondly many of them—for instance Baudrillard—espouse poststructuralism or deconstructionism without committing themselves to a post-modernist position. The connections are, again, largely made by other thinkers. Thirdly it needs to be said that their writing, especially in the case of the French thinkers, is dense and difficult; quotations, especially in translation, are not often very illuminating.

The connection between these thinkers and theories of post-modernity has mainly to do with their announcements of the 'death of man' (Foucault), or the 'death of the subject' (Derrida), or the 'death of the author' (Barthes). In Foucault's account of the development of the human sciences, man as a subject of science is not, as is commonly thought, a preoccupation going back to the ancient Greeks. It goes back only as recently as to the birth of the modern age, in the late eighteenth and early nineteenth centuries. From that time man was placed at the centre of accounts purporting to uncover the truth of his being, his history and his future destination.

For Foucault this development of knowledge was illusory, based on a false 'anthropologization' of reality. It is not man, the 'knowing subject', who should be the ground of the human sciences; what needs to be studied are the discursive practices of the human sciences that constitute and construct man. Foucault gives his unstinted admiration to Nietzsche, who 'killed man and God both at the same time'. He put into question the whole status of man as agent and subject, showing the essential issue to be a matter of language. Man is a construct of linguistic practices, not the essential ground of knowledge and value.

To all those who still wish to talk about man, about his reign or his liberation, to all those who still ask themselves questions about what man is in his essence, to all those who wish to take him as their starting-point in their attempts to reach the truth . . . to all these warped and twisted forms of reflection we can answer only with a philosophical laugh. (Foucault 1970: 342–3)

Foucault looks forward to the time when language will have regained its primacy in the study of the human condition. Then 'one can certainly wager that man would be erased, like a face drawn in sand at the edge of the sea'.

As the archaeology of our thought easily shows, man is an invention of recent date. And one perhaps nearing its end . . . Man is in the process of perishing as the being of language continues to shine ever brighter upon our horizons. Since man was constituted at a time when language was doomed to dispersion, will he not be dispersed when language regains its unity? (Foucault 1970: 386–7)

Foucault's attack on the man-centred character of the modern human sciences is paralleled by Derrida's attack on the subject-centred character of modern philosophy, and modern western thought in general. Derrida, like Foucault, expresses his debt to Nietzsche, and also to Heidegger. His target is precisely defined in the following remark of Heidegger's, in his study of Nietzsche.

That period we call modern . . . is defined by the fact that man becomes the center and measure of all beings. Man is the *subjectum*, that which lies at the bottom of all beings, that is, in modern terms, at the bottom of all objectification and representation. (In Habermas 1987: 133)

Derrida's response to the modern paradigm of knowledge is to propose a radical 'decentring of the subject'. Language does not have speakers with coherent, stable identities. Texts do not have authors with purposive design and intention. The subject or author as much as the text is a linguistic product—as Paul de Man puts it, we 'rightfully reduce' the subject to 'the status of a mere grammatical pronoun'. There is no distinction between literature and philosophy; all discourses flow into and interpenetrate each other; all are equally 'fictive', equally the products of particular signifying practices. There can be no privileged reading of a text or any other cultural practice, no universal or authentic meaning assigned to it. Texts are open, 'dialogic' structures, shot through with 'aporias' (ramifying contradictions) and 'heteroglossia' (a plurality of voices). Agreement on meaning can be reached, if at all, only in particular 'interpretive communities'—of critics or citizens—and remains internal to them. At any rate no author or reader, no agent or subject, can be the privileged carrier of meaning. Just as with Baudrillard the self is no more than the intersection of electronically-transmitted messages, and with Foucault the meeting-point in the flows (or discourses) of power, so with Derrida and the deconstructionists the self is the place where language criss-crosses in a spiralling arc (or abyss) of indeterminacy.[5]

Is there a clear connection between all this and a post-modern politics and social theory?

Some have doubted it. Deconstructionism, they allege, is so relentlessly subversive that it subverts itself. Despite its insistence on difference, it conjures up a flattened, depthless, entropic world, devoid of all energy. Its radical rejection of the concept of subject or agent leaves society and history with no directional force. It leads to an apolitical detachment and resignation, an attitude of irony and amusement at the comic human drama (Alexander 1994: 181).

Moreover, although it proclaims that the concept of 'textuality' applies to the world, not just to the book, its aestheticization of reality and its obsession in practice with written language have seemed to some to bring it closer to modernism than to post-modernism. It appears to share in the modernist principle of the autonomous, separated world of culture (Huyssen 1992: 60; cf. Connor 1989: 226). It is not surprising therefore to find a high degree of ambiguity and uncertainty in the politics of many of the principal deconstructionsist—Derrida, for instance (Poster 1990: 104–6; but cf. Derrida 1994).

Nevertheless it is not too difficult, at least in principle, to connect up poststructuralism and deconstructionism with the social theory of post-modernity. They go along with the general emphasis on fragmentation and pluralism, and on the absence of any centralizing or 'totalizing' force, that is a feature of all theories of post-modernity. What they tend to see at the individual level, post-modern theory sees at the level of society. Deconstructionism's dissolution of the subject is paralleled—whether as cause or effect—by the post-modern dissolution of the social: not in the sense of denying society as such, but in denying its power as an embodied collectivity. Just as there is no responsible or active agent in deconstructionism—no author of a text, for instance—so in post-modern theory society cannot act, not at least in the manner assumed by Marx or Durkheim.

This can lead postmodern theorists towards a radical individualism, not easily distinguishable from the individualism of the contemporary radical Right. But it has also led some theorists on the Left to reconstruct such traditional concepts as democracy. Democracy can no longer, they argue, base itself on an 'essentialist' notion of a unitary and universal rational agent, the bearer of universal rights, as in classic liberal theory. It must accept, post-modern style, the plurality of perspectives and the differentiated identities that constitute individuals (or what may be called the 'non-individuality of individuals'). Democracy must adapt itself to the fact of this irreducible pluralism—by abandoning the idea of consensual politics, for one thing, or the view that the national 'sovereign' state must be the only arena of politics. Such a concept of democracy should prove, and has proved, attractive to several groups concerned with the politics of identity and difference—feminists especially, but also those active on behalf of subordinate ethnic groups and postcolonial peoples. Its appeal is that it does not abandon traditional leftist goals of liberation, but attempts to give a new meaning to that goal and proposes different means of achieving it (Laclau and Mouffe 1985; Mouffe 1993).

Moreover, even those such as Andreas Huyssen who argue that poststructuralists are primarily modernist, in their overwhelming concern with language and culture, see a critical difference between the older and newer forms of discourse. Modernism believed in the power of art, uncontaminated by extraneous considerations of politics and commerce, to keep alive certain pure values. It contained implicitly, if not always explicitly, a critique of modern society, especially in its bourgeois form. That is why ardent champions of modernism such as Clement Greenberg could also be Marxists (Clark 1982). Poststructuralism rejects this belief in the redemptive power of culture. Art cannot save the individual or change the world. Such a vision of redemption was always illusory, and is any case no longer credible.

It is in such a 'retrospective reading' of modernism, its awareness of 'modernism's limitations and failed political ambitions', that poststructuralism shows its affinity with post-modern theory (Huyssen 1992: 61). More than this, perhaps. In its radical scepticism, its urge to deconstruct and dissolve everything, its fundamentally anti-messianic and anti-utopian character, poststructuralism connects up directly with one of the central tenets of post-modernity: what Lyotard calls the 'incredulity toward metanarratives' (1984a: xxiv). This is one of the best-known and most generally accepted attributes of post-modern theory. It unifies what would otherwise be a hopelessly diffuse and dispersed series of propositions. In doing so, it shows where the

theory of post-modernity gets its main thrust from: not in the announcement of something new, in a positive sense, but in the rejection of the old, the past of modernity.

The 'metanarratives' or 'grand narratives' that Lyotard talks about are the great historico-philosophical schemes of progress and perfectibility that the modern age threw up. Though narratives, being prescriptive and practical, are distinguished by Lyotard from 'science', which is concerned with truth and truth-claims, there cannot be any doubt that much of the appeal of the metanarratives of modernity turned on their association with science and the scientific method. From Kant to Hegel and Marx, from Saint-Simon to Comte and Spencer, the advancement of reason and freedom was linked to the progress of modern science. Science was both a way of understanding the world and a way of transforming it.

It is indeed the crisis of science that may partly account for the attraction of post-modern theory at the present time. The rejection of 'grand narratives' had started, at least in the west, some time ago. Already in the 1940s and 1950s books such as F. A. Hayek's *The Road to Serfdom* (1944), Karl Popper's *The Open Society and Its Enemies* (1945), Jacob Talmon's *The Origins of Totalitarian Democracy* (1952), and Isaiah Berlin's *Historical Inevitability* (1954) had launched powerful and highly influential attacks on the philosophical and historical presuppositions of much nineteenth-century social theory. The grand narrative of Marxism in particular, as the most conspicuous and successful survivor of nineteenth-century thought, was assailed for its theoretical shortcomings and its historical implausibility.

But not only did this leave the grand narrative of liberalism largely unscathed. More importantly science remained untouched. In fact it was further elevated as the only true method of inquiry, while its presence in society—in the form of scientists and scientific institutions—was declared by some such as Sir Charles Snow to be the sole guarantor of future progress and prosperity. Hence, though it was widely proclaimed that 'ideology', in the sense of systematic social philosophies, had been discredited, this did not prevent a quite powerful ideology of progress from attaching itself to such ideas and practices as 'modernization' and 'industrialization'. In this guise the grand narrative continued to enjoy a flourishing career, in the west and the world at large.

The downfall of communism in eastern Europe, and its retreat in most other parts of the world, has inevitably further weakened the credibility of grand narratives (though arguably nationalism was waiting in the wings to inherit the mantle). But it is perhaps more significant that modernization and industrialization are now also under attack, together with the whole idea of progress that sustained them. There are a number of reasons for this, but a principal one is the spread of ecological consciousness. Ecology throws a pall of gloom over all theories of progress through further industrialization. The crisis of confidence has extended to the scientists themselves. Not only do they now question the wholesale application of science to the world; they also raise disturbing questions about the very status of science as a privileged method of understanding (see, for example, Griffin 1988). With the rise of the 'new indeterminacy'—not to mention the repeated assaults of the sociologists—science itself seems subject to the same subjectivity and relativism that are characteristic of all narratives. 'The game of science is . . . put on a par with the others . . . Science plays its own game; it is incapable of legitimating the other language games' (Lyotard 1984: 40–1; see also 53–60).

This is a turnabout indeed, by any measure—if it is true—one of epochal proportions. Modernity was associated—even if mainly retrospectively—with the Scientific Revolution of the seventeenth century (Kolakowski 1990: 7). It was this that gave moderns the confidence that they could match and even surpass the achievements of the ancients. Out of this confidence came the grand themes and theories of Progress, Reason, Revolution and Emancipation. In one form or another, covertly or explicitly, they shored up most of the politics of the western world from the late eighteenth to the mid-twentieth centuries.

Now, if the post-modernists are right, they are empty, highsounding words, no longer capable of inspiring commitment or action.[6] It is not simply that 'there aren't any good, brave causes left' to fight for anymore, in the aggrieved tones of the protagonist of John Osborne's play of 1956, *Look Back in Anger*. The point seems to be that there *cannot* now be

any great causes left to fight for. Philosophy, whether in the form of Popper's anti-historicism or Derrida's deconstructionism, has undermined the pretensions of most social theories to be objective, scientific accounts of the world. Politics, in the form of the failure of communism as well as of other explicitly ideological experiments in social reconstruction, has undermined confidence in the power of politics to re-make the world. The rot has now spread to liberalism as well. The rational, autonomous individual of liberal theory has been dissolved—'deconstructed'—into a multiplicity of overlapping and mutually inconsistent persons possessing different identities and interests. The rational pusuit of goals by self-interested, utility-maximizing individuals becomes a chimæra. The question, whose or what interest, properly applies, it is claimed, as much to the many-headed individual as to the plural society. In these conditions 'reason' or 'truth' become impossible, because unreal, objectives (see Pangle 1992: 19–56).

The post-modernists can support their case by pointing to a widespread disengagement and disillusionment with politics, both in the newly-emergent democracies of eastern Europe and the older democracies of the west. This suggests a withdrawal and a scepticism consonant with the discrediting of 'grand narratives'. Others too, without necessarily accepting the post-modern diagnosis in its own terms, have concurred to the extent of seeing in this condition a new, more profound 'end of ideology'. Such is the position of Francis Fukuyama, whose much-discussed statement on 'the end of history' (1992) was commonly misinterpreted as a triumphalist vindication of western liberalism against all other ideologies. In fact Fukuyama finds liberalism almost as unattractive as its rivals. Its practical victory in the conflict with communism heralds not a new era of freedom and creativity but an end to the dialectic of ideas that gave history meaning. It means the reign of passive consumerism and privatized existence. In his melancholy Nietzschean vision of the 'last man', Fukuyama conjures up a future world as lacking in meaningful striving or purpose as any of the scenarios of the post-modernists (Fukuyama 1992: 287–339). The death of grand narratives may mean less fanaticism but it also means the death of passion, and the loss of the cultural creativity that comes of the struggle of ideologies.

Lyotard himself puts a brave face on all this. The lack of a universal metalanguage' that can validate the great narratives does indeed imply that we must abandon the Enlightenment goals of universal emancipation and the rational society. Nor can these goals be saved in the manner attempted by Jürgen Habermas, who looks to the achievement of a rational 'consensus' through a dialogue between free and equal actors. Such a hope still rests on the Enlightenment belief in humanity as 'a collective (universal) subject', which attempts to achieve its 'common emancipation' through finding a structure of agreed or general rules governing all forms of interaction. But there are no such universal rules of the game—of *all* games—and no prospect therefore of consensus. We have to acknowledge that 'any consensus on the rules defining a game and the "moves" playable within it *must* be local, in other words agreed on by its present players and subject to eventual cancellation' (Lyotard 1984: 66).

Here are the grounds for some kind of optimism. The abandonment of grand narratives leaves the way open for the free play of 'little narratives' (*petits récits*). Little narratives are for Lyotard the stuff of 'imaginative invention', in science as well as social life. They are forms of 'customary' or 'local' knowledge, with the contextuality, provisionality and boundedness that this suggests (cf. Geertz 1983). Little narratives—as in truth all narratives, shorn of their scientific pretensions—do not depend on external, objective validation but are internal to the communities within which they occur. They determine their own criteria of competence and define what has the right to be said and done—that is, they are self-legitimating. Unlike the scientific claims of grand narratives, which are couched in homological universals, little narratives are 'paralogical', which means that they accept what according to the canons of scientific logic would be called false reasoning and illogical arguments.[7] They show a 'sensitivity to differences' and a willingness to 'tolerate the incommensurable'. In this as in most other respects they are like the popular stories recited in traditional societies, as in Homeric Greece (Lyotard 1984: xxv, 18–23, 60).

The political vision underlying this is, as in much of Lyotard's writing, rather vague. It strives towards an ideal of an 'open community' based, among other things, on the 'tem-

porary contract'. This, says Lyotard, 'corresponds to the course that the evolution of social interaction is currently taking; the temporary contract is in practice supplanting permanent institutions in the professional, emotional, sexual, cultural, family, and international domains, as well as in political affairs' (1984: 66). This echo of post-Fordism is not altogether reassuring, as Lyotard himself admits. It leaves room for exploitation and insecurity as much as for flexibility and freedom. But it seems for Lyotard to spell out the forms of the future. No more permanent institutions and organizations, encased within the rigid framework of the nation state. No more 'totalizing' ideologies, setting distant goals within the context of pseudo-scientific blueprints for the future. Instead a network of loosely connected communities, inventing their own forms of life and finding their own means to express them. Not social systems governed by metalanguages, but 'the "atomization" of the social into flexible networks of language games' (Lyotard 1984: 17). Not scientific 'laws' of society, but local customs and usage; not 'legislators' but 'interpreters' of culture who seek to make communities mutually intelligible (cf. Bauman 1987; 1992: 1–25). Not Marx—but Proudhon? . . .

Modernity versus Post-Modernity

At the end of his series of magisterial reflections on post-modernism, Fredric Jameson writes:

I occasionally get just as tired of the slogan 'post-modern' as anyone else, but when I am tempted to regret my complicity with it, to deplore its misuses and its notoriety, and to conclude with some reluctance that it raises more problems than it solves, I find myself pausing to wonder whether any other concept can dramatize the issues in quite so effective and economical a fashion. (Jameson 1992: 418)

It is this dilemma that haunts most discussions of post-modernity. Is post-modernity simply a slogan, a fashionable dinner-party tag much deployed on the media, a catch-all concept so vague and all-embracing as to be vacuous? Or is it, or something like it, actually necessary in the current condition of contemporary western societies? Does it describe a real new state of society, one which requires a new term?

The problem does not stop there. Even if the new term is desirable, what does it purport to describe? Does it, as its name initially suggests, point to a state of things 'after' or 'beyond' modernity? Or is it rather a form of reflection on modernity, a new way, as one commentator has put it, of 'relating to modern conditions and their consequences' (Smart 1993: 152)?

We have, as seems logical, set our discussion of post-modernity against a background of the concept of modernity. Whatever meaning post-modernity may have must derive in some way from an understanding of modernity.

We have also, as have many others, made the distinction between modernity and modernism. Modernity refers to the economic, technological, political and in many respects intellectual creations of western societies in the period since the eighteenth century. ('Modernization' may then be thought to be the process by which this modernity was brought into being, and hence made imitable by other, non-western, societies). Modernism is a cultural movement that began in the late nineteenth century. Though in some ways continuing the impulse of modernity, modernism more significantly constituted a reaction against some of the dominant features of modernity.

No comparable distinction can be made between post-modernity and post-modernism, for reasons that we have indicated. But we should remember Charles Jencks's account of post-modernism as a 'double-coded' phenomenon, at once continuing and opposing (or 'transcending') the tendencies of both modernity and modernism.

It is partly because of the existence of such a plurality of terms, each with shifting meanings, that there can be so much fertile ground for disagreement: a boon to publishers but a nightmare for social theorists. We need to accept that whatever verdict we might pass on the idea of post-modernity will depend to a good extent on our highly challengeable definitions of it. Things, in other words, are not as they are with the information society or post-Fordism. In those cases there is a reasonable degree of consensus on their meanings; nothing of the kind applies to post-modernity. If, in the end, we agree with Jameson that post-modernity is a useful and even perhaps indispensable term, it will be because the account

that we have given of it in the previous chapter highlights certain aspects of the theory that appear particularly promising and valuable. Our definition of the 'field of meaning' surrounding post-modernity suggests uses and perspectives, a map of our current condition, that more conventional descriptions do not match.

The confusions of the debate on post-modernity are well illustrated in the celebrated riposte to the postmodernists by the German thinker Jürgen Habermas. Habermas accuses the post-modernists of a defeatist and escapist conservatism in face of the still unfulfilled promise of Enlightenment modernity. But the 'postmodernists' he has in mind are cultural conservatives or 'neo-conservatives' such as Daniel Bell, whose *Cultural Contradictions of Capitalism* is singled out for treatment as a postmodernist tract. Along with these neo-conservatives are nostalgic 'old conservatives' and a group Habermas labels 'the young conservatives'. This group includes Foucault and Derrida, namely, the very people normally associated with post-modernism. For Habermas though these thinkers are not so much postmodernist as anti-modernist. He sees them as following in the footsteps of the original exponents of 'aesthetic modernity' at the turn of the century. But their view of a de-centred subjectivity, and their attacks on reason, take them 'outside the modern world.' 'On the basis of modernist attitudes, they justify an irreconcilable anti-modernism' (Habermas 1981: 13).

It is probably fortunate that most commentators have not followed Habermas's usage in the debates on post-modernity. What they have rightly taken seriously, however, is his attack on post-modernity as fundamentally a conservative, anti-modern ideology. For Habermas it is too early to renounce modernity. He accepts that Enlightenment rationality contains many perils, some of them powerfully exposed by Habermas's own mentors Max Horkheimer and Theodor Adorno in their book *Dialectic of the Enlightenment* (1944). The main problem is the reliance on a concept of 'subject-centred reason', developed most influentially by Kant. This privileged the solitary, individual ego, seeking to comprehend the world in its totality from the viewpoint of the individual mind. The danger is of a solely instrumental, calculative concept of reason, which can lead to an attitude of domination and exploitation towards both nature and society. But, argues Habermas, the Enlightenment had already provided its own antidote. Already in the critics of Kant, in Schlegel, Schiller, Fichte and a whole line of thinkers culminating in the Young Hegelians and Nietzsche, this concept of reason had come under vigorous attack. Thus from the very beginning modernity supplied its own 'counterdiscourse'. Our contemporary radical critics of reason, the deconstructionists such as Foucault and Derrida, 'suppress that almost 200-year counterdiscourse inherent in modernity itself . . . The intention of revising the Enlightenment with the tools of the Enlightenment is . . . what united the critics of Kant from the start' (Habermas 1987: 302–3; cf. Giddens 1990: 48–9).

From this critical tradition Habermas develops, in opposition to subject-centred reason, the concept of what he calls 'communicative reason'. In this the perspective of the all-knowing individual subject is subordinated to the consensual agreement that is reached through communicative interaction between equals. For Habermas this avoids the potentially 'terroristic' implications of subject-centred reason, the focus of the attacks of contemporary postmodernists. Our problem is not, as they assert, reason itself but the dominance hitherto of a particular, one-sided, version of it. We suffer indeed not from an excess but 'a deficit of rationality'. The task is to disinter alternative traditions of reason buried within the legacy of the Enlightenment. Capitalism, the chief carrier of modernity, has in this respect been ambivalent. 'The communicative potential of reason has been simultaneously developed and distorted in the course of a capitalist modernization.' Habermas is the least starry-eyed of thinkers, and is aware of the immense difficulties of releasing this potential in the face of the powerful technological and bureaucratic structures of capitalist rationality. The instrumental rationality of these structures has gone far in colonizing the 'lifeworld' that is the sphere of communicative interaction. But he equally remains convinced of the greater dangers of the 'totalizing repudiations of modern forms of life'. We are not, whatever the postmodernists say, at the end of modernity, nor can we simply renounce it. To reject the 'grand narratives' of modernity is to render ourselves powerless in the face of instrumental rationality. We are in

modernity; modernity is our fate. The challenge now remains essentially what it was for Hegel, and for Marx: how to to fulfil modernity's promise of universal 'self-consciousness, self-determination and self-realization' (Habermas 1987: 338; see also Bernstein 1985; Ashley 1990).

Habermas's view that Enlightenment modernity itself offers us the tools with which to deal with its perplexities ('aporias') is shared by a number of other writers who are equally hostile to theories of post-modernity. Albrecht Wellmer, who comes from the same school of Critical Theory as Habermas, argues that what appears today as a rejection or supersession of modernity is mainly a form of 'self-critical' modernism. The critique of modernity has been implicit in the modern project since its inception; at most postmodernism has 'redirected' this critique, removing the remaining vestiges of utopianism and scientism. Thus cleansed, we are left with a 'post-metaphysical modernism', a modernism that Wellmer regards as 'an unsurpassable horizon in a cognitive, aesthetic and moral-political sense'. Moreover the denial of the utopian component does not detract from the persisting moral or political appeal of the original promise of modernity. 'A postmetaphysical modernity would be a modernity without the dream of ultimate reconciliations, but it would still preserve the rational, subversive and experimental spirit of modern democracy, modern art, modern science and modern individualism' (Wellmer 1991: viii; see also 91–4; and cf. Bürger 1992: 44–5).

The most spirited defence of modernity, and the most defiant rejection of post-modernity, is to be found in Marshall Berman. For Berman, like Habermas, modernity is double-edged. Its very power and dynamism means that it destroys as much as it creates. 'To be modern is to find ourselves in an environment that promises adventure, power, joy, growth, transformation of ourselves and the world— and, at the same time, that threatens to destroy everything we have, everything we know, everything we are.' Modernity unites all mankind, but it is 'a paradoxical unity, a unity of disunity: it pours us all into a maelstrom of perpetual disintegration and renewal, of struggle and contradiction, of ambiguity and anguish' (Berman 1983: 15).

But whether we are more impressed by modernity's destructive or its creative capacities, we have no choice but to live with it. It is 'the only world we have got.' Both anti-modernism and what is claimed as postmodernism are doomed attempts to escape our fate. Berman has some sympathy for the exuberant 'postmodernism' of 1960s America, as expressed by Leslie Fiedler and other exponents of the pop and counter-culture. As against the official custodians of modernism, they had in fact a better claim to the 'spirit and honour of modernism'. But he is scathing about the French thinkers of the 1970s and 1980s who represent the second wave of postmodernism. He accuses them of a retreat into an esoteric intellectual world divorced from all political and social reality. 'Derrida, Roland Barthes, Jacques Lacan, Michel Foucault, Jean Baudrillard, and all their legions of followers, appropriated the whole modernist language of radical breakthrough, wrenched it out of its moral and political context, and transformed it into a purely aesthetic language game.' Contemporary postmodernists are the heirs of the failed hopes of May 1968 in France. They have 'dug themselves into a grand metaphysical tomb, thick and tight enough to furnish lasting comfort against the cruel hopes of spring' (Berman 1992: 42–6).

In any case, says Berman, the postmodernists are irrelevant. They are a side-show. The main drama on the world stage is still modernity, and it is destined to hold its place for as long as we can see. We are in fact most likely still only in the early stages of modernization. Large sections of the world are only just beginning to feel its full impact. It is for this reason that Berman thinks we can still draw inspiration from the great nineteenth-century writers on modernity—Marx, Nietzsche, Baudelaire, Dostoevsky. Living in the earliest and most formative years of modernity, they were able to grasp its contradictions—the losses and the unprecedented possibilities—more profoundly than we seem able to. 'To appropriate the modernities of yesterday can be at once a critique of the modernities of today and an act of faith in the modernities . . . of tomorrow and the day after tomorrow' (Berman 1983: 36; see also 345–8). What links the positions of Habermas, Wellmer, Berman and similar thinkers is the conviction that modernity is still unfinished business—an 'unfinished project', as Habermas puts it. It has potential still to be realized. One can make this point in a spirit of celebra-

tion, as with Berman, or in a more guardedly hopeful way, as with Habermas. Or one can simply be pragmatic about it. One might make the point that, as a matter of empirical fact, modernity—seen as an expression of Enlightenment rationality—is what most of the world seems to want, to the exclusion of other modes of thought and practice.

Ernest Gellner, for instance, is quite prepared to concede that belief in Enlightenment reason is ultimately a form of faith. Enlightenment rationalism is the product of a particular culture at a particular time: eighteenth-century western civilization. By virtue of its success in conferring enormous economic and political power on those who adopted it, it has become the preferred mode of thought of most educated people in the world. 'Enlightenment Secular Fundamentalism' has become the path to scientific-industrial civilization, and that is the path chosen by the majority of the world's societies. The relativism of the postmodernists may be philosophically tenable but apart from the fact that it leads to nihilism it is practically irrelevant. It remains the fashionable plaything of western intellectuals. The attacks on 'rationalist fundamentalism' fall on deaf ears. 'We happen to live in a world in which one style of knowledge [Enlightenment rationality], though born of one culture, is being adapted by all of them, with enormous speed and eagerness, and is disrupting many of them, and is totally transforming the milieu in which men live. This is simply a fact' (Gellner 1992: 78).

It is important to see that there is a certain correspondence between these views of modernity and the position of at least one important strand of postmodern theory. Clearly for the champions of modernity—whether in Gellner's stoical acceptance of it as a matter of fact, or in the more desire-laden conviction of Habermas and Berman that modernity still has to fulfil its emancipatory promise—modernity cannot be declared over, at least in a temporal or historical sense. But that is not the same as saying that it has not changed. Such an understanding is especially implicit in Habermas's and Berman's account of modernity as driven by the process of capitalist industrialization. Two hundred years may not be a long time in civilizational terms, but it is long enough for modernity to reveal a good deal of its character. This is particularly so with a social form as inherently unstable and dynamic as all agree is the case with modern capitalist civilization. We should remember the position of postmodernists such as Bauman and Huyssen. They do not regard post-modernity as a new historical stage but rather as the culmination of modernity, a vantage point from which critically to assess its performance and, presumably, its remaining potential, if any. Post-modernity on this view is a modernity become conscious of its principles and practice, a self-conscious modernity. Such an interpretation accords well with that of thinkers such as Agnes Heller, who is generally hostile towards theories of post-modernity. If the concept of post-modernity has any meaning it cannot, she says, refer to 'a new period that comes after modernity'. It should be understood rather as equivalent to 'the contemporary historical consciousness of the modern age'. 'Post-modern is not what follows after the modern age, but what follows after the unfolding of modernity. Once the main categories of modernity have emerged, the historical tempo slows down and the real work on the possibilities begin' (Heller 1990: 168–9; see also Heller and Feher 1988:1) . . .

I hope I have shown that these theories do speak to our current condition. Like all theories they are one-sided and exaggerated. That is why they are useful and stimulating. No doubt they leave out much that needs to be considered. Arising as they do out of the recent experiences of western societies, they may carry too much the marks of their origins in particular cultures and even particular classes. The changes of the present decade, and their still uncertain outcomes, may also throw a different light on these theories in the years to come. Nevertheless, what seems to me remarkable is how much of the present state of the world they manage to capture. We do live in a world saturated with information and communication. The nature of work and industrial organization is truly changing with unnerving speed. Modern societies have indeed reached a point where, even if they have not given up on modernity, many of its classic attitudes and assumptions have become seriously questionable.

There is finally another aspect to these theories that is also highly appealing. They are ambitious in their scope, sensitive to historical change, and unwilling to be limited by the boundaries of academic disciplines. At a time when powerful professional and political forces are encouraging the social sciences to become ever more narrowly technical, these are all features to be welcomed. Post-industrial theory seeks, almost by definition, to break with the classic inheritance of nineteenth-century sociology, at least so far as concerns the content of ideas. But it continues the spirit of that tradition, and deserves our attention and respect even if only for that.

Notes

1. Cf. Paul Blumberg: 'Much to the dismay of the post-industrialists, the clock of history seems to be turning counterclockwise' (1980: 217).
2. It is remarkable how frequently, when once you have expounded the postmodernist idea to them, people see postmodernism all about them, with a more or less excited sense of illumination (or of disenchantment).
3. For these characteristics of post-modernity, variously linked to theories of post-industrialism, post-Fordism, the information society, 'disorganized' or 'late' capitalism, see Lash and Urry 1987: 5–16, 285–300; 1994: 279–313; Harvey 1989: 293–6, 302–3, 338–42; Hassan 1985: 125–7; Jencks 1989: 43–52; 1992: 33–5; Soja 1989: 157–89; Huyssen 1992: 68–9; Crook et al. 1992: 32–41, 220–3.
4. There has been considerable discussion of the urban styles and forms of post-modernity, especially with reference to American cities. In addition to Soja, see Cook 1988; Zukin 1991, 1992; Davis 1992; Lash and Urry 1994: 193–222; Brain 1995.
5. The literature on poststructuralism and deconstructionism is enormous. For clear and helpful summaries of some of the main concepts, see Selden 1985: 72–105 and Abrams 1985, both of which also contain good bibliographies.
6. Cf. Hassan: 'God, King, Father, Reason, History, Humanism have all come and gone their way, though their power may still flare up in some circles of faith. We have killed our gods—in spite of lucidity, I hardly know—yet we remain ourselves creatures of will, desire, hope, belief. And now we have nothing—nothing that is not partial, provisional, self-created—upon which to found our discourse' (Hassan 1992: 203).
7. In view of the importance of 'paralogical' thinking in much post-modern theory it should perhaps be pointed out that the medical definition of 'paralogia' is 'illogical or incoherent speech, as in delirium or schizophrenia' (*OED*).

References

Abercrombie, N., Hill, S., and Turner, B. S. (1986), *Sovereign Individuals of Capitalism* (London: Allen and Unwin).

Abrams, M. H. (1985), *A Glossary of Literary Terms*, (6th edn., Fort Worth, Tex.: Harcourt Brace Jovanovich).

Alexander, J. (1994), 'Modern, Anti, Post, and Neo: How Social Theories Have Tried to Understand the "New World" of "Our Time" ', *Zeitschrift für Soziologie*, 23/3: 165–97.

Anderson, P. (1984), 'Modernity and Revolution', *New Left Review*, 144: 96–113.

Ashley, D. (1990), 'Habermas and the Completion of the "Project of Modernity" ', in Turner, B. S. (ed.), *Theories of Modernity and Postmodernity* (London: Sage).

Baudrillard, J. (1983), 'The Ecstasy of Communication', in Foster, H. (ed.), *The Anti-Aesthetic: Essays on Postmodern Culture* (Port Townsend, Washington: Bay Press).

—— (1987b), *Forget Foucault and Forget Baudrillard: An Interview with Sylvère Lotringer* (New York: Semiotext(e)).

—— (1988b), 'Simulcra and Simulations', in *Selected Writings*, ed. M. Poster (Cambridge: Polity Press).

—— (1989), *America* (London: Verso).

Bauman, Z. (1987), *Legislators and Interpreters: On Modernity, Post-Modernity and Intellectuals* (Cambridge: Polity Press).

—— (1992), *Intimations of Postmodernity* (London: Routledge).

Bell, D. (1973), *The Coming of Post-Industrial Society* (New York: Basic Books).

Berman, M. (1983), *All That Is Solid Melts Into Air: The Experience of Modernity* (London: Verso).

—— (1992), 'Why Modernism still Matters', in Lash, S. and Friedman, J. (eds.), *Modernity and Identity* (Oxford: Basil Blackwell).

Bernstein, R. J. (ed.) (1985), *Habermas and Modernity* (Cambridge: Polity Press).

Blumberg, P. (1980), *Inequality in An Age of Decline* (New York: Oxford Univ. Press).

Brain, D. (1995), 'From Public Housing to Private Communities', in Weintraub, J., and Kumar, K. (eds.), *Public and Private in Thought and Practice* (Chicago: Univ. of Chicago Press).

Bürger, P. (1992), 'The Decline of Modernism', in *The Decline of Modernism*, transl. N. Walker (Cambridge: Polity Press), 32–47.

Clark, T. J. (1982), 'Clement Greenberg's Theory of Art', *Critial Inquiry*, 9/1: 139–56.

Connor, S. (1989), *Postmodernist Culture: An Introduction to Theories of the Contemporary* (Oxford: Basil Blackwell).

Cook, P. (1988), 'Modernity, Postmodernity and the City', *Theory, Culture and Society*, 5: 475–92.

Crook, S., Pakulski, J., and Waters, M. (1992), *Postmodernization: Change in Advanced Society* (London: Sage Publications).

Davis, M. (1992), *City of Quartz: Excavating the Future in Los Angeles* (London: Vintage).

Derrida, J. (1994), *Specters of Marx* (London and New York: Routledge).

Drucker, P. (1969), *The Age of Discontinuity* (London: Heinemann).

Eco, U. (1987), *Travels in Hyperreality* (transl. W. Weaver, London: Picador).

Foucault, M. (1970), *The Order of Things: An Archaeology of the Human Sciences* (London: Tavistock Publications).

Fukuyama, F. (1989), 'The End of History?', *The National Interest*, 16: 3–18.

Geertz, C. (1983), *Local Knowledge: Further Essays in Interpretive Anthropology* (New York: Basic Books).

Gellner, E. (1992), *Postmodernism, Reason and Religion* (London: Routledge).

Gershuny, J. I. (1978), *After Industrial Society? The Emerging Self-Service Economy* (London: Macmillan).

Gibson, W. (1984), *Neuromancer* (New York: Ace Books).

Giddens, A. (1990), *The Consequences of Modernity* (Cambridge: Polity Press).

Griffin, D. R. (ed.) (1988), *The Re-enchantment of Science: Postmodern Proposals* (Albany: State Univ. of New York Press).

Habermas, J. (1981), 'Modernity versus Postmodernity', *New German Critique*, 22: 3–14.

—— (1987), *The Philosophical Discourse of Modernity: Twelve Lectures*, transl. F. Lawrence (Cambridge: Polity Press).

Harvey, D. (1989), *The Condition of Postmodernity: An Inquiry into the Origins of Cultural Change* (Oxford: Basil Blackwell).

Hassan, I. (1985), 'The Culture of Postmodernism', *Theory, Culture and Society*, 2/3: 119–31.

—— (1992), 'Pluralism in Postmodern Perspective', in Jencks, C. (ed.), *The Post-Modern Reader* (London: Academy Editions).

Heller, A. (1990), *Can Modernity Survive?* (Cambridge: Polity Press).

——, and Feher, F. (1988), *The Postmodern Political Condition* (Cambridge: Polity Press).

Hirsch, F. (1977), *The Social Limits to Growth* (London: Routledge).

Huyssen, A. (1992), 'Mapping the Postmodern', in Jencks, C. (ed.), *The Post-Modern Reader* (London: Academy Editions).

Jameson, F. (1992), *Postmodernism, or, The Cultural Logic of Late Capitalism* (London: Verso).

Jay, M. (1993), 'Apocalypse and the Inability to Mourn', in *Force-Fields: Between Intellectual History and Cultural Criticism* (London: Routledge), 84–98.

Jencks, C. (1989), *What is Post-Modernism?* (3rd edn., London: Academy Editions).

Kolakowski, L. (1990), 'Modernity on Endless

Trial', in *Modernity on Endless Trial* (Chicago and London: Univ. of Chicago Press), 3–13.

Kumar, K. (1978), *Prophecy and Progress: The Sociology of Industrial and Post-Industrial Society* (Harmondsworth: Penguin Books).

Laclau, E., and Mouffe, C. (1985), *Hegemony and Socialist Strategy* (London: Verso).

Lash, S. (1994), *Economies of Signs and Space* (London: Sage Publications).

—— and Urry, J. (1987), *The End of Organized Capitalism* (Cambridge: Polity Press).

Lyotard, J.-F. (1984), *The Postmodern Condition: A Report on Knowledge* transl. G. Bennington and B. Massumi (Manchester: Manchester Univ. Press).

Marin, L. (1984), 'Utopic Degeneration: Disneyland', in *Utopics: The Semiological Play of Textual Spaces*, transl. R. A. Vollrath (Atlantic Highlands, NJ: Humanities Press International), 239–57.

McLuhan, M. (1967), *Understanding Media: The Extensions of Man* (London: Sphere Books).

Mouffe, C. (1993), *The Return of the Political* (London and New York: Verso).

Pangle, T. L. (1992), *The Ennobling of Democracy: The Challenge of the Postmodern Age* (Baltimore and London: Johns Hopkins Univ. Press).

Poster, M. (1990), *The Mode of Information: Poststructuralism and Social Context* (Cambridge: Polity Press).

Ross, G. (1974), 'The Second Coming of Daniel Bell', in Miliband, R. and Saville, J. (eds.), *The Socialist Register 1974* (London: Merlin Press), 331–48.

Selden, R. (1985), *A Reader's Guide to Contemporary Literary Theory* (Brighton: Harvester Press).

Smart, B. (1993), *Postmodernity* (London and New York: Routledge).

Soja, E. W. (1989), *Postmodern Geographies: The Reassertion of Space in Critical Social Theory* (London: Verso).

Stretton, H. (1976), *Capitalism, Socialism and the Environment.* (Cambridge: Cambridge Univ. Press).

Toffler, A. (1970), *Future Shock* (New York: Random House).

Wellmer, A. (1991), *The Persistence of Modernity: Essays on Aesthetics, Ethics and Postmodernism*, transl. D. Midgley (Cambridge: Polity Press).

Zukin, S. (1991), *Landscapes of Power: From Detroit to Disney World* (Berkeley and Los Angeles: Univ. of California Press).

6

Crossing the Boundaries of Educational Discourse: Modernism, Postmodernism, and Feminism

Henry Giroux

We have entered an age that is marked by a crisis of power, patriarchy, authority, identity, and ethics. This new age has been described, for better or worse, by many theorists in a variety of disciplines as the age of postmodernism (e.g. Foster 1983; Hassan 1987; Hebdige 1986, 1989; Huyssen 1986; Hutcheon 1988a, 1988b, 1989; Appignanesi and Bennington 1986; Aronowitz 1987/8; Connor 1989; Jameson 1990; Lash 1990; and Flax 1990). It is a period torn between the ravages and benefits of modernism; it is an age in which the notions of science, technology, and reason are associated not only with social progress but also with the organization of Auschwitz and the scientific creativity that made Hiroshima possible (Poster 1989). It is a time in which the humanist subject seems to no longer be in control of his or her fate. It is an age in which the grand narratives of emancipation, whether from the political right or left, appear to share an affinity for terror and oppression. It is also a historical moment in which culture is no longer seen as a reserve of white men whose contributions to the arts, literature, and science constitute the domain of high culture. We live at a time in which a strong challenge is being waged against a modernist discourse in which knowledge is legitimized almost exclusively from a European model of culture and civilization. In part, the struggle for democracy can be seen in the context of a broader struggle against certain features of modernism that represent the worst legacies of the Enlightenment tradition.

And it is against these features that a variety of oppositional movements have emerged in an attempt to rewrite the relationship between modernism and democracy. Two of the most important challenges to modernism have come from divergent theoretical discourses associated with postmodernism and feminism.

Postmodernism and feminism have challenged modernism on a variety of theoretical and political fronts, and I will take these up shortly, but there is another side to modernism that has expressed itself more recently in the ongoing struggles in Eastern Europe. Modernism is not merely about patriarchy parading as universal reason, the increasing intensification of human domination over nature in the name of historical development, or the imperiousness of grand narratives that stress control and mastery (Lyotard 1984). Nor is modernism simply synonymous with forms of modernization characterized by the ideologies and practices of the dominating relations of capitalist production. It exceeds this fundamental but limiting rationality by offering the ideological excesses of democratic possibility. By this I mean that, as Ernesto Laclau and Chantal Mouffe (1985) have pointed out, modernism becomes a decisive point of reference for advancing certain and crucial elements of the democratic revolution.

Beyond its claims to certainty, foundationalism, and epistemological essentialism, modernism provides theoretical elements for

Extracts from *Border Crossings: Cultural Workers and the Politics of Education* (Routledge, 1992), 39–88. Reprinted with permission.

analyzing both the limits of its own historical tradition and for developing a political standpoint in which the breadth and specificity of democratic struggles can be expanded through the modernist ideals of freedom, justice, and equality. As Mark Hannam (1990) points out, modernism does have a legacy of progressive ambitions, that have contributed to substantive social change, and these ambitions need to be remembered in order to be reinserted into any developing discourses on democracy. For Hannam, these include: 'economic redistribution towards equality, the emancipation of women, the eradication of superstition and despotism, wider educational opportunities, the improvement of the sciences and the arts, and so forth. Democratization was one of these ambitions and frequently was perceived to be a suitable means towards the realization of other, distinct ambitions.' . . .

I want to argue that modernism, postmodernism, and feminism represent three of the most important discourses for developing a cultural politics and pedagogical practice capable of extending and theoretically advancing a radical politics of democracy. While acknowledging that all three of these discourses are internally contradictory, ideologically diverse, and theoretically inadequate, I believe that when posited in terms of the interconnections between *both* their differences and the common ground they share for being mutually correcting, they offer critical educators a rich theoretical and political opportunity for rethinking the relationship between schooling and democracy. Each of these positions has much to learn from the theoretical strengths and weaknesses of the other two discourses. Not only does a dialogical encounter among these discourses offer them the opportunity to re-examine the partiality of their respective views. Such an encounter also points to new possibilities for sharing and integrating their best insights as part of broader radical democratic project. Together these diverse discourses offer the possibility for illuminating how critical educators might work with other cultural workers in various movements to develop and advance a broader discourse of political and collective struggle. At stake here is an attempt to provide a political and theoretical discourse, that can move beyond a postmodern aesthetic and a feminist separatism in order to develop a pro-

ject in which a politics of difference can emerge within a shared discourse of democratic public life. Similarly at issue is also the important question of how the discourses of modernism, postmodernism, and feminism might be pursued as part of a broader political effort to rethink the boundaries and most basic assumptions of a critical pedagogy consistent with a radical cultural politics. . . .

Mapping the Politics of Modernism

To invoke the term 'modernism' is to immediately place oneself in the precarious position of suggesting a definition that is itself open to enormous debate and little agreement (Lunn 1982; Kolb 1986; Larsen 1990; Giddens 1990). Not only is there a disagreement regarding the periodisation of the term, there is enormous controversy regarding to what it actually refers. To some it has become synonymous with terroristic claims of reason, science, and totality (Lyotard 1984). To others it embodies, for better or worse, various movements in the arts (Newman 1985; 1986). And to some of its more ardent defenders, it represents the progressive rationality of communicative competence and support for the autonomous individual subject (Habermas 1981; 1982; 1983; 1987). It is not possible within the context of this essay to provide a detailed history of the various historical and ideological discourses of modernism even though such an analysis is essential to provide a sense of the complexity of both the category and the debates that have emerged around modernism (Habermas 1983; 1987; Berman 1988; Richard 1987/88). Instead, I want to focus on some of the central assumptions of modernism. The value of this approach is that it serves not only to highlight some of the more important arguments that have been made in the defense of modernism, but also to provide a theoretical and political backdrop for understanding some of the central features of various postmodernist and feminist discourses. This is particularly important with respect to postmodernism, which presupposes some idea of the modern and also various elements of feminist discourse, which have increasingly been forged largely in opposition to some of the major assumptions of modernism, particularly as these relate to notions such as rationality, truth, subjectivity, and progress.

The theoretical, ideological, and political complexity of modernism can be grasped by analyzing its diverse vocabularies with respect to three traditions: the social, the aesthetic, and the political. The notion of social modernity corresponds with the tradition of the new, the process of economic and social organization carried out under the growing relations of capitalist production. Social modernity approximates what Matei Calinescu (1987: 41) calls the bourgeois idea of modernity, which is characterized by:

The doctrine of progress, the confidence in the beneficial possibilities of science and technology, the concern with time (a measurable time, a time that can be bought and sold and therefore has, like any other commodity, a calculable equivalent in money), the cult of reason, and the ideal of freedom defined within the framework of an abstract humanism, but also the orientation toward pragmatism and the cult of action and success.

Within this notion of modernism, the unfolding of history is linked to the 'continual progress of the sciences and of techniques, the rational division of industrial work, which introduces into social life a dimension of permanent change, of destruction of customs and traditional culture' (Baudrillard 1987: 65). At issue here is a definition of modernity, that points to the progressive differentiation and rationalization of the social world through the process of economic growth and administrative rationalization. Another characteristic of social modernism is the epistemological project of elevating reason to an ontological status. Modernism in this view becomes synonymous with civilization itself, and reason is universalized in cognitive and instrumental terms as the basis for a model of industrial, cultural, and social progress. At stake in this notion of modernity is a view of individual and collective identity in which historical memory is devised as a linear process, the human subject becomes the ultimate source of meaning and action, and a notion of geographical and cultural territoriality is constructed in a hierarchy of domination and subordination marked by a center and margin legitimated through the civilizing knowledge/power of a privileged Eurocentric culture (Aronowitz 1987/88: 94–114).

The category of aesthetic modernity has a dual characterization that is best exemplified in its traditions of resistance and formal aestheticism. But it is in the tradition of opposition, with its all consuming disgust with bourgeois values and its attempt through various literary and avant-garde movements to define art as a representation of criticism, rebellion, and resistance that aesthetic modernism first gained a sense of notoriety. Fueling this aesthetic modernism of the nineteenth and early twentieth centuries was an alienation and negative passion whose novelty was perhaps best captured in Bakunin's anarchist maxim, 'To destroy is to create' (Calinescu 1987: 117). The cultural and political lineaments of this branch of aesthetic modernism are best expressed in those avant-garde movements that ranged from the surrealism and futurism to the conceptualism of the 1970s. Within this movement, with its diverse politics and expressions, there is an underlying commonality and attempt to collapse the distinction between art and politics and to blur the boundaries between life and aesthetics. But in spite of its oppositional tendencies, aesthetic modernism has not fared well in the latter part of the twentieth century. Its critical stance, its aesthetic dependency on the presence of bourgeois norms, and its apocalyptic tone became increasingly recognized as artistically fashionable by the very class it attacked (Barthes 1972).

The central elements that bring these two traditions of modernism together constitute a powerful force not only for shaping the academic disciplines and the discourse of educational theory and practice, but also for providing a number of points where various ideological positions share a common ground. These elements can be recognized in modernism's claim for the superiority of high culture over and against popular culture, its affirmation of a centered if not unified subject, its faith in the power of the highly rational, conscious mind and its belief in the unequivocal ability of human beings to shape the future in the interest of a better world. There is a long tradition of support for modernism and some of its best representatives are as diverse as Marx, Baudelaire, and Dostoevsky. This notion of the unified self based on the universalization of reason and the totalizing discourses of emancipation have provided a cultural and political script for celebrating Western culture as synonymous with civilization itself and progress as a terrain that only needed to be mastered as part of the inexorable march of science and history. Marshall

Berman (1982: 11) exemplifies the dizzying heights of ecstasy made possible by the script of modernism in his own rendition of the modernist sensibility (1982; 1988: 81–6).

Modernists, as I portray them, are simultaneously at home in this world and at odds with it. They celebrate and identify with the triumphs of modern science, art, technology, communications, economics, politics—in short, with all the activities, techniques, and sensibilities that enable mankind to do what the Bible said God could do to 'make all things new.' At the same time, however, they oppose modernization's betrayal of its own human promise and potential. Modernists demand more profound and radical renewals: modern men and women must become the subjects as well as the objects of modernization; they must learn to change the world that is changing them and to make it their own. The modernist knows this is possible: the fact that the world has changed so much is proof that it can change still more. The modernist can, in Hegel's phrase, 'look at the negative in the face and live with it.' The fact that 'all that is solid melts into air' is a source not of despair, but of strength and affirmation. If everything must go, then let it go: modern people have the power to create a better world than the world they have lost.

Of course, for many critics, the coupling of social and aesthetic modernism reveals itself quite differently. Modernist art is criticized for becoming nothing more than a commercial market for the museums and the corporate boardrooms and a depoliticized discourse institutionalized within the universities. In addition, many critics have argued that under the banner of modernism, reason and aesthetics often come together in a technology of self and culture that combines a notion of beauty, that is white, male, and European with a notion of mastery that legitimates modern industrial technologies and the exploitation of vast pools of labor from the 'margins' of Second and Third World economies. Robert Merrill (1988: 9) gives this argument a special twist in claiming that the modernist ego with its pretensions to infallibility and unending progress has actually come to doubt its own promises. For example, he argues that many proponents of modernism increasingly recognize that what has been developed by the West in the name of mastery actually indicates the failure of modernism to produce a technology of self and power that can deliver on the promises of providing freedom through science, technology, and control. He writes:

[A loss of faith in the promises of modernism] . . . is

no less true for corporate and governmental culture in the United States which displays a . . . desperate quest for aestheticization of the self as modernist construct—white, male, Christian, industrialist—through monumentally styled office buildings, the Brooks Brothers suit (for male and female), designer food, business practices which amount only to the exercise of symbolic power, and most of all, the Mercedes Benz which as the unification in design of the good (here functional) and the beautiful and in production of industrial coordination and exploitation of human labor is pre-eminently the sign that one has finally achieved liberation and master, 'made it to the top' (even if its stylistic lines thematize what can only be called a fascist aesthetics).

It is against the claims of social and aesthetic modernism that the diverse discourses of postmodernism and feminism have delivered some of their strongest theoretical and political criticism, and these will be taken up shortly. But there is a third tradition of modernism that has been engaged by feminism but generally ignored by postmodernism. This is the tradition of political modernism, which, unlike its related aesthetic and social traditions, does not focus on epistemological and cultural issues as much as it develops a project of possibility out of a number of Enlightenment ideals (Mouffe 1988: 31–45). It should be noted that political modernism constructs a project that rests on a distinction between political liberalism and economic liberalism. With the latter, freedom is conflated with the dynamics of the capitalist market place, whereas with the former, freedom is associated with the principles and rights embodied in the democratic revolution that has progressed in the West over the last three centuries. The ideals that have emerged out of this revolution include 'the notion that human beings ought to use their reason to decide on courses of action, control their futures, enter into reciprocal agreements, and be responsible for what they do and who they are' (Warren 1988: 9–10). In general terms, the political project of modernism is rooted in the capacity of individuals to be moved by human suffering so as to remove its causes, to give meaning to the principles of equality, liberty, and justice; and to increase those social forms that enable human beings to develop those capacities needed to overcome ideologies and material forms that legitimate and are embedded in relations of domination . . .

Postmodern Negations

If postmodernism means putting the Word in its place . . . if it means the opening up to critical discourse the line of enquiry which were formerly prohibited, of evidence which was previously inadmissible so that new and different questions can be asked and new and other voices can begin asking them; if it means the opening up of institutional and discursive spaces within which more fluid and plural social and sexual identities may develop; if it means the erosion of triangular formations of power and knowledge with the expert at the apex and the 'masses' at the base, if, in a word, it enhances our collective (and democratic) sense of possibility, then I for one am a postmodernist.

Dick Hebdige's guarded comments (1989: 226) regarding his own relationship to postmodernism are suggestive of some of the problems that have to be faced in using the term. As the term is increasingly employed both in and out of the academy to designate a variety of discourses, its political and semantic currency repeatedly becomes an object of conflicting forces and divergent tendencies. Postmodernism has not only become a site for conflicting ideological struggles—denounced by different factions on both the left and the right, supported by an equal number of diverse progressive groups, and appropriated by interests that would renounce any claim to politics—its varied forms have also produced both radical and reactionary elements. Postmodernism's diffuse influence and contradictory character is evident within many cultural fields—painting, architecture, photography, video, dance, literature, education, music, mass communications—and in the varied contexts of its production and exhibition. Such a term does not lend itself to the usual topology of categories that serve to inscribe it ideologically and politically within traditional binary oppositions. In this case, the politics of postmodernism cannot be neatly labeled under the traditional categories of left and right.

That many groups are making a claim for its use should not suggest that the term has no value except as a buzzword for the latest intellectual fashions. On the contrary, its widespread appeal and conflict-ridden terrain indicate that something important is being fought over, that new forms of social discourse are being constructed at a time when the intellectual, political, and cultural boundaries of the age are being refigured amidst significant historical shifts, changing power structures, and emergent alternative forms of political struggle. Of course, whether these new postmodernist discourses adequately articulate rather than reflect these changes is the important question.

I believe that the discourse of postmodernism is worth struggling over, and not merely as a semantic category that needs to be subjected to ever more precise definitional rigor. As a discourse of plurality, difference, and multinarratives, postmodernism resists being inscribed in any single articulating principle in order to explain either the mechanics of domination or the dynamic of emancipation. At issue here is the need to mine its contradictory and oppositional insights so that they might be appropriated in the service of a radical project of democratic struggle. The value of postmodernism lies in its role as a shifting signifier that both reflects and contributes to the unstable cultural and structural relationships that increasingly characterize the advanced industrial countries of the West. The important point here is not whether postmodernism can be defined within the parameters of particular politics, but how its best insights might be appropriated within a progressive and emancipatory democratic politics.

I want to argue that while postmodernism does not suggest a particular ordering principle for defining a particular political project, it does have a rudimentary coherence with respect to the set of 'problems and basic issues that have been created by the various discourses of postmodernism, issues that were not particularly problematic before but certainly are now' (Hutcheon 1988*a*: 5). Postmodernism raises questions and problems so as to redraw and re-present the boundaries of discourse and cultural criticism. The issues that postmodernism has brought into view can be seen, in part, through its various refusals of all 'natural laws' and transcendental claims that by definition attempt to 'escape' from any type of historical and normative grounding. In fact, if there is any underlying harmony to various discourses of postmodernism it is in their rejection of absolute essences. Arguing along similar lines, Laclau (1988: 10–28) claims that postmodernity as a discourse of social and cultural criticism begins with a form of epistemological, ethical, and political awareness based on three fundamental negations.

The beginning of postmodernity can . . . be conceived as the achievement of multiple awareness: epistemological awareness, insofar as scientific progress appears as a succession of paradigms whose transformation and replacement is not grounded in any algorithmic certainty; ethical awareness, insofar as the defense and assertion of values is grounded on argumentative movements (conservational movements, according to Rorty), which do not lead back to any absolute foundation; political awareness, insofar as historical achievements appear as the product of hegemonic and contingent—and as such, always reversible—articulations and not as the result of immanent laws of history.

Laclau's list does not exhaust the range of negations that postmodernism has taken up as part of the increasing resistance to all totalizing explanatory systems and the growing call for a language that offers the possibility to address the changing ideological and structural conditions of our time. . . .

Postmodernism and the Negation of Totality, Reason, and Foundationalism

A central feature of postmodernism has been its critique of totality, reason, and universality. This critique has been most powerfully developed in the work of Jean-Francois Lyotard. In developing his attack on Enlightenment notions of totality, Lyotard argues that the very notion of the postmodern is inseparable from an incredulity toward metanarratives. In Lyotard's view (1984: 24), 'The narrative view is losing its functors, its great hero, its great dangers, its great voyages, its great goal. It is being dispersed in clouds of narrative language elements—narrative, but also denotative, prescriptive, descriptive, and so on.' For Lyotard, grand narratives do not problematize their own legitimacy; rather, they deny the historical and social construction of their own first principles and in doing so wage war on difference, contingency, and particularity. Against Habermas and others, Lyotard argues that appeals to reason and consensus, when inserted within grand narratives that unify history, emancipation and knowledge, deny their own implications in the production of knowledge and power. More emphatically, Lyotard claims (1984: 82) that within such narratives are elements of mastery and control in which 'we can hear the mutter-

ings of the desire for a return of terror, for the realization of the fantasy to seize reality'. Against metanarratives, which totalize historical experience by reducing its diversity to a one-dimensional, all-encompassing logic, Lyotard posits a discourse of multiple horizons, the play of language games, and the terrain of micropolitics. Against the formal logic of identity and the transhistorical subject, he invokes a dialectics of indeterminacy, varied discourses of legitimation, and a politics based on the 'permanence of difference.' Lyotard's attack on metanarratives represents both a trenchant form of social criticism and a philosophical challenge to all forms of foundationalism that deny the historical, normative, and the contingent. Nancy Fraser and Linda Nicholson (1988: 86–7) articulate this connection well:

For Lyotard, postmodernism designates a general condition of contemporary Western civilization. The postmodern condition is one in which 'grand narratives of legitimation' are no longer credible. By 'grand narratives' he means, in the first instance, overarching philosophies of history like the Enlightenment story of the gradual but steady progress of reason and freedom, Hegel's dialectic of Spirit coming to know itself, and, most important, Marx's drama of the forward march of human productive capacities via class conflict culminating in proletarian revolution. . . . For what most interests [Lyotard] about the Enlightenment, Hegelian, and Marxist stories is what they share with other non-narrative forms of philosophy. Like ahistorical epistemologies and moral theories, they aim to show that specific first-order discursive practices are well formed and capable of yielding true and just results. True and just here mean something more than results reached by adhering scrupulously to the constitutive rules of some given scientific and political games. They mean, rather, results that correspond to Truth and Justice as they really are in themselves independent of contingent, historical social practices. Thus, in Lyotard's view, a metanarrative . . . purports to be a privileged discourse capable of situating, characterizing, and evaluating all other discourses, but not itself infected by the historicity and contingency that render first-order discourses potentially distorted and in need of legitimation.

What Fraser and Nicholson imply is that postmodernism does more than wage war on totality, it also calls into question the use of reason in the service of power, the role of intellectuals who speak through authority invested in a science of truth and history, and forms of leadership that demand unification and consensus within centrally administered chains of command. Postmodernism rejects a notion of reason that is disinterested, transcendent, and universal. Rather than separating reason from the terrain of history, place, and desire, post-modernism argues that reason and science can only be understood as part of a broader histor-ical, political, and social struggle over the rela-tionship between language and power. Within this context, the distinction between passion and reason, objectivity and interpretation no longer exist as separate entities but represent, instead, the effects of particular discourses and forms of social power. This is not merely an epistemological issue, but one that is deeply political and normative. Gary Peller (1987: 30) makes this clear by arguing that what is at stake in this form of criticism is nothing less than the dominant and liberal commitment to Enlightenment culture. He writes:

Indeed the whole way that we conceive of liberal progress (overcoming prejudice in the name of truth, seeing through the distortions of ideology to get at reality, surmounting ignorance and supersti-tion with the acquisition of knowledge) is called into question. Postmodernism suggests that what has been presented in our social-political and our intellectual traditions as knowledge, truth, objec-tivity, and reason are actually merely the effects of a particular form of social power, the victory of a particular way of representing the world that then presents itself as beyond mere interpretation, as truth itself.

By asserting the primacy of the historical and contingent in the construction of reason, authority, truth, ethics, and identity, post-modernism provides a politics of representa-tion and a basis for social struggle. Laclau argues that the postmodern attack on founda-tionalism is an eminently political act because it expands the possibility for argumentation and dialogue. Moreover, by acknowledging questions of power and value in the construc-tion of knowledge and subjectivities, post-modernism helps to make visible important ideological and structural forces, such as race, gender, and class. For theorists such as Laclau, the collapse of foundationalism does not suggest a banal relativism or the onset of a dangerous nihilism. On the contrary, Laclau (1988a: 79–80) argues that the lack of ultimate meaning radicalizes the possibilities for human agency and a democratic politics. He writes:

Abandoning the myth of foundations does not lead to nihilism, just as uncertainty as to how an enemy will attack does not lead to passivity. It leads, rather, to a proliferation of discursive interventions and arguments that are necessary, because there is no extradiscursive reality that discourse might sim-ply reflect. Inasmuch as argument and discourse constitute the social, their open-ended character becomes the source of a greater activism and a more radical libertarianism. Humankind, having always bowed to external forces—God, Nature, the neces-sary laws of History—can now, at the threshold of postmodernity, consider itself for the first time the creator and constructor of its own history.

The postmodern attack on totality and foun-dationalism is not without its drawbacks. While it rightly focuses on the importance of local narratives and rejects the notion that truth precedes the notion of representation, it also runs the risk of blurring the distinction between master narratives that are mono-causal and formative narratives, that provide the basis for historically and relationally plac-ing different groups or local narratives within some common project. . . .

Postmodern Feminism as Political and Ethical Practice

Feminist theory has always engaged in a dialectical relationship with modernism. On the one hand, it has stressed modernist con-cerns with equality, social justice, and free-dom through an ongoing engagement with substantive political issues, specifically the rewriting of the historical and social construc-tion of gender in the interest of an emancipa-tory cultural politics. In other words, feminism has been quite discriminating in its ability to sift through the wreckage of mod-ernism in order to liberate its victories, partic-ularly the unrealized potentialities that reside in its categories of agency, justice, and poli-tics. On the other hand, postmodern femi-nism has rejected those aspects of modernism in which universal laws are exalted at the expense of specificity and contingency. More specifically, postmodern feminism opposes a linear view of history, that legitimates patriar-chal notions of subjectivity and society; more-over, it rejects the notion that science and reason have a direct correspondence with objectivity and truth. In effect, postmodern feminism rejects the binary opposition between modernism and postmodernism in favor of a broader theoretical attempt to situate both discourses critically within a feminist political project.

Feminist theory has both produced and profited from a critical appropriation of a number of assumptions central to both modernism and postmodernism. The feminist engagement with modernism has been taken up primarily as a discourse of self-criticism and has served to radically expand a plurality of positions within feminism itself. Women of color, lesbians, and poor and working-class women have challenged the essentialism, separatism, and ethnocentricism that have been expressed in feminist theorizing and in doing so have seriously undermined the Eurocentricism and totalizing discourse that has become a political straitjacket within the movement. Fraser and Nicholson (1988: 92, 99) offer a succinct analysis of some of the issues involved in this debate, particularly in relation to the appropriation by some feminists of 'quasi-metanarratives.'

They tacitly presuppose some commonly held but unwarranted and essentialist assumptions about the nature of human beings and the conditions for social life. In addition, they assume methods and/or concepts that are uninflected by temporality or historicity and that therefore function *de facto* as permanent, neutral matrices for inquiry. Such theories, then, share some of the essentialist and ahistorical features of metanarratives: they are insufficiently attentive to historical and cultural diversity; and they falsely universalize features of the theorist's own era, society, culture, class, sexual orientation, and/or ethnic or racial group.... It has become clear that quasi-metanarratives hamper, rather than promote, sisterhood, since they elide differences among women and among the forms of sexism to which different women are differentially subject. Likewise, it is increasingly apparent that such theories hinder alliances with other progressive movements, since they tend to occlude axes of domination other than gender. In sum, there is a growing interest among feminists in modes of theorizing that are attentive to differences and to cultural and historical specificity.

Fashioning a language that has been highly critical of modernism has not only served to make problematic what can be called totalizing feminisms, but has also called into question the notion that sexist oppression is at the root of all forms of domination (Malson, O'Barr, Westphal-Wihl, and Wyer 1989a: 1–13). Implicit in this position are two assumptions that have significantly shaped

the arguments of mostly Western white women. The first argument simply inverts the orthodox Marxist position regarding class as the primary category of domination with all other modes of oppression being relegated to a second rate consideration. Here, patriarchy becomes the primary form of domination, while race and class are reduced to its distorted reflection. The second assumption recycles another aspect of orthodox Marxism that assumes that the struggle over power is exclusively waged between opposing social classes. The feminist version of this argument simply substitutes gender for class and in doing so reproduces a form of 'us' against 'them' politics that is antithetical to developing community building within a broad and diversified public culture.

Both of these arguments represent the ideological baggage of modernism. In both cases, domination is framed in binary oppositions, which suggests that workers or women cannot be complicit in their own oppression and that domination assumes a form that is singular and uncomplicated. The feminist challenge to this ideological straitjacket of modernism is well expressed by bell hooks (1989: 22), who avoids the politics of separatism by invoking an important distinction between the role that feminists might play in asserting their own particular struggle against patriarchy as well as the role they can play as part of a broader struggle for liberation.

Feminist effort to end patriarchal domination should be of primary concern precisely because it insists on the eradication of exploitation and oppression in the family context and in all other intimate relationships.... Feminism, as liberation struggle, must exist apart from and as a part of the larger struggle to eradicate domination in all of its forms. We must understand that patriarchal domination shares an ideological foundation with racism and other forms of group oppression, that there is no hope that it can be eradicated while these systems remain intact. This knowledge should consistently inform the direction of feminist theory and practice. Unfortunately, racism and class elitism among women has frequently led to the suppression and distortion of this connection so that it is now necessary for feminist thinkers to critique and revise much feminist theory and the direction of the feminist movement. This effort at revision is perhaps most evident in the current widespread acknowledgement that sexism, racism, and class exploitation constitute interlocking systems of domination—that sex, race, and class, and not sex alone, determine the nature of any female's identity, status, and circumstance, the degree to which she will or will not be dominated, the extent to which she will have the power to dominate.

I invoke the feminist critique of modernism to make visible some of the ideological territory it shares with certain versions of postmodernism and to suggest the wider implications that a postmodern feminism has for developing and broadening the terrain of political struggle and transformation. It is important to note that this encounter between feminism and postmodernism should not be seen as a gesture to displace a feminist politics with a politics and pedagogy of postmodernism. On the contrary, I think feminism provides postmodernism with a politics, and a great deal more. What is at stake here is using feminism, in the words of Meaghan Morris (1988: 16), as 'a context in which debates about postmodernism might further be considered, developed, transformed (or abandoned)'. Critical to such a project is the need to analyze the ways in which feminist theorists have used postmodernism to fashion a form of social criticism whose value lies in its critical approach to gender issues and in the theoretical insights it provides for developing broader democratic and pedagogical struggles.

The theoretical status and political viability of various postmodern discourses regarding the issues of totality, foundationalism, culture, subjectivity and language are a matter of intense debate among diverse feminist groups . . . [1]

Feminism's relationship with postmodernism has been both fruitful but problematic (Ann Kaplan 1988: 1–6). Postmodernism shares a number of assumptions with various feminist theories and practices. For example, both discourses view reason as plural and partial, define subjectivity as multilayered and contradictory, and posit contingency and difference against various forms of essentialism.

At the same time, postmodern feminism has criticized and extended a number of assumptions central to postmodernism. First, it has asserted the primacy of social criticism and in doing so has redefined the significance of the postmodern challenge to founding discourses and universal principles in terms that prioritize political struggles over epistemological engagements. Donna Haraway (1989: 579) puts it well in her comment that 'the issue is ethics and politics perhaps more than epis-

temology'. Second, postmodern feminism has refused to accept the postmodern view of totality as a wholesale rejection of all forms of totality or metanarratives. Third, it has rejected the postmodern emphasis on erasing human agency by decentering the subject; it has also resisted defining language as the only source of meaning and has therefore linked power not merely to discourse but also to material practices and struggles. Fourth, it has asserted the importance of difference as part of a broader struggle for ideological and institutional change rather than emphasizing the postmodern approach to difference as either an aesthetic (pastiche) or as a expression of liberal pluralism (the proliferation of difference without recourse to the language of power). . . .

Towards a Postmodern Pedagogy

As long as people are people, democracy in the full sense of the word will always be no more than an ideal. One may approach it as one would a horizon, in ways that may be better or worse, but it can never be fully attained. In this sense, you too, are merely approaching democracy. You have thousands of problems of all kinds, as other countries do. But you have one great advantage: You have been approaching democracy uninterrupted for more than 200 years. (Havel 1990: 16)

How on earth can these prestigious persons in Washington ramble on in their subintellectual way about the 'end of history?' As I look forward into the twenty-first century I sometimes agonize about the times in which my grandchildren and their children will live. It is not so much the rise in population as the rise in universal material expectations of the globe's huge population that will be straining its resources to the very limits. North-South antagonisms will certainly sharpen, and religious and national fundamentalisms will become more intransigent. The struggle to bring consumer greed within moderate control, to find a level of low growth and satisfaction that is not at the expense of the disadvantaged and poor, to defend the environment and to prevent ecological disasters, to share more equitably the world's resources and to insure their renewal—all this is agenda enough for the continuation of 'history'. (Thompson 1990: 120)

A striking character of the totalitarian system is its peculiar coupling of human demoralization and mass depoliticizing. Consequently, battling this system requires a conscious appeal to morality and an inevitable involvement in politics. (Michnik 1990: 120)

All these quotations stress, implicitly or explicitly, the importance of politics and ethics to democracy. In the first, the newly elected president of Czechoslovakia, Vaclav Havel, addressing a joint session of Congress reminds the American people that democracy is an ideal that is filled with possibilities but one that always has to be seen as part of an ongoing struggle for freedom and human dignity. As a playwright and former political prisoner, Havel is the embodiment of such a struggle. In the second, E. P. Thompson, the English peace activist and historian, reminds the American public that history has not ended but needs to be opened up in order to engage the many problems and possibilities that human beings will have to face in the twenty-first century. In the third, Adam Michnik, a founder of Poland's Workers' Defense Committee and an elected member of the Polish parliament, provides an ominous insight into one of the central features of totalitarianism, whether on the Right or the Left. He points to a society that fears democratic politics while simultaneously reproducing a sense of massive collective despair. All of these writers are caught up in the struggle to recapture the Enlightenment model of freedom, agency, and democracy while simultaneously attempting to deal with the conditions of a postmodern world.

These statements serve to highlight the inability of the American public to grasp the full significance of the democraticization of Eastern Europe in terms of what it reveals about the nature of our own democracy. In Eastern Europe and elsewhere there is a strong call for the primacy of the political and the ethical as a foundation for democratic public life, whereas in the United States there is an ongoing refusal of the discourse of politics and ethics. Elected politicians from both sides of the established parties complain that American politics is about 'trivialization, atomization, and paralysis.' Politicians as different as the late Lee Atwater, the former Republican Party chairman, and Walter Mondale, former vice president, agree that we have entered into a time in which much of the American public believes that 'Bull permeates everything . . . (and that) we've got a kind of politics of irrelevance' (Oreskes 1990: 16). At the same time, a number of polls indicate that while the youth of Poland, Czechoslovakia, and Germany are extending the frontiers of democracy, American youth are both unconcerned and largely ill-prepared to struggle for and keep democracy alive in the twenty-first century.

Rather than being a model of democracy, the United States has become indifferent to the need to struggle for the conditions that make democracy a substantive rather than lifeless activity. At all levels of national and daily life, the breadth and depth of democratic relations are being rolled back. We have become a society that appears to demand less rather than more of democracy. In some quarters, democracy has actually become subversive. What does this suggest for developing some guiding principles in order to rethink the purpose and meaning of education and critical pedagogy within the present crises? In what follows, I want to situate some of the work I have been developing on critical pedagogy over the last decade by placing it within a broader political context. That is, the principles that I develop below represent educational issues that must be located in a larger framework of politics. Moreover, these principles emerge out of a convergence of various tendencies within modernism, postmodernism, and postmodern feminism. What is important to note here is the refusal to simply play off these various theoretical tendencies against each other. Instead, I try to critically appropriate the most important aspects of these theoretical movements by raising the question of how they contribute to creating the conditions for deepening the possibilities for a radical pedagogy and political project that aims at reconstructing democratic public life so as to extend the principles of freedom, justice, and equality to all spheres of society.

At stake here is the issue of retaining modernism's commitment to critical reason, agency, and the power of human beings to overcome human suffering. Modernism reminds us of the importance of constructing a discourse that is ethical, historical, and political. At the same time, postmodernism provides a powerful challenge to all totalizing discourses, places an important emphasis on the contingent and the specific, and provides a new theoretical language for developing a politics of difference. Finally, postmodern feminism makes visible the importance of grounding our visions in a political project, redefines the relationship between the margins and the center around concrete political struggles, and offers the opportunity for a politics of voice that links rather than severs the relationship between the personal and the political as part of a broader struggle for justice and social transformation. All the principles developed below touch on these issues and recast the relationship between the pedagogical and the political as central to any social movement that attempts to effect emancipatory struggles and social transformations.

1. Education needs to be reformulated so as to give as much attention to pedagogy as it does to traditional and alternative notions of scholarship. This is not a question of giving pedagogy equal weight to scholarship as much as it is of assessing the important relationship between them. Education must be understood as the production of identities in relation to the ordering, representation, and legitimation of specific forms of knowledge and power. As Chandra Mohanty reminds us, questions about education cannot be reduced to disciplinary parameters, but must include issues of power, history, self-identity, and the possibility of collective agency and struggle (Mohanty ch. 36). Rather than rejecting the language of politics, critical pedagogy must link public education to the imperatives of a critical democracy. Critical pedagogy needs to be informed by a public philosophy defined, in part, by the attempt to create the lived experience of empowerment for the vast majority. In other words, the language of critical pedagogy needs to construct schools as democratic public spheres.

In part, this means that educators need to develop a critical pedagogy in which the knowledge, habits, and skills of critical citizenship, not simply good citizenship, are taught and practiced. This means providing students with the opportunity to develop the critical capacity to challenge and transform existing social and political forms, rather than simply adapt to them. It also means providing students with the skills they will need to locate themselves in history, find their own voices, and provide the convictions and compassion necessary for exercising civic courage, taking risks, and furthering the habits, customs, and social relations that are essential to democratic public forms.

In effect, critical pedagogy needs to be grounded in a keen sense of the importance of constructing a political vision from which to develop an educational project as part of a wider discourse for revitalizing democratic public life. A critical pedagogy for democracy cannot be reduced, as some educators, politicians, and groups have argued, to forcing students to either say the pledge of allegiance at the beginning of every school day or to speak and think only in the language of dominant English. A critical pedagogy for democracy does not begin with test scores but with questions. What kinds of citizens do we hope to produce through public education in a postmodern culture? What kind of society do we want to create in the context of the present shifting cultural and ethnic borders? How can we reconcile the notions of difference and equality with the imperatives of freedom and justice?

2. Ethics must be seen as a central concern of critical pedagogy. This suggests that educators attempt to understand more fully how different discourses offer students diverse ethical referents for structuring their relationship to the wider society. But it also suggests that educators go beyond the postmodern notion of understanding how student experiences are shaped within different ethical discourses. Educators must come to view ethics and politics as a relationship between the self and the other. Ethics, in this case, is not a matter of individual choice or relativism but a social discourse that refuses to accept needless human suffering and exploitation. Ethics becomes a practice that broadly connotes one's personal and social sense of responsibility to the Other. Thus, ethics is taken up as a struggle against inequality and as a discourse for expanding basic human rights. This points to a notion of ethics attentive to both the issue of abstract rights and those contexts that produce particular stories, struggles, and histories. In pedagogical terms, an ethical discourse needs to be taken up with regard to the relations of power, subject positions, and social practices it activates. This is an ethics of neither essentialism nor relativism. It is an ethical discourse grounded in historical struggles and attentive to the construction of social relations free of injustice. The quality of ethical discourse is not simply grounded in difference but in the issue of how justice arises out of concrete historical circumstances and public struggles.

3. Critical pedagogy needs to focus on the issue of difference in an ethically challenging

and politically transformative way. There are at least two notions of difference at work here. One, difference can be incorporated into a critical pedagogy as part of an attempt to understand how student identities and subjectivities are constructed in multiple and contradictory ways. In this case, identity is explored through its own historicity and complex subject positions. The category of student experience should not be limited pedagogically to students exercising self-reflection but opened up as a race, gender, and class specific construct to include the diverse ways in which students' experiences and identities have been constituted in different historical and social formations. Two, critical pedagogy can focus on how differences between groups develop and are sustained around both enabling and disabling sets of relations. In this instance, difference becomes a marker for understanding how social groups are constituted in ways that are integral to the functioning of any democratic society. Examining difference in this context does not only focus on charting spatial, racial, ethnic, or cultural differences structured in dominance, but also analyzes historical differences that manifest themselves in public struggles.

As part of a language of critique, teachers can make problematic how different subjectivities are positioned within a historically specific range of ideologies and social practices that inscribe students in various subject positions. Similarly, such a language can analyze how differences within and between social groups are constructed and sustained within and outside of the schools in webs of domination, subordination, hierarchy, and exploitation. As part of their use of a language of possibility, teachers can explore the opportunity to develop knowledge/power relations in which multiple narratives and social practices are constructed around a politics and pedagogy of difference that offers students the opportunity to read the world differently, resist the abuse of power and privilege, and construct alternative democratic communities. Difference in this case cannot be seen as simply either as a register of plurality or as a politics of assertion. Instead, it must be developed within practices in which differences can be affirmed *and* transformed in their articulation with historical and relational categories central to emancipatory forms of public life: democracy, citizenship, and public spheres.

In both political and pedagogical terms, the category of difference must not be simply acknowledged but defined relationally in terms of antiracist, antipatriarchal, multicentric, and ecological practices central to the notion of democratic community.

4. Critical pedagogy needs a language that allows for competing solidarities and political vocabularies that do not reduce the issues of power, justice, struggle, and inequality to a single script, a master narrative that suppresses the contingent, the historical, and the everyday as serious objects of study. This suggests that curriculum knowledge should not be treated as a sacred text but developed as part of an ongoing engagement with a variety of narratives and traditions that can be reread and reformulated in politically different terms. At issue here is how to construct a discourse of textual authority that is power-sensitive and developed as part of a wider analysis of the struggle over culture fought out at the levels of curricula knowledge, pedagogy, and the exercise of institutional power. This is not merely an argument against a canon, but one that refigures the meaning and use of canon. Knowledge has to be constantly re-examined in terms of its limits and rejected as a body of information that only has to be passed down to students. As Laclau has pointed out, setting limits to the answers given by what can be judged as a valued tradition (a matter of argument also) is an important political act. What Laclau is suggesting is the possibility for students to creatively appropriate the past as part of a living dialogue, an affirmation of the multiplicity of narratives, and the need to judge those narratives not as timeless or as monolithic discourses, but as social and historical inventions that can be refigured in the interests of creating more democratic forms of public life. Here is opened the possibility for creating pedagogical practices characterized by the open exchange of ideas, the proliferation of dialogue, and the material conditions for the expression of individual and social freedom.

5. Critical pedagogy needs to create new forms of knowledge through its emphasis on breaking down disciplinary boundaries and creating new spheres in which knowledge can be produced. In this sense, critical pedagogy must be reclaimed as a cultural politics and a form of social-memory. This is not merely an epistemological issue, but one of power,

ethics, and politics. Critical pedagogy as a cultural politics points to the necessity of inserting the struggle over the production and creation of knowledge as part of a broader attempt to create a number of diverse critical public cultures. As a form of social-memory, critical pedagogy starts with the everyday and the particular as a basis for learning. It reclaims the historical and the popular as part of an ongoing effort to critically appropriate the voices of those who have been silenced and to help move the voices of those who have been located within narratives that are monolithic and totalizing beyond indifference or guilt to emancipatory practice. At stake here is a pedagogy that provides the knowledge, skills, and habits for students and others to read history in ways that enable them to reclaim their identities in the interests of constructing more democratic and just forms of life.

This struggle deepens the pedagogical meaning of the political and the political meaning of the pedagogical. In the first instance, it raises important questions about how students and others are constructed as agents within particular histories, cultures, and social relations. Against the monolith of culture, it posits the conflicting terrain of cultures shaped within asymmetrical relations of power, grounded in diverse historical struggles. Similarly, culture has to be understood as part of the discourse of power and inequality. As a pedagogical issue, the relationship between culture and power is evident in questions such as, 'Whose cultures are appropriated as our own? How is marginality normalized?' (Popkewitz 1988: 77) To insert the primacy of culture as a pedagogical and political issue is to make central how schools function in the shaping of particular identities, values, and histories by producing and legitimating specific cultural narratives and resources. In the second instance, asserting the pedagogical aspects of the political raises the issue of how difference and culture can be taken up as pedagogical practices and not merely as political categories. For example, how does difference matter as a pedagogical category if educators and cultural workers have to make knowledge meaningful before it can become critical and transformative? Or what does it mean to engage the tension between being theoretically correct and pedagogically wrong? These concerns and tensions offer the possibility for making the

relationship between the political and the pedagogical mutually informing and problematic.

6. The Enlightenment notion of reason needs to be reformulated within a critical pedagogy. First, educators need to be skeptical regarding any notion of reason that purports to reveal the truth by denying its own historical construction and ideological principles. Reason is not innocent, and any viable notion of critical pedagogy cannot exercise forms of authority that emulate totalizing forms of reason that appear to be beyond criticism and dialogue. This suggests that we reject claims to objectivity in favor of partial epistemologies that recognize the historical and socially constructed nature of their own knowledge claims and methodologies. In this way, curriculum can be viewed as a cultural script that introduces students to particular forms of reason, that structure specific stories and ways of life. Reason in this sense implicates and is implicated in the intersection of power, knowledge, and politics. Second, it is not enough to reject an essentialist or universalist defense of reason. Instead, the limits of reason must be extended to recognizing other ways in which people learn or take up particular subject positions. In this case, educators need to understand more fully how people learn through concrete social relations, through the ways in which the body is positioned through the construction of habit and intuition, and through the production and investment of desire and affect.

7. Critical pedagogy needs to regain a sense of alternatives by combining a language of critique and possibility. Postmodern feminism exemplifies this in both its critique of patriarchy and its search to construct new forms of identity and social relations. It is worth noting that teachers can take up this issue around a number of considerations. First, educators need to construct a language of critique that combines the issue of limits with the discourse of freedom and social responsibility. In other words, the question of freedom needs to be engaged dialectically not only as one of individual rights but also as part of the discourse of social responsibility. That is, whereas freedom remains an essential category in establishing the conditions for ethical and political rights, it must also be seen as a force to be checked if it is expressed in modes of individual and collective behavior that

threaten the ecosystem or produce forms of violence and oppression against individuals and social groups. Second, critical pedagogy needs to explore in programmatic terms a language of possibility that is capable of thinking risky thoughts, that engages a project of hope, and points to the horizon of the 'not yet'. A language of possibility does not have to dissolve into a reified form of utopianism; instead, it can be developed as a precondition for nourishing convictions that summon up the courage to imagine a different and more just world and to struggle for it. A language of moral and political possibility is more than an outmoded vestige of humanist discourse. It is central to responding not only with compassion to human beings who suffer and agonize but also with a politics and a set of pedagogical practices that can refigure and change existing narratives of domination into images and concrete instances of a future that is worth fighting for.

There is a certain cynicism that characterizes the language of the Left. Central to this position is the refusal of all utopian images, all appeals to 'a language of possibility.' Such refusals are often made on the grounds that 'utopian discourse' is a strategy employed by the Right and is therefore ideologically tainted. Or the very notion of possibility is dismissed as an impractical and therefore useless category. In my mind, this represents less a serious critique than a refusal to move beyond the language of exhaustion and despair. What is central to develop in response to this position is a discriminating notion of possibility, one that makes a distinction between a language that is 'dystopian' and one that is utopian. In the former, the appeal to the future is grounded in a form of nostalgic romanticism that calls for a return to a past, which more often than not serves to legitimate relations of domination and oppression. Similarly, in Constance Penley's terms (1989: 122), a 'dystopian' discourse often 'limits itself to solutions that are either individualist or bound to a romanticized notion of guerrilla-like small-group resistance. The true atrophy of the utopian imagination is this: we can imagine the future but we *cannot* conceive the kind of collective political strategies necessary to change or ensure that future.' In contrast to the language of dystopia, a discourse of possibility rejects apocalyptic emptiness and nostalgic imperialism and sees history as open and

society worth struggling for in the image of an alternative future. This is the language of the 'not yet,' one in which the imagination is redeemed and nourished in the effort to construct new relationships fashioned out of strategies of collective resistance based on a critical recognition of both what society is and what it might become. Paraphrasing Walter Benjamin, this is a discourse of imagination and hope that pushes history against the grain. Nancy Fraser (1989: 107) illuminates this sentiment by emphasizing the importance of a language of possibility for the project of social change: 'It allows for the possibility of a radical democratic politics in which immanent critique and transfigurative desire mingle with one another.'

8. Critical pedagogy needs to develop a theory of educators and cultural workers as transformative intellectuals who occupy specific political and social locations. Rather than defining teacher work through the narrow language of professionalism, a critical pedagogy needs to ascertain more carefully what the role of teachers might be as cultural workers engaged in the production of ideologies and social practices. At one level this suggests that cultural workers first renounce the discourse of objectivity and decenteredness and then embrace a practice that is capable of revealing the historical, ideological, and ethical parameters that frame its discourse and implications for the self, society, culture, and the other. Cultural workers need to unravel not only the ideological codes, representations, and practices that structure the dominant order, they also need to acknowledge 'those places and spaces we inherit and occupy, which frame our lives in very specific and concrete ways, which are as much a part of our psyches as they are a physical or geographical placement' (Borsa 1990: 36). The practice of social criticism becomes inseparable from the act of self-criticism; one cannot take place without the other; nor does one have priority over the other, instead they must be seen as both relational and mutually constitutive.

At another level, cultural workers need to develop a nontotalizing politics that makes them attentive to the partial, specific, contexts of differentiated communities and forms of power. This is not a call to ignore larger theoretical and relational narratives, but to deepen power of analyses by making clear the specificity of contexts in which power is operationalized, domination expresses itself, and resistance works in multiple and productive ways. In this case, teachers and cultural workers can undertake social criticism within and not outside of ethical and political discourses; they can address issues that give meaning to the contexts in which they work, but at the same time relate them to broader articulations that recognize the importance of larger formative narratives. Critique, resistance, and transformation in these terms is organized through systems of knowledge and webs of solidarity that embrace the local and the global. Cultural workers need to take seriously Foucault's model of the specific intellectual who acknowledges the politics of personal location. This is important, but not enough; cultural workers must also actively struggle as public intellectuals who can relate to and address wider isssues that affect both the immediacy of their location and the wider global context. Transformative intellectuals must create webs of solidarity with those that share localized experiences and identities but must also develop a politics of solidarity that reaches out to those others who live in a global world whose problems cannot be dismissed because they do not occupy a local and immediate space. The issues of human rights, ecology, apartheid, militarism, and other forms of domination against both humans and the planet affect all of us directly and indirectly. This is not merely a political issue; it is also a deeply ethical issue that situates the meaning of the relationship between the self and the other, the margins and the center, and the colonizer and colonized in broader contexts of solidarity and struggle. Educators need to develop pedagogical practices that not only heighten the possibilities for critical consciousness but also for transformative action. In this perspective, teachers and other cultural workers would be involved in the invention of critical discourses, practices, and democratic social relations. Critical pedagogy would represent itself as the active construction rather than transmission of particular ways of life. More specifically, as transformative intellectuals, cultural workers and teachers can engage in the invention of languages so as to provide spaces for themselves, their students, and audiences to rethink their experiences in terms that both name relations of oppression and also offer ways in which to overcome them.

9. Central to the notion of critical pedagogy is a politics of voice that combines a postmodern notion of difference with a feminist emphasis on the primacy of the political. This engagement suggests taking up the relationship between the personal and the political in a way that does not collapse the political into the personal but strengthens the relationship between the two so as to engage rather than withdraw from addressing those institutional forms and structures that contribute to forms of racism, sexism, and class exploitation. This suggests some important pedagogical interventions. First, the self must be seen as a primary site of politicization. That is, the issue of how the self is constructed in multiple and complex ways must be analyzed both as part of a language of affirmation and a broader understanding of how identities are inscribed in and between various social, cultural, and historical formations. To engage issues regarding the construction of the self is to address questions of history, culture, community, language, gender, race, and class. It is to raise questions regarding what pedagogical practices need to be employed that allow students to speak in dialogical contexts that affirm, interrogate, and extend their understandings of themselves and the global contexts in which they live. Such a position recognizes that students have several or multiple identities, but also confirms the importance of offering students a language that allows them to reconstruct their moral and political energies in the service of creating a more just and creditable social order, one that undermines relations of hierarchy and domination.

Second, a politics of voice must offer pedagogical and political strategies that affirm the primacy of the social, intersubjective, and collective. To focus on voice is not meant to simply affirm the stories that students tell, nor to simply glorify the possibility for narration. Such a position often degenerates into a form of narcissism, a cathartic experience that is reduced to naming anger without the benefit of theorizing in order to both understand its underlying causes and what it means to work collectively to transform the structures of domination responsible for oppressive social relations. Raising one's consciousness has increasingly become a pretext for legitimating hegemonic forms of separatism buttressed by self-serving appeals to the primacy of individual experience. What is often expressed in such appeals is an anti-intellectualism that retreats from any viable form of political engagement, especially one willing to address and transform diverse forms of oppression. The call to simply affirm one's voice has increasingly been reduced to a pedagogical process that is as reactionary as it is inward looking. A more radical notion of voice should begin with what bell hooks calls a critical attention to theorizing experience as part of a broader politics of engagement. In referring specifically to feminist pedagogy, she argues that the discourse of confession and memory can be used to 'shift the focus away from mere naming of one's experience . . . to talk about identity in relation to culture, history, and politics' (1989: 110) For hooks, the telling of tales of victimization, or the expression of one's voice is not enough; it is equally imperative that such experiences be the object of theoretical and critical analyses so that they can be connected rather than severed from a broader notions of solidarity, struggle, and politics.

Conclusion

This chapter attempts to analyze some of the central assumptions that govern the discourses of modernism, postmodernism, and postmodern feminism. But in doing so, it rejects pitting these movements against each other and tries instead to see how they converge as part of a broader political project linked to the reconstruction of democratic public life. Similarly, I have attempted here to situate the issue of pedagogical practice within a wider discourse of political engagement. Pedagogy is not defined as simply something that goes on in schools. On the contrary, it is posited as central to any political practice that takes up questions of how individuals learn, how knowledge is produced, and how subject positions are constructed. In this context, pedagogical practice refers to forms of cultural production that are inextricably historical and political.

Pedagogy is, in part, a technology of power, language, and practice that produces and legitimates forms of moral and political regulation, that construct and offer human beings particular views of themselves and the world. Such views are never innocent and are always implicated in the discourse and relations of ethics and power. To invoke the importance of pedagogy is to raise questions not simply about how students learn but also how educators (in the broad sense of the term) construct the ideological and political positions from which they speak. At issue here is a discourse that both situates human beings within history and makes visible the limits of their ideologies and values. Such a position acknowledges the partiality of all discourses so that the relationship between knowledge and power will always be open to dialogue and critical self-engagement. Pedagogy is about the intellectual, emotional, and ethical investments we make as part of our attempt to negotiate, accommodate, and transform the world in which we find ourselves. The purpose and vision that drives such a pedagogy must be based on a politics and view of authority, that links teaching and learning to forms of self- and social empowerment that argue for forms of community life that extend the principles of liberty, equality, justice, and freedom to the widest possible set of institutional and lived relations.

As defined within the traditions of modernism, postmodernism, and postmodern feminism, pedagogy offers educators an opportunity to develop a political project that embraces human interests that move beyond the particularistic politics of class, ethnicity, race, and gender. This is not a call to dismiss the postmodern emphasis on difference as much as it is an attempt to develop a radical democratic politics that stresses difference within unity. This effort means developing a public language that can transform a politics of assertion into one of democratic struggle. Central to such a politics and pedagogy is a notion of community developed around a shared conception of social justice, rights, and entitlement. Such a notion is especially necessary at a time in our history in which the value of such concerns have been subordinated to the priorities of the market and used to legitimate the interests of the rich at the expense of the poor, the unemployed, and the homeless. A radical pedagogy and transformative democratic politics must go hand in hand in constructing a vision in which liberalism's emphasis on individual freedom, postmodernism's concern with the particularistic, and feminism's concern with the politics of the everyday are coupled with democratic socialism's historic concern with solidarity and public life.

We live at a time in which the responsibilities of citizens extend beyond national borders. The old modernist notions of center and margin, home and exile, and familiar and strange are breaking apart. Geographic, cultural, and ethnic borders are giving way to shifting configurations of power, community, space, and time. Citizenship can no longer ground itself in forms of Eurocentrism and the language of colonialism. New spaces, relationships, and identities have to be created that allow us to move across borders, to engage difference and otherness as part of a discourse of justice, social engagement, and democratic struggle. Academics can no longer retreat into their classrooms or symposiums as if they were the only public spheres available for engaging the power of ideas and the relations of power. Foucault's notion of the specific intellectual taking up struggles connected to particular issues and contexts must be combined with Gramsci's notion of the engaged intellectual who connects his or her work to broader social concerns that deeply affect how people live, work, and survive.

But there is more at stake here than defining the role of the intellectual or the relationship of teaching to democratic struggle. The struggle against racism, class structures, sexism, and other forms of oppression needs to move away from simply a language of critique, and redefine itself as part of a language of transformation and hope. This shift suggests that educators combine with other cultural workers engaged in public struggles in order to invent languages and provide critical and transformative spaces both in and out of schools that offer new opportunities for social movements to come together. By doing this, we can rethink and re-experience democracy as a struggle over values, practices, social relations, and subject positions that enlarge the terrain of human capacities and possibilities as a basis for a compassionate social order. At issue here is the need for cultural workers to create a politics that contributes to the multiplication of sites of democratic struggles. Within such sites cultural workers can engage in specific struggles while also recognizing the necessity to embrace broader issues that enhance the life of the planet while extending the spirit of democracy to all societies.

Far from being exhaustive, the principles offered are only meant to provide some fleeting images of a pedagogy that can address the importance of democracy as an ongoing struggle, the meaning of educating students to govern, and the imperative of creating pedagogical conditions in which political citizens can be educated within a politics of difference that supports rather than opposes the reconstruction of a radical democracy.

Note

1. A number of feminist theorists take up these issues while either rejecting or problematizing any relationship with postmodernism (Hartsock 1989–90; Felski 1989). For a range of feminist theoretical analyses concerning the construction of gender and modes of social division, see the two special issues of *Cultural Critique*, 13 (1989), 14 (1989–90).

References

Ann Kaplan, E. (1988), 'Introduction', in E. Ann Kaplan (ed.), *Postmodernism and its Discontents* (London: Verso Press), 1–6.

Appignanesi, L., and Bennington, G. (1986) (eds.), *Postmodernism*, ICA Documents 4 (London: Institute of Contemporary Arts).

Aronowitz, S. (1987/8), 'Postmodernism and Politics', *Social Text*, 18: 94–114.

Barthes, R. (1972), *Critical Essays* (New York: Hill and Wang).

Baudrillard, J. (1987), 'Modernity', *Canadian Journal of Political and Social Theory*, 11/3.

Berman, M. (1982), *All that is Solid Melts Into Air: The Experience of Modernity* (New York: Simon and Schuster).

——(1988), 'Why Modernism Still Matters', *Tikkun*, 4/11: 81–6.

Calinescu, M. (1987), *Five Faces of Modernity: Modernism, Avant-Garde, Decadence, Kitsch, Postmodernism* (Durham: Duke Univ. Press).

Connor, S. (1989), *Postmodernist Culture: An Introduction to Theories of the Contemporary* (New York: Basil Blackwell).

Felski, R. (1989), 'Feminism, Postmodernism, and the Critique of Modernity', *Cultural Critique*, 13 (Fall), 33–56.

Flax, J. (1990), *Thinking Fragments: Psychoanalysis, Feminism, and Postmodernism in the Contemporary West* (Berkeley: Univ. of California Press).

Foster, H. (1983) (ed.), *The Anti-Aesthetic: Essays on Postmodern Culture* (Port Townsend, Wash.: Bay Press).

Fraser, N., and Nicholson, L. (1988), 'Social Criticism Without Philosophy: An Encounter Between Feminism and Postmodernism', in A. Ross (ed.), *Universal Abandon? The Politics of Postmodernism* (Minneapolis: Univ. of Minnesota Press).

Giddens, A. (1990), *The Consequences of Modernity* (Stanford: Stanford University Press).

Habermas, J. (1981), 'Modernity Versus Postmodernity', *New German Critique*, 8/1: 3–18.

——(1982), 'The Entwinement of Myth and Enlightenment', *New German Critique*, 9/3: 13–30.

——(1983), 'Modernity—An Incomplete Project', in H. Foster (ed.), *The Anti-Aesthetic: Essays on Postmodern Culture* (Port Townsend, Wash.: Bay Press), 3–16.

——(1987), *The Philosophical Discourse of Modernity*, trans. F. Lawrence (Cambridge, Mass.: MIT Press).

Hannam, M. (1990), 'The Dream of Democracy', *Arena*, 90.

Haraway, D. (1989), 'Situated Knowledges: The Science Question in Feminism and the Privilege of Partial Perspective', *Feminist Studies*, 14/3.

Hartsock, N. (1989–90), 'Postmodernism and Political Change: Issues for Feminist Theory', *Cultural Critique*, 14 (Winter), 15–33.

Hassan, I. (1987), *The Postmodern Turn: Essays in Postmodern Theory and Culture* (Columbus, Oh.: Ohio State Univ. Press).

Havel, V. (1990), in M. Oreskes, 'America's Politics Loses Way as its Vision Changes World', *New York Times*, 16.

Hebdige, D. (1968), 'Postmodernism and the Other Side', *Journal of Communication Inquiry* 10/2: 78–99.

——(1989), *Hiding in the Light* (New York: Routledge).

Higgdens, A. (1990), *The Consequences of Modernity* (Stanford: Stanford Univ. Press).

hooks, b. *Talking Back* (Boston: Southend Press).

Hutcheon, L. (1988a), 'Postmodern Problematics', in R. Merrill (ed.), *Ethics/Aesthetics: Post-Modern Positions* (Washington DC: Maisonneuve Press).

——(1988b), *The Poetics of Postmodernism* (London: Routledge).

——(1989), *The Politics of Postmodernism* (London: Routledge).

Huyssen, A. (1986), *After the Great Divide* (Bloomington, Ind.: Indiana Univ. Press).

Jameson, F. (1990), *Postmodernism or, the Cultural Logic of Late Capitalism* (Durham: Duke Univ.).

Kolb, D. (1986), *The Critique of Pure Modernity* (Chicago: Univ. of Chicago Press).

Laclau, E., and Mouffe, C. (1985), *Hegemony and Socialist Strategy* (London: Verso Press).

Laclau, E. (1988a), 'Politics and the Limits of Modernity', in A. Ross (ed.), *Universal Abandon? The Politics of Postmodernism* (Minneapolis: Univ. of Minnesota Press).

——(1988b), 'Building a New Left: An Interview with Ernesto Laclau', *Strategies*, 1/1: 10–28.

Larsen, N. (1990), *Modernism and Hegemony* (Minneapolis: Univ. of Minnesota Press).

Lash, S. (1990), *Sociology of Postmodernism* (New York: Routledge).

Lunn, E. (1982), *Marxism and Modernism* (Berkeley: Univ. of California Press).

Lyotard, J.-F. (1984), *The Postmodern Condition* (Minneapolis: Univ. of Minnesota Press).

Malson, M., O'Barr, J., Westphal-Wihl, S., and Wyer, M. (1989), 'Introduction', in M. Malson, J. O'Barr, S. Westphal-Wihl, and M. Wyer (eds.), *Feminist Theory in Practice and Process* (Chicago: Univ. of Chicago Press), 1–13.

Merrill, R. (1988), 'Forward-Ethics/Aesthetics: A Post-Modern Position', in R. Merrill (ed.), *Ethics/Aesthetics: Post-Modern Positions* (Washington DC: Maisonneuve Press).

Michnik, A. (1990), 'Notes on the Revolution', *New York Times Magazine* (11 March), 44.

Morris, M. (1988), *The Pirate's Fiancee: Feminism, Reading, Postmodernism* (London: Verso).

Mouffe, C. (1988), 'Radical Democracy: Modern or Postmodern?', in A. Ross (ed.), *Universal Abandon? The Politics of Postmodernism* (Minneapolis: Univ. of Minnesota Press).

Newman, C. (1985), *The Post-Modern Aura* (Evanston: Northwestern Univ. Press).

——(1986), 'Revising Modernism, Representing Postmodernism', in L. Appignanesi and G. Bennington (eds.) (1986), *Postmodernism: ICA Documents 4* (London: Instit. of Contemporary Arts), 32–51.

Peller, G. (1987), 'Reason and the Mob: The Politics of Representation', *Tikkun*, 2/3.

Penley, C. (1989), *The Future of an Illusion: Film, Feminism and Psychoanalysis* (Minneapolis: Univ. of Minnesota Press).

Poster, M. (1989), *Critical Theory and Poststructuralism* (Ithaca: Cornell Univ. Press).

Richard, N. (1987/8), 'Postmodernism and Periphery', *Third Text*, 2: 5–12.

Thompson, E. P. (1990), 'History Turns on a New Hinge', *The Nation* (29 Jan.), 120.

Warren, M. (1988), *Nietzsche and Political Thought* (Cambridge, Mass.: MIT Press).

7

Having a Postmodernist Turn or Postmodernist Angst: A Disorder Experienced by an Author Who is Not Yet Dead or Even Close to It

Jane Kenway

There is a defiant spirit in my title to this chapter. However, I don't feel defiant and I do feel more close to death than I'd like to. I'm not dying—at least not 'by chocolate' unfortunately—but I do feel a certain political unease, wariness and weariness; if not a sense of hopelessness then at least a reduced optimism with regard to feminism in and maybe beyond education.[1] I am disturbed but not surprised at the recent backlash against feminism in Australian education and health systems (this is most evident in the rise of the boys' and the men's rights movements[2]), but I am also unsettled, agitated and anxious about some of the current directions in feminism in education and I want to publish my anxieties and see if others share them.[3] I say I am anxious, others say I am paranoid. I say there is a range of reasons to be both and others say some of these reasons are more my problem than feminism's. I say maybe that is true, but let me at least express my anxieties and see if they strike a chord—publish and be damned. Others say if you do publish, you will be damned; you will experience a feminist backlash. Yet others say that, in these current backlash times, I should defend feminism, not criticize it. They say that feminists, 'progressive educators' (whatever that means) and 'Left academics' (whatever that means) should promote feminist (and other) worthy causes, and that criticism should be directed particularly at those who

detract from, and undermine, such causes and who benefit most from current inequitable social and educational arrangements.

I agree to some considerable extent with this last imperative. How could I do otherwise when I live in the Australian state of Victoria, a state governed by radical conservatives who, since coming to power less than two years ago, have vandalized the school system, removed 8,200 teaching positions, closed or amalgamated over 230 schools, wound back the provision of educational support services, pushed schools into a market mode, instituted a model of management which has turned educational leadership into a form of institutional management devoid of educational concerns, undermined the morale of teachers, almost totally destroyed the teachers' unions, officially removed the concept of social justice from the educational agenda, shaved $300 million off the state education budget and increased aid to private schools by 15 per cent in real terms (see further Marginson, forthcoming). I agree that there is an urgent and pressing need for educators to speak out strongly and courageously against those types of educational manoeuvres, to deconstruct the truth claims which have been mobilized to justify and legitimate such moves and to name them for what they are. I also think it is equally important that the broader national and global political, cultural and economic shifts which

From R. Smith and P. Wexler (eds.), *After Postmodernism: Education, Politics and Identity* (Falmer Press, 1995), 36–55. Reprinted with permission.

have helped to provide the conditions for this great leap backwards are identified and critically named. And here comes the rub, or at least one of them, with regard to much work by feminist academics in education. I have to be critical of such work in order to encourage more feminists to become critical education activists not just with regard to the obvious gender politics of education but with regard to these and other current directions which often have more subtle implications for girls and women. In the third part of this chapter I will suggest some directions that feminism in education may take if it is to accept my implicit challenge.

I believe that in recent times feminism in and for education has become so preoccupied with its own 'internal' theoretical and political difficulties and differences that it has not paid due and proper attention to what is going on in the rest of the 'restructured' educational world. I also believe that it has become so infatuated with various versions of poststructuralism and/or postmodernism, so influenced by the concerns and interests and intrigued by the debates and challenges of these fields that it has, in many senses, let the educational policy world go by.[4] Certainly exploring the implications of these theories for education policy has not been high on the agenda. This is not to say that any of its postmodernist concerns are unimportant, rather it is to say that a great deal of other really important educational ground is being lost and that feminism seems to be sacrificing much of its critical edge in those Political (the big P is intentional) circles where education policy is made. It seems to be off in a space by itself somewhere, meanwhile something is burning, and it's not Rome.

If I am correct, a matter always open to dispute as my friends eagerly and constantly tell me, then the obvious question to be asked is 'why?'. I attribute part of the reason to the 'nature' (for want of a better word) of popular or dominant versions of postmodernism, to the selective appropriations from the fields that some feminists in education have made and to the ways in which they have translated these ideas into the worlds of education. I also believe that feminist educators have not deployed certain insights from postmodernism as wisely and strategically as they might have in current times and that their engagement with postmodernism has not

been as critical as it should have been. I know these are harsh words and in saying them I do not wish to imply that I am innocent or that I am on higher moral or political ground than others. Far from it. I have been just as infatuated and uncritical as the next person, as some of my recent feminist research and writing indicates (see for example, Kenway, Willis, Blackmore, and Rennie 1994). Indeed, it hasn't been my feminist work that has led me to be as concerned as I am. It has been my work examining the rise of market forms in education in association with other major policy shifts and in the context of the commodification and technologization of western culture.[5] This complex world of practice, commentary and analysis in and beyond but connected to education is barely touched by the ideas of feminists in education and yet it is this world which is largely shaping education's future. Feminists from outside of education have not been quite so tardy with regard to matters associated with the commodity and technology, although the volume of their work is not great.

One way to proceed from here would be to go back through the literature and carefully document and substantiate my claims. This would fit comfortably within the cleverer and 'holier than thou' traditions of academic scholarship. I could add to this a 'humbler than thou' dimension and identify the deep flaws in my own recent research and writing. Certainly, I could develop a catalogue of sinners and write myself into it, and this would be one route towards making the case that feminism needs to consider either moving past the post or into a more politically astute relationship with it. However, I am not inclined to take this route (call me irresponsible or cowardly if you will). Rather, what I will do is offer a short satirical piece which fondly but irreverently names what I see as some of the problems and issues. This involves what Rosemary Hennessy calls a 'double move between solidarity and critique' (1993 p. xviii). When I feel the overwhelming urge to make a 'scholarly' aside, I will resort to a footnote.

In many senses feminist postmodernism has become 'The New Way' to approach feminist research, pedagogy and politics. However, when one takes this new way, one confronts many confusions, difficulties, dilemmas and dangers. Here I will discuss postmodernism in a metanarrativizing way fully anticipating a reaction of incredulous 'othering' from the mini narrativists who read it. In postmodernist terms what I am about to do is scandalous. I will talk of postmodernism as IT not ITS, as singular not plural. Can I get away with this if I say that what I am discussing is the cultural logic of late postmodernism? (Just a little intertextual joke there.[6])

Postmodernism tells us that all that we once thought was solid has 'melted into air'[7]

- all certainties are to be replaced by uncertainties,
- all stabilities are to be replaced by instabilities.

That's what it *definitely* says! It has ordered us to recognize the disorderly.

Postmodernism talks to us, with great *authority*, about endings and death:

- the death of the author;
- the death of the subject;[8] and
- the end of the Enlightenment project.

It has discursively either killed off or at least seriously wounded all epistemologically and politically incorrect (PI) 'isms' such as:

- structuralism;
- functionalism;
- humanism;
- realism;
- binarism;[9] and
- essentialism.[10]

It has killed off all metanarratives to allow difference and plurality to thrive.[11] It has made way for the 'return of the repressed'.

It has voiced the 'unvoiced' but then it made problematic their voices and, indeed, the notion of 'voice'.

When, subsequently, the 'unvoiced' tried to speak, or to unvoice the voiced, (including the poststructuralist voice), postmodernism pointed to the problem of authority and to their multiple subjectivities/positionalities and therefore to the impossibility of their politics of identity and location.

Indeed, postmodernism has told us all that we can have no political home; it has sent us into exile, named us nomads, dubbed us diasporic. But, ironically, at the same time it talks up prime real-estate theory and almost fetishes position, position, position.

Postmodernism is, indeed, anti-structure but it is terribly interested in the spatial:

- in centres and margins and borders,
- in decentring and recentring; and
- in being central, i.e., in being 'The Theory' which positions all other theories as 'other'. (Doing as well as recognizing 'othering' is an 'essential' skill of the postmodernist.)

Despite postmodernism's 'lack' of support for a politics of location, it will support a politics of affinity. Indeed, it has a strong affinity with the building industry—hence its obsession with construction and deconstruction, fixing and unfixing, and bricollage spelt brick etc.

The Federated Union of Postmodernists will nail you to the wall and 'other' your very foundations if you talk about truth of any kind except the truth that postmodernism tells about no truth and other related non-truths.

Postmodernism tells us not to try to tell the truth. It tells us that as soon as we become a truth teller we become a power monger—an authoritative/authoritarian author who is by no means as dead as we should be. While postmodernism believes in the freedom and playfulness of the signifier and the lively reader—in general (but not in a metanarrativizing way, of course), it also believes that power mongers' signifiers are much less playful than those of their 'others'.

Amongst such power mongers are university teachers/researchers—those who are supposedly employed, in part, to seek the truth, test the truth and tell the truth to those who:

- won't pass the Course without it;
- want it;
- need it;
- deserve it;
- pay for it; or
- get it anyway (because they bought the book in a hurry and didn't read the blurb on the back cover).

For some university teachers/researchers, the postmodernist 'truth' is a non event, a perverted nonsense, an intellectual wank, a lie—a silly lie.

They ignore it, ridicule it in the newspaper or at parties or spend a lot of effort telling their own truths about postmodernism; preferably, of course, in referred journals or well reviewed popular but scholarly books. Deconstructing deconstruction is a popular game amongst some aspiring and expired academics. It allows them to show off, to appear to be cutting at the cutting edge.[12]

For other academics, hearing the 'truth' about 'truth' is a very disturbing experience. No longer feeling the bearable rightness of being an academic, they recognize 'the unbearable lightness of being' an academic. They wonder what to do. They search for a purpose in the now purposeless world of the academy.

Some find their comfort in posing as simulacra (now that is tricky), or in untruthing others; in pigging out on incredulity, deconstruction and genealogy.

Piously hexing and vexing the text (and there is no such thing as a text-free zone—that *is* 'all there is', tell Peggy Lee) or textual terrorism is their new academic purpose. This sometimes involves a lot of self-righteousness and sneering and has led some other people (i) to consider the development of a post-Marxist theory of alienation which will help to explain why poststructuralists can be such a turn off at times (well, to be honest, lots of the time) and (ii) to refuse to watch TV with them because they won't let them enjoy such 'simple' pleasures like *Roseanne* without hexing and vexing and speaking in tongues (to please Donna Harraway).

The incredulists get a great deal of pleasure out of deconstructing pleasure—which means they are not much fun to be around—unless you are one of them. And sometimes, even then, they're not much fun. You now hesitate to show your writing to your postie friends because, too often in the past, their pleasure in deconstruction has become your work's unpleasant destruction. You cringe at the memory of rereading your writing after their friendly (read terroristic) 'look at it for you'. How did you miss its residual humanism, its subtle but oppressive binary logics and its embarrassing shades of essentialism? But, after all, what are friends for if not to save you from your 'self'? (Of course you don't have a 'self', at least not a stable self, certainly not now anyway; not after what they said about your book draft which has also melted into air—cyber-space actually!)

Yet other academics, often those with a politically incorrect socialist feminist background, which, through guilt, they attempt to repress, try to divest themselves totally of authority, voice, reason and all P.I isms.[13]

They search for new ways of continuing to work as feminist teachers and researchers. (After all they have mortgages on more than exposing 'truth').

These people tell tales, and tales about tales. They get into performance, parody, and pastiche.[14]

Through these means they seek to disrupt, destabilize, and unsettle.

They seek to be seriously mischievous, naughty but nice, playful but political and most of all pure and correct—good, fun, poststructuralist feminists who even in their dreams never have an essentialist moment and who couldn't possibly even ask their daughter to tell the truth about where she has been till four o'clock in the morning and why is she coming in looking like *that*! (Indeed, for mothers of adolescent daughters who might like to have a little order in their lives, exert a little authority, clarify a few matters, like for instance 'what happened to my shirt that you borrowed two weeks ago?', postmodernism does not hold out much possibility or hope. But postmodernism is not 'into' hope, not really. Certainly it is not into making 'hope practical' but it thrives on making 'despair convincing'—as if we needed help in this respect.[15])

Yet others say 'Hang on a minute, if I'm to live up to the paradoxes inherent in postmodernism, if I am to have any useful relationship to contemporary emancipatory movements then I can't simply obey its imperatives. But at the same time, I can no longer think the way I once thought or work the way I once worked'.

These people tend to do one of two things. They either leave the University, lock themselves in a dark room and wait for Foucault and Derrida to re Kant, or refuse the:

- deathism;
- endism;
- pessimism;
- negativism;
- relativism;[16] and
- authoritarian anti-authoritarianism

of postmodernism and start exploring post, post ways of thinking and doing epistemology, methodology, pedagogy and their associated politics. They look back but only to help them to look forward. Scavenging carefully through the mess and clutter of postmodernism and its critical predecessors, they salvage that which will help them to think anew and renew their work for change. They try to work 'with and out of' (Yeatman 1994: 3), through and beyond postmodernism.

Spelling out an adequate feminist postmodernist politics for/in education is clearly not an easy or unambiguous task. And, it is a task easily avoided or rejected on the grounds that to undertake it would be to go against the central tenets of postmodernism. However, it is just this sort of faint-hearted response to the challenge which becomes dangerous for feminism and other emancipatory movements in the difficult times we are going through. Fortunately for feminism, not all feminists subscribe to this form of postmodern paralysis. Let me now note some ways in which the thought of the not-so-faint-hearted is proceeding.[17]

In my view, materialist feminists are first past the post by a long way when it comes to explicating the political. (I include under this title Donna Haraway, Anna Yeatman and Rosemary Hennessy. Whether they would all agree to this is another matter.) Materialist feminists try to identify and clarify what it means to undertake what Yeatman (1994) calls 'postmodern emancipatory politics' *in the postmodern age*. They are concerned to 'rewrite feminism for and in the postmodern moment confronting its contradictory positionality under late capitalism and in relation to an array of oppositional knowledges' (Hennessy 1993: 13). They are interested in the mechanics *and the politics* of signification and subjectivity. They are concerned about the social effects of the modes of intelligibility offered by various aspects of postmodern theorizing. They are concerned to remap the postmodern in order to clarify its political implications—to criticize and extend it.[18] This remapping almost invariably involves some discussion of the relationship between modernism and postmodernism, for the two come together in materialist feminism. And, as I will go on to explain, materialist feminism is in some very real sense past the post. Of course this raises the obvious question about the meaning of the term 'post' which to some implies total rupture and discontinuity— even antagonism, and to others implies continuity but difference. In this instance it implies the latter. As Yeatman points out she is not 'anti but post'.

Materialist feminist politics revolves around the interplay of difference and dominance. To Yeatman, such politics (which she calls critical, postmodern/feminist) are about 'a democratic politics of voice and representation where the ideal state is not the overcoming of domination once and for all but ongoing imaginative and creative forms of positive resistance to various types of domination' (p. 9). Yeatman makes the important point that such a form of politics does not 'abandon modern universalism and rationalism but enters into a deconstructive relationship with them' (vii). Indeed, she goes so far as to say that 'The kind of emancipatory politics of difference which critical postmodern/feminist theorising pursues is weakly developed unless it understands its dependency on the values of modern universalism, rationalism, justice and individualism.' (x) and more specifically with 'the modern tradition of emancipatory discourse', (p. 10). She continues:

it concerns the authority and nature of reason. Where moderns turn their enquiry on the question of the conditions of right reason, postmoderns interrogate the discursive economies of the different versions of right reason that we have inherited. Postmoderns insist on the exclusions which these different economies effect. They desacralise reason, they do not reject it. Specifically, they attempt to work reason and difference together. (Yeatman 1994; vii–iii)

Like other materialist feminists, Yeatman is not frightened to explore the extent to which feminism still needs to claim normative grounds in order to stake out its emancipatory politics. As Hennessy says, 'holding on to normative grounds does not mean embracing master narratives or totalising theories. But it does mean rewriting them' (1993: 3). While postmodernism has made notions of authority, accountability, vision and emancipation problematic this does not necessarily mean their abandonment. Rather what it means is their reinvention after having interrogated such concepts with a view to unmasking their particular 'economy of inclusions and exclusions' (Yeatman 1994: ix).

This view of politics moves clearly beyond the notion that negative struggle or play can be the only form of struggle. That such a view of contestation is limited is increasingly being recognized. For example, Biddy Martin (1988), argues that, while acknowledging the limitations of modernist feminisms, they must also be recognized as providing certain conditions of political possibility. She points out that feminism faces something of a paradox which she characterizes as the historical and political necessity 'for a fundamentally deconstructive impulse and a need to construct the category woman and to search for truths, authenticity, and universals', thus necessitating a 'double strategy'. In so saying, she asks, 'How do feminists participate in struggles over the meaning(s) of woman in ways that do not repress pluralities without losing sight of the political necessity for fiction and unity?' How do we avoid establishing 'a new set of experts who will speak the truth of ourselves and our sex in categorical terms, closing our struggle around certain privileged meanings and naturalising the construct woman?' She concludes by saying: 'We cannot afford to refuse to take a political stand "which pins us to our sex" for the sake of an abstract theoretical correctness, but we can refuse to be content with fixed identities or to universalize ourselves as revolutionary subjects' (pp. 13–18).

Other feminists also emphasize the importance of being practical. They too reject the claims by some postmodernist feminists that negative critique, deconstruction or parody is the best we have to offer and note the importance both of feminist utopias and visions and of political mobilization. However, they also point to the necessity for organizations, strategies, and visions which, as Sawicki (1991: 12) puts it, are 'sensitive to the dangers of authoritarianism, ethnocentricism and political vanguardism'. With regard to political mobilization dialoguing across difference becomes the strategy to adopt with a view to reaching what Yeatman calls a 'negotiated and provisional settlement; one which, draws on, deconstructs and reinvents according to the circumstances, concepts associated with modernist emancipatory projects, rights, democracy, justice and so forth'.

Let me expand this point a little by looking at the issue of difference. Drawing from the work of Audre Lorde, Sawicki invites us to explore the many dimensions of difference. She asks us to consider 'How power uses difference to fragment opposition and to divide individuals within themselves' (p. 18). But she also insists that we must uncover the distortions in our understandings of each other and in the process, both redefine what differences mean and seek to preserve them. Further, she says we must search for ways of utilizing difference as a multisource both of resistance to various modes of domination and of change. In this sense, then, feminism becomes a broad-based, diverse struggle which combines an 'appreciation of the limits of individual experience' (p. 12) with an appreciation of our commonality. But of necessity part of this struggle is to redefine and learn from our differences. In this regard, Sawicki makes the case for radical pluralism and coalition politics built on shifting allegiances and interests, rather than on the ahistorical illusion of stable coalitions. The benefit of this approach to difference is that it does not slip into the vapid celebration of difference for its own sake but it locates its systems of exclusion and exploitation.

As I see it, this way of thinking about difference has important implications for feminist teachers in universities, for curriculum and pedagogy. Rather than implying the necessity of abandoning certain modernist feminisms, it implies the need for an education in different feminisms, for an exploration of their different weaknesses and strengths in particular circumstances in educational institutions and beyond, and for a view of them as strategies rather than truths for pedagogy. Feminist university teachers could help students to see different feminisms as strategies for change to be selectively and judiciously deployed. They could then also help students to see that feminism itself is a discursive field of struggle, not only with different 'horses for different courses' but also with different dividends for different punters. This is not by any means a call for a pluralist view of feminisms, rather it is a recognition of the strategic merits of different feminisms but one which should not blind teachers to their dangers. A feminist politics of difference has alerted other feminisms to their particular dominating tendencies; to their potential dangerousness, as Foucault would say.

Another feature of a materialist feminist politics is its insistence not so much on the materiality of discourse but that discourse has material effects; that discourse constitutes and is constituted by wider social power dynamics. It recognizes that the politics of discourse is often overdetermined by the power relationships which exist beyond the moment and the specific locality, indeed that times and places cannot be isolated from their wider contexts. As Sawicki (1991) and others point out, the postmodernisms which arise from Foucault do not necessarily deny broad patterns of domination and subordination. What they do deny, however, is that one theory fits all situations. To be more specific, they deny that all power is possessed by one particular group or set of institutions, that it is dispersed from a centre, and that is primarily repressive. Their focus however, is on the 'myriad of power relations at the micro level of society' (Sawicki 1991: 20). When they do widen the lens they none the less show the ways in which the micro-physics of power contribute to more widescale sets of relationships. However, for Foucault, understanding the local is what is important in developing strategies of resistance, which, he feels, of necessity, must also be local.

Along with other materialist feminists such as Rosemary Hennessy and Nancy Fraser I do not entirely agree with Foucault on these matters. Indeed, the distinguishing feature of materialist feminism is that it articulates important insights from postmodernism with an analysis of social totalities. It articulates an analysis of struggles over meaning with an analysis of struggles over other resources. From postmodernism it draws on ideas about signification, textuality, subjectivity and difference. It also insists that 'modes of intelligibility [including theory] are closely tied to economic and political practices' (Hennessy 1993: 8). It stresses materiality and historical specificity—including the historical specificity of its own theories. It also articulates a commitment to the possibility of transformative social change. (Call it old fashioned or maybe the new fashion.)

I find it useful, despite their differences, to use Antonio Gramsci alongside Foucault, for it was Gramsci (1971) who, through his notion of hegemony, developed a most persuasive account of the ways in which social groups and collective identities and sociocultural hegemonies are formed and reformed through discourse (see further Kenway 1988; Fraser 1992). As Nancy Fraser (1992) explains:

The notion of hegemony points to the intersection of power, inequality and discourse. However, it does not entail that the ensemble of descriptions that circulate in society comprise a monolithic or seamless web, nor that dominant groups exercise on absolute top-down control of meaning. On the contrary, 'hegemony' designates a process wherein cultural authority is negotiated and contested. It

presupposes that societies contain a plurality of discourses and discursive sites, a plurality of positions and perspectives from which to speak. Of course not all of these have equal authority. Yet conflict and contestation are part of the story. (Fraser 1992: 179)

The concept 'hegemony' has the benefit of helping us to recognize the unruly but patterned nature of systemic and widescale asymmetrical power relations. It allows for a recognition of social totalities without abandoning a recognition of their specific manifestations in different places and times and their different implications for the positionality of different women. Or, as Hennessy (1993) says in developing an argument for systemic analysis,

it makes it possible to acknowledge the systematic operation of social totalities . . . across a range of interrelated material practices. These totalities traverse and define many areas of the social formation—divisions of labour, dimensions of state intervention and civil rights, the mobility of sites for production and consumption, the reimagination of colonial conquest, and the colonisation of the imagination (Hennessy 1993: xvii).

The social totalities Hennessy refers to are capitalism, patriarchy, and colonialism.

Of course Gramsci developed his theory of hegemony during what has been dubbed the historical period of modernity and any discussion of hegemony these days needs to take into account the particularities of what is often called the postmodern age or postmodernity. And here we meet another distinguishing feature of materialist feminism which as I suggested above locates itself firmly within the historical period of postmodernity which requires a little explanation beginning with a few quick qualifications.

Firstly, when I talk of postmodernity in the next few paragraphs, I am focusing on broad material, social and cultural shifts and conditions. I am not focusing on the philosophical/intellectual shifts I have called postmodernism and parodied earlier in this chapter. Nor am I referring to the artistic/cultural products defined as postmodernist or postmodern. Of course these are not unrelated although exactly how and why is difficult to specify. Secondly, I acknowledge that as a descriptor of current times postmodernism or the postmodern age are highly contentious and contested terms, particularly when used to imply a sharp distinction between the historical periods of modernity and postmodernity, a global applicability without different implications for different regions, and when they suggest that all the defining characteristics are historically unique. As Featherstone (1991: 3) points out, 'the post-modern is a relatively ill-defined term as we are only on the threshold of the alleged shift, and not in the position to regard the post-modern as a fully fledged positivity which can be defined comprehensively in its own right'. In this sense then, postmodernity emerges from or 'feeds off' (p. 6) rather than dramatically breaks with modernity. While I acknowledge a certain discomfort in using the concept, I none the less find it useful as a shorthand which points to the 'cultural logic' or 'cultural dominant' (Jameson 1984) or to key features of contemporary times in the 'first-world' countries of the West—features which clearly also have an impact on 'third-world' countries. So what am I referring to here and why is it pertinent to education?

The key 'logics' or features of postmodernity include the techno-scientific and communications revolutions, the production of what can be called 'techno' or 'media' culture, the development of a form of techno-worship, the collapse of space and time brought about by the application of new technologies, the cultural dominance of the commodity and the image, the internationalization and postindustrial technologization of the economy (at least in western economies), and an identity crisis for nation states accompanied by the decline of the welfare state and the intensification of state-inspired nationalism. And, of course all of this has implications for human relationships and subjectivities and for cultural 'sensibilities' or 'moods' as do the new social movements and philosophical and artistic/cultural trends which are part of post-modernity and which are also under discussion in this chapter (see further Hinkson 1991).

A particular feature of postmodernity is the development of what can be called the global economic and technological village. Significant changes in international economies, including the growth of world trading blocks and supernational corporations, the internationalization of the labour market and the money market and the rapid growth, and, again, the extensive application of new information and communications technologies have facilitated these 'developments'.

The mode of production associated with this 'village' has been called post-Fordism and post-Fordism commonly, although not unproblematically, refers to an unevenly emerging movement away from the mass manufacturing base and assembly line practices of the Fordist era towards 'flexible' and decentralized labour processes and patterns of work organization brought about by the rapid growth, development and application of new information and communications technologies.[19] This is accompanied by 'the hiving off and contracting out of functions and services; a greater emphasis on choice and product differentiation, on marketing packaging and design, on the "targeting" of consumers by lifestyle, taste and culture, . . . a decline in the proportion of the skilled, male, manual working class, the rise of the service and white collar classes and the "feminisation" of the work force' (Hall 1988: 24).

These changes are said to have resulted in crises both for the nation-State which loses much of its capacity to control its economy and culture and for certain segments of capital which seek out new and often very exploitative ways to survive in times which threaten their annihilation. Needless to say, as the unemployment figures and the attack on unions indicate, these changes have in many instances been disastrous for workers (see Levidow 1990). The Australian government's particular approaches to addressing these crises and gaining some control over its economy and culture can be seen to arise from the profoundly successful discursive and interdiscursive work of disparate but powerful social and political groupings who have reshaped public and political opinion in favour of economic rationalism (see Pusey 1991), corporate managerialism (see Yeatman 1990) and market forms in public services and vocationalism in education (see Kenway with Bigum and Fitzclarence 1993). As a result all sectors of education have been dramatically restructured leading, in the worst cases, to the sorts of vandalism of the education system that I described at the beginning of this chapter.

Universities are certainly being redefined by the postmodern condition. Here is how Hennessy understands this process.

Computer technology has intensified capital's reach, proliferating opportunities for investment, speeding up shifts in production and refining divisions of labour. The accompanying fragmentation and dislocation of communities and the increasingly anonymous corporate structure have made the operations of exploitation in the age of information ever more insidious even as inequalities between women and men, minorities and dominant racial and ethnic groups have intensified. As the terms of economic power veer more and more towards control over information, knowledge is being stripped of its traditional value as product of the mind making it a commodity in its own right whose exchange and circulation helps multiply new divisions of Labor and fractured identities. Politically the 'ruling class' is being reconfigured as a conglomerate of corporate leaders, high level administrators and heads of professional organisations. An accompanying reinscription of the bourgeois 'self' as a more complex and mobile subjectivity inextricably bound up in myriad circuits of communication is unfolding in multiple cultural registers. One of them is the academy. (Hennessy 1993: 10)

Indeed it is becoming unavoidably obvious that universities are reorienting themselves more and more in line with the demands of the corporate State and, in turn, with the needs of the service-based economy, capital's expanding global markets and consumer culture. Universities now increasingly concentrate on providing both scientific and technological information tailored to the needs of multinational capitalist production and professional training for middle-level managers and the professions. It is important to note here though that at the same time, this historical moment has produced other political discourses which also have had an impact on the knowledge taught in the academy hence the rise of those subordinate knowledges associated with new social movements such as feminism and multiculturalism, and with new media forms such as cultural studies. And as many commentators observe, the extent to which these knowledges perform a counter-hegemonic function or become neutralized and sabotaged within the academy remains open to question. Meanwhile I will briefly note the ways in which materialist feminists are attending to the postmodern condition.

According to Hennessy (1993) feminist politics today require a systemic, critical, 'global analytic'. This, she argues, attends to multinational capital with its 'dense grid of information and highly refined international divisions of labor' (p. 15) and insists on a sys-

tematic reading of the global. This involves an attempt to delineate the relations between the highly fluid ideological processes and economic and political arrangements which characterize the complex social arrangements of postmodernity. It understands the social in terms of 'systems and structures of relations' (p. 16) and multiple registers of power. These are the sorts of matters which Hennessy believes should come under scrutiny here: shifting centres of production, the formation of new markets through colonization, the relationship between political alliances, state formations and disciplinary technologies and the global power relations that local arrangements sustain and vice versa. More generally, she is concerned with the ways in which postmodernism produces new 'material conditions of alienation and exploitation', 're-scripts systems of domination and opens up new frontiers for capitalism, patriarchy and colonisation' and reforms subjectivities. Let me say a few words on the question of postmodern subjectivities.

Materialist feminism both draws on and extends the postmodern conceptualization of subjectivity. It recognizes the subject as fragmented, dispersed and textualized but draws attention to the fact that this occurs within the workings of globally dispersed and state controlled multinational capitalism and consumer culture. As Hennessy (1993: 6) says, 'In the "age of information", cybernetics, instantaneous global finance, export processing zones, artificial intelligence and hyper-realities an atomised socius affords an increasingly fluid and permeable capital its products, its work-force and its new markets.' Donna Harraway offers the cyborg as metaphor for women's subjectivity in the conditions of postmodernity. Focusing on the informatics of domination and the polyvocal information systems which characterize these times, she gives us the cyborg as an 'ironic myth which is faithful to feminism, socialism and materialism' (p. 65) — a myth both produced through technocratic domination and scientific discourses and also through the politics of counter identity.

From what I have said it should be clear that the crisis of knowledge in the academy is the complex result of both postmodernity and postmodern philosophy (postmodernism). Equally, students in the postmodern university are the subjects of postmodernity and postmodern philosophy. Feminists who focus on one side of the coin without the other, fail to understand their own historical location and equally, again, they fail to help students reach an understanding of the ways in which their identities are structured through their engagement within global relationships of difference and dominance. This is only one of the issues at stake here and I will now briefly pick up on some others pertinent to my parody later.

Clearly postmodernism has destabilized the professional authority of feminist teachers and researchers in universities and clearly this is a good thing to the extent that such authority made sweeping unsustainable claims and unvoiced the unvoiced in the name of feminism. However, as I implied above, some now seem to believe that this gives them permission to simply wave away their professional authority by either denying or playing with it. To do so, in my view, is to ignore many important 'what next?' questions associated with the relationship of feminist academics both to the politics of the state (as I implied above) and to feminists in associated fields outside the academy, not to mention their wider constituencies who are particular groups of women and girls and women and girls in general. As I see it, three key questions are as follows: firstly 'What is the nature of such professional authority after postmodernism?', secondly, 'How are feminists to be accountable?' and thirdly 'To what purpose do feminists participate in the politics of the state?' In what remains of this chapter, I will begin to address these questions.

Let me begin with the question of knowledge and authority. The point to be made here is that postmodernism does not require that feminists stop making knowledge claims or asserting truths. Indeed, participating in the politics of discourse, i.e. in the disarticulation and rearticulation of meaning without recourse to closure, is at the heart of postmodernist feminism and materialist feminism. Yeatman (1994: 14) makes the case that 'there is no privileged position "outside" the semiosis of a particular representational formation. Contestation, thus, does not explore an autonomous alternative representational space. Instead it works with the contradictions, heteroglossia, and historically contingent features of a specific representational or discursive formation.' However, a condition of such participation in the politics of discourse is that knowledge claims are recognized, always, as embodied and particular. Yeatman talks about perspectival and positioned views of knowledge, which are 'governed by the view of those who are the knowers', and are 'historically variable and specific' (p. 19). Harraway talks similarly of 'situated knowledges', of 'partial, locatable and critical knowledges'. She notes Sandra Harding's 'multiple desire' for both a 'successor science project and a post-modern insistence on irreducible difference' and for 'a radical multiplicity of local knowledges' and points out that 'All components of the desire are paradoxical and dangerous and their combination is both contradictory and necessary' (Haraway 1991: 187). Hennessy (1993: 25) argues that 'claims to truth are historical and inescapably inscribed in theoretical frameworks'.

It is in the context of these qualifications that it becomes possible to talk of feminist versions of authority and accountability. Indeed, Yeatman insists on the 'provisional exercise of authority'. She develops a notion of accountability which is tied to the work of what she calls subaltern intellectuals—those who develop an intellectual 'narrative which is ordered by metaphors of struggle, contest, forced closure, strategic interventions and contingent openings of public spaces for epistemological politics' (p. 31). She notes how such intellectuals are positioned across complex lines of intellectual and political authority and accountability which have the potential to result in them both mediating and domesticating the claims of their constituencies outside of the academy. This contradictory set of demands for accountability do make her authority problematic and challenge her to self-consciously negotiate them. Yeatman continues,

Subaltern intellectuals are positioned in a contradictory relationship to intellectual authority. As intellectuals and as evidenced especially when they are directing their intellectual claims upwards, as it were to the ruling elites of academy they are drawn within the culture of intellectual authority and use its conventions unproblematically. At the same time as subaltern intellectuals they are not only positioned as outsiders in respect of these ruling elites, which can foster a tendency to call into question the reliance of these elites for their status on intellectual authority, but they are positioned with loyalties and ties both to fellow subaltern intellectuals . . . and to subaltern non intellectuals. (Yeatman 1994: 35)

In a similar vein, Hennessy (1993) points to the responsibilities of the oppositional intellectual. Drawing on Stuart Hall she talks of the 'alienation of advantage', of identifying the ways in which knowledge, and indeed the knowledge we use as intellectuals, supports unfair advantage. To her, the responsibility of the oppositional intellectual is to put a hegemonic system of knowledge in the service of counter-hegemonic projects and to help the non-dominant to develop counter-hegemonic knowledges.

Social institutions such as universities and schools and education bureaucracies, cultural products such as curriculum texts, and interpersonal processes such as pedagogy (teaching-learning) are made up of many different and often contradictory discourses and discursive fields. Some of these are dominant, some subordinate, some peacefully coexisting, some struggling for ascendancy. Universities and schools can be seen to consist of fragile settlements between and within discursive fields and such settlements can be recognized as always uncertain; always open to challenge and change through the struggle over meaning, or what is sometimes called the politics of discourse; that is, interdiscursive work directed towards the making and remaking of meaning. Materialist feminists participate in this struggle over meaning but recognize more fully than do postmodernist feminists that this struggle is overdetermined by the distribution of other resources. It is neither naive nor voluntaristic.

What is important is to what end and *how* feminists practise their authority as intellectuals, whether they make it problematic to themselves and others and whether and how they make themselves accountable and to whom. The question about accountability to whom leads back to the point that feminists in universities are split across contradictory lines of accountability. Their work has many different audiences. As Yeatman notes these include the academic world, students generally and female and feminist students particularly and women generally. For those in professional faculties they also include service-delivery practitioners (such as teachers, bureaucrats and policy makers) generally and oppositional service-delivery practitioners particularly. Clearly the feminist academic's position is highly ambiguous but this does not mean that she should abandon her authority which for various reasons and in various ways can play a powerful supportive role for the non-dominant. Indeed, in some senses the feminist academic should 'hold onto her authority as an intellectual and place it in the service of the non-dominant' (Yeatman 1994). A similar point applies to her relationship with oppositional service-delivery practitioners who to some extent depend on her authority and expertise for the legitimacy and development of their own projects. The ironical twist here is that those who are on the receiving end of such service delivery may well need some protection from it and again the role of the independent subaltern intellectual comes into play if, through independent research, he or she is in the position to respond to the voices of non professionals and feed it back into the process of policy development. So, in discussing the professional authority which accrues to feminist academics by virtue of their institutional location, Yeatman argues that this should not be surrendered; that 'feminists should not abandon too readily the authority which resides in scholarly erudition and expertise'.

However, to Yeatman the notion of public or audience is crucial and she insists that feminist academics examine the ways in which they construct their actual and potential audiences—their 'strategies of public address'—so as to 'avoid deauthorising the voice of less credentialled feminists and nonfeminist others'. Haraway (1990) talks of the political and strategic necessity for the development of webs of communication called solidarity in politics, . . . 'shared, power sensitive conversations' and for a 'positioning which implies responsibility for enabling practices'. She argues that this become a basis for 'making rational knowledge claims in feminist terms'.

Returning to the subject of my *angst*, in conclusion let me say that it is a fascinating paradox that postmodernism has assumed such a hegemonic status amongst feminists in universities; a new and sneaky disciplinary technology which, by handing around the tools for its own dismantling, reasserts its discipline. (Audre Lorde, you got it right about 'the masters' tools'!) Clearly moving past this post is a very difficult and risky business. But, in my view, it is necessary if feminism is to remain a viable force for change in the post-modern university, in the postmodern state, and in the postmodern age.

Notes

1. I am aware that feminism is best discussed in the plural and I am also aware that, despite the addition of an 's', feminism/s is/are still undergoing an identity crisis with regard to who to be, how to be and what to value. Too soon, in my view, the addition of an 's' lost its radical potential and became a lazy way of being inclusive.
2. In education policy circles this has taken the form of a boys' movement which, by and large seeks to reign in the feminist policy agenda. Proponents of the boys make the case that boys' education has been neglected and that boys have been disadvantaged as a result of policies directed towards the education of girls.
3. Being unsettled and disturbed by certain directions in feminism in education is by no means unusual for me, particularly with regard to dominant directions in feminist policy and curriculum (see for example Kenway *et al.* 1994).
4. For the rest of this chapter I will use the term 'postmodernism' to include poststructural-ism. It seems to be the case that a great deal of the education literature in the US collapses the two and for the sake of space and conve-nience I will do so here. However, like Roman (1994), I do not think this is good enough and I refer readers to her excellent paper given at the American Association for Research in Education conference in 1994 for a discus-sion of the conceptual and political differ-ences.
5. I refer here to a research project I am conduct-ing with some colleagues called 'Marketing Education in the Information Age' (see fur-ther Kenway with Bigum and Fitzclarence 1993).
6. Jameson got away with it when he talked about 'Postmodernism or the cultural logic of late capitalism' (Jameson 1984) or the 'cultural dominant', i.e. the key features of contempo-rary times.
7. Actually, it was Marx who developed this metaphor.
8. It is interesting to speculate about the geneal-ogy of this focus on endings and death. In more sociological terms it relates to the decline in popularity of causality theses and to the shift from theories which focus on social and cultural production to those which focus on social and cultural reception. Exploring these shifts in the historical context of the life of intellectuals would be an interesting and no doubt revealing project.
9. Spotting dualisms and naming them as hierar-chical and oppressive has been fashionable in certain educational circles for some time. However, it has not usually been the case that the relationship between the two sides of the binary has been well theorized. Yeatman (1994) offers a useful discussion of the ways in which binary differences both divide and unite or as she says 'exist within each other' (pp. 17–18). Drawing on Trinh Minh-ha's notions of outsider on the inside and insider on the outside she points to the implications of this insight for a politics of difference *and* commonality thus leading to the notion of hybridized identity and to the possibility of affinity politics which accommodate differ-ences.
10. Diana Fuss (1989) wrote an excellent geneal-ogy of the essentialism debate at the beginning of which she pointed to the often mindless and politically unhelpful demonizing of essential-ism.
11. Hennessy (1993: 7) makes the point that 'it is increasingly important for feminists to come to terms with the difference between theory as a mode of intelligibility and theory as a totalizing or master narrative'.
12. Brodribb (1992) is an annoying feminist example of this.
13. It is this particular strand of postmodernism of which I am most critical. In my view it has shades of nihilism and contributes to a form of anomie that takes us nowhere fast.
14. Yeatman (1994: 3) argues that such a position is 'a more or less ironically inflected, sceptical, playful but fundamentally quietistic relation-ship to the postmodern condition'. She calls it a 'positivistic' relationship.
15. Thanks to Raymond Williams for these turns of phrase.
16. Postmodernism is commonly accused of rela-tivism and in some instances it is an easy target and in others not so. Liz Grosz (1988: 100) makes a useful distinction between relativist theories of knowledge in feminism and rela-tional theories which she sees as those that are connected to other practices rather than being free-floating and available to any subject. But there is a further point to be made here. As Yeatman (1994: 30) points out, relativism develops an 'ideological fiction of a horizon-tally integrated community of differently val-ued-oriented intellectuals'. It thus fails to attend to the assymetrical relationships of power within which different knowledges are intricated.
17. If I had more space here and time in my life I

would do more than 'note'. A more elaborated discussion will have to wait.

18. A number of political cartographies of the postmodern have emerged from feminists (and others) in recent times. See e.g. Ebert 1991 *a* and *b*. Interestingly, these almost invariably map the postmodern along a positive (i.e., critical, resistant)/negative grid.

19. For an extensive discussion both of post-Fordism in its different variations, and of its implications for education see Kenway, 1993.

References

Alcoff, L. (1988), 'Cultural feminism versus post-structuralism', in Minnich, E., O'Barr, J., and Rosenfield, R. (eds.), *Reconstructing the Academy: Women's Education and Women's Studies* Chicago: (University of Chicago Press).

Brodribb, S. (1992), *Nothing Mat[t]ers: A Feminist Critique of Postmodernism* (North Melbourne, Victoria, Australia: Spinifex Press).

De Lauretis, T. (1990), 'Eccentric Subjects: Feminist Theory and Historical Consciousness', in *Feminist Studies*, 16/1, (Spring).

Ebert, T. (1988), 'The Romance of Patriarchy: Ideology, Subjectivity, and Postmodern Feminist Cultural Theory', *Cultural Critique*, 10: 19–58.

—— (1991*a*), 'The (Body) Politics of Feminist Theory', *Phoebe*, 3/2: 56–63.

—— (1991*b*), 'The "Difference" of Postmodern Feminism', *College English*, 53/8: 886–904.

Featherstone, M. (1991), *Consumer Culture and Postmodernism* (Sage Publications).

Foucault, M. (1977), *The Archaeology of Knowledge* (London: Tavistock).

Fraser, N. (1992), 'The Uses and Abuses of French Discourse Theories/or Feminist Politics', in Fraser, N., and Bartky, S. L. (eds.), *Revaluing French Feminism: Critical Essays on Difference Agency and Culture* (Bloomington and Indianapolis: Indiana Univ. Press).

Fuss, D. (1989), *Essentially Speaking: Feminism, Nature and Difference* (New York: Routledge).

Gramsci, A. (1971), *Selections from the Prison Notebooks*, Hoare, Q., and Nowell-Smith, G. (eds.), (New York: International Publishers).

Grosz, E. (1988), 'The In(ter)vention of Feminist Knowledges', in Caine, B., Grosz, E., and de Lepervance, M. (eds.), *Crossing Boundaries: Feminisms and the Critique of Knowledge*, (Sydney: Allen and Unwin).

Hall, S. (1988), 'Brave New World', in *Marxism Today* (Oct.): 24–9.

Haraway, D. (1990), 'The Actors are Cyborg, Nature is Coyote and the Geography is Elsewhere: Postscript to "Cyborgs at Large" ', in Penley, C., and Ross, A. (eds.), *Technoculture*

(Oxford and Minneapolis: Univ. of Minnesota Press).

—— (1991), *Simians, Cyborgs and Women: The Reinvention of Nature* (London: Free Association Books).

Hennessy, R. (1993), *Materialist Feminism and the Politics of Discourse* (New York: Routledge, Chapman and Hall).

Hinkson, J. (1991), *Post-modernity, State and Education* (Victoria, Australia: Deakin Univ. Press).

Jameson, F. (1984), 'Post-modernism, or the Cultural Logic of Late Capitalism', *New Left Review*, 146: 53–93.

Kenway, J. (1988), *High Status Private Schooling in Australia and the Production of an Educational Hegemony* (Ph.D. thesis, Murdoch Univ., Western Australia).

—— (1993), *Economizing Education: The Post-Fordist Directions* (Geelong, Victoria: Deakin Univ. Press).

——, Bigum, C., and Fitzclarence, L. (1993), 'Marketing Education in the Postmodern Age', *Journal of Education Policy*, 8/2: 105–23.

——, Willis, S., Blackmore, J., and Rennie, L. (1994), 'Making Hope Practical rather than Despair Convincing: Feminism, Post-structuralism and Educational Change', in *British Journal of the Sociology of Education*, 15/2: 187–210.

——, and Willis, S., with Education of Girls Unit, SA (1993), *Telling Tales: Girls and Schools Changing Their Ways* (Canberra: Australian Government Publishing Service).

Levidow, L. (1990), 'Foreclosing the Future', *Science as Culture*, 8: 59–79.

Marginson, S. (forthcoming), *Schooling What Future?: Balancing the Education Agenda* (Deakin Centre for Education and Change, Deakin University, Geelong, Australia).

Martin, B. (1988), 'Feminism, Criticism and Foucault', in Diamond, I., and Quinby, L. (eds.), *Feminism and Foucault: Reflections on Resistance* (Boston: North Eastern University Press).

Pusey, M. (1991), *Economic Rationalism in Canberra: A National Building State Changes Its Mind* (Sydney: Cambridge University Press).

Roman, L. (1994), 'Postmodernism Relativism and Feminist Materialism as Issues of Importance to Science Education', Paper given at the American Association for Research in Education conference, New Orleans.

Rosenau, P. (1992), *Post-modernism and the Social Sciences* (Princeton, NJ: Princeton Univ. Press).

Sawicki, J. (1991), *Disciplining Foucault: Feminism, Power and the Body* (New York: Routledge).

Yeatman, A. (1990), *Bureaucrats, Technocrats, Femocrats: Essays on the Contemporary Australian State* (Sydney: Allen and Unwin).

Yeatman, A. (1994), *Postmodern Revisionings of the Political* (New York: Routledge).

8

Feminisms and Education

Gaby Weiner

Introduction

Many people think of feminism as a comparatively recent phenomenon—a rather 'hippy'
and utopian vision left over from the 1960s
and 1970s. Some have even termed the 1980s
onwards as a 'post-feminist' era in which
women can relax at last, safe in the knowledge
that all the necessary gains (the vote, equal
pay, opportunities in the labour market, sexual freedom and so on) have been safely
secured (Rumens 1985).

In fact, feminism has a very long history
even though the term is of more recent origin.
It derives from the Latin *femina* (woman),
feminism initially meaning 'having the quality of females', and came into use as a perspective on sexual equality in the 1890s. Rossi
(1974) traced its first usage in print to a book
review published in *The Athenaeum*, 27 April
1895 although this does not signal the beginning of feminism as a movement since, prior to
this 'womanism' was more commonly used to
describe interest in sex equality issues.
According to Tuttle (1986: 349), nineteenth-
century usage of the term 'The Woman Question' to denote interest in the condition of
women signalled 'a pre-feminist consciousness' rather than feminism as a political movement, as it is conceived today. To purloin Dale
Spender's book title, indeed, 'There's Always
Been a Women's Movement' (Spender
1983*b*). As feminist historians have found, if
you look hard enough, every era has had its
share of women complaining of their lot in
relation to their male contemporaries. From
Sappho in the seventh century BC, through the
middle ages to the modern (and even the post-

modern) period, there has been a distinctive
feminist presence in history.

However, different feminisms have priori-
tized different aspects of women's struggle
against oppressive forces. It has been common
in recent years to categorize each feminism
according to its particular ideological source
in order to show the differences within feminism as well as the shared commitment to
women's advancement. In 1987, Madeleine
Arnot and I identified three perspectives on
feminism which, we argued, had made the
most impact on education: these we termed
'Equal Rights in Education' (namely liberal
feminism), 'Patriarchal Relations' (radical
feminism) and 'Class, Race and Gender:
Structures and Ideologies' (marxist/socialist
feminism) (Arnot and Weiner 1987). We were
later rightly criticized for rendering as marginal those feminisms on the fringes of our
three categories, in particular, black feminism
and lesbian feminism. Measor and Sikes catalogue four main strands of feminism in their
book on gender and schooling—liberal, radical, socialist and psychoanalytic—(Measor
and Sikes 1992), while Tong in her introduction to feminist thought published in 1989,
distinguishes liberal, marxist, radical, psychoanalytic, socialist, existentialist and postmodern feminisms, seven in all. As
poststructuralism rightly identifies, it is proving ever more difficult to categorize the
amoeba-like changes in feminism, due to the
shifting nature of terminology, say of 'woman'
or 'feminism' or 'femininity' and the discursive frameworks which have helped shape the
'normalizing' processes for generations of
women. Indeed hooks (1984) argues that feminist thought is always a 'theory in the mak-

From *Feminisms in Education: An Introduction* (Open Univ. Press, 1994), 51–67. Reprinted with permission.

ing', always open to re-examination and new possibilities. Moreover, if there is any agreement about feminism, as Mitchell points out, it is likely to be of a general and diffuse nature.

If feminism is a concern with issues affecting women, a concern to advance women's interests, so that therefore anyone who shares this concern is a feminist, whether they acknowledge it or not, then the range of feminism is general and its meaning is equally diffuse. (Mitchell 1986: 12)

However, what has clearly marked out modern feminism has been its emphasis on the need for feminist *consciousness*; that is, the concern to understand what has caused women's subordination in order to campaign and struggle against it. Because such theoretical understandings (of the causes of women's oppression) are dependent on ideological and political value positions, however, and also because feminism as 'theory in the making' is resistant to any one dominant discourse, any attempts to summarize differences in feminist perspective are necessarily hazardous and vulnerable to criticism. Nevertheless, in this chapter I shall attempt (perhaps unwisely) to consider, as far as it is possible, the various shifts in modern feminist thought and their impact on education, at the same time as emphasizing feminism's 'harmonious' goals of equality and sisterhood, and its discordant tones of difference and identity.

Feminisms and Feminist Thought

We tend to be familiar with the two most recent feminist 'waves': the first, in the nineteenth century stretching into the first two decades of the twentieth century, and the second, from the late 1960s onwards.

The 'first wave' movement was associated with the emergence of liberal individualism and Protestantism at the time of the Enlightenment (at the end of the eighteenth and beginning of the nineteenth centuries), drawing specifically on ideas about natural rights, justice and democracy. Not surprisingly given its origins, the movement was *liberal, bourgeois* and highly *individualistic*, principally concerned with extending legal, political and employment rights of middle-class women. Whilst different class interests such as Owenites, Chartists, Unitarians and middle-class reformers united in campaigning on 'The

Woman Question' (often as part of a pattern of reforms that embraced universal suffrage and a national system of education), improvement of the marriage property laws, greater access to education and the professions, wider employment opportunities and participation of women in government and public life undoubtedly yielded greater benefits for middle-class women.

Liberal feminism, which has arguably been the most enduring and accepted of all the feminisms (visible currently in the campaigns in the UK for more women members of parliament and for the rights of women to become Church of England clerics on an equal basis with men) asserts that individual women should be as free as men to determine their social, political and educational roles, and that any laws, traditions and activities that inhibit equal rights and opportunities should be abolished. Access to education is fundamental to this perspective since it claims that by providing equal education for both sexes, an environment would be created in which individual women's (and men's) potential can be encouraged and developed. Liberal feminists also assume that equality for women can be achieved by democratic reforms, without the need for revolutionary changes in economic, political or cultural life, and, in this, their views are in sharp contrast to those of other feminist campaigners.

The 'second wave' women's movement had more dissident origins and aims, although was initially much influenced by the liberal feminism of Betty Friedan whose 1963 publication, *The Feminine Mystique* has been popularly regarded as signalling its beginnings. The Women's Liberation Movement (WLM, also called the modern or new feminist movement) was born in the USA in the 1960s out of other movements of the political 'new' Left, particularly the Civil Rights and anti-Vietnam war movements. A group of women, thoroughly disenchanted with the male domination of political organizations ostensibly committed to democratic/egalitarian practices, began to explore ideas about women-centredness in political organizations and to organize their own autonomous movement for women's liberation. Though its debt to marxism is clearly evident in the terminology used, for example Shulamith Firestone's *Dialectic of Sex* (1970) sought to define society in terms of a sex/class system and offered the case for a feminist revolution, the ideas developed came to be known as those characterizing *radical feminism*.

First, the concept of 'patriarchy' was used to analyse the principles underlying women's oppression. Its original meaning—the rule of the father—was altered to describe the historical dominance of men over women, this being seen as the prototype of all other oppressions and necessary for their continuation.

Male supremacy is the oldest, most basic form of domination. All other forms of exploitation and oppression . . . are extensions of male supremacy . . . All men have oppressed women. (*Redstockings Manifesto*, quoted in Bouchier 1983)

Further, Millett (1971) argued that patriarchy is analytically independent of capitalist or other modes of production and Firestone (1970) defined patriarchy in terms of male control over women's reproduction.

However, whilst the concept of patriarchy has been crucial to modern feminism because as Humm (1989: 159) puts it 'feminism needed a term by which the totality of oppressive and exploitative relations which affect women could be expressed', different feminist discourses produce different versions of how patriarchy is constituted, as we shall see later in this chapter.

Another related assumption of radical feminism is that of the 'universal oppression of women'. It necessarily follows that if all men oppress women, women are *the* oppressed class, though there has been some disagreement about how patriarchal relations were/are created and sustained. Firestone (1970) argued that the fundamental inequality between men and women is traceable to the physical realities of female and male biology (particularly their roles in reproduction) and their consequences. Ortner (1974) in contrast, saw the relegation of women to the private sphere arising out of the *interpretation* of biology in terms of women's association with nature and men's, with culture and civilization.

The third main assumption of radical feminism is that, to be aware of the effects of male domination, women have to undergo a process of women-focused education (or re-education) known as 'consciousness raising'. Developed in the 1960s, consciousness raising is a means of sharing information about female experience and was used as a means of education for women in the absence of a comprehensive knowledge-base on women.

We wanted to get the truth about how women felt, how we viewed our lives, what was done to us and how we functioned in the world. Not how we were *supposed* to feel but how we really did feel. This knowledge, gained through honest examination of our personal experience, we would pool to help us figure how to change the situation of women. (Shulman 1980: 154)

For a time, during the 1970s, radical feminist goals dominated the 'second-wave' women's movement as it drew in women from a wide range of backgrounds and interests. In Britain, Rowbotham remembers that there seemed to be small groups in most large towns, loosely connected together through national conferences; thus, 'the movement was sufficiently concerted to back national campaigns, for example on abortion' (Rowbotham 1989: xii).

Feminists grouped to address one or more of the numerous concerns of women characterizing the last quarter of the twentieth century: issues such as sexuality, women's health, abortion and reproductive rights, pornography, male violence, and also access to and conditions of employment, child-care provision, sexual harassment in the workplace and so on. The need to create a knowledge-base that illuminated the experiences of women resulted in a burgeoning feminist scholarship and also the emergence, particularly in the United States, of a proliferation of Women's Studies courses. Further, the perceived need to create a more effective, female, political power-base led to increased interest in the development of women-friendly organizations and practices (non-hierarchical, cooperative etc). This was characterized by 'the refusal of formal delegated structures of political organisation, a stress on participation rather than representation' (Mitchell 1986: 26).

Further, as Mitchell (1986) points out, radical feminism not only sought to challenge contemporary sexual relations and politics; it also produced a new language and a new discursive framework based on liberation and collectivism.

One of the most striking features of women's liberation and radical feminism was their recourse to a new language—the language of liberation rather than emancipation, of collectivism rather than individualism. (Mitchell 1986: 26)

However, by the end of the 1970s, a number of different feminist perspectives surfaced to challenge the hegemonic position of radical (and to some extent, liberal) feminism, both as a critique and an extension of the feminist project. For example, women within *marxist* and *socialist* organizations began, in a sense, to strike back at the sisters who had originally defected, although in Britain, as early as the 1950s, Juliet Mitchell had begun to articulate feminist ideas within the British Left. Because she was criticized by male comrades for ideological incorrectness, she began to develop a feminist position that demanded changes outside conventional marxist economic and social policy. These included changes in: *production*—women's place in the labour market; *reproduction*—sexual divisions within the family; *sexuality*—in the views of women as primarily sexual beings and sex-objects; and *socialization*—in the way in which the young were reared and educated (Mitchell 1971).

Later, other marxist and socialist feminists attempted to incorporate ideas about women's oppression and patriarchal relations into classic marxism, focusing in particular, on the relationship between production (the labour market) and reproduction (the family); the interrelationship of capitalism and patriarchy; and the complex interplay between gender, culture and society (see, for example, Barrett 1980; Davis 1981; Segal 1987).

Accordingly, patriarchy has a materialist and historical basis in that capitalism is founded on a patriarchal division of labour. Hartmann (1976) for example, defined patriarchy as a set of social relations with a material base underpinned by a system of male hierarchical relations and solidarity.

An important emphasis was that of the impact of class on gender formation exemplified in MacDonald's claim that gender and class are inexorably drawn together within capitalism:

both class relations and gender relations, while they exist within their own histories, can nevertheless be so closely interwoven that it is theoretically very difficult to draw them apart within specific historic conjunctures. The development of capitalism is one such conjuncture where one finds patriarchal relations of dominance and control over women buttressing the structure of class domination. (MacDonald 1981: 160)

Whilst this feminist perspective had greater explanatory power, it appeared to be less suc-

cessful than radical feminism in attracting large numbers of women to its political position, possibly because in seeking to incorporate feminist ideas within marxism, its complexities posed an obstacle to all but the most theoretically sophisticated.

In many ways, the most important challenge to radical feminism came from *black feminism* which criticized not only the white, patriarchal society for triply oppressing black women (on the basis of sex, colour and class) but also the oppressive nature of the white women's movement which had glossed over economic and social differences between women in its attempt to articulate an authentic, overarching female experience. Moreover, in the United States, both waves of feminism were associated with black political campaigns: in the nineteenth century, around the abolition of slavery and in the twentieth, around the Civil Rights movement. The apparently new black feminist presence was to shatter irreparably the notion of universal sisterhood—though as Tuttle points out, black feminism has been in existence as long as white feminism 'although [it has] ... suffered the fate of most women of being "lost" to history' (Tuttle 1986: 41).

Black feminists challenged the idea that a feminism that ignores racism can be meaningful. As bell hooks wrote in 1984:

Feminist theory would have much to offer if it showed women ways in which racism and sexism are immutably connected rather than pitting one struggle against the other, or blatantly dismissing racism. (hooks 1984: 52)

Moreover, it mounted a challenge to some of the most central concepts and assumptions of the white women's movement. Carby argues, for example, that the concept of 'patriarchy' has different meanings for black women.

We can point to no single source of our oppression. When white feminists emphasize patriarchy alone, we want to redefine the term and make it a more complex concept. Racism ensures that black men do not have the same relations to patriarchal/capitalist hierarchies as white men. (Carby 1982, rep. 1987: 65)

hooks further argued that the concentration of the white feminist movement on identifying white middle and upper-class men as the 'enemy' and the 'oppressor' let other men off the hook.

The labelling of the white male patriarch as 'chauvinist pig' provided a convenient scapegoat for black male sexists. They could join with white and black women to protest against white male oppression and divert attention away from their sexism, their support of patriarchy and their sexist exploitation of women. (hooks 1982: 87–8)

Black feminists pioneered the concept of identity politics, of organizing around a specific oppression, which allowed for both difference and equality to become issues within feminist politics. Hill Collins adds a commitment to a humanist vision in her definition of black feminism as 'a process of self-conscious struggle that empowers women and men to actualize a humanist view of community' (Hill Collins 1990: 39). She also draws on standpoint theory to articulate a specific black woman's position in the political economy, in particular, their ghettoization in domestic work enabling them to see white élites from a position not available to black men.

Interestingly, British black feminists retain stronger links with marxist and socialist feminism than their North American counterparts due to the specific experience of British imperialism and colonialism. For example, Brah and Minhas present their feminist position as follows:

We start from the position that any discussion [of education] . . . must be understood in the context of the complex social and historical processes which account for the subordination of black groups in British society. Social relations between white and black groups in Britain today are set against a background of colonialism and imperialism. (Brah and Minhas 1985: 14)

In particular, British black feminists emphasized the exploitation and unjust treatment of black immigrants (women and men) from the Caribbean and the Asian subcontinent from the 1950s onwards, for example, concerning overt discrimination such as the use of the 'colour bar' in housing, employment and education (Bryan et al. 1985). The state was further viewed as having created new forms of racism (termed 'institutional racism') within the bureaucracies and institutions for which it was responsible; thus 'contemporary racism now needs to be seen as a structural feature of the social system rather than a phenomenon merely of individual prejudice' (Brah and Minhas 1985: 15).

Furthermore, the possibility of making generalizations across all groups derived, say, from theories based on the white family as a site of sexual oppression, was heavily criticized. Phoenix (1987) argues that in the light of the endemic and unremitting racism of British society, the black British family is more likely to be a source of strength and a haven, than a site of oppression for black women.

Simultaneously, radical feminism began to exhibit divisions as breakaways championing a *separatist* feminist position were taken up by the 'new age' philosophies of Mary Daly and her followers on the one hand, and political lesbianism on the other. Mary Daly, in her 1979 volume *Gyn/Ecology* offers a new, metaphysical *spiritual feminism* in which men are depicted as evil and death-loving, parasitical on the energies of good, life-loving women. Daly argued that patriarchy is itself the world's prevailing religion and that women need to withdraw from men in order to create a new, women-centred universe with a new philosophy and theology, and even a new language.

Lesbian feminism, in sharp contrast, took a much more overtly political stand, arguing that lesbianism is not simply a matter of sexual preference or an issue of civil rights but rather a whole way of life combining the personal with the political. The concept of *political lesbianism* was developed as a critique of the ideology and practices of heterosexuality. According to Charlotte Bunch,

Lesbian-feminist politics is a political critique of the institution and ideology of heterosexuality as a cornerstone of male supremacy. It is an extension of the analysis of sexual politics to an analysis of sexuality itself as an institution. It is a commitment to women as a political group, which is the basis of a political/economic strategy leading to power for women, not just an 'alternative community'. (quoted in Tuttle 1986: 180–1)

The argument was made that since sexual orientation is a matter of personal preference, lesbianism should not be stigmatized. Furthermore, that lesbianism should be made more visible within the women's movement, in history and in society as a whole. Moreover, because political lesbianism constitutes a major challenge to male domination in its commitment to an autonomous, women-centred society, it has a legitimate and central place in any movement which seeks to redress the power balances between the sexes.

Significantly, the more 'radical' feminist

groupings were remarkably successful in achieving societal attitudinal change, particularly given their relatively small numbers. Their public campaigns, for instance, concerning the seriousness of rape and the establishment of rape crisis centres, the revelation of hitherto unacknowledged incidence of child sexual abuse and male violence in the family, the establishment of havens for battered wives, and campaigns against pornography as a violation of women's civil rights, all fundamentally affected the societies within which they were active (see, for example, Brownmiller 1975; Dworkin 1981).

Another form of feminism to emerge in the 1970s, drawing to some extent on both marxist and radical feminism but also with its own specific knowledge-base was that of *psychoanalytic feminism*. Its main concern was to place greater emphasis within feminism on how the oppression of women affects their emotional life and their sexuality (as opposed, say, to their employment prospects or position within the family). It argued, for instance, that the roots of women's oppression are deeply embedded in the psyche and that for women to free themselves, an 'interior' (as well as societal) revolution is necessary so that women are able to challenge their own oppression. Extending her earlier ideas on the necessary prerequisites for women's liberation (see earlier in this chapter) Mitchell (1982) continued to articulate her concern about the ideologies underlying women's position, this time taking Freud's theories about the unconscious and the construction of femininity and demonstrating their importance as tools for analysing and challenging patriarchal society.

Criticisms of the phallocentric nature of Freud's work led other feminists into alternative ways of theorizing women's position in the family and in child-rearing. Chodorow, for example, explored mother/daughter relationships. Rejecting the notion that women's universal primary role in child-care could be explained in purely biological or social terms, Chodorow claims that women become mothers because they were themselves mothered by women. In contrast, the fact that men are parented by women psychically reduces their potential for parenting. Women's exclusive mothering, Chodorow asserted:

creates a psychology of male dominance and fear of women in men. It forms a basis for the division of the social world into unequally valued domestic and public spheres, each the province of a different gender. (Chodorow 1978)

According to this view, patriarchy stems from the gender formation of females and males, uniting psychic and property relations (Dinnerstein 1976). Thus to achieve women's liberation, the family must be reorganized so that women and men share parenting responsibilities equally and children grow up dependent upon both women and men from their earliest days. Not surprisingly given other radical feminist perspectives, major criticisms of Chodorow's thesis includes her prioritization of psychic dynamics over social structures in women's liberation, and her failure to appreciate the diversity of family structures inter- and intra-culturally (Tong 1989).

Other, more complex (and often more confusing!) critical feminisms emerged in the 1980s to challenge and critique both the women's movement and patriarchal relations, developing out of the general disillusionment with science and macro-political theory in the post-Chernobyl and post-Communist/Cold War eras. They were grounded, as Lather writes, in 'the disappointed hopes engendered by optimistic confidence in the continuing progress and imminent triumph of Enlightenment reason' (Lather 1991: 87).

They arose out of theories of poststructuralism and postmodernism, increasingly popular and influential in the social sciences towards the end of the 1980s. However, there was much confusion about what poststructuralism and postmodernism brought to the understanding of social relations. In fact, Hudson reveals the extent to which characterizations of postmodernism differ: seen alternatively as a myth, periodization, condition or situation, experience, historical consciousness, sensibility, climate, crisis, episteme, discourse, poetics, retreat, topos, and task or project (Hudson 1989: 140). Calinescu (1985) suggests however that postmodernism is principally used in two ways: as a historical category (namely defining a post-modern era) and as a systematic or ideal concept (namely a theoretical, analytic framework). Also, its relationship to poststructuralism lies in the acceptance by poststructuralists of the analytic framework but not the sense of periodization.

Thus, if postmodernist critiques aim to

deconstruct philosophical claims generally, and the very idea of possible unitary theories of knowledge, *post-modern feminism* also concentrates on such critiques but within feminism (Nicholson 1990). Accordingly, feminism is perceived as having much in common with postmodernism in questioning the 'foundationalism and absolutism' (Hekman 1990: 2) of the modern historical period (from the late eighteenth century onwards); in criticizing the claims to objectivity and rationality of modern (male) western scholarship; and in asserting that this epistemology must be displaced and a different way of describing human knowledge and its acquisition must be found.

Feminism, like postmodernism, poses a challenge to modern thought in every discipline from philosophy to physics, but the cutting edge of both critiques is to be in those disciplines that study 'man'. Both feminism and postmodernism are especially concerned to challenge one of the defining characteristics of modernism, the anthropocentric [male-centred] definition of knowledge. (Hekman 1990: 1–2)

However, Hekman makes the point that feminism is also tied to the universalisms of Enlightenment epistemology, both because of its modernist legacy (namely the emergence at the end of the eighteenth century of liberal feminism as part of Enlightenment thinking in, say, the work of Mary Wollstonecraft, 1792), and because of radical feminism's adherence to dichotomies and absolutes connected with revealing an essential nature of womanhood. Accordingly, a post-modern approach to feminism must necessarily reject outright the epistemological categories that have created and sustained the female-male dualism and also aim to reveal some of the flaws in contemporary feminism, such as the attempt to define an essential female nature (such as by Mary Daly), the failure to recognize the historical and cultural embeddedness of its own assumptions, or to replace the current 'masculinist' epistemology with a similarly flawed 'feminine-ist' epistemology. Moreover, if all knowledge (including that created by feminism) is perceived as interpretive and open to criticism this will add considerable substance and power to the overall feminist critique.

In contrast, *poststructural feminism* has placed more emphasis on the creation of new ways of seeing and knowing. Drawing on the work of the French philosopher Michel Foucault among others, poststructural *feminism* seeks to analyse in more detail the workings of patriarchy in all its manifestations—ideological, institutional, organizational and subjective. Moving away from the universals of liberal and radical feminism, social relations are viewed in terms of plurality and diversity rather than unity and consensus, enabling an articulation of alternative, more effective ways of thinking about or acting on issues of gender (Wallach Scott 1990).

A poststructural analysis, it is argued, differs fundamentally from structuralist analyses such as that of the linguist Saussure in that it recognizes the importance of 'agency' as well as structures in the production of social practices:

It recognizes not only the constitutive force of discourse and the social structures emerging through those discourses, but accords the possibility of *agency* to the subject. For children and anyone else not accorded full human status within society, agency stems from a critical awareness of the constitutive force of discourse. (Davies and Banks 1992: 3)

Thus people are not socialized into their personal worlds, not passively shaped by others but rather, each is active in taking up discourses through which he or she is shaped.

Moreover, feminist poststructuralism argues that what it means to be a 'woman' and/or to be acceptably 'feminine' shifts and changes as a consequence of discursive shifts and changes in culture and history. If the meanings of concepts such as 'womanhood' or feminism, for that matter, are necessarily unstable and open to contestation and redefinition, then they require continual scrutiny; according to Wallach Scott (1988: 5):

they require vigilant repetition, reassertion and implementation by those who have endorsed one or another definition. Instead of attributing transparent and shared meaning to cultural concepts, poststructuralists insist that meanings are not fixed in a culture's lexicon but are rather dynamic, always potentially in flux.

What poststructural feminism claims to be able to do, then, even if it lacks any substantive powerbase, is to offer discursive space in which the individual woman is able to resist her subject positioning (a specific fixing of identity and meaning). According to Weedon (1987: 105):

A constant battle is being waged for the subjectivity of every individual—a battle in which real interests are at stake, for example, gender-based social power—dominant, liberal-humanist assumptions about subjectivity mask the struggle.

As a 'reverse-discourse', feminism is positioned to challenge meaning and power, enabling the production of new, resistant discourses. Weedon suggests, however, that radical feminism has failed to do this thus far since it has run parallel to the hegemonic, male discourse, rather than subverting its power. On the other hand, while privileging the interests of women, feminist poststructuralism, Weedon argues, is more analytical and illuminating in revealing how power is exercised through discourse, how oppression works and how resistances might be possible.

Criticisms of postmodernism and poststructuralism have largely been concerned with questioning their appropriateness, although theoretically strong, for political action. Thus the charge that postmodernist (and indeed poststructuralist) feminism cannot provide a viable political programme because it rejects absolute values and verges on relativism, needs seriously to be addressed even though its rejection of male-defined knowledge and action is one of the most obvious goals of feminism.

The range of feminisms described above, I suggest, are those that have been of most influence to British feminism; however, other forms have had greater prominence in other cultures. In France, for example, different forms of feminism have emerged both out of *existentialism* and *poststructuralism/postmodernism*—indeed Tong claims that until recently, post-modern feminism was popularly referred to as 'French feminism' (1989: 217).

In the first instance, drawing on the work of the French existential philosopher Jean-Paul Sartre in her 1949 book *Le Deuxième Sexe*, Simone de Beauvoir (1953) conceptualized woman's oppression as unique, derived from her position as the Other, not only separate from man but inferior to him. Her perception of the effects on women of having and caring for children suggested to de Beauvoir that it was harder for a woman to become and remain 'a self', especially as a mother. Writing at a time when feminism was at a low point, de Beauvoir argued the case for cultural factors in women's oppression, seeing causes and reasons beyond those suggested by female biology and physiology to account for why woman is invariably selected by society to play the role of the Other (de Beauvoir 1953). At the time of writing *Le Deuxième Sexe*, de Beauvoir declared that she was not a feminist, believing the class struggle to be more important and that women's rights would come with the achievement of socialism. In the 1970s, however, she joined the Women's Liberation Movement, latterly convinced of the need for women to unite to fight against the manifest continuation of sexual inequality in revolutionary, leftist societies.

Later, in the 1980s, younger French feminist writers such as Cixous, Irigaray and Kristeva drew on the work of de Beauvoir as well as the philosophical writings of Foucault, Derrida and Lacan, to develop a philosophy of *deconstructionism* which aims to illuminate the internal contradictions of the predominant systems of thought and also to reinterpret Freudian psychoanalytic theory and practice (Tong 1989). Cixous (Cixous 1971), for instance, applies Derrida's notion of 'differance' to writing, contrasting feminine writing (*l'écriture féminine*) with masculine writing (*literatur*) and arguing that these differences are psychically constructed. For a variety of socio-cultural reasons, masculine writing has reigned supreme over feminine writing with the consequence that man has been associated with 'all that is active, cultural, light, high or generally positive and women with all that is passive, natural, dark, low or generally negative' (Tong 1989: 224). However, the legacy of de Beauvoir is also clearly evident in this strand of French feminist thought since Cixous also asserts that man is the self and woman is his Other; and woman exists in man's world on his terms. She further argues that women need to write themselves out of the world men have constructed for them by putting into words the unthinkable/unthought, and by using women's own particular forms of writing.

As feminism has become more fractured, and identity politics more possible, other feminisms have continued to emerge: for example, *Christian feminism* (concerned with the creation of a feminist theology—e.g. Maitland 1983); *humanist feminism* (advocating equality that judges women and men by a single standard—e.g. Young 1985); *Muslim feminism* (which sees women's liberation as both more threatening to Islam than it is in the West but also more broadly based—e.g. Mernissi 1985); *eco-feminism* (another broadly-based movement with aims ranging from a quest for a new spiritual relationship with nature to concern to empower women in developing countries—e.g. Vidal 1993) and so on. Conflicts within feminism led also to the use of labels of a more derogatory nature for the activities and beliefs of certain forms of feminism by those holding alternative views: for example, the terms 'revisionist', 'bourgeois', 'career' have all been applied to liberal feminism (Tuttle 1986) which has often been viewed by more radical feminist perspectives as conservative and conformist.

If anything is certain, it is that new feminisms will continue to emerge in the decades to come to reflect the different cultural, psychological and material concerns of new generations of women, rather than any terminal decline of feminism or entry into any post-feminist era.

References

Amos, V., and Parmar, P. (1984), 'Challenging Imperial Feminism', *Feminist Review*, 17: 3–18.

Arnot, M., and Weiner, G. (eds.) (1987), *Gender and the Politics of Schooling* (London: Hutchinson).

Barrett, M. (1980), *Women's Oppression Today: Problems in Marxist Feminist Analysis* (London: Verso).

Bouchier, D. (1983), *The Feminist Challenge* (London: Macmillan).

Brah, A., and Minhas, R. (1985), 'Structural Racism or Cultural Difference: Schooling for Asian Girls', in Weiner, G. (ed.), *Just a Bunch of Girls: Feminist Approaches to Schooling* (Milton Keynes: Open University Press).

Brownmiller, S. (1975), *Against Our Will: Men, Women and Rape* (New York: Simon and Schuster).

Bryan, B., Dadzie, S., and Scarfe, S. (1985), *The Heart of the Race: Black Women's Lives in Britain* (London: Virago).

Calinescu, M. (1985), 'Introductory Remarks', in Calinescu, M., and Fokkema, D. (eds.), *Exploring Postmodernism* (Amsterdam: John Benjamins Publishing Company).

Carby, H. (1987), 'Black Feminism and the boundaries of sisterhood', in Arnot, M., and Weiner, G. (eds.), *Gender and the Politics of Schooling* (London: Hutchinson).

Chodorow, N. (1978), *The Reproduction of Mothering: Psychoanalysis and the Sociology of Gender* (Berkeley: Univ. of California Press).

Cixous, H. (1971), 'Sorties', in Marks, E., and de Courtivron, I. (eds.), *New French Feminisms* (New York: Schocken Books).

Clarricoates, K. (1978), 'Dinosaurs in the Classroom: A Re-Examination of Some Aspects of the "Hidden Curriculum": in Primary Schools', *Women's Studies International Quarterly*, 1: 353–64.

Daly, M. (1979), *Gyn/Ecology* (London: The Women's Press).

David, M. (1980), *The State, the Family and Education* (London: Routledge and Kegan Paul).

Davies, B., and Banks, C. (1992), 'The Gender Trap: A Feminist Post-Structuralist Analysis of Primary-School Children's Talk about Gender', *Journal of Curriculum Studies*, 24/1: 1–25.

—— (1989), *Frogs and Snails and Feminist Tales: Pre-school Children and Gender* (Sydney: Allen and Unwin).

Davis, A. (1981), *Women, Race and Class* (London: The Women's Press).

de Beauvoir, S. (1953), *The Second Sex*, (transl. and ed.) H. M. Parshley (London: Jonathan Cape).

Deem, R. (ed.) (1984), *Coeducation Reconsidered* (Milton Keynes: Open Univ. Press).

Dinnerstein, D. (1976), *The Mermaid and the Minotaur: Sexual Arrangements and Human Malaise* (New York: Harper and Row).

Dworkin, A. (1981), *Pornography: Men Possessing Women* (New York: Pedigree Books).

Firestone, S. (1970), *Dialectic of Sex* (New York: Paladin).

Griffin, C. (1985), *Typical Girls* (London: Routledge and Kegan Paul).

Hartmann, H. (1976), 'Capitalism, Patriarchy, and Job Segregation by Sex', in Blaxall, M., and Reagan, B. (eds.), *Women in the Workplace: The Implications of Occupational Segregation* (Chicago: Univ. of Chicago Press).

Hekman, S. J. (1990), *Gender and Knowledge: Elements of Postmodern Feminism* (Boston: Northeastern Univ. Press).

Hill Collins, P. (1990), *Black Feminist Thought* (New York: Routledge).

hooks, b. (1982), *Ain't I a Woman: Black Women and Feminism* (1992 edn., London: Pluto Press).

—— (1984), *Feminist Theory: From Margin to Center* (Boston: South End Press).

Hudson, W. (1989), 'Postmodernity and Contemporary Social Thought', in Lassman, P. (ed.), *Politics and Social Theory* (London: Routledge).

Humm, M. (1989), *The Dictionary of Feminist Theory* (Hemel Hempstead: Harvester/Wheatsheaf).

Jones, A. (1993), 'Becoming a "Girl": Post-Structuralist Suggestions for Educational Research', *Gender and Education*, 5/2: 157–66.

Jones, C., and Mahony, P. (1989), *Learning Our Lines: Sexuality and Social Control in Education* (London: The Women's Press).

Lather, P. (1991), *Getting Smart: Feminist Research and Pedagogy Within the Postmodern* (New York: Routledge).

Macdonald, M. (1981), 'Schooling and the Reproduction of Class and Gender Relations', in Dale, R. *et al.* (eds.), *Politics, Patriarchy and Practice* (London: Falmer/Open Univ. Press).

McRobbie, A. (1978), 'Working-Class Girls and the Culture of Femininity', in Women's Studies Group, Centre of Contemporary Cultural Studies (ed.), *Women Take Issue* (London: Hutchinson).

McWilliam, E. (1993), ' "Post" Haste: Plodding Research and Galloping Theory', *British Journal of Sociology of Education* 14/2: 199–206.

Maitland, S. (1983), *A Map of the New Country: Women and Christianity* (London: Routledge and Kegan Paul).

Measor, L., and Sikes, P. (1992), *Gender and Schooling* (London: Cassell).

Mernissi, F. (1985), *Beyond the Veil: Male-Female Dynamics in Muslim Society* (London: Al Saqi Books).

Millett, K. (1971), *Sexual Politics* (London: Hart Davis).

Mirza, H. (1992), *Young, Female and Black* (London: Routledge).

Mitchell, J. (1971), *Woman's Estate* (Harmondsworth: Penguin).

—— (1982), *Psychoanalysis and Feminism* (Harmondsworth: Penguin).

—— (1986), 'Reflections on Twenty Years of Feminism', in Mitchell, J., and Oakley, A. (eds.), *What is Feminism?* (Oxford: Blackwell).

Nicholson, L. J. (1990), *Feminism/Postmodernism* (New York: Routledge).

Ortner, S. (1974), 'Is Female to Male as Nature to Culture?', in Rosaldo, M. Z., and Lamphere, L. (eds.), *Women, Culture and Society* (Stanford: Stanford Univ. Press).

Phoenix, A. (1987), 'Theories of Gender and Black Families', in Weiner, G., and Arnot, M. (eds.), *Gender Under Scrutiny* (London: Hutchinson).

Rossi, A. (1974) (ed.), *The Feminist Papers: From Adams to de Beauvoir* (New York: Bantam).

Rowbotham, S. (1989), *The Past is Before Us: Feminism in Action since the 1960s* (London: Pandora).

Rumens, C. (1985) (ed.), *Making for the Open: The Chatto Book of Post-Feminist Poetry 1964–1984* (London: Chatto and Windus).

Segal, L. (1987), *Is the Future Female? Troubled Thoughts on Contemporary Feminism* (London: Virago).

Shulman, S. (1980), 'Sex and Power: Sexual Bases of Radical Feminism', *Signs*, 5/4: 590–604.

Spender, D. (1983b), *There's Always Been a Women's Movement* (London: Pandora Press).

Tong, R. (1989), *Feminist Thought: A Comprehensive Introduction* (Sydney: Unwin and Hyman).

Tuttle, L. (1986), *Encyclopedia of Feminism* (London: Arrow Books).

Vidal, J. (1993), 'And the Eco-Feminists shall Inherit the Earth', The *Guardian* (supplement, 9 August), 10.

Walkerdine, V. (1990), *School Girl Fictions* (London: Verso).

Wallach Scott, J. (1988), *Gender and the Politics of History* (New York: Columbia Univ. Press).

—— (1990), 'Deconstructing Equality-Versus-Difference; Or the Uses of Poststructural Theory for Feminism', in Hirsch, M., and Fox Keller, E. (eds.), *Conflicts in Feminism* (New York: Routledge).

Weedon, C. (1987), *Feminist Practice and Poststructuralist Theory* (Oxford: Basil Blackwell).

Williams, J. (1987), 'The Construction of Women and Black Students as Educational Problems: Re-evaluating Policy on Gender and "Race" ', in Arnot, M., and Weiner, G. (eds.), *Gender and the Politics of Schooling* (London: Hutchinson).

Willis, P. (1977), *Learning to Labour* (Farnborough: Saxon House).

Wollstonecraft, M. (1985), *Vindication of the Rights of Women* (orig. publ. 1792; London: Penguin).

Wolpe, A. M. (1988), *Within School Walls: The Role of Discipline, Sexuality and the Curriculum* (London: Routledge).

Wright, C. (1987), 'The Relations between Teachers and Afro-Caribbean Pupils: Observing Multiracial Classrooms', in Weiner, G., and Arnot, M. (eds.), *Gender Under Scrutiny* (London: Hutchinson).

Young, I. M. (1985), 'Humanism, Gynocentrism and Feminist Politics', *Women's International Studies Forum*, 8/3.

PART TWO

EDUCATION, THE GLOBAL ECONOMY, AND THE LABOUR MARKET

Part Two: Introduction
Education, the Global Economy, and the Labour Market

No sophisticated theory of education can ignore its contribution to economic development (Durkheim 1977; Bowles and Gintis 1976). Indeed, throughout the twentieth century the relationship between education and the economy has constantly assumed greater significance. This is not only due to the increasing importance attached to knowledge as a condition for wealth creation, but because of the economic theory of human capital developed in the 1960s (Schultz 1961; Becker 1964). The attraction of human-capital theory is that investments in education and training are viewed as profitable for both the individual and for society (Marginson 1993). The main tenets of human-capital theory, and the controversy which surround its empirical findings, are summarized in the contribution by Maureen Woodhall, who notes the problems involved in trying to calculate the 'rate of return' from investment in human, rather than physical, capital and other methodological problems. Such concerns have not deterred either private or public investment in education. In 1992 the OECD countries, including Australia, Canada, Japan, the United States, and the United Kingdom, spent between 4.8 and 7.9 per cent of GDP to support their educational institutions (OECD 1995: 71).

The fact that human-capital theory has lost none of its salience in the minds of politicians and policymakers can, to a considerable extent, be explained by political responses to economic globalization (discussed in the Introduction). Globalization is assumed to weaken the power of nation states to control the outcome of economic competition, as Robert Reich argues in his chapter here. He suggests that in a global economy it is no longer possible for countries to protect domestic workers from the full force of international competition. Hence, the development of human capital is the main weapon that individuals and governments now have in the fight for economic prosperity. Moreover, economic globalization is also associated with a change in the nature of economic competition. In the future, Reich argues, the only way the advanced Western economies in North America and Europe can maintain a high standard of living is to compete within niche markets for customized goods and services, which depend on the ability of nations to exploit the skills, knowledge, and insights of what he calls the 'symbolic analysts' (Reich 1991).

The main difference between Reich's argument and earlier theories of human-capital theory is one of context rather than substance, given that he assumes a global rather than a national focus. Indeed, the protagonists of human-capital theory may see this as its extension, by viewing national labour markets as an impediment to the operation of a global market for labour, within which workers are rewarded according to their contribution, based on skills and productivity rather than political settlements between government, employers, and trade unions. It is in these terms that Reich explains why the 'rich are getting richer and the poor, poorer'. He explains the income polarization which has occurred in countries including the United States, Britain, and Australia as a reflection of the relative ability of workers to sell their skills, knowledge, and insights in the global labour market. Reich explains the increased incomes of the top 20 per cent of earners in terms of their ability to break free from the constraints of local and national labour markets. The global labour market offers far greater rewards to 'symbolic analysts' precisely because the market for their services has grown, whereas those workers who remain locked into national or local markets have experienced stagnation or a decline in income (see Murnane and Levy 1993).

Reich's argument not only draws on human-capital theory, but also impinges on established debates about skill and the occupational structure (Block 1990). In the 1970s this debate centred on alternative accounts of trends in skill forma-tion. The technocratic view which dominated the sociology of education in the postwar decades asserted that the logic of industrial development was towards an inexorable process of upskilling, reflected in the increasing demand for labour-market entrants with tertiary level qualifications (Kerr *et al.* 1973). The neo-Marxists, on the other hand, argued that the logic of capitalist development led to a process of deskilling the workforce (Braverman 1974; Bowles and Gintis 1976). The chapter by Aronowitz and De Fazio reflects the way in which the 'deskilling' debate has been superseded by that of 'skill polarization'. This draws on empirical evidence which shows that there has been a complex process of deskilling, reskilling and upskilling (Gallie 1991). However, this does not necessarily support the idea of a polarization of skills, although this is what Aronowitz and De Fazio assume to be the result of what they call the 'scientific-technological revolution of our time'. They argue that this revolution, is transforming the nature of managerial and professional work, leading to mass proletarianization and mass unemployment. Only a small occupational élite (which appear to share much in common with Reich's symbolic analysts) seem able to preserve their personal autonomy and fulfilment through their work.

Moreover, whereas Reich maintains the idea of social mobility through invest-ment in education and training, Aronowitz and De Fazio assert that middle-class occupations have become as insecure as those long associated with working-class employment. Hence, official statements about the growing demand for techni-cal, managerial, and professional workers obscure the fact that employment con-tracts, conditions, and relations in postwar Western capitalist societies no longer hold with the demise of bureaucratic work (Brown Ch. 45). There is already clear evidence of a mass process of corporate restructuring (Peterson 1994; Heckscher 1995). There is little doubt that restructuring has led to large-scale redundancy among the middle class, and has created conditions of insecurity and uncertainty amongst all categories of white-collar workers. This represents a profound change from the 1970s, where it has been calculated that approximately half the men in the US workforce were in jobs which effectively offered lifetime security (Hall 1982). The question of whether there has been an absolute decline in the numbers of jobs offering extensive 'career' opportunities, as well as that of the changing relationship between education, the labour market, and employment must await detailed empirical investigation. What also needs to be acknowledged is that our knowledge about the issues raised in recent debates over globalization, technological innovation, corporate restructuring, and new forms of knowledge and skill remains highly contentious. This is clearly illustrated in the paper by Blackmore on the gendering of skill, and that by Levin and Kelly on skills, income, and productivity.

Blackmore argues that the human-capital model is based on an a-historical and gender-blind view of the relationship between education and work, ignoring the fact that skill is a social construct, involving conflicts over the definition of what 'skilled' work really is. This leads her to reject the view that skills are essentially technical and therefore open to measurement. Blackmore would also reject the assumption made by human-capital theorists that income is directly determined by the skill and productivity of employees. Several studies, for instance, have shown how professional associations, trade unions, and employers are involved in power struggles over definitions of 'skill' and the way skill levels are used to legitimate differences in remuneration, which typically disadvantage women, young workers, and ethnic minorities in the labour market (Dex 1985; Ashton and Green 1996). Therefore, if we are going to understand how skill differentials have been used to establish initial occupational segregation and how they have been used to maintain gendered divisions of labour (p. 357), skill, like gender, needs to be understood as a relational concept. This requires consideration of how 'skills' are embedded in different forms of social and cultural capital, and how such differences advantage or disadvantage different individuals and social groups. Hence, Blackmore suggests, if we are going to achieve a better understanding of the relationship between education, skill, and occupational inequalities, detailed case-studies will need to be conducted in order to investigate the micro-politics of occupations, organizations, and worksites.

Blackmore also shows how the idea of upskilling has played centre stage in the vocationalism of Australian education, whose changing discourse has been linked to issues of democracy and social justice. Skilling, through education and training, is now seen to be the key to improving the position of the traditionally disadvantaged working-class, rural, Aboriginal, and female students. This is premised on the idea that there has been a fundamental shift from a Fordist to a post-Fordist economy, within which there is much greater demand for employees who are multi-skilled, creative, and flexible. The debate about post-Fordism will be considered below, but what is of interest here is Blackmore's account of the shift from 'situation-specific' towards 'generic' social and personal skills. In curriculum terms this has led to a greater emphasis on critical thinking, competencies, and problem-solving rather than content. Learning is work, and work now depends on learning (Zuboff 1989). Blackmore's response to this change in the discourse of vocationalism is ambiguous in terms of its significance for female students. On the one hand she suggests that it has not significantly altered the view that 'skill is a fixed and measurable attribute defined by the technical needs of the workplace', and therefore gender divisions on the basis of 'skill' will continue to be reproduced between the sexes despite an increasing emphasis on personal and social skills. However, it is also recognized that 'whilst women may no longer be destined only for motherhood and family, their "feminine qualities" (caring, interpersonal relations, and communication) have now been "co-opted" for managerialist ends'.

The importance of education in meeting the changing demand for technical, personal, and transferable skills again raises the question of the relationship between skills, income, and productivity. It also raises questions about the efficacy of education to deliver economic growth and prosperity. It is this which provides the focus of the contribution from Levin and Kelly. They question the exaggerated claims which are made about the contribution which the educational system can make to overcoming social and economic problems including healthcare, crime, overpopulation, inequality, and economic growth. The main reason given for the overstatement of educational outcomes is that longitudinal consequences of educational investment have been inferred from cross-sectional studies of the relation between education and various social and economic outcomes. They show, for instance, that the income returns to education in the 1980s have been exaggerated because it is assumed that the incomes of those leaving college or university will be the same as those already in the labour market with commensurate qualifications. However, when the incomes of credential holders are studied longitudinally, it can be clearly shown that in the US the incomes of most categories of credential holders have fallen during the last two decades. Although Levin and Kelly do not attempt to explore other factors which could explain why the educational system is treated as a universal panacea, it may also be seen to reflect the fact that education remains one of the few areas of social policy over which national governments are able to exert a decisive influence. In other words, educational policy has become an important test of 'statecraft', where governments can demonstrate their power to improve the conditions of everyday life. Exaggerated claims about education also reflect political ideology. The New Right have strenuously argued that unemployment, poor productivity, and sluggish economic growth are essentially supply-side problems. If education were more in tune with the needs of industry, and there was greater flexibility within the labour market, countries such as the US and the UK could soon be on the road to recovery. This failure to consider the importance of the demand for highly skilled workers is addressed by Levin and Kelly when they suggest that education can work to improve productivity only if there are employment opportunities for more productive workers.

However, their argument is not that education is irrelevant, but rather that it is one factor, which requires a range of 'complementary conditions' in order to provide a significant payoff. Hence, a key question is how to maximize these complementary conditions in order to realize the full potential of investment in education and training. This in turn opens a rich field of interdisciplinary enquiry into why some employing organizations (or countries) have been able to utilize their human resources more effectively than others, even when the educational levels are similar. The importance of this work, which goes some considerable distance beyond human-capital theory, is illustrated by the performance of Japanese plants in the United States. Levin and Kelly use the example of a joint venture between General Motors and Toyota. In 1982 General Motors closed their plant in Fremont, California because of poor productivity, high absenteeism, poor product quality, and labour–management conflict. With Toyota responsible for production and General Motors for marketing, the plant was reopened in 1985. Toyota redesigned the plant, and over 80 per cent of employees were hired from the ranks of those laid off when GM had closed it. The point Levin and Kelly draw from this example is that by changing the complementary conditions productivity was 50 per cent higher than in the old GM plant, and was equal to a similar plant in Takaoka City, Japan.

The idea of complementary conditions is also a central theme of the paper by Ashton and Sung, who argue that the relationship between education and economic development is historically specific. They distinguish three phases or waves of development which are reflected in different national systems of education and training. Firstly, countries such as England and the United States industrialized relatively early, but the impact of this on the educational system was seen to be minimal, given that there was little demand for a formally educated workforce, although there was an increased emphasis on the 'three Rs' in order for employees to follow basic instructions concerning rules of conduct. The second wave included countries such as Germany and Japan, where the vocational role of education was more clearly emphasized as a condition for economic growth. Thirdly, these authors argue that the success of the 'Asian Tiger' economies, of which they take Singapore as an exemplar, is premised on a new approach to skill formation. This approach challenges the way in which debates about education and the economy in the West have been couched in terms of the state versus the market. Ashton and Sung argue that Singapore does not conform to a free-market or a command economy, but rather that it offers a 'third' way, where the competing demands of both employers and the trade unions are subordinated to the state 'vision' of economic development, which is to make Singapore as affluent as Switzerland by the year 2020. A key element of this strategy is to target resources for education and training in preparation for the demand for skills in specific areas of economic activity. Ensuring an adequate demand for skilled workers is based on close collaboration between government and employers, which includes giving 'incentives' to companies to upgrade their product range in ways which exploit the productive potential of highly skilled workers. Indeed, Singapore may be the first advanced capitalist economy where Bowles and Gintis's (1976) concept of a 'direct correspondence' between education and production may actually apply.

    This contribution from Ashton and Sung raises crucial questions about the education–work relationship. They imply that competitive advantage in the new global economic competition will depend upon the close articulation between education and the labour market. They also suggest that it depends on a strong state, capable of keeping both the employers and trade unions at arms' length in order to pursue a state-defined vision of the national 'interest'. But what are the consequences for democratic participation and the role of schooling? Their argument also challenges the idea of an inherent technological or capitalist logic pushing to a convergence of national educational and training systems, and they show that the state is still able to play a profound role in both the education system and in shaping national economic development. This is an issue examined in the paper by Brown and Lauder.

    These authors return to the question of globalization and its implications for education and economic development. They suggest that although globalization processes weaken the power of the state to control economic competition, they believe that this still leaves considerable room for manoeuvre in how nation states respond to these conditions. It is for this reason that Brown and Lauder distinguish two ideal typical routes from 'walled' Fordist economies in North America and Europe. The political project of the New Right has led to a neo-Fordist route characterized by greater market flexibility through a reduction in social overheads and the power of trade unions, the privatization of public utilities and the welfare state, as well as a celebration of competitive individualism. Alternatively, a post-Fordist trajectory is premised on the development of the state as a 'strategic trader' (Krugman 1993), shaping the direction of the national economy through investment in key economic sectors in a bid to move to high-value-added, customized production and services using multi-skilled workers. They also suggest that whereas a lot has been written about the failure of the New Right's 'neo-Fordist' strategy, far less has been written about the strategies of the centre-left 'Modernizers' in the US and UK who espouse the principles of post-Fordism. At the heart of the Modernizers' agenda is a set of assumptions about the global economy, skill, and education. It is argued that these assumptions do not stand up to critical evaluation. For instance, although the Modernizers recognize the importance of increasing educational standards for all, they assume that this can be achieved without tackling the issue of inequalities of educational opportunities. Indeed, the relationship between equity and efficiency at the end of the twentieth century not only rests on the reassertion of meritocratic competition in education, but on a recognition that the wealth of a nation's human resources is inversely related to social inequalities, especially in income and opportunities. Hence, an attempt to narrow such inequalities is an essential condition for the shift to a post-Fordist economy. Brown and Lauder's critique of the Modernizers raises a further issue which is likely to have profound implications for education, economic, and social policy in the future, namely, that regardless of how much the educational system can be attuned to the needs of the economy, distributional justice can no longer be resolved through the labour market. They argue that the introduction of a basic income or citizen's wage is a necessary condition both for social justice and for the creation of a 'learning' society (Halsey and Young Ch. 49; Parijs 1992).

References

Ashton, D., and Green, F. (1996), *Education, Training and the Global Economy* (Cheltenham: Edward Elgar).

Becker, G. (1964), *Human Capital: A Theoretical and Empirical Analysis, with Special Reference to Education* (New York: Columbia Univ. Press).

Block, F. (1990), *Postindustrial Possibilities: A Critique of Economic Discourse* (Berkeley: Univ. of California Press).

Bowles, S., and Gintis, H. (1976), *Schooling in Capitalist America* (London: Routledge).

Braverman, H. (1974), *Labor and Monopoly Capital: The Degradation of Work in the Twentieth Century* (New York: Monthly Review Press).

Dex, S. (1985), *The Sexual Division of Work* (Brighton: Wheatsheaf).

Durkheim, E. (1977), *The Evolution of Educational Thought* (London: Routledge).

Gallie, D. (1991), 'Patterns of Skill Change: Upskilling, Deskilling or the Polarization of Skills?' *Work, Employment and Society*, 5: 319–51.

Hall, R. (1982), 'The Importance of Lifetime Jobs in the US Economy', *American Economic Review*, 72/4: 716–24.

Heckscher, C. (1995), *White-Collar Blues: Management Loyalties in an Age of Corporate Restructuring* (New York: Basic Books).

Krugman, P. (1993), *Peddling Prosperity: Economic Sense and Nonsense in the Age of Diminished Expectations* (New York: W. W. Norton).

Marginson, S. (1993), *Education and Public Policy in Australia* (Cambridge: Cambridge Univ. Press).

Murnane, R., and Levy, F. (1993), 'Why Today's High-School Educated Males Earn Less than their Fathers Did: The Problem and an Assessment of Responses', *Harvard Educational Review*, 63/1: 1–19.

OECD (1995), *Education at a Glance: OECD Indicators* (Paris: OECD).

Parijs, V. P. (1992), *Arguments for Basic Income: Ethical Foundations for a Radical Reform* (London: Verso).

Peterson, W. (1994), *Silent Depression: The Fate of the American Dream* (New York: W. W. Norton).

Reich, R. (1991), *The Work of Nations* (New York: Simon and Schuster).

Schultz, T. (1961), 'Investment in Human Capital', *American Economic Review*, 51: 1–17.

Zuboff, S. (1989), *In the Age of the Smart Machine: The Future of Work and Power* (Oxford: Heinemann).

9

Why the Rich Are Getting Richer and the Poor, Poorer

Robert B. Reich

[T]he division of labour is limited by the extent of the market.

ADAM SMITH, *An Inquiry into the Nature and Causes of the Wealth of Nations* (1776)

Regardless of how your job is officially classified (manufacturing, service, managerial, technical, secretarial, and so on), or the industry in which you work (automotive, steel, computer, advertising, finance, food processing), your real competitive position in the world economy is coming to depend on the function you perform in it. Herein lies the basic reason why incomes are diverging. The fortunes of routine producers are declining. In-person servers are also becoming poorer, although their fates are less clear-cut. But symbolic analysts—who solve, identify, and broker new problems—are, by and large, succeeding in the world economy.

All Americans used to be in roughly the same economic boat. Most rose or fell together, as the corporations in which they were employed, the industries comprising such corporations, and the national economy as a whole became more productive—or languished. But national borders no longer define our economic fates. We are now in different boats, one sinking rapidly, one sinking more slowly, and the third rising steadily.

The boat containing routine producers is sinking rapidly. Recall that by midcentury routine production workers in the United States were paid relatively well. The giant pyramidlike organizations at the core of each major industry coordinated their prices and investments—avoiding the harsh winds of competition and thus maintaining healthy earnings. Some of these earnings, in turn, were reinvested in new plant and equipment (yielding ever-larger-scale economies); another portion went to top managers and investors. But a large and increasing portion went to middle managers and production workers. Work stoppages posed such a threat to high-volume production that organized labor was able to exact an ever-larger premium for its cooperation. And the pattern of wages established within the core corporations influenced the pattern throughout the national economy. Thus the growth of a relatively affluent middle class, able to purchase all the wondrous things produced in high volume by the core corporations.

But, as has been observed, the core is rapidly breaking down into global webs which earn their largest profits from clever problem-solving, -identifying, and brokering. As the costs of transporting standard things and of communicating information about them continue to drop, profit margins on high-volume, standardized production are thinning, because there are few barriers to entry. Modern factories and state-of-the-art machinery can be installed almost anywhere on the globe. Routine producers in the United States, then, are in direct competition with millions of routine producers in other nations. Twelve thousand people are added to the world's population every hour, most of whom, eventually, will happily work for a small fraction of the wages of routine producers in America.[1]

The consequence is clearest in older, heavy industries, where high-volume, standardized

The Work of Nations: A Blueprint for the Future (London: Simon and Schuster, 1991), 208–24. Reprinted with permission.

production continues its ineluctable move to where labor is cheapest and most accessible around the world. Thus, for example, the Maquiladora factories cluttered along the Mexican side of the U.S. border in the sprawling shanty towns of Tijuana, Mexicali, Nogales, Agua Prieta, and Ciudad Juárez— factories owned mostly by Americans, but increasingly by Japanese—in which more than a half million routine producers assemble parts into finished goods to be shipped into the United States.

The same story is unfolding worldwide. Until the late 1970s, AT&T had depended on routine producers in Shreveport, Louisiana, to assemble standard telephones. It then discovered that routine producers in Singapore would perform the same tasks at a far lower cost. Facing intense competition from other global webs, AT&T's strategic brokers felt compelled to switch. So in the early 1980s they stopped hiring routine producers in Shreveport and began hiring cheaper routine producers in Singapore. But under this kind of pressure for ever lower high-volume production costs, today's Singaporean can easily end up as yesterday's Louisianan. By the late 1980s, AT&T's strategic brokers found that routine producers in Thailand were eager to assemble telephones for a small fraction of the wages of routine producers in Singapore. Thus, in 1989, AT&T stopped hiring Singaporeans to make telephones and began hiring even cheaper routine producers in Thailand.

The search for ever lower wages has not been confined to heavy industry. Routine data processing is equally footloose. Keypunch operators located anywhere around the world can enter data into computers, linked by satellite or transoceanic fiber-optic cable, and take it out again. As the rates charged by satellite networks continue to drop, and as more satellites and fiber-optic cables become available (reducing communication costs still further), routine data processors in the United States find themselves in ever more direct competition with their counterparts abroad, who are often eager to work for far less.

By 1990, keypunch operators in the United States were earning, at most, $6.50 per hour. But keypunch operators throughout the rest of the world were willing to work for a fraction of this. Thus, many potential American data-processing jobs were disappearing, and the wages and benefits of the remaining ones were in decline. Typical was Saztec International, a $20-million-a-year data-processing firm headquartered in Kansas City, whose American strategic brokers contracted with routine data processors in Manila and with American-owned firms that needed such data processing services. Compared with the average Philippine income of $1,700 per year, data-entry operators working for Saztec earn the princely sum of $2,650. The remainder of Saztec's employees were American problem-solvers and -identifiers, searching for ways to improve the worldwide system and find new uses to which it could be put (Maxwell Hamilton 1989).

By 1990, American Airlines was employing over 1,000 data processors in Barbados and the Dominican Republic to enter names and flight numbers from used airline tickets (flown daily to Barbados from airports around the United States) into a giant computer bank located in Dallas. Chicago publisher R. R. Donnelley was sending entire manuscripts to Barbados for entry into computers in preparation for printing. The New York Life Insurance Company was dispatching insurance claims to Castleisland, Ireland, where routine producers, guided by simple directions, entered the claims and determined the amounts due, then instantly transmitted the computations back to the United States. (When the firm advertised in Ireland for twenty-five data-processing jobs, it received 600 applications.) And McGraw-Hill was processing subscription renewal and marketing information for its magazines in nearby Galway. Indeed, literally millions of routine workers around the world were receiving information, converting it into computer-readable form, and then sending it back—at the speed of electronic impulses—whence it came.

The simple coding of computer software has also entered into world commerce. India, with a large English-speaking population of technicians happy to do routine programming cheaply, is proving to be particularly attractive to global webs in need of this service. By 1990, Texas Instruments maintained a software development facility in Bangalore, linking fifty Indian programmers by satellite to TI's Dallas headquarters. Spurred by this and similar ventures, the Indian government was building a teleport in Poona, intended to make it easier and less expensive for many other firms to send their routine software design specifications for coding (Gupta 1989).

This shift of routine production jobs from advanced to developing nations is a great boon to many workers in such nations who otherwise would be jobless or working for much lower wages. These workers, in turn, now have more money with which to purchase symbolic-analytic services from advanced nations (often embedded within all sorts of complex products). The trend is also beneficial to everyone around the world who can now obtain highvolume, standardized products (including information and software) more cheaply than before.

But these benefits do not come without certain costs. In particular the burden is borne by those who no longer have good-paying routine production jobs within advanced economies like the United States. Many of these people used to belong to unions or at least benefited from prevailing wage rates established in collective bargaining agreements. But as the old corporate bureaucracies have flattened into global webs, bargaining leverage has been lost. Indeed, the tacit national bargain is no more.

Despite the growth in the number of new jobs in the United States, union membership has withered. In 1960, 35 percent of all nonagricultural workers in America belonged to a union. But by 1980 that portion had fallen to just under a quarter, and by 1989 to about 17 percent. Excluding government employees, union membership was down to 13.4 percent (US Government Printing Office 1989). This was a smaller proportion even than in the early 1930s, before the National Labor Relations Act created a legally protected right to labor representation. The drop in membership has been accompanied by a growing number of collective bargaining agreements to freeze wages at current levels, reduce wage levels of entering workers, or reduce wages overall. This is an important reason why the long economic recovery that began in 1982 produced a smaller rise in unit labor costs than any of the eight recoveries since World War II—the low rate of unemployment during its course notwithstanding.

Routine production jobs have vanished fastest in traditional unionized industries (autos, steel, and rubber, for example), where average wages have kept up with inflation. This is because the jobs of older workers in such industries are protected by seniority; the youngest workers are the first to be laid off. Faced with a choice of cutting wages or cutting the number of jobs, a majority of union members (secure in the knowledge that there are many who are junior to them who will be laid off first) often have voted for the latter.

Thus the decline in union membership has been most striking among young men entering the work force without a college education. In the early 1950s, more than 40 per cent of this group joined unions; by the late 1980s, less than 20 per cent (if public employees are excluded, less than 10 percent) (Katz and Revenga 1989). In steelmaking, for example, although many older workers remained employed, almost half of all routine steelmaking jobs in America vanished between 1974 and 1988 (from 480,000 to 260,000). Similarly with automobiles: During the 1980s, the United Auto Workers lost 500,000 members—one-third of their total at the start of the decade. General Motors alone cut 150,000 American production jobs during the 1980s (even as it added employment abroad). Another consequence of the same phenomenon: The gap between the average wages of unionized and nonunionized workers widened dramatically—from 14.6 per cent in 1973 to 20.4 per cent by end of the 1980s.[2] The lesson is clear. If you drop out of high school or have no more than a high school diploma, do not expect a good routine production job to be awaiting you.

Also vanishing are lower- and middle-level management jobs involving routine production. Between 1981 and 1986, more than 780,000 foremen, supervisors, and section chiefs lost their jobs through plant closings and layoffs (US Dept of Labor 1986). Large numbers of assistant division heads, assistant directors, assistant managers, and vice presidents also found themselves jobless. GM shed more than 40,000 white-collar employees and planned to eliminate another 25,000 by the mid-1990s (*Wall Street Journal* 1990). As America's core pyramids metamorphosed into global webs, many middle-level routine producers were as obsolete as routine workers on the line.

As has been noted, foreign-owned webs are hiring some Americans to do routine production in the United States. Philips, Sony, and Toyota factories are popping up all over— to the self-congratulatory applause of the nation's governors and mayors, who have lured them with promises of tax abatements and new sewers, among other amenities. But as these ebullient politicians will soon discover, the foreign-owned factories are highly automated and will become far more so in years to come. Routine production jobs account for a small fraction of the cost of producing most items in the United States and other advanced nations, and this fraction will continue to decline sharply as computer-integrated robots take over. In 1977 it took routine producers thirty-five hours to assemble an automobile in the United States; it is estimated that by the mid-1990s, Japanese-owned factories in America will be producing finished automobiles using only eight hours of a routine producer's time (International Motor Vehicles Program 1989).

The productivity and resulting wages of American workers who run such robotic machinery may be relatively high, but there may not be many such jobs to go around. A case in point: In the late 1980s, Nippon Steel joined with America's ailing Inland Steel to build a new $400 million cold-rolling mill fifty miles west of Gary, Indiana. The mill was celebrated for its state-of-the-art technology, which cut the time to produce a coil of steel from twelve days to about one hour. In fact, the entire plant could be run by a small team of technicians, which became clear when Inland subsequently closed two of its old cold-rolling mills, laying off hundreds of routine workers. Governors and mayors take note: Your much-ballyhooed foreign factories may end up employing distressingly few of your constituents.

Overall, the decline in routine jobs has hurt men more than women. This is because the routine production jobs held by men in high-volume metal-bending manufacturing industries had paid higher wages than the routine production jobs held by women in textiles and data processing. As both sets of jobs have been lost, American women in routine production have gained more equal footing with Amercian men—equally poor footing, that is. This is a major reason why the gender gap between male and female wages began to close during the 1980s.

The second of the three boats, carrying in-person servers, is sinking as well, but somewhat more slowly and unevenly. Most in-person servers are paid at or just slightly above the minimum wage and many work only part-time, with the result that their take-home pay is modest, to say the least. Nor do they typically receive all the benefits (health care, life insurance, disability, and so forth) garnered by routine producers in large manufacturing corporations or by symbolic analysts affiliated with the more affluent threads of global webs.[3] In-person servers are sheltered from the direct effects of global competition and, like everyone else, benefit from access to lower-cost products from around the world. But they are not immune to its indirect effects.

For one thing, in-person servers increasingly compete with former routine production workers, who, no longer able to find well-paying routine production jobs, have few alternatives but to seek in-person service jobs. The Bureau of Labor Statistics estimates that of the 2.8 million manufacturing workers who lost their jobs during the early 1980s, fully one-third were rehired in service jobs paying at least 20 per cent less (US Dept of Labor 1986). In-person servers must also compete with high school graduates and dropouts who years before had moved easily into routine production jobs but no longer can. And if demographic predictions about the American work force in the first decades of the twenty-first century are correct (and they are likely to be, since most of the people who will comprise the work force are already identifiable), most new entrants into the job market will be black or Hispanic men, or women—groups that in years past have possessed relatively weak technical skills. This will result in an even larger number of people crowding into in-person services. Finally, in-person servers will be competing with growing numbers of immigrants, both legal and illegal, for whom in-person services will comprise the most accessible jobs. It is estimated that between the mid-1980s and the end of the century, about a quarter of all workers entering the American labor force will be immigrants (Federal Immigration and Naturalization Service 1986–7).

Perhaps the fiercest competition that in-person servers face comes from labor-saving machinery (much of it invented, designed, fabricated, or assembled in other nations, of course). Automated tellers, computerized cashiers, automatic car washes, robotized vending machines, self-service gasoline pumps, and all similar gadgets substitute for the human beings that customers once encountered. Even telephone operators are fast disappearing, as electronic sensors and voice simulators become capable of carrying on conversations that are reasonably intelligent, and always polite. Retail sales workers—among the largest groups of in-person servers—are similarly imperiled. Through personal computers linked to television screens, tomorrow's consumers will be able to buy furniture, appliances, and all sorts of electronic toys from their living rooms—examining the merchandise from all angles, selecting whatever color, size, special features, and price seem most appealing, and then transmitting the order instantly to warehouses from which the selections will be shipped directly to their homes. So, too, with financial transactions, airline and hotel reservations, rental car agreements, and similar contracts, which will be executed between consumers in their homes and computer banks somewhere else on the globe (Deutsch 1989).

Advanced economies like the United States will continue to generate sizable numbers of new in-person service jobs, of course, the automation of older ones notwithstanding. For every bank teller who loses her job to an automated teller, three new jobs open for aerobics instructors. Human beings, it seems, have an almost insatiable desire for personal attention. But the intense competition nevertheless ensures that the wages of in-person servers will remain relatively low. In-person servers—working on their own, or else dispersed widely amid many small establishments, filling all sorts of personal-care niches—cannot readily organize themselves into labor unions or create powerful lobbies to limit the impact of such competition.

In two respects, demographics will work in favor of in-person servers, buoying their collective boat slightly. First, as has been noted, the rate of growth of the American work force is slowing. In particular, the number of younger workers is shrinking. Between 1985 and 1995, the number of eighteen- to twenty-four-year-olds will have declined by 17.5 per cent. Thus, employers will have more incentive to hire and train in-person servers whom they might previously have avoided. But this demographic relief from the competitive pressures will be only temporary. The cumulative procreative energies of the postwar baby-boomers (born between 1946 and 1964) will result in a new surge of workers by 2010 or thereabouts (Johnson, Packer et al., 1987). And immigration—both legal and illegal—shows every sign of increasing in years to come.

Next, by the second decade of the twenty-first century, the number of Americans aged sixty-five and over will be rising precipitously, as the baby-boomers reach retirement age and live longer. Their life expectancies will lengthen not just because fewer of them will have smoked their way to their graves and more will have eaten better than their parents, but also because they will receive all sorts of expensive drugs and therapies designed to keep them alive—barely. By 2035, twice as many Americans will be elderly as in 1988, and the number of octogenarians is expected to triple. As these decaying baby-boomers ingest all the chemicals and receive all the treatments, they will need a great deal of personal attention. Millions of deteriorating bodies will require nurses, nursing-home operators, hospital administrators, orderlies, home-care providers, hospice aides, and technicians to operate and maintain all the expensive machinery that will monitor and temporarily stave off final disintegration. There might even be a booming market for euthanasia specialists. In-person servers catering to the old and ailing will be in strong demand.[4]

One small problem: The decaying baby-boomers will not have enough money to pay for these services. They will have used up their personal savings years before. Their Social Security payments will, of course, have been used by the government to pay for the previous generation's retirement and to finance much of the budget deficits of the 1980s. Moreover, with relatively fewer young Americans in the population, the supply of housing will likely exceed the demand, with the result that the boomers' major investments—their homes—will be worth less (in inflation-adjusted dollars) when they retire than they planned for. In consequence, the huge cost of caring for the graying boomers will fall on many of the same people who will be paid to care for them. It will be like a great sump pump: In-person servers of the twenty-first century will have an abundance of health-care jobs, but a large portion of their earnings will be devoted to Social Security payments and income taxes, which will in turn be used to pay their salaries. The net result: no real improvement in their standard of living.

The standard of living of in-person servers also depends, indirectly, on the standard of living of the Americans they serve who are engaged in world commerce. To the extent that *these* Americans are richly rewarded by the rest of the world for what they contribute, they will have more money to lavish upon in-person services. Here we find the only form of 'trickle-down' economics that has a basis in reality. A waitress in a town whose major factory has just been closed is unlikely to earn a high wage or enjoy much job security; in a swank resort populated by film producers and banking moguls, she is apt to do reasonably well. So, too, with nations. In-person servers in Bangladesh may spend their days performing roughly the same tasks as in-person servers in the United States, but have a far lower standard of living for their efforts. The difference comes in the value that their customers add to the world economy.

Unlike the boats of routine producers and in-person servers, however, the vessel containing America's symbolic analysts is rising. Worldwide demand for their insights is growing as the ease and speed of communicating them steadily increases. Not every symbolic analyst is rising as quickly or as dramatically as every other, of course; symbolic analysts at the low end are barely holding their own in the world economy. But symbolic analysts at the top are in such great demand worldwide that they have difficulty keeping track of all their earnings. Never before in history has opulence on such a scale been gained by people who have earned it, and done so legally.

Among symbolic analysts in the middle range are American scientists and researchers who are busily selling their discoveries to global enterprise webs. They are not limited to American customers. If the strategic brokers in General Motors' headquarters refuse to pay a high price for a new means of making high-strength ceramic engines dreamed up by a team of engineers affiliated with Carnegie-Mellon University in Pittsburgh, the strategic brokers of Honda or Mercedes-Benz are likely to be more than willing.

So, too, with the insights of America's ubiquitous management consultants, which are being sold for large sums to eager entrepreneurs in Europe and Latin America. Also, the insights of America's energy consultants, sold for even larger sums to Arab sheikhs. American design engineers are providing insights to Olivetti, Mazda, Siemens, and other global webs; American marketers, techniques for learning what worldwide consumers will buy; American advertisers, ploys for ensuring that they actually do. American architects are issuing designs and blueprints for opera houses, art galleries, museums, luxury hotels, and residential complexes in the world's major cities; American commercial property developers, marketing these properties to worldwide investors and purchasers.

Americans who specialize in the gentle art of public relations are in demand by corporations, governments, and politicians in virtually every nation. So, too, are American political consultants, some of whom, at this writing, are advising the Hungarian Socialist Party, the remnant of Hungary's ruling Communists, on how to salvage a few parliamentary seats in the nation's first free election in more than forty years. Also at this writing, a team of American agricultural consultants are advising the managers of a Soviet farm collective employing 1,700 Russians eighty miles outside Moscow. As noted, American investment bankers and lawyers specializing in financial circumnavigations are selling their insights to Asians and Europeans who are eager to discover how to make large amounts of money by moving large amounts of money.

Developing nations, meanwhile, are hiring American civil engineers to advise on building roads and dams. The present thaw in the Cold War will no doubt expand these opportunities. American engineers from Bechtel (a global firm notable for having employed both Caspar Weinberger and George Shultz for much larger sums than either earned in the Reagan administration) have begun helping the Soviets design and install a new generation of nuclear reactors. Nations also are hiring American bankers and lawyers to help them renegotiate the terms of their loans with global banks, and Washington lobbyists to help them with Congress, the Treasury, the World Bank, the IMF, and other politically sensitive institutions. In fits of obvious desperation, several nations emerging from communism have even hired American economists to teach them about capitalism.

Almost everyone around the world is buying the skills and insights of Americans who manipulate oral and visual symbols—musicians, sound engineers, film producers, makeup artists, directors, cinematographers, actors and actresses, boxers, scriptwriters, songwriters, and set designers. Among the wealthiest of symbolic analysts are Steven Spielberg, Bill Cosby, Charles Schulz, Eddie Murphy, Sylvester Stallone, Madonna, and other star directors and performers—who are almost as well known on the streets of Dresden and Tokyo as in the Back Bay of Boston. Less well rewarded but no less renowned are the unctuous anchors on Turner Broadcasting's Cable News, who appear daily, via satellite, in places ranging from Vietnam to Nigeria. Vanna White is the world's most watched game-show hostess. Behind each of these familiar faces is a collection of American problem-solvers, -identifiers, and brokers who train, coach, advise, promote, amplify, direct, groom, represent, and otherwise add value to their talents.[5]

There are also the insights of senior American executives who occupy the world headquarters of global 'American' corporations and the national or regional headquarters of global 'foreign' corporations. Their insights are duly exported to the rest of the world through the webs of global enterprise. IBM does not export many machines from the United States, for example. Big Blue makes machines all over the globe and services them on the spot. Its prime American exports are symbolic and analytic. From IBM's world headquarters in Armonk, New York, emanate strategic brokerage and related management services bound for the rest of the world. In return, IBM's top executives are generously rewarded.

The most important reason for this expanding world market and increasing global demand for the symbolic and analytic insights of Americans has been the dramatic improvement in worldwide communication and transportation technologies. Designs, instructions, advice, and visual and audio symbols can be communicated more and more rapidly around the globe, with ever-greater precision and at ever-lower cost. Madonna's voice can be transported to billions of listeners, with perfect clarity, on digital compact disks. A new invention emanating from engineers in Battelle's laboratory in Columbus, Ohio, can be sent almost anywhere via modem, in a form that will allow others to examine it in three dimensions through enhanced computer graphics. When face-to-face meetings are still required—and videoconferencing will not suffice—it is relatively easy for designers, consultants, advisers, artists, and executives to board supersonic jets and, in a matter of hours, meet directly with their worldwide clients, customers, audiences, and employees.

With rising demand comes rising compensation. Whether in the form of licensing fees, fees for service, salaries, or shares in final profits, the economic result is much the same. There are also nonpecuniary rewards. One of the best-kept secrets among symbolic analysts is that so many of them enjoy their work. In fact, much of it does not count as work at all, in the traditional sense. The work of routine producers and in-person servers is typically monotonous; it causes muscles to tire or weaken and involves little independence or discretion. The 'work' of symbolic analysts, by contrast, often involves puzzles, experiments, games, a significant amount of chatter, and substantial discretion over what to do next. Few routine producers or in-person servers would 'work' if they did not need to earn the money. Many symbolic analysts would 'work' even if money were no object.

At midcentury, when America was a national market dominated by core pyramid-shaped corporations, there were constraints on the earnings of people at the highest rungs. First and most obviously, the market for their services was largely limited to the borders of the nation. In addition, whatever conceptual value they might contribute was small relative to the value gleaned from large scale—and it was dependent on large scale for whatever income it was to summon. Most of the problems to be identified and solved had to do with enhancing the efficiency of production and improving the flow of materials, parts, assembly, and distribution. Inventors searched for the rare breakthrough revealing an entirely new product to be made in high volume; management consultants, executives, and engineers thereafter tried to speed and synchronize its manufacture, to better achieve scale efficiencies; advertisers and marketers sought then to whet the public's appetite for the standard item that emerged. Since white-collar earnings increased with larger scale, there was considerable incentive to expand the firm; indeed, many of America's core corporations grew far larger than scale economies would appear to have justified.

By the 1990s, in contrast, the earnings of symbolic analysts were limited neither by the size of the national market nor by the volume of production of the firms with which they were affiliated. The marketplace was worldwide, and conceptual value was high relative to value added from scale efficiencies.

There had been another constraint on high earnings, which also gave way by the 1990s. At midcentury, the compensation awarded to top executives and advisers of the largest of America's core corporations could not be grossly out of proportion to that of low-level production workers. It would be unseemly for executives who engaged in highly visible rounds of bargaining with labor unions, and who routinely responded to government requests to moderate prices, to take home wages and benefits wildly in excess of what other Americans earned. Unless white-collar executives restrained themselves, moreover, blue-collar production workers could not be expected to restrain their own demands for higher wages. Unless both groups exercised restraint, the government could not be expected to forbear from imposing direct controls and regulations.

At the same time, the wages of production workers could not be allowed to sink too low; lest there be insufficient purchasing power in the economy. After all, who would buy all the goods flowing out of American factories if not American workers? This, too, was part of the tacit bargain struck between American managers and their workers.

Recall the oft-repeated corporate platitude of the era about the chief executive's responsibility to carefully weigh and balance the interests of the corporation's disparate stakeholders. Under the stewardship of the corporate statesman, no set of stakeholders—least of all white-collar executives—was to gain a disproportionately large share of the benefits of corporate activity; nor was any stakeholder—especially the average worker—to be left with a share that was disproportionately small. Banal though it was, this idea helped to maintain the legitimacy of the core American corporation in the eyes of most Americans, and to ensure continued economic growth.

But by the 1990s, these informal norms were evaporating, just as (and largely because)

the core American corporation was vanishing. The links between top executives and the American production worker were fading: An ever-increasing number of subordinates and contractees were foreign, and a steadily growing number of American routine producers were working for foreign-owned firms. An entire cohort of middle-level managers, who had once been deemed 'white collar,' had disappeared; and, increasingly, American executives were exporting their insights to global enterprise webs.

As the American corporation itself became a global web almost indistinguishable from any other, its stakeholders were turning into a large and diffuse group, spread over the world. Such global stakeholders were less visible, and far less noisy, than national stakeholders. And as the American corporation sold its goods and services all over the world, the purchasing power of American workers became far less relevant to its economic survival.

Thus have the inhibitions been removed. The salaries and benefits of America's top executives, and many of their advisers and consultants, have soared to what years before would have been unimaginable heights, even as those of other Americans have declined.

Notes

1. The reader should note, of course, that lower wages in other areas of the world are of no particular attraction to global capital unless workers there are sufficiently productive to make the labor cost of producing *each unit* lower there than in higher-wage regions. Productivity in many low-wage areas of the world has improved due to the ease with which state-of-the-art factories and equipment can be installed there.
2. US Department of Commerce, Bureau of Labor Statistics, 'Wages of Unionized and Non-Unionized Workers', various issues.
3. The growing portion of the American labor force engaged in in-person services, relative to routine production, thus helps explain why the number of Americans lacking health insurance increased by at least 6 million during the 1980s.
4. The Census Bureau estimates that by the year 2000, at least 12 million Americans will work in health services—well over 6 per cent of the total work force.
5. In 1989, the entertainment business sum-

moned to the United States $5.5 billion in foreign earnings—making it among the nation's largest export industries, just behind aerospace. US Department of Commerce, International Trade Commission, 'Composition of US Exports', various issues.

References

Deutsch, C. H. (1989), 'The Powerful Push for Self-Service', *The New York Times* (9 April), 3:1.

Federal Immigration and Naturalization Service (1986, 1987), *Statistical Yearbook* (Washington DC: US Government Printing Office).

Gupta, U. (1989), 'US-India Satellite Link Stands to Cut Software Costs', *The Wall Street Journal* (6 March), B2.

International Motor Vehicles Program (1989: MIT).

Johnson, W., Packer, A., *et al.* (1987), US Bureau of the Census Current Population Reports Series P23/138, Tables 2.1, 4.6, in *Workforce 2000: Work and Workers for the 21st Century* (Indianapolis: Hudson Institute).

Katz, L., and Revenga, A. (1989), 'Changes in the Structure of Wages: US and Japan', *Calculations of Current Population Surveys* (National Bureau of Economic Research, Sept.).

Maxwell Hamilton, J. (1989), 'A Bit Player Buys Into the Computer Age', *The New York Times Business World* (3 December), 14.

The Wall Street Journal (16 February 1990), A5.

US Department of Labor, Bureau of Labor Statistics (1986), 'Re-employment Increases Among Displaced Workers', *BLS News* (USDL, 14 October), 86–414: Table 6.

US Government Printing Office (1989), *Statistical Abstract of the United States* (Washington DC), 416: Table 684.

10

Education, Globalization, and Economic Development

Phillip Brown and Hugh Lauder

Since the first oil shock in the early 1970s western societies have experienced a social, political, and economic transformation that is yet to reach its conclusion. At its epicentre is the creation of a global economy that has led to an intensification of economic competition between firms, regions, and nation states (Dicken 1992; Michie and Smith 1995). The globalization of economic activity has called into question the future role of the nation state and how it can secure economic growth and shared prosperity. At first sight this may appear to have little to do with educational policy; however, the quality of a nation's education and training system is seen to hold the key to future economic prosperity. This paper will outline some of the consequences of globalization and why education is crucial to future economic development. It will also show that, despite the international consensus concerning the importance of education, strategies for education and economic development can be linked to alternative 'ideal typical' neo-Fordist and post-Fordist routes to economic development which have profoundly different educational implications.

These neo-Fordist and post-Fordist routes can also be connected to alternative political projects. Since the late 1970s American and Britain have followed a neo-Fordist route in response to economic globalization, which has been shaped by the New Right's enthusiasm for market competition, privatization, and competitive individualism. However, with the election of the Democrats in the 1992 American presidential elections and the resurgence of the British Labour Party there is

increasing support for a post-Fordist strategy. Although much has already been written about the flaws in the New Right's approach to education and national renewal, far less has yet been written on what we will call the 'left modernizers'. It will be argued that whilst the left modernizers present a promising programme for reform *vis-à-vis* the New Right, their account of education, skill formation, and the global economy remains unconvincing. An important task of this paper is therefore to highlight the weaknesses in the left modernizers' account to show that, if post-Fordist possibilities are to be realized, it will be essential for those on the left to engage in a more thoroughgoing and politically difficult debate about education, equity, and efficiency in late global capitalism.[1]

Globalization and the New Rules of Economic Competition

The significance of globalization to questions of national educational and economic development can be summarized in terms of a change in the rules of eligibility, engagement, and wealth creation (Brown and Lauder forthcoming). Firstly, there has been a change in the rules of eligibility. In the same way that sports clubs run 'closed' events where club membership is a condition of entry, they may also run tournaments 'open' to everyone. Likewise there has been a shift away from the closed or walled economies of the postwar period towards an open or global economy. As a result of this change in the rules of eligibility,

From *Journal of Education Policy*, 11 (1996), 1–24. Reprinted with permission.

domestic economies have been exposed to greater foreign competition (Reich 1991; ILO 1995). Changes in the rules of eligibility have also enhanced the power of the multinational corporations (MNCs). The MNCs not only account for a growing proportion of cross-border trade, but are a major source of new investment in technology, jobs, and skills. Since the mid-1970s the MNCs have grown more rapidly than the world economy. In 1975, the fifty largest industrial corporations worldwide had sales of $540 billion, and received $25 billion in profits. In 1990, sales figures for the top fifty had climbed to $2.1 trillion and their profits had reached $70 billion. In real terms, whereas the US economy was growing at an annual rate of 2.8 per cent (the OECD average was 2.9 per cent), the MNCs' annual sales growth was in the region of 3.5 per cent during the period between 1975 and 1990 (Carnoy *et al.* 1993: 49).

Moreover, the old national 'champions' such as Ford, IBM, ICI, and Mercedes Benz have tried to break free of their national roots, creating a *global auction* for investment, technology, and jobs. As capital has become footloose, the mass production of standardized goods and services has become located in countries, regions, or communities which offer low wage costs, light labour-market legislation, weak trade unions, and 'sweeteners' including 'tax holidays' and cheap rents. Such investment has significantly increased in the New Industrial Countries (NICs) such as in Singapore, Taiwan, China, and Brazil (Cowling and Sugden 1994). It is estimated that, in the 1980s, some 700 American companies employed more than 350,000 workers in Singapore, Mexico, and Taiwan alone, and that 40 per cent of the jobs created by British MNCs were overseas (Marginson 1994: 64).

In reality, the global auction operates like a Dutch auction. In a Dutch auction corporate investors are able to play off nations, communities, and workers as a way of increasing their profit margins, and bidding spirals downwards, impoverishing local communities and workers by forcing concessions on wage-levels, rents, and taxes in exchange for investment in local jobs. In order to persuade Mercedes to set up a plant in Alabama the company received an initial $253 million, with tax breaks over 25 years estimated to be worth an extra $230m. The Swiss Bank Corporation will receive some $120m of incentives over the next 10 years from Connecticut for moving its US headquarters from Manhattan to the city of Stamford.[2]

In America and Britain the creation of a global auction has also been linked to the breakdown of the Fordist rules of engagement between government, employers, and workers. Although some writers have restricted their definition of Fordism to refer exclusively to the system of mass production, Fordism is a label that can equally be applied to Keynesian demand management in the postwar period, referring to the expansion of mass consumption as well as of mass production (Lipietz 1987; Harvey 1989). The rapid improvement in economic efficiency which accompanied the introduction of mass-production techniques necessitated the creation of mass markets for consumer durables, including radios, refrigerators, television sets, and motor cars. In order for economic growth to be maintained, national governments had to regulate profits and wage levels to sustain the conditions upon which economic growth depended. Hence, the development of the welfare state in western industrial societies was seen to reflect efforts on the part of national governments to maintain the Fordist compromise between employers and organized labour. The combination of increased welfare-state protection for workers, coupled with full employment and a degree of social mobility, temporarily 'solved' the problem of distribution (Hirsch 1977) under Fordism. The problem of distribution is that of determining how opportunities and income are to be apportioned. Under capitalism this is an ever-present problem, because it is a system which is inherently unequal in its distribution of rewards and opportunities. However, during the Fordist era the combination of the rewards of economic growth being evenly spread across income levels with increasing social security and occupational and social mobility according to ostensibly meritocratic criteria generated a high degree of social solidarity. However, over the last 20 years America and Britain have introduced 'market' rules of engagement. Here the nation-state is charged with the role of creating the conditions in which the market can operate 'freely'. Therefore, rather than trying to engineer a compromise between employers and the trade unions, the state must prevent the unions from using their 'monopoly' powers to bid up wages which are not necessarily reflected in productivity gains. Hence, according to the market rules of engagement the prosperity of workers will depend on an ability to trade their skills, knowledge, and entrepreneurial acumen in an unfettered global marketplace.

Finally, the transformation in western capitalism has entailed new rules of wealth creation. These have undermined the viability of building national prosperity on the Fordist mass production of standardized goods and services.[3] Fordist mass production was based on the standardization of products and their component parts. Many of the tasks previously undertaken by skilled craftsmen, such as making door panels or parts of the car's engine 'by hand', were mechanized by designing jigs, presses, and machines able to perform the same operations hundreds if not thousands of times a day, with the use of a semi-skilled operative. The Fordist production line was characterized by a moving assembly line, where the product passes the workers along a conveyor, rather than the worker having to move to the product as in nodal production. A further feature of Fordism was a detailed division of labour, within which the job tasks of shop-floor workers were reduced to their most elementary form in order to maximize both efficiency and managerial control over the labour process. Hence, Fordism was based on many of the principles of 'scientific management' outlined by Frederick Taylor, who offered a 'scientific' justification for the separation of *conception* from *execution*, where managers monopolized knowledge of the labour process and controlled every step of production.

However, in the new rules of wealth creation economic prosperity will depend on nations and companies being able to exploit the skills, knowledge, and insights of workers in ways which can no longer be delivered according to Fordist principles. Enterprise which can deliver a living wage to workers now depends on the quality as much as the price of goods and services, and on finding new sources of productivity and investment. Such 'value added' enterprise is most likely to be found in companies offering 'customized' goods and services in microelectronics, telecommunications, biotechnology, financial services, consultancy, advertising, marketing, and the media.[4]

In response to these new rules all western nations, in their domestic economies and foreign affairs, have had to look to their own social institutions and human resources to meet the global challenges they confront (OECD 1989). Lessons learnt from Japan and the Asian Tigers suggest that the 'human side of enterprise' is now a crucial factor in winning a competitive advantage in the global economy. Advantage is therefore seen to depend upon raising the quality and productivity of human capital. Knowledge, learning, information, and technical competence are the new raw materials of international commerce:

Knowledge itself, therefore, turns out to be not only the source of the highest-quality power, but also the most important ingredient of force and wealth. Put differently, knowledge has gone from being an adjunct of money power and muscle power, to being their very essence. It is, in fact, the ultimate amplifier. This is the key to the power shift that lies ahead, and it explains why the battle for control of knowledge and the means of communication is heating up all over the world. (Toffler 1990: 18).

Although such statements greatly exaggerate the importance of knowledge in advanced capitalist economies, without exception, national governments of all political persuasions have declared that it is the quality of their education and training systems which will decisively shape the international division of labour and national prosperity. Therefore the diminished power of nation states to control economic competition has forced them to compete in what we call the global *knowledge wars*. In Britain, for instance, the National Commission on Education suggests:

For us, knowledge and skills will be central. In an era of world-wide competition and low-cost global communications, no country like ours will be able to maintain its standard of living, let alone improve it, on the basis of cheap labour and low-tech products and services. There will be too many millions of workers and too many employers in too many countries who will be able and willing to do that kind of work fully as well as we or people in any other developed country could do it—and at a fraction of the cost. (1993: 33)

But how the problem of education and training policies are understood, and how the demand for skilled workers is increased, is subject to contestation and political struggle. There is no doubt, for instance, that the introduction of new technologies has expanded the range of strategic choice available to employers and managers. However, this has exposed increasing differences, rather than similarities, in organizational cultures, job design, and training regimes (Lane 1989, Green and Steedman 1993). There are few guarantees that employers will successfully exploit the potential for 'efficiency', precisely because they may fail to break free of conventional assumptions about the role of management and workers, and cling to the established hierarchy of authority, status, and power. As Harvey (1989) has recognized, new technologies and coordinating forms of organization have permitted the revival of domestic, familial, and paternalistic labour systems, given that, 'the same shirt designs can be reproduced by large-scale factories in India, cooperative production in the "Third Italy", sweatshops in New York and London, or family labour systems in Hong Kong' (p. 187). This should alert us to the fact that the demise of Fordism

in the West does not necessarily mean that the majority of workers will find jobs which exercise the range of their human capabilities. The interests of employers seeking to maximize profits and workers seeking to enhance the quality of working life and wages remain an important source of cleavage, given that it is still possible for companies to 'profit' from low-tech, low-wage operations. There is no hidden-hand or post-industrial logic which will lead nations to respond to the global economy in the same way, despite the fact that their fates are inextricably connected. Indeed, we would suggest that the universal consensus highlighting education and training systems as holding the key to future prosperity has obscured fundamental differences in the way nations are responding to the global economy.

Therefore, while recognizing that some of the key elements of Fordism in western nations are being transformed in the global economy, it is important not to prejudge the

Table 10.1. Post-Fordist possibilities: alternative models of national development

Fordism	Neo-Fordism	Post-Fordism
Protected National Markets.	Global Competition through: productivity gains, cost-cutting (overheads, wages).	Global Competition through: innovation, quality, value-added goods and services.
	Inward investment attracted by 'market flexibility' (reduce the social cost of labour, trade union power).	Inward investment attracted by highly skilled labour force engaged in 'value added' production/services.
	Adversarial market orientation: remove impediments to market competition. Create 'enterprise culture'. Privatization of the welfare state.	Consensus based objectives: corporatist 'industrial policy'. Co-operation between government, employers and trade unions.
Mass production of standardized products/ low skill, high wage.	Mass production of standardized products/low skill, low wage 'flexible' production.	Flexible production systems/ small batch/niche markets; shift to high-wage, high-skilled jobs.
Bureaucratic hierarchical organizations.	Leaner organizations with emphasis on 'numerical' flexibility.	Leaner organizations with emphasis on 'functional' flexibility.
Fragmented and standardized work tasks.	Reduce trade union job demarcation.	Flexible specialization/ multi-skilled workers.
Mass standardized (male) employment.	Fragmentation/polarization of labour force. Professional 'core' and 'flexible' workforce; (i.e. part-time, temps., contract, portfolio careers).	Maintain good conditions for all employees. No 'core' workers receive training, fringe benefits, comparable wages, proper representation.
Divisions between managers and workers/low trust relations/collective bargaining.	Emphasis on 'managers' right to manage'. Industrial relations based on low trust relations.	Industrial relations based on high trust, high discretion, collective participation.
Little 'on the job' training for most workers.	Training 'demand' led/ little use of industrial training policies.	Training as an national investment/state acts as strategic trainer.

direction of these changes, which must remain a question of detailed empirical investigation (see Block 1990). For analytical purposes it is useful to distinguish two 'ideal typical' models of national economic development in terms of neo-Fordism and post-Fordism (see Table 10.1). Neo-Fordism can be characterized as creating greater market flexibility through a reduction in social overheads and the power of trade unions; as encouraging the privatization of public utilities and the welfare state; and as celebrating competitive individualism. Alternative post-Fordism can be defined in terms of the development of the state as a 'strategic trader', shaping the direction of the national economy through investment in key economic sectors and in the development of human capital. Post-Fordism is therefore based on a shift to 'high value' customized production and services using multi-skilled workers (see also Allen 1992).

In the 'real' world, the relationship between education and economic development reveal examples of contradiction as much as correspondence. Moreover, although it is true to say that countries such as Germany, Japan, and Singapore come closer to the model of post-Fordism, and the USA and Britain approximate neo-Fordist solutions, we should not ignore clear examples of 'uneven' and contradictory developments within the same region or country. Such a relationship also highlights the fact that there are important differences in the way nation states may move towards a post-Fordist economy, with far-reaching implications for democracy and social justice.

Nevertheless, these models represent clear differences in policy orientations, both in the dominant economic ideas which inform them, and in their underlying cultural assumptions about the role of skill formation in economic and social development (Thurow 1993). We will begin by assessing the New Right's interpretation of education as part of a neo-Fordist strategy, before undertaking a detailed account of the left-modernizers' vision of a post-Fordist, high-skill, high-wage economy.

The New Right: Education in a Neo-Fordist 'Market' Economy

The New-Right interpretation of the Fordist 'crisis' is based on what we will call the 'welfare-shackle' thesis. In the nineteenth century it was the aristocracy and the *ancien régime* in Europe who were blamed for 'shackling' the market and free enterprise. In the late twentieth century it is the welfare state.[5] The New Right argue that the problem confronting western nations today can only be understood in light of profound changes in the role of government during the third quarter of the twentieth century. They assert that it is no coincidence that at the same time as western governments were significantly increasing expenditure on social welfare programmes there was high inflation, rising unemployment, and economic stagnation (Murray 1984). Western societies have run into trouble because of extensive and unwarranted interference by the state. Inflation, high unemployment, economic recession, and urban unrest all stem from the legacy of Keynesian economics and an egalitarian ideology which promoted economic redistribution, equality of opportunity, and welfare rights for all. Hence, the overriding problem confronting western capitalist nations is to reimpose the disciplines of the market.

According to the New Right, the route to national salvation in the context of global knowledge wars is through the survival of the fittest, based on an extension of parental choice in a market of competing schools, colleges, and universities (Ball 1993). In the case of education, where funding, at least during the compulsory school years, will come from the public purse, the idea is to create a quasi-market within which schools will compete (Lauder 1991). This approximation to the operation of a market is achieved by seeking to create a variety of schools in a mixed economy of public and private institutions. In some cases they will aim at different client groups, such as ethnic minorities, religious sects, or 'high flyers'. This 'variety', it is argued, will provide parents with a genuine choice of different products (Boyd and Cibulka 1989; Halstead 1994). Choice of product (type of school) is seen to be sufficient to raise the standards for all, because if schools cannot sell enough desk space to be economically viable, they risk going out of business. Moreover, the economic needs of the nation will be met through the market, because when people have to pay for education they are more likely to make investment decisions which will realize an economic return. This will lead consumers to pick subjects and courses where there is a demand for labour, subsequently overcoming the problem of skill shortages. Equally, there will be a tendency for employment training to be 'demand-led' in response to changing market conditions (Deakin and Wilkinson 1991).

Critics of the marketization of education therefore argue that the introduction of choice and competition provides a mechanism by which the middle classes can more securely gain an advantage in the competition for credentials (Brown 1995). This is because not all social groups come to an educational market as equals (Collins 1979); cultural and material capital are distributed unequally between classes and ethnic groups. In particular, it is the middle classes which are more likely to have the cultural capital to make educational choices which best advantage their children (Brown 1990; Brown and Lauder 1992). In consequence, the introduction of parental choice and competition between schools will amount to a covert system of educational selection according to social class, as middle-class children exit schools with significant numbers of working-class children. The consequence will be that the school system will become polarized in terms of social class, ethnic segregation, and resources. As middle-class students exit from schools with working-class children, they will also take much-needed resources from those schools and effectively add to already well-off middle-class schools.

What evidence there is about the workings of educational markets suggests that they are far more complex than its critics suggest (Lauder *et al.* 1994). Nevertheless, the evidence so far confirms the prediction that choice and competition tend to lead to social-class and ethnic polarization in schools (Willms and Echols 1992; Lauder *et al.* 1994). In nations like America and Britain, the overall effect will be to segregate students in different types of school on the basis of social class, ethnicity, and religion. The net result will again be a massive wastage of talent as able working-class students once more find themselves trapped in schools which do not give them the opportunity of going to university (Halsey *et al.* 1980). If this is the overall effect, then it can be argued that the marketization of education, while appearing to offer efficiency

and flexibility of the kind demanded in the post-Fordist era, will in fact school the majority of children for a neo-Fordist economy which requires a low level of talent and skill.

The marketization of education will inevitably have an inverse effect on the ability of nation states to compete in the global auction for quality inward investment, technology, and jobs. Although multinational organizations are always on the lookout to reduce their overheads, including labour costs, investment in 'high-value' products and services crucially depends upon the quality, commitment, and insights of the workforce, for which they are prepared to pay high salaries. The problem that nation states now confront is one of how to balance commercial pressures to reduce labour costs and other overheads with the mobilizing of an educated labour force and maintaining a sophisticated social, financial, and communications infrastructure. This problem has been exacerbated by the fact that the low-skill, high-wage jobs associated with Fordism in North America and Europe are either being transplanted to the NICs (Newly Industrializing Countries), where labour costs are much lower, or are leading to a significant deterioration in working conditions in the low-skilled jobs remaining in the West (Wood 1994).

In the context of the global auction, the market reforms in education are likely to leave a large majority of the future working population without the human resources to flourish in the global economy. Here the link between market reforms and neo-Fordism is barely disguised in countries which have been dominated by New Right governments in the 1980s. The principal objective of economic policy is to improve the competitiveness of workers by increasing labour-market flexibility by restricting the power of trade unions, especially in order to bring wages into line with their 'market' value. This philosophy led Britain to reject the Social Chapter of the Maastricht Treaty, which provided legislative support for workers, because it was argued that it would undermine Britain's competitiveness in attracting inward investment, despite the poor work-conditions this would inflict on employees. In contradistinction, market reforms in education and the economy have ensured conditions in which highly paid middle-class professionals and élite groups are able to give their children an 'excellent' (*sic*) education in preparation for their bid to join the ranks of Reich's (1991) 'symbolic analysts'.

A different critique, albeit coming to the same conclusion, can be mounted against the introduction of market mechanisms in post-compulsory education and training. A key area of the post-compulsory sector for a post-Fordist economy is that concerned with the education of skilled tradespeople and technicians (Streeck 1989). The New Right has argued that the introduction of market mechanisms into this area will ensure a closer matching of supply and demand for trained labour and hence greater efficiency in the allocation of skilled labour. The argument rests on the assumptions that individuals and employers should bear the cost and responsibility for training. It is assumed that individuals gain most of the benefits from such a training, and that they should therefore bear much of the cost (Lauder 1987). Moreover, since they are paying substantially for their training they will choose to train in an area in which there is market demand. In so far as employers should help bear the cost of training and the responsibility for the type of training offered, it is argued that employers are in the best position to assess the numbers of skilled workers required and the kind of skills they should possess. Underlying this observation is an appreciation of employers' short-term interests. Given the assumption that they 'know best' what the levels and nature of skilled labour should be, it follows that they will be reluctant to pay taxes or levies for training undertaken by a third party, such as the state.

While this view, as with other New Right views, is plausible, it has come in for sustained criticism. One of the most cogent is that of Streeck (1989, 1992). He argues that under a free-labour contract of the kind found in liberal capitalist societies, giving workers the right to move from one firm to another, skills become a collective good in the eyes of employers. This is because the rewards of training individuals can easily be 'socialized' by the expedient of trained workers moving to another job while the costs of training remain with the original employer. Since employers face a clear risk in losing their investment they are unlikely to invest heavily in training. Streeck argues that, as a result, western economies are likely to face a chronic skill shortage unless the state intervenes to ensure that adequate training occurs.

Moreover, without state intervention employers will reduce the training programmes they do have when placed under intense competitive pressure and/or during a recession. Streeck (1989) notes that in the prolonged economic crisis of the 1970s, western economies, with the exception of Germany, reduced their apprenticeship programmes. In Germany government and trade-union pressure ensured that the apprenticeship programme was extended. Two consequences followed: the apprenticeship system helped to alleviate youth unemployment, and it contributed to the technical and economic advantage enjoyed by German industry in the early 1980s.

There are further criticisms that can be made of a market-determined training system. From the standpoint of the individual, it is unlikely that those working- and lower-middle-class school leavers who would potentially enter a skilled trade or technical training could either afford the costs of such a training or take the risks involved. The risks are twofold: firstly, given the time lag between entering a training programme and completing it, market demand for a particular type of training may have changed with a resulting lack of jobs. In the competitive global market, such an outcome is all too likely. If the training received were of a sufficiently general nature to produce a flexible worker that may be less of a problem. However, in an employer-led training system the pressure will always exist for training to meet employers' specific and immediate needs. The consequence is that such a training system is likely to be too narrowly focused to meet rapidly changing demand conditions. Secondly, a further point follows from this, namely that the industries of today are likely to be tomorrow's dinosaurs. As a result, employer-led training schemes may not contain the vision and practice required in order to maintain the high skill-base necessary for a post-Fordist economy. Clearly the structure of Germany's training system offers an example of an alternative which can begin to meet the requirements of a post-Fordist economy. This, as Streeck (1992) notes, involves a partnership between the state, employers, and trade unions. It is a system which ensures that employers' immediate interests are subsumed within a system concerned with medium- and longer-term outcomes. Therefore the outcome of the reassertion of market discipline in social and economic institutions has been the development of a neo-Fordist economy characterized by insecurity and the creation of large numbers of temporary, low-skilled, and low-waged jobs. We have also argued that the appeal to 'self-interest' and 'free enterprise' serves to mask the political interests of the most privileged sections of society. Indeed, the very notion of a national system of education is called into question as professional and élite groups secede from their commitment to public education and the ideology of meritocracy upon which public education in the twentieth century has been founded.

Left Modernizers: Education in a Post-Fordist 'Magnet' Economy

Over the last decade a new centre-left project has emerged in response to the ascendancy of the New Right. These 'left modernizers' reject much that was previously taken for granted amongst their socialist predecessors, contending that the transformation of capitalism at the end of the twentieth century had significantly changed the strategies that the left need to adopt in its pursuit of both social justice and economic efficiency. This involves a recognition that the left must develop a credible response to the global economy which will include economic policy and management as well as dealing with issues of distribution, equity, and social policy (Rogers and Streeck 1994: 138). At the top of their agenda is a commitment to investment in human capital and strategic investment in the economy as a way of moving towards a high-skilled, high-waged, 'magnet' economy. Underlying these economic forms of investment is a vision of a society permeated by a culture of learning; for it is the knowledge, skills, and insights of the population that is the key to future prosperity. The ideas of the 'left modernizers' are to be found in books such as Reich (1991) and Thurow (1993) in the United States, and the Commission on Social Justice (1994) and Brown (1994) in Britain. The ideas represented in these works are also consistent with Democratic politics in the United States and have informed the direction of Labour Party policy in Britain.[6]

The modernizers' account of how to create a post-Fordist economy can be summarized in the following way. It begins with a recognition that it is impossible to deliver widespread prosperity by trying to compete on price rather than the quality of goods and services. They therefore advocate a change in policy relating to investment in both physical and human capital. They advocate what has become known as producer capitalism (Dore 1987; Thurow 1993; Hutton 1995) in which low-cost, long-term investment is linked to the development of human capital. Producer capitalism stands in stark contrast to market capitalism, in which price and short-term profit are the key criteria for enterprises. Not surprisingly, they reject the assertion made by the acolytes of market capitalism that the only route to prosperity is through the creation of greater market 'flexibility' by lowering labour costs or by repealing labour-protection laws. The modernizers see that, in the new economic competition, making those at the bottom end of the labour market more insecure and powerless against exploitative employers is not the way for workers and nations to confront the challenge of the global auction. They recognize that the provision of a floor of protective rights, entitlements, and conditions for workers in the context of the global auction is both socially desirable and economically essential. In practice what this means is reinforcing labour laws against the worst excesses of unscrupulous employers and the vagaries of the global auction. This will include a minimum wage and various forms of government intervention to get the long-term unemployed back into work. For modernizers, this is part of building a new high-trust partnership between government, employers, and workers; for, they argue, it is only through such a partnership that a high-skill, high-wage economy can be created. The role of the state in such a partnership is that of a 'strategic trader' (Krugman 1993) selecting 'winners' or guiding industrial development where appropriate and, most importantly, providing the infrastructure for economic development. Here the development of a highly educated workforce is seen as a priority.

The importance the modernizers attach to education stems from a belief that the increasing wage inequalities in America and Britain over the last decade are a reflection of the returns to skill in a global auction for jobs and wages. The essence of this idea was captured by Bill Clinton in a major address on education:

The key to our economic strength in America today is productivity growth . . . In the 1990s and beyond, the universal spread of education, computers, and high-speed communications means that what we earn will depend on what we can learn and how well we can apply what we learn to the workplaces of America. That's why, as we know, a college graduate this year will earn 70 per cent more than a high-school graduate in the first year of work. That's why the earnings of younger workers who dropped out of high school, or who finished but received no further education or training, dropped by more than 20 per cent over the last ten years alone.[7]

Hence for all western societies the route to prosperity is through the creation of a 'magnet' economy capable of attracting high-skilled, high-waged employment within an increasingly global labour market. This is to be achieved through sustained investment in the national economic infrastructure including transportation, telecommunications, research and development, and so forth, alongside investment in education and training systems. In the modernizer's account it is nevertheless acknowledged that there are unlikely to be enough skilled and well-paid jobs for everyone. However, flexible work patterns are assumed to lead to greater occupational mobility, permitting people to move from low-skilled jobs when in full-time study, to high-skilled jobs in mid-career, back to low-skilled jobs as retirement age approaches. Of course, such a view depends on substantial mobility in both an upwards and downwards direction (Esping-Andersen 1994). Therefore, in the same way that unemployment is tolerable if it only lasts for a few months, being in a low-skilled, poorly paid job is also tolerable as long as it offers progression into something better.

Education and training opportunities are therefore pivotal to this vision of a competitive and just society. For not only can education deliver a high-value-added 'magnet' economy, but it can also solve the problem of unemployment. However, it is a mistake for nation states to 'guarantee' employment, because this harbours the same kind of vestigial thinking that led to previous attempts to protect uncompetitive firms from international competition; they simply become even less competitive. The only way forward is to invest in education and training to enable workers to become fully employable. In this account, social justice inheres in providing all individuals with the opportunity to gain access to an education that qualifies them for a job. Clearly there is a tension here between the idea of flexibility and the need to guarantee a minimum wage, so protecting labour from exploitation. All the indications are that the modernizers will err on the side of caution and provide what could only be described as minimal protection. In the end, the difference between the modernizers and the New Right on this issue may be marginal; although, as we shall see, there are good economic reasons why adequate social protection is desirable.

There are several features of the modernizers' account with which we concur, including the need to introduce a version of 'producer' capitalism; but as a strategic policy for education and economic development it is flawed. Our purpose in exposing these flaws is to set the scene for a more radical and thoroughgoing debate about education, economy, and society in the early decades of the 21st century. Our criticisms cluster around four related problems. First, the idea of a high-skilled, high-wage, magnet economy; second, whether reskilling the nation can solve the problem of unemployment; third, whether it is correct to assume that income polarization is a true reflection of the 'value' of skills in the global labour market; and finally, the problem of how the modernizers propose upgrading the quality of human resources so that all are granted an equal opportunity to fulfil their human potential.

How Can a High-Skilled, High-Wage, 'Magnet' Economy be Created?

Their view that the future wealth of nations will depend on the exploitation of leading-edge technologies, corporate innovation, and the upgrading of the quality of human resources can hardly be quarrelled with. Nations will clearly need to have a competitive advantage in at least some of the major industrial sectors, such as telecommunications, electronics, pharmaceuticals, chemicals, and automobiles (Porter 1990; Thurow 1993). There is also little doubt that this will create a significant minority of jobs requiring highly skilled workers. However, the problem with the modernizers' account is that they assume that highly skilled and well-paid jobs will become available to all for at least a period of their working lives. Indeed, this is an essential tenet of their argument, given that they suggest that widening inequalities can be overcome through upskilling the nation, and that full employment remains a realistic goal. In other words, the modernizers continue to believe that the labour market can act as a legitimate mechanism (through the occupational division of labour) for resolving the distributional question in advanced capitalist societies.

The plausibility of this account hangs on the idea that the global auction for jobs and enterprise offers the potential for western nations to create 'magnet' economies of highly skilled and well-paid jobs. This is an idea which has obvious appeal to a broad political constituency. It serves to replenish the spirits of those who see the US following Britain in a spiral of economic decline after a period of global dominance. We are presented with the comforting picture of a global economy which, although no longer likely to be dominated by American and European companies, is characterized by prosperous Western workers making good incomes through the use of their skills, knowledge, and insights. In reality, however, this characterization represents an imperialist throwback to the idea that innovative ideas remain the preserve of the advanced western nations (with the possible exception of Japan). Reich, for example, assumes that as low-skilled work moves into the NICs and third-world economies, America, the European EC countries, and Japan will be left to fight amongst themselves for the high-value-added jobs. The problem with this view is that it completely misunderstands the nature of the economic strategies now being implemented by the Asian Tigers, who have already developed economic and human capital infrastructures which are superior to those of many western countries (Ashton and Sung 1994). This is partly reflected in the international convergence in education systems, at least in terms of expanding their tertiary sectors. Therefore, whilst we should not rule out the possibility that MNCs (Multinational Corporations), when making inward and outward investment decisions, will judge the quality of human resources to be superior

in particular countries, it is extremely unlikely that a small number of nations will become 'magnets' for high-skilled, high-waged work.

They have also overestimated the extent to which even the most successful modern economies depend on the mass employment of highly skilled workers. Indeed, an unintended consequence of the massive expansion of tertiary education may be to create a substantial wastage of talent amongst college and university graduates unable to find a demand for their skills, knowledge, and insights. This new 'wastage of talent' is likely to be especially acute in countries which have pursued the neo-Fordist trajectory of labour-market deregulation, corporate downsizing, and the growth of temporary, casual, and insecure work, conditions which are hardly conducive to the production of high-quality jobs distinguished by worker autonomy and cognitive complexity.

The difficulty for the modernizers is that by concentrating on the question of skill formation rather than on the way skills are linked to the trajectory of economic development, they obscure some of the fundamental problems relating to educated labour. Piore (1990), for example, has argued that where labour-market regulation is weak, there is no incentive for employers to invest and use the new technology in a way which raises the value added and the quality of work. Rather, weak labour-market regulation leads to a vicious circle whereby profit is extracted through sweatshop labour, low wages, and low productivity. In effect, what regulated labour markets do is to create an incentive for entrepreneurs to invest in capital-intensive forms of production in order to generate the high-value-added to pay for the wage levels set by regulated labour markets (Sengenberger and Wilkinson 1995). If Piore is correct, then we would expect the patterns of future work to develop along different trajectories depending on the degree to which their labour markets are regulated. While projections of labour supply and occupational change need to be viewed with some scepticism, the recent OECD (1994) report on this subject certainly supports Piore's position when the United States is compared with Holland. On all indices of social protection and labour-market regulation, Holland provides an example of far greater social protection for workers, yet the vast majority of new jobs being created could be classified as 'skilled' (OECD 1994). In the United States approximately half the jobs being created were in service occupations requiring little formal training. The lesson here is obvious: the route to a high-value-added economy must involve an analysis of factors affecting the demand for educated labour. The implicit assumption, harboured by the modernizers, that through investing in the employability of workers employers will automatically recognize this potential and invest in upgrading the quality of their human resources is clearly naïve.[8] The historical record in both America and Britain shows that while there are firms that recognize investment in people to be vital to the medium-term success of their companies, there are many others who equally recognize that fat profits can still be made off the backs of semi-skilled and unskilled, low-waged workers. Equally, the idea that western nations can compensate for the failings of local employers by attracting inward investment from blue-chip MNCs is clearly not going to be sufficient to move from a neo-Fordist to a post-Fordist economy. Therefore, there seems little doubt that although in some important respects the modernizers will succeed in producing some improvement in the quality of employment opportunities, they will not achieve the goals of post-Fordist development because investment in education and training as the focal point of their policy will not lead to the creation of a high-skill, high-wage economy.

Can Reskilling the Nation Solve the Problem of Unemployment?

The focus on employability rather than employment also leaves the modernizers accused of failing to offer a realistic return to full employment. Indeed, the high-skill, high-wage route may be pursued at the price of high unemployment. This is because neo-classical economists argue that labour-market deregulation is the only way to solve unemployment. The theory is that the regulation of the labour market favoured by the modernizers bids up the price of those in work and discourages employers from taking on more workers. With deregulation the price of labour would fall and employers would 'buy' more workers. The debate over labour-market deregulation has given rise to the view that

all advanced societies are now on the horns of a dilemma regarding unemployment. Either labour markets are deregulated, as in America, where official unemployment is below 5 per cent but where there is extensive poverty because wages at the bottom end of the labour market are insufficient to live off, or they are more regulated, as in the producer-capitalist route pursued by Germany, where unemployment is higher, but so is the compensation paid to the unemployed (European Commission 1993; Freeman 1995). The problem this poses to the modernizers is that, on the one hand, a majority of workers can expect good-quality jobs and a reasonable standard of living, but that, on the other, the polarization of market incomes avoided by the producer-capitalist route is reproduced between those in work and those unemployed. The divisions in society remain, but their sources is different.

Unemployment at the low levels achieved during the postwar period was historically unique, depending on a contingent set of circumstances (Ormerod 1994). Attempting to create similar circumstances for the early part of the 21st century is likely to prove impossible, something of a political hoax perpetrated by political parties who promise it or something close to it. It is, perhaps, for this reason that the modernizers translate full employment into full employability, thereby throwing the onus on the individual to find a job.

If we examine the profiles of several OECD countries, there are two striking observations that can be made. Firstly, Gross Domestic Product (GDP) has been divorced from employment in the past 20 years, just as growth has not led to a shared prosperity during the same period. In Spain the economy grew by 93 per cent between 1970 and 1992, and 2 per cent of its jobs were lost (*Financial Times*, 2 Oct. 1993). This is in stark contrast to the postwar period, when both incomes and jobs were linked to economic growth. Growth delivered an even rise in income for all occupational groups. Secondly, the trajectories taken by OECD countries in terms of their main indicators, inflation, growth, and balance of payments, vary dramatically, yet unemployment remains around or above 7 per cent, according to official statistics, for every country with the exception of America and Japan. This includes countries with high levels of growth such as Canada, New Zealand, and Australia.[9]

What appears to have happened in the past 25 years is that a set of economic and social forces have pushed the lower limit of unemployment up substantially from an OECD average well below 5 per cent in the postwar period to an average well above 7 per cent. Clearly the oil-price hikes of the early 1970s had much to do with the initial jump in unemployment, but since then a series of contingent factors have conspired to lock unemployment in at this high level. The introduction of new technology which has enabled machines to replace workers could have had a significant impact on unemployment for both blue- and white-collar workers, as the jobless growth in Spain suggests. Similarly, the number of blue-collar jobs lost to the developing nations has added to the problem (Wood 1994). However, these factors have to be placed within the wider context of economic regulation in relation to the global economy. It is worth noting that current economic orthodoxy ensures that interest rates rise with economic growth, thereby potentially choking off further investment in productive capacity, and hence employment. It may also reduce demand, especially in countries like America and Britain with a high proportion of families with mortgages.

There are two mutually consistent explanations for the link between rising interest rates and growth. The first is that in a deregulated global finance market there is a shortage of investment funds, especially at times of growth. After all, with the potential to invest in developing nations as well as the developed nations, the competition for investment has increased dramatically. Moreover, in a global economy the business cycles of the developed and developing nations are likely to be more synchronized, so that an upturn in the global economy is likely to be met by a global demand for increased investment (Rowthorn 1995). The second is that, within nations, the key instrument for the control of inflation is interest rates. As economies overheat, interest rates are raised by central banks to choke off demand. The use of interest rates is claimed to be successful in controlling inflation in a way in which other measures tried in the 1970s and 1980s, incomes policies and control of the money supply, were not. Again, however, we should note the role of the new global economy in defining the control on inflation as a key element in any successful national competitive strategy. If inflation in any one country rises to appreciably higher levels than in competitor countries, its goods are likely to be priced out of the market: hence the significance accorded to the control of inflation in a global economy. But the cost of using interest rates to this end is that economies are permanently run under capacity (ILO 1995: 163). The rise in interest rates simply chokes off demand before it can appreciably affect unemployment levels.

More recently, studies have argued that it is declining economic growth (and hence demand) among the OECD countries since 1973 which is the fundamental cause of unemployment (ILO 1995; Eatwell 1995). While the trend is that economic growth in all OECD countries has declined (ILO 1995: 133) it is unclear whether raising levels to those in the period between 1960 and 1973 would have the same impact on unemployment now as it did then, as the examples of Australia and Canada show. The problem is that in a global economy, growth may be achieved through exports and the benefits of growth spent on imports rather than home-produced goods. Whereas in the postwar Fordist economies a rise in demand would percolate through the economy, thereby creating jobs, a rise in demand now may simply create jobs in some other part of the world. This may be especially so in countries where increases in incomes are accruing to the wealthy who spend their money on luxury goods from overseas.

The alternative to this macroanalysis of the causes of unemployment is the microanalysis of some neo-classical economists, who argue that it is labour-market rigidities, of the kind discussed above, especially the power of trade unions and highly regulated labour markets, which cause unemployment and sustain inflation. There are two elements to their explanation. The first is that these rigidities bid up the price of labour and maintain it at a level higher than desirable, to clear the labour market of the unemployed. The second is that they allow the 'insiders' who are employed to bid up their wages even when others are unemployed (Lindbeck and Snower 1986). There are two problems with this theory. Firstly, there appears to be no strong relationship between the degree of social protection, labour-market regulation, and unemployment, with the exception of America (although see Freeman 1995). Historically the lowest levels of unemployment, from 1950 to 1973, have been associated with the highest levels of social protection and labour-market regulation, while the present period represents one of the lowest levels of protection and regulation and the highest levels of unemployment. Moreover, even within the current period, differences between nations relating to regulation, protection, and economic performance hardly bear out this thesis. For example, the UK has one of the lowest levels of labour protection in the OECD and an unemployment rate of 8.4 per cent (OECD 1994: 155). In contrast Holland, which has an above-average level of protection and regulation, has an unemployment rate of 7.3 per cent. Moreover, their inflation rates are not substantially different. Britain has had an annual rate of 2.4 per cent in the past year, and Holland 3 per cent. Secondly, where labour markets have been deregulated, it is doubtful whether they have genuinely achieved the benefits that appear to have resulted. For example, poverty amongst those on low wages in the United States is high, and it has been argued that there is a *de facto* policy of incarceration of the unemployed (Freeman 1995).

Overall, it seems extremely unlikely that the problem of unemployment can be solved by any of the conventional remedies, and to pretend otherwise merely holds out false promises to a generation of unemployed. The New Right solution was to price people back into jobs. The modernizers' solution is to create a high-skill, high-wage, 'magnet' economy. Neither solution is adequate. The New Right solution manifestly has not worked and it threatens a new cycle of low-wage job creation. The modernizers, whilst having a more sustainable approach to global economic competition, have no answer to unemployment. Therefore, the most important conclusion to be drawn from this discussion is that the modernizers lack an adequate account of how all will share in the future prosperity accrued from investment in education and national economic growth. Unemployment will remain a structural feature of Western societies, and the 'distributional' question (Hirsch 1977), temporarily solved under Fordism through full employment and the even spread of the fruits of growth across the occupational structure, must now be addressed by the modernizers. Consequently,

we argue elsewhere (Brown and Lauder forthcoming) that the distributional problem can only be remedied by the introduction of a 'basic income' (Parijs 1992) and that occupational opportunities will have to be shared. Moreover, the question of unemployment is not only one of social justice, but one of economic efficiency. If the economic fate of nations increasingly depends upon the quality of their human resources, it will not be possible to write off a large minority of the population to an 'underclass' existence. Indeed, the issue of long-term unemployment is part of a wider problem of social and economic polarization. Therefore, we need to examine the modernizers' account of skill and income polarization before asking how those people living in poverty are going to acquire the appropriate skills to get high-skilled, high-waged jobs, when research has demonstrated that social deprivation has a profoundly negative impact on academic performance.

Does Income Polarization Reflect the 'Value' of Skills, Knowledge, and Insights in the Global Labour Market?

Considerable doubt must be cast on the way the modernizers have understood the 'high skill equals high wage' equation. This is important to our discussion because growing income inequalities are seen to reflect individual differences in the quality of their 'human capital'. Here their argument is based on trend data which shows a widening of income inequalities, in which there has been a dramatic increase in both America and Britain since the late 1970s. Such evidence is taken to reflect the relative abilities of workers to trade their knowledge, skills, and insights on the global labour market. According to the modernizers, as low-skilled jobs have been lost to developing economies with cheaper labour, the wages of less skilled workers in the West have declined. By the same token, in the new competitive conditions described above, those workers who have the skills, knowledge, and insights that can contribute to 'value added' research, production, consultancy, or service delivery in the global labour market have witnessed an increase in their remuneration. Hence analysis and remedy are closely related in the modernizers' account: if so many workers are in low-paying jobs or unemployed because they lack skills, the solution is to give them the skills. It's an appealing analysis, but at best it is based on a partial truth.

If increasing income polarization was a consequence of the neutral operation of the global economy we should find the same trend in all the advanced economies. However, the evidence suggests that the increasing polarization in income is far more pronounced in America and Britain than in any other OECD country (Gardiner 1993: 14; Hills 1995). In Germany there has actually been a decline in income differentials (OECD 1993).

It could also be expected that if the increased dispersion of income was a result of the changing cognitive and skill demands of work, then nations with the highest levels of technology and investment in research and development would lead the table of income inequalities. Yet the evidence that does exist suggests quite the opposite. Wood (1994) notes that 'Japan and Sweden are leaders in applying new technology, while the USA and UK are laggards' (p. 281). He also notes that the work of Patel and Pavitt (1991) suggests that civilian research and development as a proportion of GDP in the 1980s was higher in Sweden and Japan than in the USA and the UK. Equally, in terms of patenting in the USA, Germany, which experienced declining inequalities of income during this period, greatly outperformed the UK.

One conclusion to be drawn from these considerations is that rather than the returns to skill becoming more responsive to the operation of the global auction, the relationship between skill and income is less direct than the modernizers assume. The reason for this is that the relationship between income and skills is always mediated by cultural, political, and societal factors. This is of course obvious when unpaid child care, undertaken primarily by women, is taken into consideration. Moreover, despite its use in the current debate about income inequalities and economic performance, it has proved extremely difficult to arrive at an agreed definition of skill, which explains why studies comparing labour markets in neighbouring countries like Germany and France show that the process of training, career progression, and reward for skills is intricate, subtle, and substantially different in the two countries (Maurice *et al.* 1986). Another study (Dore 1987) has highlighted

differences in the way rewards are distributed for work in America as opposed to Japan. In America it is assumed by neo-classical economists that there is a direct relationship between skill and income. However, Japanese industry, the exemplar of producer capitalism, has not organized the relationship between skill and income in this way, but has based income on loyalty to the company and length of service rather than on 'skill' in any pristine sense. As Dore has noted, in Japan there is a remarkable 'lack of consciousness of the market price of a skill' (p. 30). This being the case, it could be expected that even if the polarization of income in America was a response to the changing demand for skill, this would not be the case in Japan. A further glance at the OECD (1993) data also tells us that while there has been some widening of income differentials in Japan, it does not reflect the polarization characteristic of the United States and Britain.

What this evidence suggests is that the modernizer's assumption that by raising skill levels there will be a commensurate increase in income regulated through the global labour market is clearly incorrect. The answer is to be found not in the neutral operation of the global labour market, as Reich and others have suggested, but in the way the United States and Britain have *responded* to global economic conditions. This response, like the global economy itself, has been shaped by the New Right political projects of Reagan and Thatcher (Marchak 1991). Although the debate over what is distinctive about America and Britain takes us beyond the confines of this paper, the polarization in income can be explained more convincingly in terms of differences in labour-market power than in returns to skills (although they are not mutually exclusive). A major consequence of market deregulation has been to enhance the power of 'core' workers in downsized organisations. This is supported by the fact that the most dramatic changes in income distribution are to be found at either end of the income parade. What income polarization in the US and UK also reveals is the way in which the 'casino' economies of these countries in the 1980s enabled company executive and senior managers, along with those who worked in the financial markets, to engage in 'wealth extraction' rather than the development of sustainable forms of 'wealth creation' (Lazonick

1993). This largely explains why a study reported by Bound and Johnson (1995) found that in America a large part of the increase in the returns to a university degree was due to an increased premium put to use in the business and law fields. The wages of computer specialists and engineers actually fell relative to high school graduates.

But if the rising incomes of the work-rich is explicable in terms of 'paper entrepreneurialism' (Reich 1984) and corporate restructuring, can the decline in the wages of the unskilled be explained in terms of the neutral operation of the global economy? In addressing this question there is the problem of measuring the extent to which semi- and unskilled work have been transplanted to the developing nations. One estimate is that up to 1990 changes in trade with the South has reduced the demand for unskilled relative to skilled labour in the North by approximately 20 per cent (Wood 1994: 11). However, it is not only that industrial blue-collar jobs were lost, but that the perennial threat of relocation to developing world countries ensured that wages were depressed for remaining unskilled workers. It is of course hard to measure the degree to which this threat has been material in keeping down wages. Nevertheless, it is worth noting that there is little correlation between manufacturing competitiveness and low wages. In the most successful industrial economies, Germany and Japan, manufacturing wages are higher than anywhere else. However, New Right governments in America and Britain took the 'lesson' to heart and helped to drive down wages by labour-market deregulation. Estimates for the UK (Gosling and Machin 1993) and the USA (Blackburn, Bloom, and Freeman 1990), for instance, calculate that the decline in unionization in the 1980s accounts for 20 per cent of the increase in wage inequality. In addition, making it easier to hire and fire workers enabled companies to achieve numerical flexibility in their wages bills (Atkinson 1985). At times of economic boom workers could be hired, while in times of downturn they could be fired. In Britain, for example, in the last three months of 1994, 74,120 full-time jobs disappeared and 173,941 part-time jobs were created. This is a clear example of how to organize a labour market for short-term expedience, but it also suggests that companies have externalized not only the risks associated with unstable market conditions but also their labour costs, especially among low-skilled workers. In such circumstances it is difficult to see how the modernizers can resolve the problem of widening income inequalities when they are judged to reflect the neutral operation of the global economy.

Indeed, high levels of income inequalities are interpreted by the modernizers as a reflection of educational and corporate inefficiency in a global labour-market which can only be narrowed through investment in education and training. If inequalities persist it is because the latter are failing to upgrade the quality of human resources. With respect to national systems of education, inequalities become a useful measure of their effectiveness. However, this raises a set of questions and problems for the modernizers with respect to the social conditions under which education can achieve greater equality of opportunity and higher levels of educational achievement for all. It is to this fourth problem that we now turn.

How can the Quality of Human Resources be Upgraded where All are Granted an Equal Opportunity to Fulfil their Human Potential?

In answering this question the modernizers recognize that the wealth of nations depends upon upgrading the quality of human resources. They recognize that ways must be found to develop the full potential of a much larger proportion of the population than prevailed in the Fordist era. They point to the need to widen access to tertiary education and to create the institutional framework necessary to offer lifelong learning to all. They also recognize a need to improve overall educational standards as American and British students appear to be falling behind in international comparative tests. A national commitment to investment in the 'employability' of present and future workers is understood by the modernizers to represent a new social contract between the individual and the state, given that such investment is viewed as a condition for economic efficiency and social justice. However, their interpretation of how equity and efficiency are to be achieved in the global economy is politically impoverished. In part, this is because the question of equity has been subsumed within a debate about how to upgrade the overall quality of education and training systems based on an assumption that domestic inequalities of opportunity are largely irrelevant if a nation can win a competitive advantage in the global knowledge wars, permitting all to compete for high-skilled, high-waged jobs. Therefore, the old national competition for a livelihood, based on the principles of meritocratic competition, is of far less importance than that of how to upgrade the quality of the education system as a whole. Again we find the idea of a high-skill, high-wage, magnet economy used to extract the political sting from questions of social and educational inequalities.

The reality is that questions of social justice cannot be resolved through the operation of the global labour market. Indeed, if the creation of a post-Fordist economy depends on a general upgrading of the skills of the labour force, tackling the problem of domestic inequalities in income and opportunities has become more rather than less important with economic globalization. There are at least two related reasons for this. Firstly, the use of education and training institutions to raise technical standards for all does not resolve the question of 'positional' advantage (Hirsch 1977). In other words, access to élite schools, colleges, and universities, along with the credentials they bestow, remains a key factor in determining labour-market power. In addition, if our analysis of income inequalities is correct, labour-market power has, if anything, become more important as a result of corporate restructuring and the decline of graduate careers (Brown and Scase 1994). Therefore, the question of social justice will continue to depend on how individual nation states frame the competition for a livelihood.

The question of positional competition has also become more important because there has been a change in the nature of educational selection. Today the institutional expression of a commitment to meritocratic competition in education has been suffocated under the grip of the New Right. A commitment to a unified system of schooling within which students will be educated according to ability and effort has been abandoned in favour of consumer sovereignty based on parental 'choice' and a system of education based on market principles. A consequence of this change in the organization of educational selection from that based on 'merit' to the 'market' (Brown 1995) is that, as argued above, it serves to encourage the creation of underfunded sink schools for the poor and havens of 'excellence' for the rich. Therefore, the school system in both America and Britain no longer reflects a commitment to open competition, but shows gross inequalities in educational provision, opportunities, and life chances. In Washington the wealthy are queuing up to pay as much as $12,000 a year to send their five-year-old children to private schools whilst Washington DC is virtually bankrupt and severe cuts to the educational budget are inevitable.[10]

Therefore, although equality of opportunity is recognized as a condition of economic efficiency, the modernizers have effectively avoided perhaps the most important question to confront the Left at the end of the twentieth century, of how to organize the competition for a livelihood in such a way that a genuinely equal opportunity is available to all. Avoiding the positional problem by appeals to the need to raise educational standards for all in the global market not only fails to address this question, but also offers little insight into how the foundations for social solidarity—upon which the institutional expression of meritocratic competition rests—are to be rebuilt. Indeed, their focus on increasing the 'employability' of workers reinforces a sense of the insecure nature of work at the end of the twentieth century (Newman 1993; Peterson 1994). It encourages people to constantly watch their backs and to put their child first in the educational and labour-market jungle. Without an adequate foundation for material and social security, the emphasis on enhanced employability within a culture of competitive individualism becomes translated into the Hobbesian condition of 'all against all'. When education becomes a positional good and where the stakes are forever increasing in terms of income, life-chances, and social status, powerful individuals and groups will seek to maximize their resources to ensure that they have a stake in the game by whatever means.[11] Therefore, how the state intervenes to regulate this competition in a way which reduces the inequalities of those trapped in lower socio-economic groups must be addressed, not only as a matter of economic efficiency but also for reasons of social justice in a post-Fordist economy.

The relationship between equity and efficiency at the end of the twentieth century does not only rest on the reassertion of meritocratic competition in education, but on a recognition that the wealth of the nation's human resources is inversely related to social inequalities, especially in income and opportunity. Therefore, narrowing such inequalities is likely to be a cost-effective way of investing in human capital, which in turn should lead to improvements in economic efficiency. Hence, we would predict that the polarization of income in nations like the United States and Britain during the 1980s will have led to a wider dispersal of educational achievement than in nations with little or no widening of incomes. We are currently analyzing the comparative evidence in order to examine the hypothesis that relative deprivation has an absolute effect on the quality of a nation's human resource (Wilkinson 1994). If our hypothesis proves to be supported by the empirical evidence, this will come as little surprise to sociologists, who have consistently found a close relationship between inequality and academic performance.[12] The fact that at least a fifth of children in both America and Britain now live in poverty is inevitably going to have a detrimental impact on the ability of these children to respond to educational opportunities and to recognize the relevance of formal study when living in neighbourhoods with high unemployment, crime, and deprivation. Indeed, the importance of equity to the question of social learning is graphically illustrated in Julius Wilson's (1987) study of the urban underclass in America. He suggests that 'a perceptive ghetto youngster in a neighbourhood that includes a good number of working and professional families may observe increasing joblessness and idleness but he [sic] may also witness many individuals going to and from work; he may sense an increase in school dropouts but he can also see a connection between education and meaningful employment' (1987: 56). He goes on to argue that the exodus of 'respectable' middle- and working-class families from the inner-city neighbourhoods in the 1970s and 1980s removed an important 'social buffer' that could deflect the full impact of prolonged and increasing joblessness, given that the basic institutions in the area (churches, schools, stores, recreational facilities, and so on) are viable so long as more economically stable and secure families remain. Hence, the more social groups become isolated from one another, the fewer opportunities exist for the kind of learning which could offer role models to children other than those created by the 'political economy of crack' (Davis 1990).

Moreover, the impact of widening social inequalities is not restricted to children from ghetto or poor backgrounds, but also infects the social learning of the wealthier sections of the population. In a characteristically perceptive discussion, John Dewey noted that every expansive period of social history is marked by social trends which serve to 'eliminate distance between peoples and classes previously hemmed off from one another' (1966: 100). At times where the opposite happens, the range of contacts, ideas, interests, and role-models is narrowed. The culture of the privileged tends to become 'sterile, to be turned back to feed on itself; their art becomes a showy display and artificial; their wealth luxurious; their knowledge over-specialized; their manners fastidious rather than humane' (Dewey 1966: 98).

Hence the modernizers' assumption that inequalities will narrow once there is proper investment in education and training fails to recognize that the future wealth of nations depends upon a fundamental challenge to inequalities of power underlying the distribution of income and educational opportunities. Therefore, the role of the nation state must increasingly become one of balancing the internal competition for a livelihood with a strategy geared towards upgrading the quality of education for all through a reduction in relative inequalities. Moreover, a commitment to equality of opportunity is not only vital to the life-blood of a high-skill economic strategy, but it provides a clear message to all sections of society that they are of equal worth and deserve genuine opportunities to fulfil their human potential.

Conclusion

The increasing importance attached to education in the global economy is not misplaced in the sense that nations will increasingly have to define the wealth of nations in terms of the quality of human resources among the population. The creation of a post-Fordist economy will depend upon an active state involved in investment, regulation, and strategic planning in the economic infrastructure alongside a commitment to skill formation through education and training. We have argued that such an economic strategy is necessary because it is the best way of creating a social dividend which can be used to fund a 'basic income' for all, given that the 'distributional' problem can no longer be solved through employment within the division of labour. A social wage which delivers families from poverty thereby becomes an important foundation of a learning society, designed to follow the post-Fordist trajectory to a globally competitive economy and to a socially just society (see Brown and Lauder forthcoming). Hence, if the potential and limitations of educational reform in the creation of a post-Fordist economy are to be adequately addressed by the modernizers, there is an urgent need for those on the Left to grapple with the issues explored in this paper.

Notes

1. This paper develops a number of themes outlined in earlier papers (Brown and Lauder 1992, 1995). It also serves to clarify our interpretation of the relationship between education and post-Fordism which has been criticized by Avis (1993) and Jones and Hatcher (1994).
2. Figures from *Financial Times* Survey 'North American Business Location', 19 Oct. 1994.
3. Antonio Gramsci (1971) used the term Fordism to describe a new system of mass-production introduced by the American car manufacturer, Henry Ford. Gramsci recognized that the introduction of mass production also required a new mode of social regulation 'suited to the new type of work and productive process' (p. 286). Ford's rise to prominence at the time stemmed from the market success of the Model T motor car which was launched in 1916. The system of mass production enabled him to capture 55 per cent of the US market in the early 1920s by selling the Model T at a tenth of the price of a craft-built car (Braverman 1974; Murray 1989).
4. As it is more difficult for competitors to mass-produce the same goods or to offer customers tailored services. See Schumpeter (1961); Collins (1986); Blackwell and Eilon (1991). In such companies improvements in productivity depend upon the 'organic' integration of applied science, technological innovation,

free-flow information networks, and high-trust relations between management and multi-skilled workers. The increasing costs of errors, demand for quality control, and for multi-skilled workers with a conceptual grasp of a large section of the production process or office activities has made the specialized division of labour in Fordism a source of organizational inefficiency.
5. The idea of a 'Feudal' shackle is discussed by Hirschman (1986).
6. Given such a diverse range of publications there will inevitably be differences in focus and policy emphasis. The extent to which the Clinton administration in America has attempted to introduce a viable industrial policy has been clearly limited (see Shoch, J. (1994), 'The Politics of the US Industrial Policy Debate, 1981–1984 (With a Note on Bill Clinton's "Industrial Policy")', in D. Kotz, T. McDonough, and M. Reich (eds.), *Social Structures of Accumulation* (Cambridge: Cambridge Univ. Press)).
7. 'They are All Our Children', speech delivered at East Los Angeles College, Los Angeles, 14 May 1992. The modernizers' view clearly contrasts with the rhetoric, if not the practice, of the New Right. There is clearly a tension between New Right views regarding the expansion of tertiary education and the practice of the Conservative Party in the UK, where there has been a rapid expansion of tertiary provision despite the views of influential theorists and journalists like Friedman, Hayek, and Rees-Mogg, suggesting that it is only a small élite that needs a university education. It is also worth noting that in terms of imagery, the New Right do not present the future in terms of a 'learning society' but of an enterprise culture, in which a few outstanding captains of industry and commerce, the Bill Gateses and Richard Bransons of this world, are fêted as the leaders of an economic renaissance.
8. The floor of protective rights for workers as envisaged by the modernizers is, for example, likely to be too weak to act as an incentive to employers to upgrading the quality of work opportunities. Moreover, see Kuttner's response to Rogers and Streeck (1994).
9. Data compiled from the *Independent on Sunday*'s economic indicators, 1994–5.
10. The question of equality of opportunity needs to be addressed head-on, as it is not only essential to economic efficiency, but to the legitimation of a system of educational and occupational selection which is inherently stratified in terms of income, status, work-styles, and life-styles. In postwar western societies the reason why a menial labourer is paid $17,000 and a private-sector manager

$85,000 was legitimated in terms of the outcome of a meritocratic competition based on individual ability and effort. The commitment to open competition found expression in the idea of the mixed-ability high or comprehensive school. There remained deprived inner-city districts where children especially from African-American and Hispanic backgrounds were clearly not getting equality of opportunity, but even here 'head-start' programmes were launched to try to create a level playing-field.

11. Moreover, the exclusion of those in lower socio-economic circumstances from decent academic provision is compounded by deindustrialization, which has created a rust belt across the heartlands of both America and Britain, sometimes destroying vibrant communities (Bluestone and Harrison 1982). Therefore, although the modernizers assume greater flexibility in the occupational structure as a response to the employment needs of men and woman at different stages of their lives, the reality seems more likely to lead to intensive competition, highly restricted opportunities to enter the professional core, and a constant flux restricted to jobs which are low-skilled, low-waged, and inherently insecure. This outcome may well be reinforced by the fact that, as employers place a premium on employees with the appropriate social and interpersonal skills alongside their technical know-how, the cultural capital of job-seekers assumes greater importance. Without the financial and social resources required to invest in cultural capital, those from poorer backgrounds who are more likely to attend less prestigious halls of learning will be at a distinct disadvantage (Brown and Scase, 1994).

12. For a discussion of the definition of relative deprivation and poverty see Townsend, P. (1993), *The International Analysis of Poverty* (New York: Harvester/Wheatsheaf).

References

Allen, J. (1992), 'Post-Industrialism and Post-Fordism', in S. Hall *et al.* (eds.), *Modernity and its Futures* (Cambridge: Polity).

Ashton, D. N., and Sung, J. (1994), *The State, Economic Development and Skill Formation: A New Asian Model, Working Paper No. 3* (Centre for Labour Market Studies, Univ. of Leicester).

Atkinson, J. (1985), 'The Changing Corporation', in D. Clutterbuck (ed.), *New Patterns of Work* (Aldershot: Gower).

Avis, J. (1993), 'A New Orthodoxy, Old Problems: Post-16 Reforms', *British Journal of Sociology of Education*, 14: 245–60.

Ball, S. (1993), 'Education Markets, Choice and Social Class: The Market as a Class Strategy in the UK and the USA', *British Journal of Sociology of Education*, 14: 1, 3–19.

Blackburn, M., Bloom, D., and Freeman, R. (1990), 'The Declining Economic Position of Less Skilled American Men', in G. Burtless (ed.), *A Future of Lousy Jobs?* (Washington DC: Brookings Institute).

Blackwell, B., and Eilon, S. (1991), *The Global Challenge of Innovation* (Oxford: Butterworth Heinemann).

Block, F. (1990), *Postindustrial Possibilities: A Critique of Economic Discourse* (Berkeley: California Univ. Press).

Bluestone, B., and Harrison, B. (1982), *The Deindustrialization of America* (New York: Basic Books).

Bound, J., and Johnson, G. (1995), 'What Are the Causes of Rising Wage Inequality in the United States?' *Economic Policy Review*, (Federal Reserve Bank of New York, Jan.) 1/1: 9–17.

Boyd, W., and Cibulka, J. (eds.) (1989), *Private Schools and Public Policy* (London: Falmer).

Braverman, H. (1974), *Labour and Monopoly Capital* (London: Jessica Kingsley).

Brown, G. (1994), 'The Politics of Potential: A New Agenda for Labour', in D. Miliband (ed.), *Reinventing the Left* (Cambridge: Polity).

Brown, P. (1990), 'The 'Third Wave': Education and the Ideology of Parentocracy', *British Journal of Sociology of Education*, 11: 65–85.

—— (1995), 'Cultural Capital and Social Exclusion: Some Observations on Recent Trends in Education, Employment and the Labour Market', *Work, Employment and Society*, 9/1: 29–51.

—— and Lauder, H. (1992), 'Education, Economy and Society: An Introduction to a New Agenda', in P. Brown and H. Lauder (eds.), *Education for Economic Survival: From Fordism to Post-Fordism?* (London: Routledge).

—— and —— (forthcoming), *The Stakeholder Society in a Global Age*.

—— and Scase, R. (1994), *Higher Education and Corporate Realities* (London: UCL Press).

Carnoy, M., Castells, M., Cohen, S., and Cardoso, F. H., *The Global Economy in the Information Age* (Pennsylvania: Penn State Univ.).

Collins, R. (1979), *The Credential Society* (New York: Academic Press).

Collins, R. (1986), *Weberian Sociological Theory* (New York: Cambridge Univ. Press).

Commission of the European Communities (1993), *Growth, Competitiveness, Employment: The Challenges and Ways Forward into the 21st Century, White Paper*, Bulletin of the European Communities 6/93.

Commission on Social Justice (1994), *Social Justice: Strategies for National Renewal* (London: Vintage).

Cowling, K., and Sugden, R. (1994), *Beyond Capitalism: Towards a New World Economic Order* (London: Pinter).

Davis, M. (1990), *City of Quartz* (New York: Verso).

Deakin, S., and Wilkinson, F. (1991), 'Social Policy and Economic Efficiency: The Deregulation of the Labour Market in Britain', *Critical Social Policy*, 11/3: 40–61.

Dewey, J. (1966), *Democracy and Education* (New York: Free Press).

Dicken, P. (1992), *Global Shift: The Internationalisation of Economic Activity* (London: Paul Chapman).

Dore, R (1987), *Taking Japan Seriously* (Athlone Press, London).

Eatwell, J. (1995), 'The International Origins of Unemployment', in J. Michie and J. G. Smith (eds.), *Managing the Global Economy* (Oxford: Oxford Univ. Press).

Esping-Andersen, G. (1994), 'Equity and Work in the Post-Industrial Life-Cycle', in D. Miliband (ed.), *Reinventing the Left* (Cambridge: Polity).

Freeman, R. (1995), 'The Limits of Wage Flexibility to Curing Unemployment', *Oxford Review of Economic Policy*, 11/1: 63–72.

Gamble, A. (1988), *The Free Market and the Strong State* (London: Macmillan).

Gardiner, K. (1993), *A Survey of Income Inequality Over the Last Twenty Years—How Does the UK Compare?* Welfare State Programme 100 (Centre for Economics and Related Disciplines, London School of Economics).

Gosling, A., and Machin, S. (1993), *Trade Unions and the Dispersion of Earnings in UK Establishments, 1980–90*, Centre for Economic Performance Discussion paper 140 (London School of Economics, London).

Gramsci, A. (1971), *Selections from Prison Notebooks* (London: Lawrence and Wishart).

Green, A., and Steedman, H. (1993), *Education Provision, Educational Attainment and the Needs of Identity: A Review of Research for Germany, France, Japan, the USA and Britain* (London: NIESR).

Halsey, A. H., Heath, A., and Ridge, J. (1980), *Origins and Destinations* (Oxford: Clarendon).

Halstead, M. (ed.) (1994), *Parental Choice and Education* (London: Kogan Page).

Harvey, D. (1989), *The Conditions of Postmodernity* (Oxford: Blackwell).

Henderson, A., and Parsons, T. (eds.) (1974), *Max Weber: The Theory of Social and Economic Organisation* (New York: Oxford Univ. Press).

Hills, J. (1995), *Income and Wealth: Volume Two, A Summary of the Evidence* (York: Joseph Rowntree Foundation).

Hirsch, F. (1977), *Social Limits to Growth* (London: Routledge).

Hirschmann, A. (1986), *Rival Views of Market Society and Other Essays* (London: Viking).

Hutton, W. (1995), *The State We're In* (London: Jonathan Cape).

International Labour Organization (ILO) (1995), *World Employment 1995* (Geneva: ILO).

Jones, K., and Hatcher, R. (1994), 'Education, Progress and Economic Change: Notes on Some Recent Proposals', *British Journal of Educational Studies*, 42: 245–60.

Krugman, P. (1993), *Peddling Prosperity: Economic Sense and Nonsense in the Age of Diminished Expectations* (New York: W. W. Norton).

Lane, C. (1989), *Management and Labour in Europe* (Aldershot: Edward Elgar).

Lauder, H. (1987), 'The New Right and Educational Policy in New Zealand', *New Zealand Journal of Educational Studies*, 22: 3–23.

—— (1991) 'Education, Democracy and the Economy', *British Journal of Sociology of Education*, 12: 417–31.

—— and Hughes, D. (1990), 'Social Inequalities and Differences in School Outcomes', *New Zealand Journal of Educational Studies*, 23: 37–60.

—— et al. (1994), *The Creation of Market Competition for Education in New Zealand* (Wellington: Ministry of Education).

Lazonick, W. (1993), 'Industry Clusters Versus Global Webs: Organisational Capabilities in the American Economy', *Industrial and Corporate Change*, 2: 1–24.

Lindbeck, A., and Snower, D. (1986), 'Wage Setting, Unemployment and Insider-Outsider Relations', *American Economic Review*, 76: 235–9.

Lipietz, A. (1987), *Mirages and Miracles: The Crises of Global Fordism* (London: Verso).

Marchak, M. P. (1991), *The Integrated Circus: The New Right and the Restructuring of Global Markets* (Montreal: McGill-Queen's Univ. Press).

Marginson, P. (1994), 'Multinational Britain: Employment and Work in an Internationalized Economy', *Human Resource Management Journal*, 4/4: 63–80.

Maurice, M., Sellier, F., and Silvestre, J. (1986), *The Social Foundations of Industrial Power* (Cambridge, Mass.: MIT).

McGregor, D. (1960), *The Human Side of Enterprise* (New York: McGraw-Hill).

Michie, J., and Smith, J. G. (eds.) (1995), *Managing the Global Economy* (Oxford: Oxford Univ. Press).

Murray, C. (1984), *Losing Ground: American Social Policy 1950–1980* (New York: Basic Books).

Murray, R. (1989), 'Fordism and Post-Fordism', in S. Hall and M. Jacques (eds.), *New Times* (London: Lawrence & Wishart).

National Commission on Education (1993), *Learning to Succeed* (London: Heinemann).

Newman, K. (1993), *Declining Fortunes* (New York: Basic Books).

OECD (1989), *Education and the Economy in a Changing World* (Paris: OECD).
—— (1993), *Employment Outlook* (Paris: OECD).
—— (1994), *Employment Outlook* (Paris: OECD).
Ormerod, P. (1994), *The Death of Economics* (London: Faber & Faber).
Parijs, P. V. (1992) (ed.), *Arguments for Basic Income: Ethical Foundations for a Radical Reform* (London: Verso).
Parkin, F. (1979), *Marxism and Class Theory: A Bourgeois Critique* (London: Tavistock).
Patel, P., and Pavitt, K. (1991), 'Europe's Technological Performance', in C. Freeman, M. Sharp, and W. Walker (eds.), *Technology and the Future of Europe* (London: Pinter).
Peterson, W. (1994), *Silent Depression: The Fate of the American Dream* (New York: W. W. Norton).
Piore, M., and Sabel, C. (1984), *The Second Industrial Divide: Possibilities for Prosperity* (New York: Basic Books).
Piore, M. (1990), 'Labor Standards and Business Strategies', in S. Herzenberg and J. Perez-Lopez (eds.), *Labor Standards and Development in the Global Economy* (Washington DC: US Department of Labor).
Porter, M. (1990), *The Competitive Advantage of Nations* (London: Macmillan).
Reich, R. (1984), *The Next American Frontier* (Harmondsworth: Penguin).
—— (1991), *The Work of Nations* (London: Simon and Schuster).
Rogers, J., and Streeck, W. (1994), 'Productive Solidarities: Economic Strategy and Left Politics', D. Miliband (ed.), *Reinventing the Left* (Cambridge: Polity).
Rowthorn, R. (1995), 'Capital Formation and Unemployment', *Oxford Review of Economic Policy*, 11/1: 26–39.
Sabel, C. F. (1982), *Work and Politics* (Cambridge: Cambridge Univ. Press).
Schumpeter, J. (1961), *The Theory of Economic Development* (New York: Oxford Univ. Press).
Sengenberger, W., and Wilkinson, F. (1995), 'Globalization and Labour Standards', in J. Michie and J. G. Smith (eds.), *Managing the Global Economy* (Oxford: Oxford Univ. Press).
Snower, D. (1995), 'Evaluating Unemployment Policies: What do the Underlying Theories Tell us?' *Oxford Review of Economic Policy*, 11: 110–35.
Streeck, W. (1989), 'Skills and the Limits of Neo-Liberalism: The Enterprise of the Future as a Place of Learning', *Work, Employment and Society*, 3: 90–104.
Streeck, W. (1992), *Social Institutions and Economic Performance* (London: Sage).
Thurow, L. (1993), *Head to Head: The Coming Economic Battle Among Japan, Europe and America* (London: Nicholas Brealey).
Toffler, A, (1990), *Powershift* (New York: Bantam).
Wilkinson, R (1994), *Unfair Shares: The Effect of Widening Income Differences on the Welfare of the Young* (Ilford: Barnardo's Publication).
Willms, J., and Echols, F. (1992), 'Alert and Inert Clients: The Scottish Experience of Parental Choice of Schools', *Economics of Education Review*, 11: 339–50.
Wilson, W. (1987), *The Truly Disadvantaged* (Chicago: Univ. of Chicago Press).
Wood, A. (1994), *North-South Trade, Employment and Inequality: Changing Fortunes in a Skill-Driven World* (Oxford: Clarendon).

11

The New Knowledge Work

Stanley Aronowitz and William De Fazio

Overview

In 1992 the long-term shifts in the nature of paid work became painfully visible not only to industrial workers and those with technical, professional, and managerial credentials and job experience but also to the public. During the year, 'corporate giants like General Motors and IBM announced plans to shed tens of thousands of workers' (Lohn 1993). General Motors, which at first said it would close twenty-one U.S. plants by 1995, soon disclaimed any definite limit to the number of either plant closings or firings and admitted the numbers of jobs lost might climb above the predicted 70,000, even if the recession led to increased car sales. IBM, which initially shaved about 25,000 blue- and white-collar employees, soon increased its estimates to possibly 60,000, in effect reversing the company's historic policy of no layoffs. Citing economic conditions, Boeing, the world's largest airplane producer, and Hughes Aircraft, a major parts manufacturer, were poised for substantial cuts in their well-paid workforces. In 1991 and 1992 major retailers, including Sears, either shut down stores or drastically cut the number of employees; in late January 1993, Sears announced it was letting about 50,000 employees go. The examples could be multiplied. Millions, worldwide, were losing their jobs in the industrialized West and Asia. Homelessness was and is growing.

Also in 1992, twelve years of a Republican national administration came to an end. Presidential candidate Bill Clinton successfully made the economy the central issue, eradicating the seemingly unassailable popularity President George Bush won during the brief Gulf War of the previous year. Among the keystones of his campaign, Clinton promised federal action to create new jobs through both direct investment in roads and mass transit and a tax credit to encourage business to invest in machinery and plants. Did this signal a return to presumably antiquated Keynesian policies and fiscal policies to encourage private investment? An important part of Clinton's approach to recovery was more money for education and stepped-up training and retraining programs, the assumption of which is that development of 'human capital' was a long ignored but important component of the growth of a technologically advanced economy.[1] According to this argument, a poor educational system and inadequate apprenticeship and retraining programs would inevitably result in a competitive disadvantage for the United States in an increasingly competitive global economy.

The peculiar feature of the latest economic recovery is that while the economic indicators were turning up, prospects for good jobs were turning down. Even before Clinton took office, the trend toward more low-paid, temporary, benefit-free blue- and white-collar jobs and fewer decent *permanent* factory and office jobs called into question many of the underlying assumptions of his campaign. For if good jobs were disappearing as fast as 'unstable and mediocre'[2] jobs were being created, more education and training geared to a shrinking market for professional and technical labor might lead nowhere for many who bought the promise. As in many manufacturing sectors, labor-displacing technological

From *The Jobless Future: Sci-Tech and the Dogma of Work* (Minneapolis, University of Minnesota Press, 1994), 13–23 and 46–56. Reprinted with permission.

change has reached the construction industry. Unless public and private investment is specifically geared to hiring labor rather than purchasing giant earth-moving machines, for example—which would imply changing a tax structure that permits write-offs for technology investments—it seems dubious that Clinton's plan to plow $20 billion a year into infrastructure could result in a significant net employment gain even as it generated orders for more labor-saving equipment. Machine tool and electrical equipment industries are leaders in the use of computer-mediated labor processes. Labor-saving technologies combined with organizational changes (such as mergers, acquisitions, divestitures, and consolidation of production in fewer plants, a cost saving made possible by the technology) yield few new jobs.

The central contention of this book lies somewhere between common sense and new knowledge. We discuss what should already be evident to all but those either suffering the political constraints of policy or still in the thrall of the American ideology and blind belief in the ineluctability of social mobility and prosperity in the American system. The two are linked: no politician who aspires to power may violate the unwritten rule that the United States is the Great Exception to the general law that class and other forms of social mobility are restricted for the overwhelming majority of the population. Our first argument—that the Western dream of upward mobility has died and it is time to give it a respectful funeral—may have at long last seeped into the bones of most Americans, even the most optimistic economist.

The dream has died because the scientific-technological revolution of our time, which is not confined to new electronic processes but also affects organizational changes in the structure of corporations, has fundamentally altered the forms of work, skill, and occupation. The whole notion of tradition and identity of persons with their work has been radically changed.

Scientific and technological innovation is, for the most part, no longer episodic. Technological change has been routinized. Not only has abstract knowledge come to the center of the world's political economy, but there is also a tendency to produce and trade in symbolic significations rather than concrete products. Today, knowledge rather than traditional skill is the main productive force. The revolution has widened the gap between intellectual, technical, and manual labor, between a relatively small number of jobs that, owing to technological complexity, require more knowledge and a much larger number that require less; as the mass of jobs are 'deskilled,' there is a resultant redefinition of occupational categories that reflects the changes in the nature of jobs. As these transformations sweep the world, older conceptions of class, gender, and ethnicity are called into question. For example, on the New York waterfront, until 1970 the nation's largest, Italians and blacks dominated the Brooklyn docks and the Irish and Eastern Europeans worked the Manhattan piers. Today, not only are the docks as sites of shipping vanishing, the workers are gone as well. For those who remain, the traditional occupation of longshoreman—dangerous, but highly skilled—has given way, as a result of containerization of the entire process, to a shrunken workforce that possesses knowledge but not the old skills (De Fazio 1985). . . .

As jobs have changed, so have the significance and duration of joblessness. Partial and permanent unemployment, except during the two great world depressions (1893–1898 and 1929–1939) largely episodic and subject to short-term economic contingencies, has increasingly become a mode of life for larger segments of the populations not only of less industrially developed countries, but for those in 'advanced' industrial societies as well. Many who are classified in official statistics as 'employed' actually work at casual and part-time jobs, the number of which has grown dramatically over the past fifteen years. This phenomenon, once confined to freelance writers and artists, laborers and clerical workers, today cuts across all occupations, including the professions. Even the once buoyant 'new' profession of computer programmer is already showing signs of age after barely a quarter of a century. The shape of things to come as well as those already in existence signals the emerging proletarianization of work at every level below top management and a relatively few scientific and technical occupations.

At the same time, because of the permanent character of job cuts starting in the 1970s and glaringly visible after 1989, the latest recession has finally and irrevocably vitiated the traditional idea that the unemployed are an 'industrial reserve army' awaiting the next phase of economic expansion. Of course, some laid-off workers, especially in union workplaces, will be recalled when the expansion, however sluggish, resumes. Even if one stubbornly clings to the notion of a reserve army, one cannot help but note that its soldiers in the main now occupy the part-time and temporary positions that appear to have replaced the well-paid full-time jobs.

Because of these changes, the 'meaning' (in the survival, psychological, and cultural senses) of work—occupations and professions—as forms of life is in crisis. If the tendencies of the economy and the culture point to the conclusion that work is no longer significant in the formation of the self, one of the crucial questions of our time is what, if anything, can replace it. When layers of qualified—to say nothing of mass—labor are made redundant, obsolete, *irrelevant*, what, after five centuries during which work remained a, perhaps *the*, Western cultural ideal, can we mean by the 'self'? Have we reached a large historical watershed, a climacteric that will be as devastating as natural climacterics of the past that destroyed whole species?

Some of these new epochal issues have been spurred by a massive shift in the character of corporate organization. Beginning in the 1970s much of the vertical structure of the largest corporations began to be dismantled. New kinds of robber barons appeared; among them, Bernard Cornfeld and James Ling were perhaps the most prominent pioneers in the creation of the new horizontal corporate organizational forms we now call conglomerates. Ling's empire, for example, spanned aircraft, steel, and banking. Textron, once a prominent textile producer, completely divested itself of this product as its business expanded to many different sectors. U.S. Steel became so diversified that it replaced *steel* with X in its name shortly after it bought Marathon Oil in 1980. And Jones and Laughlin, a venerable steel firm, became only one entry in Ling's once vast portfolio of unconnected businesses. Every television watcher knows that Pepsi-Cola has gone far beyond producing soft drinks to operating a wide array of retail food services; by the 1980s it owned Pizza Hut and several other major fast-food chains.

New forms of organization such as mergers and acquisitions, which have intensified centralized ownership but also decentralized production and brought on the shedding of whole sections of the largest corporations, have spelled the end of the paternalistic bureaucracy that emerged in many corporations in the wake of industrialization and, especially, the rise of the labor movement in the twentieth century.

Large corporations such as IBM and Kodak, for example, have reversed historic no-layoffs policies that were forged during the wave of 1930s labor organization as a means of keeping the unions out. Equally important, layoffs as a mode of cost cutting have been expanded to include clerical, technical, and managerial employees, categories traditionally considered part of the cadre of the corporate bureaucracies and therefore exempt from employment-threatening market fluctuations. The turnover of ownership and control of even the largest corporations combined with technological changes undermines the very concept of job security. The idea of a lifetime job is in question, even in the once secure bastions of universities and government bureaucracies. Thus, the historic bargain between service workers and their employers, in which employees accepted relatively low wages and salaries in return for security, has, under pressure of dropping profit margins and a new ideology of corporate 'downsizing,' been abrogated.

For the corporate conglomerate, the particular nature and quality of the product no longer matter since the ultimate commodity, the one that subsumes and levels all others, is the designating language, the representing language in the terms of forms of credit. That is to say, along with the technical changes, which are knowledge changes, the changes in representation are not only parallel, but in conflict. Knowledge itself, once firmly tied to specific labor processes such as steelmaking, now becomes a relatively free-floating commodity to the extent that it is transformed into information that requires no productive object. This is the real significance of the passage from industry-specific labor processes to computer-mediated work as a new universal technology.

Science and technology (of which organization is an instance) alter the nature of the labour process, not only the rationalized manual labor but also intellectual labor, especially the professions. Knowledge becomes ineluctably intertwined with, even dependent on, technology, and even so-called labor-intensive work becomes increasingly mechanized and begins to be replaced by capital- and technology-intensive—*capitech-intensive*—work. Today, the regime of world economic life consists in scratching every itch of everyday life with sci-tech: eye glasses, underarm deodorant, preservatives in food, braces on pets. Technology has become the universal problem solver, the postmodern equivalent of deus ex machina, the ineluctable component of education and play as much as of work. No level of schooling is spared: students interact with computers to learn reading, writing, social studies, math, and science in elementary school through graduate school. Play, once and still the corner of the social world least subject to regimentation, is increasingly incorporated into computer software, especially the products of the Apple corporation. More and more, we, the service and professional classes, are chained to our personal computers; with the help of the modem and the fax we can communicate, in seconds, to the farthest reaches of the globe. We no longer need to press the flesh: by E-mail, we can attend conferences, gain access to library collections, and write electronic letters to perfect strangers. And, of course, with the assistance of virtual reality, we can engage in electronic sex. The only thing the computer cannot deliver is touch, but who needs it, anyway?[3]

Each intrusion of capitech-intensiveness increases the price of the product, not makes it cheaper, because the investment in machines has to be paid off. For example, getting on E-mail is not free; in 1993 dollars it costs about ten dollars a month for the basic service. Joining a conference or forum network might cost an additional ten or fifteen dollars, and each minute on the E-mail line carries an additional charge, although it is not as high as the charge for traditional voice-based telecommunications. Like the 900 number used to get vicarious sexual experience or esoteric information, computer-driven information is not free. Of course, as scientific, technical, academic, and other professionals feel that they 'need' access to information that, increasingly, is available only through electronic venues, the cost of being a professional rises, but the privileges are also more pronounced.

The new electronic communication technologies have become the stock-in-trade of a relatively few people because newspapers, magazines, and television have simply refused to acknowledge that we live in a complex world. Instead, they have tended to *simplify* news, even for the middle class. Thus, an 'unintended' consequence of the dissemination of informatics to personal use is a growing information gap already implied by the personal computer. A relatively small number of people—no more than ten million in the United States—will, before the turn of the century, be fully wired to world sources of information and new knowledge: libraries, electronic newspapers and journals, conferences and forums on specialized topics, colleagues, irrespective of country or region around the globe. Despite the much-heralded electronic highway, which will be largely devoted to entertainment products, the great mass of the world's population, already restricted in its knowledge and power by the hierarchical division of the print media into tabloids and newspapers of record, will henceforth be doubly disadvantaged.

Of course, the information gap makes a difference only if one considers the conditions for a democratic, that is, a participatory, society. If popular governance even in the most liberal-democratic societies has been reduced in the last several decades to *plebiscitary* participation, the potential effect of computer-mediated knowledge is to exacerbate exclusion of vast portions of the underlying populations of all countries.

The problem is not, as many have claimed, that the US economy has gone global. Not only has *every* economy become global, but in fact economies have been 'global' for centuries.[4] International trade and investment were part of the impetus that brought Columbus to these shores more than five hundred years ago. The movement of both capital and labor across geographic expanses has been, since 1492, a hallmark of US, Caribbean, and Canadian economic development. From its days as a series of English, French, and Spanish colonies, the geographic expanse that, eventually, became the United States and later Canada was, because of fertile agricultural and horticultural production, a valuable source of food, raw materials, and tobacco for Europe. Only after 1850, more than three centuries after Columbus, did the US economy enter the industrial era, the major products of which—textiles, iron, steel, and later machine tools, for example—were closely intertwined with the European economy.

In fact, the era of US international economic dominance began, at the beginning of the twentieth century, with its leadership in the development of industrial uses for electricity, oil, and chemicals. The application of electricity to machinery and chemical manufacturing eliminated vast quantities of industrial labor and accelerated the process whereby science, rather than craft, drove the production process. The primacy of knowledge is reflected as well in the rationalization, by assembly-line methods, of automobile production even though, at least until the late 1970s, this type of mass production required vast quantities of semiskilled labor. Needless to say, under pressure from growing international competition, the introduction of computer-mediated robotics and numerical controls has, since the late 1970s, enabled auto corporations to substantially reduce their labor forces and impose other efficiencies in production.

In retrospect we can see how temporary US domination of world industrial markets really was. Despite truly remarkable industrial development, agricultural products are still the most important US export commodities today. In the wake of the rise of Middle Eastern, Soviet, and Latin American oil production in the interwar period, the rapid recovery of European industrial capacity by the 1960s, especially in conventional mechanized industries such as autos and steel, and the truly dramatic development of Japanese export industries in consumer durable goods such as cars, electronics, and computer hardware as well as basic commodities, the US economy had little else besides agriculture and its substantial lead in the development of informatics to commend it to foreign markets. Only France and Canada were able to offer significant farm competition, and Japan was the only significant competitor in computer hardware, though the explosion of the personal-computer market was initiated by IBM. The major industrial commodities in which the United States still enjoys an uncomfortable lead are computer chips and software. Japanese-made IBM clones have outdistanced the parent in the production and sales of personal computers. And it has taken the alliance of Intel, the world's premier chip pro-

ducer, and Microsoft, whose lead in software is quite wide, to fend off Japanese and European competition.

What is new is that after a century of expansion and then world economic, political, and military dominance after World War II, the US lead remains only in these sectors—and in military production. The United States is now the only military superpower. Still a formidable economic and political force, the United States nevertheless no longer commands, in terms of either production or, increasingly, consumption, anything like its former authority. Moreover, the United States has lost its great historical leadership and ability to mobilize science in the service of technological change. Today, not only Japan, Korea, and Germany but also China and India are producing engineers and scientists who compare favorably with those employed in the West.[5] Consequently, US companies engaged in the production of high technologies such as robotics, lasers, and other computer-mediated industries are either relocating in these regions—not for their cheap manual labor, but for their cheap technically and scientifically trained labor—or are in fact communicating with this labor.

New uses of knowledge widen the gap between the present and the future; new knowledges challenge not only our collectively held beliefs but also the common ethical ground of our 'civilization.' The tendency of science to dominate the labor process, which emerged in the last half of the nineteenth century but attained full flower only in the last two decades, now heralds an entirely new regime of work in which almost no production *skills* are required. Older forms of technical or professional knowledge are transformed, incorporated, superseded, or otherwise eliminated by computer-mediated technologies—by applications of physical sciences intertwined with the production of knowledge: expert systems—leaving new forms of knowledge that are *inherently* labor-saving. But, unlike the mechanizing era of pulleys and electrically powered machinery, which retained the 'hands-on' character of labor, computers have transferred most knowledge associated with the crafts and manual labor and, increasingly, intellectual knowledge, to the machine. As a result, while each generation of technological change makes some work more complex and interesting and raises the level of training or qualification required by a (diminishing) fraction of intellectual and manual labor, for the overwhelming majority of workers, this process simplifies tasks or eliminates them, and thus eliminates the worker.

The specific character of computer-aided technologies is that they no longer discriminate between most categories of intellectual and manual labor. With the introduction of computer-aided software programming (CASP), the work of perhaps the most glamorous of the technical professions associated with computer technology—programming— is irreversibly threatened. Although the 'real' job of creating new and basic approaches will go on, the ordinary occupation of computer programmer may disappear just like that of the drafter, whose tasks were incorporated by computer-aided design and drafting by the late 1980s. CASP is an example of a highly complex program whose development requires considerable knowledge, but when development costs have been paid and the price substantially reduced, much low-level, routine programming will be relegated to historical memory.

The universal use of computers has increased exponentially the 'multiplied productive powers' of labor (Marx 1973). In this regime of production, the principal effect of technological change—labor displacement— is largely unmitigated by economic growth. That is, it is possible for key economic indicators to show, but only for a short time, a net increase in domestic product without significant growth of full-time employment. On the other hand, growth itself is blocked by two effects of the new look to working in America. Labor redundancy, which is the main object of technological change, is, indirectly, an obstacle to growth. In the wake of the shrinking social wage, joblessness, the growth of part-time employment, and the displacement of good full-time jobs by mediocre badly paid part-time jobs tend to thwart the ability of the economic system to avoid chronic overproduction and underconsumption.

The Global Metastate

Thus, for many employers the precondition of weathering the new international economic environment of sharpened competition is to ruthlessly cut labor costs in order to reverse the free fall of profits. The drop of profits over the past five years may be ascribed to a number of factors including declining sales; increased costs of nearly all sorts, but especially of borrowing; and the high price of expensive technologies used to displace even more expensive labor. But many corporations experience profit loss in terms of falling prices, a telltale sign of *overproduction* in relation to consumption. Along with labor-displacing technological change aimed at reducing the size of the labor force, wages must be reduced and benefits cut or eliminated, especially those that accrue on the basis of length of employment. And, wherever possible, employers are impelled to export production to areas that offer cheap labor and, like Mexico, free plants, water, and virtually no taxes. These measures produce chronic overproduction of many commodities that formed the foundation of postwar domestic growth: cars, houses, and appliances. Consistent cost cutting leads to a domestic labor force that suffers short-term—that is, security-free—jobs. This situation is exacerbated by the accelerated globalization of production and the current international recession, so that raising the level of exports as a means to overcome the structural crisis within the national economy is much more difficult to achieve even as it plays a greater role in foreign policy. In fact, the very notion of 'exports,' just like the notion of a purely national working class in a global economy, is problematic if not already anomalous.

Here, from the economic perspective, we can observe the effective breakdown of the purely 'national' state and the formation of what might be called the 'metastate,' in which the intersection of the largest transnational corporations and the international political directorates of many nations constitute a new governing class. Institutional forms of rule— multi-lateral trade organizations such as the General Agreement on Tariffs and Trade (GATT) and the North American Free Trade Agreement; proliferating international conferences on terrorism, technological change, and new forms of international economic arrangements in which business leaders, diplomats, academics, and other 'experts' regularly consult; and increasingly frequent summits among government leaders of the key national states, usually flanked by trade representatives recruited from the international business establishment—are taking over.

Until recently, from the perspective of these metastates, to the extent that currency regulation remained a national affair, national states were important as the major means for valorization of capital. Labor was regulated within the framework of national law, and police forces and armies were raised in this way. Of course, the nation, with or without the state, remained the context within which culture and ideology are produced, itself an aspect of control, at least from the perspective of international business. Although these functions are still partially served by national states, we may discern, in the various forms of spurious capital formation made possible by informatics, a definite decline in the valorization functions of national treasuries; the emergence of a de facto international currency undermines the power of the dollar, the yen, and the mark as universal media of exchange. Further, international capital has forced many states to relax enforcement of protective labor codes if not the law itself, leaving employers freer to pay lower wages, export jobs, and import (undocumented) labor. The very idea of national 'border' in all except its most blatant geographic connotation is becoming more dubious as labor flow becomes heavier between formally sovereign states. Finally, while elements of national culture remain, the past quarter century is definitively the era of media and cultural internationalization, precisely because of available technologies as well as the proliferation of transnational production and distribution companies for (primarily) U.S. cultural products. The international culture industry has destroyed all but a few national film industries (in Europe, in France and Germany but not in Britain and Italy; in Asia, in India; and in Latin America, Argentina's is dead, Mexico's weak, and Brazil's almost nonexistent). American television syndication has reached deeply into the world market, and only Great Britain and, to a lesser degree, France have achieved transnational dissemination in Western countries.

The pressure on profits and the imperative to subsume labor under the new global arrangements is the 'rational' basis for the decimation of the industrial heartlands—of the United States as well as European countries such as France and Great Britain—manifested in plant closings, drastic workforce reductions, and the definitive end of the social compact that marked the relationship between a significant portion of industrial labor and corporations since the New Deal and the postwar European compromise between capital and labor. Ronald Reagan's dramatic and highly symbolic firing of 11,000 air traffic controllers in 1981 may be remembered as the definitive act that closed the book on the historic compromise between a relatively powerful, if conservative, labor movement and capital. As the American unions whimpered but offered little concrete resistance, employers' groups quickly perceived that it was possible to undertake a major frontal assault on labor's crucial practice, collective bargaining. The ensuing decade witnessed rapid deterioration in union power and *therefore* a decline in real wages (what income can actually buy) for a majority of workers. Millions of women entered the wage-labor force in part to mitigate the effects of a fairly concerted employer/conservative campaign to weaken unions and to reduce wages and salaries beginning in the 1970s.[6]

In the 1980s, the two-paycheck family became a commonplace. Of course, the entrance of large numbers of women into the wage-labor force was also a sign of their growing refusal to accept subordination within the male-dominated family. At the same time, as the computerization of the labor process accelerated, millions of well-paid industrial jobs were eliminated by technological change and others migrated to the global South, both within the United States and in other parts of the world. . . .

Things Fall Apart

After two decades of dramatic economic growth, Western Europe began to experience the scourge of stagnation. By the late 1960s Great Britain was, measured by the criterion of growth, already in a long-term decline, and Germany and France were not far behind. By the early 1970s it was generally acknowledged that Europe was in the throes of a recession, the most distressing manifestation of which was the nearly permanent two-digit unemployment rates. From the middle of the 1970s to the present, no major European country has succeeded in reducing its joblessness much below 10 per cent; frequently, Europe has suffered 15 per cent rates. But there were other economic disasters in this decade as well. From 1973 to 1977, the world was beset with an oil crisis, reflecting chronic overproduction and falling prices but also the effort by the leading oil-producing nations of the Third World to limit production in order to rescue profits. The instability of the Middle East, reflected in the breakup of the Metternichian deal between Israel, the Arab world, and the great powers, intensified the crisis. Arab sheiks took their oil to Western banks. The giant banks were, at the same time, beginning the process of reorganizing international money exchanges to reflect the increasing internationalization of capital. In these new arrangements, the leading oil companies were quick to see their advantage: they boosted prices and became the behind-the-scenes partners of the Organization of Petroleum Exporting Countries (OPEC).

Buoyed by high levels of military spending both during and following the Vietnam War as well as world leadership in agricultural production, the United States, despite oil-soaked surging inflation, managed, for a decade after Europe's relative bust, to avoid the outward appearances of stagnation and the concomitant high unemployment rates. But in 1980 it was apparent that the United States was ready to fall into line. During the 1981–83 recession, American workers suffered the highest official jobless rates since the Great Depression, nearly 12 per cent. At the same time, millions of workers were on short weeks or could secure only part-time employment.

Even after the recession ended, owing in large measure to the rapid growth of debt and the expansion of financial and other service industries, many remained out of work or found that part-time labor had become a permanent fact of life. When the official unemployment rate dipped to slightly more than 5 per cent between 1985 and 1988, the extent of actual underemployment was disguised by the growth of part-time work and the sharp decline of real wages in many sectors. The erosion of living standards corresponded to the relative decline of unions during the 1970s and especially the 1980s, precipitous capital flight that rendered much of the industrial

heartland and the Northeast economically prostrate.

The already familiar tales of plant shutdowns in industrial towns and cities was ascribed, at first, by employers and conservative economists for whom blaming the victim is always a ready explanation to noncompetitive high union wages and benefits, and then to the lack of worker productivity. What caused lagging productivity? Were American workers lazy during the booming 1950s and 1960s? How was it that the United States and Britain, during the postwar era the leading developers of computer-mediated technologies—robotics, numerical controls, and lasers—fell behind Europe and Japan?

At the same time, the major developers of the new computer technologies, the United States and Britain, were using computers extensively in military production, introduced them in the clerical workplace, and, especially in the United States, developed a consumer computer market or were exporting software as well as hardware to other countries. Europe was a wonderful market for US and British technological innovation. The effects of the destruction visited upon major European industries by Allied bombings were nothing short of devastating. But with the help of the U.S.-sponsored Marshall Plan and the cooperation of European unions and socialist parties (including the communists) to moderate wage demands, European economies were rebuilt at a time when automation and cybernation, especially computer-mediated technologies, could be applied to production industries. In the late 1950s and 1960s, numerical controls, robotization, and lasers were widely introduced into key industries such as steel and autos in West Germany, Italy, and Japan at a time when US civilian industries were mired in the old mechanical technologies or had barely introduced the transfer machine, the basic technology of automation.

The major employers in the U.S. steel, auto parts, and machine tool industries, among others, did not introduce these technologies until the late 1970s. The largesse of the federal government's defense establishment provided few if any incentives to productive civilian investment; during the war boom of the 1960s even civilian products benefited from this bounty. When the boom was over and some investment in basic technologies finally occurred, the era of global competition had arrived in the late 1970s; US industry was no longer a net exporter of steel and cars, but had become a net importer of these crucial commodities. Consequently, by the early 1980s, it was almost too late to save older plants and smaller companies. Of course, the companies and the plants that remained were, given the globalization of the US economy, obliged to undertake serious modernization, especially to introduce computer mediation into almost every aspect of life, it seemed. Combined with world economic stagnation and a veritable epidemic of mergers and acquisitions, computerization meant that millions of workers were permanently displaced from industrial production. For example, employment in the steel industry declined from 600,000 production and maintenance workers in 1960 to fewer than 200,000 by 1992; most of the reduction occurred in the 1980s. Auto jobs were slashed by half, and machine tools and electrical machinery have lost some 40 per cent of their workforces. At the same time, with the exception of autos, industrial production has, despite accelerating imports, maintained and in some sectors increased its levels.

Of course, the introduction of computer-mediated technologies in administrative services—especially banks and insurance companies and retail and wholesale trades—preceded that in goods production. From the early days of office computers in the 1950s, there has been a sometimes acrimonious debate about their effects. Perhaps the Spencer Tracy–Katharine Hepburn comedy *Desk Set* best exemplifies the issues: when a mainframe computer is introduced into the library of a large corporation, its professional and technical staff is at first alarmed, precisely because of their fear of losing their jobs. The film reiterates the prevailing view of the period (and ours?) that, far from posing a threat, computers promise to increase work by expanding needs. Significantly, the film asserts that the nearly inexhaustible desire for information inherent in human affairs will provide a fail-safe against professional and clerical redundancy. In contradistinction to these optimistic prognostications, new information technologies have enabled corporations, large law firms, and local governments to reduce the library labor force, including professional librarians. In turn, several library

science schools have closed, including the prestigious library school at Columbia University.

By the 1980s many if not most large and small businesses used electronic telephone devices to replace the live receptionist. A concomitant of these changes has been the virtual extinction of the secretary as an occupational category for all except top executives and department heads, if by that term we mean the individual service provided by a clerical worker to a single manager or a small group of managers. Today, at the levels of line and middle management, the 'secretary' is a word-processing clerk; many middle managers have their own answering machines or voice mail and do their own word processing. They may have access to a word-processing pool only for producing extensive reports. Needless to say, after a quarter of a century during which computers displaced nearly all major office machines—especially typewriters, adding machines, and mechanical calculators—and all but eliminated the job category of file clerk, by the 1980s many major corporations took advantage of the information 'revolution' to decentralize their facilities away from cities to suburbs and exurbs. Once concentrated in large urban areas, date processing now can be done not only in small rural communities but also in satellite- and wire-linked, underdeveloped offshore sites. This has revived the once scorned practice of working at home. Taken together, new forms of corporate organization, aided by the computer, have successfully arrested and finally reversed the steady expansion of the clerical labor force and have transferred many of its functions from the office to the bedroom.

Visiting a retail food supermarket in 1992, President George Bush was surprised to learn that the inventory label on each item enabled the checkout clerk to record the price by passing it through an electronic device, a feature of retailing that has been in place for at least fifteen years. This innovation has speeded the checkout process but has also relieved the clerk of punching the price on the register, which, in turn, saves time by adding the total bill automatically. The clerk in retail food and department stores works at a checkout counter and has been reduced to handling the product and observing the process, but intervenes only when it fails to function properly. Supermarket employers require fewer employees and, perhaps equally important, fewer workers in warehouses: an operator sits at a computer and identifies the quantity and location of a particular item rather than having to search for its location and count the numbers visually. The goods are loaded onto a vehicle by remote control and a driver operating a forklift takes them to the trucking dock, where they are mechanically loaded again. Whereas once the warehouse worker required a strong back, most of these functions are now performed mechanically and electronically.

Some of the contraction of clerical and industrial employment is of course a result of the general economic decline since the late 1980s. But given the astounding improvements in productivity of the manual industrial and clerical work force attributable to computerization, as we argued earlier, there is no evidence that a general economic recovery would restore most of the lost jobs in office and production sites—which raises the crucial issue of the relationship between measures designed to promote economic growth and job creation in the era of computer-mediated work. Many economists, most notably Robert Solow, who won a Nobel Prize for his views, have argued that technological innovation is the key to economic growth because of its relevance to productivity gains that enable employers to reduce costs and prices and thereby increase profits and expand markets. In the standard measure, growth is defined as an increment in the value of goods and services, in real terms, within a given time frame. The prevailing assumption is that for every unit of investment, particularly in capital goods (machines and raw materials), a multiplier effect produces a concomitant increase in employment for those who operate the machinery, those who produce, distribute, and sell the machines and raw materials, and those who produce, distribute, and sell the product made by the labor that operates the machine.

If the rate of economic growth lags behind the productivity increases, however, technological investment will displace more workers than the jobs produced by its application. For, from the individual employer's perspective, the real purpose of technological innovation is labor displacement as a vital component of reducing costs. This is precisely what occurred in the late 1980s. While the absolute number of jobs appeared to rise, most of the increases were in the service sector, and many of them were offered on a part-time basis. As the steel, auto, steel fabricating, clothing, and machinery industries introduced robots, lasers, and numerical controls on a wide scale, their workforces continued to shrink even as production remained at previous levels or, as in the case of steel, increased.

The corporate, neoliberal program to persuade displaced blue- and white-collar workers to adapt to the post-Fordist regime, which, among other things, proposed to disrupt the social compact, met with considerable success during the Reagan years. Surely, some workers were not resigned to capital flight, union busting, and other signs of the disappearing compact. But many others made a surprisingly rapid adjustment to the new situation, owing in part to the debt-induced boom that masked the decline of real wages and the partial breakup of the old wage-labor system. Consumerism generated a vast expansion of service jobs, especially in finance and retailing. As millions of women entered the labor force to occupy these niches during the 1980s, family income actually rose and many households increased their consumption of homes, cars, and appliances as well as health and education services even as well-paid factory jobs were disappearing forever. The two-paycheck family, for a time, sustained the vitality of the cultural ideal.

But all is not well in the post-Fordist era. The end of the Reagan boom has produced considerable political and economic instability. In 1992 the twelve-year right-wing hold on the White House was broken, even as the new administration indicated that it would retain many of the Reagan-Bush economic policies. At the same time, the Democrats rode to power not on stasis but on the theme of change, which policy parlance translates into the promise to produce more jobs. Needless to say, there is no substantial economic turnaround, nor have the feeble signs of slow recovery in some sectors produced more jobs. In fact, any hope of a substantial recovery may, for this reason, be thwarted. For it is not difficult to understand why investments may rise without job creation if the existing labor force works harder and labor-saving equipment continues to take its toll.

The American cultural ideal is tied not only to consumer society but also to the expectation that, given average abilities, with hard work and a little luck almost anyone can achieve occupational and even social mobility. Professional, technical, and managerial occupations perhaps even more than the older aspiration of entrepreneurial success are identified with faith in American success, and the credentials acquired through postsecondary education have become cultural capital, the necessary precondition of mobility. Put another way, if scientifically based technical knowledge has become the main productive force, schooling becomes the major route to mobility. No longer just places where traditional culture is disseminated to a relatively small elite, universities and colleges have become the key repositories of the cultural and intellectual capital from which professional, technical, and managerial labor is formed.

For the first quarter century after World War II, the expansion of these categories in the labor force was sufficient to absorb almost all of those trained in the professional and technical occupations. In some cases, notably education, the health professions, and engineering, there were chronic shortages of qualified professionals and managers. Now there is growing evidence of permanent redundancy within the new middle class . . . whole professional occupations are in the process of changing: some are disappearing, and others are being massively restructured. . . . In some instances, knowledge inextricably intertwined with traditional professional practice is being transferred to the computer. In others, the organization of the workplace renders obsolete previously acquired cultural capital. In still others, 'science' has been definitively transformed into *technoscience*: the work cannot be separated from its mechanical aspects, which, in the light of the drift of the field, seem to dominate all so-called intellectual problems.

While it is important to examine these changes and their implications for what it means to be a 'professional' or an 'intellectual' today and tomorrow, we need to go beyond description to draw the consequences of these changes for economic, political, and cultural life. For if becoming a professional or a manager has become one of the central elements of the cultural ideal of advanced industrial societies, for millions of working people and their children the earthquake has already occurred and we are living its aftershocks.

In the two decades beginning in the mid-1960s the United States experienced the largest-scale restructuring and reforming of its industrial base in more than a century. Capital flight, which extended beyond U.S. borders, was abetted by technological change in administration and in production. Millions of workers, clerical and industrial, lost their high-paying jobs and were able to find employment only at lower wages. Well-paid union jobs became more scarce, and many, especially women, could find only part-time employment. But the American cultural ideal, buttressed by ideological—indeed, sometimes mythic—journalism and social theory, was barely affected in the wake of the elimination of millions of blue- and white-collar jobs. As C. Wright Mills once remarked in another context, these public issues were experienced as private troubles.

The persistence, if not so much the real and exponential growth, of poverty amid plenty was publicly acknowledged, even by mainstream politicians, but, like alienated labor, it was bracketed as a discrete 'racial problem' that left the mainstream white population unaffected. Job creation precluded serious consideration of the old Keynesian solutions; these had been massively defeated by the state-backed, yet ideologically antistatist, free-market ideologies. We were told that deregulation would free up the market and ensure economic growth that eventually would employ the jobless, provided they cleaned up their act. Even in the halcyon days of the Great Society programs of the war-inflated Johnson years, the antipoverty crusade offered the long-term unemployed only literacy and job training and, occasionally, the chance to finish high school and enter college or technical school. The Great Society created few permanent jobs and relied on the vitality of the private sector to employ those trained by its programs.

The concept of government as the employer of last resort was at best sporadically implemented. Even most social welfare liberals refused to acknowledge that the 'failure' of the poor to find jobs was not, in the main, a function of their personal deficits but was instead a symptom of a much broader failure of the labor market.

Talcott Parsons grounded his theory of social equilibrium on the nearly certain capacity of the cultural system to socialize the underlying population into the norms necessary to reach social balance (Parsons 1951). In Parsons's tripartite social system, the personality system, based on the structural conflict between the superego (society) and the id to capture the ego, constituted a source of instability while, on the other side, the cultural system was the social order's reliable ally. Of course, ego psychology and sociological theory sought to explain through concepts of cultural continuity how the system can maintain itself, the world-historical shocks that have characterized the twentieth century notwithstanding. For some, culture remains constant regulation, despite the end of increasingly high levels of military spending and the fierce investment program of many corporations and government agencies in labor-saving technologies. Placed next to the longer-term phenomenon of the globalization of national economies, including the emergence of a truly international production line, labor force, and scientific and technological apparatus, poverty as a public issue has been replaced by symptoms of a catastrophic future for the middle class as well as the working class in nearly all countries of late capitalism. While the economic consequences of this sea change are profound, we want to explore the political and cultural consequences as well.

In the United States, long before the current *perceived* cultural crisis, these traditions have been undermined by the process of citizenship eduction—'Americanization' or assimilation, which, in the large waves of immigration at the beginning of the twentieth century demanded the replacement of Old World culture by that of the New World. Among the leading elements of the New World cultural system were consumer society and its technological basis, electronically mediated mass communication; the emphasis on productivity, which until recently privileged quantitatively measured production over quality; and the militant assertion of American nationality as an official state culture, an identity that implies, in the hegemonic political discourse, shedding the habits of mind and body that were identified with European and subaltern cultures, and the values associated with them. This forced shedding of the older cultures has been 'exported' on a global level and becomes—the decline of the United States notwithstanding—a universal Americanization on more affluent levels while the lower and impoverished levels fragment in a frenzy of cultural and ethnic warfare.

One of the crucial features of the specifically 'American' cultural ideal is the idea that we can reinvent ourselves. From the time most immigrants arrive at an entry point and experience an instant name change because some official finds it impossible to pronounce an eastern or southern European, Asian, or Spanish surname, to school and work, when we discover our own *difference* from the model of a typical American, despite the ideology of 'family' values that represents an invocation by officially moral authorities to adhere to the cultural system, we are invited to make a personal break from family and ethnic traditions lest we lose a chance to advance in the social and occupational structure.

Paul Willis has shown how British working-class kids remained loyal to their parents' class identity, at least in the 1970s (Willis 1981). Until recently, the idea of leaving your class behind was, in many quarters, viewed with suspicion if not downright hostility. Among some immigrant groups, in both Great Britain and the United States, becoming a professional brings with it similar stigmatization; it is a betrayal to leave the family and the neighborhood. These subcultural rules are frequently broken, especially in the wake of the disappearance of good working-class jobs. Yet beyond the circumstances of economic necessity lies the frailty of working-class traditions in the United States, precisely because of the immigrant—ethnic and racial—composition of the industrial working class.

The question now is not only what the consequences of the closing of routes to mobility of a substantial fraction of sons and daughters of manual and clerical workers may be, but also whether the professional and technical middle class can expect to reproduce itself at the same economic and social level under the new, deregulated conditions. For the older and most prestigious professions of medicine, university teaching, law, and engineering are in trouble: doctors and lawyers and engineers are becoming like assembly-line clerks ... proletarians. Although thus far there are only scattered instances of long-term unemployment among them, the historical expectation, especially among doctors and lawyers, that they will own their own practices, has for most of them been permanently shattered. More than half of each profession (and a substantially larger proportion of recent graduates) have become salaried employees of larger firms, hospitals, or group practices; with the subsumption of science and technology under large corporations and the state, engineers have not, typically, been self-employed for over a century.

Similarly, the attainment of a Ph.D. in the humanities or the social or natural sciences no longer ensures an entry-level academic position or a well-paid research or administrative job. Over the past fifteen years a fairly substantial number of Ph.D.s have entered the academic proletariat of part-time and adjunct faculty. Most full-time teachers have little time and energy for the research they were trained to perform. Of course, the reversal of fortune for American colleges and universities is overdetermined by the stagnation and, in some sectors, decline of some professions; by the long-term recession; by organizational and technological changes; and by twenty years of conservative hegemony, which often takes the cultural form of anti-intellectualism. Since the 1960s, universities have been sites of intellectual as well as political dissent and even opposition. A powerful element in the long-term budget crises many private as well as public institutions have suffered is at least partially linked to the perception among executive authorities that good money should not be thrown after bad.

And, with the steep decline in subprofessional and technical jobs, universities and colleges, especially the two-year community colleges, are reexamining their 'mission' to educate virtually all who seek postsecondary education. In the past five years, we have seen the reemergence of the discourse of faculty 'productivity,' the reimposition of academic 'standards,' and other indicators that powerful forces are arrayed to impose policies of contraction in public education. . . .

In the subprofessions of elementary and secondary school teaching, social work, nursing, and medical technology, to name only the most numerically important, salaries and working conditions have deteriorated over the past decade so that the distinction, both economically and at the work-place, between the living standards of skilled manual workers and these professionals has sharply narrowed. Increasingly, many in these categories have changed their psychological as well as political relationship to the performance of the job. The work of a classroom teacher, line social worker, or nurse is, despite efforts by unions and professional organizations to shore up their professional status, no longer seen as a 'vocation' in the older meaning of the term. Put succinctly, many in these occupations regard their work as does any manual worker: they take the money and run. More and more, practicing professionals look toward management positions to obtain work satisfaction as well as improvements in their living standard since staying 'in the trenches' is socially unappreciated and financially appears to be a dead end. Consequently, in addition to a mad race to obtain more credentials in order to qualify for higher positions, we have seen a definite growth in union organization among these groups even as union membership in the private sector, especially as a proportion of the manual labor force, has sharply declined. . . .

The economic and technological revolutions of our time notwithstanding, work is of course not disappearing. Nor should it. Rebuilding the cities, providing adequate education and child care, and saving the environment are all labor-intensive activities. The unpaid labor of housekeeping and child rearing remain among the major social scandals of our culture. The question is whether work as a cultural ideal has not already been displaced by its correlates: status and consumption. Except for a small proportion of those who are affected by technological innovation—those responsible for the innovations, those involved in developing their applications, and those who run the factories and offices—most workers, including professionals, are subjugated by labor-saving, work simplification, and other rationalizing features of the context within which technology is introduced. For the subjugated, paid work has already lost its intrinsic meaning. It has become, at best, a means of making a living and a site of social conviviality.

. . . But despite the displacements of consumer society and the nebulous notions surrounding 'community,' work remains the fulcrum of our cultural aspirations—among them the values of success, well-being, self-worth—the gulf separating actual from ideal form constitutes the source of both catastrophe and the challenge to received wisdom.

206 The New Knowledge Work

Notes

1. The concept of human capital in its classic enunciation is in Becker, G. (1964), *Human Capital: A Theoretical and Empirical Analysis with Special Reference to Education* (New York: Columbia University Press). Building on the work of T. W. Schultz, Becker argues that the growth of physical capital (machinery, buildings, and so forth) accounts for 'a relatively small part of the growth of income' when compared to 'education and skills.' Hence his argument that education, which, presumably, upgrades skills and knowledge, is crucial for growth policies.
2. The words used by the secretary of labor after the Bureau of Labor Statistics reported an increase of 365,000 jobs in February 1993 (*New York Times*, 24 March 1993).
3. Dick, P. K. (1978), *The Three Stigmata of Palmer Eldritch* (London: Jonathan Cape and Granada Books). First published in 1964, Dick's novel foreshadows the development of virtual reality technology, linking it to a future when most people can no longer live on Earth but are afforded the means to simulate a life on this planet from a position somewhere in the galaxy.
4. Wallerstein, I. (1974), *The Modern World System* (New York: Academic Press). Building on the work of 'dependency' theorists such as Giovanni Arrighi, Cardozo and Faetto, Andre Gunder Frank, and, especially, the Annales school of French historiography (Braudel, Lucien Febvre), Wallerstein demonstrates that, since the sixteenth century, capitalism has been a global system, albeit one of unequal exchange.
5. In 1992, Indian engineers and computer scientists emerged as world-class players in high-tech design. American and European corporations began letting contracts to Bombay- and Delhi-based software firms.
6. In the United States, nearly 70 per cent of women had entered the labor force by 1990. In recent years, many have been able to obtain only part-time jobs.

References

De Fazio, W. (1985), *Longshoremen: Community and Resistance on the Brooklyn Waterfront* (South Hadley, Mass.: Bergin and Garvey).

Lohn, S. (1993), 'Top IBM Issue: How, Not Who', *The New York Times* (25 March).

Marx, K. (1973), *Grundrisse* (New York: Vintage), 701–5.

Parsons, T. (1951), *The Social System* (Glencoe, Ill.: Free Press).

Willis, P. (1981), *Learning to Labor* (New York: Columbia Univ. Press).

12

Education, Skill Formation, and Economic Development: The Singaporean Approach

David N. Ashton and Johnny Sung

Introduction

The aim of this paper is to show how the Asian Tigers are forging newer, closer links between education, training, and economic growth. It is argued that in the older Western countries, especially the UK and USA, the relationship between education and economic growth is very weak as the educational system developed with a high degree of independence from the requirements of the economy. Among the Asian Tigers the relationship between education and economic growth has been much stronger, with the educational system and its output exhibiting a very strong and much closer linkage to the requirements of the economy.

Education and Industrial Development: The British Approach

In Britain, the educational system was only established after the economy had reached industrial maturity. Indeed, it was not until the 1870s that Britain introduced a national system of elementary education. Green (1995) argues that we can explain the development of national education systems by reference to the process of state formation. Where the process of state formation took place rapidly and over a relatively short space of time (as in France and Prussia after the French Revolution), the national education system also developed rapidly. Where the process of state formation was more protracted or delayed, the pressure for the development of a national educational system was less intense. Green (1995) and Castells (1992) have both noted that the con-

ditions which give rise to this acceleration in the process of state formation are crises of state viability. Political conflict between nations forces a state's leaders to concentrate on political and economic reform and to encourage strong feelings of national identity among its citizens. In Britain the state had already established a dominant position in world affairs by the nineteenth century and before the development of modern industry, so the pressures from outside which had such a strong effect in accelerating the process of state formation in France and Prussia were absent. The state had little need to develop an educational system to foster a sense of national identity (Green 1990).

The absence of external pressure on the British state was complemented by the absence of any substantial internal demands from employers, at least in the early part of the nineteenth century. Industry had developed in the late eighteenth century on the basis of new forms of manufacture which harnessed water- and, later, steam-power to human labour. However, for significant parts of British industry the new system of manufacture (e.g. cotton, footwear, and clothing) utilized a large proportion of unskilled labour in the form of females and children. In sectors such as engineering, more highly skilled labour was provided by remnants of the medieval apprenticeship system. The new industrial forms of production which were developed in the UK, the first industrial nation, required little in the way of educated labour, at least in the early phases. These new industrial forms of production were able to provide the UK with a significant competitive advantage in foreign markets, even relying, as

Table 12.1. The relationship between education and industrial development in the UK

	Education	Industry
1980s	Expansion of higher education, upgrading of technical skills	Information technology, financial service
1940s	Secondary education	
1900		Chemicals, electrical engineering
1870s	National system	
1850		Industrial maturity
1780		Cotton, textiles

they did for the most part, on unskilled, illiterate labour. The skilled labour that was required could be met by the old apprenticeship system. The resulting relationship between the development of the education system and the productive system is illustrated in Table 12.1, whose aim is to show how the main phases in the development of the education system and the productive system were only loosely related (Ashton and Green 1996).

Having established an effective system of industrial production based largely on unskilled labour, there was little pressure to introduce a national system of education. When the government did introduce such a system after the economy had reached industrial maturity, its primary function was not to provide for the needs of industry, which were already being catered for, but to ensure moral control to socialize the new industrial working class in the virtues of discipline and obedience. It was not until the late nineteenth and early twentieth century, when such new industries as chemicals and electrical engineering created a demand for scientific and technical skills, that industrial development made demands on the system for educated labour. By then the educational system had been moulded in a very different form, one which was geared to producing educated gentlemen for the professions and positions of leadership in the state and empire, while at the lower levels the primary concern was to control the new industrial working class. The result was that education for industry had to be grafted onto a system designed for other purposes. Scientific knowledge was provided

through new universities, but technical education failed to obtain a firm foothold in the school system (Sanderson 1994), being provided on a part-time basis for those already in work (Lee 1968). Only in the latter decades of the twentieth century was it incorporated into the system, through the Polytechnics and Colleges of Further Education.

When the new knowledge-intensive industries of electronics, aerospace, computing, and financial and business services developed in the second half of the twentieth century, their need for an educated labour-force with both intermediate-level and higher-level skills had to be met by a system of higher education still dominated by the aristocratic institutions of Oxford and Cambridge, and a school system modelled on the nineteenth-century private ('public') schools which had produced the 'gentleman' leaders of the Empire. Only in the latter decades of the twentieth century did the introduction of a national curriculum start to service the needs of knowledge-based industries. By then the predominantly liberal academic curriculum had produced a strong reaction from those concerned with vocational education. This took the form of National Vocational Qualifications, which in turn led to the creation of an alternative 'curriculum', based only on the current skill needs of industry.

The irrelevance of much of what was transmitted through the education system for the needs of industry meant that companies and organizations were left to develop their own forms of training. During the nineteenth century this was delivered by a combination of informal on-the-job training for labour-intensive industries which required only unskilled and semi-skilled labour, and the apprenticeship system, which provided skilled labour for the various engineering industries. However, during the latter part of the twentieth century the growth of firm internal labour markets, and the increasing provision by the Colleges of Further Education of training for business in the service industries, undermined the traditional apprenticeship system. This also transferred the cost of much of the initial training required for industry to the state, which funded Further Education Colleges, and to parents, who funded the extended education of their children. Industry was left to fund only the costs of job-specific training.

Education and Industrial Development: The Singaporean Approach

In the case of the Asian Tigers, the relationship between the development of the education system and the productive system has been very different. The British and US education and training systems developed during the first wave of their industrialization as the first industrial nations. During this phase of industrialization the British and American manufacturers had a competitive advantage in world markets, because they had developed the first industrial forms of production while their competitors in world markets were still operating on the basis of handicraft production. The countries which industrialized in the second phase, in the late nineteenth and early twentieth centuries, and which included Germany, France, and Japan, had to compete against the first-phase industrial countries which already dominated world markets. However, the situation confronting the new industrial economies of the Pacific Rim (the Tigers), which industrialized in the second half of the twentieth century, was even more daunting. They faced competition in world markets not only from Britain and the USA, but also from the second-wave countries such as Germany and Japan (Ashton and Green 1996). This had a profound effect on the way in which the relationship between the education systems and the productive systems developed. Table 12.2 illustrates the way in which the relationship developed in Singapore. We use the case of Singapore to illustrate this new relationship between the two systems because it has arguably the most sophisticated training systems of the four Asian Tigers, together with an education system most closely tied to the requirements of the productive system.

In addition to having to break into highly competitive world markets Singapore, like the other Asian Tigers, faced an acute political threat to its existence (Castells 1992). In a small island state, surrounded by larger Muslim neighbours, the Singaporean leaders were acutely conscious of the need to secure and maintain the country's political independence. For this they required a strong economy and an equally strong sense of national identity and commitment among Singapore's population of 3 million. The education system therefore had to fulfil two important factors.

Table 12.2. The relationship between education and industrial development in Singapore

	Education	Industry
1980s	Expansion of higher education, upgrading of technical skills	13 key industries, e.g. financial services
1970s	Extended secondary education and vocational training	Higher-value-added produced 'Second Industrial Revolution'
1950s	Elementary education	Labour-intensive low-value added production

The first was to establish a sense of national identity and commitment, and the second was to sustain the development of the economy. The political leaders saw it as their task to ensure that, as industry developed, the human capital was in place to make effective use of the physical capital. The result was a very close relationship between the education and productive systems.

As we have seen, the relationship between the education system and the productive system in Britain was characterized by the education system expanding over time in a direction controlled by élites whose primary concern was the maintenance of the interests of an aristocratic mercantile class. The educational needs of industry, which changed with the development of the productive system, were only partially incorporated into the system. The same relationship in Singapore took a very different form. From the outset, changes in the education and training system moved in tandem with changes in production; far from the interests of industry being tangential to education, they were seen as central to its development. In this respect it is possible to identify three distinct phases in the growth of the education and training system which correspond directly to the changes which took place in the development of the economy (see Table 12.2). The synchronization of these changes in the two spheres was largely the product of a strong and efficient state bureaucracy controlled by modernizing élites with the capacity to act independently of the immediate interests of capital and labour.

FIRST PHASE

The state's ability to achieve a degree of relative autonomy from internal vested interests was connected to the political threat facing the country in its early years. As we have seen, after securing independence from British colonial rule the Singaporean political élite wanted to safeguard the political survival of Singaporean society and create a national identity in the face of possible threats from neighbouring Muslim countries. This provided the impetus for the establishment of a strong state apparatus, staffed by technically competent officials (Castells 1992; World Bank 1993). Through control of this apparatus the political élite maintained its independence from vested interests.

On the political front, the education system was charged with the task of creating a strong sense of national identity. On the economic front, Singaporean independence was to be secured through the creation of a strong industrial base. In the first phase of Singapore's development, therefore, the government sought to attract inward investment from multinational corporations (MNCs) in order to establish a strong manufacturing base (Low 1993; Tan 1995).

With a poorly educated labour force, and unemployment rates in excess of 14 per cent, the political élite had to rely initially on cheap, disciplined labour and a strong and stable political system to attract MNCs. As these labour-intensive industries required little educated labour, the fact that education was limited to provision at primary level was not a problem. The government did move to upgrade basic literacy levels and provide training in maths and science. Their main aims, however, were to maintain the discipline of the labour force and to contain labour costs, both of which were essential to the MNCs. They achieved these aims by repressing communist labour organization (Deyo 1989), and by using the People's Action Party (PAP) to persuade workers to minimize their wage demands. They argued that, by doing this, further inward investment would be attracted by the low labour costs and therefore more jobs would be generated[1]. The success of these policies was evident in the creation of full employment.

SECOND PHASE
In the late 1970s the growing availability of equally attractive low-cost labour in other parts of the region meant that Singapore was losing its competitive advantage. In addition, the political threat to Singapore's independence continued. In a move which both served the country's own interests and satisfied its rivals, the political élite sought to share its early success. Companies producing low-value-added goods on the basis of low-cost labour were persuaded to leave Singapore to take advantage of the lower cost of labour in the immediate hinterland, while the Singaporean economy was re-engineered to enter a 'second industrial revolution'. The aim was to use the resources of the state to reduce reliance on low-wage, labour-intensive industry and replace this with capital-intensive, higher-value-added industries (Wong 1993).

In order to achieve these political goals, the government had to act independently of the immediate interests of capital and entice new companies which could introduce higher-value-added production to Singapore. At the same time it cajoled and coerced companies already established there to move away from low-value-added production. Toward this end, it adopted a number of new policies aimed at increasing the cost of labour and thereby discouraging further investment in low-value-added production. Employers in low-value-added production were encouraged to relocate through the persuasion of activists from the PAP. Meanwhile, the unions were actively encouraged to push for large increases in wages, in the region of 20 per cent. The government also imposed a levy on low-paid labour to discourage companies from continuing to embark on low-value-added production (Wong 1993). This levy created the Skills Development Fund (SDF) which was then used to finance a series of programmes aimed at improving worker skills and employers' ability to train.

In detaching itself from the immediate interests of capital the government has been able to use its power to pursue its 'vision', which became of central importance in directing the country's trade and industry policy. New industries had to be encouraged and old industries relocated. If new industries were to be attracted then the human resources essential for the successful performance of those industries had to be in place. The state therefore acted once again to coordinate capital and labour at a national level, providing the basis of the dynamism which characterizes Singaporean education and training policy.

In order to attract the higher-value-added industries required for the second phase, the education system was upgraded and a new training infrastructure put in place under the auspices of the Vocational and Industrial Training Board (VITB), while within the education system there was an attempt to shift the emphasis of the curriculum away from the academic to the technical. This period also saw the establishment of the Singapore Technical Institute (Yip and Sim 1994). In 1979 the Goh report recommended the introduction of streaming into primary and secondary education and a greater emphasis to be placed on language acquisition. Central control of the curriculum was maintained, but a common curriculum only retained for the first 2 years of secondary education.

The speed of Singapore's development had meant that many of those who left the education system in the colonial era and in the early stages of Singapore's independence still had literacy and numeracy deficiencies. As late as the 1980s, 61 per cent of Singapore's non-student population had an educational level of Primary Six or less (Ministry of Trade and Industry 1991). Because they could not wait for changes in the system of initial education to increase the stock of skills slowly, the government adopted a second front and sought to act directly on the employed adult labour force to improve the basic skills of those already in work, launching a series of programmes aimed at enhancing the skills of mature workers. The programmes, delivered in modular form through institutes and employers, provided a progression route for such workers either to continue their education to secondary-school level or to provide a basis for the enhancement of their work-based skills. By 1990 illiteracy rates had been reduced to 10 per cent of the total population and 1.4 per cent for the 20–24 age group (Census of Population 1990).

The foundation programme, Basic Education for Skills Training (BEST), introduced in 1983, had by 1992 reached 78 per cent of the potential target pool of 225,000 workers, in a total labour force of 1.4 million workers (ITE 1993: 25). On the foundations laid by BEST a whole series of programmes were used to improve the basic skills of the labour force. In 1986 the Modular Skills Training programme was introduced, aimed at enhancing the skills of semi-skilled workers. In 1987 Worker Improvement through Secondary Education was introduced to General Certificate of Edu-

cation level, and by 1992 42 per cent of the target pool of 122,000 had been reached (ITE 1993: 25). The Core Skills for Effectiveness and Change programme was also introduced in 1987, aimed at service-sector workers, and this covers two-thirds of the low-income labour force.

THIRD PHASE

Towards the end of the 1980s there was a further shift in the political leaders' vision of the future of Singapore. To stay ahead of their competitors in the region, the government set out to match the economic performance of the best industrial economies. The current 'vision' is set out in the document 'The Next Lap' (Government of Singapore 1991). The implications of this vision for the economic development of the country was detailed in the Strategic Economic Plan (Ministry of Trade and Industry 1991). This established that the country was to achieve the same standard of living for the Singaporean people as that achieved by the Swiss.

To achieve the status and standard of living of the Swiss by the year 2020 or 2030 the economy was to continue to attract companies planning to invest in the production of high-value-added goods and services. However, in order to sustain economic growth it was felt necessary for Singaporean companies to move out of Singapore into the Asia Pacific region and form a 'second ring'. This would enable them not only to take advantage of cheaper labour outside Singapore, but would also place Singapore in the centre of the region's drive for economic growth. Singapore would move from 'Singapore Incorporated' to Singapore International Incorporated' (Low 1993). Thirteen industrial clusters were identified as areas where Singapore could sustain a competitive advantage in world markets, and these were to be the priority areas for development.

In order to ensure success in achieving these objectives, measures had to be taken to ensure that the human resources were in place to facilitate the establishment and development of these industries. This meant that the education system had to be upgraded to bring it in line with the most advanced systems in the older industrial countries. In addition, training policy had to be re-focused to concentrate on enhancing intermediate work-based skills as well as, crucially, improving the use of the workplace as a source of learning. This was essential if employers were to have access to the same level of skills as were available in other industrial societies.

The upgrading of the educational system focused on three areas: the identification of the basic skills required for effective participation in an advanced industrial society; the production of intermediate-level technical skills; and the expansion of higher education. To identify the basic skills the government studied education practices in Germany and Japan, which it considered to be the most advanced, and found that the teaching of the working language and mathematics amounted to 50 per cent of curriculum time in the primary school (Ministry of Education 1991). However, in Singapore the problems posed by bilingualism (English and the mother tongue) meant that if children in primary schools were to have the same exposure to languages as in Germany or Japan, there would be less time left for other subjects. The solution, introduced through the 1990 reforms, was to introduce a preparatory programme for all five-year-olds in order to compensate for the heavier demands made by the bilingual requirement. In order to ensure that school-leavers had mastered these basic skills necessary to enable them to develop further at work, it was decided that all young people should have 10 years' minimum general education. Intermediate technical skills were to be produced through an upgrading of vocational education. The VITB, renamed the Institute of Technical Education (ITE) in 1992, now only takes on young people for technical training after they have completed this basic education so as to enhance the status of technical education. The ITE now offers much higher-skill-content courses, which enables those following the vocational route to proceed to further education in the polytechnics and universities. For those already in the labour force, the lowest level of National Trade Certificate (renamed the National Technical Certificate in 1992, and roughly equivalent to the UK NVQ Level 1) disappeared in 1995. The lowest level is now equivalent to the standard of the competent craftsman. The aim of these reforms was to ensure that all those entering the labour market had the requisite base on which today's skills and those of tomorrow can be built. In line with this objective, the types of skills transmitted in the educational system are starting to shift from the 'harder' technical skills to the 'softer' office and business skills (Felstead, Ashton, Green, and Sung 1994).

Building on the high participation rates in education (with over 90 per cent of 15-to-19 year olds in education) tertiary education was expanded, and by the early 1990s was accounting for 26 per cent of 20-to-24 year olds (Felstead, Ashton, Green, and Sung 1994). The educational system's current targets by the year 2000 are to have 25 per cent of the age group either in junior colleges or universities, 40 per cent in polytechnics, and 25 per cent in Institute for Technical Education programmes, with a dropout rate of 10 per cent. However, the dropouts are not regarded as lost to the system, for they are targeted, once they have had some work experience, through government programmes aimed at enhancing their work-based skills. By the early 1990s the education system was producing levels of educational attainment comparable with those of the much older British educational system (Felstead, Ashton, Green, and Sung 1994).

This third phase also saw a continuance of the two-pronged approach. The programmes the government had established to enhance the skills of those who missed out on their primary and secondary education (BEST and MOST) have been run down as the target pool declines in size, with the emphasis moving towards enhancing the process of work-based learning. It became evident in the late 1980s that while improvement in the quantity of training undertaken by employers was important, the new growth industries of the 1990s demanded competence not just in technical skills but also in the ability of workers to achieve greater flexibility and develop the skills to tackle new, unforeseen problems. In these new circumstances, learning at work took on greater importance. Studies of the German dual system, and the Japanese and Australian systems of on-the-job training, were used to identify ways in which this might be achieved.

One of the lessons learnt from the German dual system was that on-the-job and off-the-job elements in training needed to be integrated if the training was to provide the quality of learning experience and the depth of skills required for companies to compete effectively in world markets. The significance of this policy shift is underlined by findings from a number of studies which suggest that some of the skills necessary for companies to compete in the markets for high-value-added goods and services can only be acquired through a combination of on-the-job and off-the-job experience (Streeck 1989; Kioke and Inoki 1990).

Improvements were made to the apprenticeship system by the introduction of the New Apprenticeship Scheme (NAS) in 1990. Modelled closely on the Baden–Wurttemberg version of the 'Dual System', it was targeted at employers with the ability to train their own workers. Like the German dual system, it required pedagogically qualified trainers (*Meisters*) and both on-the-job and off-the-job training. Concurrent with the launch of the NAS in 1991, the ITE introduced the Industry Trainer Programme to help companies develop pedagogically qualified trainers to support their apprenticeship courses. By 1994 the ITE had trained some 1,900 industry trainers. Based on some 600 companies that are participating in the apprenticeship scheme, this works out at an average of three trainers per company.

The same idea of integrating on- and off-the-job training has been used to inform the new 'Hybrid' apprenticeship system. This was launched in 1992, aimed at the small- and medium-sized enterprises (SMEs) which had traditionally avoided apprenticeship training. The same objective of enhancing both the on-the-job and off-the-job training of mature workers (aged between 20 and 40 years with below-O-level qualifications) was tackled by the ITE's Adult Co-operative Training Scheme, introduced in 1992. This is based on the new apprenticeship model, so workers have to be sponsored by their employers but then receive on-the-job and off-the-job training in the company's time (ITE 1993).

While the apprenticeship model was the preferred form of providing education and training, not all employers would adopt it; and therefore other forms of intervention had to be found if the labour force as a whole was to have its skills enhanced. The Skills Development Fund[2] had experience of funding company-based training through the skills programmes introduced during the second phase of economic development, with the number of training places supported by the fund increasing more than 12 times from

32,600 in 1981 to 407,900 in 1991 (NPB 1993: 44). This has been further enhanced in two ways. First, employers were provided with a series of programmes which offered help and assistance for them in learning how to organize and implement their own training. Secondly, after studying other countries, ways were found of helping firms enhance the quality of their on-the-job training.

The task of helping employers to learn how to organize and implement training was done through the Training Grants Scheme under the auspices of the National Productivity Board (NPB) and funded by the SDF. This comprises a series of schemes focused on helping employers improve particular aspects of training. The Training Grants Scheme provides grants to employers of between 30 and 90 per cent of the cost of (re)training workers through in-plant programmes to upgrade their skills. The largest of the schemes, the Worker Training Plan, encourages companies to undertake systematic training through an annual plan. This was responsible for 61 per cent of the total training places supported by the SDF in 1991, and accounted for 88 per cent of the total SDF spent (SDF 1992: 12). The trainee recipients of all these schemes tend to be workers with average or below-average educational levels; 72 per cent of training places were filled by workers with O levels or less (SDF 1992: 38).

Other schemes have been established to help companies ease cash-flow problems when investing in staff training, to enable them to embark on systematic training based on the results of a company-wide training-needs analysis, and to make the services of good-quality training providers available to small companies who do not have the resources to develop their own training programmes. In addition, other schemes are in place to enhance the training infrastructure, for example by helping managers improve their ability to train, and by providing training in delivery of quality in the service sector (Ashton and Sung 1994).

Another way to improve the quality of training identified by the NPB was the more widespread use of structured on-the-job training (OJT), seen as the most cost-effective form of training. Research by the NPB in 1986 revealed that 90 per cent of companies in Singapore engaged in some form of OJT, but that this was not necessarily structured. As a result it was found that 'more often than not, OJT meant that workers were left to chance to acquire skills during the course of their work' (NPB 1992: 9). A task force was therefore set up with the Economic Development Board (EDB) and the Institute of Technical Education to identify the core skills needed to be developed through OJT schemes, and following this the NPB introduced a programme aimed at identifying industry-based blueprints or model OJT schemes. This programme commenced in 1993, with schemes being developed with leading companies in a variety of industries which are then used as a base model for other companies to emulate. The long-term plan is to get 100,000 through OJT by the end of the decade. By May 1995 36,000 workers had successfully completed OJT programmes (NPB 1995). In addition, steps have been taken to develop OJT instructors which will complement the off-the-job training undertaken by the ITE and will be available for firms in service as well as manufacturing industries.[3]

Good-quality OJT, while providing workers with the skills required for today's companies, will not necessarily equip them to cope with the demands of the new markets and associated industrial restructuring. In line with the vision of where Singapore hopes to be by the year 2020, the focus of the government's concern with on-the-job training has shifted from the provision of flexible, multiskilled workers to the task of skills-deepening. The result is a skills-deepening programme.

Swiss workers are seen as extremely welltrained in technical skills, and 'equipped with the foundation for drastic retraining should industrial restructuring take place' (NPB 1993: 51). Following a study mission to Switzerland in 1992, the NPB is working with other government departments to identify the leading-edge companies with potential for skills-deepening. These are seen as the industries experiencing rapid growth with the potential to compete in regional and international markets. The NPB is working with such companies to develop and design training programmes to deepen core job skills using OJT techniques. The aim is to train workers in these companies not just with the technical skills but also with the deeper intellectual skills necessary to cope with the drastic retraining they will have to undergo to enable them to handle industrial change and restruc-turing. Core areas of the economy, such as precision engineering, have been targeted for the implementation of a programme of skillsdeepening.

In addition to borrowing training policies and practices from the older industrial countries, the government is also active in transferring the latest knowledge and techniques directly to the indigenous labour force. In the second phase it did this through the establishment of Joint Industrial Training Centres with MNCs and three foreign governments: Germany, France, and Japan. In the mid-1980s the EDB decided that knowledge- and technology-intensive industries would require resources in excess of those that single partners involved in the Joint Industrial Training Centres could provide. It needed to access expertise on a global rather than single-country basis, and to achieve this it sought agreements from the three governments to incorporate other MNCs into the Institutes. The successful introduction of this strategy led to the adoption of a transnational approach by the EDB. By securing the co-operation of governments and several MNCs, it proved possible to provide the necessary 'hardware, software, and teachware' required for the establishment and development of knowledge- and technology-intensive industries. In this way the EDB continues to set up training in anticipation of the needs of new and emerging industries (Wong 1993: 262).

THE CO-ORDINATION OF EDUCATION, TRAINING, AND INDUSTRIAL DEVELOPMENT

Given this close linkage between ET and economic growth we must now ask how this has been accomplished. Again, the Asian model proves distinctive. During the second wave of industrialization the Japanese and Germans had succeeded in establishing a broad correspondence between changes in the educational system and those in the structure of industry (Ashton and Green 1996), but have never achieved such a tight form of integration as that developed by the Singaporeans. The Singaporeans were so effective because of the establishment of a number of mechanisms which ensured that the education and training system responded directly to changes in the government's trade and industry policy.

The first such mechanism was the ability of government to achieve a degree of autonomy in relation to capital and labour. As we have seen, unlike the UK and US governments, which have always sought to leave the market to determine the direction taken by economic development, the Singaporean government has always taken upon itself the determination of this direction. The second mechanism was the ability to learn from the experience of older industrial nations. The Singaporean government had the model of more advanced economies, which it could use to help identify the next step in the process of economic growth.[4] As we have seen, the government also learned from joint ventures and visits to other countries.

The third mechanism was the organization of government departments. Once having identified the next stage of economic growth through its 'vision', the goals as defined in this vision provide the targets which inform the work of the Ministry of Trade and Industry and the Investment Board. The Ministry of Trade and Industry is powerful and responsible for ensuring that the economy is geared to the demands of the international market and is therefore in a position to achieve the government's vision. Other departments, such as Education and the National Productivity Board, are subordinate to the Ministry of Trade and Industry, ensuring that the requirements of industry are always taken into account when decisions about the allocation of resources for human-resource development are made.

The fourth mechanism lay in the institutional procedures put in place to facilitate the co-ordination of human-resource development with the requirements of industry, and the use of targets to monitor the performance of the agencies which have to implement policy. Thus, to identify the future human-resource needs of the country the government relies on agencies such as the Investment Board, which sells the benefits of investing in Singapore and which, in negotiating with foreign capital, is in a position to identify future demands on the country's human resources which that investment is likely to make. The Ministry of Trade and Industry then collates such information and this is mapped against projections from academics about the likely state of labour (human-resource) supply. The results provide the basis for the identification of the country's skill needs.

The Economic Development Board translates this information about the country's skill requirements into targets for the Council for Professional and Technical Education (CPTE). First established in 1979, this is a national body, chaired by the Minister responsible for Trade and Industry, which sets targets for education and training at all levels. This Council institutionalizes the link between trade and industry policy and the education and training system (Selvaratnam 1989) and thereby ensures that human-capital demands of new industries inform the targets.

The Council disaggregates the overall target into specific targets for the universities, polytechnics, schools, and the Institute of Technical Education, and ascertains whether these targets can be met within existing resources, or whether new institutions or policy initiatives will be needed. For this exercise they require feedback from the education and training authorities. If the government cannot meet the targets from indigenous institutions then they look to import the requisite skills. In this way each sector, Higher Education, Schools, and the Institute of Technical Education has its own targets for student numbers and for levels of achievement.

Other government departments and agencies are also involved in ensuring that the human resources required to achieve the government's vision are in place. Thus while the National Productivity Board has a different focus, being concerned with employer-based training, it too has its targets. One of the NPB's 'vision goals' was for organizations to double their training investment from 2 to 4 per cent of payroll by 1995, the amount which it is believed the better corporations in the world spend on training (NPB 1993).

The quotas for numbers and targets for performance are implemented by the higher-education institutions, schools, the ITE, and the NPB in their own plans. The performance of the respective institutions are then systematically evaluated against their targets. Within the ITE training plans are formulated on a 5-year basis, but these are rolled over every 2 years. When any revision occurs, the Trade and Industry Ministry has a significant input. This ensures that the future demands of the economy are constantly fed back and that they inform any revision of targets. In this way the education and training system as a whole responds to the future human-resource development needs of the economy.

The case of Singapore illustrates how the

driving force behind the technical education and training system is not the needs of individuals, or indeed of individual employers, but that of the economy as a whole. The emphasis in government programmes is on encouraging individuals to participate in training, but objectives in standards of training and education are set by what are seen as the needs of the future economy, and not by the demands of individuals. Employers play a crucial role in delivering the programmes, but such programmes are targeted just as clearly at enhancing the employers' skills to organize and deliver training as they are the individual's ability to learn. Finally, in addition to enhancing the amount and quality of training undertaken by individuals and employers, the state also plays an important part in ensuring that skills and technical knowledge are transferred from the more advanced and larger companies to the indigenous population and smaller companies. In short, the state adopts and implements a human-resource development policy for society as a whole.

Conclusion

In conclusion we return to the comparison with the first-wave industrializers, especially the British. There the government has relied on the market to determine both the direction in which the economy moves and also, in recent years, the delivery of training. In effect this means leaving the development of the productive system to be determined by the outcome of the competitive struggle between employers in the market-place: the state merely guarantees the legal framework. In the field of education the development of the system is left to the professionals who run universities and schools within a 'market framework' which is increasing educational inequalities (Brown 1990). However, there is little or no linkage between decisions which concern the overall development of the education system and those concerning the development of the productive system. Indeed, as the government claims it cannot determine the direction of development of the economy, there would be little point in such an exercise.

This is in marked contrast with Singapore, where the government has used its resources to facilitate the operation of the market and move it in the direction which the government's vision has established. This is not central planning in which the government lays down plans which then determine the allocation of resources within the productive system. The reality of the Singaporean system is very different, and is best conceptualized as a new form of government intervention, in which the government has sought to understand the operation of market forces and use them to realize its political objectives. Decisions about the allocation of the factors of production at the level of the firm and of specific markets are left to employers; but the state uses its powers to determine the type of employers who are attracted to the market. Thus in terms of its industrial and trade policy the government seeks to attract only those companies which will produce higher-value-added goods and services. In order to ensure that these companies are successful and that their costs are contained, the government seeks to provide them with the appropriate skilled labour. In this way the government uses the market to achieve its own political objectives; by structuring the context it makes sure that the operation of the market is in line with its political vision.

What the Singaporean government has done is to find a way of co-ordinating capital and labour as factors of production. In many respects this is reminiscent of the ways in which, in the US in the early twentieth century, the giant corporations which emerged found ways to co-ordinate the factors of production which had previously been co-ordinated by the market. As Chandler (1977) has shown, the corporations replaced the invisible hand of the market by the visible hand of management, by co-ordinating the sourcing of materials with the manufacture and distribution of the product, they were able to make significant efficiency gains. In many respects the Singaporean government is undertaking an analogous process at the national level.

In the late 1960s it could have left the market to determine the direction in which the economy moved. Had it done so, however, Singapore might still be producing low-value-added goods and services. Instead, the government sought to persuade such industries to leave, and set about creating the conditions which would dissuade them from staying while simultaneously putting in place measures to attract high-value-added producers. However, for this type of capital to be utilized efficiently required a labour force which was not only disciplined, but also skilled; and the education system, no matter how efficient it was, could not upgrade the labour force as a whole, only those flowing into it. To ensure that skilled labour was in place on which employers could rely to ensure that their plants operated efficiently, measures were put in place to upgrade the stock of skills. It is in this way that the state co-ordinates the inputs of capital and labour to ensure that the economy as a whole moves in the direction of its political objectives.

We can observe the same process at present. In order to make Singapore a regional centre for certain of the knowledge-based industries, the government has decided that it requires not just a significant proportion of the population to move through higher education, but also that schools must ensure the development of creativity among pupils and, crucially, that the system of higher education must produce the requisite number of scientists and engineers to provide the level of research and development required to sustain such industries. In this context the government can use a battery of measures to help ensure that these human resources are in place. For example, it can seek to influence young people's choices of subjects for study on entering higher education, or it can use its control of the quota system which determines the opportunities available to them there. Through the CPTE it has a means of creating an ongoing dialogue between the employers and decision-makers in the education system, to ensure that the requirements of employers are met. In this way the human resources necessary for the successful establishment of an industry will be put in place. Where this differs from the function of a giant corporation, and where that analogy breaks down, is that the government is not just co-ordinating the delivery of the various factors necessary to meet today's requirements, but co-ordinating to create a new set of circumstances. In this situation education can never be allowed the kind of autonomy it has experienced in the West, but will always need to be subordinated to the needs of nation-building and especially of economic development.

The result of this co-ordination of education and training with the requirements of the productive system is that we are likely to wit-ness a closer link between investment in education and training and economic growth in societies such as Singapore than we have witnessed in the older industrial societies of the West. This is not surprising, because the older industrial systems developed without the need for an educated labour force, and subsequent developments in education bore only a loose relationship to what happened in the economy (Ashton and Green 1996). What this analysis suggests is that, as the number of newly industrialized economies (NIEs) grows, statistical studies will reveal a much stronger relationship between investment in education and economic growth in these societies, precisely because they have put in place mechanisms to institutionalize the links.

Notes

1. The information on the operation of the Singaporean system has been derived from interviews with members of the political élite and government officials conducted over the period 1993–6.
2. The SDF is the levy imposed on employers who pay workers less than $750 per month, and is used to enhance work-related learning.
3. Information supplied during interviews with NPB officials, 1994.
4. This was only possible as long as the countries are 'catching up' with the older industrial nations. As the Asian Tigers are now approaching the status of advanced industrial countries this form of learning will not be available.

References

Ashton, D. N., and Green, F. (1996), *Education, Training and the Global Economy* (Cheltenham: Edward Elgar).

Ashton, D. N., and Sung, J. (1994), 'The State Economic Development and Skill Formation: a New East Asian Model', Working paper 3 (Univ. of Leicester, Centre for Labour Market Studies).

Brown, P. (1990), 'The "Third Wave": Education and the Ideology of Parentocracy', *British Journal of Sociology of Education*, 11/1: 65–85.

Castells, M. (1992), 'Four Tigers with a Dragon Head: A Comparative Analysis of the State, Economy and Society in the Asia Pacific Rim', in Appelbaum, R., and Henderson, J., *States and Development in the Asia Pacific Rim* (London: Sage).

Census of Population (1990), Singapore, Government of Singapore.

Chandler, A., Jr. (1977), *The Visible Hand: The Managerial Revolution in American Business* (Cambridge, Mass.: Harvard Univ. Press).

Deyo, F. C. (1989), *Beneath the Miracle: Labor Subordination in the New Asian Industrialism*, (Berkeley: Univ. of California Press).

Felstead, A., Ashton, D. N., Green, F., and Sung, J. (1994), *Vocational Education and Training in the Federal Republic of Germany, France, Japan, Singapore and the United States* (Leicester Univ., Centre for Labour Market Studies).

Government of Singapore (1991), *The Next Lap* (Singapore: Times Editions Pte Ltd.).

Green, A. (1990), *Education and State Formation: The Rise of Education Systems in England, France and the USA* (London: Macmillan).

—— (1995), 'Education and the Developmental State in Europe and Asia' (London Univ. Institute of Education, mimeo).

ITE (1993), *Institute of Technical Education, Annual Report 92/93* (Singapore: Institute of Technical Education).

Kioke, K., and Inoki, T. (eds.) (1990), *Skill Formation in Japan and Southeast Asia* (Tokyo: Univ. of Tokyo Press).

Lee, D. J. (1968), 'Class Differentials in Educational Opportunity and Promotion from the Ranks', *Sociology*, 2/3: 293–312.

Low, L. (1993), 'From Entreport to a Newly Industrialising Economy', in Low, L., Heng, T. M. H., Wong, T. W., Yam, T. K., and Hughes, H., *Challenge and Response: Thirty Years of the Economic Development Board* (Singapore: Times Academic Press).

Ministry of Education (1991), *Improving Primary Education* (Report of Review Committee, March, Singapore: Ministry of Education).

Ministry of Trade and Industry (1991), *The Strategic Economic Plan: Towards a Developed Nation* (Singapore: Economic Planning Committee).

NPB (1992), *Productivity Digest* (June, Singapore: National Productivity Board).

—— (1993), *Productivity Statement* (Singapore: National Productivity Board).

—— (1995), *Productivity Digest* (June, Singapore: National Productivity Board).

Sanderson, M. (1994), *The Missing Stratum: Technical School Education in England 1900–1990s* (London: Athlone Press).

Selvaratnam, V. (1989), 'Vocational Education and Training: Singapore and Other Third World Initiatives', *Singapore Journal of Education*, 10/2: 11–23.

SDF (1992), *The Skills Development Fund Annual Report 1991/1992* (11 November), 126.

Streeck, W. (1989), 'Skills and the Limits of Neo-Liberalism: The Enterprise of the Future as a Place of Learning', *Work Employment and Society*, 3/1: 89–140.

Tan, Gerald (1995), *The Newly Industrializing Countries of Asia* (2nd edn., Singapore: Times Academic Press).

Wong, S. T. (1993), 'Education and Human Resource Development', in Low, L., Heng, T. M. H., Wong, T. W., Yam, T. K., and Hughes, H., *Challenge and Response: Thirty Years of the Economic Development Board* (Singapore: Times Academic Press).

World Bank (1993), *The East Asian Miracle: Economic Growth and Public Policy* (New York: Oxford Univ. Press).

Yip, J. S. K., and Sim, W. K. (1994), *Evolution of Educational Excellence: 25 Years of Education in the Republic of Singapore*, (2nd edn., Singapore: Longmans).

13

Human Capital Concepts

Maureen Woodhall

The concept of human capital refers to the fact that human beings invest in themselves, by means of education, training, or other activities, which raises their future income by increasing their lifetime earnings. Economists use the term 'investment' to refer to expenditure on assets which will produce income in the future, and contrast investment expenditure with consumption, which produces immediate satisfaction or benefits, but does not create future income. Assets which will generate income in the future are called capital. Traditionally, economic analysis of investment and capital tended to concentrate on physical capital, namely machinery, equipment, or buildings, which would generate income in the future by creating productive capacity. However, a number of classical economists, notably Adam Smith, pointed out that education helped to increase the productive capacity of workers, in the same way as the purchase of new machinery, or other forms of physical capital, increased the productive capacity of a factory or other enterprise. Thus, an analogy was drawn between investment in physical capital and investment in human capital.

The concept was not fully developed, however, until the early 1960s when the US economist Theodore Schultz analysed educational expenditure as a form of investment (Schultz 1961), the *Journal of Political Economy* in the US published a supplement on 'Investment in human beings' in 1962, and Gary Becker published a book with the title *Human Capital* (Becker 1964; 1975) which developed a theory of human capital formation and analysed the rate of return to investment in education and training.

Since that time the concept of human capital has dominated the economics of education and has had a powerful influence on the analysis of labour markets, wage determination, and other branches of economics, such as the analysis of economic growth, as well as expenditure on health care and the study of migration. For it is recognized that these also represent investment in human capital, since they can help to determine the earning capacity of individuals, and therefore increase their lifetime incomes.

However, investment in human capital remains a controversial issue. Attempts to measure the rate of return to investment in education have been attacked by critics who argue that education does not increase the productive capacity of workers but simply acts as a 'screening device' which enables employers to identify individuals with higher innate ability or personal characteristics which make them more productive. A summary of this controversy is given below, together with a brief review of research on investment in education and some other applications of the concept of human capital.

Measuring the Rate of Return to Investment in Human Capital

When economists refer to expenditure on education and training as investment in human capital, they are doing more than pointing to analogies between education and investment in physical capital. They are asserting that it is possible to measure the

From G. Psacharopoulos (ed.), *Economics of Education: Research and Studies* (Oxford: Pergamon, 1987), 21–4. Reprinted with permission.

profitability of investment in human capital using the same techniques of cost–benefit analysis and investment appraisal that have been traditionally applied to physical capital.

The profitability, or rate of return on investment, is a measure of the expected yield of the investment, in terms of the future benefits, or income stream generated by the capital, compared with the cost of acquiring the capital asset. Cost–benefit analysis is designed to express all the costs and benefits associated with an investment project in terms of a single figure, the rate of return, which shows the rate of interest at which the present discounted value of future income is exactly equal to the present discounted value of costs. This enables different projects to be compared and an optimum investment strategy consists of identifying and investing in projects offering the highest rate of return, or profitability.

If money devoted to education, training, or health care is regarded as investment in human capital, since it raises the lifetime earnings of workers who are better educated and trained or more healthy than other workers, then techniques of cost–benefit analysis can be used to compare the economic profitability of different types or levels of education, of on-the-job compared with off-the-job training, or of different types of medical treatment. It should also be possible to compare rates of return to investment in human capital and physical capital, in order to discover whether it is more profitable to invest in men and women or machines.

Investment in human capital produces benefits both to the individual and to society as a whole. The individual who takes part in education or vocational training benefits by increasing his or her chances of employment and by increased lifetime earnings. These additional earnings, after allowance for payment of taxes, can be compared with the direct and indirect costs of education that must be borne by the individual, including fees, expenditure on books or equipment, and earnings forgone while in school, college, or university. This provides a measure of the private rate of return to investment in education or other form of human capital.

Both the costs and benefits of education also affect society as a whole, since society benefits from the increased productivity of educated workers. Throughout the world this is recognized by governments who pay some or all of the costs of education, and provide free or subsidized tuition in schools or higher education institutions. The costs and benefits to society can be compared by means of the social rate of return.

The question of the profitability of different types and levels of education and training, and the question of the relative yield of investment in human capital and physical capital, have attracted a considerable amount of research activity since the 1960s, as well as provoking fierce disagreements among economists and educational planners. Psacharopoulos has reviewed attempts to measure the social and private rate of return to investment in education in 32 countries (Psacharopoulos 1973) and more recently has updated this survey of research on the returns to education by analysing the results of cost-benefit analysis of education in 44 countries (Psacharopoulos 1981). Estimates of social and private rates of return to educational investment, based on surveys of the earnings of workers of different educational levels in 44 countries in the period from 1958 to 1978 reveal, according to Psacharopoulos (1981: 326), four underlying patterns:

1. the returns to primary education (whether social or private) are the highest among all educational levels;
2. private returns are in excess of social returns, especially at the university level;
3. all rates of return to investment in education are well above the 10 per cent common yardstick of the opportunity cost of capital;
4. the returns to education in less developed countries are higher relative to the corresponding returns in more advanced countries.

The Profitability of Human Capital versus Physical Capital

The rates of return that are reviewed by Psacharopoulos are summarized in Table 13.1, which shows the average private and social rate of return for primary, secondary, and higher education in less developed, intermediate, and economically advanced countries. These rate of return estimates refer to single years, and therefore do not show how

Table 13.1. The returns to education by region and country type (per cent)

Region or country type	N[a]	Private			Social		
		Prim.[b]	Sec.[c]	High.[d]	Prim.	Sec.	High.
Africa	9	29	22	32	29	17	12
Asia	8	32	17	19	16	12	11
Latin America	5	24	20	23	44	17	18
LDC average	22	29	19	24	27	16	13
Intermediate	8	20	17	17	16	14	10
Advanced	14	[e]	14	12	[f]	10	9

[a] N: Number of countries in each group. [b] Prim.: primary educational level. [c] Sec.: secondary educational level. [d] High.: higher educational level. [e] Not computable because of lack of a control group of illiterates. [f] Source: Psacharopoulos (1973: 86).

rates of return change over time, although the average rate of return is calculated from estimates for years which range over a 20-year period. However, there are very few countries for which it is possible to calculate rates of return on an historical time-series basis. Data exist on earnings of workers in the USA classified by educational level since 1939. Estimates of rates of return to secondary and higher education between 1939 and 1976 suggest that the returns to education are falling, although not by a large amount. Data from Colombia also suggest that between 1963 and 1974 the returns to education declined, but still remained profitable.

The results of all these studies confirm that expenditure on education does represent investment in human capital, and that it is a profitable investment, both for the individual and for society, although some critics deny that the earnings of educated workers provide an adequate measure of the economic benefits of education. It is difficult, however, to answer the question of whether human or physical capital represents the more profitable form of investment.

An early attempt to answer this question was called 'Investment in men *versus* investment in machines' (Harberger 1965), and this is still a question that is of vital concern to economists and planners. Psacharopoulos examined estimates of the returns to physical

capital in both developed and developing countries and concluded: (a) the returns to both forms of capital are higher in developing countries, which reflects the differences in relative scarcities of capital in either form in developed and developing countries; and (b) human capital is a superior investment in developing countries but not in developed countries, as indicated by the reversal of the inequality signs in Table 13.2 (Psacharopoulos 1973: 86).

How does Human Capital Increase Workers' Productivity?

The earliest explanations of the concept of human capital suggested that education or training raised the productivity of workers, and hence increased their lifetime earnings, by imparting useful knowledge and skills. However, this assumption was soon attacked by critics who argued that the higher earnings of educated workers simply reflected their superior ability, rather than the specific knowledge and skills acquired during the educational process. In addition, it was argued that highly educated workers are more likely to come from higher social class groups in society, and to work in urban rather than rural areas. Many estimates of rates of return to

Table 13.2. The returns to alternative forms of capital by level of economic development

Level of development	Physical capital		Human capital
Per capita income under $1,000 (7 countries)	15.1	<	19.9
Per capita income over $1,000 (6 countries)	10.5	>	8.3

Source: Psacharopoulos (1981: 329).

education therefore adjust the observed earnings differentials of educated people to allow for the influence of other factors on earnings.

Since ability is one of the main factors that may determine earnings, this is often called the 'ability adjustment' or alternatively the 'alpha coefficient', where 'alpha' (α) represents the proportion of the extra earnings of the educated, which is assumed to be due to education. Regression analysis and earnings functions suggest that an appropriate value for the α coefficient is between 0.66 and 0.8 (Psacharopoulos 1975).

More recently, however, critics have gone further, and have argued that education does not improve productivity by imparting necessary knowledge and skills, but simply acts as a screening device, which enables employers to identify individuals who possess either superior innate ability or certain personal characteristics, such as attitudes towards authority, punctuality, or motivation, which employers value and which are therefore rewarded by means of higher earnings.

This argument is called by various names in the literature, including the 'screening' or 'filtering' hypothesis, or alternatively the 'certification' or 'sheepskin' argument, since it is suggested that education simply confers a certificate, diploma, or 'sheepskin', which enables the holder to obtain a well-paid job without directly affecting his or her productivity. This argument has attracted considerable controversy, but has been refuted by a number of economists who argue that while a 'weak' version of the screening hypothesis is undoubtedly true, since employers do use educational qualifications in selecting employees, as a proxy for other characteristics, there is no evidence to support the 'strong' versions of the hypothesis, that education has no direct effect on productivity. The fact that employers continue to pay educated workers more than uneducated workers throughout their working lives refutes this (Psacharopoulos 1979).

Even if the 'strong' version of the screening hypothesis is rejected, and it is difficult to see why no cheaper means of identifying workers with desired characteristics has not been developed if education really had no effect on productivity, it is nevertheless true that the idea of education as a screen or filter has been important in influencing recent directions in research in the economics of education. Blaug

(1976) in a review of research on investment in human capital, which he describes as a 'slightly jaundiced survey' of the empirical status of human capital theory, predicts that:

in time, the screening hypothesis will be seen to have marked a turning point in the 'human investment revolution in economic thought', a turning point to a richer, still more comprehensive view of the sequential life cycle choices of individuals. (Blaug 1976: 850)

The reason why the screening hypothesis is important is that it has focused attention on the precise way in which education or other forms of investment in human capital influence productivity, and has served as a reminder that education does far more than impart knowledge and skills. The reason why employers continue to prefer educated workers is that not only does the possession of an educational qualification indicate that an individual has certain abilities, aptitudes, and attitudes, but the educational process helps to shape and develop those attributes. In other words, it is now increasingly recognized that education affects attitudes, motivation, and other personal characteristics, as well as providing knowledge and skills.

This means that the concept of investment in human capital is still valid, but it must be extended to include activities which affect personal attributes as well as skills, and it must recognize that such activities increase workers' productivity in complex ways.

Other Forms of Investment in Human Capital

Other forms of investment in human capital also develop the personal attributes that help to determine a worker's productivity. On-the-job training and work experience and the process of job search, including migration, as well as health care, can all increase earning capacity, and can therefore be regarded as investment in human capital. Blaug's survey of research on human capital links all these activities together.

The concept of human capital, or 'hard core' of the human-capital research program is the idea that people spend on themselves in diverse ways, not for the sake of present enjoyments, but for the sake of future pecuniary and non pecuniary returns. . . . All these phenomena—health, education, job search, information retrieval, migration and in-service training—may be viewed as investment rather than consumption, whether undertaken by individuals on their own behalf or undertaken by society on behalf of its members. What knits these phenomena together is not the question of who undertakes what, but rather the fact that the decision-maker, whoever he (*sic*) is, looks forward to the future for the justification of his present actions. . . . The human-capital research program has moved steadily away from some of its early naive formulations . . . [but] it has never entirely lost sight of its original goal of demonstrating that a whole range of apparently disconnected phenomena in the world are the outcome of a definite pattern of individual decisions having in common the features of forgoing present gains for the prospect of future ones. (Blaug 1976: 829, 850)

Not only does research in human capital now link those apparently disparate activities together, but many programmes that have been developed in recent years in response to high levels of unemployment among young people are increasingly concerned to forge closer links between education, training, and work experience. Programmes such as the Youth Opportunities Programme and Youth Training Scheme in the United Kingdom and a number of programmes for young people in Europe are designed to provide alternating periods of vocational education, training, and work experience, recognizing that all these

activities represent investment in human capital (CEDEFOP 1982).

References

Becker, G. S. (1964, 1975), *Human Capital: A Theoretical and Empirical Analysis, with Special Reference to Education* (1st edn., 1964; 2nd edn., 1975, Princeton, NJ: Princeton Univ. Press).

Blaug, M. (1976), 'The Empirical Status of Human Capital Theory: A Slightly Jaundiced Survey', *J. Econ. Lit.*, 14: 827–55.

CEDEFOP (European Centre for the Development of Vocational Training) (1982), *Alternance Training for Young People: Guidelines for Action* (Berlin: CEDEFOP).

Harberger, A. C. (1965), 'Investment in Men Versus Investment in Machines: The Case of India', in Anderson, C. A., and Bowman, M. J. (eds.), *Education and Economic Development* (Chicago: Aldine).

Psacharopoulos, G. (1973), *Returns to Education: An International Comparison* (Amsterdam: Elsevier).

—— (1975), *Earnings and Education in OECD Countries* (Paris: Organization for Economic Co-operation and Development).

—— (1979), 'On the Weak Versus the Strong Version of the Screening Hypothesis', *Econ. Letters*, 4: 181–5.

—— (1981), 'Returns to Education: An Updated International Comparison', *Comp. Educ.*, 17: 321–41.

Schultz, T. W. (ed.) (1961), *Investment in Human Beings* (Chicago: Univ. of Chicago Press).

14

The Gendering of Skill and Vocationalism in Twentieth-Century Australian Education

Jill Blackmore

Central to the numerous educational and economic reform reports which have emerged during the 1980s and early 1990s, both at the state and national level in Australia, is the notion of skilling. Rapid change in the workplace is seen to require recurrent training and upgrading of the skill base of the Australian labour force. For example, in the federal policy statement, *Skills for Australia* (Dawkins and Holding 1987), it is argued that, in order to improve Australia's internal market competitiveness in manufacturing and the service sector, Australia will 'require a more highly skilled and better educated workforce' (Dawkins and Holding 1987: 8). Education and training are seen to be the keys to developing this skills base. Statements about 'the skill demands of new technology' and 'skilling for the national interest' are now starting points from which policy is developed. (See Department of Employment, Education and Training 1989; Ministry of Education and Youth Affairs 1988; Finn 1991.) This 'language of skills', which has assumed different formulations in different times, has largely been translated uncritically into educational policy, usually without clarification. It has provided the rationale for state and federal governments' restructuring of tertiary education, post-compulsory school reorganization as well as curriculum and assessment reform. While intended to link education more closely to the economy and the labour market, this reorganization of school and work is also couched in terms of equity and fairness, 'as preserving and extending the national commitment to democracy and social justice'

(Commonwealth Schools Commission 1987: 8; see also Dawkins 1988; *Australia Reconstructed* 1987). Skilling (through education, training and specific skill programmes, e.g., Skillshare) is therefore rhetorically linked to improving the position of the traditionally disadvantaged (working class, rural, Aboriginal and female students).

The 'language of skills' of the 1980s is based on a number of assumptions. First, that Australia is moving into a post-industrial society which, in turn, requires a new type of productive worker who is 'flexible', 'adaptable' and 'multi-skilled'. In a 'post-industrial society', it is assumed that there has been a shift away from the Fordist organization of work which accompanied industrialization (Matthews *et al.* 1988). Fordism is characterized by a vertical and hierarchical organization of work, distinguishing between management and labour on the basis of the separation of the conception from the execution of labour power. This strict division of labour permeates the organization, with a high degree of specialization and routinized labour. Post-Fordism, by contrast, is premised on the view that quality, innovation and production control can best be handled by front-line producers and not centralized managers. Post-Fordism emphasizes decentralization, support teams and localized decision making. The emphasis is not on top-down control but on horizontal communication between relatively autonomous production units which can, because of their flexibility and adaptability, meet the needs of the consumers better (Murray 1991). The post-Fordist worker

From *Journal of Education Policy*, 7 (1992), 351–8 and 367–77. Reprinted with permission.

must therefore be an adaptable, innovative problem solver possessing a package of generic skills which are transferable across different worksites (Watkins 1990). Different views of skill implicit in the Fordist or non-Fordist perspectives, therefore, carry with them differing implications about how education should prepare youth for work and further training for adults (Meyer 1991).

Second, the 'language of skills' tends to assume a technologically progressivist and determinist stance. It is progressivist in that technology is presumed to bring positive benefits to society in general in that it requires a higher level of technological sophistication and expertise from all members of society (e.g., Myer Committee 1980). It is determinist in that it assumes that technology 'determines' the way in which work is organized. That is, skills are technically defined, rather than the position that technology, as skill, is socially constructed in ways which suit particular interests, whether it be male labour or capital.

Third, while education and training focus on individualized skills, there is the assumption that skilling the individual will have national benefits through aggregation. Since 1987, the notion of skills has been central to the arguments about education making Australia more productive and competitive internationally through 'restructuring' as laid down in *Australia Reconstructed* (1987). This involves changes in the workplace regarding both the roles and skill requirements of workers and is critical to the renegotiation of wages awards. New awards in the 'education industry' link productivity gains to the upgrading of skills with the creation of the Advanced Skills Teacher. The assumption is that there is a direct link between credentials and skilling, between individual skills and national productivity. More people, it is argued, are gaining higher credentials in order to meet the demands of more skilled occupations (Myer 1980: 102), although it is more likely that the credentialing spiral is a consequence of scarcity of educational places and jobs (in February 1992, unemployment ran at 10–11 per cent and up to 30,000 qualified students did not gain tertiary places (*The Age*, 20 February 1992)).

The language and logic of 'skilling' is a particularly well-articulated strand of the discourse of vocationalism which has been loudly

articulated in various periods of economic and social dislocation in Australia and other western welfare capitalist states during the 20th century. This discourse has invariably linked schools to work at the macro level in a more instrumental, economically functional manner. As a set of organized systematic meanings represented through state policy, the media, education—and which become part of common sense—the *discourse of vocationalism* shapes everyday practices, it encourages certain possibilities and limits others by defining concepts in particular ways. For example, at the macro level, during each of the economic recessions of the 1890s, 1930s and 1970s, education was initially blamed for its failure to prepare youth adequately for work, both attitudinally and skillwise. Yet there emerged in the latter phases of each economic downturn the view that education could also provide a solution for the economic ills of the nation through the upgrading of the skills of youth (Bessant 1988). The tension over whether education is the problem or the solution has in some instances led to a shift away from the general notion of 'education for citizenship' (usually associated with liberal education) during the prosperous 1950s and 1960s towards an instrumental and economic view of education serving the economy through the development of individualized skills in the 1980s. What differs in each of these periods is the extent to which the state has been prepared to intervene and, more specifically, to fund the 'upgrading' of the skill of the individual, specific groups or the population at large, although the state has been active in contributing to the discourse (Blackmore 1991).

At the micro level, whilst skill definitions shape in concrete ways the experiences and opportunities of specific groups of youth, the language of skill utilized in the policy discourse tends to use the term in a universal and all-inclusive manner to include a range of activities, from using a cash register to using a lathe. This lack of clarity is in part due to uncertainty as to *actual* technical skill requirements arising from rapid changes in the labour process as well as the gap between policy and what actually occurs in practice. But the universal claims of the skilling thesis at the macro level also obscure the political and social aspects of skill—about who acquires what skills and to whose benefit—and thus serves an ideological function. This ideological aspect is critical at times of scarcity of educational places and employment due to the social selection function of credentials (which supposedly signify skills). Debates which tend to focus on the vocational function of education (and how it should respond to the skill demands of the workplace) are really about who is taught what curriculum, how and by whom. Invariably vocational education is seen to be the lesser alternative to the hegemonic academic curriculum, an alternative which targets 'disadvantaged' or 'at risk' groups (Blackmore 1986).

This article, which is informed by a larger historical and empirical study, looks at the notion of skill as it has altered since the late 19th century; of how, as a major element of the wider discourse of vocationalism, historically and gender-specific notions of skill were produced and maintained as 'givens' (Blackmore 1986). Whereas vocationalization tends to mean the formal linking of education to work (apprenticeship, vocational and career guidance, work education), the discourse of vocationalism refers to how the education–work relationship is discursively constituted in ways which shape the activities of individuals and social groups. In the article, I first critique from a feminist perspective two dominant theoretical frameworks, that of human capital and labour process theory, because of their emphasis on skill and the implications this has for education. Second, I illustrate how, despite the common elements which are present in the discourse of vocationalism (to 'upgrade the skills of school leavers' and to make the curriculum 'more vocationally relevant') there are important differences in what is meant by key concepts such as 'skills' and 'vocational' in specific historical contexts, differences premised on how work is seen to be organized, on different perceptions as to the 'needs' of the nation and the 'needs' of the individual according to their class and gender. In turn these presume particular notions of the learner and the worker. Finally, I consider how the language of skills is framing the reshaping of secondary and tertiary education since the mid-1980s, with particular reference to the implications of this for women and girls. My analysis focuses on the conceptualization of skill in the official rhetoric or policy text in the light of commercial education which provided for girls an occupation which was 'feminized' at the turn of the century. I argue that despite the post-Fordist rhetoric, government reports on labour markets, the economy and education still carry with them many common-sense 'Fordist' assumptions about the nature of skills: that skills are concrete, can be readily categorized, are technically defined and neutral.

Theoretical Frameworks Informing the Education and Skills Debate

Two opposing theoretical frameworks have tended to dominate the ways in which the education–work nexus has been conceptualized—human capital theory derived from mainstream neo-classical economics and labour process theory derived from Marxism. In each the notion of skill has been central. 'Human capital' theory has tended to dominate the official view of the school–work link during the 20th century. It presumes an instrumental view of the relationship between school and work. At a macro level, human capital theory assumes an essentially structuralist-functionalist view of the education–society relationship. It presumes a direct, linear and positive correlation between education and technology, education and individual productivity, education and national economic productivity. At the micro level, the model can be summarized thus: education is an investment which benefits both the individual (and the nation) in that education proportionally increases the potential for individual effort (productive work) and the economic rewards gained from this effort. Individual gain is then aggregated to produce national productivity. Education is viewed as an investment, a matter of individual choice. Skills acquired through education are transferable to work. Educational credentials indicate the level and nature of these skills. The individual is rewarded in proportion to the amount of that investment in education as signified by credentials. The longer one invests in education, the greater the economic rewards. In this model, women's lower economic rewards are a consequence of individual 'choice' not to invest in longer periods of training as they give priority to their family responsibilities rather than due to discrimination or structured disadvantage (Woodhall 1973; Strober 1990).

But the human capital model which has increasingly informed educational policy is empirically and historically inaccurate as a depiction of the choices, options and experiences available to many men, largely working class and/or non-Anglo Celtic, and most women. The emphasis on the labour market and the role of education in supplying labour-market needs assumes, first, that there *is* a labour market in which individuals freely compete on the basis of their skills as signified by the educational credentials they possess. Second, human capital theory argues that discrimination by employers on the basis of gender, race or class is 'irrational' because unprofitable, as the most qualified candidate would not necessarily be employed. That is, there is a direct correlation between the level of education and life chances (Rumberger 1987: 324–6). Third, the mechanism of the labour market, it is argued, is neutral. Criticisms of human capital theory have focused first on the failure to recognize the screening, symbolic and cultural value of credentials, which undermines any notion of them as neutral mechanisms of fair selection; second, on the fact that the problem is as much one of demand as of supply; and, third, that human capital theory has ignored the *sexual* division of labour as central to the workings of the labour market and of capital itself (O'Donnell 1984; Marginson 1990). Indeed, labour-market research has indicated that girls and women, who are more successful educationally and whose work is often more cognitively complex, do not achieve the same economic rewards and promotional opportunities as their male counterparts with equivalent qualifications, a factor exacerbated by labour-market segmentation and employer discrimination (Strober 1990).

The major critique of this 'skilling thesis' has been undertaken by labour process theorists, initiated largely by the work of Harry Braverman in *Labour and Monopoly Capital* in 1974. Braverman argued that, despite the demand for higher education qualifications in general, close historical analysis suggested that technology had in fact led to a general *trend* of deskilling or dispossession of 'the mass of workers from the realms of science, knowledge and skill' since 1900 whilst at the same time increasing the specialization and skills of a small segment of the work-force, the managers and technicians (Braverman 1974:

426). Moreover, he argued that this polarization between those who conceived the organization of work and technology and those who executed these plans on the workshop floor facilitated the process of accumulation of wealth by the few, generally white male middle-class professionals. Certainly, labour-market research has supported some aspects of Braverman's account. Future labour-market demands in the USA, UK and Australia suggest the increasing polarization of labour between the majority of workers, most of them women, being concentrated in increasingly semi-skilled or unskilled labour and a minority of 'highly skilled' technicians, professionals and managers, usually male (Rumberger 1987). Australian research indicates that the demand for skilled workers, particularly in hi-tech industries and engineering, is not as great or universal as the skilling thesis claims (Marginson 1990; Sweet 1987). Employment trends indicate that the greatest area of expansion in employment is in casual and part-time labour for women in jobs not requiring skills or an upgrade in skills, in what could be described as Fordist work organization in which there is little worker autonomy and more repetitive work. This deskilling is also evident in the peripheral labour markets facilitating more 'flexible manufacturing' (Watkins 1990).

Both Braverman's deskilling hypothesis and labour process theory, as well as human capital theory, have been criticized for their claims of universality and determinism. The proliferation of empirical and historical evidence arising from Braverman's publications suggests that the processes of 'deskilling' and 'reskilling' often occur simultaneously, affecting individuals, worksites and social groups differently and often in contradictory ways.

The major points of the critique revolve around Braverman's romantic view of labour, his neglect of class consciousness, his neglect of valorisation, his neglect of gender issues, his neglect of trade union resistance, his failure to see the possibility of re-skilling and hyperskilling—indeed his poor conception of skill itself—his over emphasis on Taylorism and de-emphasis on other forms of job design and his universalistic view of the de-skilling process. (Burrell 1990: 277)

Added to this could be the failure to recognize other 'hegemonic' regimes which elicit workers' consent (Vallas 1990). Braverman's definition of skill is equally limited because it is tuned to the 'craftsman' and is wary of 'relativist' definitions.

Feminists, meanwhile, have critiqued human capital (Woodhall 1973; Strober 1990) and labour process theory (West 1990; O'Donnell 1984) for their assumptions as to the universality of the white middle-class male experience. In particular human capital theorists and psychologists look at skill as the objective property of the worker which can be measured, what Attewell calls the positivist approach to skill. Feminist critiques draw largely from the social constructivist approach to skill which suggests that skill is socially and historically constructed in ways which favour particular individuals and social groups (Attewell 1990). 'Skill' should be seen as being relative, for example, to previous experience; and context bound in that it does not exist without prior knowledge and a framework within which it is defined. Indeed, skill takes on new meanings in specific historical contexts and different worksites. For example, we may think of someone being skilled in the use of a lathe, sewing machine or computer. But empirical research indicates that each of these 'skills' is judged differently according to how the skills are acquired (training/experience), who possesses the skills (male/female, adult/youth) and in what context these skills are used (public/private). Individuals are generally only seen to have expertise or 'skill' when such a skill is associated with paid work and when such skills have been acquired through training. Particular types of skills such as social skills (e.g., interpersonal and emotional management) and operational skills (carrying out routine tasks), which are generally possessed by women, are less highly valued (and paid) or defined as being a lesser skill than other types of skills. Manual, strength-related skills and technical skills which have connotations of expertise, those generally possessed by men, receive higher remuneration and status.

These dichotomies have developed historically, largely because it has been male workers who have had the opportunity and capacity, primarily through guild activity in the 16th century which institutionalized male-dominated craft skills through the law and then more recent union activity, to demand recognition for the types of skills they have acquired and frequently monopolized to

the exclusion of women. Indeed, male unionists have been complicit with male management in excluding women's acquisition of the more valued skills (craft, management and technological). Women's work has therefore generally been stereotyped and statistically and legally categorized as unskilled as much because they have lacked the industrial strength to define it otherwise and not due to any real difference in actual content or technical knowledge. As Nancy Jackson comments:

> The concept of skill involves a complex interplay of technical and social forces. 'Skill' is an idea that serves to differentiate between different kinds of work and workers and to organise relations among them. It has been used for many years to protect the interests of those who have power, and so has come to express the interweaving of the technical organisation of work with hierarchies of power and privilege between men and women, whites and non-whites, old and young. (Jackson 1991)

What historians and social constructionists have come to understand and feminists argue is that people take for granted what they are capable of doing and do not view it as a skill. Indeed, the more widely shared the skills tend to be the more they are devalued perceptually, a relevant issue for women's labour (Attewell 1990: 431).

At the same time, it needs to be recognized that skill is not merely a social or ideological construct, but is often based on material differences in what men and women do. For example, men tend to work in more capital-intensive work whilst women work in labour-intensive work, although both work with technology (Armstrong 1982; Wacjman 1991). Skill, as Cynthia Cockburn has shown in the printing trade, is also bound up with 'the material of male power' in the workplace in which jobs are gendered because of the actual manifestation of the male physical presence as well as the exclusionary power of the male work culture. Hegemonic masculinity in any particular instance is therefore closely associated with technological competence or linked to images of being the male family provider. Changes in skill definitions and boundaries, therefore, are often actively resisted by male unionists as threatening not only their material situation but also their gendered identity (Cockburn 1983).

Furthermore, what is seen to be skilled is as much a factor of supply and demand, and much of the activity of professionals is to restrict supply of their expertise to a select few and by so doing exclude others, thereby maintaining their position as possessors of highly valued skills (Attewell 1990). The feminization of an occupation is often synonymous with deskilling and the displacement of women by men leads to an upgrading of skills, as men have many more horizontal and vertical escape exits. Professionalism and craft unionism have largely been built on the power of an elite group of male experts to claim unique skills. Appealing to such notions therefore has ambiguous implications for women. Finally, deskilling is not uniform for all women. The introduction of new information technologies did not necessarily adversely affect women due to a reduction in office jobs, the deskilling of typists whilst increasing productivity, and the incorporation of the monitoring of work into the machinery itself. Empirical studies have indicated that information technology has been incorporated into existing patterns of work and did not lead to a significant deskilling. This is because any universal theory of deskilling ignores the ways in which women workers actively organize to gain greater satisfaction and control, on how they use the machine within specific contexts (Wacjman 1991).

Occupational case studies and historical research have indicated the complexity of the interaction between patriarchy and capital, education and work, suggesting that the interests of one can indeed work in contradictory ways at some points and converge in other instances. Just because men, both as employers and workers, have in the past and now continue to shape work to protect their labour interests, it does not mean that the gender order is not multidimensional and internally inconsistent in ways which provide space for women workers' resistance and gain, both individually and collectively. What can no longer be denied is that:

far from being an objective economic fact, skill is often an ideological category imposed on certain types of work by virtue of the sex and power of the workers who perform it. Skill has become saturated with sex. It is not that skill categories have been totally subjectified: in all cases some basis was found in the content of the work to justify the distinction between men's and women's work. But the equations—men/skilled and women/unskilled—are so powerful that the identification of a particular job with women required that the skill content of the work would be downgraded. (Phillips and Taylor 1980: 79, 85).

Skill is therefore a relational concept, just as is gender. It is how one activity, attribute or form of knowledge is compared with others. What is at issue is not whether deskilling occurs, or whether reskilling is possible, but rather why the gender stereotyping of jobs, with men largely controlling the more highly skilled (and technological) jobs and women the less skilled (social) jobs, has not altered given the inconsistent findings to support more universal and totalizing theories. We need to distinguish between the ways in which skill was used to establish initial occupational segregation and how it has been used to maintain gendered divisions of labour.

Likewise, education does not instrumentally serve the economy or organize itself in correspondence to production. The role education plays in either the deskilling or reskilling theses has also been oversimplified and deterministic. Whilst human capital theory emphasizes supply-side forces of the labour market (e.g., skills possessed by individual workers) with little reference to the production process, labour process theory has tended to ignore the labour market. In the former perspective, education is an individual investment; in the latter, education systematically reproduces social inequalities based only on class. Neither has a sense of the contradictory relationships in the education–work relationship, nor how work and education must be linked to the family and the gendered subject. Nor do they recognize how various discourses or policies seeking to produce equity (equality of opportunity, vocational education) are translated differentially, even subverted, at the level of practice within specific locations and contexts. This requires investigating small-scale, localized relationships within occupations, organizations and worksites and points to the need for further historical and process-type case studies (Fincher 1989). Work of this type is already under way. Studies of vocational education in 20th-century Britain (Schilling 1989); corporation schools in early 20th-century USA (Nelson-Rowe 1991); unemployed youth in Victoria in the 1930s (Holbrook 1987); adolescent girls' career choices in 1950s Victoria (Blackmore 1986); work experience programmes in the 1970s (Watkins 1987) indicate how vocational schemes intending to produce more malleable and productive workers have often meant targeted youth were less likely to be involved in the workplace in the area in which they were 'trained'.

I have emphasized the human capital model of the education–work relationship and its critics because it underpins the economic, award and educational restructuring in Australia in the late 1980s and early 1990s negotiated between the Federal Labor government with the complicity of the male-dominated peak union organization (the Australian Council of Trade Unions) within the framework of the Economic Accord (1983) (Campbell 1990). Indeed, current trends appear to have assumed what Attewell has described as a positivist approach to skill. This view has dominated economic, sociological, psychological and educational theory for much of the 20th century in the search for more sophisticated and technical ways to categorize and measure skills so that they can be standardized and compared across work situations, rather than questioning the very notion itself.. . .

Skilling for the National Economy from the 1970s to the 1990s

Despite expansion of the service sector and the collapse of agriculture and mining during the 1970s, the solution to Australia's economic crisis was seen to rest with developing a manufacturing and science infrastructure. Education was to assist by focusing on science, maths and applied technology and technical education, as previously, in the 1930s and 1900s, it was promoted as the main avenue for developing the skills base for the economic infrastructure. In 1974, the Technical and Further Education (TAFE) colleges were established to meet directly the immediate training needs of industry. But the TAFE system was saturated with masculine bias and skill training was modelled on the male craftsman. Not only did apprenticeship continue to absorb its resources but the training, rather than educational emphasis, reflected the interest, experience and energy of its predominantly male staff. Women's access programmes intended to act as bridging courses for women between generalist education and

specialist technical courses were secondary to the legal commitment to apprenticeship monopolized by males (Pocock 1988: 18). As unemployment increased, the technical versus general education debate within the TAFE sector intensified and 'equity' (often equated with access to women) lost out to efficiency. Vocational relevance in the context of declining resources in the TAFE sector meant providing training which had immediate economic benefit (job-specific skills) which met workplace demand rather than more general prevocational education oriented towards interpersonal and life skills (women's access programmes). And, as has been the pattern since 1900, women tended to pay for their vocational training in specialist skill areas such as hairdressing and clerical work whilst the federal government maintained high levels of funding for apprenticeships and in areas which were traditionally male fields (electronics and engineering).

Schools initially also responded to the growing youth unemployment after 1974 in traditional ways, largely because state schools and individual youth were again blamed for job shortages which were a consequence of global and structural factors. For example, there was concern to upgrade skill formation in new technology with the introduction of computers and word processing. Specific courses were developed for 'at risk' youth which were more vocationally relevant, e.g., word processing and corporate secretarial work (see also Gaskell 1986 for a Canadian example). Sandra Taylor argues that in fact in Australia this was training girls in job-specific skills at a time when the introduction of word processing was in fact reducing the demand for female school leavers with clerical skills by over a half during the period 1971–76 (Taylor 1986; Sweet 1980). Whilst the rationale for such business courses at secondary and tertiary level was to impart job-specific vocational skills, the courses themselves, as in the past, were more concerned first, about the socialization of the female students into 'good' secretarial practice which was premised on the acquisition of social and highly gendered constructs of femininity rather than technical skills and, second, a 'life skills' emphasis due to the high possibility of unemployment (Gaskell 1986; Claydon 1986). As in the past, the emphasis on social rather than cognitive or technical skills for 'at risk' students virtually guarantees their unemployability, although within this 'skilling' is couched as a means of promoting equity through improving at-risk youth's access to the market. Schools are not directly catering for labour-market demand, but as much meeting political pressure to address wider social issues of youth unemployment.

Likewise the first youth employment schemes of the Liberal Government focused on the mismatch between youth's skills and those required by the labour market resulting from the perceived failure of schools (Williams report 1979: 88–9). Again, youth policy initially relied heavily on the private business sector, voluntary organizations and community-based programmes to create solutions for this youth crisis, e.g., Community Youth Support Scheme. At the same time major policy initiatives kept the responsibility for vocational training with the public educational sector, e.g., the Transition Education Program which encouraged 'at risk' youth to stay on at school. TEAC rejected narrow vocational training in favour of a more integrated studies curriculum designed to encourage the development of a wide set of skills broadly related to work and human relations (coping and survival skills) and 'self reliance'. Whilst this did produce many worthwhile curricular practices in schools it still individualized the youth problem by emphasizing self-help and social skilling to increase 'juvenile productivity' (Dwyer *et al.* 1984).

So by the 1980s two competing educational ideologies existed—the vocational manpower perspective on transitional education exemplified in such community and non-school programmes as CYSS, which focused on social and survival skills, and a 'liberal approach in which schools supplied general skills transferable to a range of circumstances (Kemmis *et al.* 1983: 114–16). The latter direction was extended with the Labor Party's election to Federal Government between 1983 and 1987 and the Participation and Equity Program which sought to 'mainstream' educational reform and make the curriculum more inclusive and less academic, and hopefully, therefore, more attractive to more students. Whilst TEAC had been content driven (teaching job skills to meet employer demands for 'school leaver with relevant skills'), PEP moved on to examine the concept

of a common curriculum (Rizvi and Kemmis 1988: 237–8).

Whilst there is a high level of continuity in how vocational education is seen to be the panacea for youth unemployment, and how 'vocational' for working-class youth and girls implies the imparting of social and attitudinal skills rather than technical or high-level cognitive skills, the 1980s witnessed significant changes in ways in which the discourse of vocationalism is framing educational policy (Seddon 1991). First, there has been a move away from the view that the state should fully fund education because the state benefits from the skilling of its citizens, towards a market philosophy which asserts that the individual also benefits from education and training and should contribute financially as well through a graduate tax in tertiary education (1989) and user-pay fees in TAFE (1991). This is a good indicator of the level to which economic rationalism became orthodoxy within a federal Labor Party which abolished university fees in 1972. Employers are also expected to fund some small part of the costs of upgrading skills with the industry training levy of 1 per cent, although Australian industry has historically invested little in research and training. The hegemony of human capital view is also clearly evident in the various national reports on education, training and technology (Myer 1980; Dawkins 1988; Finn 1991) with their 'rejection of Keynesian economics' and 'reversion to classical political economics' (Freeland and Sharp 1984: 215–16). Hence the emphasis on educational production functions (which presumes an input-output industrial model) and cost effectiveness as a means to measure educational output and reduce the wastage of human capital. Recent reports invoke the capacity of 'market forces' to allocate efficiently labour power and the distribution of educational opportunities for individuals. That is, the market will apportion rewards according to merit and therefore deliver equity, a claim now challenged with high white-collar unemployment. A second difference which emerged with the *Kirby Report on the Labour Market* in 1985 is the desire to minimize labour-market segmentation, as it impeded the creation of a 'flexible and highly skilled workforce' able to adapt quickly to the changing needs of a rapidly changing and more technologically sophisticated post-Fordist workplace. The gendered division of labour is now seen to be unprofitable and unproductive (and not just unfair). Women are now the 'wasted resource' to be encouraged to enter areas which suffer a skill shortage—science, engineering, technology and the trades (Blackmore and Kenway 1988; Kenway 1989).

Third, past dichotomies are disappearing from the discourse of vocationalism as they lose their power when confronted with the perceived needs of the post-Fordist worker. This is most obvious in the oft-repeated statement that the 'artificial distinction between "general" and "vocational" has long outlived its usefulness.... The Schools Commission does not see a "necessary conflict between general educational goals and vocationally useful education" ... nor a necessary dichotomy between the needs of the individuals and the interests of the nation as a whole' (Commonwealth Schools Commission 1987: 3). Again, in 1991, the Finn *Review on Post-compulsory Education and Training* stated 'both individual and industry needs are leading towards a convergence of general and vocational education. There is an increasing realism internationally that the most successful forms of work organization are those which encourage people to be multi-skilled, creative and adaptable' (Finn 1991: ix). Both reports presume a more instrumental view of education directing education towards national economic priorities as we move into a post-Fordist society.

The post-Fordist worker, therefore, is expected to display flexibility and adaptability (Watkins 1990). Job continuity is no longer the norm. The language of skill now focuses on 'multiskilling' and 'broadbanding': the transferability of 'generic' skills across a broad band of work situations. 'Multiskilling' is seen to be distinct from job-specific training, the latter now relegated to specialist courses in TAFE. Skilling in this context has taken on an abstract quality. Whereas skills in the early and mid-20th century referred more narrowly to what were seen to be specific technical or manual competencies, skilling now also refers more broadly to social, affective and intellectual competencies as well, e.g., entrepreneurial and creative skills in the search for a 'clever country'. Field (1990: 1) in *Skilling Australia*, for example, defines skill formation as 'a holistic concept that includes "education", "personal development", "formal training", "on

the job learning" and "experimental learning" '. Likewise, education, as the means to acquiring the necessary skills, has also to become 'flexible' (Watkins 1991). For example, *In the National Interest* states: 'the object of education is the development of educated persons who have the breadth of knowledge, useful and readily refocused skills, a commitment to continue learning, and competencies which make them effective persons in the various facets of their social and working lives' (Commonwealth Schools Commission 1987: 8). These sentiments are echoed in the Finn Review.

The educational response in curriculum terms, as in *Strengthening Australia's Schools: A Consideration of the Focus and Content of Schooling* (Department of Employment, Education and Training 1989), has been to emphasize critical thinking, competencies and problem solving rather than content; what could be described as learning about learning. Knowledge, skills and capacities are therefore seen to be discrete. Indeed the language of skills of the 1980s implies that skilling itself is 'content free'. Out of this, a new 'curriculum of employability' for the majority has emerged, defined by the Finn Review as a 'general vocational' education which is 'broad and balanced' with an 'appropriate mix of vocational and general education', 'theoretical and applied studies'. Learning is work, and work is learning in this new curriculum. Literacy and numeracy are now joined by computer literacy and communication skills as the key elements of vocational literacy. Specific subject fields (language and communication, mathematics, scientific and technological understanding, cultural understanding, problem solving, personal and interpersonal) are being broken down into 'key competencies'. This is a further shift in the direction started by the Australian Education Council's Hobart Statement on National Curriculum Objectives towards finding common definitions of work-related key competencies (skills) in specific fields of knowledge or learning areas so that they too can be assessed and compared across sites, across time and across individuals.

A number of dilemmas exist for educationalists here. First, the highly generalized 'language of skills' is problematic for educators because it lacks specific criteria for translating policy into practice. Skills can mean minimal literacy and numeracy, can refer to specific skills or more generic skills of comprehension and problem solving, skills in emotional management or high-level cognitive expertise, or can imply the capacity to increase ability in an area and gain mastery or excellence. There now appears to be a shift towards clarification of what is meant by skill. This creates new problems, given that the new competency-based approach to curriculum is both controlling of students and teachers, not only because it has a particularly narrow behaviourist view of pedagogy, but also because it can be linked to standardized assessment. Second, the introduction of problem solving includes the traditions of liberal progressivist educational thought with its focus on analysis, critical thinking, decision making and creative thinking but offers a new competency: 'skill transfer to new contexts'.

Third, the construction of skill is no less gendered in this new reading of the language of generic skills, despite the apparent inclusion of equity. Rather, it has assumed different nuances and produced new ironies. For example, women's work has traditionally been associated largely with the emotional management skills (caring and sharing) and therefore not seen to 'skill'. The notion of the multi-skilled manager in corporate management has effectively captured, without the same commitment, these emotional management, communication, interpersonal team-work skills in management and marketing (Yeatman 1990). This is most evident in the way in which the Finn Review perceives interpersonal and personal key competencies which include personal management and planning, negotiation and team skills, initiative and leadership, adaptability to change, self-esteem and ethics, all expectations of what may be required of the post-Fordist worker (or androgynous manager?) in the corporate state. And, as with previous appeals to vocational education, the Finn Review links the skilling of Australia to disadvantage (rather than equity or discrimination). In seeking to promote mass secondary education until the age of 19, and in so doing raise the status of technical education, the Finn Review glibly slips across the essentially male-based power structure of TAFE, and the possibility of making it (and the traineeships) more accessible to women. Furthermore, the Mayer Committee (1992), which is expected to operationalize the specific meaning of 'work-related key competencies' has been belatedly asked to consider 'competencies relating to family and household management as a way of ensuring gender equity in employment opportunities' (Department of Employment, Education and Training 1992: 7). Thus shifts in the meaning of 'skill' signify changing social relationships within the labour process and between the public and private in ways which do not necessarily alter power relationships.

Indeed, I would suggest that, despite the theoretical shift from the notion of 'situation-specific' towards 'generic' skills, the current national agenda for skill formation and all its educational implications has not significantly altered the underlying positivist and common-sense view embedded in human capital theory that skill is a fixed and measurable attribute defined by the technical needs of the workplace. And this is clear in the way in which the social constructivist position assumed by feminists has been marginalized. Increasingly, skilled work has been more closely associated with mental and esoteric rather than the physical and everyday activities. The social constructionist position, one largely assumed by feminists working in this field, is that skill is a relational phenomenon which depends not only on the relation of one kind of task to another (e.g., mental/manual work) but the supply and demand for people to do these tasks (e.g., local labour market) and the capacity of the incumbents to exclude others (e.g., male jobs/female jobs) as well as the material and technical aspects of work. Feminist theories of skill perhaps point to the need to consider different ways of judging skill—ones which value different types of skills, which are less individualized and more experientially based (Wacjman 1991).

So why has the skilling thesis of human capital theory become part of Labor orthodoxy? My argument suggests that it can be attributed partly to the poor database on skill classifications and how skills are linked to education, as well as to the lack of comprehensive research on the labour market in Australia. But there are other factors which must be considered. First, the focus on skills has much to do with the maintenance of particular gendered power relations in the workplace. Whilst there has been some sensitivity to the notion of skill as a social construct, it has been marginalized as a women's issue, because to view skill as other than an objective criterion for job evaluation is to undermine the position, historically developed, of male unionists in the skilled trades. In current award restructuring there is only token acknowledgement of the social constructionist approach to skill which tries to understand the conditions under which some occupations are marked as more skilled than others when trying to comprehend the anomaly of women (Attewell 1990). Because the male craft worker is still the benchmark for skill definition in award restructuring, it is in the interests of negotiators not to do otherwise: the trade unions who cannot negate past notions of skill which have been historically constructed to favour male skilled trades; the business groups who seek to reduce costs through redefinitions of skill and have always benefited from women's lower pay rate; and the male managers who seek to maintain the status of mental over manual skill and be sure that skill is measured by how many you have authority over and how much money you manage rather than degree of autonomy or actual cognitive activity. No wonder women's interests in this process have largely been perceived as particularistic and marginal. Second, there is relative empirical ignorance of the complexity of factors which influence the individual's educational and occupational decisions and how these are impacted by gender, race and class. Third, the lack of criticism indicates the power of the hegemonic discourse of vocationalism in a period of economic uncertainty, about how schools should better serve the economy, and how this ideology has assumed a commonsense view of the school–work nexus which is ahistorical, inaccurate and deterministic.

The Language of Skills and its Educational Implications

What are the educational consequences of the uncritical acceptance of the language of skills in education? First, the language of skills conflates the acquisition of menial, trivial and routinized tasks by subdividing and labelling, thereby converting 'tasks' into 'skills'. In so doing, such tasks become 'meaningful and productive work' (Jonathon 1991). In Australia, the conflation of skill in the educational discourse is evident with the introduction of

work education as a cross-curriculum activity in many states. Now mental, manual and social skills acquired in classrooms can be related in all courses to future work. Study skills are now defined as productive work, such valuable intellectual skills being construed to lead to more creative and flexible workers.

Second, by using the 'language of skills' as a justification for education, training *and* skilling, it 'rationalizes' the connection of welfare payments to what appears to be the acquisition of skills which are supposedly beneficial to both the individual and the community. In this way, it is generally the working-class student who is forced to undergo 'upskilling' in menial work or acquisition of 'life' or social skills rather than technical or cognitive skills in order to receive welfare benefits through such programmes, which means the recipients of such 'skilling' will remain 'outsiders' in terms of the mainstream skill formation.[1]

Third, there is increasingly a skills-based approach to curriculum formation away from a curriculum based on teacher-pupil interaction according to needs towards a mechanistic, standardizing approach. The new Victorian Certificate of Education finalized in 1992 emphasizes a broad range of problem-solving skills or learning about learning. The generalist liberal curriculum (as opposed to the classical liberal curriculum) has been 'vocationalized' in that it is seen to provide each individual with a set of skills which will supposedly broaden their post-school options in an idealized conception of the nature of skills, of work and the operation of the labour market: that is, the multiskilled student. I have suggested that the competency-based approach to learning being taken up by the Finn Review, a report written by non-educationalists, despite its claim to produce the post-Fordist worker, assumes essentially a behaviourist (if not Taylorist) approach to pedagogy, in which curriculum is treated as a technology, the teacher as a facilitator in transmitting an agreed package of competencies; in which competencies are concrete and measurable products of a linear learning process transferable to the workplace (Brown 1991). In so doing, it still adheres to the craft-based view of skill of the late 19th century. Unfortunately, in the search for key competencies within a national curriculum and assessment framework, competencies which are testable and comparable, whichever view of skill dominates has critical implications for curriculum and assessment, and therefore for pedagogy.

Fourth, it is the state system of education which has been blamed for education's failure to prepare youth with the necessary vocational skills given that the public education system has historically been expected to 'warehouse' potentially disruptive youth, thus allowing the private system its uninterrupted monopoly of the liberal-academic curriculum. Thus the 'language of skills' is ideologically powerful to conservative governments seeking to further privatize education at the cost of residualizing state education.

Finally, new dilemmas arise out of the discourse of vocationalism and the skilling debate for women and girls in the current educational context. The skilling thesis has been closely linked to arguments for greater equality of opportunity. Historically, girls and women have benefited from state interventionism, e.g., Equal Opportunity Policy and the funding of vocational initiatives. Working-class girls, for example, have been funded by the state whilst acquiring job-specific training in stenography and typing in the period after 1945 until the 1970s when such skills became redundant. This has promoted the social mobility of many working-class girls into white-collar jobs, in relatively more pleasant work environments than factories. At the same time, these gender-specific vocational skills slotted them effectively into female-type jobs (e.g., secretarial). In this way, the vocationalization of schooling reinforced rather than challenged the gender relations of the workplace, whilst allowing limited social mobility for a few. Likewise, youth traineeships in the 1980s (a watered-down version of apprenticeship), which specifically targeted girls to broaden their skill base, succeeded primarily only in the public sector whereas the private sector failed to respond. So, in one sense, women continue to benefit from state intervention.

But the state is also determining the direction and therefore redefinition of equity. Current national policy initiatives (*Higher Education: A Policy Statement* (Dawkins 1980) and the *National Policy on the Education of Girls*) also favour an unsegmented and free labour market, undifferentiated by sex in which the multiskilled individual can move within broad bands of related occupations, acquiring new skills and updating old, with a particular focus on non-traditional fields (science, maths and technology). These vocational arguments are fired by a particularly narrow view of equality and an ill-informed notion of how the labour market works and so may be a disservice in the long run to most women's and girls' interests. Such policies continue to ignore the relationship between the public domain of paid work and the 'private' aspect of individual lives. Instead, women are being 'repackaged' for the service of the market (Weiner 1988). It is incorrectly assumed, for example, that the skills held by women will receive the same economic and social rewards in the labour market. The notion of equity, is also redefined, linking it to individual choice in a free market rather than to the group disadvantage constructed through a gendering process embedded in the interactions between the labour market, the labour process, education and the family. The needs of the individual are also redefined narrowly in terms of skill and not more broad human attributes.

Furthermore, the emphasis on women gaining access to the science and technology labour market privileges, even if by default, cognitive and technical skills over social and affective skills, which are the 'traditional' skills associated with women's work (Kenway 1989). And where social skills *are* valued, as with the 'multiskilled manager', they are encouraged merely for their instrumental value in increasing productivity and not for their intrinsic human value (Yeatman 1990). Whilst women may no longer be destined only for motherhood and family, their 'feminine qualities' (caring, interpersonal relations, communication) have now been 'co-opted' for managerialist ends. Because of other complexities, it has, therefore, become increasingly difficult at a practical level to distinguish between 'liberal/progressive ideas concerning the freedom for girls and women to move upwards in educational and occupational hierarchies and "liberal"/laissez-faire ideas about labour market freedom, "the myth perpetrated by the New Right" ' (Seddon 1991).

In conclusion, at a macro level, other contradictions follow if the technological progressivist 'skilling thesis' is taken to its logical conclusion in an uncritical manner. The introduction of technology as a social good leads to temporary employment dislocation which demands constant reskilling and retraining. Consequently, there is a continual 'drain' on public expenditure acquired by the state through taxes on capital accumulation, which in turn reduces profitability and restricts capital accumulation (Freeland and Sharp 1984). This puts pressure on Labor governments to privatize and individualize skill acquisition. Furthermore, if education systems were more effective in producing the well-educated students as the upskilling thesis implies and in reducing the sexual inequalities of the labour market, the result would be socially critical employees (half of them women) who would be more disruptive and demanding in terms of conditions of employment, a trend which would be detrimental to capital's and/or male control over the workplace. But such contradictions are generally submerged through the persuasive power of the hegemonic discourse of vocationalism and the language of skills.

Note

1. The raising of the unemployment benefit minimum age to 18 years in Australia in 1989 and maintaining the benefit at a lower level than Austudy has forced many students who would previously have left to stay on in school.

References

Apprenticeship Commission, Victoria (1941–58), *Annual Reports* (Melbourne: Victorian Government Printer).

Archer, L. J. (1952), 'What do Employers Expect from Secondary Schools with Regard to Pre-Employment Commercial Education?' (B.Ed. investigation, Melbourne Univ.).

Armstrong, P. (1982), 'If it's Only Women it Doesn't Matter so Much', in J. West (ed.), *Work, Women and the Labour Market* (London: Routledge and Kegan Paul).

Attewell, P. (1990), 'What is Skill?' *Work and Occupations*, 17/4: 422–48.

Australian Council of Trade Unions (1987), *Australia Reconstructed* (Canberra: AGPS).

Bacchi, C. (1990), *Same Difference: Feminism and Sexual Difference* (Sydney: Allen and Unwin).

Baxter, F. (1937), 'Commercial Education in High Schools in a Metropolitan, Industrial District and in Country Districts' (B. Ed. Investigation, Melbourne Univ.).

Bessant, B. (1971), 'Education and Politics in the Development of Educational Customs of N. S. W. and Victoria, 1900–1940' (unpubl. Ph.D. thesis, Monash).

Bessant, J. (1988), 'Meeting the Demands of the Corporate Sector: Unemployment, Education and Training', *Journal of Australian Studies* (May): 22–34.

Blackmore, J. (1986), 'Schooling for Work: Vocationalism in Victorian State Secondary Education 1920–60' (unpubl. Ph.D. thesis, Stanford Univ.).

—— (1987), 'Schooling for Work: Gender Differentiation in Commercial Education in Victoria 1930–60', *History of Education Review*, 17/1: 31–50.

—— (1991), 'Education and the Marketplace', *Education Links*, 41 (Spring): 22–6.

—— and Kenway (1988), 'Rationalisation, Instrumentalism and Corporate Managerialism: The Implications of the Green Paper for Women', *Australian Universities Review*, 31/1: 42–8.

Blaug, M. (1976), 'The Empirical Status of Human Capital Theory: A Slightly Jaundiced Survey', *Journal of Economic Literature*, 13/2: 47–55.

Braverman, H. (1974), *Labor and Monopoly Capital: The Degradation of Work in Twentieth Century America* (New York: Monthly Press).

Brown, M. (1991), 'Competency Based Training: Skilled Formation for the Workplace or Classroom Taylorism' (paper presented to the Australian Curriculum Studies Association Conference, Adelaide, July).

Browne, K. (1981), 'Schooling, Capitalism and the Mental/Manual Division of Labour', *Sociological Review*, 29/3: 445–73.

Burrell, G. (1990), 'Fragmented Labours', in D. Knights and D. Wilmott (eds.), *Labour Process Theory* (London: Macmillan).

Campbell, I. (1990), 'The Australian Trade Union Movement and Post-Fordism', *Australian Political Economy*, 26 (April): 1–26.

Claydon, L. (1986), 'Closing the Gap Between Technical Education and the Occupationally Disoriented: A Case Study', *Discourse*, 6/2: 32–45.

Cockburn, C. (1983), *Brothers: Male Dominance and Technological Change* (London: Pluto Press).

Commonwealth Schools Commission (1987), *In the National Interest: Secondary Education and Youth Policy in Australia* (Canberra: Australian Government Printing Service).

Connell, R. W., and Irving, I. (1980), *Class Structure in Australian History* (Melbourne: Longman).

Crompton, R., and Mann, M. (eds.) (1986), *Gender and Stratification* (Cambridge: Polity Press).

Dawkins, J. (1988), *Higher Education: A Policy Statement*, The White Paper (Canberra: Australian Government Printing Service).

—— and Holding, C. (1987), *Skills for Australia* (Canberra: Australian Government Printing Service).

Deacon, D. (1985), 'Political Arithmetic: The Nineteenth Century Australian Census and the Construction of the Dependent Woman', *Signs*, 11/1: 27–47.

—— (1989), *Managing Gender: The State, the New Middle Class and Women Workers 1830–1930* (Melbourne: Oxford Univ. Press).

Department of Employment, Education and Training (1987), *The National Policy for the Education of Girls in Australia* (Canberra: Australian Government Printing Service).

—— (1989), *Strengthening Australia's Schools: A Consideration of the Focus and Content of Schooling* (Canberra: Australian Government Printing Service).

—— (1992), *National Collaborative Curriculum and Assessment Program: A Commonwealth Information Paper* (Canberra: Schools and Curriculum Policy Branch).

Dwyer, P., Wilson, B., and Woock, R. (1984), *Confronting School and Work* (Sydney: George Allen and Unwin).

Education Reform Association (1945), *Better Education Campaign*, Pamphlet 4 (Melbourne: ERA).

Eltham, E. P. (1935), *A Report on Technical Education in Other Countries* (Sydney: Government Printer).

Feinberg, W., and Horowitz, B. (1990), 'Vocational Education and Equality of Opportunity', *Journal of Curriculum Studies*, 22/2: 188–92.

Field, L. (1990), *Skilling Australia* (Melbourne: Longman, Cheshire).

Fincher, R. (1989), 'Class and Gender Relations in the Local Labor Market and the Local State', in J. Wolch and M. Dear (eds.), *The Power of Geography* (London: Unwin and Hyman).

Fink Commission (1901), *Royal Commission on Technical Education in Victoria Second Report* (Melbourne: Victorian Government Printer).

Finn, B. (1991), *Young People's Participation in Post Compulsory Education and Training. Report of the Australian Education Council Review Committee* (Canberra: Australian Government Printing Service).

Freeland, J., and Sharp, R. (1984), 'The Williams Report on Education, Training and Employment: The Decline and Fall of Karmelot', in P. Watkins, *Youth Schooling and Work* (Geelong: Deakin University Press).

Garner, C. (1982), 'Educated and White Collar Women in the 1880s', in E. Windschuttle, *Women, Class and History* (Sydney: Fontana): 112–31.

Gaskell, J. (1986), 'The Changing Organisation of Business Education in the High School: Teachers Respond to School and Work', *Curriculum Inquiry*, 16/4: 417–37.

—— (1991), 'Conceptions of Skills and the Work of Women: Some Historical and Political Issues', *Network of Women in Further Education* (Dec.): 10–17.

Holbrook, A. (1987), 'Slotting them into the Right Niche: Adolescence and Vocational Guidance', in B. Bessant, *Mother State and Her Little Ones* (Melbourne: Centre for Youth and Community Studies).

—— and Bessant, B. (1986), 'Responses to Youth Unemployment in the 1930s and the 1980s', paper presented at Anzhes Conference, Adelaide.

Jackson, N. (1991), *The Politics of Skill* (Geelong: Deakin University Press).

Jonathon, R. (1987), 'The Youth Training Scheme and Core Skills: An Educational Analysis', in G. Esland (ed.), *Education, Training and Employment*, ii: *The Educational Response* (Milton Keynes: Addison Wesley).

Keeves, J., and Read, J. (1974), 'Sex Differences in Comparing for Scientific Occupations', *Educational Administration Report* (Hawthorn: ACER).

Kemmis, S. *et al.* (1983), *Transition and Reform in the Victorian Transition Education Program* (Geelong: Deakin Institute for Studies in Education).

Kenway, J. (1989), 'Non-Traditional Pathways: Are They the Way to Go?' (unpubl. paper, Geelong: Deakin University).

Kirby Report (1985), *Committee of Enquiry into Labour Market Programs Report* (Canberra: Australian Government Printing Service).

Lowe, G. S. (1987), *Women in the Administrative Revolution* (Cambridge: Polity Press).

Maglen, L. R. (1990), 'Challenging the Human Capital Orthodoxy: The Education–Productivity Link Re-examined', *Economic Record*, 195: 281–94.

Marginson, S. (1990), 'Labor's Economic Policies in Higher Education', *The Australian Quarterly Review* (Spring): 256–66.

Martindale, J. (1939), 'The Vocational Aspect of a Secondary School in a Rural Community' (B. Ed. Investigation, Melbourne Univ.).

Matthews, J., Hall, G., and Smith, H. (1988), 'Towards Flexible Skill Formation and Technological Literacy: Challenges Facing the Education System Economic and Industrial Democracy', *Economic and Industrial Democracy*, 9: 497–522.

Mayer Committee (1992), *Employment Related Key Competencies for Post Compulsory Education and Training. A Discussion Paper*.

McCallum, D. (1989), *The Social Production of Merit* (Sussex: Falmer Press).

McQueen, H. (1983), 'Higgins and Arbitration', in E. Wheelwright and K. Buckley (eds.), *Essays in the Political Economy of Australian Capitalism* (NSW: Australian and New Zealand Book Co).

Medley, J. (1943), *Education for Democracy* (Melbourne: ACER).

Meyer, T. (1991), 'Post-Fordist Ideologies and Education', *Melbourne Studies in Education 1991*, ed. D. Stockley (Bundoora: Latrobe Univ. Press).

Miller, P. (1984), 'Efficiency, Stupidity and Class Conflict in South Australian Schools, 1875–1900', *History of Education Quarterly* (Fall): 32–43.

Ministry of Education and Youth Affairs, NSW (1988), *Discussion Paper on the Curriculum in New South Wales Schools*, Carrick Report (Sydney: NSW Government Printer).

Morey, E. (1946), *The School Leaving Age* (Hawthorn: Australian Council of Educational Research).

Murray, R. (1991), 'The State after Henry', *Marxism Today* (May): 24–8.

Musgrave, P. W. (1964), *Technical Change and the Labour Force and Education* (London: Pergamon Press).

Myer Committee (1980), *Technological Change in Australia*, i. (Canberra: Australian Government Printing Service).

Nelson-Rowe, S. (1991), 'Corporation Schooling and the Labour Market at General Electric', *History of Education Quarterly*, 31/1: 27–45.

O'Donnell, C. (1984), *The Basis of the Bargain: Gender, Schooling and Jobs* (Sydney: Allen and Unwin).

Phillips, A., and Taylor, B. (1980), 'Sex and Skill: Notes Towards a Feminist Economics', *Feminist Review*, 6: 79–88.

Pocock, B. (1988), *Demanding Skill: Women and Technical Education in Australia* (Sydney: Allen and Unwin).

Pringle, R. (1988), *Secretaries Talk: Sexuality, Power and Work* (Sydney: Allen and Unwin).

Reiger, K. (1985), *The Disenchantment of the Home* (Melbourne: Oxford Univ. Press).

Rizvi, F., and Kemmis, S. (1988), *Dilemmas of Reform* (Geelong: Deakin Institute of Studies in Education).

Rowse, T. (1978), *Australian Liberalism and National Character* (Melbourne: Kibble Books).

Rumberger, R. (1987), 'The Potential Impact of Technology on the Skill Requirements of Future Jobs in the United States', in G. Burke and R. Rumberger (eds.), *The Future Impact of Technology on Work and Education* (Lewes: Falmer Press): 23–41.

Ryan, E. (1987), 'Women and Production', in N. Grieve and A. Burns (eds.), *Australian Women: New Feminist Perspectives* (Melbourne: Oxford Univ. Press).

Schilling, C. (1989), *Schooling for Work in Capitalist Britain* (Lewes: Falmer Press).

Seddon, T. (1991), 'Educating the Clever Country', paper presented to Royal Australian Institute of Public Administration and Australian College of Education, Canberra, July.

Selleck, R. J. (1987), 'State Education and Culture', *Australian Journal of Education*, 26/1: 1–15.

Shields, J. (1982), 'A Dangerous Age: Bourgeois Philanthropy, the State and the Young Unemployed in NSW in the 1930s', in Sydney Labour History Group, *What Rough Beast? The State and Social Order in Australian History* (Sydney: George Allen and Unwin), 151–170.

Strober, M. (1990), 'Human Capital Theory: Implications for HR Managers', *Industrial Relations*, 29/2: 239–46.

Sweet, R. (1980), 'An Analysis of the Trends in the Teenage Labour Market in NSW 1971–6', *TAFE Research Report*, Sydney.

—— (1987), 'Australian Trends in Skill Requirements', in G. Burke and R. Rumberger (eds.), *The Future Impact of Technology on Work and Education* (Lewes: Falmer Press), 42–55.

Tate, F. (1908), 'School Power: An Imperial Necessity', address to the Imperial Federation League, Melbourne.

Taylor, S. (1986), 'Teenage Girls and Economic Recession in Australia: Some Cultural and Educational Implications', *British Journal of Sociology of Education*, 7/4: 379–95.

Vallas, S. (1990), 'The Concept of Skill: A Critical Review', *Work and Occupations*, 17/4: 379–98.

Victorian Teachers Union (1934), *Minutes, Annual Conference* (Melbourne: Victorian Teachers Union Archives).

Wacjman, J. (1991), 'Patriarchy, Technology, and Conceptions of Skill', *Work and Occupations*, 18/1: 29–45.

Watkins, P. (1987), 'Student Participation in the Contested Workplace: The Policy Dilemmas of In-School Work-Experience', *Journal of Education Policy*, 2/2: 27–42.

—— (1990), 'Flexible Manufacturing, Flexible Technology and Flexible Education: Visions of the Post-Fordist Solution', in Sachs (ed.), *Technology Education in Australia* (Canberra: Commonwealth Schools Commission).

—— (1991), 'Satisfying the Needs of Industry: Vocationalism, Corporate Culture and Education', in G. Esland (ed.), *Education, Training and Employment*, ii: *The Educational Response* (London: Addison Wesley).

Weiner, G. (1988), 'Feminism, Equal Opportunities and Vocationalism: The Changing Context', in V. Millman and H. Burchett (eds.), *Equal Opportunities in the New Initiatives* (Milton Keynes: Open Univ. Press).

Wellington, J. (1987), 'Skills for the Future', in M. Holt (ed.), *Skills and Vocationalism: The Easy Answer* (Milton Keynes: Open Univ. Press).

West, J. (1990) 'Gender and the Labour Process', in D. Knights and H. Willmott (eds.), *Labour Process Theory* (London: Macmillan).

Wheelwright, E. L., and Buckley, K. (eds.) (1980), *Essays in the Political Economy of Australian Capitalism*, i–iv (Sydney: Australian and New Zealand Book Company).

Williams, B. (1979), *Education, Training and Employment, Report* (3 vols., Canberra: AGPS).

Womens Employment Branch (1990), *Women and Award Restructuring: Skill* (Melbourne: Department of Labour).

Woodhall, M. (1973), 'Investment in Women: A Reappraisal of the Concept of Human Capital', *International Review of Education*, 27–34.

Yeatman, A. (1990), *Bureaucrats, Technocrats and Femacrats* (Sydney: Allen and Unwin).

—— (1991), 'Talking With Each Other: Women and the System', *Networking of Women in Further Education Newsletter* (June), 11–15.

15

Can Education Do It Alone?

Henry M. Levin and Carolyn Kelley

Introduction

Economists and other social scientists have long viewed education as the solution to many social challenges including productivity, inequality, economic growth, health status, overpopulation, political participation, reduction of criminal behavior, and welfare dependency (e.g. Haveman and Wolfe 1984). Education is viewed as an investment in human capital that has both direct payoffs to the educated individual as well as external benefits for society as a whole. In the eighties education has become a special focus for resurrecting the US economy. Such reports as that of a national panel appointed by the US Secretary of Education have even asserted that we are a 'nation at risk' because we are not producing students who meet the rigorous educational requirements of school systems in other countries (National Commission on Educational Excellence 1983). This report concludes that unless we raise the achievement of US students as represented by standardized test scores, the US economy will not be able to compete with those of Western Europe and Japan. The educational solution to the economic malaise is to establish higher standards on examinations for high school graduation as well as more required courses, longer school days and longer school years.

In this paper we wish to make a point that is so obvious that it would hardly seem worth emphasizing. Education can work to improve productivity only if there are employment opportunities for more productive workers. The same is true for reducing criminal behavior and welfare dependency. Only if education translates into opportunities which can reduce the need for welfare dependency or the incentives for criminal activity, can education be effective in diminishing these outcomes. Education may also mean better informed voters and ones who are more able to master the complex issues on the ballot, but it will not increase voting behavior if potential voters feel that they cannot influence policy through electoral politics.

The theme of this paper is that education is potentially effective in accomplishing much of what is claimed for it. Yet, that effectiveness depends crucially on the existence of complementary inputs. In the absence of complementary inputs, education is not likely to be as potent as the promises of its advocates. Unfortunately, the complementary inputs that determine the effectiveness of education are being largely ignored by both policy makers and economists who focus on education. It is not so much that the potential importance of education is overstated: it is only that the conditions under which education can reach that potential are increasingly ignored as education is viewed as a magic bullet to cure all that ails society. In this paper we will discuss some of the dangers in overstating the impact of education without considering the supportive or complementary conditions that must prevail for education to be successful.

Are Education's Effects Overstated?

If the economy is to grow rapidly and American companies are to reassert their world leadership, the educational standards that have been established in the nation's schools must be raised dra-

From *Economics of Education Review*, 13/2 (1994), 97–108.

matically. Put simply, students must go to school longer, study more, and pass more difficult tests covering more advanced subject matter (Johnston and Packer, 1987).

This quote from a US Department of Labor Report called *Workforce 2000: Work and Workers for the 21st Century* is representative of the views of not only the US Department of Labor, the US Department of Education, and most of the national commissions on educational reform. It is also the perspective of the preponderance of US business leaders who argue that if our workforce is not as well educated as those of Germany and Japan, we cannot compete effectively in the world economy. And they cite evidence of lower test scores for US students than for other countries as the proof of their perspective.

But there are at least two problems with what seems to be such a logical and self-evident conclusion. The first is that test scores have never shown a strong connection with either earnings or productivity. The second is that Japanese firms that establish manufacturing plants in the US are able to produce far more efficiently than US plants, and one case has shown that their production is comparable to that of plants in Japan producing the same product. Let us review these briefly.

TEST SCORES AND PRODUCTIVITY
It is very appealing to believe that simply raising the test scores of the labor force—or at least new entrants to the labor force—will have profound effects on worker productivity. As *Nation At Risk* implies, the strong performance of the West German and the Japanese economies must surely be attributable to the fact that students in those countries have test scores that are among the highest in international comparisons of educational achievement (Bishop 1989) and their students go to school for much longer school days and school years than those in the US. However, two types of direct evidence suggest that raising test scores may not have much impact on worker productivity. First, economists have been able to estimate earnings functions that include as explanatory variables the test scores of workers. Second, there is a considerable literature on the use of test scores to predict both worker productivity and supervisory ratings of workers.

EMPIRICAL EVIDENCE ON TEST SCORES AND PRODUCTIVITY
Several decades of research have shown a very limited connection between test scores and earnings for workers at a given level of education. Typically, even a very large difference in test scores for workers of the same educational level and race is associated with a very small difference in earnings. For example, a rise from the 50th to the 84th percentile has typically been associated with only a 3–4 per cent gain in earnings or less (Bishop 1989).

Recent empirical work by Murnane, Willett and Levy (1992) on test scores and earnings has found that the relation has grown in magnitude in recent years. However, a close examination of the new findings shows that the connection between test scores and earnings is still exceedingly modest, particularly from the perspective of educational reform. Murnane, Willett and Levy estimated equations on the log of hourly wages for samples of high school graduates, six years after graduation, for 1978 and 1986. The equations controlled for multiple measures of family background, race, and work experience. They found that the wage difference associated with a one standard deviation difference in mathematics test scores went from about 3 per cent in 1978 to 7.4 per cent in 1986 for males and from 8.5 per cent to 15.5 per cent for females.

Since real wages and annual earnings fell in the US over the seventies and eighties, we might explore how rising test scores might have reversed that trend. Murnane, Willett and Levy calculated the average wage for males in the 1978 group at $9.49 an hour in 1988 dollars, an average that had *fallen* to $7.92 an hour in 1986 for similar males. Even a 1986 male whose test score was one standard deviation higher than the mean would have been earning about one dollar an hour *less* than the *average* 1978 male.

And, consider that there is no educational reform in any country that has been shown to systematically raise test scores of high school graduates by even one standard deviation. Indeed, much of the call for educational vouchers is based upon the reported test score performance of private schools as reported by Coleman and Hoffer (1987). They found that by their senior year, high school sophomores in Catholic schools had gained about a 0.06 standard deviation advantage over public school students with similar initial test scores, race, and socioeconomic indicators. This accounts for an hourly wage difference in the Murnane. Willett, and Levy study of about 4 cents an hour.

Researchers who assume that the productivity implications are greater than this argue that profit-maximizing employers are ignorant of the true relation between productivity and test scores, and they use studies by industrial psychologists to buttress their claims (Bishop 1989). However, as we will note below, disinterested appraisals of the research on the predictive validity of test scores conclude that there is only a very modest connection between test scores and productivity ratings by supervisors (Hartigan and Wigdor 1989). Indeed, an overall summary of the potential economic gains from using test scores for employment selection suggests that the economic claims of industrial psychologists are flawed and highly exaggerated (Levin 1989).

Alternatively, there are a variety of other educational characteristics of workers that are important in predicting productivity, if workers meet minimal threshold levels of achievement. For example, an inquiry into the Toyota automobile plant in Kentucky revealed that that firm devoted about 26 hours to testing and interviewing its job applicants in 1990. Of this, less than 3 hours was devoted to cognitive testing, and only to make sure that workers met threshold levels. In contrast, about 23 hours was devoted to the other selection criteria, including evidence of work commitment and the ability of the workers to engage productivity in work teams. Brown, Reich, and Stern (1990) report on a very successful, multi-national electronics firm that set minimal test scores for hiring that are equivalent to a seventh grade level in reading and fifth grade in mathematics. Further, they report that test score performances of employees did not correlate with 'team skills' and 'work habits', two important ingredients of productivity in that firm.

The same authors found that employment criteria at a very productive Japanese automobile assembly plant in the US did not require high school graduation, but relied primarily on previous work experience. Workers took a 30 minute mechanical aptitude test and a 20 minute basic math test out of an overall assessment that takes three half-days. That assessment includes simulations of teamwork and performing jobs similar to those on the assembly line. Candidates are scored in team orientation, interpersonal skills, and task orientation in teamwork and on efficiency and quality in production. Scores on simulations are used by the company to assess worker trainability and future productivity. These results also comport well with a study of five firms specializing in high technology products in which workers needed to meet only relatively low threshold criteria in mathematics and reading skills (Levin, Rumberger, and Finnan 1990).

Berlin and Sum (1988) found that among a nationally representative sample of youth who were 18–22 years old in 1979, who were no longer enrolled in school, and who had 12 years or less of schooling, annual earnings between 1979 and 1981 were about $5,100. Using a multivariate analysis that controlled for demographic characteristics of the individuals and local labor market conditions, an additional grade-equivalent of basic skills as measured by test scores was associated with about $185 in additional annual earnings, about 3.6 per cent. But an additional grade level completed was associated with $715 in additional earnings, about 14 per cent: and a high school diploma was associated with an additional $927, or 18 per cent. Roughly speaking, completing the last year of high school was associated with an increase in annual earnings of 10 times as much as an additional grade equivalent of test score gain.

The weakness of the observed connections between test scores and earnings is supported by an equally weak empirical link between test scores and estimates of worker productivity. For example, the US Employment Service uses the General Ability Test Battery (GATB) to refer candidates to prospective employers. That test has been used to predict direct measures of productivity in a few occupations and supervisory ratings of workers in hundreds of different jobs. It is based upon sub-tests of intelligence, verbal aptitude, and numerical aptitude as well as a range of other measures. The simple correlation of GATB with supervisory ratings of employees among different jobs is on the order of 0.25, even when adjusted for sampling error and reliability (Hartigan and Wigdor 1989) according to a study of the research literature on GATB by a National Research Council panel.

Indeed, this finding is similar to that of

other studies that attempt to summarize the empirical results of the predictive validities of employment tests and job performance. Correlations tend to be in the 0.2 to 0.3 range (e.g. see Schmitt, Gooding, Noe, and Kirsch 1984). This implies that only about 4–9 per cent of the variance in observed productivity by supervisors is associated with test scores, hardly a solid base for suggesting that future labor force productivity will depend crucially on increases in student achievement. But, even these simple correlations overstate the case because they do not take account of the fact that educational attainments *are not controlled for* in the validity studies that constitute the research base. That is, some of the observed correlation between the test scores and the measure of productivity is likely attributable to the fact that the higher education of persons with higher test scores has not been included in the studies. Thus, the simple correlation between test scores and productivity which form the 'predictive validities' attributed to test scores is inflated by the covariance with educational attainment of the workers.

The empirical evidence from employer studies suggests that workers do need to meet a minimum threshold of achievement in order to perform adequately on the job. There is no precise agreement on what this threshold is, although a National Research Council report on what is needed by high school graduates who enter the labor market is very informative. That particular panel was made up primarily of employer representatives who obtained data directly from their firms (National Academy of Sciences 1984). It suggests that competence in computational skills, communication skills (including listening, speaking, reading, and writing), and reading skills should be required of all workers. Presumably this threshold must be met even in lower-level jobs in order to obtain regular employment, to benefit from training, and to have access to some job mobility.

While this is hardly a high level of achievement, it is not a level that is being achieved by perhaps one third of present US students, so-called at-risk students. This group is composed predominantly of students who are from minority and immigrant families as well as those in poverty (Pallas *et al.* 1989). These pupils are increasing as a proportion of the total student population (Pallas *et al.* 1989);

they account for a disproportionately high share of high school dropouts (Rumberger 1983); and they have much lower test scores than other students, many with achievement that probably does not meet the threshold that is necessary for stable employment, additional training, and occupational mobility.

In summary, the general notion that the competitive economic position of the US can only be sustained if we can out-compete students from other countries in scores on achievement tests is naive and hardly supported by the overall empirical data. Test performance is more of a concern for those students in at-risk categories where a special effort must be made to bring such students into the educational mainstream. These overall findings are less surprising when one considers what the tests measure. To a large degree they assess the ability of the students to succeed at basic skill levels in which facts must be memorized rather than to understand or to use that information. It is not clear that repositories of information have a considerable payoff in an age of almost unlimited access to electronic memories; it is how that information is used to solve problems and to make resource allocation decisions that is more crucial once a threshold in terms of solid basic skills is reached. We will return to this theme below, but it is also noteworthy that test specialists are now focusing on more authentic assessment while international comparisons are based on the very tests that are not useful predictors of productivity (Office of Technology Assessment of the US Congress 1991).

A final note on this point is the rhetoric that is common about rapidly rising cognitive skill requirements of jobs in the 'information economy' (Berryman and Bailey 1992). Counter to that claim, the most comprehensive study undertaken of changes in skill requirements of jobs does not support the view that the demand for cognitive skills has accelerated over time. Howell and Wolff (1991) have evaluated the changes in skill requirements of the labor force between 1960 and 1985 by studying the detailed change in occupational composition and the skill requirements found in the Dictionary of Occupational Titles. They found that the average growth rate of cognitive skills in the economy required by occupations *fell* considerably from an increase of about 0.7 per cent a year in the sixties to less than 0.5 per cent in the seventies to less than 0.3 per cent in the first half of the eighties.

JAPANESE PRODUCTION IN THE UNITED STATES
Strong counter-examples to the view that the relatively poor performance of the US economy is due to its poor labor force is provided by the success of Japanese automobile and electronics manufacturers in their US factories. One of the largest selling automobiles in the US in recent years has been the Honda Accord (Honda: is it an American car? 1991). Most of these are produced in Marysville. Ohio where 10,000 workers are employed of which only about 300 are Japanese. The quality of the Honda Accord and a new minivan produced in Marysville is so high that the Accord is being shipped to 18 countries including Europe and Japan. According to the President and CEO of Honda, '. . . the quality of cars produced in Ohio is superior to those made in Japan' (Castillo, 1991). In addition, Nissan, Mazda, and Toyota have also established profitable assembly plants in the US using local labor forces.

Substantial research has been carried out on the productivity of the joint venture of General Motors and Toyota called the New United Motor Manufacturing, Incorporated (NUMMI) plant in Fremont, California (Brown and Reich 1989; Krafcik 1986; New United Motor Manufacturing Inc. 1991). That plant was closed by General Motors in 1982 because of poor productivity, high absenteeism, poor product quality, and labor-management conflict. It was ranked at the bottom of GM plants in productivity and had absentee rates of over 20 per cent and a backlog of more than a thousand grievances.

The NUMMI plant began production in 1985, producing the Chevrolet Nova, a car that was the equivalent of the four door model of the imported Toyota Corolla. It later manufactured the Toyota Corolla FX and has been producing the Geo Prizm since 1988 and Toyota pickup trucks since August 1991. The plant produced its millionth vehicle in January 1991.

Toyota had responsibility for production and GM was responsible for marketing. Toyota redesigned the plant completely and, by agreement with the United Auto Workers, over 80 per cent of the workers hired by NUMMI were drawn from the laid-off workers from the closed GM plant. Production began in December 1984, and by the spring of 1986 the plant had reached its full capacity output of over 20,000 cars per month.

The NUMMI production process is built around the use of teams of four to eight members. Teams set out the work tasks and rotate them among members. They also meet periodically to discuss how to improve the work process and product quality. Whenever possible, it is expected that the teams will solve production problems rather than calling in engineering or management representatives. Workers have the right to stop the assembly line at any time to solve an assembly problem. Emphasis is on worker flexibility and involvement in the work process.

NUMMI uses a just-in-time system of inventory, and an emphasis on 100 per cent quality requirement at the team level of production. The management organization of the plant is based upon a flattened hierarchy in which major supervisory and quality control functions are handled by the work teams rather than by line supervisors.

From a human capital perspective, the employment contracts are long term. That is, there is a no lay-off policy as long as the firm is not threatened by economic catastrophe. The result is that both workers and management view human capital investment as having a long-term payoff, and there is a great incentive for both to invest in specific training. All workers received considerable on-the-job training, and one-fifth of the workers—the team leaders and group leaders—were sent to Japan for three weeks of classroom and on-the-job training in the Toyota production system. A policy of flexible work roles was adopted jointly by NUMMI and the United Auto Workers to give each team member greater responsibility and make each team member multi-functional.

The results of these arrangements on productivity were remarkable. Productivity was 50 per cent higher than in the old GM plant and was equal to that of its sister plant in Takaoka City, Japan (Krafcik 1986). Unexcused absences were only about one-half of one per cent, and the level of quality was found to be comparable to the imported Toyota Corolla by both consumer and industry analyses. What is most remarkable about all of this is that these extraordinary gains in productivity between the old plant and the new one were not due to a more educated workforce. Over

80 per cent of the workers at NUMMI were drawn from the old GM workforce, one that GM had considered among the worst in its entire production system.

Cost of Ignoring the Complementary Inputs

What we have tried to show in this section is that the present view that education, almost single-handedly, can solve problems of productivity and competitiveness of the US economy is at odds with the empirical evidence. This view suggests that the success of the Japanese and West Germans is due to their rigorous school systems and high examination scores. Therefore, policies to raise student test scores to 'world levels' will be necessary to compete effectively in the world economy.

But, with the exception of at-risk students who do not meet threshold levels of achievement, this view is hopelessly naive and even dangerous. It is naive because research on the connections between test scores and earnings or productivity show very modest statistical associations. Further, Japanese firms that have established automobile production plants in the United States have found that they are able to manufacture their products efficiently, according to world standards, with the existing work force.

The view is dangerous because it ignores the other conditions or complementary inputs that are necessary for education to provide a higher payoff. What are some of these?

1. New investment is clearly a major requirement in order to take advantage of more productive approaches and new technologies. The US has a rate of new investment and capital formation that is only a fraction of that of our competitors.

2. New methods of work organization are necessary to take advantage of the greater productive capacity of educated workers (Levin 1987). That is, firms must provide opportunities based upon work teams and other participative approaches that enable workers to use their discretion to make decisions and that support those opportunities with the information, incentives, and accountability that are integral to such approaches (Levin 1987). In many respects these new forms of work organization are based upon creating the potential

for workers to make allocative decisions in an information-rich environment, probably the area of greatest potential for educated workers to improve productivity of the firm (Schultz 1975; Welch 1970). The Commission on the Skills of the American Workforce (1990) claims that only about 5 per cent of employment is found in what Osterman (1992) has termed the 'High Performance Work Organization'.

3. New managerial approaches must be undertaken to provide support for productive approaches to worker participation as well as to create more integrated approaches to research, training, product development, marketing, production and finance. General Motors attempted to adopt the use of work teams in one of its plants on the basis of the NUMMI system, but it did not incorporate the NUMMI management organization, employment contracts, training, product development and other features of NUMMI (Brown and Reich 1989). The attempt failed, and the plant is now slated for closure. A better replication seems to have been achieved by General Motors for its Saturn automobile which is produced in an independent plant in Tennessee. However, the larger GM organization as well as the other auto-makers are not able to approach the results for the US based plants of the Japanese automakers because of their piece-meal approaches to change (for a discussion of the failures of incremental change, see Levy and Murnane 1992).

The danger is that American firms are being reinforced in their beliefs that the main obstacle to their success is the poor education of the workforce. Not only does this ignore consideration of the other changes that must be made to make such firms competitive. It also promotes a self-fulfilling prophecy that only by producing in other countries can multi-national firms obtain a productive workforce. Thus, the single-factor approach to improving productivity—raising educational levels and test scores—serves to distort both national and industry policies in directions that are unlikely to improve national productivity and that delay the day of reckoning. What we should be doing is acknowledging the entire range of changes that are necessary to increase national productivity and placing education in that context as only one of a constellation of related and complementary factors in the policy mix. Changes in education should be coordinated with changes in these other dimensions rather than as an independent phenomenon that is largely disconnected.

Overstating Education's Effects in Research

It is not only politicians, educational policy-makers, and business spokespersons who have overstated the role of education in creating a more productive society. Economists and other social scientists have also played this role by estimating the payoffs to increased education while ignoring the complementary inputs and conditions on which their estimates are premised. Almost all analyses of the effects of education on improving income, health, political participation, and reducing such areas of public cost as crime and public assistance are based on cross-sectional studies that relate the education of individuals to individual economic and other outcomes. But cross-sectional studies of these relations assume that the apparent impact of differences in education at a point in time can be used to assess the impact of changes in education over time. Indeed, any policy to improve education can only take place over time, so an evaluation of a social investment in education

is one that must necessarily interpret results across education within a cross-sectional sample as being predictive of the impact of educational changes over time. In this section, we will suggest that cross-sectional studies will inevitably overstate the effects of rising educational levels over time, if education is increased without a comparable expansion in the complementary inputs and conditions which determine education's payoff. In order to discuss concrete results, we will provide three brief examples.

PUBLIC ASSISTANCE

It is well-known that persons with less education are more likely to be unemployed, employed at low wages, and in poverty. Since low income is the major criterion for receiving public assistance, it is not surprising that the probability of receiving such assistance is negatively related to education. For example, a study of black women in their mid-thirties in 1967 found that each additional year of schooling was associated with a reduction of between 3 and 4 per cent in the probability of receiving public assistance (Owens 1990). Since the black female population in that age group had a slight increase in education in subsequent years, we would expect to find that the probability of receiving public assistance would have fallen. Instead, as Table 15.1 shows, despite gains in educational attainment over the 15 year period, welfare inci-

Table 15.1. Effects of educational attainment on welfare incidence and single-parent status (black women in their mid-thirties, National Longitudinal Survey Data; data in percentages)

Years of schooling	Welfare incidence	Single-parent status	Welfare incidence	
			Single parent	Not single
A. Early cohort (1967)				
Less than 9	43.0	24.7	79.8	31.0
9 to 11	34.3	27.3	64.4	23.0
12	18.1	23.3	39.9	11.5
More than 12	9.2	22.3	15.4	7.4
16 or more	5.4	22.0	4.3	5.0
Average	29.5	24.9	57.6	20.3
N	1190	1190	305	885
B. Late cohort (1982)				
Less than 9	81.5	56.4	97.0	61.1
9 to 11	62.4	54.1	80.1	41.9
12	42.4	43.7	65.2	24.2
More than 12	24.3	34.8	44.1	14.3
16 or more	10.4	23.2	18.7	8.3
Average	46.2	45.1	69.0	27.5
N	916	916	402	514

Source: Owen (1990).

dence of black females increased from 29.5 per cent in 1967 to 46.2 per cent in 1982. In addition, the welfare incidence increased at all levels of educational attainment (Owens 1990).

Why was a rise in education not associated with a decline in public assistance dependency? A logical hypothesis is that in later years the probability of receiving public assistance had become less sensitive to education. However, Owens (1990) found that in 1982 an increase of one year in education was associated with a 7 per cent decline in the probability of being on public assistance. That is, the marginal probability of being on welfare for a difference in education of one year was twice as great in 1982 as in 1967. Thus, participation in public assistance had become considerably more education-dependent rather than less education-dependent.

Unfortunately, the data available to Owen for his analysis compared a relatively prosperous economic year, 1967, with a recessionary one, 1982. Therefore, it is not possible to separate out the effects of the poor economy from structural changes in poverty and education. However, it is unlikely that the effects were only attributable to recession. The poverty rate overall in the US was as high in 1989 at the height of economic recovery as it was in 1967, despite the substantial increase in education of the US labor force over that period (US Department of Commerce 1991: 11).

What if we had estimated the economic value of education in terms of reducing payments on public assistance (admittedly a transfer payment) or done a benefit-cost study of educational investment in terms of its reduction in welfare payments? If we had used

the 1967 data, we would have vastly overstated the benefits of increased education in future years relative to actual benefits. Indeed, this is the hazard that we face in these types of studies by not taking into account the complementary conditions that are needed to replicate over time the within-population results at a point in time. In order for more education to reduce public assistance by the amount reflected in the 1967 data, we would need to replicate the cross-sectional conditions for longitudinal changes in society among the population under scrutiny with respect to such factors as: welfare eligibility, probabilities of employment, earnings levels, probabilities of marriage to husbands with given earnings levels, and so on. These are virtually never taken into account in the longitudinal projections of effects.

EDUCATION AND EARNINGS

A second area that we might consider is the projection of the effects of educational investments on earnings. Rates of return and benefit-cost studies are invariably based on cross-sectional analysis of earnings patterns and their application to longitudinal changes in education. Eckhaus (1973) has shown that such approaches are based on assumptions about future earnings patterns that may be totally invalid. Although we may acknowledge such possibilities, they are soon forgotten when we do the analysis.

Table 15.2 shows the annual income in constant 1987 dollars by educational attainment for 25–34-year-old males. The median income in 1968 was almost $24,000 in constant 1987 dollars. If we assume that the

Table 15.2. Annual income of males 25 to 34 years of age, by educational level, 1968 and 1987[a]

Education level	1968 Educational attainment	1968 Median income	1987 Educational attainment	1987 Projected income	1987 Median income
0 to 7 years	6.2%	$13.611	2.8%	$13.611	$9978
8 years	6.0%	$18.100	1.5%	$18.100	$9843
9 to 11 years	16.5%	$20.457	9.6%	$20.457	$12.990
12 years	39.3%	$24.166	40.4%	$24.166	$18.366
13 to 15 years	13.2%	$25.753	20.7%	$25.753	$20.920
16 years	10.8%	$30.568	16.0%	$30.568	$27.423
>16 years	8.0%	$29.736	8.9%	$29.736	$30.035
Total	100.0%	$23.934	100.0%	$25.267	$20.112

[a] All incomes are reported in 1987 dollars
Sources: US Department of Education, OERI, NCES, Digest of Education Statistics: US Department of Commerce, Bureau of the Census, Current Population Reports, Series P-20, Nos. 182 and 428; US Department of Commerce, Bureau of the Census Statistical Abstract of the United States, 1990. Table No. 756.

payoff to each level of education would have remained the same, but the education distribution shifted to higher levels, the expected median income in 1987 would have risen to about $25,267. In fact, the median income of males in this age group declined to $20,112, almost $4,000 below the 1968 level, and over $5,000, or 20 per cent below the predicted value. Moreover, every education group experienced declines in real income over this period with the exception of the highest category (post-graduate studies) which had about a 1 per cent improvement over the 19 years.

According to the 1968 earnings differences shown in Table 15.2 social investments in education would be expected to have a high positive return when in actuality they had a negative payoff. The present values of benefits and costs to increased investment in education were estimated using the 1968 earnings levels for estimating benefits: 1974 educational expenditures for direct educational costs, and 1972 earnings for 18–24–year-old males with high school education for foregone earnings of college. With an 8 per cent discount rate, the present value in 1968 of upgrading the male educational distribution to 1987 educational attainment levels was equal to about unity. That is, the internal rate of return on this investment would have been 8 per cent had the earnings pattern from 1968 been retained in 1987. It would have been on the order of about 10 per cent if historic improvments in labor force productivity had taken place. In fact, the deterioration in earnings between 1968 and 1987 meant that the increment to education over this period was associated not with a gain, but a *loss* in value as

well as approximately $58 billion in direct costs and foregone earnings. Cross-sectional results suggested that the same market conditions for each category of education in 1968 could also be used to estimate the payoff to improved education over time. But instead, those conditions changed over time in a way that reduced the social returns, even though the private returns were high because the differentials between educational categories remained large in 1987. The social investment required to raise the education level of the labor force was actually associated with a substantial social cost rather than benefit.

EDUCATION AND POLITICAL PARTICIPATION

A final example might be drawn from the area of education and political participation. An important social benefit of education is considered to be its impact on raising the knowledge of the electorate as well as political participation. A common finding in studies of voting behavior is that the probability of voting is an increasing function of education (Wolfinger and Rosenstone 1980). Table 15.3 shows voter turnout among voters in the 1968 and 1988 presidential elections by educational level. As the 1968 results show, there is a fairly considerable rise in the probability of voting from the lowest to the highest educational categories. For example, the proportion of college graduates who voted in the 1968 presidential election was about 20 percentage points higher than for high school dropouts.

When these percentages are applied to the distribution of education in the 1988 population 25 years and older, we would expect the proportion of the population that voted to

Table 15.3. Voter turnout in the 1968 and 1988 US presidential elections among individuals 25 years of age and older by education level

Educational level	1968 Educational attainment	% voting in 1968 pres. election	1988 Educational attainment	Projected % voting in 1988	Actual % voting in 1988
0 to 4 years	5.6%	38.5%	2.5%	38.5%	25.2%
5 to 7 years	8.9%	53.2%	4.3%	53.2%	35.7%
8 years	13.7%	63.2%	5.1%	63.2%	46.7%
9 to 11 years	17.7%	64.2%	11.3%	64.2%	46.7%
12 years	33.0%	75.5%	38.4%	75.5%	59.1%
13 to 15 years	10.1%	81.2%	17.6%	81.2%	68.7%
16 years	6.7%	84.4%	12.1%	84.4%	75.8%
>16 years	4.2%	86.0%	8.6%	86.0%	82.7%
Total	100.0%	69.4%	100.0%	74.7%	61.0%

Sources: US Department of Commerce, Bureau of the Census Current Population Report Population Characteristics, Series P-20. nos. 192 and 440.

have risen from 69.4 per cent to almost 75 per cent. In fact, the actual proportion of the population that voted in the 1988 election was only 61 per cent. This difference is not a function of the year that was chosen, since the long-term trend has shown a decline in participation in presidential elections throughout this period. One hypothesis is that differences in education have become less important for determining differences in voting behavior. In actuality, the opposite is the case. That is, the 1988 results show greater responsiveness to differences in education than the 1968 results. However, all education groups were less likely to participate in 1988 than in 1968. Even though there was a slight rise in voter turnout in the 1992 election, experts attribute the increase to poor economic conditions, increased use of alternative forms of media to cover the campaign, and interest generated by the presence of a viable third party candidate rather than to a permanent change in historical trends in participation. Despite the increase, turnout in 1992 was still eight percentage points lower than in 1960 (Teixera 1993).

Again, one must think of the complementary conditions that are assumed when one looks at the relation between education and voting behavior. Any extrapolation of the earlier results assumes that individuals will have the same incentives for political participation and will face the same costs in the future as in the present. In fact, these incentives may have changed drastically with the population feeling that voting is less meaningful in their lives or that the cost of voting (e.g. in terms of gaining knowledge of complex issues) has risen considerably.

WHAT IS MISSING?
What is missing from the wide range of studies that attempt to ascertain the effects of educational investment on earnings as well as other social outcomes such as those summarized by Haveman and Wolfe (1984)? First, each study makes claims about the effects of education by modeling the phenomenon and estimating effects using cross-sectional data. Little or no attention is given to the possible impact of changes in the complementary conditions or inputs that are assumed by the cross-sectional comparisons.

Second, there is virtually no attempt in the literature to evaluate systematically the accuracy of the implied predictions of these studies for the actual changes that have taken place in educational levels. That is, we know that education has risen over time, in part inspired by the human capital story that economists like to tell (Becker 1964). But, we are much quicker to publish our results than to test their predictive validity over time. Since education has risen, we can compare retrospectively the actual changes in earnings, crime, public assistance, family size, political participation, and so on, with those that would be predicted by the educational coefficients in earlier studies. This is a neglected area of research with virtually no extant literature.

Third, from these comparisons we could begin to study the causes of divergences between actual and predicted results. From these we could attempt to isolate the factors that were either not accounted for or not properly accounted for in the previous research, and we could incorporate new methodologies in the studies that might consider their impacts. For example, on the basis of a preliminary scrutiny of data on earnings, crime, health, public assistance, and political participation, we believe that cross-sectional studies have overstated the impact of education. Some of this may have been due to the generalization from individual effects for a marginal individual to social effects for larger groups, that is the error of aggregating from marginal changes. However, other errors have surely been induced by ignoring the potential effects of historical changes in other inputs and conditions that affect the payoff to education.

Summary

We have tried to show that there is a social and scientific zeal about the potential of education for addressing many of our most important social needs. What is lost in this zeal is a more careful analysis of the potential of education within the constellation of conditions and complementary inputs that are necessary for education to pay off. National policy is presently predicated on an assumption that higher test scores will rescue the economy. Clearly, the evidence on the connections between test scores and productivity raises serious questions about the assumption. Clark

Kerr (1991) examined a range of evidence that is related to the contention that education is the key to the Nation's competitiveness. He concluded, 'Seldom in the course of policy-making in the United States have so many firm convictions held by so many based on so little proof'.

Unfortunately, most economists have either been silent on the matter or have supported the view that the complementary conditions for a large educational payoff are already in place and that the onus remains on schools to deliver the goods (e.g. Bishop 1989; Berryman and Bailey 1992; Johnston and Packer 1989). For example, a 1992 publication on changing skills in the US work force interprets the rising gap between earnings for high school and college graduates as evidence of a 'skills shortage' (Johnston and Wirt 1992). The authors fail to recognize that as Table 15.2 shows, real incomes of young college graduates fell over the long run. During the same period, the US Bureau of Labor Statistics found that about one of five college graduates had to settle for jobs that do not require college degrees for entry, and the proportion is expected to rise over time (Hecker 1992; Shelley 1992). Even the larger economic literature on the social returns to education has based its results mainly on cross-sectional analyses which tend to inflate the predicted longitudinal impacts of education. Yet there has been little interest in examining the predictive validity of our methods and providing a corrective feedback loop to our knowledge base and methodology.

The fact of the matter is that education is just one factor, albeit an important one, in an overall melange of conditions that determines productivity and economic competitiveness as well as the levels of crime, public assistance, political participation, health, and so on. Education has the potential for powerful impacts in each of these areas if the proper supportive conditions and inputs are present. It has the potential for a very nominal impact when the complementary requirements are not in place. By ignoring this set of facts in both policy and in our research, we tend to overstate the potential of education for improving society. We need to be realistic about what education can do and what other changes are necessary to maximize the effects of education and to realize our aspirations for economic and social betterment.

References

Becker, G. S. (1964), *Human Capital* (1st edn., New York: Columbia Univ. Press).

Berlin, G., and Sum. A. (1988), *Toward a More Perfect Union: Basic Skills, Poor Families and Our Economic Future*. Occasional Paper 3. Ford Foundation Project on Social Welfare and the American Future (New York: Ford Foundation), 41.

Berryman, S. E., and Bailey, T. R. (1992), *The Double Helix of Education and the Economy* (New York: Institute on Education and the Economy, Teachers College, Columbia Univ.).

Bishop, J. (1989), 'Incentives for Learning: Why American High School Students Compare so Poorly to their Counterparts Overseas', in Commission on Workforce Quality and Labor Market Efficiency, *Investing in People*. Background Papers, i (Washington DC: US Department of Labor), 1–84.

Brown, C., and Reich, M. (1989), 'When does Union-Management Cooperation Work? A Look at NUMMI and GM', Van Nuys, *California Management Rev*, 31: 26–44.

—— , —— , and Stern, D. (1990), *Skills and Security in Evolving Employment Systems: Observations from Case Studies*. Paper prepared for presentation at the Conference on Changing Occupational Skill Requirements: Gathering and Assessing the Evidence (5–6 June, Providence, RI: Brown Univ.).

Castillo, C. (1991), 'Honda Boss Talks at GSB about 'World Car' Concept', *Campus Report* 24/8 (13 Nov., Stanford Univ.), 4.

Coleman, J. M., and Hoffer. T. (1987), *Public and Private High Schools* (New York: Basic Books).

Commission on the Skills of the American Workforce (1990), *America's Choice: High Skills or Low Wages* (Rochester, NY: National Center on Education and the Economy).

Eckaus, R. S. (1973), *Estimating the Returns to Education: A Disaggregated Approach* (Berkeley, Calif.: Carnegie Commission on Higher Education).

Hartigan, J. A. and Wigdor, A. K. (eds.) (1989), *Fairness in Employment Testing: Validity Generalization, Minority Issues, and the General Aptitude Test Battery*. (Committee on the General Aptitude Test Battery, Commission on Behavioral and Social Sciences and Education, National Research Council, Washington DC: National Academy Press).

Haveman. R. H., and Wolfe. B. L. (1984), 'Schooling and Economic Well-Being: The Role of Nonmarket Effects', *J. of Human Res.*, 19: 377–407.

Hecker, D. E. (1992), 'Reconciling Conflicting Data on Jobs for College Graduates', *Monthly Labor Rev*. (July), 3–12.

'Honda: Is It An American Car?' (1991), *Business Week* (18 Nov.), 105–112.

Howell, D. R., and Wolff, E. N. (1991), 'Trends in Growth and Distribution of Skills in the US Workplace, 1960–1985', *Industrial and Labor Relations Rev.* 44/4 (April), 3–13.

Johnston, W. B. and Packer, A. (1987), *Workforce 2000: Work and Workers for the 21st Century* (Indianapolis, Ind.: Hudson Institute).

Kerr, C. (1991), 'Is Education Really all that Guilty?' *Ed.Week* (27 Feb.), 30.

Krafcik, J. (1986), *Learning from NUMMI* (International Vehicle Program Working Paper, Cambridge, Mass.: Massachusetts Institute of Technology).

Levin, H. M. (1987), 'Improving Productivity through Education and Technology', in *The Future Impact of Technology on Work and Education*, ed. by Burke, G., and Rumberger, R. W. (New York: Falmer Press).

—— (1989), 'Ability Testing for Job Selection: Are the Economic Claims Justified?', in *Test Policy and the Politics of Opportunity Allocation: The Workplace and the Law* ed. by Gifford, B. R. (Boston: Kluwer Academic Publishers).

——, Rumberger, R. W., and Finnan, C. (1990), *Escalating Skill Requirements or New Skill Requirements?* Paper prepared for presentation at the Conference on Changing Occupational Skill Requirements: Gathering and Assessing the Evidence (5–6 June, Providence, RI: Brown Univ.).

Levy, F., and Murnane, R. J. (1992), 'Where Will all the Smart Kids Work?' *J. Am. Planning Assoc.*, 58: 283–7.

Murnane, R. J., Willett, J. B., and Levy, F. (1992), *The Growing Importance of Cognitive Skills in Wage Determination* (October, Cambridge: Harvard Graduate School of Education).

National Commission on Educational Excellence (1983), *Nation At Risk* (Washington DC: US Government Printing Office).

National Academy of Sciences (1984), *High Schools and the Changing Workplace*, Report of the Panel on Secondary School Education for the Changing Workplace (Washington DC: National Academy Press).

New United Motor Manufacturing, Inc. (1991), Fremont, CA: New United Motor Manufacturing, Inc.

Office of Technology Assessment of the US Congress (1991), *Testing in American Schools* (Washington DC: US Government Printing Office).

Osterman, P. (1992), *How Common is Workplace Transformation and How Can We Explain Who Adopts It?* Results from a National Survey: Draft (December, Cambridge: Sloan School, Massachusetts Institute of Technology).

Owens, J. D. (1990), 'The Social Benefits of Education: An Intertemporal Analysis' (Detroit, MI: unpubl. manuscript, Economics Dept. Wayne State Univ.).

Packer, A. H., and Wirt, J. G. (1992), 'Changing Skills in the US Work Force: Trends of Supply and Demand', in *Urban Labor Markets and Job Opportunity*, ed. by Peterson, G. E., and Vroman, W. (Washington DC: Urban Institute Press), 31–65.

Pallas, A. M., Natriello, G., and McDill, E. L. (1989), 'The Changing Nature of the Disadvantaged Population: Current Dimensions and Future Trends', *Ed. Researcher, 5* (June–July), 16–22.

Rumberger, R. W. (1983), 'Dropping out of School: The Influences of Race, Sex and Family Background', *Am. Ed. Research J.*, 20: 199–220.

Schmitt, N., Gooding, R. Z., Noe, R. A., and Kirsch, M. (1984), 'Meta-analyses of Validity Studies Published between 1964 and 1982 and the Investigation of Study Characteristics', *Personnel Psychology*, 37: 407–22.

Schultz, T. W. (1975), 'The Value of the Ability to Deal with Disequilibria', *J. of Econ. Lit.* 13/3 (September), 827–46.

Shelley, K. J. (1992), 'The Future of Jobs for College Graduates', *Monthly Labor Review* (July), 13–21.

Teixeira, R. A. (1993), 'Turnout in the 1992 Election', *The Brookings Review* (Spring), 47.

US Department of Commerce, Bureau of the Census (1990), *Statistical Abstract of the United States*, (Washington DC: US Government Printing Office), Table 756.

—— *Poverty in the United States: 1988 and 1989.* Current Population Reports. Series P-60, 171 (Washington DC: US Government Printing Office).

—— selected years. Current Population Reports. Series P-20, 182, 192, 428 and 440 (Washington DC: US Government Printing Office).

US Department of Education, OERI, selected years. *Digest of Education Statistics* (Washington DC: US Government Printing Office).

Welch, F. (1970), 'Education in Production', *J. of Pol. Econ.*, 78/1 (Jan. Feb.) 35–59.

Wolfinger, R. E., and Rosenstone, S. J. (1980), *Who Votes?* (New Haven: Yale Univ. Press).

PART THREE

THE STATE AND THE RESTRUCTURING
OF TEACHERS' WORK

The State and the Restructuring of Teachers' Work

The state is central to an understanding of the nature of educational systems. As Dale (Ch. 17) notes, it is the funder and regulator of education, and has been the major provider of educational services. During the 1950s and 1960s the state was seen by liberals as a neutral arbiter in the competition for educational resources. It was assumed that the state would allocate resources fairly and would ensure that all had equality of opportunity. In part, these assumptions reflected the consensus of the day as to the role and aims of education. A further assumption of that era was that social scientific knowledge in the hands of experts would provide unbiased policy advice to governments about education.

However, by the early 1970s these benign assumptions about the state and the role of education were under attack. There were several reasons for this. During the 1960s, it became a truism in Western Europe and the United States that for certain groups in society—working-class, women, and people of colour—education could not solve the problem of inequality of opportunity. The traditions of 'political arithmetic', represented by Floud and Halsey (1961), and Halsey, Heath, and Ridge (1980) in Britain, and methodological empiricism, represented by Coleman (1966) and Jencks (1972; 1979) in the United States, all served to demonstrate that there were systematic class inequalities rooted in the structures of society for which education, in Bernstein's phrase, could not compensate. Educational policies designed to address these inequalities during the 1960s and 1970s, such as Project Headstart in the United States and the Educational Priority Areas in Britain, appeared to have failed.[1]

One inference to be drawn from this research and experience was that rather than being a neutral arbiter, the state (and, by extension, education) was active in the maintenance of class inequalities in society. This inference was drawn in particular by the developing tradition of neo-Marxist educators. The work of the French Marxist Althusser (1972) and that of Bowles and Gintis (1976) was most influential at the time in arguing that the state acted as the 'servant' of capitalism. In this capacity, education was designed to reproduce the privileges of the ruling class and to reproduce the skills and attitudes required to maintain a capitalist economy. Far from promoting progress by reducing inequalities and preparing individuals for democracy, the education system was an instrument of oppression.

This view was soon considered too deterministic. Dale (1982) and Carnoy and Levin (1985) argued that the state had a greater degree of autonomy than these early theorists had suggested, and that the capitalist state was also constrained by the democratic process: there were limits to the inequalities that would be tolerated in a democratic society. Moreover, the rhetoric of an education for democracy was not entirely empty, and this constituted a contradiction for schools, since an education for democracy was quite different from that designed to socialize students for the Fordist assembly line.

This critical approach to the state and education was soon taken up by feminists and anti-racists. Their argument was that processes of socialization and selection similar to those which militated against working-class students also militated against girls and students of colour. These analyses have been particularly cogent in relation to the New-Right inspired changes in education and society (see, for example, Arnot and Weiler (1993), Eisenstein (1982), Troyna and Williams (1986), and Troyna (1992)). Such critical theories of the state have made considerable inroads into explaining the links between capitalist, patriarchal, and postcolonialist societies and inequality.

However, they also contributed to a general scepticism, which dates back to at least 1968, about the role of the state in the development of progressive policies in Western liberal democracies. This scepticism left the door open for the most influential theory of the state and education in recent years, derived from what has become known as Public Choice theory (Buchanan and Tullock 1962). Since Public Choice theory has clearly played a significant role in guiding the restructuring of education, it is worth spending some time spelling out its fundamental tenets. Its explanatory scope is most ambitious, since it is a theory which seeks to explain the Western economic crisis of the past two decades and how it can be solved. Fundamental to this explanation is the idea that the roots of this crisis are political and relate to the growth of state activity. The welfare state has grown, according to this theory, because the democratic process has enabled pressure groups to assert their interests over the wider and more prudent economic interests of state. They have done this by demanding increases in state expenditure, ultimately in return for votes. They have been abetted in this process by middle-class state workers who have an interest in the expansion of jobs and opportunities in the public sector. The result has been increased government expenditure and debt ending in high levels of inflation.

A further premiss of this theory is that the increase in welfare-state expenditure has not been beneficial to the very people it was designed to help. In the area of welfare, support for this view is taken from Murray's (1984) highly controversial claim that increased welfare expenditure has exacerbated rather than alleviated the problem of poverty. In education, support for this view is garnered from Chubb and Moe (1990, and Ch. 24) and from Hanushek (1986). The latter's research, which purports to show that the cost of education has risen while educational standards have declined, provides an excellent illustration of the application of Public Choice theory to education. The clear inference of Hanushek's research is that while most of the increase in educational expenditure has been as a result of rises in teacher income, such rises have been unwarranted in terms of results. He marshals evidence to show that educational expenditure on schools does not have a significant impact on outcomes, nor does class size or teacher qualifications. Moreover, teachers are protected by complex regulations and powerful unions which bid up their price while deterring schools from firing poor teachers and hiring good ones. In other words, while expenditure has risen, the students it was designed to help remain, if anything, less advantaged than they might have been. Hanushek's claims are controversial, and evidence for quite the opposite conclusions regarding the training and qualifications of teachers is adduced by Darling-Hammond (Ch. 22), while others[2] have taken Hanushek to task on other aspects of his case. Arguably, the significance of his work lies not in his specific claims but in the application of Public Choice theory to education.

The consequence of Public Choice theory applied to education is that it assumes that middle-class professionals, like teachers, have been unjustifiably privileged because they have not been subject to the spurs and sanctions of market disciplines; that is, they are not suitably rewarded when successful, nor are they threatened with unemployment when unsuccessful. Consequently, it assumes that educational expenditure can be contained or reduced if education is deregulated and market disciplines imposed.

Clearly Public Choice theory is a powerful explanatory instrument, and its recommendations to introduce market mechanisms into education appealed to the New Right governments of the 1980s. There are some elements of Public Choice that are of theoretical interest. For example, it roots the causes of economic crisis in the political economy of the state, for it is the way the state and democracy are structured that has caused the economic crisis. It also sees the state and education as a site of struggle, which can explain why educational outcomes are systematically biased in favour of some groups (the middle class) and not others (the working class and ethnic minorities: see Lauder, Ch. 25); and it can be fruitful in guiding empirical analysis (Glennester and Low 1990). But as a general theory of capitalist crisis and the restructuring of education it can be subject to a series of criticisms.

The first is that it assumes that the economic crisis has been caused by a set of conditions peculiar to the postwar period of economic nationalism. However, as neo-Marxists will be quick to point out, periodic crises are endemic to capitalism and have been so throughout the various phases of industrialization.

The second is that it fails to see the exercise of power as intrinsic to the state, education, and the economy. Rather it defines the exercise of unwarranted power in terms of insulation from the market-place. This is not surprising, because the theory is derived from neo-classical economics and it sees the source of unwarranted power as arising out of monopolies. The solution to all problems is, therefore, to remove monopoly power, open up individuals to the disciplines of the market, and thereby approximate to the conditions of perfect competition. Perfect competition acts, in this context, rather like a communist utopia in unreconstructed Marxist theory.

A further consequence of this view is that New Right Public Choice theorists redraw the map of social division and conflict in society. In their view, primary social divisions are not the product of social class, gender, or ethnic conflict; rather, divisions are created between producers (teachers, in the case of education) who seek to 'capture' state resources for their own advantage, and consumers who are denied the resources and services they merit. Similarly, the privileged are defined as those who are sheltered from market forces. This provides the impetus for what Dale (Ch. 17) describes as 'mainstreaming', that is, to subject all workers to similar market conditions, almost as a matter of social justice as well as efficiency.

The third follows from this, for as Lauder (Ch. 25) argues, it doesn't follow that standards will be raised merely by organizing education according to market conditions. The fundamental reason for this is that market conditions are always mediated in capitalist societies by issues of class. Fundamentally, the class structure is determined not only by the market but by changes in the technical and power relations of work. As such, social classes do not come to the market as equals, and hence market systems in education are likely to exacerbate educational inequalities.

The fourth concerns the underlying assumption of the theory that individuals are self-seeking, and that they are driven primarily by the lures of wealth and status. This ignores the possibility that teachers, for example, are motivated by professional ideals as much as by income. Market disciplines in this respect may be a low-trust way of motivating teachers, for they fail to provide the autonomy that teachers may need in order to perform to the highest levels. This is a point to which we shall return shortly because it has become a key issue in the debate over the restructuring of education.

The fifth point is that Public Choice theorists have an impoverished view of democracy and hence of the role of education in promoting the dispositions and qualities appropriate to a democracy. The logical consequence of the Public Choice position is that education should be privatized. Several of the chapters in this section (Dale, Whitty, Grace) are concerned about the dangers of losing the long-held principle that education is a public good (see also Grace 1989). However, for Public Choice theorists the political processes of democracy are not where human freedom is best expressed; rather, the natural home of human freedom is the market. Indeed, the politics of democracy are seen as the source of injustice and inefficiency, in which the most powerful interest-groups win. But, again, it is important to note that this view is only plausible if it is assumed that the market is the best arena for reconciling conflict peacefully and efficiently.

An alternative explanation for the restructuring of education which eschews the myth of perfect competition and which takes inequalities of power to be endemic to capitalist societies is that of more recent neo–Marxist theories of the state, such as that of Codd, Gordon, and Harker (Ch. 16). Whereas Public-Choice accounts see the political system as a cause of economic crisis, Codd, Gordon, and Harker see causality as operating in the other direction: it is economic crises which lead to a crisis in the state.

Their work, based on the theories of Gramsci, Habermas, and Offe, represents a significant departure from the early theories of Althusser and Bowles and

258   **Introduction to Part Three**

Gintis, in ascribing greater autonomy to the state from the demands of a capitalist ruling class. Indeed, their work makes no reference to a ruling class *per se*, but
rather to the structural properties of a capitalist economy and in particular its
propensity to enter periods of crisis. According to Codd, Gordon, and Harker,
when faced with an economic crisis the capitalist state in liberal democracies has
also to contend with a legitimation crisis. The essence of the problem is that in
the light of economic demands for a reduction in state expenditure, such as
that advocated by the New Right, the state has to (i) restructure the way
demands on education are made so as to weaken and control them more effectively, and (ii) 'sell' what may be a significant reduction in educational services to
the voting public. The idea of what amounts to self-managing schools, coupled
with a rhetoric of community and individual choice, they argue, fits the bill. If
schools have the ability to set wages, hire, and fire, trade-union solidarity is
broken and with it union power to press for more educational resources. Indeed,
a rhetoric of community participation and choice over children's schooling is
seen as legitimating the state's enhanced potential to reduce educational expenditure while claiming greater parental empowerment. In this view the state is
devolving responsibility, but not power, to parents and communities. The
preservation of state power rather than community democracy is what educational restructuring is really all about. The net result is that whereas New Right
Public-Choice theorists see such measures as increasing educational efficiency
and effectiveness, Codd, Gordon, and Harker see the same process as a structural
problem anchored in the economy to which educational decentralization is an
answer.

Dale (Ch. 7) observes that the restructuring of education has led to a fundamental set of changes in the state–education relationship, from direct state
bureaucratic control to a set of what he terms governance relationships, in which
the former state activities of funding, provision, and regulation are turned
over to other agencies. He argues that the task now is to map these changes to
compare the effects of restructuring in different societies. Dale's early work
represented a sophisticated neo-Marxist reading of the state and education,
which has informed the work of writers including Codd, Gordon, and Harker.
However, this paper marks a significant change in Dale's thinking. He notes,
for example, that while the shift to market forms of education has been the
predominant change in the state–education relationship, it is not the only
one; between bureaucracy and the market there is a third form, of co-ordination
and delivery, which he terms community. In part, the development of this third
category does reflect the aspirations for culturally autonomous schooling,
although how much of the devolution of education is designed to meet the
aspirations of identifiable cultural groups, and how much it pays lip service to
them, is another matter. Dale also argues that many of the responses made by
the state have more to do with the limits of its capacity to act than with its
power to enforce. However, in the end the state must address the questions of
democratic accountability and equality of opportunity in devolved systems of
education, at a time when the particularisms of private wealth and community

are reasserting themselves, if the progressive role of education in a civilized society is to be preserved.

The paper by Green throws further light on the motivations and possible outcomes of the decentralization of education in Anglophone societies. Green's starting point is to ask the straightforward question of whether highly centralized education systems produce higher overall educational achievement than decentralized systems. The question may be straightforward, but obtaining answers is not. There is some tentative evidence for the conclusion that it is the most centralized systems that produce the best outcomes for all children. However, in considering this question, Green raises some further questions for consideration. The first is that, as he notes, it is those countries that have been or are in a process of accelerated nation-building that have the most centralized education systems. The second is that it appears to be the culture underpinning the education system which affects high overall achievement as much as the system itself. If this is the case, the idea that the radical individualism of the Anglophone countries can recreate high-achieving systems of education by importing the techniques of more centralized systems is clearly dubious. The third is that Green's paper raises two possible explanations of the decentralization of education in Anglophone countries. The first is to follow Codd, Gordon, and Harker in arguing that decentralization is not about raising overall standards *per se*, but about maintaining standards within what is seen by the New Right as an affordable budget. The second is to argue that decentralization and the emphasis on choice is part and parcel of what Bernstein (Ch. 3) calls the shift from individual to personalized forms of social solidarity. Finally, Green's highly suggestive paper raises perhaps one of the great issues to emerge at the end of the twentieth century. If centralized state education systems are intimately related to the history of nation-building, what do highly decentralized systems say about the meaning and significance of nationhood in the countries of which they are a part?

Whitty's paper (Ch. 19) introduces a further dimension to the debate over the restructuring of education. One of the fundamental issues concerning the relationship of New Right changes in education to fundamental post-modern change in society. The question, as Whitty puts it, is whether the restructuring of education represents the 'transitory policies of the New Right' or a more profound change in the relationship of education to the state and civil society, occasioned by the shift from a modern to a post-modern society. Education in a post-modern society would be understood in this context as a shift to more collaborative decision-making in education, flexibility between subject boundaries, greater diversity of provision, and responsiveness to local communities. Whitty argues that the reforms have reinforced hierarchy and distinction rather than diversity and collaboration, and he supports this view by reference to the international literature on the impact of restructuring on teachers. He concludes by raising the possibility of new forms of public association, in which education is seen as a public good integral to the renewal of democracy.

The starting point to Grace's chapter is a critique of Chubb and Moe's (1992) view that the self-managed school, headed by a strong leader, is the way forward for education. In a strong critique of Chubb and Moe's position which relates to his previous work in defence of education as a public good (Grace 1989), Grace points out that the self-managed school may not be in the interests of all parents, nor indeed in the national interest. He raises the question of why a 'strong' leadership style is seen as desirable, when it flies in the face of the call for greater democracy in educational decision-making. In addressing this question he raises one of the fundamental issues in educational restructuring, which is how to achieve consensus over innovation when it is implemented at speed and on the assumption that the key 'players' i.e., teachers, will be hostile to it. According to Public-Choice adherents such as Chubb and Moe, their recommendations for change will subject teachers to market disciplines and hence entail the loss of their privileged monopoly position. Like Whitty, Grace concludes by exploring the prospects for an alternative form of educational decision-making based on community democracy.

A fundamental problem with highly devolved systems of education is how to control them at arm's length. Most states in which education has been fundamentally restructured have sought to link accountability to assessment as a key lever of control, as Harry Torrance points out in Chapter 21. But assessment has also been used to achieve a variety of other ends simultaneously. These include the use of assessment as an instrument to provoke change in the teaching profession and as a means of raising standards to meet the demands of global competition. Precisely because assessment is being used to play so many different roles, the debates about it have been complex and overlapping. Torrance takes us carefully and incisively through these debates, and concludes that modernizing the curriculum and assessment methods in response to economic need is at variance with the emphasis on the use of assessment as market signals to aid parental choice. The latter is driving assessment towards the use of simplistic instruments which will constrict the curriculum and pedagogy in ways antithetical to the complex demands of a modern society.

Underlying these issues is a fundamental tension between the interests and impositions of the state in seeking to control and measure the activities of teachers, and research which emphasizes the importance of the particular interests and dispositions of learners. For example, individuals and groups may have different learning styles and needs (see Delpit Ch. 35) and we know from research that sensitivity to the learning context is vital if assessment is to provide a reliable guide to what has been learnt. If these findings are not taken into account, assessment is likely to abet the maintenance of inequality rather than promote greater opportunities for educational achievement (Gipps and Murphy 1994).

The particular tension between the interests of the state and that of students is broadened into a more general debate about the appropriate conditions necessary to bring education into the twenty-first century in the contributions by Darling-Hammond (Ch. 22) and Hargreaves (Ch. 23). Both have a vision of post-bureaucratic/post-modern schooling. Darling-Hammond explicitly links her criticisms of current restructuring strategies in an analysis of bureaucratic schooling. The latter was designed to educate an élite for the top corporate positions, and schooling therefore comprised strategies for efficiently sorting and selecting students, to ration the scarce resources of expert teachers and rich curricula. This enabled a greater routinization of teaching into semi-skilled work. She argues that now, however, the strategies of bureaucratic education are no longer viable and teaching must become a highly skilled profession. She gains credence for her views by drawing parallels between highly successful firms organized along post-Fordist lines and schools (see Brown and Lauder 1992). When judged against these successful models, she argues that there has been a woeful underinvestment in teachers, and that little has been done to address the dramatic inequalities of resourcing of education in the United States, graphically documented in a recent OECD report (OECD 1994).

Hargreaves's chapter provides an appropriate conclusion to the section, for he locates the dilemmas of restructuring within a broader vision of the fundamental changes in society. He also argues that the failure of states to take into account new social and economic realities will mean that the new generation of students will be short-changed in their education. These realities are ones which emphasize the importance of the local and particular as society becomes increasingly diverse. Paternalistic, bureaucratic state policies are simply inappropriate under these conditions. His case rests on the assumption of high-trust educational policies which will give teachers a high degree of professional autonomy to respond appropriately to local conditions. Like Dale, Grace, and Whitty he regards it as imperative that in the attention to diversity and local community the wider common purpose of society is not lost. He recognizes the risk that unless diversity can be reconciled with the public good, chaos may ensue. This is perhaps the most fundamental theme and challenge to emerge from the debates over the restructuring of education.

Notes

1. There has since been some revision of this view see Lazar (1977) and Banting (1985).
2. For discussion of aspects of cost effectiveness see Mortimore (Ch. 31), and for criticisms of Hanushek's paper in terms of the impact of educational expenditure on outcomes see Hedges, Lane, and Greenwald (1994).

References

Althusser, L. (1972), 'Ideology and Ideological State Apparatuses', in Cosin, B. (ed.), *Education, Structure and Society* (Harmondsworth: Penguin Books).

Arnot, M., and Weiler, K. (eds.) (1993), *Feminism and Social Justice in Education* (London: Falmer Press).

Banting, K. (1985), 'Poverty and Educational Priority', in McNay, I., and Ozga, J. (eds.), *Policy-Making in Education* (Oxford: Pergamon Press).

Bowles, S., and Gintis, G. (1976), *Schooling in Capitalist America* (London: Routledge and Kegan Paul).

Brown, P., and Lauder, H. (eds.) (1992), *Education for Economic Survival: From Fordism to Post-Fordism?* (London: Routledge).

Buchanan, J., and Tullock, G. (1962), *The Calculus of Consent* (Ann Arbor: Univ. of Michigan Press).

Carnoy, M., and Levin, H. (1985), *Schooling and Work in the Democratic State* (Stanford, Calif.: Stanford Univ. Press).

Chubb, J., and Moe, T. (1990), *Politics, Markets and America's Schools* (Washington DC: Brookings Institution).

—— (1992), *A Lesson in School Reform from Great Britain* (Washington DC: Brookings Institution).

Coleman, J., *et al.* (1966), *Equality of Educational Opportunity* (Washington DC: Government Printing Office).

Dale, R. (1982), 'Education and the Capitalist State', in Apple, M. (ed.), *Cultural and Economic Reproduction in Education* (London: Routledge).

Eisenstein, Z. (1982), 'The Sexual Politics of the New Right: Understanding the "Crisis of Liberalism" for the 1980s', in Keohane, N., *et al.* (eds.), *Feminist Theory: A Critique of Ideology* (Brighton: Harvester Press).

Floud, J., and Halsey, A. (1961), 'English Secondary Schools and the Supply of Labour', in Halsey, A. H., Floud, J., and Anderson, J. (1961), *Education, Economy and Society* (New York: Free Press).

Glennerster, H., and Low, W. (1990), 'Education and the Welfare State: Does it Add Up?' in Hills, J. (ed.), *The State of Welfare* (Oxford: Clarendon Press).

Gipps, C., and Murphy, P. (1994), *A Fair Test? Assessment, Achievement and Equity* (Buckingham: Open Univ. Press).

Grace, G. (1989), 'Education: Commodity or Public Good?' *British Journal of Educational Studies*, 37/3: 207–21.

Halsey, A. H., Heath, A., and Ridge, J. (1980), *Origins and Destinations* (Oxford: Clarendon Press).

Hanushek, E. (1986), 'The Economics of Schooling: Production and Efficiency in Public Schools', *Journal of Economic Literature*, 24 (September), 1141–77.

Hedges, L., Laine, R., and Greenwald, R. (1994), 'Does Money Matter? A Meta-Analysis of Studies of the Effects of Differential School Inputs on Student Outcomes', *Educational Researcher*, 23/3: 5–14.

Jencks, C., *et al.* (1972), *Inequality: A Reassessment of the Effects of Family and Schooling in America* (New York: Basic Books).

—— (1979), *Who Gets Ahead? The Determinants of Economic Success in America* (New York: Basic Books).

Lazar, I., Hubbell, V., Murray, H., Rosche, M., and Royce, J. (1977), *The Persistence of Pre-School Effects: A Long Term Follow-Up of Fourteen Infant and Pre-School Experiments*, DHEW Publication No. (OHDS) 78–30129.

Murray, C. (1984), *Losing Ground: American Social Policy 1950–1980* (New York: Basic Books).

OECD (1994), *Economic Surveys: The United States* (Paris: OECD).

Troyna, B. (1992), 'Can You See the Join? An Historical Analysis of Multicultural and Anti-Racist Education Policies', in Gill, D., Mayor, B., and Blair, M. (eds.), *Racism and Education: Structures and Strategies* (London: Sage).

——, and Williams, J. (1986), *Racism, Education and the State* (London: Croom Helm).

16

Education and the Role of the State: Devolution and Control Post-Picot

John Codd, Liz Gordon, and Richard Harker

... As the education system has expanded, the role of the state as major funder and provider of education has been largely unchallenged. This situation, however, no longer prevails. Educational policy has been linked so closely to economic policy in recent times that any attempt to analyze the former without regard to the influences of the latter would be inevitably deficient. This raises a number of important issues concerning the inter relationship between the economic, political and cultural spheres of governmental activity. Any analysis of these issues, therefore, must examine contemporary theories of the state and its role in each of these spheres.

This chapter examines the political/economic conditions that appear to be shaping New Zealand educational policy. In particular, we argue that current educational policy directions enunciated in *Tomorrow's Schools* are indicative of a state that is facing dual crises of capital accumulation and legitimation. The central role of the state at present is clearly directed towards improving conditions for the accumulation of capital. However, the effects of this, particularly in terms of unemployment and reducing real wages, require the state to legitimate not only capital, but also the effects of its own policies on the production and maintenance of social inequality.

Our analysis rejects economic determinism and adopts a Gramscian position on the political role of the state similar to that developed in several recent neo-Marxist accounts (Habermas 1976; Offe 1984; O'Connor 1984). These accounts have rejected the orthodox Marxist model in which the state is a mechanistic servant of capital reproduction and have reconceptualized the state as an 'independent' mediator between the economic imperatives of capital and the political imperatives of civil society. Within this more recently developed model, state education policies can be seen as attempts by agents of the state to deal with the complex and contradictory problems of fiscal management and political legitimation. In the current New Zealand situation, this becomes an attempt on the one hand to reduce or contain government expenditure, while on the other to produce educational policies which will address the legitimation problems stemming from youth unemployment and Maori underachievement. In this chapter we contend that the Picot Report's advocacy of economic efficiency and devolution and subsequent *Tomorrow's Schools* policy is a response to these conflicting imperatives and will have contradictory effects.

Theorizing the State

Although the state in contemporary society has become increasingly powerful and pervasive, surprisingly little attention has been given, until relatively recently, to developing adequate theories of its role and relationship to other aspects of society. Few would now disagree with Wolfe's claim that:

If state power is ever to be understood, the term itself must be brought back into existence; to resurrect the state is to make a political declaration about

From H. Lauder and C. Wylie (eds.), *Towards Successful Schooling* (London: Falmer Press, 1990), 15–32.
Reprinted with permission.

the centrality of organised political power in modern societies. (Wolfe 1977: ix)

The virtual absence of theories of the state in educational policy analysis is largely a reflection of the liberal ideology within which such analysis is generally undertaken. This ideology embodies a political theory of possessive individualism, which has a long history within the Western intellectual tradition beginning with philosophers such as Hobbes and Locke (MacPherson 1962). According to this view, the state comprises a set of institutions produced by the consensual collective actions of individuals in order to protect their general interests and to make provisions for common social goods such as education, defence and the protection of property. With the rise of capitalism, this liberal view of the state became more deeply entrenched. Carnoy and Levin (1985) summarize this trend as follows:

With Bentham and Mill in the early nineteenth century, 'classical' theories of the State, which had been premised on a relatively homogeneous rural society of smallholders, shifted to a utilitarian view of democracy that incorporated the newly emerged capitalist class structure and provided an intellectual rationale for it. Utilitarians adopted Adam Smith's argument in *The Wealth of Nations* that, because of the guiding 'invisible hand' of the market-place, unfettered individual economic activity would maximise social welfare, that indeed there was no inconsistency between the unlimited pursuit of individual gain and social good, and that the State should thus limit itself only to the production of such public goods as defense, education, and the enforcement of laws. (p. 28)

During the twentieth century, mainly in response to economic crises in the accumulation of capital, the state has become more and more involved in the provision of services and in the operation of the economy. Different liberal economic theories have emerged to account for these developments. Keynesian theories are based upon the assumption that the market lacks the capacity to secure favourable profit conditions without regulatory state interventions, whereas monetarist theories assume that the accumulation process is self-regulating and therefore that the state should not intervene in the free market. Both these views, however, are considered by Marxist theorists to be false because they do not recognize the class-based nature of capitalist society.

Within the Marxist tradition, differing conceptions of the state have been advanced. The classical view, taken from Marx himself, defines the state as an essential means of class domination in a capitalist society (Carnoy 1984: 44–64). Within this view, the state is seen to be an instrument of the capitalist class, necessary to the maintenance of its control over the relations of production. Because of instability in the capitalist production process, giving rise to periodic crises of over- or under-production, the dominant class needs to extend its power to the state and its various agencies and institutions. Hence the primary role of the state is to avert, resolve or prevent the economic crises that are endemic to capitalist society.

For neo-Marxists, this orthodox economistic view of the state is unable to explain sufficiently the complex functions of state institutions and the diverse effects of state policies in advanced capitalist societies. Nor can it explain adequately, in their view, the role of the state in relation to economic, political and social crises (O'Connor 1987). In contrast to both liberal theories and the orthodox Marxist view,

Neo-Marxism stresses that politics and state policy are deeply enmeshed in modern capitalist accumulation. The deep interpenetration between state and capital, policies and the market, means that modern 'political capitalism' is inexplicable in terms of conventional economic and political theory. Instead, it is argued that we need new kinds of political economic theories which explain economic crisis in relation to political processes and dynamics. (O'Connor 1987: 127)

A major contributor to this new wave of state theory is Claus Offe (1984 and 1985) who has been influenced by the Frankfurt School, particularly Habermas (1976), and, to some extent, by Weber's analysis of bureaucracy. Offe (1984) argues that the modern capitalist state has two simultaneous and often contradictory roles. These are (i) to support the process of capital accumulation (e.g. by providing transport systems, business subsidies, etc.); and (ii) to legitimate this role by maintaining electoral support and by endeavouring to enhance the value of labour (for example, through education and training policies) and to ameliorate the social costs of private accumulation (for example, through welfare policies, environmental protection policies etc.).

In performing these roles, the institutions of the state are 'independent' of any direct or systematic control by the capitalist class, but these institutions tend to support capitalist interests mainly because they are dependent upon capital accumulation for their continued existence. In other words, although the institutional form of the state is not determined by the interests of capital, state policies will tend to shape capitalist development and reproduce the capitalist mode of production. At the same time, however, the state also responds to and attempts to mediate a range of other political demands from various social movements and from state bureaucrats themselves. Thus, the political power of the state depends, indirectly, on the private accumulation of capital which, through taxation, provides the state with its resources. But to remain in power, the state must also be legitimate, that is it must maintain a certain level of popular support. This legitimation is achieved through the democratic processes of election and representation, and through the production of mass loyalty to the existing system of administrative and political power.

The capitalist welfare state, in Offe's view, 'seeks to implement and guarantee the *collective* interests of all members of a *class society, dominated by capital*' (Offe 1984: 120). This means that state agencies and policies will tend to have contradictory purposes. Some policies have the purpose of redistributing resources to various groups who are systematically disadvantaged by market exchange processes while, at the same time, other policies have the primary purpose of supporting the commodity production and exchange relationships of the capitalist economy. Such an economy works most effectively, according to Offe, when all forms of both capital and labour power take on the *commodity form*, i.e. are able to be exchanged within an open and unrestricted market.

Problems arise within the capitalist economy when values cease to exist in the commodity form. This occurs when there is over-production of certain goods or when conditions of unemployment prevent the free exchange of labour power. Such problems lead to interventions by the state which in turn tend to paralyze further the commodity form of value. For example, during conditions of high youth unemployment, the state intervenes with work-skill training programmes (for example, Access programmes) not to provide the necessary labour power for certain industries, but to enhance the opportunities for the exchange value of labour. In order to achieve this, however, the state must channel resources (taxation) into supporting a vast training system (including the salaries of tutors and trainers) which is exempt from the commodity form. Thus, according to Offe, 'the state's attempts to maintain and *universalize* the commodity form require organizations whose mode of operation is no longer subject to the commodity form' (Offe 1984: 127). This produces a structural contradiction in state policies which adopt non-market or *decommodified* means for achieving specific social goals, while being dependent upon the processes of commodity production and exchange for their continued viability. Welfare state education policies have traditionally been fraught with this contradiction. Decommodified services (early childhood provisions, advisory and support services, special education agencies, etc.) have been developed and expanded on the basis of demand and educational value regardless of the capacity of the commodified economic sector to support such expansion.

Offe argues (ibid. 51–61) that the self-paralyzing and disorganizing tendencies of the capitalist economy necessitate regulatory state policies while, at the same time, threatening the effectiveness and fiscal viability of those policies. As the state's institutions extend their sphere of activity in order to sustain capitalist expansion, there is a parallel expansion of state budgets with increasing problems of fiscal management. The accumulation process depends upon the state to provide such forms of support as transportation and communication systems, subsidized energy resources, and research and development programmes. These costs are added to those arising from the provision of social services in health education and welfare, causing state expenditure to exceed state revenues and producing the familiar problem of persistent budget deficits. The borrowing and taxation capacities of the state then begin to cause serious contractions in the accumulation of capital, resulting in what O'Connor (1973) called 'the fiscal crisis of the state'. This crisis can be resolved only by savage reductions in state expenditure, but the policies required to bring this about tend to undermine mass loyalty, producing what Habermas (1976) and others have called a 'legitimation crisis'.

In neo–Marxist theory, 'legitimation crisis' is defined as the tendency of state institutions to lose popular political support and sometimes to invoke popular opposition and resistance. Legitimation is what persuades the mass of the population that the status quo is the common sense way to organize society: it converts power into authority. Traditionally, the free market economy is legitimated through common sense beliefs such as 'the protestant work ethic', but in advanced capitalism the legitimation of the state itself is maintained by what Habermas (1976) calls 'scientific–technical rationality'. Social institutions are rationalized by technical experts and political problems are converted into technical ones, with technical solutions. Hence, increasingly, people are being depoliticized, according to Habermas, because decisions are taken over by 'experts', and democracy is reduced to occasional choice between administrative teams.

Legitimation problems arise when state institutions cannot function normally and/or when they cannot inspire sufficient public confidence or loyalty. Clearly, this situation is more likely to arise at times of economic crisis because, as O'Connor (1987) points out:

legitimation depends on the capacity of the political system to secure a consensus of political policies from groups which either will not benefit or will be harmed by capitalist accumulation—a task which typically requires that policies be defined and presented to the 'public' in ways that conceal their true nature. (pp. 110–11)

Thus, a crisis of legitimation will tend to coincide with a crisis of accumulation (especially where the latter is manifested as a fiscal crisis), further limiting the state's capacity to redistribute resources and opportunities. Wolfe suggests that this loss of legitimacy in advanced capitalist society 'reinforces public cynicism towards government', because of the 'basically correct' perception that the state only helps the rich. Thus, according to Wolfe (1977):

the problem of legitimacy and problems of accumulation reinforce each other . . . The legitimacy crisis is produced by the inability of the late capitalist state to maintain its democratic rhetoric if it is to preserve the accumulation function, or the ability to spur further accumulation if it is to be true to its democratic ideology. (p. 329)

This is a dilemma that we have seen clearly evidenced in New Zealand government policies of the late 1980s. The political storm over the sale of state assets is a prime example. What this illustrates is the close interdependence between the political dimensions of state policy and the wider economic conditions of a welfare capitalist society such as New Zealand. We want to argue, with reference to the *Tomorrow's Schools* policy, that this kind of analysis is useful for explaining the conditions that have shaped such a policy initiative. We shall go on to argue, however, that the state–capital relationship is less useful for explaining the cultural, social and political effects of such policies. At this point, we need to use the theories discussed so far to outline briefly the nature of the present crisis concerning the role of the state in New Zealand.

The Fiscal Crisis of the New Zealand State

. . .The dominant ideology guiding current state policies in New Zealand holds that increased government spending is a prime cause of the economic crisis. It is claimed that state employment is inherently 'unproductive' and stultifies economic growth by keeping taxation levels too high. The assumption is that lowering taxes increases the incentive for people to work harder and longer. Such claims do not recognize that the economic problem is not due to insufficient physical output per worker, but rather to a decline in surplus value production per worker. Describing the popular promotion of these doctrines in the United States, O'Connor (1987) comments as follows:

These views by monetarist and neo–classical economists were underpinned by the dogmatic belief that economic problems in the USA and the rest of the world were remediable through the normal mechanisms of the market. Unemployment, austerity, and a purge of the system's fat tissues, especially the heavy layer of 'unreal' popular expectations created by 'irresponsible' and 'weak' politicians and bureaucrats would 'create a new prosperity' (in Reagan's words). Government policy would be brought into line with these views on the causes and consequences of the economic crisis; the 'new' supply-side economics was transparently the ancient economics of *laissez faire*. (pp. 36–7)

The current fiscal crisis of the New Zealand state is fully described in the Treasury document, *Government Management* (1987). The figures show that 'total net government expenditure . . . has risen steadily as a share of GDP from 31.1 per cent in 1973/74 to reach 43.6 per cent in 1986/87' (Treasury 1987 1: 223). This increase 'does not reflect an increased demand for real goods and services' (ibid. 224) but it mainly reflects the growing cost of debt servicing and transfer payments to such areas as national superannuation and unemployment benefits. The effect has been a succession of fiscal deficits which have led to continued overseas borrowing and a situation in which New Zealand has become the fourth most indebted country in the OECD (p. 230). In attempting to contain this increasing fiscal crisis, the government has exercised stringent controls on all areas of state expenditure, including education, and more recently, has embarked upon a programme of corporatization followed by privatization of a growing number of state institutions. Despite these policies of desperation, the fact remains that the 1988 budget produced a fiscal deficit (excluding asset sales) of $ 1.4 billion.

. . .Economic restructuring and corporatization policies have driven unemployment to record levels, caused severe problems of social dislocation, and generally increased inequalities between groups and communities. In these circumstances, state institutions, especially the education systems, are unable to satisfy public expectations and they become predictable targets for frustration and anxiety. For the past decade in New Zealand, there have been expressions of concern by some pressure groups about such issues as declining educational standards, contentious curriculum developments, incompetent teachers, high levels of illiteracy, ineffective schools, inefficient bureaucrats, and a host of other perceived problems and deficiencies. More recently, the state education system has been strongly attacked also by the new monetarists. Until the 1980s, education was broadly identified as a means for generating the wealth of the nation. However, the monetarists have convinced many people that public expenditure on education is a drain on the nation's resources, keeping investment money away from the market and providing benefits mainly to the individuals who receive it rather than the nation as a whole. This argument was put forward in the Treasury's brief to the 1987 incoming government.

This Treasury document on 'Education Issues' (*Government Management*, 1987/2) presents a graphic account of an education system that is relentlessly squeezed between fiscal and political pressures. The analysis reveals a crisis in which state policy-makers, faced with absolute limitations of resources, can no longer meet public expectations and political demands for further extension and improvement of educational provision. As the Treasury brief points out:

In recent years a number of pressures on the state system have become discernible. They are not just pressures for more and better of the same (such pressures always exist), but for different types of education service and, in some respects, a different kind of education structure. (Treasury 1987/2: 15)

Given these pressures, and the political acceptance of fiscal constraints argued for by Treasury, it is predictable that the responses of state policy-makers will be fraught with underlying contradictions. This is indeed the case with *Tomorrow's Schools* and the Picot Report which preceded it. These documents, we contend, should be interpreted within the context of their production. They are ideological texts that can be used to legitimate political decisions that will effectively reduce educational expenditure and fragment existing structures and patterns of interest representation. The main effect, we argue, will be to reduce pressures upon the state for continued expansion and improvement of educational provision and to decentralize and disorganize the existing arena of political contestation as it relates to education.

The Picot Report: Context, Contradictions, and Consequences

. . . The Picot Task Force was announced in 1987. Its terms of reference set an agenda in which two concepts were to be central: devolution and efficiency. All matters relating to curriculum or the nature of teaching and learning were excluded. The task force was requested to report directly to the Ministers of Education, Finance and State Services and it was specifically asked to 'identify any costs and benefits of its recommendations and recommend the nature and timing of any necessary transitional arrangements' (Picot Report 1988: p. ix).

How much influence Treasury had in the preparation and writing of the Picot Report is a matter for further research, but it should be noted that a Treasury officer was seconded to the task force as one of its part-time secretaries. It should also be noted that the Treasury released its own document on education towards the end of 1987, before the task force would have commenced writing its report. A careful analysis and comparison of the two texts reveals some interesting similarities.

The Treasury's analysis identifies three issues which are said to underlie recent public concerns about education. The first is the issue of *choice* which is juxtaposed against 'state direction'. The second is the issue of *equity* which is linked to funding and what is called the 'middle-class capture effect'. The third issue is *efficiency* which is linked to 'levels of performance'.

By couching the issues in this way, Treasury's ideological agenda is revealed. It is an agenda in which equity becomes redefined in individualistic consumerist terms (user-pays) and the role of the state is reduced to that of guarantor of individual rights and liberties. There is no doubt that the same ideology lies behind the Picot statement (1988: 4) that, 'we see the creation of more choice in the system as a way of ensuring greater efficiency and equity.' This assumption that equity can be achieved by increasing individual choice and the further assumption 'that nearly everyone will have a genuine commitment to doing the best job possible for all learners' (ibid.) are central to the Picot rationale for devolution. It is a rationale that has the same ideological origins as the rationale given by Treasury for reducing the state's role in education. Indeed, the full weight of monetarist doctrine lurks behind Treasury's statement that:

government intervention is liable to reduce freedom of choice and thereby curtail the sphere of responsibility of its citizens and weaken the self-steering ability inherent in society to reach optimal solutions through the mass of individual actions pursuing free choice without any formal consensus. (Treasury 1987/2: 41)

This 'free market' ideology readily coheres with some popular common sense beliefs about government interference in the lives of individuals. It can become, therefore, a powerful source of legitimation. To this end, the Picot Report begins with a highly critical description of the education system, endorsing the popular belief that all bureaucracy is inherently and fundamentally bad. The Report presents a cynical and highly negative image of a system which is alleged to be inflexible, unresponsive and weighed down with unnecessary rules and regulations. It suggests that the bureaucracy is largely self-serving and that most of the rules and procedures governing the allocation and use of resources exist only to frustrate or prevent decision-making at the level of individual institutions. The Report proposes, therefore, that as far as possible, all such rules and procedures should be abolished and each institution should be given discretion over how it spends its funds. The proposal that the Ministry of Education dispense a bulk grant annually to the Board of Trustees of each institution subsequently became central to the *Tomorrow's Schools* policy.

Thus, the rationale for devolution is that it produces greater flexibility and responsiveness, but it also produces a structure in which decisions can be more effectively controlled. This latter outcome is implicit in Picot but it is made explicit in the Treasury document, where it states that:

With central planning, mistakes tend to be excessively costly and impact on everyone, with few alternatives being available when things go wrong. The bounded rationality of central planners and the complexity of the world creates strains for the relative efficacy of centrally determined solutions. (Treasury 1987/1: 42)

The new structure entails a devolution of decision-making in a wide range of administrative areas, including resource allocation, staff appointments, support services and staff development. Boards of Trustees are given some discretion in these areas but control is firmly invested in the two central state agencies: the Ministry itself, and the Review and Audit Agency. This control is to be manifested, not in the form of directives, but in the form of tightly circumscribed limits and constant surveillance.

Removing formal administrative structures from the local and district level produces a situation in which highly centralized control is exercised through legal contracts, in the form of institutional charters, and regular review and auditing processes. In this way, the state can more effectively control educational expenditure in the form of bulk grants, while shifting responsibility for the way funds are spent to the institutional level. Most public dissatisfaction with education, therefore, is to be vented at the local level and thus diverted from central government. The legitimation crisis is transported downwards.

Another implication of this strategic manoeuvre is that pressures for increased expenditure in education can no longer be as readily applied through established channels at the national level. The new structure effectively removes most of the institutional routes by which claims have been made on central government for qualitative improvements in education. Teacher organizations, for example, can no longer press for reduced class sizes, more professional support, curriculum resources or in-service training. Responsibility for these matters is to reside in each institution.

What is it then about Picot and *Tomorrow's Schools* that is different from most other educational policies? In Offe's terms, it is a 'structural' as opposed to a 'conjunctural' policy. A 'structural policy' is one that:

follows the imperative of keeping output constant, that is at levels that are considered reasonable or affordable, while channelling demand inputs in a way that appears compatible with available resources. (Offe 1985: 224)

Such policies are based upon a different form of political rationality from the more common 'conjunctural' policies which 'seek to maximize the adequacy of policy responses to problems as they emerge and appear on the agenda' (ibid. 226). Policies to expand early childhood provisions, to reduce pupil/teacher ratios, to introduce bilingual schools, to increase student teacher intakes, are all examples of 'conjunctural' policies.

Whereas 'conjunctural' policies intervene in order to satisfy demands or anticipate developments, 'structural' policies aim to shape and channel demands 'so as to make them satisfiable' (ibid. 225). Structural policies, according to Offe,

are adopted in response to conditions of economic and institutional crises. In response to such crises, the physical and economic parameters of production and the institutional parameters of interest representation, which together constitute the nature of the problem, become subject to redesign. The shift is from policy output and economic

demand management to the shaping of political input and economic supply—from 'state intervention' to 'politicization'. (Offe 1985: 226)

Offe argues that a shift from 'conjunctural' to 'structural' policies 'has been a dominant trend in advanced capitalist nations since the late sixties' (ibid.).

As a 'structural' policy, *Tomorrow's Schools* represents a strategic response to the fiscal crisis of the New Zealand state. If it succeeds, its major effects would be (i) to give the central agencies of the state more control over economic supply and political demand; and (ii) to shift the locus of legitimation problems away from central government. However, because of the contradictions inherent in the policy itself, particularly the contradiction between choice and equity, there is a very real prospect that it will fail. Its failure would inevitably lead to a further deepening of the legitimation crisis. In a characteristically elliptical way, Habermas points to the dilemma, when he comments that:

a legitimation crisis can be avoided in the long run only if the latent class structures of advanced-capitalist societies are transformed or if the pressure for legitimation to which the administrative system is subject can be removed. (Habermas 1976: 93)

Tomorrow's Schools will certainly not change the latent class structures of New Zealand society; it remains to be seen whether it can remove the pressure for legitimation.

State, Capital, and Civil Society

The discussion to this point has focused on state policy formation and the political/economic conditions that have produced a policy such as *Tomorrow's Schools*. Drawing upon the theories of Offe, Habermas and O'Connor, we have argued that it represents a policy response to the dual crises of accumulation and legitimation. Because these theories focus primarily on the state–capital relationship, they have proven useful in examining the dynamics of policy production, but they are clearly limited when it comes to considering the social/political *effects* of a policy such as *Tomorrow's Schools*. What this requires is a theoretical framework which embraces all spheres of society and which explains why certain state policies will produce political contestation or resistance. In this final section of the paper, we shall outline a Gramscian framework for such analysis, which recognizes the complex interrelationship between the state, capital and civil society.

Most neo-Marxist theorists have been influenced in one way or another by Gramsci but few have examined the intricacies and subtleties of his theory of the state. Essentially, Gramsci argued that the state cannot be understood independently of *civil society*. In reconstructing a Gramscian notion of civil society from the numerous scattered comments in his writing, Simon describes it as:

all the 'so-called private' organizations such as churches, trade unions, political parties and cultural associations which are distinct from the process of production *and* from the coercive apparatuses of the state. All the organizations which make up civil society are the result of a complex network of social practices and social relations. (Simon 1982: 69)

From a Gramscian perspective then, a capitalist society is composed of three sets of social relations:

1. the relations of production (capital-labour);
2. the coercive relations of the state (the term 'political society' is used for the coercive relations in the state apparatuses); and
3. all other relationships that make up civil society. (ibid.)

It is in his use of the concept of *hegemony* that Gramsci is able to maintain both a contrast and a continuity between these sets of relationships. According to Carnoy (1984, pp. 69–70), Gramsci's concept of hegemony has two principal meanings. At one level, it is 'a process within civil society whereby a fraction of the dominant class exercises control through its moral and intellectual leadership over other allied fractions of the dominant class' (ibid. 70). At another level, hegemony 'involves the successful attempts of the dominant class to use its political, moral, and intellectual leadership to establish its view of the world as all-inclusive and universal, and to shape the interests and needs of subordinate groups' (ibid.). Thus, hegemony is not an alternative to coercion but it is a synthesis of consent and coercion, taking different forms, and extending throughout both the state and civil society.

Carnoy suggests that:

the function of hegemony in civil society, where the ideological apparatuses are much less obvious, and therefore much more effective in mystifying the dominance of class rule, differs from the State's hegemonic apparatuses, which are much more apparent in their reproductive role, especially since they carry coercion's armour (the juridical system and the school, for example). (ibid. 73)

Thus schools are prime examples of institutions that manifest both the coercive relations of the state (for example, compulsory attendance, core curriculum, national credentials) and the hegemonic relations of civil society (for example, pedagogy, reward systems, hierarchies). They cannot be said to 'belong' in one sphere or the other; schools are institutional constituents of both the state *and* civil society (Codd, Harker and Nash, 1985).

The recognition that the relations of domination are the same in both the state and civil society led Gramsci to the following major proposition:

by 'state' should be understood not only the apparatus of government, but also the 'private' apparatus of 'hegemony' or civil society. (Gramsci 1971: 261)

This he came to call the *integral state*, i.e. 'hegemony protected by the armour of coercion' (ibid. 262). Thus, Gramsci distinguishes the state from civil society, but then brings them together in his notion of the integral state.

According to Simon, this ambiguity within Gramsci's theory of the state arises because he uses the term 'state' in its everyday use, and as a synonym for power. Gramsci sought to explain why capturing the 'political' state did not in itself change the basis of power within society. Gramsci's argument is that:

the social relationships of civil society are relations of power just as much (though in a different way) as are the coercive relations of the state. A hegemonic class exercises power over subordinate classes in civil society in addition to state power which it exercises through its predominance in the state. (Simon 1982: 72)

This Gramscian analysis raises important questions about the social effects of a policy such as *Tomorrow's Schools* which shifts certain aspects of the administration of schools from the central agencies of the state to small organizational units within civil society in the form of Boards of Trustees. The declaration that each board should 'properly reflect the composition of its community' is based upon assumptions that are contradicted by social realities. The fact is that in an unequal society particular kinds of competence, including administrative skills, are distributed unequally among individuals and between communities.

Bourdieu's concept of 'cultural capital' is relevant here (Harker, 1985). Just as economic resources are distributed unequally, so too are cultural resources and some kinds of cultural competence bestow social power upon those who have that competence. The power of a small formally organized group such as a Board of Trustees would be derived from the cultural capital of its members. Predictably, therefore, in a situation where learning institutions are in competition with each other some will dominate over others.

By removing bureaucratic administrative structures from the local and district level, *Tomorrow's Schools* effectively reduces the coercive power which can enable the state to protect some of the interests of less powerful groups. Without these structures, the forces of hegemonic domination in civil society are given a free rein. Although institutional charters are intended to have coercive force, by placing boundaries on areas of discretion, these too will be cultural texts, open to interpretation and with hegemonic effects.

Any comprehensive analysis of such a policy should consider not only the political context of its production but also the social context of its implementation. Drawing on Gramscian concepts, we can begin to develop a theory which recognizes the state's central role in the reproduction of the relations of production without restricting that explanation to a form of economic reductionism. The theory we are suggesting identifies the state as a sphere of political activity with its own dynamic, influenced but not determined by the dynamic of capital, and also influenced by the dynamics of various political forces and coalitions located within civil society (Dale 1983).

This gives us a theoretical framework which defines the role of the state in terms of *limits* and *capacity*. The notions of the limits and capacity of the state recognize the plural pressures that arise from the state's location in a contradictory and unstable mode of production, a social context of conflicting cultural forms resulting both from the relations of production and the demands of non-dominant groups, and its own political sphere with agendas that are often blatantly 'political' and bear little resemblance to capital's 'needs'. Whilst the capitalist mode of production clearly both influences and constrains all of these spheres, we cannot understand the politics of education without examining the limits which each sphere sets on the others, the capacity of the state to ensure consent for its own agenda, and the nature of the hegemonic settlement within civil society (Gordon, 1989).

As Jessop (1983) notes, as long as capitalism continues, we know by definition that there is an 'economically dominant' class. But this does not tell us:

whether capital (or one of its fractions) enjoys political, intellectual and moral hegemony. Given the possibilities for dislocation between economic domination and/or economic hegemony and hegemony in broader terms, these issues can only be settled in the light of specific overdetermined conjunctures. Clearly only concrete analyses of concrete situations will resolve these issues. (p. 106)

The notion of limits refers to all those aspects of the state that prevent it from acting in its own interests. These limits originate in the state's relations to both capital and civil society; it is limited by its very position *within* civil society. The central contradiction for the state is that, while it must work for its own reproduction, it must at the same time appear to be working as a popular-democratic state, that is in the interests of 'the people' (however these are conceived); and also for the reproduction of the mode of production (for example, in education it must provide vocationally oriented courses if these are demanded by the labour-market).

Conclusion

The role of the state in the current crisis has been to maintain the existing power relations enshrined within the education system, while dramatically altering the fiscal and bureaucratic 'inputs'. This has required a reordering and restructuring of agencies within the state, through the abolition of regional bodies and the conversion of the central Department of Education into a Ministry.

The ideological justification for the reform of educational administration obscures the reality that the hegemonic power relations have been merely relocated from the central state towards the boundary of state/civil society, that is the individual school in its local community. The establishment of the Review and Audit Agency, which must be seen, in Offe's terms, as a coercive agency, is there to ensure that any deviations from the existing power relationships do not occur. Thus, the state remains, finally, as guardian of existing social relations.

The structural reorganization of the administration of education must be understood, then, as a response to crises occurring in other sectors of society, underpinned by particular ideological views of the role of the state. Few of the explanations that have been given for these changes, for example, more choice, parent-power, simplification of administration, clearer lines of accountability, etc., actually reflect the real changes that have taken place. The deep economic crisis of the state and the government's monetarist response to it have placed severe limits on state action in education, and have necessitated the structural reforms contained in *Tomorrow's Schools*. At the same time, the capacity of the state has been constrained by the ideological rhetoric of the free market that has emanated from Treasury and permeated the bureaucracy.

We have argued that *Tomorrow's Schools* is the product of a particular set of historical, economic and political forces. It is a policy that has been formed at a time when the New Zealand state's capacity to promote redistributive policies is severely limited by a crisis of capital accumulation. Behind an ideological 'free market' rhetoric of devolution and efficiency, we have a policy that will tighten the state's control over educational expenditure, shift the arena of political contestation towards the periphery of civil society, and exacerbate the problem of 'middle class capture'. It heralds a new era of hegemonic domination in New Zealand schools.

References

Booth, P. (1988), 'David Lange on Education: Is He Giving or Taking Away?' *North and South* (April), 53–60.

Carnoy, M. (1984), *The State and Political Theory* (Princeton, NJ: Princeton Univ. Press).

—— and Levin, H. M. (1985), *Schooling and Work in the Democratic State* (Stanford, Calif.: Stanford Univ. Press).

Codd, J. A. (1988), 'The Construction and Deconstruction of Educational Policy Documents', *Journal of Education Policy*, 3/3: 235–47.

Codd, J., Harker, R., and Nash, R. (eds.) (1985), *Political Issues in New Zealand Education* (Palmerston North: Dunmore Press).

Dale, R. (1983), 'The Politics of Education in England 1970–1983: State, Capital and Civil Society', paper presented to the Symposium on Marxism and Sociology of Education (Madrid, December).

Department of Education (1987), *The Curriculum Review* (Wellington: Department of Education).

Gordon, L. (1989), 'Beyond Relative Autonomy Theories of the State in Education', *British Journal of Sociology of Education*.

Gramsci, A. (1971), *Selections from Prison Notebooks* (London: Lawrence and Wishart).

Habermas, J. (1976), *Legitimation Crisis* (London: Heinemann).

Harker, R. (1985), 'Schooling and Cultural Reproduction', in Codd, J., Harker, R., and Nash, R. (eds.), *Political Issues in New Zealand Education* (Palmerston North: Dunmore Press).

Jessop, B. (1983), 'Accumulation Strategies, State Forms, and Hegemonic Projects', *Kapitali State*, 10/11: 89–111.

MacPherson, C. B. (1962), *The Political Theory of Possessive Individualism* (Oxford: Clarendon Press).

Minister of Education (1988), *Tomorrow's Schools* (Wellington: Department of Education).

O'Connor, J. (1973), *The Fiscal Crisis of the State* (New York: St Martin's Press).

—— (1984), *Accumulation Crisis* (Oxford: Blackwell).

—— (1987), *The Meaning of Crisis* (Oxford: Blackwell).

Offe, C. (1984), *Contradictions of the Welfare State* (London: Hutchinson).

—— (1985), *Disorganized Capitalism* (Oxford: Polity Press).

Simon, R. (1982), *Gramsci's Political Thought* (London: Lawrence and Wishart).

Task Force to Review Education Administration, Report of (1988) (Picot Report), *Administering for Excellence* (Wellington: Government Printer).

Wolfe, A. (1977), *The Limits of Legitimacy: Political Contradictions of Late Capitalism* (New York: Free Press).

17

The State and the Governance of Education: An Analysis of the Restructuring of the State–Education Relationship

Roger Dale

Introduction

The past decade has seen far-reaching changes in the education systems of most Western countries. There is broad agreement at a rather general level about the causes and nature of these changes. They are seen as part of the wider decline of the postwar welfare-state settlement, and that in turn is increasingly linked to changes in the global economy. This explanation is, however, very general, and if we are to make progress in understanding the specifics of any case we need above all to be able to spell out the mechanisms through which these changes have been installed. Of course, considerable and valuable work has been carried out in many countries on these issues which has enabled a fairly broad consensus to develop about the nature of the changes, including shifts away from 'state control' towards 'privatization' and 'decentralization' as the commonest responses to the new problems that education systems are facing. However, there has been little investigation of the precise mechanisms of these schemes, and it frequently appears to be assumed that what is 'privatization' or 'decentralization' in one country is the same in another. Recognizing, though, that education systems have nowhere (with the possible example of Chile) literally been privatized, and that there are numerous and very different possible interpretations of decentralization, delegation, devolution, and so on, should give us pause before assuming that we are talking about the same phenomenon.

What I intend to do in this chapter is to develop a basis for understanding and comparing the restructuring of the education–state relationship in Western societies. This involves isolating and analysing the relationships between the various mechanisms crucial to the new relationships between the state and education. Such an enterprise involves a considerable degree of discussion which, though rather abstract, is necessary if these changes to education are to be mapped and their likely effects in terms of equality, democracy, and participation assessed and compared. It is only if a sound basis for comparision can be developed that we can determine what policies are most likely to be effective in meeting the public aims of education.

In doing this I will argue that far from being weakened, the state's role in the control of education has actually been strengthened, if transformed; however, one very serious consequence of the change in the state's role in education is that the public–good functions of education, of which the state is the only reliable guarantor are being withdrawn. There are two reasons for this. The first and perhaps primary reason concerns the ideological commitments of neo-liberalism, which rejects the view that the state has a significant responsibility in supporting the public-good functions of education. The second is more complex and relates to Offe's (1990) view that in certain policy areas the state's capacity to act is severely limited in the present social and economic context.

Most existing theories of the government and control of education have tended to take for granted that education systems are state-controlled and state-run. The question has been 'why the state and education?' rather than 'whether the state and education'. In *The State and Education Policy* (1989) I argued that the education system, like all state organizations, could not avoid addressing the three central problems confronting the state in capitalist societies; (i) supporting the capital accumulation process, (ii) guaranteeing a context for its continued expansion, and (iii) legitimating the capitalist mode of accumulation, including the state's own part in it, especially in education. The paper by Codd, Gordon, and Harker (Ch. 16) provides one example of the application of this approach.

The fact that these core problems are permanently on the agenda of all Western states provides a framework for comparision, although it does not mean that each state will interpret, address, or seek solutions to those problems in the same way. The core problems set limits to state actions, but they do not determine them wholly; the form of state activity can not be read off from its functions.

The central problematic of this approach remains as important as ever. However, the nature and consequences of changes in the global economy and the development of 'pluralist' societies in which ethnic communities are asserting the right to cultural (if not always political and economic) sovereignty means that this framework for comparision needs development.

Education has been affected both directly and indirectly by the changes in the global economy. The direct impact is clearly seen in the case of those developing countries whose education systems have been shaped increasingly by the lending policies of the World Bank and the demands of 'structural adjustment' (i.e. the diminution of the public sector and the expansion of the private) that organizations like the IMF make conditions of support. More indirect effects are seen in those advanced countries that have been striving to cope with the aggregated effects of the decline of the Keynesian welfare-state settlement to the point where public funding of services like education seems no longer feasible at previous levels.

From State Control to Governance

Some elements of the reaction to these changes have been common to many Western countries. What they amount to is a 'hollowing out' of the state (see Jessop 1993) with the loss of some activities 'upwards' to supranational bodies and the loss of others 'downwards' to sub-national or non-state bodies. Thus we see apparently rather similar moves to various forms of 'decentralization' and 'privatization' of education in many Western countries. We might therefore say that while education remains a public issue, in common with many other state activities its co-ordination has ceased to be (at least formally) the sole preserve of the state or government. Instead it has become co-ordinated through a range of forms of *governance*, among which decentralization and privatization figure prominently. Hirst and Thompson (1995) distinguish the key terms in the following way:

the tendency in common usage (is) to identify the term 'government' with the institutions of the state that control and regulate the life of a territorial community. Governance—that is, the control of an activity by some means such that a range of desired outcomes is attained—is, however, not just the province of the state. Rather, it is a function that can be performed by a wide variety of public and private, state and non-state, national and international, institutions and practices. (p. 422)

It is crucial to note that the state does not 'go away' in this process. Rather, I will argue that its continuing role as overwhelmingly the major funder and regulator of education enables it to remain very much in the driving seat. True, the nature of the work it does has changed, very broadly speaking, from carrying out most of the work of the co-ordination of education itself to determining where the work will be done and by whom. This devolution and detachment demonstrate strength rather than weakness (albeit over a policy terrain considerably reduced by the consequences of states' changing relationships to the global economy). The comparative theoretical issue then becomes one not so much of witnessing the banishment of the state as of 'locating' it and disaggregating its activities.

The Governance of Education

In focusing on the governance of education two sets of issues must be distinguished: what is involved in the governance of education, and how and by whom these activities are carried out. It is in this area that the assumptions of students of education systems are most starkly revealed. It had been effectively taken for granted, firstly, that 'running education' was a single activity and, secondly, that it was carried out by the state. It is necessary to examine these two issues before the consequences for what does and can go on in schools can be specified.

Much recent work on the economics and politics of the welfare state has distinguished three forms of what is usually referred to as 'state intervention'. These relate to three distinct and separable *activities* involved in welfare policy: how it is *funded*, how it is *provided* (or delivered), and how it is *regulated* (or controlled). It is argued that it is not necessary for the state to carry out all of these activities, while remaining in overall control of education.

These activities have to be co-ordinated, and in line with the hollowing-out thesis it has become common for three major *institutions of social coordination* to be distinguished (see e.g. Thompson *et al.* 1991). Several versions of these distinctions appear, but common to them all is the identification of the state and the market as two of the three key institutions of social co-ordination. The third, community, is always a residual category to the state and market and is conceptualized differently (though usually implicitly) according to the conception of state and market taken.[1] Once again, it should be noted that the 'traditional' assumption has been that all the activities involved in the co-ordination of education were carried out by the state. However, a moment's thought shows us that the state has never done all these things alone; the market and especially the community have been indispensable to the operation of the education systems. The difference now is that the areas of their involvement have been greatly expanded and formalized as the area of direct state involvement has contracted. Combining these two sets of variables into a three-by-three table, then, sheds some new light on the governance of education.

In particular, the table demonstrates the inadequacy of a simple 'public–private' distinction and shows how confusing, even misleading, that distinction can be. Only if and when funding, regulation, and provision were all carried out by the state alone could we speak of a 'public' system. Only if and when

they were all carried out by 'non-state' bodies could we speak of a 'private' system, and even then 'private' would have to be interpreted as 'non-state'. Table 17.1, is, therefore, salutory because it begins to show the potential complexity of recent educational reforms and hence the dangers of oversimplified arguments about the 'privatization' or 'marketization' of education. It requires us not only to ask what activities are being privatized or handed over to the market or the community, but what this means. The table also fulfils the aim of providing an initial basis for international comparisons of the nature and effects of educational reform.

Table 17.1. A simple representation of the governance of education

	Coordinating Institutions		
Governance Activities	State	Market	Community
Funding			
Regulation			
Provision/Delivery			

However, in this form the table has rather limited value, largely because the categories are too coarse to register the kinds of changes that have been taking place in education systems in recent years. For instance, in recent years we have seen the state remain as principal funder of compulsory education in the Anglophone-dominated societies while using choice- and market-co-ordinating institutions. But even then there are differences in the purposes or aims underlying choice and market mechanisms, and hence different modes of regulation which determine the rules of the choice regimes and markets that have been created. For example, in England and New Zealand market mechanisms have been introduced with the primary aim of creating efficiency, arguably at the expense of equity. In contrast, a controlled-choice regime has been established in Boston. Here the aim is to reconcile parents' preferences with the provision of socially well-balanced schools. The evidence suggests that socially mixed schools are likely to enhance the educational performance of lower socio-economic-status students, hence there is an equity consideration in this system. In Boston parental choice is, therefore, mediated by a central agency which sorts and reorders the preferences for schools. We can call the differing aims underlying the institutions of co-ordination and the regulatory framework they generate their *modes of operation*.

A further difficulty with Table 17.1 is that it doesn't capture the subtlety and complexity of many of the forms of decentralization that have taken place, such as the changes entailed by the Grant Maintained Schools initiative in England, or the raft of reforms that have enabled much greater inter-school contestability in New Zealand. In both cases the state remains the only (formal) funder and operates a regulatory role, through a National Curriculum and assesment regimes, that is more powerful than has traditionally been the case. At the same time, market modes of contestability between schools have been introduced, while ostensibly schools are governed by community forms of management, through the establishment of Boards of Trustees in New Zealand and Boards of Governors in England.

In comparative terms, therefore, we need to pay very close attention to the complexities of the relationships between governance activities and co-ordinating institutions if we are to assess their effects. In order to do so we need to look more carefully at the governance activities, for it is they which ultimately shape and invest the co-ordinating institutions with specific purposes.

Governance Activities

FUNDING

I will begin by setting out very briefly some different forms taken by funding, regulation, and provision. One useful example of the historic existence of a multiplicity of funding sources in education is the English public (i.e. private) schools. These are funded in part directly by fees paid by parents, i.e. 'privately'. Many are also funded in part by religious or other voluntary organizations, i.e. directly 'community' funded. They also receive various forms of state subsidy—through tax relief on various forms of charitable giving from which they are able to benefit, and through rates relief deriving from their charitable status. Private schools also benefit from direct state funding of the academic and professional education of their teachers. All this makes it difficult to state categorically that we are dealing here with a 'private' institution; in terms of funding British 'private' schools

share elements of all three kinds of institution. Funding then can be made up of direct, fee, payments, of direct or tax-subsidized gifts, of direct state funding, of community or parent-raised funds, of international funds for education, whether 'public' (and mediated through state and/or voluntary bodies) or 'private', provided by transnational companies or by international voluntary or 'not-for-profit' organizations, or, of course, by any combination of these sources and types of funding.

It is, though, useful to set out the principles of distribution of funding:

1. Funding may be directed to organizations or to individuals (e.g. in the form of scholarships or vouchers) or to combinations of both.
2. Funding may be available to all members of, and/or organizations within, a given population (a territory for the state, an income bracket or 'pooled insurance risk' for the market, 'recognized members' for the community), or targeted at particular groups or individuals (whether on the basis of virtue—e.g. scholarships—or need, as in the case of compensatory funding).
3. Funding may be made subject to conditions (e.g. some form of payment by results).
4. It may be available only on a competitive basis.
5. It can take the form of grants, loans, investment, or subsidy.

All these principles of distribution of funding, which can be combined into a wide range of alternatives, cross the three sets of institutions. It is only when we focus on the sources of funding that significant variation between the institutions is apparent. So only the state can fund education through taxation, whatever combination of central and local, general and specific taxation may be employed. Taxation remains overwhelmingly the dominant source of educational funding, certainly in the compulsory sector. However, one very important feature of educational funding in recent years has been the state-induced (whether through the stick of reduced state funding or the carrot of increased organizational autonomy) proliferation of 'non-state' funding of education. For instance, in an increasing minority of cases tax-derived funds for educational expansion have been augmented by 'community' (typically religious) funds.[2] We should also note the English City Technology College scheme, however, where the set-up costs of schools were to be met largely by industry (see Whitty *et al.* 1993). User fees continue to grow as a proportion of educational funding in 'state' schools, as well as in the private schools, where they have always been indispensable. In addition to the traditional fundraising activities of parent organizations, schools are increasingly encouraged to profit from their own commercial activities, such as renting out their premises, selling computer programs, or enrolling foreign full-fee-paying students. Sponsorship and donations, from whatever source, take on even greater importance than previously.

The restructuring of funding does not only (and all too frequently) entail 'brute' cuts in the public funding of education and the encouragement to look to other sources of funding, but it also assumes a greater 'efficiency' in the use of funds for education. That is to say, the educational 'reforms' in most Anglophone-dominated societies have affected both the level and the disbursement of funding, and point to the removal of barriers preventing the more 'efficient' use of funds. In practice this has meant efforts to diminish the influence of the 'provider' unions on maintaining existing levels of educational expenditure and pressure, in some cases backed up by legislation (see Dale and Jesson 1994), to have public organizations run more like private ones. Such actions are the source of the widespread view that in recent years education has been to a greater or lesser extent 'deregulated'; this is symbolized in the frequent tendency to shift responsibility for the day-to-day running of schools to the schools themselves.

REGULATION
Perhaps the greatest, and certainly the most important, range of variations comes in the area of regulation. It is the ultimate ability of the state to determine policy and sanctions through law that shapes the whole area of regulation. Together with funding, regulation provides the framework within which provision is possible. Funding and regulation combine in different ways to create the context for educational policy, provision, and practice.

However, it is worth probing this a little more deeply, since, as Prosser (1995) points out, the tendency towards greater marketization and 'privatization' of education seems to be seen by policy-makers as the resolution of technical issues of economic principle which are assumed to be similar in any market-oriented economy, so neglecting the particular constraints of legal and political culture. Part of the point of much economic literature (from which Prosser excepts the public-choice school) is to bracket out such cultural factors in favour of an 'acultural form of rational behaviour' (1995: 509). This emphasizes the crucial point, widely acknowledged since Polanyi's *The Great Transformation*, that markets are in no sense 'natural' institutions, but are always shaped by patterns of state regulation (see Waslander and Thrupp Ch. 29). In looking at what might shape education 'markets', therefore, it is essential to pay close attention to the regulations that frame the attempted move towards them; this includes, of course, 'deregulation', the removal of existing regulations that are perceived to act as barriers to greater consumer choice of schools, and all that it is assumed will flow from it in the way of responsiveness, efficiency, and so forth. Such policies typically seek to remove bureaucratic/democratic controls and minimize the areas over which professionals have discretion.

There are three aspects of the processes by which states have shaped the governance of education that are germane to this discussion. These are deregulation, juridification, and the New Public Management. They are closely linked, though they vary considerably both individually and in the ways they combine; together they provide the framework whereby the state retains, even enhances, its strength while divesting itself of a significant range of activities which will, it is anticipated, also thereby become more efficient and responsive.

In Christopher Hood's words, 'Regulation . . . ultimately comes from government's traditional role in providing a basis for trading, by setting standards and rules for the operation of markets' (1995: 19). However, as both Hood and Majone (1990) point out, there are significant differences between national traditions of regulation. As Majone puts it, 'In Europe there is a tendency to identify regulation with the whole realm of legislation, governance, and social control' (p. 1), whereas in America it refers much more to control over activities by specific regulatory agencies; 'regulation is not achieved simply by passing a law but requires detailed knowledge of, and intimate involvement with, the regulatory activity' (p. 2). Majone argues that 'these differences in meaning reflect significant ideological differences between the American and European approach to the political control of markets' (p. 2). The American system 'expresses a widely held belief that the market works well under normal circumstances and should be interfered with only in cases of market failure, such as monopoly power, negative externalities or inadequate information' (ibid.), whereas the traditional response of most European governments to market failure was not regulation but various forms of direct intervention; where regulation has been employed it has typically been assigned to traditional ministries rather than specialized regulatory agencies.

What we may be witnessing then, alongside economic deregulation and the encouragement of markets which includes education, is not just a move to deregulate but to shift the pattern of regulation much more in the American direction. This is especially clear in the New Zealand case, where, following the 1989 education reforms, not only was formal responsibility switched to individual school Boards of Trustees, but the old multi-purpose Department of Education was split up into a policy-orientated Ministry, and a range of specialist agencies such as the Education Review Office and the New Zealand Qualifications Authority. Bureaucratic generalists were everywhere replaced by agencies set up to regulate particular aspects of a formally deregulated and decentralized system. So talking merely of 'deregulation' does not tell the whole story, either in New Zealand or other countries that have followed a similar policy path.[3]

The second state strategy has been juridification, which may be defined loosely as the use of law in structuring social, political, cultural, and economic life (see Cooper 1995: 507). The effect of juridification has been to remove particular, often politically contentious, issues from the political agenda, making them subject to legal and not political dispute. In this, juridification can be seen to draw on some central precepts of Public Choice theory (see

Lauder Ch. 25), which emphasizes the importance of constraining political actors by constitutional means. The creation of Reserve banks with responsibility for controlling inflation, irrespective of, or indifferent to, political consequences is one example of this strategy; legislation requiring a balanced budget is another. This applies not just, for instance, to matters like National Curricula (common though these have become), but to teachers' training, their conditions of service, and the basis on which schools are to be run; this is typically to be based on legislation which, as pointed out above, is designed to enable commercial enterprises to run more efficiently.

The third strategy has been the introduction of various versions of the New Public Management which is the policy expression of Public Choice theory. Its central feature is the stress which it places on the importance of public accountability. As Hood (1995) puts it, 'The basis of NPM lies in . . . lessening or removing differences between the public and the private sector and shifting the emphasis from process accountability towards a greater element of accountability in terms of results' (p. 94). Hood lists seven major elements of the NPM: disaggregation of public organizations; greater competition between public-sector organizations as well as between public and private; greater use of private-sector management practices; greater stress on discipline and parsimony in resource use; a move towards more 'hands-on' management; a move towards explicit and measurable standards of performance for public-sector organizations; and attempts to control public organizations according to preset output measures (ibid. 96–7). A major target of this initiative was the level and use of professional discretion, which many of these measures were designed to routinize. It also entails a 'mainstreaming' of state activities, removing claims to special treatment on the grounds of distinct (and unique) sectoral needs and traditions, for instance that teachers' work, conditions, and patterns of reward are different from those of production workers (see Dale and Jesson 1994).

One consequence of the changes to regulation is the effective creation of two different sets of principles by which regulatory and accountability procedures can be determined. We may call these principles 'rule-governed' and 'goal-governed'. Rule-governed forms of regulation operate *ex ante*, before the fact. They seek to control resource *inputs* to activities and to shape and channel *demands* on them. Agents' discretion is constrained by the *legal framework* within which they operate.

Goal-governed forms, by contrast, are designed to control institutions by means of judging how closely they have conformed to their performance targets. That is, they operate *ex post* and focus on the organization's *outputs*, which they aim to influence by controlling the supply of the organization's products or services. Agents' discretion is constrained by the relevant operational procedures.

It is possible to point to two clear targets of these new patterns of regulation. One has certainly been the assumedly malign effects of provider capture in education. These strategies seem designed to limit the influence of teachers over education, atomizing the system by decentralization, introducing tighter controls over curriculum and assessment, and limiting the scope for the political discussion of education. The other aim has been to create regulatory frameworks that encourage new 'providers' to enter the 'educational market', and it is to this issue that we now turn.

PROVISION AND DELIVERY
I do not intend to spend much space on the question of provision and delivery. One reason for the relatively brief treatment is that, as I have argued above, it is shaped by, and largely results from, those changes in funding and regulation that I have just been discussing. Another is that it has been the subject of far more discussion in the literature than either funding or regulation. In this section, therefore, I want to draw attention to just one of the key dimensions of this governance activity: the way provision relates to the question of entitlement. Ralf Dahrendorf, in *The Modern Social Conflict* (1984), refers to policies that seek to make products and services available to consumers, even if that means they are not available to everyone, while entitlement-based policies place the emphasis on ensuring the widest possible distribution of a basic minimum, even if that means curtailing the range of choice for some. The distinction when applied to education concerns that between consumers and citizens (Ranson 1987; 1993). Market forms of provision which

have as their aim efficiency arguably play down or exclude issues of equity. Consumers who have material and cultural capital are likely to gain high-quality educational services while those that do not have these forms of capital may be excluded even from a basic education in inner-city areas with low funding and where schools are experiencing a spiral of decline. In a system of education designed for citizens, an attempt is made through the mechanisms of funding and regulation to ensure that everyone has access to a sound education. The clearest examples of these systems tend to be highly centralized bureaucratic forms of education such as that found in Japan (see Green Ch. 18).

The difficulty with the distinction between consumers and citizens in this context is that it doesn't easily fit with elements of community co-ordination and provision of education. For consumers the principle on which education is provided is that of *ability to pay*. For citizens, education is provided as a *universal entitlement* for all who are citizens of a society. Universalism entails treating all members of a population on the same basis. The relevant population for the state is theoretically the whole population under its jurisdiction. However, as Nancy Fraser (1989) has pointed out more decisively than most, in practice if not in principle states' definitions of the population entitled to benefit from 'universally' provided services do not include every citizen but are typically based on class, gender, and racial categories. However, where the state has failed in living up to the principle of universalism it can be challenged in the public arena, although of course as Nancy Fraser (1994) has also pointed out, the public arena itself is a contestable concept.

For community forms of co-ordination and provision, the principle on which education is provided is *eligibility for membership*. In the case of systems of culturally autonomous schooling, such as Kura Kaupapa (Maori) education, the entitlement is based on a subset of citizens with a particular history and culture. The principle underlying provision, which is based on ensuring that benefits go only to members recognized by the community, is explicitly and intentionally particularistic (i.e. designed to exclude non-members). In terms of changes to the state–education relationship, the emergence of a pluralist society with community education provision is perhaps the most novel aspect of the changes that have taken place. This crucial distinction between the state and community modes can be extended through arguments put forward by the Portuguese sociologist Boaventura de Sousa Santos, whose comments, although he is writing about the Portuguese context, have wider applicability. I take the 'welfare society' formulation he uses to be very close to what I intend by the notion of 'community mode'. A pluralist society distinguished by culturally autonomous education would approximate to De Santos's notion of a welfare society. Funds may be devolved to identifiable groups for education, or, indeed, any other welfare function, but how they are then distributed may then be a matter for those groups. He writes:

Welfare society is hostile to equality, or at least it does not distinguish as clearly as the welfare state between legitimate and illegitimate inequalities . . . it is hostile to citizenship and legal entitlements, since welfare relations are concrete, multiplex, and based on the concrete long-term reciprocity of sequences of unilateral benevolent actors. (Santos 1991: 39)

This distinction points up the issue of accountability within the new state–education relationship. For the complexity involved in the shift from state control to governance also involves different modes of accountability to different constituencies. Many of the current debates in education over, for example, the marketization of education turn on the question of who education is provided for and who is to be held to account for problems of provision. Underlying these debates is the fundamental question of how the public-good purposes of education relating to democracy and equity can be addressed when the governance of education is so fragmented.

Some readers will detect a paradox in the formulation of this problem, because at the outset it was argued that while the nature of the state–education relationship had changed, state power had increased through the shift from state control to governance. State control of funding, the curriculum, and the teaching profession has clearly been strengthened, as the preceding arguments make clear, but it can also be argued that the state's grip is also tightened by decentralized, multiple modes of accountability.

Accountability and the Limits to State Action

Claus Offe (1990: 247) has argued powerfully that the state's capacity to act effectively is severely limited, particularly 'in policy areas where the passions, identities, collectively shared meanings, and moral predispositions within the "life-world" of social actors (rather than their economic interests) are the essential parameters that need to be changed in order to achieve a solution'. He suggests that there are 'clear absolute limits' to all three forms of governmental intervention that he identifies: regulation, manipulation of fiscal resources, and the use of information and persuasion. Bureaucratic regulation is limited by its inflexibility and by the possibility of powerful interests being able to resist it. Economic forms have little impact on people who 'refuse to act according to some utility-maximizing economic calculus' (p. 247). The value of the use of information tends to fall as people become suspicious that it is being used to manipulate rather than to inform them.

Under these circumstances the ability of a government to keep at a distance from being held accountable can clearly be expedient. In the case of devolution to a community it not only shifts accountability onto the community but it appears a particularly 'potent' solution in cases where shared meanings and moral dispositions count for more than the economic calculus. But we should note that while governments may devolve accountability onto communities, the limitations of this devolution may have more to do with appearances than reality. Culturally autonomous schooling can be seen as a 'licensed departure' of a very limited kind, rather than the actions of a genuinely liberal state in a pluralist society.

The case of devolution to choice regimes and quasi-markets in education appears to be a rather more straightforward response to the inflexibilities of bureaucratic forms of organization identified by Offe. The attempts to introduce greater choice into the allocation of public services, through the creation of quasi-markets, for instance, does indicate that the scope-choice regimes may be greater than a simple profit-motive calculation may suggest, for instance in increasing the responsiveness, effectiveness, and efficiency of services. However, the question of accountability in choice regimes remains open and contentious because, inevitably, choice regimes involve decentralization, and where there are many different loci of power it is more difficult to mark out a clear audit trail to those ultimately responsible, as repeated questions about the scope of ministerial responsibility in the new public sector demonstrate.

Conclusion

While specific community or quasi-market policies may go some way to addressing the 'poverty of policy' as articulated by Offe, while keeping the state firmly in the driving seat, the fundamental problem still remains to be addressed. Overall, the state can be seen to be responding to three different sets of pressures. The first is economic and relates to the changing role of the state in the global economy. The second concerns the shift from a welfare state to a welfare society in which the presumption of universalism has been replaced by new forms of particularism based either on the social-class privileges of material and cultural capital, or on membership of an identifiable group in society. The third concerns the limits of state action in the modern context. The shift from state control to governance in education, with all its attendant complexities, can be explained in these terms.

In this paper I've tried to locate some[4] of the key mechanisms involved in this shift so that a comparative analysis of the various effects of the new state–education relationship can be studied. However, there are some broad trends that are now discernible and their effects can be predicted. Essentially, I want to suggest that the most common broad pattern of state withdrawal has been motivated by a wish to reduce public expenditure, limit the extent of provider capture, encourage possessive individualism (Apple 1982), and improve the efficiency and responsiveness of the education system. What has been less frequently attempted, scarcely attempted at all, in fact, has been a commitment by the state to ensure the perpetuation of the public-good qualities of education that it alone can guarantee. The tasks confronting Western states are twofold. Firstly, they need to address the question of how equality of resources and outcomes can be achieved under a complex system of governance in which particularism rather than uni-

versalism is an important guiding factor in the provision of education. Secondly, they need to address the question of how effective democratic accountability can be introduced into the system. By addressing these problems rather than resorting to an expedient arms'-length form of accountability, states would be attempting to resolve the dilemma posed by Offe of how to bring about social change in areas resistant to policy intervention of the traditional kind. In doing so, they may create the basis for shared responsibility for education. Finding answers to these challenges is essential to a civilized society.

Notes

1. In a recent paper I distinguished twenty different combinations of 'state, market and network/community/civil society/the family, etc.' (see Dale 1994)). This is not a trivial matter, as will become clear.
2. See Fowler (1994) on the French case.
3. The rationale for creation of multiple agencies has probably been inspired by the New Public Management, which sees the creation of contestability of advice to government from different agencies as a key to the restructuring of the public sector.
4. For further discussion of the mechanisms which are likely to be influential in the new state–education relationship see Dale (1996).

References

Apple, M. (1982), 'Curricular Form and the Logic of Technical Control; Building the Possessive Individual', in Apple, M. (ed.), *Cultural and Economic Reproduction in Education* (London: Routledge).
Cooper, D. (1995), 'Local Government Legal Consciousness in the Shadow of Juridification', *Journal of Law and Society* 22/4: 506–26.
Dahrendorf, R. (1984), *The Modern Social Conflict* (Berkeley: Univ. of California Press).
Dale, R. (1994), 'Locating "The Family and Education" in the Year of the Family'. Keynote address to Australia and New Zealand Comparative Education Society Conference, Melbourne, December.
—— (forthcoming), *Markets and Education* (Milton Keynes: Open Univ. Press).
—— (1996), *Governance* (Auckland: Education Department, Univ. of Auckland).
Dale, R., and Joce, J. (1992), ' "Mainstreaming" Education: the role of the State Services Commission' in Manson, H. (ed.), *Annual Review of*

Education in New Zealand (Wellington: Victoria Univ.), 2: 7–33.

Fowler, F. C. (1992), 'School Choice Policy in France: Success and Limitations', *Educational Policy*, 6/4: 429–43.

Fraser, N. (1989), *Unruly Practices: Power, Discourse and Gender in Contemporary Social Theory* (Minneapolis: Univ. of Minnesota Press).

—— (1994), 'Rethinking the Public Sphere: A Contribution to the Critique of Actually Existing Democracy', in Giroux, H., and McLaren, P. (eds.), *Between Borders: Pedagogy and the Politics of Cultural Studies* (New York: Routledge).

Hirst, P., and Thompson, G. (1995), 'Globalization and the Future of the Nation State', *Economy and Society*, 24/3: 408–42.

Hood, C. (1994), *Explaining Economic Policy Reversals* (Milton Keynes: Open Univ. Press).

—— (1995), 'The New Public Management in the 1980s: Variations on a Theme', *Accounting, Organizations and Society*, 20/2–3: 93–109.

Jessop, B. (1993), 'Towards a Schumpeterian Workfare State? Preliminary Remarks on post-Fordist Political Economy', *Studies in Political Economy*, 40: 7–39.

Majone, G. (ed.) (1990*a*), *Deregulation or Regulation? Regulatory Reform in Europe and the United States* (London: Pinter).

—— (1990*b*), 'Analyzing the Public Sector: Shortcomings of Policy Science and Policy Analysis', in Kaufman, F. (ed.), *The Public Sector* (New York: de Gruyter), 29–45.

Offe, C. (1990), 'Reflections on the Institutional Self-Transformation of Movement Politics: A Tentative Stage Model', in Dalton, R. J., and Koehler, M. (eds.), *Challenging the Political Order: New Social and Political Movements in Western Democracies* (New York: Oxford Univ. Press), 233–50.

Prosser, T. (1995), 'The State, Constitutions and Implementing Economic Policy: Privatization and Regulation in the UK, France, and the USA', *Social and Legal Studies*, 4: 507–16.

Ranson, S. (1987), 'Citizens or Consumers? Policies for School Accountability', in Barton, L., and Walker, S. (eds.), *Changing Policies, Changing Teachers* (Milton Keynes: Open Univ. Press).

—— (1993), 'Markets or Democracy for Education?' *British Journal of Educational Studies*, 41/4: 333–52.

Santos, B. (1991), *State Wage Relations and Social Welfare in the Semi-Periphery: The case of Portugal* (Universidade de Coimbra: Centro de Estudos Sociaias).

Thompson, G., and Levacic, R. (eds.) (1991), *State, Market and Networks* (London: Sage).

Whitty, G., Edwards, T., and Gewirtz, S. (1993), *Specialisation and Choice in Urban Education: The City Technology College Experiment* (London: Routledge).

18

Educational Achievement in Centralized and Decentralized Systems

Andy Green

School decentralization arguments have been widely adopted in the rhetoric (if less in the practice) of educational reform in many countries around the world, and particularly in the English-speaking states. Claims that decentralization will enhance the effectiveness of school systems have formed the central plank in the work of many prominent school reform advocates (Chubb and Moe 1990; Sexton 1987). However, the logical arguments advanced to support these claims are much contested (Ball 1990; Carnoy 1993; Green 1994; Whitty 1992) and the empirical evidence, such as it is, has yet to substantiate the case. Decentralizing measures, such as 'school choice' and 'local management' policies in England, New Zealand, and the USA are too partial and too recent in origin to permit any definitive analysis of their effects on aggregate national outcomes; and the evidence proffered by advocates from within-country cross-school comparisons only weakly supports their case, if at all. Chubb and Moe (1990), for instance, find that private (i.e. less centralized) schools in the USA rate higher than state schools on school–effectiveness traits, but this could be simply the result of their ability to select pupils with whom it is easier to display effective schooling. Comparative studies have not adequately established that they can achieve higher levels of 'value-added' than the supposedly more centralized schools in the public systems (Carnoy 1993). Furthermore, international comparisons, which decentralization advocates rarely cite, provide more evidence, if anything, for the effectiveness of more 'centralized systems', depending on what one means by these categories.

The purpose of this paper is to review some of the evidence from international comparisons on the relative effectiveness of 'centralized' and 'decentralized' education systems in the advanced industrialized nations, and to construct a number of hypotheses, relating to characteristics of centralism and decentralism, to explain variations in educational outcomes between countries. This will entail comparing outcomes for a sample of nations for which we have comparable data; isolating certain 'clusters' of institutional (and cultural) characteristics which seem to be common to a number of high achieving systems; and analyzing how these may be affecting aggregate national levels of attainment as measured by qualifications.

This procedure is clearly highly provisional, and the hypotheses cannot be fully tested empirically since we have insufficient data currently to do this. To perform any analytical statistical analysis of the factors underlying variations in national outcomes, we would need a large sample of countries for which we had reliable comparative data on outcomes and institutional and cultural characteristics. The latter would need to be precisely defined and susceptible to valid measurement by proxy indicators. At present none of these conditions are met. Datasets on national outcomes for a wide range of countries are also not entirely reliable, either because the outcome definitions used are insufficiently precise or not fully comparable (as with the ISCED levels in OECD 1995) or because the national survey samples used are not always representative (as often with the IEA studies). Fully comparable quantitative data on national institutional characteristics are scarce. The OECD has begun to define indicators and assemble comparative data for a range of characteristics, but the work is still in its early stages and the indicators will require a great deal more refinement before they can be used for these purposes.

However, for a small sample of countries we do have quite robust comparative data on educational outcomes and a wealth of analytical comparative work on institutional structures. The comparative dataset on outcomes relates to qualifications, and has been constructed by benchmarking the major qualifications in each country at given levels and collecting data on the stocks and flows of these qualifications for a series of years. It affords the most reliable comparisons for a group of countries which have national qualification systems, reliable official records of qualifications awarded by year and age of recipient, and Labour Force Survey data on highest qualifications held. The countries include France, Germany, Singapore, and the UK. Although they have less comprehensive national systems of qualifications, and thus present greater problems for comparison, a number of other countries have been extensively studied in terms of their achievement levels and these can also be included in our comparisons. These include Japan, Sweden, and the USA.

Comparative studies of these countries have consistently shown that France, Germany, Japan, Sweden, and, in recent years, Singapore, achieve relatively high average levels of educational qualification, whereas the UK and the USA seem to lag somewhat behind. France, Germany, Japan, Sweden, and Singapore are traditionally accredited with having relatively centralized educational systems, although in the German case it is more proper to talk about centralization at the regional level. The UK and the USA have traditionally been seen as classic examples of educational decentralization, although their systems are now changing (Archer 1979; Green 1990).

Educational Outcomes in France, Germany, Japan, Singapore, Sweden, UK, and USA

Data for educational outcomes for the seven countries are taken from three sources: the International Evaluation of Achievement Studies (IEA 1988); the recent International Adult Literacy Survey (IALS) (OECD Statistics Canada 1995); and the author's own research with Hilary Steedman (Green and Steedman 1993; and forthcoming).[1] These studies are based on different methodologies and compare different things amongst different age groups. The IEA studies used here are based on tests of knowledge and skills in Maths and Science administered between 1981 and 1986 to sample school populations aged 10, 13/14, and 18 years in a large range of countries. The IALS study was based on various tests of literacy administered in 1994 to samples of adults in Canada, Germany, Netherlands, Poland, Sweden, Switzerland, and the USA. The Green and Steedman studies are based on analyses of the stocks and flows of qualifications in the sample countries for various years. These disparate methodologies limit the degree to which the results of the different studies can be compared. The national comparisons made here, therefore, will be largely based on the qualifications evidence. However, where this is less conclusive, as with the data for Japan, Sweden, and the USA, the survey/test evidence will also be used.

The Green and Steedman research on national qualification attainment has included France, Germany, Singapore, the UK, and the USA, with Japan included in the earlier study (Green and Steedman 1993). The methodology involved benchmarking the major national qualifications awarded in each of these countries against UK levels, and subsequently comparing the stocks and flows of these qualifications in each country, using official data sources on qualification awards and labour-force survey data on highest qualifications held by different age groups in the 16 to 65 populations. The focus of the research was on qualifications normally taken at the end of compulsory education (i.e. at about 15 or 16 years) and at the end of upper secondary education, including foundation training (at between 17 and 19 years) and which were judged to be equivalent to the UK NCVQ qualification levels 2 and 3 respectively. NCVQ level 2 represents attainment of 5 GCSEs at grades A to C or better; a General National Vocational Qualification (GNVQ) level 2; or a National Vocational Qualification (NVQ) level 2. NCVQ level 3 represents attainment of 2 or more A levels or a (G)NVQ level 3. These levels are roughly equivalent to the OECD's ISCED level 3 and 4, although the latter are only defined in very general terms and utilize equivalences based on reports made by individual governments, rather than through any benchmarking of standards, as employed here.

For each country the major national (i.e. state-recognized) qualifications were selected and benchmarked against the UK levels. Judgements about levels of qualifications were made by subject experts drawn from each of the countries and through analysis of syllabuses, test criteria, and examination papers. Level judgements were based on a range of criteria including:

1. the position of the qualification in the relevant national hierarchy of qualifications;
2. the duration and mode of study of the course concerned;
3. the typical age of students entering and qualifying;
4. the entry requirements for admission to the course;
5. the range and level of the contents specified for the course;
6. the types of assessment used and standards required;
7. the rights of access to other courses conferred by the qualification; and
8. the typical destinations of graduates in employment or further education or training.

The survey was not able to include qualifications awarded by private bodies and not recognized by the state, nor could it assess skills acquired but not certificated. Consequently, in countries where skills are frequently acquired informally and not certificated, or where they are attested in certificates not recognized by the state, the data on qualifications may underestimate the true prevalence of skills. Inevitably, establishing level equivalence between qualifications in different countries involved making normative judgements, as for instance where the range and breadth of knowledge attested in one qualification had to be balanced against the depth and complexity of knowledge in another. The final evaluations thus represent judgements made against a range of criteria and agreed amongst a body of expert assessors.

The results of the evaluations for qualifications deemed equivalent in level to the UK NCVQ level 2 were as follows: for France, the *Brevet*, the CAP (*certificat d'aptitude professionnelle*) and the BEP (*brevet d'études professionelles*); for Germany the *Hauptschulabschluss* and the *Realschulabschluss* (and assuming this level for those with the *Abitur* who had bypassed the earlier qualification); and for Singapore, 5 O levels, the Certificate of Office Studies, and the National Trade Certificate level 2. The level 3 equivalents were: for France, the *Baccalauréats* (including the general, technological, and vocational *baccalauréats*); for Germany, the *Abitur*, the *Fachhoschulreife*, and the Apprenticeship certificate (excluding those completed in 2 years or less); and for Singapore, 2 or more A levels, the Certificate in Business Studies, the Industrial Technician Certificate, and the National Trade Certificate level 1. In each country, these qualifications represent the vast majority of awards made to young people at this general level.

Japan and the USA present a greater problem for comparisons, since there are few national qualifications at this level in either country. The High School Certificate in the USA, awarded by individual schools, attests completion of a number of courses, but does not guarantee the attainment of a given level in a range of subjects, and cannot therefore be used for these comparisons. In this case we can only use data for degrees and associate degrees, which, although also issued by individual institutions, are deemed to involve a more consistent standard. Like the USA, Japan also uses high-school completion certificates as the measure of attainment at the end of upper secondary education. However, although these are issued by individual schools without external moderation, and also involve variability in standards between institutions, the latter appears to be less pronounced than in the USA. Furthermore, a study of vocational upper-secondary schools in Japan in 1982 by the NIESR compared textbooks and syllabuses with those for vocational courses in similar areas in the UK, and came to the conclusion that the standard and range of studies (in vocational areas and Maths) were close to those in the National Diploma, a level 3 qualification (Prais 1987). Data for high-school graduation in Japan are thus presented, but must be treated with caution. On the basis of this set of qualification equivalences, and with particular caution in relation to two of the countries, we can now compare qualification levels for seven countries using data on flows and stocks for recent years.

Information on stocks of qualification held is contained in the annual labour-force survey reports for France, Germany, Singapore, the UK, and the USA (the Japanese LFS data is available, but has not yet been analyzed). These reports generally contain data on the highest qualifications held by the adult population, down to the level of the major individual qualifications. The data for Singapore cannot be disaggregated to the level of individual qualifications, and the broad 'secondary' classification does not correspond directly with our level 2 category, and therefore cannot be used for comparisons. However, the higher 'post-secondary' classification is comprised of precisely the same qualifications as were designated to be level 3 equivalent, and can be the basis for valid comparisons. For the USA the only categories which can be used are those described as 'degree' and 'associate degree'. The LFS data allow comparisons across countries for levels of qualifications of the active, inactive, and total population by age band, gender, and occupation. Taking the data for 1994 for the 25-to-28-year-olds in the total population (the youngest age band capturing the majority of awards made at this level), we can see that there are marked differences in the proportions of the age group in each country having obtained at least level 2 and at least level 3 qualifications (Table 18.1). Compared with the UK and Singapore, both France and Germany would appear to have a considerably higher proportion of their 25- to-28-year-olds qualified at level 2 or higher and at level 3 or higher. However, in the Singapore case, the younger 19 to 24 age group is considerably better qualified than the older age group, reflecting the speed of improvement in rates of qualification in recent years. The overall German advantage against the other countries is considerable, due to the large numbers gaining the apprentice qualification through the Dual System, and it may be objected that not all of these apprentices have attained a level 3 standard. However, even if we exclude those apprentice graduates whose highest previous qualification was the *Hauptschulabschluss* (i.e. from the lower-ranking secondary schools),

52 per cent of the age group could still be said to have reached level 3, compared with 36 per cent in the UK.

Table 18.1. Proportion of 25–28 year olds qualified to levels 2 and 3 or higher in 1994

	Level 2 or Higher	Level 3 or Higher
France	79	42
Germany	80	75 (52)
Singapore (25–29)	—	35
(19–24)	—	41
UK	53	36
USA	—	(32)[a]

[a] Degree and Associate Degree only

Data on stocks is perhaps the most straightforward basis for comparisons of national qualification levels. However, it has the disadvantage that it is always presenting a historical picture of the rate at which a country is generating qualified people. The persons included in the data for 25- to-28-year-olds would normally have gained their level 3 qualifications at 18 or 19, i.e. between 1980 and 1984. Comparative data on qualification flows, on the other hand, can generally be assembled for the previous year, which at the time of writing is for 1994. This allows us to see more clearly the results of recent changes in policies and rates of qualification in different countries. The data is also based on total body counts, not sample surveys, and therefore avoids the potential errors associated with the latter.

However, there is no one agreed method for calculating qualification flows as a proportion of a country's relevant age cohorts. The simplest method is probably that used in the French national statistics, which involves dividing the total number of qualifications (or equivalent groups of qualifications) awarded in a given year by the size of the most typical year-group taking them (i.e. 18-year-olds for level 3 qualifications). This so-called 'age cohort qualification rate' is a statistical abstraction which does not refer to the rate of qualification of actual people of a given age in a particular year. However, it does offer a reasonable proxy for the accumulated qualification rates of actual people in a given year-cohort. (If the quantity and age-spread of awards remained stable over a number of years equal to the year-span of the spread of awards, then the rate would be the same as the accumulated qualification rates for each individual age-group within that age-span at the end of the period). The measure can also be used as a fair basis for comparison, providing that each country uses it in the same way, that care is taken to include individuals who have bypassed a given level of qualification and attained a qualification at a higher level, and that double-counting individuals who have gained two qualifications at the same level is avoided.

This method is applied in Table 18.2, but with some modifications necessitated by the different kinds of data available in each country. For Germany we include as level 3 qualifications the *Abitur*, the *Fachhoschulreife* and the (higher) apprentice qualifications. For the *Abitur* and *Fachhoschulreife*, a figure is used

which is based on the proportion of those leaving school in a given year with particular levels of qualification. For the apprenticeship figure, discounts are made for those passing who already have a level 3 qualification or whose previous qualification is the *Hauptschulabschluss* or less. For Singapore we include as level 3 two or more A levels, level-3-equivalent vocational qualifications, and polytechnic diplomas gained by those who do not already have a level 3 qualification. In each case the rates are calculated by dividing total awards by the age-cohort number for 18-year-olds. For England we use the official DFEE A level qualification rate, which is calculated in terms of the proportion of those reaching 18 in a given year who gain two A levels in that year or a previous year. This method will give a somewhat deflated age-cohort qualification

Table 18.2. Age cohort qualification rate at level 3 in 1994

England		
2 more A levels	(England)	28.0
GNVQ Advanced	(England, Wales and NI)	0.34
BTEC National Diplomas	(E, W and NI)	7.36
BTEC National Certificates	(E, W and NI)	1.16
BTEC Level 3 NVQs[a]	(E, W and NI)	0.07
City and Guilds level 3	(UK)	2.28
Other	(UK)	1.05
Total		**40.26**
France		
Baccalauréat[b]		**58**
Germany (western Lander)		
Abitur or Fachhochschulreife (1993)		31.7
Apprenticeship[c]		31.6
Total		**63.3**
Singapore		
2 or More A Levels		23.5
Higher Technical[d]		5.3
Diploma[e]		21.7
Total		**50.5**
Japan (1992)[f]		**92.2**
Sweden (1992)[g]		**83**

[a] This includes NVQs, City and Guilds and other occupationally specific qualification judged to be at level 3. The figures are stocks figures for the 19–21 population taken from the LFS. (See Helm and Redding 1992, for methodology.)

[b] Includes general, vocational and technological *baccalauréats*. Data from Ministry of National Education, Notes d'Information.

[c] Excludes those passing the apprenticeship who already have an *Abitur* or *Fachhoschulreife* (20 per cent) or whose previous qualification was below the *Realschulabschluss* (25.7). Data from Statistisches Bundesamt.

[d] This includes the Certificate in Business Studies, The National Trade Certificate Level 1 and the Industrial Technician Certificate. Data collected from Singapore Ministry of Education and Institute for Technical Education. Data on Polytechnic awards to those without prior level 3 qualifications from individual Singapore Polytechnics.

[e] These are Polytechnic diplomas normally taken at 19. The figure excludes all those who already had a level 3 qualification.

[f] This is the upper secondary graduation rate for 1992 from OECD, Education at a Glance (1995), 214.

[g] The upper secondary graduation rate as above.

rate, since it excludes those over 19 gaining two A levels. However, these are few in number in England, as compared with France for instance, where, due to frequent grade repeating, some 30 per cent of *baccalauréat* candidates are over 18. To minimize the comparative discrepancy for the total level 3 rate for England we have included 19-year-olds gaining GNVQs and NVQs in the English figure.

For Japan and Sweden, for which we have no national qualifications at this level, we can only present rates of matriculation from upper-secondary high schools. This is not a very safe basis for comparison, since standards at matriculation from high schools in these countries will vary between vocational and general streams and, to some extent, between institutions. However, for Japan at least, we have some evidence that the standard expected in the vocational high schools (mostly ranked below the general high schools) is generally at least as high as that for our benchmark level-3 vocational course in the UK (Prais 1987).

Using these methods we find that the level 3 age-cohort qualification rates vary considerably by country. Again, Germany and France come out with high rates of qualification at this level, and this time Singapore comes close behind France. England (and Wales for vocational qualifications) lags considerably behind. If we accept high-school graduation as level 3 equivalent, Sweden and Japan would both come out with high rates compared with all the other countries.

Further comparisons of national attainments can be made using the data from the IEA studies and the recent IALS survey on adult literacy. The IEA study *Science Achievement in Seventeen Countries* (1988) was based on tests carried out on samples on children aged 10, 14, and 18. The national results for the 18-year-olds cannot really be compared, since the populations in school at this age are more highly selected in some countries than others; but one can compare the average national results for the 10 and 14 year olds, and Table 18.3 shows the ranking of each country for each age group for all the countries in the survey. Japan and Sweden come out with high-average scores for both age-groups, whereas the scores for Britain and the USA are relatively low. Singapore also comes out low, which is consistent with the picture

emerging from the stocks and flows data about the relatively recent improvement in rates of qualification. What is also notable from the IEA study is that there was a high degree of dispersal in the scores recorded for the UK and the USA, with the bottom 25 per cent doing particularly badly in both those countries. This confirms the conclusions drawn by Postlethwaite from the 1965 IEA Maths study that England showed the largest differences between students' attainments of any country in the study (Postlethwaite 1982).

Table 18.3. Rank order of countries for achievement at each level

Country[a]	Rank for 10-year-olds	Rank for 14-year-olds
England	12	11
Japan	1	2
Singapore	13	14
Sweden	4	6
USA	8	14

[a] From IEA, *Science Education in Seventeen Countries, A Preliminary Report* (Pergamon Press, 1988: 3).

The IALS study was based on tests of literacy carried out on adult populations in eight countries including Germany, Sweden, and the USA. The tests were designed to ascertain proficiency in three areas (defined as Prose Literacy, Document Literacy, and Quantitative (arithmetic) Literacy) and were scored against a scale with five ascending bands, from levels 1 to 5. The report of the study does not produce a national rank order, but one can be produced by averaging, for each country, the percentages scoring at each level. On this basis it is calculated that 36.96 per cent of the Swedish sample were scoring at levels 4 and 5 (the highest levels) across the range of criteria, compared with 29.44 for Germany and 26.26 for the USA. On the other hand, 21.83 per cent of the US sample only scored at an average of level 1, compared with 9.98 for Germany and 6.75 for Sweden (Canada Statistics/OECD 1995: 84).

The relatively low ranking of the UK and the USA in aggregate level of attainment, as compared with a range of countries (including, variously, Germany, France, Japan, and Sweden) is confirmed by other studies which have reviewed the available evidence (Finegold and Soskice 1988; Ashton and Green 1996).

Factors Influencing Educational Achievement in High-Attaining Countries

The data presented above suggest that one group of countries (France, Germany, Japan, Sweden, Singapore), whose education systems have been traditionally characterized as 'centralized' (Archer 1979; Boucher 1982; Gopinathan 1994; Green 1990; Schoppa 1991), appear to obtain better aggregate attainments than another pair of countries (UK and USA) which are traditionally characterized as 'decentralized' (Archer 1979; Green 1990; Kaestle 1983). Does this demonstrate that centralized education systems generally achieve better average educational results than decentralized ones? Clearly, the answer to this is no. Firstly, the sample of countries is too small for deriving any general rules: a larger sample would no doubt include some counter-examples of more centralized systems which performed relatively poorly, and some more decentralized systems (such as, perhaps, the Netherlands) which obtain relatively high average standards. Secondly, the terms 'centralization' and 'decentralization' are themselves too vague to yield much insight into the system factors that affect national rates of achievement. The countries traditionally designated as centralized in our sample here differ considerably in the ways in which central control is utilized. In Germany, 'central' control over the school system (as opposed to the apprentice system) is exercised at the level of the individual *Länder* and not at the federal government level, although the policies of the *Länder* are co-ordinated with each other by inter-state bodies. In Japan, there is indeed strong central-government control over the school system—Monbushō controls the curriculum and textbooks—but there is a large number of private schools, including Juku, high schools, and universities; the Juku are fully independent, and the private high schools and universities, although part financed and regulated by the state, have a greater degree of autonomy in certain areas than the public institutions. Historically, Sweden and France have both had highly centralized educational systems, but this is now changing to some extent, although too recently to have had much impact on the outcomes reported above. Both operate a degree of 'school choice', although this is still limited in France; Sweden has given more discretion to schools concerning the curriculum; and France has transferred some responsibilities from the central to regional and municipal levels (although not much to individual schools). Each of these countries may still be reckoned to have relatively 'centralized' systems, but saying so does not tell us very much. So what can be deduced about the factors affecting achievement in the higher-attaining countries?

The causes of educational attainment amongst nations, as with individuals, are complex. Comparative researchers have sought in vain for particular characteristics of education systems which might explain the different average levels of attainment between countries; but the only factor which systematically correlates with national educational outcomes appears to be the time spent studying by children (IAEP 1992; Inkeles 1979). Many of the factors which appear to dominate national debates about standards, like school organization, class size, and levels of finance seem to have little explanatory power in relation to the causes of differences in national standards.

No significant statistical relationship has been found between levels of educational expenditure within advanced industrial nations and national educational outcomes (Lynn 1988). Of the countries in this study, Japan has the second-lowest public expenditure per student, after Singapore, and arguably the highest educational outcomes. The USA has the highest public expenditure per school student and among the lowest educational outcomes (data for educational expenditures in OECD 1995).

High average levels of achievement in different countries are not consistently associated with any particular form of school organization. Some countries with comprehensive schools during the compulsory years have very high average outcomes (Japan, France, and Sweden); others do not (UK, USA). Equally, there are examples of both successful and less successful selective systems. The IAEP study (1992) found no consistent relationship between average national attainments and policies on streaming. It would appear that in high-achieving countries teachers are generally held in high public esteem, but there is no statistically significant correlation between national educational outcomes and levels of teacher pay relative to other professions in the same country. Nor can any statistical correlation be established between average class sizes and national standards of attainment (Lynn 1988). Japan has considerably larger average class sizes than most of the other countries in this study, apparently without negative effects on its levels of achievement.

The outcomes of the educational process in different countries would seem to be the result of a host of factors, some relating to the internal features of the education system (institutional structures; curriculum design; teaching methods; forms of assessment and certification), and others relating to the social context in which it is set (societal and parental attitudes and expectations; employment opportunities; the nature of the labour market). It is the interaction of these factors, rather than any particular practices in education, which would seem to determine the levels of achievement characteristic of different systems (IAEP 1992; Altback *et al.* 1982).

The countries which achieve higher standards in education and training, like Germany, France, Japan, and Singapore (in recent years), would appear to have one fundamental thing in common: as nations they place great emphasis on educational achievement, engendering high educational aspirations amongst individual learners. They tend to have a 'learning culture', in which parents and teachers have high expectations of their children's educational achievements, where the education systems are designed to provide opportunities and motivation for learners of all abilities, and where the labour market, and society in general, rewards those who do well in education.

Education has played a particularly important role in the historical development of Germany, France, Japan, and Singapore as modern nation states. It was a critical factor in the industrialization of each of these countries: in France after the Revolution; in Prussia after the Napoleonic invasions; in Japan after the Meiji Revolution; and more recently in Singapore (Green 1995). In Japan and Germany it was also seen as crucial to the process of political and economic restructuring after the Second World War. For these and other historical reasons, these societies place an exceptionally high value on education both for its potential contribution towards national development and for its enhancement of individual opportunities.

The effects of this cultural stress on education are now manifested in a number of different ways in each of these countries: the majority of young people are willing to defer wage-earning until 18 and beyond in order to extend their education and gain higher qualifications; parents are willing to maintain their children through extended secondary education and, in the Japanese case, to devote considerable resources to paying fees for Juku and upper secondary schools; and employers are willing to invest heavily in training and to reward young people who gain qualifications.

High expectations in these countries are also institutionalized within the education systems. Prescribed curricula govern the content of education in different types of school and for different ages. These establish norms and expectations for all children, and give clarity and purpose to the educational process. Curriculum development and pedagogical research have been more systematically organized and focused than in countries like Britain; and this, together with prescribed curricula and teaching methods and the extensive use of professionally designed materials and textbooks, has tended to encourage a more uniform practice within education, with shared understandings of aims and objectives amongst teachers, parents, and students. In his evaluation of the IEA data (1982), Postlethwaite has concluded that the importance of systematic curriculum development and evaluation could not be overemphasized.

In each of these systems, whether comprehensive or selective in structure, there is a clear identity and purpose for each institution, and at each stage children appear to know what is expected of them. Norms are established for all children, in whichever stream, and they are reinforced through regular assessment and reporting. The practice of grade repeating, which is widespread in Germany and France, serves to underline the expectation that certain standards are required at each level for all children. The practice has been criticized for the supposedly damaging effects that such 'labelling' may have on pupil confidence and motivation. However, recent research in France indicates that, at the secondary stage, redoublement does not noticeably damage pupils' self-esteem, and that for a proportion of those repeating a class, subsequent progress is better than for those of similar attainments who do not repeat (Robinson, Tayler, and Piolat 1992). Grade-repeating may been seen, therefore, as a practice which embodies an important and empowering educational principle: whilst some children may take longer than others, all are capable of achieving.

Tightly regulated structures and institutionalized norms would also seem to have effects in classroom practices. British and US observers of classrooms in Germany, France, and Japan (HMI 1986, 1991, and 1992; White 1987) frequently note the relative orderliness and purposefulness of lessons. This may be partly a result of teaching methods which tend to stress whole-class activities; but it may also be attributable to the clarity of aims and purpose afforded by the structures described above. In either case it would appear that the teachers' work in these countries may be made easier through the use of whole-class teaching, and by the supportive structures provided by national curricula, standardized assessment procedures, recommended methods and textbooks, and so on. Where less energy is expended on planning lesson content, producing learning materials, and organizing individualized learning in class, more time and effort can be given to the learning process.

In support of this, Postlethwaite's review of the IEA data (1982) suggested that there was some evidence of a correlation between the average proportion of lesson time spent 'on task' in different countries and both aggregate national attainments and the dispersal of attainments. He cites Japan, using Cummins's evidence, as an example of a country with high levels of attainment, where students tend to be actively engaged for a high proportion of classroom time. According to Cummings, the average proportion of actively engaged classroom time in Japan was 90 per cent, compared with about 65 per cent in some Chicago schools tested. Higher rates of time spent 'on task' is one of the effects one might expect to be associated with the relative 'orderliness' of lessons, as reported by observers of classrooms in Japan and Germany (see Postlethwaite 1982).

High aspirations are encouraged for all students in these systems not only by the institutionalization of shared norms and standards, but also by the structure of incentives and rewards offered to students. At the end of compulsory schooling there are appropriate examinations or awards for all children, in whichever type of institution or stream. These are invariably grouped examinations and awards, requiring passes in all major subjects, and they have the effect of encouraging children to do well in all subject areas. Even in Singapore, where the single-subject British GCE exams are taken, these are offered to students in groups whereby each student is required to take a prescribed combination of subjects. Qualifications tend to form part of a well-understood hierarchy, having genuine currency in the labour market or giving rights of access to higher levels of education and training. (The system in Japan works somewhat differently and will be considered later.) Each educational track, therefore, has progression possibilities built into it, so the majority of children have incentives to achieve. This is reinforced, typically, by the structure of the labour market, which rewards those who gain qualifications.

The Failure to Institutionalize High Expectations in the England and the USA

Compared to the higher achieving countries discussed above, both England (and Wales)[2] and the USA have been relatively unsuccessful in institutionalizing high expectations for all their pupils. They have both been consistently successful in educating their élites to the highest international standards, but have failed to generalize the high aspirations of their élites to the generality of their populations. In recent years commentators in both countries, including governments, have frequently bemoaned the lack of a 'learning culture' throughout society, and have made unfavourable comparisons on this between their own countries and other countries like Japan and Germany (National Commission on Excellence in Education 1984; National Commission on Education 1994; Ball 1991). Not only do their cultures appear to fail to generalize sufficiently the desire to excel in education, but their education systems would appear to lack many of the features which in other countries appear to institutionalize high expectations.

In accordance with their common liberal traditions—and in the US case also because of its federal structure—neither country has traditionally favoured giving central government too much power in education. This has made it difficult to enforce common structures, practices, and standards across the whole of each system. Uniquely amongst European education systems, England did not have a national curriculum until very recently. In the USA there are mandatory school curricula prescribed by some state Boards of Education, but there is still no national curriculum. Nor does either country have a national system of qualifications in the continental European sense of the term. The UK has recently developed a national system of vocational qualifications (overseen by the National Council for Vocational Qualifications), but its academic qualifications are awarded by numerous private examining boards which have only recently become subject to significant levels of government regulation, and this falls far short of a state guarantee of the standards of individual awards. The awards are also for elective single-subject examinations which make no requirement of students to perform to a given standard over a range of core subjects, as in the typical continental 'grouped' awards. The USA has no national awards guaranteed by state at all. High-school graduation requirements typically allow a large degree of choice in subjects taken, and diplomas may be gained without reaching any specified standard (National Commission on Excellence in Education 1984).

There are other important areas where light central regulation has allowed a diversity of practices. Neither country can claim to have a common institutional structure of schools across its entire territory, as is the case in countries like France, Germany, and Japan. Arrangements vary by state in the USA and by Local Education Authority in the UK. Funding is also far from uniform. School-funding systems in both countries involve degrees of discretionary local funding which lead to considerable regional disparities, particularly in the USA (Winkler 1993). Lastly, in both countries there has been a tradition of relatively low levels of central-government regulation and intervention as regards teaching styles and materials and modes of assessment, although at certain periods in the USA State Boards have been quite active. While this is now changing to some extent in both countries, it would seem likely that there is a greater variety in pedagogic practices across schools in England and Wales and the USA than is the case in some of the more regulated systems like France and Japan (HMI 1990).

Whilst in some areas, as in the prescription of textbooks, there may be powerful democratic and human-rights objections to overly strong central regulation (see Horio 1988 on Japan), it is not hard to see that low levels of regulation across a number of fields is likely to increase the variability of practices and standards across schools and regions within a given country. As we have seen, there is evidence from the IEA studies that this is the case for the UK; it is also a common perception from observers both inside (National Commission on Excellence in Education 1994; Moore 1990) and outside the country (HMI 1990) that this is also the case for the USA. This may, of course, result from other social and cultural factors in these countries—both, for instance, have relatively high levels of inequality of wealth and income as compared with the majority of European and, indeed, developed Asian states as measured on the Gini scale (Wade 1990). However, it would seem highly plausible that low levels of regulation also contribute to this effect. It is in the nature of markets, if unregulated, to produce differentiation. As recent research has suggested (Adler, Petch, and Tweedie 1986; Carnoy 1993; Moore 1990), the adoption of school-choice policies in both the UK and the USA already shows signs of exacerbating the differences in quality and standards across schools.

The essential difference between the compulsory school-systems of the high-achieving countries as compared with the lower-achieving countries would appear to be that the former have both a culture and certain institutional mechanisms which encourage high aspirations and achievement amongst a wide majority of children, whereas the latter are successful only with their élites, whether they are the children with the higher abilities or those from the higher social groups. Whereas in all countries you will find some low-status schools and educationally marginalized social groups, in the lower-achieving countries this is relatively more widespread. As every teacher in the USA and the UK knows, the gap between the schools in deprived inner-city areas and those in the prosperous suburbs and rural areas can be immense. The argument here is that this is exacerbated by the liberal or 'laissez-faire' traditions which have prevailed historically in these countries. Whilst the affluent schools, drawing on deep pools of cultural and social capital amongst their constituents, have prospered when left to their own devices, other less-advantaged schools have not. There seems as yet to be little in the policy armoury of the liberal states that can counter this effect.

The irony is that it is these systems, which traditionally pride themselves on their concern for the individual student, which seem to leave so many without hope or self-confidence, whereas in some other systems, which are often characterized as less humanistic because of their more regimented and uniform nature, fewer students are so marginalized. Robinson and Taylor (1989) report on a survey of attitudes to self, school, and school-work by samples of English, Japanese, and French low-attainers. They found that 'the depressed level of self-esteem is most pronounced for the English', and comment, 'The [English] system, which explicitly claims to be child-centred rather than curriculum-led, and which is concerned "to meet the needs of individual children" and to match the subject, level and methods to these needs, is in fact the system which shows the greatest gradient in general self-esteem and in commitment to school.'

Factors Affecting Attainment in Post-Compulsory Education and Training

By the end of compulsory schooling some of our seven countries are already quite clearly differentiated in terms of average levels of attainment. However, it is during the post-compulsory phase of education and training (PCET) that the differences in qualification rates become most apparent. This is because PCET is the most critical phase as regards qualification attainment. The 15-to-20-years phase of PCET is where most young people gain their terminal and highest qualification and it is where they transport this qualification to their differential positions in the labour market. It is also the phase where the different levels of participation in different countries begin to impact on rates of qualification.

Although in all our seven countries the majority now stay on into PCET, it is a smaller proportion in the UK, for instance, than in the other six countries (Green and Steedman 1993). What happens in the PCET phase should therefore be relatively important in explaining differential national rates of attainment.

At first sight there would appear to be no obvious institutional characteristics common to the higher-attaining countries which are not shared by the lower-attaining countries. Institutional structures in PCET fall into three broad types. There are systems which are based primarily on the apprentice model, with a minority set of élite educational institutions running parallel. Germany offers the pre-eminent example of this (and is the only one in our sample) with its Dual System of apprentice training representing the dominant mode of PCET, and with the *Gymnasien* reserved for a minority (although a growing one). There are predominantly school-based systems with a variety of institutions offering different kinds of provision. France, Japan, and Singapore fall into this category: France with its general, technical, and vocational lycées; Japan with its general and vocational high schools; and Singapore with its academic junior colleges, vocational polytechnics, and technical training centres. England and Wales now have a predominantly school-based system, although the different institutions—school sixth forms and further education colleges—are not clearly differentiated in the curriculum which they offer. Each of these systems maintains a residual form of apprentice training. Lastly, there are the predominantly school-based systems in which one dominant type of institution offers comprehensive provision. The USA with its high schools exemplifies one version of this, and Sweden with its comprehensive *Gymnasieskola* another (OECD 1985). Whatever their institutional structures, each of these systems incorporates different tracks, some of which are academic and some vocational. The balance between the two varies by country. In the USA and Japan, general or academic education is dominant. In the other countries the majority of participants are on vocational courses, although in France, Germany, and Sweden these contain a large element of general education (OECD 1990). England and Wales, and Singapore, which adapts British qualifications, are somewhat unusual in having relatively little general education in their vocational programmes.

These different institutional models show no obvious correlations with national outcomes. Clearly, it is possible for systems which are predominantly employment-based, like Germany's, to achieve high average outcomes, just as some school-based systems (Japan) can do. The highest-achieving systems tend to place great stress on general education in all the tracks (except perhaps Singapore), but then so does the system in the USA, at least in quantitative terms, and this appears to perform less well. It is still, of course, true that the higher-achieving systems are mainly distinguished by having curricula largely specified by central or state government, whereas in the UK and the USA there is still no national curriculum for the post-compulsory phase. However, it is more difficult to argue, for this phase, that the institutionalization of normative expectations is crucial for high average attainments, because education and training provision are here necessarily more specialized and differentiated, it being the stage where young people are beginning to make choices about careers. In PCET it is the labour market which begins to exercise the predominant influence on determining norms and expectations, and it is to this which we should now turn.

The most obvious feature common to the higher-achieving systems (and not to the USA and the UK) is the high degree of articulation between education and training systems and labour markets. In each of the higher-achieving countries there are mechanisms which ensure that job entry and pay are tightly linked with qualifications held or educational levels attained (in those countries without national qualifications). How these mechanisms function varies between countries. France and Germany are both historically highly credentialist societies. A large number of jobs in each country are reserved by law for those with particular qualifications. In Germany this extends beyond the normal range of professional occupations to craft work as well, since federal legislation forbids those without Dual System qualifications to employ others and provide services in areas such as plumbing, building maintenance, and so on (CEDEFOP 1987). Even where statutory regulations do not apply, in both countries national sectoral agreements between employer organizations and unions determine entry requirements and pay levels for a wide range of jobs where these are explicitly linked to qualifications.

In Japan, as in several other Asian countries, the system works somewhat differently. Job attainment is governed not by qualifications but by the networks of association which link educational institutions to firms. Access to high-status positions in prestigious firms is dependent, to a large extent, on gaining access by competitive exams to the best high schools and the best universities, and then on being recommended by them to the best firms. The prevalence of internal labour-markets in Japan, at least in the large firms, means that promotion depends less on qualifications than on seniority and job performance. The latter involves performing well in training and showing the ability to acquire new skills, all of which may be facilitated by earlier educational success. Singapore, with its large proportion of foreign multinationals, tends to have more occupational labour markets, as in Europe, and here too the labour market is becoming fiercely credentialist.

Both Britain and the USA diverge markedly from the above patterns. Although there is a degree of credentialism and network influence operating in both countries, neither display the same degree of articulation between education and training and the labour market. Historically, both countries have been relatively less credentialist than continental Europe, having relatively more open labour markets, where employers often place greater stress on experience than qualifications. Criteria for job entry and pay determination are less pervasively regulated by government and national and sectoral agreements between unions and employer organizations. Qualifications clearly count in both countries, but there are other avenues open for building successful careers which are not so dependent on qualifications and formal schooling. Succeeding at school and acquiring qualifications figure highly for a proportion of young people in the UK and the USA, but a large proportion appears to give up aspiring for these things at a relatively early age. In France, Germany, and Japan there is also a marginal group who give up, but it would seem to be smaller. One reason for this may be that in these countries there is practically no secure employment available to those who do not graduate from high school or gain formal qualifications. In Britain and the USA, with their more open labour markets, there are more second chances for those without qualifications (Wolf 1992).

The close articulation between education and training attainment and the labour market in the higher-achieving countries is to a large extent the result of statist and corporatist influences which have historically played a greater role in continental European countries than in Britain and the USA (in Asia we may talk of statism but less of corporatism). These influences have also affected the supply of work-based training, whose relative prevalence has also contributed to differences in national levels of qualification. In general terms, the higher-achieving countries, with their higher level of state or corporatist regulation, have tended to achieve higher levels of employer and individual investment in training than countries like Britain which are less regulated and more prone to market failure in training (MSC 1985). The reasons for this have been exhaustively analyzed in a number of studies (Carnoy 1993; Finegold and Soskice 1988; Streeck 1989; and Marsden and Ryan 1995).

Put simply, the argument is as follows. Society benefits economically from a well-trained population above and beyond the gains captured by individuals and their families. These social gains, or economic externalities, accrue, as Carnoy writes, 'through the lower costs of social and economic infrastructure, a better social environment (higher public consumption), a more effective political system, and even, under certain organizational arrangements, higher productivity' (Carnoy 1993: 166). However, because many of the gains are 'external' to individuals, in unregulated market situations both employers and individuals are likely to underinvest in training. Employers may make rational choices not to train because they fear the loss of their investment due to the likelihood of other employers poaching the employees they have trained, or because they calculate they can make better profits in the short term by operating a low-cost, low-skill business strategy (Finegold and Soskice 1988). Individuals may also underinvest in training for a number of reasons. They may lack sufficient information and maturity to calculate the long-term marginal benefits of training, or they may lack access to funds to invest in training (Carnoy 1993; Streeck 1989).

The higher-achieving countries in our sample have generally used some form of regulation to overcome these problems of market failure. In France, Singapore, and Sweden training taxes are levied on employers to encourage them to train. This either takes the form of a payroll tax, which can be recouped by employers who demonstrate sufficient effort in training (France), or a punitive tax on firms employing people on low wages (Singapore). The latter provides an incentive for employers to pay higher wages and thus to train to recoup their costs through higher productivity (Ashton and Green 1996). In Germany training levies only apply in a few sectors, although there are small compulsory levies payable to the Chambers (*Kammern*) which play a major role in regulating the apprentice system. However, more importantly, there are national sectoral agreements which keep apprentice wages low (thus reducing employer-training costs) and which govern pay at different levels. The latter prevents firms paying higher wages for the same job and thus being able to poach employees trained at another employer's expense (CEDEFOP 1987; Marsden and Ryan 1995). Japan does not need to operate any of these forms of regulation because its system of internal labour markets and lifelong employment in the larger companies ensures that firms are unlikely to lose their training investments through trained employees moving to other companies (Green 1995*b*). In each of these countries the individual's incentive to train is enhanced by the tight linkage between achievement in formal education and training, and access to jobs.

The USA and the UK are exceptional in our group of countries since they neither have pervasive internal labour markets nor forms of regulation to stimulate training. This has allowed the perennial problem of employers free-riding by poaching trained employees rather than training themselves. In addition to this, both countries have traditions of short-termism in business decision-making. The nature of company ownership law and financial markets in both countries tend to place great pressure on firms to deliver short-term profits and dividends to shareholders or face takeover (Hutton 1995). This has also increased the disincentives to train. The result is that in both countries company training tends to be widespread and systematic only in the larger companies. Individuals are likewise less inclined to invest in training where they know that the labour markets allow employment opportunities, at least in the short term, which do not involve personal costs of training.

Conclusions

Comparisons across a small range of countries clearly cannot provide any definitive answers regarding the causes of national differences in average levels of attainments. Even with a larger sample of countries and with adequate empirical measures of system characteristics, this would be difficult because of the sheer complexity of factors which affect outcomes. However, the comparisons made above do indicate certain factors which are common to a range of more successful countries and not shared by the less successful ones, and this may be at least suggestive of certain avenues for fruitful investigation.

What emerges from the above is that there are certain very broad cultural characteristics which seem to underlie national education achievement, and that these can be seen to be manifested in a set of related institutional characteristics. Put at its most simple (and, arguably, simplistic) level, the high-achieving countries appear to have an 'inclusive learning culture' which is characterized by the high premium which society places on learning *for all groups*. High aspirations for the majority are reinforced by the way in which the education and training systems institutionalize norms and expectations for everyone, and not just the élites, and the way in which the labour markets reward those doing well in education and training. To achieve inclusive norms and opportunities, systems generally have to employ a number of devices which act to standardize certain practices which would otherwise, in a unregulated market situation, become highly differentiated as a result of unequal market endowments. These typically involve, *inter alia*, the specification of fairly uniform institutional structures and standardized funding systems; the use of national curricula and a degree of prescription in methods of assessment and teaching; and the

existence of national systems of qualification (or some alternative means for recognizing attainment and allocating rewards which is transparent and predictable). In the PCET sector it also involves means of articulating education and training with the labour market which provide incentives for individuals and employers to train.

Such structures and practices do not necessarily require all decisions to be made at the central government level and nor, indeed, do they require that government alone make all the decisions. Germany has a federal system of education, which devolves power down to the local level, and a corporatist system of training and labour-market control which gives the social partners substantial control. Japan allows semi-private bodies substantial roles in its education system. However, it does seem to require a high degree of state 'regulation', where government acts in a concerted fashion at different levels to define and operationalize the system, including defining and enabling the roles of the different social partners within it. Although not invariably 'centralized', the most effective systems do indeed all appear to shows signs of 'tight regulation' in the critical areas, with high levels of policy coherence, institutional systematization, and close articulation between levels of the education and training system and between this system and the labour market. Such systems are clearly not 'market' systems or even 'quasi-market' systems.

Coherent structures and 'concerted' social action in education and training has been achieved in recent years in a number of countries with quite different cultural traditions and political systems. However, their state forms, broadly speaking, seem to fall into two types. There are the 'corporatist' continental European states, like France, Germany, and Sweden, which have combined high levels of state regulation and intervention (at different levels) with encompassing institutional structures for integrating social partners in decision-making. And there are the more purely 'statist' countries in developed Asia, which have a relatively low density of corporate organization in 'civil society' and where the only 'partner' of big government is 'Big Business'. Each state form can be associated with certain common institutional characteristics as regards education, although there are, of course, also myriad differences resulting from different national cultures and histories. Both types of state seem capable of generating high-achieving educational systems in ways that the 'neo-liberal' states, like the UK and the USA, are not.

Any explanation of why these states are as they are, and why they are associated with certain educational outcomes, would require a historical analysis of state formation which is well beyond the scope of this article. However, it is worth noting, in conclusion, that there is a strong historical connection between the emergence of particular state forms and the emergence of particular kinds of national education system. National education systems were the historical product of the process of state formation, and, arguably, it is in nation-building that organized public education found its first and main purpose and rationale. Education systems have tended to develop fastest in countries undergoing intensive or accelerated processes of state formation, usually prompted by external military threats (as in early nineteenth-century Prussia and late nineteenth-century Japan), or by the need to reconstruct after revolution (as in eighteenth-century France and the USA) or war devastation (Germany and Japan after the Second World War). Countries undergoing these concerted and accelerated processes of nation-building have usually employed the full machinery of the state to develop both their economies and their education systems. They have also tended to cultivate a 'learning culture', in which educational aspiration is closely linked with broader notions of nation-building and citizen-formation (Green 1990).

At various periods in each of the high-achieving countries here such historical conditions appear to have driven educational development, creating both the cultural and institutional conditions for rapid educational development. We can see this process in Singapore now. In the other high-achieving countries, it exists as a historical sediment, visible in the cultural norms and institutional practices of the 'learning society'.

Notes

1. Current research conducted by Hilary Steedman and Andy Green for the UK Department for Education and Training project: 'International Comparisons of Skills Supply and Demand'. To be published by the Centre for Economic Performance, London School of Economics.
2. The education system in Scotland is considerably different from that in England and Wales and is not discussed here.

References

Adler, M. E., Petch, A. J., and Tweedie, J. W. (1986), *Parental Choice in Education Policy* (Edinburgh: Edinburgh Univ. Press).
Archer, M. (1979), *The Social Origins of Educational Systems* (London: Sage).
Ashton, D., and Green, F. (1996), *Education, Training and the Global Economy* (London: Elgar).
Ball, C. (1991), *Learning Pays* (London: Royal Society of Arts).
Ball, S. J. (1990), 'Education, Inequality and School Reform', King's College Memorial Lecture.
Boucher, L. (1982), *Tradition and Change in Swedish Education* (London: Pergamon).
Carnoy, M. (1993), 'School Improvement: Is Privatization the Answer?' in J. Hannaway and M. Carnoy (eds.), *Decentralization and School Improvement* (San Francisco: Jossey-Bass).
CEDEFOP (1987), *The Role of the Social Partners in Vocational Training and Further Training in the Federal Republic of Germany* (Berlin: CEDEFOP).
Chubb, J., and Moe, T. (1990), *Politics, Markets and American Schools* (Washington DC: Brookings Institution).
Her Majesty's Inspectorate (1986), *Education in the Federal Republic of Germany: Aspects of Curriculum and Assessment* (London: HMSO).
Finegold, D. and Soskice, D. (1988), 'The Failure of Training in Britain: Analysis and Prescription', *Oxford Review of Economic Policy*, 4/3: 21–53.
Green, A. (1990), *Education and State Formation* (London: Macmillan).
—— (1994), 'Postmodernism and State Education', *Journal of Education Policy*, 9/1, 67–83.
—— (1995a), 'Education and State Formation in Europe and Asia', in A. Heikkinnen (ed.), *Vocational Education and Culture: Prospects for Theory and Practice* (Finland: Univ. of Tampere).
—— (1995b), 'The Role of the State and Social Partners in VET Systems', in L. Bash and A. Green (eds.), *World Yearbook of Education: Youth Education and Work* (London: Kogan Page), 92–108.
—— and Steedman, H. (1993), *Educational Provision, Educational Attainment and the Needs of Industry: A Review of the Research for Germany, France, Japan, the USA and Britain*, Report no. 5 (London: NIESR).

Gopinathan, S. (1994), *Educational Development in a Strong-Developmentalist State: The Singapore Experience*, paper presented to the Australian Association for Research in Education Annual Conference.

HMI (1990), *Aspects of Education in the USA: Teaching and Learning in New York Schools* (London: HMSO).

—— (1991), *Aspects of Primary Education in France* (London: HMSO).

—— (1992), *Teaching and Learning in Japanese Elementary Schools*, (London: HMSO).

Horio, T. (1988), *Educational Thought and Ideology in Modern Japan: State Authority and Intellectual Freedom*, ed. and trans. by S. Platzer (Japan: Tokyo Univ. Press).

Hutton, W. (1995), *The State We're In* (London: Jonathan Cape).

Inkeles, A. (1979), 'National Differences in Scholastic Performance', *Comparative Education Review*, October, 386–407.

International Assessment of Achievement (1988), *Science Achievement in Seventeen Countries* (London: Pergamon).

International Assessment of Educational Progress (1992), *Learning Mathematics* (New Jersey: Educational Testing Service).

Lynn, R. (1988), *Educational Achievement in Japan: Lessons for the West* (London: Macmillan).

Kaestle, C. (1983), *Pillars of the Republic: Common Schools and American Society, 1780–1860* (Toronto: Hill and Wang).

Manpower Services Commission (1985), *Competence and Competition* (Sheffield: MSC).

Marsden, D. and Ryan, P. (1985), 'Work, Labour Markets and Vocational Preparation: Anglo-German Comparisons of Training in Intermediate Skills', in L. Bash and A. Green (eds.), *World Yearbook of Education: Youth, Education and Work* (London: Kogan Page), 67–79.

Moore, D. (1990), 'Voice and Choice in Chicago Schools', in W. Clune and J. Witte (eds.), *Choice and Control in American Education*, ii (London: Falmer Press).

National Commission on Education (1994), *Learning to Succeed* (London: Heinemann).

National Commission on Excellence in Education (1984), *A Nation at Risk* (Washington, DC: US Government).

OECD (1985), *Education and Training Beyond Basic Schooling*, (Paris: OECD).

—— (1989), *Pathways to Learning*, (Paris: OECD).

—— (1995), *Education at a Glance*, (Paris: OECD).

OECD/Statistics Canada (1995) *Literacy, Economy and Society: Results of the First International Survey* (Paris: OECD).

Postlethwaite, N. (1982), 'Success and Failure in Schools', in P. Altback, R. Arnove, and G. Kelly, *Comparative Education* (New York: Macmillan).

Prais, S. J. (1987), 'Education for Productivity: Comparisons of Japanese and English Schooling and Vocational Preparation', *National Institute Economic Review* (February), 40–56.

Robinson, W. P., and Taylor, C. A. (1989), 'Correlates of Low Academic Attainment in Three Countries: England, France and Japan', *International Journal of Educational Research*, 13: 585–96.

—— —— and Piolat, M. (1992), 'Redoublement in Relation to Self-Perception and Self Evaluation: France', *Research in Education*, 47 (May.)

Schoppa, J. (1991), *Education in Japan: A Case of Immobilist Politics* (London: Routledge).

Sexton, S. (1987), *Our Schools: A Radical Policy* (London: Institute of Economic Affairs).

Streeck, W. (1989), 'Skills and the Limits of Neo-Liberalism: The Enterprise of the Future as a Place of Learning', *Work, Employment and Society*, 3/1: 89–104.

Wade, R. (1990), *Governing the Market: Economic Theory and the Role of Government in East Asian Industrialization* (Princeton: Princeton Univ. Press).

White, M. (1987), *The Japanese Educational Challenge* (London: Macmillan).

Winkler, D. (1993), 'Fiscal Decentralization and Accountability: Experience in Four Countries', in J. Hannaway and M. Carnoy (eds.), *Decentralization and School Improvement* (San Francisco: Jossey-Bass).

Whitty, G. (1992), 'Education, Economy and National Culture', in R. Bocock and K. Thompson (eds.), *Social And Cultural Forms of Modernity* (Buckingham: Open Univ. Press).

Wolf, A. (1992) *Mathematics for Vocational Students in France and England: Contrasting Provision and Consequences*, 23 (London: National Institute of Economic and Social Research).

19

Marketization, the State, and the Re-Formation of the Teaching Profession

Geoff Whitty

Introduction

A great deal of recent policy discourse about education blames teachers for poor educational standards. Education reforms in countries as different as England and Nicaragua have limited the autonomy of teachers and curbed the power of teacher trade unions. Even in other countries, such as the USA, where the rhetoric of reform has put more emphasis on the empowerment of teachers, there has been an attempt to make teachers less the servants of local bureaucracies and more responsive to the demands of their clients. This paper considers how far such developments represent the transitory policies of particular New Right governments and how far a more fundamental repositioning of education in relation to the state and civil society. It begins by discussing the significance of recent education reforms and the extent to which they can be considered a post-modern phenomenon; goes on to suggest that, while there has been no clearly discernible post-modern 'break', the marketization of education has involved changes in the relationship between the state and civil society; and then reviews some evidence about the effects of recent reforms on the teaching profession and considers how far it is useful to characterize teachers as operating in a post-modern age. The final section considers whether there are viable alternatives to state control or market accountability for the future regulation of the teaching profession.

Education Reform: A Post-Modern Phenomenon?

In recent years, there has been a discernible trend in many parts of the world to restructure and deregulate state education. Central to these initiatives have been moves to disempower centralized educational bureaucracies and create in their place devolved systems of schooling, entailing significant degrees of institutional autonomy and a variety of forms of school-based management and administration. In many cases, these changes have been linked to an increased emphasis on parental choice and on competition between diversified and specialized forms of provision, thereby creating 'quasi-markets' in educational services (Le Grand and Bartlett 1993).[1]

Although such policies have received particular encouragement from New Right governments in Britain and the USA in the 1980s, and have subsequently been fostered by the IMF and the World Bank in Latin America and Eastern Europe (Arnove 1996), the political rhetoric of parties of the left has also begun to place increasing emphasis on diversity and choice in education. Even though these directions in education policy have not penetrated all countries (Green 1994), and they have been mediated differently by the traditions of different nation states and different political parties, the similarity between the broad trends in many parts of the world suggests that education policy may be witnessing something more significant than the passing political fashion that has come—in Britain and beyond—to be termed 'Thatcherism'.

It is therefore sometimes suggested that these shifts in the ways in which education is organized reflect broader changes in the nature of advanced industrial societies, characterized by some commentators as post-Fordism and by others as post-modernity.[2]

Thus, some observers suggest that the reforms can be understood in terms of the transportation of changing modes of regulation from the sphere of production into other arenas, such as schooling and welfare services. They point to a correspondence between the establishment of differentiated markets in welfare, and a shift in the economy away from Fordism towards a post-Fordist mode of accumulation which 'places a lower value on mass individual and collective consumption and creates pressures for a more differentiated production and distribution of health, education, transport and housing' (Jessop *et al.* 1987). Ball (1990), for example, has claimed to see in new forms of schooling a move away from the 'Fordist' school towards a 'post-Fordist' one—the educational equivalent of flexible specialization driven by the imperatives of differentiated consumption replacing the old assembly-line world of mass production. These 'post-Fordist schools' are designed 'not only to produce the post-Fordist, multi-skilled, innovative worker but to behave in post-Fordist ways themselves; moving away from mass production and mass markets to niche markets and "flexible specialization" . . . a post-Fordist mind-set is thus having implications in schools for management styles, curriculum, pedagogy, and assessment' (Kenway 1993).

However, Kenway herself regards the rapid rise of the market form in education as something much more significant than post-Fordism; she therefore terms it a 'postmodern' phenomenon (Kenway 1993). In her own pessimistic version of postmodernity, 'transnational corporations and their myriad subsidiaries . . . shape and reshape our individual and collective identities as we plug in . . . to their cultural and economic communications networks' (Kenway 1993). Her picture is one in which notions of 'difference', far from being eradicated by the 'globalization of culture', are assembled, displayed, celebrated, commodified, and exploited (Robins 1991). Such trends can be detected in the current emphasis on both tradition and diversity in education policy.

In other accounts the rhetoric of 'new times' seems to offer more positive images of choice and diversity, reflecting the needs of communities and interest groups brought into prominence as a result of complex contemporary patterns of political, economic, and cultural differentiation, which intersect the traditional class divisions upon which common systems of mass education were predicated. From this perspective, it is possible to contrast post-modernity to the oppressive uniformity of much modernist thinking—as 'a form of liberation, in which the fragmentation and plurality of cultures and social groups allow a hundred flowers to bloom' (Thompson 1992). Some feminists, for example, have seen attractions in the shift towards the pluralist models of society and culture associated with post-modernism (Flax 1987). The possibilities for community-based rather than bureaucratically controlled welfare are also viewed positively by some minority ethnic groups, and many of the advocates of quasi-market systems of public education regard them as particularly beneficial for the urban poor (Moe 1994; Pollard 1995).

Part of the appeal of the recent education reforms thus lies in their declared intention to encourage the growth of different types of school, responsive to the needs of particular communities and interest groups. They also link to concepts of multiple identities and radical pluralism, and can thus seem more attractive than unidimensional notions of comprehensive schooling and, indeed, of citizenship. Some aspects of the rhetoric of the new policies thus seem to connect to the aspirations of groups who have found little to identify with in the 'grand narratives' associated with class-based politics. In this sense, the reforms might be viewed as a rejection of all totalizing narratives and their replacement by 'a set of cultural projects united [only] by a self-proclaimed commitment to heterogeneity, fragmentation and difference' (Boyne and Rattansi 1990). In other words, support for schools run on a variety of principles reflect a broader shift from the assumptions of modernity to those of postmodernity.

However, there are various problems with these 'new times' theses. They are not only 'notoriously vague' (Hickox 1995) but also tend to exaggerate the extent to which we have moved to a new regime of accumulation. Moreover, in the field of education, it is certainly difficult to establish a sharp distinction between mass and marketized systems. For example, the so-called 'common school' in the USA or the 'comprehensive system' in Britain were never as homogeneous as many commentators claim. Nor have there been decisive changes in the prevailing character of schools as institutions. In so far as recent changes in management practices represent an '*adjustment* to the problems of Fordism' rather than signifying an entirely new direction, neo-Fordism may be a more appropriate term than post-Fordism (Allen 1992).

Although the changes may thus not be as momentous as Kenway and others suggest, her pessimistic analysis of what changes have taken place has rather more credibility than would an optimistic one. There does seem to have been an intensification of social differences, together with their celebration in a new rhetoric of legitimation. However, as the new discourse of choice, specialization, and diversity replaces the previous one of common and comprehensive schooling, there is a growing body of empirical evidence that, rather than benefiting the disadvantaged, the emphasis on parental choice and school autonomy is further disadvantaging those least able to compete in the market (Smith and Noble 1995; Gewirtz *et al*. 1995: Lauder *et al*. 1995). At the same time, it is increasing the differences between popular and less popular schools on a linear scale, reinforcing a vertical hierarchy of schooling types rather than producing the promised horizontal diversity (Whitty 1994). For most members of disadvantaged groups, as opposed to the few individuals who escape from schools at the bottom of the status hierarchy, the new arrangements seem to be just a more sophisticated way of reproducing traditional distinctions between different types of school and between the people who attend them.

To regard the current espousal of heterogeneity, pluralism, and local narratives as indicative of a new social order may be to mistake phenomenal forms for structural relations. Marxist critics of theories of postmodernism and postmodernity, such as Callinicos (1989), who reassert the primacy of the class struggle, certainly take this view. Even Harvey, who does recognize significant changes, suggests that postmodernist cultural forms and more flexible modes of capital accumulation may be shifts in surface appearance, rather than signs of the emergence of some entirely new post-capitalist or even post-industrial society (Harvey 1989). At most, current reforms would seem to relate to a version of post-modernity (PM1) that emphasizes 'distinction' and 'hierarchy' within a

fragmented social order, rather than one (PM2) that positively celebrates 'difference' and 'heterogeneity' (Lash 1990). Thus, despite new forms of accumulation, together with some limited changes in patterns of social and cultural differentiation, the continuities seem as striking as the discontinuities.

The State and Civil Society

Nevertheless, new arrangements for managing education and other public services can be seen as new ways of resolving the problems of accumulation and legitimation facing the state, in a situation where the traditional Keynesian 'welfare state' is no longer deemed to be able to function effectively (Dale 1989). But even if current policies are new ways of dealing with old problems, there clearly have been changes in the state's mode of regulation. City Technology Colleges (CTCs), grant-maintained schools, and LEA schools with open enrolment and local management in England—and equivalent quasi-autonomous institutions in other parts of the world—are now operating alongside, and increasingly in place of, collective provision by elected bodies with a mandate to cater for the needs of the whole population. Similar reforms have been introduced into the health and housing fields.

With the progressive removal of tiers of democratically elected government or administration between the central state and individual institutions, conventional political and bureaucratic control by public bodies is replaced by quasi-autonomous institutions with devolved budgets competing for clients in the marketplace—a system of market accountability sometimes assisted by a series of directly appointed agencies, trusts, and regulators. Such quasi-autonomous institutions, state-funded but with considerable private and voluntary involvement in their operation, appear to make education less of a political issue. The political rhetoric accompanying the educational reforms in Britain certainly sought to suggest that education had been taken out of politics as normally understood (Riddell 1992). For Chubb and Moe (1990) in the USA, the removal of schools from the local political arena is a *sine qua non* of their success.

So, although the extent of any underlying social changes can easily be exaggerated by various 'post-ist' forms of analysis, both the discourse and the contexts of political struggles in and around education *have* been significantly altered by recent reforms. Not only have changes in the nature of the state influenced the reforms in education, but the reforms in education are themselves beginning to change the way we think about the role of the state and what we expect of it. Green (1990) has pointed to the way in which education had not only been an important part of state activity in modern societies, but also played a significant role in the process of state formation itself in the eighteenth and nineteenth centuries. The current changes in education policy may similarly be linked to a redefinition of the nature of the state and a reworking of the relations between state and civil society.

The new education policies foster the idea that responsibility for welfare, beyond the minimum required for public safety, is to be defined as a matter for individuals and families. As a result, not only is the scope of the state narrowed, but civil society becomes increasingly defined in market terms. Although one of the many origins of the concept of civil society was the attempt by late eighteenth-century liberal economists to protect an autonomous economic sphere from the growing administrative power of the state (Foucault 1988), political radicals used it as a context for democratic debate and the fostering of active citizenship. However, Meehan (1995) suggests that, by the mid-twentieth century in Britain and some other countries, the establishment of political democracy and a concern that 'private interests might overwhelm the public good' led to a view in many countries that state bureaucratic regulation itself might serve as 'a tool to improve the collective life of society'. This reliance on the state led to a decline in the autonomy and vitality of civil society. McKenzie (1993) argues that, as a result, education has increasingly been excluded from the public sphere.

As many of the responsibilities adopted by the state during the postwar period begin to be devolved to an increasingly marketized version of civil society, consumer rights prevail over citizen rights. Some aspects of education have been 'privatized' not so much in the strictly economic sense as in that of transferring them to the private sphere; others have become a matter of state mandate rather than local democratic debate. This can be seen as part of that broader project to create a free economy and a strong state (Gamble 1988) which, as far as democratic citizenship is concerned, seems to produce the worst of both worlds—reducing the opportunities for democratic debate and collective action about education within both the state and civil society.

Meanwhile, in many countries certain aspects of state intervention have been maintained, indeed strengthened. Recent education reforms in England, notably the National Curriculum, are themselves actually as much to do with transferring power from the local to the central state as with giving autonomy to the schools. While some of the extreme neo-liberals of the New Right would have liked to see the curriculum itself left to the market, the government seems to have been more persuaded on this score by the argument of neo-conservative pressure groups such as the Hillgate Group. This group argued that, even if market forces should ultimately be seen as the most desirable way of determining a school's curriculum, central-government imposition of a National Curriculum on all state schools was a necessary interim strategy to undermine the vested interests of a 'liberal educational establishment' which threatened educational standards and traditional values. McKenzie (1993) claims that 'British governments have actually increased their claims to knowledge and authority over the education system whilst promoting a theoretical and superficial movement towards consumer sovereignty'. This is also the case, though to differing degrees, elsewhere (Harris 1993; Arnove 1996).

In terms of educational decision-making, the example of the National Curriculum suggests that the contemporary state has not merely devolved responsibility to a remarketized civil society. In the British case, it may have abdicated some responsibility for ensuring social justice by deregulating major aspects of education, but in increasing a limited number of state powers it has actually strengthened its capacity to foster particular interests while appearing to stand outside the frame.

The Teaching Profession Re-Formed

To what extent, then, have these developments impacted upon the position of teachers? Are teachers, as Hargreaves (1994) suggests, caught in struggle between the forces of modernity and post-modernity in which the latter are winning out? And, even if we are sceptical about his postmodern thesis, is he right in suggesting that, despite the pressures currently being experienced by teachers in Canada and elsewhere, there is potentially much that could be positive in recent developments?

Le Grand (1996) suggests that in England, during the so-called 'golden age of teacher control' from 1944 to the mid-1970s (Lowe 1993), parents of children in state schools were expected to trust the professionals and accept that teachers knew what was best for their children. This usually involved accepting a degree of uniformity in the system. He goes on to argue that the assumptions underlying what he calls the 'democratic socialist welfare state' have now been questioned, and that 'the notion that, for the sake of the collectivity, everyone would passively accept standardized, relatively low levels of services was challenged by studies showing that in key areas of welfare the middle classes extracted at least as much if not more than the poor in terms of both the quantity and quality of service'. The belief that professionals are concerned only with the welfare of their clients has increasingly been challenged, with Public-Choice theorists arguing that the behaviour of public servants and professionals could be better understood if they were assumed to be largely self-interested (Glennerster 1995; Lowe 1993).

The teachers of the 'swollen state' of postwar social democracy are thus now regarded as ill-adapted to be either agents of the narrowed state or entrepreneurial service-providers in a marketized civil society. In the light of this and the broader changes outlined above, there has now been something of a move away from the notion that the teaching profession should have a professional mandate to act on behalf of the state in the best interests of its citizens, to a view that teachers (and, indeed, other professions) need to be subjected to the rigours of the market and/or greater control and surveillance on the part of the re-formed state. As with the Hillgate Group's view of the purposes of the National Curriculum, the latter approach may be transitional, in that it is partly concerned with the reconstitution of

teacher subjectivities to accord more closely with the demands of education in a society where the prevailing mode of regulation is changing. Even in countries like Britain and the USA, where professions have traditionally enjoyed considerable autonomy from the central state, there have been similar attempts to increase surveillance and supervision in earlier periods of transition and social upheaval (Popkewitz 1994).

In the current context, control strategies have taken a variety of forms. In many countries the power of the teaching unions has been challenged, both through the dismantling of former 'corporatist' styles of education decision-making and through the decentralization of education systems. In England, the reforms have been accompanied by swingeing attacks on the integrity of the teaching profession in general and the teachers' unions in particular. The unions' traditional involvement in policy-making, and even in negotiating teachers' pay, was systematically undermined by the Thatcher government during the 1980s, so that even some of the less militant unions expressed strong reservations about the government's reforms.

Nevertheless, research carried out by Sinclair *et al.* (1993) suggests that the atomization associated with school self-management has not yet entirely succeeded in breaking down the traditional power of teacher unions within the state education system. Many of the district-wide networks are still in place, and legal confusion about who is technically the employer in LEA schools operating under local management means that there are a number of issues which remain to be tested in the courts. However, in some grant-maintained schools and CTCs, where the legal issues are more clear-cut, unions are being forced to strengthen their plant bargaining capacity or are being marginalized by management. Only one grant-maintained school has so far derecognized teacher unions and withdrawn from national pay agreements, but some CTCs, which operate outside both national and local agreements, have established in-house staff associations within individual schools, or offered the less militant unions 'no-strike' agreements in return for recognition.

More generally, the notion that teachers are part of an 'education establishment', representing producer interests against those of the newly empowered consumer, has led to a questioning of both the altruism and the neutrality of teachers. Strategies for challenging the supposed self-interest of the profession are particularly evident in attempts to reform initial teacher education, especially in England. One strategy favoured by the neoliberals is deregulation of the profession, to allow schools to go into the market, recruit graduates (or even non-graduates) without professional training, and prepare them on an apprenticeship basis in school. This also has some appeal to neo-conservative critics who have detected collectivist (and even Marxist) ideological bias among teacher educators in higher education.[3] Thus, a recurring theme in the pamphlets of New Right pressure groups is the need to challenge the liberal educational establishment, which is seen to have been behind the 'progressive collapse' of the English educational system. This educational establishment is seen as prey to ideology and self-interest and no longer in touch with the public. It is therefore 'time to set aside . . . the professional educators and the majority of organised teacher unions . . . [who] are primarily responsible for the present state of Britain's schools' (Hillgate Group 1987).

Neo-conservative concerns with 'enemies within', possibly combined with vocationalist concerns with international competitiveness (Hickox 1995), have meant that the British government has not pursued a policy of total deregulation. Instead, it has introduced a common list of competences to be required of beginning teachers, regardless of the nature of the route by which they have achieved them. This has given rise to the suspicion that the government wants to 'deprofessionalize' teaching by ensuring that, wherever they are trained, teachers focus on the development of craft skills rather than professional understanding. Just as basing training in particular schools can limit the development of broader perspectives on education, so might specifying particular competences encourage restricted rather than extended notions of professionalism and professionality (Hoyle 1974).[4] It is also sometimes suggested that competence-based teacher education is undermining the dominant discourse of liberal humanism within the teaching profession and replacing it with one of technical rationality (Jones and Moore 1993). Neither, though, involves the abandonment of notions of rationality associated with the Enlightenment pro-

ject, which might be expected if these changes represented an abandonment of the dominant assumptions of modernity.

Similar trends have been detected within schools. In New Zealand, Sullivan (1993) has suggested that lack of consultation with teachers over the reforms is in danger of creating a low-trust, hierarchical system rather than a high-trust, collegial one. In England, Grace (1995) posits a shift from a social democratic to a market phase of school leadership, which Gewirtz and Ball (1996) suggest is similar to the broader erosion of 'bureau-professional' regimes of institutional regulation in favour of 'new managerial' ones (Clarke and Newman 1992). Gewirtz and Ball themselves outline two 'ideal-type discourses of school headship', which they term 'welfarism' and 'new managerialism'. Welfarism denotes 'a primary ideological commitment to the material and emotional well-being of individuals and to the creation of a better and fairer society', though Fabian and Radical Welfarists differ about what this might involve. New Managerialism, on the other hand, is 'untainted' by the dominant welfarist values of the postwar era; the New Management discourse is essentially technicist in character, and good management involves 'the smooth and efficient implementation of aims set elsewhere within constraints also set elsewhere'. Although the real cases they discuss introduce 'some messiness into the neat polarization of these pristine binaries', they believe that they have identified a discursive shift of some significance. But here again, as Blackmore (1995: 45) points out, the self-managing school retains 'strong modernist tendencies for a top-down, executive mode of decision-making . . . [alongside its] "weaker" post-modern claims to decentralise and encourage diversity, community ownership, local discretion, professional autonomy and flexible decision-making'. And, although particular management strategies, such as flattened hierarchies and TQM, are entering some fields of education, they are used in a context which is more neo-Fordist than post-Fordist in character.

Teachers' Professional Lives

Nevertheless, those changes that are taking place in the nature of educational governance and in management practices in schools clearly impact upon the character of teachers' professional lives. To date, empirical evidence from various countries provides more support for Hargreaves' assertion that the reforms are leading to an intensification of teachers' work than for his claim that they have potential for developing more rewarding forms of teacher culture (Hargreaves 1994). A survey conducted by Campbell and Neill (1994) on the effects of the National Curriculum on primary school teachers in England and Wales concluded that there had been no overall improvement in standards but that teachers had been driven to burnout. They found that a 54-hour week was now the norm for teachers of children aged 4 to 7, with one in ten working more than 60 hours, and respondents talked of tiredness, irritability, and depression, of sleeping badly, increased drinking, occasional crying in the staffroom, and a sense of guilt that they were neglecting their own families.

Studies in New Zealand (Bridges 1992; Wylie 1994; Livingstone 1994), where the National Curriculum loading is a less significant factor but school self-management has gone further, have produced similar figures. New Zealand teachers have reported high levels of stress, declining job satisfaction, and a desire to leave the profession, even where they felt the reforms had brought some benefits. In another study of those schools with the greatest degree of autonomy, although principals still saw themselves as curriculum leaders, teachers stressed 'the current role as being more of a business manager' (Hawk and Hill 1994: 97).

Some of the small-scale ethnographic evidence from Britain and New Zealand chronicles in more detail the effects of the intensification of teachers' work and its consequences for industrial relations in schools. In England, Bowe et al. (1992) point to real problems with both self-management and the National Curriculum as they are working out on the ground in secondary schools, and see them as contributing to a growing gulf between senior managers and teachers, and a clash between managerial and educational values. Laughlin et al. (1993), however, report evidence from other schools that the demands of LMS were (initially at any rate) absorbed by a core 'coping group' of senior managers whose efforts were able to leave the core educational values of the school relatively unscathed.

While headteachers themselves often claim that local management has increased the involvement of teaching staff in decision-making, a study of the effects of self-management on industrial relations in schools by Sinclair et al. (1993) suggests that the very logic of the reforms is that 'headteachers are no longer partners in the process of educating pupils—they become allocators of resources within the school, managers who are driven to ensure that the activities of employees are appropriate to the needs of the business, and givers of rewards to those whose contribution to the business is most highly regarded'.

When schools were managed from a more distant bureaucracy, there was often a sense of headteacher and teachers being the professionals fighting a common cause against the distant bureaucracy. With self-management, there has sometimes been a much sharper sense that the school governors and the senior management team are 'management' and teaching and other staff the 'workers'. Halpin et al. (1993) suggest that, in the case of grant-maintained schools, the very process of running a self-managing unit can result in an increase in the distance of headteachers from classroom teachers, although in some cases headteachers themselves are coming under pressure from governing bodies acting like Boards of Directors.

Classroom teachers face a number of new pressures—increased workloads, attempts to use them more flexibly to counter the effects of budget restrictions, performance-related pay, and the substitution of full-time, permanent, qualified, and experienced staff by part-time, temporary, less-qualified and less-experienced (and therefore less-expensive) alternatives. Women teachers, traditionally concentrated in the lower ranks of the teaching workforce, are particularly vulnerable to exploitation in these circumstances. A recent report by the National Foundation for Educational Research confirms that many of these trends have accelerated since the introduction of local management (Maychell 1994). This, of course, has potential implications for teachers' conditions of service and poses new challenges for the teacher unions.

There have been suggestions, for example by Kerchner and Mitchell (1988) in the USA and Barber (1992) in the UK, that the teaching unions need to develop a new mode of operation, sometimes termed 'third generation' or 'professional' unionism, in which they negotiate educational as well as industrial issues and potentially become partners with management in educational decision-making to serve the best interests of learners. Self-management has been seen to pose a threat to traditional styles of trade unionism, but to provide real opportunities for this new-style version. It could also be a way of giving classroom teachers a voice in management without diverting them from their primary role.

Barber, Rowe, and Whitty (1995) mounted a small research project, with funding from a national teachers' union, to see how far union representatives in England were actually involved in school-based decision making on the ground. Only about 15 per cent of school union representatives had ever been consulted about the budget, the curriculum, or the school development plan. Subsequent fieldwork suggested that even these figures exaggerated the extent of genuine consultation, let alone formal involvement of unions in school management. We found little evidence of union representatives participating in issues other than those associated with 'second generational unionism', that is, giving advice to members, negotiating with management over grievances, and campaigning on issues related to pay and conditions of work. Many felt that there was a fine line to be drawn between third-generation trade unionism and the sort of collaboration that makes it difficult for unions to bargain for their members' interests. Flexibility and claims of enhanced professionalism could sometimes become a cover for exploitation of teachers and worsening conditions of service.

The rhetoric of reform in the USA has often made far more reference to school-based shared decision-making (SBDM) as a way of enhancing teacher professionalism than has hitherto been the case in England. Yet, although much of the rhetoric of the American reform movement has emphasized the importance of empowering teachers, this has often not come about in practice. Wohlstetter *et al.* (1994) have suggested that site-based management will only have positive effects if it is implemented in accordance with what, drawing upon the literature of private-sector management, they term the 'high-involvement model'. This requires teacher involvement in decision-making, good information, knowledge and skills, and power and rewards.

However, even the more participatory forms of teacher involvement in decision-making can have unintended consequences. In Minnesota charter schools, for example, 'as much as teachers appreciated being board members and making administrative decisions, wearing two hats required a great deal of time and effort' from which they would eventually require some relief (Urahn and Stewart 1994: 51). Even in this context, it may therefore be important to take seriously the political insights of those teachers who resist attempts to engage them in management without addressing the broader meaning and consequences of the reforms (Gitlin and Margonis 1995).

Citizenship Rights in Education

If, as much of the initial research evidence suggests (Whitty 1997), recent reforms are encouraging advantaged schools and advantaged families to maximize their advantage, then it is particularly important that there is an arena in which such broader issues can be considered not only by teachers but by other stakeholders in public education. As Henig (1994: 222) says of the USA, 'the sad irony of the current education-reform movement is that, through over-identification with school-choice proposals rooted in market-based ideas, the healthy impulse to consider radical reforms to address social problems may be channeled into initiatives that further erode the potential for collective deliberation and collective response'.

Yet, if social relations are increasingly accommodated in the notion of the strong state and the free economy, then *neither* the state *nor* civil society will be the context of active democratic citizenship through which such broader issues can be addressed and social justice pursued. The reassertion of citizenship rights in education would seem to require the development of a new public sphere *between* the state and a marketized civil society, in which new forms of collective association can be developed. However, given what has been dismantled by New Right governments, creating a new public sphere in which educational matters can even be debated—let alone determined—poses considerable challenges. Foucault points out that what he called new forms of association, such as trade unions and political parties, arose in the nineteenth century as a counterbalance to the prerogative of the state, and that they acted as the seedbed of new ideas (Foucault 1988). We need to consider what might be the modern versions of these collectivist forms of association to counterbalance not only the prerogative of the state, but also that of the market.

Part of the challenge must be to move away from atomized decision-making to the reassertion of collective responsibility, without recreating the very bureaucratic systems whose shortcomings have helped to legitimate the current tendency to treat education as a private good rather than a public responsibility. We need to ask how can we use the positive aspects of choice and autonomy to facilitate community empowerment rather than exacerbating social differentiation. In England, the increasingly centrist Labour Party seems to have adopted many rightist policies, while the Left has done little yet to develop a concept of public education which looks significantly different from the state education so often criticized in the past for its role in reproducing and legitimating social inequalities (Young and Whitty 1977). And even if the social democratic era looks better in retrospect, and in comparison with current policies, than it did at the time, that does not remove the need to rethink what might be progressive policies for the next century. This is particularly important if, as Dale (1994) implies, neo-Keynesianism is not even on the agenda.

If new approaches are to be granted more legitimacy than previous ones, what new institutions might help to foster them—initially within a new public sphere in which ideas can be debated, but potentially as new forms of democratic governance themselves? Clearly, such institutions could take various forms and they will certainly need to take different forms in different societies. They will no doubt be struggled over, and some will be more open to hegemonic incorporation than others. Some may actually be created by the state, as the realization dawns that a marketized civil society itself creates contradictions that need to be managed. Thus, there is likely to be both a bottom-up and a top-down pressure to create new institutions within which struggles over the control of education will take place.

Careful consideration will need to be given to the composition, nature, and powers of new institutional forms if they are to prove an appropriate way of reasserting democratic citizenship-rights in education in the late twentieth century and beyond. They will also need to respond to critiques of the gender bias of conventional forms of political association in most modern societies. Paradoxically, current forms of democracy in England may be even less appropriate than those associated with directly elected School Boards in the nineteenth century, which used 'an advanced form of proportional representation [which] ensured that all the major political and religious groupings could be represented on the School Boards, so that positive policies at this level achieved a genuine consensus' (Simon 1994: 12). We now have to ask: what are the appropriate constituencies through which to express community interests in the late twentieth century? What do we mean by communities? What forms of democracy can express their complexity? How do we develop a radical pluralist conception of citizenship that involves creating unity without denying specificity (Mouffe 1992)?

Similar issues face the teaching profession. As Keith (1996: 70) puts it, in calling on teachers to foster the emergence of hitherto 'silenced voices', 'we need a new discourse that joins the themes of collaboration, care, commitment and community to those of difference, equity, rights, dialogue, and a wider sense of community'. Hargreaves (1994: 19) suggests that the conventional notion of professionalism is one 'which is grounded in notions of esoteric knowledge, specialist expertise and public status' and that this is being superseded by one which involves 'the exercise of discretionary judgement within conditions of unavoidable and perpetual uncertainty'. It is certainly the case that teachers will need to be responsive to changing demands, but it is also the case that there will be an expectation of accountability to constituencies that have tended to be ignored.

Both state control and market forces imply a 'low trust' relationship between society and its teachers, of the sort which currently exists in England and which Sullivan (1993) suggests is developing in New Zealand. Media characterizations of teacher unions often tend to encourage popular suspicion of teachers. Furthermore, the defence of the education service has too often been conducted within the assumptions of the 'old' politics of education, which involved consultation between government, employers, and unions but excluded whole constituencies—notably parents and business—to whom the New Right has subsequently successfully appealed (Apple and Oliver 1996). We need to ask some fundamental questions about who has a legitimate right to be involved in defining teacher professionalism. It is perhaps indicative of the paucity of thinking on this that some of the Left teacher educators who, 20 years ago, were criticizing the élitism of the professions, should now be amongst those suggesting that teachers should adopt the modes of self-regulation traditionally associated with the conservative professions of medicine and the law. Are state control, market forces, or professional self-governance the only models of accountability—or can we develop new models of teacher professionalism, based upon more participatory relationships with diverse communities?

In the Australian case, Knight *et al.* (1993) argue for what they call 'democratic professionalism', which seeks to demystify professional work and facilitate 'the participation in decision-making by students, parents and others'. They acknowledge a tension between the profession's claim to particular and specialist knowledge and expertise and a degree of relative autonomy, and a requirement that it be open to the needs and concerns of other groups in a democratic society. They also concede that 'the practice of open or democratic professionalism is largely lacking in formal teacher education' as it has traditionally been conducted.

Interestingly, they go on to posit alternative forms of teacher education that stress flexibility and diversity for a 'post-Fordist future'. In a way, this takes us back to where we began. Whether or not the changes that are taking place in education do reflect fundamental changes in modes of accumulation and modes of social solidarity, signalled by terms such as post-Fordism and post-modernity, they do need to be confronted. At the level of rhetoric (though not reality), the recent reforms of the New Right *have* probably been more responsive than their critics usually concede to those limited, but none the less tangible, social and cultural shifts that have been taking place in modern societies. A straightforward return to the old order of things would be neither feasible nor sensible. Social democratic approaches to education which continue to favour the idea of a common school are faced with the need to respond to increasing specialization and social diversity.

However, this does not necessarily mean that the only future for public education lies with the particular marketized forms that are currently fashionable. If we are to avoid the atomization of educational decision-making, and associated tendencies towards fragmentation and polarization between schools and within schools, we need to create new contexts for determining appropriate institutional and curricular arrangements on behalf of the whole society. This will require new forms of association in the public sphere within which citizen rights in education policy—and indeed other areas of public policy—can be reasserted against current trends towards both a restricted version of the state and a marketized civil society. Otherwise education will become merely a private consumption good rather than a public issue.

Acknowledgements

I am grateful to Hugh Lauder and Sally Power for their helpful comments on an earlier version of this paper.

Notes

1. For further discussion of the nature of these changes and their impact, see Whitty (1997).
2. This section of the paper draws on ch. 7 of Whitty *et al.* (1993).
3. For an extended discussion of this see Whitty (1993).
4. Whether this is actually happening is being investigated by the Modes of Teacher Education (MOTE) project, funded by the Economic and Social Research Council and designed to compare the nature, costs, and outcomes of different ways of training teachers.

References

Allen, J. (1992), 'Post-Industrialism and Post-

Fordism', in S. Hall, D. Held, and T. McGrew (eds.), *Modernity and its Futures* (Cambridge: Polity Press).

Apple, M. W., and Oliver, A. (1996), 'Becoming Right: Education and the Formation of Conservative Movements', in Apple, M. W., *Cultural Politics and Education* (New York: Teachers College Press).

Arnove, R. (1996), 'Neo-Liberal Education Policies in Latin America: Arguments in Favor and Against', paper delivered to the Comparative and International Education Society, Williamsburg, March 6–10.

Ball, S. (1990), *Politics and Policy Making: Explorations in Policy Sociology* (London: Routledge).

Barber, M. (1992), *Education and the Teacher Unions* (London: Cassell).

——, Rowe, G., and Whitty, G. (1995), 'School Development Planning: Towards a new Role for Teaching Unions?'

Blackmore, J. (1995), 'Breaking out from a Masculinist Politics of Education', in B. Limerick and B. Lingard (eds.), *Gender and Changing Education Management* (Rydalmere, NSW: Hodder Education).

Boyne, R., and Rattansi, A. (eds.) (1990), *Postmodernism and Society* (London: Macmillan).

Bowe, R., Ball, S., with Gold, A. (1992), *Reforming Education and Changing Schools* (London: Routledge).

Bridges, S. (1992), *Working in Tomorrow's Schools: Effects on Primary Teachers* (Christchurch: Univ. of Canterbury).

Broadbent, J., Laughlin, R., Shearn, D., and Dandy, N. (1993), 'Implementing Local Management of Schools: A Theoretical and Empirical Analysis', *Research Papers in Education*, 8/28: 149–76.

Callinicos, A. (1989), *Against Postmodernism: A Marxist Critique* (Cambridge: Polity Press).

Campbell, J., and Neill, S. (1994), *Curriculum at Key Stage 1: Teacher Commitment and Policy Failure* (Harlow: Longman).

Centre for Contemporary Cultural Studies (CCCS) (1981), *Unpopular Education* (London: Hutchinson).

Chubb, J., and Moe, T. (1990), *Politics, Markets and America's Schools* (Washington: Brookings Institution).

Clarke, J., and Newman, J. (1992), 'Managing to Survive: Dilemmas of Changing Organisational Forms in the Public Sector', paper presented to the Social Policy Association, Univ. of Nottingham, July.

Dale, R. (1989), *The State and Education Policy* (Milton Keynes: Open Univ. Press).

—— (1990), 'The Thatcherite Project in Education: The Case of the City Technology Colleges', *Critical Social Policy*, 9/3: 4–19.

—— (1994), 'Neo-Liberal and Neo-Schumpeterian Approaches to Education', paper presented

to a conference on '*Education, Democracy and Reform*', Univ. of Auckland, 13–14 August.

Flax, J. (1987), 'Postmodernism and Gender Relations in Feminist Theory', *Signs* 12/4: 621–43.

Foucault, M. (1988), *Politics/Philosophy/Culture*, ed. L. D. Kritzman (New York: Routledge).

Gamble, A. (1988), *The Free Economy and the Strong State* (London: Macmillan).

Gewirtz, S., Ball, S. J., and Bowe, R. (1995), *Markets, Choice and Equity* (Buckingham: Open Univ. Press).

—— and Ball, S. J. (1996), 'From Welfarism to New Managerialism: Shifting Discourses of School Leadership in the Education Quasi-Market'. Paper to Parental Choice and Market Forces Seminar, King's College, London.

Gitlin, A., and Margonis, F. (1995), 'The Political Aspect of Reform: Teacher Resistance as Good Sense', *American Journal of Education*, 103.

Glennerster, H. (1995), *British Social Policy since 1945* (Oxford: Blackwell).

Grace, G. (1995), *School Leadership: Beyond Education Management: An Essay in Policy Scholarship* (London: Falmer Press).

Green, A. (1990), *Education and State Formation* (London: Macmillan).

—— (1994), 'Postmodernism and State Education', *Journal of Education Policy*, 9/1: 67–84.

Halpin, D., Power, S., and Fitz, J. (1993), 'Opting into State Control? Headteachers and the paradoxes of Grant-maintained Status', *International Studies in the Sociology of Education*, 3/1: 3–23.

Hargreaves, A. (1994), *Changing Teachers, Changing Times: Teachers' Work and Culture in the Postmodern Age* (London: Cassell).

Harris, K. (1993), 'Power to the People? Local Management of Schools', *Education Links*, 45: 4–8.

Harvey, D. (1989). *The Condition of Postmodernity: An Enquiry into the Origins of Cultural Change* (Oxford: Basil Blackwell).

Hawk, K., and Hill, J. (1994), *Evaluation of Teacher Salaries Grant Scheme Trial: The Third Year* (Palmerston North: Massey Univ.).

Henig, J. R. (1994), *Rethinking School Choice: Limits of the Market Metaphor* (Princeton: Princeton Univ. Press).

Hickox, M. (1995), 'Situating Vocationalism', *British Journal of Sociology of Education*, 16/2: 153–63.

Hillgate Group (1987), *The Reform of British Education* (London: Claridge Press).

Hoyle. E. (1974), 'Professionality, Professionalism and Control in Teaching', *London Education Review*, 32

Jessop, B., Bonnett, K., Bromley, S., and Ling, T. (1987), 'Popular Capitalism, Flexible Accumulation and Left Strategy', *New Left Review*, 165: 104–23.

Jones, L., and Moore, R. (1993), 'Education, Competence and the Control of Expertise', *British Journal of Sociology of Education*, 14: 385–97.

Keith, N. Z. (1996), 'A Critical Perspective on Teacher Participation in Urban Schools', *Educational Administration Quarterly*, 32/1: 45–79.

Kenway, J. (1993), 'Marketing Education in the Postmodern Age', *Journal of Education Policy*, 8/1: 105–22.

Kerchner, C., and Mitchell, D. (1988), *The Changing Idea of a Teachers' Union* (London: Falmer Press).

Knight, J., Bartlett, L., and McWilliam, E. (eds.) (1993), *Unfinished Business: Reshaping the Teacher Education Industry for the 1990s* (Rockhampton: Univ. of Central Queensland).

Lash, S. (1990), *Sociology of Postmodernism* (London: Routledge).

Lauder, H., Hughes, D., Watson, S., Simiyu, I., Strathdee, R., and Waslander, S. (1995), *Trading in Futures: The Nature of Choice in Educational Markets in New Zealand* (Smithfield Project, Victoria: Univ. of Wellington).

Le Grand, J., and Bartlett, W. (1993), *Quasi-Markets and Social Policy* (London: Macmillan).

Le Grand, J. (1996), 'Knights, Knaves or Pawns? Human Behaviour and Social Policy', unpublished paper, School of Policy Studies, Univ. of Bristol.

Livingstone, I. (1994), *The Workloads of Primary School Teachers: A Wellington Region Survey* (Wellington: Chartwell Consultants).

Lowe, R. (1993), *The Welfare State in Britain since 1945* (London: Macmillan).

Maychell, K. (1994), *Counting the Cost: The Impact of LMS on Schools' Patterns of Spending* (Slough: National Foundation for Educational Research).

McKenzie, J. (1993), 'Education as a Private Problem or a Public Issue? The Process of Excluding "Education" from the "Public Sphere" ', paper presented at the International Conference on the Public Sphere, Manchester, 8–10 January.

Meehan, E. (1995), *Civil Society: Contribution to an ESRC/RSA seminar series on The State of Britain* (Swindon: Economic and Social Research Council).

Moe, T. (1994), 'The British Battle for Choice', in Billingsley, K. L. (ed.), *Voices on Choice: The Education Reform Debate* (San Francisco: Pacific Institute for Public Policy).

Mouffe, C. (ed.) (1992), *Dimensions of Radical Democracy: Pluralism, Citizenship, Democracy* (London: Verso).

Pollard, S. (1995), *Schools, Selection and the Left* (London: Social Market Foundation).

Popkewitz, T. S. (1994). 'Professionalization in Teaching and Teacher Education: Some Notes on its History, Ideology and Potential', *Teaching and Teacher Education*, 10/1:

Riddell, P. (1992), 'Is it the End of Politics?' *The Times*, 3 August.

Robins, K. (1991), 'Tradition and Translation: National Culture in its Global Context', in J. Corner and S. Harvey (eds.), *Enterprise and Heritage: Crosscurrents of National Culture* (London: Routledge).

Simon, B. (1994), *The State and Educational Change* (London: Lawrence and Wishart).

Sinclair, J., Ironside, M., and Seifert, R. (1993), 'Classroom Struggle? Market Oriented Education Reforms and their Impact on Teachers' Professional Autonomy, Labour Intensification and Resistance', paper presented to the International Labour Process Conference, 1 April.

Smith, T., and Noble, M. (1995), *Education Divides: Poverty and Schooling in the 1990s* (London: Child Poverty Action Group).

Sullivan, K. (1994), 'The Impact of Education Reform on Teachers' Professional Ideologies', *New Zealand Journal of Educational Studies*, 29/1: 3–20.

Thompson, K. (1992), 'Social Pluralism and Postmodernity', in S. Hall, D. Held, and T. McGrew (eds.), *Modernity and its Futures* (Cambridge: Polity Press).

Urahn, S., and Stewart, D. (1994), *Minnesota Charter Schools: A Research Report* (St Paul, MN: Research Department, Minnesota House of Representatives).

Whitty, G. (1989), 'The New Right and the National Curriculum: State Control or Market Forces?' *Journal of Education Policy*, 4/4: 329–41.

—— (1993), 'Education Reform and Teacher Education in England in the 1990s', in P. Gilroy and M. Smith (eds.), *International Analyses of Teacher Education* (JET Papers One) (Oxford: Carfax).

—— (1994), 'Devolution in Education Systems: Implications for Teacher Professionalism and Pupil Performance', in National Industry Education Forum: *Decentralisation and Teachers: Report of a Seminar* (Melbourne: National Industry Education Forum).

—— (1997), 'Creating Quasi-Markets in Education: A Review of Recent Research on Parental Choice and School Autonomy in Three Countries', *Review of Research in Education*, 22.

——, Edwards, T., and Gewirtz, S. (1993), *Specialisation and Choice in Urban Education: The City Technology College Experiment* (London: Routledge).

Wohlstetter, P., Smyer, R., and Mohrman, S. A. (1994), 'New Boundaries for School-Based Management: The High Involvement Model', *Educational Evaluation and Policy Analysis*, 16/3: 268–86.

Wylie, C. (1994), *Self Managing Schools in New Zealand: The Fifth Year* (Wellington: New Zealand Council for Educational Research).

Young, M. and Whitty, G. (eds.) (1977), *Society, State and Schooling* (Lewes: Falmer Press).

20

Politics, Markets, and Democratic Schools: On the Transformation of School Leadership

Gerald Grace

> The whole world is being swept by a realisation that markets have tremendous advantages over central control and bureaucracy.
> (CHUBB AND MOE 1992: 46)

The Market and Strong Leadership as Salvationist Symbols

In reporting to Americans on *A Lesson in School Reform From Great Britain*, Chubb and Moe (1992) are convinced that the radical education reforms of the 1980s and 1990s in Britain have much to teach the American educational system about decentralization, competition, and choice. From their perspective, direct democratic control of schooling in America exercised by communities, state legislatures, and school boards has simply resulted in bureaucratic domination rather than democratic responsiveness or effective scholarly performance. For Chubb and Moe, democracy as a system of governance for schools has failed. The salvation of America's schools in the future will be found not in the culture and procedures of democracy, but in the culture and dynamics of the market democracy. Market 'democracy' by the empowerment of parents and students through resource-related choices in education has the potential, according to Chubb and Moe, to produce greater responsiveness and academic effectiveness. British educational reform, and in particular the strong contemporary emphasis upon choice in an educational market, is seen to be the way forward for American reform. Britain has 'boldly' implemented a market democracy in education through various mechanisms for the empowerment of choice, but within government guidelines:

Choice is not a free market system. Its educational markets operate within an institutional framework and the government's job is to design the framework ... If this framework is designed with care and

concern markets can be allowed to work their wonders with it—for everyone's benefit. (Chubb and Moe 1992: 10–11)

This 1992 report to the American people, reinforced by interviews with a small and unrepresentative sample of English headteachers,[1] gives the impression that market democracy in schooling is already 'working its wonders' for the transformation of English schooling culture. This being so, Americans are encouraged not to be left behind:

In fundamental respects then Britain is not unique. What is happening here is happening in the United States: the problems, the reforms, the conflict, and the alliances are all roughly the same. The only real difference is that Britain, owing to its parliamentary form of government, has been able to move further and faster toward a radical overhaul of its educational system—and is far more likely to succeed. (Chubb and Moe 1992: 50)

There are four issues arising out of Chubb and Moe's enthusiastic advocacy of policy importation from England to the United States. The first concerns the underlying assumptions that self-managed schools in a market context will deliver educational outcomes of the kind they envisage. The second turns on the question of why they place so much emphasis on *leadership* in delivering these outcomes; and the third relates to the *uncritical* importation of policy from England to the United States. The fourth is the most crucial of all, for it involves an exploration of the possibilities for an alternative, community-based democratic model of school rather than the flawed market model favoured by Chubb and Moe. These issues are dealt with in turn.

The Assumptions Underlying the Concept of the Self-Managed School

Chubb and Moe represent the strong form of the self-managed school, in a market context, as follows:

Schools would be legally autonomous; free to govern themselves as they want, specify their own goals and programmes and methods, design their own organisations, select their own student bodies, and make their own personnel decisions. Parents and students would be legally empowered to choose among alternative schools. (1990: 226)

Thus the vision for the future has been a scenario of varied and free-standing schools, characterized by strong leadership at the individual-site level, and responsive to the market democracy of consumer choice.

What is the problem with this vision of American education in the twenty-first century? The advocates of market policies in education like Chubb and Moe tend to conflate two contradictory sets of interests in setting out their claims for the advantages of choice and competition in education by arguing that educational markets get the incentives right for parents *and* teachers. Chubb and Moe emphasize the ability of schools to select their students; and this is at the heart of the problem for, in principle, schools' ability to select means that their interests are opposed to those of parents in an educational market. In a competitive context in which official results and unofficial reputations count, the logic of the market generates pressure on schools to recruit the students most likely to succeed academically. Here, social class and ethnicity stand as good predictors of subsequent academic achievement (see Lauder Ch. 25). For parents the aim is to be able to enrol their children in the school of their choice irrespective of the judgements schools make about which type of student is most likely to succeed academically. Research shows that where schools have the power to select their students, bias on the basis of social class and ethnicity become more pronounced (Moore and Davenport 1990; Lauder *et al*. 1995).

Given this documented bias in schools that are able to select their students, what are the grounds for arguing for self-managed schools able to select their students? Lauder *et al*. (1995) suggest there are two arguments that have been used to defend the ability of schools to select their students. The first is based on efficiency, the second on a form of academic élitism. Researchers like Chubb and Moe establish their position on the basis of the first argument. According to them, efficiency derives from the opportunity schools have to define their core business (just as a firm in private enterprise might) and to select students on that basis. So, in principle, some schools may decide to specialize in high academic levels of achievement while others will specialize in alternative philosophies and teaching methods which eschew credential success. There are two central problems with this view. The competition for academic credentials, reinforced by school results and reputations, makes it difficult for 'alternative' schools to survive. In such a competitive context schools with less credential success will generally be considered less desirable, and the effect will be to ghettoize children in specific schools according to social class or ethnicity.

As a result of giving schools the power to select there is a contradiction between what may be considered in the interests of specific schools and what is in the public interest. Selecting the most able students may serve the interests of a school that can do so, but only at a cost to the system as a whole. The creation of schools with few highly achieving students is certainly not in the public interest. In effect, what enrolment schemes in a market context do is to create the potential for a covert system of selection on the basis of class and ethnicity.

For advocates of academic élitism there may seem to be little wrong with such a system of selection. Indeed, in England the claim has been made (see Brown Ch. 26) that the introduction of educational markets was designed to break down the comprehensive system in favour of a return to the former selective system, albeit by other means. The aim of such a system of selection is to improve academic standards of excellence by concentrating the most able students together in a few élite institutions. However, the view that a concentration of such students leads to better subsequent academic performance at university is doubtful. The research conducted in this field, although still in the early stages of development, does not support such a view (Hughes, Lauder, and Strathdee 1991; 1996). At the same time, the costs of such a creaming off of 'talent' is likely to be high if, as is likely, better-balanced schools in terms of social-class mix create better results for the majority of students in them (see McPherson and Willms Ch. 42).

The fundamental difficulty for the proponents of marketization rests in conflating the interests of individual schools with the interests of the system as a whole and hence the national interest. Neither efficiency nor élitism are likely to be able to act as justifications for the marked differences in school selection caused by the freedom individual schools have to determine student selection. Clearly the basis for their enthusiasm for the English market system of education needs, at best, to be heavily qualified and at worst is irredeemably flawed.

However, this is but the first of the problems with their position.

The Questionable Merits of 'Strong' Leadership

In their earlier work Chubb and Moe (1990: 229) argue that 'there are many paths to democracy and public education' and do not argue for any particular form of school organization so long as schools are subject to market competition. However, by the time they come to write *A Lesson in School Reform from Great Britain* their view has changed to one in which they see leadership embodied in one strong person as the key to change. The subtext is clearly that they envisage a hierarchical form of executive leadership driven by the vision of the self-managed, market-oriented school. Why the change? The answer lies in the quotation cited earlier, where they refer to 'conflicts and alliances' being the same in England as in the United States. Chubb and Moe are advocates of public-choice theory which predicts that teachers will resist the introduction of market forces into education because it will mean that their jobs are threatened if they and their schools don't perform (see Lauder Ch. 25). Clearly if this view is taken then the type of educational 'reform' advocated by Chubb and Moe must be imposed, and it is principals who are cast in the role of the vanguard of the new order. But this conflict approach to educational change raises the question of whether the means justify the ends. The ends we have seen are dubious,

the means even more so. As Whitty (Ch. 19) notes, where educational change has been imposed it has led to a lowering of morale, offending the canons of management which claim that it is through participation in decision-making that the vision for a school is 'owned' by all its members. Therefore, imposing a new system of education on unwilling participants does not augur well for its success; however, the problem is compounded when it is based on the importation of a model from a context the authors clearly do not understand. To understand the difficulties of importing policy models we need to appreciate the historical and comparative dimensions of the question of educational leadership, something Chubb and Moe manifestly fail to do.

The English Context of School Leadership and the Problems of Policy Importation

Research undertaken with more extensive samples of headteachers (Ball 1994; Grace 1995) suggests a more complex picture than Chubb and Moe care to paint. It is far from obvious that English schooling culture is being swept by the realization that market democracy has tremendous advantages. The majority of English headteachers have experienced a much more contradictory matrix of changes, involving the simultaneous impact of increased central control and bureaucracy on the one hand and moves towards a deregulated education market on the other, a recognition that markets in education intensify the 'winner'—'loser' syndrome, and an acute sense of the moral, ethical, and professional dilemmas which markets generate for school leaders.

English headteachers, as school leaders, have deplored the action of a strong state in the 1980s in attempting 'bold and rapid' transformation of schooling culture without due processes of professional and democratic consultation. While the majority of headteachers have welcomed the greater freedom for manoeuvre involved in local management of schools, they have wished to operate that freedom in a responsible relationship with reformed local democracy in education, and not as individual cultural entrepreneurs in the marketplace. It is a misrepresentation of the present state of schooling culture in England to imply that the market vision has been endorsed either by the majority of English school leaders (governors and headteachers) or by a majority of parents and community members.[2]

It is possible to represent headteacher resistance to market democracy as professional conservatism, vested interest, and 'fear of freedom', as Public Choice theorists like Chubb and Moe would. On the other hand, it is possible to interpret it as an informed professional judgement about the limitations of market values when applied in schooling.

Whatever interpretation is adopted, it cannot be denied that the historically autonomous tradition of English school leadership does not articulate easily with either democratic control (as realized in the local education authority, empowered governing bodies, or community forum) or with market control (as realized in greater inter-school competitiveness and empowered educational consumers). Nevertheless, these are the challenges which face contemporary headteachers.

At this historical juncture, English school leadership is at a major cultural turning point. The established cultural practices and the old leadership settlements are breaking up and new patterns are emerging. The critical question is, what will shape these new patterns and what form will they take?

English school leadership has moved historically from being the property of a dominant class to being the practice of a dominant leader. It has moved again from being the practice of a dominant leader to being a shared enterprise with teachers and school governors (Grace 1995). Now, in an era of enhanced accountability in schooling, it has to construct new relationships and a new sense of vision. If headteachers are, as educational leaders, the facilitators of a strategic vision and the articulators of fundamental principles, then it is clear that they have a crucial role in the transition of English schooling to greater democratic accountability in some form. At present the strategic choice appears to be consumer accountability mediated by a relationship with an educational market, or a democratic accountability mediated by a relationship with the whole community of citizens. The question for educational judgement and for

educational leadership is, which is the best path?

English headteachers are cautious about taking the path of consumer 'democracy' in education. Their professional caution as educational leaders arises in most cases because they believe that market forces and market values in education will be inimical to educational and professional values. Consumer accountability has, in their view, the potential to distort values and relationships and the nature of education itself. How could schooling in England, which has at its heart a concern for religious, moral, ethical, and value issues, and for the equitable nurture of all children and young people, become accountable to market 'democracy' which cannot give a special place to any of these considerations? Can an essentially moral enterprise be accountable to an essentially amoral agency?

Most headteachers do not believe that markets will work miracles. They recognize that markets might work wonders for a minority of schools, but to the disadvantage of other schools and communities. Observing the potential effects of market accountability from a professional standpoint which endorses the serious pursuit of equality of educational opportunity results in deep scepticism that social equity in education will be an outcome of market forces in practice.

However, if English headteachers are cautious about the path of consumer accountability and market 'democracy', they are also cautious about that of greater community accountability. There is an ambivalence towards the new partnerships with empowered school governors as providing the first stage towards a fuller realization of community involvement in educational decision-making. A long historical concern to protect the proper sphere of professional autonomy in education has resulted in a generally defensive stance to ideas for greater community involvement in the setting of the educational mission of the school. English teacher professionalism has been constructed at a distance from political, economic, and community interests. This has been its particular form of legitimated professionalism (Grace 1987).

While, in principle, the dilemma in the 1990s for English headteachers as school leaders is whether they should take the path of market or community accountability in schooling,[3] this formulation of the leadership dilemma is over simplified. In the first place, the 'options' are heavily constrained by government empowerment of, and advocacy for, market accountability. This, in political terms, is the option of the 'real world'. Once a group of school leaders begins to operate upon market principles in their locality, it becomes difficult for other adjacent schools to opt out of competitive marketing relationships. This means that despite professional reservations about market accountability, the responsibility of educational leaders to ensure institutional survival in competitive conditions removes the notion that there is a policy option. English headteachers are not unfamiliar with a political discourse which simultaneously articulates 'choice' and the injunction 'there is no alternative'.[4]

For those headteachers who are attracted to market accountability, generally from the base of a strongly resourced school, new forms of executive and entrepreneurial leadership have their rewards. These rewards may be immediate and tangible in salary and status enhancements, or micro-political in strengthening the power relations of their executive school leadership. In other words, democratic accountability to an *external* market need not result in greater *internal* democracy in a school, as Chubb and Moe appreciate, but rather to a renaissance, in modern form, of earlier hierarchical traditions of headship. The 'headmaster tradition' becomes transposed into the new chief-executive mode (still largely patriarchal). Both have strong leadership connotations.

Against such structural empowerment, external pressures, and internal inducements to take the path of market accountability in schooling, the 'option' for greater democratic accountability to the community seems theoretical, a construct of the educational seminar rather than of the culture of practical school leadership. Such a view arises, however, only if school leaders in England remain parochial in outlook, immune to the moral and social principles which should inform education. If Gutmann's (1987) argument for the moral primacy of democratic education is accepted, then the moral primacy of accountability to the community rather than to the market can be asserted. From this perspective 'democratic community' is the larger and morally prior concept, which subsumes market relations as one sector of its activities and field of opera-

tion. Education's responsibilities are therefore primarily to the democracy of citizens rather than to the democracy of consumers.

However, it is one thing to claim moral primacy for an educative relationship; but quite another thing to show that such a relationship can be realized in practice. It is here that the comparative study of already existing forms of democratic education and of democratic educational leadership assumes importance. Although different models of educational practice cannot be simplistically transposed from one cultural setting to another, the critical examination of such models can provide the basis for appropriate cultural adaptation. If educational leadership in England, for instance, is to make any serious move in the direction of greater democratic accountability, then lessons must be learned from other historical and cultural settings—and there are models from which to learn (see Jensen and Walker 1989).

One of these settings is the United States, for while Chubb and Moe (1990; 1992) have suggested that constitutional democratic control has been the pattern of American schooling and that it has clearly failed, it is by no means obvious that their assertions represent a consensus of American educators or of American citizens. There are other claims, that the schooling system of the USA demonstrates various types of democratic control and leadership, and that some of these types are associated with greater responsiveness and greater educational effectiveness (e.g. Rollow and Bryk 1994). In other words, the suggestion that America can learn from Britain about educational markets, rather than Britain learning from America about educational democracy in action, seems premature. The schooling system of the USA has historically been a vast and complex setting for the realization of forms of democratic leadership in education. There is much to be learned from this democratic culture of schooling, and it is premature to conclude that it has been tried and that it has failed.

In the debates which must take place about the future of education and of educational leadership, existing school leaders have a particular responsibility. In England, for instance, school governors and headteachers are strategically placed to be the providers of a vision for the future. It is important that they resist complete immersion in day-to-day management concerns to find the spaces and the settings for the exercise of reflective leadership and to consider the alternatives to market accountability. However, it will not be easy to do so. As Ball (1994: 59) has noted, the present government has sought to put the tenets of Public Choice theory into practice:

the ethical and ideological position of the head-teacher is crucial. It seems undeniable that the government intended to capture and reconstruct the headteacher as the key actor in the process of reform and redefinition.

There are rewards in collaborating with this powerful ideological transformation, and there are stark institutional consequences for those who do not, as has been noted. What the present conjunction demonstrates is the historical isolation and vulnerability of the professional culture of English headteachers. Formed in the contexts of an insulated professional autonomy, headteachers have had little experience of working in sustained democratic relationships, either within the school or within the wider community; but the democratization of school headship is now the only alternative to its reworking as the chief executive of 'education plc. (school division)'.

Towards An Alternative Community-Based Democratic Model of Educational Administration

The work of Stewart Ranson (1993; 1994*a*; 1994*b*) suggests a counter-hegemonic agenda to the commodification of schooling:

The creation of a moral and political order that expresses and enables an active citizenship within the public domain is the challenge of the modern era. The task is to regenerate or constitute more effectively than ever before a public—an educated public—that has the capacity to participate actively as citizens in the shaping of a learning society and polity. (Ranson 1994*a*: 105)

Such a project can be achieved, according to Ranson, if community participation in education is supported, educated for, and encouraged by politicians, policy-makers, and education professionals, particularly headteachers. The creation of the political, structural, and ideological conditions for such a transformation will only be found if there are radical changes in the constitution and control

of the central and the local state. Even if such transformations were to come about by the political process, the cultural and moral consolidation of a new order of active citizenship would be a key responsibility of schooling and a key responsibility for headteachers. There is little precedent for this in English schooling culture or in the traditions of English school headship. However it does seem evident that headship itself is already in a process of transformation. If English headteachers do not want, in the main, to be recontextualized as strong leader-entrepreneurs, then it would seem that, collectively, through their local and regional associations and their national organizations, they must clearly set for themselves an alternative project.

There is evidence that in reaction against market forces and market culture in education some headteachers are perceiving a valuable democratic potential in recent changes in school governance in England:

Even after ten years' headship in English schools, I have never quite got to grips with the concept of 'my' school and the inherent autocracy encapsulated in it . . . Too many English schools were ruled by none-too-benevolent despots! Many working-class governors have real power in school now. I applaud this.   (Secondary headteacher)
There are potential conflicts, but only those irked by the diminution of the illegitimate power that headteachers have wielded in the past find these threatening.   (Secondary headteacher)
There may have been a golden age of English headship—but only because heads were able to lead, govern, and rule without any real challenge to their authority . . . it would be great to see real community power taking over.

            (Secondary headteacher)
            (Grace 1995: 84–5)

While such responses are not typical of head-teacher reactions in general, they may demonstrate the beginning of a process whereby headteachers are prepared to embrace conceptions of an active public culture in education rather than simply seeing this as a source of 'interference' in their own professional jurisdiction.[5] However, it is also clear that such possibilities will not be realized on any significant scale unless continuing professional development and continuing adult-education programmes are available to resource these new conceptions and working relationships. As both White (1982; 1983) and Rizvi (1989) have pointed out, democratic leadership and more organizational democracy in schools must be educated for. At present English headteachers are being 'trained' to deal with finance, management, public relations, and markets. They have yet to be seriously educated for working in a democratic, public culture of schooling. Similarly, newly empowered school governors require an induction into conceptions of community education as well as into their responsibilities in school-site and budget management.[6]

The realization of active citizenship at child, youth, and adult levels in education, as a serious practice (rather than a political rhetoric), requires major cultural and resource inputs, just as the oppositional project to realize active consumership has commanded such resources from many agencies.

A serious culture of active citizenship in education would have the potential to prioritize community before market, citizen before consumer, and public good before individual self-interest. Thus stated, this appears to be an agenda for civic virtue rather than for the dynamics of the 'real world'. However, this is a false dichotomy. English schooling culture has always attempted moral, spiritual, and civic formation of various types and for various social and political ends. One of the socio-historical problems with this is that English schools have often constituted themselves too much as insulated 'museums of virtue' (Waller 1965). Their moral culture has focused upon the shaping of the individual and of the member of the 'school community', but not in any explicit sense upon the moral or the political shaping of the citizen for democratic public culture and public participation.[7]

There can be little doubt that the reworking of the school as an entrepreneurial enterprise and the reworking of the position of headteacher as chief executive is bringing the era of the school as a museum of virtue to a rapid end. Ranson's (1994a) project for a new moral and social mission, constructed in partnership with local democratic community, provides an alternative destiny for English schools. In the realization or impeding of that project, headteachers as school leaders will have a crucial role to play.

There is evidence that in reaction against the individualizing and competitive tendencies of the market in education, headteachers in some areas have strengthened their already existing local professional networks to provide support groups to deal with the intensification of external pressures of various types:

It is probably because so many demands are being put upon us . . . that we have started to pull together more. Local heads have tended to start grouping . . . they have been morally supportive . . . we are fighting against it (the market).

(Primary headteacher, Grace 1995: 134)

There is an interesting paradox and contradiction emerging in English schooling culture. Whereas the introduction of local management of schools and of market forces in education is clearly premised upon a construct of the individual, empowered headteacher, the intensification of external pressures is causing some headteachers to combine together in local and regional groupings more intensively than before. While these groupings exist to fulfil a range of purposes, it is clear that they provide a countervailing professional community setting in which the worse excesses of market culture in education can be resisted. Similar developments have been noted in the reaction of New Zealand school principals to the growth of competitive market culture (see Waslander and Thrupp Ch. 29).[8] Such professional community groupings among headteachers and principals could make an important contribution to the empowerment of a public culture in education if they extended their remit and their terms of reference to include members of the wider community in discussion of developments in education policy and practice. This would require headteachers to go beyond a 'professional community' grouping to embrace a more radical notion of a Community Forum on Education. The idea of a Community Forum was first articulated in 1988 in New Zealand during the education reform processes of the fourth Labour government. The Forum was intended to be a setting in which all interested citizens in a given locality could meet with education professionals and policy-makers, to give added strength to the notion of a public culture in education and to have opportunities to exercise active citizenship in education through discussion of salient issues. As was noted at the time:

the potential empowerment of communities through the agency of Community Forum marked a distinct shift from Labour's traditional reliance upon educational bureaucracy. (Grace 1990: 181).

In the event, such potential was not realized in New Zealand because of the defeat of the Labour government and the coming to power of a different political and ideological order. However, the concept of a Community Education Forum is potentially fruitful for the development of a serious public culture in education, as opposed to either a professional culture ('provider capture') or a market culture ('consumer capture').[9] Existing groupings of headteachers and principals could provide the growth point for such democratic developments. With the incremental weakening of the local education state as a countervailing force against central state power, with the scepticism about educational bureaucracy, the alternative is not, as Chubb and Moe (1992) suggest, an uncritical celebration of market forces in education. This only leaves the state stronger than ever. A serious alternative is the reform of local democracy in education (Cordingley and Kogan 1993), part of which could include the establishment of Community Education Forums working with the local and regional networks of headteachers and school governors. If New Right ideological agencies are currently attempting to rework the position of the headteacher as market innovator, there is no reason why Centre Left agencies should not support the project of reworking the position of the headteacher as community innovator.[10] For English schooling culture this would be a radical conception which might 'work wonders for everyone's benefit', including observers from across the Atlantic, like Chubb and Moe.

Notes

1. The number of headteachers interviewed by Chubb and Moe (1992) is not stated but appears to be between 6 and 10, most of whom were heads of grant-maintained schools.
2. Despite massive government publicity in favour of the grant-maintained school, for instance, only 1,000 schools have opted for this relatively autonomous status. As a proportion of Britain's 25,000, schools this suggests that English parents are not endorsing the breakup of the local education community service in favour of individual school advantage.
3. In formal terms, this is a decision for school governing bodies, in so far as they have any discretion within the strong parameters of government policy. However, it is posed as a dilemma for headteachers because in most cases school governing bodies are still likely to look to the professional leader for guidance on this issue.
4. One of the contradictions of English political and policy discourse is that 'choice' is celebrated while at the same time there is a resourced 'right answer'.
5. English headteachers, in the early stages of shared leadership with school governors, are still using the language of 'interference' in some cases, rather than of 'partnership' (see Grace 1995: 83–4).
6. The culture of training puts an emphasis upon specific skills and competences. The culture of education focuses upon issues of principle and of values. While both are clearly necessary, the culture of training is currently in the ascendant position in headteacher professional development.
7. The cultural inhibition here has resulted from a fear that citizenship education could easily become an instrument for indoctrination. However, it may be noted that much contemporary indoctrination on the superiority of market solutions is currently in progress.
8. For an important analysis of New Right ideology and of its educational implications in New Zealand, see Lauder (1990).
9. New Right ideological critiques of state education make constant use of a discourse of 'provider capture'. However, there is much less attention given to the counterphenomenon of 'consumer capture'. The education service of a given community should clearly be 'captured' by neither providers nor consumers; rather, it should be in the possession of local citizens.
10. It could be countered that English headteachers in general showed little enthusiasm for notions of community education in the 1960s and 1970s. However, this was the period when social democratic and legitimated professionalism gave them strong protection from external influences and little incentive to open themselves to the wider community.

References

Ball, S. J. (1994), *Education Reform: A Critical and Post-Structural Approach* (Buckingham: Open Univ. Press).

Chubb, J., and Moe, T. (1990), *Politics, Markets and America's Schools* (Washington DC: Brookings Institution).

—— (1992), *A Lesson in School Reform from Great Britain* (Washington DC: Brookings Institution).

Cordingley, P., and Kogan, M. (1993), *In Support of Education: Governing the Reformed System* (London: Jessica Kingsley).

Grace, G. R. (1987), 'Teachers and the State in Britain: A Changing Relation', in Lawn, M., and Grace, G. (eds.), *Teachers: The Culture and Politics of Work* (London: Falmer Press).

—— (1990), 'Labour and Education: The Crisis and Settlements of Education Policy', in Holland, M., and Boston, J. (eds.), *The Fourth Labour Government: Politics and Policy in New Zealand* (Auckland: Oxford Univ. Press).

—— (1995), *School Leadership: Beyond Education Management: An Essay in Policy Scholarship* (London: Falmer Press).

Gutmann, A. (1987), *Democratic Education* (Princeton: Princeton Univ. Press).

Hughes, D., Lauder, H., and Strathdee, R. (1991), 'University Performance of Pupils from State and Independent Schools in New Zealand', *Access*, 10/1: 1–7.

—— (1996), 'First-Year University Performance as a Function of Type of Secondary School Attended and Gender', *New Zealand Journal of Educational Studies*, 31/1 (Forthcoming).

Jensen, K., and Walker, S. (1989) (eds.), *Towards Democratic Schooling: European Experiences* (Milton Keynes, Open Univ. Press).

Lauder, H. (1990), 'The New Right Revolution and Education in New Zealand', in *New Zealand Education Policy Today: Critical Perspectives* (Wellington: Allen and Unwin).

—— Hughes, D., Watson, S., Simyu, I., Strathdee, R., and Waslander, S. (1995), *Trading in Futures: The Nature of Choice in Educational Markets in New Zealand* (Wellington: Ministry of Education).

Moore, D., and Davenport, S. (1990), 'Choice: The New Improved Sorting Machine', in Boyd, W., and Walberg, H. (eds.), *Choice in Education: Potential and Problems* (Berkeley, Calif.: McCutchan).

Ranson, S. (1993), 'Markets or Democracy for Education', *British Journal of Education Studies*, 41/4: 333–52.

—— (1994a), *Towards the Learning Society* (London: Cassell).

—— and Stewart, J. (1994b), *Management for the Public Domain: Enabling the Learning Society* (London: Macmillan).

Rizvi, F. (1989), 'In Defence of Organisational Democracy', in Smyth, J. (ed.), *Critical Perspectives on Educational Leadership* (London: Falmer Press).

Rollow, S., and Bryk, A. (1994), 'Democratic Politics and School Improvement: The Potential of Chicago School Reform', in Marshall, C. (ed.), *The New Politics of Race and Gender* (London: Falmer Press).

Waller, W. (1965), *The Sociology of Teaching* (New York: Wiley).

Waslander, S., and Thrupp, M. (1995), 'Choice, Competition and Segregation: An Empirical Analysis of a New Zealand Secondary School Market 1990–93', *Journal of Educational Policy*, 10: 1–26.

White, P. (1982), 'Democratic Perspectives on the Training of Headteachers', *Oxford Review of Education*, 8/1: 69–82.

—— (1983), *Beyond Domination: An Essay in the Political Philosophy of Education* (London: Routledge and Kegan Paul).

21

Assessment, Accountability, and Standards: Using Assessment to Control the Reform of Schooling[1]

Harry Torrance

Introduction

Over recent years governments around the world, but perhaps particularly in the United Kingdom, have alighted upon assessment as a key mechanism for both monitoring and improving standards of educational achievement in schools. Of course, student scores, derived in various ways from various sorts of tests and examinations, have traditionally provided a fairly *ad hoc*, taken-for-granted indication of overall standards within a school system, as well as indicating the particular achievements of individual students within that system. But such tests and exams were developed first and foremost to generate evidence about individuals for purposes of certification and selection rather than to provide data on the system as a whole. It is only much more recently that changes in assessment practices and procedures have been undertaken in order to monitor school systems *as systems*, and, furthermore, that such changes in assessment have been used to intervene directly in the operation of school systems through the underpinning of specific curriculum changes, or through the impact of accountability pressures invoked by the publication of test results, or both.

These developments beg some severe questions about the logic, practicality, and actual impact of such intervention strategies. Are standards falling? What exactly do we mean by standards anyway? Can more testing raise standards? If so, how? If not, why not, and how else might changes in assessment assist in improving the quality of educational provision in our schools? With respect to the UK,[2] the government's basic position seems to be that improving educational standards is of paramount importance in improving economic competitiveness within an increasingly competitive global economy, and that a new national assessment framework will help to raise standards by setting publicly accessible targets; measuring whether or not they have been met; encouraging schools to compete with each other by publishing the results; and allowing parents to choose their children's schools and tying finance in part to student numbers, while at the same time using the new assessment regime to underpin the introduction of a National Curriculum. However, these various elements of the government's strategy are not in themselves 'a proven and essential way towards raising standards' (DES 1987: 10), despite the government's oft-repeated claims; nor do they form a coherent and compatible whole. The purpose of this chapter is to review both the rationale for such a strategy and the evidence, such as it is, that has been generated about changes in educational standards, before going on to a broader discussion about the ways in which changes in assessment might be used more positively to underpin curriculum change and the pursuit of higher standards.

What do we Mean by Standards?

A first step in such a review is briefly to acknowledge that the terms of the debate are usually dominated by a view of standards as defined by scholarly, academic, subject-based achievement, and measured by traditional forms of timed, written tests (essays and multiple-choice formats). There are two basic issues here: first, such measures pay no regard to the many other personal, practical, and social outcomes of schooling that most governments (and individuals) would claim are important. It is not the purpose of this chapter to develop such a critique further, although the unanticipated consequences of focusing too narrowly on test and examination results as indicators of achievement will be returned to. Such criticism must be acknowledged, however, since even if and when we find evidence of rising or falling academic standards we would need far wider evidence before making claims about the quality of overall educational provision and educational achievement (see Gray and Wilcox (1995) for a discussion of other elements, such as the quality of teacher–student relationships).

Second, we must ask whether or not the academic goals which exams do measure, are worthwhile in their own terms. The content of traditional school-curriculum subjects is constantly changing (often to incorporate aspects of the practical and the social aspects of knowledge within subject boundaries). Thus standards could be said to be changing (and perhaps becoming more socially and economically 'relevant'), but whether or not this means they are being raised or lowered involves a value-judgement about the role and purpose of contemporary schooling. However, change in the curriculum usually involves expansion rather than contraction, in the area of skills and processes as well as content (witness the still-continuing debate about 'slimming down' the National Curriculum, Dearing 1993a; b). Thus far more investigation, understanding, analysis, application, and communication are included in the school curriculum than hitherto, and one would be justified in claiming that our goals for the school system are expanding in both scope and scale. We are demanding that more students learn more things about more complex topics than ever before.

Rising or Falling Standards?

We may be demanding more, but is more being achieved? If one were to take the public and political debate about standards at face value over the last 25 years, starting with the 'Black Paper' critics of comprehensivization (Cox and Dyson 1968) and continuing through the 'Great Debate' of the 1970s up to and beyond the introduction of the National Curriculum, the answer would be a resounding 'no'. In fact, however, the evidence is far more positive. A key element in the rhetoric that has been used to justify government intervention is a general belief that educational standards in the UK are not only too low, but falling. Standards have been consistently, if anecdotally, identified as low and getting lower, with schools being blamed for young people's lack of qualifications, skills, and overall employability. It is little coincidence that these criticisms were voiced at the same time as youth unemployment became a major social concern and issues of global economic competition came to dominate political and economic debate (see Brown and Lauder 1992). Of course this is not to say that coincidence equates to cause and effect; for example, one could hardly blame the primary schools of the late 1970s and early 1980s for the concurrent problems of school leavers who had first entered their primary schools more than 10 years before. Nevertheless it was not just the upper years of secondary schools, but the education system as a whole which became the focus of concern throughout the 1980s, and clearly, the government perceived both a real problem in terms of skills, attitudes, and competitiveness, and a political problem in terms of being seen by the electorate to be 'doing something' about it.

Thus the DES booklet which first outlined the thrust of the 1988 legislation introducing National Curriculum and Testing asserted that progress on raising educational standards 'has been variable, uncertain and often slow' (DES 1987: 2). More recently, the first report issued by HMI under new inspection arrangements has been seized on (not least by the Chief Inspector himself in an associated lecture) as evidence that standards are, if anything, still getting worse rather than better (*Guardian* 1 February 1995; *TES* 27 January 1995). Actually the report included much the same sort of figures as HMI reports often include, with 30 to 40 per cent of observed lessons judged as 'good or very good', another 40 per cent 'satisfactory', and 20 to 30 per cent 'unsatisfactory or poor'; overall, a more considered review published a week later suggested that 'educational standards were starting to rise' (*TES* 3 March 1995: 4). In similar vein, the 1995 GCSE results attracted front-page headlines suggesting a 'slump' in standards (*The Times* 24 August 1995) despite reflecting very marginal changes over the previous year. Clearly there are issues here concerning the political and commercial agenda of newspapers as well as the legitimatory rhetoric of government. More recently still, it has been in the political interests of the parliamentary opposition to raise further doubts about educational standards in order to discredit the government's reforms.

In fact, if the evidence in terms of examination results is to be believed—supposedly the ultimate measure of effectiveness for a government which has placed such emphasis upon them over two decades—standards of achievement have been rising over many years. The percentage of 16-year-olds gaining 5 or more GCSE grades of A to C (or their equivalent, GCE O-level and CSE grade 1) has increased from around 25 per cent in 1980 (when the Conservative government first made publishing results mandatory) to 43 per cent in 1995 (DE Statistical Bulletins 15/92, 7/94; *TES* 24 November 1995). Results in English and Maths for the years 1987 and 1988, i.e. immediately before and after the introduction of GCSE, and then again for 1991, 1992, 1993, 1994, and 1995 (the first five cohorts of students to complete the whole of their secondary education under GCSE regulations and syllabuses) also show steady and marked improvement up to 1994, with a marginal downturn (the 'slump') in 1995 which nevertheless still leaves the figures above their 1992 levels, as shown in Table 21.1.

Of course, overall percentages can hide wide variations between schools and groups of students within the system; thus, for example, girls are currently gaining more high grades than boys at GCSE, though still not succeeding as well at A level (Gipps and Murphy 1994; Elwood 1995). Nor do such figures tell us anything in absolute terms about the standards being achieved in these examinations. Arguments still ensue about Britain's place in international 'league tables' of educational performance (35th, according to a recent speech by Geoffrey Holland, a former permanent secretary to the DE, *Guardian* 4 January 1996), and some critics query whether or not GCSE is indeed of a similar standard to the more traditionally academic O level. Rather, the suggestion is that greater numbers of students are simply passing an easier exam. Equally, however, an argument could be made (as above) that the emphasis placed in GCSE on practical work, the design and conduct of investigations, and problem-solving, renders the examination more rather than less difficult: a larger number of more complex educational goals are being pursued through GCSE. A key issue here is that because of the introduction of the new single examining system of GCSE and continuing changes in curriculum content, we are not comparing like with like over time. However, this point cuts both ways—comparisons of standards will always have to confront such problems, and analysis of data can only be at best indicative and provisional. This is even more the case with comparative international surveys. Reports from such surveys often appear many years after the initial data is gathered (because of the scale and complexity of the research), and are derived from attempts to compare achievement across different curricula, cultures, and (as is often also the case) age groups, which again raises issues of whether like is really being compared with like (Gipps and Murphy 1994; McLean 1990).[3] Thus it is important to recognize that such evidence as we have suggests educational standards are rising: more students are passing more examinations based upon more up-to-date (and hence, the implication is, more demanding) syllabuses. But such evidence is neither con-

Table 21.1. Percentage of entrants gaining GCSE grades A–C or O level/CSE equivalent in English and Maths[a]

	1987	1988	1991	1992	1993	1994	1995
English	46.2	48.9	55.2	55.3	57.1	58.2	56.9
Maths	37.1	41.9	43.7	44.7	45.3	45.9	44.8

[a] *Sources:* Department for Education 1992*a*, *b*; 1994*a*; SCAA 1994; SEAC 1993; *Guardian* 24 August 1995.

clusive—the trend, for what it is worth, is upwards, but it may yet turn down again—nor does it suggest that educational standards are high enough or could not be improved still further.

Can Testing Raise Standards?

So, given that complacency is certainly not in the national interest, nor in the interest of individual children, can the current focus on assessment and testing contribute to raising standards still further? The British government is not alone in focusing on changes in assessment as a key mechanism in attempts to reform the school system and raise educational standards. Academics and policy-makers in the United States have become increasingly attracted by the idea (see OTA 1992; Gifford and O'Connor 1992), as have similar personnel in Europe, and educational analysts and planners who take a particular interest in developing countries (Weston 1990; Kellaghan and Greaney 1992; Lockheed 1992). Indeed, a recent review of secondary examinations in eight countries indicated that the role of assessment in system control and reform is a key factor in why examinations have not merely persisted in recent years, despite all the criticisms levelled at them, but 'have positively flourished' (Eckstein and Noah 1993: 9). However, not all discussions of the role of assessment in reforming schools derive from similar analyses of the nature of the problem; and far less do they agree on uniform solutions. Thus the UK government has asserted that educational standards are too low and that a new, wide-scale programme of testing, linked to the publication of results, is what will raise them. Others would argue that it is all too often programmes of testing themselves that are the cause of poor standards—because they narrow the focus of teaching, and result as much in student failure and demotivation as student success. Thus what is required is improved forms of assessment, which may or may not include improved forms of testing: broaden the goals and methods of assessment, and you will broaden the curriculum and raise standards (Resnick and Resnick 1992; Weston 1990). Two basic positions thus seem to be adopted with respect to using assessment to raise standards: using assessment *results* to

influence or manage the system in some way; and using changes in assessment *processes* to improve teaching directly by underpinning curriculum change and providing exemplary models of what good teaching and assessment tasks should look like.

In practice the UK government has tried to operationalize a combination of both these approaches, as political interest in mobilizing accountability pressures and inter-school competition through the publication of results has been combined with and mediated by the educational ambitions of those professionals charged with implementing policy (e.g. TGAT 1988).[4]

Testing and League Tables

To take issues of accountability and competition first, debate in the UK has been focused on the proposed publication of so-called 'league tables' of National Curriculum test results, though in fact these have actually been manifest through the publication of secondary school examination results (i.e. GCSE), something which was legislated for well before the enactment of National Curriculum and Assessment policy. Thus secondary schools have had to publish their examination results in reports and prospectuses for parents since 1980. While these have often been picked up and published comparatively by local newspapers it is only since the Education Reform Act of 1988 that figures have been compiled and published nationally (in the late autumn, for the previous summer's examination results). Comparative figures are generated and reported school by school, and local authority by local authority (school district) for the percentage of the relevant age cohort gaining 5 or more 'higher grade' GCSEs (i.e. grades A to C), 5 or more grades A to G (i.e all grades awarded), and 1 or more A to G-grade certificate.[5] This indicates what percentage of students are doing particularly well (5 + A–Cs) as well as to what extent all students are making at least some progress. Figures for unauthorized absences (truancy) are also reported. As noted earlier, the current national average for 5 + A to C grades is 43 per cent. A typical 'profile' for a comprehensive school near the national average might thus be 5 + A to Cs: 48 per cent; 5 + A to Gs: 93 per cent; 1 + A to G: 94 per cent, indicating that 6 per cent of students in that school gained no certificates whatsoever (actual example taken from 1995 figures published in *TES* 24 November 1995).

While this represents a mammoth statistical undertaking by government, and one that has attracted sustained criticism, to which I will return below, it is still a far cry from the original discussion document outlining the 1988 National Curriculum legislation, which implied that league tables of performance would be produced for all schools (primary and secondary), in all National Curriculum subjects (English, Maths, Science, Technology, History Geography, a Modern Language, Art, Music, Physical Education, and, in Wales, Welsh), at four separate age groups (7, 11, 14 and 16):

A national curriculum backed by clear assessment arrangements will help raise standards of attainment by . . . [] . . . setting clear objectives for what children . . . should be able to achieve . . . [] . . . checking on progress toward those objectives . . . [] . . . Parents will be able to judge their children's progress against agreed national targets . . . [] . . . parents . . . will be able to pinpoint deficiencies . . . from information about objectives and performance provided to them. (DES 1987: 3–5, 23)

The formal assessment, reporting, and publishing of results was quickly restricted to the three 'core' subjects of English, Maths, and Science, but the above agenda is still expected to be delivered to individual students and parents via teachers' coursework assessments and reports. Even restricting publication to three subjects did not allay criticisms of the both the policy and the logistics of testing, however, such that a teacher boycott of the testing programme (from 1992 to 1994) led to disruption of the government's plans. Up to the end of 1995 only four reports on National Curriculum Test results had been published (on 7-year-olds in 1991, 1992, and 1994, and 14-year-olds in 1994) comprising a total of only 121 pages of statistics across all four reports: hardly value for money, given the vast amounts of political and material resources poured into the enterprise (DES 1991; DfE no date; DfE 1994*b*, *c*). Furthermore, these reports have focused on aggregate figures broken down by profile component and sex rather than individual school results (e.g. percentage of boys and girls at age 7 gaining level 2 in reading and writing in English, or space, shape, and data handling in Mathematics).

Publication of the first test results for 11-year-olds in January 1996 caused a furore because large numbers of students did not gain the grades expected of them, given the assumed age-related progression through National Curriculum levels. That is, it was assumed by the architects of the system (TGAT 1988) that, on a ten level scale, the average 11-year-old would reach level 4. In fact 52 per cent of pupils got less than level 4 in English, 56 per cent got less than level 4 in Maths, and there was 'Uproar over Test Failures by 11-Year-Olds' (*The Times* 26 January 1996: 1). Inherent in the furore is a misunderstanding and conflation of norm-referenced and criterion-referenced judgements, not to mention the fact that the results might have reflected problems of validity and reliability in the testing process. However the key point to underline is that once again reporting focused on aggregate results rather than school-level data: we are still in the realms of national monitoring rather than school-by-school competition.

Nevertheless, the intention is still to produce school-level results, as is the case with GCSE results, so it is important to review the more general criticisms of the validity of such an endeavour.[6] Apart from the crucial problem of test results not reflecting the full, or even the main, goals of schooling, the major problem with publishing comparative lists of results is that it gives no indication of what achievements and aptitudes students had when they began at a particular school and thus what we might expect them to achieve anyway; that is, raw results give no indication of the specific 'value-added' by a particular school. Extensive research demonstrates that the most significant predictor of exam success at 16 is previously measured achievement at 11 (see Gray and Wilcox 1995). This is an issue of particular importance for schools in poorer neighbourhoods, since research also demonstrates the correlation of socio-economic status with student achievement and such school are thus likely to come out at the bottom of the list (and do). However it could also be of crucial concern for individual parents in schools which are apparently doing quite well, but should be doing much better: in such cases the socio-economic status of the students and their parents could well be masking relatively poor teaching (again, see Gray and Wilcox 1995 for a fuller discussion of these and related issues). Thus for example the 1995 GCSE results demonstrated that private schools achieved better results than government-maintained schools, selective schools achieved better than non-selective, and schools in suburban local authorities did better than those in inner city authorities (*TES* 24 November 1995). Surprise, surprise.[7]

This is not to say that the correlation of performance with socio-economic background, and thus the overall *explanation* of why comparisons may be unfair, should be taken as an enduringly legitimate *excuse* for poor performance in individual cases; nor that individual parents within a reasonably homogenous locality (be it suburban or inner-city) might not learn something of interest about their local schools (as indeed might the teachers within those schools). Some suburban schools will do better than others, as will some inner-city schools. If, within a locality, one secondary school out of the four or five that parents might reasonably be able to choose from is doing particularly well, or particularly badly, then such information may be of use to parents (and teachers). However, results can swing enormously from year to year,[8] and it would take a consistent trend over 3 or more years before one could say with some certainty that things were indeed going better or worse than elsewhere. Furthermore, even supposing that such a trend could be established and a particularly effective school identified, such a school could not expand indefinitely without significant additional capital investment, nor, presumably, would it wish to, since such expansion would threaten the delicate balance of whatever constellation of factors were responsible for its success—expanding the school more than marginally would change it. The school could thus begin to choose its students, rather than vice-versa. Evidence from the 1995 figures demonstrates that this can indeed be the case (*TES* 24 November 95: 7). Conversely, schools cannot contract indefinitely either, but if, say, within a local economy, one school out of four or five were perceived to be particularly unsuccessful and started to lose students to other schools, the educational experience of its remaining students could be severely damaged before remedial action were taken by the school or its local authority.

There are also broader educational issues

about how distorting an over-concentration on grades A to C might become. Within highly competitive 'local economies' of four or five similar schools it might well be in a school's interest to focus additional teaching resources on 'borderline' candidates, to maximize the percentage gaining five or more grades from A to C. Whether such cramming, even if it leads to an improvement in results, can be taken to indicate a general improvement in educational standards is one issue; another is that such cramming would inevitably be at the expense of other groups within the school, especially perhaps low achievers. And indeed, an aspect of the 1995 results which drew particular comment was the increase in students gaining no grades whatsoever from 7 per cent in 1994 to 8.1 per cent in 1995.

Using Assessment Processes to Reform Schooling

While most of the political rhetoric has focused on setting tests and publishing results, much of the detail of implementation of National Curriculum Assessment—particularly the school-based 'teacher assessment' element, i.e. the assessment of routine classwork and homework by teachers—has been concerned with using changes in assessment processes and procedures to underpin changes in the curriculum and teaching methods. Indeed, this approach to the role of assessment in school reform predates the National Curriculum and was central to the introduction of more coursework assessment and practical assessment in GCSE. This more educational argument for using assessment to underpin change derives from concerns with the validity of results produced as well as the quality of educational interaction in the classroom. Thus it is argued that as the curriculum changes and new educational objectives are introduced such as planning, carrying out, and writing up extended tasks, or speaking and listening effectively, they cannot be validly assessed by traditional written tests. At the same time, it is recognized that traditional testing formats will inhibit such curriculum change and thus changes in assessment should be introduced in tandem with changes in curriculum (DES 1985; TGAT 1988; Kellaghan and Greaney 1992).

The extent to which governments appreciate the complexities of such arguments is a moot point, of course, but it is worth interrogating them in a little more detail, since more recently it has come to be suggested that changes in assessment do not simply have to follow changes in curriculum, but could come *first*, and lead (or even 'drive') the curriculum in desirable directions. Such arguments clearly had an impact on the educational ambitions of the implementers of policy, if not the policy-makers themselves.

The argument in favour of using assessment to improve standards has been most explicitly developed in the United States, where it has become known as 'Measurement-Driven Instruction' (MDI) (Popham 1987*a*). Proponents claim that MDI 'occurs when a high-stakes test of educational achievement, because of the important contingencies associated with the students' performance, influences the instructional program that prepares students for the test' (Popham 1987*a*: 680). In other words, when tests are seen by teachers and students to be important—perhaps for teacher accountability, but more significantly when they carry consequences for students' future life-chances—they will directly influence teaching and learning; teachers will teach to the test and students will practise for it. Thus the better the test—the higher the standards encapsulated within it—the better the teaching and learning. This is quite a tall order for test designers, of course, and as a mechanism for school improvement it places great emphasis (and responsibility, and resources) on getting the test 'right', on the assumption that the teaching will automatically follow.

Not surprisingly, such an argument has not gone unchallenged. In practice much MDI development has been based on defining curriculum objectives and developing criterion-referenced tests to ascertain whether or not the objectives have been met:

The chief virtue of MDI stems from the clarity with which instructional targets—that is the skills and knowledge being tested—are described. . . . Thus criterion-referenced tests . . . must be employed . . . because the descriptive clarity of well-constructed criterion-referenced tests gives teachers comprehensible descriptions of what is being tested. (Popham 1987*a*: 680)

This is easier said than done. The sorts of multiple-choice tests commonly associated with the testing industry in the United States have come in for considerable criticism; far from improving educational standards, it is argued, they trivialize and narrow teaching into little more than test preparation; tests, moreover, which do not demand any extended writing, analysis, or problem solving (Bracey 1987). Considerable empirical evidence from the US supports this view, indicating that setting minimum standards to be met by all, especially when directly related to school and teacher accountability, can all to often lead to those minima becoming *de facto* maxima, as teachers strive to ensure that as many students as possible reach the minimum, rather than stretching many students beyond it (Atkin 1979). Similarly, coaching and practice can lead to improvements in test scores without there being any real or lasting impact on educational quality (Corbett and Wilson 1988; Shepard 1991). There are echoes here of the sort of cramming for borderline GCSE candidates that was identified earlier. Perhaps an even more important point for the UK context is that (currently, at least) only GCSE examinations could be said to be genuinely 'high-stakes tests', especially from the point of view of the individual student. It may be a matter of concern for a primary school that their overall National Curriculum test scores at Key Stage 1 (age 7 years) or Key Stage 2 (age 11 years) are below the national average, but the individual scores of the children will be of little concern to the children themselves—at least in the short term. It remains to be seen whether recent policy announcements about the reintroduction of a significant element of selection in entry to secondary schools (i.e. the selection of students by schools) 'raises the stakes' of tests at 7, and especially at 11 (*Guardian* 9 January 1996); but such a policy hardly accords with a general concern for raising the educational standards of all children, or indeed with the principle of consumer choice which underpins so much else of recent educational (and economic) policy.

Supporters of a more sophisticated approach to MDI counter that good tests can be developed, and that the issue is really one of improving the quality and validity of the assessment process:

advocates of new ways to test often argue that since tests can play a powerful role in influencing learning, they must be designed to support educational goals. These advocates disparage 'teaching to the test' when a test calls for isolated facts from a multiple-choice context, but endorse the concept when the test consists of 'authentic' tasks. (OTA 1992: 11)

Thus, as Resnick and Resnick (1992: 59) argue, 'if we put debates, discussions, essays, and problem-solving into the testing system, children will spend time practising those activities'. However, even reviews which are broadly pragmatic, and sympathetic to the possibilities of MDI, recognize the problems of adequately conceptualizing and articulating 'higher-order' skills and understandings in a teaching and testing programme, along with the practical problem of whether or not teachers are willing and able to implement new subject-matter and associated teaching methods (Airasian 1988). As Stake (1991: xxiv–xxv) has put it:

one key assumption behind reform based on assessment policy is that people can agree on which educational outcomes are desirable . . . A second assumption is that we have a language for the specification of educational goals . . . A third . . . is that we can measure the attainment of those [goals] . . . a fourth . . . is that . . . we can use the information to improve teaching.

All of these assumptions seem to be present in the UK government's approach to using testing to raise standards, although, as noted above, their complexity is not necessarily appreciated by the government itself. In many respects the debate which has been played out in the United States in education journals and state-level pilot developments has been played out 'for real' in the UK—British schools, and more particularly British children, have been subjected to an unprecedented 'natural experiment'.

It was the TGAT Report (TGAT 1988: paras. 3–4) that put educational meat on the political bones of the government's programme. The report stated that:

Promoting children's learning is a principal aim of schools. Assessment lies at the heart of this process . . . it should not simply be a bolt-on at the end. Rather it should be an integral part of the educational process, continually providing both 'feedback' and 'feedforward'. It therefore needs to be incorporated systematically into teaching strategies and practices at all levels.

From these propositions flowed the detail of the Report's recommendations: for teacher assessment (TA) to be used alongside nationally comparable Standard Assessment Tasks

(SATs); for both TA and SATs to be as valid as possible and to support good teaching by employing 'a wide range of modes of presentation, operation and response' (para. 50; cf. also para. 60); and for the system to be formative as well as summative, i.e. for it to contribute to improving the process of learning, as well as measuring the outcomes of the process. The TGAT Report made one other crucial recommendation, however, one which survived longest and certainly caused the most problems: 'the assessment results should give direct information about pupils' achievement in relation to objectives: they should be criterion-referenced' (para. 5). Here is where the report borrowed most from the American literature but learned least from American experience. At the same time as Popham (1987*a*) was advocating the use of MDI, he was also advising educational evaluators and decision-makers to avoid producing overly detailed lists of objectives, and instead to 'focus on a manageable number of broad-scope objectives' (Popham 1987*b*: 39). His definition of 'well-constructed criterion-referenced tests' included similar advice, though then implied that the solution was to be found in narrowing the focus of the test:

Too many instructional targets turn out to be no targets at all . . . Teachers who are inundated with endless litanies of miniscule instructional targets will pay heed to none. A high-stakes test must focus on only a reasonable number of important skills or knowledge targets. (1987*a*: 680)

In fact the UK experience is that when 'miniscule instructional targets' are backed up by force of law, and underpinned still further by in-service material stressing the need to assess each and every one (e.g. SEAC 1990), teachers attempt to pay heed to all of them—and the system is stretched to breaking point as a result.

It is not that members of TGAT and related National Curriculum Working Groups were unaware of the problems. Margaret Brown, for example, a close colleague at King's College of the TGAT Chairman, Professor Paul Black, and herself a member of the Mathematics National Curriculum Working Group, very clearly recognized the danger of attainment targets 'multiplying like vermin' (Brown 1988: 19). Yet somehow, once the Holy Grail of criterion-referencing was invoked it proved extremely difficult to keep the scope of the search under control, especially since the solution offered by advocates such as Popham (select key objectives and narrow the test to focus on them) takes us right back to all the criticisms of testing that TGAT was attempting to avoid: too narrow a test will give an invalid measurement, narrow the curriculum, and restrict teaching to coaching for the test. The logic of using the *content* of testing to underpin good teaching (as opposed to the method) implies that everything you think is important (and thus should be taught) must also be assessed, otherwise it may get ignored if only certain things are selected for inclusion in the testing programme. TGAT and SEAC's interventions served to drive the system first of all towards including all desirable objectives in the first round of SATs—making them far too complicated (Torrance 1991)—then subsequently towards including them in TA, which led to classroom overload (SEAC 1990; Dearing 1993a and b). Gipps et al. (1995) suggest that TA in particular has also had positive consequences, but equally point to the dangers of the new simplified Standard Tests undermining these gains.

What Assessment Can and Cannot Achieve

So, standards are not falling; on the contrary, the evidence suggests that they are rising, and certainly that our ambitions for what school systems should deliver are rising. We expect vastly more of our school system, in terms of both the scale and scope of its endeavours, than we did even 10 years ago. We expect getting on for 50 per cent of 16-year-olds to achieve the sorts of results that a selected élite of 20 per cent once achieved, and we expect them to achieve these results on syllabuses and examinations that stress the understanding and application, as well as the recall, of knowledge. But in an increasingly competitive economic environment it would be imprudent to suggest that standards are high enough, or cannot be improved still further.

The role that changes in assessment can play in this is complex, far more complex than the political rhetoric of market accountability allows. Clearly testing will have an impact on teaching, learning, and the standards of achievement in a school system. However, this impact can be negative as well as positive, and the available evidence suggests that the simple initiative of imposing tests on a school system cannot, of itself, improve standards of achievement. Indeed, if anything, the reverse is the case. The key issue here must be the question of standards of what, and for whom, which in turn connects with the rapidly changing purposes of education.

The logic of attempting to raise standards by imposing a testing programme is essentially twofold: first, the publication of results combined with the financial consequences for schools of gaining or losing students is intended to raise standards by engendering competition—between students, between teachers, and between schools. But competitions, even supposing they are 'fair' and involve meaningful substantive activity, as opposed to 'market manipulation', involve losers as well as winners, and this seems a very high-risk strategy for trying to improve educational standards across the system as a whole. The practices which are starting to emerge from the UK GCSE 'league tables' suggest that such competition focuses attention on too narrow a range of educational outcomes and, despite overall improvements in results, masks differential performance across groups within the system and increases the gap between better- and worse-performing schools rather than bridging it.

Second, if we assume that the ambitions for the programme are serious and meaningful, the intention must be for the tests to encapsulate the highest-quality versions of the key goals of the system—do well on these tests and you really will have demonstrated high-level educational achievement and be capable of significant educational and/or vocational performance in the future. As we have already seen, this is a very demanding ambition, and it must be questionable whether or not high-quality educational goals such as planning, analyzing, communicating, problem-solving, and the like, goals which in other contexts of discourse are claimed to be essential for future economic competitiveness, can truly be captured in a testing programme, let alone one which is intended to include all students at four different age groups, but in only three subjects (English, Maths, and Science). The scale of the endeavour must push the technology of testing towards over-simplistic paper-and-pencil methods, while the focus on only three subjects runs the risk of distorting the activity of the system as a whole: combined with the use of league tables, the implication is that if we design the wrong 'performance indicators', and place too much emphasis upon them, then the system will veer off course very quickly.

The danger, then, of using testing too narrowly and mechanistically in pursuit of higher standards is that the technology simply cannot cope with the task. If our definition of higher standards and our goals for the system involve developing the capacity for creativity, flexibility, and innovation, the supposed 'high skill/high wage' activities of the post-industrial future, then these activities must be manifest in the school curriculum and its attendant assessment procedures. A major part of the problem is lack of understanding about the history of assessment and lack of clarity about what assessment can and cannot achieve. Assessment and certification practices were developed in the context of taken-for-granted assumptions about high-quality schooling being the same as academic schooling. The issue for assessment was to select the most able students for exposure to this demanding regime, then in turn to certificate and legitimate their entry into leadership roles in the labour market. Whether or not they (or anyone else) learned useful skills along the way was hardly questioned—it was simply assumed that they would. More recently such assumptions have been severely questioned, by the competency movement in vocational education as well as by critics of the school system (cf. Butterfield 1995; Wolf 1995). Developments in assessment theory and practice over the last 10 years or so can thus be seen as part of a continuing debate about the economic and social functions of schooling. The curriculum has been seen to be in need of modernization, and assessment has been seen as both supporting this modernization and contributing to the longer-term emancipatory project of schooling through maximizing the learning opportunities of pupils (rather than restricting such opportunities through selection). This trend of modernization has involved a shift away from only assessing knowledge, towards assessing skills and understandings; from only assessing products towards assessing processes; from only assessing at the end of the course through external means towards assessing during courses, internally; from only using written methods

towards the use of a variety of methods and evidence; from norm-referencing towards criterion-referencing; from pass/fail summative assessment (for selection) towards identifying strengths and weaknesses formatively, and recording positive achievement. The trend has been most fully represented in the Record of Achievement movement (Broadfoot *et al.* 1988) but was also very evident in the design of GCSE and in the first round of Standard Assessment Tasks (see Torrance 1995 for a fuller discussion).

This debate about modernization has overlapped with market mechanisms introduced to render the system more sensitive to consumer needs. However, while the government has been riding both horses, in many respects they are pulling in different directions. Modernizing the curriculum and assessment methods suggests an analysis of economic need and the development of educational planning which is at variance with the 'hidden hand' of the market manifested through parental choice of their children's schools. Assessment is being used as the key mechanism of both approaches, but the pressure to produce simple indicators of educational output is clearly antithetical to the possibilities of developing more flexible and demanding methods of assessment which would underpin rather than undermine good teaching. Furthermore, even broader and more flexible approaches to assessment are still struggling with the legacy of producing a definitive 'result', a 'true score', which derives from and adheres to the individual, rather than describing the different performances of individuals and groups generated by undertaking a variety of tasks in a variety of contexts. Yet the challenge for (post-modern?) assessment must lie with this latter task—how to produce descriptions of diverse outcomes which are informative both to the individual learner and to a wide variety of third parties.

In the short term, policy-makers must recognize that tools designed to measure the output of the system will have an impact on it, and that the simpler the tools, the narrower and more constricting the impact. Likewise, those who would use changes in assessment to attempt to broaden the curriculum must recognize that this also raises issues of scale and of impact on teachers at classroom level. The more ambitious the new assessment procedures are, and the larger the overall programme is, the more distant is its genesis and development likely to be from individual schools and classrooms. This raised immense problems with respect to the original SATs. Thus just because poor assessment can narrow the curriculum and depress standards, it does not follow that better assessment will automatically enhance the curriculum and raise standards. Better assessment should proceed in tandem with curriculum development, but cannot 'drive' it; it is a necessary but not sufficient condition for the improvement of educational provision and performance. In the longer term, the challenge is to build on this understanding and ensure that assessment responds to the demands for creativity and flexibility in the system, for a diversity of context-specific information, and for self-development and equity in a pluralist society.

Notes

1. Parts of this article are adapted from Torrance, H. (1996), 'Can Testing Raise Educational Standards?' forthcoming in Watson, K., Modgil, C., and Modgil, S., *Educational Dilemmas: Debate and Diversity*, iv: *Quality in Education* (Cassells).
2. I refer throughout the article to the 'UK government'; in fact the details of policy have been developed and implemented in different ways in England and Wales, Northern Ireland, and Scotland, but the principles and broad thrust of political intervention are common to all.
3. Similar debates are played out in other contexts (e.g. the United States) where the news media also rarely prevent the facts getting in the way of a good story about educational decline; cf. Stedman 1994; Westbury 1992.
4. Mediating policy is both an inevitable part of the process of implementation (cf. Ball and Bowe 1992) and in some cases was probably an overt intention of at least some of those involved; however, educational ambition combined with political intransigence led to massive overload of the system (cf. Black 1988, 1994; Dearing 1993).
5. Publication is in alphabetical order, not rank order, but direct comparisons are quickly constructed by the press (cf. *TES* 24 November 1995: 6).
6. Because of the irregularity of reporting over time, comparisons of results are not yet possible; and, because of continual changes in the curriculum, they are unlikely to be valid when they are possible.

7. Thomas (1995) reviews similar research evidence for younger children and demonstrates that pupil characteristics such as age, gender, home language, and social background make a significant difference to results at Key Stage 1.
8. For example, St Francis Xavier, in North Yorkshire, was featured on the front page of the *TES* as having improved its 5 + A to C results from 29 per cent in 1994 to 61 per cent in 1995 (*TES* 24 November 1995: 1). One can only hope that the pendulum doesn't swing back again just as quickly.

References

Airasian, P. W. (1988), 'Measurement-Driven Instruction: A Closer Look', *Educational Measurement: Issues and Practice* 7/4: 6–11.

Atkin, M. (1979), 'Educational Accountability in the United States', *Educational Analysis*, 1/1: 5–21.

Ball, S., and Bowe, R. (1992), 'Subject Departments and the "Implementation" of the National Curriculum', *Journal of Curriculum Studies* 24/2: 97–115.

Black, P. (1988), 'The Task Group on Assessment and Testing', in Torrance, H. (ed. op. cit.).

—— (1994), 'Performance Assessment and Accountability: The Experience in England and Wales', *Educational Evaluation and Policy Analysis* 16/2: 191–203.

Bracey, G. (1987), 'Measurement-Driven Instruction: Catchy Phrase, Dangerous Practice', *Phi Delta Kappan*, 68: 683–6.

Broadfoot, P., *et al.* (1988), *Records of Achievement: Report of the National Evaluation of Pilot Schemes* (London: HMSO).

Brown, M. (1988), 'Issues in Formulating and Organizing Attainment Targets in Relation to their Assessment' in Torrance, H. (ed. op. cit.).

Brown, P., and Lauder, H. (eds.) (1992), *Education for Economic Survival* (London: Routledge).

Butterfield, S. (1995), *Educational Objectives and National Assessment* (Buckingham: Open Univ. Press).

Corbett, H., and Wilson, B. (1988), 'Raising the Stakes in Statewide Mandatory Minimum-Competency Testing', *Journal of Education Policy*, 3/5: 27–39.

Cox, C. B., and Dyson R. F. (eds.) (1968), *Fight for Education* (London: Critical Quarterly).

Dearing, R. (1993a), *The National Curriculum and its Assessment: An Interim Report* (London: NCC/SEAC).

—— (1993b), *The National Curriculum and its Assessment: Final Report* (London: SCAA).

Department of Education and Science (1985), *General Certificate of Secondary Education: A General Introduction* (London: HMSO).

—— (1987), *The National Curriculum 5–16: A Consultation Document* (London: DES/Welsh Office).

—— (1991), *Testing 7-Year-Olds in 1991: Results of the National Curriculum Assessments in England* (London: DES).

Department for Education (no date), *Testing 7-Year-Olds in 1992: Results of the National Curriculum Assessments in England* (London: DE).

—— (1992*a*), *Statistical Bulletin 15/92* (London: DfE).

—— (1992*b*), *Statistics of Education School Examinations GCSE and GCE 1991* (London: DfE).

—— (1994*a*), *Statistical Bulletin 7/94* (London: DfE).

—— (1994*b*), *Testing 7-Year-Olds in 1994: Results of the National Curriculum Assessments in England* (London: DfE).

—— (1994*c*), *Testing 14-Year-Olds in 1994: Results of the National Curriculum Assessments in England* (London: DfE).

Eckstein, M., and Noah, H. (1993), *A Comparative Study of Secondary School Examinations*, Research Working Paper No. 7 (London: International Centre for Research on Assessment).

Elwood, J. (1995), 'Gender Differences in A level Examinations: The Reinforcement of Stereotypes', Paper presented to the British Educational Research Association, Bath, September 1995.

Gifford, B., and O'Connor, M. (eds.) (1992), *Future Assessments: Changing Views of Aptitude, Achievement and Instruction* (Boston: Kluwer).

Gipps, C., and Murphy, P. (1994), *A Fair Test? Assessment, Achievement and Equity* (Buckingham: Open Univ. Press).

—— Brown, M., McCallum, B., and McAllister, S. (1995), *Intuition or Evidence? Teachers and National Assessment of Seven Year Olds* (Buckingham: Open Univ. Press).

Gray, J., and Wilcox, B. (1995), *Good School, Bad School: Evaluating Performance and Encouraging Improvement* (Buckingham: Open Univ. Press).

Guardian (1995), ' "Ignorant" Teachers Faulted' (1 January), 2.

—— (1996), 'Plan to Lift UK from Place as "Dunce of the World" ' (4 January), 6.

—— (1996), 'Schools Face Court Test' (9 January), 1.

Kellaghan, T., and Greaney, V. (1992), *Using Examinations to Improve Education* (Washington DC: World Bank).

Lockheed, M. (1992), *World Bank Support for Capacity Building: The Challenge of Educational Assessment* (Washington DC: World Bank).

McLean, L. (1990), 'Possibilities and Limitations in Cross-National Comparisons of Educational Achievement', in Broadfoot, P., Murphy, R., and Torrance, H. (eds.), *Changing Educational Assessment: International Perspectives and Trends* (London: Routledge).

Popham, W. J. (1987*a*), 'The Merits of Measurement-Driven Instruction', *Phi Delta Kappan*, 68: 679–82.

—— (1987*b*), 'Two-Plus Decades of Educational Objectives', *International Journal of Educational Research*, 11/1: 31–41.

Office of Technology Assessment (Congress of the United States) (1992), *Testing in American Schools: Asking the Right Questions* (summary report) (Washington DC).

Resnick, L., and Resnick, D. (1992), 'Assessing the Thinking Curriculum', in Gifford, B., and O'Connor, M. (eds.), School Curriculum and Assessment Authority (1994), *GCSE Examinations Results 1993 (ref: KS4/94/066)* (London, SCAA).

Schools Examination and Assessment Council (1990), *A Guide to Teacher Assessment, Packs A, B and C* (London: Heinemann Educational).

—— (1993), *GCSE Examinations Results 1992 (ref: B/067/L/93)* (London: SEAC).

Shepard, L. (1991), 'Will National Tests Improve Student Learning?' *Phi Delta Kappan* (November), 232–8.

Stake, R. E. (ed.) (1991), *Advances in Program Evaluation: Using Assessment Policy to Reform Education* (Greenwich: JAI Press).

Stedman, L. (1994), 'Incomplete Explanations: The Case of the U.S. Performance in the International Assessments of Education', *Educational Researcher*, 23/7: 24–32.

Task Group on Assessment and Testing (1988), *A Report* (London: DES).

Thomas, S. (1995), 'Considering Primary School Effectiveness: An Analysis of 1992 Key Stage 1 Results', *The Curriculum Journal*, 6/3: 279–95.

The Times Educational Supplement (1995*a*), 'Woodhead Castigates Progressives' (27 January), 3.

—— (1995*b*), 'Reform is Working, Says Chief Inspector (3 February), 4.

—— (1995*c*), 'Table Talk Centres on Fears of Great Divide' (24 August), 6; and 'State High-Flyers are Selecting Now', 7; and 'School and College Performance Tables', extra supplement.

Torrance, H. (ed.) (1988), *National Assessment and Testing: A Research Response* (Kendal: British Educational Research Association).

—— (1991), 'Evaluating SATs: The 1990 Pilot', *Cambridge Journal of Education*, 21/2: 129–40.

—— (ed.) (1995), *Evaluating Authentic Assessment* (Buckingham: Open Univ. Press).

Westbury, I. (1992), 'Comparing American and Japanese Achievement: Is the United States Really a Low Achiever?' *Educational Researcher*, 21/5: 18–24.

Weston, P. (ed.) (1990), *Assessment, Progression and Purposeful Learning in Europe: A Study for the Commission of the European Communities* (Slough: NFER).

Wolf, A. (1995), *Competence Based Assessment* (Buckingham: Open Univ. Press).

22

Restructuring Schools for Student Success

Linda Darling-Hammond

To make a difference in American education, we must rethink how schools are designed, how teaching and learning are pursued, and how resources are allocated. If we want schools not merely to 'deliver instruction' but to ensure that all students learn in more powerful and effective ways, we must create schools that are sufficiently personalized to know their students well, that are managed and staffed by teachers who are professionally prepared and supported, and that are funded equitably in ways that invest in the front lines of teaching and learning. This three-part agenda requires a paradigm shift in how we think about the management and purpose of schools: from hierarchical, factory model institutions where teachers, treated as semi-skilled assembly line workers, process students for their slots in society, to professional communities where student success is supported by the collaborative efforts of knowledgeable teachers who are organized to address the needs of diverse learners.

Today's schools were designed when the goal of education was not to educate all students well but to process a great many efficiently, selecting and supporting only a few for 'thinking work'. Strategies for sorting and tracking students were developed to ration the scarce resources of expert teachers and rich curricula, and to standardize teaching tasks and procedures within groups. This, in turn, enabled greater routinization of teaching work, and less reliance on professional skill and judgment, a corollary of the nineteenth-century decision to structure teaching as semi-skilled labor.

The goal was to instill in the masses of students the rudimentary skills and the basic workplace socialization needed to follow orders and conduct predetermined tasks neatly and punctually. As recent national and international research on US education has demonstrated, the rote learning needed for these early twentieth-century objectives still predominates in today's schools, reinforced by top-down prescriptions for teaching practice, mandated curriculum packages, standardized tests that focus on low-level cognitive skills, and continuing underinvestment in teacher education that would enable more ambitious teaching (Boyer 1983; Goodlad 1984; McKnight *et al.* 1987; ETS 1989*a*; ETS 1989*b*).

The school structure created to implement this conception of teaching and learning is explicitly impersonal, a function of both its size and organization. Students move from one teacher to the next, from grade to grade, and from class period to class period, with little opportunity to become well known to any adults who can consider them as whole people or as developing intellects. Secondary school teachers may see 150 or more students a day. Teachers work in isolation from one another, stamping students with lessons. Students, too, tend to work alone and passively, listening to lectures, memorizing facts and algorithms, and engaging in independent work at their separate desks (Goodlad 1984).

In urban areas, schools are huge warehouses, with three thousand or more students. They are focused substantially on the control of behavior rather than the development of community. With a locker as their only stable point of contact, a schedule that cycles them through a series of seven to ten overloaded

From *Daedalus*, 124 (1995), 153–62. Reprinted with permission.

teachers, and a counselor who struggles to serve the 'personal' needs of several hundred students, teenagers have little to connect to. Most students are likely to experience such high schools, heavily stratified within and substantially dehumanized throughout, as non-caring or even adversarial environments where 'getting over' becomes important when 'getting known' is impossible. For adults, the capacity to be accountable for the learning of students is reduced by the departmentalized structure that gives them little control over or connection to most of what happens to the students they see only briefly.

It is becoming increasingly clear that the task of educating very diverse learners to much higher standards of learning in a world with rapidly changing educational demands will require more skillful teaching and more responsive schools than current educational bureaucracies allow. New school organizations—like the new organizations that are being created to replace ossified bureaucracies in business and industry—will need to rely on much greater knowledge, skill, and judgment on the part of all 'front line' workers (teachers), along with flexible planning and problem-solving more responsive to the needs of students and the realities of change.

Just as many businesses have been flattening hierarchies, decentralizing decision-making, and placing more responsibility in the hands of front line work teams, schools have been restructuring to reduce the over-specialization and bureaucratization that have proved increasingly problematic. These changes are increasing schools' capacities to connect with families and to succeed with students (Darling-Hammond, forthcoming; Lieberman 1995). As reforms in business and education mature, striking parallels emerge between the organizational strategies of 'high performance, high involvement' corporations and those of extraordinarily successful schools. Such schools feature smaller, more personalized, and less fragmented structures with less departmentalization, stronger relational bonds between and among students and teachers, greater use of teaching teams, and substantial teacher participation in school redesign and decision-making (Braddock and McPartland 1993; Wehlage et al. 1989; Lee et al. 1993). Teacher collaboration in these settings promotes knowledge sharing and communication that focuses 'a faculty's collective technical expertise on specific problems within the school' (Lee et al. 1993).

Small size is one important factor. A substantial body of research shows that, all else equal, smaller schools and school units (in the range of three hundred to five hundred students) are associated with higher achievement (Howley 1989; Howley and Huang 1992; Haller 1992a), as well as better attendance rates (Lindsay 1982), fewer dropouts (Pittman and Haughwout 1987), and lower levels of student misbehavior (Garbarino 1978; Gottfredson and Daiger 1979; Haller 1992b). They are more effective in allowing students to become bonded to important adults in a learning community, who can play the role that families and communities find it harder and harder to play. They are also more effective in creating good interpersonal relationships, and in providing opportunities for students to participate in extracurricular activities and to take leadership roles. (Fowler 1992; Green and Stevens 1988; Haller 1992b; Howley 1989; Lindsay 1982; 1984).

Size is not the only factor at work here, however. The most effective schools or school units are those that create structures for caring—forms of organization that enable close, sustained relationships among students and teachers—rather than structures determined by bureaucratic divisions of labor. Structures that enable teachers to know students and their families well are associated with increased student achievement, more positive feelings toward self and school, and more positive behavior (Gottfredson and Daiger 1979; Wehlage et al. 1989). Typically this is achieved by restructuring teaching and grouping assignments so that teachers work for longer periods of time with a smaller total number of students, for example, by teaching a core interdisciplinary curriculum to one or two groups of students rather than a single subject to five groups, and/or by teaching the same students for more than one year.

In smaller schools or 'houses' within a school, students may work with the same group of teachers and advisors over several years, thus making students' and teachers' work less fragmented and disjointed. This enables a more holistic view of students, and a more in-depth approach to teaching and learning. In short, successful schools focus on more powerful and more coherent learning for all students, in settings that are structured as learning organizations for adults and students alike.

Although these strategies require creative rethinking of staffing, scheduling, and personnel assignments, they do not cost substantially more money (Darling-Hammond, forthcoming). The greatest barriers to these kinds of changes are the forces of conventional thinking and the geological dig of regulations and work rules that currently define the parameters of schooling. Many schools that have substantially restructured their work exist on waivers from various state and local requirements governing uses of time and personnel, facilities, and the organization of curriculum and teaching. Until these regulatory obstacles are removed, widespread change is unlikely to occur.

Despite the fact that they must exist 'against the grain', schools with these features show much greater levels of student success. These include schools affiliated with the Coalition of Essential Schools in New York City that have graduation and college enrollment rates of over 90 per cent for students often considered 'at risk' (Darling-Hammond *et al.* 1995); Philadelphia's charter schools (Fine 1994); and schools associated with restructuring initiatives in Louisville, Kentucky; Hammond, Indiana; Dade County, Florida; and Southern Maine (Elmore 1990; Lieberman 1995). Their outcomes should not be surprising, since teaching involves much more than conveying subject matter to passive recipients. Effective teaching requires knowledge of students, their experiences, and the ways in which they learn. It also requires continuing opportunities for teachers to learn from one another, to evaluate the outcomes of their work, and to invent new practices.

The idea that teachers should be involved in planning and evaluating their own work confronts Tayloristic job structures and the 'trickle-down' theory of knowledge prominent in bureaucracies. Structures and assumptions that de-skill teaching are well established in school systems that have sought to standardize and simplify jobs through age grading, tracking, and specialization, and that have created elaborate administrative and supervisory structures for designing and overseeing the work in each cell of an elaborate organizational matrix. Expertise is presumed to reside at the top of the system and is used to design work specifications (curricula, textbooks, and tests, and decision rules for

grading, promotion, and grouping of students, etc.) for routine implementation.

Such an approach can work when tasks are predictable and unvaried. However, teaching is not this kind of work. Teaching decisions are many; teaching strategies must be continually adapted to different subject areas, learning goals, and student approaches and needs. To teach successfully, teachers must have both the knowledge about teaching and learning needed to manage the complex process of getting diverse students to learn well and the discretion to practice variably rather than routinely. Successful education can occur only if teachers are prepared to meet rigorous learning demands *and* the different needs of students.

This is not the conception of teaching that has informed US policy. In contrast to other industrialized countries, teacher education in the United States has been thin, uneven, and badly underfunded. Schools of education are typically funded less well than any other school or department on campus, and school districts spend less than one half of 1 per cent of their resources on staff development, as compared to 8 to 10 per cent of expenditures in most corporations and in other countries' schools. As a result, many US teachers enter the profession with inadequate preparation, and most have very few opportunities to enhance their knowledge and skills over the course of their careers.

Despite this unevenness, teacher education makes a substantial difference when it is available. Dozens of studies have found that better prepared teachers are more effective with students (Darling-Hammond 1992) and that the single most important determinant of student achievement is the quality of teachers and the extent of their knowledge about teaching and learning (Ferguson 1991; Armour-Thomas *et al.* 1989).

School systems in Germany, France, Switzerland, the Netherlands, and Japan invest in a greater number of well-prepared, well-paid, and well-supported teachers, rather than in a large bureaucracy populated by non-teaching staff hired to manage, inspect, and control the work of teachers. Teacher education and ongoing professional development are much more extensive in these countries than in the United States; substantial time for learning and collegial work are built into the school day; and teachers make most school and curriculum decisions (Darling-Hammond 1994). This is fiscally possible because classroom teachers comprise 80 per cent of the education employees in these countries, as compared to under 50 per cent in the United States (OECD 1992). By investing in large administrative superstructures to control the work of teachers rather than in teachers themselves, we have sucked resources out of classrooms where they could make a difference.

The importance of transforming teaching is becoming ever more clear as schools are expected to find ways to support and connect with the needs of all learners. Responsive teaching cannot be produced through teacher-proof materials or regulated curricula. In order to create bridges between common, challenging curriculum goals and individual learners' experiences and needs, teachers must be able to develop learning experiences that accommodate a variety of cognitive styles, with activities that broaden rather than reduce the range of possibilities for learning. They must understand child development and pedagogy as well as the structures of subject areas and a variety of alternatives for assessing learning. And they must have a base of knowledge for making decisions traditionally reserved for others in the educational hierarchy.

The implications for teacher education, licensing, and advanced certification are many: Teachers will need to be prepared to teach for understanding and have a deeper knowledge of their disciplines and their students. They will need to be prepared to address the wide range of languages, cultures, learning styles, talents, and intelligences that children bring with them to school. They will need to look at and listen to children, and be knowledgeable about how children learn and develop, in order to understand what their students know and can do, as well as how they think and how they learn.

This will require major investments in pre-service and in-service teacher education and major transformations in the way teachers are recruited, licensed, hired, inducted, certified, and supported. Teachers will need more rigorous and tightly coupled theoretical and clinical preparation in schools of education, preferably in graduate level programs that provide sustained internships integrated with coursework. They will also need job-based professional development opportunities that involve them in collegial planning, curriculum work, and study throughout their careers. Hiring more teachers and fewer administrative staff will provide more time for teachers to learn and work together and more resources for their professional development. In restructured schools that have done this, teachers have large blocks of time for joint planning and professional development as well as for a wide variety of professional roles as school leaders, mentors for beginning teachers, and curriculum developers.

These changes must be supported by more meaningful standards for teacher licensing and more sophisticated and authentic assessments of teaching, such as those developed by the new National Board for Professional Teaching Standards and the Interstate New Teacher Assessment and Support Consortium (Darling-Hammond *et al.* 1995). States like Vermont, Indiana, Maine, and Ohio have begun to enact policy changes in teacher education, licensing, and ongoing professional development that will ensure that there are highly-qualified teachers in every classroom. Meanwhile, school networks in New York, Philadelphia, and elsewhere have begun to provide models of schools structured for teacher and student learning.

Their efforts will be strengthened by improvements in salary structures, working conditions, and recruitment incentives that will entice qualified teachers into all teaching fields and all communities, rather than lowering standards wherever shortages occur. The chronic shortages of teachers in fields like mathematics, science, and special education have undermined education in these fields for decades, just as the hiring of tens of thousands of unqualified entrants has undermined the education of children in poor rural and urban areas.

Finally, in contrast to the dramatic inequalities in school spending that characterize this country, other industrialized nations fund education centrally and equally, thereby ensuring an even starting point for their students and the capacity for all districts to hire well-prepared teachers. On this equitable foundation, they build smaller, more personalized schools staffed with highly competent teachers whose work is organized to allow them to know and teach students well. These schools attain higher standards of student learning for more students because they focus on what makes a difference: the relationship between knowledgeable teachers and their students in a supportive, caring environment. That is what we must do if we are to invent schools that will help all students learn well.

References

Armour-Thomas, E., Clay, C., Domanico, R., Bruna, K., and Allen, B. (1989), *An Outlier Study of Elementary and Middle Schools in New York City: Final Report* (New York: New York City Board of Education).

Boyer, E. L. (1983), *High School: A Report on Secondary Education in America* (Princeton, NJ: Carnegie Foundation for the Advancement of Teaching).

Braddock, J. H., and McPartland, J. (1993), 'Education of Early Adolescents', in Darling-Hammond (ed.), *Review of Research in Education*, 19 (Washington DC: American Education Research Association).

Darling-Hammond, L. (1992), 'Teaching and Knowledge: Policy Issues Posed by Alternate Certification for Teachers', *Peabody Journal of Education*, 67/3: 123–54.

——— (1994), *The Current Status of Teaching and Teacher Development* (New York: National Commission on Teaching and America's Future).

——— (forthcoming), 'Beyond Bureaucracy: Restructuring Schools for High Performance', in O'Day, J., and Fuhrman, S. (eds.), *Incentives and School Reform* (San Francisco, Calif.: Jossey-Bass).

———, Ancess, J., and Faulk, B. (1995), *Authentic Assessment in Action: Studies of Schools and Students at Work* (New York: Teachers' College Press).

———, Wise, A. E., and Klein, S. (1995), *A License to Teach: Building a Profession for Twenty-First-Century Schools* (Boulder, Colo.: Westview).

Educational Testing Service (1989), *Crossroads in American Education* (Princeton, NJ: Educational Testing Service).

Elmore, R. F., and associates (1990), *Restructuring Schools: The Next Generation of Educational Reform* (San Francisco, Calif.: Jossey-Bass).

Ferguson, R. F. (1991), 'Paying for Public Education: New Evidence on How and Why Money Matters', *Harvard Journal on Legislation*, 28/2 (Summer), 465–98.

Fine, M. (1994), *Chartering Urban School Reform* (New York: National Centre for Restructuring Education, Schools, and Teaching, Teachers' College, Columbia Univ.).

Fowler, W. J. (1992), 'What Do We Know About School Size? What Should We Know?', paper presented at the annual meeting of the American Educational Research Association (April, San Francisco, Calif.).

Garbarino, J. (1978), 'The Human Ecology of School Crime: A Case for Small Schools', in Wenk, E. (ed.), *Theoretical Perspectives on School Crime* (Davis, Calif.: National Council on Crime and Delinquency), 122–33.

Goodlad, J. I. (1984), *A Place Called School* (New York: McGraw Hill).

Gottfredson, G. D., and Daiger, D. C. (1979), *Disruption in Six Hundred Schools* (Baltimore: Johns Hopkins Univ. Centre for Social Organization of Schools).

Green, G., and Stevens, W. (1988), 'What Research Says About Small Schools', *Rural Educators*, 10/1: 9–14.

Haller, E. J. (1992a), 'Small Schools and Higher Order Thinking Skills', paper presented at the annual meeting of the American Education Research Association (San Francisco, Calif.).

——— (1992b), 'High School Size and Student Indiscipline: Another Aspect of the School Consolidation Issue?', *Education Evaluation and Policy Analysis*, 14/2: 145–56.

Howley, C. B. (1989), 'Synthesis of the Effects of School and District Size: What Research Says about Achievement in Small Schools and School Districts', *Journal of Rural and Small Schools* 4/1: 2–12.

——— and Huang, G. (1992), *Extracurricular Participation and Achievements: School Size as Possible Mediator of SES Influence among Individual Students* (January, Washington DC: Resources in Education).

Knight, C. C., Crosswhite, F. J., Dossey, J. A., Kifer, E., Swafford, J. O., Travers, K. J., and Cooney, T. J., *The Underachieving Curriculum: Assessing US School mathematics from an International Perspective* (Champaign, Ill.: Stipes).

Lee, V. A., Bryk, A. S., and Smith, J. B., 'The Organization of Effective Secondary Schools', in Darling-Hammond (ed.), *Review of Research in Education*, 19 (Washington DC: American Education Research Association).

Lieberman, A. (1995), *The Work of Restructuring Schools: Building from the Ground Up* (New York: Teachers College Press).

Lindsay, P. (1982), 'The Effect on High School Size on Student Participation, Satisfaction, and Attendance', *Education Evaluation and Policy Analysis*, 4: 57–65.

——— (1984), 'High School Size, Participation in Activities, and Young Adult Social Participation: Some Enduring Effects of Schooling', *Educational Evaluation and Policy Analysis*, 6/1: 73–83.

OECD (1992), *Education at a Glance: OECD Indicators* (Paris: OECD).

Pittman, R., and Haughwout, P. (1987), 'Influence of High School Size on Dropout Rate', *Educational Evaluation and Policy Analysis*, 9: 337–43.

Wehlage, G. G., Rutter, R. A., Smith, G. A., Lesko, N., and Fernandez, R. R. (1989), *Reducing the Risk: Schools as Communities of Support* (Philadelphia: Falmer).

23

Restructuring Restructuring: Postmodernity and the Prospects for Educational Change

Andy Hargreaves

Introduction

In 1986, the Carnegie Forum of 'Education and the Economy', in their report, *A Nation Prepared*, announced the need to 'restructure schools' (Carnegie Forum on Education and the Economy 1986). This restructuring, it was thought, would respect and support the professionalism of teachers to make decisions in their own classrooms that best met local and state goals, while also holding teachers accountable for how they did that.

In this article, I will examine some of the meanings of restructuring, along with a number of key choices and dilemmas that restructuring poses for educators, particularly with regard to teacher development and professional growth. The paper begins by distinguishing restructuring from its antecedent of educational reform. Two different scenarios of restructuring are then explored, as represented by the writings of Sarason and Schlechty. Together, it is argued, these scenarios highlight tensions in restructuring between bureaucracy and professionalism. Such tensions, I go on to show, are not specific to education but are rooted in wider tensions in society as a whole as it moves into the restructured era of postmodernity. Finally, the implications of these tensions in restructuring are explored in the form of four fundamental dilemmas between:

- vision and voice;
- mandates and menus;
- trust in persons and trust in processes;
- structure and culture.

The Context and Meaning of Restructuring

Change by *restructuring* has followed quickly on the heels of change by *reform* which sought to mandate improvement on teachers by bureaucratic control and compliance, rather than supporting teachers to improve themselves and creating structured opportunities for them in ways that respected their professionalism. Within the era of reform, the USA placed substantial emphasis on teacher certification and on basic competency tests for teachers. In many states and school districts, initiatives to motivate the teaching force followed through such measures as merit pay, career ladders and differentiated staffing. In the UK, central controls over teacher preparation were exerted at the national level through procedures of accreditation for teacher education programmes. These accredited programmes devoted more attention to practical teaching experience and subject-matter mastery and, by implication, less attention to critical reflection on the purposes, ethics and social consequences of different versions of teaching (Rudduck 1989). In 1988, a newly legislated teacher contract also enumerated the number of hours for which teachers would be minimally contracted including what was termed 'directed time' out of class: to be directed according to the wishes of the headteacher or principal.

Within the context of change through reform, measures designed to motivate teachers were paralleled by ones aimed at improving curriculum and instruction. In the UK,

From *Journal of Education Policy*, 9 (1994), 47–65. Reprinted with permission.

the increased prominence given to subject-matter knowledge in teacher education, and the governmental imposition of a subject-based National Curriculum, betrayed a shift from broad sponsorship of teachers and school self-education, self-evaluation and critical reflection to training and induction in contents and principles already determined elsewhere—at the national level (Hargreaves 1989). In the USA, many career ladder and teacher leadership programmes selected, rewarded and evaluated teachers not according to multiple criteria of excellence and professional growth, but according to those teachers' adherence to approved models of instruction, often ones that placed a premium on mastery of basic skills (Hargreaves and Dawe 1990; Popkewitz and Line 1989; Smyth and Garman 1989). In these cases, the reform of teaching and the reform of instruction went together. Teacher development was not self-development. It was development directed toward the goals of others within a bureaucratic context of regulation and control.

It did not take long for problems of the reform paradigm to surface. It under-estimated the divisive effects of career ladders among teachers, misunderstood the basis of teacher motivation as one rooted not in extrinsic career 'carrots' but in intrinsic work rewards, and did not appreciate that because of teachers' control over the sanctuaries of their own classrooms, teacher improvement could not be mandated by bureaucratic control. More than this, as the US debt crisis mounted, and the responsiveness of the corporate world to global competitiveness began to look sluggish, there were growing concerns that young people leaving high school needed more than the traditional minimum competences and basic skills that had preoccupied reformers' thinking hitherto. Problem solving, higher order thinking skills, risk taking, teamwork and co-operation: these were emerging as the skills and competencies that young people would require as America entered the global information society. Tinkering and quick fixes within the bounds of the existing system, it seemed, could not bring about significant improvements even in terms of the basic skills and academic achievements that comprised the traditional goals of schooling. Certainly, they could not meet the still greater educational challenges now being posed by the new information society. Reform

within the bounds of the existing system was not enough. Something more fundamental was called for: nothing short of a complete *restructuring* of the organization of teaching and learning to meet the challenges of the 21st century.

In the space of just a few years, restructuring has become common currency in educational policy vocabulary, right up to the office of President in the USA and among Ministers and civil servants in other national and regional policy contexts too (O'Neil 1990). Yet its meanings are various, conflicting and often ill-defined. As Tyack observes, where restructuring is concerned, vague is vogue (Tyack 1990).

The possible components of restructuring are many and various. According to Murphy and Everston, they comprise school-based management, increased consumer choice, teacher empowerment and teaching for understanding (Murphy and Everston 1991). For the National Governors' Association, they include curriculum and instruction redesigned to promote higher order thinking skills; the decentralization of authority and decision making to site level; more diverse and differentiated roles for teachers; and broadened systems of accountability (National Governors' Association 1989). While the specific components of restructuring vary from one writer to another, most seem to agree that what is centrally involved is a fundamental redefinition of rules, roles, responsibilities and relationships for teachers and leaders in our schools (Schlechty 1990). Beyond this point, though, the desire for consensus about and commitment to restructuring in general has left its specific meaning inchoate.

But the broader meanings of restructuring are not infinite. While the particulars vary from scheme to scheme, certain general patterns of restructuring are becoming evident which embody quite distinct principles of power and control and which serve very different purposes. Two scenarios of restructuring offer an initial flavour of some of the important contrasts here.

The first is drawn from Seymour Sarason's account of *The Predictable Failure of Educational Reform* (Sarason 1990). Sarason argues that, by the criterion of classroom impact, most educational reform has failed. This failure, he says, is predictable. He identifies two factors as responsible for this. First, he notes that the different components of educational reform have neither been conceived nor addressed as a whole, in their inter-relationships, as a complex system. If components like curriculum change, or professional development or new teaching strategies are tackled in isolation while others are left unchanged, the success of the reforms will almost certainly be undermined. Sarason supplies numerous historical examples of such failed reforms. That such patterns are not merely a matter of historical record, but persist as a chronic feature of our present systems, is strikingly revealed in recent studies of the implementation of manipulative problem-solving approaches to mathematics teaching in California. These evaluations show that teachers commonly fail to implement the programmes because of the persistence of other programmes that emphasize direct instruction in basic skills, and because the dominant forms of evaluation and testing continue to be of a conventional, paper-and-pencil kind. Sarason's argument has two important implications. First, significant change in curriculum, assessment or any other domain is unlikely to be successful unless serious attention is also paid to teacher development and the principles of professional judgement and discretion contained within it. Second, teacher development and enhanced professionalism must also be undertaken in conjunction with developments in curriculum, assessment, leadership and school organization.

Sarason's second, and arguably more radical contention is that major educational change is unlikely to be successful unless it addresses school power relationships. 'Schools . . . remain intractable to desired reform as long as we avoid confronting their existing power relationships', he argues (Sarason 1990: 5). These include relationships between administrators and teachers, between teachers and parents and between teachers and students. Sarason argues for a radical rethink of how schools and classrooms are run. His vision of restructuring entails change that is comprehensive in scope, accompanied by significant, not superficial redistributions of existing power relationships among principals, teachers, parents and students. It is a vision that is rooted in a sociopsychological understanding of schools as places not only devoted to teaching and learning, but also defined through relation-ships of power and control. Restructuring means redefining these relationships in fundamental ways.

In a second scenario, Philip Schlechty also sets out a comprehensive restructuring agenda (Schlechty 1990). Like Sarason, Schlechty's advocacy of restructuring springs from a concern about the inappropriateness of most school structures for the needs of modern society. With their single classroom, single lesson, single teacher formats, such structures are more suited to late 19th- and early 20th-century preoccupations with mass education in basic skills, and with rigid educational selection for future work roles that are expected to remain fixed over time, than to the complex needs of the postindustrial order.

Both Schlechty and Sarason see a need for new skills and qualities in postindustrial society, and for new structures to generate them. Sarason defines these in a socially and politically broad way. For him they are the skills and problem-solving capacities needed to cope with and respond to a complex, changing and threatened social world. They are cultural and political skills as well as occupational ones. For Schlechty, though, the purposes of education in the 21st century are driven by more specifically corporate concerns. For him, the challenge is that of the global information society. Children are construed as 'knowledge-workers' and schools are defined as being in the business of 'knowledge-work'.

It is reasonable to expect that, as the American economy becomes more information based, and as the mode of labour shifts from manual work to knowledge work, concern with the continuous growth and learning of citizens and employees will increase. Moreover, the conditions of work will require one to learn to function well in groups, exercise considerable self-discipline, exhibit loyalty while maintaining critical faculties, respect the rights of others and in turn expect to be respected . . . .This list of characteristics could as well be a list of the virtues of a citizen in a democracy. (Schlechty 1990: 39)

While many of these contents are similar to Sarason's, the corporate context of Schlechty's agenda none the less narrows the range of the qualities and characteristics thought appropriate as outcomes in the schools of the future. There is talk of respect, but not of care—either for other persons or for the environment. Justice and equity are also absent. Productivity is paramount. This does not distort, but it does restrict what it is seen as appropriate for schools to do.

The corporate context of Schlechty's advocacy has especially striking implications for his views of power and leadership in restructured schools. Participatory leadership *is* advocated but not on the grounds of truth, beauty or justice. The grounds of organisational effectiveness are the ones that are invoked. While, superficially, Schlechty appears to support changes in power relationships, in practice it is only the 'symbols of power' that are to be rearranged. Much of the mechanics of leadership may change but ultimately control of the organization is vested in 'strong leaders'; leaders who are the architects of their organizations' visions.

This is a view of power and leadership that is quite different from Sarason's more democratic view and is instead deeply rooted in the corporate perspective. Schlechty advises administrators to read more widely outside education, but all the references he lists are in the corporate and economic domain. Moral philosophy, organizational politics and human development are excluded from that list. Moreover, he instructs his readers that 'those who are leading the restructuring of schools and those who are leading the restructuring of America's enterprises are in the same business' (Schlechty 1990: 14–15). Restructuring for Schlechty is therefore restructuring in a corporate context—corporate in its proposed structures for schooling and corporate in its desired outcomes for learning. This corporate perspective gives Schlechty a limited purchase on power relationships and teacher empowerment—one where bold rhetoric disguises balder realities; where professional growth is subsumed into a framework of administrative control.

Together these two scenarios remind us that there is nothing inevitably good or inherently bad about restructuring. Much depends on who controls it, who is involved in it and the purposes to which it is to be put. The agenda of restructuring comprises many important dilemmas, dilemmas that involve profound ethical and political choices about values and purposes.

At the heart of these is a fundamental choice between restructuring as bureaucratic control, where teachers are controlled and regulated to implement the mandates of others, and restructuring as professional empower-

ment, where teachers are supported, encouraged and provided with newly structured opportunities to make improvements of their own, in partnership with parents, principals and students. Our wish for consensus and our desire to maintain the momentum of change often deflects us from addressing these fundamental and difficult dilemmas. Yet if we do not grapple with them ourselves and resolve them to our own satisfaction, others will only resolve them for us later and perhaps in ways that jar with and undermine our own values and commitments. In the remainder of this paper, I want to scratch beneath the current consensus of restructuring, and expose the dilemmas of value, of purpose and of control which I believe we must now confront and resolve as we meet the educational challenges of the coming century.

Dilemmas of Restructuring

Restructuring involves many choices and dilemmas. Some of these, like the choice between centralization and decentralization, are familiar ones and have already been widely discussed. Here I want to review what I consider to be four equally important but less widely discussed dilemmas of restructuring; ones that have powerful implications for the purposes of restructuring and the directions it will take, as well as for the processes of teacher development contained within it. We shall see that tensions between bureaucracy and professionalism run through all of these.

VISION OR VOICE
One of the key tensions in restructuring is between vision and voice. It is not specific to restructuring in education, but has its roots in the restructuring of contemporary society more generally.

There is a burgeoning literature now on the transitions currently being experienced within and across many societies from industrial to postindustrial, modern to postmodern, or liberal to postliberal forms. The outcome of these transitions is, for most analysts, uncertain. As the prefix 'post' itself suggests, there is more clarity about what we are moving beyond than what we are moving towards (Fleming 1991). Most writers agree, though, that at the heart of the transition is the globalization of information, communication and technology (Giddens 1990; Harvey 1989; Menzies 1989; Naisbett and Aberdene 1990). With it has come a compression of time and space and an increase in the pace of productivity and decision making. Computerization, along with satellite communication and fibre-optic telecommunications, has made international trading in information and currency markets ceaseless. Turnover time of goods and services has shortened and economic corporations have been able to spread their interests and expertise across national boundaries, utilizing local markets, labour resources and land opportunities, and maintaining instantaneous connection and co-ordination across the whole network of operations through modern communications technology.

The globalization of trade and of economic activity is weakening the significance of national boundaries as the world reorganizes into a smaller number of larger, more robust economic units. By the end of 1992, all customs and trade barriers will have been removed in the European Community. The once unthinkable goal of a common European currency has been agreed in principle. And the opening of the Channel Tunnel will merely complete a physical and technological union that will already have been achieved economically. Free Trade agreements already secured between the USA and Canada, and now Mexico, have similarly elevated economic unity and flexibility above national identity on the other side of the Atlantic.

In many respects, the globalization of economic life is coming to mean that the nation-state as a separate economic, political and cultural entity is under threat and in decline. In response to these threats, attempts have emerged to protect and reconstruct national identities, not least through the development of national curricula as described by Goodson, in which elements of national culture and heritage figure strongly (Goodson 1990).

Goodson sees, within the reassertion of traditional academic subjects prescribed by the National Curriculum of England and Wales, an attempt to revive and reconstruct a floundering national identity.

The globalization of economic life, and more particularly of communication, information and technology, all pose enormous challenges to the existing modes of control and operation of nation-states. In this sense, the pursuance of a new cen-tralized national curriculum might be seen as the response of the more economically endangered species among nations. (Goodson 1990: 220)

Dealing with the specific case of history, he continues.

[T]he balance of subjects in the national curriculum suggest [sic] that questions of national identity and control have been pre-eminent, rather than industrial or commercial requirements. For example, information technology has been largely omitted, whilst history has been embraced as a 'foundation subject', even though it is quite clearly a subject in decline within the schools. (Goodson 1990: 221)

This is particularly so, he argues, given the high emphasis accorded to British history within the history curriculum. British history, Canadian content—these are the stuff of national cultural reconstruction, where the burden of reinvented traditions is placed, like most other social burdens, on the shoulders of education. More important still, as globalization intensifies, as McDonald's opens in Moscow and sushi bars prosper in New York, as international urban landscapes become ever more alike in the global commodification of community living, we are witnessing the resurgence of ethnic, religious and linguistic identities and attachments in the face of globalization, as seen in the struggles of Latvians, Lithuanians and Estonians to secure secession from the Soviet Union. It can also be seen on Canadian soil, in the collapse of constitutional accords, in the fights of francophones to secure recognition for themselves as a distinct society and for the province of Quebec as a politically autonomous unit, and in the struggles of First Nation peoples for self-determination as 'nations-within-a-nation'.

What we are witnessing here is the emergence in the context of postmodernity of the voices of those who have previously been unheard, neglected, rejected, ignored—the voices of those who have formerly been marginalized and dispossessed. Gilligan's influential book, *In a Different Voice*, draws attention to the undervalued women's perspective on moral development, for instance (Gilligan 1982). As Harvey (1989: 48) puts it, 'The idea that all groups have a right to speak for themselves, in their own voice accepted as authentic and legitimate is essential to the pluralistic stance of postmodernism.' In the educational change and educational research literature, the formerly unheard or undervalued teacher's voice has been accorded increasing respect and authority in recent years. And there, especially in elementary schools, the teacher's voice is also usually the woman's voice. Elbaz notes how much of the emergent work on teachers' knowledge, thinking and empowerment is centrally concerned with the notion of voice. Where the notion of voice is used, she says, 'the term is always used against the background of a previous silence, and it is a political usage as well as an epistemological one' (Elbaz 1991: 10). Goodson argues that teachers' voices are rooted in their lives, their lifestyles and their point in the life cycle (Goodson 1991). The teacher's voice, says Goodson, articulates the teacher's life and its purposes. To understand teaching, therefore, either as a researcher, an administrator or a colleague, it is not enough merely to witness the behaviour, skills and actions of teaching. One must also listen to the voice of the teacher, to the person it expresses and to the purposes it articulates. Failure to understand the teacher's voice is failure to understand the teacher's teaching. For this reason, our priority should be not merely to listen to the teacher's voice, but also to sponsor it as a priority within our teacher development work.

Yet, the rise of dissident voices threatens traditional centres of power and control. Struggles for regional autonomy and linguistic or ethnic separatism, for instance, challenge long-standing patterns of central domination. Similarly, in education, the bureaucratic impetus to guide the process of change and improvement from the centre may lead the teacher's voice that doubts the change or disagrees with it to go unheard, or be silenced or be dismissed as 'mere' resistance. In this respect, as the forces of bureaucratic control and teacher development wrestle with one another, one of the greatest challenges to the emergence of teacher *voice* is the orchestration of educational *vision*.

The development of a common vision, commitment to shared goals or developing clarity in understanding the goals being implemented by others are commonly advocated components of the change and improvement process. They are seen as essential to developing confidence and consistency among a community of teachers. Educational leaders are viewed as vital to the development

of motivating visions. According to Achilles (1987: 18), for instance, leaders 'must know what is needed to improve schools, they must know how to administer the schools to achieve the desired results. As a starting point, principals must envision better schools, articulate this vision to others, and orchestrate consensus on the vision'. There is a strong sense here that the vision is primarily the principal's vision, a vision to be articulated to (not developed with) others, a vision around which the orchestration of consensus will follow later.

These criticisms are not intended to dispute the importance of vision, of shared purpose and direction among a school's staff. The crucial question, though, is 'whose vision is this?'. For some writers, the principal's role in promoting school improvement and helping develop the culture of the school becomes one of manipulating the culture and its teachers to conform to the principal's own vision. Deal and Peterson, for example, urge that once principals have come to understand their school's culture, they should then ask, 'If it matches my conception of a "good school", what can I do to reinforce or strengthen existing patterns?'; 'If my vision is at odds with the existing mindset, values or ways of acting, what can be done to change or shape the culture?' (Deal and Peterson 1987). For Deal and Peterson, who write very much from a corporate perspective, this is part of the solution to the challenge of school leadership. In many respects, though, it can be seen as part of the problem.

The corporate folly of vision building being spearheaded by strong and single-minded leaders is revealed in an account of how Air Canada's new president, Claude Taylor, tried to turn the company around.

To show the new way, Taylor wrote a mission statement for the airline, framed it on his private meeting room wall and sent a copy to every employee's home. (*The Globe and Mail Report on Business*, February 1991)

Part of the solution? Or part of the problem?

'My company', 'my vision', 'my teachers', 'my school'—these proprietary claims and attitudes suggest an ownership of the school and of change which is individual rather than collective, imposed rather than earned, and hierarchical rather than democratic. The ownership is also most usually male ownership, in which power is exercised over women.

With *visions* as singular as this, teachers soon learn to suppress their *voice*. Management becomes manipulation. Collaboration becomes co-optation. Worst of all, having teachers conform to the principal's vision minimizes the opportunities for principals to learn that parts of their own vision may be flawed: that some teachers' visions may be as valid or more valid than theirs!

This does not mean that principals' visions are unimportant. The quality and clarity of their visions may have helped mark them out for leadership. But principals have no monopoly on wisdom. Nor should they be immune from the questioning, inquiry and deep reflection in which we have asked teachers to engage. Principals' visions should therefore be provisional visions: ones that are open to change. They should be part of the collaborative mix. The authority of principals' views should not be presumed because of whose views they are, but because of their quality and richness.

Ultimately, the responsibility for vision building should be a collective, not an individual one. Collaboration should mean creating the vision together, not complying with the principal's own. All stakeholders should be involved in illuminating the mission and purposes of the school. Leithwood and Jantzi describe a practical example of developing shared school goals for school improvement, where the responsibility for the task was delegated to school improvement teams. This, they note, 'prevented the principal's goals from dominating the process', although the authors add ominously in parentheses 'or from being seen to dominate the process'! (Leithwood and Jantzi 1990).

Exclusive emphasis on vision or voice alone is constructive neither for restructuring nor for professional development in particular. A world of voice without vision is a world reduced to chaotic babble where there are no means for arbitrating between voices, reconciling them or drawing them together. This is the dark side of the postmodern world, a world from which community and authority have disappeared. It is a world where the authority of voice has supplanted the voice of authority to an excessive degree. Research studies which go beyond merely understanding teachers' stories to endorsing and celebrating them, and research traditions which give arbitrary credence to teacher accounts over

(neglected) accounts of parents or students, for instance, illustrate some of the difficulties of this postmodern perspective. Voices need to be not only heard, but also engaged, reconciled and argued with. It is important to attend not only to the aesthetics of articulating teacher voices, but also to the ethics of what it is those voices articulate!

We have seen that a world of vision without voice is equally problematic. In this world where purposes are imposed and consensus is contrived, there is no place for the practical judgement and wisdom of teachers; no place for their voices to get a proper hearing. A major challenge for educational restructuring is to work through and reconcile this tension between vision and voice; to create a choir from a cacophony.

MANDATES OR MENUS

The paradox of postmodernity is that with the globalization of information, communication and economic life come tendencies and capacities to adapt, respond to and emphasize local and immediate production needs and consumer wants. This move from massification to diversity in economic activity, together with the localized and regionalized revitalizations of cultural, ethnic and linguistic identity described in the previous section, has profound implications for knowledge and belief systems and the expertise that rests upon them. What we are witnessing here at the societal level is a shift from a small number of stable singularities of knowledge and belief to a fluctuating, ever changing plurality of belief systems.

Confidence in universalizing, all-encompassing belief systems is in decline. Our growing understanding of the imminence of environmental catastrophe on a global scale has seriously undermined our faith in technology as a way of accurately and reliably predicting and controlling our world in the rational pursuit of progress. The spread of information along with the globalization of economies has also threatened beliefs in the scientifically predicted inevitability of socialist transformation, a change both symbolized and stimulated by the collapse of the Berlin Wall. Such meta-theories and meta-narratives of human understanding are in disrepute (Harvey 1989). Even narrative knowing itself, as something which seeks to understand the allegedly inherent 'narrative unities' that make up people's lives, has been subjected to vigorous criticism on the grounds that people's lives and biographies are characterized as much by inconsistency, contradiction and fragmentation as they are by any purported unity (Willinsky 1989).

The movement from vision to voice is therefore being accompanied by a movement from single and relatively stable belief systems to multiple and rapidly shifting ones. This is because of the globalization of information and understanding. It is also occurring because such globalization compresses space and time, leading to an increasing pace of change in the world we seek to know and in our ways of knowing it—a flux which continually threatens the stability and endurance of our knowledge bases, making them irretrievably provisional. In addition, the diversification of knowledge and belief is due to the expansion of travel and of multicultural migration, bringing different belief systems into increasing contact. Lastly, the shift is also due to an ever-tightening and recursive relationship between social research and development, where the social world changes even as we study it, not least as a response to the very inquiries we make of it (Giddens 1990)!

This transformation in our ways of knowing in many respects marks a movement from cultures of certainty to cultures of uncertainty. This diminishing credibility of traditional knowledge bases along with declining certainty attached to research expertise has immense implications for education and its restructuring. These implications are expressed in an emerging tension between *mandates* and *menus* as preferred ways of delivering and developing educational improvement. They are tensions that make themselves felt in a number of areas, two of which I will explore here. These are the implementation of new teaching strategies, and the development of different kinds of collegiality.

In teaching strategies, as in other areas, a key issue is whether to recognize and sponsor single or multiple versions of excellence; whether to acknowledge only one route to salvation or to concede that many such routes are possible. Many, perhaps most of our reform efforts over recent years have been predicated on single models of excellence. These have been grounded in and legitimated by the allegedly incontrovertible findings of educational research. Madeline Hunter's renowned

model of *Elements of Instruction* is one example (Hunter 1984). This model organizes training in effective teaching around closely prescribed principles of 'direct instruction'. For a time, the model was widely adopted and mandated in many American and Canadian school districts, as a required focus for staff training in methods of supposedly 'proven' effectiveness. In many districts, adherence to the model has been used as a basis for teacher evaluation. In at least one district, effective compliance with the model has also been used to evaluate teachers' suitability to be mentors of new entrants to the profession (Popkewitz and Line 1989).

Direct instruction has subsequently been criticized on the grounds that it is not universally applicable but effective only in particular settings—especially those emphasizing basic skills (Hallinger and Murphy 1987), on the grounds that its widespread adoption in a school prejudices the growth of more risk-taking, open-ended teaching strategies (see articles in the *Educational Evaluation and Policy Analysis* issue of Fall 1990), and on the grounds that it fosters dependency and inflexibility among those who use it (Smyth and Garman 1989). It would seem, therefore, that efforts to improve teacher effectiveness, and to implement policies of evaluating and promoting teachers on the basis of their presumed effectiveness, have actually been based not on broad criteria of effectiveness at all but on particular and limited versions of it; indeed on versions that may actually inhibit the growth of effective characteristics and behaviours of other kinds among teachers.

Similar criticisms have been directed at the models of teaching reviewed by Joyce and Weil, and used as a basis for programmes of in-service teacher training through peer coaching (Joyce and Weil 1986). In *Staff Development for Student Achievement*, Joyce and Showers promote strategies of peer coaching to secure the adoption of preferred teaching strategies such as co-operative learning and mastery teaching, whose usefulness and effectiveness are said to be solidly grounded in the findings of educational research (Joyce and Showers 1988). Joyce and Showers's work, which has also been used widely in school systems, has been criticized on the grounds that it undervalues the practical insight and wisdom of teachers and requires teachers to comply with the knowledge, expertise and prescriptions that are the property and prerogative of a small cadre of scientific 'experts' (Hargreaves and Dawe 1990). Robertson (1992: 46) sees in their technologically optimistic claims to scientific certainty, not only an unjustified warrant for bureaucratic intervention in teachers' work, but also an overconfidence in the authority of 'hard research' that has strong gender connotations. As she puts it:

One can hear a stereotypically masculine overconfidence when the authors quote Ron Edmonds in their introduction: 'We can, whenever and wherever we want, successfully teach all children whose schooling is of interest to us. We already know more than we need to do that.' Such certainty and predictability are familiar aspects of a masculine view of reality, as is the dependence on external rather than internal inquiry. The 'we' to whom Edmonds is referring is assuredly not classroom teachers; this claim for the power of knowledge and instrumentalism refers only to those whose expertise is validated within hierarchical systems. The authors give no indication that they believe teachers might already know enough to teach more children better, but rather that experts can train teachers in observable and tested behaviours which will produce predicted results.

Reliance on the imposition of singular models of teaching expertise can create inflexibility among teachers and make it hard for them to exercise proper discretionary judgements in their classrooms. It can lead to teacher resistance because of implicit rejections of the worth and value of the rest of a teacher's repertoire, and of the life and the person that has been invested in building it up. It can also lead to an overly narrow focus on particular techniques just when we are beginning to understand that effective instruction in real classroom settings involves teachers possessing a wide repertoire of teaching strategies which they apply flexibly according to the needs of the child and the moment.

The pathways of educational reform are strewn with the discarded certainties of the past. Reading schemes, language laboratories, programmed learning, even open classrooms—reforms such as these would be appropriate exhibits for any museum of innovation. Today's solutions often become tomorrow's problems. Future exhibits in the museum of innovation could easily include whole-language, co-operative learning or manipulative maths. We do not know yet. The

point is, our knowledge and understanding of the effectiveness of these methods is often provisional, and contingent on their being used in particular circumstances. Singular models of expertise that rest on an allegedly dependable research base are built on epistemological sand. Multiple models of excellence are grounded in and arise from collective wisdom in the community of teachers and other educators (including but not confined to research). They acknowledge the provisional and context-dependent character of the knowledge base of teaching. They respect and leave space for teachers' discretionary judgements in their own classrooms. And by endorsing the possession and application of broad teaching repertoires, they permit gradual and selective adaptation and integration of new approaches without this necessarily implying wholesale rejection of the old.

In addition to all this, multiple models of instructional excellence also foster greater collegiality among teachers by acknowledging that teachers have complementary instructional expertise as a basis for partnership. In a study of elementary teachers' use of preparation time, Wignall and I found that teachers generously acknowledged their colleagues' complementary expertise when it was rooted in subject-matter (Hargreaves and Wignall 1989). They readily acknowledged they might need help and could get support in, say, art or physical education or music. They were less likely to acknowledge complementary expertise in classroom management or in styles of instruction, however. This may be because, among teachers, there is an easier acceptance of a legitimate range of alternative teaching styles. For many teachers, to acknowledge expertise in another's teaching style is not to acknowledge the value of another version of teaching, but to defer to someone else's superior skills as a teacher and therefore to cast doubts on the adequacy of one's own. For all these reasons, multiple models of classroom excellence are to be preferred over singular ones. Menus from which to choose are to be preferred to mandates which have to be implemented.

A second area in which menus should prevail over mandates is that of teacher collaboration and collegiality. Collaborative work among teachers can take many different forms. Teachers can collaborate, for instance, on developing school goals or mission statements. They can collaborate in curriculum and other kinds of planning. They can collaborate through structured systems of help and support in the forms of peer coaching or mentor programmes. They can collaborate in systematic inquiry or action research. And they can collaborate in classroom practice through team teaching. Yet, administrative systems sometimes assume or act as if collaboration takes only one form, then pressurize teachers to adopt it. Mandatory peer coaching, compulsory team teaching, required collaborative planning—measures as inflexible and insensitive as these rest on singular models of collaborative excellence. They fail to recognize the diverse forms that collaborative work can take. They prescribe narrow techniques that may not suit some people or contexts, and lose sight of the broad collaborative principle which gives rise to them and which could command wider support. They therefore offend the discretionary judgement of teachers that is at the core of teacher professionalism. Despite administrative rhetoric, mandating specific kinds of collaboration is not empowering but disempowering.

Where such singular models of collaborative excellence are adopted, what transpires is what I have elsewhere called *contrived collegiality* (Hargreaves 1991): a form of collaboration which is forced rather than facilitated, which meets the implementation needs of bureaucratic systems rather than the development needs of teachers and schools, which is designed to be administratively predictable rather than unpredictable in its outcomes, and which, as a result, might be viewed as stereotypically male rather than female in its style of operation. *Collaborative* teacher *cultures*, meanwhile, comprise many different and interconnected forms of collaborative work, some quite informal; they offer teachers high discretion over the kinds of collaborative work with which they want to be involved; they evolve more slowly around the trust and patience that is needed to build supportive relationships; and, because of the levels of teacher involvement and control, they are more unpredictable in terms of their specific outcomes. This can cause particular difficulty for bureaucratic and hierarchical systems of administration seeking to incorporate collaborative work into existing systems of administrative control.

Putting menus before mandates means not forcing through one particular approach. It means developing awareness of, commitment to and experience in the general collaborative principle. Administratively, it is important to commit to the collaborative principle, but to empower teachers to select from the wide range of practice the ones that suit them best. However, while commitment to collaboration is important, over-commitment or compulsion can be damaging. Increasing the commitment to collaborative work and having most teachers try some aspects of it is probably vital. But working for a 100 per cent adoption rate is unrealistic and undesirable. Most teachers will plan for or teach some things better alone than together. And there are some who teach better entirely alone. The solitary mode has its place (Hargreaves 1993).

Not all individualistic teachers are weak teachers. A few are strong, even excellent classroom practitioners. They may be eccentric, prima donna-ish, difficult to work with as colleagues, but skilled in their own classrooms none the less. The idiosyncratic excellence of such teachers should not be punished in pursuit of the collegial norm.

While commitment to collaboration is important, therefore, it should not be pursued with administrative and ideological inflexibility. Above all else, even above collaboration, respect for teacher discretion is paramount, providing this does no harm to students. This is why menus should prevail over mandates. The struggle in making that choice is ultimately a struggle for professional, discretionary control among the community of teachers at school level, against the retention and reconstruction of bureaucratic control by administrators and their system.

TRUST IN PEOPLE OR TRUST IN PROCESSES?
In the struggle between bureaucratic control and personal empowerment that marks the transition to postmodernity, collaborative relationships and the particular forms they take are central. Such relationships, I have argued, can help give vent to the voice of the people, or they can contribute to the reconstitution of central control. They are at the core of the restructuring agenda and all its contradictory possibilities.

A pervasive theme that runs throughout the literature of shared leadership and collaborative cultures is the truism of trust. The establishment of trust, it is argued, is essential to the build-up of effective and meaningful collaborative work relationships. For Lieberman and colleagues, 'trust and rapport . . . are the foundation for building collegiality in a school' (Lieberman *et al.* 1988). Louden (1991: 14), for instance, describes the importance of trust in the establishment of a collaborative relationship between himself as a researcher, and the teacher with whom he worked.

The trust we developed was quite personal in character. We found that we liked each other, we became friends and the project became more than a piece of work for both of us. I enjoyed working with Johanna and participating in the life of the school, she liked having me around and hoped my study would go well.

The value of such trust in collaborative working relationships is so widely acknowledged and understood that we rarely probe more than superficially into its meaning and nature. One exception is Nias and her colleagues who note that 'to talk of trust as if it explained everything is . . . to make it into a "black box", an abstract word packed with individual meanings' (Nias, Southworth, and Yeomans 1989). They argue that trust has two dimensions—predictability and common goals. 'For trust to exist,' they argue, 'people must find one another highly predictable and share substantially the same aims' (Nias *et al.* 1989: 81). To paraphrase Nias *et al.*, we might say that trust is a process of personal and predictable mutuality.

This understanding of trust and the social-psychological heritage from which is springs certainly helps illuminate our understanding of the dynamics of interpersonal relationships in the context of small-group collaboration. But it is an understanding that does not illuminate all forms of trust; only trust in particular circumstances. These are ones of interpersonal relationships that remain relatively stable and persistent over time. As Gidden observes, however, there are also other variants of trust. These can be found in contexts where interpersonal relationships are much less stable and persistent over time. Giddens (1990: 34) alludes to these contrasts in his core definition of trust.

Trust may be defined as confidence in the reliability of a person or system, regarding a given set of outcomes or events, where that confidence expresses a faith in the probity or love of another, or in the correctness of abstract principles.

Trust in other words, can be invested in persons or in processes—in the qualities and conduct of individuals, or in the expertise and performance of abstract systems. It can be an outcome of meaningful face-to-face relationships, or a condition of their existence.

The movement from small and simple to massified and modernistic societies brought with it transformations in the forms of trust that were dominant in people's lives. These transformations can be seen particularly clearly in the changing relationships between these two things. There is a reciprocal relationship between trust and risk. In simple societies, risk was associated with permanent danger; with threats of wild beasts, marauding raiders, famines and floods. Personal trust in family, friends and community helped people cope with these persistent risks. Risk in simple societies was something to be minimized or avoided. In modern, mass organizations and societies, risk and trust took on different qualities. In modern, mass secondary schools, for instance, there were often too many adults to know everyone well. Personnel could change frequently, including leaders. Trust in individuals was no longer sufficient. When key individuals left or leaders moved on, exclusive reliance on personal trust could cause massive instability. In part, these sorts of problems in societies of growing industrial complexity explained the rise of and constituted a persuasive case for bureaucratic forms of organization. Advancing change and complexity led to a decline in traditional forms of authority. Even innovative schools spearheaded by charismatic leaders often reverted to mediocrity when they left. In modern, mass societies and organizations, another kind of trust was therefore called for: trust in processes and abstract systems.

Tragically and ironically, though, as Max Weber's work reveals so clearly, the iron grip of modern bureaucracy simply perverted the course of system trust (Weber 1968). Predictability turned into inflexibility. Relationships and responsiveness became strangled by rules and regulations. Once they had grown and become established, modern bureaucratic organizations became too inflexible and self-serving to respond to local circumstances and changing needs. The interests of persons were blocked by the inertia of procedure. Trust in impersonal authority and technical expertise therefore declined. Confidence in abstract principles was undermined.

Modern secondary schools, for instance, were and still are criticized for being vast bureaucratic organizations unable to build a sense of community, to secure loyalty and attachment among their students, and to be responsive to the changing social world around them. Secondary schools, that is, were an integral part of the malaise of modernity. Similarly, prevailing patterns of educational change and reform have been criticized for their top-down, standardized, bureaucratic application across entire systems in ways that neglect the purposes and personalities of individual teachers and the context in which they work.

The transition form modernity to postmodernity marks the emergence of new kinds of process trust along with the reconstruction of more traditional kinds of personal trust. In postmodern societies, the form and articulation of corporate activity changes from the large mass factory to smaller, dispersed centres of enterprise, connected by rapid communications and efficient means for processing information. These developments give rise to two important trends in the reconstruction of trust.

First, there is the reconstruction of personal trust. There is extensive and increasing advocacy in the corporate and educational worlds for making the local unit of enterprise more meaningful to those working within it and more empowered to respond to the needs of its local environment. Emphasis is placed on the reconstruction of intimacy, warmth and personal trust in the building of rewarding and also productive collaborative work relationships. With these ends in view, many school districts have initiated programmes of school-based management. Large and impersonal secondary schools are also looking increasingly generously at the possibilities for creating smaller, self-contained mini-schools or subschools within them that are more meaningful and self-determining for students and teachers alike (Hargreaves and Earl 1990).

This reinvention of personal trust is double-edged, however. Personal trust can build loyalty, commitment and effectiveness in the enhanced capacity that comes from shared decision making. But it can also reintroduce problems of paternalism and dependency and characterized traditional forms of authority and organization. Indeed, a number of writers have noted that what appear to be collabora-

tive school cultures seem to prosper most in smaller organizations under conditions of exceptionally strong leadership of a personalized nature (Nias *et al.* 1989). As Acker notes, this can transform internal collective confidence into collective complacency, carrying with it reduced capacity and willingness to network and learn from other kinds of expertise from outside that are not grounded in immediate and trusted personal relationships (Acker 1989). Too much reliance can be placed on the principal to be responsible for external linkages.

Exclusive reliance on personal trust and the forms of collaboration that are built upon it can lead to paternalism and parochialism, then. Additional trust in expertise and processes helps postmodern organizations develop and solve problems on a continuing basis in an environment where problems and challenges are continuous and changing. Processes to be trusted here are ones that maximize the organization's collective expertise and improve its problem-solving capacities. These include improved communication, shared decision making, creation of opportunities for collegial learning, networking with outside environments, commitment to continuous inquiry and so on. Trust in people remains important, but trust in expertise and processes supersedes it. Trust in processes is open-ended and risky. But it is probably essential to learning and improvement.

This means that in postmodern school systems, risk is something to be embraced rather than avoided. Risk taking fosters learning, adaptability and improvement. The trust it presumes may need to extend beyond the close interpersonal understandings that make up the collaborative cultures described earlier. These understandings and cultures are important, especially in smaller schools and teams. But larger and more rapidly changing schools require teachers who can invest trust in processes too; who can trust their colleagues provisionally, even before they know them well. This is not to advocate contrived collegiality, which can substitute managerial tricks for organizational trust. But it is to advocate a kind of trust that extends beyond the deep knowledge of interpersonal relationships.

The establishment of trust is central to the restructuring of education. The challenge of trust is to reconstruct collaborative working relationships among close colleagues that enhance personal meaning without reinforcing paternalism and parochialism. It is also the challenge of building confidence and connectedness among teachers who may not know each other quite so well, by investing mutual trust in complementary expertise—without this also leading to burgeoning bureaucracy. The challenge of trust is one of restructuring and ultimately choosing between enhancing genuine empowerment or reconstructing administrative control.

STRUCTURE OR CULTURE?
A fourth tension in educational restructuring and the way it is organized is that between *structure* and *culture* as a proper focus for change. This tension is highlighted by Werner in an incisive analysis of recent restructuring efforts within the province of British Columbia in Canada. Werner refers to the provincial minister's call in 1989 for 'a fundamental restructuring of the provincial curriculum with a focus on the development of problem solving and creative thinking' (Werner 1991). This proposed restructuring included an ungraded primary curriculum, an integrated, common curriculum; and a strengthening of assessment and accountability procedures.

Werner dismisses the proposed restructuring for British Columbia as 'a classic curriculum fix', reflecting a pervasive and deep-rooted belief in the power of curriculum reform to secure effective change (especially if supported by some in-service training and supervision). Against this structural orientation to change, Werner, drawing on a submission by the British Columbia Principals' and Vice-Principals' Association, suggests an alternative strategy: 'to encourage teacher development, strengthen school culture, and build upon those good practices already in place in schools' (Werner 1991: 236). In effect, Werner supports the strategy of improving schools from within rather than reforming them from without. More significant than centralized control of curriculum development and implementation, he argues, 'will be groups of teachers who search out and discuss ways to better understand and organize their programs, and who take action in and within the structure of their own schools' (1991: 236). Werner's concern is that, despite rhetorics of empowerment along with an appearance of

devolving power to teachers by giving them more responsibility for planning and organizing curriculum integration, the British Columbia ministry 'retained control of curriculum by strengthening student testing and program evaluation. In essence, this meant that power relations around the curriculum would change little' (Werner 1991: 234).

What is being counterposed here by Werner are politically popular *structural* solutions to educational change against less fashionable but more enduring and effective *cultural* ones. The contrast is a striking and persuasive one. Structural changes of the sort initially proposed for British Columbia underestimate the traditions, assumptions and working relationships that profoundly shape existing practice. Consequently, they also over-estimate the power of structural changes to alter such practice, even with the support of in-service training for teachers. The image is of a powerful, determining structure acting on a relatively malleable body of practice. The important thing about change here is therefore to get the structures right so they support your educational goals, then have practice conform to them.

The cultural view, by contrast, sees existing practice as heavily determined by deeply rooted beliefs, practices and working relationships among teachers and students that make up the culture of the school and the traditions of the system. In this pattern of deep cultural determination, structural reforms are perceived as small, transient and ineffective: little match for the power of the existing culture. Change, in this view, is brought about by acting on and supporting the culture itself so that teachers are more able to make change as a community in the interests of the students they know best. Promotion of change in this cultural view is achieved by what Werner has elsewhere called policy support strategies—ones which create release time for teachers to work together, assist them in collaborative planning, encourage teachers to try new experiences (like a new practice or grade level), involve teachers in goal-setting, create a culture of collaboration, risk and improvement, and so on (Werner 1982).

While there are growing indications that deep cultural changes of this sort are much more likely to be effective in improving classroom practice than quick structural fixes, there are nevertheless limits to the effectiveness and applicability of Werner's cultural model. Werner's writing, like a good deal of other writing on teacher development and the culture of the school, treads a fine line between respecting the beliefs and perspectives of teachers and romanticizing them. In the quest for collaborative professional development and improvement, the inherent generosity and altruism of all teachers cannot always be presumed. Teachers' beliefs and practices are grounded not only in expertise and altruism, but also in structures and routines to which they have become attached and in which considerable self-interest may be invested. Such structures, we have seen, have often evolved historically to meet political and moral purposes that are very different from those which many of us would now consider important. Effective teacher development in the building of collective improvement therefore depends on more than the release of moral virtue. It also depends on controlling vested interests. For example, stronger forms of collegiality in the teacher work culture may require modifications to the subject-specialist, departmentalized secondary school curriculum that currently isolates teachers from many of their colleagues and ties them to the balkanized domain of departmental politics and self-interest (Hargreaves, forthcoming; Fullan and Hargreaves 1991).

In some cases, therefore, especially in larger secondary schools, it is not possible to establish productive school cultures without prior changes being effected in school structures that increase the opportunities for meaningful working relationships and collegial support among teachers. The importance of the structural option of restructuring, therefore, may be less in terms of its direct impact on curriculum, assessment, ability grouping and the like, than in terms of how it creates improved opportunities for teachers to work together on a continuing basis. The challenge of restructuring along the lines of changed power relationships proposed by Sarason, therefore, is not one of choosing between structure and culture as targets of reform. Nor is it one of 'managing' school cultures so that teachers cheerfully comply with structural goals and purposes already fixed by the bureaucratic centre. Rather, it is a challenge of redesigning school structures away from 19th- and early 20th-century models so as to help teachers work together more effec-

tively as a community in collaborative cultures of positive risk and continuous improvement. As an essential precondition for productive interaction, this much at any rate may need to be mandated!

Conclusion

Restructuring, I have argued, has no single, agreed definition. Its meaning, rather, is to be found in the context and purpose of its use. In the centralization of curriculum change and assessment demands, where restructuring is a camouflage for reform, it can support intensification of bureaucratic control. Strong, singular visions and imposed, inflexible mandates—these are the stuff of such control. Equally, though, restructuring can also propel us into a world of postmodern indeterminacy and ephemerality—into a cacophony of voices of undistinguished moral validity, without any common vision or purpose: a world in which the decision-making power invested in school cultures is arbitrarily shaped by the inertia of historical tradition and ingrained interest rather than the virtue of collective moral choice.

The challenge of restructuring in education and elsewhere is a challenge of abandoning bureaucratic controls, inflexible mandates, paternalistic forms of trust and quick system fixes in order to hear, articulate and bring together the disparate voices of teachers and other educational partners. It is a challenge of opening up broad avenues of choice which respect teachers' professional discretion and enhance their decision-making capacity. It is a challenge of building trust in the processes of collaboration, risk and continuous improvement as well as more traditional kinds of trust in people. And it is a challenge of supporting and empowering school cultures and those involved in them to develop changes themselves on a continuing basis. But in relaxing and relinquishing administrative control, the challenge of restructuring in postmodern times is also one of not losing a sense of common purpose and commitment with it. In trading bureaucratic control for professional empowerment, it is important we do not trade community for chaos as well.

This paper is not a litany of solutions to

these complex dilemmas, but has sought to sketch out ways of approaching them. Its purpose has been to show that the resolutions are not ideologically simple but profoundly complex; that they involve more than straight choices between restructuring and reform. Restructuring is not an end to our problems but a beginning. In this paper, I have tried to point to ways in which the concept and practice of restructuring may itself already need to be restructured, if the purposes of professionalism and empowerment are to be pursued with seriousness and integrity.

References

Achilles, C. M. (1987), 'A Vision of Better Schools', in W. Greenfield (ed.), *Instructional Leadership: Concepts, Issues and Controversies* (Boston: Allyn and Bacon), 18.

Acker, S. (1989), 'It's What we Do Already But . . . Primary Teachers and the 1988 Education Act', paper presented at a conference on Ethnography, Education and Policy, St Hilda's College, Oxford, September 1989.

Carnegie Forum on Education and the Economy (1986), *A Nation Prepared: Teachers for the 21st Century*, Report of the Carnegie Task Force on Teaching as a Profession (Washington DC: Carnegie Forum).

Deal, T., and Peterson, K. (1987), 'Symbolic Leadership and the School Principal: Shaping School Cultures in Different Contexts', unpublished paper, Vanderbilt Univ.

Educational Evaluation and Policy Analysis (Fall 1990) (see the collection of papers, 12[3]).

Elbaz, F. (1991), 'Research on Teachers' Knowledge', *Journal of Curriculum Studies*, 23/1: 10.

Fleming, T. (1991), 'Canadian School Policy in Liberal and Post-Liberal Eras: historical perspectives on the changing social context of schooling 1846–1990', *Journal of Education Policy*, 6(2), pp. 183–199.

Fullan, M., and Hargreaves, A. (1991), *What's Worth Fighting For?: Working Together for your School* (Toronto: Ontario Public School Teachers' Federation).

Giddens, A. (1990), *The Consequences of Modernity* (Oxford: Polity Press), 34.

Gilligan, C. (1982), *In a Different Voice: Psychological Theory and Women's Development* (Cambridge, Mass.: Harvard Univ. Press).

Goodson, I. (1990), 'Nations at Risk and National Curriculum: Ideology and Identity', in *Politics of Education Association Yearbook* (London, New York, Philadelphia: Taylor and Francis), 219–52.

Hallinger, P., and Murphy, J. (1987), 'Instructional Leadership in the School Context', in W. Greenfield (ed.) *Instructional Leadership: Concepts, Issues and Controversies* (Boston, Mass. Allyn and Bacon), 179–303.

Hargreaves, A. (1989), *Curriculum and Assessment Reform* (Milton Keynes: Open Univ. Press).

—— (1991), 'Contrived Collegiality: A Micropolitical Analysis', in J. Blase (ed.), *The Politics of Life in Schools* (New York: Sage).

—— (1993), 'Individualism and Individuality: Reinterpreting the Culture of Teaching', *International Journal of Educational Research*, 18/1.

—— (1994), *Changing Teachers, Changing Times: teachers' work and culture in the postmodern age* (London: Cassell; New York: Teachers' College Press; Toronto: OISE Press).

—— and Dawe, R. (1990), 'Paths of Professional Development: Contrived Collegiality, Collaborative Culture, and the Case of Peer Coaching', *Teaching and Teacher Education*, 6/3, 227–41.

—— and Earl, L. (1990), *Rights of Passage* (Toronto: Queen's Printer).

—— and Wignall, R. (1989), 'Time for the Teacher: A Study of Collegial Relations and Preparation Time among Elementary School Teachers', final research report (Toronto: The Ontario Institute for Studies in Education).

Harvey, D. (1989), *The Condition of Postmodernity* (Oxford: Polity Press).

Hunter, M. (1984), 'Knowing, Teaching and Supervising', in P. Hosford (ed.), *Using What we Knew About Teaching* (Alexandria, Va. Association for Supervision and Curriculum Development), 169–92.

Joyce, B., and Showers, B. (1988), *Student Achievement Through Staff Development* (New York: Longman).

—— and Weil, M. (1986), *Models of Teaching* (3rd edn. Englewood Cliffs, NJ: Prentice-Hall).

Leithwood, K., and Jantzi, D. (1990), 'Transformational Leadership: How Principals can Help Reform School Culture', paper presented at the Annual Conference of The American Educational Research Association, Boston, Mass. April 1990.

Lieberman, A., Saxl, R., and Miles, M. B. (1988), 'Teachers Leadership: Ideology and Practice', in A. Lieberman (ed.), *Building a Professional Culture in Schools* (New York: Teachers' College Press), 148–66.

Louden, W. (1991), *Understanding Teaching* (London: Cassell; New York: Teachers' College Press).

Menzies, H. (1989), *Fast Forward and Out of Control: How Technology is Changing our Lives* (Toronto: Macmillan).

Murphy, J., and Everston, C. (eds.) (1991), *Restructuring Schools: Capturing the Phenomena* (New York: Teachers' College Press).

Naisbett, J., and Aberdene, P. (1990), *Megatrends 2000* (New York: William Morrow).

National Governors' Association (1989), *Results in Education* (Washington, DC: NGA).

Nias, J., Southworth, G., and Yeomans, A. (1989), *Staff Relationships in the Primary School* (London: Cassell), 78.

O'Neil, J. (April 1990), 'Piecing Together the Restructuring Puzzle', *Educational Leadership*, 47/7: 4–10.

Popkewitz, T., and Lind, K. (Summer 1989), 'Teacher Incentives as Reforms: Teachers' Work and the Changing Control Mechanism in Education', *Teachers College Record*, 90/4: 575–94.

Robertson, H. (1991), 'Teacher Development and Gender Equity', in A. Hargreaves and M. Fullan (eds.), *Understanding Teacher Development* (London: Cassell; New York: Teachers' College Press).

Rudduck, J. (1989), 'Accrediting Teacher Education Courses: The New Criteria', in A. Hargreaves and D. Reynolds (eds.), *Education Policies: Controversies and Critiques* (Philadelphia: Falmer Press); 178–90.

Sarason, S. (1990), *The Predictable Failure of Educational Reform* (San Francisco: Jossey-Bass).

Schlechty, P. (1990), *Schools for the Twenty-First Century* (San Francisco: Jossey-Bass).

Smyth, J., and Garman, N. (1989), 'Supervision as School Reform: A Critical Perspective', *Journal of Education Policy*, 4/4: 343–61.

The Globe and Mail Report on Business (February 1991), *Hello Cruel World: Claude Taylor Fought for a Decade for Privatization. Now he Confesses Air Canada Wasn't Ready*, 7/8: 36.

Tyack, D. (1990), 'Restructuring in Historical Perspective: Tinkering Toward Utopia', *Teachers College Record*, 192/2: 170–91.

Weber, M. (1968), 'The Types of Legitimate Domination', in G. Roth and C. Wittich (eds.), *Economy and Society: An Outline of Interpretive Sociology* (New York: Bedminster Press).

Werner, W. (1982), 'Evaluating Program Implementation (School Based)', final project report (Centre for the Study of Curriculum Instruction, Vancouver, Univ. of British Columbia).

Werner, W. (1991), 'Defining Curriculum Policy Through Slogans', *Journal of Education Policy*, 6/2: 225–38.

Willinsky, J. (Fall 1989), 'Getting Personal and Practical with Personal and Impractical Knowledge', *Curriculum Inquiry*, 9/3: 247–64.

PART FOUR

POLITICS, MARKETS, AND SCHOOL EFFECTIVENESS

Part Four: Introduction

Politics, Markets, and School Effectiveness

The introduction of market competition in public education has led to the rapid development of a new field of analysis. The intellectual impetus for the development of educational markets originally derived from neo-classical economics and the cognate discipline of Public Choice theory. The original arguments advanced for the marketization of education by neo-classical economists and their supporters focused on improving educational provision and outcomes by giving parents greater consumer sovereignty in their choice of public schools. They assumed that the motivation of parents to ensure that their children had a sound education would be enhanced by increasing consumer choice, while teachers' motivation would also be improved by the spurs and challenges of the competition for students that choice would create. More recently, this argument has been strengthened by hypotheses which have associated the introduction of choice and market competition with improved equality of opportunity. It is argued that choice could lead to the establishment of centres of educational excellence within impoverished city centres, and that the removal of zoning could enable children in the inner cities to escape ghetto schools for more successful middle-class suburban schools (Coons and Sugarman 1978; Coleman 1990). Therefore, while the agenda of marketizing education has been advanced by the New Right, the idea that markets in education can have a significant impact in promoting equality of opportunity is also one that has been taken up by advocates across the political spectrum.

Chubb and Moe (Ch. 24) state what has now become the 'classic' argument in favour of choice and competition in schools. Their argument is consistent with the tenets of Public Choice theory (see the Introduction to Part Three) and comprises three theses. First, the hierarchy of democratic and bureaucratic constraints imposed on public schools impairs their performance because schools lack the ability to set their own goals; the administrative ability to hire and fire; and the ability to determine curriculum, instruction, discipline. Secondly, the greater the absence of external constraint the more schools can set their own goals, use the initiative and autonomy of teachers, and create a team spirit which sets a positive ethos for the school. Thirdly, they assume that market modes of control provide the kind of autonomy that teachers need to raise school performance, citing the performance of Catholic schools as evidence for this claim. Having set out their theory, Chubb and Moe then attempt to test it empirically. Overall, their contribution to the debate both in this paper and in their subsequent book is imaginative (Chubb and Moe 1990). Yet the very imaginative nature of the thesis is also its weakness; and their findings are, to say the least, controversial.[1] To give one example, as Rosario, Barnett, and Franklin (1992) note, Chubb and Moe use the term 'bureaucratic control' so widely that virtually any systematic, non-market form of control of schools can be so labelled. But school systems are highly complex organizational structures which use a variety of control systems, not all of which are bureaucratic (Weiss 1990). This leads to the problem of knowing precisely which control system causes which outcomes in any school organization. Moreover, the general proposition that systems of education which are considered highly centralized and bureaucratic necessarily restrict teacher autonomy is false.[2]

However, while Chubb and Moe's paper merits the attention it has received, there are clearly problems with the proposition that schools, driven by parental choice and teacher 'autonomy', will raise educational standards.[3] There is an opposing position to that of Chubb and Moe and their colleagues, suggesting that rather than improving the efficiency and effectiveness of schools, the intro-duction of choice and competition in public education represents a crucial shift in the *class mechanisms of exclusion*. Lauder (Ch. 25) argues that the Public Choice assumption that by insulating teachers from market mechanisms schools are likely to underperform is false. This is because Public Choice theory ignores the class-determined nature of choice in education. The consequence of marketization is likely to be the polarization of school intakes, since middle-class parents will have the material and cultural capital to exercise choice in a way denied to working-class parents. Market reforms in education also affect both the role of schools in a democracy and outcomes. In terms of democracy, the polarization of intakes means that students from different social-class and ethnic backgrounds are unlikely to mix. Hence, the possibility for the kinds of mutual understanding between students from different backgrounds envisaged by Dewey (1916) as the basis for the democratic qualities of tolerance and respect for persons will be lost. A further consequence of polarization is that it will lead to an overall decline in standards, since unpopular schools will suffer a decline in resources and morale.

The issue of the class-determined nature of educational markets is taken a stage further by Brown (Ch. 26), who argues that the marketization of education reflects a change in the principles of provision and selection from those based on the ability and effort of the child to the wishes and wealth of the parents. In ideo-logical terms this change signifies a shift from 'meritocracy' to what Brown calls 'parentocracy'. He argues that this New-Right-driven policy amounts to the reintroduction of selection by stealth. The idea that students from different social classes should attend different kinds of school is anathema to notions of equality of opportunity, hence New Right governments have chosen to reintro-duce selection covertly. In making this claim, Brown assumes that markets will generate a greater social-class polarization between school intakes. The tentative explanation Brown gives for the introduction of this form of covert selection is that, at a time of youth unemployment, an educational system based on the

wealth and wishes of parents will minimize the risk of middle-class student failure. He has subsequently extended this analysis (see Ch. 45) in the light of the
increased insecurity of middle-class work, since credentials are the best insurance against job insecurity and long-term unemployment.

The view that educational markets will be class-divided is also taken up and
extended by Ball, Bowe, and Gewirtz (Ch. 27). In this qualitative study of an educational market they provide a wealth of detail as to how class mechanisms of
exclusion work. They suggest that schools within markets can be seen in terms
of circuits, divided according to the status of schools and the social-class clientele
they serve. Following Bourdieu's lead they point out, for example, that working-
class ways of life remain organized around the practical business of getting by. In
this context, locality and family organization are key elements in choice-making.

They found that working-class families, especially those from low-income
households, were less likely to chose to send their children out of the immediate
locality than those from higher socio-economic groups. The fact that many
working-class families do not have readily accessible transport reinforces the
emphasis on the local. The issue here, as the researchers emphasize, is not merely
one of limited resources, but also that families are interwoven into a network of
social obligations and reciprocal favours. Care-givers, usually mothers, have to
ensure that their children go to schools where they can be dropped off and picked
up by relatives and neighbours when, as is often the case, they themselves are
unable to do this. In contrast, for their middle-class respondents the interweaving of social networks and obligations is not so closely textured. They may have
similar social obligations, but their networks are more widely dispersed; and they
have another essential advantage: time horizons and 'the imagination of time'.
According to the authors, their middle-class interviewees were more likely to
imagine their children's futures in terms of the professions they took up.

Two key insights into the operation of markets in education emerge from this
study. The first concerns the *way* parents make choices. In contrast to the
accounts of choice given by proponents of marketization, Ball, Bowe, and
Gewirtz draw attention to the complexity of the processes involved in choice. It is
not merely a matter of selecting the best school: issues of class culture, networks
of reciprocal obligations, and the capacity for children to travel some distance to
schools, all play a part. In essence, parents are engaged in a juggling exercise of
permutations of possibility within the limits afforded by their class position.

The second insight concerns the way middle-class material and cultural capital is *translated* into advantage within the market context. The significance of this
study lies in the fact that it elaborates upon the mechanisms by which the changing rules of engagement established to mediate the competition for credentials
(Brown, Ch. 45) are capitalized by them. If, as Ball, Bowe, and Gewirtz predict,
market 'opportunity' structures will enhance the power of the middle class to
gain an advantage for their children, we should expect to see similar results from
other studies.

Stuart Wells examines the impact of choice regimes in St Louis by interviewing thirty-seven African-American high-school students and thirty-four of their

parents and grandparents. Drawing on the work of Bourdieu and Passeron (1977) and Willis (1977), she suggests that, theoretically, the complex ways in which students interact and redefine their experience in the educational system are neither predictable nor deterministic. Such an outcome is likely for those who, traditionally, have been excluded from the essentially middle-class assumptions, messages, and curricula of schools. Translated into the racial context of St Louis, she finds that there are three overlapping and intertwined factors affecting school choice: the degree of parental involvement in the initial choice of school; students' acceptance or rejection of the achievement ideology of schools; and students' and parents' racial attitudes, their fear and distrust of whites, and the degree to which they accept the dominant view of whites as higher status.

In one sense, the most interesting group of those she interviewed were students that had transferred from nearby inner-city schools to middle-class white schools in the suburbs. Of this group, some remained in the suburban schools while others returned to inner-city schools. Some (but not all) of those who remained in the suburban schools came from higher social-class backgrounds, which suggests that some working-class parents are able to take advantage of choice schemes. Clearly, the degree to which markets can work for those on low incomes is dependent on how they are structured. Even so, Stuart Wells's research shows that there is likely to be a racial as well as a class dynamic to the issue of school choice. Of those that returned to inner-city schools, having started in the suburbs, a majority cited factors that in one way or another could be attributed to a complex of class and racial issues.

Overall, the low-income minority students in her study reacted in different ways to the opportunity to exercise choice. In doing so, many confounded the assumption of neo-classical economists that all will, rationally, seek to maximize their children's advantage, and they throw doubt on the claim that choice can be used as a mechanism to promote greater equality of opportunity for people of colour in the inner cities.

The assumptions of neo-classical economists are also confounded in the study by Waslander and Thrupp (Ch. 29). This study is of interest for two reasons. In contrast to many studies of educational markets, it is able to compare the degree of social class and ethnic polarization in schools under zoned and de-zoned regimes. Much of the case against educational markets rests on studies which observe social-class and ethnic inequalities of choice. However, the mere observation of inequalities of choice is not a persuasive argument against markets unless it can be shown that these create greater polarization than occurred under a zoned system. It is clear that, at least in the market studied by Waslander and Thrupp, the professional middle-class parents were exercising 'choice' while zones were in place. They note, however, that with de-zoning the trend is towards greater polarization. The second aspect of interest concerns what they call the 'lived market', the combination of formal rules and informal arrangements which determine the flow of students within the market. The assumption that markets will enhance school performance is only plausible if genuine competition takes place; but, as these authors show, schools will seek by processes of political manipulation and collusion to mitigate the effects of competition on them. In addition, the formal rules of the market they study are such that the schools least able to compete, those in low socio-economic areas, have to spend more time and money trying to recruit students, while élite single-sex middle-class schools are able to concentrate on the business of teaching as their customer base is guaranteed. The implication from this study is that schools which are oversubscribed choose their students on the basis of social class.

Whatever the hopes of those who have initiated market policies in education, the fact is that questions of decentralization, choice, and competition cannot be divorced from those of power. Fine (Ch. 30) tellingly reinforces this point by her study of programmes of parental involvement in three American cities, Baltimore, Philadelphia, and Chicago. She notes that, in a variety of ways, parents are being brought into the discourse of educational restructuring and improvement. The point of this discourse is to invite parents to succeed where others have failed to repair or reconstruct public education.

Her case studies show, however, that parents cannot do this alone; the asymmetries of power at all levels of educational administration are such that projects of parental and community collaboration and concerted action break down. Part of the problem is that, for her vision of community-based democracies of difference to flourish, the public sphere needs to be expanded. But she argues that in the 1990s the state has constrained the debate, resources, and work of those involved in schooling.

In an important sense, Fine is using her case-studies as a litmus test of the health of democratic participation in and around schooling in America. In this endeavour she rejects the meagre view of democracy of the New Right and its privatizing agenda for education. In arguing that public education can flourish within a wider and more vibrant democratic community, she is eloquently joining common cause with many other contributors to this volume, who argue that democratic education depends on a rich, diverse, and vibrant public sphere. The problem is to find the theory, practice, and political will to engage in such renewal.

If Fine is clear that schools and their outcomes cannot be divorced from the wider public and political context, the current reality is that the restructuring of education has left individual schools to carry the aspirations of students and their parents. The question addressed by Mortimore (Ch. 31) is to what extent effective schools can compensate for the inequalities of society. Can they, in other words, compensate low-income students by providing them with similar levels of educational opportunity and achievement to those enjoyed by their middle-class counterparts? In seeking to answer this question Mortimore carefully analyzes the knowledge gained from a tradition of school-effectiveness research which has been established for some 20 years. His conclusion is that schools can make an important difference. However, because they are part of the wider society 'they will always be inefficient and partial mechanisms for compensation'. This balanced conclusion is timely, because it counters the more extravagant claims that schools can be effective irrespective of their intakes, that it is a matter of management and incentive structures rather than the interrelationship between student intakes and the ethos and practices of the school that determines outcomes.

Overall, the chapters in this section do not support the frequently expressed view that the marketization of education is a panacea for raising standards. By the same token, it remains an open question as to whether the degree of polarization predicted by its critics will eventuate. Part of the difficulty of research into the effects of markets is that it is hard to generalize. As Bowe, Ball, and Gold (1992) have insisted, identifiable educational markets have their own peculiar socio-geographic and historical conditions which may have a significant impact on their outcomes. The debate over educational markets is likely to remain intense, because its impact on the lives of parents (and especially mothers[4]) and their children is profound in many ways. However, it is clear from the chapters in this section in what direction educational progress is to be made. On the one hand, support for public education based on strong principles of equality of opportunity, embedded in a vibrant democratic culture, is clearly necessary; on the other, the painstaking work of communities, schools, and educational researchers is required to raise and maintain the performance of individual schools.

Notes

1. See, for example, the powerful criticisms of their (1990) book by Glass and Matthews (1991) and Rosario, Barnett, and Franklin (1992).
2. For example, prior to 1989 New Zealand had a highly centralized and, by common definitions of the word, bureaucratic system of education. Yet teachers had a high degree of professional autonomy. See Lauder and Yee (1987).
3. Grace (Ch. 20) discusses some of the conceptual and empirical problems involved in this claim.
4. See the research by David (1993), David, M., Edwards, R., Hughes, M., and Ribbens, J. (1993), and David, M., West, A., and Ribbens, J. (1994), for a discussion of the repositioning of mothers in the discourse and practice of choice.

References

Bourdieu, P., and Passeron, J.-C. (1977), *Reproduction* (London: Sage).

Bowe, R., Ball, S., and Gold, A. (1992), *Reforming Education and Changing Schools* (London: Routledge).

Chubb, J. and Moe, T. (1990), *Politics, Markets and America's Schools* (Washington DC: Brookings Institution).

Coleman, J. (1990), *Equity and Achievement in Education* (Boulder: Westview Press).

Coons, J., and Sugarman, S. (1978), *Education By Choice: The Case for Family Control* (Berkeley: Univ. of California Press).

David, M. (1993a), *Parents, Gender and Education Reform* (Cambridge: Polity Press).

—— Edwards, R., Hughes, M., and Ribbens, J. (1993b), *Mothers and Education: Inside Out? Exploring Family-Education Policy and Experience* (London: Macmillan).

—— West, A., and Ribbens, J. (1994), *Mother's Intuition? Choosing Secondary Schools* (London: Falmer Press).

Dewey, J. (1916), *Democracy and Education* (New York: Macmillan).

Glass, G., and Matthews, D. (1991), 'Are Data Enough? Review of Politics, Markets and America's Schools', *Educational Researcher* (April), 24–7.

Lauder, H., and Yee, B. (1987), 'Are Teachers Being Proletarianized? Some Theoretical, Empirical and Policy Issues', in Walker, S., and Barton, L. (eds.), *Changing Policies, Changing Teachers* (Milton Keynes: Open Univ. Press).

Rosario, J., Barnett, W., and Franklin, B. (1992), 'On Politics, Markets and America's Schools', *Journal of Educational Policy*, 7/2: 223–35.

Weiss, J. (1990), 'Control in School Organisations: Theoretical Perspectives', in Clune, W., and Witte, H. (eds.), *Choice and Control in American Education*, i (London: Falmer Press).

Willis, P. (1977), *Learning to Labour* (Farnborough: Saxon House).

24

Politics, Markets, and the Organization of Schools

John E. Chubb and Terry M. Moe

Virtually all public schools in the United States are governed by democratic institutions of the same basic form. This form is now taken for granted. There is a broad consensus that democratic control of the public schools is a good thing and that democratic control means control through local school boards, superintendents, central office bureaucracies, and corresponding apparatuses at the state and (increasingly) the federal levels. However heated the conflict over educational policy and practice, however intense the struggle for influence and resources, the 'one best system' stands above it all (Tyack 1974).

In recent years, educational politics has centered on the quality of the public schools. Long-simmering discontent about declining test scores, loose academic standards, and lax discipline—fueled by a series of national studies—has engendered a widespread reaction against the 'rising tide of mediocrity' (National Commission on Excellence in Education 1983), and state legislatures around the country have responded with reforms ranging from stricter academic requirements to merit pay plans for teachers (Doyle and Hartle 1985). Throughout this period, the 'one best system' has provided the institutional framework within which problems have been identified and policy responses chosen. It structures criticism and reform, but it is never their target.

Much the same is true within educational research, which has generally taken institutions as given. Studies of school effectiveness have focused directly on the schools, asking about those aspects of organization and imme-diate environment that explain school performance. Taken as a whole, this work has promoted a loose consensus on factors that appear to enhance effectiveness, among them, clear school goals, rigorous academic requirements, an orderly climate, strong instructional leadership by the principal, teacher participation in decision making, cooperative principal-teacher relations, active parental involvement, and high expectations for student performance (Boyer 1983; Brookover et al. 1979; Goodlad 1984; Powell, Farrar, and Cohen 1985; Rutter et al. 1979; Sizer 1984).

This research has shaped the contours of public debate by suggesting traits good schools ought to have. But it is the institutional system itself, accepted by one and all, that tells us how these desirable features are to be transmitted to the schools: they are to be imposed from above. For many objectives—tougher academic requirements, say—reform simply calls for new legislative or district policy. Not coincidentally, these have been among the more popular reforms. Other objectives are less amenable to formal imposition—cooperative relations within the school, for example. But these tend to be regarded as matters of good management and training, and thus as reforms that can be delegated to the professional side of the control structure. Whether the means are formal or professional, then, the rationale of democratic control is to 'make' schools more effective by imposing desirable traits on them (Campbell et al. 1985).

These reforms are likely to fail. To see why, it is useful to begin with a curious feature of

From *American Political Science Review*, 82 (1988), 1065–87. Reprinted with permission.

the way schools are conventionally understood. Among those who study education, it is received doctrine that schools are open systems and thus products of their environments (Scott and Meyer 1984; Weick 1976). By this logic it should follow that the organization and performance of schools are largely explainable by the environments that surround them. Different types of environments should tend to produce different types of schools. When schools turn out to have undesirable characteristics, the logical culprit is the environment—not the schools.

Yet studies of school effectiveness have rarely taken the environment seriously. They tend to explain poor performance in terms of variables inside and immediately outside the school—and then they turn to our institutions of democratic control to make the necessary changes. Our institutions, however, are core components of the very environment that by open systems reasoning is likely to have caused the problems in the first place. These studies should be asking, Which is the relationship between democratic control and the organization of schools? Might there be something inherent in these institutions that systematically promotes organizations of a type no one really wants?

We do not pretend to have all the answers. We do think, however, that institutions are fundamental to an understanding of schools. Here we try to make a plausible case for this view by developing a theoretical argument and presenting some new evidence from a recent survey.

Our basic argument is that the organization of schools is largely endogenous to the system of institutional control in which the schools are embedded. Different systems of institutional control should tend to produce schools with distinctive patterns of characteristics. While we will specify these patterns in some detail, our most general claim is simply that the hierarchy of democratic control, the 'one best system,' puts its stamp on the organization of our public schools and that this stamp holds the key to school quality and school reform.

Institutional issues are often difficult to explore through empirical research. This is especially true in studying the 'one best system.' How can we study institutional effects if there is only one, all-encompassing institution? An instructive way to proceed, we

believe, is to compare public schools to those schools that fall outside the hierarchy of democratic control: private schools.

That is what we do here. We explore the logic of institutional control in the two sectors and derive implications for schools. This line of reasoning suggests that schools should indeed look different across sectors and, most importantly, that democratic control should inhibit the emergence of 'effective school' characteristics. Using data obtained from a representative sample of public and private high schools, we compare them on a range of characteristics commonly associated with effective academic performance. These results consistently suggest that institutions are important determinants of school organization—and that, in consequence, public schools are quite literally at a systematic disadvantage.

Politics, Markets, and Control

Public schools are controlled by democratic authority and administration. The specifics vary from district to district and state to state, but the basic framework is remarkably uniform throughout the country. The private sector might seem to lack any comparable uniformity. Most private schools are affiliated with a church; some are elite preparatory schools; some are military academies; and there are other types as well (Kraushaar 1972). But they all have two important institutional features in common: society does not control them directly through democratic politics, and society does control them—indirectly—through the marketplace. Rather than marvel at diversity, we find it useful to think about schools in terms of these alternative institutions of social control. As a shorthand, we will refer to them as politics and markets.

We want to provide a little background on how these institutions operate and what they imply for schools. We will not yet relate them to specific aspects of school organization. This will be done later when we turn to a discussion of the survey data.

CONSTITUENTS AND CONSUMERS
Popular myth lauds the role of local citizens and their elected school boards in governing the public schools. But the fact is that the

schools are not locally controlled and are not supposed to be. The state and federal governments have legitimate roles to play in financing schools, setting standards, and otherwise imposing their own policies. This means that US citizens everywhere, whether or not they have children in school and whether or not they live in the district or even the state, have a legitimate hand in governing each school (Campbell *et al.* 1985; Wirt and Kirst 1982).

The proper constituency of even a single public school is a huge and heterogeneous one whose interests are variously represented by formally prescribed agents—politicians and administrators—at all levels of government. Parents and students, therefore, are but a small part of the legitimate constituency of 'their own' schools. The schools are not meant to be theirs to control and are literally not supposed to provide the kind of education they might want. Public education is shaped by larger social purposes as defined by larger constituencies.

Private schools determine their own goals, standards, and methods. These may reflect the values of owners or patrons, or perhaps a collective such as a diocese. But the market imposes a fundamental constraint. Private schools provide services in exchange for payment, and unless heavily subsidized from the outside, they must please their consumers—students and parents—if they are to prosper. Whatever the constituency of the private school, therefore, it will surely be much smaller and more homogeneous than the democratic constituency of the public school, and students and parents will occupy a much more central position within it.

EXIT AND VOICE

In the private marketplace, educational choice is founded on what has come to be called, following Hirschman (1970), the *exit* option. If parents and students do not like the services they are being provided, they can exit and find another school whose offerings are more congruent with their needs. This process of selection promotes a match between what educational consumers want and what their schools supply. Matching is reinforced by the population effects (Alchian 1950) of selection: schools that fail to satisfy a sufficiently large clientele will be weeded out (or, if subsidized, become an increasing burden).

Selection also forges a strong bond between consumer satisfaction and organizational well-being. This gives schools incentives to please their clientele, as well as to set up *voice* mechanisms—committees, associations—that build a capacity for responsiveness into organizational structure. These incentives, too, promote a match—but they are not necessary for success. A school might rigidly adhere to purist doctrine yet succeed because that is what enough consumers happen to want. Either way, the result tends to be the same: a match.

In the public sector, popular control is built around voice. Exit plays a minimal role. The public school is usually a local monopoly, in the sense that all children living in a given area are assigned to a particular school. This does not eliminate choice, since parents can take account of school quality in deciding where to live. But residential decisions involve many factors in addition to education, and once they are made, sunk costs are high.[1] Low or declining quality need not keep parents from moving into an area, and it is even less likely to prompt existing residents to pick up and leave.

It might prompt them to consider a private school. But here they confront a major disincentive: public schools are free, private schools are not. Due to this cost differential, the perceived value of private schools must far outweigh that of public schools if they are to win students. To put it the other way round, public schools, because they are relatively inexpensive, can attract students without seeming to be particularly good at educating them.

Lacking a real exit option, many parents and students will choose a public school despite dissatisfaction with its goals, methods, or personnel. Having done so, they have a right to voice their preferences through the democratic control structure—but everyone else has the same rights, and many are well armed and organized. Voice cannot remedy the mismatch between what parents and students want and what schools provide. Conflict and disharmony are built into the system.

AUTONOMY AND CONTROL

In the private sector, the exit option not only promotes harmony and responsiveness, it also promotes school autonomy. This is true even for schools that are part of a hierarchy, as the Catholic schools are. The reason is that most of the technology and resources needed to please clients are inherently present at the bottom of the hierarchy—in the school—since educational services are based on personal relationships and interactions, on continual feedback, and on the knowledge, skills, and experience of teachers. The school is thus in the best position to know how to enhance its own organizational well-being. Hierarchical control, or any external imposition, tends to be inefficient and counterproductive.[2]

Central direction is important when superiors have an agenda of their own that cannot be pursued simply by pleasing clients. In the private sector, imposition of such an agenda involves a trade-off: if schools are constrained in their efforts to please clients, dissatisfied clients can leave. In some hierarchies—notably, those associated with churches—superiors may consider this an acceptable price; they may prefer 'pure' schools to growing, prosperous ones. But it is still a price, one that threatens organizational well-being—and one that in the limit can be fatal. Thus, even if there are higher-order values to be pursued, the exit option discourages tight external control in favor of school autonomy.

In the public sector the institutional forces work in the opposite direction. The raison d'être of democratic control is to impose higher-order values on schools and thus limit their autonomy. Exit is an obstacle to control: when the governance structure imposes a policy on parents and students who disagree, exit allows them to avoid compliance by 'voting with their feet,' thus defeating the purpose of the policy. But public officials do not have to take exit as a given. They can simply pass laws restricting its availability. While private decision makers value autonomy because it helps them cope with problems of exit, public officials eliminate exit in order to facilitate their imposition of higher-order values.

The drive to restrict autonomy is built into the incentive structures of politicians and bureaucrats. Politicians seek political support by responding to various constituency groups, particularly those that are well organized and active. These include teachers' unions and associations of administrators, but also a vast array of groups representing more specialized interests—those of minorities, the handicapped, bilingual education, drivers' education, schools of education, book publishers, and accrediting and testing organiza-

tions, among others. These groups typically have financial or occupational stakes in existing educational arrangements, and their policy positions reflect as much. They all want a share of the public's educational resources. They want to influence educational programs. They want to have a say in how the schools are organized and operated. And politicians are only too happy to oblige—this is the path to political popularity (Masters, Salisbury, and Eliot 1964; Iannaccone 1967; Peterson 1976; Wirt and Kirst 1982).

Bureaucrats play both sides of the governmental fence. Their power rests on the fact that bureaucracy is essential to direct democratic control. The imposition of higher-order values is hardly automatic, particularly given the built-in dissatisfaction of parents and students and the inevitable pressures from teachers and principals for autonomy. Control requires rules and regulations, monitoring, incentive structures, and other means of ensuring that those engaged in the educational process behave as they are supposed to behave. It requires bureaucracy—and bureaucrats.[3]

As public officials they have incentives to expand their budgets, programs, and administrative controls. These are the basics of bureaucratic well-being, and their pursuit is an integral part of the job. But bureaucrats also belong to important interest groups—of administrators, of professionals—that lobby government from the outside (ostensibly) as well. Although traditionally they have portrayed themselves as nonpolitical experts pursuing the greater good, they are in fact a powerful special interest—an interest dedicated to hierarchical control (Knott and Miller 1987; Tyack 1974).

The system, in short, is inherently destructive of autonomy. Politicians have the authority to shape the schools through public policy, and, precisely because they have this authority, they are consistently under pressure from interest groups to exercise it. It is in their own best interests to impose choices on the schools. The same is true of bureaucrats, who have occupational and professional stakes in control: a world of autonomous schools would be a world without educational bureaucrats. Thus, while principals and teachers may praise the virtues of autonomy, the 'one best system' is organized against it. Politicians, bureaucrats, and virtually the full spectrum of interest groups tend to see autonomy for what it is: a transfer of power and a threat to their interests.[4]

PURPOSE AND PERFORMANCE

Public schools are products of public policy. With a huge constituency, there is inevitably dissension over what constitutes 'good' policy—and many of the contending groups have their own stakes in public education and are not simply struggling to provide us with 'good' policy anyway. Even if they were, there is no guarantee they could implement it very effectively, for bureaucratic control is an inherently difficult and costly means of engineering educational outcomes.

Reform grows naturally out of all this. When important groups signal their dissatisfaction with what the schools are doing, politicians and bureaucrats spring into action. They respond to group demands by doing what they are institutionally empowered and motivated to do: they seek remedies through new policies and new controls. This is the characteristic way in which the public schools are 'improved.' And because administrative problems, value conflicts, and shifts in power alignments are endemic to the system, reform is a never-ending process.

Private schools operate in a wholly different institutional environment. Reform occurs when schools find it in their own best interests to make adaptive adjustments, when new schools enter the educational marketplace, and when unpopular schools fail. All are closely tied to the interests of parents and students.

Are private schools also likely to be better than public schools? In an important sense, the answer is *yes*. Parents and students who choose a private school are revealing their judgment of quality: the private school is not only better, it is better by an amount that exceeds the cost differential. Since there is clearly an objective basis for their judgment— they directly experience private education and are free to return to the public sector at any time—we have good reason to believe that private schools are in fact more effective at providing the types of educational services their clients care about.

But are they better at the important things schools ought to be doing? This question cannot be answered without substituting our value judgments for those of parents and students. A church school that attracts students on the basis of religious and moral training almost surely outperforms the local public school on this dimension. But this says nothing about their relative effectiveness in transmitting democratic values or an appreciation of cultural diversity. Performance is only desirable if the goals are desirable.

This, of course, is the justification for democratic control. In principle, our institutions are set up to articulate important social goals and to ensure that schools act effectively on them. If private schools do a better job of providing certain services or of pleasing parents and students, this does not mean that society must therefore prefer private to public education. Any evaluation has to depend on a more fundamental judgment about what the schools ought to be doing.

In objective terms the two institutional systems are simply very different, and they give rise to schools that reflect these differences— providing different services in different ways to please different constituencies.

Data and Method

High School and Beyond (HSB), first administered in 1980, is the most comprehensive survey of secondary schools to date. The original data base, pertaining to some 60 thousand students in more than one thousand public and private schools, provided a rich source of information about student achievement, attitudes, activities, and family background. This was the empirical foundation for Coleman, Hoffer, and Kilgore's (1982) *High School Achievement*, which set off shock waves in the educational community with its conclusion that private schools are academically more effective than public schools.[5]

High School and Beyond included certain information about the schools, but important aspects of organization and environment were not part of the study. To augment the data base, we helped design the Administrator and Teacher Survey (ATS), which went back to about five hundred HSB schools and administered questionnaires to the principal, a sample of 30 teachers, and selected staff members in each. Their responses tell us a good deal more about the schools as organizations—about their external relationships, their leadership, their structure and goals, their patterns of influence and interaction, and their educational practices. We put the ATS data to use in exploring how education is organized in the public and private sectors.[6]

Because private schools are so diverse, empirical work on student achievement has frequently clarified sectoral comparisons by distinguishing two relatively homogeneous types of private schools in the HSB sample—Catholic and élite—from all the rest. Catholic schools have played the central role in these analyses. They are the majority of private schools, and their students are very similar on socioeconomic and ethnic grounds to students in the public sector. The elite schools are the handful of top private schools in the nation as judged by the proportion of seniors who were semifinalists in the National Merit Scholarship competition. The remaining schools, 'other private,' vary from tiny religious groupings to large college prep schools.[7] We will maintain these distinctions—and despite their marked diversity, we will expect a uniformity across the three types. For by virtue of their shared institutional context, they should give evidence of something that approaches a common syndrome of organization.

In the analysis, we simply regress each organizational or environmental characteristic against dummy variables representing the three types of private schools.[8] Specifically, if C is the characteristic in question, we estimate the following equation:

$$C = B0 + B1 \text{ Catholic} \\ + B2 \text{ other private} + B3 \text{ élite} \\ + \text{error.}$$

The constant, B0, measures the public school mean on C. *Catholic, other private*, and *élite* are dummy variables taking on the value 1 if the school is of that type, 0 otherwise. B1 measures the difference between the Catholic school mean and the public school mean on characteristic C. B2 and B3 measure the same private-public comparison for the other private and élite categories.

These comparisons are made without the usual laundry list of statistical controls. It is an easy matter to include controls for school size, student background, and countless other factors, but we think it would be inappropriate and possibly very misleading to do so at this point. In estimating relationships among variables, the purpose of statistical controls is to remove covariation due to prior or exogenous influences. An institutional perspective on the organization of schools, however, suggests that all major variables are probably endogenous.

It may be, for instance, that private schools are more likely to exhibit certain characteristics—happy teachers, perhaps—because they tend to be smaller organizations than public schools. But it is no accident that private schools tend to be smaller, since small size is a major basis on which they appeal to students, parents, and teachers. Small size and happy teachers are integral parts of the same syndrome. Similarly, private schools may seem to have desirable organizational traits—more orderly climates, say—because their students come from families that care more about education. But these families have chosen their schools in the first place precisely because they like the way the schools are organized. So what causes what? Do motivated students make for a good school, or do good schools attract motivated students? The most reasonable view is that causality flows both ways and thus that both variables are endogenous.

Analogous arguments apply for virtually any variables of interest. To control for them as though they are exogenous is to remove from the sectoral comparisons—and to remove in a methodologically inappropriate way (via additive terms in recursive equations)—factors that are integrally woven into the very fabric of each system. For now, prudence argues for getting a clear look at how basic aspects of environment and organization differ across sectors. Investigation of the causal structure—and with it, informed thinking about statistical controls—can proceed most usefully once this sort of foundation has been laid.

The Findings

EXTERNAL AUTHORITIES

If the operation of politics and markets suggests anything, it is that the control of schools should differ systematically across sectors. Public schools should find themselves operating in larger, more complex governing systems that tend to exert greater influence over school policy, educational practice, and per-

Table 24.1. Types of outside authorities (%)

Outside Authorities Present	Public[b]	Catholic[c]	[P]Other Private	Elite Private
School board and administrators[a]	99.3 (287)	69.0 (20)	52.9 (9)	28.6 (2)
School board only	.0 (0)	24.1 (7)	41.2 (7)	57.1 (4)
Administrators only	.3 (1)	3.4 (1)	.0 (0)	.0 (0)
None	.3 (1)	3.4 (1)	5.9 (1)	14.3 (1)
Total	99.9 (289)	99.9 (29)	100 (17)	100 (7)

Note: Numbers in parentheses are the unweighted number of schools in each sector.
[a] Administrators include superintendent or central office.
[b] Excludes several special public schools oversampled in ATS.
[c] Excludes exclusively black Catholic schools oversampled in ATS.

sonnel decisions. Private schools should tend to enjoy more autonomy with respect to their structure, goals, and operation. Of course, these tendencies are well documented when they derive from higher levels of government authority: public schools are part of state and federal hierarchies, integrated financially and programmatically, while private schools generally are not (Coleman, Hoffer, and Kilgore 1982). But what about immediate outside authorities? What kind of governing system operates at the local level to distinguish the sectors?

Table 24.1 presents summary figures on the extent to which the various schools are hierarchically subordinate to school boards or to outside administrative superiors (in the form of a superintendent or central office of some kind). Not surprisingly, virtually all public schools in the sample are governed by both; only two of nearly three hundred schools depart from this pattern. The private sector is far more diverse. Almost all private schools, regardless of type, have a school board of some sort, but often there is no accompanying administrative apparatus. Such an apparatus is quite rare among the élite schools, and nearly half of the 'other privates' are similarly unencumbered. It is the Catholic schools that most resemble the publics in this regard, with some two-thirds of Catholic schools having both school boards and administrative superiors; even here, however, there is a good deal of hierarchic diversity by comparison to the public sector. Fully a quarter of the Catholic schools are overseen only by a school board, the Church's reputation for hierarchy notwithstanding.

Because administrative authorities are often absent from the environments of private schools, many of these schools will operate relatively free from bureaucratic control. But what about the control exercised by the political and administrative authorities that public and private schools often have in common? In Table 24.2 control by school boards as perceived by principals is compared along five basic policy dimensions: curriculum, instructional methods, discipline, hiring, and firing. The results are striking in their consistency.

Table 24.2. The influence of school boards on school policies

Areas of Influence	Catholic	Other Private	Elite Private
School board			
Curriculum	−.27 (1.33)	−.24 (1.52)	−.07 (.04)
Instruction	−.03 (.14)	−.003 (.02)	−.03 (.01)
Discipline	−.80 (4.02)	−.35 (2.24)	−1.16 (.56)
Hiring	−.98 (5.16)	−.80 (5.31)	−1.11 (.56)
Firing	−.76 (3.83)	−.41 (2.63)	−.86 (.42)
School board vs. principal			
Curriculum	−.40 (1.96)	−.26 (1.63)	.05 (.03)
Instruction	−.06 (.31)	.41 (2.50)	.17 (.08)
Discipline	−.72 (3.59)	−.28 (1.75)	−.92 (.44)
Hiring	−.97 (4.89)	−.42 (2.67)	−1.30 (.63)
Firing	−1.08 (5.65)	−.72 (4.72)	−1.23 (.62)

Note: Reports regression coefficients and t–scores (in parentheses) for dummy variable regression models in which the dependent variable is standardized.

On all five dimensions school boards in the public sector appear to have more influence over school policy than they do in the private sector, regardless of the type of private school. The differences between public and private are consistently greater (and statistically significant) for personnel and disciplinary policy than for matters pertaining to educational practice and content.[9] They amount on the average to between one and two points on a six-point influence scale. But in view of the uniformity of the overall pattern, there is reason to suspect that even the small estimated differences for curriculum and instruction are indicative of a greater role by school boards in the public sector generally. This is reinforced by the perceived influence of school boards relative to principals. As outlined in the lower half of Table 24.2, the sectoral differences are repeated and sometimes amplified. Relative to their school boards, private principals play a more autonomous role in setting and implementing policy—especially as it pertains to personnel and discipline—than public principals do.

Relative to their administrative superiors, private principals appear to be similarly autonomous. At least this is true of principals in Catholic schools, the only type of private school with enough administrative supervision to make a comparison with public schools valid and instructive. The figures, presented in Table 24.3, suggest an interesting conclusion: that the famed Catholic hierarchy (although see Greeley 1977) plays a comparatively small role in governing Catholic schools. On all five dimensions, the influence of administrative superiors is far less in Catholic than in public schools. These differences are again greatest in the area of personnel policy, but here the other policy areas reflect substantial differences as well. When we explore the school's autonomy a bit further by comparing the principal's influence to that of administrative superiors, the same pattern emerges. Relative to administrators, Catholic principals enjoy more freedom than public principals in setting school policy.

To be sure, the differences in school autonomy that seem to distinguish the public and private sectors are based on simple measures of perceived influence and not on actual behaviour. But the patterns these measures yield are quite uniform and entirely consistent with our expectations for external control.

The authorities that are so ubiquitous in the democratic context of the public school are often simply absent from private school settings—and even when they are an acknowledged part of the private governing apparatus, they play less influential roles in the actual determination of school policy. Private schools, it would appear, have more control over their own destinies.

Table 24.3. The influence of administration on school policies

Areas of Influence	Catholic	
Administration		
Curriculum	−1.51	(8.19)
Instruction	−1.01	(5.12)
Discipline	−1.23	(6.39)
Hiring	−1.82	(10.28)
Firing	−2.11	(12.65)
Administration vs. principal		
Curriculum	−1.57	(8.44)
Instruction	−1.23	(6.33)
Discipline	−1.11	(5.66)
Hiring	−1.56	(8.39)
Firing	−2.00	(11.57)

Note: Administration includes superintendent or central office. Table reports regression coefficients and t-scores (in parentheses) for dummy variable regression models in which the dependent variable is standardized.

EXTERNAL CONSTRAINTS: CHOOSING THE ORGANIZATION'S STAFF

Among the controls that any organization seeks to exercise over its operations, perhaps none is as important as control over its staff—in the case of a school, its teachers. To what extent does the school have flexibility in recruiting the kinds of teachers it wants and getting rid of those who do not live up to its standards? We have already seen that public schools are at a disadvantage in this regard, for external authorities have much more influence over hiring and firing in the public sector than they do in the private sector. The sectoral differences are not limited to the role of external authorities, however. They become still more dramatic when we consider two additional constraints on the choice of personnel: tenure and unions.

Tenure systems in public schools are special cases of the civil service systems that exist at all levels of government. Historically, these systems arose to prevent politicians from rewarding their supporters with public jobs. Reformers recognized that the widespread use of patronage was inconsistent with the kind of expertise, professionalism, and continuity so necessary to effective government, and—in a halting process that took decades to accomplish—they brought about the pervasive adoption of civil service systems built around objective qualifications and designed to protect employees judged to be qualified. Tenure is one of these protections (Peterson 1985).

Teacher unions (or 'associations'), although initially resisted by politicians wedded to patronage, eventually found political allies of their own. Organized teachers could offer money, manpower, and votes to politicians. In state and local elections, where turnout is typically very low, these are attractive inducements indeed. As teacher unions thrived, they gained not only economic concessions but also contractual guarantees of job security and other limitations on responsibilities that reinforced the protections of the civil service system and introduced wholly new constraints into personnel decisions affecting the local school (Grimshaw 1979).

Although there is nothing to prevent unions from gaining a foothold in private schools nor to keep private schools from adopting tenure and other civil service-like protections, there is nothing comparable to government that drives them in that direction. Whether unions and tenure systems take hold in the private sector is determined much less by politics and much more by markets. Schools may choose to offer tenure and other protections as a means of attracting good teachers, particularly given that public schools offer that benefit. But private schools may also decide, especially if the supply of teachers is high, that they can offer a very attractive set of benefits—such as good students, orderly atmosphere, and collegial decision making—without offering tenure at all.

Similarly, as in any market setting, unions may or may not succeed in organizing teachers. But they cannot count on symbiotic relationships with the authorities, as public unions can, to help their cause.

The ATS data suggest that the public and private sectors are in fact enormously different in these respects. While 88 per cent of public schools offer tenure, only a minority of the private schools do: 24 per cent of the Catholics, 39 per cent of the élites, and 17 per cent of the 'other privates.' Among the schools that do offer tenure, moreover, the proportion of teachers who have actually been awarded it reflects the same asymmetry: 80 per cent of the eligibles in public schools have tenure, while the figure is some 10 to 16 per cent lower in the private sector. The differences in unionization are even more substantial. The vast majority of public schools are unionized—some 80 per cent—almost all of them by either the National Education Association or the American Federation of Teachers. In the private sector, by contrast, teachers are rarely represented by unions. Only about 10 per cent of the Catholic schools are unionized, and virtually none of the élites and 'other privates' are.

To assess whether school control over personnel is perceptibly constrained by tenure, unions, and other proximate external authorities, we asked principals to evaluate an assortment of potential barriers to hiring excellent teachers and firing incompetent ones. On the hiring side, principals in the two sectors agreed on the severity of several obstacles, including applicant shortages and low pay. But public school principals were far more likely to complain about obstacles administrative in origin: 'central office control' and 'excessive transfers from other schools' (see Table 24.4).

Table 24.4. School personnel policy and process

Personnel Constraints	Catholic	Other Private	Elite Private
Barriers to Hiring			
Too many transfers	−.57 (2.72)	−.56 (3.36)	−.43 (.20)
Central office control	−.51 (2.43)	−.25 (1.51)	−.47 (.22)
Barriers to Firing			
Complex procedures	−.59 (3.35)	−1.47 (10.51)	−1.26 (.69)
Tenure rules	−.93 (5.08)	−1.36 (9.39)	−1.55 (.82)
Hours involved in firing someone	−.85 (4.01)	−.75 (4.47)	−.90 (.41)

Note: Reports regression coefficients and t-scores (in parentheses) for dummy variable regression models in which the dependent variable is standardized.

The obstacles to dismissing teachers for poor performance differ similarly. In the public schools the procedures are far more complex, the tenure rules more constraining, and the preparation and documentation process roughly three times as long (Table 24.4). The complexity and formality of dismissal procedures is the highest barrier to firing cited by public school principals. For private school principals, of every type, the highest barrier is 'a personal reluctance to fire.' These responses provide a rather poignant statement of the differences between the sectors: while the public school principal is bound most by red tape, the private school principal is bound most by his or her conscience.

Principals do, of course, have other forms of control over their staffs. They can encourage undesirable staff to resign, retire, or transfer. They can offer good teachers special assignments or relieve them of onerous duties. They can recognize high performance with awards.[10] But none of these practices differs systematically across the sectors. Public principals simply have less power than private principals to mold and manage their teaching staffs.

Even if public superintendents or central offices wanted to delegate such power to the school—and, in general, there is no reason to think they have incentives to do this—many personnel decisions cannot in practice be delegated. Tenure protections are usually guaranteed through laws that are written by school boards or state legislatures, and these laws are then enforced by administrators. Union contracts are typically bargained at the district level, not at the school level, and are enforced from above. Tenure and unionization tend to settle the question of where and how the basic personnel decisions will be made in the public sector. They will be centralized. Schools in the private sector, largely free of such constraints, have far greater flexibility to choose their own members and chart their own paths.

PARENTS

In most respects, private schools would seem to have ideal parental environments. Parents, after all, have made a positive choice to send their children to a private school, presumably because they care about education and have a high appraisal of the school. And, if at any time they change their views, they can simply exercise their exit option. This means that the school is likely to enjoy significant gains: they gain children whose family lives encourage education, and parents who not only will facilitate school objectives by monitoring homework and the like but will be informed and supportive when they take an active interest in school decision making. Parents who may cause problems on these scores are precisely the ones most likely to drop out of the school's environment voluntarily.

Public schools are not so fortunate. Many of their students come from families that put little or no emphasis on education; the students come to school with poor attitudes and orientations, and the parents do little to facilitate the school's efforts. Because exit is often not a viable option, many parents who do not support the school's goals, methods, or activities will remain in its environment nevertheless; and some—perhaps many—will use the democratic mechanisms at their disposal, as well as interactions with principal and staff, to express their dissent and press for change. Far from gaining sustenance from a supportive parental environment, the public school may often find itself dealing as best it can with conflict, disappointment, and apathy.

Not all public and private schools will neatly fit these molds, of course. But it seems clear that characteristics inherent in the two sectors—characteristics anchored in politics

Table 24.5. Parental relationships with schools

Parental Role	Catholic	Other Private	Elite Private
Monitoring students	.90 (4.69)	.43 (2.82)	1.30 (.65)
Expectations of students	1.24 (6.85)	.91 (6.33)	2.62 (1.39)
Involvement in school	.74 (3.81)	.52 (3.39)	.64 (.32)
Cooperativeness	.43 (2.13)	.18 (1.14)	.47 (.22)
Freedom from constraint	.57 (2.81)	.22 (1.35)	.49 (.23)

Note: Reports regression coefficients and t-scores (in parentheses) for dummy variable regression models in which the dependent variable is standardized.

and markets—encourage the kinds of environmental differences outlined here. And results from the ATS study, detailed in Table 24.5, are consistent with this line of reasoning. Parents in the private sector, regardless of the type are less constrained by the kinds of formal rules and norms that due to democratic governing structures impinge on the flexibility of public school principals.

Parents are uniformly more supportive of their schools. They have higher expectations about their children's educational performance, they are more active in monitoring their children's behavior outside of school, and they are more deeply involved with the school as an organization. Private school principals, not surprisingly, also express greater satisfaction with their parental environments. Relationships with parents are more cooperative than they are in the public sector.

The operation of politics and markets, then, appears to put public schools at a real disadvantage. Because of forces largely beyond the control of the individual school, parents in the public sector tend to be less supportive of the school's general educational efforts and more likely to promote organizational conflict—and, to make matters worse, the school has less flexibility in seeking solutions to these problems. By comparison, private schools have fewer such problems and yet more flexibility for dealing with them.

BETWEEN ENVIRONMENT AND ORGANIZATION:
THE PRINCIPAL

The principal operates at the boundary of the organization and is, more than any other single person, responsible for negotiating successfully with the environment—responding to demands and pressures from parents, unions, administrators, and school boards, and dealing with external disruptions such as budget cuts, policy conflicts, and demographic changes. The principal may also hold a key to school effectiveness. Evidence increasingly suggests that educational excellence is promoted by a principal who articulates clear goals, holds high expectations of students and teachers, exercises strong instructional leadership, steers clear of administrative burdens, and effectively extracts resources from the environment (e.g., Blumberg and Greenfield 1980; Brookover et al. 1979; Goodlad 1984).

It is seldom stressed, however, that the school environment can have a lot to say about whether the principal is able to practice these precepts of effective leadership—or, for that matter, is even motivated to practice them. Effective leadership does not simply inhere in the individual filling the role; it is unavoidably contingent upon the demands, constraints, and resources that the principal must deal with. Depending on the nature and strength of these forces, even the 'best' principal may have only a marginal effect on school performance. We must also remember that principals do not possess or lack leadership qualities by accident. Both environment and organization tend to ensure that there will be selective attraction to the job: certain schools will tend to attract certain kinds of principals. Similarly, principals will be socialized on the job, and internal and external factors will ensure that principals at distinctly different schools will be socialized differently. Thus, while it is one thing to point to certain qualities that appear conducive to effective leadership, it is quite another to suggest that principals are free to develop them.

It should not be surprising, then, to find differences between public and private school

Table 24.6. Characteristics of school principals

Characteristics	Catholic	Other Private	Elite Private
Teaching experience	.43 (2.21)	.56 (3.59)	.58 (.28)
Motivations			
Policy control	.61 (3.04)	.46 (2.92)	.31 (.15)
Preference for administrative duties	−.33 (1.63)	−.49 (3.08)	−.14 (.07)
Career advancement	−.69 (3.52)	−.61 (3.91)	−.48 (.23)
Desire further advancement	−.76 (3.95)	−.71 (4.69)	−1.04 (.52)
Leadership as perceived by teachers	.41 (2.12)	.74 (4.84)	.64 (.32)
Instructional leadership	.66 (3.67)	1.28 (8.98)	.82 (.44)

Note: Reports regression coefficients and t-scores (in parentheses) for dummy variable regression models in which the dependent variable is standardized.

principals, both in terms of their own characteristics and in terms of their performance. Consider first what the ATS data (see Table 24.6) have to say about how they came to their jobs. Private school principals have quite a bit more teaching experience than their public counterparts—the gap is almost four years for principals in Catholic schools, and over five years for those in the élites and 'other privates.'[11] This is consistent with the hierarchic organization of public sector education: its career ladder offers teachers early opportunities for moving into a host of subordinate administrative positions (such as assistant principalships), followed by subsequent opportunities for moving up in status and salary. As this implies, principals also come to their jobs with different motivations. Private principals are more likely to stress 'control over school policies,' while public principals place greater emphasis on 'preference for administrative responsibilities,' a 'desire to further [their] career[s],' and an interest in advancing 'to a higher administrative post.'

The typical career orientations of principals in the two sectors thus appear to be quite different. Public principals tend to disembark from teaching relatively early, get on an administrative track, and take the job of principal to keep the train rolling. Private principals are scarcely on a track at all. They stay in teaching longer, and their view of the principalship focuses more on its relation to the school than on its relation to their movement up the educational hierarchy.

How the principal performs on the job is a function of many things, not just the values and experiences noted here. They would, however, appear to have a direct bearing on one aspect of performance consistently singled out in the effective schools literature: instructional leadership. Teachers in the ATS study were asked questions about the quality of the assistance they received in regard to instructional problems, and their responses indicate strong differences across the sectors. As judged by their own teachers, private principals are more effective in this important area of leadership than public principals are. Again, this may be due to a variety of factors. But the simple fact that the public principal has far less teaching experience (which itself has roots in his or her distinctive career orientation) is in itself likely to affect rapport with teachers, self-perception of instructional role,

and other aspects of the job as they pertain to teaching. It is not surprising to find that instructional leadership is more effective in private schools.

Finally, the ATS teachers were asked to evaluate their principal with regard to a range of leadership-related qualities bearing on knowledge of school problems, communication with the staff, clarity and strength of purpose, and willingness to innovate. Constructing a general index of leadership from these items, we find that by these criteria teachers rate private principals to be better all-around leaders than public principals. This result is more likely to reflect the operation of general environmental conditions than the earlier one on instructional leadership. Principals in the public sector are forced to operate in much more complex, conflictual circumstances in which educational success is more difficult to achieve regardless of the principal's (perhaps considerable) abilities and qualifications. If anything, however, it is plausible to suggest that the public principal's lack of teaching experience and a hierarchic career orientation probably contribute to these leadership problems.

While these findings only begin to scratch the surface, it does appear that public and private school principals are quite different in important respects. They have different backgrounds, different career orientations, and—whatever the true constraints on their performance might be—they are evaluated differently by their teachers: principals in private schools are more highly regarded as leaders.

THE ORGANIZATION: GOALS AND POLICIES
Given what we know of their environments, there is every reason to expect that public and private schools should adopt very different orientations toward the education of their students. Because public schools must take whoever walks in the door, they do not have the luxury of being able to select the kind of students best suited to organizational goals and structure—it is the latter that must do virtually all the adapting if a harmonious fit is to be achieved. In practice, this means that the pursuit of educational excellence must compete with much more basic needs—for literacy, for remedial training, for more slowly paced instruction. In addition, there is the hierarchic structure of democratic control to ensure that

a range of actors and diverse, often-conflicting interests are brought to bear in decisions about what the public school ought to be pursuing and how. As in other areas of politics, the thrust is toward compromises and 'solutions' (see also Powell, Farrar, and Cohen 1985) that reflect the lowest common denominator—and often a great deal of ambiguity and internal inconsistency as well. This is to be expected when an important function of the decision-making process is conflict resolution. The process is unavoidably a political exercise, not an analytical attempt at problem solving.

Private schools are largely unconstrained in comparison, both in the selection of students and in the determination of organizational goals. It is only reasonable to suggest that a given private school is likely to have clearer and more homogeneous goals than a given public school. Aggregate comparisons, however, are more uncertain because the private sector is comprised of so many different types of schools; an elite school will emphasize academic excellence, but a religious or military school may have quite different priorities—although we would still expect them to be relatively clear and homogeneous compared to the publics.

Despite such uncertainties, the comparisons across sectors are quite uniform (see Table 24.7). In terms of general goals, public schools place significantly greater emphasis on basic literacy, citizenship, good work habits, and specific occupational skills, while private schools—regardless of type—are

more oriented by academic excellence, and personal growth. For the most part, these sorts of differences are what we should expect in view of the more fundamental differences in student bodies and governing structures. Most obviously, public schools would ordinarily find it politically and organizationally very difficult to place high priority on academic excellence.

Whether these goals become reflected in school structure and performance depends on whether they are upheld by specific policies and clearly discerned by the staff. As Table 24.7 suggests, there are definite differences across sectors in these respects. To begin with, the private schools have more stringent minimum graduation requirements; their students, regardless of track, must take significantly more English and history, science and math, and foreign language than must public school students in order to graduate. In science, math, and foreign language the differences range up to two years.

Private schools also have stricter homework policies. This is particularly true of the élites and 'other privates,' most of which establish schoolwide daily minimums per subject, strongly encourage homework, or, in cases where faculty are overzealous, set daily maximums per subject. In contrast, 90 per cent of all public schools leave the amount of homework entirely up to teachers. Catholic schools fall in between these extremes.

These differences in goals and policies are accompanied by differences in their clarity and their acceptance by organization

Table 24.7. School structure

Characteristics	Catholic	Other Private	Elite Private
Goals			
Basic literacy	−1.59 (8.83)	−.83 (5.81)	−1.10 (.59)
Citizenship	−1.12 (6.06)	−1.04 (7.11)	−.96 (.50)
Good work habits	−.92 (4.68)	−.52 (3.37)	−.26 (.13)
Occupational skills	−.89 (4.60)	−.77 (5.01)	−.98 (.49)
Academic excellence	.10 (.48)	.41 (2.57)	.94 (.45)
Personal growth	.47 (2.33)	.12 (.78)	.69 (.33)
Human relations	.24 (1.19)	.11 (.71)	.34 (.16)
General graduation requirements			
English and history	.61 (3.09)	.51 (3.26)	.57 (.28)
Science and mathematics	.34 (1.73)	.88 (5.77)	1.78 (.88)
Foreign language	1.28 (7.88)	1.61 (12.47)	3.33 (1.96)
School-wide homework policy	.13 (.65)	.48 (3.06)	.90 (.44)
Goal clarity	.64 (3.32)	.80 (5.24)	.80 (.40)
Goal disagreement	−.35 (1.80)	−.85 (5.59)	−.55 (.27)

Note: Reports regression coefficients and t-scores (in parentheses) for dummy variable regression models in which the dependent variable is standardized.

members—key factors in their translation into organizational action. Private teachers uniformly report school goals as clearer—and more clearly communicated by the principal—than public teachers report. In addition, there is less disagreement among the school priorities reported by teachers in private schools. In general, private schools tend to possess a clarity and homogeneity of educational purpose that does set them apart from public schools, at least on average. They place more emphasis on academic excellence, have stricter graduation requirements, and have tougher homework policies. And their staff members have clearer, more consistent conceptions of what their organizations are supposed to be achieving. These are, of course, stereotypical characteristics of 'effective schools.' They are also characteristics that, due to the differential operation of politics and markets, would seem extremely difficult for public schools to develop in the same degree.

THE ORGANIZATION: PEOPLE, DECISIONS, OPERATION

What should public and private schools look like on the inside? What might we expect in general about their structures, processes, and personnel? A widely accepted notion in organization theory is that environmental complexity is reflected in organizational complexity (Lawrence and Lorsch 1967). For rather obvious reasons, then, public schools should prove far more complex than their private counterparts; and existing studies indicate that this is actually the case (Scott and Meyer 1984). Moreover, their very complexity of structure and heterogeneity of goals suggest that public schools may often be 'loosely coupled,' characterized by relatively autonomous centers of activity and decision making. Private schools, on the other hand, would seem to approximate classical notions of organization. They have simpler, more stable, less threatening environments, and goals that are fewer in number, clearer, and more narrowly based—characteristics that facilitate the centralized direction of goal pursuit. This would seem to be consistent with the private schools' reputation for rigid curricula, traditional instructional methods, and strong principals.

A politics-and-markets perspective cannot hope to tell us everything we might want to know about organizational structure and process, but it does tend to point us in a different direction. The critical fact about the public school environment is not just that it is complex but that it literally imposes decisions about policy, structure, personnel, and procedure on the school. Thus, while the school may well adapt to environmental complexity by developing an internal complexity of its own, its range of choice is severely constrained—for a great many potential adaptive adjustments are simply ruled out by environmental fiat. Conversely, the private school is not only blessed with a relatively simple environment but with a much broader range of organizational options in adapting to it.

Consider, in particular, the most crucial agent of organizational performance: the teacher. As we have seen, the public school principal is far less able than the private school principal to staff the organization according to his or her best judgment. The public principal may value expertise, enthusiasm, collegiality, communication skills, creativity, or any number of qualifications related to the school's goals but simply has less power to obtain teachers who possess them or eliminate ones who do not. This should tend to promote staff heterogeneity and conflict. Teachers may reject the principal's leadership, dissent from school goals and policies, get along poorly with their colleagues, or fail to perform acceptably in the classroom—but the principal must somehow learn to live with them. When these teachers are represented by unions, as they normally are, leadership difficulties are magnified and an important wedge is driven between the principal and the staff, a wedge that promotes formalized decision procedures, struggles for power, and jealousies over turf. 'Professionalism' takes on new meaning—as a justification for placing decision power in the hands of teachers rather than the principal.

Private schools are not immune from personnel problems and struggles for power. But the principal, having much greater control over hiring and firing, can take steps to recruit the kinds of teachers he or she wants and weed out the rest. It also means that teachers have a strong inducement to live up to the principal's criteria on a continuing basis. By comparison to the public school counterpart, then, the private school principal is in a position to create a 'team' of teachers whose values, skills, and willingness to work together tend to mirror those qualifications the principal deems conducive to the pursuit of organizational goals. At the same time, the principal is in a position to make teacher professionalism work for, rather than against, him or her. Without real threat to his or her own authority or control, the principal can encourage teacher participation in decision making, extend teachers substantial autonomy within their own spheres of expertise, and promote a context of interaction, exchange of ideas, and mutual respect.

The data from the ATS study seem to provide strong support for this general line of reasoning. As outlined in Table 24.8, principals and teachers simply have higher opinions of one another in the private sector. Private principals consistently claim that a larger percentage of their schools' teachers are 'excellent,' suggesting that they are more confident in the abilities of their own staff members than public school principals are. Private sector teachers, in turn, have better relationships with their principals. They are consistently more likely to regard the latter as encouraging, supportive, and reinforcing; and, as we saw earlier, they have higher regard for their principals as effective organizational leaders.

Private school teachers also feel more involved and efficacious in important areas of

school decision making that bear on their teaching. In particular, they feel more influential over schoolwide policies governing the curriculum, student behavior, teacher in-service programs, and the grouping of students of differing abilities. Regarding issues of special relevance to the classroom, they believe they have more control over text selection, course content, teaching techniques, disciplining students, and, in the Catholic schools, determining the amount of homework to be assigned. (The non-Catholic private teachers feel constrained by the schoolwide homework policies identified earlier.) Even on matters of hiring and firing, private teachers believe they are more influential—this, despite the almost complete absence of unions in their sector.

Relative harmony between private principals and private teachers is matched by relative harmony among the private teachers themselves. On a personal level, relationships are more collegial in the private sector. Stated in the plain terms of the survey, private teachers are more likely to believe that they 'can count on most staff members to help out anywhere, anytime—even though it may not be part of their official assignment' and ultimately that 'the school seems like a big family.' On a professional level, private teachers give

Table 24.8. Staff Relations

Characteristics	Catholic		Other Private		Elite Private	
Per cent excellent teachers	.40	(2.07)	.78	(5.05)	1.16	(.58)
Principal–teacher relations	.44	(2.29)	.90	(5.93)	.96	(.48)
Teacher influence and control						
Student behavior codes	.95	(5.15)	1.00	(6.84)	1.04	(.54)
In-service programs	.32	(1.64)	.77	(5.05)	.41	(.20)
Ability groupings	1.24	(7.20)	1.32	(9.69)	1.37	(.76)
Curriculum	1.01	(5.66)	1.22	(8.59)	1.22	(.66)
Text selection	.66	(3.46)	.78	(5.11)	.74	(.37)
Topics taught	.50	(2.62)	.94	(6.23)	.53	(.27)
Techniques	.70	(3.58)	.40	(2.61)	1.06	(.52)
Discipline	1.34	(7.17)	.46	(3.12)	.83	(.42)
Homework	.63	(3.19)	.33	(2.14)	−1.16	(.57)
Hiring	.54	(2.63)	.38	(2.38)	.93	(.44)
Firing	.55	(2.75)	.16	(1.04)	.21	(.10)
Teacher–teacher relations						
Curriculum coordination	.60	(3.11)	.67	(4.37)	.96	(.48)
Teaching improvement	.60	(3.21)	1.06	(7.21)	1.03	(.53)
Collegiality	.90	(5.34)	1.58	(11.82)	.82	(.47)
Success not beyond personal control	.79	(4.19)	.54	(3.59)	1.23	(.62)
Doing best not waste of time	1.12	(5.39)	.96	(5.85)	1.78	(.82)
Job satisfaction	.57	(3.37)	.54	(4.06)	1.01	(.58)
Teacher absenteeism	.58	(3.00)	.73	(4.74)	.49	(.24)
Lowest teacher salary	−.75	(3.92)	−.86	(5.72)	.39	(.19)
Highest teacher salary	−.76	(3.87)	−.57	(3.65)	.91	(.45)

Note: Reports regression coefficients and t-scores (in parentheses) for dummy variable regression models in which the dependent variable is standardized.

greater evidence of mutual involvement and support. They are more likely to know what their colleagues are teaching, to coordinate the content of their courses, and to observe one another's classes. They also spend more time meeting together for the purpose of discussing curriculum and students.

It is no surprise, then, that private school teachers also feel more efficacious than public school teachers. Unlike their public counterparts, they do not believe their success is beyond their control, and they do not feel it is a waste of time to do their best. Overall, private school teachers are much more satisfied with their jobs. It is no wonder, then, that private school teachers have better attendance records nor that they tend to work for less money. Private school teachers are trading economic compensation and formal job security for superior working conditions, professional autonomy, and personal fulfilment. Public school teachers are doing precisely the opposite.

In short, private schools do tend to look more like 'teams.' By their own account, teachers have better relationships with principals, are more integrally involved in decision making, interact more frequently and productively with their colleagues, and feel more positively about their jobs and their organization. According to their principals, they are higher-quality teachers as well. As professionals, it appears they are given much greater reign in a private setting, which gives them opportunities to put their ideas and skills to use through a level of active involvement and a sharing of power that teachers in the public sector generally cannot expect. The key to explanation is anchored in a more fundamental feature of the sectors: private leaders have the freedom to chose their own professionals, public leaders do not.

Conclusion

The Administrator and Teacher Survey provides the first opportunity to document public-private differences by means of a large, representative sample of schools, and its findings dovetail nicely with major lines of argument in the education literature. If it is true, as Coleman, Hoffer, and Kilgore (1982) and Coleman and Hoffer (1987) have claimed, that private schools outperform public schools on academic grounds, and if the effective schools research is basically correct in the characteristics it tends to associate with effectiveness, then we should find that private schools disproportionately possess these characteristics.

That is just what we find. Private schools have simpler, less constraining environments of administrators, school boards, and parents. They are more autonomous and strongly led. They have clearer goals and stricter requirements, and they put greater stress on academic excellence. Relations between principals and teachers and among teachers themselves are more harmonious, interactive, and focused on teaching. Teachers are more involved in policy decisions, have greater control over their work, and are more satisfied with their jobs.

We have tried to do more here than present findings and relate them to existing work, however. We have tried to develop an institutional perspective that suggests why schools should be expected to differ across the sectors. This perspective arises from our belief that institutional context has pervasive consequences for the organization and operation of all schools, consequences more far-reaching than most of the literature tends to suggest (Pfeffer and Salancik 1979).

Public schools are products of our democratic institutions. They are subordinates in a hierarchic system of control in which diverse constituency groups and public officials impose policies on local schools. It is no accident that public schools are lacking in autonomy, that principals have difficulty leading, and that school goals are heterogeneous, unclear, and undemanding. Nor is it an accident that weak principals and tenured, unionized teachers struggle for power. These sorts of characteristics constitute an organizational syndrome whose roots are deeply anchored in democratic control as we have come to know it.

Private schools are controlled by society too, but not through politics or bureaucracy. They make their own decisions about policy, organization, and personnel subject to market forces that signal how they can best pursue their own interests. Given their substantial autonomy—and given the incentives for autonomy that are built into the system—it is not surprising to find that principals are stronger leaders; that principals have greater control over hiring and firing; that principals and the teachers they choose have greater respect for, and interaction with, one another; and that teachers—without conflict or formal requirement—are more integrally involved in policy-making. These sorts of characteristics are bound up with one another, and they jointly arise from the institutional environment. Different institutions promote different organizational syndromes.

If this is essentially correct, the standard proposals for reforming public schools are misconceived. It is easy to say, for instance, that schools should have greater autonomy or that principals should be stronger leaders. But these sorts of reforms are incompatible with the 'one best system' and cannot succeed. Politicians and bureaucrats have little incentive to move forcefully in these directions. Their careers are tied to their own control over the schools, and they are unavoidably responsive to well-organized interests that have stakes in the system's capacity to impose higher-order values on the local schools. Restricting autonomy is what democratic control is all about.

It is also about power, about who gets to have how much say in the control of schools. Reformist notions that the various actors should work together in the best interest of the schools are doomed by the institutions of democratic control, which guarantee conflict of interest, struggle for advantage, and resort to formally enforced 'cooperation.' Reforms calling for even the simplest changes—testing veteran teachers for minimum competence, say—will normally fail if they threaten established interests. Their bearing on school effectiveness has little to do with their political feasibility.

Reformers must reckon with the possibility that the measures they support, particularly those arising from the effective schools research, are often inconsistent with our current framework of democratic control. The public schools cannot be anything we might want them to be. They must take organizational forms compatible with their surrounding institutional environments. It may well be, then, that the key to school improvement is not school reform, but institutional reform—a shift away from direct democratic control.

This does not mean that the public schools must be freed from all democratic governance. But it is instructive that the private schools, which are products of an institutional system that decentralizes power to the producers and immediate consumers of educational services, tend to develop precisely the sorts of organizational characteristics reformers want the public schools to have. Some sort of voucher system, combining broad democratic guidance with a radical decentralization of resources and choice, is at least a reasonable alternative to direct control—one that might transform the public schools into different, more effective organizations, while still leaving them truly public.

Even if this or some other alternative is someday shown to have compelling features, however, democracy probably cannot get us from here to there. Any proposal to shift away from prevailing institutions is so threatening to established interests that it stands little chance of political victory. Because a shift in institutional control may be the one reform that makes all the others possible, the uncomfortable reality may simply be that all the others are not possible.

Notes

An earlier version of this paper was presented at the 1987 annual meeting of the American Political Science Association, Chicago. The first draft appeared as the Brookings Institution's Governmental Studies Discussion Paper No. 1.

1. The responsiveness of residential decisions to differences in the quality of public services, including education, has been extensively investigated and generally found to be quite imperfect (Rose-Ackerman 1983).

2. This is not to say that intelligent guidance from the center—e.g., about important innovations in curriculum and methods—is unimportant, only that education appears to benefit from a balance of control and autonomy favoring the teachers and the school (e.g., Carnegie Forum on Education and the Economy 1986).

3. On the logic of control and its implications for bureaucratic forms of organization, see e.g. Williamson 1975. For a review with applications to politics, see Moe 1984. On the historical development of the educational bureaucracy, see Tyack 1974 and Peterson 1985.

4. There are some interesting complications that we cannot dwell on here without getting too far afield. Mayors, for instance, sometimes attempt to avoid the risks and pressures of educational politics by minimizing their own

roles and shifting authority to others (e.g. members of the school board). More generally, politicians sometimes find it advantageous to create agencies that are insulated in some measure from political influence, including their own influence. These maneuvers, however, never put an end to politics or political control—and the maneuvers themselves are reversible through subsequent political maneuvers. Through it all, the authority to impose higher-order values is still there, and those with access to it still have incentives to use it to get what they want.

5. This study has been pummeled from all angles. See e.g. Bryk 1981; Goldberger and Cain 1982; Guthrie and Zusman 1981; Heyns and Hilton 1982; Murnane 1981. It seems to us, however, that the thrust of the Coleman-Hoffer-Kilgore argument has largely withstood these attacks. In more recent research by Coleman and Hoffer (1987) it has also been strongly reinforced.

6. When the ATS data are merged with those from HSB and its follow-ups (the details of which are available from the National Center for Education Statistics), they offer a unique foundation for exploring the connections among environment, organization, and student achievement. That is the purpose of our larger project, of which this paper is a part.

7. Studies of organization, as opposed to student achievement, have dealt almost entirely with public schools. Most of what is known about the organization of private schools is derived from case studies or studies of limited samples (Cibulka, O'Brien, and Zewe 1982; Erickson 1982; Greeley 1966; Peshkin 1986; Sanders 1981). Systematic national surveys are rare (Abramowitz and Stackhouse 1980; Kraushaar 1972).

8. The procedures employed in constructing indexes and measures of the variables are detailed in an appendix available from the authors.

9. Throughout this paper coefficients will be called 'statistically significant,' or simply 'significant,' if they satisfy a two-tailed t-test at a probability level of .05. The results for the élite schools will not, however, be evaluated in this fashion. The élite schools are not a sample, but a population—the schools with the most National Merit semi-finalists in 1978. As such, it is arguably inappropriate to make statistical inferences from the 'sample' to the population. In any case, the number of élite schools is too small, especially after weighting, to produce t-scores in the necessary range of 2.0.

10. Private schools may also offer merit pay; however, only the 'other private' sector makes significantly greater use of it. Catholic schools do

not differ from public schools in providing merit pay.

11. Recall that the coefficients reported in the tables are based on standardized measures of the dependent variables. When converted back to their original metric, the coefficients for teaching experience are equivalent to the years reported in the text.

References

Abramowitz, S., and Stackhouse, E.A. (1980), *The Private High School Today* (National Institute of Education: Washington).
Alchian, A. A. (1950), 'Uncertainty, Evolution, and Economic Theory', *Journal of Political Economy*, 58: 211–21.
Blumberg, A., and Greenfield, W. (1980), *The Effective Principal: Perspectives on School Leadership* (Boston: Allyn and Bacon).
Boyer, E. (1983), *High School: A Report on American Secondary Education* (New York: Harper and Row).
Brookover, W. B., Beady, C., Flood, P., Schweitzer, J., and Wisenbaker, J. (1979), *School Social Systems and Student Achievement: Schools Can Make a Difference* (New York: Praeger).
Bryk, A. S. (1981), 'Disciplined Inquiry or Policy Argument?' *Harvard Educational Review*, 51: 497–509.
Campbell, R. I., *et al.* (1985), *The Organization and Control of American Schools* (5th edn., Columbus, Ohio: Charles E. Merrill).
Carnegie Forum on Education and the Economy (1986), *A Nation Prepared: Teachers for the Twenty-first Century* (Washington: Carnegie Forum).
Cibulka, J. G., O'Brien, T. J., and Zewe, D. (1982), *Inner City Private Elementary Schools* (Milwaukee: Marquette Univ. Press).
Coleman, J. S., and Hoffer, T. (1987), *Public and Private High Schools* (New York: Basic Books).
——, and Kilgore, S. (1982), *High School Achievement* (New York: Basic Books).
Doyle, D. P., and Hartle, T. W. (1985), *Excellence in Education: The States Take Charge* (Washington: American Enterprise Institute).
Erickson, D. A. (1982), 'Disturbing Evidence About the "One Best System" ', in *The Public School Monopoly*, (ed.) Robert B. Everhart (San Francisco: Pacific Institute for Public Policy Research).
Goldberger, A. S., and Cain, G. G. (1982), 'The Causal Analysis of Cognitive Outcomes in the Coleman, Hoffer, and Kilgore Report', *Sociology of Education* 55: 103–22.
Goodlad, J. I. (1984), *A Place Called School:*

Prospects for the Future (New York: McGraw Hill).

Greeley, A. M. (1966), *The Education of Catholic Americans* (Chicago: Aldine).

—— (1977), 'Who Controls Catholic Education?' *Education and Urban Society*, 9: 146–66.

Grimshaw, W. J. (1979), *Union Rule in the Schools* (Lexington, Mass.: Lexington Books).

Guthrie, J. W., and Zusman, A. (1981), 'Unasked Questions', *Harvard Educational Review*, 51: 515–18.

Heyns, B., and Hilton, T. H. (1982), 'The Cognitive Tests for High School and Beyond: An Assessment', *Sociology of Education*, 55: 89–102.

Hirschman, A. O. (1970), *Exit, Voice, and Loyalty* (Cambridge: Harvard Univ. Press).

Iannaccone, L. (1967), *Politics in Education* (New York: Center for Applied Research in Education).

Knott, J. H., and Miller, G. J. (1987), *Reforming Bureaucracy: The Politics of Institutional Choice* (Englewood Cliffs, NJ: Prentice-Hall).

Kraushaar, O. F. (1972), *American Nonpublic Schools: Patterns of Diversity* (Baltimore: Johns Hopkins Univ. Press).

Lawrence, P. R., and Lorsch, J. W. (1967), *Organization and Environment* (Homewood, Ill.: Richard D. Irwin).

Masters, N. A., Salisbury, R., and Eliot, T. H. (1964), *State Politics and the Public Schools* (New York: Knopf).

Moe, T. M. (1984), 'The New Economics of Organization', *American Journal of Political Science*, 28: 739–77.

Murnane, R. J. (1981), 'Evidence, Analysis, and Unanswered Questions', *Harvard Educational Review*, 51: 483–89.

National Commission on Excellence in Education (1983), *A Nation at Risk* (Washington: NCEE).

Peterson, P. E. (1976), *School Politics, Chicago Style* (Chicago: Univ. of Chicago Press).

—— (1985), *The Politics of School Reform: 1870–1940* (Chicago: Univ. of Chicago Press).

Peshkin, A. (1986), *God's Choice: The Total World of the Christian School* (Chicago: Univ. of Chicago Press).

Pfeffer, J., and Salancik, G. R. (1979), *The External Control of Organizations: A Resource Dependence Perspective* (New York: Harper and Row).

Powell, A. G., Farrar, E., and Cohen, D. K. (1985), *The Shopping Mall High School: Winners and Losers in the Educational Market place* (New York: Houghton Mifflin).

Rose-Ackerman, S. (1983), 'Beyond Tiebout: Modeling the Political Economy of Local Government', in *Local Provision of Public Services: The Tiebout Model after Twenty-five Years*, (ed.) G. R. Zodrow (New York: Academic).

Rutter, M., Maughan, B., Mortimer, P., Ouston, J., and Smith, A. (1979), *Fifteen Thousand Hours: Secondary Schools and Their Effects on Children* (Cambridge, Mass.: Harvard Univ. Press).

Sanders, J. W. (1981), *The Education of an Urban Minority: Catholics in Chicago, 1822–1965* (New York: Oxford Univ. Press).

Scott, W. R., and Meyer, J. W. (1984), 'Environmental Linkages and Organizational Complexity', Stanford University Institute for Research on Educational Finance and Governance Project Report No. 84–A16.

Sizer, T. R. (1984), *Horace's Compromise: The Dilemma of the American High School* (Boston: Houghton Mifflin).

Tyack, D. (1974), *The One Best System* (Cambridge: Harvard Univ. Press).

Weick, K. E. (1976), 'Educational Organizations As Loosely Coupled Systems', *Administrative Science Quarterly*, 21: 1–19.

Williamson, O. (1975), *Markets and Hierarchies* (New York: Free Press).

Wirt, F., and Kirst, M. (1982), *Schools in Conflict* (Berkeley: McCutchan).

25

Education, Democracy, and the Economy

Hugh Lauder

The 'conviction politics' of Mrs Thatcher's period in office has brought the question of democracy to the fore. In education, alone, there is a catalogue of examples where it could be argued the spirit of democracy, if not the law, has been abused; to cite but four: the abolition of the ILEA for political rather than educational reasons; the absence of adequate debate prior to the Education Reform Act; the manner in which the prolonged dispute with teachers was prosecuted; and the subsequent loss of teachers' negotiating rights. It is, of course, difficult in the cut and thrust of politics to distinguish the personality and style of a leader like Mrs Thatcher from the theories that drove her attempt to create an 'enterprise culture'. Nevertheless, there is a strong case to be made for the view that the neo-liberal theory behind much of Mrs Thatcher's politics provided a rationale and guidance for her authoritarianism. For example, a similar kind of neo-liberal conviction politics has been practised in New Zealand despite the personalities involved being of a quite different stripe to Mrs Thatcher.[1] If this argument holds then the authoritarian legacy of the Thatcher years will far outlive her political demise because the principles corrosive of democratic practices are implicit in the neo-liberal restructuring of British society.

In this paper I shall argue that neo-liberal political economy licenses an authoritarian approach to politics. When this political economy is applied to education it severs the connection, made in the modern context since Dewey (1916), between education and democracy. Within neo-liberal political economy there is a trade-off between democracy and economic well being (Buchanan & Tul-

lock 1962) which may be appealing at times of economic crisis; after all, the (temporary?) erosion of democracy may be considered a small price to pay for economic health. A similar argument can be discerned in education, where the restructuring of education has been 'sold', in part, on the grounds that it will lead to greater economic efficiency and productivity. However, a further argument of this paper will be that neo-liberal political economy of education will create an education system with lower overall standards and lower morale—precisely the kind of system appropriate to a low trust, low skill economy. This outcome is of a piece with the application of neo-liberal economic principles which have served to produce a low wage, low technology economy (Jessop et al. 1990).

The establishment of these arguments provides some of the necessary preliminary work for the larger task of developing policies which will recreate the links between education and democracy, and which will provide an education system appropriate to a high wage, high technology economy. However, this enterprise is likely to fail unless it is recognised that while neo-liberal educational and economic policies may produce unacceptable outcomes they are a response to fundamental changes in the world economy (Brown and Lauder 1991a) and related changes in the social structure. It is equally important to acknowledge that the political catchcries of 'choice', 'diversity' and 'excellence' used to 'sell' the key elements of neo-liberal education policy have struck a popular chord because they appear to speak to interests and concerns created by changed social circumstances. 'Choice' and 'diversity' in some ways mirror the interests created by

From *British Journal of Sociology of Education*, 12 (1991), 417–31. Reprinted with permission.

the fragmentation of a largely Anglo-Saxon male class based social order while 'excellence' addresses a concern with the question of economic decline.

Democracy and Neo-Liberal Political Economy of Education

The main ingredients in this political economy are a normative theory of individual freedom, which distinguishes freedom of choice from democratic participation—Hayek's (1960) appears to have been most influential in Britain; public choice theory pioneered by Buchanan and Tullock (1962),[2] from which a theory of provider capture has been developed; and a theory of educational provision and consumption loosely based on market theories of competition. What binds this 'family' of theories into an apparently coherent political economy is a common set of underlying assumptions that individuals are rational-egoists, fundamentally concerned with the pursuit of self-interest, and that it is in the marketplace that individuals can best realise the freedom to pursue their self-interest. A corollary of this view is that the same pursuit of self-interest in the political arena can lead to economically and socially undesirable consequences. Hence, so long as education is politically controlled rather than determined by market forces it is likely to produce less than optimal outcomes.

Hayek's Normative Theory of Individual Freedom

In the opening pages of *The Constitution of Liberty* (1960) Hayek defines individual freedom as involving an absence of coercion by the arbitrary will of others. However, he rapidly makes it clear that this kind of freedom should be distinguished from political freedom, which he defines as the participation of men in the choice of their government, in the process of legislation, and in the control of administration. Of this kind of freedom he says, 'A free people in this sense is not necessarily a people of free men; nor need one share in this collective freedom to be free as an individual' (p. 13). However, political liberty of this kind is no guarantee of individual liberty for, he

argues, we have seen millions this century vote for a tyrant, e.g. Hitler. However, there is a further set of reasons why Hayek does not want to relate individual liberty to political freedom. This concerns the relationship between liberty, viewed as a positive power to achieve certain ends, the role of the state and the promotion of equality. Hayek rejects the notion, he attributes to Dewey, that 'liberty is power, effective power to do specific things' (p. 17) because liberty, in this sense, can be used to destroy individual liberty defined as the absence of coercion. Clearly, this positive notion of freedom is connected to Hayek's suspicion of state intervention and coercion. For Hayek, the only justified type of state intervention is based on:

Coercion according to known rules, which is generally the result of circumstances in which the person to be coerced has placed himself, then becomes an instrument assisting the individuals in the pursuit of their own ends and not as a means to be used for the ends of others. (p. 21)

These 'known rules' should be equally applied to everyone. In consequence he argues that the equality before the law that freedom requires leads to material inequality. Hence, the 'desire of making people more alike in their condition cannot be accepted in a free society as a justification for further and discriminatory coercion' (p. 87). Hayek then elaborates on this argument by rejecting the idea that liberty can be identified with wealth and, hence, that a condition of liberty is that wealth be redistributed to those on low income or benefits.[3]

By contrasting his view of liberty to rival views which relate liberty to democratic participation, political power and wealth, Hayek is then able to give a clearer characterisation of his own position. This involves five elements: legal status as a protected member of the community; immunity from arbitrary arrest; the right to work at whatever one desires to do; the right to movement according to the individual's choice; and the right to private property. These elements constitute the basic rights required for the untrammelled operation of a 'free' market.

The importance of this theory of individual liberty is that it licenses a series of policy initiatives in both education and the labour market predicated upon the separation of individual freedom and choice; from power and wealth. In education this means that a system of education can be constructed in which the most impoverished state school can co-exist in the same 'market' with the most heralded public school precisely because wealth and power are unrelated to individual liberty. Similarly, in the labour market, de-regulation can be presented as supporting individual choice because the exercise of the latter is unrelated to power and wealth.[4]

Hayek's separation of wealth and power from economic and educational arrangements reinforces the view that his theory of liberty should not be confused with democracy. For example, Hayek would clearly reject the idea of an education for democratic citizenship in which the understandings and skills necessary for democratic participation were taught to all children. Such a policy would entail the equalising of educational provision at least to the minimum standard required to ensure that all children gained the relevant understandings and skills: a policy which would clearly contravene Hayek's strictures against redistribution. By the same token, Hayek is skeptical about giving political rights to those who are on benefits, i.e. not in the market.[5] He would certainly reject the idea that citizenship required an adequate level of material well being for all, including those who, for whatever reason, cannot find paid employment. Indeed, Hayek himself is clear that liberty and democracy are, at best, contingently related:

However strong the general case for democracy, it is not an ultimate or absolute value and must be judged by what it will achieve. It is *probably* the best method of achieving certain ends, but it is not an end in itself. (1960: 106; my italics.)

If Hayek sets the normative framework for the development of a neo-liberal state it is Buchanan who provides the sharpest critique of liberal democracies, particularly those concerned to promote greater equality and democratic participation. His work, therefore, paves the way for Hayekian neo-liberal policies in education and the economy.

Buchanan's Theory of Public Choice

Buchanan's project is to apply the postulates of neo-classical economics to political behaviour and in particular to analyse the constraints imposed by voter and interest group behaviour on the way governments and state bureaucracies operate. One neo-liberal commentator (Brittan 1988) has described Buchanan as a modern Hobbesian because, starting from similar premises, about human nature, to those of Hobbes, he argues that the constitution of the modern state has to be redefined to take into account the self-interested activities of the major players in the political arena—pressure groups, bureaucrats and politicians. In pursuit of their self-interest these players have endangered the workings of the capitalist economy by increasing government expenditure which is likely to crowd out private sector investment and fuel inflation:

The activities and the importance of special interest groups in the political process are not independent of either the overall-size or the composition of the governmental budget . . . interest group activity, measured in terms of organisational costs, is a direct function of the 'profits' expected from the political process by functional groups. (Buchanan and Tullock 1962: 286)

The pressure applied by interest groups is answered by bureaucrats who seek to increase their departmental budgets and power and by politicians who buy votes with promises of greater expenditure. To quote one commentator on public choice theory:

Following this approach, voters can be likened to consumers; pressure groups can be seen as political consumer associations or sometimes as co-operatives; political parties become entrepreneurs who offer competing packages of services and taxes in exchange for votes; political propaganda equates with commercial advertising; and government agencies are public firms dependent upon receiving or drumming adequate political support to cover their costs. (Self 1985: 51.)

In their early work Buchanan and Tullock (1962) allowed the possibility of a Kantian morality in which considerations of what ought to be the case were divorced from the pursuit of self-interest. However, the whiff of idealism in their work was inconsistent with their fundamental hypothesis that self-interest can explain political behaviour in just the way it can economic behaviour. In more recent work (Buchanan and Wagner 1977), the inconsistency has been removed and Buchanan has argued that because 'budgets cannot be left adrift in a sea of democratic politics' (p. 175) the constitution governing democratic politics would have to be changed so that monetary policy designed to reduce inflation and maintain a stable currency is taken out of the sphere of public choice.

Clearly, Buchanan and his colleagues assert the primacy of economic interests over considerations of democracy. While they argue that the pursuit of self-interest in the economic sphere can typically have socially desirable outcomes the same pursuit in the political sphere creates damaging consequences for the economy and, hence, it is the political sphere that has to be curtailed. There are three specific senses in which public choice theory subjugates a concern for democracy in the interests of a 'free market' economy. First, the consequence of public choice theory is to strengthen the hand of the state by taking a major set of policy instruments, i.e. monetary policy, out of the public sphere. This is one element in the paradox whereby the creation of a 'free market' is accompanied by an authoritarian state (Gamble 1988). Secondly, as Wolfe (1989) notes, such a state is necessary, in theory and practice, to maintain social order precisely because in Buchanan's Hobbesian society the social bonds of love, respect for others and collective memory are stripped away in the struggle for resources.[6] The consequence is that the necessary values and experiences relating to democratic life are denied. For as Dewey (1916: 101) argued, 'A democracy is more than a form of government; it is primarily a mode of associated living, of conjoint communicated experience.' Thirdly, the assumption that particular groups can engage in what Buchanan *et al.* (1980) describe as rent-seeking behaviour, what has become more popularly known as provider capture,[7] has in practice created an arbitrary politics of exclusion. This is because governments can choose to exclude any group from the decision-making process likely to resist their policies on the grounds that the group has a vested interest. Even where the charge of vested interest can be made legitimately, the doctrine of provider capture assumes that all knowledge is tied to social interests and it is, therefore, to be judged not by the normal canons of rationality, but by where people 'come from'. The net consequence of this doctrine is that the essential link between democracy and rationality is lost. For modern democracy has been founded on the

assumptions that arguments and evidence can be assessed with a degree of impartiality[8] and that all citizens should be able to contribute to political debate.

In addition to the politics of exclusion, the effect of provider capture has been to attempt to render impotent those groups most likely to engage in rent-seeking behaviour. It is at this point that Buchanan and Hayek's work forcefully combine to rationalise Thatcherite 'conviction' politics. For they see trade unions, in particular, as bastions of unwarranted privilege which use that privilege to bid up wages, thereby fuelling inflation and creating unemployment (Gamble 1986); hence, the uncompromising stance of the Thatcher government against the teacher unions. However, the concern expressed by Buchanan and Hayek about rent seeking activity underscores the more general themes to emerge from an examination of their political economy: both reject a rich notion of participatory democracy, as suggested by Dewey, because both consider the successful working of a largely unregulated market economy to be of paramount importance in relation to the exercise of human freedom and economic efficiency. In essence, market choice replaces democratic participation as the touchstone of human freedom. The question, then, to be raised is, what is the likely impact of the application of the concepts of neo-liberal political economy on education?

In order to answer this question I shall examine one application of what neo-liberals would consider a paradigm case of provider capture in education: zoning. According to neo-liberals, the latter epitomises the major problems created by provider capture in education and should, therefore, be abolished. I shall then consider the extent to which the marketisation of education, the neo-liberal antidote to the provider captured policy of zoning, provides better grounds for raising educational performance.

A Paradigm Case of Provider Capture— Zoning?

We should begin by noting that the concept of provider capture is a pejorative term—it denotes a state of affairs which is unwarranted and undesirable. It follows, therefore, that it can only be appropriately applied in those cases where (a) it can be shown that the arrangements described as 'capture' produce undesirable outcomes and (b) that there is an alternative which can provide better outcomes. In other words, implicit in the claim that provider capture exists in a particular context is a counterfactual assumption that an alternative set of arrangements will produce more desirable outcomes (Bertram 1988).

There are, no doubt, several ways in which the concept has apparently plausible application in education. For example, Whitty (1990) has raised the possibility that it may be applied to teachers' 'capture' of the curriculum, which, from a neo-liberal perspective may, in turn, suggest the need for a centralised state-directed curriculum. However, Whitty also notes that the politics involved may not conform to such a neat explanation. Moreover, it takes us a considerable way from the source concept in economics, of monopoly, which has generated the notion of provider capture. In contrast, zoning provides a clear example of what could be taken for provider capture since it involves the application of the notion of monopoly which, in turn, generates a set of clear 'predictions' about the nature of privilege created by the monopoly. The critique of zoning is also essential to the neo-liberal project because zoning offends the dogma that competition and choice are always, and everywhere, desirable. Given the criteria articulated above does zoning constitute provider capture?

On the face of it, there does appear to be a case to answer. For what zoning does is to guarantee a group of 'consumers' to a school irrespective of the educational 'product' delivered. It effectively creates a monopoly for the school which means that it is not subject to the normal market disciplines created by competition and, hence, according to neo-liberals, is likely to become inefficient. It privileges, therefore, a group of workers, i.e. teachers, by guaranteeing a source of income and work for them. In consequence, it can be 'predicted' that schools will (1) become wasteful of resources and (2) that the quality of their product, educational standards, is likely to decline. Moreover, zoning creates among parents what in the public choice literature is called rational ignorance, a concept derived from Tullock (1976). According to this idea, one reason why parents do not take an informed interest in their children's schooling

is because state intervention, through zoning, denies them the incentive to think about education. Through zoning their children will automatically go to the in-zone school, and the question of choice and, hence, involvement in education, does not arise. Consequently, their children are likely to underperform.

Before testing these claims it is worth noting the highly contentious foundations on which the notion of provider capture is built. In economic theory the notion of a monopoly is contested as are predictions about their undesirable consequences (Auerbach 1988). Moreover, there are clear difficulties in modelling educational organisations and processes on those designed to produce goods and services, in the tradeable sector.[9] For example, Handy and Aitken (1986), note that it is difficult to translate the educational language of students and teachers into the language of the tradeable sector. They ask whether children should be considered as workers, clients or products, and through a process of tortuous reasoning eventually conclude that the different descriptions are appropriate to children, but at different times in their educational careers. Now the very fact that there is no easy or convincing way in which the language of education can be translated into that of the tradeable sector suggests that the organisations and processes of the two sectors are dissimilar in important respects. In turn, this must cast doubt on the uncritical application of economic concepts, such as the notion of 'monopoly' and its cousin 'provider capture', to the educational domain.

Let us assume, however, that the notion of provider capture can be applied, in principle, to education. Does zoning produce undesirable outcomes and would a market-led system improve educational outcomes? One important undesirable outcome predicted by 'provider capture' is that educational standards are likely to decline in a non-competitive system of education. If we take credentials gained as a measure of educational standards we can test the claim in two ways. First, we can ask the general question has a zoned comprehensive education system increased the number and level of credentials attained? Second, does a comprehensive system of education penalise the most able? In other words while the general number and level of educational qualifications may have risen, those deemed 'most able' may still have been handicapped by a system which caters for the 'average' student.

The most important historical evidence addressing the first question has come from Scotland where McPherson and Willms' (1988) research strongly suggests that comprehensivisation has improved the number and level of qualifications attained; and, that a significant factor in this improvement has been the more balanced social class intakes that comprehensive education has been able to create. This view is supported by most studies in the effective schools literature[10] and has recently been further established by Willms (1990). Moreover, in answer to the second question, there is evidence that a balanced school mix will do little to penalise the 'most able' students while raising the academic achievements of the 'least able' (Lauder and Hughes 1990). In other words, academic excellence and policies designed to promote greater equality may not be mutually exclusive. If, then, zones are drawn to produce a well balanced social class mix it is likely that this will produce the highest *overall* standard of education possible, within the limits set by the social class structure and the sociogeographic distribution of schools within that structure.

This conclusion suggests that the charge of provider capture is unwarranted. However, before we rest on this conclusion we need to consider the counterfactual condition that a market system of education, as the antidote to monopoly conditions, could produce higher standards of education. In other words, we need now to examine the nature of the concept of an educational market and assess its likely 'outcome'.

The Nature and Outcome of Educational Markets

We should begin by noting that the creation of an educational market is an attempt to take education out of the political sphere, where the pursuit of self-interest leads to socially undesirable outcomes, e.g. provider capture, and situate it in the economic sphere where the same pursuit of self-interest will have socially desirable outcomes. In order for this claim to hold, it would be a requirement placed upon the proponents of marketisation that they specify in an intellectually rigorous

way the conditions under which educational markets would operate to produce socially desirable outcomes, e.g. higher educational standards. One way of testing whether this demand can be fulfilled would be to take the paradigm case of educational competition identified by proponents of marketisation, public schools (Hillgate Group 1987), and ask whether it conforms to the most rigorous of models of competition, perfect competition.[11] Such a test may seem unfair either because it is too rigorous or because the notion of perfect competition is, in its own terms, highly problematic (Auerbach 1988; Best 1990). However, as Block (1990: 46) has noted, despite the problems involved in the notion of perfect competition it is an ideal that neo-liberal economists aspire to:

They insist that whatever gains in economic efficiency have occurred over the past two centuries are the result of an institutional framework that has increased market freedom, and that had we moved even closer to full market freedom, the gains would have been even greater.

Space does not permit a full demonstration of the ill fitting relationship between the postulates underpining the theory of perfect competition and the 'market' for public schooling. However, enough points of contrast can be noted to suggest that the market for public schooling operates *in spite* of the postulates of perfect competition rather than in conformity with them.

Consider a scenario for a perfectly competitive market in education. In this market parents would be free to send their children to whatever school they considered 'best'. What counted as the 'best' would be determined by a set of price and quality indicators which would act as market signals for parents. All other things being equal, parents would choose the school which had the highest quality 'output', e.g. credentials for the lowest price. According to these criteria 'good' schools would enrol more students while 'bad' schools would improve or close down. However, the moment a school's performance indicators declined parents would switch schools thereby sending a signal to the school that if it doesn't improve it will perish. As a proxy for the governing, perfectly competitive, concepts of marginal utility and marginal product, a school will only expand to the point where the quality of its education doesn't suffer; similarly, a school will only alter its staff: student ratio to improve its educational 'outputs'. If it seeks to cut costs by reducing staff and this leads to poorer educational performances the market mechanism will ensure that more staff are hired. It is through mechanisms of this kind that the providers of education are kept honest and standards are maximised; or so the argument goes. Now let us turn to the reality of the market.

For a start, unlike a spot market which perhaps best approximates to a perfectly competitive market, the exchange which characterises an education market takes place over a prolonged period. Now in cases where services are provided over a long period buyer and seller must establish a relationship, expressed explicitly or implicitly, by some form of contract. In an education market the contract is implicit and is one in which the school 'guarantees' to provide the standard of education expected by the parents, and the parents, for the sake of continuity in their child's schooling, 'guarantee' to keep their child at the school. The nature of the school's guarantee is determined by reputation and tradition, what the latter connote to parents is that by buying into the reputation of the school they are likely to reduce the risk of their children failing. Part of the reputation, of course, is determined by social class intake, for in essence the guarantee the school provides is that it will only recruit from the appropriate social class to ensure high performance in terms of credentials. For example Halsey *et al.* (1984) have shown that in England the difference in credential success between public and state schools can largely be explained by the social class background of parents and that the social class mix of public schools is different to the social class mix of state schools.

The factors relating to the implicit contract combine to reduce risk for both the school and the parents, under these conditions price will not operate as if in a perfectly competitive market or anything approximating to it. For example, schools with high reputations may charge a premium and parents may pay in order to reduce the risks on *both* sides.

Of course, parents are not only paying to reduce the risk of their children failing they are also paying for the class badge or status that students can then cash in when entering the labour market. These points suggest that the market for public schooling can only be understood in class cultural terms. It works precisely because of the nature of the class structure, not because it approximates to the tenets of perfect competition. As Brown (1990) has noted, there is an absurdity in the idea of attempting to provide schooling for all as suggested by the Hillgate Group (1987) because the status attached to public schooling would then diminish.

The point in demonstrating why the public school market does not conform to the tenets of perfect competition is in part to establish that increased efficiencies and gains in educational standards do not follow from the marketisation of education. This is because the market for public schooling can only be understood to work because of its class cultural context. In terms of the overall argument of this paper this is perhaps the more significant point. A key argument for public choice theorists is that the removal of education from the political to the economic realm will see improved educational performances. Implicit in the distinction between the political and economic realms is the assumption that the market is the natural realm of human freedom when it is undistorted by politics and culture. As Levine (1981: 168) puts it:

the market appears 'natural' both in the sense that it is the institutional form proper to our nature as free human beings and, more importantly, in the sense that whatever constrains economic agents where market relations pertain is conceptually of a piece with the constraints of bare nature.

As the discussion of the market for public schools shows this underlying assumption is simply untenable. Since this is the case it follows that the distinction between the political and the economic cannot be sustained. There is then no *prima facie* case for asserting the superiority of market determined outcomes in education over any other.[12]

The central issue concerning the likely effects of an educational market come down to the question of how the market is politically and culturally constructed. In relation to the aims of an education for a high wage high technology economy and democratic citizenship there are at least three major tests of its likely efficacy. The first concerns the question of choice: will parents have genuinely enhanced choices in a market led system and will this promote greater and more informed parental participation in education, thereby countering the effects of rational ignorance created by zoning? Secondly, will a market-led system create schools with well balanced social class mixes? Thirdly, will a market-led system of education promote an education for democratic citizenship?

Turning to the first question, it is unclear that the marketisation of education will lead to increased choice. Ball (1990) notes that it takes only a small number of parents to switch their preferences from one school to another for a school's economic viability to be placed in jeopardy. In other words, the educational preferences of a majority may be determined by a minority. Moreover, even if parents do exercise choice it doesn't follow that they will provide the kind of educational support necessary for their children's educational success: choice can involve a 'one-off' decision.

More importantly, different groups enter the market on vastly different terms in both material and cultural capital. Which groups will operate successfully in the market will be determined, not so much by participation *per se*, but by the cultural capital, the knowledge of the rules of the game, that 'consumers' bring to the market. Therefore, there is no good reason for supposing that the so-called consumer power in education will lead to greater educational equality of achievement or higher educational standards.

However, it is most likely that the marketisation of education will lead to a decline in overall educational standards. Schools are likely to become sharply differentiated, with élite schools for the rich and a gradation of less prestigious and less 'successful' schools beneath them. The less successful schools are likely to enter a spiral of decline in which the loss of students will be accompanied by a loss of income and a consequent decline in morale as teachers become constrained in their pedagogical methods (Bowe and Ball 1991) and curriculum offerings. These less 'successful schools' will inevitably create the personalities for a low trust low skill economy. The mechanism by which schools will be differentiated into a hierarchy of this kind will be middle class white flight. In a 'free market' education will become an even more powerful means for translating material capital into cultural capital. The net effect will be to further polarise the social class mix of schools and, hence, educational attainment.[13]

It should be apparent that the emphasis on consumer choice in education should not be equated with an education for democratic citizenship. The ostensible function of choice in a market system is to raise educational standards. Indeed, neo-liberal theory severs the connection between education and democracy both conceptually and empirically. Conceptually, it does so by asserting that in a 'free market' for education knowledge should be seen a private good, a commodity like any other (Grace 1989). This means that access to it is determined by the vagaries of the market. Given the predicted decline in educational standards in some schools as a result of market forces it is hard to see how a market-led education system can deliver on what Amy Gutman (1988: 115) argues is a necessary minimum requirement for an education for democratic citizenship. Namely, that 'democratic institutions allocate sufficient resources to education to provide all children with an ability adequate to participate in the democratic process'. In a democratic society education is intimately linked to the notion of democracy through the concept of rationality. While the precise nature of rationality and its connection to democracy has been hotly debated in recent years[14] the underlying assumption that there are important connections to be made between education, rationality and democracy has provided a justification for considering education a public good. For it is only if education is seen in this way that any imperative exists to ensure that all students can acquire the rationality and knowledge necessary for citizenship.

Conclusion: Towards An Alternative Democratic System of Education

The preceding argument has been designed to show that neo-liberal political economy privileges the imperative of the market over democratic participation. However, the 'free market' economics advocated by neo-liberals is likely to create a low wage, low technology economy. As Jessop *et al.* (1990) argue, the neo-liberal rejection of corporatism in favour of largely market determined outcomes has led to the use of high interest rate, high exchange rate and high unemployment rates as policy instruments which have failed because they have stripped the industrial bases of the economies they have been applied to. However, in the wastelands that have been created, labour market policies guided by Hayek's insistence that freedom in the market is unrelated to wealth and power will inevitably produce a low wage skill low wage economy. Precisely because employers have greater power over employees, especially in a deregulated labour market, they will be able to bid down wages. However, under these conditions employers will have no incentive to invest in high technology because profits can be made out of cheap labour (Lauder *et al.* 1990). In essence a market system of education is entirely consistent with a low wage, low technology economy precisely because it is likely to produce the low skilled low trust personalities for such an economy.

In contrast, a high wage, high technology economy requires overall high levels of skill and worker autonomy (Zuboff 1988)[15] and an education system which produces an *overall* high level of educational achievement. Such a system needs to promote equality of opportunity in its strongest form, i.e. equality of results, for not only would skilled occupations expand in a sophisticated economy, but a wider range of talents and abilities than was the case in bureaucratically organised forms of work (Brown and Lauder 1991*b*) would be required.

The requirements of an education for democracy are similar: high overall level of achievement so that students have the understandings and skills required to participate in a democratic society and an open, non-selective system of education which promotes equality of results. A strong notion of equality of opportunity of this kind is required[16] because in a society differentiated by ethnicity, gender and class in which those who conceive policy are nearly always highly educated, a voice needs to be given to those groups who do not traditionally succeed in education.[17]

The general principles of an education system which has the aims of creating the skills and understandings necessary for life in an economically sophisticated, democratic society are then clear. These aims require a non-selective, non-competitive, i.e. zoned, state system of education. However, within these general parameters tensions exist. In the introduction to this paper I noted that neo-liberal political economy has touched a popular chord in terms of the concepts of choice

and diversity. However, choice and diversity in a democratic system of education need to be genuinely linked to the aspirations of ethnic minorities, women and the working class, rather than being used as code words designed to enhance the 'social wage' of the wealthy and powerful. The challenge, then, is to devise a system of education which can accommodate the necessity for schools to have well balanced social class intakes, with aspirations for genuine choice and diversity. What I have attempted to demonstrate in this paper is that so called 'choice' is unlikely to fulfil the promise held out for it by proponents of marketisation. Where 'choice' does exist, it will only advantage the privileged sectors of society. However, the cost of increasing the advantage of the privileged is to reduce the overall standard of education, thereby helping to create the personnel for a low skill low trust economy. By the same token, a market system of education neither intends to, nor can it meet the demands for an education for democratic citizenship.

Notes

1. Roger Douglas, former Labour Minister of Finance and architect of neo-liberal reforms in New Zealand is also a supporter of 'conviction' politics. In an address to the Australian Education Council Conference, Adelaide, Dec 1990 he said: 'implement reform in quantum leaps. Moving step by step lets vested interests mobilise. Big packages neutralise them. Speed is essential . . . Once you start the momentum rolling never let it stop'.

2. Buchanan and Hayek share similar views regarding the relationship of vested interests to democratic government. However, Buchanan's analysis is more thorough going. It should be noted though that Hayek and Buchanan do differ in relation to the question of the redistribution of wealth. See Brittan (1988). Buchanan typically works with others, but I refer to it as *his* theory because he is usually the major author.

3. Hayek has little or no concern regarding disparities in wealth. In his *Constitution of Liberty* (1960) he says, 'It is difficult to see, however, in what sense it could ever be legitimate to say that any one person is too far ahead of the rest or that it would be harmful to society if the progress of some greatly outstripped that of others' (p. 46).

4. For a cogent critique of Hayek's separation of

liberty from power, wealth and education, see Norman (1982).
5. See the remarks in Hayek (1960), 105.
6. I am indebted to Wolfe's (1989) analysis of public choice theory. For anyone concerned with the social underpinnings to democracy Wolfe's paper is particularly important.
7. Provider capture can be defined as the ability of specific groups to insulate themselves from market disciplines and consequences by exerting political pressure. Provider capture should be distinguished from Stigler's (1970) notion of 'Director's Law' or middle class capture. It is quite unclear to me how the notion of class is compatible with neo-liberal ontology, which denies the notion of society.
8. This is not to underestimate the difficulties in finding an epistemological basis for such judgements. See note 14. It is, however, to suggest a degree of openness is possible in seeking grounds for an impartial assessment of arguments, evidence, etc.
9. I use the term tradeable rather than private sector because there are still a few state trading organisations left! The use of the term here should not be confused with its use on money markets where it typically refers to the export sector.
10. There is one notable, partial exception. Chubb and Moe (1990) find a weak statistical relationship between social class mix and school performance. However, they do acknowledge parental background to be an important factor in school success. Unfortunately, they fail to take social class background and the consequent asymmetries in parental power and knowledge into account in recommending a market system of education. To my knowledge, theirs is the strongest attempt, to-date, to provide a rationale for the marketisation of education.
11. Hayek is a critic of the theory of perfect competition. However, Hayek's own theory appears to be based on the faith (Auerbach 1988) that in nearly all cases the introduction of competition will create 'progress'. For Hayek (1979) competition is the way we have acquired much of the skills and knowledge we possess. Markets, then, are the most efficient way of learning and problem solving. However, as Bredo (1988) notes, when applied to education there is a vital distinction to be made between short- and long-term adjustments to choice and knowledge. See the following discussion.
12. Indeed, economists are now rejecting the various analytical models of competition in favour of an historical and social understanding of how they work. *Contra* Hayek, this suggests that the 'success' of market economies in the twentieth century should be seen as the

product of a particular set of social and political conditions, rather than as the inevitable result of their intrinsic rationality or of human nature. See Best (1990).
13. The only extant, largely private provider system of education is Holland's. There is evidence from Holland which supports this prognosis. See Seashore *et al.* (1990/1991).
14. There has been a major three-cornered debate in recent years on this issue between the 'London School' of philosophers of education, and Marxist and feminist theorists of education. See, respectively, Hirst (1974), Harris (1979) and Walker (1981); Gilligan (1982) and Martin (1985).
15. This is to suggest that political struggle can have a determinate effect on economic structures. See Esping-Andersen (1990).
16. While a strong notion of equality of opportunity is important it should be noted that, in general terms, the concept has strong connections to the demands of bureaucratic education, and strategies of class incorporation. In a democratically organised education system, a strong notion of equal rights to participation in decision-making at the school level is also necessary. In other words, the notion of equality needs to be applied in a plurality of ways in a democratic education system. See Lauder (1988).
17. It can be argued that one way of providing that voice is through separate schooling. If various groups within society find comprehensive schools alienating, then it would seem to be a requirement, in terms of an education for democratic citizenship, that those groups are provided with an educational context in which the skills and critical understandings required for citizenship can be learnt.

References

Auerbach, P. (1988), *Competition: The Economics of Industrial Change* (Oxford: Blackwell).
Ball, S. (1990), 'Education, Inequality and School Reform: Values in Crisis!' An Inaugural Lecture, Centre for Educational Studies, King's College, London.
Bertram, G. (1988), 'Middle Class Capture: A Brief Survey', *Royal Commission on Social Policy*, 3/2: *Future Directions* (Wellington, N.Z.: Government Printer).
Best, M. (1990), *The New Competition: Institutions of Industrial Restructuring* (Cambridge: Polity Press).
Block, F. (1990), *Post Industrial Possibilities: A Critique of Economic Discourse* (Berkeley: Univ. of California Press).
Bowe, R., and Ball, S. (1991), 'Doing What Comes

392

Education, Democracy, and the Economy

Naturally: An Exploration of LMS in One Secondary School', Centre for Educational Studies, King's College, London.

Bredo, E. (1988), 'Choice, Constraint and Community', in W. Lowe Boyd, W. L., and Kerchner, C. (ed.), *The Politics of Excellence and Choice in Education* (London: Falmer Press).

Brittan, S. (1988), *A Restatement of Economic Liberalism* (London: Macmillan).

Brown, P. (1990), 'The Third Wave: Education and the Ideology of Parentocracy', *British Journal of Sociology of Education*, 11: 65–85.

—— and Lauder, H. (1991a), 'Education, Economy and Social Change', *International Journal of Sociology of Education*, 1: 3–23.

—— (1991b), 'Education, Economy and Society: An Introduction to a New Agenda', in Brown, P., and Lauder, H. (eds.), *Education for Economic Survival* (London: Routledge).

Buchanan, J., and Tullock, G. (1962), *The Calculus of Consent* (Ann Arbor: Univ. of Michigan Press).

—— Wagner, R. (1977), *Democracy in Deficet* (New York: Academic Press).

—— Tollison, R., and Tullock, G. (eds.) (1980), *Toward A Theory of the Rent-Seeking Society* (Texas; A and M Univ. Press).

Chubb, J., and Moe, T. (1990), *Politics, Markets and America's Schools* (Washington DC: Brookings Institution).

Dewey, J. (1916), *Democracy and Education* (New York: Macmillan).

Esping-Andersen, G. (1990), *The Three Worlds of Welfare Capitalism* (Princeton, N.J.: Princeton Univ. Press).

Gamble, A. (1986), 'The Political Economy of Freedom', in Levitas, R. (ed.), *The Ideology of the New Right* (Cambridge: Polity Press).

—— (1988), *The Free Market and the Strong State* (London: Macmillan).

Gilligan, C. (1982), *In a Different Voice* (Cambridge: Harvard Univ. Press).

Grace, G. (1989), 'Education: Commodity or Public Good?' *British Journal of Educational Studies*, 37: 207–21.

Gutman, A. (1988), 'Distributing Public Education', in Gutman, A. (ed.), *Democracy and the Welfare State* (Princeton, N.J.: Univ. of Princeton Press).

Halsey, A., Heath, A., and Ridge, J. (1984), 'The Political Arithmetic of Public Schools', in Walford, G. (ed.), *British Public Schools: Policy and Practice* (London: Falmer Press).

Handy, C., and Aitken, R. (1986), *Understanding Schools as Organisations* (London: Penguin).

Harris, K. (1979), *Education and Knowledge* (London: Routledge and Kegan Paul).

Hayek, F. (1960), *The Constitution of Liberty* (Chicago: Univ. of Chicago Press).

—— (1979) *Law, Legislation and Liberty*, 3 (Chicago, Univ. of Chicago Press).

Hillgate Group (1987), *The Reform of British Education* (London: Claridge Press).

Hirst, P. (1974), *Knowledge and the Curriculum* (London: Routledge and Kegan Paul).

Jessop, B., Bonnett, K., and Bromley, S. (1990), 'Farewell to Thatcherism? Neo-Liberalism and "New Times" ', *New Left Review*, 179: 81–102.

Lauder, H. (1988), 'Traditions of Socialism and Educational Policy', in Lauder, H., and Brown, P. (eds.), *Education in Search of a Future* (London: Falmer Press).

—— and Hughes, D. (1990), 'Social Inequalities and Differences in School Outcomes', *New Zealand Journal of Educational Studies*, 25: 37–60.

—— Brown, P., and Hughes, D. (1990), 'The Labour Market, Educational Reform and Economic Growth', *New Zealand Journal of Industrial Relations*, 15: 203–18.

Levine, A. (1981), *Liberal Democracy; A Critique of its Theory* (New York: Macmillan).

McPherson, A., and Willms, D. (1987), 'Equalisation and Improvement: Some effects of Comprehensive Reorganisation in Scotland', *Sociology*, 21: 509–39.

Martin, J. (1985), *Reclaiming a Conversation: the Ideal of the Educated Woman* (New Haven: Yale Univ. Press).

Norman, R. (1982), 'Does Equality Destroy Liberty?' in Graham, K. (ed.), *Contemporary Political Philosophy: Radical Studies* (Cambridge: Cambridge Univ. Press).

Seashore, K., Boudewijn, A., and van Zelzen, M. (1990/91), 'A Look At Choice in the Netherlands', *Educational Leadership* (Dec/Jan), 66–72.

Self, P. (1985), *Political Theories of Modern Government: Its Role and Reform* (London: Allen and Unwin).

Stigler, G. (1970), 'Director's Law of Public Income Redistribution', *Journal of Law and Economics*, 13.

Tullock, G. (1976), *The Vote Motive* (London, IEA).

Walker, J. (1981), 'Autonomy, Authority and Antagonism: A Critique of Ideology in the Philosophy of Education' (Ph.D. thesis, Univ. of Sydney, Australia).

Whitty, G. (1990), 'The New Right and the National Curriculum: State Control or Market Forces?' in Flude, M., and Hammer, M. (eds.), *The Education Reform Act, 1988: Its Origins and Implications* (London: Falmer Press).

Willms, D. (1990), 'Do Scottish Education Authorities Differ in their Examination Results? Findings from the Scottish School Effectiveness Study' (Centre for Educational Sociology, Univ. of Edinburgh).

Wolfe, A. (1989), 'Market and Society as Codes of Moral Obligation', *Acta Sociologica*, 32: 221–36.

Zuboff, S. (1988), *In the Age of the Smart Machine* (New York: Basic Books).

26

The 'Third Wave': Education and the Ideology of Parentocracy

Phillip Brown

Introduction

The social basis of educational selection has been an important area of sociological concern, particularly since the Second World War.[1] This interest not only reflects the importance attached to education as a determinant of future life chances, but also the growing commitment to generating equality of educational opportunity. These concerns have led sociologists to examine the extent to which educational change had actually generated a more 'open' and 'equal' society. Liberal and Marxist accounts of post-war reforms have arrived at very different conclusions.[2] Nevertheless, the idea of the educational 'meritocracy' in advanced industrial/capitalist societies had become part of the taken-for-granted landscape of the sociologist. Indeed, the popularity of Marxist accounts of education in the late 1970s were largely a product of the frustrations of those who felt that liberal-democratic reforms had not led to an immediate and significant improvement in the life-chances of children from working-class origins (Lauder and Brown 1988). From a Marxist perspective, liberal reforms were seen as a legitimate target for criticisms, because they were perceived as a *necessary* feature of late capitalist development, serving the interests of capital. The possibility that the welfare state would be dismantled or comprehensive education scrapped was not foreseen.

In Britain, a Conservative reaction to post-war reforms was however, recognised in Anthony Crosland's *The Future of Socialism* (1956: 27):

it was always obvious that the Conservatives would do reactionary things, and peel off several layers of what had been achieved: that they would alter the priorities, withdraw the frontiers of social control and ownership, and above all redistribute real income from poor to rich. . . . All these things have in fact been done, and more will be done in the future. But it was never likely that the Conservatives would destroy the hard core of the achievement; and even if we suffer several more years of Conservative rule, I should still expect 75% of the reforms to remain intact.

With the benefit of hindsight, Crosland was clearly correct to expect a Conservative reaction to post-war social democratic reforms, but he was over-optimistic about the obdurate qualities of these and subsequent reforms. Although it is difficult to predict the final outcome, radical change in both educational ideology and practice is now occurring (Ball 1987; Demaine 1988; Brown 1989; Jones 1989).

The argument I want to develop here is that we are entering a 'third wave' in the socio-historical development of British education which is neither part of a final drive towards the 'meritocracy', nor the result of a socialist victory for educational reform. To date, the 'third wave' has been characterised by the rise of the educational *parentocracy*, where a child's education is increasingly dependent upon the *wealth* and *wishes* of parents, rather than the *ability* and *efforts* of pupils. However, it does not preclude the possibility of further educational expansion. Indeed it seems likely that there will be further expansion of post-compulsory education in the near future.[3]

From *British Journal of Sociology of Education*, 11 (1990), 65–85. Reprinted with permission.

The defining feature of an educational parentocracy is not the amount of education received, but the social basis upon which educational selection is organised. It will be argued here that the existing 'third wave' policies will not only reinforce but increase educational inequalities. It is also important to note that the ideology of parentocracy has not emerged as a result of a ground swell of popular demand for radical educational reform among a majority of parents, and does not imply an increase in 'parent power' over the school curriculum. On the contrary, it has been the State and not parents who have strengthened their control over what is taught in schools.

To use the 'wave' analogy popularised by Toffler (1981), it will be argued that the 'first wave' involved the development of elementary state education for the 'lower orders'. This schooling of the working-class was primarily concerned with the inculcation of basic information and knowledge seen to be appropriate for their predetermined (ascribed) place in society. This Dewey (1916) once described as the 'feudal dogma of social predestination'. The 'second wave' can be characterised as one involving a shift in educational ideology and policy from that based upon social ascription to one based upon 'age, aptitude and ability'. Paramount importance is placed upon individual merit and achievement as a determinant of one's educational and occupational career. It must however be remembered that although the liberal-democratic reforms since 1944 have been consistent with the ideology of meritocracy, and important advances in working-class performance have been found, equality of educational opportunity has never been achieved (Halsey *et al.* 1980).

The 'third wave' can be characterised in terms of the rise of the ideology of parentocracy. This involves a major programme of educational reform under the slogans of 'parental choice', 'educational standards' and the 'free market'. In this paper these three 'waves' of educational ideology and policies will be briefly outlined in order to provide a general picture of educational change in England.[4] As a contribution to subsequent debates this paper will also address the question of why the ideology of parentocracy has dominated policy debates in the late twentieth century, and consider what implications it may have for our understanding of the relationship between education and the State.

The 'First Wave'

The 'first wave' is characterised by the development of mass schooling in the nineteenth century. It was intended to *confirm* rather than *transcend* existing social divisions (Hurt 1981). The education a child received had to conform to his or her predetermined place in the social order. Floud and Halsey (1958: 177) note that in such a society 'education serves primarily a differentiating function, maintaining the styles of life of different strata and the supply of appropriately socialised recruits to them'. This principle of educational organisation was clearly expounded by the Bishop of Norwich in 1755:

There must be drudges of labour (hewers of wood and drawers of water, the Scriptures call them) as well as Counsellors to direct, and Rulers to preside. . . . To which of these classes we belong, especially the more inferior ones, our birth determines . . . . These poor children are born to be daily labourers, for the most part to earn their bread by the sweat of their brows. It is evident then that if such children are, by charity, brought up in a manner that is only proper to qualify them for a rank to which they ought not to aspire, such a child would be injurious to the Community. (Bendix 1956: 64)

As the provision of education developed for the masses during the nineteenth century, it was not only 'by charity', but also the disruptive potential 'by education', which concentrated the minds of the ruling classes (Simon, 1966). Such concerns were reinforced by the pace of industrialisation and urbanisation, which generated the need for new forms of social control, new manufacturing methods, and new social and economic arrangements.

In Booth's study of London in the 1880s, for example, it was found that 80 per cent of the population were between the ages of 15 and 25 and many were living in absolute poverty. Coupled with the Factory Acts of the 1860s and 1870s, which accelerated the decline in child labour and heightened fears among employers about Britain's ability to compete economically, there was considerable concern about the 'untutored masses' and 'dangerous classes', and a growing belief that the school offered a potential solution. However, due in part to the antagonism which existed between Church and State, even in the late nineteenth century, England was still educationally a very underdeveloped society (Glass 1961; Lawson and Silver 1973).[5]

Elementary education was largely defined in terms of instruction to meet the minimum requirements perceived to be necessary in order for the labouring poor to fulfil their future roles in a changing society. The school was seen as a device to reform manners, promote religion and ensure discipline (Johnson 1976). This 'gentling of the masses' was to be achieved by exposing them to superior influences; therefore it is hardly surprising that H. G. Wells referred to Forster's 1870 Education Act as one designed to 'educate the lower classes for employment on lower class lines, and with specially trained, inferior teachers' (in Glass 1961: 394).

Secondary education, which remained a preserve of the middle classes until well into the twentieth century, existed primarily to provide an education perceived to be suitable for a 'gentleman', and in order to ensure the reproduction of social and economic élites. The curriculum of the public schools and the endowed grammar schools in the late nineteenth century was academic in content and intended to set its incumbents apart from the masses in preparation for entry into the professions. The relationship between the secondary schools and the professional organisations was, as Glass has noted, 'not simply to recruit members who would confer distinction upon the profession, but also to have a profession which would confer social prestige upon its members' (p. 396). If social class was the dominant organising principle during the 'first wave', it was cross-cut in a vitally important way by gender. Fig. 26.1 shows the ways in which the ascribed attributes of class and gender gave rise to different interpretations of what was to count as an appropriate 'education'.

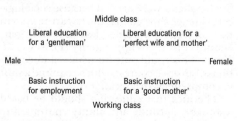

Fig. 26.1. Class and gender inequalities in the 'first wave'

Note: The phrase 'perfect wife and mother' is used by Purvis (1983) to distinguish the concerns of middle-class women with the learning of complex rituals of etiquette, the management of the household and domestic servants, and the participation in 'good' works in the locality. The working-class 'good mother' refers to the importance attached to learning practical domestic skills without any of the frills!

The education of the male was seen to be of primary importance given the patriarchal structure of the family, and there was a commonly held assumption at the time that women were biologically inferior to men, both in physique and intellect:

It is evident that the man, possessing reasoning faculties, muscular power, and courage to employ it, is qualified for being a protector: the woman, being little capable of reasoning, feeble, and timid, requires protection. Under such circumstances, the man naturally governs: the woman as naturally obeys. (Alexander Walker 1840, in Purvis 1983)

Deem (1978) and Purvis (1983), among others, have also noted the importance of education for girls, which identified a woman's role with the domestic sphere regardless of social class. Therefore this typology highlights the fact that schooling during the 'first wave' was structured on the basis of ascription for one's predetermined future social, occupational *and* domestic roles.

The 'Second Wave'

The 'second wave' involved an ideological shift in organising principle, from an education determined by an accident of birth (ascription) to one based upon one's age, aptitude and ability (achievement). In a 'meritocratic' system of education (Young 1961), all must be given an equal opportunity of gaining access to jobs concomitant with their abilities. However, the meritocracy never promised equality, only that inequalities would be distributed more fairly.

The importance attached to individual achievement as a determinant of one's educational and occupational career was particularly evident in the writings of Parsons (1961) and informed much of the debate about education in the post-war period 1944–76 (Bernbaum 1977). Parsons argued that in an advanced industrial society the school confronted a dual problem of selecting the most able individuals and facilitating their educational and social advancement, as well as the problem of internalising the commitment and capacities necessary for the successful performance of their future adult roles (Davis and Moore 1967).

The perceived nature and consequences of the rapid social and economic changes which confronted all Western industrial societies following the Second World War had a powerful impact on the direction of educational change, although Britain was much slower than the USA in shifting from what Turner (1961: 122) described as a system of 'sponsored' mobility to a system of 'contest' mobility. The system of educational sponsorship in Britain increased in significance as the 'first wave' began to lose its ideological domination. Sanderson (1987: 75) has noted:

The first concept which broke down the assumption that elementary and secondary education should relate to different social classes was that of the ladder of opportunity. This envisaged by its narrow imagery, a difficult steep climbing relationship whereby a few very able children clambered in small numbers from one level to another.

Although such ideas existed in the 1870s it was only very slowly that they gained increasing acceptance, and it was not until the inter-war years that the idea of an educational ladder was extended to a call for 'secondary education for all'. Tawney (1931), a leading commentator at the time, argued that social justice and a common culture required that equality of educational opportunity be extended:

The goal to be aimed at is simplicity itself. The idea that differences of educational opportunity among children should depend upon differences of wealth among parents is a barbarity.... A special system of schools, reserved for children whose parents have larger bank accounts than their neighbours, exists in no other country on the same scale as in England. It is at once an educational monstrosity and a grave national misfortune. It is educationally vicious, since to mix with companions from homes of different types is an important part of the education of the young. It is socially disastrous, for it does more than any other single cause, except capitalism itself, to perpetuate the division of the nation into classes of which one is almost unintelligible to the other. (p. 145)

Yet even after the passing of the 1944 Education Act, it was the tripartite system which flourished, allowing sponsorship to continue, although a larger number of academically able pupils from a deprived social background were now able to enter the academic grammar schools.

The shift towards a system of 'contest' mobility in Britain (which necessitates a system of comprehensive education) was not ultimately achieved on an appeal to social justice or the acquisition of a common culture, but on the grounds that educational expansion was necessary in order to ensure Britain's economic prosperity. This argument was based on the assumption that the general level of skill and knowledge required for most occupations would increase as the number of unskilled jobs declined rapidly. It was also assumed that an investment in education was both a sure way of maintaining economic competitiveness, and, for the individual, an insurance policy against unemployment. The implications of the economic argument for educational expansion was outlined by Floud and Halsey (1961: 40):

The notion that an advanced industrial economy requires a well-educated, adaptable, and fluid, i.e. geographically and occupationally mobile—labour force is implicit in our account of the growing involvement of education and economy. Ideally, runs the implication, talent should find its own level in the market, and the only guarantees that it may possibly do so lie in a high rate of social mobility and the minimizing or elimination of social factors in educational selection and occupational recruitment.

Consequently they were able to conclude that:

We have seen that a technological society has little use for social-class or other rigidities in the supply of labour, and that the principle of equality of opportunity in education serves an important economic function in such a society. (p. 9)

A logical outcome of this argument was the development of educational policies aimed at ending the restrictive practices which prevented able working-class pupils from realising their educational and economic potential. Such policies were needed because sociological evidence showed that the tripartite system was not freeing working-class talent and generating equality of opportunity (Halsey et al. 1961). This could only be achieved in conditions of an open contest, which required a shift to comprehensive education.

The idea that education should be based upon age, aptitude and ability continued to assume that there were 'natural' differences between the sexes for much of the 'second wave'. Differences in subjects studied and in examination results were seen to reflect a process of natural differentiation, which was reinforced by the assumption that girls and boys would ultimately perform different adult roles (Deem 1980). During the later stages of the 'second wave', gender (and to a lesser extent race) issues have received considerable attention, particularly among feminist writers who have attacked a class-focused, but gender-blind sociology (Acker 1981). The somewhat belated extension of meritocratic principles to the education of the sexes has been particularly noticeable in recent policy statements (Arnot 1987). Moreover, despite continuing differences in subjects studied and inequalities confronting young women in the market for jobs, the examination performance of girls has significantly improved (Central Statistical Office 1989). There have also been increasing attempts to break down gender differentiation and inequalities in the school curriculum (Whyte *et al.* 1985; Burchell and Millman 1989).

The expansion of comprehensive education in the 1960s and 1970s has led to a general improvement in educational standards, although the working classes have not significantly improved their relative educational or life chances. It also needs to be recognised that during the 'second wave', gender inequalities have declined, despite the fact that important gender divisions remain (Arnot and Weiner 1987). During the 'second wave', gender divisions in the organisation and process of schooling have become less explicit, more open to question and subject to policy reform. The scale of the decline in social inequalities need not detain us here (see Halsey *et al.* 1980; Swann 1985; Beechey and Whitelegg 1986). What is in need of discussion are the reasons for the attack on the comprehensive school, which resulted from the changing economic conditions outside the school and the growing disillusionment with the results of liberal reforms evident across the political spectrum.

The 'Third Wave'[6]

If the dual objectives of 'equality of opportunity' and 'economic efficiency' were the two-edged sword thrust at the heart of élite educational sponsorship, it has been turned against the advocates of comprehensive edu-

cation, because on both counts the educational system has failed to live up to its promise. The massive investment in education during the 1960s did not prevent the economic recession signalled by the Oil Crisis of 1973 and the subsequent increase in youth unemployment, which in the early 1980s amounted to the virtual collapse of the youth labour market in many parts of Britain. By the mid-1970s the educational consensus was dead, and James Callaghan's Great Debate on Education which was launched in 1976 signalled 'noise of crisis' (Donald 1981) which was yet to be fully articulated or understood. There were a growing number of complaints from employers, which blamed the school for the rising levels of youth unemployment and for generally failing to meet the needs of industry (Hopkins 1978). The political ascendancy of the Right also gave credence to the idea that the attempts to 'tap the pool of ability' believed to exist among the working-class in the 1960s were now a source of economic liability (Brown 1987; Finn 1987).

Equally, the proponents of comprehensive education could find little comfort from the research evidence concerning the extent to which the 'meritocracy' had become a reality, and little support from the academic community which by the time of the Great Debate was coming to grips with what Marxists were telling them about the role of education in a capitalist society. The Marxist message was that the 'meritocracy' was largely symbolic, given the structural correspondence which was assumed to exist between education and production (Bowles and Gintis 1976). The educational system was therefore treated as a 'dependent agency of social control, reproducing recruits to the class structure through pedagogical relations of authority which correspond to, and, for the child, anticipate relations of authority in work' (Halsey *et al.* 1980: 2).

In these terms the educational system was seen to be as much an enemy of the working-class as that which existed during the 'first wave', but now it resembled the forbidden fruit in the Garden of Eden—it was there to tempt the working classes but it would ensure their damnation as they were duped into believing that the competition for credentials was fair, rather than fixed, in order to reproduce and legitimise existing inequalities (Brown 1987).

Similar 'black papers' on the state of comprehensive education were being produced by the Right, which also saw liberal reforms as a betrayal of the working-class.

The radical Right's account of the educational crisis (see Cox and Dyson 1968; Cox and Boyson 1977) has asserted that the comprehensive 'experiment' had not only failed, but was the cause of a decline in educational standards. They argued that the spirit of competition and excellence had been sacrificed in order to make the educational system conform to a socialist notion of social justice. Therefore, 'merit' and 'standards of excellence' need to be defended against those who promote mediocrity in the name of social justice (Cox and Boyson 1977; Hillgate Group 1986; 1987):

It must always be remembered that the deterioration in British education has arisen partly because schools have been treated as instruments for equalizing, rather than instructing, children. Merit, competition and self-esteem have been devalued or repudiated; the teaching of facts has given way to the inculcation of opinion; education has often been confounded with indoctrination; and in many places there is a serious risk of disciplined study being entirely swamped by an amorphous tide of easy-going discussion and the idle play. (Hillgate Group 1987: 2)

The Right also present the shift to comprehensive education as a radical transformation which Flew (1987) has compared with the Bolshevik Revolution in 1917:

This truly radical reorganisation has sometimes been described as a great experiment; just as, in the 1920s and the 1930s, the operations of the regime established by the Bolshevik coup of October 1917 were regularly characterised as 'that great social experiment in Russia'.

Certainly the continuing effects of the Comprehensive Revolution are both very extensive and extremely important. (Flew 1987: 27)

The difficulty faced by the Right in their attempt to impute a socialist revolutionary character to the shift towards comprehensive education is of course, the participation of post-war Conservative governments in their establishment.

Such difficulties do not affect their contention that the comprehensive experiment has failed. Indeed, because of the hopelessly optimistic belief that comprehensive education could overcome broader social inequali-

ties and Britain's economic troubles, the proponents of liberal-democratic reforms have found it difficult to counteract the Right's critique. The Right have argued that the comprehensive experiment has not only failed the working-class, but betrayed it. This view is premised on the dubious assertion that only a small proportion of pupils from working-class origins can benefit from the demands of an academic education. Despite such problems they assert that comprehensive reorganisation has both eroded the standards of our élite schools because of their contamination by the masses, and led the masses to receive an education which is not suited to their 'needs' (see Bantock 1977).

The issue of declining educational standards has been at the heart of the Right's attack on comprehensive education for many years (Cox and Dyson 1968; Jones 1989). However, the lack of credible evidence to support the assertion that educational standards have declined,[7] let alone to show that any decline is the result of comprehensive reorganisation, has not prevented the question of 'standards' from remaining at the centre of what the Right define as the educational crisis. This is because 'standards' are as much a moral as an educational issue. The main concern of the authoritarian Right is to regain traditional authority, leadership and the reproduction of élite culture, in which the educational system is seen to have a key role to play. For them, it is the very idea of comprehensive education which violates their notion of standards, not only its imputed consequences (Brown 1989). It is the shift from élite to mass culture, and the erosion of respect for authority, which they oppose. This desire often contradicts the goals of the 'free marketeers', whose ideas derive from classical liberalism (see Scruton 1984; Belsey 1986; Green 1987). Here, emphasis is placed on the 'free market economy' and 'individual liberty'. An uneasy alliance between the authoritarian Conservatives and the 'market' men and women has been possible due to their mutual disdain of 'collective social reform'. Classical liberals oppose such reforms because they 'consider them to be menaces to freedom, conservatives, because they consider them to be egalitarian in tendency' (Phillips 1978: 12).

The potential conflict among the Right has so far been limited because despite their ideological differences both groups serve the political and material interests of the powerful and privileged (Gamble 1988). In a free market society, although we may have formal equality before the law, we do not have substantive equality. Moreover, the privatisation of education has an appeal to the authoritarian conservatives, because the latter believe that, if left to the free market, not only would the élite schools be preserved, but also the schooling for different social groups would 'diversify as society required' (Scruton 1984: 160).

If the educational parentocracy were to become a reality, we would witness the establishment of an 'independent education for all' (Flew 1987; Hillgate Group 1987). This would mean that the Local Education Authorities (LEAs) would no longer be the main providers of 'education' and the comprehensive system would be scrapped. In order to establish an 'independent education for all' it is necessary to think of schools as separate educational firms, subject, like the presently existing independent schools, to the incentives and discipline of the market. It is argued that a major advantage of this kind of educational arrangement is that it maximises variety and choice while rejecting all attempts to impose and sustain what its proponents see as a state 'monopoly' and a 'uniform service' for all its consumers. Hence two conditions need to exist in order to achieve an 'independent education for all'. First, all parents should be free and able to move their children from one school to another if they so desire, and secondly, every school should have strong financial incentives to attract and to hold custom, and have sufficient reason to fear disaster if it fails (Flew: 7). This system of *survival by results* involves the privatisation of education:

The aim . . . is to offer an independent education to all, by granting to all parents the power, at present enjoyed only by the wealthy, to choose the best available education for their children. This aim can be accomplished only by offering schools the opportunity to liberate themselves from Local Authority control. (The Hillgate Group 1987: 2)

Therefore any fetter to the supply and demand for education should be removed because it is assumed that open competition between schools will raise standards for all and offer real choices to parents. However, those schools which fail to recruit enough pupils (sell desk space for the services they have on offer) should be allowed to go out of business.

An 'independent education for all' has yet to be introduced, although many of the ideas which inform it are currently shaping the future direction of British education (they are also having an important impact in other countries: see Shor 1986; Botstein 1988; Lauder *et al.* 1988). Already the Educational Reform Act in England and Wales (1988), which includes the financial delegation to schools, open enrollment, charging for school activities and opting out (to become grant maintained schools), are further steps towards educational privatisation (Pring 1987) and the establishment of an 'independent education for all'[8].

Simon (1988) has noted that the main thrust of the Education Reform Act is towards 'destabilising locally controlled "systems" and, concomitantly, pushing the whole structure of schooling towards a degree, at least, of privatisation, so establishing a base which could be further exploited later' (p. 48). What Simon is hinting at here is the possibility of moving towards the introduction of educational vouchers. The 'opting out' proposal as envisaged by Margaret Thatcher is not quite a voucher system but it is similar to it (Wilby and Midgley 1987)[9].

A further element of the Education Reform Act is the introduction of formal testing and assessment of pupils at the ages of 7, 11, 14, and 16. This represents part of the attempt to provide parents with the necessary consumer information to decide to which school to send their child. Formal testing and the imposition of a 'core curriculum' are also seen as ways of increasing standards. But, as Simon (1988) has correctly stated, while the Right want a variety of schools they also demand a 'strict *uniformity* in the curriculum where, they now claim, there is too much "variety" '(emphasis in the original, p. 17). Therefore, despite the rhetoric of 'choice' and 'individual freedom', in practice the educational system is becoming *more* centrally controlled, and both teachers and parents will have less control over the school curriculum[10].

The Sociological Context of the 'Third Wave'

The 'third wave' is still in its nascent form, and although it is legitimate to talk about the ideology of parentocracy, it is important to note that there is nothing inevitable about the direction of educational change (Simon 1985). Indeed, there are genuine possibilities that education in the 'third wave' will be based on an alternative politics of education to that currently directing policy because of the inherent contradictions within a market system of education. The social and economic transformation of Western industrial societies, which we are currently experiencing, will make the need for an alternative to the ideology of parentocracy all the more urgent. It will be argued elsewhere that there are new historical possibilities for the emergence of a more democratic, efficient and equitable system of formal education in the 'third wave' (Brown and Lauder 1992).

Moreover, when policies are applied in practice intentions and outcomes are rarely the same, as anyone who has studied the recent history of educational reforms will testify (Shilling 1989). Policy implementation often results in unintended consequences which are often difficult to predict, and which may mitigate the worst excesses of 'third wave' policies (Whitty 1989). Such policies are also likely to meet with considerable resistance from working-class parents and children, who have most to lose from these reforms. Indeed, when the realities of 'parental choice' become clearer, the demand for *real* choices and opportunities for their children is likely to increase (David 1980). With these caveats in mind, I want to tentatively consider two questions; first, why the ideology of parentocracy has come to dominate the educational agenda during the late twentieth century, and secondly, what its implications are for educational selection and legitimation.

To answer the question of why we are abandoning comprehensive education will require a broader framework than that outlined above. In particular there appear to be at least three points which need elaboration. First, the ideology of parentocracy and the introduction of 'third wave' policies have developed against a background of high youth unemployment and economic recession. In this respect the 'third wave' has been a response to traditional concerns about the social consequences of youth unemployment, particularly those who live in urban areas, and the failure of the school to meet the needs of industry (Dale 1985). Such

political concerns are not unique to Britain. The enhanced role of technical and vocational education in secondary education has been almost universal (Lauglo and Lillis 1988). However, the OECD (1985) report, *Education in Modern Society*, was able to conclude that, 'The essentially moral—and certainly ambitious—objective that each child should be educated to the limits of his of her ability appears to have survived the economic thunder' (p. 11). This has not been the case in Britain because the relationship between education and industry, and the social control and containment of youth, has been incorporated into a larger political debate about the relative merits of selective versus comprehensive education, and a State monopoly of education versus a market system of education. Those opposed to post-war reforms in education have not been slow to exploit the disquiet expressed about the products of education, and to support a powerful (and largely successful) lobby which has undermined the ideological foundations of the 'second wave'. A major concern of the Right has been to ensure a much clearer relationship between educational and social hierarchy and authority, which is why it has demanded more selection and greater diversity (*sic*). However, the attempt to reorganise the educational system explicitly on the basis of social ascription is politically unacceptable, which is why they have opted for *social selection by stealth*, through market solutions. Beneath the rhetoric of 'parental choice', 'academic excellence' and 'individual freedom' is the belief that opening up the educational system to the discipline of the market will solve the problem of social authority and hierarchy, that different types of schools would emerge for different types of mind/people. Flew (1987) has candidly admitted that the break-up of the comprehensive system in favour of different types of specialist schools is what 'the radical right in education has been begging for years, and which would very soon emerge if once the existing individual state schools had to compete for custom' (p. 22). Yet to seek to explain the 'third wave' in terms of political ideology is inadequate. My second point is that although it is difficult to refute the ideological foundations of the educational parentocracy, its development has been inextricably connected to the question of 'statecraft' which Bulpitt has defined as 'the art of winning elections and, above all, achieving a necessary degree of governing competence in office' (1986: 19; see also Harris 1989).

There is little doubt that in the context of rising unemployment, economic decline and the escalation in educational expenditure, a commitment to extending 'equality of educational opportunities' was difficult to maintain. Comprehensive education had become a political liability to Callaghan's Labour government, especially because, unlike the situation in a number of other countries such as Sweden (Ball and Larsson 1989), the principle of comprehensive education had never gained unquestioning political or public support. The working classes did not embrace the comprehensive school as the road to their liberation, and the Left held out little hope that the educational system would or could significantly improve the life chances of working-class people (Bowles and Gintis 1976; Bourdieu and Passeron 1977).

By the time Mrs Thatcher became Prime Minister in 1979, there was little political mileage to be gained by the attempt to bolster the post-war educational consensus, especially as the Labour Party under James Callaghan had already brought into question the performance of comprehensive schooling. Leaving aside ideological preference, the Thatcher government has been fully aware of the problems associated with implementing equal opportunities in education, and because education had become a scapegoat for Britain's social and economic problems, it was an area of social policy about which something had to be done. Therefore, purely in terms of Conservative statecraft, a governing competence over education was facilitated by identifying post-war liberal-democratic reforms as the cause of our current troubles, which provided the government with an argument for radical educational change.

My third point is based on a more general observation of the relationship between education, certification and social change. The relationship between social class and educational performance has long been a 'central life interest' of the educational sociologist. This interest has overwhelmingly been directed at working-class responses to school and the question of how educational inequalities are legitimated to those the system rejects and ejects as failures. Sociologists have recently noted the problems of legitimating school

practices when there are few occupational opportunities available, and have conducted a number of studies of the 'new vocationalism'. Although this research is important I want to argue that the more significant challenge to the comprehensive school has come from the middle classes.

The 'third wave' is in part a manifestation of a power struggle for educational certification which is undermining the principles of 'equality of educational opportunity'. Whereas the social élite have continued to enjoy the benefits of private education throughout the twentieth century, the demand to equip their incumbents with academic credentials has increased (Walford 1986). The changing demand for academic credentials among the middle-class as a whole has been noted by Bourdieu and Boltanski (1978: 198), who argue that the increasing demand for education is closely linked to broader changes in social structure:

the combined transformation of the system of the means of reproduction (and in particular of the system of inheritance) and of the method of appropriation of economic profit is the source of the intensified use made of the education system by those sections of the ruling and middle classes who previously assured the perpetuation of their position by the direct transmission of economic capital. Consequently it is also the origin of the steady inflation of academic qualifications, a process triggered off and continually maintained by their correlative devaluation. This is such as to impose on all classes and class fractions, beginning with the greatest users of the school, a continued intensification of their use of the school.

Here Bourdieu and Boltanski are talking about the bureaucratisation and rationalisation of the recruitment practices used by large corporations and professional organisations. This has resulted in the growing demand for certification among the middle classes in order to reproduce their social advantage. This shift towards the 'credential society' (Collins 1979; but see also Murphy 1984) has further intensified in the 1980s and is likely to continue, despite the decline in youth unemployment. The increasing instrumentalism among middle-class pupils and students has been a response to economic recession and high rates of youth unemployment. In some parts of the country the consequences of educational failure was not a question of trading down into a less desirable job but more one of getting a job or being unemployed. The acquisition of educational credentials has become an even more important insurance policy, minimising the likelihood of unemployment. Worries about downward social mobility were also fuelled by the expenditure cuts in higher education, making it that much more competitive to get a place, particularly at university (Burnhill *et al.* 1988).

An equally important change has resulted from the restructuring of occupations and economic life (Sabel 1982; Piore and Sabel 1984; Gallic 1988; Pahl 1988). Those in white collar and managerial jobs are not immune from these changes. The overall impact of these changes remains to be seen and is likely to vary from country to country (Lane 1988). One outcome, however, has been to undermine traditional patterns of career progression within public and private sector organisations. Career advance through internal labour markets has become an increasingly risky strategy, especially in private companies, given the increasing propensity for corporations to be 'taken-over', 'broken-up', or 'rationalised'. The consequences for employees are frequently enforced 'career moves', 'redundancy', or 'early retirement'. The acquisition of externally validated qualifications is being used as a way of insulating managers and company executives against the vagaries of the global market and corporate restructuring. This trend not only helps us to explain the growing demand for business studies at both undergraduate and postgraduate levels (e.g. the massive expansion of MBA programmes in Britain), but also the increasingly instrumental attitudes of middle-class parents concerning the education of their children.

The onslaught against comprehensive education by the popular press, coupled with the teachers' industrial action in the mid-1980s, added to the anxieties of many middle-class parents, which resulted in an increasing propensity to send their children to private (Independent) schools, especially between the ages of 16 and 18. In England almost 20 per cent of pupils between these ages were already in private education in 1986.

In the present political climate, where we are told that there is 'no such thing as society, only families and individuals' (see Harris 1989), those parents who can afford to buy a competitive advantage for their children are increasingly likely to do so, because the Right have claimed a moral legitimacy for a privatised education system under the rhetorical slogans of 'parental choice', 'standards of excellence' and 'economic freedom'. The bare facts however are that a growing section of the 'old' and 'new' middle classes are undermining the principle of 'equality of opportunity', in the sense that educational outcomes should be determined by the abilities and efforts of pupils, not the wealth and preferences of parents. This form of 'social closure' is the outcome of an evaluation by the middle classes that educational success has become too important to be left to the chance outcome of a formally open competition (despite what the research evidence has taught us about social class and patterns of achievement). The fact that potentially more able students who do not have the same financial means will lose out just becomes another hard fact of life, because it is not the responsibility of the State to regulate the competition for education in a fair and equal manner, but to ensure the sovereignty of 'parental choice'. It is this change in the relationship between education and the state which I now want to consider.

Education and the State: Control Without Responsibility

The rise of an educational parentocracy clearly has important implications for the way sociologists have interpreted the role of education in advanced capitalist societies, and more specifically the relationship between education and the State (Dale 1989). Liberal accounts have emphasised the importance of State control of education in order to ensure its organisation on meritocratic principles. This form of State involvement has been taken for granted because it is assumed that if society is to function efficiently it is essential to get the best people in the most demanding jobs irrespective of class, gender or racial attributes. Marxist accounts have alternatively emphasised the role of the State in securing the reproduction of social inequalities by legitimating the predetermined outcomes of educational selection as a fair rather than a fixed contest. It is the implications of the 'third wave' for educational selection and legitimation that I want to consider here.

What underlies the educational parentocracy is a number of ideological supports which assert that the State cannot successfully equalise educational opportunities through its attempts to standardise educational experience, and that the State monopoly of education is an infringement of individual freedom. The view that State intervention in education cannot generate greater equality of opportunity is supported by the assertion that there is a relatively small proportion of pupils who can benefit from an academic education due to differences in innate abilities and deep-seated cultural predisposition which, once formed, are largely impervious to change (Bantock, 1977). Moreover, as noted earlier, it is assumed that recent attempts to impose egalitarian ideals have done so at the expense of standards of educational excellence which are believed to have declined. In Botstein's (1988) analysis of similar educational reforms in the USA, he suggests that a minimalist view of education harbours an implicit 'social Darwinism' with regard to educational ability. He also notes that:

in the view of the Reagan Administration, the universal acceptance of proper standards, in the name of objective merit, must result inevitably in creating a sanctioned but unequal system of educational achievement. In this view, since the crux of equality lies in educational opportunities and not results, and since the school is a limited instrument, the educationally disenfranchised have no one but themselves to blame. This becomes just another hard fact of life . . . More money and programs will not solve the problem. Therefore, the social fact that the poor and the non-white populations do not achieve well enough by measurable standards in sufficient numbers cannot be held against the government. (p. 5)

It is argued that the State's attempt to equalise opportunities not only threatens social and educational standards, but it is also an infringement of individual freedom (Adam Smith Institute 1984). The educational system should therefore be exposed to market forces, which will both allow a greater expression of parental choice, and also ensure that the system will be organised for the benefits of the consumers rather than the providers. Here we find the link between 'standards' and free market solutions. The ideology of parentocracy, therefore, involves a significant change in political objectives, most important of which is the abandonment of educational

policies geared towards generating 'equality of opportunity' (see also Apple 1989). The State has, nevertheless, extended its control over the organisation and content of the educational system but reduced its responsibility for educational selection and outcomes. Selection will be determined by market forces as the State abandons the attempt to monitor the competition for education. Opting for market solutions to the problem of educational selection is consistent with Conservative statecraft, which has decisively moved away from the post-war consensus and has taken some of the key decisions about the distribution of education 'out of politics' (Bulpitt 1986).

An attendant consequence of the shift to market education is a change in the site of educational legitimation. This is of sociological significance because it raises interesting questions about the way in which Marxists have characterised the legitimation functions of the State, and, in particular, the tendency to assume that the ideology of meritocracy has been necessary for the State to legitimate the educational and social inequalities found in advanced capitalist democracies.

The deregulation and privatisation of schools shifts the responsibility for educational outcomes squarely on the shoulders of the schools and parents. If the school did not produce 'the goods' it was a poor school, and another should have been selected (assuming that a better alternative was available). Therefore, if one's child did not perform and achieve to the expected level, then one, as a parent, must look to oneself for the reason. Perhaps it was because one did not give sufficient attention to the 'choice' of school, or perhaps it was because any additional cash one had was spent on a holiday in Spain, rather than invested in education. There is nothing morally wrong with the former course of action, it demonstrates consumer sovereignty, but of course it is no good looking to blame the State for personal decisions: one cannot have freedom without responsibility!

To summarise, it can be seen that the State has extended its control over the organisation and content of schooling in order to ensure that adequate educational standards are met. However, such intervention will stop short of ensuring that educational selection is based on 'equality of opportunity'. This 'selective minimalism' is justified on the grounds that egalitarian principles have already been tried and found wanting. In the educational parentocracy, selection will be determined by the free play of market forces, and because the State is no longer responsible for overseeing selection, inequalities in educational outcome, at least in official accounts, cannot be blamed on the State. Such inequalities (the Right prefer the term 'diversity') will be viewed as the legitimate expression of parental preferences, differences in innate capacities, and a healthy 'diversity' of educational experience.

Conclusion

I have argued that we are now beginning to see, in its nascent form, a 'third wave' in the socio-historical development of British education (other capitalist societies, most notably the USA, Australia and New Zealand, have witnessed similar educational debates and policy initiatives).

Despite the speculative and undeveloped nature of much of this discussion, it does raise sociological issues about the relationship between education and the State, and the way sociologists and educationalists have understood the development of 'State'-sponsored comprehensive education.

We have noted that, early in the twentieth century, Tawney mounted a concerted campaign for an educational system which sought to eliminate social ascription as the determining factor of educational experience. Yet, despite the reforms of the following 50 years, we seem set to end the century as we began, with the 'heredity curse' of its organisation upon lines of social class, and with significant differences in the educational performance of girls and boys, and among pupils from different ethnic backgrounds (Troyna 1987).[11] Recent educational reforms will lead to increasing racial segregation of our schools, and equal opportunities policies aimed at breaking down gender and racial inequalities will suffer, given the lack of time and resources for co-ordinated planning, as schools try to live within their financial budgets.

We can also see the continuity with the past, particularly concerning the question of 'who shall be educated?' (Warner *et al.* 1946). This is not a question to be answered by the free play of market forces, because it is a political question concerning the distribution of knowledge, power and life chances. It is a question which also draws our attention to the role of the State in the production and reproduction of educational and social inequalities. This paper barely touches upon these issues, but it does seek to offer some conceptual apparatus for beginning to think about education in the 'third wave'.

Acknowledgements

I would like to thank Clyde Chitty, Rosemary Crompton, Krishan Kumar, Hugh Lauder, David Marsland, Mollie Roots, and Richard Scase for their comments on an earlier draft of this paper.

Notes

1. The idea of a 'third wave' is, of course, lifted from Toffler's book *The Third Wave*.
2. One of the most cherished sociological assumptions of the twentieth century has been the view that as industrial societies became more complex in their organisation, technology, and division of labour, they inevitably became more meritocratic (Parsons 1961; Kerr 1973). The educational system in an advanced industrial society was therefore perceived in liberal accounts to perform a pivotal role, both in terms of teaching the knowledge and skills which were needed in order to fulfil future adult roles, and because a large proportion of jobs were assumed to be more technically and intellectually demanding. Economic survival was therefore seen to depend upon the educational system selecting the most talented individuals without prejudice to class, gender or racial differences. Although Marxists have strongly criticised this characterisation of capitalist society and the role of the educational system, they have nevertheless recognised a shift in the structure of schooling from one where working-class exclusion was immediate, and based upon ascribed characteristics, to exclusion on the basis of examination performance in an obstensibly 'open' competition. Bourdieu (1974) argued, for example, that the concern about equality of opportunity is *necessary* in order to legitimate inequalities in advanced capitalist societies by mystifying the primary concern of the educational system with social reproduction 'by operating a selection procedure which,

although apparently formally equitable . . . schools help both to perpetuate and legitimate inequalities' (p. 42).

3. An expansion of higher education is already beginning to take place, given the need to take a broader range of students because of the further decline in the number of 16–18-year-olds. This is likely to lead to a larger proportion of middle- and working-class students entering higher education (assuming that the latter are willing and able to pay off substantial financial debts at the end of their studies), but this does not represent an equalisation of opportunities. It simply means that differences between institutions of higher education will increase, rather like those found in the United States. Nevertheless, assuming that there will not be a serious world recession in the near future, the rate of occupational mobility will increase in the 1990s, due partly to changes in the occupational structure and the decline in the numbers of school leavers. A significant proportion of young people will however, get locked into a 'poor school, poor work' continuum (Brown and Scase 1990). The inequalities which underlie 'third wave' policies will become more apparent in the medium rather than the short-term. If academic qualifications are to remain a significant determinant of labour market position, then academic performance will always be *relative*, and it is when supply exceeds the demand for labour that the consequences of social inequalities in educational access, and ultimately performance, become most evident. Moreover, if the educational parentocracy is increasingly important to our understanding of educational selection during the compulsory years at school, it is perhaps going to become even more significant to our understanding of educational selection in further and higher education.

4. Obviously such a broad canvas cannot hope to do justice to the full complexity of the socio-historical development of education in England. It does however, help us to understand the similarities and differences in the historical arguments and sociological accounts of the role and content of State education over the last 150 years.

5. In reality, compulsory elementary education for the masses did not arrive until the 1902 Education Act (Lawson and Silver 1973), although from the 1830s private philanthropy and funds provided by the State supported a considerable number of schools, given a further impetus by Forster's 1870 Education Act.

6. For an extended version of this discussion on New Right educational reforms and the Thatcher government, see Brown 1989.

7. Objective evidence of declining standards is difficult to come by, Wright (1983), for example, has noted that 'in 558 pages of Black Papers so far published, not one piece of sound evidence has been produced to show that standards are declining' (p. 175), and the same can be said of more recent claims about declining educational standards. Recent evidence has also shown that comprehensive education may well be benefiting pupils from a working-class background (McPherson and Willans 1987).

8. Shortage of space makes it impossible to discuss the Education Reform Act in any detail. There are a number of good accounts of the Act, including Simon (1988) and Maclure (1988).

9. There is a complication when talking about educational vouchers because such a system has been advocated by those on the Left as well as the Right. The re-emerging interest in educational vouchers is often associated with Milton Friedman, although the original notion is attributed to Adam Smith in the late eighteenth century. The kind of educational voucher system which is being advocated by the Right is one which approximates that favoured by Friedman—a straightforward system which gives every child the same 'pupil entitlement' (Hillgate Group 1987: 41). Goldberg has described this type of voucher scheme as the 'unregulated market ideal', in which all vouchers are of equal value and schools charge at the market rate (Snook 1987; Le Grand and Robinson 1984). Parents will therefore be left to pay any additional sum beyond the value of the voucher out of their new-found economic freedom provided by tax cuts.

10. The Education Reform Act is estimated to give the Secretary of State for Education over 175 new powers. For a general discussion of the role of the State, see Gamble (1988), Hall (1988), and Dale (1989).

11. In this paper I have deliberately avoided a detailed discussion of the likely consequences of the 'third wave', and what an alternative politics of education would look like. These tasks have been attempted, in an albeit undeveloped way, elsewhere (Brown 1988; 1989). A more developed discussion of these ideas will be presented in Brown and Lauder (1992).

References

Acker, S. (1981), 'No-Woman's-Land: British Sociology of Education 1960–1979', *Sociological Review*, 29: 77–104.

Adam Smith Institute (1984), *The Omega File: Education* (London: Adam Smith Institute).

Apple, M. W. (1989), 'How Equality has been Redefined in the Conservative Restoration', in W. G. Secada (ed.), *Equality in Education* (Lewes: Falmer Press).

Arnot, M. (1987), Political Lip-Service or Radical Reform? Central Government Responses to Sex Equality as a Policy Issue', in: Arnot, M., and Weiner, G. (eds.), *Gender and the Politics of Schooling* (London: Hutchinson).

—— and Weiner, G. (eds.) (1987), *Gender and the Politics of Schooling* (London: Hutchinson).

Ashton, D. N. (1988), 'Educational Institutions, Youth and the Labour Market', in Gallie, D. (ed.), *Employment in Britain* (Oxford: Blackwell).

Ball, S. J. (1987), *The Micro-Politics of the School* (London: Methuen).

—— and Larsson, S. (eds.) (1989), *The Struggle for Democratic Education: Equality and Participation in Sweden* (Lewes: Falmer Press).

Bantock, G. H. (1977), An Alternative Curriculum', in Cox, C. B., and Boyson, R. (eds.), *Black Paper 1977* (London: Temple Smith).

Beechey, V., and Whitelegg, E. (eds.) (1986), *Women in Britain Today* (Milton Keynes: Open Univ. Press).

Belsey, A. (1986), 'The New Right, Social Order and Civil Liberties', in Levitas, R. (ed.), *The Ideology of the New Right* (Cambridge: Polity Press).

Bendix, R. (1956), *Work and Authority in Industry* (New York: Wiley).

Bernbaum, G. (1977), *Knowledge and Ideology in the Sociology of Education* (London: Macmillan).

Botstein, L. (1988), 'Education Reform in the Reagan Era: False Paths, Broken Promises', *Social Policy*, 18: 3–11.

Bourdieu, P. (1974), 'The School as a Conservative Force: Scholastic and Cultural Inequalities', in Eggleston, J. (ed.), *Contemporary Research in the Sociology of Education* (London: Macmillan).

—— and Passeron, J. C. (1977), *Reproduction: In Education, Society and Culture* (London: Sage).

—— and Boltanski, L. (1978), 'Changes in Social Structure and Changes in the Demand for Education', in Giner, S., and Archer, M. (eds.), *Contemporary Europe: Social Structure and Cultural Change* (London: Routledge and Kegan Paul).

Bowles, S., and Gintis, H. (1976), *Schooling in Capitalist America* (London: Routledge and Kegan Paul).

Brown, P. (1987), *Schooling Ordinary Kids* (London: Routledge and Kegan Paul).

—— (1988), 'Education and the Working-Class: A Cause for Concern', in Lauder, H., and Brown, P. (eds.), *Education: In Search of a Future* (Lewes: Falmer Press).

—— (1989), 'Education', in Brown, P., and Sparks, R. (eds.), *Beyond Thatcherism* (Milton Keynes: Open Univ. Press).

—— and Lauder, H. (eds.) (1992), *Education for Economic Survival* (London: Routledge and Kegan Paul).

—— and Scase, R. (eds.) (1990), *Poor Work* (Milton Keynes, Open Univ. Press).

Bulpitt, J. (1986), 'The Discipline of the New Democracy: Mrs Thatcher's Domestic Statecraft', *Political Studies*, 34: 19–39.

Burchell, H., and Millman, V. (eds.) (1989), *Changing Perspectives on Gender* (Milton Keynes: Open Univ. Press).

Burnhill, P., Garner, C., and McPherson, A. (1988), 'Social Change, School Attainment and Entry to Higher Education 1976–1986', in Raffe, D. (ed.), *Education and the Youth Labour Market* (Lewes: Falmer Press).

Central Statistical Office (1989), *Social Trends* (London: HMSO).

Collins, R. (1979), *The Credential Society: An Historical Sociology of Education and Stratification* (New York: Academic Press).

Crosland, A. (1956), *The Future of Socialism* (London: Jonathan Cape).

Cox, C. B., and Boyson, R. (eds.) (1977), *Black Paper 1977* (London: Temple Smith).

——, and Dyson, A. E. (eds.) (1968), *Fight for Education* (London: Critical Quarterly).

Dale, R. (ed.) (1985), *Education, Training and Employment* (Oxford: Pergamon).

—— (1989), *The State and Education Policy* (Milton Keynes: Open Univ. Press).

David, M. (1980), *The State, the Family and Education* (London: Routledge and Kegan Paul).

Davis, K., and Moore, W. E. (1967), 'Some Principles of Stratification', in Bendix, R., and Lipset, S. (eds.), *Class, Status and Power* (London: Routledge and Kegan Paul).

Deem, R. (1978), *Women and Schooling* (London: Routledge and Kegan Paul).

—— (1980), *Schooling for Women's Work* (London: Routledge and Kegan Paul).

Demaine, J. (1988), 'Teachers' Work, Curriculum and the New Right', *British Journal of Sociology of Education*, 9: 247–64.

Dewey, J. (1916), *Democracy and Education* (New York: Macmillan).

Donald, J. (1981), 'Green Paper: Noise of Crisis', in Dale, R., Esland, G., Ferguson, R., and MacDonald, M. (eds.), *Schooling and the National Interest* (Lewes: Falmer Press).

Durkheim, E. (1938), *L'Evolution Pedagogique en France*, transl. (1977) as *The Evolution of Educational Thought* (London: Routledge and Kegan Paul).

Finn, D. (1987), *Training without Jobs* (London: Macmillan).

Flew, A. (1987), *Power to the Parents* (London: The Sherwood Press).

Floud, J., and Halsey, A. H. (1958), 'The Sociology

of Education: A Trend Report and Bibliography', *Current Sociology*, 3: 165–93.
—— (1961), 'Introduction', in Halsey, A. H. *et al.* (eds.), *Education, Economy and Society* (Glencoe: Free Press).
Gallie, D. (ed.) (1988), *Employment in Britain* (Oxford: Blackwell).
Gamble, A. (1988), *The Free Market and the Strong State* (London: Macmillan).
Glass, D. V. (1961), 'Education and Social Change in Modern England', in Halsey, A. H. *et al.* (eds.), *Education, Economy and Society* (Glencoe: Free Press).
Green, D. G. (1987), *The New Right: The Counter-Revolution in Political, Economic and Social Thought* (Brighton: Wheatsheaf).
Hall, S. (1988), *The Hard Road to Renewal* (London: Verso).
Halsey, A. H., Floud, J., and Anderson, C. A. (eds.) (1961), *Education, Economy and Society* (Glencoe: Free Press).
——, Heath, A. F., and Ridge, J. M. (1980), *Origins and Destinations* (Oxford: Clarendon Press).
Harris, C. C. (1989), 'The State and the Market', in P. Brown and R. Sparks (eds.), *Beyond Thatcherism* (Milton Keynes: Open Univ. Press).
Hillgate Group (1986), *Whose Schools? A Radical Manifesto* (London: Claridge Press).
—— (1987), *The Reform of British Education* (London: Claridge Press).
HMSO (1987), *Education Reform Bill* (London: HMSO).
Hopkins, A. (1978), *The School Debate* (Harmondsworth: Penguin).
Hurt, J. (ed.) (1981), *Childhood, Youth and Education in the late Nineteenth Century* (Leicester: History of Education Society).
Johnson, R. (1976), 'Notes on the Schooling of the English Working-Class 1780–1850, in: R. Dale, G. Esland, and M. MacDonald (eds.), *Schooling and Capitalism* (London: Routledge and Kegan Paul).
Jones, K. (1989), *Right Turn: The Conservative Revolution in Education* (London: Hutchinson Radius).
Kerr, C., Dunlop, J., Harbison, F., and Myers, C. (1973), *Industrialism and Industrial Man* (Harmondsworth: Penguin).
Lane, C. (1988), 'Industrial Change in Europe: The Pursuit of Flexible Specialization in Britain and West Germany', *Work, Employment and Society*, 2: 141–68.
Lauder, H. (1987), 'The New Right and Educational Policy in New Zealand', *New Zealand Journal of Educational Studies*, 22: 3–23.
—— and Brown, P. (eds.) (1988), *Education: In Search of a Future* (Lewes: Falmer Press).
——, Middleton, J., Boston, J., and Wylie, C. (1988), 'The Third Wave: A Critique of the New Zealand Treasury's Report on Education',

New Zealand Journal of Education Studies, 23: 15–33.
Lauglo, J., and Lillis, K. (eds.) (1988), *Vocationalizing Education: An International Perspective* (Oxford: Pergamon).
Lawson, J., and Silver, H. (1973), *A Social History of Education in England* (London: Methuen).
Le Grand, J., and Robinson, R. (eds.) (1984), *Privatisation and the Welfare State* (London: Allen and Unwin).
Lowe, R. (1988), *Education in the Post-War Years: A Social History* (London: Routledge and Kegan Paul).
Maclure, S. (1988), *Education Reformed* (London: Hodder and Stoughton).
McPherson, A., and Willams, J. D. (1987), Equalisation and Improvement: Some Effects of Comprehensive Reorganisation in Scotland, *Sociology*, 21: 509–40.
Moore, R. (1988), 'Education, Production and Reform', in Lauder, H., and Brown, P. (eds.), *Education: In Search of a Future* (Lewes: Falmer Press).
Murphy, R. (1984), 'The Structure of Closure: A Critique and Development of the Theories of Weber, Collins and Parkin', *British Journal of Sociology*, 35: 547–67.
OECD (1985), *Education in Modern Society* (Paris: OECD).
Pahl, R. (ed.) (1988), *On Work* (Oxford: Blackwell).
Parsons, T. (1961), 'The School Class as a Social System: Some of its Functions in American Society', in Halsey, A. H. *et al.* (eds.), *Education, Economy and Society* (Glencoe: Free Press).
Phillips, N. R. (1978), *The Quest for Excellence* (New York: Philosophical Library).
Piore, M. J., and Sabel, C. F. (1984), *The Second Industrial Divide* (New York: Basic Books).
Pring, R. (1987), 'Privatization in Education', *Journal of Educational Policy*, 2: 289–99.
Purvis, J., (1983), 'Towards a History of Women's Education in Nineteenth-Century Britain: A Sociological Analysis', in Purvis, J., and Hales, M. (eds.), *Achievement and Inequality in Education* (Milton Keynes: Open Univ. Press).
Sabel, C. F. (1982), *Work and Politics* (Cambridge: Cambridge Univ. Press).
Sanderson, M. (1987), *Equal Opportunity and Social Change in England* (London: Faber and Faber).
Scruton, R. (1984), *The Meaning of Conservatism* (London: Macmillan).
Shilling, C. (1989), *Schooling for Work in Capitalist Britain* (Lewes: Falmer Press).
Shor, I. (1986), *Culture Wars* (London: Routledge and Kegan Paul).
Simon, B. (1966), *Studies in the History of Education 1780–1870* (London: Lawrence and Wishart).
—— (1985), *Does Education Matter?* (London: Lawrence and Wishart).

Simon, B. (1988), *Bending the Rules: The Baker 'Reform' of Education* (London: Lawrence and Wishart).

Snook, I. (1987), 'The Voucher System: An Alternative Method of Financing Education', *New Zealand Journal of Educational Studies*, 22: 25–34.

Swann, Lord (1985), *Education for All: A Brief Guide* (London: HMSO).

Tawney, R. H. (1931), *Equality* (repr. 1983) (London: Allen and Unwin).

Toffler, A. (1981), *The Third Wave* (London: Pan Books).

Troyna, B. (ed.) (1987), *Racial Inequality in Education* (London: Routledge and Kegan Paul).

Turner, R. H. (1961), 'Modes of Social Ascent Through Education: Sponsored and Contest Mobility', in A. H. Halsey *et al.* (eds.), *Education, Economy and Society* (Glencoe: Free Press).

Walford, G. (1986), *Life in Public Schools* (London: Methuen).

Warner, W. L., Havighurst, R. J., and Loeb, M. B. (1946), *Who Shall be Educated?* (London: Kegan Paul).

Whitty, G. (1989), 'The New Right and the National Curriculum: State Control or Market Forces', *Journal of Education Policy*, 4: 329–41.

Whyte, J., *et al.* (eds.) (1985), *Girl-Friendly Schooling* (London: Methuen).

Wilby, P., and Midgley, S. (1987), 'The Future of Schooling Lies with the Tory Radicals', *Guardian*, 23 July.

Wright, N. (1983), 'Standards and the Black Papers', in Cosin, B., and Hales, M. (eds.), *Education, Policy and Society* (London: Open Univ. Press).

Young, M. (1961), *The Rise of the Meritocracy* (Harmondsworth: Penguin).

27

Circuits of Schooling: A Sociological Exploration of Parental Choice of School in Social-Class Contexts[1]

Stephen J. Ball, Richard Bowe, and Sharon Gewirtz

Introduction

This paper has two purposes. One is substantive; to present an account of class related patterns of schooling in the context of the new 'market' in education. The other is theoretical; to move beyond the simple empiricism of much parental choice research and begin to develop a conceptual system within which parental choice can be analysed sociologically. Thus the paper is an attempt to break from the abstract and de-contextualised forms of analysis which currently predominate in research on parental choice of school.

The paper draws upon a set of 70 in-depth, loosely-structured interviews with parents of year 6 children in the throes of choosing a secondary school. The interviews were conducted in late 1991 and early 1992. A sub-set of those interviews (16) are quoted from below. The data relate primarily to three adjacent LEAS—Riverway, Westway and Northwark.[2] The social class categorisation employed (working-class and middle-class) is derived from a composite of parents' occupations and education and housing—equivocal cases have been excluded from the class related generalisations and tendencies.[3] This is a first analytical foray into our parental data.

The extracts from interviews quoted below are more than usually inadequate in what they can convey, they are very much ripped out of context and lose impact and effect as a result. Choice making is typically accounted for by parents in terms of long narratives or a complex social calculus of compromises and constraints. The quotations are representative examples only—to provide a sense of things (see Gewirtz, Ball and Bowe 1992). Both presences and absences in the data are important to our argument, what is said and what is not said by families in different class groups. And it is important to stress that we are trying to convey a sense of the dynamic between wants and constraints, values and deprivations—this is not intended to be either a one sided social pathology or a one sided structural deprivation argument.

The Circuits

Research on parental choice in the Greater London area provides the opportunity to examine the workings of a complex school market system. This is a system which in many respects pre-dates the 1988 Education Act. Competition between schools here is not new and neither is the willingness of some parents to explore to the full the possibilities of choice available to them. But these processes have been given a decisive new edge and greater impetus by the provisions of the 1988 Act. In particular our data point up the interplay between social class, cultural capital and choice within the differentiated circuits of schooling in this market system. This analysis is related to our general argument that while there maybe certain general principles of

From *The Sociological Review*, 43 (1995), 52–78. Reprinted with permission.

choice and market relations, the dynamics of choice and market relations are local and specific. The principles have to be related to local conditions, possibilities and histories.

Across the three Local Education Authorities (LEAs) and adjacent areas in which this research is situated there are three clear circuits of schooling which relate differently to choice, class and space. (Different groups of parents 'plug into' each of the circuits and each circuit empowers its students differently in terms of life chances). First, there is a circuit of local, community, comprehensive schools (A) which recruit the majority of their students from their immediate locality, have highly localised reputations and which have policies and structures which relate to a comprehensive school identity. They are oriented to fairly definite locales, which is in Giddens' terms a 'physical region involved as the setting of interaction, having definite boundaries which help to concentrate interaction in one way or another' (1984: 375). Some newly 'opted-out', Grant Maintained (GMS) schools, at present part of this circuit, may be beginning to move between this and the next category. Second, there are cosmopolitan, high-profile, élite, maintained schools (B) which recruit some or often many of their students from outside their immediate locale, which have reputations which extend well beyond their home LEAs, some of which are (overtly) selective, i.e. grammar schools, others of which have 'pseudo-selective' or limited catchment criteria. These schools are usually considerably oversubscribed.

Third, there is the 'local' system of day, independent schools (C). These are schools which in effect compete with the maintained sector and which provide alternatives or possibilities for parents who also make a choice to maintained schools; although of course they also attract parents who are interested exclusively in the private sector. There is also a fourth parallel but separate circuit of Catholic schools (D), which has its own hierarchy, pattern of competition and spatial structure. We have little to say about the fourth circuit here.

The schools in each of these categories which fall into the remit of our study and which are regularly mentioned by parents in interview are listed below. Most of these schools are referred to in the extracts from data quoted later.

(A) Trumpton, Milton, St Ignatius (D), Oak Glade, Martineau, Ramsay Macdonald, Corpus Christi, Parsons, Overbury, Flightpath, Parkside, Gorse, Blenheim, Lymethorpe and Goddard.

(B) Suchard Grammar, Princess Elizabeth, Arthur Lucas, Fletcher, Hutton, Pankhurst, the CTC, Nancy Astor Girls, Florence Nightingale, Cardinal Heenan (D).

(C) Trinity, Camberwick High, Madeley High, Harrod.

Several of the schools in the B circuit are typically considered together by middle class parents when it comes to choosing a secondary school. They are perceived as being schools 'of a kind', although their differences are also understood. They are often considered alongside the C circuit. The A circuit schools are less often considered by the middle class parents we interviewed and then usually only for reasons of propinquity or special interest (e.g. single sex schooling) or as fallbacks in case other choices are unsuccessful.

We went to Martineau (single sex girls), Pendry, Camberwick High and Madeley High and Princess Elizabeth. We went to the CTC (City Technical College), but it wasn't quite . . . it's actually having an open day next week. Trumpton I didn't go to though. I had been going to because I felt I ought to being as it was on the doorstep . . . I wasn't really interested and at the same time felt I ought to go, but it didn't work out. (Mrs K)

She's down for Pendry but we'd actually prefer her to go to Princess Elizabeth. Lisa is more academic than Robert, although she is also quite artistic, she is an all rounder, she loves the sciences, she's good at maths, though she's not keen on it. (Mrs Q)

We applied to two independents, Camberwick High and Madeley High, and to the CTC college and to Princess Elizabeth. I really wanted her to go to one of the independents, you know, the results were that much better . . . and then Princess Elizabeth . . . she didn't get in there . . . and then CTC and Northwark schools were bottom of the list. (Mrs D)

However, the boundary between A and B is not absolute and fixed and there are borderline schools. And the arrival of the CTC, which 'opened for business' in September 1991, has 'disturbed' local system, as it is intended to do. Similarly some families in a sense also hover on the borderline or move between circuits, particularly between B and C, the cosmopolitan state and private schools.

We're going to have a look at the CTC college . . . but that worries me because I feel that in a way it's like a guinea pig school . . . you don't know how it's going to work out, and I worry about Lisa being one of the first, in case it doesn't work out. But we're going to go and have a look, I'm not shutting my mind to the possibilities of CTC. (Mrs G)

Martineau for a while when they first amalgamated they didn't have a good reputation, and I suppose it was all the . . . a settling down period and all that sort of thing but I've heard some good reports from that recently, and that's an all girls school. And for Sara I do like the idea of all girls . . . a single sex school for girls. (Mrs G)

We had a look at Milton and thought that was probably the best of . . . I mean I didn't go to Trumpton school, but I've been past there at lunchtime and I didn't like what I saw, so decided that that definitely wasn't to be looked at. If he had not been successful in choosing the CTC, then we were going to pay for him, because we didn't consider anything else. (Mrs M)

Very much, he came and looked at Pendry and he liked it a lot, and he came and looked at CTC and liked it even better, so the choice came down to Pendry and CTC and we were rather hopeful that CTC would come up trumps, which it did. (Mrs M)

We've come from a family where the tradition has been for the boys to go to the local grammar school, which is now an independent school. So brothers, uncles, cousins are all there and have been there. So there was a very strong inclination for the first son to go to the independent school, Harrod, do you know it . . . and if he failed that, my only other, or our only other consideration was a local church school . . . out of the LEA, because I wouldn't consider Parsons. It had a very bad reputation and had had for many years and . . . it would not have been my choice. (Mrs R)

Despite the element of tautology we refer to those families who engage with the education market in this strategic fashion as 'cosmopolitans' and those who make a deliberate choice for their neighbourhood school as 'locals'. Empirically the former are likely to be middle class, but not all middle class families are market strategists and some working-class families are. Equally, the 'locals' are typically working-class, although there are one or two middle-class examples. Nonetheless exceptions are exceptions; the pattern of class-related orientations to choice in the whole data set is strong. Altogether middle-class 'choosers' are much more active in the education marketplace (see also Echols, McPherson and Williams 1990; Moore 1990; and Blank 1990 for similar findings).

Historical reputations have a key role in

sustaining the circuits outlined above, at least for 'cosmopolitan' parents. *The point is that these reputations (or the existence of this circuit of schools) are not even apparent to other 'local choosers'.* This knowledge of the system is part of the cultural capital that immediately separates out many middle-class parents (see Gewirtz *et al.* 1992) and orients them differently to school choice. But also many working class parents want and value different things from their schools, localness is often a value in its own right. The priorities and possibilities of choice are significantly different for middle class and working class choosers. Choice fits into their lives and life-plans in very different ways. Different class strategies of reproduction are involved, as we shall see.

Working Class 'Locals'

In the case of the working class respondents choice of secondary school was a contingent decision rather than an open one. Ideas about school were often subordinated to consideration of the constraints of family and locality; 'we find individual consciousness, language and social identity interacting in a dialectical fashion with the immediate social context of people's lives' (Dickens 1990: 11). As Dickens also notes: 'According to Bourdieu, working class ways of life remain largely organised around the "practical order" of simply getting by' (p. 17). Thus, 'choice' of school fits into the practicalities of 'getting by' rather than into some grander social agenda of 'new, rarer and more distinct goods' (Bourdieu 1984: 247). School has to be 'fitted' into a set of constraints and expectations related to work roles, family roles, the sexual division of labour and the demands of household organisation. And the material and cultural aspects of this are difficult to separate. For our middle-class respondents it was much more common to find family roles and household organisation being accommodated to school. But it is not simply a matter of education being of less importance for working class families, our interviewees were very concerned that their children get a good education. Rather the competing pressures of work and family life made certain possibilities difficult or impossible to contemplate and others seem obvious and appropriate. Choice of school as 'embedded' in a complex pattern of family demands and structural limitations. This is not a matter of cultural deficit but rather pragmatic accommodation.

Among our working-class respondents social reproduction takes on a more immediate quality, it is more closely tied to a sense of locale and community, of which the family is a co-extensive part. The local school is in Cremin's (1976) terms part of a 'functional community', it is chosen positively for this reason. That is to say, reproduction is defined and constrained and achieved within a spatial framework. Family life, and things such as school choice, are played out within, and over and against, a space and time budget. As Harvey (1989) suggests spatial practices 'take on their meanings under specific social relations of class, gender, community, ethnicity, or race and get "used up" or "worked over" in the course of social action' (223). For the working-class choosers space and family organisation were very often the key elements in choice-making.

They catch the bus . . . there's a few children that go to the school, they live in the other road . . . in the morning, my parents . . . they take them, because they have to go that way, they go past the school at half past eight, so they take them . . . then they come home on their own or I go and pick them up . . . if I'm picking Ian up, I'll pick them up as well. But I think you have to think of that now . . . where they go. (Mrs E)

Twenty past 3 . . . the other one finishes at half past three . . . so you know what I mean . . . she [Mrs W] has to fetch him first, the other one makes his way home . . . he's a bit sensible . . . and then she has to run down to go and fetch the one at Gorse school, you see . . . by the time . . . the other one has to wait . . . out there till their mum comes back home . . . so . . . makes it very difficult for her. I'll appreciate it if they go to the same school. It's easier for her and for the boys . . . at least . . . because . . . the reason that's true . . . the education that he's doing . . . when the second one will go there . . . Yes, they went to Windsor Primary and then to Parsons, then I bought this house . . . it's about four years now . . . so we decided to move here . . . the nearest school . . . would be handy more for my wife than to run back to. (Mr W)

Too far. I mean . . . it's not . . . I mean, supposing something was to happen, god forbid, that means I would have to go miles to get her, do you know what I mean or . . . get any of the children. I'd rather have a quick way of getting there, you know . . . (Mrs H)

Really only because her brother goes there and its local as well, cos she'll have to pick up her sister as well, so she's got to have something local . . .

Because my husband really wanted him to go to Crawford Park, because he'd come from there, but we thought it was too far for him to go . . . that we wanted something really local and by having Trumpton, like my husband said, they can all go there, because it's a mixed school, which is good. (Mrs N)

Here space, travel and family organisation are tightly tied into the choice of school. In transport studies, activity analysis research, which 'examines inter-dependencies within the household in respect of the scheduling and time-space constraints placed upon individual household members' (Grieco, Jones and Polak 1991: 1), suggests that 'household organisation lies at the heart of the understanding of travel behaviour' (p. 4). Among low-income households on time-constrained budgets, the limitations of private and public transport play a key role in a whole range of decision-making. And, as above, these constraints and the forms of household organisation which develop as a result are particular associated 'with the gender roles of women' (Grieco 1991: 4). 'Women in many such households are able to meet their daily domestic responsibilities and to respond to crises only by "borrowing" time and other resources from other houses (principally kin) in their social network' (Grieco and Pearson 1991: 4). Where transport deprivation leads to the social isolation and segregation of particular social groups in particular localities social enclaves are created. The existence of such enclaves reinforces the importance of *the local* and the need for complex intra and inter-household dependencies. Research has also related the existence of enclaves to informational dynamics and local information structures (Weimann 1982). Our work on parents' knowledge about schools underlines this. These patterns and processes of time and space management and the existence of social enclaves and social networks are of prime importance in understanding school choice making for certain class groups. And such an analysis begins to point up the important interrelationships between market schooling and the other deregulation policies of the current UK government; like transport, housing, health, social welfare and employment training (Carlen, Gleeson, and Wardhaugh 1992).

The information networks of local choosers are limited in scope but nonetheless rich and useful. These networks themselves are indicative of the relationship between local schools, families and community.

Well Parsons . . . my sister-in-law's children go to Flightpath and each one has done very very well. I've known children to go to Parsons and they haven't done well. (Mrs H)

Time and space are important in the analysis of choice in another, related, sense. The schooling of children of these working class families is not normally related to long range planning, it is not about other places and other times but very much about the here and now. Parental aspirations are often vague and typically limited by the wants and needs of the children themselves. (We return to this below). Thomas and Dennison (1991) in a questionnaire study of inner-city students found 60 per cent reporting that *they* had made the decision about secondary school choice and both Thomas and Dennison and Coldron and Boulton (1991) found the 'happiness' of their children to be a major organising principle in parents' approach to choice of school. It is not about who they might become but who they are. Now in traditional terms this might be interpreted as working class short-termism, as against the deferred gratification of the middle-classes, but alternatively we might see these differences in relation to conceptions of or use of space (and place) and time, that is as the relationship between locality and moral careers (Dickens 1990).

but we always said that they could choose the school they wanted to go to . . . so . . . she was quite adamant that she was going to Flightpath, she wanted to go there . . . we went to the open evening . . . and that's where she wanted to go and so we left it, I mean we just let them choose, even though it's probably not our choice, but it's not us that's got to go. (Mrs E)

Yes, yes. I hadn't forced her. I'd never force a child into going somewhere where they didn't want to go, you know. (Mrs H)

Again we might see this in relation to horizons; time horizons and the imagination of time. The middle-class 'cosmopolitan' families are more likely to 'imagine' their children as dentists or accountants or artists, at university, in the sixth form; whereas the working-class, 'locals' will 'wait and see' they are less likely to speculate about the future of their offspring.

I'm not educated and I'd really like them to be a bit more than me. I don't expect them to be miracle workers but I expect them to have a decent educa-

tion . . . just pass their exams really, I mean I wouldn't be disappointed if they didn't, but I don't tell them that . . . I wouldn't force them to go on sixth form, but I mean my son at the moment is talking about staying on to the sixth form, but you don't know until it comes to it really. (Mrs N)

Again though these limited horizons may be in good part a matter of confidence and knowledge. By virtue of their own experiences cosmopolitan parents are more likely to be able to envisage their child in yet to be realised contexts. Again this may be a question of imagination (see below). Thus, in terms of 'getting by', the working-class parents were more likely to start with priorities related to family (or the child's preferences) or propinquity whereas middle-class parents typically started with finding the right school as their priority. But these perceptual differences are related to differences in 'Finite time resources and the "friction of distance" (measured in time or cost taken to overcome it) (which) constrain daily movement' (Harvey 1989: 211). The distribution of 'time-space biographies' is class related—and in this way 'the organisation of space can indeed define relationships between people, activities, things, and concepts' (Harvey: 216). Access to a car, the pattern of bus, tube and train routes, the local transport timetables, the pattern of busy roads and open spaces and the physical location of schools all affect the possibility and the perception of choice. To reiterate, what the interviews reveal are differences both in the ability (or willingness) to overcome 'the friction of distance' and perceptual differences in spatial horizons. These differences have specific implications for the construction of futures for children. 'Spatial and temporal practices, in any society, abound in subtleties and complexities. Since they are so closely implicated in processes of reproduction and transformation of social relations' (Harvey: 218). In part these horizons (and the complex relationship of space to distance) relate what Harvey calls the 'representations of space' to 'spaces of representation' or imagination; particularly in the latter 'unfamiliarity' and 'spaces of fear' are important.

Mrs H: She'd go . . . across the crossing . . .
RB: Through the Park?
Mrs H: Oh no, she won't go through the park, definitely not . . . there's a pathway . . . it goes all the way round, past the library . . . and then under that footway bridge . . . then round the corner. She's

been taught . . . she don't go in parks . . . no way.

The closeness of a school is an important value (as well as practicality) for many parents and will be a major priority or limitation in the making of choices. Most working class respondents were clearly reticent about choosing schools for their children that would involve them in lengthy travel and expose them to the 'unfamiliar'. But clearly, again, this reticence is not unrelated to the availability of public transport; although in a number of cases 'closeness' meant within walking distance.

I think Parsons school is too far away. I mean I know you can get the bus, but . . . I mean there's a zebra crossing across the road, which you can cross and it's just about 15 minutes, 20 minutes walk . . . (Mrs H)

Mainly because it's one of the easiest to get to for him, by bus . . . and it's just one bus . . . and it is the easiest one to get to. (Mrs G)

But while for some working class families distance and locality is almost the only significant factor in choice for others space is interwoven with other factors. There is a trade-off between this and other concerns.

I considered Pankhurst girls' school, that's only across the road . . . but I went to an all girls school, and I think it's a good idea for them to mix, and as her brother goes to Overbury we just straight away said Overbury. (Mrs J)

Yes, I did see the exam results and my sister . . . she lives in . . . and her daughter and son have been in that school . . . and secondly . . . the education of that school and the principal . . . it's very strict, you know . . . like the kids, if they're not in uniform or they haven't done their homework, things like that, if they muck about . . . they'll be told off and at the end of the day they're not so . . . know all the time misbehaving in the school, things like that. (Mr W)

And while middle-class choosers appeared more confident about their use of space and their children's ability to manage travel and less constrained by unfamiliarity they were still often concerned about distance:

We did think a little bit, not for very long, about Lockmere, mainly because a colleague at my school, her husband was the deputy head, and she always considered that it was sort of 100 per cent better than our school, but again . . . I'm not sure that I really wanted them to travel sort of an hour or so a day . . . morning and night . . . not with home-work and dark evenings so really it entered our head

but then quickly went out again. (Mr P)

Actually Princess Elizabeth is not really that far away. I didn't feel it was . . . well it is a bit of a distance, it's a tube journey, but it's only three stops on the tube, and for one reason or another, it has quite a good reputation. Though I don't like to take too much notice of reputations, but . . . she liked the idea of it. (Mrs K)

I couldn't put a figure on my radius because it was fairly flexible, because it wasn't just a circle . . . we also took into account the ease of transport . . . so perhaps . . . a school over in Westing wouldn't be possible because the transport would be difficult . . . but Pendry wouldn't be too bad because it's one bus . . . it's a long walk but then it's one bus ride to Pendry . . . so the radius changed depending on the transport arrangements. (Mrs D)

Some middle-class parents went to considerable lengths to make distance possible and safe for their children. But the point is that for many middle-class parents travel and distance emerge as contingent factors, not priority or determinate ones.

When Robert came home from Fletcher on the first day, what I did was . . . I didn't actually stand at the bus stop with him, cos he would have felt a bit silly, but I followed the bus on my bicycle behind and checked everything was okay, and watched him get off the bus, and met him at home. So summing up it's not a major consideration but obviously you have to take it into account. (Mr Q)

We'd have to for the first couple of years be fetching her and taking her, then obviously with both of us working, we'd have to reconsider it. But it's an easy enough journey, which was something I looked at, it's not just the distance, but do they travel in unlit parks or have to go under bridges or alleyways . . . its something I take into consideration. (Mrs Q)

The complexities of 'choice', and the term must be used with care, for the working-class parents reported here are created by the intersection of the values and constraints of locality. There are vestiges apparent here of the 'localism' which Clarke (1979: 240) refers to as 'a pervasive mode of working class culture'. But there are also a set of frictions and limitations and fears and concerns which tie working class students to their local schools.

Middle-Class 'Cosmopolitans'

The cosmopolitans sometimes 'touch base' with the local system (A) but often express doubts (or different ambivalences) about these schools:

Yes, I don't know whether it was just the impression, but it seemed there were more boys there than girls, I don't know what the split is. But . . . it appeared quite a liberal sort of school . . . but a parent last year spoke to me, whose sons went there and she was full of praise of Milton. (Mrs K)

The use of the term liberal is significant here (see below).

Obviously the nearest is Trumpton school. I suppose living very near to the school it's quite off putting, I didn't look at the school . . . when my daughter was changing. In fact she had just come out of hospital and we didn't drag her around so many of the schools, but I did take Alex to see Trumpton and we were very very impressed with the school. I couldn't see him there but I was very impressed with what they had to offer there. (Mrs K)

Through the interviews it is clear that the priorities of the cosmopolitan choosers are both more educationally specific and longer-term than the working-class respondents. None the less, some parents who are primarily oriented to the maintained/élite circuit (B) are willing to consider the local/comprehensives (A), while others are oriented exclusively to the B circuit. Some of the latter are making a deliberate choice out of the local, comprehensive system, particularly in the case of Northwark LEA. This is partly based on an historic antipathy to Northwark (ex-ILEA) schools—an interesting class-related perception that the ILEA was engaged in social engineering not in the interests of aspiring middle-class parents:

We only went to Pendry for Robert . . . yes, that was the only one we went to for Robert, I just refused point blank to consider the schools in Northwark . . . It was very soon after the change as well, and things like that and I thought they wouldn't have had time to settle down anyway. (Mrs Q)

Oh yes, my neighbour across the road has three daughters who've done very well, they're taking A levels at Trumpton school . . . so yes, I mean we did speak to other people locally . . . I was just going to say that a lot of people . . . particularly . . . that I've found parents very locally here, tended to send their children out of LEA anyway, unless they were very very worried about their travelling at eleven. (Mrs B)

The exact opposite seems to be the case in Riverway, the LEA system is well perceived on the whole. For many Riverway parents the

Riverway schools have many of the qualities of those schools sought after by aspiring parents elsewhere. They can be pretty confident about *who their child will go to school with*, and about the long-range outcomes of choice.

I suspect all schools in Riverway are not really that different, and I do not believe they're going to go to one school and get into Oxford and go to another school . . . and get no GCSEs. I really don't believe that round here . . . it's terribly easy to get absolutely bogged down in it all, and I think to some extent I'm falling into that trap at the moment. (Mrs L)

None the less, even in Riverway there are still some 'markers' of comprehensivism—like mixed-ability grouping and teaching schemes like SMILE mathematics—which are regarded with suspicion by middle class parents and there is still a large private sector in Riverway, plenty of parents are not content to choose state schools. (More than 20 per cent of secondary age children in Riverway are in the independent sector).

Overbury we just didn't like that much really. I think I didn't like the way they taught their maths. They all sort of taught out of books. It wasn't set until after two years, they were very late in setting in the subjects. (Mrs L)

Reputation and image are key to understanding the position of the élite schools and for individual parents general reputations are often supported by first-hand reports. The middle-class respondents were likely to refer to multiple sources of information relating to the reputations and practices of the schools they were considering and those they had dismissed.

I like the idea of uniform, and I must admit . . . Pendry in the summer with the girls in their cycling shorts, so long as they're blue . . . I think they could be stricter on the uniform . . . but children are happy there and things like that, whereas at Corpus Christi, one friend of mine had sent three of her children there and her third child she pulled out after two terms, because the bullying was getting so bad, and they haven't got a strict policy on how to deal with it, and yet at Pendry it's something that comes up at least every week in assembly . . . how verbal bullying and physical bullying will not be tolerated . . . it's an infringement of each other's rights and . . . you know, they wouldn't like it done to them and . . . it's something that they act on, they don't just pay lip service to . . . they actually act on it. I mean verbal bullying I think in a way is worse than physical because it's something that's very hard to prove, and very very upsetting for the children. (Mrs Q)

Some classes have 35 . . . I just can't understand how teachers can cope, I find it hard coping with two. And they're mine. I couldn't cope with 35 of someone else's. But also at Princess Elizabeth's they have an HMI report which they photocopied and distributed to the parents, and one of the things that the inspectors found there was the attitude of the staff and the girls towards each other, was very caring and very supportive. (Mrs Q)

It happened over a period of time somehow . . . you sort of hear things from people, but at the same time you want to make up your own mind . . . I knew one family whose daughter's probably in the third year now at Pendry, who had been to Trumpton for a year, but didn't like it at all, and he'd changed her in the second year . . . and I'd also heard from one or two other parents that it had quite a good reputation. We also had an evening session with Mr Allison, the headmaster at St Josephs (primary), he organised a chat . . . going through various local schools . . . here and there giving his opinion but . . . um . . . it's hard to sort of remember everything, it seemed a very busy time. (Mrs K)

Also in some cases the reputation of a school has some specificity, that is they are perceived to have or not to have some particular strength or quality; e.g. cricket at Lucas, art and pastoral care at Pendry, technology at the CTC. Aspects of reputation interact with other choice concerns.

That was one of the bad points really. There is a family who have four daughters and their youngest one is going there this year, Nicki could have travelled with them. But it would have been quite time consuming really, I wasn't very keen. The music didn't seem quite as strong as some of the other schools either. (Mrs K)

These market niches appear to be matters of marginal academic or curricular difference between schools rather than indicators of significantly different kinds of education (except perhaps at the CTC). But they are part of the 'matching' of the specific qualities or needs of children to the specific qualities or programmes of schools. This was of great importance to middle class choosers but rarely mentioned by working class ones. This is part of what Slaughter and Schnieder (1986) call 'holistic' choosing, the parents are concerned with the 'configuration of education' (Cremin, 1976) on offer in any institution. The size of the school can often play an important role here.

I suppose from first looking at the school, they are dressed immaculately, and that's a very important thing as far as we're concerned. The discipline was always very good there, and I feel that they are secure, in a disciplined school. Also at that time I was very much looking for an extension of St Josephs . . . I don't know if it's easy to explain . . . it's . . . trying to find somewhere where she's been happy for the last seven years, that was important to me. Because Florence Nightingale was on a split site . . . again that was important to us, because it made it into a very small girls church school, and that's really what we wanted for her, and she was very happy . . . I mean she was happy there, but she just wasn't able to work, lots of distractions. (Mrs B)

Milton, we went to Milton as well actually, yes . . . We were quite impressed by chatting to some of the teachers, they seemed very dedicated in what they were trying to do, but I felt the size of the school and . . . it seemed a bit daunting . . . (Mrs M)

I don't think she took too much notice of what her friends were doing . . . her best friend isn't going to the same school, and . . . she's happy with Lady Margarets, she liked it, she liked the feeling of the small school . . . I was a bit unsure about the lack of options possibly, that there is in a smaller school, but I feel it suits her better. (Mrs K)

Furthermore, some middle-class parents were aware of established patterns of transfer from certain primaries to particular secondaries, almost a preparatory school system related to the secondary circuits. Thus, for cosmopolitan parents the choice of primary school is often the first of several strategic decisions involved in the careful construction of their child's school career. And the primary Headteacher often plays a key role in influencing or deflecting parental choices and in providing crucial 'access' and application information. For example, knowing which schools only consider 'first choices' is extremely important. Some of the cosmopolitan schools also have difficult or obscure systems of entry, which are 'known' to the cosmopolitan parents. They are also often aware of the problem of over subscription.

We looked at Martineau, in fact because she had just come out of hospital I had missed the open day . . . and . . . they didn't seem very keen to accommodate us at any other time, whereas Nancy Astor Girls welcomed us with open arms, even the second time around. I mean they're always very oversubscribed. It's a very happy school.

Such parents are often able to employ forms of direct contact and negotiation which can be vital in accessing these schools (see Gewirtz *et al.* 1992). This is where cultural capital plays a crucial role, knowing how to approach, present, mount a case, maintain pressure, make an impact, be remembered (Edwards, Fitz, and Whitty 1989: 215 make a similar point).

Well we went to see her because . . . originally we were thinking of Lisa doing the scholarship and we were thinking of getting in a tutor because . . . we realised that you have to approach these tests in a certain way and things like that . . . which ordinary school I don't think prepares you for. And then a friend of mine said to me . . . oh I know someone who is an educational consultant and if you pay . . . if you go to see her, basically she gives you advice on what your child would need tutoring on, if she did, what schools would be suitable, she's independent . . . and so rather than sort of paying out for tutors for across the board education, go and have a look to see what Lisa would actually need if she went for a scholarship. And then when we went she recommended a couple of schools, which she thought would be suitable for Lisa, and which Lisa would probably get into . . . and . . . what was it, it was only maths that she needed help on really . . . (Mrs Q)

I'd like to talk to him . . . (Lisa's primary Head) I'd just like to say to him, Princess Elizabeth want two referees . . . one is fine from the head teacher, but they want another one. All her extra curricular activities are associated with the school, so we can't actually give another one, I'd just like to ring him up and say; 'look, is this a problem with Princess Elizabeth?'; because he obviously knows the head teacher there pretty well (Mr Q)

Both schools were terribly over-subscribed. Florence Nightingale didn't make a big sort of fuss about joining the school, they just said that . . . obviously if you fill the criteria do apply to the school. We were refused entry initially and then about 48 hours after we had a place at the school. (Mrs B)

I got Corine to agree to my phoning up on the Wednesday, to see if she could go and have another look, and any fears that she had had over it, hopefully dispelled, because she'd obviously got something in her mind about it. But they were ever so kind, and we had the admission secretary who showed us round on a personalised tour, the day before we had to accept or reject the offer and she was shown round with a friend of hers who had been at St Josephs and had moved to the Madeley High junior school . . . (Mrs D)

In terms of image, the iconography of the parents own schooling often plays a part in perception and in choice, they want this for their children. The image of a school is also conveyed powerfully through its students. Clearly, as noted already, part of choosing and not choosing is concerned with who your child will go to school with.

He loves his computer and all that kind of thing . . . yes, that was a sort of . . . that was a feature in our choice, but it wasn't the over-riding one. What we were looking for was a good, safe school for him to go to, and we particularly wanted a uniform because I didn't want to get into this . . . £80 pair of trainers thing . . . which I think . . . it's hard not to if you go to a school that doesn't have a uniform. And the thought that there were only going to be 300 children at this new CTC because they've only been open two years, I thought would be wonderful for Simon because he's at a small school now, and he would transfer to a small school and start and build up . . . which . . . he'd get his foot in the door with not so many children then. We thought maybe that would be ideal, touch wood. (Mrs M)

In this respect for those families oriented to particular 'markers' of image the local school can come off badly because they can see too much of it; e.g. the students leaving school.

Well they come out and I mean the uniform thing. They actually look not badly turned out but girls of 13 and 14 were wearing make up to school . . . then their manner was sometimes very aggressive . . . and their language was foul . . . and Princess Elizabeth I've seen girls coming out of there before, and I've always been impressed, and certainly their manner and their attitude on the night of the parents' evening. (Mrs Q)

We had a look at Milton and thought that was probably the best of . . . I mean I didn't go to Trumpton school, but I've been past there at lunchtime and I didn't like what I saw, so decided that that definitely wasn't to be looked at. (Mrs M)

Examination production is a crucial part of the reputation of the élite/maintained schools, but this is not the exclusive or even primary basis for parental choice. There is a package of cultural indicators and class advantage embedded in these schools, including 'feeling of the atmosphere' which is fundamental to choice making. 'I don' really know what it was, it's more a sort of feeling of the atmosphere and . . . what sort of options there are after school, that sort of thing' (Mrs K). The parents are making a choice for the whole package, they do not want an examination factory; although they recognise the relationship between recruitment, atmosphere and performance. Quality and ethos rather than academic variety seem to be the concerns of the strategic choosers (Sosniak and Ethington 1992). They are concerned much more with what Bernstein calls the expressive order of the school, i.e. the complex of behaviour and activities in the school which are to do with conduct, character and manner. This expressive order is the medium for the recontextualisation of the student's out-of-school-life and is often 'a formalization, crystallisation, even idealisation, of an image of conduct, character and manner reflected by some, but not all, groups in the wider society' (Bernstein 1975: 30, 38, and 49). There are relationships here with Maddaus' (1990) and Slaughter and Schnieder's (1986) research in the United States. Both studies found that school ethos and climate were of greater primary importance to parents in their choice of school than were indicators of academic achievement, which were secondary considerations.

I mean somebody said to me, I hated Blenheim, it was just like a grammar school. Well that wouldn't put me off, because it was just like a grammar school necessarily, if I liked the school. (Mrs L)

Thus, the perception and labelling of schools within these different circuits often seems to be directly class/culturally related.

Clifford (Mr Q) went to Northwark boys, and I think that was one of the better schools in the area . . . and then they changed that and they amalgamated with Crawford Park, which one, the distance, two the fact that it's in the middle of an estate is something I'm not overkeen on, I think that school should be in separate environments. (Mrs Q)

We have a school very near here called Trumpton, and the acid test that I use, and it's probably not a very good one, other than their academic records, is to stand outside the school and have a look at the kids coming out and see how they behave and how they dress and that . . . and I did that at a number of schools in the borough and none of them were suitable. It's a sad fact that Pendry, being in a predominantly middle class area, does tend to have a more supportive PTA, the kids are better encouraged at home, it's generally a better school academically than what was on offer round here . . . (Mr Q)

It was the first choice for the Riverway school . . . although Arthur Lucas was the first choice, overall . . . so I think . . . when we actually went to Arthur Lucas . . . because . . . again it's a very small school, and the boys are beautifully dressed, which is unusual to find, and the academic side of things, as well as the musical side of things are very much for us . . . the sports side of things . . . I think they do play cricket, again that was another factor for us, among the other things, but it just sort of pieced the whole jigsaw together. A complete picture. (Mrs B)

Again, the iconography of traditional, selective schooling are valued whereas markers of comprehensivism, like mixed-ability, non-uniform are also reasons for avoidance.

And another thing I was pleased to learn about was that there is still an element of streaming in the school. They don't have mixed ability classes for the main subjects, for the core curriculum. (Mr Q)

I think the other major factor for us was the fact that they do set them at Arthur Lucas, as they do at Coombe, and we haven't found this to be the case with any other school. And they are set within the first two weeks of starting the school. (Mrs B)

Because I don't think mixed ability works when they change school . . . I think that was a great problem at Florence Nightingale. (Mrs B)

We were a little bit disappointed in the sense that . . . I'd been to an old fashioned grammar school, in the sixties, where it was blazers and caps and berets and things like this and very strict discipline and so on, and so did my husband. We were a bit upset when we went to the parents' evening, or the prospective parents' evening, and they said well we are actually phasing blazers out. (Mrs P)

As part of all this the fact that certain schools are more difficult to gain admission to is significant in itself; this serves as some sort of surrogate guarantee of quality. But also, particularly, as a mechanism of social exclusion, selection provides an assurance of continuity and to some extent commonality.

Further, the middle-class cosmopolitan choices are often based, in contrast to the working-class choices on long-range expectations about a child's education and/or career

But I think Lisa is the kind of child as well . . . I think she'd do what she had to do to get by, whereas at Princess Elizabeth they give that extra bit of encouragement and she needs that, and also they can stay on to do A levels there, whereas Robert isn't intending to do A levels, he wants to go on to art college. (Mrs Q)

All through his junior school he's wanted to go on to art college and do something in fashion or design or . . . something in the arts, definitely. I mean when he does change his mind it's . . . he wants to be a screen writer, or wants to be a director, but it's always in the arts. (Mrs Q)

Results are an important part, yes, because without qualifications you don't have much of a chance in . . . and also my daughter is reasonably bright, and I didn't want her secondary school to be wasted. You know, if she's got the ability at eleven, then I don't want it to be killed in secondary school . . . for her not to achieve her potential (Mrs D)

Again here the keynote is complexity. The political simplicities of *The Parents Charter* and the simplicities of some of the existing parental choice research (see Bowe, Gewirtz and Ball, 1994) simply do not capture the messiness, compromise and doubt which infuse the process of choosing a school.

Discussion: Complexities of Choice

The 1988 Act has enhanced competition between schools and between parents and in particular it has raised the stakes for success and failure in the market place (for schools and parents). In all this, we argue, certain sorts of choices and concerns are privileged, in a variety of ways, and certain parents have advantages in and through choice. (But these data also point up the mismatch between crude government notions of choice-making and the complexities of parents' actual choice-making—parents' choice-making is humanistic rather than technological—as noted also by Adler, Petch, and Tweedie 1987: 134.) Parents are oriented culturally and materially differently towards the education market. They expect different things from it. Some see it as a market and others do not.

What we are describing here was an already highly complex and differentiated system of schools—with hierarchy, specialisms, selection, and over-subscription all present. Within this system space, distance and transport all play a part in making some schools more 'get-at-able' than others. History and reputation make some schools more desirable to some choosers. Schools are more or less well placed in spatial terms and so are families. Patterns of choice are generated both by choice preferences and opportunities and capacities. Thus in making choices, reputation and desirability are played off against other factors, like distance, and like matching. For some parents it is not the general characteristics of a school that are important but the specific match or fit between the school and their child. For working class parents the child's wishes are more often decisive but family organisation is a constraint. For middle class parents family organisation seems to be less of a constraint but the child's input into the choice process is more limited. The individualisation of choice is different in each case. In all the ways noted above the market is strongly related to social class differences. There are two distinct discourses of choice in evidence. A working class discourse dominated by the practical and the immediate and a middle class discourse dominated by the ideal and advantageous.

We want now to attempt to 'place' the education market sociologically in more general terms by applying to it an analysis developed in relation to a somewhat different but related set of changes by Bourdieu and Boltanski. In Bourdieu and Boltanski's (1979: 197) language the use of the market by 'cosmopolitan', middle class families, as outlined above, is a particular strategy of reproduction. That is, a strategy by which members of classes or class fractions 'tend, consciously or unconsciously, to maintain or improve their position in the structure of class relations' (198). In our case, three factors 'trigger' or provide for the increased emphasis on strategic choice within the middle class families reported here. First, there is the steady inflation of academic qualifications and their correlative devaluation. Second, and related, is the increased democratisation of schooling, by comprehensivisation. Both of these pose threats to the maintenance of class advantage by reducing educational differentiation and by changing patterns of access to higher education and the labour market. Third, is the new possibilities offered in and by the policies of school specialisation and increasing selection and choice within a market framework, being pursued by the Conservative government. That is to say, the middle classes here are making the most of the new opportunities which these policies offer to re-establish their historic economic advantages or newly achieved status position. Or, in other words, changes in educational opportunity have 'compelled the classes and class fractions whose reproduction was chiefly or exclusively assured by the school to increase their investments in order to maintain the relative scarcity of their qualifications and, in consequence, their position in the class structure' (Bourdieu and Boltanski 1979: 220). All of this might be taken as a perverse example of the arguments made by Halsey, Heath, and Ridge (1980). They suggest that educational growth, at least initially, tended to increase inequality because new opportunities are taken up first and disproportionately by the middle classes. Further, they argued that in relation to inequality, 'scarcity of places was the crucial factor' (217). The market is a new 'opportunity' for the middle classes, particularly related in its operation to the conversion of their habitus; and its infrastructure of 'desire', is driven by patterns of scarcity. It must also be noted that all of these factors are set within a context of financial retrenchment in education and general economic depression and unemployment. In relation to both relative educational advantage takes on added significance. What is important here then is the 'utilisation of the specific powers of the educational system as an instrument of reproduction' (Bourdieu and Boltanski 1979: 205). Furthermore, within the education marketplace this 'mechanism of class transmission' is 'doubly hidden'; it is obscured first of all by the continuing assumptions about the neutrality of patterns of achievement in education, and second, by assumptions about the neutrality of the market itself and by the model and distribution of the 'good parent' upon which it trades. The working-class families are also engaged in a process of social reproduction; but their 'use' of the school system is driven by a different set of purposes, values and objectives. Their utilisation of the specific powers of the education system is accommodative rather than strategic.

The market orientations of the cosmopolitan, middle class families quoted above involve the reinvestment of cultural capital for a return of educational capital.

The educational market thus becomes one of the most important loci of the class struggle . . . Strategies of reconversion are nothing but the sum of the actions and reactions by which each group tries to maintain or change its position in the social structure or, more precisely, to maintain its position by changing . . . the reproduction of the class structure operates through a *translation* of the distribution of academic qualifications held by each class or section of a class . . . which can conserve the *ordinal ranking* of the different classes. (Bourdieu and Boltanksi: 220–1)

While this analysis of the role and functioning of the market in education undoubtedly needs further test and development it begins to bring policy, agency, class relations and social structure together in a powerful way. It allows us to see the link between the ideological and structural aspects of a public service market and the reproduction of class relations and relative economic advantage. These are the beginnings of a sociological analysis of parental choice.

Notes

1. This paper is an edited version of a presentation to the 1992 British Educational Research Association Annual Conference. It draws upon the work of an ESRC funded research study of market forces in education; award number R000 232858.
2. Northwark is an inner, metropolitan area with a Conservative controlled council. It has a diverse ethnic and socio-economic population; although over the past ten years there has been a steady process of gentrification. The housing stock ranges from detached mansions to council high-rise. It is an ex-ILEA education authority. Riverway and Westway are outer metropolitan areas. Riverway is predominantly middle/upper middle class and has a Social Democrat controlled council. The housing stock is dominated by terraced, semi-detached and detached Victorian and Edwardian villas. There is a large tract of parkland and many social amenities. This is primarily a residential/commuter area. Westway, especially in the southern area covered by our research, is predominantly working class. And there is a large, well-established south Asian community. The housing stock is dominated by 1950s urban sprawl and 1960s low and high-rise council housing. Local employment is provided by light industry and international transport facilities.
3. Data was collected in each interview on both parents' occupations, both parents' educational careers and qualifications, and housing status (ownership, council rented, housing association rented). Using a simple Registrar General's classification of occupations, a categorisation of educational careers into those terminated at the end of compulsory schooling and those with further education and qualifications (using both parents in each case) and housing status—a middle class/working class division was arrived at. Contrary to our expectations all but a few families could be straightforwardly allocated in this way. However, in further analysis we intend to employ a more sensitive classification of class fractions.

References

Adler, M., Petch, R., and Tweedie, J. (1989), *Parental Choice and Educational Policy* (Edinburgh: Edinburgh Univ. Press).

Bernstein, B. (1975), *Class, Codes and Control*, iii (London: Routledge).

Blank, R. (1990), 'Educational Effects of Magnet High Schools', in Clune, W., and Witte, J. (eds.), *Choice and Control in American Education*, ii (Lewes: Falmer Press).

Bourdieu, P. (1984), *Distinction: A Social Critique of the Judgement of Taste* (Cambridge, Mass.: Harvard Univ. Press).

—— and Boltanski, L. (1979), 'Changes in Social Structure and Changes in the Demand for Education', in *Information Sur Les Sciences Sociales*, 12 (5 October), 61–113.

Bowe, R., Gewirtz, S., and Ball, S. J. (1994), 'Captured by the Discourse? Issues and Concerns in Researching "Parental Choice" ', *British Journal of Sociology of Education*, 15/1: 63–78.

Carlen, P., Gleeson, D., and Wardhaugh, J. (1992), *Truancy: The Politics of Compulsory Schooling* (Buckingham: Open Univ. Press).

Clarke, J. (1979), 'Capital and Culture: The Postwar Working Class Revisited', in Clarke, J., Critcher, C., and Johnson, R. (eds.), *Working Class Culture* (London: Hutchinson).

Coldron, J., and Boulton, P. (1991), ' "Happiness" as a Criterion of Parents' Choice of School', *Journal of Education Policy*, 6/2: 169–78.

Cremin, L. A. (1979), *Public Education* (New York: Basic Books).

Dickens, P. (1990), *Urban Sociology: Society, Locality and Human Nature* (Hemel Hempstead: Harvester/Wheatsheaf).

Echols, F., McPherson, A., and Wilms, J. (1990), 'Parental Choice in Scotland', *Journal of Education Policy*, 5/3: 207–22.

Edwards, T., Fitz, J., and Whitty, G. (1989), *The State and Private Education: An Evaluation of the Assisted Places Scheme* (Lewes: Falmer Press).

Gewirtz, S., Ball, S. J., and Bowe, R. (1992), 'Parents, Privilege and the Education Market Place', *Research Papers in Education*, 9/1: 3–29.

Giddens, A., (1984) *The Constitution of Society* (Oxford: Polity Press).

Grieco, M. (1991) *Low Income Families and Inter-Household Dependency: The Implications for Transport Policy and Planning* (Oxford University Transport Studies Unit).

—— Jones, P., and Polack, J. (1991), *Time to Make the Connection* (Oxford University Transport Studies Unit).

—— and Pearson, M. (1991), *Spatial Mobility Begins at Home? Rethinking Inter-Household Organisation* (Oxford University Transport Studies Unit).

Halsey, A. H., Heath, A., and Ridge, J. (1980), *Origins and Destinations* (Oxford: Clarendon).

Harvey, D. (1989), *The Condition of Post Modernity* (Oxford: Blackwell).

Maddaus, J. (1990), 'Parental Choice of School: What Parents Think and Do', (ed.) Cazden, C. B., *Review of Research in Education*, 16 (Washington, DC: AERA).

Moore, D. (1990), 'Voice and Choice in Chicago', in Clune, W., and Witte, J. (eds.), *Control and Choice in American Education*, ii (Lewes: Falmer Press).

Slaughter, D. T. and Schnieder, B. L. (1986), *Newcomers: Blacks in Private Schools* (Evanston, Ill.: Northwestern University).

Sosniak, L. A., and Ethington, C. A. (1992), 'When Public School "Choice" is not Academic: Findings from the National Education Longitudinal Study of 1988', *Educational Evaluation and Policy Analysis*, 14/1: 35–52.

Thomas, A., and Dennison, B. (1991), 'Parental or Pupil Choice—Who Really Decides in Urban Schools?', *Educational Management and Administration*, 19/4: 243–9.

Weimann, G. (1982), 'On the Importance of Marginality: One More Step in the Two Way Flow of Information', *American Sociological Review*, 47: 764–73.

28

African-American Students' View of School Choice

Amy Stuart Wells

The political debate over the merits of deregulated school-choice plans that give parents publicly funded vouchers to spend at private schools promises to continue throughout the decade, as more states hold elections and engage in legislative battles on the issue. Meanwhile, in the absence of any widespread voucher plans in the US, policymakers and voters can only speculate about the impact of such programmes on the distribution of educational resources.[1] Arguments on both sides of the issue include large assumptions about how parents and students would respond to such policies. Proponents of deregulated voucher-plans generally assume that all parents and students will respond to such programmes in a similar goal-oriented and self-interested fashion, systematically seeking the highest quality schools. Opponents of private-school-choice plans, on the other hand, often over-emphasize the extent to which low-income families of colour will passively withdraw from competition within the educational free market.

In this way, voucher advocates and opponents alike offer simplistic views of families' responses to changes in the structure and governance of educational systems. Both sides tend to under-estimate the role of human agency—the freedom of individuals to act independently—in creating a wide array of reactions to such massive deregulation. As a result there is little meaningful discussion of the complex ways in which the cultural context of individual actors guides decision making.

This lack of attention to agency and culture in debates concerning educational choice is all the more surprising given recent findings in educational research. In sociology of education, for instance, 'resistance theorists' including Willis (1977) and Everhart (1983) have shown that students from lower-class families are not passively shuffled through the educational system and consigned to the lowest-paying jobs, as structural Marxists (Bowles and Gintis 1976) would lead us to believe. Rather, according to these sociologists, lower-class students are active agents in their own social reproduction, resisting the dominant culture and the achievement ideology that inform school life.

Apple (1985: 95) argues that researchers and theorists must challenge beliefs about the passivity of students in social reproduction: 'This assumption tends to overlook the fact that students . . . are creatively acting in ways that often contradict these expected norms and dispositions which pervade the school and the workplace'. Apple and others have shown that, though students act out their opposition in inherently contradictory and relatively disorganized ways, these practices 'will exist. To ignore them is to ignore the fact that in any real situation there will be elements of resistance, of struggle and contradiction.' (p. 93).

Critical theorists, building on the neo-Marxist theories of cultural domination and resistance, have demonstrated the role that students can play in the educational system. Fine's research (1991), for instance, illustrates

From B. Fuller, R. Elmore, and G. Orfield (eds.), *Who Chooses? Who Loses? Culture, Institutions, and the Unequal Effects of School Choice* (Teachers College Press, 1996). Reprinted with permission.

the 'complicated, contradictory conscious-ness' operating within the minds and lives of poor and minority adolescents (p. 107). She found that students who succeed academically and graduate from high school 'seem to deny, repress or dismiss the stories of failure, and persist undaunted in their personal crusade against the odds' (p. 134). Meanwhile, the students who fail in school and eventually drop out were 'more critical of social and economic circumstances'. These dropouts also retained strong connections to their community, kin, peers, and racial/ethnic identity, and resisted the dominant culture's emphasis on individualism and the achievement ideology—that those who work hard in school will get ahead.

Similarly, Ogbu's research has illustrated what he calls paradoxical behaviour among African-American students. On the one hand, Ogbu writes, black parents and black communities emphasize the importance of education in getting ahead in life, but on the other hand, black parents and students are very aware of the 'job ceiling' in the labour market that prevents many blacks from getting high-paying jobs despite their degrees. These conflicting messages lead many black students to adopt an oppositional culture, rejecting the traditional achievement ideology and labelling black students' commitment to school achievement as 'acting white'. For these students, black culture becomes a symbol of identity and a basis of self-worth that stands in opposition to the dominant culture (Ogbu 1988, and Stevenson and Ellsworth 1993).

Along with this increased emphasis on human agency and cultural resistance, the last 15 years has seen the growing influence of Pierre Bourdieu's notions of *cultural capital* and *habitus*. According to Bordieu, *cultural capital* is a system of implicit and deeply internalized values passed down by generations and influenced by social class, ethnicity, and parents' education. For example, the kinds of books that parents read to their children or the type of entertainment they expose them to—film, theatre, music, or museums—provides students with different bases of knowledge, upon which they draw when trying to create new meanings in relation to material presented to them in school. Educators tend to perceive the cultural capital of those who control the economic, social, and political resources as the natural and only proper sort,

and thus favour students who possess the cultural capital of the dominant group or groups (Harker 1984).

Bourdieu argues that degrees of economic and cultural capital are not perfectly correlated. For example, university teachers generally have far greater cultural than economic capital, and members of the capitalist class generally have more economic than cultural capital (Bourdieu 1977). Bordieu's theory thus shifts emphasis from more deterministic structural models of social reproduction, based on class conflict in the economic realm, and introduces a cultural dimension of stratification that can apply to racial and ethnic group conflict as well. Furthermore, Bourdieu highlights the role of agency in his description of the various ways in which students who do not have the dominant groups' cultural capital interact with the educational system. Some try to bluff their way through, picking up bits and pieces of the valued cultural capital along the way; others simply give up when they realize that they lack the cultural capital which schools reward (Bourdieu and Passeron 1979).

This variability in how individual students make sense of the world and of the opportunities presented to them is perhaps best illustrated by Bourdieu's concept of *habitus*, or the way in which a culture is embodied in the individual (Harker 1984: 118). Bourdieu and Passeron (1977) define *habitus* as a system of 'schemes of perception, thought and action', usually generated by objective conditions but tending to persist even after alteration of those conditions. For example, some African Americans view themselves as inferior to whites years after the abolition of slavery and legal segregation. More simply put, *habitus* is how one's view of the world is influenced by the traditional distribution of power and status in society.

According to Bourdieu, and others who have employed the concept, members of different groups—whether classes, races, or religions—can share a *group habitus*, or set of dispositions which shape conduct and opinion.[2] Group *habitus* is then redefined and incorporated within a family *habitus* and finally within the *habitus* of the individual. A person's social class, race, and religion thus strongly affect his or her *habitus*, or matrix of perceptions and appreciations; but family influence and encounters with the world make each person's *habitus* unique (see DiMaggio 1979 and Robbins 1991).

The concepts of resistance, opposition, cultural capital, and *habitus* all suggest that the complex ways in which schools and students interact and redefine students' experiences in the educational system are not predictable or deterministic. Without ignoring the very real correlation between students' social class or race and their educational opportunities, most sociologists of education now agree that social reproduction within the educational system is not a neat or uncontested process. Allowing for human agency explains why individual students, despite demographic similarities, react to the same set of circumstances and opportunities quite differently.

In order to predict accurately the impact of deregulated school-choice policies, policy-makers need to pay more attention to this body of research and theory. In doing so they will better understand why changing the structure of the educational system will not empower all parents and students to compete for seats in high-quality schools— why, among demographically similar families, some will choose not to participate in this competition because they resist the dominant culture it symbolizes or they perceive their chances of winning to be slim, while others may choose to participate in a school-choice plan seeking upward mobility through access to higher-status schools.

In an effort to contribute to the small body of research addressing some of these issues as they pertain to choices of social services and educational institutions, I interviewed 71 African-Americans—37 high school students and 34 of their parents or grandparents—who live in inner-city St Louis and have several urban and suburban school choices available to them. My study demonstrates that the school-choice process for these students is neither predictable nor uniform; wide variations within racial and social-class groups exist. Students' and parents' views are filtered through a *habitus* that is informed by a shared group perspective as well as by family and experience.

Choosing Schools: A Closer Look at the Process

African-American students who reside in the city of St Louis have the option of participating in an inter-district transfer programme—a desegregation plan that allows black students to attend 120 predominantly white suburban or county schools instead of the all-black schools in their neighbourhoods. Students receive brochures and other information on the transfer programme and the 16 participating suburban school districts in the mail and at their schools. The programme is also publicized through radio, newspaper, and television public-service announcements. African-American students who want to transfer to a county school simply fill out an application form and send it to the state-funded agency that administers the transfer process.[3]

Currently, about 13,500 black students participate in the voluntary city-to-county transfer programme. Under a Federal District Court order, the suburban districts are not allowed to turn away prospective transfer students on the basis of prior school achievement. Because this is choice-centred, voluntary desegregation, black students are not compelled to participate. From the black students' perspective, the transfer plan is semi-regulated school choice skewed in their favour to assure them the greatest number of options. Although the St Louis transfer programme is not a deregulated voucher plan in which parents are given public funds to spend at private schools, it does provide thousands of students with school choices, and researchers with an opportunity to test assumptions concerning how these choices are made. In fact, I would argue that black students in the city of St Louis have more real choice under this desegregation plan that than they would under a voucher plan that would not provide free public transportation, cover the expenses for every receiving school, or require predominantly white schools to increase their black enrolment.

We interviewed three groups of black high-school students and their parents for this study. The *city* group consisted of those who chose to remain in all-black city high schools. The *transfer* group included those who transferred to county schools and were still enrolled in these schools at the time of the interview. The *return* group was comprised of those who had transferred to a county school but had since returned to all-black city schools or dropped out of school all together. Samples

Table 28.1. Demographic differences between city, transfer, and return students

	12 City Students	12 Transfer Students	13 Return Students
Students behind in school	7	1	7
Average years behind	2	1	1.4
Average number of siblings	4.8	2.5	2.2
Parents with high school degrees	5	9	9
Parents unemployed	4	1	5
Parents work in the county	0	5	5

of students from each of these three categories were drawn from three predominantly black, city neighbourhoods identified as *middle-income*, *working-class*, and *low-income*, based on Census Bureau descriptions of the residents' education, employment, and income. The final sample consisted of 17 boys and 20 girls, all between the ages of 15 and 19, and 34 parents or grandparents. This chapter focuses primarily on the student interviews, drawing on the parent responses only to illustrate parent–child relationships (see Wells 1993 for details on parent interviews).

Choosers and Non-Choosers

Although this study's focus is on individual families and how they approach school choice, some general description of the students and their parents helps to set the scene. The distinctions between families of the city, transfer, and return students were more pronounced than those between the families from the three different neighbourhoods—middle-income, working-class, and low-income. The city and return students in this sample were, as a group, further behind in school than the transfer students (see Table 28.1). City students in this sample have more siblings, and their parents have fewer years of education. More city and return students' parents were unemployed at the time of the interview, and not one of the city students' parents held a job that took him or her across the city–county colour line.

This small sample suggests that city students who stay behind in the urban schools and return students who end up back in urban schools (or out of school altogether) tend to be more disadvantaged in terms of parental education and employment than the transfer students who chose to enrol in predominantly white suburban schools. Furthermore, a quantitative evaluation of the St Louis desegregation plan (Lissitz 1992) found that, in a comparison of 2,350 African-American tenth-graders who remained in all-black, non-integrated city schools with 864 students who transferred to county schools, the parents of the transfer students had completed more years of education. For instance, 29 per cent of the mothers of the transfer students, as opposed to 21 per cent of the mothers of students attending non-integrated city schools, had at least some years of college (pp. 28–46). Also, the students in the non-integrated city schools tended to be, on average, 4 months older than the transfer students in their same grade. There were no differences, however, between the transfer and city students in the percentage which qualified for free or reduced-price lunch. For both groups, the percentage was 58 (pp. 24–46). Certainly, other research supports the notion that non-choosers are more disadvantaged in terms of parents' education and social class than choosers in most educational choice programmes (see Wells 1991 for a review). But the main point of this research was to get past simplistic and deterministic generalizations and try to make sense of the complex school-choice process from the perspective of the people making the decisions. In the students' explanations of how and why they chose the schools they did, there lies the impact of culture and human agency.

Our interviews illustrate that for these African-American students, three overlapping and intertwined factors strongly affect school choices:

1. the degree of parent involvement in the initial school choice;
2. students' acceptance or rejection of the achievement ideology, or what it takes to get ahead in the world; and

3. students' and parents' racial attitudes—their fear or distrust of whites and the degree to which they accept the dominant view of whites as higher-status. All three factors are heavily influenced by both students' and parents' *habitus* as it relates to their understanding of the kind of cultural capital needed to succeed in a predominantly white suburban school.

The first two factors—parent involvement and the achievement ideology—were closely linked, both because students tended to adopt their parents' ideology with regard to achievement, and because there appears to be a link between the parents' ideology and their involvement. Researchers have demonstrated a positive correlation between the degree of parent involvement in education and parent SES (see Lareau 1989 and Epstein 1987), but there are exceptions. In St Louis many low-income, poorly educated parents are very involved in their children's education and the school choice process. Thus, it is important to look more carefully at the human-agency side of the equation. How do individual students and parents' perceptions of where they fit into the larger social structure—their *habitus*—affect their interpretation of the achievement ideology, and how does that interpretation play a role their school choices?

With few exceptions, the overall parent involvement in the students' education, and the degree to which parents directed and controlled their children's' educational decisions, varied greatly between the city students who remained in all-black neighbourhood schools and the transfer students who chose to attend predominantly white, suburban schools. City parents, in almost every case, absolved themselves of the school-choice responsibility, leaving the entire decision to the students. Transfer parents, on the other hand, pushed their children onto buses heading for the suburbs. Parents of the return students were frequently involved in the initial choice of a suburban school, but less involved in helping their children cope in the predominantly white setting, and eventually had little say in their children's final decision to leave the suburban schools.

Achievement ideology was closely linked to parents' involvement. Parents who were more involved in their childrens' choices tended to accept the dominant achievement ideology, an acceptance they generally passed to their children. Transfer students thus tended to believe that school status and the right cultural capital would help them to succeed in the world. City students, on the other hand, adopted a 'learn-anywhere' ideology that downplayed the significance of attending higher-quality schools. The achievement ideology of return students was more vexed; some accepted the dominant achievement ideology, but felt that they could not live comfortably with it; others rejected it outright.

City Students: Comfort and Learn-Anywhere Ideology

Eight out of the 11 city parents (or guardians)[4] interviewed said that the student alone made the decision to remain in a city school. Half of these parents said that they did not even discuss this decision with their child. Only one parent in the sample, a teacher in the city-school system who maintains a strong black separatist attitude, said she had actually decided which school her son would attend (Wells 1993). These parents appeared particularly withdrawn and alienated from the educational system. They spoke as if they could be of no help to their children regarding educational decisions (Wells 1993).

Left to their own devices, city students opted for the nearby and the familiar—the all-black, neighbourhood school. Interviews reveal that what city students were really choosing was the sense of kinship and shared culture that pervades their all-black schools. Because their parents did not insist that they ride a bus to the suburbs, city students remained in schools in which they felt more comfortable.

When asked what they like most about their city high schools, 9 of the 12 city students gave responses that had nothing to do with learning, the quality of the school, or their goals. Familiarity with students or teachers, tradition and pride associated with certain extracurricular activities, or closeness to home clearly dominated the responses. Veronica said that what she like most about her neighbourhood high school was being on the pompon squad. Leander said that what he liked most was that he knew everybody, and Cherrine said there was nothing that she liked about her city high school except that it was close to home. Sabrina, who is 19 years old and still in the tenth grade, said that what she enjoyed most about her city school were the pep rallies, the choir, and the glee club. Corey noted that the teachers and students were all right and the bus ride was short.

Erica, a friendly young woman who talked a great deal about the importance of being well-liked by her peers, described her favourite aspect of the city high school in her low-income neighbourhood: 'I know a lot of people up there . . . and I don't feel lost.' Erica's life, like that of many high-school students, seemed to evolve around the social events at her school. She noted that she was not excited about a special internship programme she was selected to participate in during junior year because it would take her away from the school and her friends for half of each school day. Luckily, she said, the programme would allow her to miss work for school events, such as 'Colors Day', when all the seniors dress up and 'you vote for the best couple, class clown, best-dressed, athletes, and stuff like that'.

Only three city students gave answers related to school achievement: Anjeanette said the teachers at her neighbourhood school helped her learn; Gina said that the teachers at her school 'want to see us make it'; and Patricia said that what she liked best about her high school was that it was close to home and that she knew some of her teachers, also adding that these teachers would 'really be on me about my work. You need teachers like that, that care about what you do'.

Yet even those whose responses were achievement-oriented discuss a sense of belonging to the school, a degree of attachment to the teachers and students in the city schools, and an acknowledgement that their cultural capital will be recognized and valued in an all-black institution. Virtually all of the city students' responses concerning what they like about their high schools incorporated this sense of shared culture, much like the shared-culture capital that DiMaggio and Mohr (1985) found to be so important in choosing marriage partners. The traditions of their all-black schools, for instance, the songs the choir sang, or the more rhythmic, less stiff style of cheerleading, reflected the history and culture of the students in ways that these activities at predominantly white suburban schools did not. These and other city-student responses are consistent with a phenomenon found in

other studies of school-choice situations— that cultural familiarity or shared values frequently dominate over school-quality factors *per se* (Henig 1990; Holloway and Fuller 1992; Madders 1990).

When asked if they ever considered attending a county school and if so, why they did not transfer, the city students responded in ways that once again suggest the importance of the cultural unity they experienced at an all-black school, as well as their lack of information about the transfer programme. Veronica said, 'I wanted to go, but I didn't. I don't know why . . . I didn't want to leave the pom squad . . . I didn't want to go that far.' Karen also said that she wanted to go, but her father told her that information on the transfer programme came too late.

Several students gave more than one answer; some students gave disjointed, rambling answers that were scattered throughout responses to various other questions. This lack of coherence suggests that, for many city students, remaining in an all-black neighbourhood school was less of a conscious decision than a subconscious avoidance of the unknown. Interestingly enough, only two respondents—Leander and Patricia—defended their choice to remain in a city school by insisting that the quality of the education in their school was comparable to that of a county school. According to Patricia, 'Some say the work is harder in the county school; I don't think so.' Leander said he never considered going to a county school. 'The education is the same here . . . I think the county schools are intentionally taking city students to tear them down—keep people confused, keep them under control.'

Four of the city students' responses to questions concerning transfers to county schools were laden with insecurity and fear of the unknown—Cherrine not wanting to meet new people, Michael not wanting to go 'way out', Sabrina worrying about not understanding what is not taught, and Erica wanting to stay where 'I know a lot of people'. None of these students discussed his or her decision in terms of the quality of the school attended or the quality of the school not attended. Once again, the comfort of the familiar was a deciding factor in the school choices.

With little parent involvement in their school choices, and little emphasis on school-quality factors in discussing their choice, most of the city students have adopted a 'learn-anywhere' achievement ideology. Thus city students most frequently responded to any question concerning the transfer programme or a comparison of city and county schools by saying that the school doesn't matter; it's the student's ability and motivation that counts. 'You have to want to learn, then you're gonna learn. It doesn't matter who might be teaching,' said Patricia. According to Erica, there is no difference between the city and the county schools: 'If you're going to learn something, you do your best anywhere you go.' Similarly, Veronica downplayed any differences between city and county schools: 'It doesn't really matter where you go . . . if you want to learn—you got the ability, you will.'

Interestingly enough, despite the city parents' lack of direct involvement in the school choice process, they have obviously had an impact on the way in which their children think about schools and achievement. The learn-anywhere achievement ideology that city students espouse echoes their parents' responses to questions concerning the quality of the city versus the suburban schools (see Wells 1993).

In short, the evidence suggests that when parents left the choice to them, the students followed the path of least resistance to a familiar, nearby school where they fitted in and felt comfortable. In an attempt to rationalize this choice in the face of popular opinion that country schools are better than city schools, the city students have adopted an achievement ideology that minimizes the importance of school quality.

This is not the portrait of families that carefully evaluated their options and their long-term goals and decided that a city school would better serve their needs than a county school. Offering these students the choice of higher-status schools did not free them from a *habitus* of fear and insecurity in a world that places them at the bottom of the social structure and devalues the culture capital of their race and community.

Transfer Students: Parent Involvement and Sacrificing

Where city parents were withdrawn and seemingly resigned to fate, transfer parents tended to be much more aggressive and bent on making the lives of their children better than their own. In contrast to the responses from 8 city parents who said the school-choice process was left entirely up to the students, only one of the 11 transfer parents said she had left the school-choice up to her daughter. Meanwhile, 6 of the 11 transfer parents said that they had made the decision for their children to attend a county school themselves, and 3 said that the decision had been made jointly with their children (Wells 1993).

Because of their parents' more active involvement, transfer students had far less control over the school-choice process than the city students, and they appeared to have very different parent–child relationships. Transfer parents are assertive, demanding, and not easily intimidated (see Wells 1993). And their children, with one exception, seem to enjoy this high level of parent involvement and accept their parents' attitudes about city versus county schools and the transfer programme.

Thus, of the three groups of students and parents interviewed, the transfer parents and their children best fitted the vision of school choosers that seems to drive proposals for greater choice in education. They were more goal-oriented and focused on school quality as an important variable in the school-choice process, although they admitted to having little first-hand knowledge of the quality of particular schools before making their choices. The parents were highly involved in their children's education, and the students, for the most part, respected their parents' decisions. These were the 'rational choosers'—intent on making the most of themselves in a highly instrumental and goal-oriented fashion (see Becker 1986)—the type of educational consumer who, in theory, will demand more of the educational system once given school choices.

Interestingly, transfer parents and their children seemed less concerned about which county school they attended, so long as it was a county school. In this sense these parents and students are not the ideal educational consumers they appear to be. Transfer parents and students lacked information about the 16 county districts and their 120 schools, suggesting they were not making the best choice but rather making the best choice possible given the limited amount of information available to them.

Factors such as perceived status or popularity of a school—the 'designer label'—played a major role in the choices these families made. 'I heard a lot of people talking about Westridge, wanting to go to Westridge,' said one transfer student. 'I'd always wanted to go to Westridge, I just like the name,' said another. Despite the vast differences between the various county school districts in terms of resources, class sizes, teacher qualifications, and so forth, the transfer parents and students indicated that the major choice was between a city school and a county—any county—school. The choice of a specific county district was usually secondary and often inconsequential.

Due to lack of transportation or time, the transfer families had not shopped for the highest-quality county school. In fact, none of the parents or students had ever been to the schools they chose. Despite their lack of information, transfer students are highly motivated to attend predominantly white schools many miles from their own home. In the way they speak to a white interviewer, in the way they carry themselves, and in the way they explain why they get up at 5 a.m. to get to their county schools every day, the transfer students as a group are by far more confident and goal-oriented than their counterparts in the city schools. With few exceptions, the transfer students drew on the parental support available to them and propelled themselves forward on their parents' hopes and dreams for their success. They were for the most part steeped in an achievement ideology stressing the importance of going to the 'best' school in order to get ahead in life. Unlike the city students, who argued that schools don't make a difference, that it's up to the individual to achieve, the transfer students perceived a more complex opportunity structure—one in which school status and perceived academic quality would make a difference in their lives.

When asked what they liked most about their suburban high schools, 5 of the 12 students cited factors that would help them attain long-term goals: 'classes that will help you with college', 'good teachers and good counsellors', and 'they give you the freedom to be grown up, young adults'. Three of the transfer students cited their involvement in a variety of extracurricular activities, including the computer club. One transfer student said he could not think of anything specific that he liked most, although he did enjoy his involvement on the basketball team; and the remaining three students cited more social factors: 'a lot of people know who I am', 'the people—the teachers, my friends', and 'meeting other transfer students from different parts of the city'. Yet even these less-academic factors differ to some degree from those cited by the city students. The transfer students are not talking about the comfort or familiarity associated with attending a predominantly white suburban school.

In fact, their responses to questions concerning what they like least about their county high schools reveal that they are willing to put up with a great deal of discomfort—including racial prejudice, a lack of respect for their cultural capital, and long bus rides—because most of them believe this sacrifice will pay off in the long run. Mitchell, for instance, when asked what he liked least about his county high school, said, 'I have to try to be two people instead of just being myself—I have to act one way in school and another way in my neighbourhood.' Toya commented that black students are not as involved in certain high-status activities—particularly those for girls, such as cheerleading and pompons—at her county high school. 'We feel like we are visitors and not part of the school,' she said. In fact, Toya, more than any of the other transfer students, is keenly aware of the subtle and not-so-subtle racism that transfer students confront in their predominantly white schools. She said the labelling of black students as 'Voluntary Transfer Students', or 'VTS' is degrading and makes them feel as though they don't belong:

We *hate* that. I mean, they will call a meeting then on the loud speaker and they will always go 'voluntary transfer students please come to the gym', and really what they are saying is all the black students come here . . . . I mean even though we're coming out there and it's supposed to be our school too . . . whenever blacks and whites get into it, the first thing they (white students) say is this is *our* school, you're coming out to *our* school.

Two other transfer students noted that some of the teachers in their county schools were prejudiced, while a third said that some of the teachers would not help if you get the wrong answer. Virgil noted that what he liked least were the racial comments, such as 'whites stereotyping blacks as street people'.

When asked, 'In what ways would you

rather have gone to the city school in your neighbourhood?' transfer students talked about additional sacrifices they had made in transferring to a school 20 or more miles from their home: Cleo said she would have had more time to do her homework and study; Toya, Antonnie, and Ursolon stated that they would have been more 'comfortable'—they would have fitted in better and would have known more people—in their neighbourhood schools.

Similarly, transfer students' responses to the question of whether or not they ever considered returning to their neighbourhood schools demonstrate the level of discomfort they frequently experience in white suburbia and their awareness of the sacrifice they are making in order to achieve a long-term goal. For instance, Toya noted that when she was in the seventh grade she thought to herself, 'Why put up with this when I can go to a neighbourhood school and be treated equal?' She added that her mother would not allow her to return to the city schools because she thought Toya was receiving a better education in the county schools. Virgil noted that he had thought about returning to the city schools, 'but I thought that would be the easy way out. I have skills now that I wouldn't have till I was 25 in the city schools.'

Several of the transfer students acknowledged, throughout their interviews, that the coursework in the county schools was more difficult than that of the city schools, that the students in county schools 'learn a little bit faster', and that the county schools have more resources. Students see their discomfort as the price they must pay for the opportunity to attend 'better', more challenging schools. And because of an achievement ideology that tells them they will be able to cash in on these opportunities in the long run, that schools indeed make a difference in their lives and chances for future success, nearly all of the transfer students, with the notable exception of Toya, believe in what their parents decided for them.

Even Toya, the one transfer student with a strong critique of the white schools, understood why her mother believed that the transfer programme would pay off in the long run.

She'll tell you that when you fill out an application [for a job], when you put Washington [the city school] down or you put Plymouth [the county school] down, it's a better chance that they will pick a Plymouth student . . . because it [the county school] like means a good opportunity.

Return Students: Resisting the Achievement Ideology

Unlike the circumstances and attitudes of the city and transfer families, which are fairly distinct, the sample of return families provide a more diffuse blend of experiences and perspectives. A few of the parents in this group were assertive and demanding, similar to the transfer parents. Others were as withdrawn and alienated as many of the city parents (see Wells 1993). The return students also varied widely from bold and outspoken to meek and soft-spoken. The return students were also more complicated in terms of the school-choice process because they had actually made two choices—first to transfer to the county schools, and then to return to their neighbourhood schools or drop out altogether. Yet what is more interesting about the return students is that how they view themselves in relation to the rest of the world—i.e. their *habitus*—has everything to do with why they left the county schools.

Where the city students were safely tied to their familiar neighbourhood schools, and the transfer students were pushed toward what were perceived to be better schools by their parents, the return students appeared to be caught between their need for comfort and positive reinforcement and the realization that the county schools represent something they once wanted but were unable to attain. With less support from their parents, return students had more trouble tolerating the stresses of attending a largely white county school. Some of these students were intimidated by the dominant culture, and withdrew from competition; others rejected that culture outright.

As a group, return students were more likely to have begun transferring to a county school at an older age than the transfer students. Seven return students did not begin transferring to the county until high school, compared to only one transfer student. These age differences suggest less parental involvement in the return-students' choices, since students who begin transferring to a suburban school during elementary or middle grades are more likely to be pushed by a parent.

In fact, 5 of the 12 return parents said they left the school choice entirely up to their sons or daughters, as opposed to 8 of 11 city parents and 1 of 11 transfer parents. Four of these return parents—as opposed to 2 city parents and 6 transfer parents—took full responsibility for the original county versus city school choice, with one mother saying that she sent her son against his wishes. But when asked whose decision it was for their son or daughter to quit the transfer programme and leave the county school, 6 of the return parents said their children made the choice on their own.

Return students' answers to why they quit the transfer programme fit into four distinct categories:

1. Four return students said that they were 'put out' or 'pushed out' of their county schools as a result of disciplinary actions by white administrators.[5] All four of these students said they felt that these actions were the result of racial bias on the part of the white administrators in the suburban schools. These students were generally bolder that the other return students; they, like Toya, were the resisters—similar in many respects to Willis's (1977) lads or Fine's (1991) dropouts—who offered a critique of the system. Although these resisters had originally been sent to the county schools by domineering parents, they were not willing to put up with the suburban schools' disciplinary codes or the perceived attitudes of the white educators who enforced them.

2. Five return students said that they left the county schools for comfort/convenience reasons, which included everything from not liking the bus ride to finding the white county students unfriendly, of whom four cited cultural factors that had to do with perceived prejudice in the county schools. These students, with one exception, tended to be the quieter return students, the ones who did not cause a lot of trouble but who wanted to return to a school environment in which they felt more comfortable. They resembled the city students who liked their neighbourhood high schools because they were close to home and full of people they knew. Their parents, meanwhile, like many of the city parents, were less involved in their educational decisions.

3. Three return students said they left the county schools for academic reasons—one said she was skipping class too much in the county school, and the other two said that they came back to the (admittedly less difficult) city schools so that they could improve their grades. The latter two of these students were clearly going through a 'cooling-off' process, during which they come to internalize their lower social status and lack of cultural capital and therefore remove themselves from the competition within the educational system. The parents of two of these three students had pushed their children to go to the county school in the first place, and all three said they wished their children had not returned from county schools. But the parents seems to lack the strength to give the kind of support, guidance, and a strong dose of achievement ideology which transfer parents gave their children.

4. The remaining return student said he had no choice but to return from the county after he had missed several months of school to take care of his ailing stepfather. He said he had been hoping to continue in the county high school and make up what he had missed, but that the principal had strongly discouraged him and told him to seek out a vocationally oriented programme elsewhere.

Given this host of reasons why return students leave the county schools, a more focused picture of who these students are and how their achievement ideology differs from the city and the transfer students is needed.

Gwendolyn, a shy 19-year old with a 2-year-old son, was pregnant with her second child at the time she was interviewed. She said she withdrew from the county school and returned to the all-black high school in her low-income neighbourhood so that she could earn better grades. Although she considers the city school to be inferior to the county school she had attended, she said she disliked the county school:

because you know how they break down the work for you, they don't really explain it to you. Some teachers they explain and others let you go on your own . . . . I didn't do so good—walked out with a 1-point grade average and I went back to public [city] school, and my grades went back up to normal. I'm a B student, but I was between a C and a D [in the county], and I didn't like that. I knew I was better than that. I knew I could function better than that . . . . It's just that you have to be real . . . your mind had to be real wise to be out there [in the county school].

At the time of the interview, Gwendolyn still had a year of coursework to complete before graduating from her neighbourhood high school; she said that this 'ain't so hot, but it'll do. It's trouble, I go there now and . . . it's trouble . . . you're around a lot of blacks, and they're just fighting.'

Reginald, from the same low-income neighborhood as Gwendolyn, first went to a county school in the fourth grade and reported that he was very popular in each of the county schools he attended. He was the quarterback of the freshman football team at his suburban high school and had made it onto the basketball team when he and his friends started getting into trouble. According to Reginald, 'The principals were prejudiced to two people in the school—me and my best friend. Every time something happened, they came and got us. They don't like us. I feel like they didn't want us in their school.'

He said he and his friend were accused of stealing a leather jacket out of a locker—an accusation he denied. And finally, he was 'put out' for fighting with a white student. Reginald enrolled in the high school in his neighbourhood, where he made straight F's and was eventually asked to leave there as well. Thus, in less than a year, Reginald had gone from being a 'popular' football quarterback with a C average to a very angry high-school dropout. His two best friends were also 'out of school'. His first child was due in a few months.

Reginald recalled that once he felt he had been treated unfairly by the administrators in the county school he began to act out and resist the educational system as a whole. His final comment on the transfer programme was, 'They need to change their attitude. Principals' attitudes gonna get them into trouble. Just a whole lot of brothers like to punch them clean in the face.'

Christian, an outspoken student from a middle-class family, represents a cross between Gwendolyn and Reginald. He quit the transfer programme to enroll in his neighbourhood high school in part because he found the work too difficult in the county school, and in part because he was resisting the culture of the mostly white environment—an environment that devalued the cultural capital he brought with him from his all-black neighbourhood. First, in talking about the curriculum and the level of the work, he noted:

I thought I could hang tough with it. You know, going to bed early and getting up and . . . but I didn't expect all those science projects and reading all this history. Work on top of work, on top of work . . . In the city they give you more lectures, and they talk to you like . . . you just got so many chapters . . . In the county, they go too fast.

He then shifted on to issues of cultural domination and his critique of what the county schools were trying to do to the black students:

They brainwash you to go out there—that they teach you more. Then you get there. Oh, you're integrated. You're not yourself no more. Your voice changes like you are a little nerd or something. I felt like I was not myself anymore.

He added that he had not had any discipline problems in the county school because 'I was totally brainwashed. You think you're smart. I went with the system and I thought, "I go to a county school." You just think you are better than everybody else. Then you find out you are not.'

In general, the return students' reasons for coming back to city schools had much to do with how they viewed themselves in relation to the larger social structure. The eight return students who cited either comfort/convenience or academic reasons for returning tended to be more like Gwendolyn in terms of their unwillingness to compete with higher-status students either socially or academically. Reginald typifies the resistance of the four return students who were 'put out' of their county schools and who now reject the legitimacy of the reward system that they feel offers them no chance of success—in high school or beyond.

When asked to compare the city to the county high schools, all 13 return students stated that the county high schools were more difficult. Meanwhile, 10 of these students stated that their city schools were more 'fair' in the way students were treated than the county schools had been. Realizing, however, that the city schools were not preparing them as well for entry into a whiter, higher-status world as the county schools did, these students' decisions to return to neighbourhood all-black schools were profound statements of their perceived long-term chances of competing for places in post-secondary educational institutions and adult employment.

Although a greater number of transfer than return students cited prejudice as what they liked least about their county high school—five versus four—the transfer students were steeped in an achievement ideology that their parents had ingrained in them. This, I believe, helped them tolerate the racial prejudice they encountered, viewing it as a sacrifice that would pay off in the long run. This longer-term focus no doubt helped the transfer students cope with the inherent injustice of a society that values the cultural capital of white, upper-middle-class students far more than that of lower-income, African-American students. Thus, their ability to deal with prejudice and discomfort became a key factor for both the transfer and the return students, as each weighed the pros and cons of remaining in a predominantly white school.

Yet for the return students, it seems as though their parents had one set of beliefs concerning racial issues in the county schools and their children were living another reality. For instance, return parents had very few complaints concerning the county schools. All twelve return parents agreed that the county schools were 'better' than the city schools and, in fact, were less critical of the county schools than the transfer parents. This is somewhat surprising, considering transfer parents still have children enrolled in these schools and return parents have children who left them—mostly because of perceived prejudice. Similarly, according to the transfer students, transfer parents were more likely to talk to their children about prejudice and what to expect from whites in the county, whereas only a few of the return students said their parents had talked to them about these topics. These findings suggest less assertiveness and support on the part of return parents in regard to potential problems and injustices which their students might face in county schools.

With little or no discussion between the parents and students, the return students' decisions to leave the county schools won out in the long run. Transfer students, mostly because of their parents, were more likely to internalize a reward structure that values academic achievement over comfort or a strong oppositional attitude. The return students, on the other hand, drew different conclusions, and ended up either lowering their own expectations—'cooling off'—or rejecting the transfer students' concept of the achievement ideology. In either case, returning to an all-black, inner-city high school does not appear

to be the way for these students to make the most of themselves, but rather the preferred choice in a no-win situation.

Racial Attitudes and School Choice

City, transfer, and return students were all aware that the status of African-Americans is at the bottom of the social hierarchy. And there was some evidence that they had internalized some of these beliefs in their fear of competing with white students and their criticisms of all-black schools. In this way they share a group *habitus*; but this common understanding of how blacks are viewed by the rest of society plays itself out differently between and within the three groups of students.

CITY STUDENTS—SAFELY SEGREGATED
The extent to which racial attitudes and fear of competing with whites affected the city students' perceptions of the transfer programme and the suburban schools is encapsulated in the concern of one city student, Sabrina, who was afraid of not understanding what is *not* taught in the suburban schools. Her comment suggests that Sabrina, like the lower-class French students studied by Bourdieu and Passeron (1979), senses she lacks the kind of cultural capital rewarded in suburban schools. Sabrina's school choice (or non-choice), like most of the city students, is informed by her sense that she will not be able to keep up with white students.

Leander's assertion that the county schools are just taking city students to 'tear them down' and 'keep people under control' demonstrates his views on white dominance in American society. In fact, his critique of black–white relations—a black separatist ideology he shares with his mother—coloured every angle of his perspective on the transfer programme. When asked what he thought of black students who go to county schools, he replied that the transfer students are 'confused'—'They let themselves be programmed by people.'

Most of the city students, however, said black students who want to go to county schools were 'doing the right thing' by transferring. 'I have no disagreement with kids who go to the county. They should have the freedom to go wherever they want to,' said

Sabrina. Other responses to the question of whether transfer students were doing the right thing contained hints of defensiveness: 'If they think they can handle it, they should go,' said Veronica. 'They're just trying to show off. They are not better,' said Cherrine.

When asked the more general questions, 'What are the benefits of going to an all-black school?' and 'What are the benefits of going to an integrated school?' the responses of city students revealed that while they may feel far more comfortable there, society has also taught them that these all-black schools lack the cultural capital associated with whiter, wealthier schools. Thus, seven of the city students responded to questions about the benefits of an all-black school with a criticism of either black schools or blacks in general.

According to Veronica, 'There isn't any benefit—any benefit at all; it's just an all-black school.' Likewise, Corey said he really could not think of any benefits. Karen said that all-black schools were a good idea because when black students are around white students they pick on them. 'When they get around white people, they get worse. . . . I'm a good person, the rest are like animals.'

Trenton noted that there was 'nothing' good about all-black schools—'there's lots of fights over silly stuff.' Gina said, 'When us black people get together, we don't know how to act. We try to appear more than ourselves when with our own kind.' According to Cherrine, in all-black schools, 'The teachers care, but the students just don't want to learn—they be carrying on and partying too much.'

Only two of the city students had anything remotely positive to say about all-black schools. Leander said there were fewer problems with racial tension in an all-black school, and Michael said that students who attend all-black schools have a 'good chance of getting into a nice college and getting some financial aid.'

Furthermore, two of the city students' responses to the question concerning the benefits of going to an integrated school denoted a sense of racial inferiority and insecurity. Sabrina, for instance, said the benefit of going to an integrated school is that 'Whites are more mature. Black students play in the halls, skip class.' Anjeanette stated that she would like to go to a 'mixed' school, but added, 'I don't know how they would react to me.'

Guided by a view of race that leads them to believe that black students are more unruly and less mature than white students, city students talk of being more hesitant and even fearful of interaction with the more mature and well-behaved white students. Clearly these concepts have affected their school choices.

TRANSFER STUDENTS—WHITE IS RIGHT

As noted above, not one of the transfer parents or students actually visited a county district before listing the three top choices on the transfer application. In fact, discussions of the school-choice process never include the degree to which one county school district might better serve the educational needs of a particular transfer student. While this finding does not say much about the effectiveness of the educational market-place, it does suggest that school preferences are frequently defined more by the race and social class of the students within them than by the academic offerings in one school versus another. Transfer parents and students appear to have automatically assumed that any of the predominantly white suburban schools were better than any of the all-black city schools. Their decision to transfer is also guided by their perception of the superiority of the white students; but, unlike city students, transfer students believe they can attain a higher status.

In terms of black–white interactions, transfer students tended to be much less fearful of whites and less likely to suggest that they themselves feel inferior to whites than their counterparts who attend city schools. But this does not mean that transfer students possessed a greater sense of black pride, or that they held a higher opinion of blacks in general. In fact, like the city students, many of the transfer students find fault with the behaviour of other blacks—either those in the city schools or their fellow-black-transfer students. In fact, some of these upwardly mobile transfer students suggest that one of the reasons they attend predominantly white schools is to acquire the white and wealthy cultural capital so valued in our society.

When asked what she considered to be the benefits of going to an integrated school, Cleo said she thought 'white kids can offer you more'. She then cited the example of a white girl who had let a close friend use her car when she went off to college. 'If it was a black person they would probably let the car sit there.' Cleo explained that she did not want to go to an all-black school because black people were always trying to prove a point by saying something that they knew they could have kept to themselves, and blacks stereotyped each other because of the way they look or dress.

Seven of the twelve transfer students responded to the question concerning the 'benefits' of going to an all-black school negatively by citing the problems they would encounter. Typical answers included 'more trouble', 'gangs fighting', and 'I would not learn as much.' Only three of the transfer students actually cited potential benefits of going to an all-black school: Toya said she would be more comfortable; Tracy said, 'It wouldn't be so boring'; and Antonnie stated that she would 'be able to learn more about black people and black history.'

When asked about the benefits of attending an integrated school, eight of the twelve transfer students gave extremely positive answers. Five of these eight stated that they could meet people of different races and backgrounds. According to Virgil, 'I get to know people, friends who will get into the business world.' Derrick said that there was less peer pressure to get in trouble in an integrated school, and Charlesetta and Tracy cited academic factors—that the teachers 'teach more' in integrated schools. Three of the transfer students said they could not think of any benefits or that they had never really thought about it. Only Toya gave a negative response:

In some things they (the integrated schools) are much better than a city school—learning techniques are better. But I mean what's the purpose? For whites and blacks to get along? White students keep it separate cause in the beginning they had control over everything.

That students who choose integrated over segregated schools are less fearful of interaction with whites and see more academic and social benefits in attending a predominantly white school than do black students who remain in all-black schools is not surprising, but it does imply a sorting process between choosers and non-choosers that is related to racial attitudes and students' willingness to interact with people of other races. Unlike the city students of this study, and unlike the lower-class French students who withdraw from the competition for a higher-status education because of their *habitus* (Bourdieu and

Passeron 1979), the transfer students act more like MacLeod's (1987) 'brothers' or Willis's (1977) 'earoles'. They seek to separate themselves from members of their own race who signify the lower status of their group.

Some of what the transfer students believed to be better about the county schools had to do with real, objective information on what they were learning or what the teachers and administrators expected from students. But much of what was perceived to be better about a county school had to do with the higher status of the students, the cultural capital that they would learn there, and a racial attitude that said, if it is black and in the city, it's not as good as a county school.

RETURN STUDENTS—COOLING OFF

The racial attitudes of the return students, like every aspect of this diverse group, are difficult to define. Some put down members of their own race and want to separate themselves from all-black schools and the students within them. Still, return students as a group tended to report more fear of whites—or at least fear of competition with whites—than transfer students, and in this regard they more closely resemble the city students. Their anxiety about competing with white students, however, was more sophisticated than that of the city students, due to their first-hand experiences.

Karen, a shy but perceptive young woman, said that she went to her county school with high expectations because of 'all the good things' she had heard about the school—'how people are friendly', adding that she was immediately surprised by the coldness of the white students. 'If you asked them where was the classroom, they act like they did not want to tell you,' she said.

Karen also explained subtle ways in which the teachers made her feel more uncomfortable in the county school:

So basically, when the teacher was teaching and they would make an example about something . . . like they would say something like that was out in the county, and I wouldn't know what they were talking about. But the white students would, because they are out there . . . you know like a shopping mall or something, and I wouldn't know what they were talking about.

Although Bourdieu and Passeron's theory of cultural capital entails a much richer definition of culture, when applied to American suburban teenagers the knowledge of shopping malls or retail outlets is valuable shared knowledge. If these stores and their expensive merchandise symbolize wealth, familiarity with their location is a form of cultural capital. Similarly, the use of this shared knowledge between the county teachers and white, county students parallels the French teacher's validation of the upper-class students' cultural capital, which leads to higher-status students gaining more self-confidence and to lower-status students feeling less capable.

Karen recalled other classroom situations in which she felt uncomfortable, like the time her English teacher showed a film that 'was like putting blacks down', or when she gave a speech in her public speaking class.

I was the only black, and . . . you had to get up and speak in front of the class. And I got so I felt real uncomfortable because of my speech. All the white kids you know just stared at me. And when like the speech was over you try to be nice and applause for somebody—they would not applause for me.

Feeling that the white students rejected her and people of her colour was reason enough for Karen to remove herself from the higher-status school, despite the objections of her mother, who was sceptical about the poor treatment of black students in county schools.

Still, return students' fear, distrust, and even resistance towards whites does not lead them to adopt a strong pro-black stance. Only four of the thirteen students said they could think of a possible benefit of attending an all-black school and, of these, three students spoke of the familiarity of the people who went to the school—'I know most of the people up there,' 'people are more outgoing; I feel more comfortable', and so on. Only Christian cited as a benefit the fact that an all-black school dealt with black culture: 'You're around your own culture, your own people—you can keep up with things and the trends in your neighbourhood.'

Six of the return students made derogatory comments when asked about the benefits of an all-black school. For example, Bruce, who was not allowed to continue at his county high school, said, 'I hate black schools . . . I don't hate them, just don't like being with same people—acting out and getting written up by teachers.' Durand, who was 'put out' of the county school for fighting, said, 'None [no

benefits to an all-black school] . . . it's a downfall. Classes with black students and white teachers—don't want to learn.' And Reginald, who was also 'put out' of his county school, noted that there was 'nothing challenging' about all-black schools. 'I'm not saying that black people are dumb, but most don't know shit. They all want to go sell drugs all their life.'

This deprecation of other African-Americans by three students who were basically thrown out of their county schools indicates that their anger and resistance toward the white educators and students in the county has not been translated into an appreciation of those they left behind when they made the initial choice to attend a county school. These and other comments suggest that the all-black city schools and the students within them serve to remind return students of their own failure to attain higher social status by succeeding in the mostly white county schools.

Despite their negative experiences in county schools, nine of the thirteen return students responded positively to the question concerning the benefits of an integrated school. Four of these students spoke of the teaching and the quality of education in the county schools, three referred to meeting different people in the integrated schools, one student said there was more freedom in the integrated schools, and one student simply said she enjoyed it.

The racial attitudes of the return students imply that, like the transfer students, they prefer mostly white schools to mostly black ones. And, like the transfer students, much of what they perceived to be better about county schools had to do with the higher status of the students and their cultural capital. Hence, the return students' first school choice—to transfer to a county school—was at least partly affected by their racial attitudes. Paradoxically, their negative experiences in the predominantly white schools appear to have done little to change these views.

Implications

The impact of human agency on the school-choice process incorporates far more student and parent attitudes and perceptions than can ever be accurately predicted. Policy-makers must understand that students and parents do not act monolithically, responding to changes in the structure of the educational system in a predetermined, goal-oriented fashion.

The less-than-systematic responses to structural changes will cut across racial, ethnic, and class boundaries, although students from white and higher SES families will no doubt be in a position to take greater advantage of the educational market. After all, they will have the most resources and the fewest reasons to resist the dominant school culture. And while both race and class affect students' *habitus*, and therefore the way they perceive school choice opportunities, not all low-income minority students and parents will react to choice options in the same way. Some will actively seek out schools that they believe will help them attain higher status; others who fear competition or failure in a higher-status school and those who have lost faith in the educational system will most likely 'choose' not to choose.

What will happen to these children in an educational free-market predicated on the existence of both winners and losers? Who will advocate for them? Who will respond to their sense of injustice or their need for the security and cultural familiarity of a neighbourhood school? These are important policy questions. In a truly deregulated system, there is no guarantee and no safety-net for these students.

Research on the relationship between culture and human agency and how students and parents mediate this relationship through their *habitus* should alert policy-makers and educators that we know very little about how individuals react to structural changes. To the extent that we can craft school-choice policies that are inclusive rather than exclusive, policies which make sure every student and parent must choose a school, we will minimize the potential negative effect of exclusive school-choice programmes on students like Sabrina, Veronica, and Reginald.

Notes

1. The type of school-choice policy proposals I am referring to are those calling for deregulated private-school-choice plans in which families compete in the free market for seats in desirable schools. These deregulated plans are quite different in scope and potential effect from the more structured-choice plans, restricted to the public schools or those limited to low-income students only, as in Milwaukee.

2. Bourdieu's work has focused on strictly class-based *habitus*, which reflects the more classist French society. But when the concept is applied to the study of schooling in the US, researchers such as MacLeod (1987) have employed the concept of *habitus* as it relates to racial and ethnic group identities.

3. The terms *suburban* and *county* are used interchangeably throughout this paper because in the St Louis metropolitan area, St Louis County contains all of the suburbs participating in this desegregation plan.

4. The term *guardian* is used loosely here, not in its official legal sense, but rather to describe whoever was taking care of the students at the time of the interview. In every case in this study, a grandparent filled this role when the parent was not present.

5. Returning transfer students are rarely out-and-out expelled from their county schools. More frequently, they receive a number of suspensions of increasing lengths—a 10-day suspension, followed by a 30-day suspension, followed by a 90-day suspension—until they have missed so much school work that it is no longer feasible for them to catch up. This is what is meant by being 'put out' or 'pushed out' of a county school.

References

Apple, M. (1985), *Education and Power* (Boston: ARK Paperbacks).

Becker, G. (1986), 'The Economic Approach to Human Behavior', in Elster, J. (ed.), *Rational Choice* (Oxford: Basil Blackwell).

Bourdieu, P. (1971), 'Intellectual Field and Creative Project', in Young, M. K. D. (ed.) *Knowledge and Control: New Directions for the Sociology of Education* (London: Collier Macmillan).

—— (1977), 'Cultural Reproduction and Social Reproduction', in Karabel, J., and Halsey, A. H. (eds.), *Power and Ideology in Education* (New York: Oxford Univ. Press).

—— and Passeron, J.-C. (1977), *Reproduction in Education, Society and Culture*, transl. Richard Nice (London Beverly Hills: Sage).

—— (1979), *The Inheritors: French Students and Their Relations to Culture*, transl. Richard Nice (Chicago: Univ. of Chicago Press).

Bowles, S., and Herbert, G. (1976), *Schooling in Capitalist America* (New York: Basic Books).

DiMaggio, P. (1979), 'Review Essay: On Pierre Bourdieu', *American Journal of Sociology*, 84/6: 1460–74.

——and John Mohr (1985), 'Cultural Capital, Educational Attainment, and Marital Selection', *American Journal of Sociology*, 90/6: 1231–61.

Epstein, J. L. (1987), 'Parent Involvement: What Research Says to Administrators,' *Education and Urban Society*, 19/2: 119–36.

Everhart, R. B. (1983), *Reading, Writing, and Resistance* (Boston: Routledge and Kegan Paul).

Fine, M. (1991), *Framing Dropouts* (Albany, NY: SUNY Press).

Harker, R. R. (1984), 'On Reproduction, Habitus and Education', *British Journal of Sociology*, 5/2: 117–27.

Henig, J. R. (March, 1990), 'Choice in Public Schools: An Analysis of Transfer Requests among Magnet Schools', *Social Science Quarterly*, 71/1: 69–82.

Holloway, S. D., and Fuller, B. (October, 1992), 'The Great Child-Care Experiment: What are the Lessons for School Improvement?' *Educational Researcher*, 21/7: 12–19.

Lareau, A. (1989), *Home Advantage* (New York: Falmer Press).

Lissitz, R. W. (January, 1992), *Assessment of Student Performance and Attitude: St. Louis Metropolitan Area Court Ordered Desegregation Effort* (St. Louis, Missouri: Voluntary Interdistrict Coordinating Council).

Maddaus, J. (1990), 'Parental Choice of Schools: What Parents Think and Do', in Cazden, C. B. (ed.), *Review of Research in Education* (Washington DC: American Educational Research Association).

MacLeod, J. (1987), *Ain't No Making It* (Boulder, Colo.: Westview Press).

Ogbu, J. (1988), 'Class Stratification, Racial Stratification, and Schooling', in Weis, L. (ed.), *Class, Race, and Gender in American Education* (Albany: State Univ. of New York).

Robbins, D. (1991), *The Work of Pierre Bourdieu* (Boulder, Colo.: Westview Press).

Stevenson, R. B., and Ellsworth, J. (1993), 'Dropouts and the Silencing of Critical Voices', in Weis, L., and Fine, M. (eds.), *Beyond Silenced Voices: Class, Race, and Gender in United States Schools* (Albany, NY: State Univ. of New York Press).

Wells, A. S. (1991), 'Choice in Education: Examining the Evidence on Equity', *Teachers College Record*, 93/1: 156–73.

——(1993), 'The Sociology of School Choice: Why Some Win and Others Lose in the Educational Marketplace', in Rasell, E., and Rothstein, R. (eds.), *School Choice: Examining the Evidence* (Washington DC: Economic Policy Institute).

Willis, P. (1977), *Learning to Labor* (New York: Columbia Univ. Press).

29

Choice, Competition, and Segregation: An Empirical Analysis of a New Zealand Secondary School Market, 1990–93

Sietske Waslander and Martin Thrupp

Introduction

In recent years the introduction of market solutions to educational problems has become the subject of intense debate (Brown 1990; Chubb and Moe 1990; Maddaus 1990; Clune and Witte 1990; Lauder 1991; Hogan 1992; Ball 1993; Marginson 1993). This highly theoretical debate now needs to be advanced through empirical research which is able to test the various hypotheses which have been developed. The marketization of education is a relatively recent phenomenon and there have been few detailed studies of the actual operation of educational markets. Some aspects of marketization have been addressed in empirical studies, especially parental choice (Adler and Raab 1988; Echols *et al.* 1990; Willms and Echols 1992) and the clash of professional educational values with those of the market (Ball 1990; Bowe *et al.* 1992). However, to our knowledge there has not been any research to date which analyses the outcomes of choice and competition for parents, students and schools within a specific market context. This paper reports part of a research programme in New Zealand which is attempting to examine comprehensively the effects of the market in education in this way.[1]

Markets need to be studied in context because the outcomes generated by educational markets will be determined by both the formal properties of a market and informal arrangements within that market. Formal properties of a market are typically established by legislation. Informal arrangements within a market are created by the actors, in this case especially schools, who seek to change or modify the nature of the competition which confronts them. Schools may do this either because market forces conflict with educational principles and practice or to gain individual or collective advantage. Our view of the informal workings of the market is derived from a key insight in the sociology of economics (Nohria and Eccles 1992) that market behaviour can only be understood in terms of the specific cultural contexts in which markets are located and the practices of cooperation and collusion which emerge from those contexts. We can hypothesize, therefore, that the outcomes of any specific market will be determined by the combination of formal properties and informal arrangements within the market. We call this combination of formal properties, informal arrangements and outcomes the *lived* market.[2]

This study documents the construction of a lived market and examines its impact on two related issues: (i) parental and school *choice*, and (ii) the size and composition of *school intakes*. These two issues, which have been extensively canvassed in the literature, underlie the key questions of whether the marketization of education will promote or retard equality of opportunity and concurrently promote or retard school effectiveness.

Debate over *choice* has turned primarily on questions about which parents will gain from choice policies. Proponents of market policies

From *Journal of Education Policy*, 10 (1995), 1–26. Reprinted with permission.

often argue that choice empowers those traditionally disadvantaged in education to escape what has been called the 'iron cage of zoning' which traps them in inferior, often inner-city ghetto, schools (Coons and Sugarman 1978; Coleman 1990). Market critics, on the other hand, usually argue that choice will be limited to parents with greater material capital and appropriate cultural capital who are able to capitalize on their income and knowledge in exercising choice (Brown 1990). The evidence thus far suggests that the critics are right: that it is those with the material and cultural capital who are most likely to take advantage of 'choice' (Willms and Echols 1992).

Another dimension of the debate over choice turns on the question of who in fact does the choosing in an educational market, parents or schools? Here the key question is whether or not 'popular' schools would take in traditionally disadvantaged students. One reason they might note is that, as Ball (1992) has noted, disadvantaged students are likely to lower the overall credential achievement of the school. Since the success of schools in the market is influenced by their credential success, it goes against the logic of the market that popular schools would take such students. The evidence supports Ball's argument: it seems that in schools where demand outstrips places available, schools choose on the basis of socio-economic status because this acts as a signal of likely achievement (Moore and Davenport 1990).

The issue of the impact of market policies on the size and composition of *school intakes* has also generated considerable debate. Will market policies redistribute the raw numbers of students between schools so that the rolls of popular schools rise while those in unpopular schools fall? Along with changes in intake size, changes in the composition of school intakes may also warrant concern for two reasons. One is that, since Dewey (1916), there has been a view shared by social democrats, at least until recently, that schools have an important role to play in creating the foundations for democracy by bringing together children from different social and ethnic backgrounds so that in learning together they can also foster the attitudes and understandings necessary to live in a democracy. Increased between-school segregation of students from different backgrounds would clearly threaten this perceived role.

The second reason why changes in the composition of school intakes may be important relates to the possible effect of intake composition on student achievement. There is a body of evidence which suggests that the socio-economic composition of school intakes—or what we call school mix may have a significant contextual effect on student achievement. Working-class students in particular may be advantaged by attending schools with a reasonable number of middle-class students (Thrupp, forthcoming). However, the idea of a school-mix effect is contested by proponents of the marketization of education who argue that, rather than school mix, it is school organization which is the key to school effectiveness and educational outcomes (Chubb and Moe 1990).

Clearly, then, there is much at stake in the debate over the effects of educational markets. In this study we test these rival hypotheses in the context of a secondary school market in a New Zealand city we call Greencity. Initially we provide background information on the formal policy changes which have signalled the development of an educational market in the New Zealand context, along with details of the sample and methodology used in the study. We are able to chart the flow of students between schools prior to the inception of the market (1990) as well as through two phases in the establishment of the lived market: the first year of the market (1991) in which rationing to oversubscribed schools was initially undertaken through balloting, and the two subsequent years (1992 and 1993), when oversubscribed schools have been able to establish enrolment schemes which effectively enable them to choose which students they will accept.

We then examine the lived market by addressing three key questions. First we ask *'Which parents are exercising choice and what kind of choices are they making?'*. We answer this question by identifying those students, in terms of parental social class and ethnicity, who do not attend the schools for which they would have been zoned prior to 1991 and trace them to their out-of-zone school destination. This approach will show whether the parents who have gained by choice in this market are those already advantaged or those who may have been trapped in the 'iron cage of zoning'.

The second question addresses the impact of market policies on the student composition of schools; we ask: '*Does choice generate polarizing or integrating tendencies in the socioeconomic and ethnic composition of schools?*'. In this section we look at changes in between-school segregation which occurred over the period 1990–93. The key aim here is to disentangle the complex relationship between neighbourhood and school segregation in terms of socio-economic status (SES) and ethnicity. If we are to assess the impact of choice on school segregation we need to measure the degree to which schools are more or less segregated in comparison with the neighbourhoods they serve. The comparison of residental and school segregation is in aggregate terms. However, if a difference between the two types of segregation is shown to exist, this then licenses further investigation to see how choice operates to either increase or reduce the effects of residential segregation. These analyses also bring us somewhat closer to providing an account of whether schools or parents are choosing and on what basis these choices are being made.

The work of Bowe *et al.* (1992) suggests that schools are not passive in the face of market competition. The third and final question we therefore examine is: '*How have schools responded to their respective situations under market competition?*'. In order to provide a clearer picture of the impact of the marketization of education on our sample schools, we answer this question by supplementing our analysis of school rolls with qualitative data taken from interviews with school principals. Their accounts highlight the way in which the lived market incorporates informal arrangements and suggests that there are various kinds of responses schools can make when confronted with competition. Broadly speaking we can classify four different kind of responses: (i) overt responses in terms of marketing; (ii) non-responses or avoiding decisions which schools judge their local market would find unacceptable; (iii) political responses which seek to change the rules or terms on which schools compete; and (iv) networked responses which involve collusion or 'co-operation'. These responses have important consequences for whether and how schools survive in a competitive market. As our case studies will illustrate, examples of all these responses were evident in our sample.

Introducing Market Competition: The New Zealand Context

From the 1950s until the late 1980s, the New Zealand government played a steadily increasing role in determining urban secondary school enrolment schemes (McCulloch 1991; Rae 1990). Officially, zoning policies were geared towards what was seen at the time as the continuing development of a largely egalitarian society. Yet, both by intent and default, zoning policies upheld selective educational practices amongst schools and supported the intensification of between-school socio-economic and ethnic segregation.[3]

In 1988 the Picot Task Force signalled a market approach to secondary school enrolments by recommending the abolition of zoning on the grounds that it 'diminish(ed) the autonomy of schools' (Picot *et al.* 1988: 17). However, the reforms that followed (Lange 1988) retained a measure of state control over enrolment policy. Maximum rolls were set for all schools although these were based on a very liberal interpretation of the capacity of schools in order to encourage market competition. Zones were retained by schools where there was an excess of demand over capacity. Local students were guaranteed attendance through home zones while 'out of zone' enrolments were decided by ballot.

The Tomorrow's Schools reforms only had one year of operation, 1991, before being superseded by reforms under the 1991 Education Amendment Act following a change of government. These later reforms were intended to reduce state involvement in enrolment policy and open the way to intensified school competition. Home zones were abolished and enrolment schemes are now only put in place where schools are at serious risk of overcrowding. The details of enrolment schemes are currently left up to the discretion of individual oversubscribed schools although they must not breach the requirements of the Race Relations Act (1971), the Human Rights Commission Act (1977) and the Bill of Rights Act (1990). The introduction of school-chosen enrolment schemes has a potentially decisive impact on the lived market because it allows oversubscribed schools to choose their students. Since there is no compulsion to take local students, the stakes here for schools are high. In case it is schools with high- and middle-class intakes that are oversubscribed, and selection is more class-based than achievement-based, it could be predicted that enrolment schemes serve the function of exacerbating existing inequalities between schools. In that case the market proponents' assumption of a level playing field is cast into further doubt and their critics' view that marketization is simply designed to increase the privilege of the already privileged is confirmed.

Sample and Methodology

Our study examines the market positions of 11 state and integrated (Catholic) secondary schools in Greencity.[4] The 11 schools include some from the central city area and others from a wedge of the city which includes both middle- and working-class suburbs. In principle, the schools in this study can be seen as comprising a local market because, although the suburbs are some miles from the city centre, proximity to public transport does afford the opportunity for students to travel in both directions. This group of schools, therefore, allows us to test the polarization hypothesis by seeing whether the creation of 'choice' produces a domino effect with the more advantaged in each class group gravitating closer to the élite schools. Approximately 80 per cent of all students attending schools in the centre of Greencity attended the schools in our study while for the suburban region we had a higher coverage of about 90 per cent. The more comprehensive coverage in the suburbs usefully allows us to track shifts from one school to another. As we shall see, this is a key requirement for uncovering the overt and covert processes of an educational market.

The study involved developing a dataset on the first year (3rd Form) student intakes in the 11 secondary schools over the four years just prior to, during, and following the dezoning reforms (1990–93). The principals of the 11 schools were also interviewed over 1992–93: we draw on these interviews for the case studies in the latter part of this paper. For the (8870) students in the quantitative dataset the following information was collected: occupations of both parents or caregivers, ethnicity, gender and residential address. In a limited number of cases, particularly where students

had already left school, not all of this information was available. However, the only real difficulty we struck was gathering reliable occupational data in some schools. This problem was addressed on a school-by-school basis in ways that eventually secured adequate data.[5] Occupations were coded into the most recent version of the Elley and Irving Socio-economic Index (Irving 1991).[6] Coding of residential addresses was based on a division into 15 geographical areas, drawn along the boundaries of former school zones. Where these zones were particularly large, the areas were further subdivided.[7]

Table 29.1. Basic descriptors of the students in the schools, 1990–93

3rd-form intake	1990	1991	1992	1993
Total numbers	2017	2015	1971	1929
Ethnicity (%)				
Maori	13	14	14	12
Pacific Island	15	13	13	13
Pakeha	66	67	66	68
Mean SES	3.12	3.66	3.29	3.40
Unemployed (%)	7	5	7	7

Some overall characteristics of the students in the quantitative dataset are given in Table 29.1. An assumption that underlies our study is that changes in school composition did not result from substantive demographic shifts. Although we have no independent demographic data to justify this assumption, it can be seen that the overall characteristics of the first-year intakes for the 11 schools remained stable throughout the period studied. The total number of students dropped only slightly over the years, following the national trend (Ministry of Education 1992). Proportions of Maori, Pacific Island Polynesian and Pakeha[8] students also remained very stable. The socio-economic background of students fluctuates marginally over the period but the level of parental unemployment was almost constant. The general picture then is one of stability from year to year which makes it most likely that any compositional changes experienced by schools were primarily the result of between-school processes rather than underlying demographic shifts.

Choice in Greencity

The first question to be examined is, '*Which*

parents are exercising choice and what kind of choices are they making?. Proponents of market policies in education argue that it is parents who choose schools, thereby acting as the driving force for educational progress. Critics, however, make the point that it is the schools with strong market positions which have market power on their side. The data reported here do not allow us to address the issue of whether it is schools or parents who make the choice. Rather our data must be seen as the outcome of both parental choice and school selection: we call this *school choice*.

To track down changes in patterns of school choice, a distinction needed to be drawn between local and non-local schools according to the area students live in. On an area-by-area basis we categorized the different schools as being either *local, adjacent* or *distant*. Schools were considered *local* when students lived within the traditional zone boundaries of the school. Schools which were clearly not the local school and for which travel was required were considered *adjacent*. To get to *distant* schools, students bypassed their local school and at least one other in a way that involved considerable travel.

The percentages of students who attended local, adjacent or distant schools are given in Table 29.2. The figures for 1990 confirm that zoning did not always prevent students from attending out-of-zone schools: as many as one in five students did not attend their local school.

Table 29.2. Percentage of students by locality of school

Locality	1990	1991	1992	1993
Local	78	69	71	71
Adjacent	12	20	20	18
Distant	10	11	9	11

Looking at the patterns since 1991 we note that the majority of students attend their local school regardless of the reforms. The question of whether these numbers testify to considerable satisfaction with the local school or to a lack of alternatives must be left unanswered at this stage. The percentage of students travelling to a distant school has remained very stable and is apparently hardly affected by dezoning. The flow that has increased over the years is the one from local to adjacent schools thereby indicating that

schools close to one another are facing intensified competition from their neighbours.[9]

ETHNIC ATTENDANCE PATTERNS

An ethnic breakdown of attendance patterns (Table 29.3) shows that in the last year of zoning the figures are fairly similar for Maori and Pacific Island Polynesian students, but Pakeha students attend distant schools more often. After the abolition of zoning, there are few changes with regard to attendance of distant schools. However, the number of students attending adjacent schools has grown, in particular for Maori and Pacific Island Polynesian students. But the inference that it is Maori and Pacific Island Polynesian students who have benefited most from the changes would be incorrect. The dynamics behind exit out of the local schools will come into focus when the socio-economic background of the students is also taken into account.

Table 29.3. Percentage of students by ethnicity and locality of school

Ethnicity/locality	1990	1991	1992	1993
Maori				
Local	82	71	75	69
Adjacent	12	24	21	25
Distant	6	5	4	6
Pacific Island				
Local	87	72	65	67
Adjacent	10	22	32	28
Distant	3	6	4	5
Pakeha				
Local	75	69	71	72
Adjacent	12	17	18	16
Distant	13	14	11	12

SOCIO–ECONOMIC ATTENDANCE PATTERNS

The privileged nature of school choice under zoning is shown in Table 29.4 by a gradually higher SES rating for students as they travel further from home to school. It was mainly the well off who managed to send their children to other than local schools under zoning.

Table 29.4. Mean SES of students by locality of school

Locality	1990	1991	1992	1993
Local	3.20	3.22	3.26	3.19
Adjacent	3.02	3.27	3.40	3.36
Distant	2.70	2.59	2.51	2.56

However, it is what happened after zoning was abolished that is of more importance here.

Who has benefited from greater parental choice? Taking the figures at face value, local attendance seems to have remained stable over time while changes took place between the background of students going to adjacent and distant schools. In combination with Table 29.2 these results are puzzling as it was shown that changes in numbers of students occurred between local and adjacent schools. It is likely therefore that we are dealing with different underlying processes which counteract each other.

Looking at the figures it would seem that students going to adjacent schools appear to come from families with a lower SES than students going to their local school. Results like this have also been found elsewhere (Williams et al. 1983). Proponents of marketization might therefore claim that those who benefit most from dezoning are the deprived. Yet the method applied above has come under attack for obfuscating the real outcomes of dezoning through analysing data at a level which is too highly aggregated. Maddaus (1990), for instance, argues that the more pertinent issue to be addressed is whether there are ethnic or SES differences 'in the propensity to pursue enrolment options *within the same attendance area*' (Maddaus 1990: 284). This argument is important for it offers a lead to unpack the different underlying processes that lie behind the figures in Table 29.4.

Our data allow us to take neighbourhood characteristics into account and to monitor trends closely both within and between suburbs. In order to focus on enrolment processes for a given attendance area, we relate the student's SES to that of the neighbourhood the student lives in. The SES of neighbourhoods is computed on a year–by–year basis to ensure greater accuracy. A positive score now refers to students who are relatively well off in comparison with their neighbourhood; a negative score means the student's SES is lower than that of the neighbourhood as a whole.

Using this adjusted measure, the pattern is confirmed for 1990 (Table 29.5). During zoning, students going to non-local school came most often from families who were relatively well off. However the pattern for subsequent years contrasts sharply with the picture painted above. The results show clearly that differences between students attending local or adjacent schools increased after dezoning. Whereas students attending an adjacent

school tended to come from families who were relatively well off compared with the area in which they lived, local schools were populated by students who were relatively worse off compared with their neighbourhoods. The relative SES of students going to distant schools remained very stable over the years, again indicating that little seems to have changed for students travelling long distances from home to school.

By taking neighbourhood characteristics into account an ecological fallacy is avoided, and a very different process of socio–economic exit is shown. The mechanism behind school choice within each area becomes more transparent: it is the relatively well off who are more likely to send their children to adjacent or distant schools, while those relatively worse off are most likely to send their children to their local school.

Table 29.5. Mean of relative SES of students by locality of school

Locality	1990	1991	1992	1993
Local	-0.12	-0.20	-0.18	-0.19
Adjacent	0.14	0.17	0.29	0.24
Distant	0.65	0.65	0.67	0.63

Relative SES refers to a student's own SES substracted from that student's neighbourhood SES.

Table 29.6. Mean of relative SES of students by ethnicity and locality of school

Ethnicity/locality	1990	1991	1992	1993
Maori				
Local	-0.60	-1.06	-0.97	-1.13
Adjacent	-0.09	-0.43	-0.25	-0.07
Distant	.35	.70	.14	.43
Pacific Island				
Local	-0.46	-0.73	-0.87	-0.83
Adjacent	-0.11	-0.14	-0.25	-0.14
Distant	.80	.55	.94	.48
Pakeha				
Local	.22	.10	.15	.09
Adjacent	.23	.38	.41	.35
Distant	.51	.62	.72	.64

The method of using a student's own SES compared with the neighbourhood SES can also be applied to examine the SES dimension of ethnic attendance patterns. Although a process of SES exit is apparent for all students, it is further accentuated for Maori and Pacific Island Polynesian students (Table 29.6). The conclusion is plain: choice of non-local schools is primarily dependent on the socio-economic background of students with the relatively better off families, regardless of ethnicity, sending their children out of local schools.

Between-School Segregation in Greencity

Changes in attendance patterns may have implications for the mix of the intake in the respective schools. The question it raises is: *'Does choice generate polarizing or integrating tendencies in the socio-economic and ethnic composition of schools?'*. We examine this question by looking at changes in socio-economic and ethnic segregation between schools.

Our measures of between-school segregation need mentioning at the outset. We use the most commonly used measure for segregation: the dissimilarity index (D).[10] D is interpreted as the difference between the distributions for two defined groups, for example high and low SES students.[11] Where all schools have exactly the same composition as each other, D has a minimum value of 0. Conversely, when D reaches its maximum value of 100 there are no mixed schools: each school is attended by either high or low SES students. D can also be read as the proportion of students from one group that would need to change schools to establish the same distribution over schools as students from the other group.

Quite clearly, the way groups are defined will have an impact on the outcomes of the measures. To provide a more sensitive analysis, therefore, we use two different groupings for both ethnic and socio-economic segregation. Ethnic segregation is looked at by comparing the distribution of (i) Maori and Pakeha students, and (ii) Pacific Island Polynesian and Pakeha students attending the schools.[12] Socio-economic segregation is studied by (iii) noting the difference in distribution between high and low SES students,[13] and (iv) comparing the distribution of students from families living on a benefit with students from families where at least one parent is in paid employment. The advantage of (iv) is that it specifically addresses the issue of parental unemployment whereas (iii) does not.

As the distinction between ethnic and socio-economic segregation is not clear-cut,

one important question to be asked is whether results should be interpreted in terms of ethnic differences or whether socio-economic differences between ethnic groups are the real issue. In an attempt to unravel racial/cultural and socio-economic factors, we divided students into three SES strata and then computed dissimilarity indices for ethnic segregation for each stratum separately.[14] For both Maori and Pacific Island Polynesian students the indices dropped as SES increased so that the difference between, for example, high SES Maori and Pakeha students was less than that between low SES Maori and Pakeha students. These outcomes indicate that at least part of the ethnic segregation between schools must be interpreted in terms of the social class of the students. More will be said about the relative importance of class and ethnicity later.

SCHOOL SEGREGATION

We begin by documenting the magnitude of ethnic and socio-economic segregation between schools in 1990 *prior* to the removal of zoning which took effect at the beginning of the 1991 school year. We then examine the changes that have occurred since. We look first at ethnic segregation and then at social class segregation.

Dissimilarity indices for ethnic segregation are listed in Table 29.7. From the 1990 figures it is evident that there was school segregation between Pakeha students and both Maori and Pacific Island Polynesian students under zoning. The table also shows that Pacific Island Polynesian students were more concentrated in particular schools than Maori. In order to

Table 29. 7. Dissimilarity indices for ethnic segregation between the 11 schools

Indicator	1990	1991	1992	1993
Maori/Pakeha	46.2	47.0	39.1	53.0
Pacific Island/Pakeha	52.0	52.5	56.8	53.5

make any comments about the amount of segregation we need material for comparison. In the High School Achievement study, Coleman *et al.* (1982) use a much debated standardized segregation index (r).[15] For the public education system in America in 1980, r reaches 0.49 for Blacks and Whites and 0.30 for Hispanics and Whites. Applying the same method to our 1990 data shows an r of 0.25 for

Pakeha and Maori students, and 0.39 for Pakeha and Pacific Island Polynesian students. Although these values are somewhat lower than those reported by Coleman *et al.* (1982), we would have to conclude that ethnic segregation between Greencity schools under zoning was substantial.

Following the abolition of zoning, D for both groups rises over the years 1991–93 indicating increasing ethnic segregation. The difference in distribution between Maori and Pakeha students rose more sharply than that between Pacific Island Polynesian and Pakeha so that by 1993 they were almost equal. However, in 1992 the index for Maori/Pakeha students dropped sharply which does not seem to fit the overall pattern of increasing segregation. A closer look at the data can explain the dynamics behind both a drop and a later increase in the Maori/Pakeha segregation index. Two schools saw their intake of Maori students fall after 1991 in the context of a general roll decline. Initially these Maori students were spread over almost all the other schools, with a more even distribution over schools as a result. A year later many Maori students began to enrol at a school which was now increasingly marketing itself as a bicultural school in the area. The rising Maori intake at this school led to Maori students becoming more concentrated so that the difference in distribution between Maori and Pakeha students increased in 1993.

The process described above coupled with the general increase in segregation poses the question of whether ethnic segregation may be the result of a deliberate and positive choice by some Maori families. Certainly the recent Maori cultural renaissance and the high profile accorded the recent development of Kura Kaupapa Maori[16] suggests that positive choice by Maori parents in favour of schools which offer, to a greater or lesser extent, the possibility of a Maori education should not be discounted. However, we should note that no such dynamic was found for Pacific Island Polynesian families. As we shall see there is evidence that some of these families were bypassing Pacific Island Polynesian dominated schools.

As the 1990 figures in Table 29.8 reveal, before dezoning socio-economic segregation between Greencity schools was even more marked than ethnic segregation. SES segregation is more difficult to compare internation-

ally than ethnic segregation because the Elley and Irving index is a peculiarly New Zealand measure.

Table 29.8. Dissimilarity indices for socio-economic segregation between the 11 schools

Indicator	1990	1991	1992	1993
SES	58.3	48.1	49.3	53.4
Unemployed	58.2	51.6	52.6	55.2

Even so, the amount of socio-economic segregation in Greencity seems substantial when compared with overseas data. Willms (1986) used a correlation ratio to establish the amount of SES segregation for Scottish schools in 1980. (The SES measure used was the Registrar General's classification.) Using this method for our 1990 data shows that for the two highest SES categories, the amount of SES segregation between schools is very similar in Scotland (0.16) and Greencity (0.17). However, when focusing on the lower SES categories, this picture changes. For Scotland only 0.05 was found, whereas in Greencity this was 0.19. Willms's conclusion that lower SES categories seem to be spread more evenly across schools than higher SES categories certainly does not apply to Greencity.

If we make allowance for the Maori/Pakeha figure in 1992, socio-economic segregation was of fairly similar levels to ethnic segregation after the abolition of zoning but followed a different pattern. Socio-economic segregation appears to have decreased in 1991 as a result of students from somewhat lower socio-economic backgrounds attending non-local schools in higher numbers. This may have been as a result of the balloting policy which was in force in 1991. From 1992 segregation increased again but it can be seen that by 1993 it was still not as pronounced as before dezoning. The overall reduction in socio-economic segregation therefore seems to provide tentative support for the desegregation thesis. Such a conclusion could be incorrect for two reasons. First, findings at this level of aggregation are misleading, a point which we will return to later. Second, the 1992 and 1993 figures are tending to rise so that, if this continues, in the next year or two segregation may be greater than in 1990.

RESIDENTIAL SEGREGATION
Clearly the findings above suggest that there is

a high degree of school segregation in terms of ethnicity and socio-economic status. We now need to compare school with residential segregation. Such a comparison is crucial to an understanding of the extent to which educational policy can have an impact on the interdependence of school and residential segregation (Menahem *et al.* 1993). To address this issue we needed the best possible indicator for neighbourhood segregation. Ideally, we would have obtained information on all students living in the areas under consideration who enrolled in a secondary school. However, as noted earlier, this study did not include all Greencity's secondary schools and the data indicated that some of the students living in certain areas must attend schools not included in this study. An indicator for neighbourhood segregation based on data for the whole area covered by the study would therefore have to be questioned.

For the suburban region of our study, however, we covered about 90 per cent of all the students who lived in the area and attended a secondary school. The six adjacent schools in the suburbs all had clearly defined local catchment areas so that a segregation index based on the areas students live in can be useful in two ways. First, it provides an insight into the magnitude of residential segregation in the suburbs. Second, it tells us what school segregation would have been like if all the students had attended their local school. As they refer to only six schools, the results in this section need to be read with caution.

Table 29.9 confirms that residential segregation along ethnic lines is substantial in the suburbs, although an index based on the suburbs may overestimate the segregation for the whole area.[17] A useful comparison can be made here with some American cities. The residential segregation of Greencity is most likely to be higher than that of New York (49.2), for instance, but probably lower than that for cities like Chicago (69.7) or Los Angeles (65.9) (Logan and Schneider 1984).

Table 29.9 also shows that residential segregation along ethnic lines is higher than school segregation in the suburbs for all years. In other words, had all the students gone to their local school, ethnic school segregation would have been even higher. This indicates that some Maori and Pacific Island Polynesian students living in areas with high concentrations of Maori and Pacific Island Polynesian

students go to schools outside their own suburbs. School segregation therefore does not add to residential segregation regardless of zoning or other policies.

Table 29.9. Dissimilarity indices for ethnic segregation in suburbs between six schools with clear local zones

Indicator	1990	1991	1992	1993
Maori				
School	48.4	48.7	43.0	55.7
Residential	49.6	52.3	46.0	56.3
Pacific Island				
School	64.8	63.8	67.0	63.1
Residential	66.6	66.2	67.9	65.1

If we now turn to Table 29.10 we see that socio-economic segregation follows a different pattern. Starting with 1990, the results show that socio-economic segregation between schools would have been smaller if every student had attended the local school. In other words, school segregation added to residential segregation. This pattern of school socio-economic segregation being greater than residential socio-economic segregation is evident in 1993 after the removal of zoning. However, in 1991 both indicators point to segregation between neighbourhoods exceeding school segregation. As mentioned earlier, 1991 was an unusual year as far as zoning policies were concerned. Schools which were able to retain zones selected their out-of-zone enrolments that year by ballot. Our results therefore suggest the possibility that balloting was a more equitable policy that began to break through the socio-economic differences between neighbourhoods. Conversely, both zoning and the current policy of oversubscribed schools developing their own enrolment policies allow socio-economic segregation between schools to intensify the effects of socio-economic segregation between suburbs.

Table 29.10. Dissimilarity indices for socio-economic segregation in suburbs between six schools with clear local zones

Indicator	1990	1991	1992	1993
SES				
School	69.7	49.2	54.9	63.6
Residential	61.9	54.2	56.8	58.7
Unemployed				
School	59.3	44.2	57.2	61.6
Residential	57.2	55.8	52.5	57.0

How Schools Respond: Four Case Studies

In this section we ask: '*How have schools responded to their respective situations under market competition?*'. Of particular interest is the way schools have been affected by the formal market structure and how they have attempted to create informal arrangements to mitigate the threat posed by marketization either to the schools or to what is considered a 'good education'.

The four schools for the case studies were chosen on the basis of their initial market position and their relationship to one another within the market. Totara College is in the suburbs straddling a white middle-class and a multiethnic working-class area. Kauri College, which is in relatively close proximity to Totara College, is in the working-class area. Manuka College, in a largely middle-class suburb, occupies a midpoint in the communications corridor to the central city. Miro College is a high SES school within the central city. In theory, then, if our initial hypothesis concerning the idea of a domino effect in the flow of students from a predominantly working-class suburb through the middle-class corridor to the high SES central city schools is correct, it should be observed at work in the schools chosen for this case study. As we shall see, stemming the *potential* flow turns out to be crucial to the fortunes of three out of the four schools.

We start by examining Kauri and Totara colleges which have been hard hit by dezoning, albeit in different ways and to varying extents. Kauri College, already in difficulty by 1990, suffered an intensified exodus of students to nearby schools after the abolition of zoning. Totara has received much of Kauri's former intake and has seen its ethnic composition change drastically as a result. The responses of both Totara and Kauri colleges illuminate tensions between educational and marketing needs under dezoned conditions.

According to the data, Manuka and Miro colleges, by comparison, have been relatively unaffected by the dezoning reforms. This seems surprising in the case of Manuka which is also near Kauri's former zone. However, we will see that the school was able to quickly and effectively introduce a strategy to insulate itself from the market. The different impact of dezoning on schools becomes very apparent.

In the case of Miro College, a strong market position, a stable intake of mainly high SES students and a formal market structure which ensures its insulation from competition have left the school virtually untouched.

KAURI COLLEGE: A SPIRAL OF DECLINE?

At Kauri College, the abolition of zoning has resulted in an exodus of students to the extent that its 3rd Form intake has almost halved in size from 1990–93. Placed in the heart of a large state housing area, the school was mostly composed of working-class Pacific Island Polynesian and Maori students for some years prior to dezoning.[18] Kauri College has been 'at the bottom of the heap' for a long time according to local principals. It is the sort of school that would appear at or near the bottom of annual academic league tables published in the local papers.

When zoning was abolished in 1991, students from Pakeha families were the quickest to avoid the school. However, their loss was fairly insignificant as they were already only a small proportion of the school's intake. Maori and Pacific Island Polynesian families did not abandon the school quite so quickly, a fact that local principals put down to a lack of knowledge about the abolition of zoning:

It's my impression that there wasn't necessarily a wide awareness in the Polynesian community that this was an option. (Principal, Manuka College)

We are three years into it now and we still get people, almost all of them, from [Kauri]'s old zone saying 'We are moving . . . ,' you know, starting to tell us a lie. We have to tell them, 'it doesn't matter, you don't have to tell us a story.' (Principal, Rimu College)

Nonetheless it did not take long before the school also lost large numbers of first Pacific Island Polynesian and then Maori students. Three neighbouring schools in particular, here known as Totara, Rimu and Manuka, seemed set to receive the students. The actual destinations, however, varied according to the ethnic background of students as well as the actions taken by the receiving schools.

Many Pacific Island Polynesian and Maori students went to the nearest alternative, Totara College:

There's certainly a number of Island families have said they're going to Totara College and some of them have sat in this office this year and said, 'Well, there are too many Samoans here,' so they are going to send their Samoan children there. (Principal, Kauri College)

Other students, mainly Maori, went to Rimu College which has been developing an image as a bicultural school in Greencity. It has attracted Maori students because of this and conversely because Kauri College, for a variety of reasons not entirely of its own making, has a less adequate Maori programme.

Manuka College, in the adjacent middle-class suburb, also looked set to receive many students from Kauri's former zone. However, the school was able to impose an enrolment scheme based on overcrowding. This action has prevented enrolments from Kauri and other lower status local schools and protected Kauri from even more decline if not complete demise.[19] The effect this action has had on Manuka College itself will be shown later on.

The shift away from Kauri College has had a major impact on the daily running of the school. The number of classes taught has almost halved and a large number of teaching positions has been lost. Moreover, the exit has had a qualitative dimension as well because the mean SES of the student intake has dropped from a low 5.3 to an even lower 5.7. The relative SES of the students compared with the neighbourhood also dropped from −0.24 to −0.68, indicating that it was the lowest SES students who stayed. The class dimension of the exit out of the area was noted by one principal we spoke to:

It took a year or two for people at the lower socio-economic end to realize what was happening, that they had a choice. Then the more upwardly mobile, if you like, of that lower socio-economic group picked up on the idea more quickly. (Principal, Rimu College)

The exit of potential students from the school has not been without response. Given the seriousness of the situation, marketing has been seen as a matter of survival. The primary concern is to enlarge the intake to retain both staff and the viability of course structures as well as ultimately the existence of the school. In this survival mode, it is the number rather than the type of students enrolled that has become most important: 'The fact of the matter is that we have to target everyone who comes' (Principal, Kauri College). A strong drive is being made to increase the roll and to set up a publicity committee to coordinate marketing activities. Initially the strategy has been dam-

age control through some highly visible means. These have included a new discipline system to reduce parental fears of violence and unruliness at the school, the introduction of an attractive yet inexpensive new uniform and improving promotional resources and activities.

There are things which can be done which probably needed changing anyway but they are always good shots to gain publicity and turn things around. I mean the discipline system, even though it is less rigorous than before in that you fire kids out less easily, the parents see you being firm and addressing what they see as a discipline problem. You can always change the uniform—that goes down well— . . . [and] change the prospectus and do some promotional things in [the local shopping centre]. (Principal, Kauri College)

However, these kinds of activities are not enough. The school also needs to turn around its academic vision and performance:

I've told the Board and the teachers that we have played all our cheap, easy cards now, the only thing which can make a difference is what happens in the classrooms. (Principal, Kauri College)

In this respect some new initiatives have been developed. The major innovation is to respond to the low levels of prior achievement of students entering the school by retaining them for an extra year in the junior school before they reach the examination-orientated senior classes. By retaining students for an extra year the school hopes usefully to increase the size of its roll by an entire year group and also meet worthwhile educational aims. These aims include ethnic language programmes in which students take two hours per week in their own ethnic language and a life skills programme.

Another innovation has been to employ management consultants. This is not only for the merits of their advice. By showing the school to be 'progressive' in using Total Quality Management consultants it is also a useful publicity device, one with the possibility of bringing in resources from a variety of interested corporate and government sources:

We came across this programme which in philosophy is stuff all different from what we are doing anyway. We've got the inside running and a lot of help from a number of consultants associated with the school so we decided that we would try and make that a part of the reforms we put in place because we can significantly improve staff and student practice. I'm not at all worried about the fact that it is a bandwagon at the moment, it's likely to be a bandwagon that can push quite a lot of training and resources our way. (Principal, Kauri College)

Kauri College's attempts to increase its intake are not without problems however. Staff are facing increasing demands at a time when permanent staff numbers have been reduced severely. The context in which this is occurring puts substantially greater daily demands on teaching and working than in most schools, so that marketing comes at a great cost. There is no fat in the system and the strain tells:

Most of the teachers are on side although I guess there must be some that are not comfortable. I mean the system is set up to make them work a lot harder. We are at the bottom of the heap, we have to put in extra hours in order to get kids here. That's what we want to do in order to preserve jobs. Some [staff] I think are uncomfortable with it [marketing efforts], I expect a backlash at some stage. (Principal, Kauri College)

In discussing the dilemmas faced by schools in a competitive environment, Bowe *et al.* (1992) draw a distinction between *image* and *vision*. Image is what schools need to project in order to survive; it is essentially a public relations exercise. Vision refers to what schools consider to be educationally desirable. Ball argues that image and vision pull in different directions and pose professional and ethical dilemmas for teachers. In the case of Kauri College, this is clearly so. Precious resources have to be placed at the service of 'image' to the detriment of 'vision'. Nevertheless, it is worth noting that the attempt to retain students for an extra year in the junior school is an instance where, arguably, good educational practice is consistent with the school's attempts at survival. But, in terms of influencing the market, Kauri College has no political power. Given the urgency with which it needs to turn its situation around, improving its 'image' is its only option. Note, however, that Kauri College has been strongly adversely affected by the instability of student intakes. If such instability or turnover is outside the influence of the school, as we hypothesize it is, then even improving its image is likely to be of limited value. There is a general point behind these observations concerning the inappropriateness of market competition in areas such as the one served by Kauri College to which we shall return.

TOTARA COLLEGE: THE EFFECTS OF FLIGHT

Totara College is located on the boundary between a state housing area and a developing high-status suburb. Owing to the way its zone was drawn and redrawn across these two catchments during the 1980s, the school grew as a mainly middle-class school with a fairly stable 25–30 per cent Maori and Pacific Island Polynesian intake. Under a series of 'progressive' principals, attempts were made to cater for pupils from both catchments through a mixed ability, multicultural approach to teaching.

Following a sudden increase in Pacific Island Polynesian and Maori enrolments from Kauri College's former zone, Pakeha families have bypassed the school. The percentage of non-Pakeha students has increased from 38 per cent in 1990 to 54 per cent in 1993, while the roll had grown by 14 per cent over those years. It is therefore ethnic composition rather than intake size that has been most affected by dezoning in the case of Totara College. The speed with which the school's non-Pakeha roll has grown after 1990 is due to the combination of a number of factors.

First, there is a belief amongst many Pacific Island Polynesian parents that their children will do better at schools less dominated by non-Pakeha students, a view not endorsed by the principal of Totara College:

[It is a] perception based on the fact that our School Certificate results very much reflect our ethnic composition . . . all those people who are moving here because they think we do better, all they are basically doing is transferring Kauri College kids into Totara College . . . we can do reasonably well as Kauri College can do reasonably well. (Principal, Totara College)

Second, the school is located in such close proximity to Kauri College's traditional catchment that for many families it is just as easy to send their children to Totara College. Prior to 1991, zoning constrained local enrolments so that when it was lifted, the response of local non-Pakeha families was immediate.[20]

As the non-Pakeha roll has increased, Pakeha enrolments have declined markedly. It is difficult to tell whether this exit out of the school should be read as white flight that happens to be higher SES or class flight that happens to be white, for the growing intake from Kauri College's former zone is composed of the higher SES Pacific Island Polynesian and Maori families from that area so that the mean SES of the school has hardly changed.[21]

The principal of Totara College had little doubt that the white flight that has followed the increased Maori and Pacific Island Polynesian enrolments has both racial and socio-economic dimensions. According to the principal, racism played a part in this white flight so that if he is to keep an ethnically well-balanced school: 'We need to be able to demonstrate that we are not going to be over-run by "blacks" ' (Principal, Totara College). Related to this are fears about the academic standard of the school and its mixed ability approach:

[There] is a perception abroad in the community that we don't stretch and extend the top academic group and that they should probably go elsewhere and that's probably true because it takes an awful lot of specialized effort to bring up the bottom group. Parents of, what they think are reasonably academic kids . . . see their kids as being sacrificed to less able kids who take more attention and are more likely to be disruptive and more demanding of teachers' time. (Principal, Totara College)

Given its situation, marketing for Totara College might be seen as a matter of attracting the kinds of white, able, middle-class students the school needs to signal its quality to the Pakeha community and prevent further white flight. Yet marketing to this audience presents massive ethical dilemmas for the school:

I suppose the question really is, are we going to drastically change our approach, try and get rid of our [former Kauri College zone] clientele and market ourselves as a middle-class school or do we say we are a state school and educate everyone who comes through the door? . . . So we are in the situation . . . do we compromise our basic principles for the sake of marketing ourselves [with the Pakeha community] or do we say well we are educational-ists and we are going to do what is best for our total clientele and if some people suffer and want to go elsewhere, well tough? (Principal, Totara College)

One solution to Totara's problems would be to stream the school. This was seen as being likely to increase middle-class Pakeha enrol-ments but such a move would go against the ethical and educational values the school has followed since inception. Furthermore, given the current context it would segregate the school on an ethnic basis:

Totara College was premised on the fact that we would be a non-streamed school, there is a strong

commitment to that amongst the staff but whether it will stand up to the pressures I don't know . . . If we broad-banded or streamed we would end up pretty much with a school that had three or four Pakeha upper stream classes. The proportion of Pakeha kids in the bottom stream classes would be very small . . . (Principal, Totara College)

A more satisfactory solution from the princi-pal's point of view would be to get the maxi-mum roll reduced in order to impose an enrolment scheme that would reduce the non-Pakeha enrolments from Kauri College's for-mer zone and retain the closer, predominantly Pakeha students. However the principal found that this strategy was unlikely to work under a National Government in 1992:

The unofficial word I've had from the Ministry yesterday is that they wouldn't see much mileage in this—they are totally committed to non-zoning and if a school goes to the wall, well, tough bikky. (Principal, Totara College)

By 1993 the school was still, 'trying to become proactive in taking control' of its market posi-tion by attempting to get the roll reduced on the grounds of inadequate space in specialist areas of the school, but again with little luck.

MANUKA COLLEGE: HOLDING THE LINE

At the top of the local hierarchy, it was clear that under open market conditions Manuka College stood to grow rapidly in size. The likely increase in the size of the school was a concern to the school's principal in two respects:

The Board and I had discussed the whole question of the size of the school and I put the view very strongly to the Board that I was sick of big schools, that I did not think they did as good a job as smaller schools and other things being equal it's better to have a smaller school than a larger school. Sec-ondly, that the Board had a social responsibility to Totara, Rimu and Kauri Colleges and that they ought not to be making this school a big school at the risk of perhaps closing other schools. (Princi-pal, Manuka College)

The principal gave several grounds for being concerned about this situation and the lack of resources, skills and knowledge to cope:

We were suddenly in the position of having absolutely no control over who came here and peo-ple came to the school with a range of educational problems for which we had no solutions because we had no special or discretionary staffing to deal with them. . . . As for us thinking that we could educate the kids from that area better than the teachers at

Rimu College can, that is a ludicrous notion! (Principal, Manuka College)

The principal at Manuka College thought the popularity of his school, as against other schools in the area, could be based on an element of racism:

I seriously wonder how much of the decisions people make about schools is actually related to their perception of the race situation at a particular school. And sadly some people do have some justification, or some way to justify the view that schools which have too large a proportion of this group or that might be unsafe for their children ... I reckon, and I suppose this could be taken as a totally racist statement, that given the state of play of Maori education, Maori SES, Pacific Island education, Pacific Island SES, once you get past a school balance which is 70 per cent European, 30 per cent Polynesian, you start to run into difficulties. That is a 'rule of thumb' thing but I reckon that is the case, both at the school and the parent choice level. (Principal, Manuka College)

In 1991 intensified exit from the former zones of Totara, Rimu and Kauri Colleges increased Manuka College's intake by 12 per cent. Prompt action was therefore taken. This centred around getting the maximum roll of the school reduced by the Ministry of Education so that the school could apply for overcrowding status and develop an enrolment scheme. Here, Manuka College was very successful because of the strength of its principal and Board who negotiated with the Ministry and lobbied the local politician:

We were originally told that this school with all its facilities could house 1800 students if we really had to. That was a crazy notion. They graciously then allowed us to take 1400 and then when we had a seizure over that they said well 1200. ... And then [the Board] argued very strongly for the lowest number the Ministry might agree to which was 1050. ... That indicated we were prepared to take an increase, because you know, the Government view was that parents ought to have a choice of school so we were saying, 'OK, let's take another 40 or so'. But the Ministry said no, 1200 so we had another standoff. Then [the local MP] intervened on our behalf so we were offered 1080 and we figured that's as low as they would go at the moment so that's our maximum roll and that's more than enough. (Principal, Manuka College)

Manuka College's action was extremely successful by any measure. By 1992 the school was clearly likely to exceed its new maximum roll so that it was able to impose a zone-based enrolment scheme with few out-of-zone

places. This was a crucial step to retain the stability of the school and it even increased enrolments from families who would otherwise have bypassed the school:

Since it has become known that we have an enrolment scheme and that it's hard to get into this school, it's interesting to notice how many people are now trying to get into this school from other schools. ... So it's a fascinating exercise in community psychology. Maybe there is some truth in the notion that where something is seen to be a scarce commodity people want it. (Principal, Manuka College)

Manuka College has had few marketing problems. Since imposing a zone, its exclusivity has intensified and its reputation consolidated. It has reinforced its dominant position in the local hierarchy and has become more competitive with the high SES schools further afield. The main requirement now is to remain competitive with the more high SES schools, something that has prompted renewed emphasis on academic acceleration and general excellence. In particular, the school has some streamed junior classes and it is unlikely that the school could move to mixed-ability groupings even if it thought it educationally desirable to do so.

It is a case like this which illustrates the potential confusion between educational vision and image. Within certain communities, of which Manuka College may be an example, educational vision is linked to rhetoric about educational standards and the role of practices like streaming in maintaining 'standards'. If the school seeks to maintain a reasonable proportion of middle-class students, it clearly needs to model its practice according to rhetoric. Whether the views of Manuka College's teachers are consistent with this rhetoric is really beside the point. In this community, given the market position of Manuka College, they have little choice in the matter. We stress that this kind of potential dilemma for educators is contingent on the views of the local community. In another school in our sample, which draws on a large lower middle-class/upper working class intake, the introduction of mixed-ability teaching was well received because parents perceived it to offer greater opportunities for their children; banding was considered élitist.

MIRO COLLEGE: WHAT COMPETITION?

Miro College is a long-established and prestigious state school with a high SES and mainly Pakeha intake. Many of its students come from the 'leafy' suburbs surrounding the school while almost a third of the intake travel considerable distances to attend. These distant students have a relatively high SES compared with the residential areas in which they live.[22]

For this school at the upper end of Greencity's educational market, little has changed under the dezoning reforms. Oversubscription is the norm:

We are in a position where we get more children than we can take, so whatever our enrolment policy is of the day or any directive from on high, we always have more than enough. (Principal, Miro College)

However, the school has been trying not to grow for two reasons. First, it already has a space shortage and, second, there would be little advantage in further growth, even if space were available:

Once you are much bigger than we are you would need a different administrative structure. We would spoil ourselves. We would lose the personal relationships you can have under a certain size. We need to keep the school person-centred. (Principal, Miro College)

Given this situation, the maximum roll provided to the school by the Ministry in 1990 was considered to be too large and, like Manuka College, the school fought successfully to get it reduced. Nonetheless, combined with the balloting system for out-of-zone enrolments, the school was still forced to increase its intake in 1991:

We were given a very high roll and were very angry about that and negotiated it down a bit but even so, because zoning of any kind was abolished . . . and there was a ballot . . . we have a rather big bulge of 4th Formers going through which of course makes it difficult in planning your school. (Principal, Miro College)

Following the 1991 Act, the school has been able to take more control. It has put its own enrolment scheme in place under the overcrowding provision and has managed its intake down to a more sustainable level. The school decided largely to retain its former zoning arrangements; in-zone students are always given priority regardless of their characteristics while out-of-zone students are enrolled, when space is available, at the principal's dis-

cretion. These enrolments are apparently selected on the basis of whether their subject choices can be accommodated by the school. Overall, then, Miro College has been largely unaffected:

We still offer the same thing, we still get kids wanting to do the same things, we still get more than we can take, our geographical zone is [the same]. (Principal, Miro College)

The principal noted the irony of parental 'choice' in a situation where popular schools are oversubscribed:

You don't really get any choice because we cannot accommodate. Last year we turned away about 150 [3rd Form enrolments]. It goes right against the National party policies because of the constraints we are under. (Principal, Miro College)

Given the situation where the school has far more enrolments than it can accept, marketing activities are unnecessary:

I do not spend a single cent on publicity. I have the plainest, simplest prospectus. I do not do anything public at all except have an open night and it is so packed you can't fit into the hall. I say quite publicly that our advertising is what goes out of the school gate and that's where it stops . . . I don't have to market the school, the product is there, people know it's there, marketing is a non-issue. (Principal, Miro College)

DISCUSSION OF THE CASE STUDIES
These case studies have illustrated how the impact of market competition on individual schools has differed markedly. Kauri College, already in difficulty, was hardest hit by the reforms both in terms of its intake size and the disadvantaged nature of the intake that remained. The onset of competition effectively ensured it entered a spiral of decline which, against the odds, it is trying to reverse through the overt strategy of marketing. Totara College has been affected less by changes in intake numbers or SES composition than by changes in ethnic composition. Manuka College was threatened in much the same way but has been able to hold its own through imposing a zone. Lastly, Miro College, with a strong initial position and a continuing zoning arrangement, has been hardly touched by the reforms. Clearly the reforms have had the greatest impact on working-class schools.

Although many of the differences between

the case study schools can be explained by their different initial positions, it is also apparent that the impact of dezoning has been contingent upon the characteristics and actions of the four schools. As indicated by the quantitative analysis, school competition is centred around adjacent schools rather than distant schools. Thus, the fact that Kauri College lost so much of its intake was encouraged by the presence of a higher SES school, Totara College, nearby. Yet, had another higher SES neighbour (Manuka College) not zoned, Kauri College might have lost even more. Conversely, the compositions of Totara and Manuka colleges would arguably not have been changed and threatened respectively if they had not been located so close to Kauri College. Meanwhile, through its enrolment scheme, Miro College could accept the higher SES students from out of zone.

The means and degree to which schools responded to market competition were also important variables. The overt marketing response anticipated by neo-liberals was that of Kauri College. Totara College provided a clear example of how the external pressures of ethnic/social class flight threatened to compromise the school's educational philosophy and ethos. It is genuinely hard to understand how the introduction of choice and competition addressed the question of raising educational standards in this case.

In order to preserve its philosophy and ethos as a multicultural state school with a reasonably well-balanced social class mix, Totara College sought the advantage given to the high SES schools of being able to control the nature of its intake by getting its maximum roll limited so that it could claim it was oversubscribed and introduce an enrolment scheme. For whatever reason, the school did not have the political influence to achieve this aim and it now has to rethink its philosophy and ethos in the light of the realities of ethnic flight. In this context, the idea of creating an attractive image would not solve the educational dilemmas it now confronts. It is a case where there is a clear hiatus between image and vision: no amount of 'image' can bridge the gap between what is educationally possible and desirable. It is precisely this point that led the principal from Totara College to note the futility of marketing:

The evidence from a place like [School XX], they spent literally thousands of dollars on promoting it, their magazine and prospectus and so on would be too good for Eton. They were on the radio last year. It has not made one wit of difference. The kids are still going off to [schools with better reputations]. People just don't believe you, it's a waste of time. (Principal, Totara College)

In contrast, Manuka and Miro colleges did not see much value in spending time and resources on marketing in a context of oversupply.

If Totara College was unsuccessful in its attempts to alter the terms of the educational market in a way consistent with its professional philosophy, Manuka College's success led to a quite different experience. Yet both Totara College and Manuka College started from much the same position as true community schools. Manuka's political ability to change the terms of the competition in its favour had some ironic consequences. On the one hand, this action averted the threat of middle-class flight to the central city while, on the other, it held the line for the schools in the adjacent working-class suburb. In essence, it probably preserved one of the schools from extinction. But, in the act of preserving its middle-class roll, it potentially tied its own hands with respect to the issue of streaming versus mixed-ability teaching. Market structures impose limits to action so that some consequences may never be observed.

In successfully introducing an enrolment scheme, Manuka College raises a further element in the study of schools in a competitive context which needs attention in subsequent studies: namely the notion of networking between organizations which are ostensibly in competition (Nohria and Eccles 1992).[23] We have no information on whether Manuka College's intention to introduce an enrolment scheme and its likely impact was known to the adjoining schools but clearly, in some respects, it was to their advantage. Certainly the lived educational market is far more complex than its advocates have recognized.

Lastly, the case study of Miro College shows that high SES schools have been insulated from the reforms: in effect they enjoy close to a monopoly position. The school was forced to grow in 1991 as a result of the balloting system but then, because it has always been oversubscribed, it was able to reimpose a zone. This has allowed it to stabilize its roll and ensure a favourable intake by restricting in-zone enrolments to high-status areas and selecting out-of-zone enrolments. Whereas all the other schools have been forced to engage in the market in one way or another, at Miro College the impact of dezoning has been largely a non-issue.

Conclusions and Discussion

Two issues lie at the heart of the marketization debate: the impact of the market on choice and on school intakes. Proponents of marketization have argued that, given the opportunity, parents from whatever ethnic or social class background will exercise choice over their child's schooling. On the other hand, critics of marketization have predicted that those already endowed with material and cultural capital will simply add to their existing advantages through choice policies. They have also argued that 'choice' in turn will lead to increasing polarization between schools in terms of the socio-economic and ethnic composition of their student bodies.

We have put these hypotheses to the test in a specific market context in one New Zealand city. The concept of a *lived* market has been introduced, based on the idea that it is the combination of formal properties and informal arrangements within a market that accounts for the outcomes of choice and competition for both parents and schools. The importance of studying a market in context has been further stressed by elaborating on the contingencies between neighbouring schools. By integrating quantitative and qualitative methodologies we have been able to paint a more complete picture of the lived market in Greencity than would otherwise have been possible.

In general terms our study has found that the concerns of market critics are justified. The choice to travel out of what was defined as the local zone prior to 1991 *is* more likely to be made by those from the upper end of each social stratum, irrespective of the ethnic background of the parents. Socio-economic segregation between schools *has* been exacerbated more than would be predicted simply on the basis of residential segregation. The formal market structure *does* give rise to a range of informal market responses which confound the predictions of market proponents. With respect to this last point, we saw in particular that, in the three schools most threatened by the introduction of competition, market responses were weighed against what was seen as educationally desirable. The tension between image and vision was ever present.

Ironically, the most advantaged, high SES, schools seem insulated from market competition by virtue of their own popularity. The fact that they continue to be vastly oversubscribed illustrates that, unlike other markets, there is no tendency towards an equilibrium between supply and demand in education. This is because while parents may often want their children to attend the schools with the best reputations, providers of education see little advantage in growth beyond a level dictated by physical space or organizational considerations (Astin 1992). (An added irony in the New Zealand context is that popular schools are not allowed to expand if a neighbouring school has spare capacity.) The fact that popular schools are not expanding also raises questions about how these schools select the out-of-zone students they *do* accept. Our data suggest that they may, wittingly or unwittingly, give value to the socio-economic status of students in the selection process because in 1991, the year when students gained entry to oversubscribed schools by ballot, socio-economic segregation between schools was reduced.

It could be argued that the ultimate goal of marketization, improving educational standards, is left untouched by our study. However, it would be hard to see how standards could have improved as a result of dezoning. For the problem faced is not 'the need to educate the best better, but how to cope with the needs of the rest' (Sernau 1993: 90). It is unlikely that popular schools insulated from competition have been pressed to improve their standards. Given that market policies were intended to do away with provider-capture, the insulation of popular schools from the market is truly ironic. The situation for schools which have been affected by choice should, however, be of even greater concern. The paradox of the New Zealand education market is that schools with the most educational needs are being forced to waste time and resources on marketing in order to survive, thus further disadvantaging their already disadvantaged students.

While the extent of middle-class flight under the previous dispensation should warn us against looking back to a golden age of zoning, our study suggests that, at the very least, the current situation can be improved somewhat by moderating the effects of the market through state intervention. For instance, our findings suggest that balloting should not be underestimated as a useful policy tool. Although balloting has been criticized by McCulloch (1991) for being based on a 'minimalist notion of what equity entails', it nevertheless appears to have had a significant influence on the extent of between-school segregation in Greencity. This kind of finding, along with the policy measures suggested by Adler (1993) hold some promise that, given careful intervention, it may be possible to develop policies which allow some parental choice without further polarizing school intakes. At the same time, there are no easy answers as to how schooling should be best delivered because neither bureaucratic nor market mechanisms have demonstrated that they can meet the aims of equality of opportunity and high educational standards.

Notes

1. The research reported here forms part of the Smithfield Project, a longitudinal study of the effects of market reforms on schools and families, funded by the New Zealand Ministry of Education under Contract No. 35/314/5. We want to acknowledge the support of all members of the Smithfield team, in particular Hugh Lauder for his support, criticism and help in writing this paper, David Hughes for his worthwhile comments and suggestions, and Ruth Huckelsby and John Molloy for their impressive data collection and coding work.

2. The concept of the 'lived' market is outlined in more detail in Lauder et al. (1994).

3. A cursory examination of the policy and practice of zoning in New Zealand during the postwar years suggests that urban secondary education was selective during zoning. First, after the 1950s state-sanctioned 'out-of-zone' quota policies allowed the established state schools to recruit up to a third of their intake from the same zones as the suburban schools on the grounds of maintaining their 'special character'. Second, where out-of-zone quotas were full, other formal methods could be used by zoned schools to top up their rolls with desirable students. Third, partly due to their

complexities, enrolment schemes were frequently poorly administered and monitored so that poaching was not uncommon. Also, after a number of legal challenges during the 1980s, departmental officials became increasingly reluctant to impose the constraints of a zone against parental wishes. Fourth, for those with sufficient financial resources, private schools were always an option for exit away from local state schools (McCulloch 1990).

4. State and integrated schools form over 90 per cent of Greencity's secondary provision. Although private schools were not included in our study, it should be noted that in New Zealand the more élite state and integrated schools are not dissimilar from private schools in their social class composition and reputation. Indeed one state school principal in our study, when asked to name the school's market peers, gave a list of élite state and private schools in New Zealand and public schools in the United Kingdom.

5. Where data on parental occupations from computer records were unavailable or unclear, card files or electoral rolls were used. In one school data were gathered directly from students. A reliability check was performed on differences between different sources for occupational data. The check was based on 56 cases in a school with the poorest computer records. For these cases we coded parental occupations from computer records, card files and electoral rolls. The correlations of around 0.75 are very reasonable when compared with other reliability tests with regard to occupations (e.g. Bielby et al. 1977). Considering that this reliability check refers to the worst situation we had to deal with, we consider the data robust enough to believe that the results will not be biased because of the differences between the data sources used. See Waslander et al. (1994) for a more extensive discussion of this issue.

6. We extended the index, for our purposes with categories for (a) beneficiaries and unemployed, and (b) home makers or retired. The added categories are not included in the computation of mean SES, however, so that the range of the scale is still from 1 (highest SES) to 6 (lowest SES).

7. Further details on data collection, coding and analysis of both the quantitative and qualitative data may be found in Waslander et al. (1994).

8. We use the Maori term 'Pakeha' for students of broadly European descent. The category 'Pacific Island Polynesian' is also a general one which includes students of mainly Samoan but also (e.g.) Cook Island, Tokelauan and Tongan descent. Finally, students of Asian descent

also formed some 5 per cent of the sample which is why the figures reported in table 1 do not add up to 100 per cent (see also note 12).

9. Owing to the way zones were drawn students were not always in-zone for the school nearest to them. Therefore, after zoning was abolished, a shift may have occurred to formerly out-of-zone schools which in fact were the nearest schools. Close examination of our data shows that this explanation only applies to a very small number of students who attend adjacent schools. Furthermore, it seems to depend on characteristics of the nearest school whether attendance at nearest but formerly out-of-zone schools actually occurs.

10. The dissimilarity index is defined as:

$$D_{xy} = (0.5) [\Sigma \mid (x_i/X)-(y_i/Y) \mid],$$

where x_i is the number of students in a category defined as X in school i, and X is the total number of students in that category;
y_i is the number of students in a category defined as Y in school i, and Y is the total number of students in that category.
For our purposes, we multiplied the index by 100 so that the range is from 0 to 100.

11. Other aspects of segregation can be measured by other indices (see, e.g. Logan and Schneider 1984, Paterson 1991). Some researchers have argued that the measure used here is not sensitive enough to capture certain changes and have used alternative measures, such as the Gini coefficient (Johnston 1981). The Gini can be interpreted as the surface area between a diagonal and a Lorentz curve based on cumulative percentages of two different categories. We computed both dissimilarity indices and Gini coefficients showing similar results leading to similar conclusions. Preference is given to the dissimilarity indices because of their more common use and more straightforward interpretations.

12. The overall proportion of Asian students (about 5 per cent) makes the group rather small for comparisons. The segregation indices, ranging from 14 to 30, imply however that the difference between the distribution of Asian and Pakeha students across schools is smaller when compared with Maori and Pacific Island students.

13. High SES is defined as Elley and Irving categories 1 and 2; low SES is defined as Elley and Irving categories 5 and 6.

14. See also Denton and Massey (1989) for the procedure used here and Waslander et al. (1994) for more details on method and outcomes.

15. The segregation index used by Coleman et al. (1982) captures another aspect of segregation

and must be read as the amount of interracial contact. See Coleman et al. (1982: 231–3) for details.

16. Kura Kaupapa Maori are kura (schools) centred on a kaupapa (philosophy) of teaching and learning through the medium of Maori language and culture. These schools developed as an autonomous initiative of the Maori community because of dissatisfaction with state provision for Maori students. Over the last few years these schools have received state recognition and funding (see for further information Smith 1992).

17. Limiting our analysis to the suburbs possibly overestimates the amount of segregation for the city as a whole. Based on all the students who entered one of our secondary schools in 1993, the indices for residential segregation are 52 for Maori and Pakeha students, and 58 for Pacific Island and Pakeha students.

18. Our findings confirm claims made by opponents of marketization that differences in ethnic composition between schools have increased over the years. The range of proportions of Maori students across the 11 schools went from 4.2–35 per cent in 1990 to 0.8–46.8 per cent in 1993 and the Pacific Island Polynesian range increased from 0.7–63.2 per cent to 1.3–68.8 per cent over the same period. Furthermore they tentatively support the notion of an ethnic tipping point (Fitzpatrick and Hwang 1990; Ottensmann and Gleeson 1992). Schools with proportions of Maori or Pacific Island students around or higher than 20 per cent have seen the proportions of these students increase while schools with proportions of Maori or Pacific Island students lower than 20 per cent have seen these proportions decrease. Close reading of the data also shows that growing proportions of Maori or Pacific Island students in schools are without exception the result of either (a) local Pakeha students attending adjacent and distant schools in higher numbers, or (b) Maori and/or Pacific Island students from adjacent areas attending the school in higher numbers. Given that both processes have been largely facilitated by the abolition of zoning, at least part of this ethnic polarization may be attributed to market policies.

19. Local opinion has it that Manuka's actions 'saved' Kauri College from emptying out completely. However, it is important to note that the lowest SES families have not shown any sign of moving out, suggesting that Kauri College may have been even a little smaller and less viable than at present, rather than completely bypassed. It is worth pointing out that this school is also competing with post-compulsory providers especially with respect to their non-academic senior students who are

offered the enticement of a weekly income by the Government for attending courses such as those in life skills.

20. In the early 1980s Totara's zone was drawn to include the part of Kauri College's traditional catchment nearest to it. This was because Totara College was a new school and was seen to need a large catchment area in order to gather momentum and viability. By the mid-1980s, however, Totara College was growing at the expense of Kauri College so the 1986 zone boundary was moved back to nearer the traditional catchment boundary. This had the effect of excluding enrolments from many of the non–Pakeha families close to Totara College. This was bitterly resisted by many local parents at the time: the local paper records charges of racism laid against the school and 'the system'. The effect of dezoning was to take immediately the mainly non–Pakeha families on the edge of traditional Kauri College zone from Kauri College to Totara College.

21. The mean SES of students enrolling in Totara College has dropped only slightly from 3.7 in 1990 to 3.9 in 1993.

22. The mean of the relative SES (a student's own SES substracted from that student's neighbourhood SES) for these distant students is around 0.7.

23. An informal agreement with respect to recruiting students was also undertaken between a high SES school in our sample and a (non-sample) school nearby thereby maintaining a higher SES mix for the non-sample school than would most likely have been the case had the agreement not been made.

References

Adler, M. (1993), *An Alternative Approach to Parental Choice*. Briefing No. 13, March (London: National Commission on Education).

—— and Raab, G. M. (1988), 'Exit, Choice and Loyalty: The Impact of Parental Choice on Admissions to Secondary Schools in Edinburgh and Dundee', *Journal of Educational Policy*, 3/2: 155–179.

Astin, A. W. (1992), 'Educational "Choice": Its Appeal May be Illusory', *Sociology of Education*, 65: 255–9.

Ball, S. J. (1990), *Education, Inequality and School Reform: Values in Crisis!* Inaugural Lecture (London: Centre for Educational Studies King's College).

—— (1993), 'Education markets, Choice and Social Class: The Market as a Class Strategy in the UK and the US', *British Journal of Sociology of Education*, 14: 3–19.

——, Bowe, R., and Gewirtz, S. (1992), *Circuits of Schooling: a Sociological Exploration of Parental Choice in Social Class Contexts*, Working Paper (London: Centre for Educational Studies King's College).

Bielby, W. T., Hauser, R. M., and Featherman, D. L. (1977), 'Response Error of Black and Non-Black Males in Models of Intergenerational Transmission of Socioeconomic Status', *American Journal of Sociology*, 82: 1242–88.

Bowe, R., Ball, S. J., and Gold, A. (1992), *Reforming Education and Changing Schools* (London: Routledge).

Brown, P. (1990), 'The Third Wave: Education and the Ideology of Parentocracy', *British Journal of Sociology of Education*, 11: 65–85.

Chubb, J., and Moe, T. (1990), *Politics, Markets and America's Schools* (Washington DC: Brookings Institution).

Clune, W., and Witte, J. (1990), *Choice and Control in American Education*: i. *The Theory of Choice and Control in American Education* (Philadelphia: Falmer).

Coleman, J. (1990), *Equality and Achievement in Education* (Boulder: Westview Press).

—— (1992), 'Some points on choice in education', *Sociology of Education*, 65, 260–2.

—— Hoffer, T., and Kilgore, S. (1982), *High School Achievement: Public, Private and Catholic Schools Compared* (New York: Basic).

Coons, J. E., and Sugarman, S. D. (1978), *Education by Choice: The Case for Family Control* (Berkeley: Univ. of California Press).

Denton, N. A., and Massey, D. S. (1989), 'Residential Segregation of Blacks, Hispanics and Asians by Socio-Economic Status and Generation', *Social Science Quarterly*, 69: 797–817.

Dewey, J. (1916), *Democracy and Education* (New York: Macmillan).

Echols, F., McPherson, A., and Willms, J. D. (1990), 'Parental Choice in Scotland', *Journal of Educational Policy*, 5: 207–22.

Elley, W. B., and Irving, J. C. (1985), 'The Elley-Irving Socio-Economic Index 1981 Census Revision', *New Zealand Journal of Educational Studies*, 20: 115–28.

Fitzpatrick, K. M., and Hwang, S. S. (1990), 'Bringing Community SES Back In; Reanalyzing Black Suburbanization Patterns, 1960–1980', *Social Science Quarterly*, 71: 766–73.

Hogan, D. (1992), 'School Organisation and Student Achievement', *Educational Theory*, 42: 83–105.

Irving, J. C. (1991), *Update of the Elley & Irving Scale* (Wellington: Ministry of Education).

—— and Elley, W. B. (1977), 'A Socio-Economic Index for the Female Labour Force in New Zealand', *New Zealand Journal of Educational Studies*, 12: 154–63.

Johnston, J. N. (1981), *Indicators of Education Systems* (Paris: Unesco).

Lange, D. (1988), *Tomorrow's Schools: the Reform of Educational Administration in New Zealand* (Wellington: Government Printer).

Lauder, H. (1991), *The Lauder Report: Tomorrow's Education, Tomorrow's Economy*, report commissioned by the education sector standing committee of the New Zealand Council of Trade Unions (Wellington: PPTA).

——, Hughes, D., Waslander, S., Thrupp, M., McGlinn, J., Newton, S., and Dupuis, A. (1994), *The Creation of Market Competition in New Zealand*, an empirical analysis of a New Zealand secondary school market, 1990–1993 (Wellington: Victoria University).

Logan, J. R., and Schneider, M. (1984), 'Racial Segregation and Racial Change in American Suburbs, 1970–1980', *American Journal of Sociology*, 89: 894–88.

Maddaus, J. (1990), 'Parental Choice of School: What Parents Think and Do', in C. Cazden (ed.), *Review of Research in Education*, 16 (American Educational Research Association), 267–96.

Marginson, S. (1993), *Education and Public Policy in Australia* (Melbourne: Cambridge Univ. Press).

McCulloch, G. (1990), Secondary School Zoning: The Case of Auckland', in J. Codd, R. Harker, and R. Nash (eds.), *Political Issues in New Zealand Education* (Palmerston North: Dunmore), 283–302.

—— (1991), 'School Zoning, Equity, and Freedom: The Case of New Zealand', *Journal of Educational Policy*, 6: 155–68.

Menahem, G., Spiro, S. E., Goldring, E., and Shapira, R. (1993), 'Parental Choice and Residential Segregation', *Urban Education*, 28: 30–48.

Ministry of Education (1992), *Education Statistics of New Zealand 1992* (Wellington: Ministry of Education).

Moore, D., and Davenport, S. (1990), 'Choice: The New Improved Sorting Machine', in W. Boyd and H. Walberg (eds.), *Choice in Education: Potential and Problems* (Berkeley: McCutchan).

Nohria, N., and Eccles, R. (1992), *Networks and Organisations: Structure Form and Action* (Boston: Harvard Business School Press).

Ottensmann, J. R., and Gleeson, M. E. (1992), 'The Movement of Whites and Blacks into Racially Mixed Neighborhoods; Chicago, 1960–1980', *Social Science Quarterly*, 73: 645–62.

Paterson, L. (1991), *Segregation Indices and Multilevel Modelling* (Edinburgh: Centre for Educational Sociology, Edinburgh University).

Picot, B., Rosenergy, M., Ramsay, P., Wise, C., and Wereta, W. (1988), *Administering for Excellence: Effective Administration in Education* (The Picot Report) (Wellington: Government Printer).

Rae, K. (1990), 'Secondary School Enrolment Schemes: A Case Study of Policy Change and its Implementation', in L. Gordon and J. Codd (eds.), *Education Policy and the Changing Role of the State*, Delta Studies in Education 1 (Palmerston North: Department of Education, Massey University).

Sernau, S. (1993), 'School Choices, Rational and Otherwise: A Comment on Coleman', *Sociology of Education*, 66: 88–90.

Smith, G. (1992), 'Kura Kaupapa Maori: Contesting and Reclaiming Education in Aotearoa', in R.Douglas and D. H. Poonwassie, *Education and Cultural Differences: New Perspectives* (London: Garland).

Thrupp, M. (forthcoming), 'The School Mix Effect: The History of an Enduring Problem in Educational Research, Policy and Practice', *British Journal of Sociology of Education*, 16/2.

Waslander, S., Hughes, D., Lauder, H., McGlinn, J., Newton, S. and Thrupp, M. (1994), *The Smithfield Project Phase One: An Overview of Research Activities* (Wellington: Victoria University).

Williams, M. F., Hancher, K. S., and Hutner, A. (1983), *Parents and School Choice: A Household Survey* (Washington DC: US Department of Education).

Willms, J. D. (1986),'Social Class Segregation and its Relationship to Pupils' Examination Results in Scotland', *American Sociological Review*, 51: 224–41.

Willms, D., and Echols, F. (1992), 'Alert and Inert Clients: The Scottish Experience of Parental Choice of Schools', *Economics of Education Review*, 11: 339–50.

30

[Ap]parent Involvement: Reflections on Parents, Power, and Urban Public Schools

Michelle Fine

> Organizing for parent involvement is like bringing the ocean to a boil.
>
> DON DAVIES

As discourse on 'parent empowerment' floods the 1990s, I find myself suspicious about my own work and that of others. Parents are being promiscuously invited into the now deficit-ridden public sphere of public education, invited in 'as if' this were a power-neutral partnership. Many would argue that parents in urban districts are being asked in when it is too late, asked in to 'fix' the damage of racism and an economy with the bottom carved out. Conservatives' call for parental involvement only thinly drapes a strategy of victim blaming, yoked to a federal retreat from the public sphere, a concerted effort at union busting, and an energetic agenda for privatization. When not reifying 'choice' and private-sector vouchers, the Right has committed to disinvesting in 'those' schools and 'those' children. But it is not only the Right that is mobilized.

Progressives and conservatives alike are appropriately distressed by a failing public sector, by broken promises of 'professionalism' and empty dreams of reform 1980s style. Together, perhaps oddly, they are pressing parental involvement/empowerment in the vanguard of educational reform. Sometimes parents are being organized as advocates for their children, other times as teacher bashers, often as bureaucracy busters, more recently, as culture-carriers, increasingly, as consumers. Parents enter the contested public sphere of public education typically with neither resources nor power. They are usually not welcomed, by schools, to the critical and serious work of rethinking educational structures and practices, and they typically repre-

sent a small percent of local taxpayers. It is, then, an opportune time to take a critical look at what role(s) parents might play, with whom, and toward what ends.

In this article three major parental involvement projects are described from urban school districts across the country—Baltimore, Philadelphia, and Chicago. In each city, there is a political movement under way to strengthen parental presence inside schools, and around concerns of education, through some form of 'collaboration.' Each case reflects the hard work of activists, parents, educators, and often friends. Across cases we have an opportunity to dissect, closely, what it is parents say they want from this work. These cases are presented along a continuum of increasing power, control, and activism by parents. For each case, practitioners, organizers, parents, and activists have been good enough to respond to drafts of this text. As you will see, their comments have been spliced into the article; they are 'in conversation' with me. With this article, I hope to provoke a broad-based conversation about urban public school reform—asking how parents are being positioned as subjects, but also as objects, of a struggle to resuscitate the public sphere of public education.

Framing the Politics of Parental Involvement

In 'Rethinking the Public Sphere: A Contribution to the Critique of Actually Existing

From *Teachers College Record*, 94 (1993), 682–710. Reprinted with permission.

Democracy,' Nancy Fraser (1990) borrows Habermas's notion of the public sphere as 'a theater in modern societies in which political participation is enacted through the medium of talk. It is the space in which citizens deliberate about common affairs . . . it is a site for the production and circulation of discourse that can in principle be critical of the state.' Within this frame, the public sphere has been defined, and bordered, by exclusion: 'Despite the rhetoric of publicity and accessibility, the official public sphere rested on, indeed was importantly constituted by a number of significant exclusions' (Fine 1990). And for public schools, these exclusions have been embodied by parents, community, and public interests.

Fraser (1990: 62–3) offers four assumptions she finds problematic undergirding the current conception of a public sphere. These four assumptions deserve critical unpacking, if we are to engage a truly democratic public sphere:

1. The assumption that it is possible for interlocutors in a public sphere to bracket status differentials and to deliberate 'as if' they were social equals;
2. The assumption that the proliferation of a multiplicity of competing publics is necessarily a step away from, rather than toward, greater democracy and that a single, comprehensive public sphere is always preferable to a nexus of multiple publics;
3. The assumption that discourse in the public sphere should be restricted to deliberation about the common good, and that the appearance of 'private interests' and 'private issues' is always undesirable;
4. The assumption that a functioning democratic public sphere requires a sharp separation between civil society and the State.

If we consider these four assumptions with respect to parents[1] in and with their public schools and districts, we see good reason for Fraser's concerns. First, in current school reform movements, parents do not even enter school-based discourse 'as if' social equals with educators, bureaucrats, or corporate representatives. With some exceptions, the history and contemporary face of public schooling suggest their explicit exclusion. Parents feel and are typically treated as 'less' than the professionals, particularly in low-

income neighborhoods (see Connell *et al.* 1982; Comer 1981; Epstein 1991, 1982; Lightfoot 1978). In upper-income communities, parents are often seen as overinvolved and intrusive (Connell *et al.* 1982). Second, most public school bureaucracies' appetite for diversity, plurality, and critique from parents is about as rich as schools' appetite for diversity, plurality, and critique from students and educators. Indeed, one might argue that the structures and practices of big-city educational bureaucracies serve to split teachers from parents. In such contexts, teachers and parents are set up as adversaries, fighting over inadequate resources and authority, while the grossly disproportionate share of both remains centralized within the halls of central districts. Indeed, centralized bureaucracies, in their profound alienation, fragmentation, and hierarchy, may be well served by the warring bodies of teachers and parents, each of which defers to the central district to calm the other down. This is a point to which I will return. Third, discussions of the 'common good' typically occlude the *real* reason parents come to school, which is to represent their 'private interests'—*their* children. What is justified as 'good for all' (tracking, labeling, education for employment, discipline and order) is constructed through a discourse of efficiency, privileging the interests of capital and the state rather than the needs, passions, desires, strengths, and worries of parents and their children, which are framed as if simply private. Fourth, the role of the state as monitor and controller of public education remains relatively unproblematized in current literature on public schooling. The bureaucratic apparatus of public education is seriously remote from workers' or consumers' interests.

It will be clear from the following three cases that questions of *power, authority*, and *control* must be addressed head-on within debates about parental involvement in public schools. To avoid these issues is to trivialize the rethinking of the urban public sphere. The presumption of equality between parents and schools, and the refusal to address power struggles, has systematically undermined real educational transformation, and has 'set up' parents as well as educators involved with reform.

In scenes in which power asymmetries are not addressed and hierarchical bureaucracies are not radically transformed, parents end up looking individually 'needy,' 'naive,' or 'hysterical' and appear to be working in opposition to teachers. Rarely do they seem entitled to strong voices and substantial power in a pluralistic public sphere. Rarely do they have the opportunity to work collaboratively with educators inventing what could be a rich, engaging, and democratic system for public education.

The Baltimore Story: Dilemmas of Collaboration

The Baltimore project is probably best described by its director (Garlington 1991):

In the summer of 1987, the 'With and For Parents' program opened its office in a community service center located in the heart of the community . . . The National Committee for Citizens in Education made a three and a one-half year commitment to work closely with a significant number of families of incoming middle schoolers and to remain with them through their children's entire middle school experience. We worked collaboratively with the Baltimore City schools as a community based, family resource to promote increased parent knowledge about and participation in the education of their children. We entered the community believing unquestionably in the potential for African-American inner-city parents to become confident, well-informed and influential people in the education of their children and in the educational life of the community.

Donnie Cook, on the faculty at University of Maryland, and I evaluated 'With and For Parents' over a three-year period (Fine and Cook 1991). We had a chance to watch this well-conceived program, which was designed to be collaborative with its middle school and to empower parents individually, change over time from what was called 'empowerment' into what became 'crisis intervention.' We learned that projects that focus on *individual parent advocacy* without a commitment to redistributing power and/or material resources inadvertently fall prey to the overwhelming depth of family needs. If a project does not negotiate power explicitly, at the family-school level, then the needs of family flood the work of school reform. Service replaces reform—which might be necessary, but constitutes a very different project.

THE CONTEXT
This community has all the troubles and vibrancy of a poor African-American urban community in the 1990s. Relative to itself twenty years ago, this community suffers substantially in terms of impoverished material conditions, scarred social relations, and an uncertain future.

Materially, the neighborhood is solidly low-income and African-American. The experience and talk of drugs and violence are omnipresent. Mothers report that they are 'happy I don't work outside—who would walk my child to school—it being so unsafe?' Others delight that the 'With and For Parents' project takes their children on recreational trips, away from the streets and from worries about sex and drugs. Many of these families are cut off from their kin networks. In ways historically unprecedented, and yet compatible with national literatures on concentrated poverty, they are cut off from church, neighbors, and public institutions. Most of these mothers manage creatively, alone and at the wire.

In such a context, social relations among neighbors are often cautious. In a community so homogeneously low-income, the public schools are filled with students who have been classified as low-ability. Special education rates at this school soar well above the city's average, and varied forms of discipline, ranging from disciplinary removals (ostensibly for three days) to suspensions (for forty-five days), define the school's sometimes quite hostile climate.

The situation today is most unlike that of the 1970s described by Sara Lawrence Lightfoot (1978):

The heightened cohesiveness of black communities during this period allowed a pooling of frustrations, resources and initiatives—much of which was focused on the school as the battleground, the most visible and vulnerable social institution within the community that was perceived as the only avenue that their children could take out of the hopelessness and poverty of ghetto life.

Instead, because of the federal abandonment of cities and the devastating impact of drugs and accompanying violence, one hears little of trust among neighbors, much criticism of those who live nearby, and whispers of anger at public institutions.

We hear a premium placed on privacy and

self-protection, and an ambivalent desire to believe in social institutions. Even if anger is saturating the community, self-denigration runs high and institutional critique runs low. Mobilizing an educational advocacy core proved difficult.

VOICES OF MOTHERS

We interviewed twelve women about their experiences of 'empowerment,' as defined by the project. From them we heard the biography of the Reagan and Bush administrations, voiced in talk about housing, drugs, street crime, and violence perpetrated by the state, and talk about barely getting by. . . .

Many women explained, for instance, that their personal illnesses could provoke dramatic, adverse consequences for their children's schooling, particularly in terms of attendance and grades. These women not only sit at the nexus of racist, classist, and sexist institutions and violent streets, but they know that when their own resources (e.g., health) go, there is no ease. When their fragile balancing act falls apart, everyone blames them. Low-income mothers are holding together the pieces of a society torn apart by a federal government that, over the past decade, has shown disdain for and has severely punished those living in poverty. They themselves are the only ones holding their lives together.

These mothers have woven a form of 'collective empowerment,' spreading across social contexts and within social networks. Ms Darden described how she works with other parents from the school:

There is that idea that we, by being in the black community, black parents don't care about their students, that's not true. I think they are very concerned. The fact that a lot of people, a lot of blacks do not have that education, a lot of them may not have gone to tenth, eleventh or twelfth, they dropped out of school, they feel as though the school system may not have done what it should have done for them, so I'm going to put my child in that school system and I'm not going to be bothered. I'm just going to let them teach and that's that.

Feeding and feeding, that just like you would to do a child. You have to keep saying well, we need to nurture the parents. And being a parent is not so easy as people think it is, whether you're black, whether you're white, whether you're . . . it doesn't make any difference. Being a parent is not an easy process and parents is still growing just as well as their children are.

Psychologist Brinton Lykes (1985) distinguishes social individuals from autonomous individuals when she writes:

Social individuals are active and involved in circles well beyond immediate family or neighborhood . . . They participate in a range of activities . . . which reflect both a sense of their own individuality . . . and a commitment to social change through collaborative or collective action.

In contrast, *autonomous individuals* tend to describe their current communities . . . not in terms of human relations or interconnections. Independence and autonomy are themes. . . . There is little evidence . . . of commitment to or engagement in action for social change.

Listening to Lykes, we can hear the leadership of women in 'With and For Parents' as preeminent social individuals. Working in circles together, they are committed to broadening these circles, across communities and generations, and 'with and for' other parents who could not, or would not, be as active as they. They feel best about themselves when their children and their communities are thriving. At the foundation of their work is not only a sense of reciprocity, and a deep understanding of the full lives of their neighbors, but a thoroughgoing commitment to community life in African-American communities. The members of the Parent Group echo powerfully and passionately the words of sociologist Cheryl Townsend Gilkes (1988: 75):

Four basic struggles . . . shape the consciousness of Black women—the struggle for human dignity, the struggle against white hypocrisy, the struggle for justice, and the struggle for survival. . . . No matter how high they rise, and no matter how diverse and how many places they go to build, Black women community workers are the ones who will come home to the community.

THE SHIFT FROM EMPOWERMENT TO CRISIS INTERVENTION

The early model of 'With and For Parents' vacillated between a sense of giving these women what they say they need and a commitment to empowering a critical community of educational advocates. For two reasons, the project tipped toward the former. First there was no clear strategy, a priori, for dealing critically with the school-parent partnership. In fact, the collaboration among the school, the project, and the families was seen as necessary for the project to be launched, but it inadvertently washed out the possibility of systemic critique and silenced the naming of power asymmetries. Second, the form of empowerment nurtured by the project was initially quite individual-oriented—that is, organized around the particular problems a child or parent was having with the school. The combination of a failure to negotiate power asymmetries with the school and the individualistic frame on advocacy tilted the project toward crisis intervention. Jocelyn Garlington (1991) captures this complicated turn toward service:

Parents of children who are doing poorly in school are treading water, like their children and keeping fingers crossed that each new day will not bring with it another crisis. In a very profound sense for these parents no news is truly good news. Parents, needing some part of their daily lives to be free from raging urgencies, accepted a role of not having to deal with school unless called, and yet we were on the scene daily, nudging, trying to fill relatively calm pockets with activity, concern and even alarm. Education issues for families whose kids quietly slip through the cracks is like high blood pressure; the symptoms can be quiet but deadly. Many overburdened parents understandably needed to focus on the pulsating migraine. These headaches were not dropout prevention-related. Monitoring and planning for low-range goals often got put aside.

What surfaced from the women was their needs, which the staff served responsively. But in that process systemic change of their schools moved to a back burner (Fine 1991). In being responsive, a turn from parental empowerment to crisis intervention may, ironically, feed the impression that the problem lies squarely in the family system. Much of the early work on parental involvement, prior to the 1980s, was generated explicitly from maternal blaming/supporting frameworks. At that point in time, 'parental involvement' classes, in low-income schools, involved learning how to 'parent' more effectively. Parents were offered workshops on loving the unlovable child, dealing with a latchkey adolescent, and assertive discipline, all of which derive from an implicit model of helping the (particularly low-income) parent cope with, and control better, an uncontrollable child (Garlington 1991). Even when work with parents is done well, however, power issues, among and between families, schools, and districts, usually remain buried. 'With and For Parents' explicitly resisted such strategies. Yet, over time, parents grew

beleaguered with and suspect of the politics of organizing. Quoting Garlington (1991) again:

I find myself cringing a bit when I think back on many of the conversations I have with folks truly committed to some form or type of parental involvement for low income, low achieving students in urban areas. Long lists are inevitably generated—parents need to this, this, and this. It is our mission to prod, push, beg and insist. Or is it? When parents do all of these 'essential' things—learn all there is to know about how schools work, invest endless hours in working with their own children at home while fully participating in the life of school, join all the right committees and be well-informed and active in all levels of decision-making, and make a commitment to being a continual and relentless thorn in the side of anyone of influence, all will be right. Or will it?

Garlington rightly calls the 'God question.' Nevertheless, the 'responsive turn' toward crisis intervention can reproduce the very discourses and practices that depoliticize the needs of low-income parents. If services are responsive and appropriate, individual needs may swell insatiably. While, as Anne Wheelock notes in a personal response to this chapter (1991), some services can be as seen supporting empowerment, the likelihood of collective public struggle in such contexts is often diminished. Schools slip gently off the hook, although Garlington (1991) again poignantly argues:

We did not feel we were releasing the school from any responsibility. We were hopefully helping to illuminate the process for sensitive and effective ways for families with limited resources to solve problems. We shared our lessons with the school and encouraged the school to think beyond the obvious interventions and be more thoughtful and creative about solutions when problems arise. We invited parents into every facet of the process and readily admitted that we did not have all the answers. We made suggestions. We listened, we researched, observed and came back to parents, often with different suggestions.

Only in retrospect can we see that the slip from parental involvement to service delivery is a lot like the ideological slip that argues that parental involvement will, in and of itself, transform student learning. This assertion, benign and liberal, depoliticizes educational outcomes and exempts district and school policies and practices from accountability.

To explain: For funding purposes and, I think, because we all wanted to believe it, 'With and For Parents' was originally premised as a dropout-prevention program. The logic argued that parental empowerment should produce more educationally supportive households and, in turn, improved student outcomes. To test the second assumption, we conducted statistical comparisons of the children of parental activists versus those of non-activists on indices of student achievement after three years of the program. Our data suggest that while a solid leadership core developed, over time, the assumption that *empowered and involved parents produce educated students* can simply be laid to rest. Our data demonstrate instead that while empowered parents may 'stick with a school' longer, they do not, in and of themselves, produce in the aggregate improved student outcomes in the areas of retention, absenteeism, California Achievement Test scores, or grades (Fine and Cook 1992).

Parental involvement is necessary but not sufficient to produce improved student outcomes. Without a serious national, state, and community commitment to serving children broadly, and to restructuring schools in low-income neighborhoods and their surrounds, deep parental involvement *with* schools will do little to positively affect—or sustain—low-income students or their schools or outcomes. As Comer (1981), Wheelock (1991), and Epstein (1991) note, it is not enough for families to become more like schools; schools and districts must also become more like families.

Over the past decade, federal and state governments have tried to shift responsibility and blame for educational problems onto the backs of low-income parents. Individual parental involvement projects cannot restore a rich, critical, and creative public sphere. Only with a powerful, supportive, and activist national agenda for children can parental involvement thrive—and only then if parental involvement provokes thoughtful, critical inquiry into public bureaucracy. We all need parents to become critical activists in their homes, in their schools, on the streets, and in the halls of Congress. And yet, to quote Garlington (1991):

Being an activist these days mean[s] standing out like a sore thumb among your peers. Gone forever, it seems, is the age of Afro wearing, angry, fist-raising Black folks determined to reclaim their communities and rattle this political system at its core. The rage is far more subdued. Sadly, there is no rage where so much is warranted. Unfortu-nately, we found that the activists in the community are viewed somewhat as weirdos, no matter how noble the cause or how many people in the community received direct benefit from the activist's fervor. Most parents just want to parent, love their children and experience some success in making things better for their future. They are not ready to carry placards, spend hours in planning meetings, keep vigilance in the schools, and show up at every important community event pressing the need for community response and interest in education.

In communities, there are impressive 'little engines that could' groups of parents (mostly women) with a sprinkling of community folks huffing and puffing and pushing themselves to the limit for some favorable but limited outcomes for kids. They must fight attitudes and perceptions that date back centuries and a school system whose resistance to change is unparalleled. But still these hardworking, devoted parents manage to make a dent—regardless how small. Then what? Their children leave the school (hopefully graduate) and the battle must start afresh. The system remains unchanged and the victories, while important to the parents who struggled to realize them, more often than not, are quickly forgotten when those parents are off the scene.

Without relentless attention to systemic power and critique, parental-involvement projects may simply surface the individual needs of families, which will become the vehicle to express, and dilute, struggles of power. If unacknowledged, power may hide, cloaked in the 'needs' or 'inadequacies' of disenfranchised mothers, and schools may persist unchallenged, employing practices that damage.

The Philadelphia Story: At the Table, Gaining a Voice, but not yet a Hearing

The Philadelphia story is one in which I am far more deeply involved as an activist researcher. I narrate this analysis, in part, as autobiography. Having been on half-time leave for four years (1988–1992) from the University of Pennsylvania to work as consultant with the Philadelphia Schools Collaborative,[2] I have a lot invested in what does and does not happen to the parents involved with the comprehensive high schools undergoing restructuring.

In June 1990, the School District of Philadelphia, the Philadelphia Federation of Teachers, and the Philadelphia Schools Collaborative entered into an agreement that this district would pursue shared decision making and school-based management (SD/SBM) in all schools that could generate radically innovative educational plans and then seek a 75 per cent approval vote, by the faculty, for those plans. Once such a vote is achieved, control over the resources of that school would move from central district to the school; waivers from state, district, and union policies would be considered; and shared decision making would be in place at the school site. It is this process of shared decision making, involving parents, to which our attention now turns.

As required by the guidelines of SD/SBM, all schools pursuing school-based management operate under the direction of governance councils, comprised of administrators, teachers, and parents, and established to assure that important 'decisions of educational renewal will be made by consensus and with respect for the elements of choice, diversity and risk taking that characterize a renewal effort.' The council is expected to:

1. establish processes to assure broad consultation and involvement of the school community in curriculum, instruction and educational renewal including posting of criteria and selection of personnel for posted positions;
2. provide the vehicles for assessing the effectiveness of the school program;
3. determine distribution of resources (financial and personnel) allocated to the school;
4. regularly report to the school community;
5. request waivers for changes in School District policy and/or contractual agreements and/or state regulations (School District of Philadelphia 1991).

Councils were designed to be comprised mostly of educators, but to enjoy substantial parent representation. Each fifteen-person council consists of the principal, an assistant principal, a building representative from the union, four parents selected by lottery from among those interested, one noninstructional staff member, one department head, and six teachers. While parents do not constitute half—much less a majority—of the council, they comprise a substantial block, and all decisions are to be made by consensus and not majority vote.

Early on, involvement of parents was recognized as politically imperative on the councils and throughout the school communities. It was expected that with SD/SBM, schools and their governance councils would eventually enjoy adequate resources and autonomy to become critical, struggling, public democracies of difference among and between educators and parents. These councils were to have broad decision-making power, and would therefore need representation of all members of the 'school community' in order to reinvent the structures, practices, and outcomes of urban high schools. Parents were invited not to represent exclusively their own children's interests, but to import 'parental perspectives' into critical policymaking conversations.

It was clear that it was not only necessary to have parents on these councils, but that without substantial support, parents would either feel like or come to be seen as tokens. They could be isolated or become hysterical quickly. As a player in the design of SD/SBM, I worried about all the possible problems—parents will not know all that they need to know to make serious educational decisions; parents are not represented fairly; parents will not feel empowered to speak their minds; parents will not get a hearing when they do speak their minds; educators will not work with parents as full partners.

In some schools, these concerns were realized. In other schools they were not. In many schools parents are decision makers working closely with teachers. In other schools their input is trivialized. Some parents feel absolutely entitled to speak their minds. Others feel so proud to have been selected to be on the council that they would not dare contradict the educators. James Sims, a father on the council at one high school, said early in the process: 'I am concerned about those educators making decisions alone about my child, and his schooling. But right now I also feel like who am I to tell them. They're professionals.'

Sims's initial concerns rang true for many of the forty-eight parents who represented the twelve high schools pursuing SD/SBM. Six months later, Sims is no longer ambivalent. He is co-chair of his school council, and astonished to find camaraderie—'They're just normal like the rest of us.' Echoing Sims, another parent explains: 'Teachers are just like the rest of us. They get off track, don't follow through, and nit-picking, argue about little things. You know, they have more education, but same feelings as regular people, if you know what I mean.'

On the first Saturday that we all met, in January 1991 (we being the parents, some representatives from the district and the union, and those of us from the collaborative), I was concerned that turnout would be terrible, parents would resent the 'extra' attention, or (flying to the other extreme of paranoia) they would grow too dependent on us to provide 'answers.' Of course I was wrong on all three counts. The turnout was fantastic: Thirty-six of forty-two selected representatives showed up on a beautiful Saturday morning. They appreciated the opportunity to organize, decided they had to meet one Saturday a month, with a Monday-evening dinner between meetings. By the third session, they asked me (and the rest of the district, union, and collaborative folks) to leave so that they could have some time among themselves. So much for my overprotective fantasies.

In July, interviews with these parents surfaced a number of issues, all rotating around the question of what parents are being asked to represent in the name of parental participation in schools. Parents today are getting better access to their educational communities, but to what end? To be 'better parents'? To be advisors on community issues? Or to be fully entitled partners in school decision making? Are they there to play out their private interests or to engage, with teachers, in creating a shared vision of a school community? Why have we not dealt, explicitly, with the parent-teacher/administrator struggle over power?

Among this group, it is clear that they have collectively, if unevenly, developed a rich set of voices. They enjoy a democracy of differences. Some have been, and continue to be, strongly oppositional to schools—believing that neither the district nor the union has their children's interests at heart. Most are still solid collaborators.

The issue that has emerged most frequently from these interviews concerns a distinction one woman made between 'getting a voice' and 'getting a hearing.' Here again the politics of power surface. No one among this group is inviting a shift from activism to service delivery, but quite a few complain that their activism is being ignored. Still others, however, are delighted with the opportunity to work in struggling partnership with schools. As Jerome Spearman, co-chair of his governance council, indicated:

We have the opportunity to influence the schools where our children are being educated; I'm surprised at how much work needs to be done. But we can't go in there and mouth off without knowing what we're talking about. They need us, because without parents, things get lopsided; that is, they care more about jobs than about the whole picture. But with us there, they get a dose of reality.

Parents take several but, at minimum, two stances about their role on the councils. There are those who maintain a parents' rights perspective, historically rooted in an oppositional, nontrusting, adversarial relation with the school district. They confront educators regularly and use their councils to do what they consider 'parent business'—trying to get more parents invited to participate on the councils, trying to secure more resources for parental involvement, and trying to 'get rid' of teachers they consider problematic. Given the historic marginalization of parents, such a stance may be understandable, but is not always appreciated by other council members. Then there are those who have taken this opportunity to try to work collaboratively with educators toward a collective vision of a school community. They press for more resources for parental involvement, and try to learn all they can about schools. Many provoke critical conversation about educational practice, tracking, multiculturalism and racism, and the splitting of vocational and academic curricula.

What has become difficult, however, is that school-based management in Philadelphia, as in the rest of the country, has emerged at a moment of public-sector retrenchment, not expansion. School-based resources and decision making have been narrowed, not expanded. School-based councils feel 'empowered' only to determine who or what will be cut. So fights fall along predictable lines of teachers versus parents, representatives of color versus whites, administrators versus teachers. In some contexts the tension is carried at the fault line of educator-parent. This seemingly oppositional relation of parents to educators is, however, neither inevitable nor healthy.

In retrospect, our decision to organize the

Philadelphia parents as a collective may have inadvertently reproduced the impulse to 'equip' (fix?) parents, rather than to transform the workings of bureaucracy so these oppositional interactions were not so overdetermined. In some ways we may have replayed the dilemma of the Baltimore project. In the name of empowering parents, the politics of systemic change may have been papered over.

Fraser identifies two dilemmas of the public sphere: the illusion of bracketing inequalities and the difficulties of engaging real talk among counterpublics. For Fraser (1990: 61), counterpublics

contest the exclusionary norms of the bourgeoisie public . . . which claim[s] to be *the* public . . . signal[ing] that they are parallel discursive arenas where members of subordinated social groups invent and circulate counter discourses, which in turn permit them to formulate oppositional interpretations of their identities, interests and needs.

In Philadelphia, inequalities cannot be bracketed, and those parents who are prepared to engage as counterpublics are looking for conversational partners within the central district and on their councils, although the struggles are most visibly played out on the councils. Manuel Ortiz, father and council member at one high school, sent an open letter to his school principal:

Due to the fact that the participants of the Governance Council are from a very specific situation—all are teachers/administrators, are from the same school, and have been oriented through the years to a particular system and culture—the language, thinking and dialogue left me always playing catch up ball with such important subjects as meaning of words and concepts, philosophy of education, and contextual questions that relate to [this high school]. This promotes a high level of frustration, sense of uselessness and very limited participation. When there is participation, it is difficult to know whether or not you have made your point because of the underlying homogeneity existing in the group.

In Philadelphia, given our ambivalent address of power, one might probe whether parents are being asked to 'contest exclusionary norms' as Fraser points out, or invited to engage with educators in spinning images of the common good (as if power were irrelevant). Robert Bellah and his colleagues have written (1991: 143) that 'private interests' interfere with the emergence of a common good:

The focus of public debate must move away from a concern for maximizing private interests . . . toward the central problems of a sustainable future in our own society and in the world. The focus must be on justice in the broadest sense . . . Without a healthy social and natural ecology, we put at risk everything we have received from our ancestors and threaten to have nothing but violence and decay as the inheritance of our children and grandchildren.

If parents' interests are shaped as private, and schools' interests as 'public,' then a conversation toward a common vision is nearly impossible. Parents (as well as teachers) cannot simply be added to the mix of decision making unless the structures and practices of bureaucracy—school-based and central district—are radically decentralized and democratic.

Slowly, now, within councils, teachers and parents are beginning to talk within groups, if more hesitantly across. Parents sometimes feel that they never have enough information to be truly informed, that they cannot frame the 'right questions,' that educators blame parents for students' educational difficulties, and that some educators are not committed to collaboration with parents, refusing to grant parents a hearing. Once they are snubbed, parents default to 'rights.' Oppositional politics follow.

But most parent council members, after six months, are organizing—together and with teachers. Wonderfully, they are figuring out and playing with the power dynamics. No longer waiting to be invited to speak up, they are invading the space between finding a 'voice' and getting a 'hearing,' dancing with some teachers through the politics of power. Many are working collaboratively with teachers for change. . . . On these school-based councils, parents are often among the first voices of critique, possibility, and common vision. They crack the silences of bureaucracy, prying open the questions that have historically been shut down inside schools—questions of authority, culture, and community. . . .

For most parents, the work of school reform is expressly about challenging and transforming the politics of public education. From their stance, few of these tensions are a surprise. When they joined the governance council, they anticipated that they would be treated as invaders. They understood that respect would be slow in coming, if forthcoming at all. They have been delighted, oddly

enough, to discover what one mother con-
fessed with glee, 'They [teachers] are just like
normal people.' At many of our high schools,
parents are pursuing the critical work of
restructuring through tough questioning,
probing, and persistence. They want to
believe that a common vision is possible but
they know that class, race, and status politics
will prevail unless constantly challenged.
More than they expected, they are finding
allies in teachers.

Three years into restructuring, parents are
now pressing questions of power, demanding
that the public sphere embrace their concerns—the concerns of the public. They often
feel they are being stonewalled. When they
seek to change a Eurocentric curriculum;
when they press questions about special education, ask about student outcomes, demand a
welcoming building, or question why teachers
are being bumped, they describe confronting
blank faces.

Today in bureaucratically controlled and
strongly centralized urban school systems,
parents may be voicing passion and outrage
for everyone. Like the family member who
'carries' everyone's anger, parents, citywide,
are carrying on, 'out of control.' 'They don't
act professionally.' If low-income and of
color, they may be seen as needing containment. If high-income and white, they may
parade their outrage in calls for 'parental
choice' or vouchers, in a well-dressed, regulated, controlled, élite etiquette (Walkerdine
1991). We need to hear the critique parents
carry, and mine their concerns for the rich
possibilities they embody. My point is simply
that we need to see the teacher-parent adversarial relation as largely *constructed by* and
serving the very bureaucracies (local, state,
and federal) that are underfunding and over-
controlling public education.

Indeed, we must resist relentlessly the
splitting of parents' and educators' interests in
their struggles to transform public education.
It is only through organizing parents and educators, as a democratic coalition, that both *privatization* and *controlling bureaucracy* can be
confronted.

As Chantal Mouffe has written (1991: 100):

The progressive character of a struggle does not
depend on its place of origin—we have said that all
workers' struggles are not progressive—but rather
on its link to other struggles. The longer the chain
of equivalences set up between the defense of the

rights of one group and those of other groups,
the deeper will be the democratization process and
the more difficult it will be to neutralize certain
struggles or make them serve the ends of the Right.

Mouffe aptly theorizes the socially constructed antagonisms between parents and
educators, particularly in urban areas. Both
bureaucracy and privatization may be well
served by instigating antagonisms between
educators and parents, mitigating the emergence of a democratic struggle. Three years
into our work in Philadelphia, many educators
and parents are beginning to recognize each
other as friendly critics and allies in the struggle to reinvent urban high schooling.

The Chicago Scene: Ironies of 'Doing Power'

Chicago is, today, the urban scene in which
questions of parents, community, and educator power have been taken most seriously.
The brilliance and exuberance of Chicago
school reform is unprecedented, and unparalleled nationally. Once you arrive in the city,
you can ask your cab driver or waitress, gyne-
cologist or librarian, and they will tell you, in
detail, some story about reform, or maybe
reveal that they are local school council members. Bureaucratic traditions of authority,
control, and decision making have been radically reversed through community control of
schools.

In 1989, school reform legislation passed by
the Illinois State Legislature called for each
school within the Chicago public schools to be
governed by a local school council (LSC),
comprised of six parents, two community representatives, two teachers, and the principal.
Their collective job would be the hiring and
evaluation of the principal, and working with
the principal on school improvement plans
and budgets. By systematically transforming
the nature of school-based power dynamics,
the law sought to dismantle the paternalistic
power of the central administration and to
decentralize public education in Chicago. At
the school site, power was addressed radically.
But, as we will see, the span of control held by
the central district remains relatively intact.

One might consider Chicago school reform
a poststructural dream. A multiplicity of
voices can be heard. A decentralized central

administration can be discerned. A deep community-based challenge to traditional bureaucratic power relations has been launched. By design, little unity or coherence can be found. Schools that are flourishing look very distinct from one another.

Chicago parents are, today, positioned as the primary decision makers within schools. They are intent on importing concerns of culture, class, and community into their schools, as is obvious in the rise of interest in African-centered curricula, afterschool programs, and community-service schools. So, too, they interrupt the monopoly power of 'professionals.' The Professional Practice Advisory Councils, comprised of teachers responsible for curriculum development, are advisory to the principal and to the parent-led LSCs. As Don Moore has articulated (1992: 24), parents as 'outsiders' can:

- Place new problems on the school's agenda that weren't previously acknowledged (for example, . . . the lack of sufficient substitute teachers; students' fears of physical attack in bathrooms, on playgrounds, on the way to and from school).
- Suggest and act on new ways of solving problems (for example, locating space that can be rented in the neighborhood to reduce over-crowding).
- Draw on their own political and organizational networks to get the problems solved (for example, making a major public issue of late bus arrivals through appeals to the media and to elected officials; getting their employer to donate management consulting help to the Local School Council).
- Bring to bear supportive parent and community resources that were not previously available (for example, recruiting community agencies to counsel students and families; organizing parent safety patrols).

The scene in Chicago is a radical reversal of traditional school politics.

With Michael Katz and Elaine Simon of the University of Pennsylvania, and with support of a Spencer grant, I have had the opportunity to study school reform in Chicago: attending LSC meetings; creating conversations among teachers, LSC chairpersons, parents, principals; visiting schools; talking with bureaucrats at the central district, the union representatives, and individuals in high-level policymaking positions. Most of our time has been spent with parents and other activists who helped to instigate and facilitate reform Chicago-style.

We all have been enormously impressed by the vibrant sense of democracy, responsibility, and community involvement that defines so many of Chicago's schools. With reform, parents and community constitute a social movement, often—but not always—with teachers inside and outside their schools. As Richard Elmore has written (1991: viii):

Chicago has embarked on a novel and far-reaching educational reform. This reform stands apart from virtually all others of the last decade, an unprecedented period of educational reform across the nation. First, it originated from a grass roots political movement, formed around a nucleus of business, philanthropic, and community organizations, in response to increasing evidence of chronic failure of schools to educate children. . . .

Second, the Chicago reform is, more than any other, based mainly on the theory that schools can be improved by strengthening democratic control at the school-community level. . . .

Third, the Chicago reform is probably more ambitious—some would say radical—than any other current reform in its departure from the established structure of school organization. The creation of 542 Local School Councils with significant decision making authority for schools, is, by itself, an enormous departure from established patterns of school organization. . . . Those with a concern for the future of urban public school systems are watching Chicago closely.

Before I detail the reform and its power implications for parents, I should note that even in Chicago there yawns a large space between the *ideological power* granted to parents and the *material power* still held by the central administration and the financial élites in this urban community. Should this national round of reform come to a halt, precipitated by crashes in urban and national economies, the callousness of late capitalism, and the brutalization of urban communities, we may hear that activist parents, particularly urban, low-income, African-American parents, are to blame for the failure of public education. And we will know this is a lie.

This concern between ideological and material power bubbled up one evening when Elaine Simon, Michael Katz, and I joined a group of parents and community members in one of Chicago's poorest elementary schools. At the school, parents, teachers, and community members were interviewing their top four candidates for principal of their school, in front of a gymnasium filled, from 5:00 P.M. until 8:00 P.M., with parents, community members, children, teachers, and food and drink. Over seventy people assembled, listening to each other, arguing, questioning, carrying voices of power, critique, and possibility. There were public debates over corporal punishment in school—and at home. One mother explained, 'I'm tired of hearing in our community the only way to handle a child is with a 2 × 4!' The conversation wandered thoughtfully from school to home to community life. We were moved deeply by these parents' sense that they owned this school, and their desire to struggle with the candidates for principal to improve public education. Private troubles were public issues. Former snipes or feelings of alienation were discussed publicly. The smells of democracy, in the streets and in the gymnasium, were sweet.

The next day we interviewed several top administrators in the central administration building, the union, and the Chicago Finance Authority. From all of these top-level policymakers, we heard: 'Our hands are tied. Since the legislation we have no power, and the whole thing is likely to collapse under the weight of budget cuts. But there's nothing we can do. And as you know, we expect $200–$300 million deficit' (Chicago Finance Authority 1991). From the eightieth floor of a high rise in mid-town Chicago, looking down, it was sobering to realize that *the* Chicago adults who feel most empowered around public education are those living well below the poverty line. Those who hold real power claim to be 'out of control.' Ideological power has been reversed, but the bulk of material power has yet to be relinquished.

THE REFORM LEGISLATION
William Ayres summarizes Chicago school reform when he writes:

On December 12, 1988 Governor James Thompson signed Public Act 85–1418, and the most far-reaching mandate to restructure a big-city school system in American history became law. . . . The intent of the law was crystal clear: power was to shift from a large central office to each local school site, and a bureaucratic, command-oriented system was to yield to a decentralized and democratic model. . . .
In this context the Chicago experiment is remarkable. As opposed to blue-ribbon commissions and

top-down recommendations, it is based on radical decentralization and broad popular ownership. Instead of élitism and benevolent dictatorship, it relies on significant authority and responsibility among the full range of interested parties. In place of prescription, it relies on invention and flexible structures. The reformers resisted the notion that a benevolent bureaucrat or an enlightened professional held the key to change. Instead they turned to the people with the problem, saying, in effect, that those with the problems are key to crafting adequate solutions. They explicitly noted that in a democracy the solutions to problems are generally more, not less, democracy. The reformers wanted a shift in power, and they defined, therefore, the problems as structural (not personal) and the solutions as social (not individual). Their goal was a wider sense of efficacy, agency, and initiative among those previously excluded from participation, an end to passivity and victimization. As Mrs. McFerren said, 'Poor people are the real experts on the lives of poor people' (Ayres 1991).

Three kinds of questions about parental involvement spin out of the Chicago school reform story. The first addresses the differential levels of 'cultural capital' that characterize these LSCs, including both what people bring to the LSCs and how they are received. Across schools, we have seen very different displays, and receptions, of what Pierre Bourdieu and Annette Lareau call 'cultural capital' (see Bourdieu 1988; Davies 1991; Lareau 1987). As Lareau has written (1987: 77):

Upper-middle-class parents' educational knowledge, disposition to critically evaluate teachers' professional performance and friendship networks with professionals constitute cultural capital and social capital to comply with teachers' requests for assistance. Overall, upper-middle-class parents possessed more, activated more effectively, and received more benefits from their cultural resources than did working-class parents. . . .
Working-class parents' inability to display cultural capital impedes their children's school success— not so much because of the intrinsic merit of the cultural displays—but because of teachers' definitions of the standards for success in educational organizations.

But as Fred Hess of the Chicago Panel on School Finances rightly points out (1991, 1992), schools have always been deeply stratified by class. This is not peculiar to the reform agenda and, he argues, reform is unlikely to fully destratify:

The issue really is, 'Will empowering parents, who have differential cultural capital at their disposal, increase or diminish the current differences in privilege among Chicago schools?' The centrist bureaucracy had already distributed the system's resources (dollars and staff) inequitably, giving disequalizing power and positions to the privileged (e.g., magnet schools were given the right to select staff without regard to seniority in 1981 and were given four extra teaching positions; they also, frequently without formal authorization, were given the right to select students). The reform act moved to correct these inequities by requiring an equalizing of basic program resources at all schools, extending teacher selection by merit to all schools, and reallocating resources significantly towards schools with the most low income students enrolled. Thus, the empowering of parents through LSC decision-making was only one part of the power rearrangement going on under reform.

As Hess and we have found, many LSCs are flourishing in Chicago. Indeed, many low-income schools are taking off educationally. But some schools cannot get a quorum. In some middle-class schools the LSCs are incorporating so that they can raise money. Some white working-class LSCs are considering redistricting their school boundaries to attract more 'good [read white] kids,' while others opt to become selective magnets. In some low-income schools, the technical training needs run high (how to read a budget) whereas in more affluent or magnet schools, budget expertise sits at the LSC table. In some sights, questions of cultural capital and 'safety nets' linger awkwardly in the midst of a city filled with enormous school-based energy and transformations.

Even Chicago parents live with a second chronic urban dilemma—a bloated and controlling public school bureaucracy that will not go away. This concern involves the role and persistence of bureaucracy in the midst of revolution. The central district in Chicago conveys a wait-and-see attitude—'Districts that are serious about school-based management, whether parent led or not, have not yet adequately struggled with what to do with the Central administration' (Hess 1992). It appears that not enough has changed. There is a premature move to announce that reform has failed, and always a move to recentralize. While the schools have been 'liberated' they may be quite near fiscal 'abandonment.' Since reform, the central administration has cut 840 positions, as stipulated by the legislation. But the workings of the administration—its posture, support, span of control, and trust of schools—have not been reoriented.

Indeed, if schools are 'in charge' and the central administration has changed little, schools are quite vulnerable to devastating, decentralized budget crises. One school principal, quoted by Darryl Ford of the Chicago Panel on School Finances, joked that in Chicago school-based management emerged just when the schools were about to go broke. As this principal said: 'You and I are driving in a car, arguing about which way we ought to be going. I run out of gas and say, "Damn it, you drive! You know how you get to choose the route, which is great. But until somebody puts gas in the tank it doesn't make much difference!" ' (Ford 1991). Indeed, if community control, Chicago-style, goes down the tubes, we may hear that the experiment failed because *parents* ran the schools into the ground, when they were never given all the resources needed to drive the car.

A third concern raised by Chicago, but not distinct to Chicago, is the question of how counterpublics—teachers, parents, community representatives—can possibly engage together in collective educational projects. We know from Baltimore and Philadelphia that power is never absent. In Chicago, the politics of power have been confronted and reversed. Parents call some important shots. Principals can be fired. LSCs determine school-based budgeting. Given that Chicago represents an astonishing moment of the 'public' taking back the 'public sphere,' the question that needs to be pressed is *which* contexts and practices need to be put in place, or invented, so that diverse counterpublics can engage in critical conversation and common projects. How can a democracy of differences breathe life into educational reform?

In Chicago, and to a lesser degree in Milwaukee, New York, Boston, and Philadelphia, parent and community groups do, as they should, import their politics explicitly into shared decision-making meetings. These politics are often generated out of prior, well-established adversarial relations with schools. Given that the reforms of the 1980s focused on 'professionalization,' and typically ignored and marginalized the publics of parents and community, today's activist voices of parents, educational advocates, and community-based organizations have been shaped, historically, against and in opposition to traditional educational institutions, educators, and unions. In many districts these voices are considered 'trouble.' More than anywhere else, Chicago is struggling to invent strategies that detour the automatic turn to oppositional interests and create, instead, ways for adults and adolescents to nurture trust, critique, and hold conversation within educational democracies.

So it is in Chicago, in this fantastic moment of participatory democracy within the public sphere, that we view this 'next generation' of struggles around parental empowerment—differential levels of received and imported cultural capital, the persistence of bureaucratic waste and obstruction, and the need for ongoing creative conversations among parents and teachers within a rich democracy of differences. Chicago holds unprecedented possibilities and moves us all forward, with the sense of serious engagement by and for parents, families, educators, and students.

In the Vanguard of Public Interruption and Resuscitation

The point they miss is that the classroom, and the school and school system generally, are not comprehensible unless you flush out the power relationships that inform and control the behavior of everyone in these settings. Ignore those relationships, leave unexamined their rationale, and the existing 'system' will defeat efforts at reform. This will happen not because there is a grand conspiracy or because of mulish stubbornness in resisting change or because educators are uniquely unimaginative or uncreative (which they are not) but rather because recognizing and trying to change power relationships, especially in complicated, traditional institutions, is among the most complex tasks human beings can undertake. The first step, recognition of the problem, is the most difficult, especially in regard to schools, because we all have been socialized most effectively to accept the power relationships characteristic of our schools as right, natural, and proper outcomes. (Sarason 1990: 29)

Reflecting on these three scenes of parental involvement, and the above quotation from Seymour Sarason, we can see the power of power. Typically unaddressed in and around schools, parent voices surface adversely in the shape of needs, outrage, or silence. As Michel Foucault would tell us, when power asymmetries are confronted and reversed, as in Chicago, they resurface through the stubborn persistence of dominant institutions and the

deceptive withdrawal of material power from now 'empowered' groups (Foucault 1990). So we see parents in the 1990s being thrown into a public sphere of public education that has lost democratic vibrancy, authentic representation, richness of critique, social legitimacy, and the depth of possibility that it once enjoyed, if only romantically. In this postmodern moment, the public institutions of schooling have been declared ineffective by activists from across the political spectrum. Clothed as crusaders, parents are being invited—by us all—to crack this sphere open through threatened exit (e.g., vouchers) or through critical voices in school-based decision making (e.g., restructuring, community control). Simply stated, we are, as a culture, asking parents, in the 1990s, to engage the work of interruption, intervention, and repair of the public sphere.

Public-sector bureaucracies are troubling today because they have swollen uncritically, remain staunchly committed to their shape and breadth, trust neither the educators nor the parents/students 'in the field.' They assume that their policies and practices reflect what Hess (1992) called a 'disinterested common good' (as if one could exist). This public sphere is troubling because educational data, to the extent that they are even made available to the public, demonstrate unambiguously that our schools are failing most of the nation's children. And this public sphere is troubling because although schools must be a site for engaging critical democratic participation, the state in the 1990s has constrained dramatically the talk, resources, and work of those employed in and attending schools.

In this historical context, parents are being put to use. They are among the most appropriate, but cannot be the exclusive, agents who speak for a radical interruption and transformation of the public sphere of public education. If they are alone, they will be read as marginalized and hysterical, especially if poor and of color. Unless the dynamics of power are addressed, unless the range and consequences of cultural capital are supported, and unless a deep vision of schools as community-based democracies of difference is engaged, parental involvement 'projects' will be transformed into crisis-intervention projects, into moments of having a voice but not getting a hearing, or into public contexts that slip into bankruptcy.

As Michael Katz states (1989: 30):

The failure of public institutions spreads beyond the 'underclass' or very poor. Because it touches all Americans, institutional failure represents one more link between the 'underclass' and the rest of America. Only, it impacts poor people with greater force because they lack alternatives. They cannot purchase private schooling, security systems and health care or, as the well-off have done in central Philadelphia, create their own special service districts to assure clean and safe streets. This cumulative failure of institutions degrades public life and raises the question of whether any common collective life remains possible in American cities. If privatization proves the only viable response, what will prevent the distribution of institutional resources from becoming more unequal? What happens to the definition of citizenship and the possibility of community?

Rich and real parental involvement requires a three-way commitment—to organizing parents, to restructuring schools and communities toward enriched educational and economic outcomes, and to inventing rich visions of educational democracies of difference. Unless parents are organized as a political body, parental involvement projects will devolve into a swamp of crisis intervention, leaving neither a legacy of empowerment nor a hint of systemic change. Without a commitment to democratically restructuring schools and communities, parental involvement projects will end up helping families (or not) rather than transforming public life. Without an image of parents and educators working across lines of power, class, race, gender, status, and politics, toward democracies of difference, each group is likely to feel they have gotten no hearing, and will default to their respective corners shrouded in private interests and opposition. Soon, the Right will privatize us all.

Schools, as transforming, reflective communities, need to feel more like meaningful communities—whatever romantic spin one has on churches, neighborhoods, social movements, or labor unions—contexts in which shared vision, textured solidarity, and ongoing struggles constitute the work of community life. Within parental involvement projects, we must resist the default to deficit-focused service, complacent silence, or singularly oppositional politics. The costs are far too high.

Those of us who are educators, researchers,

activists, and/or parents need to pursue the work we do with/as parents around schools. All of us, hungry for a reinvigorated public sphere, must understand that the need is far more immense and the project far more ambitious than we imagined. These days, speaking aloud about wasteful public bureaucracies and irresponsible public institutions bears substantial costs. The bodies and minds of low-income children are simply expendable in the many designs for a privatized public sphere (see Chubb and More 1990). Nevertheless, without feeding the perverse pleasures of the privatizing Right, we must reconceptualize a democratic, critical, lively public sphere within public education. And we need to do this with, but not exclusively on the backs of, parents.

Acknowledgements

I appreciate support from the W. T. Grant Foundation, the Spencer Foundation, and the Pew Charitable Trusts, and acknowledge the generous work of Jennifer Williams, and invaluable feedback from Gail Clouden, Jocelyn Garlington, Fred Hess, Annette Lareau, Manuel Ortiz, and Anne Wheelock.

Notes

1. 'Parents' will be used to designate parents and guardians.
2. The collaborative is supported by a grant from Pew Charitable Trusts to restructure the 22 comprehensive high schools in Philadelphia.

References

Ayres, W. (1991), 'If Bumble Bees Can Fly: Taking Off with the Chicago School Reform' (unpubl., Chicago: Univ. of Illinois).

Bellah, R. *et al.* (1991), *The Good Society* (New York: Alfred A. Knopf).

Bourdieu, P. (1988), *Outline of a Theory of Practice* (Cambridge: Cambridge Univ. Press).

Chicago Finance Authority (1991), interview.

Chubb, J. E., and Moe, T. M. (1990), *Politics, Markets, and America's Schools* (Washington DC: Brookings Institution).

Comer, J. P. (1981), 'New Haven's School Community Connection', *Educational Leadership* (March), 42–8.

Connell, R. *et al.* (1982), *Making the Difference: Schools, Families and Social Division* (Sydney: George Allen and Unwin).

Davies, D. (1991), *Testing a Strategy for Reform: The League of Schools Reaching Out* (Boston: Instit. for Responsive Education).

Elmore, R. (1991), 'Introduction', in *School Restructuring, Chicago Style*, (ed.) G. Hess (Newbury Park, Calif.: Corwin Press), viii.

Epstein, J. L. (1982), 'Schools in the Centre: School, Family, Peer and Community Connections for More Effective Middle Grades Schools and Students', mimeographed draft prepared for the Carnegie Task Force on Education of Young Adolescents (Johns Hopkins Univ.).

—— (1991), 'School and Family Connections: Theory, Research, and Implications for Integrating Societies of Education and Family', in *Families in Community Settings: Interdisciplinary Perspectives*, (ed.) D. G. Unger and M. B. Sussman (New York: Hayworth Press).

Fine, M. (1990), 'The "Public" in Public Schools: The Social Constriction/Construction of a Moral Community', *Journal of Social Issues*, 46: 107–9.

—— and Cook, D. (1991), *Evaluation Reports: 'With and For Parents'* (final report, Baltimore: National Committee of Citizens for Education).

Ford, D. J. (1991), 'The School Principal and Chicago's School Reform: Principals' Early Perceptions of Reform Institutions', in *Chicago Panel on Public Policy and Finance* (Chicago: Chicago Panel on Public School Policy and Finance).

Foucault, M. (1980), *The History of Servality*, i (New York: Vintage Books).

Fraser, N. (1990), 'Rethinking the Public Sphere: A Contribution to the Critique of Actually Existing Democracy', *Social Text*, 8: 56–80.

Garlington, J. (1991), *Helping Dreams Survive: The Story of a Project Involving African-American*

Families and the Education of their Children (Baltimore: National Committee of Citizens for Education, 15 November), xxi.

—— (1991), personal communication.

Gilkes, C. T. (1988), 'Going Up for the Oppressed', in *Empowerment and Women*, (ed.) A. Bookmen and S. Morgan (Philadelphia: Temple Univ. Press), 75.

Hess, G. F. (1991, 1992), personal communication.

Katz, M. B. (1989), *The Undeserving Poor: From the War on Poverty to the War on Welfare* (New York: Pantheon).

Lareau, A. (1987), 'Social Class Differences in Family-School Relationships: The Importance of Cultural Capital', *Sociology of Education*, 60: 73–85.

Lightfoot, S. L. (1978), *Worlds Apart: Relationships between Families and Schools* (New York: Basic Books).

Lykes, B. (1985), 'Gender and Individualistic versus Collectivist Bases for Notions about the Self', *Journal of Personality*, 53: 375.

Mouffe, C. (1991), 'Hegemony and New Political Subjects: Toward a New Concept of Democracy', in *Marxism and the Interpretation of Culture*, (ed.) C. Nelson and L. Grossberg (Urbana, Ill.: Univ. of Illinois Press), 100.

Moore, D. (1992), 'The Case for Parent and Community Involvement', in *Empowering Teachers and Parents*, (ed.) G. Hess (South Hadley: Greenwood Publishing).

Sarason, S. B. (1990), *The Predictable Failure of Educational Reform: Can We Change Course Before It's Too Late?* (San Francisco: Jossey-Bass).

School District of Philadelphia (1991), *Philadelphia Federation of Teachers Guidelines SBM/SDM* (June).

Walkerdine, V. (1991), *The Mastery of Reason* (New York: Routledge).

Wheelock, A. (1991), personal communication.

31

Can Effective Schools Compensate for Society?

Peter Mortimore

Why Ask This Question?

According to Silver (1994), 'Schools, and the philosophers, and providers of schooling, have always been concerned with outcomes'. Silver cites the concern of Plato that the *overseers* of the state should be prepared by the *right* education. He also notes the development of schools for specialist occupations such as bureaucrats, religious leaders, musicians, lawyers, and craftsmen over the years. Green (1990) makes the case that mainland Europe developed systems of schools at a much earlier period than did the English. The English, however, were quick to establish an inspectorate (the first of Her Majesty's Inspectors was appointed in 1839), thus initiating an interest in questions of quality judged through the learning outcomes of students. Effectiveness, although not known by that word, also underlies much of the work of the Newcastle Commission. Established as part of the 'payment by results' movement, the Commission examined the variability of standards in schools during the late nineteenth century. During the twentieth century with the provision of free and, in most cases, compulsory education for children up to the age of 14, an expectation grew that education would overcome the problems caused by ignorance and poverty. As Silver points out, there followed a period of reaction when, during the 1960s, it was found that education had not eradicated such problems.

In 1970 Bernstein stated that 'schools cannot compensate for society'. In this succinct sentence, he summarized the view that the potential effects of schools should always be compared with the totality of influences in society and that, in his judgement, many of these other influences were likely to be more powerful than those of the school. Bernstein's statement was made shortly after Coleman had reported the results of the large-scale American survey of Equality of Educational Opportunity (Coleman 1966). Coleman found no relationship between the amount of resources available to schools and the achievements of the students who had attended them. Instead he explained the differences in achievement between students in terms of their personal and family characteristics.

Subsequent work by Jencks and colleagues showed that 'if all high schools were equally effective, differences in attainment would be reduced by less than one per cent' (Ouston *et al.* 1979: 67). Similar negative conclusions were reached by those responsible for the evaluation of a series of *Head Start* programmes carried out in the 1960s although, interestingly, some gains—both short-and long-term—were noted (Ouston *et al.* 1979).

Since then, there has been a re-evaluation of the significance of Coleman's and Jencks's findings and a reappraisal of *Head Start* based on its long-term effects (Lazar *et al.* 1977). Coleman and other investigators working at that time had access only to macro-level variables, such as the size of the school site, the facilities available, and the resources provided. This inevitably restricted the questions they could ask of schools and of their effects. Had Coleman and Jencks had access to more micro-level variables, such as school climate, staff behaviour, pupil attitudes, and institutional relationships they could have tested their conclusions against these more detailed factors. It is this shift in focus from macro- to micro-variables—from the system to the individual school—that has inspired a number of researchers to consider the effects of individual schools on the learning outcomes of their own students.

As a result of this shift many studies of schools have been undertaken in the United States including, for example, studies by Brookover and Lezotte (1977); Edmonds (1979); and Teddlie *et al.* (1984 and 1989). Each of these investigations found that schools could influence the outcomes of their students. The number of such studies undertaken in the US over the last 20 or so years is now vast, filling forty-one pages of references produced in the latest review by the North West Regional Educational Laboratories (NWREL 1995). In the United States the research on the potential differential effects of individual schools has been closely bound up with concern about the plight of disadvantaged children and the limited opportunities available to them: hence the frequent use of the catch-phrase coined by the late Dr Ron Edmonds (1979), 'all children can learn'.

In the United Kingdom, detailed research into school effectiveness has included those studies carried out in South Wales (Reynolds *et al.* 1976), the pioneering study of twelve inner-city secondary schools (Rutter *et al.* 1979), the ILEA's study of primary schools (Mortimore *et al.* 1988); the study of children in infant schools (Tizard *et al.* 1988); and Smith and Tomlinson's (1989) study focusing on the progress of students from minority ethnic groups. The investigations found clear evidence of school differences in students' outcomes. Each of the research teams used this evidence to argue that these differences were not simply due to the effects of schools receiving different types of students but, rather, that they were associated with differences in the way the schools, through management and the quality of the teaching and learning environment, promoted achievement.

Similar studies have been undertaken in many other parts of the world including Australia (Fraser 1989); the Netherlands (Brandsma and Knuver 1989; and Creemers and Lugthart 1989); Norway (Dalin 1989); and Israel (Bashi and colleagues 1990). There has been particular interest in questions of methodology in the studies in the Netherlands (see, for example, Luyten (1994)). An exhaustive review of the international literature has been compiled by Reynolds *et al.* (1994).

The results of these studies provide justification for the question which forms the title of this chapter. It should be noted that, unlike Bernstein's original statement, this question focuses on *the potency of individual schools* rather than on that of education in general. The problem of how best to answer such a question, however, remains.

I shall endeavour to do so by reporting on some of the work which has taken place in this field of study over the last 20 years, and by reviewing the published evidence about school effects on a selection of student outcomes. Given the scale of activity, I will not attempt to be exhaustive, but will seek to select appropriately in order to illustrate the general picture.

The Model of School Effectiveness

In order to gauge the potential effectiveness of a school, a researcher has to find a way of taking account of the fact that—in most societies—schools do not receive uniform intakes of students. From the point of view of the researcher, random allocation of both students and teachers would be far preferable, but given an increasingly powerful trend towards providing parents with the opportunity to express a preference and, in some cases, a choice of school, this cannot easily be achieved. Instead, increasingly sophisticated statistical techniques, such as multi-level modelling (Paterson and Goldstein 1991), are used to equate for differences in the prior achievement and other relevant characteristics (such as gender, age, and socio-economic status) of students entering schools.

The research model usually involves the collection of data on the behaviour and performance of individual students at various stages of schooling. These outcomes are compared with estimates modelled from the intake information to ensure that like is being compared with like. Confidence intervals are calculated and schools with statistically significant differences in their impact on student outcomes are then noted.

Those researchers with access to appropriate data have then sought to relate these indicators of school effectiveness to information collected about the detailed life of the school. By examining the positive correlations they have endeavoured to identify the kinds of behaviours—of staff and students—typically associated with the more effective outcomes. More recent studies have progressed from correlational techniques to attempts to incorporate information about key processes in multi-level models of school effectiveness (Sammons et al. 1995). A number of common characteristics of effectiveness drawn from an international review of studies have also recently been identified (Sammons et al. 1994).

Like all research in the social sciences, the collection of valid and reliable data about individuals and institutions is challenging. Rutter (1983); Purkey and Smith (1983); Raudenbush (1989); Bosker and Scheerens (1989); and Reynolds and Cuttance (1992) have found weaknesses in procedures and have contributed to advances in methodology in this field. Further work is needed on the conceptualization of problems and the development of theory.

Outcomes of Schooling

In seeking to judge the effectiveness of schools, researchers have focused on a range of student outcomes. All studies have used some measure of academic attainment. Some have also incorporated measures of attendance and behaviour (Rutter et al. 1979). A few have included more sophisticated (and more difficult to measure) variables, such as student attitudes to their schools, or to themselves as learners (Mortimore et al. 1988).

Various studies have used one-day surveys and whole-year individual records of student attendance. Mortimore and colleagues (1988) found systematic differences between primary (elementary) schools, and Reynolds and colleagues (1976), Rutter and colleagues (1979) and Smith and Tomlinson (1989) all found clear school differences between secondary schools. Despite the characteristics of the particular students and regardless of their previous attendance records in other schools, the way the school operates appears to have a direct relationship with the attendance rates.

The collection of data on student behaviour

is far from straightforward. Interactions between teachers and students are affected by the behaviour of both parties and yet it is the one (the teachers) who rate the behaviour of the others (the students). Few researchers have found ways of modifying the ratings to take account of teacher differences. Rutter found that only half of his sample of students, identified on a teacher-rated behaviour inventory in any one year, were likely to appear in subsequent years.

Data on behaviour have nevertheless been collected by a range of researchers including Bennett (1976); Mortimore and colleagues (1988); Heal (1978); Rutter and colleagues (1979); Reynolds and colleagues (1976); Power and colleagues (1967); Cannan (1970); and Gray and colleagues (1983). Significant differences between students in both in-school and out-of-school activities, including delinquency, have been found.

The data most commonly collected in studies of schools is concerned with academic achievement. A great number of studies of schools in the United States have focused on the collection of test data: Weber (1971); New York Department of Education (1974); Edmonds (1979); Brookover and Lezotte (1977); Clark and McCarthy (1983); McCormack-Larkin and Kritek (1982); and Teddlie and colleagues (1989).

In the United Kingdom, Bennett (1976); Galton and Simon (1980); Mortimore and colleagues (1988); Tizard and colleagues (1988); Reynolds and colleagues (1976); Brimer and colleagues (1978); Rutter and colleagues (1979); Gray and colleagues (1990); Smith and Tomlinson (1989); Daly (1991); Nuttall and colleagues (1989); Blakey and Heath (1992); Thomas and Mortimore (1995); and Sammons and colleagues (1995) have all collected systematic evidence on student achievement measured by tests or in the results of public examinations. Similar data have also been collected in Australia (Fraser, (1989), the Netherlands (Brandsma and Knuver (1989); Creemers and Lugthart (1989)); Norway (Dalin (1989)); and Israel (Bashi and colleagues, (1990). Only a minority of studies, however, have attempted to collect data on attitudes (Mortimore et al. (1988); Tizard et al. (1988); Smith and Tomlinson (1989); Ainley and Sheret (1992); and NFER (1994)), but where this has been done clear differences have been found both in students' judgements about themselves and about their views of the school.

Although the studies cited here differ in their scope, methodologies, and objectives, their findings are reasonably consistent: schools vary in their general ability to promote the positive development of their students, whether this is in academic progress, attendance, behaviour, or attitude formation. The consistency of school effectiveness in promoting different student outcomes, however, is an area of considerable complexity. Sammons *et al.* (1996) discuss whether schools perform consistently on different outcomes, over time, and across different phases of schooling and differing school memberships. The authors conclude that the evidence indicates positive (though far-from-perfect) associations between school effects on different areas of cognitive development (less work has taken place in the affective or social areas). Consistency is also found in school effects on student academic achievement over the short to medium term. Interestingly, however, this appears to work at the level of the total examination score of the student and to conceal the variation between performance in separate subjects; the overall consistency at the school level is thus made up of a series of swings-and-roundabout effects. There is also some evidence that the effects in general may be stronger for primary than for secondary schools. In terms of student membership, the evidence suggests that secondary schools especially may exert differential influence on different groups of students (more or less able, more or less advantaged, and on different gender and ethnic groups). This is an area in which further research is needed. Studies which focus on the major domains of activity (academic, affective, and behavioural) and, within these, on different outcomes, are likely to prove helpful both to practitioners seeking to improve different aspects of the performance of their schools and to researchers exploring the nature of school influences.

The Size of School Differences

The crucial question being addressed by such studies—especially by those using sophisticated statistical measures—is what proportion of the variance between students is accounted for by the school once background factors have been taken into account. A typical finding is that multi-level studies account for about 30 to 40 per cent of the total variance between students' examination results. Of this, about 10 per cent can be traced directly to the school (Thomas and Mortimore 1988). In terms of the English examination system used by secondary schools, 10 per cent is the equivalent of over 14 points (GCSE points scale). This can be roughly translated into the difference between being awarded seven E grades and seven C grades. Obtaining the C grades in seven subjects will permit the student to move on to A level work and open up the possibility of working in the more prestigious occupations. In contrast, obtaining even seven subjects at E grade is seen in England as evidence of fairly low achievement.

Thus, although the variance obtained by the school is comparatively modest, its significance is considerable in a system where even minor differences may influence significantly the life chances of students. Most importantly, data from studies of school effectiveness show that the maximum impact of the school can be identified in the amount of progress exhibited by the student. In the *School Matters* study (Mortimore *et al.* 1988), for instance, it was found that the proportion of variance in reading progress accounted for by the school was approximately five times the size of that accounted for by home factors. Also of interest are the findings by Sammons *et al.* (1994) that primary school effects are not completely washed out by subsequent phases of schooling, and the argument by Goldstein and Sammons (1995) that the primary range of differences may be wider than those occurring at the end of the secondary phase.

In Australia, the analyses have now been extended to the classroom. In a recent study looking at primary students' attainments in English and Mathematics (Hill and Rowe, forthcoming) substantial variation was found between schools. School effects of between 16 and 18 per cent of the variance were identified, but these shrank to between 5 and 8 per cent once the school classes of the students were taken into account. Interestingly, the proportion of variance explained by the class ranged from 16 to 44 per cent for English and from 47 to 56 per cent for mathematics, suggesting that the impact of the school was experienced through the greater impact of the class.

In a further study Hill *et al.* (1996) have concluded that 'in Australian elementary schools, the influence of home background characteristics tends to be small once adjustments have been made for prior achievement.' The research team is now engaged in teasing out the 'myriad influences that best predict student progress'.

Current Status of School Effectiveness

Undoubtedly, this topic has been one of the growth areas in educational research in a number of different countries, and is now recognized as a legitimate field of study for academics. Not all academics, however, are supportive of this trend. Over the years some have questioned the purpose of the research (Acton 1980), while others have sought to improve its methodology (Goldstein 1987, 1995; Preece 1988). Some have questioned whether the effectiveness model has, in fact, helped schools in self-evaluation tasks (Brown 1994). The fear that research in this area provides governments with an excuse for failing to provide adequate levels of resources on the grounds that effectiveness is not necessarily affected by them has also occasionally been expressed.

Some aspects of this research, however, have been welcomed by governments and their agencies. In the United Kingdom, for instance, the Government Response to a *Report on Performance in City Schools* compiled by the House of Commons Education Committee (HMSO 1995) acknowledged that 'schools can and do make a difference'. The Secretary of States's speech to the local educational authorities at their annual conference in 1995 also focused largely on this area (Shephard 1995). In countries as diverse as Singapore, the Netherlands, and Australia, governments have shown that they are aware of—and take into account—research studies undertaken in this area. In the United States the amendment to the Elementary and Secondary Education Act of 1965 by the Hawkins-Stafford Elementary and Secondary School improvement amendments has had a major impact on the federal education block-grant programme.

Most importantly, it is clear that school effectiveness is acknowledged as important by a significant number of practitioners. Headteachers (principals) see the research as being relevant to their daily work and their engagement with day-to-day school problems. Work in a number of British, Dutch, American, German, and Australian universities is providing support for applied projects based on school-effectiveness findings. A Scottish Office Education Department project (undertaken by Strathclyde University and the Institute of Education), for instance, involves working with the staff in eighty primary and secondary schools drawn from across Scotland, and systematically endeavouring to improve the performance of their pupils (Mortimore and MacBeath 1994). There are also a number of networks involving practitioners and academics producing bulletins and disseminating information reports on this area of research.

The standing of this research, in my judgement, is reasonably high. Researchers in the field have focused on important questions about the character of schooling in modern societies, and these investigations have been aimed at both policy makers and practitioners. Furthermore, researchers have developed an appropriate methodology which uses statistical techniques such as multi-level modelling, together with more conventional qualitative and quantitative methods, in order to explore differences between schools and the correlation of these differences with their staff and student characteristic behaviour. Where the field of research has failed to develop—as noted earlier—is in the production of an adequate theory. This does not mean that no progress has been made. Ideas from a broad range of disciplines, including child development, the study of institutions, contingency theory, and public choice theory have been invoked in order to explain school differences; but despite the work of a number of researchers (Scheerens 1992; Coleman and Collinge 1991; Slater and Teddlie 1992; and Hopkins 1994), more work is needed before a distinctive theory is likely to be formulated.

The Application of Studies of School Effectiveness

The first application of knowledge about

school effectiveness has been devoted to how best to address issues of school improvement, a flourishing area of educational activity in both the United States and the United Kingdom. Stoll and Mortimore (1995) provide an account of how the two fields relate together, combining as they do a common data set but rather different aims, concepts, and methods. As part of their analysis they make a distinction between the eleven factors of school effectiveness (what they term the 'final picture') and the facilitating conditions provided by school improvement projects. Thus they link the characteristic of firm and purposeful leadership, incorporating ideas to do with the role of the head teacher (principal) as the leading professional, with a participative approach in which the head's role is that of motivator and guide, involving teachers in decision-making and seeing them as agents of change within the school.

The National Commission on Education (NCE 1995) has published a collection of eleven case studies illustrating how schools with intakes below average still manage to achieve results above it. In their collation of the findings from the case studies, Maden and Hillman (NCE 1995) emphasize the importance of a cluster of behaviours: a leadership stance which builds on and develops a team approach; a vision of success which includes a view of how the school can improve and which, once it has improved, is replaced by a pride in its achievement; school policies and practices which encourage the planning and setting up of targets; the improvement of the physical environment; common expectations about pupil behaviour and success; and an investment in good relations with parents and the community.

Reynolds (1995), Barber (1995), Stoll (1995), and Myers (1995) have all, on the other hand, addressed the question of how schools *fail* to improve, in order to complement earlier studies of success. Stoll (1995) has drawn our attention to a lack of vision, unfocused leadership, dysfunctional staff relationships, and ineffective classroom practices as mechanisms through which the effectiveness of schools can deteriorate. Myers (1995) has argued that failing schools not only permit their students to make less progress than expected, but may incur negative costs: 'In other words it is possible that the students will do worse on the measure in question by

attending the school than they would have done if they had stayed at home.'

A second issue related to school improvement concerns the need to learn more about the differential effects of effective schools. Through the ESRC (Economic and Social Research Council)-funded study, Sammons, Thomas, and I have uncovered a complex picture of schools producing differential effects for students of different prior attainments as well as those from different ethnic backgrounds. To a lesser extent we also found differences according to gender and social background. The results are reported in full in Sammons *et al.* (1995) and Thomas *et al.* (1995). Interestingly, we found that all students appear likely to perform poorly in *ineffective* schools and departments, with the exception of some minority ethnic groups who seem to be able to pull themselves up and achieve above the level of their white counterparts. Furthermore, all students seemed likely to perform *well* in generally effective schools; but those students with particularly advantaged backgrounds appear able to perform even better than their high-performing peers.

A third issue concerns the question of stability of results. In the ESRC study just cited, my colleagues and I found a relative stability in the overall GCSE value-added results. We found overall correlations of 0.8 between the total examinations score of one year and another, but the effects on individual subjects varied. History was stable, with correlations of 0.92 between 1990 and 1991 and 0.71 between 1991 and 1992, whilst the equivalent correlations for French were 0.48 and 0.38.

Studies of Cost-Effectiveness

A fourth area of general concern which is sometimes addressed by those involved with studies of school effectiveness is whether schools are worth the money spent on them. Hanushek (1986, 1989, 1991), for instance, has argued that whilst 'teachers and schools differ dramatically in their effectiveness' (1986: 1159), the results indicate that 'there is no strong or systematic relationship between school expenditures and student performance' (p. 47). In particular he has claimed that there is no strong evidence that '(low) student-teacher ratios (good) teacher education, or teacher experience have the expected positive effects on student achievement' (1989: 47).

Hanushek's conclusions have been attacked by Hedges *et al.* (1994) on the grounds of inadequate data, methods, and, most seriously, biased reporting of results. I will address simply the question of student–teacher ratios, since the issue of class size and its related costs and benefits is of considerable interest to those involved in the British education system, and has been discussed in numerous articles in the press and on television. A review of research findings and an analysis of current trends in British schools has recently been published (Blatchford and Mortimore 1994; Mortimore 1995).

The debate in the United Kingdom has been much influenced by publications about the STAR (Student-Teacher Achievement Ratio) Project, which describes how from 1985 to 1989 over 7,000 students from 328 classes in 79 primary schools in Tennessee took part in an experiment designed to ascertain the effects of class size (Finn and Achilles 1990; Nye *et al.* 1993).

Pupils were assigned randomly to classes of different sizes (small classes of between 13 and 17; regular classes of between 22 and 25; and regular enhanced classes with a teaching aide) for a period of 2 years. Their academic progress was measured in reading and mathematics using standardized tests (Stanford Achievement Tests) and curriculum-based assessments (Tennessee Basic Skills). Teachers were randomly assigned to the different-sized classes, but were not given any special training for teaching small groups or preparation for working with aides.

The statistical design of the experiment treated schools as a random dimension, nested within four locations (inner-city, urban, suburban and rural). These locations were crossed with classtype (small, regular, and aide) and race (white and minority). Means on each outcome were calculated for each class for white and minority students in each classroom.

The results of the experiment showed statistically significant benefits in both subjects for students in the reduced size classes from kindergarten through to the end of grade 3. It was also found that students from minority ethnic groups benefited most from the smaller-class environment, especially when the curriculum-based tests were used as the

learning criteria. No significant improvement occurred with the use of classroom aides. The researchers also noted that students who experienced smaller classes displayed significantly more effort to learn in the classroom, took more initiative in learning activities, and exhibited less non-participatory or disruptive behaviour than their peers (Finn and Voelkl 1992).

The progress of students involved in the STAR experiment was further monitored through the *Lasting Benefits Study* (Achilles *et al.* 1993). This found that, even after students had returned to normal size classes, they continued to score significantly above their classmates on all achievement tests even though in effect sizes were not as great as they had been during the experimental study. As a direct result of the dissemination of the research findings, recent legislation in Tennessee now prohibits class sizes of more than 20 for the youngest students.

The benefits of the smaller classes for the students revealed by *Project Star*, although consistent across types of schools and types of pupils, were relatively modest. According to Finn and Voelkl (1992) success rates on the curriculum-based tests were between 2.2 and 11.5 per cent higher in small classes in reading, and between 6.3 and 6.7 per cent higher in mathematics.

The very high cost of reducing classes to the levels found effective in Project Star has been commented upon by, amongst others, Bob Slavin, author of what is acknowledged to be one of the best intervention programmes in the United States, *Success for All*. Slavin (1990) argues that, for an equivalent amount of money, more pupils could receive better learning support through the use of 'reading recovery' or similar programmes focused on individual learners. An estimate of the cost of moving from an average of 24 pupils to one of 15 in the United States is $69 billion.

The question of the cost-effectiveness of different aspects of the education service, therefore, remains unresolved, though it is my belief that a much greater use is likely to be made of economic analyses. In one study in which I was involved (Mortimore *et al.* 1994) we adopted a cost-effectiveness analysis framework for judging the effectiveness of the use of associate staff (non-teachers employed in schools). We were able to tease out the costs and the benefits of employing classroom assistants whilst taking into account not only their salaries but also of premises, equipment, and supervision costs. In detailed interviews with all those involved in the schools, it emerged that the use of such staff was educationally sound, cost-effective, and highly popular with the teachers: features which undoubtedly help schools to be effective.

Conclusions

So: can effective schools compensate for society? The answer, in my judgement, is yes—to a certain extent. The school offers an opportunity for the individual to develop whatever talents he or she possesses. In doing so the individual is aided or hindered by a range of other personal variables to do with their temperament, their motivation, and their attitudes. They are also influenced by their family, class, gender, ethnic background, and various other social variables. Those individuals who are advantaged by these factors can enhance their situations through their schooling. Those who are disadvantaged can be supported by their school in their bid to overcome the negative effects of the other societal pressures. The evidence reported here shows that effective schools are better-equipped to help the student mount such a challenge.

The success of such schools, however, is generally likely to be both partial and limited, because schools are also part of the wider society, subject to its norms, rules, and influences. Schools are also likely to contain at least some of those students who benefit from the way things are. Because of the capacity of those who are advantaged to extract from any situation more than those who are disadvantaged, schools will always be inefficient and partial mechanisms for compensation. It is also important to ensure that schools are not blamed for all the ills of society nor held responsible, unfairly, for failing to overcome all the pre-existing differences in attainment amongst their student intakes. In some countries, one can detect a tendency to blame teachers collectively for the seemingly inadequate academic standards that developed nations, facing a complex and competitive future, realize they have tolerated for too long. There is also a tendency to make an issue of the minority of teachers who fail to come up to

scratch. These tendencies are unfair and unhelpful, since the impetus for improvement must lie with teachers.

The research has thrown up some interesting interactions between the school and the background of the student. For instance, in the *School Matters* study, in no school did we find evidence of whole groups of the disadvantaged outperforming whole groups of the advantaged. We did find, however, that disadvantaged students in the most effective schools sometimes made more progress than relatively advantaged students in the least effective ones. The school, it appeared, was acting as a mediating factor between the level of progress attained and the family background.

For families whose lives are disadvantaged in relation to their peers, schools remain one of the few mechanisms that are able to provide a compensating boost. The more effective the school, the higher the proportion of students that will get to the starting-line in the competition for favourable life-chances. How well such students will perform in the subsequent race will depend on their talents, motivation, and luck; but they will at least have a chance to compete. Their peers who have not attended effective schools are less likely to reach this stage.

There are obvious lessons from this research for those involved: parents who seek to send their children to effective schools; head teachers who are endeavouring to increase the effectiveness of their schools; and governments which are seeking to support schools in becoming more effective. Some of the lessons, however, are less obvious, and turn on the overall educational goals of societies and on whether policy-makers wish to give priority to the education of a small élite or to the majority, which will include the disadvantaged. If the priority is to sustain an élite, then it needs to be recognized that only in exceptional cases will disadvantaged students—sponsored by particularly effective schools—win through. In most cases the majority of opportunities will be won by those who have experienced most advantages. However, if the aim is to improve the lot of the majority and to lift overall standards, then ways need to be sought in which compensating mechanisms can be created or made more readily available. These may include better preschool provision, out-of-school study-support centres, fuller financial help with school meals, travel to school or college and, for older students, maintenance allowances and special programmes either to help individual students—such as reading recovery—or to help the school improve itself.

There is an ethical problem to this issue. The most effective way of closing the educational gap between the disadvantaged and the rest is through a series of specifically targeted initiatives. Should such initiatives, however, be restricted to the disadvantaged? If they work well, how can they be denied to families which, in comparative terms, are well off even though the result of free access to such programmes will undoubtedly be an increase in the gap that was originally causing concern?

A policy of lifting overall standards, however, means ensuring that educational spending is fairly distributed and, in some cases, directed towards those schools which serve the most disadvantaged students instead of the seemingly inevitable situation whereby most resources tend to end up at the disposal of the most advantaged. As has been discovered, the distribution of extra resources to chosen areas is complicated and creates problems (Acland 1973; Sammons et al. 1983). It has also been argued that extra resources alone will not guarantee effectiveness; there is no evidence, however, to show that the lack of them helps.

'Education cannot compensate for society,' as Bernstein noted in 1970; but it does appear that education is able to change certain societies in other parts of the world. In Singapore, Taiwan, and parts of the Indian subcontinent it is clearly doing this. The question of whether such change is possible in the industrially advanced (and economically deteriorating) Western societies is not yet clear. My own view is that school effectiveness provides an opportunity for this to happen. I do not believe, however, that it should be thought of as a panacea. Its methodology and its applications have developed impressively over the last 20 years and its standing and reception among practitioners maximizes its opportunity to influence the development of schools. Headteachers and their staff are unlikely to exploit the fruits of this research fully by themselves. They need the support of their students, the parents, the universities, communities, and governments.

The desire to improve schools and to lift standards is widespread. Where there are debates, these are usually over the methods to be adopted for such a task. Research on school effectiveness suggests that top-down 'command and control' systems of changing schools seldom work. More plausible is an approach which recognizes the dilemmas and the challenges of change, but nevertheless endeavours to maximize support for it by providing accurate feedback—in relation to the performance of schools with similar intakes—and ensuring that appropriate expertise to help schools facing difficulties is made available. It is the school that will be the focus of attention, and the management of the school, in the form of its principal, staff, and governors, which must be accountable for its progress. If this situation can be brought about and be supported by those who work in universities, or hold positions in public life, scope for change—both of the school and, more broadly, of society, increases. The challenge is to ensure that these changes make it more rather than less likely that schools—in whatever form they exist in the future—can better compensate for the worst ills of society.

Acknowledgements

Grateful thanks are extended to all those colleagues working in the fields of school effectiveness and school improvement with whom I have collaborated over the last 20 years.

References

Achilles, C. M., Nye, B. A., Zaharias, J. B., and Fulton, B. D. (1993), 'The Lasting Benefits Study (LBS) in grades 4 and 5 (1990–1991): A Legacy from Tennessee's Four-Year (K-3) Class-Size Study (1985–1989), Project STAR' (Paper to North Carolina Association for Research in Education).

Acland, H. (1973), 'Social Determinants of Educational Achievement: An Evaluation and Criticism of Research' (Ph.D. Thesis, Univ. of Oxford).

Acton, T. (1980), 'Educational Criteria of Success: Some Problems in the Work of Rutter, Maughan, Mortimore, and Ouston', Educational Research, 22: 163–9.

Ainley, J., and Sheret, M. (1992), Effectiveness of High Schools in Australia: Holding Power and Achievement (Paper presented to the International Congress for School Effectiveness and

Improvement, Victoria: British Columbia, January 1992).

Barber, M. (1995), *The Dark Side of the Moon: Imagining an End to Failure in Urban Education* (TES/Greenwich Lecture, May).

Bashi, J., Sass, K., Katzir, R., and Margolin, I. (1990), *Effective Schools: From Theory to Practice: An Implementation Model and its Outcomes* (Jerusalem: Van Leer Institute).

Bennett, S. N. (1976), *Teaching Styles and Pupil Progress* (London: Open Books).

Bernstein, B. (1970), 'Education Cannot Compensate for Society', *New Society*, 387: 344–7.

Blakey, L., and Heath, A. (1992), 'Differences Between Comprehensive Schools: Some Preliminary Findings', in *School Effectiveness: Research, Policy and Practice*, (eds.) D. Reynolds and P. Cuttance (London: Cassell), 121–33.

Blatchford, P. J., and Mortimore, P. J. (1994), 'The Issue of Class Size for Young Children in Schools: What Can We Learn from Research?', in *Oxford Review of Education*, 20/4: 411–28.

Bosker, R., and Scheerens, J. (1989), 'Issues and Interpretations of the Results of School Effectiveness Research', *International Journal of Educational Research*, 13/7: 741–52.

Bransdma, H., and Knuver, J. (1989), 'Effects of School and Classroom Characteristics on Pupil Progress in Language and Arithmetic', *International Journal of Educational Research*, special issue: 'Developments in School Effectiveness Research', 13: 777–88.

Brimer, A., Madaus, G., Chapman, B., Kellaghan, T., and Wood, D. (1978), *Sources of Difference in School Achievement* (Slough, Buckinghamshire: National Foundation for Educational Research).

Brookover, W., and Lezotte, L. (1977), *Changes in School Characteristics Co-incident with Changes in Student Achievement* (East Lansing Institute for Research on Teaching: Michigan State Univ.).

Brown, S. (1994), 'School Effectiveness Research and the Evaluation of Schools', *Evaluation and Research in Education*, 8/1 and 2: 55–68.

Cannan, C. (1970), 'Schools for Delinquency', *New Society*, 427: 1004.

Clark, T., and McCarthy, D. (1983), 'School Improvement in New York: The Evolution of a Project', *Educational Research*, 12: 17–24.

Coleman J. S. (1966), *Equality of Educational Opportunity* (US Department of Health, Education and Welfare, Washington: US Government Printing Press).

Coleman, P., and Collinge, J. (1991), 'In the Webb: Internal and External Influences Affecting School Improvement', *School Effectiveness and School Improvement* 2/4: 262–85.

Creemers, B., and Lugthart, E. (1989), 'School Effectiveness and Improvement in the Netherlands', in *School Effectiveness and Improvement, Proceedings of the First National Congress, London 1988*, (eds.) D. Reynolds, B. Creemers, and T. Peters (Groningen: RION Institute for Educational Research/School of Education, Univ. of Wales College of Cardiff), 89–103.

Dalin, P. (1989), 'Reconceptualising the School Improvement Process: Charting a Paradigm Shift', in *School Effectiveness and Improvement, Proceedings of the First International Congress, London, 1988*, (eds.) D. Reynolds, B. Creemers, and T. Peters (Groningen: RION Institute for Educational Research/School of Education, Univ. of Wales College of Cardiff), 30–45.

Daly, P. (1991), *How Large Are Secondary School Effects in Northern Ireland?* (Belfast: School of Education, Queens University).

Edmonds, R. (1979), 'Effective Schools for the Urban Poor', *Educational Leadership*, 37/1: 15–27.

Finn, J. D., and Achilles, C. M. (1990), 'Answers and Questions about Class Size: A State-Wide Experiment', *American Educational Research Journal*, 27/3: 557–77.

Finn, J., and Voelkl, K. (1992), *Class Size: An Overview of Research* (Buffalo: Graduate School, State Univ. of New York).

Fraser, B. (1989), 'Research Synthesis on School and Instructional Effectiveness', *International Journal of Educational Research*, 13/7: 707–20.

Galton, M., and Simon, B. (1980), *Progress and Performance in the Primary Classroom* (London: Routledge and Kegan Paul).

Goldstein, H. (1987), *Multilevel Models in Educational and Social Research* (London: Griffin; New York: Oxford Univ. Press).

—— (1995), *Multilevel Statistical Models* (2nd edn.), (London: Edward Arnold; New York: Halsted Press).

—— and Sammons, P. (1995), *The Influence of Secondary and Junior Schools on 16-Year Examination Performance: A Cross-Classified Multilevel Analysis* (A paper presented to the European Conference on Educational Research, University of Bath, September).

Gray, J., Jesson, D., and Sime, N. (1990), 'Estimating Difference in the Examination Performance of Secondary Schools in 6 LEAs', *Oxford Review of Education*, 16/2: 137–58.

Gray, J., McPherson, A., and Raffe, D. (1983) *Reconstructions of Secondary Education: Theory, Myth and Practice since the War* (London: Routledge and Kegan Paul).

Green, A. (1990), *Education and State Formation* (New York: St Martin's Press).

Hanushek, E. A. (1986), 'The Economics of Schooling: Production and Efficiency in Public Schools', *Journal of Economic Literature*, 24: 1141–77.

—— (1989), 'The Impact of Differential Expenditures on School Performance', *Educational Researcher*, 18/4: 45–65.

Hanushek, E. A. (1991), 'When School Finance "reform" May Not be a Good Policy', *Harvard Journal on Legislation*, 28: 423–56.

Heal, K. (1978), 'Misbehaviour Among School Children', *Policy and Politics*, 6: 321–32.

Hedges, L. V., Laine, R. D., and Greenwald, R. (1994), 'Does Money Matter? A Meta-analysis of Studies of the Effects of Differential School Inputs on Student Outcomes (An exchange Part 1)', *Educational Researcher*, 23/3: 5–14.

Hill, P., and Rowe, K. (in press), 'Multi Level Modelling in School Effectiveness Research', *School Effectiveness and School Improvement*.

—— and Holmes-Smith, P. (1996), '*Modelling Student Progress: School Effectiveness and Improvement*' (Minsk, Belarus).

HMSO (1995), *Performance in City Schools* (House of Commons Education Committee).

Hopkins, D. (1994), *Towards a Theory for School Improvement* (ESRC Seminar, Sheffield, October).

Jencks, C. S., Smith, M., Acland, H., Bane, M. J., Cohen, D., Gintis, H., Heyns, B., and Micholson, S. (1972), *Inequality: A Reassessment of the Effect of Family and Schooling in America* (New York: Basic Books).

Lazar, I., Hubbell, V., Murray, H., Rosche, M., and Royce, J. (1977), *The Persistence of Pre-school Effects: A Long-term Follow-up of Fourteen Infant and Pre-school Experiments* (DHEW Publication No. (OHDS) 78–30129).

Luyten, H. (1994), *School Effects: Stability and Malleability* (Enschede: Univ. of Twente, Faculty of Education).

McCormack-Larkin, M., and Kritek, W. (1982), 'Milwaukee's Project RISE', *Educational Leadership*, 40/3: 16–21.

Mortimore, J., Mortimore, P., and Thomas, H. (1994), *Managing Associate Staff: Innovation in Primary and Secondary Schools* (London: Paul Chapman Publishing).

Mortimore, P. (1995), 'The Class Size Conundrum', *Education* (September).

——, and MacBeath, J. (1994), 'Quest for the Secrets of Success', *The Times Educational Supplement* (March).

——, Sammons, P., Jacob, R., Stoll, L., and Lewis, D. (1988), *School Matters: The Junior Years* (Salisbury: Open Books).

Myers, K. (1996), *School Improvement in Practice: The Schools Make a Difference Project* (London: Falmer Press).

National Commission on Education (1995), *Success against the Odds: Effective Schools in Disadvantaged Areas* (London: Routledge).

New York Department of Education (1974)

North West Regional Educational Laboratory (NWREL) (1990), *Effective Schooling Practices: A Research Synthesis* (Portland, Ore.: Author)

Nuttall, D., Goldstein, H., Prosser, R., and Rashbash, J. (1989), 'Differential School Effective-ness', *International Journal of Educational Research*, 13/7: 769–76.

Nye, B. *et al.* (1993), 'Tennessee's Bold Experiment', *Tennessee Education*, 22/3: 10–17.

Ouston, J. *et al.* (1979), 'School Influences on Children's Development', in M. Rutter (ed.), *Developmental Psychiatry* (London: Heinemann), 67–76.

Paterson, L., and Goldstein, H. (1991), 'New Statistical Methods of Analysing Social Structures: An Introduction to Multilevel Models', *British Educational Research Journal*, 17/4: 387–93.

Power, M., Alderson, M., Phillipson, C., Schoenberg, E., and Morris, J. (1967), 'Delinquent Schools', *New Society*, 10: 542–3.

Preece, P. (1988), 'Misleading Ways of Expressing the Magnitude of School Effects', *Research Papers in Education*, 3/2: 97–8.

Purkey, S., and Smith, M. (1983), 'Effective Schools: A Review', *Elementary School Journal*, 83/4: 427–52.

Raudenbush, S. (1989), 'The Analysis of Longitudinal Multilevel Data', *International Journal of Educational Research*, 13/7: 721–40.

Reynolds, D. (1995), 'Failure-Free Schooling' *IARTV Series 49*.

——, and Cuttance, P. (eds.) (1992), *School Effectiveness: Research, Policy and Practice* (London: Cassell).

——, Jones, D., and St. Leger, S. (1976), 'Schools Do Make a Difference', *New Society*, 37: 321.

——, Teddlie, C., Creemers, B. P. M., Cheng, Y. C., Dundas, B., Green, B., Epp, J. R., Hauge, T. E., Schaffer, E. C., and Stringfield, S. (1994), 'School Effectiveness Research: A Review of the International Literature', in D. Reynolds, B. P. M. Creemers, P. M. S. Nesselrodt, E. C. Schaffer, S. Stringfield and C. Teddlie (eds.), *Advances in School Effectiveness Research and Practice* (Oxford: Pergamon).

Rutter, M., (1983), 'School Effects on Pupil Progress: Research Findings and Policy Implications', *Child Development*, 54/1: 1–29.

——, Maughan, B., Mortimore, P., and Ouston, J. (1979), *Fifteen Thousand Hours: Secondary Schools and their Effects on Children* (London: Open Books).

Sammons, P., Hillman, J., and Mortimore, P. (1994), *Key Characteristics of Effective Schools: A Review of School Effectiveness Research* (London: Office for Standards in Education).

——, Kysel, F., and Mortimore, P. (1983), 'Educational Priority Indices: A New Perspective', *British Educational Research Journal*, 9/1: 27–40.

——, Thomas, S., and Mortimore, P. (1995), *Accounting for Variations in Academic Effectiveness between Schools and Departments: Results From the "Differential Secondary School Effectiveness Project": A Three-Year Study of GCSE Performance* (paper presented at the European

Conference on Educational Research/BERA Annual Conference, Bath, 14–17 September).

——, ——, and —— (1996), *Differential School Effectiveness: Departmental Variations in GCSE Attainment* (paper presented at the School Effectiveness and Improvement Symposium of the Annual Conference of the American Educational Research Association, New York).

Scheerens, J. (1992), *Effective Schooling: Research Theory and Practice* (London: Cassell).

Shephard, G. (1995), CLEA speech (Brighton: July).

Silver, H. (1994), *Good Schools Effective Schools: Judgements and their Histories* (London: Cassell).

Slater, R., and Teddlie, C. (1992), 'Towards a Theory of School Effectiveness and Leadership', *School Effectiveness and School Improvement*, 3/4: 247–57.

Slavin, R. (1990), 'Class Size and Student Achievement: Is Smaller Better?' *Contemporary Education*, 62/1: 6–12.

Smith, D., and Tomlinson, S. (1989), *The School Effect: A Study of Multi-Racial Comprehensives* (London: Policy Studies Institute).

Stoll, L. (1995), *The Complexity and Challenge of Ineffective Schools* (research paper presented to the European Conference on Educational Research and the Annual Conference of the Educational Research Association, Bath).

—— and Mortimore, P. (1995), 'School Effectiveness and School Improvement', *View Point*, (London: Institute of Education), 2: 1–8.

Teddlie, C., Falkowski, C., Stringfield, S., Deselle, S., and Garvue, R. (1984), *The Louisiana School Effectiveness Study Phase 2* (Louisiana: State Department of Education).

——, C., Kirby, P., and Stringfield, S. (1989), 'Effective Versus Ineffective Schools: Observable Differences in the Classroom', *American Journal of Education*, 97/3: 221–36.

Thomas, S., and Mortimore, P. (1995), 'Comparison of Value Added Models for Second-ary School Effectiveness' (forthcoming), *Research Papers in Education* (paper presented at the ECER/BERA Conference, Bath).

——, Sammons, P., Mortimore, P., and Smees, R. (1995), *Stability and Consistency in Secondary School Effects on Students' GCSE Outcomes over 3 Years* (paper presented at ICSEI Leeuwarden, The Netherlands).

Tizard, B., Blatchford, P., Burke, J., Farquhar, C., and Plewis, I. (1988), *Young Children at School in the Inner City* (Hove and London: Lawrence Erlbaum Associates).

Weber, G. (1971), *Inner-City Children can be Taught to Read: Four Successful Schools* (Washington, DC: Council for Basic Education).

PART FIVE

KNOWLEDGE, CURRICULUM, AND CULTURAL POLITICS

Part Five: Introduction

Knowledge, Curriculum, and Cultural Politics

Historically, the sociology of education has focused on issues of educational inequalities in access and outcome. These were often linked to debates about education and economy, irrespective of whether they led to a view of education as the 'handmaiden' (*sic*) of industrialism (Kerr *et al.* 1973), involving the creation of a highly skilled workforce, or to the repression of human talent in the reproduction of capitalist relations (Bowles and Gintis 1976). Typically, questions of knowledge, curriculum, and cultural politics were marginalized in such debates. What was called the 'new' sociology of education (Young 1971) in the 1970s represented the first significant attempt to examine issues of school knowledge and the curriculum. But, even here, the main focus was on how school knowledge disadvantaged working-class students because it reflected the 'dominant' culture of élite social groups. Moreover, although the 'new' sociology of education rejected the idea that educational knowledge was based on a 'consensus' of normative values, attitudes, and beliefs (Parsons 1959), it did assume that a common culture could be constructed if it was inclusive of class differences in society (Williams 1961). However, in the last decade the politics of culture, knowledge, and the curriculum have moved to centre stage in the sociology of education (especially in the United States). This shift in focus has been associated with vigorous debates about democracy, knowledge, and education in a 'postmodern' society. Issues of gender, race, and ethnicity are now given at least equal billing with that of social class (Giroux, Ch. 6).

In Bloom's contribution it is argued that democracy should be based on 'natural rights', including justice, freedom, and the common good. According to Bloom, the emphasis on 'natural rights' is the best way of overcoming differences of class, race, religion, culture, or national origin, because these 'disappear or become dim when bathed in the light of natural rights'. However, the assimilationist implications of Bloom's position are clearly evident in reference to immigrants in American society: 'The immigrant had to put behind him the claims of the Old World in favor of a new and easily acquired education. This did not necessarily mean abandoning old daily habits or religions, but it did mean subordinating them to new principles. There was a tendency, if not a necessity, to homogenize nature itself.' The ethnocentrism inherent in this argument is justified by Bloom, who asserts that one's cultural heritage as a device for instilling loyalty and love for family, friends, and nation stands at the heart of the good society. It is for these reasons that the main thrust of his contribution is to condemn the transformation of democracy and its impact on American higher education.

He argues that for the last 50 years democracy has been hollowed out in the name of 'equality' and an intolerance to truth claims based on scientific reason. Hence students are taught that truth is relative, ethnocentrism is bad, and that it is undemocratic to be judgmental. The teaching of non-Western cultures and societies in American universities is not, according to Bloom, intended to give students the opportunity to analyze the history, culture, or political systems of Third World countries, but to teach American students that their way of life cannot be defined as better or worse than any other. However, this leads to a paradox, because as students discover that other cultures are ethnocentric they must inevitably be defined as inferior, since they are not as 'open-minded' as people in Western societies.

Cornell West would interpret Bloom's account of how democratic 'openness' leads to a 'closing' of student minds to the search for truth and absolute standards as an attempt to reassert the principles of 'exclusion, silence and blindness of male WASP cultural homogeneity'. Indeed, what West calls 'the new politics of difference' also rejects much of what Bloom condemns, because it has failed to 'trash the monolithic and homogeneous in the name of diversity, multiplicity, and heterogeneity; to reject the abstract, general, and universal in light of the concrete, specific, and particular; and to historicize, contextualize, and pluralize by highlighting the contingent, provisional, variable, tentative, shifting and changing'.

Moreover, the forces which have given rise to the new cultural politics are not confined to changes within Western conceptions of democracy and inequality, but are a response to what he calls the Age of Europe (1492–1945), the demise of the US as a world superpower, and the decolonization of the Third World. This has, for instance, given rise to the decolonized sensibilities that have fuelled the civil rights and black power movements, along with students', anti-war, feminist, brown, gay, and lesbian movements. Hence the fight for a voice and dignity among blacks in America is a direct response to the problem of 'invisibility' and 'namelessness' which resulted from colonization, and reinforced by assimilationist policies in the era of economic nationalism (Ch. 1).

West's account of the new cultural politics also serves to reveal the inadequacies of Bloom's ideal of universal natural rights as the foundation for democracy and education. The problem is that the common humanity 'is cast in an assimilationist manner that subordinates black particularity to a false universalism, i.e. non-black rubrics and prototypes'. Indeed, the intellectual challenge at the heart of the new cultural politics is the 'demystification' of empire, colonization, gender, race, nature, sexual orientation, and so on, in order to understand the possibilities and limitations of 'transformational praxis'.

Peter McLaren concurs with much of West's analysis as he attempts to grapple with the question of how educators can develop a progressive pedagogy of resistance and transformation. This analysis focuses on multiculturalism in a post-modern society. McLaren argues that the diversity of post-modern theories requires us to distinguish different strands of post-modern thought in terms of its potential to enhance a radical pedagogy of resistance. The strength of his contribution is that whilst recognising the need for a new cultural politics which rejects the metanarrative of natural rights in the contribution by Bloom, he also notes the need to maintain a sense of 'totality'. The importance of not losing sight of totality is based on the view that a politics of liberation must operate at both a macro- and micro-level simultaneously: 'Without a shared vision (however contingent or provisional) of democratic community, we risk endorsing struggles in which the politics of differences collapses into new forms of separatism'.

Mohanty's chapter 'on race and voice' sees the new cultural politics as a challenge to contemporary liberal education. Whilst rejecting the conservative position outlined by Bloom, given its tendency to impose a unitary world view which is an assault on the integrity, identity, and voices of Others, she is also sceptical of liberal definitions of 'cultural pluralism'. In her analysis of classroom pedagogies of gender and race and prejudice-reduction workshops Mohanty shows how the liberal view of diversity and difference has led to the erosion of the 'politics of collectivity through the reformulation of race and difference in individualistic terms'. Here everyone should be given a voice and a chance to be heard, but these voices are interpreted as an expression of personal preference rather than collective responses to cultural, social, and economic inequalities.

Mohanty does not accept institutional and pedagogical practices in the spirit of 'harmony in diversity' but, along with other radical educators (Giroux, Ch. 6), as a political and cultural site of struggle, accommodation, and transformation in the construction of race and gender. This struggle not only involves giving the power of self-definition and collective knowledge to marginalized peoples, but to the recovery of alternative, oppositional histories of domination and struggle. This she sees as central to pedagogical projects such as women's studies, black studies, and ethnic studies. However, the increasing emphasis on 'reverse discrimination' rather than 'affirmative action' in the United States has put the teachers and students involved in such programmes on the defensive. Moreover, there are other problems that may reinforce the marginal status of such programmes and blunt their potential for educational and social change. Firstly, Mohanty suggests that education for critical consciousness or critical pedagogy involves moving away from the 'knowledge-as-accumulated-capital model' of education, to focus on the link between 'the historical configuration of social forms and the way they work subjectively'.

This shift is viewed as necessary to free the individual from being locked into liberal views about education, employment, and personal progress. However, such a view is likely to meet with considerable scepticism from students who must rely on the educational system to improve their lot, especially when they are being taught by radical educators who have successfully used their credentials to great effect in the academic labour market.

Secondly, Mohanty recognizes with refreshing honesty that, within her own teaching, issues of race and gender can easily get defined in terms of personal or individual experience, such as students feeling the need to become 'more sensitive' to Third World peoples. Mohanty suggests that this response can lead to a situation where white students are constructed as marginal observers, and students of colour are the real 'knowers'. Hence, people of colour are granted a voice, but it belongs to a different 'space', separate from the 'agency of white students'; and the question of what kind of voice is allowed is vital. Thirdly, a related problem is that whilst it is possible to see how women's studies or black studies can change self-identification and enhance solidarity between course members, the question remains of how this can increase 'intersubjectivity' across society.

Equally, the problem with all forms of critical pedagogy is how it can be used to mobilize support for 'transformational praxis' (see West Ch. 33). The complexity of this question can be grasped when one reflects on the fact that the new cultural politics has gained considerable sway among academics across the United States and Europe precisely at a time when people of colour are having to deal with increasing social inequality and political indifference. However, the feminist movement, which in the last 30 years has done a great deal to raise awareness of gender inequalities, has met with considerable success in the attempt to improve the conditions of women in the family, education, and the labour market.

The contribution from Gumport highlights the relationship between cultural politics and power in higher education. Her study is based on in-depth interviews with feminist scholars who entered graduate school between 1956 and 1980. In institutions based on rigid disciplinary boundaries and academic 'disinterest' in the pursuit of knowledge, feminist scholars inevitably confronted opposition to the interdisciplinary and oppositional character of feminist scholarship. Gumport shows that impressive advances have been made since the late 1960s in terms of the number of courses and degree-granting programmes which have emerged, along with the proliferation of feminist research and publication. However, she notes that despite the institutionalization of women's studies, 'the academy has yet to accept the legitimacy of feminist scholarship as an academic vocation'.

Delpit's paper takes up some of the themes examined by Mohanty. She is particularly concerned to explain the 'silenced dialogue' between white educators and educators of colour. This dialogue is silenced because white educators seem unwilling to accept that cultural differences in learning styles may make the pedagogical practices of middle-class, liberal educators less suited to the needs of students of colour.

She suggests that imposing liberal, middle-class values and aspirations as the universal standard by which all should be educated is to ensure the reproduction of advantage in the school and society at large. Moreover, although Delpit does not draw on the work of Bernstein (Ch. 3), his work is clearly complementary to the themes and analysis she develops in this chapter. She argues, for instance, that many liberal educators hold the view that the primary goal of education is for children to become autonomous learners, to develop fully who they are in the classroom setting without having arbitrary, external standards forced upon them—in Bernstein's terms, they are advocating an 'invisible' child-centred pedagogy. Bernstein shows that 'child-centred' approaches involve implicit power relations, which make it difficult for students who do not already know the 'rules of the game' to learn what the teacher expects of them. Therefore, it is only those students who share the same cultural understandings of teachers and the school who are likely to progress. Likewise, Delpit recognizes the importance of power relations in education as she notes that 'those with power are frequently least aware of—or least willing to acknowledge—its existence. Those with less power are often most aware of its existence.' As a result, liberal educators are opposed to direct instruction in the primary-school classrooms because of the explicit control exhibited by teachers. But Delpit's argument is that the power-less deal with their lack of power more successfully in situations when the rules of the game are made explicit to the child, so that she or he knows what to do and what is expected of them; and so parents of 'disadvantaged' children disagree with liberal educators because they want to ensure that the school provides their children with 'discourse patterns, interactional styles, and spoken and written language styles that will allow them to succeed in the larger society' (p. 125).

Cultural politics therefore involves a recognition that different pedagogical approaches may be required for some black students (although these may offend middle-class, liberal sensibilities) in order to function in the dominant society. West, McLaren, and Mohanty would interpret this approach as misguided, because of its assimilationist consequences in not challenging the dominant, white, middle-class culture. However, this example reveals a conflict between those who see cultural politics as a way of developing a critical pedagogy as an oppositional response to the hegemony of white middle-class society, and those who use it to enhance the life-chances of people of colour within the existing social structure. This also raises the issue, noted by West, of a tendency for blacks to homogenize the black experience, and for black 'cultural workers' to 'speak for' black people without listening or being aware of the range of voices within the black community (see Weiner, Ch. 8). Delpit's response to the assimilationist charge is that she does not advocate a rejection of one's own language and culture, which must be preserved as a source of pride. However, she does reject the idea that political change towards meaningful diversity and black empowerment can be effected from the bottom up. The failure to teach children of colour how to live in the dominant society is to disadvantage them: 'I am certain that if we are truly to effect societal change, we cannot do so from the bottom up, but we must push and agitate from the top down. And in the meantime, we must take the responsibility to *teach*, to provide for students who do not already possess them the additional codes of power.'

Cameron McCarthy also challenges much of the existing mainstream and radical literature on racial inequality. This is due to a failure to develop theories of educational difference which recognize multidimensionality, historical variability, and subjective differences. This leads him to advance a theoretical framework which is based on the notion of 'nonsychrony' in order to highlight the fact that schools do not express the same concerns, needs or expectations at the same point in time. McCarthy suggests that the theory of nonsynchrony enables researchers to better understand the relationship between the empirical and theoretical. It also leads to a rejection of simplistic accounts of the dynamic and contradictory relations of race, class, and gender in the process of social reproduction.

The relationship between knowledge, curriculum, and power is also central to the contribution by Apple. However, Apple sees little to commend postmodernist debates about variety and difference, given that it ignores the politics of the New Right who are shaping educational policy in ways which will do little to enhance the interests of people of colour. Apple argues that the postmodernists have too readily forgotten the importance of capitalism and class relations in shaping what is to count as legitimate knowledge in universities, colleges, and schools. He accuses most postmodernist analyses of education of ignoring the political economy of high-status knowledge. Hence, in his view, they have not only failed to focus adequately on developing critical accounts of the New Right agenda, but have voluntarily removed perhaps their most important conceptual weaponry in rejecting Marxist theories of capitalism. In anticipating the likely responses postmodernists would make to such criticism, Apple also argues that there is a big difference between an analysis of class relations as an essential part of a critical discourse on the New Right and viewing any form of Marxist analysis as 'essentialist'.

Apple believes that an analysis of the power politics of the New Right stands at the heart of critical pedagogy in the 1990s. He suggests that the neo-conservative and neo-liberal (see Ch. 1) strands of the American New Right have combined forces with key business interests to form a 'power bloc' capable of imposing a significant change in educational policy. These 'interests' are aimed at 'providing the educational conditions believed necessary both for increasing international competitiveness, profit, and discipline and for returning us to a romanticized past of the "ideal" home, family and school'. The most important manifestation of this alliance in terms of knowledge and the curriculum is an increased emphasis on 'technical/administrative knowledge'. Applied technological and scientific knowledge is consequently receiving greater emphasis in terms of time in the curriculum, funding, resources, and prestige throughout the educational system. This trend is, according to Apple, undermining the educational foundation for critical citizenship.

A related debate to the new cultural politics is that of gender, knowledge, and educational performance. In the last 30 years feminist scholarship has transformed sociology by highlighting the importance of gender relations in shaping all areas of social life. Within the sociology of education, this not only led to studies of gender inequality in access, curriculum, and school practices, but to an examination of how 'feminine' identities reinforce patriarchal relations (Arnot and Weiner 1987). More recently, greater attention has also been given to our conception of 'masculinities' in shaping institutional relations in areas including the school, family, and the labour market. The process of deindustrialization, the shift from manufacturing to service-sector employment; the changing nature of the family, including the growth of female participation in the labour market; the increase in long-term male unemployment and significant improvements in the academic performance of women, have all fuelled the idea of a deepening crisis in Western models of masculinity (Mac An Ghaill 1995).

The importance of Connell's contribution is that he positions contemporary debates about masculinities within a comparative framework of world history. This leads him to reject a number of explanations for gender differences, such as the emphasis in sociology on the psychological essence of man, or 'sex-role' theories which, he asserts, are based on an inadequate theory of social structure and a superficial understanding of human personality and motivation. Locating masculinities in *discourse* has been more successful in attending to issues of power and to nuances and complexities in the representation of masculinities; but Connell is equally aware of their failure to advance significantly our understanding because 'they operate wholly within the world of discourse, they ignore their own conditions of existence in the practices of gender and in the social structuring of those practices'.

In locating the study of masculinities in its historical and comparative context, Connell draws attention to the 'startling ethnocentrism' of current approaches. This is not simply due to the dominance of a white middle-class perspective, but because such approaches are premised on no more than 5 per cent of the world's population of man. The major weakness of current scholarship is, therefore, that it underestimates the variation and the fluidity of 'masculinities' in world history. Hence, 'to speak of "masculinity" as one and the same entity across differences in place and time is to descend into absurdity'. Therefore, contemporary working-class identities which have been seen as problematic in the context of contemporary social change are, according to Connell, 'no more set in stone than are ruling-class masculinities'. Indeed, the current challenges to men's power in the form of feminism, and to institutional heterosexuality in the form of lesbian and gay men's movements, are transforming the politics of gender and sexuality in new ways. But in recognizing the potential of such changes, Connell suggests the need to distinguish between the *presence* of such movements from the operating *power* they have won, which is often 'disappointingly small'.

A key question for Weiner, Arnot, and David is whether girls and women have made significant steps towards equality in education. Their answer, based on recent evidence in England and Wales, is less clear-cut than one might imagine, given television documentaries and newspaper articles proclaiming that 'the future is female'. These authors do show that women are doing much better at all stages of education than a decade or more ago. However, significant differences in the subjects studied remain, along with enduring gender inequality in employment.

This evidence leads them to examine the discourse of gender and academic performance, which is clearly linked to the cultural politics of gender, knowledge, and social power. They suggest that there has been a major shift from the 1970s discourse on female underachievement to the 1990s version of male underachievement. The former emerged as a result of feminism and other forces, examined by Cornel West (Ch. 33). The current discourse of male under-achievement is, alternatively, explained in terms of a crisis in both working- and middle-class masculinities. Weiner, Arnot, and David show how male working-class under-achievement is interpreted as a threat to law and order, and male middle-class under-achievement as deriving from problems of 'attitude', complacency, and arrogance. However, they also note how the dominant gender discourse in relation to education has not celebrated the advances made by women, but bemoaned the failure of men. This, they suggest, is because men still appear to find the possibility of genuine equality between the sexes extremely threatening, and they conclude by suggesting that the 'hegemonic educational discourses which seek to emphasize male under-achievement might be seen as constituting a backlash to past feminist gains. What we may be seeing is, in fact, merely a new rendition of the old patriarchal refrain.'

References

Arnot, M., and Weiner, G. (1987) (eds.), *Gender and the Politics of Schooling* (London: Hutchinson).

Bowles, S., and Gintis, H. (1976), *Schooling in Capitalist America* (London: Routledge).

Kerr, C., Dunlop, J., Harbison, F., and Myers, C. (1973), *Industrialism and Industrial Man* (Harmondsworth: Penguin).

Mac An Ghaill, M. (1995), *The Making of Men: Masculinities, Sexualities and Schooling* (Buckingham: Open Univ. Press).

Parsons, T. (1959), 'The School Class as a Social System: Some of its Functions in American Society', *Harvard Educational Review*, 29: 297–318.

Williams, R. (1961), *The Long Revolution* (Harmondsworth: Penguin).

Young, M. (1971) (ed.), *Knowledge and Control: New Directions for the Sociology of Education* (London: Collier-Macmillan).

32

Our Virtue (Introduction to *The Closing of the American Mind*)

Allan Bloom

There is one thing a professor can be absolutely certain of: almost every student entering the university believes, or says he believes, that truth is relative. If this belief is put to the test, one can count on the students' reaction: they will be uncomprehending. That anyone should regard the proposition as not self-evident astonishes them, as though he were calling into question $2 + 2 = 4$. These are things you don't think about. The students' backgrounds are as various as America can provide. Some are religious, some atheists; some are to the Left, some to the Right; some intend to be scientists, some humanists or professionals or businessmen; some are poor, some rich. They are unified only in their relativism and in their allegiance to equality. And the two are related in a moral intention. The relativity of truth is not a theoretical insight but a moral postulate, the condition of a free society, or so they see it. They have all been equipped with this framework early on, and it is the modern replacement for the inalienable natural rights that used to be the traditional American grounds for a free society. That it is a moral issue for students is revealed by the character of their response when challenged—a combination of disbelief and indignation: 'Are you an absolutist?,' the only alternative they know, uttered in the same tone as 'Are you a monarchist?' or 'Do you really believe in witches?' This latter leads into the indignation, for someone who believes in witches might well be a witch-hunter or a Salem judge. The danger they have been taught to fear from absolutism is not

error but intolerance. Relativism is necessary to openness; and this is the virtue, the only virtue, which all primary education for more than fifty years has dedicated itself to inculcating. Openness—and the relativism that makes it the only plausible stance in the face of various claims to truth and various ways of life and kinds of human beings—is the great insight of our times. The true believer is the real danger. The study of history and of culture teaches that all the world was mad in the past; men always thought they were right, and that led to wars, persecutions, slavery, xenophobia, racism, and chauvinism. The point is not to correct the mistakes and really be right; rather it is not to think you are right at all.

The students, of course, cannot defend their opinion. It is something with which they have been indoctrinated. The best they can do is point out all the opinions and cultures there are and have been. What right, they ask, do I or anyone else have to say one is better than the others? If I pose the routine questions designed to confute them and make them think, such as, 'If you had been a British administrator in India, would you have let the natives under your governance burn the widow at the funeral of a man who had died?,' they either remain silent or reply that the British should never have been there in the first place. It is not that they know very much about other nations, or about their own. The purpose of their education is not to make them scholars but to provide them with a moral virtue—openness.

Every educational system has a moral goal

From *The Closing of the American Mind: How Higher Education has Failed Democracy and Impoverished the Souls of Today's Students* (New York: Simon and Schuster, 1987), 25–43. Reprinted with permission.

that it tries to attain and that informs its curriculum. It wants to produce a certain kind of human being. This intention is more or less explicit, more or less a result of reflection; but even the neutral subjects, like reading and writing and arithmetic, take their place in a vision of the educated person. In some nations the goal was the pious person, in others the warlike, in others the industrious. Always important is the political regime, which needs citizens who are in accord with its fundamental principle. Aristocracies want gentlemen, oligarchies men who respect and pursue money, and democracies lovers of equality. Democratic education, whether it admits it or not, wants and needs to produce men and women who have the tastes, knowledge, and character supportive of a democratic regime. Over the history of our republic, there have obviously been changes of opinion as to what kind of man is best for our regime. We began with the model of the rational and industrious man, who was honest, respected the laws, and was dedicated to the family (his own family—what has in its decay been dubbed the nuclear family). Above all he was to know the rights doctrine; the Constitution, which embodied it; and American history, which presented and celebrated the founding of a nation 'conceived in liberty and dedicated to the proposition that all men are created equal.' A powerful attachment to the letter and the spirit of the Declaration of Independence gently conveyed, appealing to each man's reason, was the goal of the education of democratic man. This called for something very different from the kinds of attachment required for traditional communities where myth and passion as well as severe discipline, authority, and the extended family produced an instinctive, unqualified, even fanatic patriotism, unlike the reflected, rational, calm, even self-interested loyalty—not so much to the country but to the form of government and its rational principles—required in the United States. This was an entirely new experiment in politics, and with it came a new education. This education has evolved in the last half-century from the education of democratic man to the education of the democratic personality.

The palpable difference between these two can easily be found in the changed understanding of what it means to be an American. The old view was that, by recognizing and accepting man's natural rights, men found a fundamental basis of unity and sameness. Class, race, religion, national origin or culture all disappear or become dim when bathed in the light of natural rights, which give men common interests and make them truly brothers. The immigrant had to put behind him the claims of the Old World in favor of a new and easily acquired education. This did not necessarily mean abandoning old daily habits or religions, but it did mean subordinating them to new principles. There was a tendency, if not a necessity, to homogenize nature itself.

The recent education of openness has rejected all that. It pays no attention to natural rights or the historical origins of our regime, which are now thought to have been essentially flawed and regressive. It is progressive and forward-looking. It does not demand fundamental agreement or the abandonment of old or new beliefs in favor of the natural ones. It is open to all kinds of men, all kinds of lifestyles, all ideologies. There is no enemy other than the man who is not open to everything. But when there are no shared goals or vision of the public good, is the social contract any longer possible?

From the earliest beginnings of liberal thought there was a tendency in the direction of indiscriminate freedom. Hobbes and Locke, and the American Founders following them, intended to palliate extreme beliefs, particularly religious beliefs, which lead to civil strife. The members of sects had to obey the laws and be loyal to the Constitution; if they did so, others had to leave them alone, however distasteful their beliefs might be. In order to make this arrangement work, there was a conscious, if covert, effort to weaken religious beliefs, partly by assigning—as a result of a great epistemological effort—religion to the realm of opinion as opposed to knowledge. But the right to freedom of religion belonged to the realm of knowledge. Such rights are not matters of opinion. No weakness of conviction was desired here. All to the contrary, the sphere of rights was to be the arena of moral passion in a democracy.

It was possible to expand the space exempt from legitimate social and political regulation only by contracting the claims to moral and political knowledge. The insatiable appetite for freedom to live as one pleases thrives on this aspect of modern democratic thought. In the end it begins to appear that full freedom can be attained only when there is no such knowledge at all. The effective way to defang the oppressors is to persuade them they are ignorant of the good. The inflamed sensitivity induced by radicalized democratic theory finally experiences any limit as arbitrary and tyrannical. There are no absolutes; freedom is absolute. Of course the result is that, on the one hand, the argument justifying freedom disappears and, on the other, all beliefs begin to have the attenuated character that was initially supposed to be limited to religious belief.

The gradual movement away from rights to openness was apparent, for example, when Oliver Wendell Holmes renounced seeking for a principle to determine which speech or conduct is not tolerable in a democratic society and invoked instead an imprecise and practically meaningless standard—clear and present danger—which to all intents and purposes makes the preservation of public order the only common good. Behind his opinion there was an optimistic view about progress, one in which the complete decay of democratic principle and a collapse into barbarism are impossible and in which the truth unaided always triumphs in the marketplace of ideas. This optimism had not been shared by the Founders, who insisted that the principles of democratic government must be returned to and consulted even though the consequences might be harsh for certain points of view, some merely tolerated and not respected, others forbidden outright. To their way of thinking there should be no tolerance for the intolerant. The notion that there should be no limitation on free expression unless it can be shown to be a clear and present danger would have made it impossible for Lincoln to insist that there could be no compromise with the *principle* of equality, that it did not depend on the people's choice or election but is the condition of their having elections in the first place, that popular sovereignty on the question of black slavery was impermissible even if it would enable us to avoid the clear and present danger of a bloody civil war.

But openness, nevertheless, eventually won out over natural rights, partly through a theoretical critique, partly because of a political rebellion against nature's last constraints. Civic education turned away from concentrating on the Founding to concentrating on openness based on history and social science.

There was even a general tendency to debunk the Founding, to prove the beginnings were flawed in order to license a greater openness to the new. What began in Charles Beard's Marxism and Carl Becker's historicism became routine. We are used to hearing the Founders charged with being racists, murderers of Indians, representatives of class interests. I asked my first history professor in the university, a very famous scholar, whether the picture he gave us of George Washington did not have the effect of making us despise our regime. 'Not at all,' he said, 'it doesn't depend on individuals but on our having good democratic values.' To which I rejoined, 'But you just showed us that Washington was only using those values to further the class interests of the Virginia squirearchy.' He got angry, and that was the end of it. He was comforted by a gentle assurance that the values of democracy are part of the movement of history and did not require his elucidation or defense. He could carry on his historical studies with the moral certitude that they would lead to greater openness and hence more democracy. The lessons of fascism and the vulnerability of democracy, which we had all just experienced, had no effect on him.

Liberalism without natural rights, the kind that we knew from John Stuart Mill and John Dewey, taught us that the only danger confronting us is being closed to the emergent, the new, the manifestations of progress. No attention had to be paid to the fundamental principles or the moral virtues that inclined men to live according to them. To use language now popular, civic culture was neglected. And this turn in liberalism is what prepared us for cultural relativism and the fact-value distinction, which seemed to carry that viewpoint further and give it greater intellectual weight.

History and social science are used in a variety of ways to overcome prejudice. We should not be ethnocentric, a term drawn from anthropology, which tells us more about the meaning of openness. We should not think our way is better than others. The intention is not so much to teach the students about other times and places as to make them aware of the fact that their preferences are only that—accidents of their time and place. Their beliefs do not entitle them as individuals, or collectively as a nation, to think they are superior to anyone else. John Rawls is almost a parody of this tendency, writing hundreds of pages to persuade men, and proposing a scheme of government that would force them, not to despise anyone. In *A Theory of Justice*, he writes that the physicist or the poet should not look down on the man who spends his life counting blades of grass or performing any other frivolous or corrupt activity. Indeed, he should be esteemed, since esteem from others, as opposed to self-esteem, is a basic need of all men. So indiscriminateness is a moral imperative because its opposite is discrimination. This folly means that men are not permitted to seek for the natural human good and admire it when found, for such discovery is coeval with the discovery of the bad and contempt for it. Instinct and intellect must be suppressed by education. The natural soul is to be replaced with an artificial one.

At the root of this change in morals was the presence in the United States of men and women of a great variety of nations, religions, and races, and the fact that many were badly treated because they belonged to these groups. Franklin Roosevelt declared that we want 'a society which leaves no one out.' Although the natural rights inherent in our regime are perfectly adequate to the solution of this problem, provided these outsiders adhere to them (i.e., they become insiders by adhering to them), this did not satisfy the thinkers who influenced our educators, for the right to vote and the other political rights did not automatically produce social acceptance. The equal protection of the laws did not protect a man from contempt and hatred as a Jew, an Italian, or a Black.

The reaction to this problem was, in the first place, resistance to the notion that outsiders had to give up their 'cultural' individuality and make themselves into that universal, abstract being who participates in natural rights or else be doomed to an existence on the fringe; in the second place, anger at the majority who imposed a 'cultural' life on the nation to which the Constitution is indifferent. Openness was designed to provide a respectable place for these 'groups' or 'minorities'—to wrest respect from those who were not disposed to give it—and to weaken the sense of superiority of the dominant majority (more recently dubbed WASPs, a name the success of which shows something of the success of sociology in reinterpreting the national consciousness). That dominant majority gave the country a dominant culture with its traditions, its litera-

ture, its tastes, its special claim to know and supervise the language, and its Protestant religions. Much of the intellectual machinery of twentieth-century American political thought and social science was constructed for the purposes of making an assault on that majority. It treated the founding principles as impediments and tried to overcome the other strand of our political heritage, majoritarianism, in favor of a nation of minorities and groups each following its own beliefs and inclinations. In particular, the intellectual minority expected to enhance its status, presenting itself as the defender and spokesman of all the others.

This reversal of the founding intention with respect to minorities is most striking. For the Founders, minorities are in general bad things, mostly identical to factions, selfish groups who have no concern as such for the common good. Unlike older political thinkers, they entertained no hopes of suppressing factions and educating a united or homogeneous citizenry. Instead they constructed an elaborate machinery to contain factions in such a way that they would cancel one another and allow for the pursuit of the common good. The good is still the guiding consideration in their thought, although it is arrived at, less directly than in classical political thought, by tolerating faction. The Founders wished to achieve a national majority concerning the fundamental rights and then prevent that majority from using its power to overturn those fundamental rights. In twentieth-century social science, however, the common good disappears and along with it the negative view of minorities. The very idea of majority—now understood to be selfish interest—is done away with in order to protect the minorities. This breaks the delicate balance between majority and minority in Constitutional thought. In such a perspective, where there is no common good, minorities are no longer problematic, and the protection of them emerges as the central function of government. Where this leads is apparent in, for example, Robert Dahl's *A Preface to Democratic Theory*. Groups or individuals who really care, as opposed to those who have lukewarm feelings, deserve special attention or special rights for their 'intensity' or 'commitment,' the new political validation, which replaces reason. The Founding Fathers wished to reduce and defang fanaticism, whereas Dahl encourages it.

The appeal of the minority formula was enormous for all kinds of people, reactionary and progressive, all those who in the twenties and thirties still did not accept the political solution imposed by the Constitution. The reactionaries did not like the suppression of class privilege and religious establishment. For a variety of reasons they simply did not accept equality. Southerners knew full well that the Constitution's heart was a moral commitment to equality and hence condemned segregation of blacks. The Constitution was not just a set of rules of government but implied a moral order that was to be enforced throughout the entire Union. Yet the influence, which has not been sufficiently noted, of Southern writers and historians on the American view of their history has been powerful. They were remarkably successful in characterizing their 'peculiar institution' as part of a charming diversity and individuality of culture to which the Constitution was worse than indifferent. The ideal of openness, lack of ethnocentricity, is just what they needed for a modern defense of their way of life against all the intrusions of outsiders who claimed equal rights with the folks back home. The Southerners' romantic characterization of the alleged failings of the Constitution, and their hostility to 'mass society' with its technology, its money-grubbing way of life, egoistic individuals and concomitant destruction of community, organic and rooted, appealed to malcontents of all political colorations. The New Left in the sixties expressed exactly the same ideology that had been developed to protect the South from the threat to its practices posed by the Constitutional rights and the Federal Government's power to enforce them. It is the old alliance of Right and Left against liberal democracy, parodied as 'bourgeois society.'

The progressives of the twenties and thirties did not like the Constitutional protection of private property or the restraints on majority will and on living as one pleased. For them, equality had not gone far enough. Stalinists also found the definition of democracy as openness useful. The Constitution clashed too violently with the theory and practice of the Soviet Union. But if democracy means open-endedness, and respect for other cultures prevents doctrinaire, natural-rights-based condemnation of the Soviet reality, then someday their ways may become ours. I remember my grade-school history textbook, newly printed on fine glossy paper, showing intriguing pictures of collective farms where farmers worked and lived together without the profit motive. (Children cannot understand the issues, but they are easy to propagandize.) This was very different from our way of life, but we were not to be closed to it, to react to it merely on the basis of our cultural prejudices.

Sexual adventurers like Margaret Mead and others who found America too narrow told us that not only must we know other cultures and learn to respect them, but we could also profit from them. We could follow their lead and loosen up, liberating ourselves from the opinion that our taboos are anything other than social constraints. We could go to the bazaar of cultures and find reinforcement for inclinations that are repressed by puritanical guilt feelings. All such teachers of openness had either no interest in or were actively hostile to the Declaration of Independence and the Constitution.

The civil rights movement provides a good example of this change in thought. In its early days almost all the significant leaders, in spite of tactical and temperamental differences, relied on the Declaration of Independence and the Constitution. They could charge whites not only with the most monstrous injustices but also with contradicting their own most sacred principles. The blacks were the true Americans in demanding the equality that belongs to them as human beings by natural and political right. This stance implied a firm conviction of the truth of the principles of natural right and of their fundamental efficacy within the Constitutional tradition, which, although tarnished, tends in the long run toward fulfilling those principles. They therefore worked through Congress, the Presidency, and, above all, the Judiciary. By contrast, the Black Power movement that supplanted the older civil rights movement— leaving aside both its excesses and its very understandable emphasis on self-respect and refusal to beg for acceptance—had at its core the view that the Constitutional tradition was always corrupt and was constructed as a defense of slavery. Its demand was for black identity, not universal rights. Not rights but power counted. It insisted on respect for blacks as blacks, not as human beings simply. Yet the Constitution does not promise respect for blacks, whites, yellows, Catholics, Protestants, or Jews. It guarantees the protection of the rights of individual human beings. This has not proved to be enough, however, to what is perhaps by now a majority of Americans.

The upshot of all this for the education of young Americans is that they know much less about American history and those who were held to be its heroes. This was one of the few things that they used to come to college with that had something to do with their lives. Nothing has taken its place except a smattering of facts learned about other nations or cultures and a few social science formulas. None of this means much, partly because little attention has been paid to what is required in order truly to convey the spirit of other places and other times to young people, or for that matter to anyone, partly because the students see no relevance in any of it to the lives they are going to lead or to their prevailing passions. It is the rarest of occurrences to find a youngster who has been infused by this education with a longing to know all about China or the Romans or the Jews.

All to the contrary. There is an indifference to such things, for relativism has extinguished the real motive of education, the search for a good life. Young Americans have less and less knowledge of and interest in foreign places. In the past there were many students who actually knew something about and loved England, France, Germany, or Italy, for they dreamed of living there or thought their lives would be made more interesting by assimilating their languages and literatures. Such students have almost disappeared, replaced at most by students who are interested in the political problems of Third World countries and in helping them to modernize, with due respect to their old cultures, of course. This is not learning from others but condescension and a disguised form of a new imperialism. It is the Peace Corps mentality, which is not a spur to learning but to a secularized version of doing good works.

Actually openness results in American conformism—out there in the rest of the world is a drab diversity that teaches only that values are relative, whereas here we can create all the life-styles we want. Our openness means we do not need others. Thus what is advertised as a great opening is a great closing. No longer is there a hope that there are great wise men in other places and times who can reveal the truth about life—except for the few remaining young people who look for a quick fix from a guru. Gone is the real historical sense of a Machiavelli who wrested a few hours from each busy day in which 'to don regal and courtly garments, enter the courts of the ancients and speak with them.'

None of this concerns those who promote the new curriculum. The point is to propagandize acceptance of different ways, and indifference to their real content is as good a means as any. It was not necessarily the best of times in America when Catholics and Protestants were suspicious of and hated one another; but at least they were taking their beliefs seriously, and the more or less satisfactory accommodations they worked out were not simply the result of apathy about the state of their souls. Practically all that young Americans have today is an insubstantial awareness that there are many cultures, accompanied by a saccharine moral drawn from that awareness: We should all get along. Why fight? In 1980, during the crisis with Iran, the mother of one of the hostages expressed our current educational principles very well. She went to Iran to beg for her son's release, against the express wishes of the government of her country, the very week a rescue of the hostages was attempted. She justified her conduct by explaining that a mother has a right to try to save her son and also to learn a new culture. These are two basic rights, and her trip enabled her to kill two birds with one stone.

Actually the problem of cultural difference could have been faced more easily here in America forty years ago. When I was in college, a young Mississippian was lodged in my dormitory room for a few days during a visit of the University of Virginia debating team, of which he was a member. It was my first meeting with an intelligent, educated Southerner. He explained the inferiority of blacks to me, the reasons for Jim Crow, and how all that was a part of a unique way of life. He was an attractive, lively, amiable, healthy youngster. I, however, was horrified by him because I was still ethnocentric. I took my Northern beliefs to be universal. The 'different strokes for different folks' philosophy had not yet taken full hold. Fortunately the homogenization of American culture that has occurred since that enables us to avoid such nasty confrontations. Only obviously pathological lower-class types now hold the racist views of my young visitor. Southerners helped to fashion our theoretical view of culture, but the Southern culture they intended to defend disappeared.

One of the techniques of opening young people up is to require a college course in a non-Western culture. Although many of the persons teaching such courses are real scholars and lovers of the areas they study, in every case I have seen this requirement—when there are so many other things that can and should be learned but are not required, when philosophy and religion are no longer required—has a demagogic intention. The point is to force students to recognize that there are other ways of thinking and that Western ways are not better. It is again not the content that counts but the lesson to be drawn. Such requirements are part of the effort to establish a world community and train its member—the person devoid of prejudice. But if the students were really to learn something of the minds of any of these non-Western cultures—which they do not—they would find that each and every one of these cultures is ethnocentric. All of them think their way is the best way, and all others are inferior. Herodotus tells us that the Persians thought that they were the best, that those nations bordering on them were next best, that those nations bordering on the nations bordering on them were third best, and so on, their worth declining as the concentric circles were farther from the Persian center. This is the very definition of ethnocentrism. Something like this is as ubiquitous as the prohibition against incest between mother and son.

Only in the Western nations, i.e., those influenced by Greek philosophy, is there some willingness to doubt the identification of the good with one's own way. One should conclude from the study of non-Western cultures that not only to prefer one's own way but to believe it best, superior to all others, is primary and even natural—exactly the opposite of what is intended by requiring students to study these cultures. What we are really doing is applying a Western prejudice—which we covertly take to indicate the superiority of our culture—and deforming the evidence of those other cultures to attest to its validity. The scientific study of other cultures is almost exclusively a Western phenomenon, and in its origin was obviously connected with the search for new and better ways, or at least for validation of the hope that our own culture really is the better way, a validation for which there is no felt need in other cultures. If we are to learn from those cultures, we must wonder whether such scientific study is a good idea. Consistency would seem to require professors of openness to respect the ethnocentrism or closedness they find everywhere else. However, in attacking ethnocentrism, what they actually do is to assert unawares the superiority of their scientific understanding and the inferiority of the other cultures which do not recognize it at the same time that they reject all such claims to superiority. They both affirm and deny the goodness of their science. They face a problem akin to that faced by Pascal in the conflict between reason and revelation, without the intellectual intransigence that forced him to abandon science in favor of faith.

The reason for the non-Western closedness, or ethnocentrism, is clear. Men must love and be loyal to their families and their peoples in order to preserve them. Only if they think their own things are good can they rest content with them. A father must prefer his child to other children, a citizen his country to others. That is why there are myths—to justify these attachments. And a man needs a place and opinions by which to orient himself. This is strongly asserted by those who talk about the importance of roots. The problem of getting along with outsiders is secondary to, and sometimes in conflict with, having an inside, a people, a culture, a way of life. A very great narrowness is not incompatible with the health of an individual or a people, whereas with great openness it is hard to avoid decomposition. The firm binding of the good with one's own, the refusal to see a distinction between the two, a vision of the cosmos that has a special place for one's people, seem to be conditions of culture. This is what really follows from the study of non-Western cultures proposed for undergraduates. It points them back to passionate attachment to their own and away from the science which liberates them from it. Science now appears as a threat to culture and a dangerous uprooting charm. In short, they are lost in a no-man's-land between the goodness of knowing and the goodness of culture, where they have been placed by their teachers who no longer have the resources to guide them. Help must be sought elsewhere.

Greek philosophers were the first men we know to address the problem of ethnocentrism. Distinctions between the good and one's own, between nature and convention, between the just and the legal are the signs of this movement of thought. They related the good to the fulfillment of the whole natural human potential and were aware that few, if any, of the nations of men had ways that allowed such fulfillment. They were open to the good. They had to use the good, which was not their own, to judge their own. This was a dangerous business because it tended to weaken wholehearted attachment to their own, hence to weaken their peoples as well as to expose themselves to the anger of family, friends, and countrymen. Loyalty versus quest for the good introduced an unresolvable tension into life. But the awareness of the good as such and the desire to possess it are priceless humanizing acquisitions.

This is the sound motive contained, along with many other less sound ones, in openness as we understand it. Men cannot remain content with what is given them by their culture if they are to be fully human. This is what Plato meant to show by the image of the cave in the *Republic* and by representing us as prisoners in it. A culture is a cave. He did not suggest going around to other cultures as a solution to the limitations of the cave. Nature should be the standard by which we judge our own lives and the lives of peoples. That is why philosophy, not history or anthropology, is the most important human science. Only dogmatic assurance that thought is culture-bound, that there is no nature, is what makes our educators so certain that the only way to escape the limitations of our time and place is to study other cultures. History and anthropology were understood by the Greeks to be useful only in discovering what the past and other peoples had to contribute to the discovery of nature. Historians and anthropologists were to put peoples and their conventions to the test, as Socrates did individuals, and go beyond them. These scientists were superior to their subjects because they saw a problem where others refused to see one, and they were engaged in the quest to solve it. They wanted to be able to evaluate themselves and others.

This point of view, particularly the need to know nature in order to have a standard, is uncomfortably buried beneath our human sciences, whether they like it or not, and accounts for the ambiguities and contradictions I have been pointing out. They want to make us culture-beings with the instruments that were invented to liberate us from culture. Openness used to be the virtue that permitted us to seek the good by using reason. It now means accepting everything and denying reason's power. The unrestrained and thoughtless pursuit of openness, without recognizing the inherent political, social, or cultural problem of openness as the goal of nature, has rendered openness meaningless. Cultural relativism destroys both one's own and the good. What is most characteristic of the West is science, particularly understood as the quest to know nature and the consequent denigration of convention—i.e., culture or the West understood as a culture—in favor of what is accessible to all men as men through their common and distinctive faculty, reason. Science's latest attempts to grasp the human situation—cultural relativism, historicism, the fact-value distinction—are the suicide of science. Culture, hence closedness, reigns supreme. Openness to closedness is what we teach.

Cultural relativism succeeds in destroying the West's universal or intellectually imperialistic claims, leaving it to be just another culture. So there is equality in the republic of cultures. Unfortunately the West is defined by its need for justification of its ways or values, by its need for discovery of nature, by its need for philosophy and science. This is its cultural imperative. Deprived of that, it will collapse. The United States is one of the highest and most extreme achievements of the rational quest for the good life according to nature. What makes its political structure possible is the use of the rational principles of natural right to found a people, thus uniting the good with one's own. Or, to put it otherwise, the regime established here promised untrammeled freedom to reason—not to everything indiscriminately, but to reason, the essential freedom that justifies the other freedoms, and on the basis of which, and for the sake of which, much deviance is also tolerated. An openness that denies the special claim of reason bursts the mainspring keeping the mechanism of this regime in motion. And this regime, contrary to all claims to the contrary, was founded to overcome ethnocentrism, which is in no sense a discovery of social science.

It is important to emphasize that the lesson the students are drawing from their studies is simply untrue. History and the study of cultures do not teach or prove that values or cultures are relative. All to the contrary, that is a philosophical premise that we now bring to our study of them. This premise is unproven and dogmatically asserted for what are largely political reasons. History and culture are interpreted in the light of it, and then are said to prove the premise. Yet the fact that there have been different opinions about good and bad in different times and places in no way proves that none is true or superior to others. To say that it does so prove is as absurd as to say that the diversity of points of view expressed in a college bull session proves there is no truth. On the face of it, the difference of opinion would seem to raise the question as to which is true or right rather than to banish it. The natural reaction is to try to resolve the difference, to examine the claims and reasons for each opinion.

Only the unhistorical and inhuman belief that opinions are held for no reason would prevent the undertaking of such an exciting activity. Men and nations always think they have reasons, and it could be understood to be historians' and social scientists' most important responsibility to make explicit and test those reasons. It was always known that there were many and conflicting opinions about the good, and nations embodying each of them. Herodotus was at least as aware as we are of the rich diversity of cultures. But he took that observation to be an invitation to investigate all of them to see what was good and bad about each and find out what he could learn about good and bad from them. Modern relativists take that same observation as proof that such investigation is impossible and that we must be respectful of them all. Thus students, and the rest of us, are deprived of the primary excitement derived from the discovery of diversity, the impulse of Odysseus, who, according to Dante, traveled the world to see the virtues and vices of men. History and anthropology cannot provide the answers, but they can provide the material on which judgment can work.

I know that men are likely to bring what are only their prejudices to the judgment of alien peoples. Avoiding that is one of the main purposes of education. But trying to prevent it by removing the authority of men's reason is to render ineffective the instrument that can correct their prejudices. True openness is the accompaniment of the desire to know, hence of the awareness of ignorance. To deny the possibility of knowing good and bad is to suppress true openness. A proper historical attitude would lead one to doubt the truth of historicism (the view that all thought is essentially related to and cannot transcend its own time) and treat it as a peculiarity of contemporary history. Historicism and cultural relativism actually are a means to avoid testing our own prejudices and asking, for example, whether men are really equal or whether that opinion is merely a democratic prejudice.

One might well wonder whether our historical and anthropological wisdom is not just a disguised and rather muddled version of the Romantic dilemma that seemed so compelling and tragic at the beginning of the nineteenth century and produced a longing for the distant past or exotic new lands and an art to satisfy that longing. As the heirs of science, so the argument goes, we know more than did the peoples of other times and places with their unscientific prejudices and illusions, but they were, or are, happier. This dilemma is expressed in the distinction between naive and sentimental art. Lévi-Strauss is an unwilling witness to my hypothesis. With a half-digested Rousseauism, he thinks the best culture is to be found at that moment when men have left the state of nature and live together in simple communities, without real private property or the explosion of *amour-propre*. Such a view requires science, which in turn requires developed and corrupted society, in order to emerge. Science is itself one of the modifications of *amour-propre*, the love of inequality. So this view simultaneously produces melancholy about science. But the dilemma seems so compelling only if we are certain that we know so much, which depends on science. Abandon that certainty, and we might be willing to test the beliefs of those happier peoples in order to see if they know something we do not know. Maybe Homer's genius was not so naive as Schiller thought it was. If we abandon this pride in our knowledge, which presents itself as humility, the discussion takes on a new dimension. Then we could go in one of two directions: abandonment of science, or the reestablishment of the theoretical life as both possible and itself productive of self-sufficient happiness. The Romantic posture is a way of not facing these extremes that masquerades as heroic endurance. Our shuttling back and forth between science and culture is a trivialized spin-off from that posture.

Thus there are two kinds of openness, the openness of indifference—promoted with the twin purposes of humbling our intellectual pride and letting us be whatever we want to be, just as long as we don't want to be knowers—and the openness that invites us to the quest for knowledge and certitude, for which history and the various cultures provide a brilliant array of examples for examination. This second kind of openness encourages the desire that animates and makes interesting every serious student—'I want to know what is good for me, what will make me happy'—while the former stunts that desire.

Openness, as currently conceived, is a way of making surrender to whatever is most powerful, or worship of vulgar success, look principled. It is historicism's ruse to remove all resistance to history, which in our day means public opinion, a day when public opinion already rules. How often I have heard the abandonment of requirements to learn languages or philosophy or science lauded as a progress of openness. Here is where the two kinds of openness clash. To be open to knowing, there are certain kinds of things one must know which most people don't want to bother to learn and which appear boring and irrelevant. Even the life of reason is often unappealing; and useless knowledge, i.e., knowledge that is not obviously useful for a career, has no place in the student's vision of the curriculum. So the university that stands intransigently for humane learning must necessarily look closed and rigid. If openness means to 'go with the flow,' it is necessarily an accommodation to the present. That present is so closed to doubt about so many things impeding the progress of its principles that unqualified openness to it would mean forgetting the despised alternatives to it, knowledge of which makes us aware of what is doubtful in it. True openness means closedness to all the charms that make us comfortable with the present.

When I was a young teacher at Cornell, I once had a debate about education with a professor of psychology. He said that it was his function to get rid of prejudices in his stu-

dents. He knocked them down like tenpins. I began to wonder what he replaced those prejudices with. He did not seem to have much of an idea of what the opposite of a prejudice might be. He reminded me of the little boy who gravely informed me when I was four that there is no Santa Claus, who wanted me to bathe in the brilliant light of truth. Did this professor know what those prejudices meant for the students and what effect being deprived of them would have? Did he believe that there are truths that could guide their lives as did their prejudices? Had he considered how to give students the love of the truth necessary to seek unprejudiced beliefs, or would he render them passive, disconsolate, indifferent, and subject to authorities like himself, or the best of contemporary thought? My informant about Santa Claus was just showing off, proving his superiority to me. He had not created the Santa Claus that had to be there in order to be refuted. Think of all we learn about the world from men's belief in Santa Clauses, and all that we learn about the soul from those who believe in them. By contrast, merely methodological excision from the soul of the imagination that projects Gods and heroes onto the wall of the cave does not promote knowledge of the soul; it only lobotomizes it, cripples its powers.

I found myself responding to the professor of psychology that I personally tried to teach my students prejudices, since nowadays—with the general success of his method—they had learned to doubt beliefs even before they believed in anything. Without people like me, he would be out of business. Descartes had a whole wonderful world of old beliefs, of pre-scientific experience and articulations of the order of things, beliefs firmly and even fanatically held, before he even began his systematic and radical doubt. One has to have the experience of really believing before one can have the thrill of liberation. So I proposed a division of labor in which I would help to grow the flowers in the field and he could mow them down.

Prejudices, strong prejudices, are visions about the way things are. They are divinations of the order of the whole of things, and hence the road to a knowledge of that whole is by way of erroneous opinions about it. Error is indeed our enemy, but it alone points to the truth and therefore deserves our respectful treatment. The mind that has no prejudices at the outset is empty. It can only have been constituted by a method that is unaware of how difficult it is to recognize that a prejudice is a prejudice. Only Socrates knew, after a lifetime of unceasing labor, that he was ignorant. Now every high-school student knows that. How did it become so easy? What accounts for our amazing progress? Could it be that our experience has been so impoverished by our various methods, of which openness is only the latest, that there is nothing substantial enough left there to resist criticism, and we therefore have no world left of which to be really ignorant? Have we so simplified the soul that it is no longer difficult to explain? To an eye of dogmatic skepticism, nature herself, in all her lush profusion of expressions, might appear to be a prejudice. In her place we put a gray network of critical concepts, which were invented to interpret nature's phenomena but which strangled them and therewith destroyed their own *raison d'être*. Perhaps it is our first task to resuscitate those phenomena so that we may again have a world to which we can put our questions and be able to philosophize. This seems to me to be our educational challenge.

33

The New Cultural Politics of Difference

Cornel West

In the last few years of the twentieth century, there is emerging a significant shift in the sensibilities and outlooks of critics and artists. In fact, I would go so far as to claim that a new kind of cultural worker is in the making, associated with a new politics of difference. These new forms of intellectual consciousness advance new conceptions of the vocation of critic and artist, attempting to undermine the prevailing disciplinary divisions of labor in the academy, museum, mass media, and gallery networks while preserving modes of critique within the ubiquitous commodification of culture in the global village. Distinctive features of the new cultural politics of difference are to trash the monolithic and homogeneous in the name of diversity, multiplicity, and heterogeneity; to reject the abstract, general, and universal in light of the concrete, specific, and particular; and to historicize, contextualize, and pluralize by highlighting the contingent, provisional, variable, tentative, shifting, and changing. Needless to say, these gestures are not new in the history of criticism or art, yet what makes them novel—along with the cultural politics they produce—is what constitutes difference and how it is constituted, the weight and gravity it is given in representation, and the way in which highlighting issues like exterminism, empire, class, race, gender, sexual orientation, age, nation, nature, and region at this historical moment acknowledges some discontinuity and disruption from previous forms of cultural critique. To put it bluntly, the new cultural politics of difference consists of creative responses to the precise circumstances of our present moment—especially those of marginalized first world agents who shun degraded self-representations, articulating instead their sense of the flow of history in light of the contemporary terrors, anxieties, and fears of highly commercialized North Atlantic capitalist cultures (with their escalating xenophobias against people of color, Jews, women, gays, lesbians, and the elderly). The nationalist revolts against the legacy of hegemonic party henchmen in second world excommunist cultures, and the diverse cultures of the majority of inhabitants on the globe smothered by international communication cartels and repressive postcolonial élites (sometimes in the name of communism, as in Ethiopia) or starved by austere World Bank and IMF policies that subordinate them to the North (as in free-market capitalism in Chile), also locate vital areas of analysis in this new cultural terrain.

The new cultural politics of difference are neither simply oppositional in contesting the mainstream (or *male*stream) for inclusion nor transgressive in the avant-gardist sense of shocking conventional bourgeois audiences. Rather they are distinct articulations of talented (and usually privileged) contributors to culture who desire to align themselves with demoralized, demobilized, depoliticized, and disorganized people in order to empower and enable social action and, if possible, to enlist collective insurgency for the expansion of freedom, democracy, and individuality. This perspective impels these cultural critics and artists to reveal, as an integral component of their production, the very operations of power within their immediate work contexts (i.e., academy, museum, gallery, mass media). This strategy, however, also puts them in an inescapable double bind—while linking their

First published in *October*, 53 (Summer 1990), 93–109. Reprinted with permission.

activities to the fundamental, structural overhaul of these institutions, they often remain financially dependent on them. (So much for 'independent' creation.) For these critics of culture, theirs is a gesture that is simultaneously progressive and co-opted. Yet without social movement or political pressure from outside these institutions (extraparliamentary and extracurricular actions like the social movements of the recent past), transformation degenerates into mere accommodation or sheer stagnation, and the role of the 'co-opted progressive'—no matter how fervent one's subversive rhetoric—is rendered more difficult. In this sense there can be no artistic breakthrough or social progress without some form of crisis in civilization—a crisis usually generated by organizations or collectivities that convince ordinary people to put their bodies and lives on the line. There is, of course, no guarantee that such pressure will yield the result one wants, but there is a guarantee that the status quo will remain or regress if no pressure is applied at all.

The new cultural politics of difference faces three basic challenges—intellectual, existential, and political. The intellectual challenge—usually cast as a methodological debate in these days in which academicist forms of expression have a monopoly on intellectual life—is how to think about representational practices in terms of history, culture, and society. How does one understand, analyze, and enact such practices today? An adequate answer to this question can be attempted only after one comes to terms with the insights and blindnesses of earlier attempts to grapple with the question in light of the evolving crisis in different histories, cultures, and societies. I shall sketch a brief genealogy—a history that highlights the contingent origins and often ignoble outcomes—of exemplary critical responses to the question.

The Intellectual Challenge

An appropriate starting point is the ambiguous legacy of the Age of Europe. Between 1492 and 1945, European breakthroughs in oceanic transportation, agricultural production, state consolidation, bureaucratization, industrialization, urbanization, and imperial dominion shaped the makings of the modern world. Pre-

cious ideals like the dignity of persons (individuality) or the popular accountability of institutions (democracy) were unleashed around the world. Powerful critiques of illegitimate authorities—the Protestant Reformation against the Roman Catholic Church, the Enlightenment against state churches, liberal movements against absolutist states and feudal guild constraints, workers against managerial subordination, people of color and Jews against white and gentile supremacist decrees, gays and lesbians against homophobic sanctions—were fanned and fueled by these precious ideals refined within the crucible of the Age of Europe. Yet the discrepancy between sterling rhetoric and lived reality, glowing principles and actual practices, loomed large.

By the last European century—the last epoch in which European domination of most of the globe was not substantively contested or challenged—a new world seemed to be stirring. At the height of England's reign as the major imperial European power, its exemplary cultural critic, Matthew Arnold ([1855] 1969), painfully observed in his 'Stanzas from the Grand Chartreuse' that he felt some sense of 'wandering between two worlds, one dead/the other powerless to be born' (p. 302). Following his Burkean sensibilities of cautious reform and fear of anarchy, Arnold acknowledged that the old glue-religion—that had tenuously and often unsuccessfully held together the ailing European regimes could not do so in the mid-nineteenth century. Like Alexis de Tocqueville in France, Arnold saw that the democratic temper was the wave of the future. So he proposed a new conception of culture—a secular, humanistic one—that could play an integrative role in cementing and stabilizing an emerging bourgeois civil society and imperial state. His famous castigation of the immobilizing materialism of the declining aristocracy, the vulgar philistinism of the emerging middle classes, and the latent explosiveness of the working-class majority was motivated by a desire to create new forms of cultural legitimacy, authority, and order in a rapidly changing moment in nineteenth-century Europe.

For Arnold ([1869]) 1925: 67), this new conception of culture.

seeks to do away with classes; to make the best that has been thought and known in the world current

everywhere; to make all men live in an atmosphere of sweetness and light. . . .
This is the *social idea* and the men of culture are the true apostles of equality. The great men of culture are those who have had a passion for diffusing, for making prevail, for carrying from one end of society to the other, the best knowledge, the best ideas of their time, who have laboured to divest knowledge of all that was harsh, uncouth, difficult, abstract, professional, yet still remaining the best knowledge and thought of the time, and a true source, therefore, of sweetness and light.

As an organic intellectual of an emergent middle class—as the inspector of schools in an expanding educational bureaucracy, professor of poetry at Oxford (the first noncleric and the first to lecture in English rather than Latin), and an active participant in a thriving magazine network—Arnold defined and defended a new secular culture of critical discourse. For him, this discursive strategy would be lodged in the educational and periodical apparatuses of modern societies as they contained and incorporated the frightening threats of an arrogant aristocracy and especially of an 'anarchic' working-class majority. His ideals of disinterested, dispassionate, and objective inquiry would regulate this secular cultural production, and his justifications for the use of state power to quell any threats to the survival and security of this culture were widely accepted. He aptly noted, 'Through culture seems to lie our way, not only to perfection, but even to safety' (Arnold, [1869] 1925: 200).

For Arnold, the best of the Age of Europe—modeled on a mythological mélange of Periclean Athens, late republican/early imperial Rome, and Elizabethan England—could be promoted only if there were an interlocking affiliation among the emerging middle classes, a homogenizing of cultural discourse in the educational and university networks, and a state advanced enough in its policing techniques to safeguard it. The candidates for participation and legitimation in this grand endeavor of cultural renewal and revision would be detached intellectuals willing to shed their parochialism, provincialism and class-bound identities for Arnold's middle-class-skewed project: 'Aliens, if we may so call them—persons who are mainly led, not by their class spirit, but by a general humane spirit, by the love of human perfection' ([1869] 1925: 107). Needless to say, this

Arnoldian perspective still informs much of academic practice and secular cultural attitudes today: dominant views about the canon, admission procedures, and collective self-definitions of intellectuals. Yet Arnold's project was disrupted by the collapse of nineteenth-century Europe—World War I. This unprecedented war—in George Steiner's words, the first of the bloody civil wars within Europe—brought to the surface the crucial role and violent potential not of the masses Arnold feared but of the state he heralded. Upon the ashes of this wasteland of human carnage—including some of the civilian European population—T. S. Eliot emerged as the grand cultural spokesman.

Eliot's project of reconstituting and reconceiving European highbrow culture—and thereby regulating critical and artistic practices—after the internal collapse of imperial Europe can be viewed as a response to the probing question posed by Paul Valéry in 'The Crisis of the Mind' ([1919] 1962) after World War I:

Will Europe become *what it is in reality*—that is, a little promontory on the continent of Asia? Or will it remain *what it seems*—that is, the elect portion of the terrestrial globe, the pearl of the sphere, the brain of a vast body? (p. 31)

Eliot's image of Europe as a wasteland, a culture of fragments with no cementing center, predominated in postwar Europe. And though his early poetic practices were more radical, open, and international than his Eurocentric criticism, Eliot posed a return to and revision of tradition as the only way to regain European cultural order and political stability. For Eliot, contemporary history had become, as James Joyce's Stephen declared in *Ulysses* ([1922] 1934), 'a nightmare from which he was trying to awake' (p. 35); 'an immense panorama of futility and anarchy,' as Eliot put it in his renowned review of Joyce's modernist masterpiece (Eliot, [1923] 1948: 201). In his influential essay, 'Tradition and the Individual Talent' ([1919] 1950: 4), Eliot stated that:

Yet if the only form of tradition, of handing down, consisted in following the ways of the immediate generation before us in a blind or timid adherence to its successes, 'tradition' should positively be discouraged. We have seen many such simple currents soon lost in the sand; and novelty is better than repetition. Tradition is a matter of much wider significance. It cannot be inherited, and if you want it you must attain it by great labour.

Eliot found this tradition in the Church of England, to which he converted in 1927. Here was a tradition that left room for his Catholic cast of mind, Calvinist heritage, puritanical temperament, and ebullient patriotism for the old American South (the place of his upbringing). Like Arnold, Eliot was obsessed with the idea of civilization and the horror of barbarism (echoes of Joseph Conrad's Kurtz in *Heart of Darkness*), or, more pointedly, the notion of the decline and decay of European civilization. With the advent of World War II, Eliot's obsession became a reality. Again, unprecedented human carnage (fifty million died)—including an indescribable genocidal attack on Jewish people—throughout Europe as well as around the globe put the last nail in the coffin of the Age of Europe. After 1945, Europe consisted of a devastated and divided continent, crippled by a humiliating dependency on and deference to the United States and Russia.

The second historical coordinate of my genealogy is the emergence of the United States as *the* world power (in the words of André Malraux, the first nation to do so without trying to do so). The United States was unprepared for world power status. However, with the recovery of Stalin's Russia (after losing twenty million lives), the United States felt compelled to make its presence felt around the globe. Then, with the Marshall Plan to strengthen Europe, it seemed clear that there was no escape from world power obligations.

The post-World-War-II era in the United States, or the first decades of what Henry Luce envisioned as 'The American Century,' was a period not only of incredible economic expansion but of active cultural ferment. The creation of a mass middle class—a prosperous working class with bourgeois identity—was countered by the first major emergence of subcultures among American non-WASP intellectuals; the so-called New York intellectuals in criticism, the abstract expressionists in painting, and the bebop artists in jazz music. The emergence signaled a vital challenge to an American male WASP élite loyal to an older and eroding European culture.

The first significant blow was dealt when assimilated Jewish Americans entered the higher echelons of the cultural apparatuses (academy, museums, galleries, mass media).

Lionel Trilling is an emblematic figure. This Jewish entree into the anti-Semitic and patriarchal critical discourse of the exclusivistic institutions of American culture initiated the slow but sure undoing of male WASP cultural hegemony and homogeneity. Trilling's aim was to appropriate Arnold's project for his own political and cultural purposes—thereby unraveling the old male WASP consensus while erecting a new post-World-War-II liberal academic consensus around cold war, anticommunist renditions of the values of complexity, difficulty, variousness, and modulation. In addition, the postwar boom laid the basis for intense professionalization and specialization in expanding institutions of higher education—especially in the natural sciences, which were compelled to respond somehow to Russia's successful ventures in space. Humanistic scholars found themselves searching for new methodologies that could buttress self-images of rigor and scientific seriousness. The close reading techniques of New Criticism (severed from their conservative, organicist, anti-industrialist ideological roots), the logical precision of reasoning in analytic philosophy, and the jargon of Parsonian structural-functionalism in sociology, for example, helped create such self-images. Yet towering cultural critics like C. Wright Mills, W. E. B. Du Bois, Richard Hofstadter, Margaret Mead, and Dwight MacDonald bucked the tide. This suspicion of the academicization of knowledge is expressed in Trilling's well-known essay 'On the Teaching of Modern Literature' ([1961] 1965: 10):

Can we not say that, when modern literature is brought into the classroom, the subject being taught is betrayed by the pedagogy of the subject? We have to ask ourselves whether in our day too much does not come within the purview of the academy. More and more, as the universities liberalize themselves, turn their beneficent imperialistic gaze upon what is called Life Itself, the feeling grows among our educated classes that little can be experienced unless it is validated by some established intellectual discipline.

Trilling laments the fact that university instruction often quiets and domesticates radical and subversive works of art, turning them into objects 'of merely habitual regard.' This process of 'the socialization of the anti-social, or the acculturation of the anti-cultural, or the legitimization of the subversive' leads Trilling to 'question whether in our culture the study of literature is any longer a suitable means for developing and refining the intelligence' ([1961] 1965: 26). He asks this question in a spirit not of denigrating and devaluing the academy but rather of highlighting the possible failure of an Arnoldian conception of culture to contain what he perceives as the philistine and anarchic alternatives becoming more and more available to students of the 1960s—namely, mass culture and radical politics.

This threat is partly associated with the third historical coordinate of my genealogy— the decolonization of the third world. It is crucial to recognize the importance of this world-historical process if one wants to grasp the significance of the end of the Age of Europe and the emergence of the United States as a world power. With the first defeat of a Western nation by a non-Western nation—in Japan's victory over Russia (1905); revolutions in Persia (1905), Turkey (1908), Mexico (1911–12), and China (1912); and much later the independence of India (1947) and China (1948) and the triumph of Ghana (1957)—the actuality of a decolonized globe loomed large. Born of violent struggle, consciousness raising, and the reconstruction of identities, decolonization simultaneously brings with it new perspectives on that long-festering underside of the Age of Europe (of which colonial domination represents the *costs* of 'progress,' 'order,' and 'culture'), and requires new readings of the economic boom in the United States (wherein the black, brown, yellow, red, white, female, gay, lesbian, and elderly working class live the same *costs* by supplying cheap labor at home as well as in US-dominated Latin American and Pacific Rim markets).

The impetuous ferocity and moral outrage that motor the decolonization process are best captured by Frantz Fanon in *The Wretched of the Earth* (1963):

Decolonization, which sets out to change the order of the world, is, obviously, a program of complete disorder. . . . Decolonization is the meeting of two forces, opposed to each other by their very nature, which in fact owe their originality to that sort of substantification which results from and is nourished by the situation in the colonies. Their first encounter was marked by violence and their existence together—that is to say the exploitation of the native by the settler—was carried on by dint of a great array of bayonets and cannons. . . .

In decolonization, there is therefore the need of a complete calling in question of the colonial situation. If we wish to describe it precisely, we might find it in the well-known words: 'The last shall be first and the first last.' Decolonization is the putting into practice of this sentence. . . .

The naked truth of decolonization evokes for us the searing bullets and bloodstained knives which emanate from it. For if the last shall be first, this will only come to pass after a murderous and decisive struggle between the two protagonists. (pp. 36–7)

Fanon's strong words describe the feelings and thoughts between the occupying British Army and the colonized Irish in Northern Ireland, the occupying Israeli Army and the subjugated Palestinians on the West Bank and Gaza Strip, the South African Army and the oppressed black South Africans in the townships, the Japanese police and the Koreans living in Japan, established armies and subordinated ethnic groups in the former Soviet Union. His words also partly invoke the sense many black Americans have toward police departments in urban centers. In other words, Fanon is articulating century-long, heartfelt, human responses to being degraded and despised, hated and hunted, oppressed and exploited, and marginalized and dehumanized at the hands of powerful, xenophobic European, American, Russian, and Japanese imperial nations.

During the late 1950s, the 1960s, and the early 1970s in the United States, these decolonized sensibilities fanned and fueled the civil rights and black power movements, as well as the student, antiwar, feminist, gray, brown, gay, and lesbian movements. In this period we witnessed the shattering of male WASP cultural homogeneity and the collapse of the short-lived liberal consensus. The inclusion of African Americans, Latino/a Americans, Asian Americans, Native Americans, and American women in the culture of critical discourse yielded intense intellectual polemics and inescapable ideological polarization that focused principally on the exclusions, silences, and blindnesses of male WASP cultural homogeneity and its concomitant Arnoldian notions of the canon.

In addition these critiques promoted three crucial processes that affected intellectual life in the country. First is the appropriation of the theories of postwar Europe—especially the work of the Frankfurt School (Marcuse, Adorno, Horkheimer), French/Italian

Marxisms (Sartre, Althusser, Lefebvre, Gramsci), structuralisms (Levi-Strauss, Todorov), and poststructuralisms (Deleuze, Derrida, Foucault). These diverse and disparate theories—all preoccupied with keeping alive radical projects after the end of the Age of Europe—tend to fuse versions of transgressive European modernisms with Marxist or post-Marxist left politics and unanimously to shun the term 'post-modernism.' Second, there is the recovery and revisioning of American history in light of the struggles of white male workers, African Americans, Native Americans, Latino/a Americans, gays and lesbians. Third is the impact of forms of popular culture such as television, film, music videos, and even sports on highbrow, literate culture. The black-based hip-hop culture of youth around the world is one grand example.

After 1973, with the crisis in the international economy, America's slump in productivity, the challenge of OPEC nations to the North Atlantic monopoly of oil production, the increasing competition in high-tech sectors of the economy from Japan and West Germany, and the growing fragility of the international debt structure, the United States entered a period of waning self-confidence (compounded by Watergate) and a nearly contracted economy. As the standards of living for the middle classes declined—owing to runaway inflation and escalating unemployment, underemployment, and crime—the quality of living fell for most everyone, and religious and secular neoconservatism emerged with power and potency. This fusion of fervent neoconservatism, traditional cultural values, and 'free market' policies served as the groundwork for the Reagan-Bush era.

The ambiguous legacies of the European Age, US preeminence, and decolonization continue to haunt our postmodern moment as we come to terms with both the European, American, Japanese, Soviet, and third world *crimes against* and *contributions to* humanity. The plight of Africans in the New World can be instructive in this regard.

By 1914 European maritime empires had dominion over more than half of the land and a third of the peoples in the world—almost seventy-two million square kilometers of territory and more than 560 million people around colonial rule. Needless to say, this European control included brutal enslavement, institutional terrorism, and cultural degradation of black diaspora people. The death of roughly seventy five million Africans during the centuries-long, transatlantic slave trade is but one reminder, among others, of the assault on black humanity. The black diaspora condition of New World servitude—in which people of African descent were viewed as mere commodities with production value, who had no proper legal status, social standing, or public worth—can be characterized, following Orlando Patterson, as natal alienation. This state of perpetual and inheritable domination that diaspora Africans had at birth produced the *modern black diaspora problematic of invisibility and namelessness*. White supremacist practices—enacted under the auspices of the prestigious cultural authorities of the churches, print media, and scientific academics—promoted black inferiority and constituted the European background against which African diaspora struggles for identity, dignity (self-confidence, self-respect, self-esteem), and material resources took place.

An inescapable aspect of this struggle was that the black diaspora peoples' quest for validation and recognition occurred on the ideological, social, and cultural terrains of non-black peoples. White supremacist assaults on black intelligence, ability, beauty, and character required persistent black efforts to hold self-doubt, self-contempt, and even self-hatred at bay. Selective appropriation, incorporation, and rearticulation of European ideologies, cultures, and institutions alongside an African heritage—a heritage more or less confined to linguistic innovation in rhetorical practices, stylizations of the body as forms of occupying an alien social space (e.g., hairstyles, ways of walking, standing, and talking, and hand expressions), means of constituting and sustaining camaraderie and community (e.g., antiphonal, call-and-response styles, rhythmic repetition, risk-ridden syncopation in spectacular modes in musical and rhetorical expressions)—were some of the strategies employed.

The modern black diaspora problematic of invisibility and namelessness can be understood as the condition of *relative lack of power for blacks to present themselves to themselves and others as complex human beings, and thereby to contest the bombardment of negative, degrading stereotypes put forward by white supremacist ide-*

ologies. The initial black response to being caught in this whirlwind of Europeanization was to resist the misrepresentation and caricature of the terms set by uncontested non-black norms and models and to fight for self-recognition. Every modern black person, especially the cultural disseminator, encounters this problematic of invisibility and namelessness. The initial African diaspora response was a mode of resistance that was *moralistic in content and communal in character*. That is, the fight for representation and recognition highlighted moral judgements regarding black 'positive' images over and against white supremacist stereotypes. These images 're-presented' monolithic and homogeneous black communities in a way that could displace past misrepresentations of these communities. Stuart Hall has discussed these responses as attempts to change the 'relations of representation.'

These courageous yet limited black efforts to combat racist cultural practices uncritically accepted non-black conventions and standards in two ways. First, they proceeded in an *assimilationist manner* that set out to show that black people were really like white people—thereby eliding differences (in history and culture) between whites and blacks. Black specificity and particularity were thus banished in order to gain white acceptance and approval. Second, these black responses rested upon a *homogenizing impulse* that assumed that all black people were really alike—hence obliterating differences (class, gender, region, sexual orientation) between black peoples. I submit that there are elements of truth in both claims, yet the conclusions are unwarranted owing to the basic fact that non-black paradigms set the terms of the replies.

The insight in the first claim is that blacks and whites are in some important sense alike—i.e., positively, in their capacities for human sympathy, moral sacrifice, service to others, intelligence, and beauty; or negatively, in their capacity for cruelty. Yet the common humanity they share is jettisoned when the claim is cast in an assimilationist manner that subordinates black particularity to a false universalism, i.e., non-black rubrics and prototypes. Similarly, the insight in the second claim is that all blacks are in some significant sense 'in the same boat'—that is, subject to white supremacist abuse. Yet this common condition is stretched too far when viewed in a *homogeniz-*

ing way that overlooks how racist treatment vastly differs owing to class, gender, sexual orientation, nation, region, hue, and age.

The moralistic and communal aspects of the initial black diaspora responses to social and psychic erasure were not simply cast into binary oppositions of positive/negative, good/bad images that privileged the first term in light of a white norm, so that black efforts remained inscribed within the very logic that dehumanized them. They were further complicated by the fact that these responses were advanced principally by anxiety-ridden, middle-class black intellectuals (predominantly male and heterosexual) grappling with their sense of double-consciousness—namely their own crisis of identity, agency, audience—caught between a quest for white approval and acceptance and an endeavor to overcome the internalized association of blackness with inferiority. And I suggest that these complex anxieties of modern black diaspora intellectuals partly motivate the two major arguments that ground the assimilationist moralism and homogeneous communalism just outlined.

Kobena Mercer has talked about these two arguments as the *reflectionist* and the *social engineering* arguments. The reflectionist argument holds that the fight for black representation and recognition—against white racist stereotypes—must reflect or mirror the real black community, not simply the negative and depressing representations of it. The social engineering argument claims that since any form of representation is constructed—i.e., selective in light of broader aims—black representation (especially given the difficulty for blacks to gain access to positions of power to produce any black imagery) should offer positive images, thereby countering racist stereotypes. The hidden assumption of both arguments is that we have unmediated access to what the 'real black community' is and what 'positive images' are. In short, these arguments presuppose the very phenomenon to be interrogated and thereby foreclose the very issues that should serve as the subject matter to be investigated.

Any notions of 'the real black community' and 'positive images' are value laden, socially loaded, and ideologically charged. To pursue this discussion is to call into question the possibility of such an uncontested consensus regarding them. Hall has rightly called this encounter 'the end of innocence or the end of the innocent notions of the essential Black subject . . . the recognition that "black" is essentially a politically and culturally constructed category' (Hall, 1988: 28). This recognition—more and more pervasive among the postmodern African diaspora intelligentsia—is facilitated in part by the slow but sure dissolution of the European Age's maritime empires and the unleashing of new political possibilities and cultural articulations among ex-colonized peoples across the globe.

One crucial lesson of this decolonization process remains the manner in which most third world authoritarian bureaucratic élites deploy essentialist rhetorics about 'homogeneous national communities' and 'positive images' in order to repress and regiment their diverse and heterogeneous populations. Yet in the diaspora, especially among first world countries, this critique has emerged not so much from the black male component of the left as from the black women's movement. The decisive push of postmodern black intellectuals toward a new cultural politics of difference has been made by the powerful critiques and constructive explorations of black diaspora women (e.g., Toni Morrison). The coffin used to bury the innocent notion of the essential black subject was nailed shut with the termination of the black male monopoly on the construction of the black subject. In this regard, the black diaspora womanist critique has had a greater impact than have the critiques that highlight exclusively class, empire, age, sexual orientation, or nature.

This decisive push toward the end of black innocence—though prefigured in various degrees in the best moments of W. E. B. Du Bois, James Baldwin, Amiri Baraka, Anna Cooper, Frantz Fanon, C. L. R. James, Claudia Jones, the later Malcolm X, and others—forces black diaspora cultural workers to encounter what Hall has called 'the politics of representation.' The main aim now is not simply access to representation in order to produce positive images of homogeneous communities—though broader access remains a practical and political problem. Nor is the primary goal here that of contesting stereotypes—though contestation remains a significant albeit limited venture. Following the model of the African diaspora traditions of music, athletics, and rhetoric, black cultural workers must constitute and sustain discursive and institutional networks that deconstruct earlier modern black strategies for identity formation, demystify power relations that incorporate class, patriarchal, and homophobic biases, and construct more multivalent and multidimensional responses that articulate the complexity and diversity of black practices in the modern and postmodern world.

Furthermore, black cultural workers must investigate and interrogate the other of blackness/whiteness. One cannot deconstruct the binary oppositional logic of images of blackness without extending it to the contrary condition of blackness/whiteness itself. However, a mere dismantling will not do—for the very notion of a deconstructive social theory is oxymoronic. Yet social theory is what is needed to examine and *explain* the historically specific ways in which 'whiteness' is a politically constructed category parasitic on 'blackness,' and thereby to conceive of the profoundly hybrid character of what we mean by 'race', 'ethnicity,' and 'nationality.' Needless to say, these inquiries must traverse those of 'male/female,' 'colonizer/colonized,' 'heterosexual/homosexual,' *et al.*, as well.

Demystification is the most illuminating mode of theoretical inquiry for those who promote the new cultural politics of difference. Social structural analyses of empire, exterminism, class, race, gender, nature, age, sexual orientation, nation, and region are the springboards—though not the landing grounds—for the most desirable forms of critical practice that take history (and herstory) seriously. Demystification tries to keep track of the complex dynamics of institutional and other related power structures in order to disclose options and alternatives for transformational praxis; it also attempts to grasp the way in which representational strategies are creative responses to novel circumstances and conditions. In this way the central role of human agency (always enacted under circumstances not of one's choosing)—be it in the critic, artist, or constituency, and audience—is accented.

I call demystificatory criticism 'prophetic criticism'—the approach appropriate for the new cultural politics of difference—because while it begins with social structural analyses it also makes explicit its moral and political aims. It is partisan, partial, engaged, and crisis centered, yet it always keeps open a skeptical eye to avoid dogmatic traps, premature closures, formulaic formulations, or rigid conclusions. In addition to social-structural analyses, moral and political judgements, and sheer critical consciousness, there indeed is evaluation. Yet the aim of this evaluation is neither to pit art objects against one another like racehorses nor to create eternal canons that dull, discourage, or even dwarf contemporary achievements. We listen to Laurie Anderson, Kathleen Battle, Ludwig van Beethoven, Charlie Parker, Luciano Pavarotti, Sarah Vaughan, or Stevie Wonder; read Anton Chekhov, Ralph Ellison, Gabriel García Márquez, Doris Lessing, Toni Morrison, Thomas Pynchon, William Shakespeare; or see the works of Ingmar Bergman, Le Corbusier, Frank Gehry, Barbara Kruger, Spike Lee, Martin Puryear, Pablo Picasso, or Howardena Pindell—not in order to undergird bureaucratic assents or enliven cocktail party conversations, but rather to be summoned by the styles they deploy for their profound insights, pleasures, and challenges. Yet all evaluation—including a delight in Eliot's poetry despite his reactionary politics, or a love of Zora Neale Hurston's novels despite her Republican Party affiliations—is inseparable from, though not identical to reducible to, social structural analyses, moral and political judgements, and the workings of a curious critical consciousness.

The deadly traps of demystification—and any form of prophetic criticism—are those of reductionism, be it of the sociological, psychological, or historical sort. By reductionism I mean either one-factor analyses (crude Marxisms, feminisms, racialisms, etc.) that yield a one-dimensional functionalism or hypersubtle analytical perspectives that lose touch with the specificity of an artwork's form and the context of its reception. Few cultural workers of whatever stripe can walk the tightrope between the Scylla of reductionism and the Charybdis of aestheticism—yet demystificatory (or prophetic) critics must. Of course, since so many art practices these days also purport to be criticism, this also holds true for artists.

The Existential Challenge

The existential challenge to the new cultural politics of difference can be stated simply: How does one acquire the resources to survive and the cultural capital to thrive as a critic or artist? By cultural capital (Pierre Bourdieu's term), I mean not only the high-quality skills required to engage in cultural practices but more importantly, the self-confidence, discipline, and perseverance necessary for success without an undue reliance on the mainstream for approval and acceptance. This challenge holds for all prophetic critics, yet it is especially difficult for those of color. The widespread modern European denial of the intelligence, ability, beauty, and character of people of color puts a tremendous burden on critics and artists of color to 'prove' themselves in light of norms and models set by white élites whose own heritage devalued and dehumanized them. In short, in the court of criticism and art—or any matters regarding the life of the mind—people of color are guilty (i.e., not expected to meet standards of intellectual achievement) until 'proven' innocent (i.e., acceptable to 'us').

This is more a structural dilemma than a matter of personal attitudes. The profoundly racist and sexist heritage of the European Age has bequeathed to us a set of deeply ingrained perceptions about people of color, including, of course, the self-perceptions that people of color bring. It is not surprising that most intellectuals of color in the past exerted much of their energies and efforts to gain acceptance and approval by 'white normative gazes.' The new cultural politics of difference advises critics and artists of color to put aside this mode of mental bondage, thereby freeing themselves both to interrogate the ways in which they are bound by certain conventions and to learn from and build on these very norms and models. One hallmark of wisdom in the context of any struggle is to avoid knee-jerk rejection and uncritical acceptance.

Self-confidence, discipline, and perseverance are not ends in themselves. Rather they are the necessary stuff of which enabling criticism and self-criticism are made. Notwithstanding inescapable jealousies, insecurities, and anxieties, one telling characteristic of critics and artists of color linked to the new prophetic criticism should be their capacity for and promotion of relentless criticism and self-criticism—be it the normative paradigms of their white colleagues that tend to leave out considerations of empire, race, gender, and sexual orientation, or the damaging dogmas about the homogeneous character of communities of color.

There are four basic options for people of color interested in representation—if they are to survive and thrive as serious practitioners of their craft. First, there is the Booker T. Temptation, namely the individual preoccupation with the mainstream and its legitimizing power. Most critics and artists of color try to bite this bait. It is nearly unavoidable, yet few succeed in a substantive manner. It is no accident that the most creative and profound among them—especially those who have staying power beyond being mere flashes in the pan to satisfy faddish tokenism—are usually marginal to the mainstream. Even the pervasive professionalization of cultural practitioners of color in the past few decades has not produced towering figures who reside within the established white patronage system, which bestows the rewards and prestige for chosen contributions to American society.

It certainly helps to have some trustworthy allies within this system, yet most of those who enter and remain tend to lose much of their creativity, diffuse their prophetic energy, and dilute their critiques. Still, it is unrealistic for creative people of color to think they can sidestep the white patronage system. And though there are indeed some white allies conscious of the tremendous need to rethink identity politics, it is naive to think that being comfortably nested within this very same system—even if one can be a patron to others—does not affect one's work, one's outlook, and most important, one's soul.

The second option is the Talented Tenth Seduction, namely, a move toward arrogant group insularity. This alternative has a limited function—to preserve one's sanity and sense of self as one copes with the mainstream. Yet it is, at best, a transitional and transient activity. If it becomes a permanent option it is self-defeating in that it usually reinforces the very inferiority complexes promoted by the subtly racist mainstream. Hence it tends to revel in parochialism and encourage a narrow racialist and chauvinistic outlook.

The third strategy is the Go-It-Alone Option. This is an extreme rejectionist perspective that shuns the mainstream and group insularity. Almost every critic and artist of color contemplates or enacts this option at some time in his or her pilgrimage. It is

healthy in that it reflects the presence of independent, critical, and skeptical sensibilities toward perceived constraints on one's creativity. Yet it is, in the end, difficult if not impossible to sustain if one is to grow, develop, and mature intellectually, as some semblance of dialogue with a community is necessary for almost any creative practice.

The most desirable option for people of color who promote the new cultural politics of difference is to be a Critical Organic Catalyst. By this I mean a person who stays attuned to the best of what the mainstream has to offer—its paradigms, viewpoints, and methods—yet maintains a grounding in affirming and enabling subcultures of criticism. Prophetic critics and artists of color should be exemplars of what it means to be intellectual freedom fighters, that is, cultural workers who simultaneously position themselves within (or alongside) the mainstream while clearly being aligned with groups who vow to keep alive potent traditions of critique and resistance. In this regard one can take clues from the great musicians or preachers of color who are open to the best of what other traditions offer, yet are rooted in nourishing subcultures that build on the grand achievements of a vital heritage. Openness to others—including the mainstream—does not entail wholesale cooptation, and group autonomy is not group insularity. Louis Armstrong, Ella Baker, W. E. B. DuBois, Martin Luther King, Jr., Jose Carlos Mariategui, Wynton Marsalis, M. M. Thomas, and Ronald Takaki have understood this well.

The new cultural politics of difference can thrive only if there are communities, groups, organizations, institutions, subcultures, and networks of people of color who cultivate critical sensibilities and personal accountability—without inhibiting individual expressions, curiosities, and idiosyncrasies. This is especially needed given the escalating racial hostility, violence, and polarization in the United States. Yet this critical coming together must not be a narrow closing of ranks. Rather it is a strengthening and nurturing endeavor that can forge more solid alliances and coalitions. In this way prophetic criticism—with its stress on historical specificity and artistic complexity—directly addresses the intellectual challenge. The cultural capital of people of color—with its emphasis on self-confidence, discipline, perseverance, and subcultures of criticism—also tries to meet the existential requirement. Both are mutually reinforcing. Both are motivated by a deep commitment to individuality and democracy—the moral and political ideals that guide the creative responses to the political challenge.

The Political Challenge

Adequate rejoinders to intellectual and existential challenges equip the practitioners of the new cultural politics of difference to meet the political ones. This challenge principally consists of forging solid and reliable alliances to people of color and white progressives guided by a moral and political vision of greater democracy and individual freedom in communities, states, and transnational enterprises—i.e., corporations and information and communications conglomerates. Jesse Jackson's Rainbow Coalition is a gallant yet flawed effort in this regard: gallant due to the tremendous energy, vision, and courage of its leader and followers; flawed because of its failure to take seriously critical and democratic sensibilities within its own operations.

The time has come for critics and artists of the new cultural politics of difference to cast their nets widely, flex their muscles broadly, and thereby refuse to limit their visions, analyses, and praxis to their particular terrains. The aim is to dare to recast, redefine, and revise the very notions of 'modernity,' 'mainstream,' 'margins,' 'difference,' 'otherness.' We have now reached a new stage in the perennial struggle for freedom and dignity. And while much of the first world intelligentsia adopts retrospective and conservative outlooks that defend the crisis-ridden present, we promote a prospective and prophetic vision with a sense of possibility and potential, especially for those who bear the social costs of the present. We look to the past for strength, not solace; we look at the present and see people perishing, not profits mounting; we look toward the future and vow to make it different and better.

To put it boldly, the new kind of critic and artist associated with the new cultural politics of difference consists of an energetic breed of new world *bricoleurs* with improvisational and flexible sensibilities that sidestep mere opportunism and mindless eclecticism; persons of all countries, cultures, genders, sexual orientations, ages, and regions, with protean identities, who avoid ethnic chauvinism and faceless universalism; intellectual and political freedom fighters with partisan passion, international perspectives, and, thank God, a sense of humor to combat the ever-present absurdity that forever threatens our democratic and libertarian projects and dampens the fire that fuels our will to struggle. We will struggle and stay, as those brothers and sisters on the block say, 'out there'—with intellectual rigor, existential dignity, moral vision, political courage, and soulful style.

References

Arnold, M. ([1869] 1925), *Culture and Anarchy: An Essay in Political Criticism* (New York: Macmillan).
—— ([1855] 1969), 'Stanzas from the Grand Chartreuse', in C. B. Tinker and H. F. Lowry (eds.), *Poetical Works* (London: Oxford), 299–306.
Eliot, T. S. ([1919] 1950), 'Tradition and the Individual Talent', in *Selected Essays* (New York: Harcourt), 3–11.
—— ([1923] 1948), 'Ulysses, Order, and Myth', in S. Givens (ed.), *James Joyce: Two Decades of Criticism* (New York: Vanguard), 198–202.
Fanon, F. (1963), *The Wretched of the Earth* (New York: Grove).
Hall, S. (1988), *New Ethnicities*, in K. Mercer (ed.), *Black Film, British Cinema* (ICA documents, 7, London: ICA), 27–31.
Joyce, J. ([1922] 1934), *Ulysses*, (New York: Random).
Trilling, L. ([1961] 1965), 'On the Teaching of Modern Literature', in *Beyond Culture: Essays on Literature and Learning* (New York: Viking), 3–30.
Valéry, P. ([1919] 1962), 'The Crisis of the Mind', in D. Folliot and J. Mathews (eds.), *The Collected Works of Paul Valéry*, (New York: Bollingen), 23–36.

34

Multiculturalism and the Postmodern Critique: Toward a Pedagogy of Resistance and Transformation

Peter McLaren

Social Justice Under Siege

We inhabit skeptical times, historical moments spawned in a temper of distrust, disillusionment, and despair. Social relations of discomfort and diffidence have always preexisted us but the current historical juncture is particularly invidious in this regard, marked as it is by a rapture of greed, untempered and hypereroticized consumer will, racing currents of narcissism, severe economic and racial injustices, and heightened social paranoia. The objective conditions of Western capitalism now appear so completely incompatible with the realization of freedom and liberation that it is no understatement to consider them mutually antagonistic enterprises. Situated beyond the reach of ethically convincing forms of accountability, capitalism has dissolved the meaning of democracy and freedom into glossy aphorisms one finds in election campaign sound bytes or at bargain basement sales in suburban shopping malls. The American public has been proferred a vision of democracy that is a mixture of Sunday barbecue banality, American Gladiator jocksniffery, AMWAY enterprise consciousness, and the ominous rhetoric of 'New World Order' jingoism.

The heroic cult of modernism which has naturalized the power and privilege of 'dead white men' and accorded the pathology of domination the status of cultural reason has all but enshrined a history of decay, defeat, and moral panic. As illustrated so vividly in Oliver Stone's television mini-series, *Wild Palms*, greed, avarice, and cynicism have insinuated themselves into virtually every aspect of cultural life, and have become rationalized and aestheticized as necessary resources that must be fed into a vast technological machine known as Western civilization. It is history that has installed Willie Horton into our structural unconscious and helped make possible and desirable the legal torture and dehumanization of Rodney King and peoples of color in general. That the fortified, postmodern *noir* metropolises of this fin-de-siècle era have grown more Latinophobic, homophobic, xenophobic, sexist, racist, and bureaucratically cruel is not reflective of the self-understanding of the public at large but of the way that the public has been constructed through a politics of representation linked to the repressive moralism of the current conservative political regime and current counterattacks on cultural democracy from the Right. We should not forget, as well, the spectatorial detachment of those postmodern free-floating intellectuals who, despite their claim to be part of a collective deconstructive project, often fail to mobilize intellectual work in the interest of a liberatory praxis.

The present moral apocalypse, perhaps most vividly represented by the maelstrom of anger and violence under the smoke-filled skies of Los Angeles—what Mike Davis calls the 'L.A. Intifada' (Katz and Smith 1992)— has not been brought on simply by the existence of midnight hustlers, the drug trade,

From H. A. Giroux and P. McLaren (eds.) *Between Borders: Pedagogy and Politics of Cultural Studies* (1994), 192–222.

skewered ambition, or gang members taking advantage of public outrage over the justice system but by shifting economic, political, and cultural relations that have worsened over the last two decades. We have been standing at the crossroads of a disintegrating culture for the last two decades where we have witnessed a steady increase in the disproportionate level of material wealth, economic dislocation, and intergenerational poverty suffered by African-Americans, Latinos, and other minorities. Such conditions have been brought about by the frenetic and, at times, savage immorality of the Reagan and Bush administrations, as evidenced in their direct attacks on the underclass, the disintegration of social programs, and the general retreat from civil rights that occurred during their tenure in office.

Other characteristics of this current juncture include: changes in the structure of the US economy; the declining inner-city job market; growing national unemployment rates; a drastic decline in the number of unskilled positions in traditional blue-collar industries in urban areas; the increasing numbers of youth competing for fewer and fewer entry-level unskilled jobs; the automation of clerical labour; the movement of the African-American middle class out of the once multiclass ghetto; the shifting of service-sector employment to the suburbs (Kasinitz 1988); the destructive competition among nations that results from a free-trade policy fueled by the retrograde notion that other nations can achieve economic growth by unbalanced sales to the US market; increased global competition provoking capitalist manufacturing firms to reduce costs by exploiting immigrant workers in US cities or 'out-sourcing' to Third World countries; and a post-Fordist demonopolization of economic structures and the deregulation and globalization of markets, trade, and labor as well as deregulated local markets 'that [make] local capital vulnerable to the strategies of corporate raiders' (Featherstone 1990: 7).

In addition, we are faced with an increasing assault on human intelligence by the architects of mass culture, an increasing dependency on social cues manufactured by the mass media to construct meaning and build consensus on moral issues, and the strengthening of what Piccone (1988: 9) has called the 'unholy symbiosis of abstract individualism

and managerial bureaucracies.' The white-controlled media (often backed by victim-blaming white social scientists) have ignored the economic and social conditions responsible for bringing about in African-American communities what Cornel West has called a '*walking nihilism* of pervasive drug addiction, pervasive alcoholism, pervasive homicide, and an exponential rise in suicide' (cited in Stephanson 1988: 276).

Furthermore, the white media have generated the racially pornographic term 'wilding' to account for recent acts of violence in urban centers by groups of young African-Americans (Cooper 1989). Apparently the term 'wilding', first reported by New York City newspapers in relation to the Central Park rapists, was relevant only to the violence of black male youth, since it was conspicuously absent in press reports of the attack of white male youths on Yusef Hawkins in Bensonhurst (Wallace 1991). Thus, the postmodern image which many white people now entertain in relation to the African-American underclass is one constructed upon violence and grotesquery—a population spawning mutant Willie Horton-type youths who, in the throes of bloodlust, roam the perimeter of the urban landscape high on angel dust, randomly hunting whites with steel pipes. Latino youth fare no better in the public eye.

The Dilemma of Postmodern Critique and the Debate Over Multiculturalism

I have foregrounded the social and cultural situatedness of oppression as a background for my discussion of multiculturalism since I share Michele Wallace's conviction that the debates over multiculturalism cannot afford to have their connection to wider material relations occulted by a focus on theoretical issues divorced from the lived experiences of oppressed groups. She is worth quoting on this issue:

Many individual events on the current cultural landscape conspire to make me obsessed with contemporary debates over 'multiculturalism' in both the art world and the culture at large, but my concern is grounded first and foremost in my observation of the impact of present material conditions on an increasing sector of the population. These material conditions, which include widespread homelessness, joblessness, illiteracy, crime, disease (including AIDS), hunger, poverty, drug addiction, alcoholism as well as the various habits of ill health, and the destruction of the environment are (let's face it) the myriad social effects of late multinational capitalism. (1991: 6)

A focus on the material and global relations of oppression can help us to avoid reducing the 'problem' of multiculturalism to simply one of attitudes and temperament or, in the case of the academy, to a case of textual disagreement and discourse wars. It also helps to emphasize the fact that in the United States the concoction called 'multiculturalism', which has resulted from a forensic search for equality and the political ladling of the long-brewing 'melting pot', has produced an aversion to rather than a respect for difference. Regrettably, multiculturalism has been too often transformed into a code word in contemporary political jargon that has been fulsomely invoked in order to divert attention from the imperial legacy of racism and social injustice in this country and the ways in which new racist formations are being produced in spaces culturally dedifferentiated and demonized by neoconservative platforms that anathematize difference through attacks on the concept of heterogeneous public cultures (see Ravitch 1990, 1991; Kimball 1991; Browder 1992).

In the sections that follow, I want to discuss recent articulations of the postmodern critique in order to examine the limitations of current conservative and liberal formulations of multiculturalism. In doing so, I would like to pose an alternative analysis. I shall argue that, despite its limitations for constructing an emancipatory politics, postmodern criticism can offer educators and cultural workers a means of problematizing the issue of difference and diversity in ways that can deepen and extend existing debates over multiculturalism, pedagogy, and social transformation. Certain new strands of postmodern critique that fall under the rubric of 'political' and 'critical' postmodernism deserve serious attention in this regard.

More specifically, I shall redraw the discussion of multiculturalism from the perspective of new strands of postmodern critique that emphasize the construction of 'a politics of difference.' I will conclude by urging critical educators to reclaim the importance of relational or global critique—in particular the concept of 'totality'—in their efforts to bring

history and materiality back into theoretical and pedagogical discourses.

Subaltern and Feminist Challenges to the Postmodern Critique

Enlightenment reason mocks us as we allow it to linger in our educational thinking and policies; for some of the most painful lessons provided by postmodern criticism have been that a teleological and totalizing view of scientific progress is antipathetic to liberation; that capitalism has posited an irrecuperable disjunction between ethics and economics; and that, paradoxically, modernity has produced an intractable thralldom to the very logic of domination which it has set out to contest and in doing so has reproduced part of the repression to which it has so disdainfully pointed.

The riot of contradictory perspectives surrounding the lush profusion of rival claims about what exactly constitutes the postmodern condition is perhaps one of the ironic outcomes of the condition itself. Broadly speaking, the postmodern critique concerns itself with a rejection or debunking of modernism's epistemic foundations or metanarratives; a dethronement of the authority of positivistic science that essentializes differences between what appear to be self-possessing identities, an attack on the notion of a unified goal of history, and a deconstruction of the magnificent Enlightenment swindle of the autonomous, stable, and self-contained ego that is supposed to be able to act independently of its own history, its own indigenist strands of meaning-making and cultural and linguistic situatedness, and free from inscriptions in the discourses of, among others, gender, race, and class.

Postmodern social theory has rightly claimed that we lack a vocabulary or epistemology that is able to render the world empirically discoverable or accurately mappable, and that experience and reason cannot be explained outside of the social production of intelligibility. It emphasizes the indissociability of language, power, and subjectivity. Meaning does not inhere stratigraphically within a text or in the abstract equivalence of the signified. The labyrinthian path of Enlightenment rationality has been shown to function not as an access to but rather as a detour from the iterability of meaning—from its connection to human suffering and oppression. Further, the postmodern critique has been exemplary in revealing the hopelessness of attempts by empiricists to transcend the political, ideological, and economic conditions that transform the world into cultural and social formations. While postmodern social theory has advanced our understanding of the politics of representation and identity formation, the fashionable apostasy of certain postmodern articulations and inflections of critical social theory have noticeably abandoned the language of social change, emancipatory practice, and transformative politics. In fact, many of them carry in their intoxication with the idea of cultural surplus a mordantly pessimistic and distinctively reactionary potential.

Postmodern criticism's shift in the concept of the political through its emphasis on signification and representation, its preoccupation with the dispersion of history into the afterimage of the text, and its challenge to logocentric conceptions of truth and experience has not gone uncontested. For instance, Paul Gilroy has made clear some of the problems with theorizing under the banner of postmodernism—if under such a banner one assumes one has constructed a politics of refusal, redemption, and emancipation. Gilroy writes:

It is interesting to note that at the very moment when celebrated Euro-American cultural theorists have pronounced the collapse of 'grand narratives' the expressive culture of Britain's black poor is dominated by the need to construct them as narratives of redemption and emancipation. This expressive culture, like others elsewhere in the African diaspora, produces a potent historical memory and an authoritative analytic and historical account of racial capitalism and its overcoming. (1990: 278)

What some prominent cultural critics view as the constituent features of postmodernism—depthlessness, the retreat from the question of history, and the disappearance of affect—do not, in Gilroy's view, take seriously enough what is going on in African-American expressive culture. Blatantly contradicting this supposed 'cultural dominant' of postmodernism is 'the repertoire of "hermeneutic gestures" ' emanating from black expressive cultures. Gilroy points out that widely publicized views of the postmodern condition held by such

prominent critics as Fredric Jameson may simply constitute another form of Eurocentric master narrative since black expressive cultures use all the new technological means at their disposal 'not to flee from depth but to revel in it, not to abjure public history but to proclaim it' (1990: 278). Similarly, Cornel West (1989: 96) qualifies black cultural practices in the arts and intellectual life as examples of a 'potentially enabling yet resisting postmodernism' that has grown out of

an acknowledgement of a reality that [black people] cannot *not know*—the ragged edges of the real, of necessity a reality historically constructed by white supremacist practices in North America during the age of Europe. These ragged edges—of not being able to eat, not to have shelter, not to have health care—all this is infused into the strategies and styles of black cultural practices. (1989: 93)

Important concerns about the postmodern critique have also been posed by feminist theorists. They have questioned why men, in particular, find the new gospel of postmodernism to be so significantly compelling at this current historical moment. Not the least of their objections is related to the fact that a theoretical conversion to the postmodern critique in many instances allows men to retain their privileged status as bearers of the Word precisely because it distracts serious attention from the recent concentration on feminist discourse (Kaplan 1987: 150–2). Dominant strands of the postmodern critique also tend to delegitimize the recent literature of peoples of color, black women, Latin Americans, and Africans (Christian 1987: 55). In addition, we are reminded that just at a time in history when a great many groups are engaged in 'nationalisms' which involve redefining them as marginalized Others, the academy has begun to legitimize a critical theory of the 'subject' which holds the concept of agency in doubt, and which casts a general skepticism on the possibilities of a general theory which can describe the world and institute a quest for historical progress (Harstock 1987: 1989; Di Stephano 1990).

It is difficult to argue against these calls to decapitalize the registers of Patriarchy, Manhood, and Truth as they manifest themselves within dominant variants of the postmodern critique. And with such a consideration in mind, I would ask if it is at all possible to recuperate and extend the project of postmodernist critique within the context of a critical pedagogy of multiculturalism in a way that remains attentive to the criticisms posed above. To attempt to answer such a question demands that I establish at the outset both my own convergences with and departures from the discourse genre of postmodernism.

Ludic and Resistance Postmodernism

My general sympathy with the postmodern critique does not come without serious qualifications. Postmodernist criticism is not monolithic and for the purposes of this essay I would like to distinguish between two theoretical strands. The first has been astutely described by Teresa Ebert (1991: 115) as 'ludic postmodernism'—an approach to social theory that is decidedly limited in its ability to transform oppressive social and political regimes of power. Ludic postmodernism generally focuses on the fabulous combinatory potential of signs in the production of meaning and occupies itself with a reality that is constituted by the continual playfulness of the signifier and the heterogeneity of differences. As such, ludic postmodernism (e.g. Lyotard, Derrida, Baudrillard) constitutes a moment of self-reflexivity in deconstructing Western metanarratives, asserting that 'meaning itself is self-divided and undecidable' (Ebert, forthcoming).

Politics, in this view, is not an unmediated referent to action that exists outside of representation. Rather, politics becomes a textual practice (e.g. parody, pastiche, fragmentation) that unsettles, decenters, and disrupts rather than transforms the totalizing circulation of meaning within grand narratives and dominant discursive apparatuses (Ebert forthcoming; Zavarzadeh and Morton 1991). While ludic postmodernism may be applauded for attempting to deconstruct the way that power is deployed within cultural settings, it ultimately represents a form of detotalizing micropolitics in which the contextual specificity of difference is set up against the totalizing machineries of domination. The contingent, in this case, determines necessity as ludic postmodernism sets up a 'superstructuralism' that privileges the cultural, discursive, and ideological over the materiality of modes and relations of production (Zavarzadeh and Morton 1991).

I want to argue that educators should assume a cautionary stance toward ludic postmodernism critique because, as Ebert notes, it often simply reinscribes the status quo and reduces history to the supplementarity of signification or the free-floating trace of textuality (1991: 115). As a mode of critique, it rests its case on interrogating specific and local enunciations of oppression but often fails to analyze such enunciations in relation to larger, dominating structures of oppression (McLaren, forthcoming; Aronowitz and Giroux 1992).

Ludic postmodernism is akin to what Scott Lash (1990) calls 'spectral postmodernism'—a form of critique that deals with the dedifferentiation and blurring of disciplinary knowledge and genres (e.g. literature and criticism) and involves the implosion of the real into representation, the social into the mediascape, and exchange value into sign value. For the spectral postmodernists, the social is sucked up and dissolved into the world of signs and electronic communication while depth of meaning is imploded into superficiality. Pauline Marie Rosenau (1992) refers to this as 'skeptical postmodernism'—a strand of postmodernism that reflects not only an ontological agnosticism that urges a relinquishing of the primacy of social transformation but also an epistemological relativism that calls for a tolerance of a range of meanings without advocating any one of them. Ludic postmodernism often takes the form of a triumphalistic and hoary dismissal of Marxism and grand theory as being hopelessly embroiled in a futile project of world-historical magnitude that is out of place in these postmodern new times. Such an endeavour often brings new forms of 'totalization' into the debate through the conceptual back door of antifoundationalist theorizing.

The kind of postmodern social theory I want to pose as a counterweight to skeptical and spectral postmodernism has been referred to as 'oppositional postmodernism' (Foster 1983), 'radical critique-al theory' (Zavarzadeh and Morton 1991), 'postmodern education' (Aronowitz and Giroux 1991), 'resistance postmodernism' (Ebert 1991, forthcoming) and 'critical postmodernism' (McLaren, forthcoming; Giroux 1992; McLaren and Hammer 1989). These forms of critique are not alternatives to ludic postmodernism but appropriations and extensions of this critique. Resistance postmodernism brings to ludic critique a form of materialist intervention since it is not solely based on a textual theory of difference but rather on one that is social and historical. In this way, postmodern critique can serve as an interventionist and transformative critique of US culture. Following Ebert, resistance postmodernism attempts to show that 'textualities (significations) are material practices, forms of conflicting social relations' (1991: 115). The sign is always an arena of material conflict and competing social relations as well as ideas, and we can 'rewrite the sign as an ideological process formed out of a signifier standing in relation to a matrix of historically possible or suspended signifieds' (Ebert, forthcoming). In other words, difference is politicized by being situated *in* real social and historical conflicts rather than simply textual or semiotic contradictions.

Resistance postmodernism does not abandon the undecidability or contingency of the social altogether; rather, the undecidability of history is understood as related to class struggle, the institutionalization of asymmetrical relations of power and privilege, and the way historical accounts are contested by different groups (Zavarzadeh and Morton 1991; Giroux 1992; McLaren and Hammer 1989). On this matter Ebert remarks: 'We need to articulate a theory of difference in which the differing, deferring slippage of signifiers is not taken as the result of the immanent logic of language but as the effect of the social conflicts traversing signification' (1991: 118). In other words, to view difference as simply textuality, as a formal, rhetorical space in which representation narrates its own trajectory of signification, is to ignore the social and historical dimensions of difference (Ebert, forthcoming). Ebert elaborates this point as follows:

A postmodern analytics of difference would enable us to move beyond the theory of difference as reified experience, and to critique the historical, economic, and ideological production of difference itself as a slipping, sliding series of relations that are struggled over and which produce the significations and subjectivities by which we live and maintain existing social relations. (1991: 118)

She further describes resistance postmodernism as a politics of difference, as a theory of practice and a practice of theory:

A resistance postmodern cultural critique—interrogating the political semiosis of culture—would be an oppositional political practice produced through the activity of reading, of making sense of cultural texts. However, opposition does not lie within—in other words it is not inherent in—a text or individual but is produced out of the practice of critique itself. Moreover the critic herself is always already interpellated in the hegemonic subject positions of the culture, and contestation derives not from some will to resist but again is produced through the practice of critique. (1991: 129)

Resistance postmodernism takes into account both the macropolitical level of structural organization and the micropolitical level of different and contradictory manifestations of oppression as a means of analyzing global relations of oppression. As such, resistance postmodernism bears a considerable degree of affinity to what Scott Lash has recently termed 'organic postmodernism'. Organic postmodernism tries to move beyond epistemic skepticism and explanatory nihilism to concern itself with issues related not just to the commodification of language but to the commodification of labour and the social relations of production. According to Lash, it attempts to reintegrate the cultural into the natural, material environment. From this perspective, rationality is not panhistorical or universal but is always situated in particular communities of discourse. In addition, organic postmodernism argues that high modernism articulates reality in a way that often serves as a cover for validating a Cartesian universe of discrete parts disconnected from wider economies of power and privilege. In other words, high modernism is accused of collapsing difference into the uneasy harmony we know as white patriarchal privilege—a privilege inextricably bound up with nationalism, imperialism, and the state.

Multiculturalism and the Postmodern Critique

In this section I want to bring a critical or resistance postmodernist perspective to bear on the issue of multiculturalism. For me, the key issue for critical educators is to develop a multicultural curriculum and pedagogy that attends to the specificity (in terms of race, class, gender, sexual orientation, etc.) of difference (which is in keeping with ludic postmodernism) yet at the same time addresses the commonality of diverse Others under the law with respect to guiding referents of freedom and liberation (which is in keeping with resistance postmodernism).

Viewed from the perspective of resistance postmodernism, the liberal and conservative attacks on multiculturalism as separatist and ethnocentric carry with them the erroneous assumption that North American society fundamentally constitutes social relations of uninterrupted accord. This view furthermore underscores the idea that North American society is largely a forum of consensus with different minority viewpoints simply accretively added on. This constitutes a politics of pluralism which largely ignores the workings of power and privilege. More specifically, it 'involves a very insidious exclusion as far as any structural politics of change is concerned: it excludes and occludes global or structural relations of power as "ideological" and "totalizing" ' (Ebert forthcoming). In addition, it presupposes harmony and agreement—an undisturbed space in which differences can coexist. Yet such a presupposition is dangerously problematic. Chandra Mohanty (1989/90) notes that the difference cannot be formulated as negotiation among culturally diverse groups against a backdrop of presumed cultural homogeneity. Difference is the recognition that knowledges are forged in histories that are riven with differentially constituted relations of power; that is, knowledges, subjectivities, and social practices are forged within 'asymmetrical and incommensurate cultural spheres' (1989/90: 181).

Too often liberal and conservative positions on diversity constitute an attempt to view culture as a soothing balm—the aftermath of historical disagreement—some mythical present where the irrationalities of historical conflict have been smoothed out. This is not only a disingenuous view of culture, it is profoundly dishonest. The liberal and conservative positions on culture also assume that justice already exists and needs only to be evenly apportioned. However, both teachers and students need to realize that justice does not already exist simply because laws exist. Justice needs to be continually created, constantly struggled for. The question that I want to pose to teachers is this: Do teachers and cultural workers have access to a language that allows them to sufficiently critique and

transform existing social and cultural practices that are defended by liberals and conservatives as democratic?

The Subject without Properties

The critical postmodernist critique provides us with a way of understanding the limitations of a multiculturalism trapped within a logic of democracy that is under the sway of late capitalism. One of the surreptitious perversions of democracy has been the manner in which citizens have been invited to empty themselves of all racial or ethnic identity so that, presumably, they will all stand naked before the law. In effect, citizens are invited to become little more than disembodied consumers. As Joan Copjec points out,

Democracy is the universal quantifier by which America—the 'melting pot', the 'nation of immigrants'—constitutes itself as a nation. If *all* our citizens can be said to be Americans, this is not because we share any positive characteristics, but rather because we have all been given the right to *shed* these characteristics, to present ourselves as disembodied before the law. I divest myself of positive identity, therefore I am a citizen. This is the peculiar logic of democracy. (1991: 30)

Renato Rosaldo (1989) refers to this process as 'cultural stripping', wherein individuals are stripped of their former cultures in order to become 'transparent' American citizens. While the embodied and perspectival location of any citizen's identity has an undeniable effect on what can be said, democracy has nevertheless created formal identities which give the illusion of identity while simultaneously erasing difference. David Lloyd (1991: 70) refers to this cultural practice as the formation of the 'subject without properties.' As the dominated are invited to shed their positive identities, the dominators unwittingly serve as the regulating principle of identity itself by virtue of their very indifference.

The universality of the position of dominator is attained through its literal indifference and it 'becomes representative in consequence of being able to take anyone's place, of occupying any place, of a pure exchangeability' (Lloyd 1991: 70). Such a subject without properties governs the distribution of humanity into the local (native) and the universal by assuming the 'global ubiquity of the white

European' which, in turn, becomes the very 'regulative idea of Culture against which the multiplicity of local cultures is defined' (Lloyd 1991: 70). Lloyd notes that the domination of the white universalized subject 'is virtually self-legitimating since the capacity to be everywhere present becomes an historical manifestation of the white man's gradual approximation to the universality he everywhere represents' (1991: 70).

Against this peculiar logic of democracy, resistance postmodernism argues that individuals need always to *rethink the relationship between identity and difference*. They need to understand their ethnicity in terms of a politics of location, positionality, or enunciation. Stuart Hall argues, rightly in my view, that 'there's no enunciation without positionality. You have to position yourself *somewhere* in order to say anything at all' (1991: 18). One's identity, whether as black, white, or Latino, has to do with the discovery of one's ethnicity. Hall calls this process of discovery the construction of 'new ethnicities' or 'emergent ethnicities'. Entailed in such a discovery is the

need to honor the hidden histories from which . . . [people] . . . come. They need to understand the languages which they've been taught not to speak. They need to understand and revalue the traditions and inheritances of cultural expression and creativity. And in that sense, the past is not only a position from which to speak, but it is also an absolutely necessary resource in what one has to say. . . . So the relationship of the kind of ethnicity I'm talking about to the past is not a simple, essential one—it is a constructed one. It is constructed in history, it is constructed politically in part. It is part of narrative. We tell ourselves the stories of the parts of our roots in order to come into contact, creatively, with it. So this new kind of ethnicity—the emergent ethnicities—has a relationship to the past, but it is a relationship that is partly through memory, partly through narrative, one that has to be recovered. It is an act of cultural recovery. (Hall 1991: 18–19)

While the discourse of multiculturalism has tended to oppose hierarchical exclusiveness with arguments in favour of unrestricted inclusiveness (Wallace 1991: 6), a resistance postmodernist critique further problematizes the issue of exclusion and inclusion by articulating a new relationship between identity and difference. Not only can a resistance postmodernist articulation of difference theorize a place where marginalized groups can speak *from* but it can also provide groups a place from which to move *beyond* an essentialized

and narrow ethnic identity since they also have a stake in global conditions of equality and social justice (Hall 1991).

Homi Bhabha (1990) has articulated an important distinction between 'difference' and 'diversity'. Working from a poststructuralist perspective, Bhabha breaks from the social-democratic version of multiculturalism where race, class, and gender are modeled on a consensual conception of difference and locates his work within a radical democratic version of cultural pluralism which recognizes the essentially contested character of the signs and signifying apparatuses that people use in the construction of their identities (Mercer 1990: 8).

Bhabha is critical of the notion of diversity used in liberal discourse to refer to the importance of plural, democratic societies. He argues that with diversity comes a 'transparent norm' constructed and administered by the 'host' society that creates a false consensus. This is because the normative grid that locates cultural diversity at the same time serves to *contain* cultural difference: The 'universalism that paradoxically permits diversity masks ethnocentric norms' (Bhabha 1990: 208). Differences, on the other hand, do not always speak to consensus but are often incommensurable. Culture, as a system of difference, as symbol-forming activity, must in Bhabha's view be seen as 'a process of translations' (1990: 210). From this follows the observation that while cultures cannot be simply reduced to unregulatable textual play, neither do they exist as undisplaceable forms in the sense that they possess 'a totalized prior moment of being or meaning—an essence' (1990: 210).

Otherness in this sense is often internal to the symbol-forming activity of that culture and it is perhaps best to speak of culture as a form of 'hybridity.' Within this hybridity, there exists a 'third space' that enables other discursive positions to emerge—to resist attempts to normalize what Bhabha refers to as 'the timelagged colonial moment' (1991*a*: 211). This 'third space' opens up possibilities for new structures of authority, and new political vistas and visions. Identity from this perspective is always an arbitrary, contingent, and temporary suturing of identification and meaning. Bhabha's distinction makes it clear why people such as Ravitch, Bloom, Hirsch, and Bennett are so dangerous when they talk about the importance of building a common culture. Who has the power to exercise meaning, to create the grid from which Otherness is defined, to create the identifications that invite closures on meanings, on interpretations and translations?

This essay has suggested that conservative and liberal multiculturalism is really about the politics of assimilation because both assume that we really do live in a common egalitarian culture. Such an understanding of difference implies, as Iris Marion Young (1990: 164) notes, 'coming into the game after the rules and standards have already been set, and having to prove oneself according to those rules and standards.' These standards are not seen as culturally and experientially specific among the citizenry at large because within a pluralist democracy privileged groups have occluded their own advantage by invoking the ideal of an unsituated, neutral, universal common humanity of self-formation in which all can happily participate without regard to differences in race, gender, class, age, or sexual orientation. Resistance postmodernism, in particular, unsettles such a notion of universal common humanity by exploring identity within the context of power, discourse, culture, experience, and historical specificity.

Difference and the Politics of Signification

Resistance postmodernism has been especially significant in reformulating the meaning of difference as a form of signification. Differences in this view do not constitute clearly marked zones of autointelligible experience or a unity of identity as they do within most conservative and liberal forms of cultural pluralism. Rather, differences are understood through a politics of signification, that is, through signifying practices that are both reflective and constitutive of prevailing economic and political relations (Ebert 1991). Against the conservative multiculturalist understanding of difference as 'self-evident cultural obviousness', as a 'mark of plurality', or 'the carefully marked off zones of experience—the privileged presence—of one group, one social category against another that we faithfully cultivate and reproduce in our analyses', Teresa Ebert defines difference as

culturally constituted, made intelligible, through signifying practices. [For postmodern theories] 'difference' is not a clearly marked zone of experience, a unity of identity of one social group against another, taken as cultural pluralism. Rather, postmodern differences are relations of opposing signifiers. (1991: 117)

According to Ebert, our current ways of seeing and acting are being disciplined for us through forms of signification, that is, through modes of intelligibility and ideological frames of sense making. Rejecting the Saussurian semiotics of signifying practices (and its continuing use in contemporary post-structuralism) as 'ahistorical operations of language and tropes', Ebert characterizes signifying practices as 'an ensemble of material operations involved in economic and political relations' (1991: 117). She maintains, rightly in my view, that socioeconomic relations of power require distinctions to be made among groups through forms of signification in order to organize subjects according to the unequal distribution of privilege and power.

To illustrate the politics of signification at work in the construction and formation of racist subjects, Ebert offers the example of the way in which the terms 'negro' and 'black' have been employed within the racial politics of the United States. Just as the term 'negro' became an immutable mark of difference and naturalized the political arrangements of racism in the 1960s, so too is the term 'black' being refigured in the white dominant culture to mean criminality, violence, and social degeneracy. This was made clear in the Willie Horton campaign ads for George Bush and in the current Bush and David Duke position on hiring quotas. And in my view it was evident in the verdict of the Rodney King case in Los Angeles.

Carlos Munoz (1989) has revealed how the term 'Hispanic' in the mid-1970s became a 'politics of white ethnic identity' that deemphasized and in some cases rejected the Mexican cultural base of Mexican-Americans. Munoz writes that the term 'Hispanic' is derived from 'Hispania' which was the name the Romans gave to the Iberian peninsula, most of which became Spain, and 'implicitly emphasizes the white European culture of Spain at the expense of the nonwhite cultures that have profoundly shaped the experiences of all Latin Americans' (1989: 11). Not only is this term blind to the multiracial reality of

Mexican-Americans through its refusal to acknowledge 'the nonwhite indigenous cultures of the Americas, Africa, and Asia, which historically have produced multicultural and multiracial peoples in Latin America and the United States' (Munoz 1989: 11), it is a term that ignores the complexities within these various cultural groups. Here is another example of the melting pot theory of assimilation fostered through a politics of signification. We might ask ourselves what signifieds (meanings) will be attached to certain terms, such as 'welfare mothers'. I think we know what government officials mean when they refer derisively to 'welfare mothers'. They mean black and Latino mothers.

The examples discussed above confirm the observation of resistance postmodernism that differences are produced according to the ideological production and reception of cultural signs. As Mas'ud Zavarzadeh and Donald Morton point out, 'Signs are neither eternally predetermined nor pan-historically undecidable: they are rather "decided" or rendered as "undecidable" in the moment of social conflicts' (1990: 156). Difference is not 'cultural obviousness' such as black versus white or Latino versus European or Anglo-American; rather, differences are historical and cultural constructions (Ebert 1991).

Just as we can see the politics of signification at work in instances of police brutality, we can see it at work in special education placement where a greater proportion of black and Latino students are considered for 'behavioral' placements whereas white, middle-class students are provided, for the most part, with the more comforting and comfortable label of 'learning disabled' (McLaren 1989). Here, a resistance postmodernist critique can help teachers explore the ways in which students are differentially subjected to ideological inscriptions and multiply organized discourses of desire through a politics of signification. For instance, a resistance postmodernist critique helps to understand how student identities are produced by a type of discursive ventriloquism in that they are creatures of the languages and knowledges that they have inherited and which unconsciously exert control over their thinking and behavior. As James Donald (forthcoming) points out, social norms often surface as personal and guilt-provoking desires since they have gone through a process that Foucault

referred to as *folding*. Donald points out that the

norms and prohibitions instituted within social and cultural technologies are folded into the unconscious so that they 'surface' not just as 'personal desires' but in a complex and unpredictable dynamic of desire, guilt, anxiety and displacement. Subjects have desires that they do not want to have; they reject them at the cost of guilt and anxiety.

While subjects are invariably prisoners of a male monopoly on language and knowledge production (Grosz 1990: 332), they are also active agents who are capable of exercising deliberate historical actions in and on the world (Giroux 1992). The point, of course, is that conscious knowledge is not exhaustive of either identity or agency. We need to acknowledge what is not so obvious about how difference is constitutive of *both identity and agency*.

Attempting to abandon all vestiges of the dominant culture in the struggle for identity can lead to a futile search for premodern roots that, in turn, leads to a narrow nationalism, as in the case of what Hall calls the 'old ethnicity'. Refusing to attempt to decolonize one's identity in the midst of the prevailing ideological and cultural hegemony can serve as a capitulation to assimilation and the loss of forms of critical historical agency. Needed is a view of multiculturalism and difference that moves beyond the 'either-or' logic of assimilation and resistance. To make a claim for multiculturalism is not, in the words of Trinh T. Minh-ha (1991: 232), 'to suggest the juxtaposition of several cultures whose frontiers remain intact, nor is it to subscribe to a bland 'melting pot' type of attitude that would level all differences. [The struggle for a multicultural society] lies instead, in the intercultural acceptance of risks, unexpected detours, and complexities of relation between break and closure'.

Always Totalize!

In this section I want to focus my analysis of multiculturalism on the concept of totality. I would like to emphasize that while educators must center their pedagogies on the affirmation of the 'local' knowledges of students within particular sociopolitical and ethnic locations, the concept of totality must not be abandoned altogether. Not all forms of total-ization are democratically deficient. Not all forms truncate, oppress, and destroy plural-ism. As Fredric Jameson remarks, 'Local struggles . . . are effective only so long as they remain figures or allegories for some larger systemic transformation. Politics has to oper-ate on the micro—and the macro—levels simultaneously; a modest restriction to local reforms within the system seems reasonable, but often proves politically demoralizing' (1989: 386). George Lipsitz underscores this idea, arguing that while totality can do vio-lence to the specificity of events, a rejection of all totality would likely 'obscure real connec-tions, causes, and relationships—atomizing common experience into accidents and end-lessly repeated play . . . [and that] only by rec-ognizing the collected legacy of accumulated human actions and ideas can we judge the claims to truth and justice of any one story'. (1990: 214)

Without a shared vision (however contin-gent or provisional) of democratic commu-nity, we risk endorsing struggles in which the politics of difference collapses into new forms of separatism. As Steven Best points out, poststructuralists rightly deconstruct essen-tialist and repressive wholes, yet they often fail to see how crippling the valorizing of dif-ference, fragmentation, and agonistics can be. This is especially true of ludic postmod-ernism. Best writes: 'The flip side of the tyranny of the whole is the dictatorship of the fragment. . . . [W]ithout some positive and normative concept of totality to counter-balance the poststructuralist/postmodern emphasis on difference and discontinuity, we are abandoned to the seriality of pluralist indi-vidualism and the supremacy of competitive values over communal life' (1989: 361). Best is correct in suggesting that what needs to be abandoned is the reductive use of totality, not the concept of totality itself. Otherwise, we risk undermining the very concept of democ-ratic public life.

Teresa Ebert (forthcoming) argues—bril-liantly in my mind—that we need to reassert the concept of totality not in the Hegelian sense of an organic, unified, oppressive unity, but rather 'as both a system of relations and *overdetermined structure of difference*'. Differ-ence needs to be understood as social contra-dictions, as difference in relation, rather than dislocated, free-floating difference. Systems of differences, notes Ebert, always involve patterns of domination and relations of oppression and exploitation. We need to con-cern ourselves, therefore, with economies of relations of difference within historically spe-cific totalities that are always open to contesta-tion and transformation. As structures of difference that are always multiple and unsta-ble, the oppressive relations of totalities (social, economic, political, legal, cultural, ideological) can always be challenged within a pedagogy of liberation. Ebert argues that totalities shouldn't be confused with Lyotard's notion of universal metanarratives.

Only when they are used unjustly and oppressively as all-encompassing and all-embracing global warrants for thought and action in order to secure an oppressive regime of truth, should totality and universality be rejected. We need to retain some kind of moral, ethical, and political ground—albeit a provisional one—from which to negotiate among multiple interests. Crucial to this argu-ment is the important distinction between universal metanarratives (master narratives) and metacritical narratives. The resistance postmodernist critique that I am suggesting educators consider repudiates the necessity or choice of any one master narrative because master narratives suggest that there is only one public sphere, one value, one conception of justice that triumphs over all others. Resis-tance postmodernism suggests, on the con-trary, that 'different spheres and rival conceptions of justice must be accommodated to each other' (Murphy 1991: 124). In other words, '[t]he communitarian, the liberal or social democrat, the developmental liberal or humanist, the radical, and the romantic must find ways of living together in the same social space' (Murphy 1991: 124). This does not mean trying to press them all into a homoge-neous cultural pulp but to suggest that there must be a multiplication of justices and plu-ralistic conceptions of justice, politics, ethics, and aesthetics.

Again, the crucial question here is one that deals with the notion of *totality*. While I would argue against one grand narrative, I believe that there exists a primary metadiscourse that could, in fact, offer a *provisional* engagement with discourses of the Other in a way that can be unifying without dominating and that can provide for supplementary discourses. This is the metacritical narrative of rights or freedom.

Peter Murphy distinguishes between a master discourse and a metadiscourse, arguing that 'a master discourse wants to impose itself on all the other discourses—it is progressive, they are reactionary; it is right, they are wrong. A metadiscourse, on the other hand, seeks to understand society as a *totality*' (1991: 126). Murphy, like Ebert, argues against a Lyotardian rejection of the grand narrative of emancipation. Instead, he embraces the idea of totality as set forth by Charles Jencks. This distinction is worth emphasizing.

Postmodernism, Jencks, following Venturi, argues is concerned with complexity and contradiction, and precisely because it is concerned with complexity and contradiction, it in fact has a special obligation to the whole. This is not the 'harmonious whole' of canonic classicism, but rather the 'difficult whole' of a pluralized and multi-dimensional world. Postmodernism, Jencks argues, is committed to synthesizing a 'difficult whole' out of fragments, references, and approaches. Its truth lies not in any part, but, as Venturi puts it, *in its totality or implications of totality*. (Murphy 1991: 126; italics original)

Here I am not reclaiming or rewriting totality as a synonym for political economy or suggesting that a critical postmodernism resist narrating the location of the theorist or abandon local struggles. I am not setting up a Manichean contest between the *méta récits* of liberation and social justice and the polyvocality and positionality of an antifoundational approach to difference. I also want to make clear that I am not using the concept of 'totalizing' to mean an act of generalizing from the law of intelligibility of one phenomena to the level of all social or cultural phenomena (Zavarzadeh and Morton 1991). Nor am I using it to mean some forgotten plenitude, formalized auratic experience, or bygone world that needs to be recovered for the sake of some noble nostalgia. Rather, I am using 'totalizing' in the manner that Zavarzadeh and Morton (1991) have described as 'global'. Global understanding is a 'form of explanation that is *relational* and *transdisciplinary* and that produces an account of the "knowledge-effects" of culture by *relating* various cultural series' (p. 155). It is a mode of inquiry that attempts to address how the ludic postmodernist critique serves as a strategy of political containment by privileging forms of 'local' analysis which center the subject in experience as the Archimedean site of truth and

posit ideology as the sole 'reader' of experience.

Global or relational knowledge points to the existence of an underlying logic of domination within the signifying practices that constitute the cultural products of late capitalism and for this reason it sets itself against ludic postmodernism's dismissal of knowledge as integrative and political because of the supposed incommensurability of cultural, political, and economic phenomena. It moves beyond the cognitivism and empiricism of the dominant knowledge industry by dispossessing individuals of their imaginary sense of the autointelligibility of experience. Further, it reveals that *différance* is not an inherent condition of textuality but a socially overdetermined historical effect that acquires its tropicity only within given historical and cultural modes of intelligibility. Zavarzadeh and Morton argue that

in the ludic space of playfulness, the social relations of production are posited not as historically necessary but as subject to the laws of the alea: chance and contingency. In ludic deconstruction chance and contingency perform the same ideological role that 'native' (i.e., non-logical, random, inscrutable) difference plays in traditional humanistic discourses. Both posit a social field beyond the reach of the logic of necessity and history. (1991: 194)

Resistance postmodernism offers teachers working in multicultural education a means of interrogating the locality, positionality, and specificity of knowledge (in terms of the race, class, and gender locations of students) and of generating of a plurality of truths (rather than one apodictic truth built around the invisible norm of Eurocentrism and white ethnicity), while at the same time situating the construction of meaning in terms of the material interests at work in the production of 'truth effects'—that is, in the production of forms of intelligibility and social practices. Consequently, teachers working within a resistance postmodernism are able to call into question the political assumptions and relations of determination upon which social truths are founded in both the communities in which they work and the larger society of which they are a part. Ludic postmodernism, in contrast, effectively masks the relationship between dominant discourses and the social relations that they justify through an immanent reading of cultural texts (reading texts on their own terms) in which their internal and formal coherence takes priority over the social relations of their production. In fact, Zavarzadeh and Morton (1991) go so far as to suggest that ludic postmodernism gained ascendancy in the academy just at the time when capitalism became deterritorialized and multinational. In effect, they are arguing that the ludic postmodern critique has suppressed forms of knowing that 'could explain multi-national capitalism's transterritoriality and its affiliated phenomena' (Zavazadeh and Morton 1991: 163).

Viewed from the perspective of constructing a global or relational understanding, the idea of organizing postmodern critique around the referents of freedom and emancipation is an attempt to avoid a unifying logic that monolithically suppresses or forecloses meaning. Conversely, it is a determined effort to retain and understand the 'difficult whole' of a pluralistic and global society. It is to take up a position against reactionary pluralists such as William Bennett, Diane Ravitch, and Allan Bloom, who embrace and advocate the idea of a harmonious common culture.

I have tried to argue that in order to have a liberating narrative informing our pedagogies, educators need to address the concept of totality. The idea of a master narrative's 'phallic projectory' into the telos of historical destiny needs to be discredited, yet the idea of totality as a heterogeneous and not homogeneous temporality must be recuperated. The concepts of totality and infinity need to be dialectically positioned within any pedagogy of liberation. Emmanuel Levinas (1969: 25) notes that 'the idea of infinity delivers subjectivity from the judgement of history to declare it ready for judgement at every moment' (cited in Chambers 1990: 109). Isn't this precisely what Frantz Fanon was trying to describe when he urged us to *totalize infinitely* as a communicative act (Taylor 1989: 26)? For me, spaces for rewriting dominant narratives come into being by the very fact of the patience of infinity, the diachrony of time which, observes Levinas, is produced by our situatedness as ethical subjects and our responsibility to the Other. The problem, of course, is that the remaking of the social and the reinvention of the self must be understood as dialectically synchronous—that is, they cannot be conceived as unrelated or only marginally connected. They are mutually informing and constitutive processes.

According to Patrick Taylor (1989: 25), the essential ingredient of a narrative of liberation is the recognition of freedom in necessity. In this sense, the necessity of freedom becomes a *responsible totalization*. Not in the sense of a master narrative but in the sense of a metadiscourse or discourse of possibility (Giroux 1992). If we talk about totalization in the sense of a master narrative, we are referring to a type of discursive homogenization, a premature closure on meaning, a false universalism (what Taylor calls an 'ordered totality') that leads to a categorical utopia—that leads, in other words, to various inflections of fascism. Infinite totalization, which is an asymptotical approach, refers to a hypothetical or provisional utopia. As P. B. Dauenhauer (1989) notes, the hypothetical embrace of utopian representation must be distinguished from the categorical embrace. To embrace ideology or utopia categorically is a form of 'bad infinity' by denying alternatives to the present reality. Of course, in saying this, attention must be given to the specific structural differences that exist in various national contexts today.

Teachers need to stress in their teaching (following Ernst Bloch 1986) the hypothetical or provisional and not the categorical embrace of utopia. Paradoxically, hypothetical utopias based on infinite totalization are the most concrete of all because they offer through their negative content (i.e., the concrete negation of domination) *the end of ordered totalities*. Patrick Taylor, citing Jameson, notes that 'the ultimate interpretive task is the understanding of symbolic works in relation to a demystifying, open-ended narrative of liberation that is grounded in the imperative of human freedom' (1989: 19). Ann Game makes a similar point when she locates inquiry as a 'disturbing pleasure' in which 'the risks of infinity, with hints of madness . . . are far preferable to the safety (and possibly, bad faith) of closure'. (1991: 191)

Narratives of freedom are ways of transcending those social myths (with their pre-given narrative orders) that reconcile us, through the resolution of binary oppositions, to lives of lived subordination. Narratives of liberation are those that totalize infinitely, but not by integrating difference into a monolithic executive identity produced by modernity's colonial or neocolonial situation—by forcing difference into silence precisely when it is asked to speak (Sáenz 1991: 158). They do not simply negate the difference produced by identity secreted in a situation of domination, because this simply saps the sustenance of the identity of the dominator (Sáenz 1991). Narratives of liberation do not simply construct an identity that 'runs counter Eurocentric identity; for such would be a mere resurrection of the racist European myth of the "noble savage"—a millenarianism in reverse, the expression of Eurocentric self-dissatisfaction and self-flagellation over its own disenchantment with the "modernity" produced by its project of "possessive individualism" ' (Sáenz 1991: 159). Rather, narratives of liberation point to the possibility of new, alternative identities contemporaneous with modernity but not simply through inverting its normative truths.

As historical agents, educators are positioned within the tension produced by modernist and postmodernist attempts to resolve the living contradiction of being both the subject and the object of meaning. But their mode of critical analysis needs to move beyond the tropological displacement of discursive familiarity or a highjacking of meaning in the back alleys of theory (as is the case with ludic postmodernism). Educators require narratives of liberation that can serve a *metacritical* function—that can metaconceptualize relations of everyday life—and that do not succumb to the transcendental unity of subject and object or their transfiguring coalescence (Saldivar 1990: 173). In other words, such narratives promote a form of analectic understanding in addition to a dialectical understanding. As Enrique Dussel (1985) has argued, analectics reaches exteriority not through totality (as does dialectics) but rather *beyond* it. But Sáenz (1991: 162) remarks that the 'beyond' that Dussel speaks about must not be interpreted as an absolute beyond all criticism (i.e., God) but rather as a 'beyond' that has its roots 'in the midst of domination', that is, in the suffering of the oppressed 'understood within its colonial textuality.' Analectics could be thus described as a form of 'pluritopic' dialectical critique aimed at revealing the monotopic understanding of Eurocentrism as merely contingent to its own cultural traditions (Sáenz 1991).

Through a praxis of infinite totalization educators can provide analectically a new vision of the future that is latent in the present, immanent in this very moment of reading, in the womb of the actual. Such a praxis can help us understand that subjective intentions do not constitute the apodictical site of truth. Subjectivities and identities of students and teachers are always the artifacts of discursive formations; that is, they are always the products of historical contexts and language games (Kincheloe 1991; Carspecken 1991). Students and teachers are all actors in narrative configurations and employments that they did not develop but that are the products of historical and discursive struggles that have been folded back into the unconscious. Teachers need to learn to recognize those internalized discourses that not only inform the ritualization of their teaching practices, but those that organize their vision of the future. They must recall, too, that human agency is not a substrate that props them up like the crutches in a Dali painting, but has *imperative force*. The theater of agency is *possibility*.

Agency is informed by the stereotypical ways in which subjectivities have been allegorized by historical discourses which have been gridded in the subject positions teachers and students take. These discourses differentially enable and enact specific forms of practice. Yet while there is a logos immanent to the discourses that constitute teachers that makes them functionaries within modern technologies of power, this does not mean that educators and cultural workers cannot foster and realize potentialities within the discursive and material conditions of their own communities. Educators have a heritage of possibilities from which to work. While these possibilities affect the ground of teachers' subjectivities, they do not saturate their will, nor do they prevent them from struggling against the constraints that bind freedom and justice. Identities may thus be considered both mobilely structured and structured mobilities and as such are dialectically re-initiating. David Trend speaks to this issue when he emphasizes the importance of understanding the productive character of knowledge. While one's influence on the process of knowledge production is always partial, cultural workers do exert considerable influence:

Acknowledging the role of the 'learning subject' in the construction of culture, we affirm processes of agency, difference, and, ultimately, democracy. We suggest to students and audiences that they have a role in the making of their world and that they need not accept positions as passive spectators or consumers. This is a position that recognizes and encourages the atmosphere of diverse and contradictory opinions so dreaded by the conservative proponents of a 'common culture.' It functions on the belief that a healthy democracy is one that is always being scrutinized and tested. (1992: 150)

Exerting an influence over cultural production means finding ways of speaking and acting outside the totalizing systems of logocentric thought by creating metacritical and relational perspectives linked to the imperative of a unifying project (in Sartre's sense). Educators need to get outside the admixtures and remnants of languages—the multiplicity of stereotypical voices that already populate their vocabulary and fill up all the available linguistic spaces—in order to find different ways of appropriating or mediating the real. Educators and cultural workers need to cross borders into zones of cultural difference rather than construct subjectivities that simply reassert themselves as monadic forms of totality facilitated by a consumerist ethics and marketplace logic (Giroux 1992; McLaren, forthcoming). This means developing a more effective theory for understanding pedagogy in relation to the workings of power in the larger context of race, class, and gender articulations. It means advancing a theory that does not elevate the teacher-other as individual knower and devalue the student as an objectified, unknowing entity. Students must not be constructed as the zombified ideal 'always already' open to manipulation for passive acquiescence to the status quo. We should not forfeit the opportunity of theorizing both teachers and students as historical agents of resistance.

Critical Pedagogy: Teaching for a Hybrid Citizenry and Multicultural Solidarity

'There's room for all at the rendez-vous of victory'
—Césaire

Resistance postmodernism has figured prominently in the development of new forms of pedagogical praxis concerned with rethinking educational politics in a multicultural society (Giroux 1992; McLaren and Leonard, forthcoming; McLaren, forthcoming; Aronwitz and Giroux 1991). Of particular significance is Giroux's concept of a 'border pedagogy' which enables educators to affirm

and legitimate local meanings and constellations of meanings that grow out of particular discursive communities but at the same time interrogate the interests, ideologies, and social practices that such knowledges serve when viewed from the perspective of more global economies of power and privilege.

A pedagogy informed significantly by resistance postmodernism suggests that teachers and cultural workers need to take up the issue of 'difference' in ways that don't replay the monocultural essentialism of the 'centrisms'—Anglocentrism, Eurocentrism, phallocentrism, androcentrism, and the like. They need to create a politics of alliance building, of dreaming together, of solidarity that moves beyond the condescensions of, say, 'race awareness week', which actually serves to keep forms of institutionalized racism intact. A solidarity has to be struggled for that is not centered around market imperatives but develops out of the imperatives of freedom, liberation, democracy, and critical citizenship.

The notion of the citizen has been pluralized and hybridized, as Kobena Mercer notes, by the presence of a diversity of social subjects. Mercer is instructive in pointing out that 'solidarity does not mean that everyone thinks the same way, it begins when people have the confidence to disagree over issues because they "care" about constructing a common ground' (1990: 68). Solidarity is not impermeably solid but depends to a certain degree on antagonism and uncertainty. Timothy Maliqualim Simone calls this type of multiracial solidarity 'geared to maximizing points of interaction rather than harmonizing, balancing, or equilibrating the distribution of bodies, resources, and territories' (1989: 191).

While guarding against the privileging of a false universalism, a false unity that denies the internal rifts of bodily desire, both teachers and students need to open themselves to the possibility of Otherness so that the particularity of individual being can become visible in relation to larger relations of power and privilege. Students especially need to be provided with opportunities to devise different assemblages of the self by dismantling and interrogating the different kinds of discursive segmentarity that inform their subjectivities, subverting those stratified and hierarchized forms of subjectivity that code the will, and developing nomadic forms of individual and collective agency that open up new assemblages of desire and modes of being-in-the-world (Grossberg 1988).

Educators must examine the development of pedagogical discourses and practices that demonize Others who are different (through transforming them into absence or deviance). A resistance postmodernism that takes multiculturalism seriously calls attention to the dominant meaning systems readily available to students—most of which are ideologically stitched into the fabric of Western imperialism and patriarchy. It challenges meaning systems that impose attributes on the Other under the direction of sovereign signifiers and tropes. And this means not directing all our efforts at understanding ethnicity as 'other than white', but interrogating the culture of whiteness itself. This is crucial because unless we do this—unless we give white students a sense of their own identity as an emergent ethnicity—we naturalize whiteness as a cultural marker against which Otherness is defined. Coco Fusco warns that 'to ignore white ethnicity is to redouble its hegemony by naturalizing it. Without specifically addressing white ethnicity there can be no critical evaluation of the construction of the other' (cited in Wallace 1991: 7). White groups need to examine their ethnic histories so that they are less likely to judge their own cultural norms as neutral and universal. 'Whiteness' does not exist outside of culture but constitutes the prevailing social texts in which social norms are made and remade. As part of a politics of signification that passes unobserved into the rhythms of daily life, and a 'politically constructed category parasitic on "Blackness"' (West 1990: 29), 'whiteness' has become the invisible norm for how the dominant culture measures its own civility.

With this in mind, a critical pedagogy that embraces a resistance postmodernism needs to construct a politics of refusal that can provide both the conditions for interrogating the institutionalization of formal equality based on the prized imperatives of a white, Anglo male world and for creating spaces to facilitate an investigation of the way in which dominant institutions must be transformed so that they no longer serve simply as conduits for a motivated indifference to victimization for a Euroimperial aesthetics, for depredations of economic and cultural dependency, and for

the production of asymmetrical relations of power and privilege.

Here it is important to contest the charge made by some liberal humanist educators that teachers should only speak for themselves and not for others. Those who claim that teachers can and should only speak for themselves—a claim that is at the very least implied by many critics of critical pedagogy—forget that 'when I "speak for myself" I am participating in the creation and reproduction of discourses through which my own and other selves are constituted' (Alcoff 1991–92: 21). Linda Alcoff notes that we need to promote a *dialogue with* rather than a *speaking for* others (although this does not preclude us from speaking for others under certain restricted circumstances). Drawing upon the work of Gayatri Chakravorty Spivak, Alcoff maintains that we can adopt a 'speaking to' the other that does not essentialize the oppressed as nonideologically constructed subjects. Summarizing Spivak, Alcoff stresses how important it is that the intellectual 'neither abnegates his or her discursive role nor presumes an authenticity of the oppressed but still allows for the possibility that the oppressed will produce a 'countersentence' that can then suggest a new historical narrative' (cited in Alcoff 1991–92: 23). As educators we need to be exceedingly cautious about our attempts to speak for others, questioning how our discourses as *events* position us as authoritative and empowered speakers in ways that unwittingly constitute a reinscription of the discourse of colonization, of patriarchy, of racism, of conquest—'a reinscription of sexual, national, and other kinds of hierarchies' (Alcoff 1991–92: 29). Educators also need to avoid a 'tolerance' that appropriates the difference of the Other in the name of the colonizer's own self-knowledge and increased domination.

Critical pedagogy does not work toward some grandiose endpoint of an ideologically perceived world history but rather attempts to make understandable the indefinite and to explore other modes of sociality and self-figuration that go beyond dominant language formations and social organizations. In doing so, it has often been accused of being inaccessible to rank-and-file teachers. Trinh T. Minh-ha (1991) issues a very telling warning against such calls for accessibility of language. She writes that resistance to the language of complex theory can reinstitute 'common sense' as an alternative to theory—that is, it can usher in a new dictatorship of pretheoretical nativism in which experience supposedly speaks for itself. To be 'accessible,' writes Minh-ha, often suggests

one can employ neither symbolic and elliptical language, as in Asian, African, or Native American cultures (because Western ears often equate it with obscurantism); nor poetic language (because 'objective' literal thinking is likely to identify it with 'subjective' aestheticism). The use of dialogical language is also discouraged (because the dominant worldview can hardly accept that in the politics of representing marginality and resistance one might have to speak at least two difference things at once). (1991: 228)

Minh-ha further notes, after Isaac Julien, that resistance to theory is embodied in white people's resistance to the complexity of black experience. Not only does such resistance point to the illusion that there exists a natural, self-evident language but such a call for accessibility can also lead to forms of racism and intolerance and the politics of exclusion. The 'diversely hybrid experiences of heterogeneous contemporary societies are denied' by such a form of binary thinking, which would reduce the language of analysis to white, hegemonic forms of clarity (Minh-ha 1991: 229).

Intensifying the Obvious and Accelerating the Mundane

A pedagogy that takes resistance postmodernism seriously does not make the nativist assumption that knowledge is preontologically available and that various disciplinary schools of thought may be employed in order to tease out different readings of the same 'commonsense' reality in a context of impartiality. Rather, the discourses that inform the educator's problematics are understood as constitutive of the very reality that he or she is attempting to understand. Consequently, the classroom is the site of the teacher's own embodiment in theory/discourse, ethical disposition as moral and political agent, and situatedness as a cultural worker within a larger narrative identity. In recognizing the important role played by 'place' in any critical pedagogy, it should be clear that we are talking not about the physical milieu where knowledge is

made visible within preordained and circumscribed limits but rather the textual space that one occupies and the affective space one creates as a teacher. In other words, the discursive practice of 'doing pedagogy' does not simply treat knowledge outside of the way that it is taken up by both teachers and students *as a form of dialogue*. I am referring here to the multi-voicedness of democratic discourse not in the sense of unrestrained intersubjective exchange but rather as challenging 'the logic of dialogue as equal linguistic exchange'. Such a challenge involves interrogating the ediological interests of the speaker, the social overdeterminations of utterances, and the social context in which utterances are both historically produced and culturally understood (Hitchcock 1993: 7). Knowledge can never be treated as a cultural artifact or possession that serves as a pristine, prefigurative source of cultural authenticity inviting unbiased analysis.

The project of critical pedagogy means bringing the laws of cultural representation face to face with their founding assumptions, contradictions, and paradoxes. It also means encouraging teachers to participate in the affective as well as intellectual cultures of the oppressed, and to challenge in the spirit of Ernst Bloch's 'militant optimism' ethical and political quietism in the face of operating homilies such as 'progress is inevitable' or what might seem like historical inevitability—a perspective that leads to the cult of the mausoleum. Educators can no longer project onto the student-as-Other that part of themselves that out of fear and loathing they rejected or subtracted from their identities in their attempt to become unified subjects— that 'split-off' part of themselves which prevents them from becoming whole, that disfiguring surplus that they have cast out in order to become white or live in the thrall of racelessness, that metaphysical double that guarantees their own self-regarding autonomy. From this point of view, liberation is never an encapsulated fulfillment of some prefigured end constructed in the temple of memory but a lived tension between the duration of history and the discourse of possibility. It resides in an approach to the '*Aufhebung*'— our passing *into* the 'not-yet', and seeking the immanent utopia in the crisis of meaning and the social relations that inform it. It is found, too, in the proleptic consciousness of liminality—the liberating intention of the reflective will caught in the 'subjunctive' moment of the 'ought' and disabused of metaphysical illusion. It is formed out of an ethical intent commensurate with the love that Paulo Freire and Che Guevara both argue constitutes the ground from which all revolutionary action should take place.

Neither the academy nor the public school system needs to sow the seeds of future priests of deconstruction in the desacralized institutional spaces of the postmodern scene by turning the college classroom into a prewar Europe Nietzschean café or Cabaret Voltaire for leftist educators who wish to reap no real political consequences for their semiotic revolution. Rather, the more pressing need is to transform present social practices and institutional relations because history compels us to do so, because the present historical juncture in which we witness so much misery and suffering necessitates it. History compels us because our dreams and our suffering are forged in it; it is what houses the furnace of our will. In the iron womb of history we create the shape of our longings, and to reclaim history is to be fully present in its making.

Educators need to do more than to help students redescribe or represent themselves in new ways—although the way we seek to imagine ourselves is an important step in the struggle for liberation. As Sander L. Gilman has pointed out in his study of stereotypes of sexuality, race, and madness, 'we view our own images, our own mirages, our own stereotypes as embodying qualities that exist in the world. And we act upon them' (1985: 242). More specifically, a pedagogy must be made available to teachers that will enable them along with their students to outface the barrenness of postmodern culture by employing a discourse and set of social practices that will not be content with infusing their pedagogies with the postmodern élan of the ludic metropolitan intellectual, with resurrecting a nostalgic past which can never be reclaimed, or with redescribing the present by simply textualizing it, leaving in place its malignant hierarchies of power and privilege, its defining pathologies. For these latter acts only stipulate the lineage of and give sustenance to those social relations responsible for the very injustice critical educators are trying to struggle against. Educators need to stare boldly and unflinchingly into the historical present and

assume a narrative space where conditions may be created where students can tell their own stories, listen closely to the stories of others, and dream the dream of liberation. Identity formation must be understood in terms of how subjectivity is contextually enacted within the tendential forces of history (Grossberg: 1992). The exploration of identity should consist of mapping one's subject position in the field of multiple relationships and should be preceded by a critique of hegemony (San Juan, Jr, 1992: 128). This suggests that educators and students need to uncouple themselves from the 'disciplined mobilizations' that regulate their social lives and rearticulate the sites of their affective investments in order to create new strategies and alliances of struggle.

A critical pedagogy also demands political and cultural tactics that can fight multiple forms of oppression yet achieve a cohesiveness with divergent social groups working toward liberatory goals. To this end, Chela Sandoval (1991) suggests that cultural workers develop 'tactical subjectivities' which she describes as forms of oppositional and differential consciousness and counterhegemonic praxis (which she discusses in the context of feminism). Tactical subjectivity enables teachers as social agents to recenter their multiple subjectivities with respect to the kind of oppression that is being confronted and 'permits the practitioner to choose tactical positions, that is, to self-consciously break and reform ties to ideology, activities which are imperative for the psychological and political practices that permit the achievement of coalition across differences' (Sandoval 1991: 15).

Resistance as 'La Conciencia De La Mestiza'

The invitation posed by critical pedagogy is to bend reality to the requirements of a just world, to decenter, deform, disorient, and ultimately transform modes of authority that domesticate the Other, that lay siege to the power of the margins. Educators would do well to consider Gloria Anzaldúa's (1987) project of creating *mestizaje* theories that create new categories of identity for those left out or pushed out of existing ones. Critical pedagogy calls for the construction of a praxis where peripheralized peoples such as African-Americans and Latinos are no longer induced to fear and obey the White Gaze of Power, where bonds of sentiment and obligation can be formed among diverse groups of oppressed peoples, where resistance can enable schools to become more than instruments of monitorization and social replication, where contrasting cultural styles and cultural capital among diverse groups cease to be tokens of estrangement that separate them but rather become the very impetus that invites them as liminal travelers to create an arch of social dreaming. We need to move beyond pedagogies of protest, which Houston Baker reminds us only reinforces the dualism of 'self' and 'other' and reinstates the basis of dominant racist evaluations, and preserves the 'always already' arrangements of white patriarchal hegemony (1985: 388). We need to develop a praxis that gives encouragement to those who, instead of being content with visiting history as curators or custodians of memory, choose to live in the furnace of history where memory is molten and can be bent into the contours of a dream and perhaps even acquire the immanent force of a vision.

The sites of our identity within postmodernity are various; as seekers of liberation, we recognize the heterogeneous character of our inscription into colonial texts of history and cultural discourses of empire. New sites of agency are erupting at the borderlines of cultural instability, in the transgressive act of remembering, and through the disavowal and refashioning of consciousness in the in-between spaces of cultural negotiation and translation. Marcos Sanchez-Tranquilino and John Tagg (1991) refer to this as the borderland, the 'in-between' space that Gloria Anzaldúa calls *la frontera*. It is a space of borders where teachers may be able to recognize

another narration of identity, another resistance. One that asserts a difference, yet cannot be absorbed into the pleasures of the global marketing culture. One that locates its different voice, yet will not take a stand on the unmoving ground of a defensive fundamentalism. One that speaks its location as more than local, yet makes no claim to universality for its viewpoint of language. One that knows the border and crosses the line. (1991: 105)

The rhythm of the struggle for educational and social transformation can no longer be contained in the undaunted, steady steps of the workers' army marching toward the iron gates of freedom but is being heard in the hybrid tempos of bordertown bands; in the spiraling currents of an Aster Aweke Kabu vocal, in the percussive polyrhythms of prophetic black rap, in meanings that appear in the folds of cultural life where identities are mapped not merely by diversity but through difference.

References

Alcoff, Linda (1991–92), 'The Problem of Speaking for Others.' *Cultural Critique* no. 20: 5–32. No volume no.

Anzaldúa, Gloria (1987), *Borderlands/La Frontera: The New Mestiza*. San Francisco: Spinsters/Aunt Lute.

Aronowitz, Stanley, and Giroux, Henry (1991), *Postmodern Education*. Minneapolis, Minn.: University of Minnesota Press.

Baker, Houston A. (1985), 'Caliban's Triple Play.' In Henry Louis Gates, Jr., (ed.) *'Race,' Writing and Difference*. Chicago, Illinois: The University of Chicago Press, 381–395.

Benjamin, Walter (1973), 'Program For a Proletarian Children's Theater,' *Performance* 1, no. 5 (March–April): 28–32. Trans. Susan Buck-Morss from Benjamin, 'Programm eines proletarischen Kindertheaters' (1928), in *Ober Kinder, Jugend und Erziehung*, (ed.) Suhrkamp 391. Frankfurt am Main: Suhrkamp Verlag, 1969.

Best, Steven (1989), 'Jameson, Totality and Post-Structuralist Critique.' In Doug Kellner (ed.), *Postmodernism/Jameson/Critique*. Washington: Maisonneuve, 233–368.

Bhabha, Homi (1990), 'Introduction: Narrating the Nation.' In Homi K. Bhabha (ed.), *Nation and Narration*. London and New York: Routledge. 291–322.

—— (1991*a*), ' "Race," Time, and the Revision of Modernity.' *Oxford Literary Review* 13, nos. 1–2: 193–219.

—— (1991*b*), 'The Third Space,' In Jonathan Rutherford (ed.), *Identity: Community, Culture, Difference*. London: Lawrence and Wishart. 207–37.

Bloch, Ernst (1986), *The Principle of Hope* (3 vols.) Translated by Neville Plaice, Stephen Plaice and Paul Knight. Cambridge, Mass.: The MIT Press.

Browder, Leslie H. (1992), 'Which America 2000 Will Be Taught in Your Class, Teacher?' *International Journal of Educational Reform* 1, no. 2: 111–33.

Carspecken, Phil Francis (1991), *Community Schooling and the Nature of Power: The Battle for Croxteth Comprehensive*. London and New York: Routledge.

Chambers, Iain (1990), *Border Dialogues: Journeys in Postmodernity*. London and New York: Routledge.

Christian, Barbara (1987), 'The Race for Theory.' *Cultural Critique* no. 6: 51–63.

Cooper, B. M. (1989), 'Cruel and the Gang: Exposing the Schomburg Posse.' *Village Voice* 34, no. 19: 27–36.

Copjec, Joan (1991), 'The Unvermogender Other: Hysteria and Democracy in America'. *New Formations* 14: 27–41.

Dauenhauer, P. B. (1989), 'Ideology, Utopia, and Responsible Politics.' *Man and World* 22: 25–41.

Di Stephano, Christine, (1990), 'Dilemmas of Difference: Feminism, Modernity, and Postmodernism.' In Linda J. Nicholson, (ed.), *Feminism/Postmodernism*. New York and London: Routledge. 63–82.

Donald, James (forthcoming), 'The Natural Man and the Virtuous Woman: Reproducing Citizens.' In Chris Jencks (ed.), *Cultural Reproduction*. London and New York: Routledge.

Dussel, Enrique (1980), *Philosophy of Liberation*. Maryknoll, N.Y.: Orbis Books.

Ebert, Teresa (1991), 'Political Semiosis in/of American Cultural Studies.' *American Journal of Semiotics* 8, no. ½: 113–35.

—— (forthcoming), 'Writing in the Political Resistance (Post) Modernism.'

Featherstone, Mike (1990), 'Global Culture: An Introduction.' *Theory, Culture, and Society* nos. 2–3: 1–14.

Foster, Hal (ed.) (1983), *The Anti-Aesthetic: Essays on Postmodern Culture*. Port Town-send, Wash. Bay Press.

Frank, Arthur W. (1990), 'Bringing Bodies Back In: A Decade Review.' *Theory, Culture, and Society* 7, no. 1: 131–62.

Game, Ann, (1991), *Undoing the Social: Towards a Deconstructive Sociology*. Toronto and Buffalo: University of Toronto Press.

Gilman, Sander L. (1985), *Difference and Pathology*. Ithaca, New York: Cornell University Press.

Gilroy, Paul (1990), 'One Nation under a Groove: The Cultural Politics of "Race" and Racism in Britain.' In Goldberg 1990, 263–82.

Giroux, Henry (1992), *Border Crossings*. London and New York: Routledge.

Goldberg, David Theo (1990), *Anatomy of Racism*. Minneapolis: University of Minnesota Press.

Grossberg, Larry (1988), *It's a Sin*. University of Sydney, Australia: Power Publications.

—— (1992), *We Gotta Get Out of This Place*. New York and London: Routledge.

Grosz, Elizabeth (1990), 'Conclusion: Notes on Essentialism and Difference.' In Sneja Gunew (ed.), *Feminist Knowledge: Critique and Construct*. London, Routledge, 332–44.

Hall, Stuart (1991), ' Ethnicity: Identity and Difference.' *Radical America* 23, no. 4: 9–20.

Harstock, Nancy, (1987), 'Rethinking Modernism: Minority vs. Majority Theories', *Cultural Critique* 7: 187–206.

—— (1989), 'Foucault on Power: A Theory for Women?' In Linda J. Nicholson (ed.), *Feminism/Postmodernism*. New York and London, Routledge. 157–75.

Hitchcock, Peter (1993), *Dialogics of the Oppressed*. Minneapolis and London: University of Minnesota Press.

Jameson, Fredric (1989), 'Afterword—Marxism and Postmodernism.' In Doug Kellner (ed.), *Postmodernism/Jameson/Critique*. Washington: Maisonneuve. 369–87.

Kaplan, E. Ann (1987), *Rocking around the Clock: Music, Television, Postmodernism and Consumer Culture*. New York: Methuen.

Kasinitz, P. (1988), 'Facing Up to the Underclass.' *Telos* 76: 170–80.

Katz, Cindi and Smith, Neil. (1992), 'L. A. Intifada: Interview with Mike Davis.' *Social Text*. 33: 19–33.

Kimball, Roger (1991), 'Tenured Radicals: A Postscript.' *The New Criterion* 9, no. 5: 4–13.

Kincheloe, Joe (1991), *Teachers as Researchers: Qualitative Inquiry as a Path to Empowerment*. London: Falmer.

Larsen, Neil (1990), Modernism and Hegemony: *A Materialist Critique of Aesthetic Agencies*. Minneapolis, MN: University of Minnesota Press.

Lash, Scott (1990), 'Learning from Leipzig . . . or Politics in the Semiotic Society.' *Theory, Culture, and Society* 7, no. 4: 145–58.

Levinas, Emmanuel (1969), *Totality and Infinity*. Pittsburgh: Duquesne University Press.

Lippard, Lucy R. (1990), *Mixed Blessings: New Art in a Multicultural America*. New York: Pantheon Books.

Lipsitz, George (1990), *Time Passages*. Minneapolis: University of Minnesota Press.

Lloyd, David (1991), 'Race under Representation.' *Oxford Literary Review* 13, nos. 1–2: 62–94.

McLaren, Peter (1989*a*), *Life in Schools*. White Plains, N. Y.: Longman.

—— (1989*b*), 'Schooling the Postmodern Body: Critical Pedagogy and the Politics of Enfleshment.' *Journal of Education* 170: 53–8.

—— (ed.) (forthcoming), *Postmodernism, Postcolonialism and Pedagogy*. Albert Park, Australia: James Nicholas Publishers.

—— and Hammer, Rhonda, (1989), 'Critical Pedagogy and the Postmodern Challenge,' *Educational Foundations*, 3, no. 3: 29–69.

—— and Leonard, Peter (1993), *Paulo Freire: A Critical Encounter*. London and New York: Routledge.

Mercer, Kobena (1990), 'Welcome to the Jungle: Identity and Diversity in Postmodern Politics.' In Jonathan Rutherford (ed.), *Identity: Community, Culture, Difference*. London: Lawrence and Wishart. 43–71.

Minh-ha, Trinh T. (1991), *When the Moon Waxes Red: Representation, Gender, and Cultural Politics.* New York and London: Routledge.

Mohanty, Chandra (1989/90), 'On Race and Voice: Challenges for Liberal Education in the 1990s.' *Cultural Critique* 19: 179–208.

Munoz, Carlos (1989), *Youth, Identity, Power.* London and New York: Verso.

Murphy, Peter (1991), 'Postmodern Perspectives and Justice.' *Thesis Eleven* no. 30: 117–32.

Piccone, Paul (1988), 'Roundtable on Communitarianism.' *Telos* no. 76: 2–32.

Ravitch, Diane (1990), 'Multiculturalism: E Pluribus Plures.' *The American Scholar* 59, no. 3: 337–54.

—— (1991), 'A Culture in Common.' *Educational Leadership* (December): 8–16.

Rosaldo, Renato (1989), *Culture and Truth: The Remaking of Social Analysis.* Boston: Beacon.

Rosenau, Pauline Marie (1992), *Post-Modernism and the Social Sciences: Insights, Inroads, and Intrusions.* Princeton, N. J.: Princeton University Press.

Sáenz, Mario (1991), 'Memory, Enchantment and Salvation: Latin American Philosophies of Liberation and the Religions of the Oppressed.' *Philosophy and Social Criticism* 17, no. 2: 149–73.

Saldivar, Ramon (1990), *Chicano Narrative: The Dialectics of Difference.* Madison WI: University of Wisconsin Press.

Sanchez-Tranquilino, Marcos, and Tagg, John (1991), 'The Pachuco's Flayed Hide: The Museum, Identity, and Buenas Garvas.' In Richard Griswold de Castillo, Teresa McKenna, and Yvonne Yarbro-Bejarano (eds.), *Chicano Art: Resistance and Affirmation.* Los Angeles: Wright Art Gallery. 97–108.

Sandoval, Chela (1991), 'U.S. Third World Feminism: The Theory and Method of Oppositional Consciousness in the Postmodern World.' *Genders* no. 10: 1–24.

San Juan, Jr., E. (1992), *Racial Formations/Critical Formations.* New Jersey and London: Humanities Press.

Simone, Timothy Maliqualim (1989), *About Face: Race in Postmodern America.* Brooklyn, NY: Autonomedia.

Stephanson, Anders (1988), 'Interview with Cornel West.' In Andrew Ross (ed), *Universal Abandon? The Politics of Postmodernism.* Minneapolis: University of Minnesota Press. 269–86.

Taylor, Patrick (1989), *The Narrative of Liberation: Perspectives on Afro-Caribbean Literature, Popular Culture, and Politics.* Ithaca, N.Y.: Cornell University Press.

Trend, David (1992), *Cultural Pedagogy: Art/Education/Politics.* New York: Bergin and Garvey.

Wallace, Michele (1991), 'Multiculturalism and Oppositionality.' *Afterimage* (October): 6–9.

West, Cornel (1989), 'Black Culture and Postmodernism.' In Barbara Kruger and Phil Mariani (eds.), *Remaking History.* Seattle: Bay Press. 87–96.

—— (1990), 'The New Cultural Politics of Difference.' In Russell Ferguson, Martha Gever, Trinh T. Minh-ha, and Cornel West (eds.), *Out There: Marginalization and Contemporary Cultures*, Cambridge, Mass.: MIT Press and the New Museum of Contemporary Art, New York. 19–36.

Young, Iris Marion (1990), *Justice and the Politics of Difference.* Princeton, NJ: Princeton University Press.

Zavarzadeh, Mas'ud, and Morton, Donald (1990), 'Signs of Knowledge in the Contemporary Academy.' *American Journal of Semiotics* 7, no. 4: 149–60.

—— —— (1991), *Theory, (Post)Modernity, Opposition.* Washington, D. C.: Maisonneuve.

35

Nonsynchrony and Social Difference: An Alternative to Current Radical Accounts of Race and Schooling

Cameron McCarthy

Despite its limitations, the mainstream and radical educational literature on race relations in schooling has pointed us in some very important directions. For instance, we now know where some of the most significant tensions, stresses, and gaps in our current research on social difference and inequality are. I believe that it is precisely these 'gaps', 'stresses', 'tensions', and discontinuities that must be explored if researchers are to begin to develop a more adequate account of the operation of racial inequality in education and society.

In the first part of this chapter, I will examine three areas which I consider crucial points of difference and tension between and within mainstream and radical approaches to racial inequality in the curriculum and educational literature. These areas can be summarized as follows: (a) the structure-culture distinction, (b) macro- versus micro-theoretical and methodological perspectives on race, and (c) the issue of historical variability versus essentialism in the designation of racial categories.

In the second part of this chapter, I will make the case for an alternative approach to racial inequality, which I shall call a *nonsynchronous theory* of race relations in schooling and society. In advancing the position of non-synchrony, I will argue against 'essentialist' or single-cause explanations of the persistence of racial inequality in education that are currently being offered in both the mainstream and radical curriculum and educational litera-

ture. Instead, I will direct attention to the complex and contradictory nature of race relations in the institutional life of social organizations such as schools.

Let us first look at the principal tensions within mainstream and radical accounts of racial inequality.

Areas of Tension in Mainstream and Radical Research

STRUCTURE VERSUS CULTURE

As I showed in chapter 2 of *Race and Curriculum* (McCarthy 1990), liberal educational theorists place a great deal of emphasis on 'values' as the site of the social motivation for the maintenance and persistence of racial inequality. This emphasis on values as a central explanatory variable in liberal theories of racial inequality should not be dismissed out of hand. The primary theoretical and practical merit of this liberal position resides in the fact that it seeks to restore human agency to the project of evaluating the relationship between social difference and education. Thus, for liberal theorists in their examination of racial antagonism in schooling, it is the active agency and subjectivities of students and teachers that really matter and that can make a difference in race relations.

In a related sense, liberal researchers also recognize the cultural role of education in

Originally published as ch. 5 in *Race and Curriculum: Social Inequality and the Theories and Politics of Difference in Contemporary Research on Schooling* (Falmer Press, 1990).

initiating the social neophyte into dominant values, traditions, and rituals of 'stratification' (Durkheim 1977; Ogbu and Matute-Bianchi 1986). But liberal pluralist researchers conceptualize racial values as emanating from a coherent Cartesian individual subject. When groups or social collectivities are invoked in liberal frameworks on racial inequality, they are specified in terms of aggregates of individuals. The problem here, as I indicated earlier, is that such an emphasis on individual agency also results in the under-theorization of the effectivity of social and economic structures in the determination of racial inequality.

This tension between structure and agency is also powerfully expressed within radical discourses. Neo-Marxists insist that racial domination must, in part, be understood in the context of capitalism's elaboration of macrostructures and not simply in terms of individual preferences. They draw our attention to the fact that racial domination is deeply implicated in the fundamental organization of specific human societies as well as in the evolution of capitalism as a world system. In this way, we come to understand race as a profoundly social category. Racial domination is thus conceptualized at the level of social collectivities and their differential and conflictual relationships to the means of production. This alerts us to the powerful connections among racial domination and economic inequality, differential material resources and capacities, and unequal access to social and political institutions such as schools.

But recent Marxist cultural criticism has sought to raise other issues concerning social difference and inequality in American education (Crichlow 1990; Omi and Winant 1986; Sarup 1986). These issues—of identity, subjectivity, culture, language, and agency—direct attention to the informal curriculum of schools and the subcultural practices of school youth. This theoretical development has taken place partly in response to the early work of radical school critics, such as Bowles and Gintis (1976), who tended to subordinate agency, meaning, and subjectivity to economic structures (for example, the workplace) exogenous to the school. Writers such as Apple and Weis (1983) contend that previous neo-Marxist emphasis on economic structures focuses attention on only part of the puzzle in our investigation of racial inequality. In a similar manner, liberal emphasis on social

and cultural 'values' as the primary site of racial antagonism provides us with only a partial understanding of the way in which racial dynamics operate. Marxist cultural theorists have therefore attempted to transcend the binary opposition of structure versus culture entailed in previous neo-Marxist and liberal theories by offering a more interactive view of the central contradictions in capitalist society. However, to the extent that some critical educational theorists have attempted to incorporate these more interactive perspectives into their examination of the relationship between schooling and inequality, these efforts have been directed almost exclusively toward understanding the dynamics of class, not race.

MACRO- VERSUS MICROPERSPECTIVES
There is a further bifurcation in the curriculum and educational literature on race: mainstream theorists have tended to focus more directly on microlevel classroom variables, while radical theorists have offered macroperspectives on racial inequality that have privileged areas outside the school, such as the economy and the labor process. As I indicated earlier, radical school critics have generally specified structural relations at such a high level of abstraction (the level of abstraction of the mode of production) that all human agency evaporates from their analysis of society. This abstract approach is also residually present in more recent critical curriculum studies of social difference and inequality in the institutional settings of schools (Apple 1988; Giroux 1985; Hogan 1982; Whitty 1985). As we saw in the previous chapter, these more culturalist theorists have argued that race is linked to other social dynamics, such as class and gender, in a system of multiple determinations. Sarup (1986) has quite persuasively argued that these 'additive' models of inequality have simply failed to capture the degree of nuance, variability, discontinuity, and multiplicity of histories and 'realities' that exist in the school setting. In a similar manner, both Omi and Winant (1986) and Burawoy (1981) have pointed to the fact that the intersection of race and class can lead, for example, to the augmentation or diminution of racial solidarity, depending on the contingencies and variables in the local setting such as the school. All of this points toward the need for theoretical and practical work articulated at what Hall (1986) calls the 'middle

range'. That is to say that it is important that radical theorists begin to specify more directly the ways in which race operates in the local context of schools.

Let me be clear about what is at issue here. I believe that the radical intuition that racial inequality is implicated and must be understood in the context of the development of capitalism's macrostructures is basically correct if it takes seriously the relatively autonomous workings of the state. On the other hand, unqualified liberal emphasis on individual motivation and rational action as the terms of reference for 'normal' behavior locates racism in idiosyncratic, arbitrary, and abnormal attitudes and actions. This requires us to abandon materialist explanations of racial antagonism and seek recourse in differential psychology and so on. The burden and responsibility for the oppression of racial minorities are squarely placed on the shoulders of these irrational or 'authoritarian personalities' (Henriques 1984). Even more problematic is the fact that change and transformation of these oppressive relations are made conditional upon the institutional reformation of these individuals and their return to the observance of rational norms that guide the society and its institutions. Needless to say, historical evidence and the very persistence of racial inequality in schools and society go against the grain of this thesis and the programmatic responses it has precipitated.

THE ISSUE OF HISTORY

Though both the macrological and micrological perspectives that underpin radical and liberal formulations give us a general map of racial logics, they do not tell us how movement is orchestrated, or realized along the grid of race relations. That is to say that neither current liberal nor neo-Marxist theories of schooling inform us about the historical trajectory of racial discourse and the struggles over such racial discourse within specific institutions such as education. There is indeed a tendency within mainstream and radical frameworks to treat racial definitions ('black', 'white', etc.) as immutable, *a priori* categories. Racial categories such as black and white are taken for granted within the popular common sense as well as in the writings of scholars in education. Associated with this tendency are tacit or explicit propositions about the origins of races and racism. Main-

stream theorists identify the origin of the races in physical and psychological traits, geography, climate, patterns of ancient migrations and so on (Gould 1981; Harris 1968). Radical theorists, on the other hand, link race and racism to the specific event of the emergence of capitalism and its 'need' to rationalize the super-exploitation of African slave labor and the segmented division of labor (Bonacich 1981; Williams 1964). The major methodological problem of all of these 'origins' arguments is that they presume the eternal existence of racial distinctions and incorporate them into the analysis of racial antagonism as though such distinctions were functional social categories that have remained stable throughout history. In both mainstream and radical writings, then, 'race' is historically given. (After all, says our common sense, 'we know who black people and white people are merely by observation and inspection'.) The historical variability associated with racial categories and the social purposes that racial distinctions serve are consequently undertheorized.

But as Omi and Winant (1986) have argued, race is pre-eminently a 'social historical concept'. For example, it is only through developed social practices and the particular elaboration of historical and material relations in the US that 'white consciousness', with its associated category 'white people', emerged. Likewise, it is only through similar historical and social practices that racial 'others'—who in reality have varying economic and social positions—emerged under the definition of 'black', 'Asian', etc. In this sense, racial categories and 'the meaning of race and the definitions of specific racial groups have varied significantly over time and between different societies' (Omi and Winant 1986: 61). A few examples are useful in helping to illustrate the instability and variability of racial categories.

In the United States, the racial classification 'white' evolved with the consolidation of slavery in the seventeenth century. Euro-American settlers of various 'ancestry' (Dutch, English, and so forth) claimed a common identity in relation to exploited and enslaved African peoples. As Winthrop Jordan (1968) observes:

From the first, then, vis-a-vis 'Negro' the concept embedded in the term *Christian* seems to have conveyed much of the idea and feeling of 'we' against 'they': to be *Christian* was to be civilized rather than barbarous, English rather than African, white rather than black. The term *Christian* itself proved to have remarkable elasticity, for by the end of the seventeenth century it was being used to define a species of slavery which had altogether lost any connection with explicit religious difference. In the Virginia code of 1705, for example, the term sounded much more like a definition of race than of religion: 'And for a further christian care and usage of all christian servants, Be it also enacted, *by the authority aforesaid, and it is hereby enacted,* That no negroes, mulattos, or Indians, although christians, or Jews, Moors, Mahometans, or other infidels, shall, at any time, purchase any christian servant, nor any other, except of their own complexion, or such as are declared slaves by this act.' By this time 'Christianity' had somehow become intimately linked with 'complexion' . . . Most suggestive of all, there seems to have been something of a shift during the seventeenth century in the terminology which Englishmen in the colonies applied to themselves. From the initially most common term *Christian*, at mid-century there was a marked shift toward 'English' and 'free'. After about 1680, taking the colonies as a whole, a new term appeared— 'white'. (pp. 94–5)

It is through these same practices of inclusion and exclusion that the 'others' of colonial America—the enslaved African peoples— were defined as 'negro' or 'black'. Thus, the racial category 'negro' redefined and homogenized the plural identities of disparate African people whose 'ethnic origins' were Ibo, Yoruba, Fulani, and so on.

Racial categories also vary contemporaneously between societies. For example, while the racial designation 'black' in the United States refers only to people of African descent, in England, oppressed Asian and Afro-Caribbean minorities have appropriated 'black' as a counter-hegemonic identity. In Latin America, racial categories are used and appropriated with a higher degree of flexibility than in the United States. Omi and Winant (1986), drawing on the work of cultural anthropologist Marvin Harris, foreground this variability and discontinuity in race relations in Latin America:

By contrast [to the United States], a striking feature of race relations in the lowland areas of Latin America since the abolition of slavery has been the relative absence of sharply defined racial groupings. No such rigid descent rule characterizes racial identity in many Latin American societies. Brazil, for example, has historically had less rigid conceptions of race, and thus a variety of 'intermediate' racial categories exist. Indeed, as Harris notes,

'One of the most striking consequences of the Brazilian system of racial identification is that parents and children and even brothers and sisters are frequently accepted as representatives of quite opposite racial types.' Such a possibility is incomprehensible within the logic of racial categories in the US. (p. 61)

Social practices of racial classification are elaborated and contested throughout society and within given institutions by personal and collective action. In this way racial definitions are reproduced and transformed. Historically, education has been a principal site for the reproduction and elaboration of racial meaning and racial identities. An examination of the career of racial discourses within the overall trajectory of curriculum and educational theories and practices rapidly disabuses us of the notion that education is a 'neutral' or 'innocent' institution with respect to racial struggles (JanMohamed 1987; JanMohamed and Lloyd 1987). An investigation of the genealogy of racial discourses in education would, for example, take us through the domains of:

1. Colonial/plantation America's education laws that prohibited the education of black Americans, such as the eighteenth-century statutes of South Carolina and other states (JanMohamed and Lloyd 1987: 7).
2. Jim Crow's educational policies in the North and the South that segregated and concentrated blacks and other minorities into inferior schools (Carnoy 1974; Ogbu 1978).
3. Mental measurement and human intelligence theories—from the laboratory of cranium estimates to the anthropological and biological theories of racial difference in the work of the likes of Morton (1839) and Gobineau (1915), and the genetics-based theories of race and intelligence of Eysenck and Kamin (1981) and Jensen (1969, 1981, 1984).
4. Curriculum theories of social efficiency, differential psychology and cultural deprivation that labeled black youth as 'under achievers', and have labeled black families and black communities as 'defective' and 'dysfunctional'.
5. Liberal and progressive-inspired educational programs such as Head Start, compensatory education and multicultural programs that have been aimed at helping

to close the educational and cultural gap between black and white youth.

At every historical juncture of the racialization of dominant educational institutions in the United States, African Americans and other racial minorities have contested and have sought to redefine hegemonic conceptions of racial differences in 'intelligence' and 'achievement' and the curriculum strategies of inclusion and exclusion and selection that these commonsense racial theories have undergirded. Over the years, this cultural resistance has been mobilized on two principal fronts. On the one hand, since the period of Reconstruction, African Americans have conducted a 'war of maneuver' (Gramsci 1983) outside the 'trenches' of dominant universities, schools and other educational centers by establishing parallel and alternative institutions of learning. While it is true that these institutions have not always been directed towards transformative projects, black educational institutions have provided a material basis for the nurturing of black intellectual and cultural autonomy (Marable 1985; West 1988).

Simultaneous with the elaboration of alternative institutions, African Americans and other minorities have conducted a 'war of position' (Gramsci 1983) in the courts and the schools for equality of access to education. These struggles have also been enlarged to include insurgent challenges over a redefinition of dominant university academic programs. These challenges have directly influenced the emergence of the 'new' disciplines of ethnic studies, women's studies and so on, that have helped to broaden the range of knowledge and interests in the university setting.

Education has therefore played a central role in the drama of struggles over racial identities and meaning in the United States. But any historical account of the racialization of American education must avoid the easy familiarity of linear narrative. The reproduction of hegemonic racial meanings, the persistence of racial inequality, and the mobilization of minority resistance to dominant educational institutions have not proceeded in a linear, coherent or predictable way. A systematic exploration of the history of race relations in education does, however, lead us to a recognition of the agency of oppressed minorities, the

fluidity and complexity of social dynamics, and the many-sided character of minority/majority relations in education.

The tensions and silences within mainstream and radical approaches to racial inequality discussed here underscore the need for a more relational and contextual approach to the operation of racial differences in schooling. Such an approach would allow us to understand better the complex operation of racial logics in schooling and would help us to explore more adequately the vital links that exist between racial inequality and other dynamics—such as class and gender—operating in the school setting. In the next section, I will present two related alternative approaches—the theories of *parallelism* and *nonsynchrony*—that will directly address the conceptually difficult but intriguing issues concerning (a) the structuration and formation of racial difference in education, and (b) the intersection of race, class and gender dynamics in the institutional setting of schools.

Nonsynchrony and Parallelism: Linking Race to Gender and Class Dynamics in Education

Racial inequality is indeed a complex, many-sided phenomenon that embraces both structural and cultural characteristics. But exactly how does racial difference operate in education? How are the 'widely disparate circumstances of individual and group racial identities' (Omi and Winant 1986: 169) intertwined and mediated in the formal and informal practices of social institutions such as schools? How do educational institutions 'integrate' the macro- and microdynamics of difference? One of the most significant contributions to an understanding of these difficult questions regarding the operation of racial inequality has been advanced by Apple and Weis (1983) in what they call the 'parallelist position'. Since the parallelist position not only represents a paradigm shift in the way contemporary curriculum theorists conceptualize race, but directly anticipates my reformulation of race relations in schooling, it is necessary to describe the theory in some detail.

Apple and Weis (1983) criticize the

tendency of mainstream and radical theorists to bifurcate society into separate domains of structure and culture. They argue that such arbitrary bifurcation directly informs tendencies toward essentialism (single-cause explanations) in contemporary thinking about race. Researchers often 'locate the fundamental elements of race, not surprisingly, on their homeground' (Omi and Winant 1986: 52). For neo-Marxists, then, it is necessary first to understand the class basis of racial inequality; and for liberal theorists, cultural and social values and prejudices are the primary sources of racial antagonism. In contrast, Apple and Weis contend that race is not a 'category' or a 'thing-in-itself' (Thompson 1966), but a vital social process which is integrally linked to other social processes and dynamics operating in education and society. These proponents of the parallelist position therefore hold that at least *three* dynamics—class, race and gender—are essential in understanding schools and other institutions. None are reducible to the others, and class is not necessarily primary:

A number of elements or dynamics are usually present at the same time in any one instance. This is important. Ideological form is *not* reducible to class. Processes of gender, age, and race enter directly into the ideological moment . . . It is actually out of the articulation with, clash among, or contradictions among and within, say class, race, and sex that ideologies are lived in one's day-to-day life. (Apple and Weis 1983: 24)

In addition to this critique of class essentialism, Apple and Weis (1983) also offer a re-evaluation of economically reductive explanations of unequal social relations. They acknowledge that the economy plays a powerful role in determining the structure of opportunities and positions in capitalist society, but in their view, 'the' economy does not exhaust all existing social relations in society. Rather than using the economy to explain everything, these theorists have argued for an enlarged view of the social formation in which the role of ideology and culture is recognized as integral to the shaping of unequal social relations and life chances. Apple and Weis (1983) maintain that there are three spheres of social life: economic, political, and cultural. These, too, are in continual interaction and are, in essence, arenas in which class, race, and gender dynamics operate. Unlike adherents to base-superstructure models, these propo-

nents of parallelist theory assume that action in one arena can have an effect on action in another. The parallelist position therefore presents us with a theory of *overdetermination* in which the unequal processes and outcomes of teaching and learning and of schooling in general are produced by constant interactions among three dynamics (race, gender, and class) and in three spheres (economic, political, and cultural). The parallelist model, taken from Apple and Weis (1983: 25), is presented in Figure 35. 1.

The proposition that 'each sphere of social life is constituted of dynamics of class, race, and gender' (Apple and Weis 1983: 25) has broad theoretical and practical merit. For example, it highlights the fact that it is impossible to understand fully the problem of the phenomenally high school dropout rate among black and Hispanic youth without taking into account the lived experience of race, class, and gender oppressions in US urban centers and the ways in which the intersections of these social dynamics work to systematically 'disqualify' inner-city minority youth in educational institutions and in the job market. In a similar manner, a theoretical emphasis on gender dynamics complements our understanding of the unequal division of labor in schools and society and directs our attention to the way in which capitalism uses patriarchal relations to depress the wage scale and the social value of women's labor.

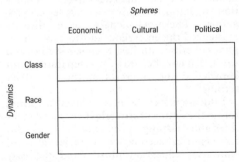

Fig. 35.1. The parallelist model
Source: Apple and Weis (1983: 25).

At a time when class-essentialist explanations still play such an important role in our thinking about schools and society, this movement toward a more relational or parallelist framework is to be welcomed. Increasingly, the work of feminist researchers in education, who argue that gender, race, and class are irreducible dynamics and that each must be taken equally seriously, is being looked upon more favorably by other radical theorists (Apple and Beyer 1988; Grant 1984; Roman, Christian-Smith, and Ellsworth 1988). Even somewhat more economistic theorists have begun to recognize how important it is to deal more thoroughly with cultural and political power and conflict within state institutions (Carnoy and Levin 1985). There has been greater recognition, as well, of the efficacy of non-class social movements and movements that cut across class, gender, and race lines, in the formation of social and educational policy. Thus the parallelist theoretical framework has proven to be a much more synthetic appraisal of how power operates than earlier accounts.

This does not mean, however, that the thesis of parallelism is without its problems. While I wish to support the validity of this model of interactions as expressing the character of the US formation at a very abstract level of generalization, there are limitations to this 'symmetrical' model at somewhat lower levels of abstraction (i.e., when applied to concrete institutional settings) that have been noted by writers such as Hicks 1981, and Sarup 1986. I will identify some of the problems with this formulation and suggest an alternative way of thinking about the operation of race and other dynamics in institutional settings.

First, it has become clear that at a conjunctural level of analysis, the parallelist model has not been adequate. It is often too general and loses cogency and specificity when applied to the actual operation of race, class, and gender in institutional settings such as schools and classrooms. While the model does serve to make us stop and think about a broader range of dynamics and spheres than before, it is difficult to account for the various twists and turns of social and political life at the microlevel if our application of theory is inappropriately 'pitched' at too high a level of abstraction (Hall 1986).

Second, this model unfortunately has often been construed in a static and simplistically additive way. Attempts to specify the dynamics of raced, classed, and gendered phenomena in education are often formulated in terms of a system of linear 'additions' or gradations of oppression (Sarup 1986). Thus, for example, Spencer (1984), in her insightful case

study of women school teachers, draws attention to their double oppression. Simply put, these women performed onerous tasks with respect to both their domestic and emotional labor in the home and their instructional labor in the classroom (pp. 283–96). In Spencer's analysis, the oppression of these women in the home is 'added' to their oppression as female teachers working in the classroom. No attempt is made here to represent the *qualitatively* different experiences of patriarchy that black women encounter in their daily lives, both in the context of the domestic sphere and within the teaching profession itself. In this essentially incremental model of oppression, patriarchal and class forms of oppression unproblematically reproduce each other. Accounts of the intersection of race, class, and gender such as these overlook instances of tension, contradiction, and discontinuity in the institutional life of the school setting (McCarthy and Apple 1988). In addition, the parallelist position does not fully address the 'mix' of contingencies, interests, needs, differential assets, and capacities in the local setting such as the school. Dynamics of race, class, and gender are conceptualized as having individual and uninterrupted effects.

Notions of double and triple oppression are not wholly inaccurate, of course. However, we need to see these relations as far more complex, problematic, and contradictory than is suggested by parallelist theory. One of the most useful attempts to conceptualize the interconnections among race, class, and gender has been formulated by Emily Hicks (1981). She cautions critical researchers against the tendency to theorize the interrelations among social dynamics as 'parallel', 'reciprocal', or 'symmetrical'. Instead, Hicks offers the thesis that the operation of race, class, and gender relations at the level of daily practices in schools, workplaces, etc., is systematically *contradictory* or *nonsynchronous*. Hick's emphasis on nonsynchrony helps to lay the basis for an alternative approach to thinking about these social relations and dynamics at the institutional level.

By invoking the concept of nonsynchrony, I wish to advance the position that individuals or groups, in their relation to economic, political, and cultural institutions such as schools, do *not* share identical consciousness and express the same interests, needs or desires 'at the same point in time' (Hicks 1981: 221). In this connection, I also attach great importance to the organizing principles of selection, inclusion, and exclusion. These principles operate in ways that affect how marginalized minority youth are positioned in dominant social and educational policies and agendas. Schooling in this sense constitutes a site for the production of politics. The politics of difference is a critical dimension of the way in which nonsynchrony operates in the material context of the school and can be regarded as the expression of 'culturally sanctioned, rational responses to struggles over scarce [or unequal] resources' (Wellman 1977: 4). As we will see, students (and teachers) tend to be rewarded and sanctioned differently according to the resources and assets they are able to mobilize inside the school and in the community. This capacity to mobilize resources and to exploit the unequal reward system and symbolic rituals of schooling varies considerably according to the race, gender, and class backgrounds of minority and majority students. White middle-class male students therefore come into schools with clear social and economic advantages and in turn often have these advantages confirmed and augmented by the unequal curriculum and pedagogical practices of schooling. However, this process is not simple, and the production of inequality in school is a highly contradictory and nonsynchronous phenomenon—one that does not guarantee nice, clean, or definitive outcomes for embattled minority and majority school actors.

But exactly how does nonsynchrony work in practice? What are the 'rules of the game' that govern the production of inequality in the school setting? And how does inequality in educational institutions become specifically classed, gendered, or raced?

There are four types of relations that govern the nonsynchronous interactions of raced, classed, and gendered minority and majority actors in the school setting. These relations can be specified as follows:

1. *Relations of competition*: These include competition for access to educational institutions, credentials, instructional opportunity, financial and technical resources, and so on.
2. *Relations of exploitation*: The school mediates the economy's demands for different types of labor in its preparation of school youth for the labor force.

3. *Relations of domination*: Power in schooling is highly stratified and is expressed in terms of a hierarchy of relations and structures—administration to teacher, teacher to student, and so forth. The school also mediates demands for symbolic control and legitimation from a racial and patriarchal state.
4. *Relations of cultural selection*: This is the totalizing principle of 'difference' that organizes meaning and identity-formation in school life. This organizing principle is expressed in terms of cultural strategies or rules of inclusion/exclusion or in-group/out-group that determine whose knowledge gets into the curriculum, and that also determine the pedagogical practices of ability grouping, diagnosing and marking of school youth. These relations also help to define the terms under which endogenous competition for credentials, resources, and status can take place in the school. It should be noted that there is considerable overlap between and among the relations of cultural selection and the other relations of competition, exploitation, and domination operating in the everyday practices of minority and majority school actors.

In the school setting, each of these four types of relations interacts with, defines, and is defined by the others in an uneven and decentered manner. For example, the principles of cultural selection embodied in codes of dress, behavior, and so forth, which help to determine the assignment of minority youth to low-ability groups (Grant 1985; Rist 1970), also help to position these youth in respect to power (domination) relations with majority peers and adults. Cultural selection therefore influences minority access to instructional opportunity as well as access to opportunities for leadership and status in the classroom and in the school (Gamoran and Berends 1986). In a similar manner, relations of cultural selection help to regulate endogenous competition for credentials and resources, thereby constraining minority and majority students to a differential structure of 'choices' with respect to the job market and ultimately to the differential exploitation of their labor power by employers. Of course, the reverse is also true in that teachers' and administrators' perceptions of the structure of opportunities for minorities (exploitation relations) can have a significant impact on the processes of cultural selection of minority and majority students to ability groups and curricular tracks in schooling (Sarup 1986; Spring 1985; Troyna and Williams 1986). By virtue of the operation of these four types of relations—of competition, exploitation, domination, and cultural selection—and their complex interaction with dynamics of race, class, and gender, schooling is a nonsynchronous situation or context. In this nonsynchronous context, racial dynamics constantly shape and are in turn shaped by the other forms of structuration, namely, gender and class (Brown 1985).

The concept of nonsynchrony begins to get at the complexity of causal motion and effects 'on the ground', as it were. It also raises questions about the nature, exercise, and multiple determination of power within that middle ground of everyday practices in schooling (Scott and Kerkvliet 1986). The fact is that, as Hicks (1981) suggests, dynamic relations of race, class, and gender do not unproblematically reproduce each other. These relations are complex and often have contradictory effects in institutional settings. The intersection of race, class, and gender at the local level of schooling can lead to interruptions, discontinuities, augmentations, or diminutions of the original effects of any one of these dynamics. Thus, for example, while schooling in a racist society like the US is by definition a 'racist institution' (Carmichael and Hamilton 1967), its racial character might not be the dominant variable shaping conflict over inequality in every schooling situation. That is to say that (a) the particular mix of history, subjectivities, interests, and capacities that minority and majority actors bring to the institutional context, and (b) the way in which these actors negotiate and 'settle' the rules of the game (the relations of competition, exploitation, domination, and cultural selection) will determine the dominant character and directionality of effects in the specific school setting.

Such a 'dominant' character refers to the relations along which 'endogenous differences' in the school are principally articulated. These dominant relations thus constitute an 'articulating principle' (Laclau and Mouffe 1982, 1985), pulling the entire ensemble of relations in the school setting into a 'unity' or focus for conflict. Such an articulating princi-

ple may be race, class, or gender. For instance, it can be argued that a sex-dominant situation exists within American university education with respect to struggles over women's studies and the very status of women in academe itself. Gender has been the articulating principle that has sharpened our focus on issues around the fundamental white male privilege operating in the university system with respect to the differentiated organization of curricular knowledge, unequal patterns of selection and appointment to tenure-track faculty positions, unequal relations between male professors and female students, and so on. The issue of gender has had multiplier effects, illuminating flash points of difference across a range of traditional male-dominated disciplines. Sexual antagonism within academe has focused our attention on the *modus operandi* of the university and its relations of competition, exploitation, domination, and cultural selection.

The powerful impact of sexual antagonism within the university has also had the effect of masking racial antagonism and or determining the political terms on which racial conflicts may be fought. (One should hasten to note that the opposite was true in the 1960s, when the balance of forces of contestation tended toward the prominence of racial difference as the articulating principle for conflicts over inequality in education.) Issues of minority failure and the under-representation of minorities at every level within the tertiary section of American education continue to be peripheral to the dominant Anglo-centric agenda in the university system. Figure 35. 2 illustrates the interaction of race, gender, and class relations in a sex-dominant situation. In this model of nonsynchrony, relations of sexual antagonism and solidarity are augmented while race and class relations are diminished. The principal sources of conflict, mobilization, and counter-mobilization within given educational institutions may then be around issues concerning gender relations: sexual harassment, women's studies, new codes of conduct within the university with regards to relations among the sexes, and so forth. This might not necessarily mean that issues around race are totally ignored. Indeed, one result might be that issues concerning minority women and their interests and aspirations would become more directly strategic and pivotal in the overall effort to secure reform in race relations in education—a situation in which it could be said that race-relations struggles in education benefited from a highly augmented focus on issues concerning gender. (Clearly the reverse was true in the 1960s.)

Within the current sociological and educational literature, there are a number of practical examples of the contradictory effects of the intersection of race, class and gender in settings inside and outside schools that can help to illustrate the nonsynchronous model I have outlined.

The work of researchers such as Omi and Winant (1986) and Sarup (1986) directs our attention to the issues of nonsynchrony and contradiction in minority/majority relations in education and society and suggests not only their complexity but the impossibility of predicting the effects of these dynamic relations in any formulaic way based on a monolithic view of race. In their discussion of educational and political institutions, Omi and Winant and Sarup have emphasized the fact that racial and sexual antagonisms can, at times, 'cut at right angles to class solidarity'.

The work of Marable (1985) and Spring (1985) focuses our attention in the opposite direction by pointing to the way in which class antagonisms have tended to undermine racial solidarity among minority groups involved in mainstream institutions. For instance,

Marable and Spring argue that since the civil rights gains of the 1960s, there has been a powerful socioeconomic and cultural division within the African American community. This has been principally expressed in terms of the evolution of an upwardly mobile black middle class which has sought to distance itself in social, educational, and political terms from an increasingly impoverished black underclass. Spring contends that such class antagonism operates as a determining variable in critical relationships between the black community and mainstream educational institutions. As we shall see, such class antagonism also influences and is vitally influenced by the endogenous relations of differentiation already existing within the school setting.

As a case in point, Spring (1985) reports on a longitudinal study of the class dynamics operating within a black suburban community ('Black Suburbia') and the way in which these dynamics get expressed in the relationship of black students and their parents to the school system. Spring's account begins in the mid-1960s, when a black professional middle-class (PMC) population moved into a midwestern suburb, formerly populated predominantly by whites. The new residents of Black Suburbia quickly embraced the predominantly white-administered school system. As the constituents of the 'new' middle class in the district, black PMC parents and

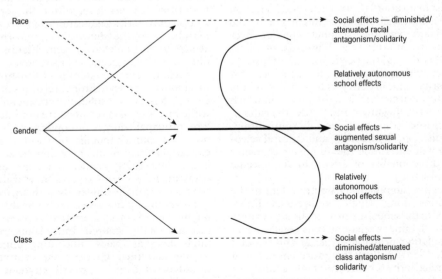

Fig. 35. 2. A schematic representation of a sex-dominant context

their children readily granted legitimacy to the existing relations of differentiation (cultural selection, competition, and so forth) operating in the schools in exchange for access to 'quality education'. They saw the schools as guarantors of continued upward mobility for their children. According to Spring:

A study of the community [Black Suburbia] in the late 1960s showed the mobility concerns and educational aspirations of the new black population . . . The study found that both the middle-aged and young middle-class black residents had high expectations of upward mobility and believed that *quality* schools were a major element in *quality* community. The population group labeled 'New, Middle-Aged, Black Middle-Class Residents' were earning more than $10,000 a year and were employed as managers, proprietors, and professionals. This group was found to have an 'extraordinarily high degree' of expectations for continuing upward mobility and concern about the quality of schools. (Spring 1985 : 105–6)

The term 'quality school' indeed summarized an ideological and strategic trade-off or 'settlement' that was tacitly implicated in the overwhelming black PMC support for the white-administered school system. But this settlement between the school system and its new PMC patrons was soon to be imperiled by a change in the demographic and cultural milieu of the Black Suburbia community and its schools. And both the expectations of upward mobility and the high educational aspirations of the black PMC residents who had arrived in the late 1960s were, by the 1970s, 'threatened by the rapid influx of a poor black population' (Spring 1985: 106). This influx of low-income blacks dramatically altered the social class composition of Black Suburbia: 'Between 1970 and 1973 the percentage of children from welfare families increased . . . from 16 to 51 percent. In other words, the migration of upwardly mobile middle-class blacks was followed by the rapid migration of black welfare families' (Spring 1985: 106).

Teachers responded negatively to the entrance of increased numbers of low-income black students into the school system and the 'standard of education' in Black Suburbia schools declined:

One of the first things to happen was that the educational expectations of the mainly white teachers and administrators in the school system began to fall. This seemed to be caused by the assumption of

the white school staff that the blacks moving into the community were not interested in education and would create major problems in the school system. (Spring 1985: 108)

These developments precipitated a crisis of legitimacy in the school system's relations to its black constituents. However, the racial response of the school system to black students was not met or challenged by a united front among the black residents of Black Suburbia. Indeed, class antagonism between the more affluent blacks and the lower class black residents intensified both in the schools and in the community. PMC black students blamed the lower class students for the sharp decline in educational standards in the schools. They complained that the teachers were incapable of controlling the 'rowdies'—a code word for low-income black students. This class antagonism spilled over into the community. Many black PMC parents expressed the fear that their children would be corrupted by the 'rowdy-culture' of welfare kids who 'were organized into natural street groupings', as one parent put it (Spring 1985: 108). As class antagonism intensified, the more affluent black parents took the further step of withdrawing their children from the public schools and sending them to private institutions. To put the matter directly, black PMC parents lost confidence in the public schools because they perceived teachers as having failed to control the 'corrupting' influence of low-income students, whom these parents blamed along with their teachers for the declining standard of education.

From the perspectives of these PMC black residents, the Black Suburbia school system had failed to deliver on its side of a tacit agreement and black students stood to suffer in competitive relations for credentials and long-term futures in the labor market. According to Spring's account, the racially motivated strategies of cultural selection that obtained in the Black Suburbia schools, had, as a response to the influx of low-income students, now come full circle to handicap black middle-class youth as well. But ultimately, in this highly provocative racial situation, the response of the residents of Black Suburbia to their school system was highly contradictory and nonsynchronous. Racial dynamics and identity were clearly 'dominated' by class interests. To say the least, the interests of black PMC residents and their low-income counterparts diverged. Resulting class antagonism undermined racial solidarity among black residents and weakened their collective ability to negotiate with the white-administered school system or challenge the racial basis of the poor quality education that the public schools were offering to their children.

Nkomo (1984), in his discussion of the dynamics of race/class relations in the South African educational system, describes an example of a nonsynchronous racial situation. In this case, Nkomo asserts that the enormous constraints placed on the aspirations and economic futures of black students and the blatant Afrikaner ideological domination of black universities have had unintended effects nonsynchronous with the interests of the apartheid state. High levels of cultural alienation experienced in South African Bantu universities by both black students from urban PMC backgrounds and working-class students from the Bantustans have heightened the bonds of racial solidarity between these youth of different class backgrounds. But racial solidarity among black students is certainly not a policy goal of the South African government. Indeed, ever since the late 1950s, the South African government has sought to balkanize South African black youth by creating highly restrictive, ethnically segregated universities in the Bantustans. The Afrikaner regime has attempted to maintain existing relations of racial domination and exploitation of South African blacks by pursuing a policy of 'separate development' (Nkomo 1984). In the area of higher education, this policy of balkanization has meant, for example, that student enrollment at the University of Zululand is limited exclusively to the Zulu and Swazi ethnic groups. And while, prior to the late 1950s, Indians and 'coloreds' could go to the University College of Fort Hare, the 1959 Transfer Act restricted enrollment at this college to Xhosa-speaking Africans only (Nkomo 1984).

The clear intent of such divide-and-conquer policies of the South African government was to promote the intensification of intra- and inter-ethnic differences among Africans, Indians, and 'coloreds' as a means of disorganizing the political capacities and the collective will of the subordinated racial groups in South Africa. But Nkomo informs us that the South African state's domination of black universities goes even further. Through the Department of Bantu Education, there is direct state control over the curriculum content, student admissions, academic staff appointments, and finances of these black universities. This abnormal state control is peculiar to the Bantu universities, since the 'European' universities in South Africa enjoy academic autonomy in consonance with the western tradition.

But it is precisely this intense racialization of the South African state's relationship to the black universities and its coercive attempt to consolidate relations of domination in these educational institutions that have led to a radical incongruity between black students' aspirations and the official university establishment. These contradictions and frustrations within the apartheid Bantu educational system have provoked a critical consciousness among urban PMC black students and their less privileged counterparts from the Bantustans that has allowed them to band together in a common struggle against the apartheid system. This development is not without its touch of irony: Bantu universities created by the South African government as part of the apartheid structure and developed to facilitate exploitation by undermining political alliances among black South African youth have had the unintended effect of galvanizing powerful cultural resistance and racial solidarity against the apartheid system. Indeed, these Bantu universities have been among the principal sites of racial mobilization and struggle against apartheid in the 1980s and now in the 1990s.

The example of the black South African university is illustrative of a race-dominant nonsynchronous situation. As Nkomo (1984) demonstrates, racial solidarity and its obverse, racial antagonism, constitute the dominant principles along which unequal social relations in these Bantu universities are ordered, organized and culturally expressed—this, despite the significant economic and social class divides that exist among black South African students.

A final example gets us closer to the nonsynchronous dynamics of unequal social relations in a number of classrooms in the United States. Based on findings from a study of 'face-to-face interactions' in six desegregated elementary school classrooms in a midwestern industrial city, Linda Grant (1984) concludes that 'Black females' experiences in desegregated schools . . . differ from those of other race-gender groups and cannot be fully understood . . . by extrapolating from the research on females or research on blacks' (p. 99).

Grant (1984) conducted detailed observations of the classrooms of six teachers (all women, three blacks and three whites) at the two schools, Ridgeley and Glendon, involved in her two–year study. Some 40 per cent of the 139 students in the first-grade classrooms studied were black. Among other things, Grant found that strategies of evaluation and cultural selection (tracking, ability grouping, and so forth) varied considerably according to 'race-gender group' (black males, black females, white females, and white males). For instance, black females were more likely than any other race-gender group to be labeled 'non-academic' (p. 102). This was particularly true of the evaluations by white teachers:

White teachers, however, gave more attention to nonacademic criteria. In fact, they made proportionally fewer comments of an academic nature about black girls than any other race-gender group. [For example,] assessments of black females contrasted markedly with these teachers' assessments of white males, for which academic criteria predominated . . . (p. 102)

While teachers identified both black and white females as more mature and 'helpful' than their male counterparts, white girls were more likely to be labeled as 'cognitively mature and ready for school' (Grant 1984: 102). In contrast, black girls were labeled as 'socially mature', and Grant contends that teachers exploited this 'social maturity'. Teachers' strategies of cultural selection also had an impact on domination relations of teacher to student and student to student in these first-grade classrooms. Thus, teachers tended to deploy black girls as 'go-betweens' when they wanted to communicate rules and convey messages informally to black boys (p. 106). Race-gender group differences were also reproduced in terms of the first graders' access to instructional opportunity as well as in the students' informal relations and orientation to teachers in the Ridgeley and Glendon elementary schools:

Although generally compliant with teachers' rules, black females were less tied to teachers than white girls were and approached them only when they had a specific need to do so. White girls spent more

time with teachers, prolonging questions into chats about personal issues. Black girls' contacts were briefer, more task related, and often on behalf of a peer rather than self. (Grant 1984: 107)

Black males were even less likely than black females—or any other race-gender group—to have extended chats with teachers. And relations between black males and their female teachers were defined by mutual estrangement. Indeed, Grant suggests in another article based on the same data (Grant, 1985) that these teachers were afraid of or 'threatened' by their black male students. Nevertheless, teachers tended to identify at least one black male in each class whom they singled out as an academic achiever or a 'superstar'. In none of the six elementary school classrooms that Grant studied was any of the black girls singled out as a high academic achiever (Grant 1984: 100). Instead, Grant maintains, black girls were typified as 'average achievers' and assigned to 'average' or 'below average' track placements and ability groups.

Ultimately, the effects of the processes of cultural selection that obtained in the classrooms that Grant (1984) observed were nonsynchronous. Teachers did not relate to their black students or white students in any consistent or monolithic way. Gender differences powerfully influenced and modified the differential ways in which teachers evaluated, assessed, diagnosed, labeled and tracked black and white students. The influence of gender on the racial response of teachers to their students was particularly evident in the case of black females. In significant ways, teachers emphasized the social, caring and nurturing qualities of the black females in their first-grade classrooms. In subtle ways, teachers encouraged 'black girls to pursue social contacts, rather than press towards high academic achievement' (p. 103). Consequently, Grant concludes that desegregated education at the elementary schools she studied had unintended negative (racial) costs for all black children. The processes of cultural selection that obtained in the desegregated classrooms she observed worked to the disadvantage of black children with respect to competition for instructional opportunity, teacher time, and resources in these schools. Grant also suggests that existing processes of cultural differentiation not only served to constrain the structure of educational opportunity available to black students within the school setting, but also helped to structure their incorporation into exploitation relations from the very start of their school careers. For black females these costs were particularly severe and were determined strongly by gender. This meant that black girls' experiences in the six desegregated classrooms were systematically nonsynchronous or qualitatively different from those of black boys or any other race-gender group:

The emphasis on black girls' social rather than academic skills, which occurs particularly in white-teacher classrooms, might point to a hidden cost of desegregation for black girls. Although they are usually the top students in black classes, they lose this stature to white children in desegregated rooms. Their development seems to become less balanced, with emphasis on social skills . . . Black girls' everyday schooling experiences seem more likely to nudge them toward stereotypical roles of black women than toward [academic] alternatives. These include serving others and maintaining peaceable ties among diverse persons rather than developing one's own skills. (Grant 1984: 109)

Conclusion

The findings of curriculum and educational researchers such as Grant (1984, 1985), Nkomo (1984) and Spring (1985) help to illustrate and clarify the complex workings of racial logics in the highly differentiated environment that exists in school settings. By drawing attention to contradiction and nonsynchrony in educational processes of cultural selection, competition, exploitation, and domination, these critical researchers directly challenge mainstream single-group studies of inequality in schooling that have tended to isolate the variable of race from gender and class. Instead, the work of Grant and others underscores the need to examine the historical specificity and variability of race and its nonsynchronous interaction with forms of class and gender structuration in education. Monolithic theories of racial inequality suppress such an understanding of these complexities and treat racial groups as biological and cultural 'unities' (Troyna and Williams 1986).

The nonsynchronous approach to the study of inequality in schooling alerts us to the fact that different race–class–gender groups not only have qualitatively different experiences in schools, but actually exist in constitutive tension, often engage in active competition with each other, receive different forms of rewards, sanctions, and evaluation, and are ultimately structured into differential futures. The critical theoretical and practical task, then, as Hall (1980) suggests, is one of 'radically decoding' the specific relations and nuances of particular historical and institutional contexts:

One needs to know how different groups were inserted historically, and the relations which have tended to erode and transform, or to preserve these distinctions through time—not simply as residues and traces of previous modes, but as active structuring principles of the present society. Racial categories *alone* will *not* provide or explain these. (Hall 1980: 339)

The work of Grant (1984), Nkomo (1984), Spring (1985), and Sarup (1986) has furthered our understanding of the complex workings of race and other dynamics in educational institutions. Their findings are also important in helping us to deconstruct the multiple determination of power in the school setting and the way in which such micropolitics can undermine the viability of conventional approaches to curriculum reform. What is abundantly clear is that monolithic or homogeneous strategies of curriculum reform that attempt to ignore or avoid the contradictions of race, class, and gender at the institutional level will be of limited usefulness to minority youth.

References

Apple, M. W. (1988), 'Redefining inequality: Authoritarian populism and the conservative restoration', *Teacher's College Record*, 90 (2), 167–84.
—— , and Beyer, L. (eds) (1988), *The Curriculum: Problems, Politics, and Possibilities* (Albany: State University of New York Press).
—— , and Weis, L. (eds) (1983), *Ideology and Practice in Schooling* (Philadelphia: Temple University Press).
Bonacich, E. (1981), 'Capitalism and race relations in South Africa: A split labor market analysis', in Zeitlin, M. (ed.) *Political Power and Social Theory* (Volume 2) (Greenwich, Ct.: JAI Press, 239–77).
Bowles, S., and Gintis, H. (1976), *Schooling in Capitalist America* (New York: Basic Books).
Brown, K. (1985), 'Turning a blind eye: Racial oppression and the unintended consequences of white non-racism', *Sociological Review* (33), 670–90.

Burawoy, M. (1981), 'The capitalist state in South Africa: Marxist and sociological perspectives on race and class', in Zeitlin, M. (ed.) *Political Power and Social Theory* (Volume 2) (Greenwich, Ct.: JAI Press, 279–335).

Carmichael, S., and Hamilton, C. (1967), *Black Power* (New York: Vintage).

Carnoy, M. (1974), *Education and Cultural Imperialism* (New York: Longman).

——, and Levin, H. (1985), *Schooling and Work in the Democratic State* (Stanford: Stanford University Press).

Crichlow, W. (1990), A social analysis of black youth commitment and disaffection in an urban high school. Unpublished Ed.D. Dissertation (School of Education and Human Development: University of Rochester).

Durkheim, E. (1977), *The Evolution of Educational Thought: Lectures on the Formation and Development of Secondary Education in France* (London: Routledge and Kegan Paul).

Eysenck, J., and Kamin, L. (1981), *The Intelligence Controversy* (New York: John Wiley and Sons).

Gamoran, A., and Berends, M. (1986), *The Effects of Stratification in Secondary Schools: Synthesis of Survey and Ethnographic Research* (Madison: National Center on Effective Secondary Schools, University of Wisconsin-Madison).

Giroux, H. (1985), 'Introduction', in Freire, P. *The Politics of Education* (South Hadley; Ma.: Bergin and Garvey).

Gobineau, J. (1915), *The Inequality of Human Races* (London: Heinemann).

Gould, S. (1981), *The Mismeasure of Man* (New York: W. W. Norton).

Gramsci, A. (1983), *Selection from the Prison Notebooks* (New York: International Publishers).

Grant, L. (1984), 'Black females' "place" in desegregated classrooms', *Sociology of Education* (57), 98–111.

—— (1985), Uneasy alliances: Black males, teachers, and peers in desegregated classroom. Unpublished Manuscript, Department of Sociology, Southern Illinois University.

Hall, S. (1980), 'Race, articulation, and societies structured in dominance', in UNESCO (eds) *Sociological Theories: Race and Colonialism* (Paris: UNESCO, 305–45).

—— (1986), 'Gramsci's relevance to the analysis of race', *Communication Inquiry* (10), 5–27.

Harris, M. (1968), *The Rise of Anthropological Theory* (New York: Thomas Crowell).

Henriques, J. (1984), 'Social psychology and the politics of racism', in Henriques, J. (ed.) *Changing the Subject* (London: Methuen, 60–89).

Hicks, E. (1981), 'Cultural Marxism: Nonsynchrony and feminist practice', in Sargent, L. (ed.) *Women and Revolution* (Boston: South End Press, 219–38).

Hogan, D. (1982), 'Education and class formation: The peculiarities of the Americans', in Apple, M. W. (ed.) *Cultural and Economic Reproduction in Education* (Boston: Routledge and Kegan Paul, 32–78).

JanMohamed, A. (1987), 'Introduction: Toward a theory of minority discourse', *Cultural Critique* (6), 5–11.

—— and Lloyd, D. (1987), 'Introduction: Minority discourse—what is to be done', *Cultural Critique* (7), 5–17.

Jensen, A. (1969), 'How much can we boost IQ and scholastic achievement?' *Harvard Educational Review* (Reprint Series No. 2), 1–23.

—— (1981), *Straight Talk About Mental Tests* (New York: Free Press).

—— (1984), 'Political ideologies and educational research', *Phi Delta Kappan* (65/7), 460.

Jordan, W. (1968), *White over Black: American Attitudes Toward the Negro, 1550–1812* (Baltimore: Penguin Books).

Laclau, E., and Mouffe, C. (1982), 'Recasting Marxism: Hegemony and new political movements', *Socialist Review* (66/12), 91–113.

—— —— (1985), *Hegemony and Socialist Strategy: Toward a Radical Democratic Politics* (London: Verso).

Marable, M. (1985), *Black American Politics* (London: Verso).

McCarthy, C., and Apple, M. W. (1988), 'Race, class, and gender in American educational research: Toward a nonsynchronous parallelist position', in Weis, L. (ed.) *Class, Race and Gender in American Education* (Albany: State University of New York, 9–39).

Morton, S. (1839), *Crania Americana or, a Comparative View of the Skulls of Various Aboriginal Nations of North and South America* (Philadelphia: John Pennington).

Nkomo, M. (1984), *Student Culture and Activism in Black South African Universities* (Wesport, Ct.: Greenwood Press).

Ogbu, J. (1978), *Minority Education and Caste* (New York: Academic Press).

—— and Matute-Bianchi, M. (1986), 'Understanding sociocultural factors in education: Knowledge, identity, and school adjustment', in California State Department of Education (ed.) *Beyond Language: Social and Cultural Factors in Schooling Language Minority Students* (Los Angeles: Evaluation, Dissemination and Assessment Center, California State University, 73–142).

Omi, M., and Winant, H. (1986), *Racial Formation in the United States* (New York: Routledge and Kegan Paul).

Rist, R. (1970), 'Social class and teacher expectations: The self-fulfilling prophecy in ghetto education', *Harvard Educational Review* (40), 441–51.

Roman, L., Christian-Smith, L., and Ellsworth, E. (1988), *Becoming Feminine: The Politics of Popular Culture* (Lewes: Falmer Press).

Sarup, M. (1986), *The Politics of Multi-racial Education* (London: Routledge and Kegan Paul).

Scott, J. C., and Kerkvliet, T. (eds) (1986), *Everyday Forms of Peasant Resistance in South East Asia* (London: Frank Cases).

Spencer, D. (1984), 'The home and school lives of women teachers', *The Elementary School Journal* (84), 293–8.

Spring, J. H. (1985), American Education: An Introduction to Social and Political Aspects (New York: Longman).

Thompson, E. P. (1966), *The Making of the Working Class* (New York: Vintage Books).

Troyna, B., and Williams, J. (1986), *Racism, Education, and the State* (London: Croom Helm).

Wellman, D. (1977), *Portraits of White Racism* (Cambridge: Cambridge University Press).

West, C. (1988), 'Marxist theory and the specificity of Afro-American oppression', in Nelson, C., and Grossberg, L. (eds) *Marxism and the Interpretation of Culture* (Urbana, Ill.: University of Illinois Press, 17–33).

Whitty, G. (1985), *Sociology and School Knowledge* (London: Methuen).

Williams, E. (1964), *Capitalism and Slavery* (London: Andre Deutsch).

36

On Race and Voice: Challenges for Liberal Education in the 1990s

Chandra Talpade Mohanty

Feminism and the Language of Difference

'Isn't the whole point to have a voice?' This is the last sentence of a recent essay by Marnia Lazreg (1988) on writing as a woman on women in Algeria. Lazreg examines academic feminist scholarship on women in the Middle East and North Africa in the context of what she calls a 'Western gynocentric' notion of the difference between First and Third World women. Arguing for an understanding of 'intersubjectivity' as the basis for comparison across cultures and histories, Lazreg formulates the problem of ethnocentrism and the related question of voice in this way:

To take intersubjectivity into consideration when studying Algerian women or other Third World women means seeing their lives as meaningful, coherent, and understandable instead of being infused 'by us' with doom and sorrow. It means that their lives like 'ours' are structured by economic, political, and cultural factors. It means that these women, like 'us,' are engaged in the process of adjusting, often shaping, at times resisting and even transforming their environment. It means that they have their own individuality; they are 'for themselves' instead of being 'for us.' An appropriation of their singular individuality to fit the generalizing categories of 'our' analyses is an assault on their integrity and on their identity. (p. 98)

In my own work I have argued in a similar way against the use of analytic categories and political positionings in feminist studies that discursively present Third World women as a homogeneous, undifferentiated group leading truncated lives, victimized by the combined weight of 'their' traditions, cultures, and beliefs, and 'our' (Eurocentric) history.[1] In examining particular assumptions of feminist scholarship that are uncritically grounded in Western humanism and its modes of 'disinterested scholarship,' I have tried to demonstrate that this scholarship inadvertently produces Western women as the only legitimate subjects of struggle, while Third World women are heard as fragmented, inarticulate voices in (and from) the dark. Arguing against a hastily derived notion of 'universal sisterhood' that assumes a commonality of gender experience across race and national lines, I have suggested the complexity of our historical (and positional) differences and the need for creating an analytical space for understanding Third World women as the *subjects* of our various struggles *in history*. Other scholars have made similar arguments, and the question of what we might provisionally call 'Third World women's *voices*' has begun to be addressed seriously in feminist scholarship.

In the last decade there has been a blossoming of feminist discourse around questions of 'racial difference' and 'pluralism.' While this work is often an important corrective to earlier middle-class (white) characterizations of sexual difference, the goal of the analysis of difference and the challenge of race was not pluralism as the proliferation of discourse on ethnicities as discrete and separate cultures. The challenge of race resides in a fundamental reconceptualization of our categories of analysis so that differences can be historically specified and understood as part of larger political

From *Cultural Critique* (1990).

processes and systems.[2] The central issue, then, is not one of merely *acknowledging* difference; rather, the more difficult question concerns the kind of difference that is acknowledged and engaged. Difference seen as benign variation (diversity), for instance, rather than as conflict, struggle, or the threat of disruption, bypasses power as well as history to suggest a harmonious, empty pluralism.[3] On the other hand, difference defined as asymmetrical and incommensurate cultural spheres situated within hierarchies of domination and resistance cannot be accommodated within a discourse of 'harmony in diversity.' A strategic critique of the contemporary language of difference, diversity, and power thus would be crucial to a feminist project concerned with revolutionary social change.

In the best, self-reflexive traditions of feminist inquiry, the production of knowledge about cultural and geographical Others is no longer seen as apolitical and disinterested. But while feminist activists and progressive scholars have made a significant dent in the colonialist and colonizing feminist scholarship of the late seventies and early eighties, this does not mean that questions of what Lazreg calls 'intersubjectivity,' or of history vis-à-vis Third World peoples, have been successfully articulated.[4]

In any case, *scholarship*, feminist, Marxist, or Third World, is not the only site for the production of knowledge about Third World women/peoples.[5] The very same questions (as those suggested in relation to scholarship) can be raised in relation to our teaching and learning practices in the classroom, as well as the discursive and managerial practices of American colleges and universities. Feminists writing about race and racism have had a lot to say about scholarship, but perhaps our pedagogical and institutional practices and their relation to scholarship have not been examined with quite the same care and attention. Radical educators have long argued that the academy and the classroom itself are not mere sites of instruction. They are also political and cultural sites that represent accommodations and contestations over knowledge by differently empowered social constituencies.[6] Thus teachers and students produce, reinforce, recreate, resist, and transform ideas about race, gender, and difference in the classroom. Also, the academic institutions in which we

are located create similar paradigms, canons, and voices that embody and transcribe race and gender.

It is this frame of institutional and pedagogical practice that I examine in this essay. Specifically, I analyze the operation and management of discourses of race and difference in two educational sites: the women's studies classroom and the workshops on 'diversity' for upper-level (largely white) administrators. The links between these two educational sites lie in the (often active) *creation* of discourses of 'difference.' In other words, I suggest that educational practices as they are shaped and reshaped at these sites cannot be analyzed as merely transmitting already codified ideas of difference. These practices often produce, codify, and even rewrite histories of race and colonialism in the name of difference. But let me begin the analysis with a brief discussion of the academy as the site of political struggle and transformation.

Knowledge and Location in the US Academy

A number of educators, Paulo Freire among them, have argued that education represents both a struggle for meaning and a struggle over power relations. Thus, education becomes a central terrain where power and politics operate out of the lived culture of individuals and groups situated in asymmetrical social and political positions. This way of understanding the academy entails a critique of education as the mere accumulation of disciplinary knowledges that can be exchanged on the world market for upward mobility. There are much larger questions at stake in the academy these days, not the least of which are questions of self and collective knowledge of marginal peoples and the recovery of alternative, oppositional histories of domination and struggle. Here, disciplinary parameters matter less than questions of power, history, and self-identity. For knowledge, the very act of knowing, is related to the power of self-definition. This definition of knowledge is central to the pedagogical projects of fields such as women's studies, black studies, and ethnic studies. By their very location in the academy, fields such as women's studies are grounded in definitions of difference, difference that attempts to resist incorporation and appropriation by providing a space for historically silenced peoples to construct knowledge. These knowledges have always been fundamentally oppositional, while running the risk of accommodation and assimilation and the consequent depoliticization in the academy. It is only in the late twentieth century, on the heels of domestic and global oppositional political movements, that the boundaries dividing knowledge into its traditional disciplines have been shaken loose, and new, often heretical, knowledges have emerged modifying the structures of knowledge and power as we have inherited them. In other words, new analytic spaces have been opened up in the academy, spaces that make possible thinking of knowledge as praxis, of knowledge as embodying the very seeds of transformation and change. The appropriation of these analytic spaces and the challenge of radical educational practice are thus to involve the development of critical knowledges (what women's, black, and ethnic studies attempt), and simultaneously, to critique knowledge itself.

Education for critical consciousness or critical pedagogy, as it is sometimes called, requires a reformulation of the knowledge-as-accumulated-capital model of education and focuses instead on the link between the historical configuration of social forms and the way they work subjectively. This issue of subjectivity represents a realization of the fact that who we are, how we act, what we think, and what stories we tell become more intelligible within an epistemological framework that begins by recognizing existing hegemonic histories. The issue of subjectivity and voice thus concerns the effort to understand our specific locations in the educational process and in the institutions through which we are constituted. Resistance lies in self-conscious engagement with dominant, normative discourses and representations and in the active creation of oppositional analytic and cultural spaces. Resistance that is random and isolated is clearly not as effective as that which is mobilized through systemic politicized practices of teaching and learning. Uncovering and reclaiming subjugated knowledges is one way to lay claim to alternative histories. But these knowledges need to be understood and defined *pedagogically*, as questions of strategy and practice as well as of scholarship, in order to transform educational institutions radi-

cally. And this, in turn, requires taking the questions of experience seriously.

To this effect, I draw on scholarship on and by Third World educators in higher education, on an analysis of the effects of my own pedagogical practices, on documents about 'affirmative action' and 'diversity in the curriculum' published by the administration of the college where I work, and on my own observations and conversations over the past three years.[7] I do so in order to suggest that the effect of the proliferation of ideologies of pluralism in the 1960s and 1970s, in the context of the (limited) implementation of affirmative action in institutions of higher education, has been to create what might be called the Race Industry, an industry that is responsible for the management, commodification, and domestication of race on American campuses. This commodification of race determines the politics of voice for Third World peoples, whether they/we happen to be faculty, students, administrators, or service staff. This, in turn, has long-term effects on the definitions of the identity and agency of nonwhite people in the academy.

There are a number of urgent reasons for undertaking such an analysis: the need to assess the material and ideological effects of affirmative action policies within liberal (rather than conservative—Bloom or Hirsch style) discourses and institutions that profess a commitment to pluralism and social change, the need to understand this management of race in the liberal academy in relation to a larger discourse on race and discrimination within the neoconservatism of the U.S., and the need for Third World feminists to move outside the arena of (sometimes) exclusive engagement with racism in white women's movements and scholarship and to broaden the scope of our struggles to the academy as a whole.

The management of gender, race, class, and sexuality are inextricably linked in the public arena. The New Right agenda since the mid-1970s makes this explicit: busing, gun rights, and welfare are clearly linked to the issues of reproductive and sexual rights.[8] And the links between abortion rights (gender-based struggles) and affirmative action (struggles over race and racism) are becoming clearer in the 1990s. While the most challenging critiques of hegemonic feminism were launched in the late 1970s and the 1980s, the present historical moment necessitates taking on board institutional discourses that actively construct and maintain a discourse of difference and pluralism. This in turn calls for assuming responsibility for the politics of voice as it is institutionalized in the academy's 'liberal' response to the very questions feminism and other oppositional discourses have raised.[9]

Black/Ethnic Studies and Women's Studies: Intersections and Confluences

For us, there is nothing optional about 'black experience' and/or 'black studies': we must know ourselves.

June Jordan

Unlike most academic disciplines, the origins of black, ethnic, and women's studies programs can be traced to oppositional social movements. In particular, the civil rights movement, the women's movement, and other Third World liberation struggles fueled the demands for a knowledge and history 'of our own.' June Jordan's claim that 'we must know ourselves' suggests the urgency embedded in the formation of black studies in the late 1960s. Between 1966 and 1970 most American colleges and universities added courses on Afro-American experience and history to their curriculums. This was the direct outcome of a number of sociohistorical factors, not the least of which was an increase in black student enrollment in higher education and the broad-based call for a fundamental transformation of a racist, Eurocentric curriculum. Among the earliest programs were the black and African-American studies programs at San Francisco State and Cornell, both of which came into being in 1968, on the heels of militant political organizing on the part of students and faculty at these institutions (Huggins 1985; Blassingame 1973). A symposium on black studies in early 1968 at Yale University not only inaugurated African-American studies at Yale, but also marked a watershed in the national development of black studies programs (Robinson, Foster, and Ogilvie 1969). In Spring 1969, the University of California at Berkeley instituted a department of ethnic studies, divided into Afro-American, Chicano, contemporary Asian-American, and Native American studies divisions.

A number of women's studies programs also came into being around this time. The first women's studies program was formed in 1969 at San Diego State University. Today 520 such programs exist across the United States (National Women's Studies Association Task Force 1990; Minnich et al. 1988). Women's studies programs often drew on the institutional frameworks and structures of existing interdisciplinary programs such as black and ethnic studies. In addition, besides sharing political origins, an interdisciplinary project, and foregrounding questions of social and political inequality in their knowledge base, women's, black, and ethnic studies programs increasingly share pedagogical and research methods. Such programs thus create the possibility of a counter-hegemonic discourse and oppositional analytic spaces within the institution. Of course, since these programs are most often located within the boundaries of conservative or liberal-white-male institutions, they face questions of co-optation and accommodation.

In an essay examining the relations among ethnicity, ideology, and the academy, Rosaura Sanchez (1987: 80–8) maintains that new academic programs arise out of specific interests in bodies of knowledge. Sanchez traces the origins of ethnic and women's studies programs, however, to a defensive political move: the state's institutionalization of a discourse of reform in response to the civil rights movement.

[E]thnic studies programs were instituted at a moment when the university had to speak a particular language to quell student protests and to ensure that university research and business could be conducted as usual. The university was able to create and integrate these programs administratively under its umbrella, allowing on the one hand, for a potential firecracker to diffuse itself and, on the other, moving on to prepare the ground for future assimilation of the few surviving faculty into existing departments. (p. 86)

Sanchez identifies the pressures (assimilation and co-optation versus isolation and marginalization) that ethnic studies programs have inherited in the 1990s. In fact, it is precisely in the face of the pressure to assimilate that questions of political strategy and of pedagogical and institutional practice assume paramount importance.

For such programs, progress (measured by institutional power, number of people of color in faculty and administration, effect on the general curricula, etc.) has been slow. Since the 1970s, there have also been numerous conflicts between ethnic, black, and women's studies programs. One example of these tensions is provided by Niara Sudarkasa. Writing in 1987 (3–6) about the effect of affirmative action on black faculty and administrators in higher education, she argues: 'As a matter of record, however, both in the corporate world and in higher education, the progress of white females as a result of affirmative action has far out-stripped that for blacks and other minorities.' Here Sudarkasa is pointing to a persistent presence of racism in the differential access and mobility of white women and people of color in higher education. She goes on to argue that charges of 'reverse discrimination' against white people are unfounded because affirmative action has had the effect of privileging white women above men and women of color. Thus, for Sudarkasa, charges of reverse discrimination leveled at minorities 'amount to a sanction of continued discrimination by insisting that inequalities resulting from privileges historically reserved for whites as a *group* must now be perpetuated in the name of "justice" for the *individual*' (p. 4). This process of individualization of histories of dominance is also characteristic of educational institutions and processes in general, where the experiences of different constituencies are defined according to the logic of cultural pluralism.

In fact, this individualization of power hierarchies and of structures of discrimination suggests the convergence of liberal and neoconservative ideas about gender and race in the academy. Individualization, in this context, is accomplished through the fundamentally class-based process of professionalization. In any case, the post-Reagan years (characterized by financial cutbacks in education, the consolidation of the New Right and the right-to-life lobby, the increasing legal challenges to affirmative action regulations, etc.) suggest that it is alliances among women's, black, and ethnic studies programs which will ensure the survival of such programs. This is not to imply that these alliances do not already exist, but, in the face of the active corrosion of the collective basis of affirmative action by the federal government in the name of 'reverse discrimination,' it is all the more urgent that our institutional self-

examinations lead to concrete alliances. Those of us who teach in some of these programs know that, in this context, questions of voice—indeed, the very fact of claiming a voice and wanting to be heard—are very complicated indeed.

To proceed with the first location or site, I attempt an analysis of the effect of my own pedagogical practices on students when teaching about Third World peoples in a largely white institution. I suggest that a partial (and problematic) effect of my pedagogy, the location of my courses in the curriculum and the liberal nature of the institution as a whole, is the sort of attitudinal engagement with diversity that encourages an empty cultural pluralism and domesticates the historical agency of Third World peoples.

Classroom Pedagogies of Gender and Race

How do we construct oppositional pedagogies of gender and race? Teaching about histories of sexism, racism, imperialism, and homophobia potentially poses very fundamental challenges to the academy and its traditional production of knowledge, since it has often situated Third World peoples as populations whose histories and experiences are deviant, marginal, or inessential to the acquisition of knowledge. And this has happened systematically in our disciplines as well as in our pedagogies. Thus the task at hand is to decolonize our disciplinary and pedagogical practices. The crucial question is how we teach about the West and its Others so that education becomes the practice of liberation. This question becomes all the more important in the context of the significance of education as a means of liberation and advancement for Third World and postcolonial peoples and their/our historical belief in education as a crucial form of resistance to the colonization of hearts and minds.

However, as a number of educators have argued, decolonizing educational practices requires transformations at a number of levels, both within and outside the academy. Curricula and pedagogical transformation has to be accompanied by a broad-based transformation of the culture of the academy, as well as by radical shifts in the relation of the academy to other state and civil institutions. In addition, decolonizing pedagogical practices requires taking seriously the relation between knowledge and learning, on the one hand, and student and teacher experience, on the other. In fact, the theorization and politicization of experience is imperative if pedagogical practices are to focus on more than the mere management, systematization, and consumption of disciplinary knowledge.

I teach courses on gender, race, and education, on international development, on feminist theory, and on Third World feminisms, as well as core women's studies courses such as 'Introduction to Women's Studies' and a senior seminar. All of the courses are fundamentally interdisciplinary and cross-cultural. At its most ambitious, this pedagogy is an attempt to get students to think critically about their place in relation to the knowledge they gain and to transform their worldview fundamentally by taking the politics of knowledge seriously. It is a pedagogy that attempts to link knowledge, social responsibility, and collective struggle. And it does so by emphasizing the risks that education involves, the struggles for institutional change, and the strategies for challenging forms of domination and by creating more equitable and just public spheres within and outside educational institutions.

Thus, pedagogy from the point of view of a radical teacher does not entail merely processing received knowledges (however critically one does this) but actively transforming knowledges. In addition, it involves taking responsibility for the material effects of these very pedagogical practices on students. Teaching about 'difference' in relation to power is thus extremely complicated and involves not only rethinking questions of learning and authority but also questions of center and margin. In writing about her own pedagogical practices in teaching African-American women's history, Elsa Barkley Brown (1989: 921) formulates her intentions and method in this way:

How do our students overcome years of notions of what is normative? While trying to think about these issues in my teaching, I have come to understand that this is not merely an intellectual process. It is not merely a question of whether or not we have learned to analyze in particular kinds of way, or whether people are able to intellectualize about a variety of experiences. It is also about coming to believe in the possibility of a variety of experiences, a variety of ways of understanding the world, a variety of frameworks of operation, without imposing consciously or unconsciously a notion of the norm. What I have tried to do in my own teaching is to address both the conscious level through the material, and the unconscious level through the structure of the course, thus, perhaps, allowing my students, in Bettina Apthekar's words, to 'pivot the center: to center in another experience.'

Clearly, this process is very complicated pedagogically, for such teaching must address questions of audience, voice, power, and evaluation, while retaining a focus on the material being taught. Teaching practices must also combat the pressures of professionalization, normalization, and standardization, the very pressures of expectations that implicitly aim to manage and discipline pedagogies so that teacher behaviors are predictable (and perhaps controllable) across the board.

Barkley Brown draws attention to the centrality of experience in the classroom. While this is an issue that merits much more consideration than I can give here, a particular aspect of it ties into my general argument. Feminist pedagogy has always recognized the importance of experience in the classroom. Since women's and ethnic studies programs are fundamentally grounded in political and collective questions of power and inequality, questions of the politicization of individuals along race, gender, class, and sexual parameters are at the very center of knowledges produced in the classroom. This politicization often involves the 'authorization' of marginal experiences and the creation of spaces for multiple, dissenting voices in the classroom. The authorization of experience is thus a crucial form of empowerment for students—a way for them to enter the classroom as speaking subjects. However, this focus on the centrality of experience can also lead to exclusions—it often silences those whose 'experience' is seen to be that of the ruling-class groups. This 'more authentic-than-thou' attitude to experience also applies to the teacher. For instance, in speaking *about* Third World peoples, I have to watch constantly the tendency to speak *for* Third World peoples. For I often come to embody the 'authentic' authority and experience for many of my students; indeed, they construct me as a native informant in the same way that left-liberal white students sometimes construct all people of color as the authentic voices of their people. This is evident in the classroom when the specific 'differences' (of personality, posture, behavior, etc.) of one woman of color stand in for the difference of the whole collective, and a collective voice is assumed in place of an individual voice. In effect, this results in the reduction or averaging of Third World peoples in terms of individual personality characteristics: complex ethical and political issues are glossed over, and an ambiguous and more easily manageable ethos of the 'personal' and the 'interpersonal' takes their place.

Thus, a particularly problematic effect of certain pedagogical codifications of difference is the conceptualization of race and gender in terms of personal or individual experience. Students often end up determining that they have to 'be more sensitive' to Third World peoples. The formulation of knowledge and politics through these individualistic, attitudinal parameters indicates an erasure of the very politics of knowledge involved in teaching and learning about difference. It also suggests an erasure of the structural and institutional parameters of what it means to understand difference in historical terms. If all conflict in the classroom is seen and understood in personal terms, it leads to a comfortable set of oppositions: people of color as the central voices and the bearers of all knowledge in class, and white people as 'observers,' with no responsibility to contribute and/or with nothing valuable to contribute. In other words, white students are constructed as marginal observers and students of color as the real 'knowers' in such a liberal or left classroom. While it may seem like people of color are thus granted voice and agency in the classroom, it is necessary to consider what particular kind of voice it is that is allowed them/us. It is a voice located in a different and separate space from the agency of white students.[10] Thus, while it appears that in such a class the histories and cultures of marginalized peoples are now 'legitimate' objects of study and discussion, the fact is that this legitimation takes place purely at an attitudinal, interpersonal level rather than in terms of a fundamental challenge to hegemonic knowledge and history. Often the culture in such a class vacillates between a high level of tension and an overwhelming desire to create harmony, acceptance of 'difference,' and cordial relations in the classroom. Potentially this implic-

itly binary construction (Third World students versus white students) undermines the understanding of co-implication that students must take seriously in order to understand 'difference' as historical and relational. Co-implication refers to the idea that all of us (First and Third World) share certain histories as well as certain responsibilities: ideologies of race define both white and black peoples, just as gender ideologies define both women and men. Thus, while 'experience' is an enabling focus in the classroom, unless it is explicitly understood as historical, contingent, and the result of interpretation, it can coagulate into frozen, binary, psychologistic positions.

To summarize, this effective separation of white students from Third World students in such an explicitly politicized women's studies classroom is problematic because it leads to an attitudinal engagement that bypasses the complexly situated politics of knowledge and potentially shores up a particular individual-oriented codification and commodification of race. It implicitly draws on and sustains a discourse of cultural pluralism, or what Henry Giroux (1988) calls 'the pedagogy of normative pluralism,' a pedagogy in which we all occupy separate, different, and equally valuable places and where experience is defined not in terms of individual *qua* individual, but in terms of an individual as representative of a cultural group. This results in a depoliticization and dehistoricization of the idea of culture and makes possible the implicit management of race in the name of cooperation and harmony.

However, cultural pluralism is an inadequate response because the academy as well as the larger social arena are constituted through *hierarchical* knowledges and power relations. In this context, the creation of oppositional knowledges always involves both fundamental challenges and the risk of co-optation. Creating counter-hegemonic pedagogies and combating attitudinal, pluralistic appropriations of race and difference thus involves a delicate and ever-shifting balance between the analysis of experience as lived culture and as textual and historical representations of experience. But most of all, it calls for a critical analysis of the contradictions and incommensurability of social interests as individuals experience, understand, and transform them. Decolonizing pedagogical practices requires taking seriously the different logics of cultures as they are located within asymmetrical power relations. It involves understanding that culture, especially academic culture, is a terrain of struggle (rather than an amalgam of discrete consumable entities). And finally, within the classroom, it requires that teachers and students develop a critical analysis of how experience itself is named, constructed, and legitimated in the academy. Without this analysis of culture and of experience in the classroom, there is no way to develop and nurture oppositional practices. After all, critical education concerns the production of subjectivities *in relation* to discourses of knowledge and power.

The Race Industry and Prejudice-Reduction Workshops

In his incisive critique of current attempts at minority canon formation, Cornel West locates the following cultural crises as circumscribing the present historical moment: the decolonization of the Third World which signaled the end of the European Age; the repoliticization of literary studies in the 1960s; the emergence of alternative, oppositional, subaltern histories; and the transformation of everyday life through the rise of a predominantly visual, technological culture. West (1987: 197) locates contests over Afro-American canon formation in the proliferation of discourses of pluralism in the American academy, thus launching a critique of the class interests of Afro-American critics who 'become the academic superintendents of a segment of an expanded canon or a separate canon.' A similar critique, on the basis of class interests and 'professionalization,' can be leveled against feminist scholars (First or Third World) who specialize in 'reading' the lives/experiences of Third World women. However, what concerns me here is the predominately white upper-level administrators at our institutions and their 'reading' of the issues of racial diversity and pluralism. I agree with West's internal critique of a black managerial class but think it is important not to ignore the power of a predominantly white managerial class (men and women) who, in fact, frame and hence determine *our* voices, livelihoods, and sometimes even our political alliances.

Exploring a small piece of the creation and institutionalization of this Race Industry, prejudice-reduction workshops involving upper-level administrators, counselors, and students in numerous institutions of higher education—including the college where I teach—shed light on a particular aspect of this industry. Interestingly, the faculty often do not figure in these workshops at all; they are directed either at students and resident counselors or at administrators.

To make this argument, I draw upon my own institution, a college that has an impressive history of progressive and liberal policies. But my critique applies to liberal/humanistic institutions of higher education in general. While what follows is a critique of certain practices at the college, I undertake this out of a commitment and engagement with the academy. The efforts of the college to take questions of difference and diversity on board should not be minimized. However, these efforts should also be subject to rigorous examination because they have far-reaching implications for the institutionalization of multiculturalism in the academy. While multiculturalism itself is not necessarily problematic, its definition in terms of an apolitical, ahistorical cultural pluralism needs to be challenged.

In the last few years there has been an increase in this kind of activity—often as a response to antiracist student organization and demands, or in relation to the demand and institutionalization of 'non-Western' requirements at prestigious institutions—in a number of academic institutions nationally. More precisely, however, these issues of multiculturalism arise as a response to the recognition of changing demographics in the United States. For instance, the fact that by the year 2000 almost 42 per cent of all public school students will be minority children or other impoverished children, and that by the year 2000 women and people of color will account for nearly 75 per cent of the labor force is crucial in understanding institutional imperatives concerning 'diversity.'[11] As Sanchez suggests, for the university to conduct 'research and business as usual' in the face of the overwhelming challenges posed by even the very presence of people of color, it has to enact policies and programs aimed at accommodation rather than transformation.

In response to certain racist and homophobic incidents in the spring of 1988 this college instituted a series of 'prejudice-reduction' workshops aimed at student and upper- and middle-level administrative staff. These workshops sometimes took the form of 'unlearning racism' workshops conducted by residential counselor and psychologists in dorms. Workshops such as these are valuable in 'sensitizing' students to racial conflict, behavior, and attitudes, but an analysis of the historical and ideological bases of such workshops indicates their limitations.

Briefly, prejudice-reduction workshops draw on the psychologically base 'race relations' analysis and focus on 'prejudice' rather than institutional of historical domination. The workshops draw on co-counseling and the reevaluation counseling techniques and theory and often aim for emotional release rather than political action. The name of this approach is itself somewhat problematic, since it suggests that 'prejudice' (rather than domination, exploitation, or structural inequality) is the core problem and that we have to 'reduce' it. The language determines and shapes the ideological and political content to a large extent. In focusing on 'the healing of past wounds' this approach also equates the position of dominant and subordinate groups, erasing all power inequities and hierarchies. And finally, the location of the source of 'oppression' and 'change' in individuals suggests an elision between ideological and structural understandings of power and domination and individual, psychological understandings of power.

Here again, the implicit definition of experience is important. Experience defined as fundamentally individual and atomistic, subject to behavioral and attitudinal change. Questions of history, collective memory, and social and structural inequality as constitutive of the category of experience are inadmissible within the framework. Individuals speak as representatives of majority or minority group whose experience is predetermined within an oppressor/victim paradigm. The questions are addressed in A. Sivanandan's incisive critique of the roots of Racism Awareness Training (RAT) in the United States (associated with the work of Judy Katz *et al.*) and its embodiment in multiculturalism in Britain.

Sivanandan draws attention to the dangers of the actual degradation and refiguration of antiracist, black political struggles as a result of the RAT focus on psychological attitudes. Thus, while these workshops can indeed be useful in addressing deep-seated psychological attitudes and thus creating a context for change, the danger resides in remaining at the level of personal support and evaluation, and thus often undermining the necessity for broad-based political organization and action around these issues.[12]

Prejudice-reduction workshops have also made their way into the upper echelons of the administration at the college. However, at this level they take a very different form: presidents and their male colleagues don't go to workshops; they 'consult' about issues of diversity. Thus, this version of 'prejudice reduction' takes the form of 'managing diversity' (another semantical gem which suggests that 'diversity' [a euphemism for people of color] will be out of control unless it is managed). Consider the following passage from the publicity brochure of a recent consultant (Prindle 1988):

Program in Conflict Management Alternatives: A team of applied scholars is creating alternative theoretical and practical approaches to the peaceful resolution of social conflicts. A concern for maximizing social justice, and for redressing major social inequities that underlie much social conflict, is a central organizing principle of this work. Another concern is to facilitate the implementation of negotiated settlements, and therefore contribute to long-term change in organizational and community relations. Research theory development, organizational and community change efforts, networking, consultations, curricula, workshops and training programs are all part of the Program.

This quote foregrounds the primary focus on conflict resolution, negotiated settlement, and organizational relations—all framed in a language of research, consultancy, and training. All three strategies—conflict resolution, settlement negotiation, and long-term organizational relations—can be carried out between individuals and between groups. The point is to understand the moments of friction and to resolve the conflicts 'peacefully'; in other words, domesticate race and difference by formulating the problems in narrow, interpersonal terms and by rewriting historical contexts as manageable psychological ones.

As in the example of the classroom discussed earlier, the assumption here is that individuals and groups, as individual atomistic units in a social whole composed essentially of an aggregate of such units, embody difference. Thus, conflict resolution is best attempted by negotiating between individuals who are dissatisfied *as individuals*. One very important ideological effect of this is the standardization of behaviors and responses so as to make them predictable (and thus manageable) across a wide variety of situations and circumstances. If complex structural experiences of domination and resistance can be ideologically reformulated as individual behaviors and attitudes, they can be managed while carrying on business as usual.

Another example of this kind of a program is the approach of a company called 'Diversity Consultants': 'Diversity Consultants believe one of the most effective ways to manage multi-cultural and race awareness issues is through assessment of individual environments, planned educational programs, and management strategy sessions which assist professionals in understanding themselves, diversity, and their options in the workplace' (Prindle 1988: 8).

The key ideas in this statement involve an awareness of race issues (the problem is assumed to be cultural misunderstanding or lack of information about other cultures), understanding yourself and people unlike you (diversity—we must respect and learn from each other; this may not address economic exploitation, but it will teach us to treat each other civilly), negotiating conflicts, altering organizational sexism and racism, and devising strategies to assess and manage the challenges of diversity (which results in an additive approach: recruiting 'diverse' people, introducing 'different' curriculum units while engaging in teaching as usual—that is, not shifting the normative culture versus subcultures paradigm). This is, then, the 'professionalization' of prejudice reduction, where culture is a supreme commodity. Culture is seen as noncontradictory, as isolated from questions of history, and as a storehouse of nonchanging facts, behaviors, and practices. This particular definition of culture and of cultural difference is what sustains the individualized discourse of harmony and civility that is the hallmark of cultural pluralism. Prejudice-reduction workshops eventually aim for the creation of this discourse of civility. Again, this is not to suggest that there are no positive effects of this practice—for instance, the introduction of new cultural models can

cause a deeper evaluation of existing structures, and clearly such consultancies could set a positive tone for social change. However, the baseline is still 'maintaining the status quo'—diversity is always and can only be added on.

So what does all this mean? Diversity consultants are not new. Private industry has been utilizing these highly paid management consulting firms since the civil rights movement. However, when upper-level administrators in higher education inflect discourses of education and 'academic freedom' with discourses of the management of race, the effects are significant enough to warrant close examination. There is a long history of the institutionalization of the discourse of management and control in American education. However, the management of race requires a somewhat different inflection at this historical moment. Due to historical, demographic, and educational shifts in the racial makeup of students and faculty in the last twenty years, some of us even have public voices that have to be 'managed' for the greater harmony of all. The hiring of consultants to 'sensitize educators to issues of diversity' is part of the postsixties proliferation of discourses of pluralism. But it is also a specific and containing response to the changing social contours of the U.S. polity and to the challenges posed by Third World and feminist studies in the academy. By using the language of the corporation and the language of cognitive and affectional psychology (and thereby professionalizing questions of sexism, racism, and class conflict) new alliances are consolidated. Educators who are part of the ruling administrative class are now managers of conflict, but they are also agents in the construction of 'race'—a word that is significantly redefined through the technical language used.

Race, Voice, and Academic Culture

The effects of this relatively new discourse in the higher levels of liberal arts colleges and universities are quite real. Affirmative action hires are now highly visible and selective; now every English department is looking for a black woman scholar to teach Toni Morrison's writings. What happens to such scholars after they are hired, and particularly when they come up for review or tenure, is another matter altogether. A number of scholars have documented the debilitating effects of affirmative action hiring policies that seek out and hire only those Third World scholars who are at the top of their fields—hence the pattern of musical chairs where selected people of color are bartered at very high prices. Our voices are carefully placed and domesticated: one in history, one in English, perhaps one in the sociology department. Clearly these hiring practices do not guarantee the retention and tenure of Third World faculty. In fact, while the highly visible bartering for Third World 'stars' serves to suggest that institutions of higher education are finally becoming responsive to feminist and Third World concerns, this particular commodification and personalization of race suggests there has been very little change since the 1970s—both in terms of a numerical increase of Third World faculty and our treatment in white institutions.

In a recent article on the racism faced by Chicano faculty in institutions of higher education, Maria de la Luz Reyes and John J. Halcon (1988: 303) characterize the effects of the 1970s policies of affirmative action:

In the mid-1970s, when minority quota systems were being implemented in many non-academic agencies, the general public was left with the impression that Chicano or minority presence in professional or academic positions was due to affirmative action, rather than to individual qualifications or merit. But that impression was inaccurate. Generally [Institutions of Higher Education] responded to the affirmative action guidelines with token positions for only a handful of minority scholars in nonacademic and/or 'soft' money programs. For example, many Blacks and Hispanics were hired as directors for programs such as Upward Bound, Talent Search, and Equal Opportunity Programs. Other minority faculty were hired for bilingual programs and ethnic studies programs, but affirmative action hires did not commonly extend to tenure-track faculty positions. The new presence of minorities on college campuses, however, which occurred during the period when attention to affirmative action regulations reached its peak, left all minority professionals and academics with a legacy of tokenism—a stigma that has been difficult to dispel.

De la Luz Reyes and Halcon go on to argue that we are still living with the effects of the implementation of these policies in the 1980s. They examine the problems associated with tokenism and the ghettoization of Third World people in the academy, detailing the

complex forms of racism that minority faculty face today. To this characterization, I would add that one of the results of the Reagan/Bush years has been that black, women's, and ethnic studies programs are often further marginalized, since one of the effects of the management of race is that individuals come to embody difference and diversity, while programs that have been historically constituted on the basis of collective oppositional knowledges are labeled 'political,' 'biased,' 'shrill,' and 'unrigorous.'[13] Any inroads made by such programs and departments in the seventies are being slowly undermined in the eighties and the nineties by the management of race through attitudinal and behavioral strategies, with their local dependence on individuals seen as appropriate representatives of 'their race' or some other equivalent political constituency. Race and gender are reformulated as individual characteristics and attitudes, and thus an individualized, ostensibly 'unmarked' discourse of difference is being put into place. This shift in the academic discourse on gender and race actually rolls back any progress made in carving institutional spaces for women's and black studies programs and departments.

Earlier, it was these institutional spaces that determined our collective voices. Our programs and departments were by definition alternative and oppositional. Now they are often merely alternative—one among many. Without being nostalgic about the good old days (and they were problematic in their own ways), I am suggesting that there has been an erosion of the politics of collectivity through the reformulation of race and difference in individualistic terms. By no means is this a conspiratorial scenario. The discussion of the effects of my own classroom practices indicates my complicity in this contest over definitions of gender and race in discursive and representational as well as personal terms. The 1960s and 1970s slogan 'The personal is political' has been recrafted in the 1980s as 'The political is personal.' In other words, all politics is collapsed into the personal, and questions of individual behaviors, attitudes, and life-style stand in for political analysis of the social. Individual political struggles are seen as the only relevant and legitimate form of political struggle.

However, there is another, more crucial reason to be concerned about (and to challenge) this management of race in the liberal academy. And the reason is that this process of the individualization of race and its effects dovetails rather neatly with the neoconservative politics and agenda of the Reagan-Bush years—an agenda that has constitutively recast the fabric of American life in a pre-1960s mold. The recent Supreme Court decisions on 'reverse discrimination' are based on precisely similar definitions of 'prejudice,' 'discrimination,' and 'race.' In an essay which argues that the U.S. Supreme Court's rulings on reverse discrimination are fundamentally tied to the rollback of reproductive freedom, Zillah Eisenstein (1990: 5) discusses the individualist framework on which these decisions are based:

> The court's recent decisions pertaining to affirmative action make quite clear that existing civil rights legislation is being newly reinterpreted. Race, or sex (gender) as a collective category is being denied and racism, and/or sexism, defined as a structural and historical reality has been erased. Statistical evidence of racial and/or sexual discrimination is no longer acceptable as proof of unfair treatment of 'black women as a group or class.' Discrimination is proved by an individual only in terms of their specific case. The assault is blatant: equality doctrine is dismantled.

Eisenstein goes on to analyze how the government's attempts to redress racism or sexism are at the core of the struggle for equality and how, in gutting the meaning of discrimination and applying it only to individual cases and not statistical categories, it has become almost impossible to prove discrimination because there are always 'other' criteria to excuse discriminatory practices. Thus, the recent Supreme Court decisions on reverse discrimination are clearly based on a particular individualist politics that domesticates race and gender. This is an example of the convergence of neoconservative and liberal agendas concerning race and gender inequalities.

Those of us who are in the academy also potentially collude in this domestication of race by allowing ourselves to be positioned in ways that contribute to the construction of these images of pure and innocent diversity, to the construction of these managerial discourses. For instance, since the category of race is not static but a fluid social and historical formation, Third World peoples are often located in antagonistic relationships to each other. Those of us who are from Third World countries are often played off against Third World peoples native to the United States. As an Indian immigrant woman in the United States, for instance, in most contexts, I am not as potentially threatening as an African-American woman. Yes, we are both nonwhite and Other, subject to various forms of overt or disguised racism, but I do not bring with me a history of slavery—a direct and constant reminder of the racist past and present of the United States. Of course my location in the British academy would be fundamentally different because of the history of British colonization, because of patterns of immigration and labor force participation, and because of the existence of working-class, trade union, and antiracist politics—all of which define the position of Indians in Britain. An interesting parallel in the British context is the recent focus on and celebration of African-American women as the 'true' radical black feminists who have something to say, while black British feminists ('black' in contemporary Britain refers to those British citizens who are of African, Asian, or Caribbean origin) are marginalized and rendered voiceless by the publishing industry and the academy. These locations and potential collusions thus have an impact on how our voices and agencies are constituted.

Critical Pedagogy and Cultures of Dissent

To conclude, if my argument in this essay is convincing, it suggests why we need to take on board questions of race and gender as they are being managed and commodified in the liberal U.S. academy. One mode of doing this is actively creating public cultures of dissent where these issues can be debated in terms of our pedagogies and institutionalized practices.[14] Creating such cultures in the liberal academy is a challenge in itself, because liberalism allows and even welcomes 'plural' or even 'alternative' perspectives. However, a public culture of dissent entails creating spaces for epistemological standpoints that are grounded in the *interests* of people and which recognize the *materiality* of conflict, of privilege, and domination. Thus creating such cultures is fundamentally about making the axes of power transparent in the context of academic, disciplinary, and institutional structures as well as in the interpersonal relationships (rather than individual relations) in the academy. It is about taking the politics of everyday life seriously as teachers, students, administrators, and members of hegemonic academic cultures. Culture itself is thus redefined as incorporating individual and collective memories, dreams, and history that are contested and transformed through the political praxis of day-to-day living.

Cultures of dissent are also about seeing the academy as part of a larger sociopolitical arena which itself domesticates and manages Third World people in the name of liberal capitalist democracy. The struggle to transform our institutional practices fundamentally also involves the grounding of the analysis of exploitation and oppression in accurate history and theory, seeing ourselves as activists in the academy—drawing links between movements for social justice and our pedagogical and scholarly endeavors and expecting and demanding action from ourselves, our colleagues, and our students at numerous levels. This requires working hard to understand and to theorize questions of knowledge, power, and experience in the academy so that one effects pedagogical empowerment as well as transformation. Racism, sexism, and homophobia are very real, day-to-day practices in which we all engage. They are not reducible to mere curricular or policy decisions—that is, to management practices.

I said earlier that what is at stake is not the mere *recognition* of difference. The sort of difference which is acknowledged and engaged has fundamental significance for the decolonization of education practices. Similarly, the point is not simply that one should have *a voice*; the more crucial question concerns the sort of voice one comes to have as the result of one's location—both as an individual and as part of collectives (Mohanty, C. T. 1987). I think the important point is that it be an active, oppositional, and collective voice which takes seriously the current commodification and domestication of Third World people in the academy. And this is a task open to all—people of color as well as progressive white people in the academy.

Acknowledgements

I would like to thank Gloria Watkins (bell hooks), Satya Mohanty, and Jacqui Alexander for numerous passionate discussions on these issues. All three have helped sharpen the arguments in this essay; all faults, however, are mine.

Notes

1. See especially my 1988 and 1987 publications. The present essay continues the discussion of the politics of location that I began in 'Feminist Encounters' and can, in fact, be seen as a companion text to it.
2. I am referring here to a particular trajectory of feminist scholarship in the last two decades. While scholarship in the 1970s foregrounded gender as *the* fundamental category of analysis and thus enabled the transformation of numerous disciplinary and canonical boundaries on the basis of the recognition of sexual difference as hierarchy and inequality, scholarship in the 1980s introduced the categories of race and sexuality in the form of internal challenges to the earlier scholarship. These challenges were introduced on both political and methodological grounds by feminists who often considered themselves disenfranchised by the 1970s' feminism: lesbian and heterosexual women of color, postcolonial, Third World women, poor women, etc. While the recent feminist turn to postmodernism suggests the fragmentation of unitary assumptions of gender and enables a more differentiated analysis of inequality, this critique was prefigured in the earlier political analyses of Third World feminists. This particular historical trajectory of the political and conceptual categories of feminist analysis can be traced by analyzing developments in feminist journals such as *Signs* and *Feminist Studies*, feminist publishing houses, and curriculum 'integration' projects through the 1970s and 1980s.
3. For instance, Jessie Bernard (1987) codifies difference as the exclusive relation of men to women, and women to women: difference as variation *among* women and as conflict *between* men and women.
4. It is clear from Lazreg's reliance on a notion like intersubjectivity that her understanding of the issue I am addressing in this essay is far from simple. Claiming a voice is for her, as well as for me, a complex historical and political act that involves understanding the interrelationships of voices. However, the term intersubjectivity, drawing as it does on a phenomenological humanism, brings with it difficult political problems. For a nonhumanist, alternative account of the question of 'historical agencies' and their 'imbrication,' see Mohanty, S. P. (1989; 1990) (forthcoming), especially the introduction and ch. 6. Mohanty

discusses the question of agency and its historical imbrication (rather than 'inter-subjectivity') as constituting the fundamental theoretical basis for comparison across cultures.

5. In spite of problems of definition, I retain the use of the term 'Third World,' and in this particular context (the U.S. academy), I identify myself as a 'Third World' scholar. I use the term here to designate peoples from formerly colonized countries, as well as people of color in the United States. Using the designation 'Third World' to identify colonized peoples in the domestic as well as the international arena may appear reductive because it suggests a commonality and perhaps even an equation among peoples with very diverse cultures and histories and appears to reinforce implicitly existing economic and cultural hierarchies between the 'First' and the 'Third' World. This is not my intention. I use the term with full awareness of these difficulties and because these are the terms available to us at the moment. In addition, in the particular discursive context of Western feminist scholarship and of the U.S. academy, 'Third World' is an oppositional designation that can be empowering even while it necessitates a continuous questioning. For an elaboration of these questions of definition, see my essay in Mohanty, C. J., Torres, L., and Russo, A. (1991).

6. See especially the work of Paulo Freire, Michael Apple, Basil Bernstein, Pierre Bourdieu, and Henry Giroux. While a number of these educational theorists offer radical critiques of education on the basis of class hierarchies, very few do so on the basis of gender or race. However, the theoretical suggestions in this literature are provocative and can be used to advantage in feminist analysis. The special issue 'On Racism and American Education,' *Harvard Educational Review* 58, no. 3 (1988) is also an excellent resource. See also Freire (1973), Freire and Macedo (1985), Apple (1979), Bernstein (1975), Giroux (1983; 1988), and Bourdieu and Passeron (1977). For feminist analyses of education and the academy, see Bunch and Pollack (eds.) (1983), Minnich *et al.* (eds.) (1988), Schuster and Van Dyne (1985), and Minnich (1990). See also back issues of the journals *Women's Studies Quarterly*, *Women's Studies International Forum*, and *Frontiers: A Journal of Women's Studies*.

7. I am fully aware of the fact that I am drawing on an extremely limited (and some might say atypical) sample for this analysis. Clearly, in the bulk of American colleges and universities, the very introduction of questions of pluralism and difference is itself a radical and oppositional gesture. However, in the more liberal institutions of higher learning, questions of pluralism have had a particular institutional history, and I draw on the example of the college I currently teach at to investigate the implications of this specific institutionalization of discourses of pluralism. I am concerned with raising some political and intellectual questions that have urgent implications for the discourses of race and racism in the academy, not with providing statistically significant data on U.S. institutions of higher learning, nor with claiming 'representativeness' for the liberal arts college I draw on to raise these questions.

8. For analyses of the intersection of the race and sex agendas of the New Right, see essays in the special double issue of *Radical America* 15, nos. 1 and 2 (1981). I have utilized Zillah Eisenstein's essay (1990). I am indebted to her for sharing this essay with me and for our discussions on this subject.

9. Some of the most poignant and incisive critiques of the inscription of race and difference in scholarly and institutional discourses have been raised by Third World scholars working outside women's studies. See West (1987), Sivanandan (1985); and S. P. Mohanty (1989).

10. As a contrast, and for an interesting analysis of similar issues in the pedagogical context of a white woman teaching multicultural women's studies, see Pascoe (1990).

11. See the American Council on Education (1988). See also *Time* (April 9, 1990), especially, William A. Henry III, 'Beyond the Melting Pot,' for statistics on changing demographics in U.S. economic and educational spheres.

12. This discussion of the ideological assumptions of 'prejudice reduction' is based on Patti De Rosa's presentation at the Society for International Education, Training, and Research Conference in May 1987.

13. This marginalization is evident in the financial cutbacks that such programs have faced in recent years. The depoliticization is evident in, for instance, the current shift from 'women's' to 'gender' studies—by all measures, a controversial reconstitution of feminist agendas.

14. Gloria Watkins (bell hooks) and I have attempted to do this in a collegewide faculty colloquium called 'Pedagogies of Gender, Race and Empire' that focuses on our practices in teaching and learning about Third World people in the academy. While the effects of this colloquium have yet to be thoroughly examined, at the very least it has created a public culture of dialogue and dissent where questions of race, gender, and identity

are no longer totally dismissed as 'political' and thus extraneous to academic endeavor, nor are they automatically ghettoized in women's studies and black studies. These questions are seen (by a substantial segment of the faculty) as important, constitutive questions in revising a Eurocentric liberal arts curriculum.

References

American Council on Education, Education Commission of the States (1988), *One-Third of a Nation: A Report of the Commission on Minority Participation in Education and American Life* (Washington, DC: American Council on Education).

Apple, M. (1979), *Ideology and the Curriculum* (London: Routledge and Kegan Paul).

Bernard, J. (1987), *The Female World from a Global Perspective* (Bloomington, Ind.: Indiana Univ. Press).

Bernstein, B. (1975), *Class, Codes, and Control*, iii (London: Routledge and Kegan Paul).

Blassingame, J. W. (ed.) (1973), *New Perspectives on Black Studies* (Urbana, Ill.: Univ. of Illinois Press).

Bourdieu, P., and Passeron, J. C. (1977), *Reproduction in Education, Society, and Culture*, transl. Richard Nice (Beverley Hills, Calif.: Sage Publications).

Brown, E. B. (1989), 'African-American Women's Quilting: A Framework for Conceptualizing and Teaching African-American Women's History', *Signs* 14/4 (Summer), 921–9.

Bunch, C., and Pollack, S. (eds.) (1983), *Learning Our Way: Essays in Feminist Education* (Trumansburg, NY: Crossing Press).

Eisenstein, Z. (1990), 'Feminism v. Neoconservative Jurisprudence: The Spring '89 Supreme Court' (forthcoming).

Frieire, P. (1973), *Pedagogy of the Oppressed*, transl. by M. B. Ramos (New York: Seabury Press).

—— and Macedo, D. (1985), *Literacy: Reading the Word and the World* (South Hadley, Mass.: Bergin and Garvey).

Giroux, H. (1983), *Theory and Resistance in Education: A Pedagogy for the Opposition* (South Hadley, Mass.: Bergin and Garvey).

—— (1988), *Teachers as Intellectuals: Toward a Critical Pedagogy of Learning* (South Hadley, Mass.: Bergin and Garvey).

Henry, W. A. III (1990), 'Beyond the Melting Pot', in 'America's Changing Colors', *Time* (9 April).

Huggins, N. I. (1985), *Afro-American Studies: A Report to the Ford Foundation* (July, n.p.: Ford Foundation).

Lazreg, M. (1988), 'Feminism and Difference: The Perils of Writing as a Woman on Women in Algeria', *Feminist Studies*, 14/1 (Spring), 81–107.

Luz Reyes, M. de la, and Halcon, J. J. (1988), 'Racism in Academia: The Old Wolf Revisited', *Harvard Educational Review*, 58/3: 299–314.

Minnich, E. *et al.* (eds.) (1988), *Reconstructing the Academy: Women's Education and Women's Studies* (Chicago: Univ. of Chicago Press).

—— (1990), *Transforming Knowledge* (Philadelphia: Temple Univ. Press).

Mohanty, C. T. (1987), 'Feminist Encounters: Locating the Politics of Experience', in 'Fin de Siecle 2000', *Copyright*, 1 (Fall), 30–44.

—— (1988), 'Under Western Eyes: Feminist Scholarship and Colonial Discourses', *Feminist Review*, 30 (Autumn), 61–88.

—— (1991), 'Cartographies of Struggle: Third World Women and the Politics of Feminism', in Mohanty, C. T., Torres, L., and Russo, A. (eds.), *Third World Women and the Politics of Feminism* (Bloomington, Ind.: Indiana Univ. Press).

Mohanty, S. P. (1989), 'Us and Them: On the Philosophical Bases of Political Criticism', *Yale Journal of Criticism*, 2/2 (Spring), 1–31.

—— (1990), *Literary Theory and the Claims of History* (Cambridge, Mass.: Blackwell).

National Women's Studies Association Task Force Report (1969), *The Women's Studies Major* (unpubl.).

Pascoe, P. (1990), 'At the Crossroads of Culture', *Women's Review of Books*, 7/5 (February), 22–3.

Prindle, S. (1988), 'Towards Prejudice Reduction: A Resource Document for Consultants, Audio/Visual Aids, and Providers of Workshops, Training and Seminars' (Oberlin, Oh.: Oberlin College).

Robinson, A. L., Foster, C. C., and Ogilvie, D. H. (eds.) (1969), *Black Studies in the University: A Symposium* (New York: Bantam Books).

Sanchez, R. (1987), 'Ethnicity, Ideology, and Academia', *Americas Review*, 15/1 (Spring), 80–8.

Schuster, M., and van Dyne, S. (1985), *Women's Place in the Academy: Transforming the Liberal Arts Curriculum* (Totowa, NJ: Rowan and Allenheld).

Sivanandan, A. (1985), 'RAT and the Degradation of Black Struggle', *Race and Class*, 26/4 (Spring), 1–34.

Sudarkasa, N., 'Affirmative Action or Affirmation of Status Quo? Black Faculty and Administrators in Higher Education', *AAHE Bulletin* (February), 3–6.

West, C. (1987), 'Minority Discourse and the Pitfalls of Canon Formation', *Yale Journal of Criticism*, 1/1 (Fall), 193–202.

37

Feminist Scholarship as a Vocation

Patricia J. Gumport

Introduction

It's harder to work when it's not fitting into one's discipline in a particular way. You can't expect to get clear judgements and rewards, although you'll get different opinions about it . . . The problem is the people who could judge it are out there and not in here in my department and my discipline.

These are the words of a feminist scholar who has struggled to gain recognition and tenure at more than one research university over the past fifteen years. That she drew from several disciplines to generate research questions and theoretical interpretations was only part of the problem. The other part stemmed from her explicit agenda for disciplinary as well as societal change. Among the first to assert in word and deed that feminist scholarship was not an oxymoron, she developed research 'for and about women' and declared her research intentions to be both 'consciousness-raising and paradigm-shifting,' asserting that 'the difference between the two are less than most people suppose'. Her primary network of colleagues lay outside her department, outside her discipline and sometimes beyond the academy altogether.

Although engaging in boundary-crossing may be rewarded academically as innovative or cutting edge, it becomes risky as a primary academic vocation, especially if the scholarship reflects a radical edge. Unlike academics who seek to explore the intersection of long-established fields (e.g. American studies, area studies, cognitive science), some scholars attempt to set up a new way of looking at the world by developing fundamental critiques of disciplinary assumptions and challenges to conventional norms of scholarly inquiry

(e.g. ethnic, Marxist, feminist perspectives). When the project is cross-disciplinary as well as oppositional in nature, both the scholars and their scholarship engage in a more ambitious struggle for legitimacy. In an effort to re-frame issues and ask new questions, they seek and find intellectual communities that cut across lines of formal structure. The formation and maintenance of such intentional communities becomes as much an organization and political endeavor as an intellectual one.

In this article, I focus on feminist scholarship as a contemporary case of struggle for recognition and resources in the American academy over the past two decades. The analysis reveals how a cohort of academic women, who received Ph.D.s in 'traditional' disciplines, came to challenge the content and organization of academic knowledge. Their intellectual biographies and career histories enable us to examine two stages of this historical process: first, how informal organizing became a motivating and sustaining basis for constructing feminist scholarship, and second, how the prevailing context of department and discipline-based peer review framed the work of scholars who chose to work in departments as well as those who sought women's studies locations.

The data are drawn from a larger two-year study with in-depth interviews of forty women faculty and thirty-five administrators and faculty as disciplinary observers who were located at ten colleges and universities in the United States (Gumport 1987). The faculty in this sample received Ph.D.s in one of three disciplines: history, sociology and philosophy. While the choice of these disciplines

From *Higher Education*, 20: (1990), 231–43. Reprinted with permission.

limits the study's potential for capturing the entire landscape of academic knowledge, the sample selection was designed to reflect a range (from more to less) in early receptivity to women and feminist work, thus suggesting epistemological or historical factors that may have shaped the context of their struggle for academic legitimacy (Gumport 1988). At the time of the study, 1985–87, the faculty in this sample were all employed full-time and evenly distributed across departments of history, sociology, philosophy and women's studies. Having entered graduate school between 1956 and 1980, the study includes retrospective data on the processes by which some women came to self-identify and contribute as feminist scholars within their disciplines or within emerging women's studies programs as well as other women who had little or no involvement but were nonetheless affected by virtue of their gender.

The analysis for this article examines the distinctive experiences of one particular cohort of academic women. These women entered graduate school roughly between 1964 and 1972; although not all of them became highly politicized, they all began graduate school in a very politicized era, which promoted a skepticism, if not a detachment, from conventional orientations to scholarly inquiry and to scholarship as a vocation. I focus on the social processes and conditions in which some of these women, whom I call the Pathfinders, made the initial fusions between political and academic interests to construct feminist scholarship.

The Emergence of Feminist Scholarship in the Academy

Pathfinders recall that they created what has since become feminist scholarship without forethought or conscious planning. They were women *in* academia, but not *of* it. Having 'backed into' graduate school with ambivalence and having experienced tension between political and academic interests, they came to generate new scholarly questions that derived from their political, personal, emotional and intellectual sensibilities.

Recalling their years as graduate students or as young faculty, many Pathfinders got the content and inspiration to carve out a new terrain in a discipline as a result of experiences in

cross-departmental networks of campus women. Increasingly supported by the momentum and language of the 1960s wave of the women's liberation movement, many Pathfinders reinterpreted their academic contexts as in need of change, the kind of change that would require collective effort.

Attending cross-departmental meetings that entailed long hours of discussion generated transformative political and academic experiences, the nature of which had not been at all apparent at the outset. One senior sociologist explained how this developed when she took the initiative to organize a group to meet at her home in the late 1960s: 'At the first meeting I asked, "do we have something in common as women?" . . . It looked as if there were some structural barrier . . . A good number of us were dropping out . . . We were in the pipeline, but could we get aboard? That was the question. Obviously all of us were wondering . . .'

Yet, when the group began, any clear expressions of a gender-based experience, such as feelings of discrimination or invisibility, were not forthcoming: 'As we went around the room, people said they were having a writer's block, having difficulty in the library, one thing and another, but not one of them gender-related. At the end of the evening, I felt, well, that we gave it a try. I called the meeting to an end and no one left for three hours afterward. They turned to the person next to them and could say privately what they couldn't say publicly'.

Gradually, people realized and disclosed their personal experiences as women in a campus environment. The process was an amazingly slow unfolding, given that the group was all women, which would more likely be a safe place. 'And so we held another meeting and a little more came out and then another meeting . . .' said the group's organizer.

Over time, the intensely private and personal nature of their conversations served as the basis for a new consciousness about their intellectual work. A critical stance emerged out of their experiences as women: 'It turned into a wonderful group in which we began to really talk about ideas. For example, what was social class, what was social mobility, and why was it determined by male occupations, what does that mean about the work women do, how should it be conceived? We began to really reconceive the whole thing. And it was intellectually an extraordinary experience'. Much to everyone's surprise, this group continued to meet regularly for eight years.

Participation in a 'women's group' or 'women's caucus' like the one just described was commonplace for Pathfinders when they were younger faculty and graduate students. The initial motivation was often to talk about their experiences of the immediate campus environment. Some women experienced it as alienating and hostile: 'There's no room for the likes of me!' or they joined 'to overcome anomie basically' and 'to share horror stories over lunch.' Others saw the campus as discriminatory and sought, for example, 'to abolish the admissions quota for women' or 'to plan a strategy to change a nepotism regulation.' In the process of validating emotional and previously private perceptions ('I always thought it was "just me" '), they used the informal meetings to determine how to survive in an inhospitable context.

Such colleagueship on campus was essential, not just for social support and validation, but for collaborating and searching for intellectual openings in the canons of their disciplines. When Pathfinders constructed questions for their research, they did so with an awareness that it entailed a risk of 'alienating powerful faculty in the department' or 'not being understood.' Pathfinders recall that campus peer networks were particularly valuable to them during graduate school, as they often found few or no faculty resources. As one now tenured sociologist recalled, 'When I wanted to write my dissertation, the faculty couldn't understand why anyone would be interested in abortion, or women . . .' Another scholar remembered that her dissertation research switched from 'a professionally promising but uninteresting topic' to a study on women; she subsequently 'dug up a new committee . . . with a woman as a chair who didn't know anything about (the topic) or feminist scholarship, but was a kind of voyeur of it . . . and two men who rubber-stamped anything'. Some Pathfinders suggested that the preferable situation for them as graduate students was to be left alone, an arrangement that would permit maximum autonomy from faculty; however, in retrospect years later, some characterized this as an unhelpful alternative in an academic system where sponsorship and colleagueship are essential elements for validating research.

The extent to which academic women needed a cross-departmental network on campus varied by department. On rare occasions, a women's group would be constituted by graduate students and faculty entirely in one department, usually history because there were more women in history. There were too few women, let alone feminists, in any other single department to form a critical mass. In philosophy, for example, the cross-departmental forum was the only option, and an attractive one at that. According to a philosopher, 'the women in philosophy who see themselves as feminist scholars will generally be the only person doing feminist work in a department and may sometimes be the only woman period. They may feel cut off or deprived of collegial relationships.'[1] In past decades, the arrangement of faculty offices by department reflected the likelihood that a philosopher could to go a colleague in the office next door to share intellectual interests, associations and audience. The emerging needs of feminist scholars called into question the premise that a department could indeed be one's primary home.

Beyond sheer numbers of women present, history and philosophy shed light on how different disciplines responded to the Pathfinders. In history, Pathfinders had to move away from their departments the least, in contrast to their colleagues in philosophy. While history as a discipline was more receptive to adding material on women and ultimately to establishing a niche called women's history, philosophy had never provided a clear space for feminist interests. Simply stated, it was easier for a feminist historian to be a historian than for a feminist philosopher to be a philosopher.

Due to the increasing popularity of social history in the late-1960s, history was more receptive to raising questions about women. Research on women seemed like a 'natural extension' of the domain of inquiry for social history, which expanded ideas of what counts as worthy subjects of historical research to include studying the lives of ordinary people, including the downtrodden and oppressed. Social history also signaled a change in notions of what counts as acceptable evidence, to include material that could reconstruct women's experiences, such as oral histories. Still, the initial tasks for a burgeoning feminist historian in the early 1970s were ambitious: 'It was damned hard to do because you didn't know where the sources were—they were so hard to find. You didn't know what the questions were. You didn't have the kind of definition by other people of what you should be looking for.'

One Pathfinder in history took a circuitous route to becoming one of the first feminist contributors to family history. She had always been interested in social history and pursued those questions because they were 'most interesting intellectually', although she recalls not having an initial intention to study women: 'The women's part passed me by at first. It simply never occurred to me that women were part of the package'. In fact, early in her graduate school experience, a professor had suggested that she write on women, which she 'took as an enormous insult, that I was pushed into that because I was a woman. So I ignored it.' She 'managed to do the entire dissertation without ever mentioning women', and yet in the end carved out a theoretical perspective that became a precursor to feminist work in family history.

The dynamics of developing her dissertation are noteworthy. She had identified a dissertation topic that entailed studying a kinship-organized revolution. She wanted to analyze how kinship structures worked, rather than how political revolutions worked. Yet her advisor and graduate student peers were more interested in conventional questions of power: 'they defined politics narrowly to mean political history of kings and other leaders of nations'. She tried to re-phrase her work on kinship in their terms, but to no avail: 'I knew if I couldn't translate it into (their) political terms, it was marginal . . . I never was told I was wrong, but no one knew what to do with it. No one would advise me'. The process left her questioning her own competence, 'I felt I didn't understand the terms of the field'. It is striking that, in retrospect, she laments that 'there was no model for me anywhere' in the canon to think about power and politics in a way that ended up taking women's experience seriously.

A social and economic historian did not begin feminist research until midway through an assistant professorship, when she 'stumbled upon' a topic in women's history 'by accident'. While working in the archives, she discovered some significant information about sexuality that was previously unre-

ported in the historical literature. That her interest was captured she attributes to always having implicitly valued women as historical agents and to the fact that women's history was becoming a hot topic at the time, the late 1970s.

Viewing this research as a dramatic departure from her earlier work as a graduate student and new assistant professor, she was now concerned about the reception it might get from her history department colleagues at the high prestige university where she worked. For a while, she considered keeping it a secret: 'I toyed briefly with not telling anyone here that I was working on it, because I was afraid of how it might be perceived, especially as I was coming up for tenure. But I decided not to. One reason was a practical reason that people would wonder what I was working on. Then it also just didn't seem right.' In spite of the risk, she presented some of this research to her colleagues in the department. She was relieved when she realized that they were intellectually engaged by her topic: 'It went very well. I was amazed. Some of the issues that I deal with are at the intersection of sex and power. They are interested in sexuality. And power they understand very well.'

In the two years following, she did receive tenure. She has made further contributions to women's history and now self-identifies as a women's historian. What began as 'an interruption', she realized, '. . . turned out to be not an interruption at all, but a major (shift) in my outlook as a historian.' Her serendipitous experience in the archives became a catalyst for a new scholarly trajectory, one which entailed a deeper intellectual and emotional involvement: 'I had realized on an intellectual level that I was uncovering some of the past . . . But it's another thing to realize how far back and how rich and how complicated and how painful some of those times are. It's like seeing a patient in a hospital beginning to recover memory. That's something that is emotionally very charged.'

She has also come to see her discipline in a different light: 'For me it is a revelation at the emotional level—to think through fully what repression of history does to people and has done to women . . . (Y)ou can see what has been done to women's history and the history of the poor and the history of all the oppressed. I was aware of the expression that history was written by the victors. And again, I could understand that on an intellectual level, but to experience it emotionally . . . I'm just beginning to understand what that means for me. It is a very enriching experience.' Now tenured in her history department, she continues to pursue this work with the understanding that ' . . . there is no going back to the way I did it before.'

In contrast to history, philosophy as a discipline was hostile to women and unreceptive to feminist analyses. 'Fifteen years ago,' a Pathfinder remembered, 'it was a major production even to have a woman hired in philosophy . . . In my first job I was told by the chairman that he had opposed my appointment because he didn't think women could do philosophy.' The substantive challenge for feminists in philosophy was first to make 'the woman question' a bona fide philosophical problem (Gould 1976). While on one level it was a struggle to establish that women constituted appropriate subject matter, on another level it was even more radical to claim that women have a unique perspective to share from their experience as women. This standpoint epistemology directly contradicted the universal, abstract, and rational assumptions of philosophical inquiry. As one feminist noted, 'Philosophy above all thinks of itself as the activity of disinterested reason. And so to have any sort of agenda is a kind of debasement of philosophy . . . Philosophy is about universals, and women are particulars which by definition doesn't count as philosophy.' Another observed that feminist philosophers continue to be discounted due to the fact that 'it's mostly women engaged in this funny kind of work which just really confirms people's initial prejudice that women can't do real philosophy . . .' A metaphor echoed by several Pathfinders is that philosophy has been 'a hard nut to crack.'

Feminists in philosophy handled this disciplinary context in one of two ways. One way was to develop two separate agendas that would parallel each other but not intersect. The other way was to move out of philosophy and into women's studies, in an effort to integrate feminist and philosophical concerns.

As an illustration of the first strategy, one Pathfinder who was trained in analytical philosophy saw herself as writing to two sets of colleagues and audiences, each requiring 'a kind of translating or re-shaping the work to fit a different set of concerns.' Her philosophy training in logic gave her a technical expertise, as she stated, 'I am equipped . . . to explore the structure of reasoning.' She has developed a research agenda that she calls 'straight philosophy'. Recalling the emergence of her feminist perspective, she explained that by the mid-1970s she began to examine the morality of abortion and affirmative action. She remembered wanting to consider these timely issues with some other women philosophers, yet she and her peers were 'puzzled about what we could do . . . I think most of us were really at a loss to see what the relation was between our work as philosophers and our political commitments as feminists.'

Over the course of her career, she has worked to develop a feminist research agenda, but she has kept it as a distinctly separate path from the 'straight philosophy.' 'When I was doing it, I didn't see it as a new direction. I mean I understood myself to be sort of doing something different, which was much more linked with my political commitments and personal inclinations. And when that was done, I'd go back to doing more standard topics.'

As a tenured professor in a philosophy department, she continues to differentiate between the two audiences. On the one hand, there is a philosophical audience, with 'narrow disciplinary boundaries.' On the other hand, a feminist audience is broader: 'if it's academic, it tends to be interdisciplinary, and sometimes (it's) not entirely academic.' A lot of 'specific disciplinary concerns' are 'totally irrelevant' to a feminist audience; 'the level of detail and the distinctions' have to 'get excised in order to keep the question alive.' In speaking to a feminist audience, she explained, ' . . . it's not that I have to drop my philosophical standards . . . it's that I have to make my work relevant in ways that I don't have to when I'm speaking to a philosophical audience that really wouldn't care about how a particular distinction is going to get applied in the world.'

Reflecting on the development of her work over the past fifteen years, she said that 'my professional ties and my intellectual ties didn't have very much to do with each other.' This is a striking comment since she clarified her sense of professional ties to be among philosophers and her intellectual ties to be in the feminist community. She saw herself as generating scholarship for both communities.[2]

Some of her feminist colleagues have chosen not to work on two separate paths. Rather they have abandoned the standard interests of the discipline in favor of developing feminist scholarship on its own terms, far from the disciplinary base yet ultimately trying to reconcile both feminist and philosophical interests. As an example of this preference, one Pathfinder in philosophy decided to work in a women's studies program rather than a philosophy department. She had two reasons for making this decision after graduate school. The first was that she found the discipline to be 'very aggressive . . . to be challenging and critical and antagonistic in breaking down others' positions.' The second reason was that she wanted to resolve 'the mind/body split', which she found problematic both in the theory and the practice of philosophy. She perceived that a philosophy department would be intolerant of her ambitions to develop 'a non-aggressive analytical stance' and 'a historical reinterpretation of spirituality': 'At the time, I felt that it was much too difficult to push my ideas into the narrow constraints of philosophy'. She also recalls having had no models in the discipline: 'It was very hard for me to begin work because the work wasn't done yet. And until it's started it's hard to know what to do. You are always challenged from people who have a defined or articulated methodology going back a couple thousand years.'

A women's studies program offered a more promising campus context in which to nurture these interests. In that setting, she would seek and find 'continuing sources of support' for her scholarship as well as 'a language from feminist theory'. She found women's studies to be a 'stimulating political, intellectual and emotional climate which has been enormously valuable' to her scholarship. She 'felt it was important for women to have some separate space and autonomy to develop on our own terms, not always tied to a male audience or male criteria . . . I feel that in my development as a thinker, as a woman thinker, a feminist and a philosopher, it's been invaluable to be able to develop my thinking freely within the context of an autonomous women's studies program.' However, her location in a women's studies program has not entirely been immersion in 'a safe harbor' for thinking, as she has been encouraged to be actively involved in local community issues about violence against women and racism. This work as 'an activist' has 'enriched' her development of 'a holistic perspective for my scholarship'.

As a Pathfinder doing feminist philosophy, her primary colleagues are outside the discipline. Although her scholarship is perceived as innovative in feminist circles inside and outside the academy, it remains unclear whether she will succeed in persuading philosophers that it indeed counts as philosophy. Having been in women's studies for ten years, she has become more interested in 'moving (her) focus back into philosophy': 'I feel ready to do this . . . partly because I've had ten years to develop my ideas and they feel real solid to me'. Initially, she 'had qualms about presenting something as unorthodox, philosophically speaking, as a talk on fertility, sexuality and rebirth . . . Although my work may be considered part of philosophy of religion, it's basically about the meaning of life. Philosophy, to me, means the pursuit of wisdom. I reach for that. But it's more a multidisciplinary approach than a strict philosophical approach'. Her attempts to re-engage in a dialogue with philosophy department colleagues have been encouraging. She is currently employed half-time in women's studies and half-time in philosophy at a state college.

Despite innovative efforts, feminist scholars' legitimacy in philosophy does not appear to be forthcoming. A Pathfinder characterized the status of feminist work as 'fairly fragile': 'There isn't a location for feminist work in philosophy, except to some extent (now) there's some recognition . . . Fifteen years ago a philosopher might have sneered at it, whereas today that same person will be careful about the company in which he or she sneers at it.'

Feminist Scholarship as a Vocation

Indeed, the increased visibility of feminist scholarship in the American academy would make its opponents less apt to sneer openly. Over the past two decades across the country, feminists have both expanded the boundaries of their disciplines and contributed to an autonomous body of work, which is now recognized as feminist scholarship, taught in women's studies programs and, although less perceptible, integrated into departmental curricula.

The magnitude of this growth is noteworthy: from 17 courses in 1969 to over 30,000 women's studies courses, 500 degree-granting programs, and 50 centers for research on women in 1980 (Howe and Lauter 1980), not to mention the ongoing proliferation of over a hundred publications and dozens of professional associations within and outside all of the disciplines (including philosophy, several physical sciences, and even engineering). Increasingly, these women's studies activities seek and obtain substantial institutional resources for teaching and research operations, including salaries for staff and academic personnel with expertise in feminist scholarship. Even Harvard in its 1986 reversal of a twelve-year-old decision established a degree-granting program in women's studies, 'after a prudent waiting period to see if it was a genuine field of scholarly inquiry' (Nelson 1987).

Although almost two decades have passed since the Pathfinders entered graduate school, and despite the major institutionalization of women's studies as interdepartmental teaching programs, the academy has yet to accept the legitimacy of feminist scholarship as an academic vocation, whether on the programmatic level or on the individual level. Women's studies programs usually lack control over faculty hiring and promotion. Relying on administrators' discretionary resources and senior academics' departmental decisions about tenure-track faculty billets, the achievement of program status does not necessarily reflect genuine or continued validation of feminist scholarship as a coherent area of expertise on which claims to authority can rest.

While in the late 1980s one does not often hear entire women's studies programs dismissed, negative sentiments about the scholarship are openly expressed in the evaluation of individual faculty, especially in hiring and promotion decisions. Involvement in feminist scholarship and in multi-disciplinary intellectual networks is often perceived by administrators and senior academics who control peer review as 'trivial', 'self-interested', 'faddish', or, perhaps more accurately, 'subversive'. Thus, whether or not the scholarly work is cutting edge, its radical edge renders it problematic.

For example, in a well-publicized case of a feminist sociologist who appealed her tenure denial, Chancellor Sinsheimer of the University of California explained that he had dismissed the testimony of outside experts in the peer review process.

It has become clear that there is an academic network of 'progressive' social scientists who will fervently support any member of this club . . . This makes even the interpretation of outside evaluations very difficult . . . Supporters of these politically committed women . . . are by definition politically motivated, by definition invalid . . . Critics of these women, on the other hand, are motivated only by a disinterested respect for scholarship. (Sternhell 1984: 97)

Sinsheimer's statement and the subsequent granting of tenure to this scholar confirmed the inherently social nature of peer review— that without a community, feminist scholars, like other academics, could not make successful claims to expertise and authority. In this fundamental sense, the advancement of feminist scholarship has been like other aspiring professional groups, engaged in an organizational and political endeavor as well as an intellectual one.

Although Sinsheimer correctly acknowledged the existence of a 'politically committed' and 'politically motivated' community of feminist scholars, he did so in such a way as to reinforce the dominant belief that those who oppose feminist scholarship are not political. While this is only one case, it is a valuable reminder of a long history perpetuating the idea that politics and scholarship are incompatible.

Even Weber, in his famous 1918 speech 'Science as a Vocation,' put forth a normative argument that the two should be separated. In asserting that 'politics is out of place . . . on the academic platform', Weber was speaking of prophets and demagogues who, he argued, should in their teaching 'abstain' from 'imposition of a personal point of view' and from fostering a dogmatic or ideological approach (Weber 1958: 145–146). At the same time, however, he also admitted that the ability to separate the two is perhaps more difficult in the practice of scholarly inquiry than in teaching.[3]

Some feminist scholars, among other contemporary critics of positivism, insist that the dichotomy between politics and scholarship is conceptually false and in practice a fiction that has been used to legitimate claims to professional expertise (Bledstein 1976; Larson 1977;

Silva and Slaughter 1984). They assert that the work of both proponents and opponents of feminist scholarship is necessarily grounded in a political if not an ontological standpoint, even when its political premises are not made explicit. In an academic context that strives for maximizing objectivity, such a critical stance exacerbates the struggle for legitimacy of feminist scholarship.

The heart of the issue lies in the extent to which feminist scholarship may succeed not just as an area of inquiry but as a vocation. At least two significant dimensions have yet to be explored, not only conceptually but also in further empirical study. The first is the problematic nature of value commitments in an organizational structure that espouses a value-free ideology. In a Weberian sense of vocation, the pursuit of feminist scholarship would strive for value neutrality, like other scholarly callings, yet simultaneously rest on 'a passionate devotion' involving 'one's "heart and soul"' (Weber 1958: 135). As the interview data suggest, the source of feminist scholarship is indeed passionate commitment, although judged to be in excess from the point of view of conventional scholars while insufficient from the point of view of radical feminists. The pursuit of feminist scholarship as a vocation has been unlike conventional scholarly callings in that the particular brand of passionate devotion is often counter-hegemonic and the scholarship quite literally often strives to integrate heart and soul by exploring the intersection of personal, political and intellectual interests. Thus, the ideological foundations of feminist scholarship as a vocation challenge and seek to transform the very premises of traditional scholarly inquiry.

A second dimension concerns the precarious structural foundations of emerging academic vocations. In the modern academic system, the social production of knowledge rests on the enduring disciplinary division of knowledge; given the premise of specialized skills and knowledge, disciplines reproduce themselves through research training in Ph.D. programs. The possibility of the reproduction of feminist scholarship in future generations of scholars would hinge on its suitability for specialized training. In one sense, that suitability would meet the exigencies of training as in other fields, such as anthropology or even auto mechanics, where the expertise of the trainer is assumed as is the

competence in evaluating progress of apprentices. In a second and equally important sense, suitability is also determined by achieving an institutional home base where training can occur. The dynamics of sustaining commitments of institutional resources will be played out differently depending on whether the institutional home for feminist scholars is an autonomous unit, as in a department of feminist scholarship, or a token position in a discipline-based department, as is the case for Marxist scholars.

Both ideological and structural foundations point to a deeper question of historical possibility: what is the likelihood of institutionalizing a political movement? The first generation of feminist scholarship emerged out of a confluence of particular social conditions, where challenges to inhospitable organizational and intellectual contexts of the academy were spurred on by a wider political movement. In consciously risking their scholarly careers, early proponents of feminist scholarship did not intend to establish a vocation. Moreover, the emerging scholarship challenged the very premises of the ideological and structural foundations of conventional scholarship, without regard for ensuring the reproduction of feminist scholarship in future academic generations. Will feminist scholarship succeed as a vocation? That will depend on the prospects for changing the existing economic and political structures of higher education institutions sufficiently to accommodate the agenda of the proponents of feminist scholarship.

Summary

The interdisciplinary and oppositional character of feminist scholarship causes scholars in departments to live out a 'personal tension' of being both insiders and outsiders, 'rooted in the contradiction of belonging and not belonging' (Westkott 1979: 422). While this tension has thus far generated a distinctive angle for scholarly critique and questions, it also entails a burden of dual loyalties, shifting audiences, and multiple sets of criteria for evaluating one's work. For those scholars not in departments but in women's studies programs, the tension takes on a different hue: these scholars are clearly in marginal organizational positions with respect to academic power and some are situated more closely to the non-academic communities from which their feminist agendas emerged.

What can be learned from the study of how feminist scholars have made their own history? Not only can we see how a new area of knowledge was socially constructed by its proponents and supporters, but we see the organizational and political ways scholars tried to gain control over the criteria and means with which to evaluate their own intellectual products.

Academia presents a double bind in constructing new scholarship. The conventional research imperative is grounded in an ideology of merit. Those who earn rewards for innovative scholarship do so by demonstrating that their work is relevant yet unique. Access to tenure, the means of decisions and power, comes from playing by, or at least near, accepted rules and expectations. To deviate too much, whether in questions or conclusions, is to run the risk of being deemed not cutting edge but over the edge.

The emergence of feminist scholarship reveals how its proponents have worked within this academic context. A cohort of academic women did organize within and across disciplines as well as within, across and beyond campuses. Their networks provided a social forum to develop and validate ideas as well as to find a convergence among political and personal and academic interests. It is a clear instance of academic change. Yet they did so without status or power in established channels of the academy. Especially for academic women who are still under-represented proportionally up the tenure ladder, involvement in feminist scholarship jeopardizes future access to power.[4]

While critical masses of like-minded colleagues and supportive wider cultural and political milieux may have been sufficient factors in establishing a scholarly niche, they are not sufficient for subsequent institutionalization *as a vocation*. Enduring academic change requires gaining control over criteria for evaluating the scholarship produced by individual faculty. At bottom, what counts as innovative is socially defined by a community of experts with claims to authority.

Since that control resides in formal organizational structures, the participation of feminist scholars in standard academic practices has become more salient. The nature and site of struggle, then, has shifted from gaining mere recognition or inclusion as academic programs to influencing such contested academic terrains as faculty hiring and promotion, peer review of publications and grants, and doctoral students' research training and dissertation advising. These are the arenas for future negotiation about the criteria for what constitutes good scholarship, for what will reconstitute the landscape of scholarly vocations, and ultimately for who can succeed as an academic.

Acknowledgements

A draft of this manuscript benefitted from comments by Yvonna Lincoln, Gary Rhoades, Karen Sacks, Sheila Slaughter, Ann Swidler and William Tierney.

Notes

1. As cross-departmental networks on campuses crystallized in the late 1960s and into the 1970s, these forums were complemented by disciplinary associations which spawned groups of feminist scholars. In these forums, one could dialogue with disciplinary and feminist colleagues. As a philosopher explains, 'Women flock to (those) meetings because those are the only places where you get both philosophical colleagueship and feminist colleagueship. You get both of them at the same time, same place, in the same sentence. And for most women that is extremely rare'.

2. The extent to which intellectual and professional stimulation is generated by separate communities requires further empirical study. It is significant that many twentieth century curricular initiatives emerged out of intellectual, political and economic ferment in the wider American society, for example World War II and area studies, civil rights and black/ethnic studies, women's liberation and women's studies, anti-Vietnam war protests and peace studies, conservation and environmental studies (Gumport 1988).

3. While Weber stated it is a responsibility to seek 'inconvenient facts', he conceded that science cannot be 'free from presuppositions' and that such presuppositions 'cannot be proved by scientific means' (1958: 147, 143).

4. Although the representation of women in the academic profession in the United States has

increased from one-fourth in 1960 to one-third in 1980, women still hold about one-fourth of all full-time positions (Bowen and Schuster 1986: 55) and only 17 per cent of the positions at research universities (Astin and Snyder 1982: 32), the top tier (3 per cent) of the institutions in the higher education system. As a general picture of differences by rank, women are one out of two instructors, one out of three assistant professors, one out of five associate professors, and one out of ten full professors (Menges and Exum 1983: 125).

References

Astin, H., and Snyder, M. (1982), 'Affirmative action 1972–1982—a decade of response', *Change* July/August: 26–59.
Bledstein, B. (1976), *The Culture of Professionalism: The Middle Class and the Development of Higher Education in America*. New York: W. W. Norton & Company, Inc.
Bowen, H., and Schuster, J. (1986), *American Professors: A National Resource Imperiled*. New York and London: Oxford University Press.
Gould, C. (1976), 'The woman question: philosophy of liberation and the liberation of philosophy', in C. Gould and M. Wartofsky (eds.), *Women and Philosophy: Toward a Theory of Liberation*. New York: G. P. Putnam and Sons.
Gumport, P. (1987), *The Social Construction of Knowledge: Individual and Institutional Commitments to Feminist Scholarship*. Unpublished Doctoral Dissertation. Stanford University.
—— (1988), 'Curricula as signposts of cultural change'. *The Review of Higher Education* 12(1): 49–62.
Howe, F., and Lauter, P. (1980), *The Impact of Women's Studies on the Campus and the Disciplines*. Washington, DC: National Institute of Education.
Larson, M. S. (1977), *The Rise of Professionalism: A Sociological Analysis*. Berkeley and Los Angeles: University of California Press.
Menges R., and Exum W. (1983), 'Barriers to the progress of women and minority faculty', *Journal of Higher Education* 54(2): 123–144.
Nelson, G. (1987), 'Harvard approves women's studies honors concentration', *Second Century Radcliffe News*. Cambridge, MA: Radcliffe College.
Silva, E., and Slaughter, S. (1984), *Serving Power: The Making of the Academic Social Science Expert*. Westport, CT: Greenwood Press.
Sternhell, C. (1984), 'The tenure battle: the women who won't disappear', *Ms. Magazine*. October: 94–98.
Weber, M. (1958), 'Science as a vocation', in H. Gerth and C. Mills, (eds.), *From Max Weber: Essays in Sociology*. New York: Oxford University Press, pp. 129–156.
Westkott, M. (1979), 'Feminist criticism of the social sciences', *Harvard Educational Review* 49(4): 422–430.

38

The Silenced Dialogue: Power and Pedagogy in Educating Other People's Children

Lisa D. Delpit

A Black male graduate student who is also a special education teacher in a predominantly Black community is talking about his experiences in predominantly white university classes:

There comes a moment in every class where we have to discuss 'The Black Issue' and what's appropriate education for Black children. I tell you, I'm tired of arguing with those White people, because they won't listen. Well, I don't know if they really don't listen or if they just don't believe you. It seems like if you can't quote Vygotsky or something, then you don't have any validity to speak about your *own* kids. Anyway, I'm not bothering with it anymore, now I'm just in it for a grade.

A Black woman teacher in a multicultural urban elementary school is talking about her experiences in discussions with her predominantly white fellow teachers about how they should organize reading instruction to best serve students of color:

When you're talking to White people they still want it to be their way. You can try to talk to them and give them examples, but they're so headstrong, they think they know what's best for *everybody*, for *everybody's* children. They won't listen, White folks are going to do what they want to do *anyway*.

It's really hard. They just don't listen well. No, they listen, but they don't *hear*—you know how your mama used to say you listen to the radio, but you *hear* your mother? Well they don't *hear* me.

So I just try to shut them out so I can hold my temper. You can only beat your head against a brick wall for so long before you draw blood. If I try to stop arguing with them I can't help myself from getting angry. Then I end up walking around praying all day 'Please Lord, remove the bile I feel for these people so I can sleep tonight.' It's funny, but it can become a cancer, a sore.

So, I shut them out. I go back to my own little cubby, my classroom, and I try to teach the way I know will work, no matter what those folk say. And when I get Black kids, I just try to undo the damage they did.

I'm not going to let any man, woman, or child drive me crazy—White folks will try to do that to you if you let them. You just have to stop talking to them, that's what I do. I just keep smiling, but I won't talk to them.

A soft-spoken Native Alaskan woman in her forties is a student in the Education Department of the University of Alaska. One day she storms into a Black professor's office and very uncharacteristically slams the door. She plops down in a chair and, still fuming, says, 'Please tell those people, just don't help us anymore! I give up. I won't talk to them again!'

And finally, a Black woman principal who is also a doctoral student at a well-known university on the West Coast is talking about her university experiences, particularly about when a professor lectures on issues concerning educating Black children:

If you try to suggest that that's not quite the way it is, they get defensive, then you get defensive, then they'll start reciting research.

I try to give them my experiences, to explain. They just look and nod. The more I try to explain, they just look and nod, just keep looking and nodding. They don't really hear me.

Then, when it's time for class to be over, the professor tells me to come to his office to talk more. So I go. He asks for more examples of what I'm talking about, and he looks and nods while I give them.

From L. Weis and M. Fine (eds.), *Beyond Silenced Voices: Class, Race and Gender in United States Schools* (Suny Press, 1993), 119–39. Reprinted with permission.

Then he says that that's just my experiences. It doesn't really apply to most Black people.

It becomes futile because they think they know everything about everybody. What you have to say about your life, your children, doesn't mean anything. They don't really want to hear what you have to say. They wear blinders and earplugs. They only want to go on research they've read that other White people have written.

It just doesn't make any sense to keep talking to them.

Thus was the first half of the title of this text born—'The Silenced Dialogue.' One of the tragedies in the field of education is that scenarios such as these are enacted daily around the country. The saddest element is that the individuals that the Black and Native American educators speak of in these statements are seldom aware that the dialogue *has* been silenced. Most likely the white educators believe that their colleagues of color did, in the end, agree with their logic. After all, they stopped disagreeing, didn't they?

I have collected these statements since completing a recently published article. In this somewhat autobiographical account, entitled 'Skills and Other Dilemmas of a Progressive Black Educator,' I discussed my perspective as a product of a skills-oriented approach to writing and as a teacher of process-oriented approaches. I described the estrangement that I and many teachers of color feel from the progressive movement when writing-process advocates dismiss us as too 'skills oriented.' I ended the article suggesting that it was incumbent upon writing-process advocates—or indeed, advocates of any progressive movement—to enter into dialogue with teachers of color, who may not share their enthusiasm about so-called new, liberal, or progressive ideas.

In response to this article, which presented no research data and did not even cite a reference, I received numerous calls and letters from teachers, professors, and even state school personnel from around the country, both Black and white. All of the white respondents, except one, have wished to talk more about the question of skills versus process approaches—to support or reject what they perceive to be my position. On the other hand, *all* of the non-white respondents have spoken passionately on being left out of the dialogue about how best to educate children of color.

How can such complete communication

blocks exist when both parties truly believe they have the same aims? How can the bitterness and resentment expressed by the educators of color be drained so that the sores can heal? What can be done?

I believe the answer to these questions lies in ethnographic analysis, that is, in identifying and giving voice to alternative world views. Thus, I will attempt to address the concerns raised by white and Black respondents to my article 'Skills and Other Dilemmas'. My charge here is not to determine the best instructional methodology; I believe that the actual practice of good teachers of all colors typically incorporates a range of pedagogical orientations. Rather, I suggest that the differing perspectives on the debate over 'skills' versus 'process' approaches can lead to an understanding of the alienation and miscommunication, and thereby to an understanding of the 'silenced dialogue.'

In thinking through these issues, I have found what I believe to be a connecting and complex theme: what I have come to call 'the culture of power.' There are five aspects of power I would like to propose as given for this presentation:

1. Issues of power are enacted in classrooms.
2. There are codes or rules for participating in power; that is, there is a 'culture of power.'
3. The rules of the culture of power are a reflection of the rules of the culture of those who have power.
4. If you are not already a participant in the culture of power, being told explicitly the rules of that culture makes acquiring power easier.
5. Those with power are frequently least aware of—or least willing to acknowledge—its existence. Those with less power are often most aware of its existence.

The first three are by now basic tenets in the literature of the sociology of education, but the last two have seldom been addressed. The following discussion will explicate these aspects of power and their relevance to the schism between liberal educational movements and that of non-White, non-middle-class teachers and communities.

1. Isues of power are enacted in classrooms.
These issues include: the power of the teacher over the students; the power of the publishers

of textbooks and of the developers of the curriculum to determine the view of the world presented; the power of the state in enforcing compulsory schooling; and the power of an individual or group to determine another's intelligence or 'normalcy.' Finally, if schooling prepares people for jobs, and the kind of job a person has determines her or his economic status and, therefore, power, then schooling is intimately related to that power.

2. There are codes or rules for participating in power; that is, there is a 'culture of power.'
The codes or rules I'm speaking of relate to linguistic forms, communicative strategies, and presentation of self; that is, ways of talking, ways of writing, ways of dressing, and ways of interacting.

3. The rules of the culture of power are a reflection of the rules of the culture of those who have power.
This means that success in institutions—schools, workplaces, and so on—is predicated upon acquisition of the culture of those who are in power. Children from middle-class homes tend to do better in school than those from non-middle-class homes because the culture of the school is based on the culture of the upper and middle classes—of those in power. The upper and middle classes send their children to school with all the accoutrements of the culture of power; children from other kinds of families operate within perfectly wonderful and viable cultures but not cultures that carry the codes or rules of power.

4. If you are not already a participant in the culture of power, being told explicitly the rules of that culture makes acquiring power easier.
In my work within and between diverse cultures, I have come to conclude that members of any culture transmit information implicitly to co-members. However, when implicit codes are attempted across cultures, communication frequently breaks down. Each cultural group is left saying, 'Why don't those people say what they mean?' as well as, 'What's wrong with them, why don't they understand?'
Anyone who has had to enter new cultures, especially to accomplish a specific task, will know of what I speak. When I lived in several

Papua New Guinea villages for extended periods to collect data, and when I go to Alaskan villages for work with Alaskan Native communities, I have found it unquestionably easier—psychologically and pragmatically—when some kind soul has directly informed me about such matters as appropriate dress, interactional styles, embedded meanings, and taboo words or actions. I contend that it is much the same for anyone seeking to learn the rules of the culture of power. Unless one has the leisure of a lifetime of 'immersion' to learn them, explicit presentation makes learning immeasurably easier.
And now, to the fifth and last premise:

5. Those with power are frequently least aware of—or least willing to acknowledge—its existence. Those with less power are often most aware of its existence.
For many who consider themselves members of liberal or radical camps, acknowledging personal power and admitting participation in the culture of power is distinctly uncomfortable. On the other hand, those who are less powerful in any situation are most likely to recognize the power variable most acutely. My guess is that the white colleagues and instructors of those previously quoted did not perceive themselves to have power over the non-white speakers. However, either by virtue of their position, their numbers, or their access to that particular code of power of calling upon research to validate one's position, the white educators had the authority to establish what was to be considered 'truth' regardless of the opinions of the people of color, and the latter were well aware of that fact.
A related phenomenon is that liberals (and here I am using the term 'liberal' to refer to those whose beliefs include striving for a society based upon maximum individual freedom and autonomy) seem to act under the assumption that to make any rules or expectations explicit is to act against liberal principles, to limit the freedom and autonomy of those subjected to the explicitness.
I thank Fred Erickson for a comment that led me to look again at a tape by John Gumperz on cultural dissonance in cross-cultural interactions. One of the episodes showed an East Indian interviewing for a job with an all-white committee. The interview was a complete failure, even though several of the

interviewers appeared to really want to help the applicant. As the interview rolled steadily downhill, these 'helpers' became more and more indirect in their questioning, which exacerbated the problems the applicant had in performing appropriately. Operating from a different cultural perspective, he got fewer and fewer clear clues as to what was expected of him, which ultimately resulted in his failure to secure the position.

I contend that as the applicant showed less and less aptitude for handling the interview, the power differential became ever more evident to the interviewers. The 'helpful' interviewers, unwilling to acknowledge themselves as having power over the applicant, became more and more uncomfortable. Their indirectness was an attempt to lessen the power differential and their discomfort by lessening the power-revealing explicitness of their questions and comments.

When acknowledging and expressing power, one tends towards explicitness (as in yelling to your 10-year-old, 'Turn the radio down!'). When de-emphasizing power, there is a move toward indirect communication. Therefore, in the interview setting, those who sought to help, to express their egalitarianism with the East Indian applicant, became more and more indirect—and less and less helpful—in their questions and comments.

In literacy instruction, explicitness might be equated with direct instruction. Perhaps the ultimate expression of explicitness and direct instruction in the primary classroom is Distar. This reading program is based on a behaviorist model in which reading is taught through the direct instruction of phonics generalizations and blending. The teacher's role is to maintain the full attention of the group by continuous questioning, eye contact, finger snaps, hand claps, and other gestures, and by eliciting choral responses and initiating some sort of award system.

When the program was introduced, it arrived with a flurry of research data that 'proved' that all children—even those who were 'culturally deprived'—could learn to read using this method. Soon there was a strong response, first from academics and later from many classroom teachers, stating that the program was terrible. What I find particularly interesting, however, is that the primary issue of the conflict over Distar has not been over its instructional efficacy—usually the students did learn to read—but the expression of explicit power in the classroom. The liberal educators opposed the methods—the direct instruction, the explicit control exhibited by the teacher. As a matter of fact, it was not unusual (even now) to hear of the program spoken of as 'fascist.'

I am not an advocate of Distar, but I will return to some of the issues that the program—and direct instruction in general—raises in understanding the differences between progressive white educators and educators of color.

To explore those differences, I would like to present several statements typical of those made with the best of intentions by middle-class liberal educators. To the surprise of the speakers, it is not unusual for such content to be met by vocal opposition or stony silence from people of color. My attempt here is to examine the underlying assumptions of both camps.

'I want the same thing for everyone else's children as I want for mine.'
To provide schooling for everyone's children that reflects liberal, middle-class values and aspirations is to ensure the maintenance of the status quo, to ensure that power, the culture of power, remains in the hands of those who already have it. Some children come to school with more accoutrements of the culture of power already in place—'cultural capital,' as some critical theorists refer to it—some with less. Many liberal educators hold that the primary goal for education is for children to become autonomous, to develop fully who they are in the classroom setting without having arbitrary, outside standards forced upon them. This is a very reasonable goal for people whose children are already participants in the culture of power and who have already internalized its codes.

But parents who don't function within that culture often want something else. It's not that they disagree with the former aim, it's just that they want something more. They want to ensure that the school provides their children with discourse patterns, interactional styles, and spoken and written language codes that will allow them success in the larger society.

It was the lack of attention to this concern that created such a negative outcry in the Black community when well-intentioned white liberal educators introduced 'dialect readers.' These were seen as a plot to prevent the schools from teaching the linguistic aspects of the culture of power, thus dooming Black children to a permanent outsider caste. As one parent demanded, 'My kids know how to be Black—you all teach them how to be successful in the white man's world.'

Several Black teachers have said to me recently that as much as they'd like to believe otherwise, they cannot help but conclude that many of the 'progressive' educational strategies imposed by liberals upon Black and poor children could only be based on a desire to ensure that the liberals' children get sole access to the dwindling pool of American jobs. Some have added that the liberal educators believe themselves to be operating with good intentions, but that these good intentions are only conscious delusions about their unconscious true motives. One of Black anthropologist John Gwaltney's informants reflects this perspective with her tongue-in-cheek observation that the biggest difference between Black folks and white folks is that Black folks *know* when they're lying!

Let me try to clarify how this might work in literacy instruction. A few years ago I worked on an analysis of two popular reading programs, Distar and a progressive program that focused on higher-level critical thinking skills. In one of the first lessons of the progressive program, the children are introduced to the names of the letter *m* and *e*. In the same lesson they are then taught the sound made by each of the letters, how to write each of the letters, and that when the two are blended together they produce the word *me*.

As an experienced first-grade teacher, I am convinced that a child needs to be familiar with a significant number of these concepts to be able to assimilate so much new knowledge in one sitting. By contrast, Distar presents the same information in about forty lessons.

I would not argue for the pace of the Distar lessons; such a slow pace would only bore most kids—but what happened in the other lesson is that it merely provided an opportunity for those who already knew the content to exhibit that they knew it, or at most perhaps to build one new concept onto what was already known. This meant that the child who did not come to school already primed with what was to be presented would be labeled as needing 'remedial' instruction from day one; indeed, this determination would be made before he

or she was ever taught. In fact, Distar was 'successful' because it actually *taught* new information to children who had not already acquired it at home. Although the more progressive system was ideal for some children, for others it was a disaster.

I do not advocate a simplistic 'basic skills' approach for children outside of the culture of power. It would be (and has been) tragic to operate as if these children were incapable of critical and higher-order thinking and reasoning. Rather, I suggest that schools must provide these children the content that other families from a different cultural orientation provide at home. This does not mean separating children according to family background, but instead, ensuring that each classroom incorporate strategies appropriate for all the children in its confines.

And I do not advocate that it is the school's job to attempt to change the homes of poor and non-white children to match the homes of those in the culture of power. That may indeed be a form of cultural genocide. I have frequently heard schools call poor parents 'uncaring' when parents respond to the school's urging, that they change their home life in order to facilitate their children's learning, by saying, 'But that's the school's job.' What the school personnel fail to understand is that if the parents were members of the culture of power and lived by its rules and codes, then they would transmit those codes to their children. In fact, they transmit another culture that children must learn at home in order to survive in their communities.

'Child-centered, whole language, and process approaches are needed in order to allow a democratic state of free, autonomous, empowered adults, and because research has shown that children learn best through these methods.'

People of color are, in general, skeptical of research as a determiner of our fates. Academic research has, after all, found us genetically inferior, culturally deprived, and verbally deficient. But beyond that general caveat, and despite my or others' personal preferences, there is little research data supporting the major tenets of process approaches over other forms of literacy instruction, and virtually no evidence that such approaches are more efficacious for children of color.

Although the problem is not necessarily inherent in the method, in some instances adherents of process approaches to writing create situations in which students ultimately find themselves held accountable for knowing a set of rules about which no one has ever directly informed them. Teachers do students no service to suggest, even implicitly, that 'product' is not important. In this country, students will be judged on their product regardless of the process they utilized to achieve it. And that product, based as it is on the specific codes of a particular culture, is more readily produced when the directives of how to produce it are made explicit.

If such explicitness is not provided to students, what it feels like to people who are old enough to judge is that there are secrets being kept, that time is being wasted, that the teacher is abdicating his or her duty to teach. A doctoral student in my acquaintance was assigned to a writing class to hone his writing skills. The student was placed in the section led by a white professor who utilized a process approach, consisting primarily of having the students write essays and then assemble into groups to edit each others' papers. That procedure infuriated this particular student. He had many angry encounters with the teacher about what she was doing. In his words:

I didn't feel she was teaching us anything. She wanted us to correct each others' papers and we were there to learn from her. She didn't teach anything, absolutely nothing.

Maybe they're trying to learn what Black folks knew all the time. We understand how to improvise, how to express ourselves creatively. When I'm in a classroom, I'm not looking for that, I'm looking for structure, the more formal language.

Now my buddy was in [a] Black teacher's class. And that lady was very good. She went through and explained and defined each part of the structure. This [white] teacher didn't get along with that Black teacher. She said that she didn't agree with her methods. But *I* don't think that White teacher *had* any methods.

When I told this gentleman that what the teacher was doing was called a process method of teaching writing, his response was, 'Well, at least now I know that she *thought* that she was doing *something*. I thought she was just a fool who couldn't teach and didn't want to try.'

This sense of being cheated can be so strong that the student may be completely turned off to the educational system. Amanda Branscombe, an accomplished white teacher, recently wrote a letter discussing her work with working-class Black and white students at a community college in Alabama. She had given these students my 'Skills and Other Dilemmas' article to read and discuss, and wrote that her students really understood and identified with what I was saying. To quote her letter:

One young man said that he had dropped out of high school because he failed the exit exam. He noted that he had then passed the GED without a problem after three weeks of prep. He said that his high school English teacher claimed to use a process approach, but what she really did was hide behind fancy words to give herself permission to do nothing in the classroom.

The students I have spoken of seem to be saying that the teacher has denied them access to herself as the source of knowledge necessary to learn the forms they need to succeed. Again, I tentatively attribute the problem to teachers' resistance to exhibiting power in the classroom. Somehow, to exhibit one's personal power as expert source is viewed as disempowering one's students.

Two qualifiers are necessary, however. The teacher cannot be the only expert in the classroom. To deny students their own expert knowledge *is* to disempower them. Amanda Branscombe, when she was working with Black high school students classified as 'slow learners,' had the students analyze RAP songs to discover their underlying patterns. The students became the experts in explaining to the teacher the rules for creating a new RAP song. The teacher then used the patterns the students identified as a base to begin an explanation of the structure of grammar, and then of Shakespeare's plays. Both student and teacher are expert at what they know best.

The second qualifier is that merely adopting direct instruction is not the answer. Actual writing for real audiences and real purposes is a vital element in helping students to understand that they have an important voice in their own learning processes. Siddle examines the results of various kinds of interventions in a primarily process-oriented writing class for Black students. Based on readers' blind assessments, she found that the intervention that produced the most positive changes in the students' writing was a 'minilesson' consisting of direct instruction about some standard writing convention. But what produced the *second* highest number of positive changes was a subsequent student-centered conference with the teacher. (Peer conferencing in this group of Black students who were not members of the culture of power produced the least-number of changes in students' writing. However, the classroom teacher maintained—and I concur—that such activities are necessary to introduce the elements of 'real audience' into the task, along with more teacher-directed strategies.)

'It's really a shame but she (that Black teacher upstairs) seems to be so authoritarian, so focused on skills and so teacher directed. Those poor kids never seem to be allowed to really express their creativity. (And she even yells at them.)'
This statement directly concerns the display of power and authority in the classroom. One way to understand the difference in perspective between Black teachers and their progressive colleagues on this issue is to explore culturally influenced oral interactions.

In *Ways With Words*, Shirley Brice Heath quotes the verbal directives given by the middle-class 'townspeople' teachers:

— 'Is this where the scissors belong?'
— 'You want to do your best work today.'

By contrast, many Black teachers are more likely to say:

— 'Put those scissors on that shelf.'
— 'Put your name on the papers and make sure to get the right answer for each question.'

Is one oral style more authoritarian than another?

Other researchers have identified differences in middle-class and working-class speech to children. Snow *et al.*, for example, report that working-class mothers use more directives to their children than do middle- and upper-class parents. Middle-class parents are likely to give the directive to a child to take his bath as, 'Isn't it time for your bath?' Even though the utterance is couched as a question, both child and adult understand it as a directive. The child may respond with 'Aw Mom, can't I wait until…,' but whether or not negotiation is attempted, both conversants understand the intent of the utterance.

By contrast, a Black mother, in whose house I was recently a guest, said to her eight-year-old son, 'Boy, get your rusty behind in that bathtub.' Now I happen to know that this woman loves her son as much as any mother,

but she would never have posed the directive to her son to take a bath in the form of a question. Were she to ask, 'Would you like to take your bath now?' she would not have been issuing a directive but offering a true alternative. Consequently, as Heath suggests, upon entering school the child from such a family may not understand the indirect statement of the teacher as a direct command. Both white and Black working-class children in the communities Heath studied 'had difficulty interpreting these indirect requests for adherence to an unstated set of rules'.

But those veiled commands are commands none the less, representing true power, and with true consequences for disobedience. If veiled commands are ignored, the child will be labeled a behavior problem and possibly officially classified as behavior disordered. In other words, the attempt by the teacher to reduce an exhibition of power by expressing herself in indirect terms may remove the very explicitness that the child needs to understand the rules of the new classroom culture.

A Black elementary school principal in Fairbanks, Alaska, reported to me that she has a lot of difficulty with Black children who are placed in some White teachers' classrooms. The teachers often send the children to the office for disobeying teacher directives. Their parents are frequently called in for conferences. The parents' response to the teacher is usually the same: 'They do what I say; if you just *tell* them what to do, they'll do it. I tell them at home that they have to listen to what you say.' And so, does not the power still exist? Its veiled nature only makes it more difficult for some children to respond appropriately, but that in no way mitigates its existence.

I don't mean to imply, however, that the only time the Black child disobeys the teacher is when he or she misunderstands the request for certain behavior. There are other factors that may produce such behavior. Black children expect an authority figure to act with authority. When the teacher instead acts as a 'chum,' the message sent is that this adult has no authority, and the children react accordingly. One reason this is so is that Black people often view issues of power and authority differently than people from main-stream middle-class backgrounds. Many people of color expect authority to be earned by personal efforts and exhibited by personal characteristics. In other words, 'the authoritative person gets to be a teacher because she is authoritative.' Some members of middle-class cultures, by contrast, expect one to achieve authority by the acquisition of an authoritative role. That is, 'the teacher is the authority because she is the teacher.'

In the first instance, because authority is earned, the teacher must consistently prove the characteristics that give her authority. These characteristics may vary across cultures, but in the Black community they tend to cluster around several abilities. The authoritative teacher can control the class through exhibition of personal power; establishes meaningful interpersonal relationships that garner student respect; exhibits a strong belief that all students can learn; establishes a standard of achievement and 'pushes' the students to achieve that standard; and holds the attention of the students by incorporating interactional features of Black communicative style in his or her teaching.

By contrast, the teacher whose authority is vested in the role has many more options of behavior at her disposal. For instance, she does not need to express any sense of personal power because her authority does not come from anything she herself does or says. Hence, the power she actually holds may be veiled in such questions/commands as 'Would you like to sit down now?' If the children in her class understand authority as she does, it is mutually agreed upon that they are to obey her no matter how indirect, soft-spoken, or unassuming she may be. Her indirectness and soft-spokenness may indeed be, as I suggested earlier, an attempt to reduce the implication of overt power in order to establish a more egalitarian and non-authoritarian classroom atmosphere.

If the children operate under another notion of authority, however, then there is trouble. The Black child may perceive the middle-class teacher as weak, ineffectual, and incapable of taking on the role of being the teacher; therefore, there is no need to follow her directives. In her dissertation, Michelle Foster quotes one young Black man describing such a teacher:

She is boring, bo:ring. She could do something creative. Instead she just stands there. She can't control the class, doesn't know how to control the class. She asked me what she was doing wrong. I told her she just stands there like she's meditating. I told her she could be meditating for all I know. She says that

we're supposed to know what to do. I told her I don't know nothin' unless she tells me. She just can't control the class. I hope we don't have her next semester.

But of course the teacher may not view the problem as residing in herself but in the student, and the child may once again become the behavior-disordered Black boy in special education.

What characteristics do Black students attribute to the good teacher? Again, Foster's dissertation provides a quotation that supports my experience with Black students. A young Black man is discussing a former teacher with a group of friends:

We had fu::n in her class, but she was mean. I can remember she used to say, 'Tell me what's in the story, Wayne.' She pushed, she used to get on me and push me to know. She made us learn. We had to get in the books. There was this tall guy and he tried to take her on, but she was in charge of that class and she didn't let anyone run her. I still have this book we used in her class. It's a bunch of stories in it. I just read one on Coca-Cola again the other day.

To clarify, this student was *proud* of the teacher's 'meanness,' an attribute he seemed to describe as the ability to run the class and pushing and expecting students to learn. Now, does the liberal perspective of the negatively authoritarian Black teacher really hold up? I suggest that although all 'explicit' Black teachers are not also good teachers, there are different attitudes in different cultural groups about which characteristics make for a good teacher. Thus, it is impossible to create a model for the good teacher without taking issues of culture and community context into account.

And now to the final comment I present for examination:

'Children have the right to their own language, their own culture. We must fight cultural hegemony and fight the system by insisting that children be allowed to express themselves in their own language style. It is not they, the children, who must change, but the schools. To push children to do anything else is repressive and reactionary.'

A statement such as this originally inspired me to write the 'Skills and Other Dilemmas' article. It was first written as a letter to a colleague in response to a situation that had developed in our department. I was teaching a senior-level teacher education course. Students were asked to prepare a written autobiographical document for the class that would also be shared with their placement school prior to their student teaching.

One student, a talented young Native American woman, submitted a paper in which the ideas were lost because of technical problems—from spelling to sentence structure to paragraph structure. Removing her name, I duplicated the paper for a discussion with some faculty members. I had hoped to initiate a discussion about what we could do to ensure that our students did not reach the senior level without getting assistance in technical writing skills when they needed them.

I was amazed at the response. Some faculty implied that the student should never have been allowed into the teacher education program. Others, some of the more progressive minded, suggested that I was attempting to function as gatekeeper by raising the issue and had internalized repressive and disempowering forces of the power élite to suggest that something was wrong with a Native American student just because she had another style of writing. With few exceptions, I found myself alone in arguing against both camps.

No, this student should not have been denied entry to the program. To deny her entry under the notion of upholding standards is to blame the victim for the crime. We cannot justifiably enlist exclusionary standards when the reason this student lacked the skills demanded was poor teaching at best and institutionalized racism at worst.

However, to bring this student into the program and pass her through without attending to obvious deficits in the codes needed for her to function effectively as a teacher is equally criminal—for though we may assuage our own consciences for not participating in victim blaming, she will surely be accused and convicted as soon as she leaves the university. As Native Alaskans were quick to tell me, and as I understood through my own experience in the Black community, not only would she not be hired as a teacher, but those who did not hire her would make the (false) assumption that the university was putting out only incompetent Natives and that they should stop looking seriously at any Native applicants. A white applicant who exhibits problems is an individual with problems. A person of color who exhibits problems immediately becomes a representative of her cultural group.

No, either stance is criminal. The answer is to *accept* students but also to take responsibility to *teach* them. I decided to talk to the student and found out she had recognized that she needed some assistance in the technical aspects of writing soon after she entered the university as a freshman. She had gone to various members of the education faculty and received the same two kinds of responses I met with four years later: faculty members told her either that she should not even attempt to be a teacher, or that it didn't matter and that she shouldn't worry about such trivial issues. In her desperation, she had found a helpful professor in the English Department, but he left the university when she was in her sophomore year.

We sat down together, worked out a plan for attending to specific areas of writing competence, and set up regular meetings. I stressed to her the need to use her own learning process as insight into how best to teach her future students those 'skills' that her own schooling had failed to teach her. I gave her some explicit rules to follow in some areas; for others, we devised various kinds of journals that, along with readings about the structure of the language, allowed her to find her own insights into how the language worked. All that happened two years ago, and the young woman is now successfully teaching. What the experience led me to understand is that pretending that gatekeeping points don't exist is to ensure that many students will not pass through them.

Now you may have inferred that I believe that because there is a culture of power, everyone should learn the codes to participate in it, and that is how the world should be. Actually, nothing could be further from the truth. I believe in a diversity of style, and I believe the world will be diminished if cultural diversity is ever obliterated. Further, I believe strongly, as do my liberal colleagues, that each cultural group should have the right to maintain its own language style. When I speak, therefore, of the culture of power, I don't speak of how I wish things to be but of how they are.

I further believe that to act as if power does not exist is to ensure that the power status quo remains the same. To imply to children or adults (but of course the adults won't believe you anyway) that it doesn't matter how you talk or how you write is to ensure their ultimate failure. I prefer to be honest with my students. Tell them that their language and cultural style is unique and wonderful but that there is a political power game that is also being played, and if they want to be in on that game there are certain games that they too must play.

But don't think that I let the onus of change rest entirely with the students. I am also involved in political work both inside and outside of the educational system, and that political work demands that I place myself to influence as many gatekeeping points as possible. And it is there that I agitate for change—pushing gatekeepers to open their doors to a variety of styles and codes. What I'm saying, however, is that I do not believe that political change toward diversity can be effected from the bottom up, as do some of my colleagues. They seem to believe that if we accept and encourage diversity within classrooms of children, then diversity will automatically be accepted as gatekeeping points.

I believe that will never happen. What will happen is that the students who reach the gatekeeping points—like Amanda Branscombe's student who dropped out of high school because he failed his exit exam—will understand that they have been lied to and will react accordingly. No, I am certain that if we are truly to effect societal change, we cannot do so from the bottom up, but we must push and agitate from the top down. And in the meantime, we must take the responsibility to *teach*, to provide for students who do not already possess them, the additional codes of power.

But I also do not believe that we should teach students to passively adopt an alternate code. They must be encouraged to understand the value of the code they already possess as well as to understand the power realities in this country. Otherwise they will be unable to work to change these realities. And how does one do that?

Martha Demientieff, a masterly Native Alaskan teacher of Athabaskan Indian students, tells me that her students, who live in a small, isolated, rural village of less than two hundred people, are not aware that there are different codes of English. She takes their writing and analyzes it for features of what has been referred to by Alaskan linguists as 'Village English,' and then covers half a bulletin board with words or phrases from the students' writing, which she labels 'Our Heritage Language.' On the other half of the bulletin board she puts the equivalent statements in 'standard English,' which she labels 'Formal English.'

She and the students spend a long time on the 'Heritage English' section, savoring the words, discussing the nuances. She tells the students, 'That's the way we say things. Doesn't it feel good? Isn't it the absolute best way of getting that idea across?' Then she turns to the other side of the board. She tells the students that there are people, not like those in their village, who judge others by the way they talk or write.

We listen to the way people talk, not to judge them, but to tell what part of the river they come from. These other people are not like that. They think everybody needs to talk like them. Unlike us, they have a hard time hearing what people say if they don't talk exactly like them. Their way of talking and writing is called 'Formal English.'

We have to feel a little sorry for them because they have only one way to talk. We're going to learn two ways to say things. Isn't that better? One way will be our Heritage way. The other will be Formal English. Then, when we go to get jobs, we'll be able to talk like those people who only know and can only really listen to one way. Maybe after we get the jobs we can help them to learn how it feels to have another language, like ours, that feels so good. We'll talk like them when we have to, but we'll always know our way is best.

Martha then does all sorts of activities with the notions of Formal and Heritage or informal English. She tells the students,

In the village, everyone speaks informally most of the time unless there's a potlatch or something. You don't think about it, you don't worry about following any rules—it's sort of like how you eat food at a picnic—nobody pays attention to whether you use your fingers or a fork, and it feels *so* good. Now, Formal English is more like a formal dinner. There are rules to follow about where the knife and fork belong, about where people sit, about how you eat. That can be really nice, too, because it's nice to dress up sometimes.

The students then prepare a formal dinner in the class, for which they dress up and set a big table with fancy tablecloths, china, and silverware. They speak only Formal English at this meal. Then they prepare a picnic where only informal English is allowed.

She also contrasts the 'wordy' academic

way of saying things with the metaphoric style of Athabaskan. The students discuss how book language always uses more words, but in Heritage language, the shorter way of saying something is always better. Students then write papers in the academic way, discussing with Martha and with each other whether they believe they've said enough to sound like a book. Next, they take those papers and try to reduce the meaning to a few sentences. Finally, students further reduce the message to a 'saying' brief enough to go on the front of a T-shirt, and the sayings are put on little paper T-shirts that the students cut out and hang throughout the room. Sometimes the students reduce other authors' wordy texts to their essential meanings as well.

The following transcript provides another example. It is from a conversation between a Black teacher and a Southern Black high school student named Joey, who is a speaker of Black English. The teacher believes it very important to discuss openly and honestly the issues of language diversity and power. She has begun the discussion by giving the student a children's book written in Black English to read.

Teacher: What do you think about the book?
Joey: I think it's nice.
Teacher: Why?
Joey: I don't know. It just told about a Black family, that's all.
Teacher: Was it difficult to read?
Joey: No.
Teacher: Was the text different from what you have seen in other books?
Joey: Yeah. The writing was.
Teacher: How?
Joey: It use more of a southern-like accent in this book.
Teacher: Uhm-hmm. do you think that's good or bad?
Joey: Well, uh, I don't think it's good for people down this a way, cause that's the way they grow up talking anyway. They ought to get the right way to talk.
Teacher: Oh. So you think it's wrong to talk like that?
Joey: Well . . . [*Laughs*]
Teacher: Hard question, huh?
Joey: Uhm-hmm, that's a hard question. But I think they shouldn't make books like that.
Teacher: Why?
Joey: Because they not using the right way to talk and in school they take off for that and li'l chirren grow up talking like that and reading like that so they might think that's right and all the time they

getting bad grades in school, talking like that and writing like that.
Teacher: Do you think they should be getting bad grades for talking like that?
Joey: [*Pauses, answers very slowly*] No . . . No.
Teacher: So you don't think that it matters whether you talk one way or another?
Joey: No, not long as you understood.
Teacher: Uhm-hmm. Well, that's, a hard question for me to answer, too. It's, ah, that's a question that's come up in a lot of schools now as to whether they should correct children who speak the way we speak all the time. Cause when we're talking to each other we talk like that even though we might not talk like that when we get into other situations, and who's to say whether it's—
Joey: [*Interrupting*] Right or wrong.
Teacher: Yeah.
Joey: Maybe they ought to come up with another kind of . . . maybe Black English or something. A course in Black English. Maybe Black folks would be good in that cause people talk, I mean Black people talk like that, so . . . but I guess there's a right way and wrong way to talk, you know, not regarding what race. I don't know.
Teacher: But who decided what's right or wrong?
Joey: Well that's true . . . I guess White people did.
[*Laughter. End of tape.*]

Notice how throughout the conversation Joey's consciousness has been raised by thinking about codes of language. This teacher further advocates having students interview various personnel officers in actual workplaces about their attitudes toward divergent styles in oral and written language. Students begin to understand how arbitrary language standards are, but also how politically charged they are. They compare various pieces written in different styles, discuss the impact of different styles on the message by making translations and back translations across styles, and discuss the history, apparent purpose, and contextual appropriateness of each of the technical writing rules presented by their teacher. *And* they practice writing different forms to different audiences based on rules appropriate for each audience. Such a program not only 'teaches' standard linguistic forms, but also explores aspects of power as exhibited through linguistic forms.

Tony Burgess, in a study of secondary writing in England by Britton, Burgess, Martin, McLeod, and Rosen, suggests that we should not teach 'iron conventions . . . imposed without rationale or grounding in communicative intent,' . . . but 'critical and ultimately cultural awarenesses'. Courtney Cazden calls for a two-pronged approach:

1. Continuous opportunities for writers to participate in some authentic bit of the unending conversation . . . thereby becoming part of a vital community of talkers and writers in a particular domain, and
2. Periodic, temporary focus on conventions of form, taught as cultural conventions expected in a particular community.

Just so that there is no confusion about what Cazden means by a focus on conventions of form, or about what I mean by 'skills,' let me stress that neither of us is speaking of page after page of 'skill sheets' creating compound words or identifying nouns and adverbs, but rather about helping students gain a useful knowledge of the conventions of print while engaging in real and useful communicative activities. Kay Rowe Grubis, a junior high school teacher in a multicultural school, makes lists of certain technical rules for her eighth graders' review and then gives them papers from a third grade to 'correct.' The students not only have to correct other students' work, but also tell them why they have changed or questioned aspects of the writing.

A village teacher, Howard Cloud, teaches his high school students the conventions of formal letter writing and the formulation of careful questions in the context of issues surrounding the amendment of the Alaska Land Claims Settlement Act. Native Alaskan leaders hold differing views on this issue, critical to the future of local sovereignty and land rights. The students compose letters to leaders who reside in different areas of the state seeking their perspectives, set up audioconference calls for interview/debate sessions, and, finally, develop a videotape to present the differing views.

To summarize, I suggest that students must be *taught* the codes needed to participate fully in the mainstream of American life, not by being forced to attend to hollow, inane, decontextualized subskills, but rather within the context of meaningful communicative endeavors; that they must be allowed the resource of the teacher's expert knowledge, while being helped to acknowledge their own 'expertness' as well; and that even while students are assisted in learning the culture of power, they must also be helped to learn about

the arbitrariness of those codes and about the power relationships they represent.

I am also suggesting that appropriate education of poor children and children of color can only be devised in consultation with adults who share their culture. Black parents, teachers of color, and members of poor communities must be allowed to participate fully in the discussion of what kind of instruction is in their children's best interest. Good liberal intentions are not enough. In an insightful study entitled 'Racism without Racists: Institutional Racism in Urban Schools,' Massey, Scott, and Dornbusch found that under the pressures of teaching, and with all intentions of 'being nice,' teachers had essentially stopped attempting to teach Black children. In their words: 'We have shown that oppression can arise out of warmth, friendliness, and concern. Paternalism and a lack of challenging standards are creating a distorted system of evaluation in the schools'.[19] Educators must open themselves to, and allow themselves to be affected by, these alternative voices.

In conclusion, I am proposing a resolution for the skills/process debate. In short, the debate is fallacious; the dichotomy is false. The issue is really an illusion created initially not by teachers but by academics whose world view demands the creation of categorical divisions—not for the purpose of better teaching, but for the goal of easier analysis. As I have been reminded by many teachers since the publication of my article, those who are most skillful at educating Black and poor children do not allow themselves to be placed in 'skills' or 'process' boxes. They understand the need for both approaches, the need to help students to establish their own voices, but to coach those voices to produce notes that will be heard clearly in the larger society.

The dilemma is not really in the debate over instructional methodology, but rather in communicating across cultures and in addressing the more fundamental issue of power, of whose voice gets to be heard in determining what is best for poor children and children of color. Will Black teachers and parents continue to be silenced by the very forces that claim to 'give voice' to our children? Such an outcome would be tragic, for both groups truly have something to say to one another. As a result of careful listening to alternative points of view, I have myself come to a viable synthesis of perspectives. But both sides do need to be able to listen, and I contend that it is those with the most power, those in the majority, who must take the greater responsibility for initiating the process.

To do so takes a very special kind of listening, listening that requires not only open eyes and ears, but open hearts and minds. We do not really see through our eyes or hear through our ears, but through our beliefs. To put our beliefs on hold is to cease to exist as ourselves for a moment—and that is not easy. It is painful as well, because it means turning yourself inside out, giving up your own sense of who you are, and being willing to see yourself in the unflattering light of another's angry gaze. It is not easy, but it is the only way to learn what it might feel like to be someone else and the only way to start the dialogue.

There are several guidelines. We must keep the perspective that people are experts on their own lives. There are certainly aspects of the outside world of which they may not be aware, but they can be the only authentic chroniclers of their own experience. We must not be too quick to deny their interpretations, or accuse them of 'false consciousness.' We must believe that people are rational beings, and therefore always act rationally. We may not understand their rationales, but that in no way militates against the existence of these rationales or reduces our responsibility to attempt to apprehend them. And finally, we must learn to be vulnerable enough to allow our world to turn upside down in order to allow the realities of others to edge themselves into our consciousness. In other words, we must become ethnographers in the true sense.

Teachers are in an ideal position to play this role, to attempt to get all of the issues on the table in order to initiate true dialogue. This can only be done, however, by seeking out those whose perspectives may differ most, by learning to give their words complete attention, by understanding one's own power, even if that power stems merely from being in the majority, by being unafraid to raise questions about discrimination and voicelessness with

people of color, and to listen, no, to *hear* what they say. I suggest that the results of such interactions may be the most powerful and empowering coalescence yet seen in the educational realm—for *all* teachers and for *all* the students they teach.

References

Apple, M. W. (1979), *Ideology and Curriculum* (Boston: Routledge and Kegan Paul).

Bernstein, B. (1975), 'Class and Pedagogies: Visible and Invisible', in B. Bernstein, *Class, Codes, and Control* (vol. 3, Boston: Routledge and Kegan Paul).

Britton, J., Burgess, T., Martin, N., McLeod, A., and Rosen, H. (1975/1977), *The Development of Writing Abilities* (London: Macmillan Education for the Schools Council, and Urbana, Ill.: National Council of Teachers of English).

Cazden, C. (1987, January), *The Myth of Autonomous Text* (Paper presented at the Third International Conference on Thinking, Hawaii).

Delpit, L. D. (1986), 'Skills and Other Dilemmas of a Progressive Black Educator', *Harvard Educational Review*, 56/4, 379–85.

Foster, M. (1987), '*It's Cookin' Now*': An Ethnographic Study of the Teaching Style of a Successful Black Teacher in an Urban Community College (unpubl. doctoral dissertation, Harvard University).

Gwaltney, J. (1980), *Drylongso* (New York: Vintage Books).

Heath, S. B. (1983), *Ways with Words* (Cambridge: Cambridge University Press).

Massey, G. C., Scott, M. V., and Dornbusch, S. M. (1975), 'Racism Without Racists: Institutional Racism in Urban Schools', *The Black Scholar*, 7/3, 2–11.

Siddle, E. V. (1986), *A Critical Assessment of the Natural Process Approach to Teaching Writing* (unpubl. qualifying paper, Harvard University).

—— (1988), *The Effect of Intervention Strategies on the Revisions Ninth Graders Make in a Narrative Essay* (unpubl. doctoral dissertation, Harvard University).

Snow, C. E., Arlman-Rup. A., Hassing, Y., Josbe, J., Joosten, J., and Vorster, J. (1976), 'Mother's Speech in Three Social Classes', *Journal of Psycholinguistic Research*, 5, 1–20.

39

What Postmodernists Forget: Cultural Capital and Official Knowledge

Michael W. Apple

Introduction

Everyone stared at the department chair in amazement. Jaws simply dropped. Soon the room was filled with a nearly chaotic mixture of sounds of anger and disbelief. It wasn't the first time she had informed us about what was 'coming down from on high'. Similar things had occurred before. After all, this was just another brick that was being removed. Yet, to each and every one of us in that room it was clear from that moment on that for all of our struggles to protect education from being totally integrated into the rightist project of economic competitiveness and rationalization, we were losing.

It was hard to bring order to the meeting. But, slowly, we got our emotions under control long enough to hear what the State Department of Public Instruction and the Legislature had determined was best for all of the students in Wisconsin—from kindergarten to the university. Starting the next year, all undergraduate students who wished to become teachers would have to take a course on Education for Employment, in essence a course on the 'benefits of the free enterprise system'. At the same time, all school curricula at the elementary and secondary levels—from five-year-olds on up—would have to integrate within their teaching a coherent program of education for employment as well. After all, you can't start too young, can you? Education was simply the supplier of 'human capital' for the private sector, after all.

I begin with this story because I think it is often better to start in our guts, so to speak, to start with our experiences as teachers and students in this time to conservatism. I begin here as well because, even though there is a new administration in Washington which may rein in some of the excesses of the rightist social agenda, the terms of debate and the existing economic and social conditions have been transformed remarkably in a conservative direction (Apple 1993). We should not be romantic about what will happen at our schools and universities, especially given the fiscal crisis of the state and the acceptance of major aspects of the conservative social and economic agenda within both political parties. The story I told a moment ago can serve as a metaphor for what is happening to so much of educational life at universities and elsewhere.

Let me situate this story within the larger transformations in education and the wider society that the conservative alliance has attempted.

Between Neo-conservatism and Neo-liberalism

Conservatism by its very name announces one interpretation of its agenda. It conserves. Other interpretations are possible of course. One could say, more wryly, that conservatism believes that nothing should be done for the first time (Honderich 1990: 1). Yet in many ways, in the current situation this is deceptive. For with the Right now in ascendancy in many nations, we are witnessing a much more activist project. Conservative politics now are very much the politics of alteration—not

From *Curriculum Studies*, 1 (1993), 301–16. Reprinted with permission.

always, but clearly the idea of 'Do nothing for the first time' is not a sufficient explanation of what is going on either in education or elsewhere (Honderich 1990: 4).

Conservatism has in fact meant different things at different times and places. At times, it will involve defensive actions; at other times, it will involve taking initiative against the *status quo* (Honderich 1990: 15). Today, we are witnessing both.

Because of this, it is important that I set out the larger social context in which the current politics of official knowledge operates. There has been a breakdown in the accord that guided a good deal of educational policy since World War II. Powerful groups within government and the economy, and within 'authoritarian populist' social movements, have been able to redefine—often in very retrogressive ways—the terms of debate in education, social welfare, and other areas of the common good. What education is for is being transformed (Apple 1993). No longer is education seen as part of a social alliance which combined many 'minority'[1] groups, women, teachers, community activists, progressive legislators and government officials, and others who acted together to propose (limited) social democratic policies for schools (e.g. expanding educational opportunities, limited attempts at equalizing outcomes, developing special programs in bilingual and multicultural education, and so on). A new alliance has been formed, one that has increasing power in educational and social policy. This power bloc combines business with the New Right and with neo-conservative intellectuals. Its interests are less in increasing the life chances of women, people of color, or labor. (These groups are obviously not mutually exclusive.) Rather it aims at providing the educational conditions believed necessary both for increasing international competitiveness, profit, and discipline and for returning us to a romanticized past of the 'ideal' home, family, and school (Apple 1993). There is no need to control the White House for this agenda to continue to have a major effect.

The power of this alliance can be seen in a number of educational policies and proposals not only at the university but in schooling in general. (In fact, it is *essential* that we see this broader picture. Without it, we cannot fully understand what is happening to institutions of higher education.) These include: (1) pro-grams for 'choice' such as voucher plans and tax credits to make schools like the thoroughly idealized free-market economy; (2) the movement at national and state levels throughout the country to 'raise standards' and mandate both teacher and student 'competencies' and basic curricular goals and knowledge increasingly now through the implementation of statewide and national testing; (3) the increasingly effective attacks on the school curriculum for its anti-family and anti-free enterprise 'bias', its secular humanism, its lack of patriotism, and its supposed neglect of the knowledge and values of the 'Western tradition' and of 'real knowledge'; and (4) the growing pressure to make the perceived needs of business and industry into the primary goals of education at all levels (Apple 1988, 1993). The effects of all this—the culture wars, the immensity of the fiscal crisis in education, the attacks on 'political correctness', and so on—are being painfully felt on the university as well.

In essence, the new alliance in favor of the conservative restoration has integrated education into a wider set of ideological commitments. The objectives in education are the same as those which serve as a guide to its economic and social welfare goals. These include the expansion of the 'free market', the drastic reduction of government responsibility for social needs (though the Clinton Administration will mediate this in not very extensive—and not very expensive—ways), the reinforcement of intensely competitive structures of mobility, the lowering of people's expectations for economic security, and the popularization of what is clearly a form of Social Darwinist thinking (Bastian *et al.* 1986).

As I have argued at length elsewhere, the political right in the USA has been very successful in mobilizing support *against* the educational system and its employees, often exporting the crisis in the economy onto the schools. Thus, one of its major achievements has been to shift the blame for unemployment and underemployment, for the loss of economic competitiveness, and for the supposed breakdown of 'traditional' values and standards in the family, education, and paid and unpaid workplaces *from* the economic, cultural, and social policies and effects of dominant groups *to* the school and other public agencies. 'Public' now is the center of all evil; 'private' is the center of all that is good (Apple 1985).

In essence, then, four trends have characterized the conservative restoration both in the USA and in Britain—privatization, centralization, vocationalization, and differentiation (Green 1991: 27). These are actually largely the results of differences within the most powerful wings of this tense alliance—neo-liberalism and neo-conservatism.

Neo-liberalism has a vision of the weak state. A society that lets the 'invisible hand' of the free market guide *all* aspects of its forms of social interaction is seen as both efficient and democratic. On the other hand, neo-conservatism is guided by a vision of the strong state in certain areas, especially over the politics of the body and gender and race relations, over standards, values, and conduct, and over what knowledge should be passed on to future generations (Hunter 1988). [2] While these are no more than ideal types, those two positions do not easily sit side by side in the conservative coalition.

Thus the Rightist movement is contradictory. Is there not something paradoxical about linking all of the feelings of loss and nostalgia to the unpredictability of the market, 'in replacing loss by sheer flux'? (Johnson 1991: 40).

At the elementary and secondary school levels, the contradictions between neo-conservative and neo-liberal elements in the Rightist coalition are 'solved' through a policy of what Roger Dale has called 'conservative modernization' (Dale, quoted in Edwards *et al.* 1992: 156–7).

Such a policy is engaged in:

simultaneously 'freeing' individuals for economic purposes while controlling them for social purposes; indeed, in so far as economic 'freedom' increases inequalities, it is likely to increase the need for social control. A 'small, strong state' limits the range of its activities by transferring to the market, which it defends and legitimizes, as much welfare [and other activities] as possible. In education, the new reliance on competition and choice is not all pervasive; instead, 'what is intended is a dual system, polarized between . . . market schools and minimum schools'.

That is, there will be a relatively less regulated and increasingly privatized sector for the children of the better off. For the rest—and the economic status and racial composition in, say, our urban areas of the people who attend these minimum schools will be thoroughly predictable—the schools will be tightly controlled and policies and will continue to be

underfunded and unlinked to decent paid employment.

One of the major effects of the combination of marketization and strong state is to remove educational policies from public debate. That is, the choice is left up to individual parents and the hidden hand of unintended consequences does the rest. In the process, the very idea of education being part of a *public* political sphere in which its means and ends are publicly debated atrophies (Education Group II 1991: 268).

There are major differences between democratic attempts at enhancing people's rights over the policies and practices of schooling and the neo-liberal emphasis on marketization and privatization. The goal of the former is to *extend politics*, to revivify democratic practice by devising ways of enhancing public discussion, debate, and negotiation. It is inherently based on a vision of democracy that sees it as an educative practice. The latter, on the other hand, seeks to *contain politics*. It wants to *reduce all politics to economics*, to an ethic of 'choice' and 'consumption' (Johnson 1991: 68). The world, in essence, becomes a vast supermarket (Apple 1993).

Enlarging the private sector so that buying and selling—in a word competition—is the dominant ethic of society involves a set of closely related propositions. It assumes that more individuals are motivated to work harder under these conditions. After all, we 'already know' that public servants are inefficient and slothful while private enterprises are efficient and energetic. It assumes that self-interest and competitiveness are the engines of creativity. More knowledge, more experimentation, is created and used to alter what we have now. In the process, less waste is created. Supply and demand stay in a kind of equilibrium. A more efficient machine is thus created, one which minimizes administrative costs and ultimately distributes resources more widely (Honderich 1990: 104).

This is of course not meant simply to privilege the few. However, it is the equivalent of saying that everyone has the right to climb the north face of the Eiger or scale Mount Everest without exception, providing of course that you are very good at mountain climbing and have the institutional and financial resources to do it (Honderich 1990: 99–100).

Thus, in a conservative society, access to a

society's private resources (and, remember, the attempt is to make nearly *all* of society's resources private) is largely dependent on one's ability to pay. And this is dependent on one's being a person of an *entrepreneurial or efficiently acquisitive class type*. On the other hand, society's public resources (that rapidly decreasing segment) are dependent on need (Honderich 1990: 89). In a conservative society, the former is to be maximized, the latter is to be minimized.

However, most forms of conservatism do not merely depend in a large portion of their arguments and policies on a particular view of human nature—a view of human nature as primarily self-interested. They have gone further; they have set out to degrade that human nature, to force all people to conform to what at first could only be pretended to be true. Unfortunately, in no small measure they have succeeded. Perhaps blinded by their own absolutist and reductive vision of what it means to be human, many of our political 'leaders' do not seem to be capable of recognizing what they have done. They have set out, aggressively, to drag down the character of a people (Honderich 1990: 81), while at the same time attacking the poor and the disenfranchised for their supposed lack of values and character.

But I digress here and some of my anger beings to show. You will forgive me I trust; but if we cannot allow ourselves to be angry about the lives of our children, what can we be angry about?

What Postmodernists Forget

Important elements of the neo-conservative and especially the neo-liberal agendas are increasingly dominating the university. The growing class and race polarization surrounding *which* universities one gets to go to (or doesn't get to go to), the funding cuts for 'unproductive' (a truly revealing metaphor), humanistic, and/or critically oriented programs, the increased pressure towards 'efficiency' and raising standards, the calls for a return to a 'common culture', and above all the growing integration of university teaching, research, funding, and many of its other functions into the industrial project—all of these and more are indicative of the effects of both strands of the complex restructuring of our daily lives.

Unfortunately, major elements of this restructuring are hardly on the agenda of discussions of some of the groups within the critical and 'progressive' communities within higher education itself. This is especially the case if we examine what kind of knowledge is now more and more being given the official imprimatur of the institution.

While the conflict over post-modern and post-structural forms continues to rage—in part because of some of the overstatements by what are affectionately known by some of my colleagues as the 'posties' as well as because of the aggressive attacks coming from movements associated with the conservative restoration (Apple 1993)—too little focus has been placed on the political economy of what knowledge is considered high status in this and similar societies. Thus, while the humanities and the social sciences are engaged in clever rhetorical and cultural 'battles' (please excuse the masculinist and militarist turn of phrase; the word is not mine) over what counts as 'appropriate' knowledge and what counts as 'appropriate' forms of teaching and knowing ('the culture wars'), what are commonsensically known as the sciences and technology—what I have called (following the lead of Walter Feinberg) technical/administrative knowledge—are receiving even more emphasis at schools at all levels in terms of time in the curriculum, funding, prestige, support from the apparatuses of the state (Apple 1985) and a new administration in Washington that is committed to technical solutions and technical knowledge.

What I shall say here is still rather tentative, but it responds to some of my intuitions that a good deal of the storm and fury over the politics of one form of textual analysis over another or even over whether we should see the world as a text, as discursively constructed, for example, is at least partly beside the point and that 'we' may be losing some of the most important insights generated by, say, the neo-Marxist tradition in education and elsewhere.

In what I say here, I hope I do not sound like an unreconstructed Stalinoid (after all I've spent all too much of my life writing and speaking about the reductive tendencies within the Marxist traditions). I simply want us to remember the utterly essential—not essentialist—understandings of the relationships (admittedly very complex) between what knowledge is considered high status and some of the relations of power we need to consider but seem to have forgotten a bit too readily. I shall not only refer to relations of power at the university but to emerging and crucial transformations that are occurring in elementary and secondary schools that educate (or don't educate) students who ultimately go (or don't go) to institutions of higher education.

The growth of the multiple positions associated with post-modernism and post-structuralism is indicative of the transformation of our discourse and understandings of the relationship between culture and power. The rejection of the comforting illusion that there can (and must) be one grand narrative under which all relations of domination can be subsumed, the focus on the 'micro-level' as a site of the political, the illumination of the utter complexity of the power-knowledge nexus, the extension of our political concerns well beyond the 'holy trinity' of class, gender, and race, the idea of the decentered subject where identity is both non-fixed and a site of political struggle, the focus on the politics and practices of consumption, not only production—all of this has been important, though not totally unproblematic to say the least (Clarke 1991; Best and Kellner 1991).

With the growth of post-modern and post-structural literature in critical educational and cultural studies, however, we have tended to move too quickly away from traditions that continue to be filled with vitality and provide essential insights into the nature of the curriculum and pedagogy that dominate schools at all levels. Thus, for example, the mere fact that class does not explain all can be used as an excuse to deny its power. This would be a serious error. Class is of course an analytic construct as well as a set of relations that have an existence outside of our minds. Thus, what we mean by it and how it is mobilized as a category needs to be continually deconstructed and rethought. Thus, we must be very careful when and how it is used, with due recognition of the multiple ways in which people are formed. Even given this, however, it would be wrong to assume that, since many people do not identify with or act on what we might expect from theories that link, say, identity and ideology with one's class position, this means that class has gone away (Apple 1992).

The same must be said about the economy. Capitalism may be being transformed, but it still exists as a massive structuring force. Many people may not think and act in ways predicted by class essentializing theories, but this does *not* mean the racial, sexual, and class divisions of paid and unpaid labor have disappeared; nor does it mean that relations of production (both economic *and* cultural, since how we think about these two may be different) can be ignored if we do it in non-essentializing ways (Apple 1992).

I say all this because of very real dangers that now exist in critical educational studies. One is our loss of collective memory. While there is currently great and necessary vitality at the 'level' of theory, a considerable portion of critical research has often been faddish. It moves from theory to theory rapidly, often seemingly assuming that the harder something is to understand or the more it rests on European cultural theory (preferably French) the better it is. The rapidity of its movement and its partial capture by an upwardly mobile fraction of the new middle class within the academy—so intent on mobilizing its cultural resources within the status hierarchies of the university that it has often lost any but the most rhetorical connections with the multiple struggles against domination and subordination at the university and elsewhere—has as one of its effects the denial of gains that have been made in other traditions or restating them in new garb (Apple 1992). Or it may actually move backwards, as in the reappropriation of, say, Foucault into just another (but somewhat more elegant) theorist of social control, a discredited and a-historical concept that denies the power of social movements and historical agents.

It is both the power of conservative social movements and the structural crisis into which they intervene which concerns me here. In our rush toward post-structuralism, we may have forgotten how very powerful the structural dynamics are in which we participate. In recognition of this, I want to focus on some of the dynamics of knowledge at the university, especially on the continued reconstruction of the role of the university towards the complex and contradictory economic and cultural 'needs' of economic rationalization, national and international competitiveness, and its associated agendas. In order to go further we need to think about the process of commodification, especially about the ways in which knowledge and institutions are reified so that they can be employed to extract surplus value. Oddly enough, I too must commodify knowledge in order to understand how it fits into the flow of capital.

The Political Economy of Cultural Capital

What I propose is somewhat dangerous. We have spent years trying to *dereify* knowledge, trying to show it as both a process of meaning construction and the embodiment of past constructions. To treat knowledge once again as a thing risks losing those gains. However, such a move is essential if we are to understand the continuing transformations that are going on in higher education. In making this case, I need to recapitulate a number of arguments I made in *Education and Power* (Apple 1985).

I want us to think of knowledge as a form of capital. Just as economic institutions are organized (and sometimes disorganized) so that particular classes and class fractions increase their share of economic capital, cultural institutions such as universities seem to do the same things. They play a fundamental role in the accumulation of cultural capital.

Now I am using the idea of cultural capital in a particular way, one that is different from that of, say, Bourdieu. For Bourdieu, for instance, the style, language, cultural dispositions, and even the bodies—the *hexus* and *habitus*—of dominant groups is the cultural capital that through a complicated process of conversion strategies is cashed in so that their dominance is preserved. Thus, students from dominant groups (and for Bourdieu these center largely around class) get ahead because of their 'possession' of this cultural capital (Bourdieu and Passeron 1977; Bourdieu 1984).

There is some strength to such a conception of cultural capital. However, it assumes that the fundamental role of educational institutions is the *distribution* of knowledge of students, some of whom are more 'able' to acquire it because of cultural gifts that come 'naturally' from their class or race or gender position. Yet, such a theory fails to catch the university's role in the production of a particular kind of cultural capital, *technical/administrative* knowledge. The production of this 'commodity' is what many universities are increasingly about, though many of the debates over the corpus of knowledge that should be taught at the university, over what is to count as 'tradition', still seem to assume that the only role the universities play is distributing knowledge (preferably after deconstructing and then reconstructing it with students) (Apple 1985; Apple 1990). This misses the structural point.

An advanced corporate economy requires the production of high levels of technical/administrative knowledge because of national and international economic competition and to become more sophisticated in the maximization of opportunities for economic expansion, for communicative and cultural control and rationalization, and so forth. Within certain limits, what is actually required is *not* the widespread distribution of this kind of high status knowledge to the populace in general. What is needed is to maximize its production (Apple 1985).

Thus, there is a complex relationship between the accumulation of economic and cultural capital. This means that it is *not* essential that everyone have sophisticated technical/administrative knowledge in their heads, so to speak. Thus, whether you or I or considerable numbers of our students have it is less important than having high levels of increasingly sophisticated forms of this knowledge *available for use*.

Broadly speaking, technical/administrative knowledge is essential in advanced industrial economies. The *way* it is employed in ours, though, is the critical factor. Given the enormous growth in the volume of production and the transformations in its organization and control, there has been a concomitant need for a rapid increase in the amount and kinds of technical and administrative information. This is coupled with the continued increase in the need for 'market research' and human relations research which each firm requires to increase the rate of accumulation and workplace control. All of this necessitates the machine production of information (and the production of more efficient machines as well). These products—the commodity of knowledge—may be non-material in the traditional sense of that term, but there can be no doubt that they are economically essential products. When one adds to this the immense role that defense related industries have played in corporate accumulation, the increasing role of agri-business in the corporate monopolization of food industries and technologies, and so forth, the importance of this kind of cultural capital increases.

In his analysis of the history of the relationship among science, technology, educational institutions, and industry, David Noble (1977: 6) earlier argued that the control of the production of technical cultural capital was an essential part of industrial strategy. Capital needed control not simply of markets and productive plant and equipment but of science as well.

Initially this monopoly over science took the form of patent control—that is the control over the products of scientific technology. It then became control over the process of scientific production itself, by means of organized and regulated industrial research. Finally, it came to include command over the social prerequisites of this process: the development of institutions necessary for the production of both scientific knowledge and knowledgeable people, and the integration of these institutions within the corporate system of science-based industry. 'The scientific-technical revolution', as Harry Braverman has explained, 'cannot be understood in terms of specific innovations . . .' Rather it 'must be understood in its totality as a mode of production in which science and exhaustive engineering have been integrated as part of ordinary functioning'. Thereby innovation is not to be found in chemistry, [bio-genetics], electronics, automatic machinery . . . or any of the products of these science-technologies, but rather in the transformation of science itself into capital.

Thus, as I have developed at greater length elsewhere, as industry tied itself more and more to the division, control, and replacement of labor and to technical innovations, if it was to expand its markets, products, and consumption it needed to guarantee a relatively constant accumulation of two kinds of capital, economic and cultural. These needs required much larger influence in the place where both agents and knowledge were produced—the university (Apple 1985).

Noble's previous statement about the importance of patent control illuminates a critical point for it is here that one can see an area where the accumulation of technical knowledge plays a significant economic role. Controlling the production of technical knowledge was important for systematic patent production and the monopolization of a market. While a primary aim of a good deal

of, say, industrial research was to find technical solutions to immediate production problems, the larger issue of the organization and control of knowledge production was essential if one was to 'anticipate inventive trends and take out patents to keep open the road of technical progress and business expansion' (Noble 1977: 128). The control of major aspects of science and technical knowledge was accomplished by use of patent monopolies and the organization and reorganization of university life (and especially its curricula and research). Thus, as Noble again shows, industry and the ideologies it has spawned played and continue to play an exceptionally important role in setting structural limits on (*not* determining) the kinds of curricula and pedagogical practices deemed appropriate for a significant portion of university and technical institute life. Given the economic crisis we currently face, one should expect an even greater influence of the (multiple and sometimes contradictory, of course) interests of capital in the future as well, especially given the Clinton Administration's neo-liberal construction of a national industrial policy in which as many aspects of the state and capital (as well as other aspects of civil society) should be integrated into rational planning models for achieving a restructured and more competitive economy for the twenty-first century.

Thus, with the Clinton Administration's move toward a corporatist model of industrial policy, we shall undoubtedly see more of an integration between universities and larger economic goals. The effects of this on what knowledge is considered to be of most worth, if I may paraphrase Spencer, will be momentous.

Henry Louis Gates, Jr puts it rather succinctly in the following quote, where he points out who some of the losers of these policies will be.

The struggle to obtain funding for research, for buildings, and for new and better programs caused the university to increasingly adapt to the priorities of corporations, foundations, government, and other élite donors. A new union emerged with business, industry, and the federal government as the principal partners of the university. At the local level, this meant that resources, human and material, were poured into programs that did research and provided services for the corporate élite. Indeed, on most campuses the resources devoted to such programs would dwarf the resources that go to programs devoted to grappling with the problems of distressed central city neighborhoods. This is also a reflection of the fact that money available for research on social issues of concern to business and industry is much greater than the money available for research on local issues of concern to blacks, Hispanics and working-class whites. (Gates 1992: 21)

Noble's and Gates's points are of course relatively economistic and essentializing. They capture neither the relatively autonomous activities of universities nor the micro-politics of science and its practitioners. They ignore the struggles that have been going on 'on the ground', so to speak, as well. Yet, they do provide an essential insight into the process by which high status knowledge is produced in a time of economic crisis and the fiscal crisis of the state.

They do help us recognize the universities are caught in a structural contradiction between the task of distributing knowledge and maximizing its production. As the institutional logic surrounding the commodification process recuperates more and more of the daily teaching and research activities at universities within its orbit, the emphasis tilts toward the latter while at the same time attempting to limit the former to only that knowledge which is economically 'essential' or to move other, more critical, forms of discourse to the margins. They, collectively, slowly become the institutionalized 'Other'.

Thus, increasingly, in the process what is *perceived* as economically useful knowledge is given the institutional imprimatur. Anything else is nice work if you can get it, but increasingly beside the point. (The neo-conservatives, however, know better. They realize that the struggle over culture and consciousness is essential. This is why the issue of language, collective memory, and how we should 'name the world' is seen by them to be so important (Apple 1993).)

I am of course speaking very generally here. This is not a smooth and rational process. There are struggles over this—over what counts as high status knowledge, over the state's role in supporting its production, and within institutions of higher education both over why these particular forms of knowledge should gain the most resources and power and over the relatively autonomous status hierarchies within the social field of the academy, hierarchies about which Bourdieu, for instance, has been so perceptive (Bourdieu 1988). Rather, I am pointing to general tendencies, tendencies I am certain have an impact on each of us in varying ways—on funding for research, fellowships, and scholarships, on the distribution of new faculty positions, and more than a little occasionally on tenure decisions and on layoffs of faculty and administrative staff.

Will our Future Students Know Better?

So far I have given an outline of my intuitions about the contradictions and dynamics surrounding the political economy of high status knowledge in the academy during a period of economic crisis. The concomitant cultural relations and authority have their own, partly independent, dynamics and struggles, of course, as we witness every day in the culture wars in our institutions. I have discussed these latter issues concerning the cultural politics of what counts as official knowledge in history, language, literature, 'the arts', and so forth at much greater length elsewhere, and do not want to rehearse them again here (Apple 1993). Rather, I now want to briefly turn to parts of the reconstruction that is occurring at the level of the elementary, middle, and secondary schools throughout the USA and what this means to what students will actually expect from their higher education.

As we witness the steady transformation of what knowledge will be converted into capital at the university—the complex conversion of cultural capital into economic capital[3]—there are similar things occurring at other levels of our educational institutions. These may have major effects on our students. Among the most important will be whether a large portion of our future students in institutions of higher education will see anything wrong with the commodification of knowledge for private gain. This is a complicated issue involving the formation of subjectivity(ies) among students. But perhaps some examples of what is happening at, say, our middle and high schools can illuminate some of the dangers we are facing.

I turn to this because one of the most crucial issues we will face will be what our students will be like—what they will know, what values they will have—when they arrive. Because of this, it is utterly essential that we focus on elementary and secondary schools as well as our institutions of higher education.

At the level of our elementary and secondary schools, the most organized and well funded curriculum reform efforts are being developed around proposed national curricula in mathematics and science. And even though the Clinton Administration has proposed making the arts the equal of more 'basic' subjects such as science and mathematics, this will have mostly rhetorical weight, not the weight of policy, especially since many large school districts such as Los Angeles are having to eliminate art instruction and lay off art teachers at all levels. Similar things are occurring in other, 'less essential' curricular areas, as well.

To take but one other example, in history it is Diane Ravitch and her relatively conservative colleagues who provided the outline for the social studies textbooks in California. Thus, because of the dominance of the textbook as the official curriculum in American schools and because nearly all publishers will *only* publish what will sell in states such as California and Texas because these states are in essence the largest guaranteed markets, the perspectives on history that the vast majority of students will receive will be a narrative of relatively self-congratulatory progress seen largely through the eyes of dominant groups (Apple 1988, 1993; Apple and Christian-Smith 1991).

Yet the cuts in particular humanities programs and the reassertion of certain narratives, while important, do not even begin to cover the entire range of transformations we are witnessing. Let me give what I believe is the best example.

There is a new generation of 'cooperative relations' between education and industry now being built. Among the most 'interesting' is something many of you may not know much about. It is called *Channel One*. Channel One is a commercially produced television news program that is now broadcast to thousands of schools in the United States. A description of it is overtly simple: ten minutes of international and national 'news' *and* two minutes of commercials produced very slickly by Whittle Communications—one of the largest publishers of material for 'captive audiences' in the world—and broadcast directly into classrooms.

In return for the use of a satellite dish (which can only receive Channel One), two VCRs, and television monitors for each classroom, schools sign a contract that over a three-to five-year period 90 per cent of all student will watch the broadcast in schools 90 per cent of the time. Compliance is monitored. For many chronically poor school districts, and an increasing number of seemingly more affluent ones, the fiscal crisis is so severe that textbooks are used until they literally fall apart. Basements, closets, gymnasiums, and any 'available' spaces are used for instruction. Teachers are being laid off, as are counselors and support staff. Art, music, and foreign language programs are being dropped. In some towns and cities, the economic problems are such that it will be impossible for schools to remain open for the full academic year. In the context of such a financial crisis, and in the context of a rhetorical strategy used by Whittle that knowledge of the world will assist students in getting jobs and in making our nation more competitive internationally (commercials for Channel One, for instance, point out that some students think that Chernobyl was Cher's original name or that silicon chips were a kind of snack food), schools throughout the nation have seen Channel One as a way of both teaching 'important knowledge' and as helping to solve their budget problems.

In *Official Knowledge* (Apple 1993), I have analyzed the strategies Whittle has employed as a rhetoric of justification, the ways Channel One enters into classrooms, the contradictions in its content and organization of the news—its linguistic codes, its constructions of the Other, etc.—and what teachers and students actually do with it. What is important here, however, is that for between 35 per cent and 40 per cent of all middle and high school students in the nation, we have *sold* our children as a captive audience to advertisers. The students themselves are positioned as consumers and commodified and purchased as a captive audience by corporations willing to spend the money for commercials on Channel One.

Now students and teachers sometimes engage in 'carnival' with material on Channel One, especially with the commercials. They ignore the news and pay attention to—and sometimes play with—the advertisements in a manner Bakhtin might enjoy. Yet, once again, our educational institutions are being reconstructed as a site for the generation of profit. For years, students will be members of that

captive audience. Their daily experience—
their common sense—will have been formed
around the transformation of knowledge (and
themselves) into a site for the production of
profit. What would seem so strange for the
same to be justifiable at universities? Thus,
why should we be surprised that particular
definitions of economically useful knowledge
increasingly dominate many institutions of
higher education when we are even now selling
students in our middle and secondary school?

Conclusion

I could say considerably more here, for I have
only touched the surface of the emerging
trends towards commodification and privatization that education is currently facing. My
major point, though, is to caution us, to correct a tendency among our 'more advanced
theorists' to marginalize concerns surrounding political economy and class relations. It is
not to ask us to revivify previous grand narratives whose 'will to know' was itself more than
a little problematic that I raise these points. It
is to remind us that this is still capitalism and
that makes a difference to our daily lives and to
the lives of those students who are not only at
our universities but who may venture into
those buildings later on. Ignoring the complex
relations between cultural capital and economic capital will not make the situation any
easier. The world may be text, but some
groups seem to be able to write their lines on
our lives more easily than others.

Notes

1. I put the word 'minority' in inverted commas
   here to remind us that the vast majority of the
   world's population is composed of persons of
   color. It would be wholly salutary for our ideas
   about culture and education to remember this
   fact.
2. Neo-liberalism doesn't ignore the idea of a
   strong state, but it wants to limit it to specific
   areas (e.g. defense of markets).
3. I do not want to romanticize the history of this.
   Universities did not have a mythical 'golden
   age' when they were cut off from the interests
   of business and industry or other élites.

Indeed, exactly the opposite is the case. See,
for example, Barrow (1990).

References

Apple, Michael W. (1985), *Education and Power*
(New York: Routledge).
—— (1988), *Teachers and Texts: A Political Economy of Class and Gender Relations in Education*
(New York: Routledge).
—— (1990), *Ideology and Curriculum* (2nd edn.,
New York: Routledge).
—— (1992), 'Education, Culture and Class
Power', *Educational Theory*, 42: 127–45.
—— (1993), *Official Knowledge: Democratic Edu-
cation in a Conservative Age*, (New York: Rout-
ledge).
—— and Christian-Smith, L. (eds.) (1991), *The
Politics of the Textbook* (New York: Routledge).
Barrow, C. (1990), *Universities and the Capitalist
State* (Madison: Univ. of Wisconsin Press).
Bastian, A., Fruchter, N., Gittell, M., Greer, C.,
and Haskins, K. (1986), *Choosing Equality*
(Philadelphia: Temple Univ. Press).
Best, S., and Kellner, D. (1991), *Postmodern Theory*
(London: Macmillan).
Bourdieu, P. (1984), *Distinction* (Cambridge,
Mass.: Harvard Univ. Press).
—— (1988), *Homo Academicus* (Stanford: Stan-
ford Univ. Press).
——, and Passeron, J.-C. (1977), *Reproduction in
Education, Society and Culture* (Beverly Hills:
Sage).
Clarke, J. (1991), *New Times and Old Enemies* (Lon-
don: Harper Collins).
Education Group II (eds.) (1991), *Education Lim-
ited* (London: Unwin Hyman).
Edwards, T., Gewirtz, S., and Whitty, G. (1992),
'Whose Choice of Schools?' in M. Arnot and L.
Barton (eds.), *Voicing Concerns* (Wallingford:
Triangle Books).
Gates, H. L., Jr. (1992), 'Redefining the Relation-
ship: The Urban University and the City in the
21st Century', *Universities and Community
Schools*, 3: 17–22.
Green, A. (1991), 'The Peculiarities of English
Education', in Education Group II (eds.), *Edu-
cation Limited* (London: Unwin Hyman).
Honderich, T. (1990), *Conservatism* (Boulder,
Colo.: Westview Press).
Hunter, A. (1988), *Children in the Service of Conser-
vatism* (Madison: Univ. of Wisconsin-Madison
Law School, Institute for Legal Studies).
Johnson, R. (1991), 'A New Road to Serfdom', in
Education Group II (eds.), *Education Limited*
(London: Unwin Hyman).
Noble, D. (1977), *America by Design* (New York:
Alfred A. Knopf).

40

The Big Picture: Masculinities in Recent World History

R. W. Connell

This article addresses the question of how we should study men in gender relations, and what view of modern world history an understanding of masculinity might give us. I start with the reasons why 'masculinity' has recently become a cultural and intellectual problem, and suggest a framework in which the intellectual work can be better done. The historicity of 'masculinity' is best shown by cross-cultural evidence on the differing gender practices of men in different social orders. The core of the paper is a sketch of the historical evolution of the forms of masculinity now globally dominant. This shows their imbrication with the military, social, and economic history of North Atlantic capitalist states, and especially with imperialism. This history provides the necessary basis for an understanding of the major institutionalized forms of masculinity in contemporary 'first world' countries, and the struggles for hegemony among them. I conclude with a brief look at the dynamics of marginalized and subordinated masculinities.

Studying 'Masculinity'

MASCULINITY AS A CULTURAL PROBLEM
The fact that conferences about 'masculinities' are being held is significant in its own right. Twenty-five years ago no one would have thought of doing so. Both the men-and-masculinity literature that has bubbled up in the interval (Carrigan *et al.* 1985; Ford and Hearn 1988; Hearn and Morgan 1990) and the

debates at conferences and seminars, testify that in some part of the Western intelligentsia, masculinity has become problematic in a way it never was before.

There is no doubt what cued the discovery of this problem. It was, first, the advent of Women's Liberation at the end of the 1960s and the growth of feminist research on gender and 'sex roles' since. Second—as important intellectually though of less reach practically—it was the advent of Gay Liberation and the developing critique of heterosexuality of lesbians and gay men.

While much of the key thinking about masculinity continues to be done by radical feminists and gay activists, concern with the issue has spread much more widely. The nature and politics of masculinity have been addressed by the new right, by heterosexual socialists, and by psychotherapists of wondrous variety. (Gilder 1975; Connell 1982; Ellis 1976; Johnson 1974). Four years ago I wrote a short essay on the 'new man' for a daily paper in Sydney, and a journalist friend commented that masculinity seemed to be the flavor of the year in journalism, with stories about men at childbirth, fathering, the 'new sensitive man,' men doing housework, and so on.

Something is going on; but what? Writers of the masculinity literature of the 1970s pictured change as a break with the old restrictive 'male sex role,' and the rapid creation of more equal relations with women. They were far too optimistic—and missed most of the politics of the process. Segal has aptly called the pace of change among heterosexual men 'slow motion,' and she has shown the political

From *Theory and Society*, 22 (1993), 597–623. Reprinted with permission.

complexities of reconstructing masculinity in the case of Britain. The leading style of gay masculinity in English-speaking countries went from camp to 'clone' in a decade, and gay politics then ran into the wall of the new right and the HIV epidemic. Commercial popular culture, in the era of Rambo movies and Masters of the Universe toys, has reasserted musclebound and destructive masculinity and has made a killing (Farrell 1975; Nichols 1975; Segal 1990; Humphries 1985).

So, to say masculinity has become 'problematic' is not necessarily to say gender relations are changing for the better. It is, rather, to say that cultural turbulence around themes of masculinity has grown. An arena has opened up. What direction gender relations move will in part be determined by the politics that happens in this arena. And this very much involves the intelligentsia. Intellectuals are bearers of the social relations of gender and makers of sexual ideology. The way we do our intellectual work of inquiry, analysis, and reportage has consequences; epistemology and sexual politics are intertwined (Connell 1987).

MASCULINITY AS AN INTELLECTUAL PROBLEM

Such awareness is not common in the English-language literature on men-and-masculinity. Indeed the implicit definitions of masculinity in this literature have limited its intellectual and political horizons quite severely.

Closest to common-sense ideas is the notion of masculinity as a *psychological essence*, an inner core to the individual. This may be inherited, or it may be acquired early in life. In either case it is carried forward into later life as the essence of a man's being. Pseudobiological versions of this concept abound. A more sophisticated version draws on psychoanalytic ideas to present masculinity as an identity laid down in early childhood by family constellations. Stoller's conception of 'core gender identity' is probably the most influential. It has had a good run in blaming mothers for transsexuality, and psychologizing the anthropology of masculinity (Tiger 1969; Stoller 1968, 1976; Stoller and Herdt 1983).

The conception of masculinity as a psychological essence obliterates questions about social structure and the historical dynamic of gender relations. At best, the formation of masculinity within the family is treated as a moment of reproduction of the gender order. At worst, an ahistorical masculine essence, as unchanging as crystal, is set up as a criterion against which social arrangements are judged, and generally found wanting. Exactly this formula is exploited by the *Rambo* films (Chodorow 1978; Sexton 1969).

The conception of a male *sex role*, the staple of American masculinity literature in the 1970s and early 1980s, promises better than this. It places definitions of masculinity firmly in the realm of the social, in 'expectations,' 'stereotypes,' or 'role models.' This allows for change. There may be role strain, conflict within or about the role, shifting role definitions. It also allows for a certain diversity. Role theorists can acknowledge that the 'black male role' may be different from the 'white male role' (David and Brannon 1976; Pleck 1976; Harrison 1979; Franklin 1987).

But these gains are slight. Sex-role theory is drastically inadequate as a framework for understanding gender. The role concept analytically collapses into an assertion of individual agency; it squeezes out the dimension of social structure. It gives no grip on the distribution of power, on the institutional organization of gender, on the gender structuring of production. Role theory rests on a superficial analysis of human personality and motives. It gives no grip on the emotional contradictions of sexuality, or the emotional complexities of gender in everyday life, which are revealed by fine-textured field research.[1]

A third book of work locates masculinity in *discourse* or treats it via cultural *representations*. Early writing on media stereotypes has now been transcended by a much more supple and penetrating account of the symbolic structures operating within particular genres. One of the best pieces of recent North American writing about masculinity, Jeffords's *The Remasculinization of America* (1989), traces the reshaping of the collective memory of the Vietnam War by novelists and filmmakers. This is a striking reversal of the slow desanitizing of the Second World War traced by Fussell in *Wartime* (1989). Theweleit's much-quoted *Male Fantasies* (1987) similarly locates sources of German fascism in discourses linking war and sexuality. These studies are politically sophisticated, even politically vibrant, in a way the discourse of 'sex roles' never has been. They attend to issues of power, to nuances and complexities in the representation of masculinity, to contradiction and change. But because they operate wholly within the world of discourse they ignore their own conditions of existence in the practices of gender and in the social structuring of those practices. Their politics is inevitably reactive. One can get from such criticism no pro-active idea of how to *change* oppressive gender relations—except perhaps to fly back in time and write a better war novel.

The limitations of our current approaches to masculinity are summed up by the startling ethnocentrism of most of the English-language literature. By this I don't only mean white, middle-class writers' habit of taking white, middle-class experience as constituting reality and marginalizing or ignoring men who work with their hands or who come from other ethnic groups. That habit exists, of course. Class and race blindness is particularly blatant in the therapeutic literature on masculinity. It has been under challenge for some time, with little effect.[2] Rather, I mean the more startling ethnocentrism by which a discourse of 'masculinity' is constructed out of the lives of (at most) 5 per cent of the world's population of men, in one culture-area, at one moment in history. Since wild overgeneralization from culturally specific custom is virtually the basis of sociobiology, it is not surprising that the literature resting on notions of masculinity as a psychological essence should be ethnocentric. It seems more remarkable that the sex-role literature, and the analysis of discourse, should be so incurious about other civilizations and other periods of history.

A cure is at hand, in a body of research that has developed quite separately from the men-and-masculinity literature. Ethnographers in a number of culture areas, doubtless sensitized to gender by feminism though rarely pursuing feminist themes, have come up with accounts of local constructions of masculinity very different from the mid-Atlantic norm. Notable examples are Herzfeld's account of the 'poetics of manhood' centering on sheep-stealing in a Cretan village; Herdt's discussion of ritualized homosexuality and the flute cult as 'idioms of masculinity' in a Melanesian culture; and Bolton's curious but evocative study of the slogans painted on their vehicles by Peruvian truck-drivers (Herzfeld 1985; Herdt 1981; Bolton 1979).

Putting such accounts together might lead

to a comparative sociology of masculinity capable of challenging many of our culture's received notions. Some studies have already been put to this use. Thus Lidz and Lidz use the Melanesian evidence to challenge conventional psychoanalytic accounts of the production of masculinity via oedipal relationships.

But the familiar comparative method rests on an assumption of intact, separate cultures; and that assumption is not defensible any more. European imperialism, global capitalism under U.S. hegemony, and modern communications have brought all cultures into contact, obliterated many, and marginalized most. Anthropology as a discipline is in crisis because of this. The dimension of *global history* must now be a part of every ethnography. And that is true for ethnographies of masculinity as well.

TOWARDS A NEW FRAMEWORK: A POLITICAL SOCIOLOGY OF MEN IN GENDER RELATIONS
To grasp the intellectual and political opportunity that is now open requires a shift in the strategic conception of research and in our understanding of the object of knowledge. The object of knowledge is not a reified 'masculinity' (as encapsulated, with its reified partner 'femininity,' in the psychological scales measuring M/F and androgyny). The object of knowledge is, rather, *men's places and practices in gender relations*. It is true that these places may be symbolically constructed (the subject of representation research); and that these practices are organized transactionally and in the life course (the subject of sex role and personality research). Thus the main topics of existing men-and-masculinity studies are included in this conception of the field. But these topics can only be understood in relation to a wider spectrum of issues that must now be systematically included in the field of argument.

First, masculinity as personal practice cannot be isolated from its institutional context. Most human activity is institutionally bound. Three institutions—the state, the workplace/labor market, and the family—are of particular importance in the contemporary organization of gender.

Thus we cannot begin to talk intelligibly about 'masculinity and power' without addressing the institutionalized masculinization of state élites, the gender differentiation of parts of the state apparatus (consider the military in the Gulf deployment), the history of state strategies for the control of populations via women's fertility. The sexual division of labor in production, the masculinized character of the very concept of 'the economic,' the levels of income and asset inequality between men and women, make it impossible to speak about 'masculinity and work' as if they were somehow separate entities being brought into relation. Hansot and Tyack have correctly emphasized the importance of 'thinking institutionally' in the case of gender and schooling, and their point has much wider relevance. It is not too strong to say that *masculinity is an aspect of institutions*, and is produced in institutional life, *as much as it is an aspect of personality* or produced in interpersonal transactions (Connell 1986; Hansot and Tyack 1987; Burton 1991: ch. 1).

Second, masculinities as cultural forms cannot be abstracted from sexuality, which is an essential dimension of the social creation of gender. Sexuality has been leeched out of much of the literature on masculinity. This perhaps reflects an assumption that sexuality is pre-social, a natural force belonging to the realm of biology. But while sexuality addresses the body, it is itself social practice and constitutive of the social world. There is no logical gap between sexuality and organizational life. Their close interconnection has been recently documented in important studies of the workplace by J. Hearn and W. Parkin and by Pringle. The sexualization of military life is evident from work on soldiers' language as well as in the more emotionally honest soldiers' autobiographies (Connell and Dowsett 1990; Hearn and Parkin 1987; Pringle 1989; Fussell 1971; Milligan 1971, 1976).

These arguments are consistent with a position in social theory that insists on the historicity of social life. Practice is situational (it responds to a particular configuration of events and relationships) and transformative (it operates on a given situation and converts it into a differently configured one). One cannot be masculine in a particular way (which is to say, engage in particular practices constructing a given form of masculinity) without affecting the conditions in which that form of masculinity arose: whether to reproduce them, intensify them, or subvert them.

Since gender relations produce large-scale inequalities—in most contemporary cultures,

collective advantages for men and disadvantages for women—masculinity understood in this way must be understood as political. I mean 'political' in the simple, conventional sense of the struggle for scarce resources, the mobilization of power and the pursuit of tactics on behalf of a particular interest. Interests are constituted within gender relations by the facts of inequality. They are not homogeneous, indeed are generally extremely complex, but they are powerful determinants of social action.

Different masculinities arise in relation to this structure of interests and embody different commitments and different tactics or strategies. I have suggested elsewhere that hegemonic masculinity in patriarchy can be understood as embodying a successful strategy for the subordination of women (Connell 1990*b*). I would now add to that formula that when the historical conditions for a strategy's success have altered, the hegemonic form of masculinity is vulnerable to displacement by other forms.

To construct such an analysis requires a standpoint, and I take the most defensible one to be the commitment to human equality. The standpoint of equality is not an end-point but a starting-point for social analysis. In relation to masculinity it defines the enterprise as one of 'studying up,' a matter of studying the holders of power in gender relations with a view to informing strategies for dismantling patriarchy. Given the interweaving of structures of inequality, it should also yield significant information on strategic questions about capitalism, race relations, imperialism, and global poverty. This is no new observation, but it bears repeating. In one of the most literate and penetrating of essays on the question of Latin American 'machismo,' the Peruvian writer Adolph argued that unchallenged male supremacy 'is one of the major obstacles to any real progress in this part of the world' (Adolph 1971). That is true of English-speaking parts of the world too.

Masculinities in History

MULTIPLE CULTURES, MULTIPLE MASCULINITIES
Ethnographies and histories of gender have now become rich enough to give us a clear view of some culture areas at least. An impor-

tant negative conclusion can be drawn immediately. The models of masculinity familiar in Euro/American discourse simply do not work for the realities of gender in other cultures, so far as these cultures can be reconstructed before colonial or commercial domination by the Euro/American world. Let me sketch, very briefly, two such cases.

In neo-Confucian China from the Song to the Qing dynasties (roughly, the thousand years before this century), the vast majority of the population were peasants working family farms, with administration in the hands of a tax-supported scholar-official class. The heavily patriarchal gender relations in the dominant class were regulated by an increasingly formal body of rules, an authoritarian development of Confucian moral and social philosophy. Peasant families were more egalitarian and less regulated, but the Confucian code remained hegemonic in the society as a whole (Wang Liu 1959; Brugger 1971; Ruhlmann 1975; Stacey 1983).

Promulgated by the state and enforced by state and clan as well as family patriarchs, the code defined conduct for men not as pursuit of a unitary ideal of masculinity, but more centrally in terms of the right or wrong performance of a network of obligations—towards emperor, parents, brothers, etc. To the extent heroic models were constructed in popular drama and fiction, they are unfamiliar types to a Euro/American sensibility. They include emperors marked not by Napoleonic agency but by a passive authority and transcendence of struggle; and scholar-politicians marked by guile, persuasiveness, and magic powers.

The difference from European culture is particularly clear in two issues important to European constructions of masculinity: soldiering, and love between men. Neo-Confucian culture deprecated military life. Soldiers were regarded more as licensed thugs than as ideals of masculinity. One set of clan rules advised men of the clan not to become soldiers, remarking that this was 'another form of loafing,' i.e., not what any responsible man would do. Fighting heroes do appear in popular literature. But, in contrast to Euro/American presumptions, this kind of heroism is unconnected with active interest in sex with women.

On the other hand, early Confucian culture seems to have been far more positive about erotic relationships between men than European culture has been. There was a well-defined literary tradition within the upper class celebrating male-to-male love, with such relationships seen as exemplary rather than decadent. Over time, however, the neo-Confucian philosophers became more hostile to homosexual relationships. In the twentieth century, the tradition affirming them has been completely broken (Hinsch 1990).

In the pre-colonial cultures of Papua New Guinea, with intergroup warfare widespread and no state culture, a marked gender division of labor in production, ritual, and fighting was usual. Male supremacy was asserted in most of these cultures, but in a context where women often had direct access to productive resources (e.g., they owned gardens). The major theme in the formation of masculinity was not entry into powerful hierarchical institutions, as in China, but a ritual and practical separation from the world of women, a symbolic construction of difference.

Lidz and Lidz (1986), reflecting on initiation practices, remark how this distinguished the course of boys' psychosexual development from European patterns, eliminating the 'oedipal' period and eroticizing the 'latency' period. Herdt's now well-known study (1984) of the 'Sambia' in the eastern highlands, reinforced by other studies of ritualized homosexuality, shows what from a conventional Euro/American perspective is an astonishing process: the construction of adult heterosexual masculinity through *homosexual* relationships in adolescence and early adulthood.

Schieffelin (1982: 155–200) and Modjeska point to a different cultural form, the 'bachelor cults' of Papua New Guinea's southern and western highlands. Rather than coercively initiating young males into the mainstream gender order, these cults provided a kind of organized exception to it. They defined an idealized masculinity in relation to *spirit* women in sharp distinction from married men's life with real women. In these cults a ritual heterosexuality glossed a strenuously homosocial reality.

These comments hardly scratch the surface for either region, but are perhaps enough to demonstrate the fact of genuinely different institutionalizations of gender in different culture areas. In the Chinese case we can also clearly see the *changing* institutionalization of masculinity through the history of the culture. Historical change is also implied by the fine detail of the Papua New Guinea research (though it is obviously more difficult to document for cultures without written records). To speak of 'masculinity' as one and the same entity across these differences in place and time is to descend into absurdity. Even a modest study of this evidence wipes out sociobiology, any scheme of genetic determination, or any ontological or poetic account of male essences, as credible accounts of masculinity.

Indeed I am forced to wonder whether 'masculinity' is in itself a culture-bound concept that makes little sense outside Euro/American culture. Our conventional meaning for the word 'masculinity' is a quality of an individual, a personal attribute that exists in a greater or lesser degree; in the mental realm an analogue of physical traits like hairiness of chest or bulk of biceps. The connection of such a concept with the growth of individualism and the emerging concept of the self in early-modern European culture is easy to see. A culture not constructed in such a way might have little use for the concept of masculinity.

Nevertheless, it is Euro/American culture that is dominant in the world now, and which must be addressed first in any reckoning with our current predicament. Imperialism was a massively important event in gender history. Some cultures' gender regimes have been virtually obliterated by imperialism. (This includes the native gender regimes of the place where I am writing: Sydney harbor foreshores had a significant Aboriginal population at the time of the white invasion.) All have been abraded by it. Surviving cultures have attempted to reconstruct themselves in relation to Euro/American world dominance, an explosive process that is perhaps the most important dynamic of gender in the contemporary world. Responses vary enormously, from the attempted dismantling of domestic patriarchy in revolutionary China to the intensification of Islamic patriarchy in response to French colonialism in Algeria (Stacey 1983; Knauss 1987).

To make this point is not to accept that gender effects simply follow from class causes. Stacey convincingly argues that Confucian China was a patriarchal class order in which the crisis of the politico-economic system was inherently also a crisis of the family and gender relations. Similarly, I argue that European imperialism and contemporary world capitalism are gendered social orders with gender dynamics as powerful as their class dynamics. The history of how European/American culture, economy, and states became so dominant and so dangerous is *inherently* a history of gender relations (as well as, interwoven with class relations and race relations). Since the agents of global domination were, and are, predominantly men, the historical analysis of masculinity must be a leading theme in our understanding of the contemporary world order.

Having made that large claim, I should back it up with a dozen volumes of evidence; and they have not yet been written. Serious historical work on themes of masculinity is extremely rare. All I can offer here is yet another sketch, a historical hypothesis about the course of events that produced contemporary Euro/American masculinities. This sketch is informed by the decent research I have been able to locate, but is necessarily very tentative.

EARLY MODERN EUROPE

Four developments in the period 1450–1650 (the 'long 16th century' in Braudel's useful phrase) mark decisive changes in European life from which we can trace the construction of modern gender regimes.

The disruption of medieval Catholicism by the spread of Renaissance culture and by the Protestant Reformation disrupted ascetic and corporate-religious ideals of men's lives, of the kind institutionalized in monasticism. On the one hand, the way was opened for a growing emphasis on the conjugal household and on married heterosexuality as the hegemonic form of sexuality. On the other hand, the new emphases on individuality of expression and on each person's unmediated relationship with God led toward the individualism, and the concept of a transcending self, which provided the basis for the modern concept of masculinity itself.

The creation of the first overseas empires by the Atlantic seaboard states (Portugal and Spain, then Holland, England, and France) was a gendered enterprise from the start, an outgrowth of the segregated men's occupations of soldiering and sea trading. Perhaps the first group who became defined as a recognizable 'masculine' cultural type, in the modern sense, were the conquistadors. They were displaced from customary social relationships, often extremely violent, and difficult for the imperial authorities to control. An immediate consequence was a clash over the ethics of conquest and a demand for controls. Las Casas's famous denunciation of Spanish atrocities in the Indies is accordingly a very significant document in the history of masculinity (Hanke 1965).

The growth of cities fuelled by commercial capitalism—Antwerp, London, Amsterdam —created a mass milieu for everyday life that was both more anonymous, and more coherently regulated, than the countryside. The changed conditions of everyday life made a more thoroughgoing individualism possible. In combination with the 'first industrial revolution' and the accumulation of wealth from trade, slaving, and colonies, an emphasis on calculative rationality began to distinguish masculinity in the entrepreneurial subculture of early capitalism. At the same time, commercial cities became the milieu (by the early eighteenth century) for the first sexual subcultures, such as the 'Molly houses' of London, institutionalizing variations on gender themes (Bray 1982). The notion that one must have a *personal identity* as a man or a women, rather than a *location* in social relations as a man or a woman, was hardening.

The onset of large-scale European civil war—the sixteenth-seventeenth-century wars of religion, merging into the dynastic wars of the seventeenth-eighteenth centuries—disrupted established gender orders profoundly. A measure of this is the fact that revolutionary struggles saw the first radical assertions of gender equality in European history, by religious-cum-political sects like the Quakers (Bacon 1981: ch. 1). At the same time, this warfare consolidated the strong state structure that is a distinctive feature of Euro/American society and has provided a very large-scale institutionalization of men's power. The centrality of warfare in these developments meant that armies became a crucial part of the developing state apparatus, and military performance became an unavoidable issue in the construction of masculinities.

We can speak of a gender order existing by the eighteenth century in which masculinity as a cultural form had been produced and in which we can define a hegemonic form of masculinity. This was the masculinity predominant in the lives of men of the gentry, the politically dominant class in most of Europe and North America.

Economically based on land ownership, gentry masculinity did not emphasize rational calculation. It was not strongly individualized, being tied to lineage and kin networks. British politics in the age of Walpole and the Pitts, for instance, generally followed family lines, and the state structure was organized by patronage. Masculinity was not strongly regulated, allowing a good deal of negotiation over its terms, to the point of public gender-switching in the celebrated case of the Chevalier d'Eon in the 1770s.

Some regulation was provided by a code of honor, both family and personal. The gentry was integrated with the state in the sense that they often were the local state (justices of the peace in Britain effectively controlled rural society), and they staffed the military apparatus. The gentry provided the officers for armies and navies and often recruited the rank and file themselves. At the intersection between this direct involvement in violence and the ethic of honor was the institution of the duel. Willingness to face an opponent in a potentially lethal one-to-one combat became a key test of gentry masculinity (Tefler 1885; for an original and convincing reinterpretation, see Kates 1991; Kiernan 1988).

TRANSFORMATIONS OF HEGEMONIC FORMS

The history of hegemonic forms of Euro/American masculinity in the last two hundred years is the history of the displacement, splitting, and remaking of gentry masculinity. Because I have limited space I am very summary at this point. Political revolution, industrialization, and the growth of bureaucratic state apparatuses saw the displacement of gentry masculinity by more calculative, rational, and regulated masculinities. The bureaucrat and the businessman were produced as social types. The economic base of the landed gentry declined, and with it the orientation of kinship and honor. Violence was split off from political power, in the core countries; Mr Gladstone did not fight duels, nor lead armies. Rather, violence became a specialty. As mass armies were institutionalized so was the officer corps. This became the repository of much of the gentry code. The Dreyfus affair in France was shaped by this code; the Prussian officer corps was perhaps its most famous exemplar. But violence was now combined with an emphasis on rationality: we see the emergence of military science. If Las Casas's

History of the Indies was a key document of early-modern masculinity, perhaps the nineteenth century equivalent was Clausewitz's *On War* (1827; 1976 edn.)—Clausewitz being one of the reformers of the Prussian army. It was bureaucratically rationalized violence as a social technique, just as much as superiority of weapons, that made European states and European settlers almost invincible in the colonial frontier expansion of the nineteenth century.

But this technique risked destroying the society that sustained it. Global war led to revolutionary upheaval in 1917–1923. In much of Europe the capitalist order was only stabilized, after half a generation of further struggle, by fascist movements that glorified irrationality and the unrestrained violence of the frontline soldier. And the dynamics of fascism soon enough led to a new and even more devastating global war.

The defeat of fascism in the Second World War cut off the institutionalization of a hegemonic masculinity marked by irrationality and personal violence. But it certainly did not end the bureaucratic institutionalization of violence. The Red Army and U.S. armed forces, which triumphed in 1945, continued to grow in destructive capability. Less technically advanced armies remained, in China, Pakistan, Indonesia, Argentina, and Chile, central to the politics of their respective states. The growth of destructive capability through the application of science to weapons development has, however, given a new significance to technical expertise.

This paralleled developments in other parts of the economy. The enormous growth of school and university systems during the twentieth century, the multiplying number of 'professional' occupations with claims to specialized expertise, the increasing political significance of technology, and the growth of information industries, are aspects of a large-scale change in culture and production systems that has seen a further splitting of nineteenth-century hegemonic masculinity. Masculinity organized around *dominance* was increasingly incompatible with masculinity organized around *expertise* or technical knowledge. 'Management' split from 'professions,' and some analysts saw power increasingly in the hands of the professionals. Factional divisions opened in both capitalist ruling classes and communist élites

between those pursuing coercive strategies towards workers (conservatives/hard-liners) and those depending on technological success and economic growth that allow integrative strategies (liberals/reformers). The emotional pattern of Reaganite politics in the United States centered on a revival of the first of these inflections of masculinity and a rejection of the second. In the 1992 U.S. presidential campaign, both Bush and Clinton image-makers seemed to be trying to blend the two (Galbraith 1971; Gouldner 1979).

SUBORDINATED FORMS

So far I have been sketching the hegemonic masculinities of the dominant class and race in the dominant countries of the world-system. But this, obviously, is far from being the whole picture. The hegemonic form of masculinity is generally not the only form, and often is not the most common form. Hegemony is a question of relations of cultural domination, not of head-counts.

On a world scale this is even more obviously true. The patterns of masculinity just outlined are formed in relation to the whole complex structure of gender relations. In terms of other masculinities, they exist in tension with the hegemonic masculinities of subordinated classes and races, with subordinated masculinities in their own class and race milieu, and with the patterns of masculinity current in other parts of the world order. To offer even a sketch of this structure, let alone analyze its dynamics, is a tall order; again I shall have to settle for indications.

The historical displacement of the gentry by businessmen and bureaucrats in core countries was plainly linked to the transformation of peasants into working classes and the creation of working-class hegemonic masculinities as cultural forms. The separation of household from workplace in the factory system, the dominance of the wage form, and the development of industrial struggle, were conditions for the emergence of forms of masculinity organized around wage-earning capacity, skill and endurance in labor, domestic patriarchy, and combative solidarity among wage earners.

The expulsion of women from industries such as coalmining, printing, and steelmaking was a key moment in the formation of such masculinity. The craft union movement can be seen as its institutionalization. The growing power of organized labor in the last decades of the nineteenth and first decades of the twentieth century was one of the main pressures on the masculinity of the dominant class that led to the splits between political alternatives (fascist, liberal, conservative) already mentioned (Seccombe 1977; Cockburn 1983).

At much the same time the masculinity of the dominant class was purged in terms of identity and object choice. As gay historians have shown, the late nineteenth century was the time when 'the homosexual' as a social type was constructed, to a considerable extent through the deployment of medical and penal power. At earlier periods of history sodomy had been officially seen as an act, the potential for which existed in any man who gave way to libertinage. From the point of view of hegemonic masculinity, this change meant that the potential for homoerotic pleasure was expelled from the masculine and located in a deviant group (symbolically assimilated to women or to beasts). There was no mirror-type of 'the heterosexual'; rather, heterosexuality became a required connotation of manliness. The contradiction between this rapidly-solidifying definition and the actual conditions of emotional life among men in military and paramilitary groups reached crisis level in fascism. It fuelled Hitler's murder of Roehm and his purge of the Stormtroopers in 1934 (Weeks 1977; D'Emilio and Freedman 1988; Orlow 1973: ch. 3).

On the frontier of settlement, regulation was ineffective, violence endemic, physical conditions harsh. Industries such as mining offered spectacular profits on a chancy basis. A very imbalanced sex ratio allowed a homosocial masculinization of the frontier. Phillips, in an important study of the New Zealand case, draws the contrast between two groups of men and two images of masculinity: the brawling single frontiersman and the settled married pioneer farmer. The distinction is familiar in the American and Canadian west too. The state, Phillips argues, was hostile to the social disorder generated by the masculine work and pub culture of the former group. Accordingly, it encouraged family settlement and might promote women's interests. It is notable that such frontier areas were the earliest where women won the vote. Nevertheless cults of frontier masculinity (Daniel Boone, the cowboys, Paul Bunyan, the diggers, the

shearers, the Voortrekkers) continued as a characteristic part of sexual ideology in former colonies of settlement such as the United States, South Africa, and Australia (Phillips 1980: 217–43).

In colonies where local populations were not displaced but turned into a subordinated labor force (much of Latin America, India, East Indies) the situation was more complex again. It is a familiar suggestion that Latin American 'machismo' was a product of the interplay of cultures under colonialism. The conquistadors provided both provocation and model; Spanish Catholicism provided the ideology of female abnegation; and oppression blocked other claims of men to power. Pearlman shows that this pattern is also a question of women's agency. Machismo is *not* the ideology governing men's relations with women in the subsistence-farming Mazatec people, where gender relations are much more egalitarian. Outmigration and commodification are changing this, but even so, the young Mazatec men who are picking up a hyper-masculine style from the wider Mexican culture are forced into code-switching at home because older women and men will not play along (Adolph 1985; Pearlman 1983).

Nevertheless, it is the Mazatec gender order that is under pressure in the interaction, not the national Mexican. Internationally it is Euro/American culture and institutions that supply the content of global mass media, design the commodities and the labor process of producing them, and regulate the accumulation of resources. This power is the strongest force redefining men's place in gender relations outside the North Atlantic world.

Contemporary Politics

THE PRESENT MOMENT

If this historical outline has some validity, it should give us purchase on what is happening in the lives of men and women in the 'first world' at the present time. It suggests, most obviously, that we should see contemporary changes in masculinity not as the softening (or hardening) of a unitary 'sex role,' but as a field of institutional and interpersonal changes through which a multilateral struggle for hegemony in gender relations, and advantage in other structures, is pursued.

The distinctive feature of the present moment in gender relations in first-world countries is the fact of open challenges to men's power, in the form of feminism, and to institutionalized heterosexuality, in the form of lesbian and gay men's movements. We must distinguish between the *presence* of these movements from the operating *power* they have won, which is often disappointingly small. Whatever the limits to their gains, and the success of the conservative backlash, the historic fact that these movements are here on the scene structures the whole politics of gender and sexuality in new ways.

These challenges are being worked out in a context of technological change and economic restructuring (e.g., the decline of heavy industry in old industrial centers), globalization of market relationships and commercial mass communication (e.g., the crumbling of Eastern-European command economies), widening wealth inequalities and chronic tensions in first-world/third-world relations (e.g., the Vietnam war, the debt crisis, the Gulf War). Each of these processes has its gender dimension.

CONTESTATION IN HEGEMONIC MASCULINITY
Earlier in the twentieth century a split began to open in the hegemonic masculinity of the dominant classes, between a masculinity organized around interpersonal dominance and one organized around knowledge and expertise. Under the pressure of labor movements and first-wave feminism, and in the context of the growing scale of mass production, dominance and expertise ceased to be nuances within the one masculinity and became visibly different strategies for operating and defending the patriarchal capitalist order. In some settings distinct institutional bases for these two variants hardened: line management versus professions, field command versus general staff, promotion based on practical experience versus university training. Political ideologies and styles—conservatism versus liberalism, confrontation versus consensus politics—also clustered around this division.

Feminism in the 1970s and 1980s often found itself allied with the liberal/professional side in this contestation, for a variety of reasons. Notions of equal opportunity and advancement by merit appealed in a techno-cratic style of management. Much feminist activity was located in universities and professions. Liberal feminism (the strongest current in feminism) as an enlightenment project found itself on the same terrain, and using much the same political language, as progressive liberalism and reformist labor.

The patriarchal counter-attack on feminism, conversely, rapidly became associated with the masculinity of dominance. Early attempts to find a scientific basis for the counter-attack, such as Goldberg's *The Inevitability of Patriarchy* (1973), were faintly ludicrous and had little influence. Much more powerful was the cultural backing given by authoritarian patriarchal churches. Perhaps the most successful of all antifeminist operations in the last 20 years has been the Catholic church's attacks on contraception, abortion, and sexual freedom for women.

The reassertion of a dominance-based masculinity has been much discussed in popular culture. To my mind its most interesting form is not Rambo movies but the 1980s cult of the 'entrepreneur' in business. Here gender imagery, institutional change, and political strategy intersect. The deregulation policies of new-right governments in the 1980s dismantled Keynesian strategies for social integration via expert macro-economic regulation. The credibility of the new policies rested on the image of a generation of entrepreneurs whose wealth-creating energies were waiting to be unleashed. That this stratum was masculine is culturally unquestionable. Among other things, their management jargon is full of lurid gender terminology: thrusting entrepreneurs, opening up virgin territory, aggressive lending, etc.

New-right ideology naturalizes these social practices, that is, treats them as part of the order of nature. But in fact the shift of economic power into the hands of this group was very conjunctural. The operations of the entrepreneurs were essentially in finance, not production. Key practices such as the leveraged management buy-out (in the United States and the construction of highly-geared conglomerates (in Australia) depended on the institutional availability of massive credit at high rates of interest (junk bonds and bank consortium loans). The political interest in sustaining a huge diversion of funds from productive investment was limited, but the 'entrepreneurs' could not stop. The growing contradiction between this particular inflection of the masculinity of dominance and the need of the rest of the dominant class for economic stability led to denunciations of greed and in the later 1980s to a virtual withdrawal of political support.

The political damage-control has generally taken the form of attempts to show these episodes were an aberration, not that they resulted from a mistaken strategy. Deregulation and the roll-back of the welfare state remains a powerful agenda in the politics of the rich countries, and neoconservative regimes continue to be electorally successful. It is in the internal politics of the state that we see most clearly the new direction in the contest between dominance and expertise. What Yeatman calls the 'managerialist agenda' in the reconstruction of the state occupies the terrain of expertise. Its ideology is provided by neoclassical economics, and its operating language is provided by a management science legitimated by university business schools and rapidly spreading through the universities themselves. But it detached the notion of expertise from the liberal/reformist politics of the Keynesian era and the humanist commitments that had allowed at least a partial alliance with feminism (Yeatman 1990; Pusey 1991).

Managerialists and technocrats do not directly confront feminist programs but under-fund or shrink them in the name of efficiency and volunteerism. Equal-opportunity principles are accepted as efficient personnel management ideas, but no funds are committed for affirmative action to make equal opportunity a vehicle of social change. Research and training funds are poured into areas of men's employment (for instance the Australian government is currently pushing science and technology) because of the perceived need to make the country 'competitive in international markets.'

Speculating a little, I think we are seeing the construction of a new variant of hegemonic masculinity. It has a technocratic rather than confrontationist style, but it is misogynist as before. It characteristically operates through the indirect mechanisms of financial administration. It is legitimated by an ideology centering on an economic theory whose most distinctive feature is its blanket exclusion from discourse of women's unpaid work—which, as Waring (1988) bitterly but accurately puts it, 'counts for nothing' in economic science.

CHALLENGES: 'ALTERNATIVE' MASCULINITIES
Contestation for the hegemonic position is familiar. What is novel, in Euro/American history, is open challenge to hegemonic masculinity as such. Such challenges were sparked by the challenge to men's power as a whole made by contemporary feminism. Feminism may not have been adopted by many men, but an *awareness* of feminism is very widespread indeed.

In the course of a recent life-history study among Australian men, this point emerged clearly. Almost all the men we interviewed had some idea of what feminism was and felt the need to take some position on it.

Their positions ranged from essentialist rejection:

I think the feminist movement's gone too far. Because women are women, they've got to be women. The feminists, as I say—the true, die-hard feminists—have taken it past the extreme, and turned women, those women, into nonentities now. They're not women any more. (Computer technician, heterosexual, 30)

via way endorsement, usually making an exception of bra-burning extremists:

I think they have a just cause, because they have sort of been oppressed. Well they certainly have been oppressed. And it would be a better world if once this equality comes. But extremists spoil it for those who want it to change. But change, so everybody can be happy. (Technical teacher, heterosexual, 40)

to full-blown acceptance of feminism:

Certain times in my life it's been the most important ideal for me and I've just done lots and lots of work on it. (Trainee nurse, heterosexual, 22)

The last kind of response is rare, though it is important in defining political possibilities. The life stories of men who reached this point via environmental politics show the importance of a direct encounter with feminist activism among women. Given the massive bias of media against feminism, more indirect acquaintance is extremely unlikely to lead to a positive response from men (Connell 1989).

The challenge to hegemonic masculinity among this group of men mainly takes the form of an attempt to re-make the self. Most of them started off with a fairly conventional gender trajectory, and they came to see a personal reconstruction as required. This turns out to be emotionally very difficult. The growth-movement techniques available to them do not deliver the political analysis, support, or follow-through that the project actually requires. Only a few, and those only marginally, have moved beyond this individualist framework to the search for a collective politics of gender among men.

A collective politics is precisely the basis of the challenge to hegemonic heterosexuality mounted by gay liberation. At one level this challenge was delivered simply by the presence of an open gay milieu based on sex and friendship. 'Coming out' is experienced as entering a social network, not just as entering a sexual practice. As a gay man in the same study put it:

Rage, rage, rage—let's do everything you've denied yourself for 25 years—let's get into it and have a good time sexually, and go out partying and dancing and drinking. (Transport worker, gay, 25)

The collective work required was to construct the network and negotiate a social presence for it. This meant dealings with the state authorities, e.g. the police; economic mobilization, the so-called 'pink capitalism'; and organizing political representation, the most famous representative being Harvey Milk in the United States (Adam 1987; Altman 1982).

Most of this went no further than a politics of pluralist accommodation, analogous, as Altman has pointed out, to claims for political space by ethnic minorities in the United States. It was this assimilationist program that was disrupted in the early 1980s by the HIV epidemic and the need for a renewed struggle against the medicalization and criminalization of homosexuality.

But in gay liberation, from very early on, was a much more radical, indeed revolutionary, challenge to hegemonic masculinity. The slogan 'Every straight man is a target for gay liberation!' jokingly catches both an open-ended libertarianism and the point that gays cannot be free from oppression while heterosexual masculinity remains as it is. Drawing on Freudian ideas, some gay theorists argued that the repression of homosexual affect among straight men was a key source of their authoritarianism and violence. These ideas have never been turned into an effective practical politics; but they remain an important moment of critique (Mieli 1980).

DECONSTRUCTIONS OF WORKING-CLASS MASCULINITY

'Rage, rage, rage' is exactly what the settled married farmer, or the respectable married working man, cannot do. Donaldson argues that the link between the family-household and the workplace, rather than the workplace itself, is the axis on which working-class masculinity is formed. It finds political expression in a community-based, formally-organized labor movement and is sustained by a sharp gender division of labor between wage-earning husband and child-raising wife. These points have been well documented in recent Australian research on sexual politics in working-class communities (Donaldson 1987; Metcalfe 1988; Williams 1981).

But with the collapse of the postwar boom, the abandonment of full employment as a policy goal by modern states, and the shift to market discipline by business strategists (an aspect of the contestation discussed earlier), the conditions of this gender regime in working-class communities have changed. Significant proportions of the working class face long-term structural unemployment. Traditional working-class masculinity is being deconstructed by impersonal forces, whether the men concerned like it or not.

Young men respond to this situation in different ways. They may attempt to promote themselves out of the working class, via education and training. They may accept their poor chances of promotion and develop a slack, complicit masculinity. Or they may fight against the powers that be, rejecting school, skirmishing with the police, getting into crime (Connell 1989, 1991).

The tattoo-and-motorcycle style of aggressive white working-class masculinity is familiar enough; Metcalfe even comments on the 'larrikin mode of class struggle.' It has generally been understood as linked with stark homophobia, misogyny, and domestic patriarchy. Our interviews with young unemployed men suggest that this pattern too is being deconstructed in a significant way. The public display of protest masculinity continues. But it can coexist with a breakdown in the *domestic* gender division of labor, with an acceptance of women's economic equality, and an interest in children, which would not be expected from traditional accounts (Metcalfe 1988; Willis 1978; Hopper and Moore 1989).

Since structural unemployment in first-world countries is most likely to affect members of oppressed ethnic groups, such a deconstruction must interweave with race politics. American discussions of masculinity in urban black ghettos show this interplay in one dramatic form. In other parts of the world it does not necessarily follow the same course. For instance, some Australian work on the making of masculinity in multi-ethnic inner-city environments suggest a more negotiated, though still racially-structured, outcome (Staples 1978, Majors 1989; Contrast Walker 1988).

What the evidence does show unequivocally is that working-class masculinities are no more set in concrete than are ruling-class masculinities—though in a bourgeois culture they are much more liable to stereotyped representation. The conscious attempts at building a counter-sexist heterosexual masculinity have mainly occurred in middle-class milieux. Some socialist explorations did occur but are now mostly forgotten. I would argue that a progressive sexual politics cannot afford to be class-blind. It must look to the settings of working-class life, and existing forms of working-class collective action, as vital arenas of sexual politics (Tolson 1977).

Afterword

To cover the territory of this article is to skate fast over dangerously thin ice. For much of the story the evidential basis is still very slight; that is why I have called it a sketch and a historical hypothesis.

But this is the scale on which we have to think, if the major problems about men in gender relations are to get sorted out. For too long the discussion of masculinity has been bogged down in psychological readings of the issue, most often in an ego-psychology based on an extreme individualism. We need to let the breezes of politics, economics, institutional sociology, and history blow through the psychology. They may puff strategies of reform away from an individualized masculinity-therapy towards a collective politics of gender equality.

At the time of writing, the most popular English-language book about masculinity is a deeply reactionary work by the American poet Robert Bly called *Iron John* (1990). The fact that significant numbers of middle-class North American men are attracted to a view of masculinity which is nativist, separatist, homophobic, and expressed through concocted myths of ancient men's rituals, is a disturbing index of current sexual politics.

Yet even here a dialectic can be seen. For Bly's 'mythopoetic men's movement' has moved beyond an individualized masculinity-therapy to emphasize collective processes, gatherings of men to enact rituals and generate solidarity. If that awareness can be connected with a pro-feminist, pro-gay agenda, we will have less drum-beating among the trees, but we may actually be moving towards gender equality.

Notes

1. For the conceptual critique see Connell (1987). Fine examples of field research are Hochschild, (1989) and Stacey (1990).
2. Attempts are now being made to take class and race issues aboard: see the recent collections Kimmel, M. S., and Messner, M. A. (eds.) (1989); Messner, M. A., and Sabo, D. (eds.) (1990).

References

Adam, B. D. (1987), *The Rise of a Gay and Lesbian Movement* (Boston: Hall).

Adolph, J. B. (1971), 'The South American Macho: Myths and Mystique', *Impact of Science on Society*, 21: 83–92.

Altman, D. (1982), *The Homosexualization of America, the Americanization of the Homosexual* (New York: St Martin's Press).

Bacon, M. H. (1986), *Mothers of Feminism: The Story of Quaker Women in America* (San Francisco: Harper and Row).

Bly, R. (1990), *Iron John: A Book About Men* (Reading, Mass.: Addison-Wesley).

Bolton, R. (1979), 'Machismo in Motion: The Ethos of Peruvian Truckers', *Ethos*, 7/4: 312–42.

Bray, A. (1982), *Homosexuality in Renaissance England* (London: Gay Men's Press).

Brugger, W. (1971), 'The Male (and Female) in Chinese Society', *Impact of Science on Society*, 21/1: 5–19.

Burton, C. (1991), *The Promise and the Price: The Struggle for Equal Opportunity in Women's Employment* (Sydney: Allen and Unwin), ch. 1: 'Masculinity and Femininity in the Organisation'.

Carrigan, T., Connell, R. W., and Lee, J. (1985), 'Toward a New Sociology of Masculinity', *Theory and Society*, 14/5: 551–604.

Chodorow, N. (1978), *The Reproduction of Mothering: Psychoanalysis and the Sociology of Gender* (Berkeley: Univ. of California Press).

von Clausewitz, K. (1827; 1975 edn.), *On War* (Princeton, NJ: Princeton Univ. Press).

Cockburn, C. (1983), *Brothers: Male Dominance and Technological Change* (London: Pluto Press).

Connell, R. W. (1982), 'Men and Socialism', in G. Evans and J. Reeves (eds.), *Labor Essays* (Melbourne: Drummond), 53–64.

—— (1987), *Gender and Power: Society, the Person and Sexual Politics* (Stanford, Calif.: Stanford Univ. Press), 253–8.

—— (1986), 'The State, Gender, and Sexual Politics: Theory and Appraisal', *Theory and Society*, 15/5: 507–44.

—— (1990), 'A Whole New World: Remaking Masculinity in the Context of the Environmental Movement', *Gender and Society*, 4/4: 452–78.

—— (1989), 'Cool Guys, Swots and Wimps: The Interplay of Masculinity and Education', *Oxford Review of Education*, 15/3: 291–303.

—— (1991), 'Live Fast and Die Young: The Construction of Masculinity Among Young Working-Class Men on the Margin of the Labour Market', *Australian and New Zealand Journal of Sociology*, 27/2: 141–71.

—— and Dowsett, G. W. (1990), 'The Unclean Motion of the Generative Parts: Frameworks in Western Thought on Sexuality' (paper to Academy of Social Sciences Workshop on Sexuality on Australia, Canberra).

David, D. S., and Brannon, R. (1976), *The Forty-Nine-Percent Majority: The Male Sex Role* (Reading, Mass.: Addison-Wesley).

D'Emilio, J., and Freedman, E. B. (1988), *Intimate Matters* (New York: Harper and Rowe).

Donaldson, M. (1987), 'Labouring Men: Love, Sex and Strife', *Australian and New Zealand Journal of Sociology*, 23/2: 165–84.

Ellis, A. (1976), *Sex and the Liberated Man* (Secaucus, NJ: Lyle Stuart).

Farrell, W. (1975), *The Liberated Man: Beyond Masculinity: Freeing Men and their Relationships with Women* (New York: Bantam).

Ford, D., and Hearn, J. (1988), *Studying Men and Masculinity: A Sourcebook of Literature and Materials* (Bradford: Univ. of Bradford Dept. of Applied Social Studies).

Franklin, C. W., II (1987), 'Surviving the Institutional Decimation of Black Males: Causes, Consequences, and Intervention', in H. Brod (ed.), *The Making of Masculinities* (Boston: Allen and Unwin), 155–69.

Fussell, P. (1989), *Wartime: Understanding and Behavior in the Second World War* (New York: Oxford Univ. Press).

Galbraith, J. K. (1971), *The New Industrial State* (Boston: Houghton Mifflin).

Gilder, G. (1975), *Sexual Suicide* (New York: Bantam).

Goldberg, S. (1973), *The Inevitability of Patriarchy* (New York: Morrow).

Gouldner, A. W. (1979), *The Future of Intellectuals and the Rise of the New Class* (New York: Seabury Press).

Hanke, L. (1965), *The Spanish Struggle for Justice in the Conquest of America* (Boston: Little, Brown).

Hansot, E., and Tyack, D. (1987), 'Gender in Public Schools: Thinking Institutionally', *Signs*, 13/4: 741–60.

Harrison, J. B. (1979), 'Men's Roles and Men's Lives', *Signs*, 4/2: 324–36.

Hearn, J., and Morgan, D. H. J. (eds.) (1990), *Men, Masculinities and Social Theory* (London: Unwin Hyman).

——, and Parkin, W. (1987), *'Sex' at 'Work': The Power and Paradox of Organization Sexuality* (Brighton: Wheatsheaf).

Herdt, G. H. (1981), *Guardians of the Flutes: Idioms of Masculinity* (New York: McGraw-Hill).

—— (ed.) (1984), *Ritualized Homosexuality in Melanesia* (Berkeley: Univ. of California Press).

Herzfeld, M. (1985), *The Poetics of Manhood: Contest and Identity in a Cretan Mountain Village* (Princeton: Princeton Univ. Press).

Hinsch, B. (1990), *Passions of the Cut Sleeve: The Male Homosexual Tradition in China* (Berkeley: Univ. of California Press).

Hochschild, A. (1989), *The Second Shift: Working Parents and the Revolution at Home* (New York: Viking).

Hopper, C. B., and Moore, J. (1989), 'Women in Outlaw Motorcycle Gangs', *Journal of Contemporary Ethnography*, 18/4: 363–87.

Humphries, M. (1985), 'Gay Machismo', in A. Metcalf and M. Humphries (eds.), *The Sexuality of Men* (London: Pluto), 70–85.

Jeffords, S. (1989), *The Remasculinization of America: Gender and the Vietnam War* (Bloomington, Ind.: Indiana Univ. Press).

Johnson, R. (1974), *He: Understanding Male Psychology* (New York: Harper and Row).

Kates, G. (1991), 'D'Eon Returns to France: Gender and Power in 1777', in J. Epstein and K. Straub (eds.), *Body Guards: The Cultural Politics of Gender Ambiguity* (New York: Routledge), 167–94.

Kiernan, V. G. (1988), *The Duel in European History: Honour and the Reign of Aristocracy* (Oxford: Oxford Univ. Press).

Kimmel, M. S., and Messner, M. A. (eds.) (1989), *Men's Lives* (New York: Macmillan).

Knauss, P. R. (1987), *The Persistence of Patriarchy: Class, Gender and Ideology in Twentieth Century Algeria* (New York: Praeger).

Lidz, T., and Lidz, R. W. (1986), 'Turning Women Things Into Men: Masculinization in Papua New Guinea', *Psychoanalytic Review*, 73: 521–39.

Majors, R. (1989), 'Cool Pose', in M. S. Kimmel and M. A. Messner (eds.), *Men's Lives* (New York: Macmillan).

Messner, M. A., and Sabo, D. (eds.) (1990), *Sports, Men and the Gender Order: Critical Feminist Perspectives* (Champaign, Ill.: Human Kinetics Books).

Metcalfe, A. F. (1988), *For Freedom and Dignity: Historical Agency and Class Structure in the Coalfields of NSW* (Sydney: Allen and Unwin).

Mieli, M. (1980), *Homosexuality and Liberation Elements of a Gay Critique* (London: Gay Men's Press).

Milligan, S. (1971), *Adolf Hitler: My Part in his Downfall* (Harmondsworth: Penguin).

—— (1976), *Monty: His Part in My Victory* (London: Michael Joseph).

Modjeska, N. (n.d.), 'The Duna Palena Nane and the Sociology of Bachelor Cults' (Macquarie Univ. School of Behavioural Sciences).

Nichols, J. (1975), *Men's Liberation: A New Definition of Masculinity* (New York: Penguin).

O'Neil, J. M. (1980), 'Male Sex-Role Conflicts, Sexism, and Masculinity: Psychological Implications for Men, Women, and the Counseling Psychologist', *The Counseling Psychologist*, 8/2: 61–80.

Orlow, D. (1973), *The History of the Nazi Party*, ii. *1933–45* (Newton Abbott: David and Charles), ch. 3.

Pearlman, C. L. (1983), 'Machismo, Marianismo and Change in Indigenous Mexico: A Case Study from Oaxaca', *Quarterly Journal of Ideology*, 8/4: 53–9.

Phillips, J. (1980), 'Mummy's Boys: Pakeha Men and Male Culture in New Zealand', in P. Bukle and B. Hughes (eds.), *Women in New Zealand Society* (Auckland: Allen and Unwin), 217–43.

Pleck, J. H. (1976), 'The Male Sex Role: Definitions, Problems, and Sources of Change', *Journal of Social Issues*, 32/3: 155–64.

Pringle, R. (1989), *Secretaries Talk: Sexuality, Power, and Work* (Sydney: Allen and Unwin).

Pusey, M. (1991), *Economic Rationalism in Canberra: A Nation-Building State Changes Its Mind* (London: Cambridge Univ. Press).

Ruhlmann, R. (1975), 'Traditional Heroes in Chinese Popular Fiction', in A. F. Wright (ed.), *Confucianism and Chinese Civilization* (Stanford, Calif.: Stanford Univ. Press), 123–57.

Schieffelin, E. L. (1982), 'The *Bau*: A Ceremonial Hunting Lodge: An Alternative to Initiation', in Herdt (ed.), *Rituals of Manhood* (Berkeley: Univ. of California Press), 155–200.

Seccombe, W. (1977), 'Patriarchy Stabilized: The Construction of the Male Breadwinner Wage Norm in Nineteenth-Century Britain', *Social History*, 2/1: 53–75.

Segal, L. (1990), *Slow Motion: Changing Masculinities, Changing Men* (London: Virago).

Sexton, P. (1969), *The Feminized Male: Classrooms, White Collars, and the Decline of Manliness* (New York: Random House).

Stacey, J. (1983), *Patriarchy and Socialist Revolution in China* (Berkeley: Univ. of California Press).

—— (1990), *Brave New Families* (New York: Basic Books).

Staples, R. (1978), 'Masculinity and Race: The Dual Dilemma of Black Men', *Journal of Social Issues*, 34/1: 169–83.

Stoller, R. J. (1968), *Sex and Gender*, i. *On the Development of Masculinity and Femininity* (London: Hogarth Press and the Institute of Psychoanalysis).

—— (1976), *Sex and Gender*, ii. *The Transsexual Experiment* (New York: Jason Aronson).

—— and Herdt, G. H. (1983), 'The Development of Masculinity: A Cross-Cultural Contribution', *American Psycho-Analytical Association Journal*, 30/1: 29–59.

Tefler, J. B. (1885), *The Strange Career of the Chevalier D'Eon de Beaumong: Minister Plenipotentiary from France to Great Britain in 1763* (London: Longmans Green).

Theweleit, K. (1987), *Male Fantasies* (Cambridge: Polity Press).

Tiger, L. (1969), *Men in Groups* (London: Nelson).

Tolson, A. (1977), *The Limits of Masculinity* (London: Tavistock).

Walker, J. (1988), *Louts and Legends: Male Youth Culture in an Inner-City School* (Sydney: Allen and Unwin).

Wang Liu, H.-C. (1959), *The Traditional Chinese Clan Rules* (New York: Association for Asian Studies and J. J. Augustin).

Waring, M. (1988), *Counting for Nothing: What Men Value and What Women are Worth* (Wellington: Allen and Unwin and Port Nicholson Press).

Weeks, J. (1977), *Coming Out* (London: Quartet).

Williams, C. (1981), *Open Cut: The Working Class in an Australian Mining Town* (Sydney: Allen and Unwin).

Willis, P. E. (1978), *Profane Culture* (London: Routledge and Kegan Paul).

Yeatman, A. (1990), *Bureaucrats, Technocrats, Femocrats: Essays on the Contemporary Australian State* (Sydney: Allen and Unwin).

41

Is the Future Female? Female Success, Male Disadvantage, and Changing Gender Patterns in Education

Gaby Weiner, Madeleine Arnot, and Miriam David

Are boys and young men falling behind in the stampede for qualifications and jobs? Are they suffering from new forms of educational disadvantage? If one is to believe the press and media of the mid-1990s, the answer to both questions is yes. What might be called a moral panic has broken out over the apparent under-achievement of boys. For example, during the examination results period of 1994 typical headlines included: 'The trouble with boys' (*The Sunday Times*, 19 June); 'Girls trounce the boys in examination league table' (*The Times*, 3 September); 'Can girls do better without the boys?' (*Daily Express*, 11 November); 'Brainy girls are top of the class' (*Today*, 22 November). A similar moral panic about boys has surfaced in other countries: for example, in Australia, Foster (1995: 54) identifies a recent 'backlash period' against gains made by girls as a result of a decade of equal-opportunities policy-making deliberately aimed at girls and young women.

It appears as if female success is viewed as a corollary to male failure. Rather than celebrating girls' achievements and aspirations, we have now a discourse of male disadvantage in which boys are viewed as falling behind in academic performance. The discourse also has powerful class and racial dimensions, with the impact of black and/or male working-class under-achievement interpreted as a threat to law and order, and male middle-class under-achievement as deriving from problems of 'attitude', complacency, and arrogance. For example, a *Sunday Times* article describes the working-class non-achiever as:

the archetypical boy at the back of the class: short-cropped hair a menacing look and a knack for disrupting his classmates' work. Being rude to teachers is his stock in trade. . . . It is a skill that . . . [he] cultivated at primary school to hide the fact that he was barely able to read or write. (19 June 1994)

In contrast, for middle-class male youth, the threat is not menace and lawlessness, but male indolence and masculine culture. A male sixth-former's account of his own poor (GCSE) examination performance provides a flavour of the perceived causes of male failure:

'After our mock exams, the teachers predicted I would get six As. No trouble, I thought. I don't need to work. So I didn't and got three As' . . . He says he is working harder to get to a decent university but still not as hard as the girls in his physics group. 'The group is mainly boys and they do almost no work at all, especially homework', he says. (*The Independent*, 18 October 1994)

In both cases, female equivalents are portrayed as more industrious and conscientious, better-behaved, more passively compliant, and, implicitly, more unimaginative and boring. Although there is little evidence that girls' improvement in examinations has been at the expense of that of boys, the predominant gender discourse in education in the mid-1990s is that of *male under-achievement*. Accompanying the hyperbole of press commentary is an escalation of conferences and seminars on male disadvantage (e.g. a one-day conference, 'The Challenge of Change', in March 1996 at Liverpool Football Club, one aim of which is to 'highlight the developing culture of under achievement of boys and its implications for male unemployment'), and the virtual eclipse of attention to issues of schooling specifically relating to girls and young women.

There is also, it must be said, some serious and important work which seeks to identify and explain the nature of masculinity, how men's lives have changed and are changing, and how this can be connected to the schooling of boys (and girls). The aims of these studies are to explore the range of masculinities that exist, and how they are produced, alongside femininities, within culture and schooling; for example, Mac An Ghaill (1994: 12) seeks to identify a 'concept of hegemonic masculinity, which . . . is constructed in relation to and against femininity and subordinated forms of masculinity' (see also Connell 1989 etc.). Sewell (1995) explores, in particular, the relationship between racism, gender, and masculine identity within schooling.

However, 20 years ago, immediately after the 1975 Sex Discrimination Act, the predominant gender discourse was that of *female under-achievement*. This was a period following the emergence of the Civil Rights and Women's Movements in the United States, and whilst changing ideas about equality swiftly crossed the Atlantic, British educationists were relatively slow in transforming these ideas into practice. Thus where girls did badly compared to boys, for example in some aspects of Mathematics and Science, prevailing explanations focused on biology and so-called innate gender differences—though this was robustly challenged by feminists of the period (Belotti 1975; Kelly 1975; Byrne 1978; Bristol Women's Studies Group 1979). Where girls appeared to do particularly well, for example in the Humanities, this was ascribed, as Walkerdine remembers from her experiences in the 1970s, to dogged hard work and conformism rather than ability.

One of the first prejudices I encountered was the consistent attempt in the research literature, as well as more popularly, to ascribe girls' good performance to hard work, diligence and good behaviour. Boys, by contrast, were held to have the kind of potential that leads to brilliance, even if their current classroom performance exhibited no tangible evidence of it. . . . To suggest that girls, too, might be rather bright seemed to be a very threatening idea. (Walkerdine 1994: 12–13)

More recently, Foster (1995) contrasts the gender educational discourses of the two periods in Australia, seeing the fervour about boys

as part of the struggle to regain ground lost to feminism in the 1980s and 1990s.

Policies and programs have reverberated to the refrain, *What about the boys!* effectively achieving a swift reassertion of male educational interests as prior, in the face of girls' perceived advances into male terrain. By contrast, male interests had earlier been strongly bolstered by a construction which emphasised girls as *lacking*, rather than viewing boys themselves as being *advantaged*. (p. 52, author's emphasis)

Against this backdrop of moral panic around boys, and confusion as to whether boys' performance has indeed deteriorated as girls' performance has improved, this article explores achievement patterns of girls and boys, and the discourses within which they have been constructed and deconstructed. It first considers a framework for looking at educational discourses of equality, then reports on past and current changes in patterns of gender achievement and in/equality, and ends with a discussion of policy implications and future possibilities.

Educational Discourses of Gender

The principal question that is explored is whether the media-constructed discourse of male disadvantage is grounded in any material evidence of change, or whether we are experiencing a fundamental shift in gender relations more generally. We also evaluate the extent to which any identified changes are due to recent policy-making directed at greater equality, disruptions to previous employment patterns, and/or wider cultural and social conditions.

In order better to understand and interpret how debates around gender equality have shifted and reproduced, a theoretical framework is needed which recognizes complexity both in interpreting gender difference and in catching hold of the slippery and sometimes erratic nature of publicly expressed concern. Foucault offers such a framework and, in particular, three aspects of his work are helpful to the analysis. First, he uses discourse to explain ways of thinking about the world that are so deeply embedded in practice that we are unconscious of their existence. Discourses are structuring mechanisms for social institutions (such as schools), modes of thought, and individual subjectivities: they are 'practices that systematically form the objects of which they speak' (Foucault 1974: 49).

Further, Foucault's understanding of power–knowledge relations allows for the relationship to be established, within any discourse, between knowledge (say, relating to the curriculum, policy, and so on) and power (who creates, controls, receives specific knowledges):

> There is no power relations without the correlative constitution of a field of knowledge, nor any knowledge that does not presuppose and constitute at that same time power relations (Foucault 1977a: 27).

This is useful because it points to the centrality of power relations within the discourse of gender in/equality itself. Questions need to be asked, for instance, about who has shaped the discourse of gender in/equality, on what evidence, and with what intention.

Another key Foucauldian notion is of the importance of the local, and of individuals or groups working for social justice at the local level:

> Working, not in the modality of the 'universal', the 'exemplary', the 'just-and-true-for-all', but within specific sectors, at the precise points where their own conditions of life or work situate them. (Foucault 1977b: 126)

Any discussion of educational in/equality therefore needs to address the 'parochial', or the specificities of local, confined settings. It also needs to be understood as enmeshed within and suffused by other, more dominant educational discourses. Thus, understanding can be enhanced about why 'equal opportunity' and 'gender equality' have had different meaning and produced different 'truths' in different historical periods and locations. The fact that many educational practitioners and

academics, such as ourselves, have lived through shifts of meaning has also enabled us to pose particular questions, and also to intervene in and shape current educational and equity discourses.

Hence, if we set the prevalent discourses of education alongside discourses of gender in/equality, in the UK from the 1950s onwards, we can detect parallel ideological and conceptual shifts (Table 41.1):

Discursive shifts are necessarily difficult to fix, therefore the terminology and the periodization used in Table 41.1 need to be interpreted flexibly. Others have chosen different points of departure. For example, David (1993) identifies similar changes in the discourse of educational reform in the United States and other industrialized nations, whilst Brown (1995) categorizes such discursive shifts according to the 'rule of engagement' in the competition for pupil credentials and qualifications.

> Whereas in the post-war period, the rules of engagement were based upon the ideology of meritocracy and the introduction of 'comprehensive' education, they are now based on 'market' principles and what has been called the 'ideology of parentocracy'. . . . As a consequence, educational selection is increasingly based on the *wealth* and *wishes* of parents rather than the individual *abilities* and *efforts* of pupils. Here the equation 'ability + efforts = merit' has been reformulated into 'resources + preferences = choice'. (Brown 1995: 44, author's emphasis)

Yet others see the impact of feminism, particularly liberal feminism, as striking at the heart of the patriarchal state which, according to Arnot (1993), has resulted in a new sensitivity to the interrelationship between gender and the state.

Table 41.1. Parallel educational discourses

Historical period	Prevalent discourses of education	Prevalent discourses of gender and education
1940s, 1950s	equality of opportunity: IQ testing (focus on access)	weak (emphasis on equality according to 'intelligence')
1960s, 1970s	equality of opportunity: progressivism/ mixed ability (focus on process)	weak (emphasis on working-class, male disadvantage)
1970s to early 1980s	equality of opportunity: gender, race, disability, sexuality etc. (focus on outcome)	equal opportunities/anti-sexism (emphasis on female disadvantage)
Late 1980s, early 1990s	choice, vocationalism and marketization (focus on competition)	identity politics and feminisms (emphasis on femininities and masculinities)
Mid-1990s	school effectiveness and improvement (focus on standards)	performance and achievement (emphasis on male disadvantage)

This sensitivity to the structuring influence of gender dynamics on state apparatuses, bureaucracies and discourses has encouraged new conceptual understandings about the relationship between patriarchy and the state. . . . A key line of argument focuses on the role that the state has played in constructing the divisions between public and private relations. (p. 191)

In Table 41.1 we show how certain shifts of emphasis concerning gender are locked into and produced by certain prevalent discourses of education at different historical periods as well as by feminist politics or movements, themselves products of wider social and cultural discursive shifts (Weiner 1994).

From the 1940s to the early 1960s, for example, there was relatively little discussion of gender and education, or of gender issues more widely. The 1944 Education Act aimed to widen the chances for working-class children by directing them to different types of schools (grammar, central, or secondary modern) according to their measured intelligence (see also David 1993, 1995). The major concern about gender of the postwar radical Labour administration, according to Dean (1991: 270) was 'that a rapidly demobilizing military machine, predominantly male, should find employment in peacetime Britain'. Education was seen as central to this endeavour.

The immediate task was to lure women back from the workplace to the home. What seemed to be required was a mixture of persuasion, education, rewards and warnings.

In her analysis of the three major reports on education spanning this period (Norwood 1943; Crowther 1959; Newsom 1963), Wolpe concludes that, though apparently grounded in reformist assumptions about an expanded system of mass education, they all 'provide an ideological basis for the perpetuation of an education system which does not open up new vistas or possibilities to the majority of girls' (Wolpe 1976: 157; see also David 1993). Similarly, in Deem's view, from the Labour government of 1944–51, through the high point of social democracy and the extension of the welfare state in the late 1960s to the breakdown of consensus about education and the decline of social democracy towards the end of the 1970s, there was little visible support for feminist goals or for any other than the broadest notions of sex equality (Deem 1981). In

this period, the educational performance of girls was generally interpreted in terms of their prime vocational destination as wives and mothers.

The discourse of progressivism that suffused especially primary education throughout the 1960s and 1970s also proved unsupportive to identification of gender inequality in education. Progressivism was premised on a notion of liberatory pedagogy where, according to Walkerdine (1983: 80) 'childhood and proper growth and development are best served by leaving children as alone, free and unencumbered as possible'. Within this discourse of 'natural' and individual development, girls' early success was viewed as transgressive, abnormal and 'not real learning'.

The real discovery and conceptualisation which form the cornerstones of modern pedagogy are contrasted with rule-following and rote-memorizing. . . . From this point of view, success in terms of attainment or correct work can be achieved *in the wrong way*. One aspect of the 'problem of female success' is that it turns out to be no success at all! Instead of thinking properly, girls *simply* work hard—if femininity is defined by passivity, good behaviour, rule-following and the other characteristics of the old methods, then the outcomes cannot be 'real learning' (Walkerdine 1983: 83–4, author's emphasis).

Thus, it seems that girls' performance *vis-à-vis* progressivism was inevitably 'not good enough', despite their obvious successes. Mixed-ability teaching in the secondary sector was framed within the discourse of comprehensive education and the reduction of social class differentials (Kelly 1973). Scant attention was paid, therefore, to pupil behaviour in mixed-sex classrooms which negatively affected girls' performance.

Discussion of gender issues within education gradually came to the fore after the passage of the Sex Discrimination Act in 1975, which included education within its remit. Feminists within education used the legislation to open up the debates about inequalities in schooling for girls, pushing for changes in pedagogy, curriculum, policy, and administration. They were backed, in the early and mid-1980s, by municipal socialism in the form of a number of Labour-controlled LEAs, which used increased support for equality initiatives as part of their challenge to New Right policies. More sharply focused, or, perhaps, 'simplistic' (Gillborn 1995: 75) policies were produced which first sought to identify and then to combine different facets of gender policymaking. Connections were made, for example, between gender, race, class, and ethnicity, as different feminisms began to make an impact on education (Minhas 1986).

Equality thus became a political football, or signifier, of the fight between the political left and right, in which the principal losers were the metropolitan left-leaning LEAs, the powers of which were sharply curtailed by the 1988 Education Reform Act and subsequent legislation (David 1993). At the same time, feminist and equality activists more generally were confronted by what seemed to be a fragmentation of political effort with the emergence of identity politics around different forms of feminist, masculine, black, and minority ethnic voices (Weiner 1994). Simultaneously, concepts of equality of opportunity and justice (recast as 'entitlement') continued to be promoted within New Right discourses, but in highly individualized and weak forms: for instance, the rough justice of the market and the aspirations of the individual were superimposed over postwar welfarism, and equality initiatives were targeted at identified social groups and communities.

By the late 1980s, as the government's increasing emphasis on achievement and standards took hold, interest in gender began to shift away from school policy and practice towards patterns of difference in examinations, and between girls and boys of different social groups. This coincided with the beginning of the British educational reform period (1988–1994) and therefore an additional interest was in the effects of the legislation, in particular the Educational Reform Act (1988), and of the National Curriculum on gender in/equality (Arnot 1989; Burton and Weiner 1990; Miles and Middleton 1990; Shah 1990; David 1993). Prevailing educational discourses of the mid-1990s were of school effectiveness, school improvement, and the best means of assessing and addressing the needs of 'good' and 'bad' schools through mechanisms of inspection, managerialism, and accountability (Gray and Wilcox 1995).

What, then, can such an analysis offer for the understanding of gender issues and the emergence of a discourse of male disadvantage in the late 1990s? The education reforms and policy-making in the UK in the 1980s and 1990s clearly produced new educational discourses which, at least in the short term, changed equality strategies within and through schooling. In particular, three long-standing strands were evident relating to gender: 'improvement in performance', 'equal-opportunities policy-making', and 'gender-fair school culture'. The scare about boys emanated from the first strand, providing an inversion of the comparisons between girls' and boys' performance made in the 1970s. Influential factors included: emphasis on examination performance as a signifier of school excellence promoted by the education reforms; particular attention given to the General Certificate of Secondary Education (implemented in 1985), the results of which were publicized in League Tables (first produced in 1993); and the timing of the release of GCSE and A level results—during the August vacation period—when there is generally little other news to report.

The equal-opportunities policy-making strand which had first emerged in 1975 as a consequence of the Sex Discrimination Act, and which was subsequently developed by municipal LEAs in the early and mid-1980s, re-emerged from 1990 onwards largely through one particular aspect of the government reforms—the requirement by OFSTED for information on equal opportunities prior to inspection visits (OFSTED 1993). The discourse concerning the promotion of a gender-fair culture within schooling, similarly, has a history stretching back to the late 1970s, deriving from the work of feminists and other social-justice activists in education, and from an overall reduction in gender divisions within the culture.

What has Changed?

In this section we examine the evidence for claims about educational in/equality, and consider in what ways the educational context that led to calls for greater gender equality in the mid- and late-1970s have changed over the two succeeding decades.

IMPROVEMENT IN PERFORMANCE
In the mid-1970s, data collection on individual and school performance and school culture was less systematic and less pervasive

than today. Any evidence of gender difference tended, therefore, to be piecemeal and fragmentary. However, it was possible to identify various more or less consistent patterns of gender difference of the period. For instance, at primary level teachers were found to treat girls and boys according to deeply held stereotypes; girls and women were under-represented or invisible in school curricula; girls and boys read sexist literature, were taught some subjects (such as crafts and PE) separately, and experienced different disciplinary codes. Variations in achievement (girls being better at reading and boys having more advanced mathematical problem-solving skills and better spatial awareness) were held to derive from biology, and were therefore viewed as 'natural', as we have seen (Walkerdine 1983).

In selective and comprehensive secondary schools of the mid-1970s, most students studied a common set of subjects (RE, English, Maths, and Physical Education), though girls and boys were taught separately for PE and sports activities, and timetabling produced sex-stereotyped choices for students at 13-plus. Indeed, subject options reflected both the resources available at the school and the sex-typed aspirations of the students. In specific subject areas, boys at 13-plus were more likely to choose Physics and Geography, and girls Biology, French, and German. Girls tended to study one science whereas boys chose two. At post-16, according to 1974 examination board data, 41.3 per cent of boys and 14.9 per cent of girls chose exclusively science-based subjects. The pattern was reversed for arts-based studies, however, with 64 per cent of girls choosing exclusively arts subjects. Significantly, girls were more likely to take science in single-sex schools (Rendel 1974).

In examinations of the 1970s overall, girls tended to do as well as boys up to O level (except in Mathematics and Science); but after this, boys had the advantage both in the numbers that stayed on at school and the number of subjects taken at A level. From CSE upwards there were fewer subject entries for girls than boys (by about 15 per cent) and at A level, subject entries for boys exceeded girls by about 10,000. This relatively lower participation of girls in examinations was reflected in their relatively lower performance in them (Rendel 1974; Weiner 1976, Bristol Women's Studies group 1979).

What is different in the 1990s?[1] First, the introduction of a National Curriculum in 1988 formalized and strengthened the set of core subjects (to which Science was added) taken by all students, and more regular and public forms of assessment and testing were introduced. There appeared to be fewer possibilities for subject choice at 13-plus, though as a consequence of the Dearing Report (1993) the number of compulsory subjects in the initial National Curriculum was reduced. At the time of writing, the outcome of the Dearing changes has yet to be evaluated, though it is anticipated that sex-stereotyping will re-emerge alongside increased choice.

At primary level in the mid-1990s, assessment focused on the core subjects (English, Mathematics, and Science) and, in the main, girls have been achieving at higher levels overall, especially in English, with boys more likely to perform at the extremes. At 16-plus the main change from previous periods was the introduction of GCSE (in 1985, first examinations in 1988) to replace the O level and CSE examinations. The resulting change in the higher examination entry and performance patterns of girls, has caused the shifts picked up by the press. Thus, there has been an increased entry and a closing gender-performance gap in most subjects at GCSE, apart from Chemistry and Economics, which are still largely taken by boys, and Social Sciences, which is largely taken by girls. Male students continue to achieve relatively less well in English and the Arts, Humanities, Modern Foreign Languages and, perhaps more unexpectedly, Technology. Single-sex girls' schools continue to be particularly successful in examination performance.

At A level, sex-stereotyped patterns of examination entry and performance tend to re-emerge. There is higher male entry into Sciences (Physics, Technology, Computer Studies, Geography, Chemistry, and Mathematics), and the level of male entry into English and Modern Foreign Languages is also higher than previously. Significantly, there is a higher female entry for Arts and Humanities. Males gain higher A level grades than females in nearly all subjects, especially in Mathematics, Chemistry, Technology, History, English, and Modern Foreign Languages.[2] However, this grade superiority is gradually being eroded, with a marked improvement in female performance at A level, particularly in Biology, Social Sciences, Art, and Design. For those students seeking vocational rather than academic qualifications, subject and course choice has remained sex-stereotyped, with girls and boys choosing different subjects and girls being less likely to gain higher awards.

EQUAL–OPPORTUNITIES POLICY–MAKING

What appears to be different from two decades previously is the relatively high level of equal-opportunities policy-making nationally in the 1990s; hitherto it had achieved a high profile only in certain metropolitan and urban areas. Given the apparent hostility of government to equality issues from 1979 onwards, an unanticipated finding of EOC Project was that in the mid-1990s most schools had equal-opportunities policies on gender (two-thirds), the majority of which (83 per cent) had been put into place after 1988. Furthermore, in the post-reform period (1994 onwards), new nomenclatures—of performance standards, value-added policies, curriculum entitlement, bullying and harassment, and others—began to shape and suffuse educational discourses of gender. There was also evidence of wide variation in awareness and application of equal opportunities or understanding of changed performance trends relating to girls and boys, with equality not perceived as a high priority by many schools.

Significantly, where equal opportunities initiatives developed locally, they tended to address the post-reform context of OFSTED inspections, indicators of 'value-addedness', raising performance, governor training, and male under-achievement. The reduction in influence of LEAs led to relative isolation in policy-making, with little attempt to disseminate beyond the immediate school cluster group or even the individual school staffroom. Thus, the equal-opportunity culture in the mid- and late 1990s has been one that has tended to have a narrow focus, and to fuse social-justice issues with performance standards and improvement, with greater emphasis on the latter.

GENDER–FAIR CULTURE

Another clear difference between the 1970s and the 1990s is in the culture of schooling. The aim of much early feminist work was to encourage a school culture in which girls could prosper and raise their aspirations and achievements. A sign of its success, perhaps, is that students in the 1990s seem more aware and sensitive to changing cultural expectations, with many girls and young women exhibiting confidence about their abilities and future, and boys and young men more sensitive to gender and equality debates. Labour-market and cultural transformation has led to changed vocational aspirations for both girls and boys, with girls tending to see improved employment possibilities in the expanding service sector. The availability of part-time work, though lower-paid, tends also to fit in with their traditional family commitments. On the other hand, the employment opportunities of young men have contracted, as conventional male manufacturing jobs have disappeared, leading to a higher degree of uncertainty about what the future has to offer, particularly for working-class youth.

However, while schools have seemed to benefit from changing pupil and student cultures, the management of education shows no equivalent changes. In fact, schools and LEAs (and also government education agencies, political parties, education quangos, universities, and so on) continue to be shaped largely by a culture of (white) male management (in staffing, governing bodies, and institutional hierarchies) which has shown little interest in equality issues. Unexpectedly, given the high ratio of female staff, this has been a noticeable feature of some primary schools.

Who Shapes the Discourse?

To what extent have the discourses of male and female disadvantage been shaped by 'facts'? Who produced the discourses of female disadvantage in the 1970s? Who has been responsible for shaping the more recent discourses of male disadvantage?

The discourse of female disadvantage in the 1970s and 1980s was enhanced by well-organized and well-informed feminist activists in education, aided by sympathetic politicians and officials at local and national levels. However, female educational disadvantage had also been highlighted by several earlier reports and research studies, the most important of which were Dale's study of the gendered outcomes of single-sex and co-education schools in the late 1960s (Dale

1969), and an influential HMI study of gender differences carried out in 1973 (published as DES 1975) which resulted in the eventual inclusion of education in the 1975 Sex Discrimination Act. Resistance to the suggestion of more gender-fair practices came from some writers, teachers, parents, and others (e.g. Hutt 1972), who tended to associate girls' poor academic performance in certain subjects with their eventual biological and vocational destinations in the home.

The discourse of male disadvantage of the 1990s has very different origins. The James Bulger murder in 1993, when a 2-year-old was abducted and killed by two boys (of 9 and 10 respectively), sent shock-waves throughout Britain, and this resulted in a media-led reappraisal of how cultural changes were affecting working-class masculinity's relationship to the family, schooling, and the labour market. As we have seen, a number of academics, some sympathetic to gender-equality issues, had also begun to examine masculinity in its various forms and its relationship to various forms of femininity within and outside schooling. As we have also seen, the publication of examination results introduced in 1993 led to a heightened media awareness of changing patterns of examination performance.

Explanations for male under-achievement tended to focus on the lack of interest and motivation of boys, and also on the collapse of working-class jobs. 'Nature' was rarely alluded to, except in the presentation of a 'laddishness' which was held to derive from a form of mischievous, harmless masculinity:

Technology lessons were only different in that the environment was unusually rich in opportunities for this type of 'play' which often involved images of war and violence, from mock Kung Fu kicks to 'sword fights' with pretty well anything 'long and straight'. (*TES* 1996)

Apparent low male performance was seen as caused in particular by the disappearance of traditional family roles (i.e. man as breadwinner, woman as homemaker). According to Arnot (1992), the family occupied a central position in New Right discourses as a defence against socialism and state power. Murray (1994), for example, argued that increases in violent crime, illegitimacy, and 'economic inactivity' (significantly, he avoided the term 'unemployment') have contributed to the creation of an underclass—the 'New Rabble'.

Illegitimacy in the lower classes will continue to rise and, inevitably, life in lower-class communities will continue to degenerate—more crime, more widespread drug and alcohol addiction, fewer marriages, more drop out from work, more homelessness, more child neglect, fewer young people pulling themselves out of the slums, more young people tumbling in. (Murray 1994: 18)

Truly, the nineteenth-century nightmare revisited, if he is to be believed! In her response to Murray, David identifies his gendered agenda as familiar, and as an implicit attack on working women:

His [Murray's] . . . proposal is that women be 'persuaded' only to have children in a proper marital situation and where they can be supported by their husbands (and so not go out to work, I presume!) This idea that men need families to civilize them and to 'force' them to do their patriarchal duty is ages old (1994: 58).

Thus it is not only boys and working-class young men who cling to the aspiration of a 'proper' job and a family wage. Traditional middle-class male management and professional career structures have been increasingly vulnerable to restructuring and 'downsizing', and to new practices arising from privatization and marketization (Brown 1995). Perhaps it is the crisis within middle-class masculinity that is fuelling the educational discourse of male disadvantage!

Notwithstanding, when 'proper' jobs do not appear, male students take refuge in a counter-culture of misbehaviour in schools. There are interesting parallels (and also differences) between these interpretations and the findings of Willis's classic 1977 study of working-class lads, where the laddish culture was viewed as bolstered by generally sexist attitudes and derogation of girls and women.

The most recent discourse of male disadvantage is simultaneously all-embracing and parochial, in the sense that it targets all schools as failing all boys, yet neglects to address the endpoint of schooling, i.e. the manifestly different class and gender patterns in vocational education and in the labour market, where males continue to hold the advantage. Significantly, differentials in pay are neglected: in 1988, for example, women's pay was still only 74.9 per cent of men's (EOC, 1990), this gap being 8 to 10 per cent wider than that in any other EC country (*Guardian* 29 Oct., 1991). The 'glass ceiling' effect, whereby women are prevented from reaching the most senior jobs, is also visible, illustrated recently in the merger of two departments, the Department for Education (DFE) and the Department of Employment (DoE), into the new Department of Education and Employment (DfEE). Appointments were overwhelmingly male at all senior levels, despite the fact that the Secretary of State was a woman. The proportion of men to women was 6: 2 in the top tier (elected members of government), 100 per cent male in the second tier (14 Director of Section posts), and 89: 23 in the third tier (excluding 4 posts, gender unknown) (DfEE, 1996).

Significantly, this pattern of *male advantage* in employment, common in both the public and private sectors, is not alluded to within the current educational discourse of male disadvantage. However, where there is the perception of an 'excess' of women, as in teaching, the need for more men is strongly asserted—as in a speech by Gillian Shepherd, the current Secretary of State for Education and Employment.

We recognise the great attraction to women of teaching as a career, but at the same time note the views repeated to us about the educational implications of the comparatively small number of male teachers in primary schools, where a growing number of children come from single-parent families with no effective male role model. (*TES* 1996: 12)

The prioritization of male issues of achievement, we suggest, constitutes a backlash against feminist successes (Faludi 1991). According to Kenway, it reflects the fact that masculinity has been forced on to the defensive and is 'in need of repair, adjustment and renewal' (1995: 62). She reasons that the feminist challenge to schooling is viewed as deeply threatening by many men:

males act as if the feminist presence in schools places masculinity under siege and that in attempting to subvert this threat, they develop a range of defensive strategies which include the mobilisation of various discourses associated with different masculinities. (Kenway 1995: 59)

To What Extent can we Say that the Future is Female?

Following our examination of shifts in the educational discourses of gender in/equality,

and in the changes in examination performance and school cultures, we suggest that it has been comparatively easy to invert gender-disadvantage discourses to focus on boys: if girls and women could be produced as victims, so also could boys and men. In fact, however, what we have is a rather more complex picture than hitherto indicated: it seems neither so bleak (for boys) nor as rosy (for girls) as has been depicted in the media and elsewhere. Girls have clearly made improvements since the 1970s in examination performance up to 16, but patterns are not nearly so clear-cut post-16. The international picture, in particular in the Western hemisphere, shows similar patterns of female success in school settings, so it is not clear to what extent national policy-making is implicated in these changes (Klein and Ortman 1994; Gipps and Murphy 1995).

Whilst the focus has switched to the so-called under-achievement of young men who might have been expected to do better in examinations, there has been conspicuous lack of attention given to students who do *not* succeed in examinations (who are they? why do they fail?) and a parallel neglect of gender patterns in vocational education and in the labour market. Meanwhile, the labour market (and vocational qualifications) is still heavily sex-divided/segregated, largely disadvantaging female workers—though, more recently, young women rather than young men have been more likely to pick up part-time, low-paid work.

More positively, changes to the culture are reflected in the expectations of young women to balance, rather than choose between, work and family. Many young men are also more aware of sex-equality issues than previous generations. Conversely, there is a strong and perhaps increasing male domination of educational management and institutional culture which is also reflected more generally in work patterns and hierarchies.

The reforms of the New Right have, to some extent, changed how we refer to and understand gender issues, but it is also clear that some changes in gender relations predated the late 1980s and 1990s. What is evident is that new educational discourses have silenced demands for increased social justice *for girls and women*, characterized by increasing resistance to policies and practices focusing specifically on them.

Future Possibilities

We suggest that positive strategies are needed, to address, through education, the continuing subordination of many women in society, to promote social justice, and to support particularly vulnerable groups, such as working-class and/or black boys. More systematic and regular systems of data collection would allow patterns of gender achievement in education to be identified speedily, and then addressed where necessary.

The school curriculum—which is but one selection of available knowledge from the culture (Lawton 1975)—implicitly produces the gender differences that it overtly seeks to eradicate. It would be possible, we suggest, to create subject clusters that defy gender stereotypes if a principal aim of schooling was to break down the gender divide.

Attention needs also to be devoted in schools to 'low-fliers', whether girls or boys, and to careers and vocational guidance. Young women might be encouraged to consider vertical career opportunities in so-called traditional 'female' occupations as well as entry into 'non-traditional' occupations. Students need to be provided with information on how women can balance family and career. In curriculum terms, students should be encouraged to look critically at male and female social positions, including those of their male and female teachers. Teachers and academics, too, need to update themselves on gender issues of the post-reform era, incorporating what can be redeemed from the old era with what can be utilized from the new. Finally, attempts need to be made to reposition and reproduce feminist and equality discourses in order to challenge new, hegemonic educational orthodoxies such as those of so-called male underachievement.

As to the question, 'is the future female?', there is little evidence to suggest that this is the case. The possibility that women may become genuinely *equal* to men still appears to be enormously threatening. Rather, the fact that we are asking this question at all suggests that current hegemonic educational discourses which seek to emphasize male underachievement might be seen as constituting a backlash to past feminist gains. What we are seeing may be, in fact, merely a new rendition of the old patriarchal refrain.

Notes

1. For this section of the article, we draw on research funded by the Equal Opportunities Commission, the report of which provides an overview of gender equality patterns in education over a 10-year period from 1984 to 1994 (Arnot, David, and Weiner 1996).
2. Male students continue to score at the extremes in examinations throughout their schooling, that is, they constitute the majority of both the weakest and the strongest students. This factor was known, too, in the 1970s.

References

Arnot M. (1989), 'Consultation or Legitimation? Race and Gender Politics and the Making of the National Curriculum', *Journal of Critical Policy*.

—— (1992), 'Feminism, Education and the New Right', in Arnot, M., and Barton, L. (eds.), *Voicing Concerns: Sociological Perspectives on Contemporary Education Reforms* (Oxford: Triangle Books).

—— (1993), 'A Crisis in Patriarchy? British Feminist Educational Politics and State Regulation of Gender', in Arnot, M., and Weiler, K., *Feminism and Social Justice in Education* (London: Falmer Press).

——, David, M., and Weiner, G. (1996), *Educational Reforms and Gender Equality in Schools* (Manchester: EOC).

Belotti, E. G. (1975), *Little Girls* (London: Writers and Readers Publishing Cooperative).

Bristol Women's Studies Group (1979), *Half the Sky: An Introduction to Women's Studies* (London: Virago).

Brown, P. (1995), 'Cultural Capital and Social Exclusion: Some Observations on Recent Trends in Education, Employment and the Labour Market', *Work, Employment and Society* 9/1: 29–51.

Burton, L., and Weiner, G. (1990), 'Social Justice and the National Curriculum', *Research Papers in Education*, 5/3: 203–28.

Byrne, E. (1978), *Women and Education* (London: Tavistock Publications).

Connell, R. W. (1989), 'Cool guys, Swots, and Wimps: The Interplay of Masculinity and Education', *Oxford Review of Education*, 15/3: 291–303.

Dale, R. R. (1969), *Mixed or Single Sex Schools* (London: Routledge and Kegan Paul).

David, M. (1980), *The State, the Family and Education* (London: Routledge and Kegan Paul).

—— (1993), *Parents, Gender and Education Reform* (Cambridge: Polity).

—— (1994), 'Fundamentally Flawed', in *Under-*

class: The Crisis Deepens (London: IEA Health and Welfare Unit), 53–8.

Dean, D. (1991), 'Education for Moral Improvement, Domesticity and Social Cohesion: Expectations and Fears of the Labour Government', Oxford Review of Education, 17/3: 269–85.

Deem, R. (1981), 'State Policy and Ideology in the Education of Women', British Journal of Sociology of Education, 2/2: 131–43.

Department for Education and Employment (DfEE) (1996), A Guide to the Department for Education and Employment (London: DfEE).

Department of Education and Science (DES) (1995), Curricular Differences for Boys and Girls: Education Survey 21 (London: HMSO).

Faludi, S. (1991), Backlash: The Undeclared War Against Women (London: Chatto and Windus).

Foster, V. (1995), 'Barriers to Equality in Australian Girls' Schooling for Citizenship in the 1990s', Lärarutbildning Och Forskning I Umea, 2, 3/4: 47–60.

Foucault, M. (1974), The Archaeology of Knowledge (London: Tavistock).

—— (1977a), Discipline and Punish: The Birth of the Prison (London: Allen Lane).

—— (1977b), 'Truth and Power', in Gordon, C. (1980) (ed.), Power/Knowledge: Selected Interviews and other Writings 1972–1977 by Michel Foucault (Brighton: Harvester Press).

Gillborn, D. (1995), Racism and Antiracism in Real Schools (Buckingham: Open Univ. Press).

Gipps, C., and Murphy, P. (1995), A Fair Test: Assessment, Achievement and Equity (Buckingham, Open Univ. Press).

Gray, J., and Wilcox, B. (1995), 'Good School, Bad School': Evaluating Performance and Encouraging Improvement (Buckingham: Open Univ. Press).

Hymas, C., and Cohen, J. (1994), 'The Trouble with Boys', The Sunday Times (19 June).

Hutt, C. (1972), Males and Females (Harmondsworth: Penguin).

Judd, J. (1994), 'The Trouble with Boys', The Independent (18 October).

Kelly, A. (1975), 'The Fate of Women Scientists', Women Speaking, (4 July).

—— (1973), Teaching Mixed Ability Classes (London: Harper and Row).

Kenway, J. (1995), 'Masculinities in Schools: Under Siege, On the Defensive and Under Reconstruction?', Discourse: Studies in the Cultural Politics of Education, 16/1: 59–79.

Klein, S. S., and Ortman, P. E. (1994), 'Continuing the Journey towards Gender Equity', Educational Researcher (November), 13–21.

Lawton, D. (1975), Class, Culture and the Curriculum (London: Routledge Kegan and Paul).

Mac An Ghaill, M. (1995), The Making of Men: Masculinities, Sexualities and Schooling (Buckingham: Open Univ. Press).

Miles, S., and Middleton, C. (1990), 'Girls' Education in the Balance: The ERA and Inequality', in Flude, M., and Hammer, M. (eds.), The Education Reform Act 1988: Its Origins and Implications (Basingstoke: Falmer Press), 187–206.

Minhas, R. (1986), 'Race, Gender and Class: Making the Connections', in ILEA (ed.), Secondary Matters (London: ILEA).

Murray, C. (1994), Underclass: The Crisis Deepens (London: IEA Health and Welfare Unit).

Office of Standards of Education (OFSTED) (1993), Handbook for the Inspection of Schools (London: OFSTED).

Rendel, M. (1974), 'What Sort of Relations Between the Sexes? Review of the Schools Council HCP Relations Between the Sexes Pack', The New Era, 53: 6.

School Curriculum and Assessment Authority (1993), The National Curriculum and its Assessment: Final Report (The Dearing Report) (London: SCAA).

Sewell T. (1995), 'A Phallic Response to Schooling: Black Masculinity and Race in an Inner-City Comprehensive', in Griffiths, M., and Troyna, B., Antiracism, Culture and Social Justice in Education (Staffordshire: Trentham Books).

Shah, S. (1990), 'Equal Opportunity Issues in the Context of the National Curriculum: A Black Perspective', Gender and Education, 2/3: 309–18.

The Times Educational Supplement (1996), 'Boys Revert to Nature when Future Looks Bleak' (12 January).

The Times Educational Supplement (1996), 'Worried About an Excess of Women' (16 February).

Walkerdine, V. (1983), 'It's Only Natural: Rethinking Child-Centred Pedagogy', in Wolpe, A. M., and Donald, J. (eds.), Is There Anyone Here From Education (London: Pluto Press).

—— (1994), 'What Makes Girls So Clever', The Independent (6 September).

Weiner, G. (1976), Girls' Education, the Curriculum and the Sex Discrimination Act (MA dissertation, London Univ. Institute of Education).

—— (1994), Feminisms and Education (Buckingham: Open Univ. Press).

Willis, P. (1977), Learning to Labour (Farnborough: Saxon House).

Wolpe, A. M. (1976), 'The Official Ideology of Education for Girls', in Flude, M., and Ahier, J. (eds.), Educability, Schools and Ideology (London: Croom Helm).

PART SIX
MERITOCRACY AND SOCIAL EXCLUSION

Part Six: Introduction

Meritocracy and Social Exclusion

Two great social principles of the Enlightenment are, firstly, that the determination of life-chances by the accidents of birth (ascription) should be driven from human society; and, secondly, that there should be mass rather than élite participants in democratic societies. Education has been seen as central to this agenda, in helping to provide the technical skills for modern society and in selecting the talented for upward mobility.

The fulfilment of these principles has been compromised by what, at root, are parental aspirations for the success of their children. Aspirations differ according to different classes and ethnic cultures. However, in the period of Economic Nationalism (see Ch. 1) a particular ideology, that of meritocracy, became the major *justification* for the process of socialization, selection, and control exercised by education systems. Meritocracy gave full expression to the twin social principles which have shaped so much of economic and social life since the Enlightenment, in the equation 'intelligence + effort = merit'. Not all subscribed to the definition of merit implicit in the equation but, more than any time before, or perhaps subsequently, there did appear to be a degree of consensus about what constituted success in society. This, as Goldthorpe *et al.* (1980) noted, was intimately related to the rise of the postwar state and corporate bureaucracies. Success was bound up with how much progress was made up the corporate ladder. Historically, there has always been an intimate link between bureaucracy and meritocracy (see Ch. 1), so that when success came to be defined in terms of promotion within a bureaucracy it was assumed to be as a result of merit: the most successful could be considered to have deserved their rewards.

However, the ideology of meritocracy had limited application in practice. The studies reported by Goldthorpe (Ch. 44) do not show that there has been the unequivocal march towards fulfilling the criteria of a meritocracy that liberals in the 1950s and early 1960s expected. Despite the rapid expansion of education, the privilege of the middle classes has remained.

However, while middle-class success may remain, the rules by which the middle classes may maintain their advantage have changed. The breakdown of bureaucracy, the increasing emphasis on market forms of capitalist organization, and the development of pluralist societies has meant that the notion of meritocracy as a justification for the socialization and selection procedures of educational systems is in doubt.

It is against this background that Goldthorpe's provocative chapter (Ch. 44) should be read. He argues that meritocracy is of doubtful value as a sociological concept, because the notion of merit is social, and is constructed in diverse ways in a market economy, and there is no one standard of 'merit'. This conclusion is reached through an initial consideration of the results of studies designed to test the Increased Merit Selection (IMS) hypothesis, which is that merit rather than social class, gender, or ethnic background is the key to access to post-compulsory education and, in turn, to a position within the division of labour. But more recent studies considered by Goldthorpe suggest that, if anything, the relationship between education and eventual class or status destination is weakening. Moreover, the overall association between social origins and class destination has remained constant over time, with little evidence to suggest that the relative influence of social origins on life-chances has diminished.

Given the lack of evidence that education is efficient in either finding talent or providing it with greater opportunities to achieve, Goldthorpe considers a range of positions and debates which have sought to explain why we are not moving closer to a meritocracy. However, his view is that this search for explanations is fundamentally misconceived. Rather, he argues that merit in a market and pluralist society has to be defined situationally, and that this will inevitably involve subjective judgements about what constitutes merit. In this way, the failure of studies to demonstrate a closer relationship between educational achievement and occupational reward can be explained. By the same token, the proposition that societies are becoming more meritocratic is difficult to formulate in an empirically testable way, precisely because what counts as merit will, at any one time, merely be the aggregation of a set context based on partially subjective judgements.

In developing this argument, Goldthorpe appears to incline to Hayek's view that meritocracy might best be understood as necessary myth, albeit double-edged, in getting people to believe that their well-being depends upon their best efforts rather than the caprice of the market. However, meritocracy may also be seen as a regulative ideal, supported in law through equal-opportunities legislation, which creates the presumption that situationally specific judgements about merit can always be challenged in public. Such a presumption will not advance us further down the road toward a meritocracy; but it may deter the excesses of a variety of forms of social exclusion in a pluralist age.

Nevertheless, a regulative ideal of this kind may leave open a high degree of latitude in the extent of opportunity available to those who have previously been the subject of exclusion and discrimination. In this context, the picture presented by post-industrial societies is complex and paradoxical. On the 'plus' side of the ledger, the development of mass tertiary education and the restructuring of secondary education into comprehensive schools has created the possibility of greater equality of opportunity. In his chapter, Halsey (Ch. 42) charts the nature of change in higher education in postwar Europe and the OECD countries. In doing so he reports on research he has undertaken adapting Wilensky's (1975) research on the welfare state. Wilensky tested the hypothesis that industrialized

countries converge in welfare provision despite differing cultures, political organizations, and ideologies, and found that economic development was a more
important predictor of welfare expenditure than political ideology. Halsey has
applied a similar analysis to test whether there is a similar convergence with
respect to access to tertiary education. This research is particularly relevant both
in the light of the claim made in the Introductory Chapter that there is now a new
consensus about the importance of education to economic development, and also
in the light of Halsey's concluding comments, pointing to the likely increase in
elements of privatization in the funding of tertiary education in Britain, which in
relation to tuition fees may increase inequality of access for students from low-
income families. This observation opens up a range of issues which suggest that
Halsey's initial work in adapting Wilensky's model may now need to be capitalized
on. For example, there is increasing variation in funding and access to tertiary
and higher education according to the different types of welfare-state regimes.
Moreover, access to higher education may also be differentiated according to the
status and wealth of universities (see Brown Ch. 48). The potential opportunities
created by the expansion of tertiary and higher education may therefore be vitiated by market forces and a status hierarchy of universities fuelled by credential
inflation.

Similar comments can be made about the position of the comprehensive or
common school. The research of McPherson and Willms (Ch. 45) is significant
because it provides an analysis of the impact of the comprehensive reorganization of secondary education in Scotland. The research shows that in the 8 years
of the study comprehensive reorganization significantly reduced social-class
inequalities in attainment. Most significantly, they found that socio-economic
status segregation was reduced nationally by the reorganization; and they
hypothesize that, among other factors, it was the increased social integration of
students which accounted for the trend towards greater equalization of attainment. This conclusion is in line with the dominant finding from the effective-
schools literature. However, as McPherson and Willms note, how more socially
balanced school-intakes improve overall school attainment is not well understood, and is clearly an avenue for further research.

Despite these results, the comprehensive school finds itself under attack. In
part this is a consequence of a developing pluralist society (see Ch. 1); but the
most immediate threat comes from the introduction of market forces into secondary education. It is claimed by opponents of marketization (see Part Four)
that the overall impact of uncontrolled choice and competition will be a polarization of school intakes—a contrary effect to that reported by McPherson and
Willms. A major debate, which will be ongoing for the foreseeable future, has
therefore been joined over the impact of market forces on elements of change and
reform in the tertiary and secondary sectors which appear to have the potential
to help equalize opportunities.

The chapters by Brown (Ch. 48), Stuart Wells and Serna (47), and Lareau (46)
form a group which seek to explain the context and mechanisms by which the
middle class is able to control the conditions which ensure the achievement of

middle-class students in secondary education. The competition for credentials is seen by these authors as a matter of power and exclusion in the service of reproducing the privilege of the middle class from one generation to another. Brown's chapter examines the major theories relating credentials to the occupation structure, and finds both technocratic and conflict theories wanting in analyzing the present context. Moreover, Brown also argues against the inevitability that middle-class cultural capital will ensure educational and occupational success. Rather, in order to ensure the success of their reproductive strategies, the middle class have had to shift the rules of engagement in the credential competition from that of merit to the market. The tension that the middle class has to negotiate is that of legitimizing its position by reference to an apparent openness of access, while resorting to techniques of closure which exclude others from the highest forms of credential success. In Chapter 48 Brown analyzes this thesis with respect to the marketization of secondary education. His chapter in this Section gives attention to the implications of the demise of the bureaucratic paradigm and the link between the expansion of higher education and management recruitment practices which explicitly include the personality characteristics most likely to be cultivated by the middle class.

Wells and Serna take one issue, that of tracking, as a case study of practices of middle-class closure. They observed ten racially mixed schools in which the decision had been made to de-track and the response of élite parents, who sought to preserve tracking as a means of preserving the privileged position of their children within the schools. The key point they make is that such parental pressure renders the idea of school autonomy in policy decisions a myth. If educators choose to pursue equity goals through policies like de-tracking, they court the danger of middle-class flight from the public school system. The dilemma is that if schools lose these students they also lose the potential, identified by McPherson and Willms, to raise overall achievement levels. In spelling out the nature of the conflict through the issue of de-tracking, Wells and Serna link their case-study analysis to broader macro-issues of class and cultural capital. In doing so they situate the particular conflict they document into the wider context articulated by Brown.

Lareau (Ch. 46) takes this process one step further by examining the way parental material and cultural capital is translated into support for their children's learning in school. Both the schools in her study promoted a family–school relationship which actively sought parental involvement in schooling, an opportunity that was fully exploited by middle-class parents in a way that could not be realized by working-class parents. In drawing this conclusion Lareau is at pains to point out that it is the way the school *defines* the proper family–school relationship which serves to exclude the contributions of working-class parents.

The focus on the chapters so far has been on the mechanisms of exclusion operated by the middle class to exclude the working class. But class structure has changed over the past 20 years in terms of employment, ethnic and gender composition, and geography. Twenty-five years ago the majority of the working class was employed; now there is talk of an underclass, in which unemployment is transmitted from one generation to another, isolated in the inner cities, and largely comprising people of colour. Heath and McMahon (Ch. 43) provide a statistical analysis of the impact of race and gender on life-chances over two generations of immigrants to Britain. The database analyzed by these authors is therefore able to provide a powerful insight into the effect of what they call the 'ethnic penalty' of not being white and British. While they show that there are important differences in the occupational and unemployment chances of non-white British people, overall the results show that ethnic penalties continue to play an important role in their life-chances even when they were born in Britain. They provide, therefore, clear evidence that issues of ethnicity remain a major obstacle to the distribution of life-chances according to merit.

William Julius Wilson (Ch. 49) marshals an elegant theory of the relationship between structural change and industrial restructuring, unemployment, culture, and situated rationality to explain the condition of what he calls the 'ghetto poor'. The theory explains the creation of the ghetto poor in terms of class rather than race or genetic endowment, and links the unemployment caused by restructuring to a theory of weak labour-force attachment, in which the socialization and discipline of family and community life, which is geared to a commitment to paid employment, is absent. In this context a culture based on risk and a transitory family life is likely to flourish. Moreover, in the ghetto life Wilson is describing there are few successful role models likely to engender the motivation to learn or to be upwardly mobile. The message conveyed by the lack of role models is reinforced by a social context in which even the schools are poor. In developing this theory, Wilson has had a dramatic impact on the debate about what is often referred to as the 'underclass', although—as he makes clear in this chapter—he now prefers the term 'ghetto poor'.

Wilson's theory is not without its critics, of whom, by implication, Ogbu (Ch. 50) is one. Ogbu's chapter provides a broad and innovative theoretical account of the persistence of racist barriers which prevent the success of Black American students. In contrast to Wilson, he argues that racism remains the chief determinant of life-chances for black Americans. In order to develop his argument, Ogbu carefully distinguishes between racial and class stratification, and in doing so is critical of Marxist analyses of class and education which seek to reduce issues of race to ones of class. In an interesting development, he also argues that different races have different class structures. He then goes on to document the way that barriers have been erected and persist in relation to the life-chances of Black Americans, especially in education. Certainly the possibility raised by Ogbu that race and class are mutually inconsistent explanatory frameworks for Black American under-achievement is a challenging one, and provokes further reflection on the nature and causes of the exclusion of people of colour from educational achievement.

However, both Wilson and Ogbu would reject the claims of hereditarians like Herrnstein and Murray, that the underclass is a function of the racial difference in genetically determined intelligence. In many ways it seems extraordinary that this explanation for poverty should resurface again, and even more extraordinary that it should attract such attention. In the face of the evidence presented by Heath and McMahon, for example, even the most convinced hereditarian would be hard-pressed to deny that there is a strong social element to the lower life-chances of some ethnic groups as opposed to others. In Chapter 51 Steven Fraser surveys the major issues regarding the debate that has been engendered by the Herrnstein-Murray thesis.

Finally, Halsey and Young (Ch. 52) draw attention to the impact of family change and poverty on children. In the debates over poverty and the state's role in mitigating it, the impact of poverty on children appears to have been over-looked. So often the debate is cast in terms of the 'deserving' and 'undeserving' poor; but children cannot be classified as undeserving, for they have no responsibility for their poverty. Yet the data clearly shows that for both the United States (Danziger and Danziger, 1993) and Britain the impact of poverty has fallen heavily on children. It is also well-established that children's education and life-chances are significantly affected by poverty. Halsey and Young map out a programme which would meet the challenge of alleviating child poverty.

References

Danziger, S., and Danziger, S. (1993), 'Child Poverty and Public Policy: Towards a Comprehensive Antipoverty Agenda', *Daedalus*, 122 (Winter), 57–84.
Goldthorpe, J., Llewellyn, C., and Payne, C. (1980), *Social Mobility and Class Structure in Modern Britain* (Oxford: Clarendon Press).
Wilensky, H. L. (1975), *The Welfare State and Equality* (London: University of California Press).

42

Trends in Access and Equity in Higher Education: Britain in International Perspective

A. H. Halsey

Introduction

The structure of access to education has shifted since the end of the 1940s. Before the Second World War the main European preoccupation with educational equity was focused on entry to secondary schools. This was the decisive point of selection in traditional education systems and remained so, for example, when OECD staged its first major review and conference on the issue of equity in 1961 at Kungalv in Sweden (OECD 1961). But in the past two or three decades, with secondary schooling becoming universal, attention has perforce shifted onto entry to higher education or, more accurately, entry into some form of post-compulsory schooling, a stage of mass tending to universal provision, whether classified as training or further or higher education. Crucial selection now occurs at the transition out of secondary education. The underlying idea of meritocratic society gives tertiary schooling a new significance.

The 'meritocratic' question itself remains in debate. Definition and measurement apart, it cannot be maintained that qualifications from schooling exactly determine market rewards. Other factors, including luck and the function of prices as signals of profitable shortages, may be in play, though a typical path analysis usually shows the highest coefficient for some measure of education where income or occupational status is the dependent variable. Market rewards accrue from occupational as well as educational experience and have no necessary relation to merit. The concept of merit is, however, more apt for analysing access to advanced forms of education than for measuring the justification or defensibility of variations in income.

Within the frame of fairness or desert, the balance of social interest has also shifted in the ensuing period of spectacular educational expansion. Rightly or wrongly the major focus of traditional concern was with social class as the largest obstacle to mobilising the productive power of nations and realising a more acceptable social equity in the distribution of opportunity. More recently attention has shifted to gender and to ethnicity. Class, gender and ethnicity are now the three giants in the path of aspirations towards equity, though awareness of other obstacles, including rurality and religion has persisted. And most significantly, there are strong signs, in discussion as well as in research, of heightened awareness that educational achievement and lifechances generally are fundamentally shaped by the structure of family upbringing. A picture of advanced industrial countries is beginning to emerge which links economic growth to regimes of low fertility. The two features of modernised society are correlated in some way with the decline of the traditional family, at least in the Western world. Research by demographers and sociologists is therefore directed onto more concentrated analysis of family background. No comprehensive attempt to cover this line of research is possible here (Coleman et al. 1991; Kiernan 1992).

From *Oxford Review of Education*, 19 (1993), 129–140. Reprinted with permission.

In the sections below we shall see some reflections of this underlying transformation of industrial society in considering the trends in access to higher education of the genders, the classes and the ethnic minorities.

The Wilensky Analysis

The enlargement of educational access, which in principle raises the chances of all social groups, is heavily concentrated in the richer countries. As part of my international study of access to higher education (funded by the Spencer Foundation) my research officer, Muriel Egerton, has carried out a path analytic study analogous to the study by Harold Wilensky of the determinants of social spending by governments (Wilensky 1975).

Comparative research on the development of welfare provision takes place against a background of competing conceptions of modernisation. Wilensky (1975) puts forward the thesis that industrialised societies, despite differing cultures, politics and ideologies, converge in welfare provision as a means of ensuring political stability and economic growth. He argues that industrial development is more important than political ideology or beliefs in determining welfare expenditure. Wilensky tested this hypothesis on a sample of 64 countries, using the following variables:

1. Social security expenditure as a percentage of gross national product (GNP) as the dependent variable.
2. GNP per capita, the average age of various social security systems, and population proportion of elderly people as independent variables, measuring industrial bureaucratic and demographic development.
3. A fourfold classification of regimes as liberal democratic, totalitarian, authoritarian oligarchic, or authoritarian populist, as the basis for independent dummy variables measuring political effects.

This political categorisation was based on the degree of coerciveness of the state, crossed with the degree of popular participation in the affairs of the state. The two most important categories for his analysis were liberal democratic and totalitarian states. Two-thirds of the

countries included in the liberal democratic category were advanced industrial ones; and all the countries included in the totalitarian category were industrial states in Eastern Europe, with the addition of the USSR as it then was. Authoritarian oligarchic states included Spain and Taiwan. Authoritarian populist states included Mexico and Iraq.

Wilensky concluded on the basis of a path analysis of these variables (Wilensky 1975: 20–7) that economic development was a more important predictor of welfare expenditure than political ideology. The effects of type of polity were minimal except among the rich countries. In so far as political system apart from economic level shaped the process of welfare state development, the two dominant modern systems, totalitarian and liberal democratic, exercised influence in the same direction (upwards) through their effects on demographic structure. Totalitarian countries, being more centralised, were slightly more effective in this limited positive influence. Wilensky excluded expenditure on education from welfare expenditure on the grounds that education expenditure redistributes opportunities rather than resources. He suggested that education systems are characteristically meritocratic, with the criteria of merit being set by the technical requirements of the state and the economy.

Of course the role of the state in determining the relation between education and the distribution of life-chances as well as the productive performance of the nation remains at issue. Thus, Hufner et al. (1987), in a wide-ranging view of comparative education research give education policy and the development of education systems a more comprehensive role than opportunity allocation. They argue that governments and international organisations concerned with development see education as the key to successful economic competition and/or modernisation. This strategy, which has its roots in the dynamics of the development of both communist and liberal democracies, values both equality and progress. So, given that both liberal democracies and centrally planned Marxist states use education policy to gain these objectives, it is to be expected that type of state will influence educational outcomes.

We have, therefore, tested Wilensky's model, using enrolment in tertiary education as the dependent variable. Data were available

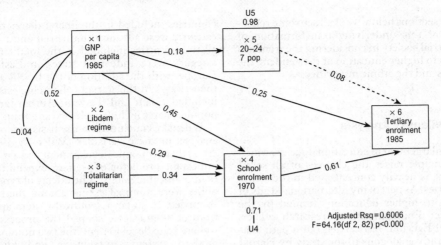

Fig. 42.1. Path diagram of direct effects on tertiary education in 85 countries

for 85 countries for this analysis. Both GNP per capita and school enrolment in 1970 have strong relationships, while the percentage of the population in the 20–24 year age cohort has weak relationship (not statistically significant at the 0.05 level), with tertiary enrolment. A path analysis of these variables was carried out following Wilensky's model and is illustrated in Fig. 42.1. School enrolment in 1970, used as a proxy for the weight of bureaucratic interests, and GNP per capita, have direct effects of 0.61 and 0.25 respectively. GNP per capita and type of polity have indirect effects through school enrolment.

Thus, this model gives a broad outline of the relationship between polity, wealth, and a universal system of primary and secondary education and the relationships are as predicted in my original research proposal to the Spencer Foundation.

Access to Higher Education in Europe

Narrowing the focus onto the European countries it appears that the period after the Second World War saw a growth in enrolment, a diversification of curricula, and a crisis in relation to the labour market destination of alumni (from both the education and the training systems and at both the secondary school and the tertiary college level) in the mid-1970s. The post-war period came to an end in the economic and political turmoil

of that time. Then there was a phase of reconstruction in the 1980s in which access and selection were increasingly influenced by manifold difficulties in the political economies of Europe, including public expenditure and unemployment and the rise or resurgence of economic-liberal doctrines of state management. Put crudely, the 1980s were the decade of the market and the expansion of higher education had to proceed under conditions of fiscal constraint which led to much redefinition of the structure and purposes of the university. Conspicuous among these developments was a pronounced weakening of the traditionally close link between the academic secondary school and educational institutions. The upper secondary school in all countries became, in effect and instead, a free-standing institution rather than a conveyance of selected minorities from common elementary schooling to élite advanced education. Most secondary pupils now leave at 18 years, many postponing entry to higher education, others choosing part-time or full-time attendance at some other form of tertiary education, and still others going straight into employment (Husen *et al.* 1992).

Nonetheless, entry to higher education in Europe and in most developed countries is still generally straight from school, sometimes from a particular type of school at which the student has concentrated in academic subjects. Italy has a very specialised structure, particular types of school leading to certain higher education categories. In the UK, as in

Japan and the USA, the examination required for higher education entry can be taken at any type of establishment which provides for post-compulsory schooling. In other countries (and in Northern Ireland and some other parts of the UK), children may be selected for entry to different types of secondary education although there is provision for transfer at later stages: the higher education entry examination is then usually taken in the more academic schools.

Each country has a specific national education qualification which forms the main basic requirement for entry to higher education. The qualification generally covers at least five subjects, some compulsory, and usually including mathematics, the native language and one modern language. England, Wales and Northern Ireland are unusual in limiting the number of subjects more narrowly and thus specialising earlier. At least five passes at GCE are required for degree level courses, of which two must be of A level standard, although most candidates for entry attempt three A-level subjects and already have at least 6 O-level passes.

Entry to higher education depends mainly on gaining the appropriate entry qualification, although limits on places may mean that a further selection process takes place either for certain types of course, or for certain institutions which experience strong demand from students. In the UK entry to all institutions is competitive.

More generally in Europe the state has increasingly controlled entry to higher education since Napoleonic times, either through defining examination content and standards or through varied means of student financial support or through special schemes of encouragement for particular social categories of student by positive discrimination or, more usually, by setting up barriers to entry. Some countries like Belgium, France or Germany use one uniform national examination. Sweden attempts the ranking of students by marks weighted according to the courses taken and work experience (which tacitly introduces age as a selective barrier). The American system of standardised attainment tests is not used in Europe. Positive discrimination in favour of candidates with working-class backgrounds has been used in Hungary, Poland and Czechoslovakia, though examination performance has also been part of the

entrance procedure. Entrance examinations have been widely used with higher requirements in medicine, science and law. Such procedures obtain in the highly prestigious institutions such as Oxford and Cambridge in the UK and the Grandes Ecoles in France, but also in the East European Communist states where, at the same time, at least a quarter of the places have been reserved for working-class students. Even the lottery is not unknown. In The Netherlands and Germany the problem of excessive demand has been overcome by its use. A lottery has been operated in which an individual's chances have been weighted by marks attained in the secondary school leaving examinations.

Nevertheless, the automatic right of entry to the university which is the privilege of those who obtain a baccalaureat or the abitur, still gives admission in France and Italy, though not to other forms of higher education. The consequences are seen in high failure or drop-out rates in the first two years of undergraduate study. Some countries, like Belgium or Spain, never granted the prerogatives of the abitur. In France, however, in spite of several university reforms, including the Loi Savary of 1984, the right of entry of a bachelier has never been modified. Of course, the highly selective Grandes Ecoles continue to cream off the best 15 per cent of the candidates. And the *numerus clausus* has been increasingly applied in France and Germany so that we can now describe the right as nominal. It gives all qualified people a place; but it does not guarantee a place in any particular faculty of any particular university.

In summary, it appears that the evolution of the admissions system since the Second World War moved the point of selection upwards from the upper secondary school and its examinations to the admissions offices of the institutions of higher education. The traditional system was essentially controlled by teachers in universities. Control now is much more in the hands of politicians and budgetary administrators. Diversity is to be found at both the secondary and tertiary levels and the unique role of the baccalaureat, the abitur and their equivalents in other European countries as the *rite de passage* to university education, is no more.

Instead there have developed alternative modes of entry to a diverse set of postcompulsory educational and training institutions with the parallel development of vocational equivalents to A level, the baccalaureat and the abitur. In France there is a technical baccalaureat with 12 options as well as the traditional one with eight sections and a proposed 30 option practical baccalaureat which, it is expected, will be taken in one form or another by 80 per cent of the secondary school leavers by the end of the century.

In all countries most students first enter higher education aged between 18 and 21. However, older students are also admitted everywhere; in Germany a quota of places is reserved for them. Reasons for starting first study in higher education later in life are many; some students pursue lower level further education full-time or enter employment; others may retake entry examinations and so increase the range of institutions which will accept them.

There has been a notable recent advance in comparable statistics arising out of the initiative of *Education at a Glance* (OECD 1992). An illustration of the comparisons now possi-

ble is shown in Table 42.1 which sets out the graduation rates in various OECD countries in 1988.

In some OECD countries, non-university tertiary education is almost non-existent. The full-time equivalent participation ratio is below 5 per cent in Austria, Italy, Luxembourg and Spain. In other countries, participation ratios reflect a substantial number of non-university students enrolled in tertiary-level institutions. The full-time non-university participation level is 20 per cent or higher in Belgium, Canada, Japan and the USA. In each of the anglophone countries with the exception of Ireland (e.g. Australia, Canada, New Zealand, the UK and the USA), part-time participation is the predominant mode for non-university tertiary education. Part-time and full-time participation levels are similar in Switzerland and Ireland. In the remainder of the countries, the part-time participation ratio is less than half the full-time level. In the Pacific area (Australia, Japan and New Zealand), as well as in Denmark and

Table 42.1. Ratio of public and private higher-education (university) graduates to population at the theoretical age of graduation (1988)

	Degree taken into account (ISCED 6)	Theoretical age of graduation	Graduation ratio		
			F+M	M	F
North America					
Canada	Bachelor	22	25.4	23.3	27.7
USA	Bachelor	22	25.6	24.4	26.9
Pacific area					
Australia	Bachelor	22	19.5	18.6	20.4
Japan	Gakushi	22	26.3	37.7	14.4
New Zealand	Undergraduate Bachelor	21	15.7	16.8	14.5
Central and Western Europe					
Austria	Diplom	23	7.2	8.1	6.3
Belgium	Licence	22	11.6	13.9	9.2
France	Licence	21	12.1	12.1	12.0
Germany	Staats-Diplomprüfung	22	13.3	16.1	10.3
Ireland	First degree	21	17.2	19.2	15.0
The Netherlands	Doctoraal examen	23	11.4	14.2	8.5
Switzerland	Licence	25	7.6	10.1	5.0
UK	Bachelor	21	16.3	17.0	15.5
Southern Europe					
Italy	Laurea	23	7.7	8.0	7.4
Spain	Diplomado/Licenciado	21/23	17.0	14.0	20.1
Turkey	Lisans	23	5.8	7.4	4.1
Northern Europe					
Denmark	Bachelor	22	10.1	12.6	7.4
Finland	Master	23	18.6	20.6	16.6
Norway	Master and Cand. mag.	22	23.6	16.3	31.4
Sweden	Undergraduate Bachelor	23	12.7	10.8	14.8

F, female;   M, male.

Source: Education at a Glance: OECD indicators (OECD, Paris: 1992).

Germany, the full-time participation level is twice as high for females as for males. The part-time participation level is only half as high for females as for males in New Zealand and a quarter as high in Switzerland.

The full-time university participation ratio is 15 or higher in eight OECD countries. Austria, Finland and Spain have the highest participation ratios. In most countries, full-time male and female participation ratios are similar. The major exceptions are Japan and Turkey where the ratios for females are only half those for males. The females ratios are also about a third lower than those for males in Belgium, Germany and Switzerland. In most countries part-time university enrolment is quite rare. The highest part-time levels are reached in Australia, Canada, New Zealand and the USA. As may be seen from Table I, the graduation rate of the UK in 1988 was behind that of Canada, the USA, Austria, Japan, Ireland and Finland. Britain's tertiary system was distinctive in the period before 1990 in that it was binary. There was a short, high-cost and efficient sector of restricted but socially open universities attended full time for three years; and a diversified, localised, part-time vocational sector with rather tenuous connections to the universities.

Reform since 1990 may bring Britain more into line with its European and American competitors. Yet the consequences for social distribution of access cannot be predicted with confidence. It may turn out that a principal historical feature of post-war higher education in Europe was the elaboration of alternatives to the university. As part of an ambitious programme of expansion, 'doubling in a decade' as the progressive slogans of the 1950s had it, the terms of entry and the definition of what was to be learned in a university were altered all over Europe. The old stereotype of entry through completion of the baccalaureat or equivalent leaving certificate from a lycée or other upper secondary school into a full-time course of three or more years in pure science or pure arts was to be transformed into a large variety of courses, typically vocational or preparatory to professional training, and offered in a wider range of institutions, residential and non-residential. The development of mass higher education was dawning in Europe, increasing participation to significant proportions of the young and, in effect, replacing the older idea of the univer-

sity in Europe by a much more expansive and, as many would argue, a diluted conception of tertiary rather than higher education.

Social Selectivity and Stratification

Walter Muller's study of nine European countries, because based on the Casmin data sets, pertains largely to the earlier post-war years (Muller and Karle 1990). Blossfield's data show the experience of young people in the 1980s as well as in the earlier years of the century (Blossfield 1990). The results of the two studies are complementary and consistent. They confirm that German higher education expanded from a low point immediately after the Second World War and that in the process there was a reduction in social selectivity for the population as a whole and for women but no serious change in the relative chances of children from the disadvantaged classes. Tertiary education remained linked characteristically to the superior and professional end of the service class with respect to recruitment and also to placement in an occupational career. This was the essential shape of meritocratic development in Europe and the role of the university within an expanding and elaborating system. The picture is complicated, not least by variation between countries in demography, the structure of the economy and the historical peculiarities of national arrangements for access to the stages of education, their curricular content, the type and availability of student financial aid, and the articulation between educational qualifications and entry to professions and trades. Thus, for example, where a country has had a large agricultural sector as in France or Poland, the significance of educational selection has been minimised for the sons of farmers. Where, as in the UK, education has been relatively loosely connected to qualifications in the labour market, it has been possible for relatively democratised access to the universities to emerge. Muller's analysis thus reveals the remarkable contrast between France and Britain that, adjusting for the difference in the shape of the occupational structure, it turns out that those who acquired a higher tertiary degree had service class origins of 55 per cent in France and only 35 per cent in England. So, at least in the earlier post-war years, the system of selection in France gave the offspring of the service classes—compared to children from other social backgrounds—better odds of surviving up to the highest educational level than they had in other countries. For his nine European countries Muller finds that, beginning at a less than 10 per cent proportion of the pupils in primary school, the service class children grew to a cross-national average of about 45 per cent among those who attained a higher tertiary degree.

England, Muller tells us, did not stand alone at the lower end of social selectivity but shared its relatively egalitarian position with Scotland and Northern Ireland. He also indicates an interesting contrast between Germany and France. By the end of compulsory schooling the proportion of service class children was highest in France and remained so through the successive stages or 'transitions'. In Germany, the proportion of service class children was lowest until the stage of an intermediate secondary degree, but then increased more than in most other countries until, at the end point of the educational career, Germany was placed in an intermediate position. Interestingly, the two command economies or Communist countries included by Muller were not among the most egalitarian from the point of view of class opportunity. Hungary in particular is near the top of the league for distributing most certificates of higher education to the higher social classes.

Like Blossfield, Muller identifies two important processes common to the countries which have inherited the European university. First education systems are organised so as to allow ever decreasing fractions of a student cohort to survive at each successive stage of education; and second, dropping out is socially selective though with decreasing severity. The outcomes are an interplay between these two processes. On the one hand the policies of expansion gradually move the systems of higher education through mass towards universal provision and *a fortiori* towards equality. On the other hand the selective forces continue to shape the composition of the student body.

Muller's study of an earlier period shows that already the European countries differed strongly in the extent to which they provided opportunities for obtaining educational qualifications to each successive cohort of young people. His data were collected in the early 1970s and the analysis relates to those aged 30 to 64, i.e. born between 1910 and 1947. They therefore had left their schools or universities mostly before 1970. Only a small proportion of them were affected in their educational careers by the reforms of the 1960s and 1970s in the Western European nations but, it must be noted, educational change in Eastern Europe had been initiated earlier. Thus, for our earlier years, Muller shows a pattern which is essentially binary. The UK and Sweden had a similar survival pattern from which Germany, Hungary, Poland and France differed. The sharpest contrast was between France and Germany. In Germany, 85 per cent of pupils were surviving beyond compulsory schooling, in France only 30 per cent. Hungary and Poland had the highest survival rates up to the end of a full secondary education. Yet, given the differences in survival rates between nations in early schooling, the remarkable feature of the systems as a whole is their similarity of outcome at the upper end. At that point, only France is distinctive with its exceptionally low fraction of the population obtaining a degree from an institution of higher education.

Within the context we have sketched, Muller draws attention to particular features of class selectivity. In Germany, Hungary and Sweden the upper service class appears to have given its children rather superior chances of educational survival. This finding fits with the observations of historians of the *Bildungsbuergertum*, a social stratum of civil servants, professionals and teachers in higher education, which has traditionally shared a set of common values associated with the experience of higher education and a relatively higher determination to pass on high standards of educational ambition and achievement to their children. The *Bildungsbuergertum* was probably most distinguished as a status group in Germany, but also existed in other countries that were influenced by the German tradition of higher education, such as Sweden and the Austro-Hungarian monarchy. English society in the early 20th century was distinctive in not having such a broad and educationally defined upper class. Entry to the upper echelons of British society was not so clearly restricted to educational channels.

In Britain, the 1970s saw little progress towards the democratisation of leisure which a modern system of higher or continuing education should represent. Instead the end of the decade saw governments, whether of the Left or of the Right, groping for solutions to external checks on economic growth, while the minority of the educated began to be more sophisticated about the nature of education as a positional rather than an investment or a consumption good, and the majority remained in blighted ignorance that education had anything seriously constructive to offer to either private or public life.

Nevertheless the story remains unfinished. Both economic fortunes and political pressure moved in the later 1980s. On the economic front, a much disputed restructuring of the economy with an also disputed movement towards integration with continental Europe had educational consequences. The achievement of competitive advantage impelled renewed educational expansion. Invidious international comparison in the preparations for '1992' excited almost hysterical reorganisation of training arrangements and reinforced pressure towards vocational education at all levels of schooling. From different standpoints and with different assumptions both the Conservative and Labour parties and the reformed Liberal Democrats began to share the view that a mass system of higher education was inevitable for 21st century Britain. In May 1991, the Conservatives, following the other parties, announced the beginning of the new educational era. Mass higher education would accommodate one school leaver in three (an extra 300,000 students over the next eight years), polytechnics could call themselves universities, the funding bodies would be dismantled and 'a single intelligence' would replace them, though with separate establishments in England, Scotland and Wales. The CNAA would be abolished. Quality would be assessed by the new academic audit unit which had recently been set up by the universities (Halsey 1992).

It must be added immediately that plans for funding the new expansion remained vague. The drive towards increasing reliance on tuition fees will remain as a governmental stimulus of market forces. The government will also encourage universities and colleges to seek funds from the private sector, particularly from industry and commerce, benefactors and alumni. A fair share of public expenditure is guaranteed to higher education but the final emphasis is on further efficiency, which the embattled dons will realistically interpret as a levelling down of standards and still further reduction of staff/student ratios. The struggle will doubtless go on as Europe seeks ways to renew economic growth and escape from current recession. But one thing is sure. The British binary line has lost its official status and a post-binary system has begun.

References

Atkinson, A. B. (1974), *The Economics of Inequality* (Oxford: Oxford University Press).

Blossfield, H. P. (1990), 'Changes in Educational Opportunities in the Federal Republic of Germany', *EUI Working Paper*, SPS: 90/4.

Coleman, J. (1991), *Resources and Actions: Parents, their Children and Schools* (Chicago: Chicago University Press).

Halsey, A. H. (1992), *Decline of Donnish Dominion* (Oxford: Oxford University Press).

—— Heath, A. F., and Ridge, J. (1980), *Origins and Destinations: Family, Class and Education in Modern Britain* (Oxford: Clarendon Press).

Hufner, K., Meyer, J. W., and Naumann, J. (1987), 'Comparative Education Policy Research: A World Perspective', in M. Dierkes, H. Weiler, and A. B. Antal (eds.), *Comparative Policy Research: Learning From Experience* (Aldershot: Gower).

Husén, T., Tuijnman, A., and Halls, W. D. (1992), *Schooling in Modern European Society: A Report of the Academia Europaea* (Oxford: Pergamon Press).

Kiernan, K. (1992), 'Family Disruption and Transitions in Young Adulthood', *Population Studies*, 46, 213–14.

Muller, W., and Karle, W. (1990), *Social Selection in Educational Systems in Europe* (paper presented to the meetings of the International Sociological Association Research Committee on Social Stratification, XIIth World Congress of Sociology, Madrid, 9–13 July).

OECD (1961), *Ability and Educational Opportunity*, (ed.) A. H. Halsey (Paris: OECD).

Wilensky, H. L. (1975), *The Welfare State and Equality* (London: Univ. of California Press).

43

Education and Occupational Attainments: The Impact of Ethnic Origins

Anthony Heath and Dorren McMahon

Introduction

In this chapter our main aims are to describe the class profiles of the different ethnic groups in Britain today, and to see how far these profiles can be explained by their differing levels of qualification. In general in Britain, the acquisition of educational qualifications has proved to be one of the major ways for people to reach the more advantaged positions in the class structure (Heath *et al.* 1992), and our interest is in whether ethnic-minority groups reach the same class positions as do native-born Whites with qualifications of the same level. For example, we shall see that Bangladeshis and Pakistanis have generally somewhat less favourable class positions than have other ethnic groups, in particular British-born Whites. But can this be explained by their lower levels of educational qualifications? Do Bangladeshis or Pakistanis with, say, a degree achieve the same occupational levels on average as do Whites with degrees?[1]

It has often been suggested that ethnic-minority-group members with exactly the same educational qualifications as native-born Whites might suffer discrimination in the labour market, or other disadvantages that lead them to achieve lower occupational levels than the native-born Whites. Thus, they might incur some sort of 'ethnic penalty' in the labour market. We use the expression 'ethnic penalty' to refer to *all* the sources of disadvantage that might lead an ethnic group to fare less well in the labour market than do similarly qualified Whites. In other words, we

use a broader concept than that of discrimination, although discrimination is likely to be a major component of the 'ethnic penalty'. We should note that statistical data of the kind available from the Census do not allow us to distinguish discrimination from other sources of disadvantage.

There has been comparatively little research on this topic so far in Britain. A number of studies have concentrated on general comparisons between Whites and Blacks (Mayhew and Rosewell 1978; McNabb and Psacharapoulos 1980; Stewart 1982; Heath and Ridge 1983; and Brennan and McGeevor 1987). In general, these studies have indeed found that an 'ethnic penalty' is incurred by ethnic-minority groups when competing for jobs with equally qualified Whites. Thus, Blacks with a given level of education tend to have lower occupational attainments than do Whites with the same qualifications.

It should be noted, however, that other studies have shown that it is important to differentiate between culturally distinctive ethnic groups. They have shown that there are considerable differences between, for example, Indian and Bangladeshi men in their educational achievements (Plewis 1988; Brennan and McGeevor 1990; Modood 1991; Drew, Gray, and Sime 1992; Cheng and Heath 1993; Jones 1993). These studies suggest that we need to be aware of such differences when looking at the education and occupation of ethnic groups.

However, the existing studies have largely focused on what we term the 'first-generation',

From V. Karn (ed.), *Education, Employment and Housing among Ethnic Minorities in Britain*, (HMSO, 1997). Reprinted with permission.

members of ethnic-minority groups, that is, people who were born overseas and subsequently migrated to Britain. Many of these people will have completed their education before coming to Britain, and it could well be argued that overseas educational qualifications will not be regarded as highly by employers as are British qualifications. It can also be argued that migrants of any ethnic group—particularly if they come from a more rural society—will have greater difficulties than the native-born, since they lack the social contacts and the knowledge of how the British labour market works. These non-educational resources may be important in securing the more privileged positions within society, and their absence may give an additional handicap to migrants (Heath and Ridge 1983).

The experience of the 'second generation', born and brought up in Britain with British educational qualifications, and presumably with greater familiarity with the British labour market, is therefore particularly interesting. The 1991 Census gives us the opportunity to look at the experience of ethnic minorities born in this country. Previous research has been hampered partly by small sample sizes, and partly by the fact that, since much migration to Britain took place in the 1950s and 1960s, few of the 'second generation' had entered the labour market at the time the research was conducted. Our analysis is directed therefore both to ethnic-group members who were born overseas, that is, to the 'first generation', and to those born in Britain, the 'second generation'.

Measuring Social Class

Our main concern in this paper is with the class positions of the ethnic minority groups. There are many alternative ways of treating social class, but the one we have selected is, we believe, particularly appropriate for studying ethnic groups. Devised by John Goldthorpe (1980), the scheme distinguishes classes according to their employment conditions. Broadly speaking, the scheme distinguishes three major groups:

1. *the salariat* (or 'service class', as Goldthorpe terms it), which consists of salaried employees such as managers, administrators, and professionals, who typically enjoy relatively secure employment, an incremental salary scale, various fringe benefits (such as pension schemes), and significant promotion chances;

2. *the petty bourgeoisie*, which consists of small employers and own-account workers. The employment conditions of these workers means that they are directly exposed to market forces; they therefore have greater insecurity, particularly with respect to income level, than do members of the salariat.

3. *the working class*, which consists of rank-and-file wage labourers in industry, services, and agriculture. These workers are employees, but lack the security, incremental salary scales, and promotion prospects of the salariat. They typically have much higher risks of unemployment and fewer fringe benefits.

Goldthorpe goes on to make some finer subdivisions within these broad classes. He distinguishes the higher from the lower salariat; the skilled from the semi-skilled working class; a routine non-manual class, in some respects marginal to the salariat; and a class of foremen and technicians marginal to the working class proper. Because of the small numbers involved, we have merged the foremen and technicians with the skilled working class. But, in view of its practical interest, we have added to Goldthorpe's schema an additional category for the unemployed.

We thus in the present chapter distinguish the following seven classes (the Roman numerals referring to the numbering in Goldthorpe's original class schema and the Arabic numerals to the version used in this chapter):

    I Higher salariat (1)
   II Lower salariat (2)
  III Routine nonmanual class (3)
  IV Petty bourgeoisie (4)
V, VI Foremen and skilled working class (5)
 VII Semi- and unskilled working class (6)
  U Unemployed (7)

From the point of view of ethnic-minority groups, our interest is in how many of their members manage to avoid unemployment, or the relatively disadvantaged and poorly paid jobs of the semi- and unskilled working class. We are interested in how many enter the petty bourgeosie, which has often been used by members of ethnic minority groups, perhaps as a way of escaping from unemployment or low-status manual work (Srinivasan 1993). And we are interested in how many reach the secure and relatively advantaged positions of the salariat.

The Class Distribution of the Ethnic Groups

We first describe the class position in 1991 of the ethnic minority groups. Table 43.1 reports the positions of the first generation men aged 21–64.

We limit ourselves to the economically active, that is, people in work or actively seeking work, and we compare the experience of the main ethnic groups covered by the Census with the Irish-born Whites, that is, with people born in the Republic of Ireland who identified themselves as White. In the first-generation tables, then, we compare the class positions of people who had all experienced migration to Britain from their countries of birth. As we noted above, migration might be expected to be disruptive and we might therefore expect that these people would not fare as well as those born and brought up in Britain. By including the Irish-born White as a comparison group, therefore, we are able to compare the fortunes of the first-generation ethnic-minority groups with those of a group of White people who had also experienced the disruptive experience of migration.

Looking at first-generation men, it can be seen that there were major variations between and within the ethnic minority groups. The most 'successful' groups were the Chinese and the Other groups (Asian): they were the most likely to be found in the managerial and professional jobs of the salariat. Next came the Black Africans and Indians, followed by the Irish-born Whites and the Black others. And we see that the Black-Caribbeans, Pakistanis, and Bangladeshis lagged substantially behind in access to the salariat.

It might be expected that Indian and Pakistani men would be relatively concentrated in the petty bourgeoisie (class IV), reflecting traditions of self-employment and their location in certain occupational sectors such as the catering trade. As can be seen, this was the case not only for these two groups but also even more markedly for first-generation Chinese men, 29 per cent of whom were in the petty bourgeoisie.

This leaves the Chinese with very few first-generation men in the working class, only 23 per cent overall, although we should note that most of these were in semi- and unskilled manual work. At the other extreme, 55 per cent of the Black-Caribbean men were in the working class, and these Black-Caribbean men were fairly evenly balanced between skilled and less-skilled manual work.

Finally, turning to unemployment, we can see that the first-generation Black-African, Pakistani, and Bangladeshi men were disadvantaged with rates of unemployment of 30 per cent or above. Given their high proportion in semi- and unskilled manual work, we can say that the first-generation Bangladeshis were the most disadvantaged group; if we combine the proportions unemployed with

Table 43.1. Class distribution: first-generation men

Ethnic Group	I	II	III	IV	V/VI	VII	U	Total	Base
				Percentage				Total	Base
Irish-born White	8	14	5	17	21	18	17	100	3333
Black-Caribbean	5	7	3	8	28	27	22	100	1439
Black-African	12	15	10	6	7	18	33	101	622
Black-Other	6	15	12	8	19	16	23	99	134
Indian	15	14	8	18	15	17	14	101	3625
Pakistani	7	7	5	19	14	18	30	100	1559
Bangladeshi	5	5	4	12	3	34	37	100	544
Chinese	18	12	5	29	2	21	12	99	664
Other groups (Asian)	21	23	10	8	9	12	17	100	874
British-born White	13	19	8	12	22	15	11	100	237335

Sample: economically active men aged 21–64.

Source: 1991 Census, 2 per cent individual SARs (ESRC/JISC purchase).

those in less-skilled manual work, we find that 71 per cent of the Bangladeshis were in what we might term 'disadvantaged positions'. None of the other groups came anywhere near this; the Black-Africans at 51 per cent, the Black-Caribbeans at 49 per cent, and the Pakistanis at 48 per cent were not nearly so disadvantaged.

The general picture that one has of these first-generation men, then, is that there were very substantial differences in the overall economic fortunes of the different groups. The Other groups—Asian, the Chinese, and the Indians—were the most advantaged groups, followed by the Irish-born White, Black-African, and Black-Other groups. The Black-Caribbean and Pakistani groups were relatively disadvantaged, but it was the Bangladeshis who were furthest behind.

It is also interesting to compare their fortunes with those of the British-born Whites. Here we find that the first three ethnic-minority groups, Chinese, Indian, and Other groups (Asian), actually surpassed the British-born Whites, with somewhat higher proportions in the salariat and with roughly similar proportions unemployed or in less-skilled manual work. All the other groups, including the Irish-born Whites, were less advantaged than the British-born Whites. It used to be argued that immigrant workers:

are usually employed in occupations rejected by indigenous workers. In a situation of full employment, the nationals of the countries concerned have taken advantage of opportunities for moving into better-paying, more pleasant jobs, usually in the white-collar or skilled sectors. The immigrants have been left with the jobs deserted by others.

Typically such jobs offer low pay, poor working conditions, little security, and inferior social status. (Castles and Kosack 1985: 112).

Such an account would appear to fit the Bangladeshis best, and it is perhaps relevant that the Bangladeshis were the most recent arrivals to Britain of the various ethnic-minority groups which the Census distinguished. But it is not an account that would appear to fit minority groups such as the Chinese, Indians, or even the Black-Caribbeans in 1991, although it may well have been more appropriate to them when they first arrived.

It is important to recognize, however, the limitations of one-dimensional comparisons such as this. A group such as the Chinese may have a similar average level of class attainment to the British-born Whites, but the profile may none the less be very different. As we have seen, in 1991 the Chinese were relatively concentrated in the petty bourgeoisie and had very few men in skilled manual work, giving them a very different profile from that of the British-born White. Again, the Black-Africans had a similar average to the British-born Whites, but they were much more polarized.

A useful summary measure of the overall differences in profile is the index of dissimilarity. This index gives the proportion of a group who would have to change their class position for their class profile to become identical to that of the British-born White. As we can see from Table 43.2, among the first-generation men, the Indian and the Irish-born White groups were the most similar in their profiles to the British-born Whites,

Table 43.2. Indices of dissimilarity from the British-born White class profiles

	First-generation men	First-generation women	Second-generation men	Second-generation women
Irish-born White	14	13	na	na
Black-Caribbean	29	20	24	17
Black-African	27	22	32	30
Black-Other	18	19	25	15
Indian	13	20	15	20
Pakistani	29	33	25	28
Bangladeshi	45	47	na	na
Chinese	29	20	na	na
Other groups (Asian)	20	12	na	na

Note: the index of dissimilarity gives the percentage of the group who would have to change their class position in order to make the class profile of that group identical to the British-born White class profile.

Source: derived from Tables 43.1, 43.3, and 43.4.

Table 43.3. Class distribution: first-generation women

Ethnic Group	I	II	III	Class IV	V/VI	VII	U	Total	Base
				Percentage					
Irish-born White	5	28	23	4	2	30	8	100	2451
Black–Caribbean	3	33	19	2	3	30	10	101	1340
Black–African	4	24	17	3	2	24	27	101	538
Black–Other	2	29	23	3	3	20	20	100	116
Indian	6	13	25	9	5	29	13	100	2445
Pakistani	4	14	14	12	3	23	31	101	356
Bangladeshi	4	11	13	4	0	14	53	99	70
Chinese	9	23	18	19	1	23	8	101	544
Other groups (Asian)	7	26	25	4	2	24	13	101	742
British-born White	5	24	34	5	3	23	6	100	173667

Sample: economically active women aged 21–59.

Source: 1991 Census, 2 per cent individual SARs (ESRC/JISC purchase).

with an index of dissimilarity of 13 and 14 respectively. The Bangladeshis were the most different, with an index of 45, but the Chinese (29), Pakistanis (29), Black–Caribbeans (29), and Black–Africans (27) also had very different profiles from the British-born Whites.

Turning next to the first-generation women, we would expect to find some general differences from the patterns among males.

As is well-known, women are more strongly concentrated in the lower salariat, routine non-manual, and semi- and unskilled manual classes than are men. Conversely, women tend to be under-represented in the higher salariat, the petty bourgeoisie, and the skilled manual class, but tend to have somewhat lower unemployment rates than men.

Table 43. 3 shows that this gender pattern

Table 43.4. Class distribution: second-generation men

Ethnic Group	I	II	III	Class IV	V/VI	VII	U	Total	Base
				Percentage					
British-born White	12	18	9	11	22	15	13	100	120418
Black–Caribbean	5	13	13	4	17	16	32	100	959
Black–African	5	14	17	4	9	14	37	100	168
Black–Other	7	16	13	4	14	11	34	99	308
Indian	9	14	15	12	14	14	22	99	484
Pakistani	6	12	12	10	14	11	35	101	205

Sample: economically active men aged 21–39.

Source: 1991 Census, 2 per cent individual SARs (ESRC/JISC purchase).

Table 43.5. Class distribution: second-generation women

Ethnic Group	I	II	III	Class IV	V/VI	VII	U	Total	Base
				Percentage					
British-born White	6	25	35	4	3	19	7	99	92953
Black–Caribbean	6	19	42	1	1	14	17	100	902
Black–African	5	16	28	2	1	11	37	148	154
Black–Other	8	18	35	1	4	15	19	100	306
Indian	8	13	41	5	1	15	18	101	364
Pakistani	2	12	33	6	2	13	33	101	122

Sample: economically active women aged 21–39.

Source: 1991 Census, 2 per cent individual SARs (ESRC/JISC purchase).

applied with few exceptions to all the ethnic-minority groups. For example, Irish-born White women were more likely to be found in the lower salariat, in the routine non-manual class, and in the semi- and unskilled manual classes than were first-generation Indian men. In other words, within each ethnic minority group there was the kind of gender differentiation familiar from previous research on the White British. (The main apparent exception to this were the Bangladeshi women, but there were so few first-generation Bangladeshi women who were economically active that any conclusions are hazardous.)

Apart from this overall gender difference, the women's profiles were rather similar to those which we have just seen for the men. In general the Chinese and Other groups (Asian) were relatively advantaged, with higher proportions in the salariat and with lower proportions unemployed. At the other extreme, it was again the Bangladeshis and the Pakistanis who were the most disadvantaged.

There were some exceptions to this general pattern. In particular, we see that the first-generation Black-Caribbean women were notable for their relatively large proportion in the lower salariat, presumably in nursing. There were many more in this class than would be expected given the overall ethnic and gender patterns. This over-representation in the lower salariat was matched by an under-representation of first-generation Black-Caribbean women in the semi- and unskilled manual class and in unemployment. In the opposite direction, we find many fewer Indian women in the lower salariat than expected, and a corresponding over-representation in skilled manual work and in unemployment.

Most of these results are familiar from previous research on the occupations of ethnic minority groups. What is of great interest, however, is the occupational distribution of the second-generation men and women. This is shown in Tables 43. 4 and 43. 5.

Since the second-generation ethnic minorities were relatively young at the time of the 1991 Census, we restrict ourselves here to economically active respondents aged between 21 and 39. We also have to exclude Bangladeshis, Chinese, and Other groups (Asian) altogether, since there were too few second-generation members in the sample to warrant detailed analysis.

The Chinese and the Bangladeshis were, of course, two of the most unusual groups among the first generation. When they are excluded, the remaining ethnic minorities appear relatively similar to each other, although all of them had higher unemployment rates and poorer chances of reaching the salariat than did the British-born Whites. But among the second-generation ethnic minority men, it was once again the Indians who appeared to be the most advantaged, with a class profile most similar to the British-born White one.

Among the second-generation ethnic-minority women we again find that, as with the first generation, the Pakistanis were particularly disadvantaged, with a high unemployment rate and poor chances of reaching the salariat, while the Indian women were again under-represented in the lower salariat. However, there was an important generational change among the Black-Caribbean women: the second-generation Black-Caribbeans did not show the over-representation in the lower salariat that was so striking in the first generation.

Modelling the Data

The interpretation of these tables is complicated by the differing age-profiles of the various groups. Unemployment tends to be higher among young people, and so the fact that the unemployment rates of the second-generation ethnic-minority groups were higher than those of the British-born Whites may simply reflect their relatively youthful age-profile. Similarly, promotion to the managerial jobs in the higher salariat tends to come somewhat later in the life-cycle, and so once again the lack of ethnic-minority groups in the higher salariat may be a consequence of their age-profile rather than of any 'ethnic penalty'. While we have mitigated these problems somewhat by selecting respondents aged between 21 and 39 for our second-generation analysis, we have by no means overcome them, since some of the groups, such as the Indians and Pakistanis, were relatively concentrated towards the lower end of this age-span in 1991.

Furthermore, and perhaps most importantly, Tables 43.1 to 43. 5 do not on their own enable us to assess whether the occupational attainments of the ethnic minorities were commensurate with their educational qualifications. As we noted in the introduction, few Pakistanis had higher qualifications and few had reached the salariat at the time of the 1991 Census, but what we want to know is whether the low proportion in the salariat can be explained by the low proportion with higher qualifications, or whether the Pakistanis had even fewer members in the salariat than their qualifications would warrant.

We therefore turn to modelling the data. Our modelling strategy is akin to Fienberg's method of log-continuation ratios (Fienberg 1977). In essence, we begin by looking at access to the salariat, the class which offers the best employment conditions and security, and which generally scores highest on measures of occupational desirability. We then look at people who had not managed to reach the salariat and consider their patterns of self-employment in the petty bourgeoisie. It has been suggested that self-employment of this kind may be regarded by first-generation members of some ethnic-minority groups as preferable to low-prestige manual work or unemployment (Srinivasan 1993). Finally, we look at people who were neither in the salariat nor in the petty bourgeoisie, and consider their success in avoiding unemployment.

More formally, we fit a series of logistic regression models in which the dependent variable is the log-odds (that is, the relative chances) of being in particular classes, and in which the explanatory variables are age, qualifications, and ethnicity.

In our analyses we dichotomize class in three different ways, giving us three different dependent variables. In model A, the dependent variable is the log-odds of employment in the salariat (classes I and II) versus employment in some other class or unemployment (classes III to VII plus U). In effect, then, in model A we explore the success of the different ethnic minorities in the competition to gain access to the salariat and to avoid the insecurity and poorer employment conditions of the other classes.

In model B we then exclude the people who were successful in reaching the salariat, and focus on those who, at the time of the Census, were in classes III to VII or were unemployed. In this model our dependent variable becomes the relative chances of self-employment in the petty bourgeoisie versus unemployment or

employment in manual or routine non-manual work.

Finally in model C we exclude people who were in the petty bourgeoisie, and we focus on the relative chances of gaining employment in classes III, V, VI, and VII versus unemployment.

The dependent variables are thus:

$$\text{(Model A)} \quad \text{LOG} \quad \frac{\{C_{1k1m} + C_{2k1m}\}}{\{C_{3k1m} + C_{4k1m} + C_{5k1m} + C_{6k1m} + C_{7k1m}\}}$$

$$\text{(Model B)} \quad \text{LOG} \quad \frac{\{C_{4k1m}\}}{\{C_{3k1m} + C_{5k1m} + C_{6k1m} + C_{7k1m}\}}$$

$$\text{(Model C)} \quad \text{LOG} \quad \frac{\{C_{3k1m} + C_{5k1m} + C_{6k1m}\}}{\{C_{7k1m}\}}$$

where C represents social class and the Arabic numerals refer to the seven-fold scheme described earlier in the text.

Our models take the general form:

$$\text{LOG} \quad \frac{\{C_{iklm}\}}{\{C_{jklm}\}} = W_o + W_{E(k)} + W_{A(l)} + W_{Q(m)}$$

Here E represents ethnic group, A represents age, Q represents qualifications, and the Ws are parameters to be estimated. As explained in previous chapters, the 1991 Census obtained information only about higher qualifications obtained after the age of eighteen. Here we simply distinguish graduates, people with higher qualifications below degree level, and people with no higher qualifications. (For further details, see the Appendix.)

Our particular interest is in the parameters associated with ethnic group. If, for example, the occupational attainments of the first-generation members of a particular ethnic group were associated with age and qualifications in the same way that they were for the Irish-born Whites, then the ethnic-group parameter would not be significantly different from zero. (If a parameter is less than twice its standard error (s.e.), we can say that it is not significantly different from zero.) A negative ethnic-group parameter would indicate that the group in question had poorer relative chances of reaching the given class than Irish-born Whites of the same age and qualification level. And of course a positive ethnic parameter would indicate that the group had superior relative chances. The parameters are technically fitted log-odds ratios, and we shall give some concrete interpretations of these parameters in the conclusion to this chapter.

Table 43.6. Logistic regression models of education and occupational attainment: first-generation men

| | Parameter Estimates | | |
	Model A	Model B	Model C
	I and II *vs.* III–VII	IV *vs.* III, V, VI, VII	III, V, VI *vs.* VII
Constant	−1.65 (.12)	−2.22 (.16)	.96 (.11)
Ethnic group			
Irish whites	0	0	0
Black Caribbean	−.61 (.10)	−1.02 (.11)	.03 (.15)
Black African	−.70 (.12)	−1.20 (.18)	−.77 (.11)
Black Other	−.27 (.25)	−.92 (.32)	−.23 (.22)
Indian	−.15 (.07)	.11 (.07)	.14 (.07)
Pakistani	−.84 (.10)	.07 (.08)	−.74 (.08)
Bangladeshi	−1.14 (.16)	−.52 (.14)	−.82 (.11)
Chinese	−.26 (.11)	.95 (.11)	.03 (.14)
Other Asian	.52 (.09)	−.54 (.14)	−.25 (.11)
Age			
21–24	0	0	0
25–34	.13 (.12)	.90 (.16)	−.01 (.11)
35–44	.06 (.12)	1.19 (.16)	.09 (.11)
45–54	.02 (.12)	1.10 (.16)	.06 (.11)
55–64	−.23 (.13)	.48 (.17)	−.13 (.11)
Qualifications			
No higher	0	0	0
Level C	2.27 (.09)	−.15 (.17)	.03 (.15)
Degree	3.02 (.07)	−.02 (.13)	−.93 (.12)
Model	3478.3	493.8	303.7
improvement (df)	(14)	(14)	(14)
N	13157	10014	8005

Sample: economically active men aged 21–64.

Figures in brackets give the standard errors.

It should be noted that the Irish-born White men themselves did not fare as well as the British-born White men in the labour market. If we control for age and qualifications, we find that the Irish-born Whites were significantly worse off than the British-born Whites in their access to the salariat (with a parameter of −0.35, s.e. 0.05) and in their avoidance of unemployment (with a parameter of −0.44, s.e. 0.06), but were somewhat more likely to take self-employment in the petty bourgeoisie.[4] When we compare the first-generation ethnic-minority-group men with the Irish-born Whites, therefore, we are comparing them with a group that was also disadvantaged when competing in the British labour market. Irish-born White women, on the other hand, seemed to compete on rather more equal terms with the British-born White women in access to the salariat (parameter of 0.10, s.e. 0.06), although they shared the disadvantages of the Irish men when it came to

avoiding unemployment (parameter of −0.43, s.e. 0.09).

First-Generation Men

Table 43.6 shows the results of our logistic modelling for the first-generation men.

We consider the results for access to the salariat (model A) first. We have treated our three explanatory variables—age, qualifications, and ethnicity—as categorical variables, and the parameters are expressed as contrasts with the baseline category for the variable. Thus, as we explained above, in the case of ethnicity we have selected the Irish-born White group as the baseline, and the parameters therefore contrast the relative success of Irish-born White men in the competition to enter the salariat with that of each of the other ethnic groups in turn (controlling for the other explanatory variables in the model). That is, the parameters for ethnic group tell us whether, compared with White migrants of similar age and qualifications from the Republic of Ireland, the first-generation men from the different ethnic-minority groups had been more or less successful in the competition for places in the salariat.

Taking our two explanatory variables of age and qualifications first, we can see that access to the salariat was only weakly related to age; this may be because qualified young people often gain direct entry to professional jobs such as teaching on completing their education, although higher-level managerial jobs usually take longer to achieve. (We should note that there was, in fact, a significant interaction between age, qualifications, and access to the salariat—less-qualified people took longer to reach it than did the more highly qualified. However, inclusion of the interaction term does not have any substantive impact on the ethnic group parameters, and we have excluded it for simplicity's sake.)

Turning to education, we see that both degrees and the higher qualifications below degree-level were strongly associated with access to the salariat, degrees giving a marked advantage over the technical and vocational qualifications below degree level (level c).

Finally we turn to the ethnic-group parameters themselves. Here we can see that every group except the Other groups (Asian) has a negative parameter. The largest negative parameters are for the Bangladeshis, Black-Africans, and Pakistanis, while the Indian, Black-Other, and Chinese groups are closer to the Irish-born Whites, with rather small negative parameters.

This is in some respects a very different story from that told by Table 43.1. There we saw for example that the first-generation Indian, Chinese, and Black-African groups all had higher proportions in the salariat than did the White-Irish migrants. However, as we have seen in previous chapters in this volume, the Indian, Chinese, and Black-African groups were all relatively highly qualified, and their high qualifications effectively masked their difficulty in gaining access to the salariat. That is, compared with similarly qualified White Irish migrants, the Indians, Chinese, and Black-Africans were less successful in converting their qualifications into salaried jobs, the Black-Africans being particularly

unsuccessful. If they had obtained the same jobs as equally qualified Irish-born Whites had done, then even more of them would have been in the salariat.[5]

Next, with model B, we restrict our attention to people who failed to reach the salariat, and we examine their relative chances of becoming self-employed in the petty bourgeoisie. The results for this model are very different from those obtained with model A. Whereas qualifications were strongly related to access to the salariat in model A, we now find that, among the respondents who failed to reach the salariat, qualifications were unrelated to self-employment in the petty bourgeoisie. Conversely, whereas age was unrelated to access to the salariat, we now find that young people aged between 21 and 24 (and to a lesser extent older people aged between 55 and 64) were relatively unlikely to take up self-employment. Clearly, self-employment is influenced by very different processes from those involved with access to the salariat.

The patterns for the various ethnic-minority groups in model B are also very different from those in model A. In model B we see that the Chinese have a very large positive parameter, indicating that they were much more likely than the comparison group of White-Irish migrants to choose self-employment in the petty bourgeoisie, rather than unemployment or non-salaried work. The Indians and the Pakistanis prove to be rather similar to the White-Irish in this respect, while all the other ethnic groups have large and statistically significant negative parameters.

Perhaps the most surprising aspect of these results is the finding that the Indians and Pakistanis do not differ significantly from the Irish in their choice of self-employment in the petty bourgeoisie (a finding which is also apparent in Table 43.1). This is perhaps due to Irish self-employment in the building trade, which may be less visible than the shopkeeping or catering in which many Indians and Pakistanis are to be found.

Moving on to the relative chances of avoiding unemployment in model C, we find different patterns again. Age does not have a statistically significant relationship with unemployment, but degrees have a strong negative association with paid work. That is to say, the graduates who failed to reach the salariat or petty bourgeoisie were *less* likely to take low-level paid employment in manual or routine clerical work than were the non-graduates. Here, perhaps, we see signs of 'overqualified graduates'. We cannot determine from these data whether the graduates' failure to take low-level paid employment instead of unemployment was caused by employers' rejection of over-qualified manpower or by the preferences of the graduates themselves. But whatever the process that generated this pattern, we can see clear evidence of polarization, with graduates being relatively likely to be found at the extremes of the class structure, in the salariat and in unemployment, rather than in routine paid work.

The ethnic parameters in model C are also of considerable interest. We can see that the Black-Caribbeans, Black-Others, Indians, and Chinese were not significantly disadvantaged compared with the White-Irish migrants in their competitive chances within this wage-labour market. None of their para-meters is significantly different from zero. But we must, of course, remember that the White-Irish-born men were themselves substantially disadvantaged compared with the British-born White men.

First-Generation Women

The patterns for the first-generation women, shown in Table 43.7, are in many respects quite different from those for the first-generation men.

While the general relationships between age and qualifications and class positions are much the same for the women as for the men, the pattern of ethnic-group parameters is rather different. In the case of access to the salariat, for example, the Black-Caribbean women have a significant positive parameter, while every other group has a substantial negative parameter. Unlike the men, there is no

Table 43.7. Logistic regression models of education and occupational attainment: first-generation women

| | Parameter Estimates | | |
	Model A	Model B	Model C
	I, II *vs.* III–VII	IV *vs.* III, V, VI, VII	III, V, VI *vs.* VII
Constant	−1.30 (.12)	−4.75 (.38)	1.56 (.13)
Ethnic group			
British-born whites	0	0	0
Black Caribbean	.30 (.08)	−.63 (.23)	−.34 (.12)
Black African	−.75 (.13)	−.32 (.28)	−1.28 (.13)
Black Other	−.59 (.25)	.14 (.48)	−.87 (.26)
Indian	−.74 (.08)	−.77 (.14)	−.36 (.10)
Pakistani	−.87 (.17)	1.26 (.20)	−1.56 (.15)
Bangladeshi	−.79 (.37)	.16 (.61)	−2.50 (.29)
Chinese	−.59 (.13)	1.99 (.16)	−.03 (.19)
Other Asian	−.25 (.12)	−.04 (.23)	−.48 (.14)
Age			
21–24	0	0	0
25–34	−.07 (.12)	1.70 (.37)	.18 (.13)
35–44	−.07 (.12)	2.21 (.37)	.45 (.13)
45–54	−.11 (.12)	1.82 (.37)	.57 (.13)
55–64	−.52 (.15)	1.43 (.42)	.54 (.17)
Qualifications			
No higher	0	0	0
Level C	2.93 (.08)	.62 (.21)	−.73 (.15)
Degree	2.80 (.09)	−.02 (.25)	−1.12 (.16)
Model improvement (df)	2611.9 (14)	342.3 (14)	376.5 (14)
N	8798	6308	5767

Sample: economically active women aged 21–64.

Figures in brackets give the standard errors.

sign here that Indian or Chinese women were more successful than women from other ethnic minorities. However, in the case of access to the petty bourgeoisie, the patterns are somewhat closer to the male ones, with a very large positive parameter for the Chinese women.

There are also some similarities in the patterns with respect to unemployment. While the absolute size of the parameters is rather different for the women, the ranking of the groups is much the same as it was for men. Thus, among men the most successful groups in avoiding unemployment were the Indians, Black-Caribbeans, and Chinese, and the same three groups of women were also the most successful in avoiding umemployment. Again, for men the three most disadvantaged groups were the Bangladeshis, the Black-Africans, and the Pakistanis, and it is the same three groups that were most disadvantaged among the women.[6]

The overall picture, then, for the first-generation women is that, relative to Irish-born Whites with similar qualifications, the Black-Caribbean, Chinese, and Indians came closest in their class positions, while the Black-Africans, Pakistanis, and Bangladeshis suffered the largest ethnic penalties in 1991.

Second-Generation Men

Previous research has suggested that first-generation White-Irish men were less successful in the labour market than were British-born Whites with similar qualifications, but that the second generation, people of Irish ancestry born in Britain, had largely caught up with their British contemporaries (McMahon 1993). Can the same success story be told about the other ethnic-minority groups?

Our analysis proceeds in essentially the same way as it did for the first generation, but because of small numbers we now have to exclude some of the smaller ethnic-minority groups, Bangladeshis, Chinese, and Other groups (Asian), and we also exclude the older age groups, just as we did in the case of Tables 43.4 and 43.5. Our baseline for comparison now becomes the British-born Whites, as we wish to compare groups who were all born and

Table 43.8. Logistic regression models of education and occupational attainment: second-generation men

	Parameter Estimates		
	Model A	Model B	Model C
	I, II vs. III–VII	IV vs. III, V, VI, VII	III, V, VI vs. VII
Constant	−1.85 (.07)	−2.38 (.10)	1.16 (.06)
Ethnicity			
British-born whites	0	0	0
Black Caribbean	−.31 (.10)	−.95 (.16)	−.95 (.09)
Black African	−.91 (.23)	−.93 (.37)	−1.24 (.18)
Black Other	−.15 (.16)	−1.00 (.29)	−1.17 (.14)
Indian	−.23 (.13)	.37 (.15)	−.55 (.13)
Pakistani	−.41 (.21)	.12 (.24)	−1.22 (.17)
Age			
21–24	0	0	0
25–29	.33 (.08)	.53 (.12)	.24 (.08)
30–34	.52 (.09)	.94 (.12)	.24 (.09)
35–39	.77 (.09)	1.03 (.13)	.22 (.11)
Qualifications			
No higher	0	0	0
Level C	2.11 (.10)	−.17 (.23)	.99 (.24)
Degree	2.87 (.09)	.07 (.22)	−.55 (.17)
Model	1844.3	187.0	294.4
improvement (df)	(10)	(10)	(10)
N	8364	6100	5296

Sample: economically active men aged 21–39.

Figures in brackets give the standard errors.

brought up in Britain. That is, we now compare people who can all be assumed to have British qualifications and to have gone through the British educational system.

Table 43.8 gives the new results for the second-generation men. Beginning with access to the salariat, we find that all the ethnic parameters are negative, although in the case of the Black (Other) group the parameter is not significantly different from zero. It is possible that the Black (Other) category includes men of Caribbean ancestry who defined themselves as 'Black British' on the Census form, and it may therefore be that these second-generation Black British had the same success in the labour market as do similarly qualified British-born Whites. The second-generation Indian, Black-Caribbean, Black-African and Pakistani men, on the other hand, quite clearly incurred significant ethnic penalties in the competition for places in the salariat.

Moving on to self-employment in the petty bourgeoisie, we find a rather similar pattern to that of the first generation. As before, there are negative parameters for the Black-Caribbean, Black-African, and Black (Other) groups, but positive parameters for the Indians and Pakistanis (the latter failing to reach statistical significance, however). Here, then, we see rather clear evidence of inter-generational continuity in traditions of self-employment. This is not a surprising result, given the considerable evidence from previous mobility surveys of the British population that membership of the petty bourgeoisie is especially likely to pass from father to son, in some cases probably through the direct inheritance of property (Goldthorpe 1980; Heath 1981).

Finally, with regard to unemployment, we once again find large and statistically significant negative parameters. The least disadvantaged group compared with the British-born Whites were the Indians, while the other four groups all suffered large and similar ethnic penalties.

The general impression, then, is that among these second-generation men ethnic penalties tended to be rather larger in the competition to avoid unemployment than they were in the competition for places in the salariat. If we look along the rows in Table 43.8, we see in every case that the ethnic-group parameters for model C are larger than those for model A, in some cases very substantially so. This suggests that recruitment to the

salariat may be somewhat more meritocratic than are recruitment practices at lower levels. We must, however, remember that the lack of educational detail provided by the 1991 Census means that we have not been able to control for lower-level qualifications, and it is possible that this could account for the results.

Second-Generation Women

The story for the second-generation women is in some respects akin to that for the second-generation men. Thus all the ethnic-minority groups have negative parameters in model A, but they tend to have even larger negative parameters in model C. That is, while the second-generation women are disadvantaged in comparison with the British-born Whites in competing for places in the salariat, they are even more disadvantaged in the competition to avoid unemployment.

As with the men, there are also some signs of inter-generational continuity. With respect to self-employment in the petty bourgeoisie, it is again the Indians and the Pakistanis who have positive parameters, just as they did in the first generation, while the other three groups have substantial negative parameters. (We should note, however, that the parameters have very large standard errors, reflecting the very small numbers of second-generation women who entered the petty bourgeoisie).

There also appears to be some inter-generational continuity in access to the salariat and in the avoidance of unemployment. The Black-Africans and the Pakistanis were the most disadvantaged in both competitions, just as they were in the first generation. And we should note that, in the second generation as in the first, the Indian women appear to be more disadvantaged than were the Indian men.

However, there is one notable exception to these patterns of inter-generational continuity—the Black-Caribbean women. Whereas in the first generation they were unusual in having a positive parameter in model A, in the second generation they have a significant negative parameter, like most of the other ethnic minority groups. In other words, the particular advantage that these women had in gaining access to the salariat in the first generation seems to have disappeared by the second generation. A possible interpretation of this is that the first-generation pattern was due to rather special recruitment efforts by the National Health Service to secure nurses from the Caribbean.

Conclusions

While the overall picture tends to be one of inter-generational continuity, with the same groups faring relatively well or relatively badly in both generations, it is naturally of considerable interest to test whether the second generation have seen any improvement in their competitive position. Given that they have been brought up in Britain and have secured British qualifications, we might expect them to be faring somewhat better than the first generation. In other words, we might expect the ethnic penalties to have reduced somewhat, even if their overall patterns are much the same.

We cannot strictly compare the ethnic-group parameters in our first- and second-generation tables—in the first-generation tables the contrast is with the White Irish-born migrants to Britain, whereas in the second-generation tables the contrast is with the White British-born population. We therefore fit some further models which formally test whether membership of the second generation is associated with an improved class position. For example, we test whether the second-generation ethnic-group members had better relative chances of gaining access to the salariat than did first-generation members from the same group, of the same age, and with the same level of qualification (but remembering that we may well be comparing British qualifications in the second generation with overseas qualifications in the first generation).

In this comparison we are necessarily limited to the groups and age-ranges in which we have an adequate number of observations. We therefore restrict ourselves in both generations to respondents who were aged between 21 and 39 at the time of the 1991 Census, and we exclude the Bangladeshis, Chinese, and Other groups (Asian). We also exclude the Whites, since we know already that the first-generation Irish-born Whites had poorer chances than the 'second-generation' British-born Whites. In essence, then, we test whether a second-generation Black-Caribbean had better relative chances of securing a place in the salariat and avoiding a lower-level class position than did a first-generation Black-Caribbean.

When we make the formal test we find that, in the case of the men from the different ethnic minority groups, 'generation' makes a negligible difference to their competitive chances of securing access to the salariat or to the petty bourgeoisie, or of avoiding unemployment. In all three cases we find that the odds of securing a place in the different classes are indistinguishable between the two generations.[7]

In the case of women, too, we find no significant generational changes. Even the reduced access of Black-Caribbean women to the salariat in the second generation just fails to reach statistical significance.[8] For both men and women, therefore, we conclude that the second generation experienced the same pattern and magnitude of ethnic penalties in the British labour-market as the first generation did.

It is important to be clear what these results do and do not tell us. They do not establish whether or not ethnic penalties have stayed the same over time. Rather, they tell us whether, in 1991, people born in this country (and therefore presumably brought up and educated in this country) had more favourable competitive chances in the British labour market than did the first generation who were born overseas. And the general answer we have obtained is that being born in this country is not associated with any improvement in competitive chances. This, of course, further suggests that the ethnic penalties which have been well-documented for the first generation should not, after all, be ascribed to their possession of overseas qualifications or to their lack of knowledge about British recruitment practices and so on.

It may be helpful to conclude by giving some interpretation of the size of these ethnic penalties. The ethnic group parameters in Tables 43.6 to 43.9 are fitted log-odds ratios. Log-odds ratios are hard to interpret, but if we exponentiate these quantities, we obtain ordinary-odds ratios without the additional complication of logarithms. These fitted-odds ratios can be interpreted as expressing the relative success of the various ethnic groups in

Table 43.9. Logistic regression models of education and occupational attainment: second-generation women

	Model A	Model B	Model C
	I, II vs. III–VII	IV vs. III, V–VII	III, V, VI vs. VII
Constant	−1.61 (.07)	−3.52 (.18)	1.79 (.08)
Ethnicity			
British-born whites	0	0	0
Black Caribbean	−.21 (.10)	−1.73 (.46)	−.80 (.11)
Black African	−1.26 (.24)	−.58 (.60)	−1.84 (.20)
Black Other	−.14 (.15)	−.86 (.51)	−.92 (.16)
Indian	−.58 (.16)	.52 (.27)	.72 (.16)
Pakistani	−.85 (.29)	.69 (.41)	−1.46 (.22)
Age			
21–24	0	0	0
25–29	.29 (.08)	.18 (.23)	.18 (.10)
30–34	.30 (.09)	.72 (.22)	.61 (.13)
35–39	.35 (.10)	1.00 (.22)	.70 (.15)
Qualifications			
No higher	0	0	0
Level C	2.70 (.11)	.85 (.32)	−.30 (.24)
Degree	2.75 (.10)	.38 (.38)	−.85 (.20)
Model	1645.7	80.0	275.4
improvement (df)	(10)	(10)	(10)
N	6646	4675	4477

Sample: economically active women aged 21–39.

Figures in brackets give the standard errors.

the competition with similarly aged and qualified British-born Whites.

A numerical example may make it clearer what the fitted-odds ratio means. It can be calculated from Model A in Table 43.8 that, among people aged between 25 and 29 with graduate qualifications, 82 per cent of British-born Whites would be found in the salariat, while the remaining 16 per cent would be found elsewhere in the class structure. These are odds of nearly five to one (more precisely 4.53: 1). In contrast, only 63 per cent of Black-Africans of the same age and qualifications are predicted to be successful in gaining a place in the salariat, while the other 37 per cent would be found in lower positions in the class structure. For the Black-Africans, then, the odds are just under two to one (more precisely 1.70: 1). The odds for the Black-Africans, therefore, are only about one-third of the odds for the British-born Whites (1.70/4.53 = 0.38). Or we can put this the other way round, and say that the odds for the British-born Whites are nearly three times as favourable as those for the Black Africans (4.53/1.70 = 2.66). We should also note that if we take the natural logarithm of 0.38 we obtain 0.98,

which is the parameter for the Black-African group in model A of Table 43.8.

In Table 43.10 we show the relative success rates of the second-generation men and women (derived from Tables 43.8 and 43.9). A figure of 1.0 in Table 43.10 would indicate that the particular ethnic group had the same success in the competition as did British-born Whites. As we can see, all the figures are below 1.0, although in a few cases the 95-per-cent confidence intervals include 1.0. For example, among men, the Black (Others) were the most successful; our model estimates that their relative success in the competition to reach the salariat was 85 per cent that of the British-born white men, and from the confidence interval we can see that they may have fared as well as or even slightly better than the White group. In the competition to avoid unemployment, however, their relative success was only one-third of that of the British-born White, and the 95-per-cent confidence interval gets nowhere near the figure of 1.0.

A somewhat similar picture emerges among the second-generation women. In the competition to reach the salariat, the Black (Other) and the Black-Caribbean women

Table 43.10. Relative success of the second generation in competition with British-born Whites

	Men		Women	
	to reach the salariat	to avoid unemployment	to reach the salariat	to avoid unemployment
Black Caribbean	0.75 (0.90–0.63)	0.43 (0.50–0.36)	0.84 (1.00–0.70)	0.47 (0.57–0.39)
Black African	0.38 (0.61–0.23)	0.33 (0.48–0.23)	0.27 (0.44–0.17)	0.17 (0.25–0.12)
Black Other	0.85 (1.17–0.62)	0.34 (0.44–0.26)	0.91 (1.23–0.68)	0.40 (0.54–0.30)
Indian	0.72 (0.93–0.55)	0.63 (0.79–0.49)	0.53 (0.72–0.39)	0.50 (0.67–0.37)
Pakistani	0.61 (0.92–0.40)	0.34 (0.47–0.24)	0.41 (0.74–0.22)	0.23 (0.34–0.15)

This table shows the fitted odds ratios derived from model A (columns 1 and 3) and model C (columns 2 and 4) in Tables 8 and 9. Figures in brackets give the 95 per cent confidence intervals for the fitted odds ratios.

Sample: economically active men and women aged 21–39 (first and second generations combined).

Source: 1991 Census, 2 per cent individual SARs (ESRC/JISC purchase).

approach parity with the White group (the confidence intervals reaching 1.0). But all the five groups fall well short of parity in the competition to avoid unemployment, the Black-African and Pakistani groups having around one-fifth of the White relative success rate.

There are some important caveats to our analyses to be remembered. In particular we should note the possible heterogeneity within the category 'no higher qualifications', and we must remember the possible role of unmeasured factors such as social-class origins. If we could take account of these, it is possible that the 'ethnic penalties' would be somewhat reduced. It is very unlikely, however, that they would in general be eliminated. On the other hand, the range in the sizes of the ethnic penalties for different minorities and for different competitions suggests that quite complex explanations will also be required for them. Both direct discrimination and cultural differences will surely play a part in explaining our findings.

APPENDIX: DATA AND CODING

Our data come from the 1991 Census of Population. For the first time, Samples of Anonymized Records (SARS) have been made available from a British Census. The SARS differ from the traditional census output of aggregated information such as the Local Base and Small Area Statistics (LBS/SAS) as abstracts of anonymized individual

records are released. This SARS information does not contain any specific information which would lead to the identification of an individual or household.

For the purpose of our analyses in this chapter we use the individual SAR. This is a 2 per cent sample of individuals in households and communal establishments in Great Britain. This file contains data on each individual, such as age and sex, and derived variables, such as socio-economic group (SEG). We include residents both in institutions and in private households (provided they meet our other criteria—see below).

The key variables that we use in our analysis are educational qualifications, social class, ethnic group, and age. These variables have been constructed as follows:

Ethnic group

The measurement of ethnic groups is problematic. The procedure used in the 1991 Census schedule was to ask respondents to tick a box beside the appropriate ethnic group. The list given to respondents was as follows:

0 White
1 Black-Caribbean
2 Black-African
   Black-Other
3 Indian
4 Pakistani
5 Bangladeshi
6 Chinese
   Any other ethnic group

Respondents ticking the Black Other or Any other ethnic group boxes were asked to describe the group to which the person thought he/she belongs or, if of mixed ethnic or racial group, to describe the person's ancestry. Thus people who considered themselves to be Black-American or Black-British, for example, might assign themselves to the Black-Other group. This procedure is not without its problems; for example, people who were born in Britain from Black-Caribbean parents might well regard themselves as Black-British and thus be included under the Black-Other category; and, indeed, we find that there were many more respondents in the Black-Other category in the second generation than there were in the first generation.

For our analysis of ethnic groups in this Chapter we have used the ten-fold classification (the ethnic group output classification) provided by OPCS (variable ETHGROUP in the 2-per-cent sample). This variable differs from the categories used in the Census schedule described above with respect to the category 'Any other ethnic group'. The variable ETHGROUP divides this into two categories: Other groups (Asian) and Other groups (Other). Given the difficulty of interpreting the meaning of the category 'Other groups (Other)', we have excluded it from the analysis. The Other groups (Asian) category is also a rather heterogeneous one, and needs to be interpreted with caution. In the first generation it contains, among others, people born in Sri Lanka, Malaysia, and Japan.

We have distinguished between the generations in our analysis with the country of birth variable (COBIRTH). We distinguish between people born in the United Kingdom and those born elsewhere. Individuals born outside the United Kingdom and who have therefore migrated to this country are regarded as first-generation, while those born in the United Kingdom are regarded as second-generation. (As described in previous volumes, there will be some anomalies, such as British citizens whose fathers were in the Armed Forces and who were born in the country overseas where their father was stationed.) Throughout, we have excluded Whites born outside the United Kingdom, with the exception of Whites born in the Republic of Ireland.

Education

The 1991 Census schedule asked questions about vocational, professional, and degree qualifications obtained by individuals after the age of 18. Thus, school qualifications such as GCSE and A level are all excluded, as are vocational and professional qualifications obtained before the age of 18.

For our analyses we used the variable QUALEVEL, which has three values:

1. no higher-level qualifications;
2. level c qualifications, that is post-A-level but

less than degree-level, such as nursing and teaching qualifications;
3. level a and b qualifications, that is first and/or higher degree.

Unlike the Labour Force Survey and General Household Survey, the Census does not enable us to distinguish between British or foreign qualifications.

Age

Since we are interested in comparing the occupational attainments of people with degrees, we employ a lower age-limit of 21. We also have an upper age-limit of 64, since relatively few older people remain in full-time work. The relationship between age and other variables of interest takes varying nonlinear forms, and it is therefore more convenient to treat age as a grouped categorical variable than as a continuous variable (for details see Tables 43.6 to 43.9).

Class

Our class variable is derived from two variables, SEGROUP (Socio-economic group) and ECONPRIM (Primary economic status). Our class categories are derived as follows:

1. Higher salariat (SEGs 1.1, 1.2, 3, 4)
2. Lower salariat (SEGs 2.2, 5.1, 5.2)
3. Routine non-manual class (SEG 6)
4. Petty bourgeoisie (SEGs 2.1, 12)
5. Foremen and skilled manual (SEGs 8, 9)
6. Semi and unskilled manual (SEGs 7, 10, 11)
7. Unemployed (ECONPRIM categories 5 and 6)

This class schema is a collapsed version of that used by Goldthorpe; but note that it is only an approximation, based on SEGs rather than coded directly from employment status and occupational unit.

The version of the class schema which we use in this Chapter excludes farmers, farm-workers, and the armed forces (SEGs 13, 14, 15, and 16), as they are small categories in which there are very small proportions of ethnic-minority-group members.

Respondents are allocated to classes only if they are currently economically active (that is, either in paid work or seeking paid work). People who describe themselves as 'looking after the home', 'retired', and so forth are excluded from all our analyses.

References

Brennan, J., and McGeevor, P. (1987), *Employment of Graduates from Ethnic Minorities* (London: Commission for Racial Equality).

Brennan, J., and McGeevor, P. (1990), *Ethnic Minorities and the Graduate Labour Market* (London: Commission for Racial Equality).

Castles, S., and Kosack, G. (1985), *Immigrant Workers and Class Structure in Western Europe* (2nd ed., Oxford: Oxford University Press).

Cheng, Y. (1994), *Education and Class: Chinese in Britain and the United States* (Aldershot: Avebury).

—— and Heath, A. (1993), 'Ethnic Origins and Class Destinations', *Oxford Review of Education*, 19/2: 151–66.

Drew, D., Gray, J., and Sime, N. (1992), 'Against the Odds: The Education and Labour Market Experiences of Black Young People', *Youth Cohort Series*, 19 (Sheffield: Department of Employment).

Fienberg, S. (1977), *The Analysis of Cross-Classified Categorical Data* (Cambridge, Mass.: MIT Press).

Goldthorpe, J. H. (1980), *Social Mobility and Class Structure in Modern Britain* (Oxford: Clarendon Press).

Heath, A. F. (1981), *Social Mobility* (Glasgow: Fontana).

—— McMahon, D., and Roberts, J. (1994), 'Ethnic minorities in the labour market', paper presented at the ECSR/ESF Research Conference on Changes in Labour Markets and European Integration, Espinho, Portugal, 22–26 October 1994.

—— Mills, C., and Roberts, J. (1992) 'Towards Meritocracy? Recent Evidence on an Old Problem' in C. Crouch and A. Heath (eds.) *Social Research and Social Reform*, (Oxford: Clarendon Press).

—— and Ridge, J. (1983), 'Social mobility of ethnic minorities', *Journal of Biosocial Science Supplement*, 8: 169–84.

Jones, T. (1993), *Britain's Ethnic Minorities: An analysis of the Labour Force Survey* (London: Policy Studies Institute).

Mayhew, K., and Rosewell, B. (1978), 'Immigrants and Occupational Crowding', *Oxford Bulletin of Economics and Statistics*, 40: 223–249.

McMahon, D. (1993), 'The Assimilation of Irish Immigrants in Britain' (University of Oxford: D.Phil thesis).

McNabb, R. and Psacharapoulous, G. (1980), 'Racial earning differentials in the UK', *Centre for Labour Economics* (London: London School of Economics).

Modood, T. (1991), *Establishing the numbers of Ethnic Minorities in Degree or Equivalent Courses to Aid Graduate Recruiters* (London: Commission for Racial Equality).

Plewis, I. (1988), 'Assessing and understanding the educational progress of children from different ethnic groups', *Journal of the Royal Statistical Society* Series A, 151: 316–26.

Srinivasan, S. (1993), 'The Asian petty bourgeoisie in Britain', (University of Oxford: D.Phil thesis).

Stewart, M. (1982), 'Racial Discrimination and Occupational Attainments in Britain', *Centre for Labour Economics* (London: London School of Economics).

44

Problems of 'Meritocracy'

John H. Goldthorpe

Introduction

Michael Young's sociological fantasy, *The Rise of the Meritocracy* (1958), provided a neologism that quickly entered into common usage. However, while the word 'meritocracy' was itself new, it served in effect to encapsulate a number of already established ideas which shared an apparent—though, as will be seen, somewhat deceptive—affinity. At least three such constituent elements need to be distinguished.

LA CARRIÈRE OUVERTE AUX TALENTS
This idea was the inspiration of the classic liberal critique, and of the eventual reform, of nineteenth-century state administration. What was demanded, most forcibly by members of the rising middle classes, was that positions of responsibility in the service of the state, both civil and military, should be allocated on the basis of demonstrated competence rather than through nepotism, patronage, bribery, or purchase. Thus, as reform proceeded, access to these positions came increasingly to depend on educational attainment, success in competitive examinations, and the completion of prescribed forms of training, while promotion was based on standards of performance in post as well as on mere seniority.

THE MATCHING OF EDUCATIONAL OPPORTUNITY TO NATURAL ABILITY
As systems of mass education developed in Western nations, the importance was emphasized of selecting from among the population at large those children who would be most likely to benefit by continuing from elementary education to secondary, and perhaps higher, levels. In this regard, an egalitarian concern for children of relatively disadvantaged backgrounds was generally less influential, at least up to the time of the First World War, than were versions of Social Darwinism, urging the need to avoid an undue wastage of the national 'stock of ability' in a context of growing economic and military competitiveness (cf. Semmel 1960). In the early decades of the twentieth century, policies of educational selection were encouraged by the rapid development of techniques of mental testing (cf. Gould 1981; Sutherland 1984) which appeared to offer the possibility of carrying out selection in an expeditious and reliable manner.

'ACHIEVEMENT' AS THE BASIS OF SOCIAL INEQUALITY IN INDUSTRIAL SOCIETY
This idea was most fully elaborated in American functionalist sociology of the 1940s and 1950s (see e.g. Davis 1942; Davis and Moore 1945; Parsons 1951, 1954). As societies make the transition from traditionalism to industrialism, it was argued, criteria of 'achievement' necessarily supersede criteria of 'ascription' in all forms of social selection. The technical and economic rationality on which industrial societies are founded demands that a close relationship be maintained between the degree of functional importance of different social positions and the capacities of their incumbents. Thus, individuals are increasingly allocated to positions according to what they have shown that they can do, rather than according to their social provenance. Furthermore,

From R. Erikson and J. O. Jonsson (eds.), *Can Education Be Equalized? The Swedish Case in Comparative Perspective* (Westview Press, 1996), 255–87. Reprinted with permission.

achievement becomes in this way the appropriate basis of reward. Different positions need to offer rewards commensurate with their functional importance in order that the more important positions should attract the more able individuals and that they should be motivated to high standards of performance. The social inequality that results can then claim legitimacy—as ascriptive inequality cannot—in that it contributes to the efficient functioning of the society as a whole and in that superior rewards, because they reflect superior achievement, are *deserved*.[1]

The relatedness of the three ideas outlined is, then, evident enough. In Young's meritocracy of twenty-first-century Britain they indeed find a closely articulated expression. Thus, the guiding model of 'rule by the cleverest people' is that provided by the Civil Service, as reconstructed after the Northcote–Trevelyan Report—though with all vestiges of the seniority principle removed. Selection for different educational 'streams', and in turn for all positions in society from the those of the governing élite downwards, is made on the basis of tests of intelligence and aptitude (objections to this practice by socialists and others having been undermined by the exigencies of international competition). Social classes are widely differentiated in their standard and style of living; but for so long as selection remains meritocratic, the élite can claim that their privileges are just reward for their achievement. Consequently, in the official ideology the family is viewed with suspicion, and the state bears responsibility for ensuring that parents in the élite do not succeed in attempts at restoring hereditary or other ascriptive tendencies.

However, on somewhat closer examination, the institutional and ideological coherence with which Young invests his doubtful Utopia can be seen to be more apparent than real—as is confirmed, it would appear, by the circumstances of its eventual demise. Most seriously, there is at its core a fateful tension, carried over from its *idées mère*, between the concept of talent—or natural ability—on the one hand, and that of merit on the other. The former refers simply to endowment, to the potential for achievement, while the latter must refer to *actual* achievement, and of some highly valued kind.

The arguments for opening up careers in the service of the state to the talented, and for

giving children an education matched to their ability, were ones advanced in a reformist spirit. They were concerned with questions of fitness for office and the proper recognition and cultivation of talent. But the argument for achievement as the basis of social inequality is of a different nature. Its focus is on the relationship between talent and reward, and this is so because it forms part of a sociological account intended to show how the functional prerequisites of modern societies are in fact met. Since it is necessary in such societies that 'human resources' should be used to the fullest advantage, then, it is held, this entails not only that talent be discovered and given opportunity, but further *that talent should be consistently converted into achievement*, and in positions of functional importance where a high level of performance matters most. Unequal rewards are essential in order to ensure that talent is so used as best to serve societal interests—or, in other words, to ensure that talent, through appropriate achievement, *becomes* merit—while at the same time being thus deserving of the privileges it attracts.

In Young's meritocracy, this problem of linking endowment to achievement, and in turn to deserved reward, finds acknowledgement in the society's leading formula: that is, in the official definition of merit as 'IQ *plus* effort'. To get from mere talent to merit, one might say, the cognitive has to be combined with the conative, or a natural with what must in the end be a moral category. ('The lazy genius is not one.') Only in this way can talent and merit be held together and thus a legitimation provided for the superior benefits that the élite enjoys. It is, though, a rather well-known difficulty of functionalist accounts of social inequality that they fail to explain just how the degree of 'importance' of different positions to societal efficiency is, or could be, determined (see e.g. Tumin 1953; Huaco 1963). In the centrally organized society depicted by Young these matters are simply decided by the élite itself; and it is evident that the effort that has to supplement IQ if merit is to be gained is effort directed towards goals that are laid down by the élite. But where such a solution by *fiat* is adopted, the danger is that the question of legitimacy reappears in a different and more radical form, in which the basis not just of social inequality but of the entire regime is challenged. And we are indeed given to understand that it was out of the ultimate arbitrariness of the élite's definition of merit—which could be exploited by both the populist and the Conservative oppositions—that the final crisis of the British meritocracy developed.[2]

Young's fantasy is thus sociologically instructive in more ways than have often been recognised. However, what for present purposes is of chief concern is that the problems of how merit is to be determined and of the relationship of merit to talent carry serious real-world implications.[3] In the following, the aim is to show, first of all, how these problems have compromised attempts by sociologists to assess empirically the extent to which actual societies are, or are becoming, 'meritocratic' in the educational and occupational selection procedures that they adopt. It is then further argued that the difficulties here encountered are not merely technical, but derive from the fact that, at least in the context of a liberal-capitalist society, it is just not possible for any one well-defined and objective conception of merit to be established. Although 'merit' may be the criterion of selection and reward that is primarily invoked, it can be defined only in ways that are situationally specific, and thus quite variable, and that further involve an inevitable degree of subjective (and often incorrigible) judgement. In exposing 'problems of meritocracy' in this way, the ultimate aim of the paper is to show that attempts to provide the structure of inequality in modern societies with a meritocratic legitimation, or to argue that such a legitimation is becoming increasingly appropriate as these societies evolve, do not succeed. In other words, not only is 'meritocracy' a sociological concept of doubtful value; it also appears unlikely to fulfil the ideological promise that it has been widely thought to hold.[4]

Measuring Meritocracy

American functionalist sociology, it has been suggested, provided one major source of the concept of meritocracy. In turn, exponents of this sociology rapidly took up 'meritocracy' as an apt description of the condition towards which they believed industrial societies were inexorably moving: that is, one in which achievement replaced ascription as the key criterion of social selection and of reward alike (cf. Wesolowski 1981). Moreover, as the idea of 'post-industrial' society developed in the 1970s, meritocratic tendencies were seen as being yet more powerfully encouraged: on the one hand, by the increasing 'knowledge-intensiveness' of all forms of economic activity; on the other, by the growth of large-scale public and private bureaucracies, especially in the services sector of the economy, within which pressures for meritocratic selection would be especially strong but would at the same time be readily accommodated.

Most influentially, Bell (1972: 30) contended, 'The post-industrial society, in its logic, is a meritocracy. Differential status and differential income are based on technical skills and higher education, and few high places are open to those without such qualifications.' And in a later formulation (1973: 409) he added, in openly functionalist fashion, 'Without those achievements one cannot fulfil the requirements of the new social division of labour which is a feature of that society.'[5] Further still, Bell made it clear that he regarded a meritocracy as capable of underwriting the pattern of social inequality to which it gave rise in moral as well as instrumental terms. A 'just' meritocracy, he maintained, is more than a mere technocracy (1973: 453): formal qualifications serve as 'an entry device into the system', but subsequent achievement then offers the possibility of both material and symbolic benefits as genuinely earned, *deserved* rewards.[6]

Not surprisingly, then, sociologists of a more empirical bent, already engaged with issues of 'ascription versus achievement' in processes of social mobility, were led to extend their investigations so that the argument of advancing meritocracy might be more directly addressed. Attention has for the most part come to focus on what Jonsson (1992*b*) has labelled the 'Increased Merit Selection' (IMS) hypothesis: that is, the claim that in modern societies merit becomes the key determinant of an individual's access to education above the basic minimum and in turn, then, of the position within the social division of labour that he or she eventually obtains—with the corollary that the influence in these respects of characteristics of individuals' families of origin will correspondingly decline. In other words, all aspects of individuals' provenance, apart from those that might contribute directly to the merit they can achieve, will be rendered increasingly irrelevant to the selection procedures at work.

In the empirical investigation of the IMS hypothesis, the way in which 'merit' is to be understood and measured must therefore take on a crucial importance. In fact, the practice that has been almost universally followed is simply to regard merit as being *indexed* by educational level actually attained—with this being then measured in terms either of time spent in education or of level of qualification reached. Justification for this practice can indeed be found in the arguments of those, such as Bell, who have maintained the IMS hypothesis, since they have themselves clearly supposed that it is educational institutions that play the leading role in discovering talent and, further, that provide the first and decisive opportunity for merit to be gained. None the less, the obvious point has to be recognised that this supposition must itself remain unexamined for so long as merit and educational attainment are not separately identified.

In Figure 44.1 stylized causal path diagrams are used in order to summarize results from a number of major enquiries that can be taken as bearing on the IMS hypothesis in so far as the indexing of merit by education is accepted— and also, it should be added, in so far as ascriptive influences are represented by individuals' class or status origins.[7] The first panel of the Figure serves to show the changes over time that would be expected in relationships among social origins (O), education (E), and eventual class or status destinations (D) if the IMS hypothesis held good. The panels below then correspondingly show the changes in these relationships that are pointed to by the results of the several enquiries represented.

As can be seen, two broadly different sets of findings emerge. Earlier studies for both the USA and England lend support to the IMS hypothesis to the extent that the influence of E on D, or at least the strength of association between them, would appear to be on the increase. However, in later studies for England and also for Sweden, essentially conflicting results are in this respect obtained: the IMS hypothesis is challenged in that the influence of E on D proves, if anything, to be weakening. This discrepancy in findings, like others that are apparent, could of course have various sources. It could follow from technical differences among the enquiries concerned, in

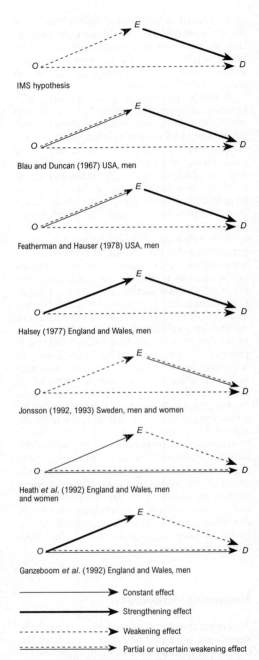

Fig. 44.1. Stylized path diagrams indicating changes expected over time in relations among origins (*O*), education (*E*), and destinations (*D*) under the IMS hypothesis, and changes found in major empirical inquiries.

data coverage and quality, analytical methods, and so on; or it could reflect real differences in trends as between periods and places. Fortunately, though, it is not for present purposes necessary to attempt to resolve this matter. While technical considerations might lead one to place greater reliance on the later studies, what is here of chief interest is the problems of interpretation that have been revealed by the critical response to the range of findings— whether at first sight favourable or unfavourable to the IMS hypothesis—that Figure 44.1 depicts.[8]

As regards results showing a closer relationship between education and individuals' eventual class or status positions, it has to be noted that the apparent confirmation of the IMS hypothesis thus provided has in fact been frequently questioned. A growing tendency on the part of employers to engage or promote employees by reference to their education does not, it is claimed, in itself imply that more meritocratic criteria of selection are in fact being adopted; nor need it be accepted that selection based on education *is* more 'functional' than other procedures that might be used. Thus, Jencks (1977: 83) has argued that just because a high level of educational attainment has become essential for obtaining some lucrative jobs, it does not follow that it ought to be so: 'If what we want is competence, for example, we might be better off dispensing with academic credentials and setting up on-the-job selection procedures for identifying incompetents.' Employers may be influenced by education because they believe it to be indicative not just of knowledge or skill but also of social and cultural background and lifestyle, with which they may be concerned for more than reasons of organizational performance. For example, senior executives may simply find it congenial to recruit new colleagues who, in background and lifestyle, are as similar as possible to themselves (cf. Collins 1971). Moreover, the imposition of formal qualifications as a condition of entry into particular occupations may come about in ways that are quite clearly *inimical* to efficiency. Most obviously, there is by now extensive evidence of employee organizations, such as professional associations or craft unions, seeking to raise entry qualifications to the jobs they cover to levels well above those required by the technical nature of the work involved as a means

of restricting labour supply and thus of protecting of improving the bargaining position of their current memberships (see e.g. Collins 1979: ch. 7; Parkin 1979: esp. 54–60; Freidson 1986: ch. 4).

At the same time, it can also be maintained that an increased emphasis on formal qualifications, whatever the motivation behind it may be, does not in itself ensure the greater equality of opportunity for individuals of differing social background that the IMS hypothesis would envisage. In so far as it becomes apparent that successful careers *are* dependent on qualifications, those families able to do so may be expected to react by devoting more of their resources, material and otherwise, to their children's education. In such circumstances, as Thurow has remarked (1972: 79), greater investment in education on the part of more advantaged families can be viewed as a 'defensive expenditure', necessary to protect their 'market share' of the more desirable forms of employment.[9]

Those who advance arguments on these lines can, indeed, also point to empirical findings that are at all events consistent with their position. Thus, the enquiries represented in Figure 41.1 that reveal an increasing influence of E on D (Blau and Duncan 1967; Featherman and Hauser 1978; Halsey 1977) do not, it can be seen, provide results so clearly favourable to the IMS hypothesis in regard to the effect of O on E (and for more recent comparative work, see Blossfield and Shavit (eds.) 1993). In the US case, the expected weakening of the influence of social origins on educational attainment was only partially found (see esp. Featherman and Hauser 1978: 240–5), while in the English case this influence appeared actually to strengthen. Halsey himself regards this result as seriously undermining the idea that a trend towards greater meritocracy is under way. Although education is 'increasingly the mediator of the transmission of status between generations' and operates in important part independently of the family, there is still no reduction within this intergenerational process in the influence that the family retains, or in the extent to which 'ascriptive forces find ways of expressing themselves as "achievement".' (1977: 184).

It is relevant, in this connection, to note further that even where some reduction is revealed in the *direct* effect of O on D, as the counterpart of the greater 'mediating' role of

E, this need not of course imply a weakening in the *overall* association between O and D. In fact, results from studies of inter-generational class or status mobility would suggest that this association (considered net of all effects of structural change) shows a high degree of constancy over time and no general tendency to diminish (see e.g. Erikson and Goldthorpe 1992: chs. 3, 9, and 10).[10]

In sum, arguments of the kind reviewed reveal, to say the least, far-from-negligible difficulties in treating evidence of an increasing influence of education on employment chances as *ipso facto* evidence of increasing selection by merit. The possibility clearly exists that the educational systems of modern societies do not in fact operate as efficiently as would need to be assumed, either in finding talent in the population at large or in providing talented individuals with more equal opportunities to gain 'merit' by the appropriate application of their abilities. If access to more desirable positions within the social division of labour is more closely governed than previously by the possession of formal qualifications, this may therefore betoken not advancing meritocracy but rather rising 'credentialism' (cf. Berg 1970; Dore 1976; Collins 1979). That is, it may be that qualifications are being used not in the interests of raising levels of individual competence and societal efficiency but, on the one hand, as an aid to relatively quick and cheap 'people processing' on the part of employing organizations and, on the other, as a means of maintaining rather than reducing disparities in relative rates of social mobility between different classes or status groups. What, then, may appear as an emergent meritocratic—and thus more legitimate—form of stratification could in fact be no more than another expression of social inequalities on a long-established pattern.

However, to revert to Figure 41.1, it has further to be acknowledged that if evidence of an increasing effect of E on D is thus open to more than one interpretation, so too are results suggesting no consistent decrease of the effect of O on E. As noted above, such results do not appear to fit well with the IMS hypothesis and could rather be taken as lending support to the 'credentialist' position. But arguments are also available through which it may be attempted to 'save' the IMS hypothesis or, at all events, to mount a counter-attack against its critics.

For example, one response to the fact that class disparities in educational attainment have shown no marked reduction has been a revival of hereditarian theories of stratification, most evident perhaps in the United States. Most notably, Herrnstein (1971, 1973) was led to claim that since educational selection procedures *are* becoming progressively more meritocratic—that is, through the use of IQ testing—the inequalities in attainment that are still revealed must primarily reflect differences in genetic endowment, the consequences of which cannot be mitigated by further, more radical educational or social reform. Indeed, Herrnstein would believe that as in modern societies the priority given to achievement over ascription continues to be thus emphasized, classes are likely to become more rigid and caste-like than previously, and that rather well-defined élite and 'residual' groupings may emerge.

Such arguments have, of course, themselves attracted forceful criticism (see e.g. Kamin 1974; Block and Dworkin (eds.) 1976; Schiff and Lewontin 1986). But for present purposes it is perhaps yet more relevant to observe that even if they could help support the IMS hypothesis, this would still be at no little ideological cost. The idea that increasing meritocracy implies a more open society would obviously have to be abandoned; and, in addition, the question is prompted of why genetic endowment should in itself be rewarded as 'meritorious'—at all events, if some connection between merit and desert is to be maintained. In Rawls's often quoted words, (1972: 104), 'It seems to be one of the fixed points of our considered judgments that no one deserves his place in the distribution of native endowments, any more than one deserves one's initial starting place in society.'

There is, though, a further way of accounting for persisting class disparities in education that would seem both more difficult to undermine empirically than hereditarian arguments and also more congenial to proponents of the IMS hypothesis in its wider implications. This has of late become a standard resort of 'revisionist' sociologists of education in Britain, who have been concerned to show that the failure of such disparities to fall—as illustrated in Figure 44.1 (Halsey 1977; cf. also Halsey, Heath, and Ridge 1980; Heath and Clifford 1990)—is not in itself compelling evidence of entrenched class biases in selection procedures or of other kinds of inequality of opportunity. What is reflected here, it is argued, may be no more than class differences in educational tastes or aspirations. Thus, working-class children and their parents may be relatively 'indifferent' to education, while middle-class children try harder to succeed educationally and receive greater parental encouragement to this end. Moreover, attempts to treat differences in tastes or aspirations as being themselves the consequences of class-linked structural or cultural influences are unconvincing, in view of the quite large absolute numbers of children of supposedly disadvantaged class origins who do achieve high educational standards (see e.g. Murphy 1981, 1990; Saunders 1989, 1990). In other words, the case made out is that no good grounds exist for regarding educational attainment as following more or less automatically from class advantage: as well as ability, it requires effort, on the part of children and of their parents, and to this extent it *is* deserving. The fact that class differentials in education show no marked decline does not, therefore, carry any direct implication that increasing selection by merit is illusory.

Finally, it may be noted here that results from the more recent studies represented in Figure 44.1 suggesting that the effect of E on D is, if anything, weakening (Jonsson 1992*b*; Heath, Mills, and Roberts 1991; Ganzeboom, Heath, and Roberts 1992) are again ones less decisive in regard to the IMS hypothesis than might at first appear. If the assumption is accepted that in modern societies educational attainment *is* the prime indicator of merit, then such results must, of course, call the hypothesis into serious doubt. But, alternatively, this assumption can itself be questioned from yet another standpoint. It is possible to argue that educational institutions are not the only means, even at a post-industrial stage of economic development, through which talent is found and merit gained; and, further, that the direct effect of O and D (that is, that not mediated through E) may in part *also* express selection by merit—as well as ascriptive influences—so that this effect has not necessarily to decline if the IMS hypothesis holds good.

What would seem to underlie the virtual equation of educational attainment with merit is the idea that in a modern, 'knowledge-intensive' economy, it is *cognitive* abilities and

skills that are crucial. But, as Jencks (1979: 83–4) among others has pointed out, this is by no means self-evident. Thus, in many kinds of sales, promotional, public relations, or personal service jobs, all of which are in expansion in post-industrial economies, more importance may attach to appropriate 'social' skills and associated styles of speech, manners, dress, and so on, or to the ability to perform what Hochschild (1983) has called 'emotional labour'—that is, work involving the management of feeling in others and oneself. And in all these respects what is learnt in the family could be of greater consequence than what is learnt in school. Similarly, in the small-business sector, which is also expanding in most modern economies, parents may well influence their children's life-chances not only 'non-meritocratically' as, say, through the inter-generational transmission of property, but also by helping them acquire relevant values and attitudes: for instance, by inducting them into an 'enterprise culture' or an individualistic work ethic.[11]

In sum, then, research findings of the kind illustrated in Figure 44.1 can only be regarded as fundamentally ambivalent in their bearing on the IMS hypothesis—and not only, or primarily, because varying results are reported from different periods or places, but because of difficulties over how merit is to be understood (and in turn represented) in empirical analyses. Unless the indexing of merit exclusively by education is accepted—and there seems to be no cogent reason why it should be—formidable problems of interpretation arise. Apparent evidence of increasing meritocratic selection can alternatively be construed as evidence of credentialism, which serves to maintain existing inequalities of opportunity and condition alike; while apparent evidence of such persisting inequalities, or of actually declining selection by merit, can be met with objections concerning what should count as merit which may be thought sufficient at least to save the IMS hypothesis from conclusive rejection.

It is, of course, possible that some of the uncertainties in question could eventually be resolved through further research. Thus, for example, instead of education being taken as a proxy for merit, more direct measures might be attempted, based, say, on IQ and other aptitude tests, taken together with some indicator of effort. However, it may still be doubted if the difficulties that arise in testing the IMS hypothesis are simply ones that could be overcome by empirical enquiry of a more sophisticated kind. The argument that will be pursued in the following section of this paper is that these difficulties are ones which face not only sociological researchers but further *social actors themselves*, and which are indeed inherent in the circumstances under which they act. That is to say, they stem ultimately from the fact that within societies (industrial or post-industrial) that possess a market economy and a pluralistic polity the concept of merit, even if widely invoked and applied, is not one that can be specified in any consistent and objective manner, but has rather to be defined in large part situationally and in ways which necessarily involve subjective judgements.

Merit, the Market and Management

The main inspiration for such an argument is to be found in the work of Hayek—which most previous sociological discussion of meritocracy has seriously neglected. Writing from what might be thought of as a European-liberal rather than an American-liberal position, Hayek (1960: esp. chs. 5 and 6, 1976: esp. ch. 9) is ready to endorse the idea of *la carrière ouverte aux talents* and, further, to accept that children should be provided with equal opportunities for education in relation to their abilities. However, he then advances a powerful critique of 'meritocracy' that starts from a rejection of what was earlier identified as its third component idea: that of—meritorious—achievement as the basis of reward.

For Hayek, it is simply not possible within a free society for the rewards gained from economic activity to be systematically related to merit in any meaningful conception. It is an essential feature of such a society that the rewards received by individuals do not have any necessary dependence on moral judgments that others may make about them; nor, moreover, that their rewards should derive from their talents and efforts *per se*. What matters is only the *value* that the goods and services that they can offer have for other individuals or organizations—as is evidenced by the readiness of the latter to pay for them. Talent and effort will only bring reward if they result in something that has such market value; unwanted talent and fruitless effort will

provide no return. Unequal rewards cannot therefore be regarded as expressing unequal merit, since they will reflect a whole range of influences on the structure of demand for goods and services that, so far as particular individuals are concerned, are simply happenstance. In fact, to speak of rewards is itself misleading in the context of a market economy in so far as there is any connotation of desert. The significance of differential returns from economic activity is prospective rather than retrospective; they serve not as rewards for what particular individuals have achieved in the past, but rather as signals to all, indicating how they should act in the future if their returns are to be maintained or improved. Thus, if oil is found under an individual's land, the riches he or she gains are not, from the standpoint of the market system—or indeed from any commonsense view—deserved; they are, rather, an encouragement to others to search for oil, for which there is an evident demand. Likewise, if workers become unemployed because the industry or occupation in which they were engaged is in decline, their plight is again not deserved; it does, however, indicate to others that they should not aim, through education, training, and so forth, to enter the industry or occupation in question.

Hayek thus stands clearly opposed to any attempt to legitimate social inequality in 'meritocratic' terms. Inequality, he maintains, has to be accepted as the inevitable outcome of a market economy, which is itself the necessary basis of a free society and, as such, needs no further defence. He does, though, go on to argue that it is also an advantage of the market that, precisely by relying on the quite impersonal processes of distribution that it involves, 'we can bring about a structure of relative prices and remunerations that will determine a size and composition of the total output which assures that the real equivalent of each individual's share that *accident or skill* assigns to him will be as large as we know how to make it' (1976: 72, emphasis added). Because, then, of this additional appeal to an apparent criterion of efficiency, Hayek's position is sometimes still seen (e.g. Marshall and Swift 1992: 43) as retaining an affinity with that of American theorists who aim to account for social stratification in functional terms. However, to grasp fully the force of Hayek's arguments it is necessary to appreciate how they are developed in a way that diverges quite radically from those of a functionalist cast.

Hayek, it must be emphasized, does not start from any notion of positions in society being differentiated in terms of their functional importance. To the contrary, he is adamantly opposed to viewing societies 'anthropomorphically' and attributing to them 'needs' or 'requirements' which can in fact be the attributes only of individuals or, perhaps, of organizations within which a clear hierarchy of ends has been established. Thus, he insists that it is meaningless to speak of economic activities as possessing 'value to society'; goods and services can have value only to individuals, or organizations, and will tend, moreover, to have very different values for different recipients (1976: 75). Achievement cannot, therefore, be calibrated as being more or less meritorious in the sense of contributing to a greater or lesser degree to fulfilling societal needs. If judgments of 'merit' *are* made, and do in fact determine rewards, then this can only be on the basis of ultimately political decision and enforcement. Hayek, one could say, would certainly regard it as no accident that Young's meritocracy was of a highly authoritarian character.

Nor, perhaps, would he find its eventual disintegration all that surprising either. For it is a further point in Hayek's case against a meritocracy that while it must necessarily be an illiberal form of society it is also likely, despite its ideology, still to be an *in*efficient one. Quite apart from the arbitrariness that he would see as being involved in determining just what kinds of achievement should be most deserving of reward, Hayek would doubt if it is in fact humanly possible to arrive at reliable assessments of individuals' 'merits', even in the more limited sense of their aptitudes and abilities, and of the uses to which they might best be put. In a free society the play of market forces substitutes for such assessments made *de haut en bas*.[12]

In sum, underlying Hayek's critique of meritocracy is a totally different understanding to that of the functionalists of how efficiency is to be sought and of the relationship that exists between efficiency and inequality. For the functionalists, it is the (supposed) fact that positions in the social division of labour differ in importance that creates the need for unequal rewards—to ensure that talented individuals perform well in the most impor-

tant positions. But here at the same time there is provided a basis for the legitimation of inequality, in so far, that is, as it conforms to the meritocratic pattern that is functionally demanded. For Hayek, in contrast, it is a category error to think of certain positions, or performance in them, as having greater or less value to society. Maximum efficiency is achieved, or rather approximated, not by seeking to meet societal needs but simply by giving individuals maximum freedom to choose and pursue their own economic activities and goals in response to market signals. Whatever inequalities then emerge can be seen as the concomitant or expression of efficiency and, more importantly, of freedom. But no grounds exist for seeking to construct and maintain some particular pattern of inequality as that which is functionally necessary to efficiency.

From Hayek's standpoint, it could then have little meaning—quite apart from technical problems of indicators and measurement—to ask whether modern societies are becoming more meritocratic. Or, at all events, if the question were to be put, it would have to be understood in a quite different sense from that of the IMS hypothesis. The issue would be not whether, in these societies, processes of selection and reward were being adapted to the exigencies of advancing technological and economic rationality, but rather, whether freedom was being eroded through the growing capacity of some élite or dominant political authority to monopolize such processes, and thus to establish its own conception of merit simply by *fiat*.[13]

There is, however, one respect in which Hayek's position is rather evidently open to challenge. His arguments would certainly be hard to resist in the case of a society in which self-employment or family-based production was the norm—a society, say, of peasants, artisans, merchants, and professionals all working on their own account. But industrial or post-industrial societies (despite the recent growth in small-scale enterprise earlier referred to) are still ones in which 80 to 90 per cent of those in the active labour force are *employees*. That is to say, they do not sell goods or services directly to consumers, but instead sell their labour to an employer, usually, in fact, an organization rather than another individual. Moreover, once organizations become relatively large and complex, it is an important consequence that the value of the contribution made by particular employees to their overall economic performance is often impossible to determine directly, and must be essentially a matter of managerial evaluation, subject to great uncertainty (cf. Offe 1970). Thus to claim, as Hayek does, that individuals' rewards reflect the market value of what they have to offer rather than judgements made about their merit by others must appear not a little unrealistic. For most members of the workforces of modern societies, precisely such judgements will play a large part in determining both the jobs they get and the remuneration they receive.

At one point Hayek openly acknowledges this difficulty in his case (1976: 99; cf. also 1960: 122–3), but he goes on to argue that it is of no great consequence provided that a situation does not arise 'in which a single comprehensive scale of merit is imposed upon the whole society'; so long as 'a multiplicity of organizations compete with each other in offering different prospects, this is not merely compatible with freedom but extends the range of choice open to the individual'. Hayek's chief concern here is clearly to preserve the idea of a market economy as the guarantor of freedom, even where 'managerial capitalism' prevails. Whether in this respect he is successful might well be debated;[14] but, for present purposes, the more relevant question is simply the factual one of whether the conceptions of merit adopted by the managements of employing organizations *are* essentially similar or possess the diversity that Hayek would hope to see. If managerial practice were highly standardized, then the IMS hypothesis could perhaps still be meaningfully pursued, with the definition and measurement of merit in empirical research being simply taken over from this practice. But if managements proceed on the basis of very variable ideas about what constitutes merit—if, in effect, merit is little more than what managements deem it to be in particular circumstances—then it is difficult to see how any *general* theory of increasing merit-selection could usefully be formulated.

There is not available, it must be said, a body of systematic research that bears directly on this issue. None the less, evidence from various kinds of enquiry that are of at least partial relevance would strongly suggest that 'a single comprehensive scale of merit' does not

in fact prevail. To the contrary, the criteria and related procedures for employee recruitment and promotion that are applied by employing organizations are revealed as quite differentiated. And one principal axis of this differentiation would appear to be precisely the extent to which educational attainment is regarded as being indicative of merit.

In some instances, especially with certain kinds of professional and technical occupations, employers do indeed find it desirable, and possible, to take employees of the kind they want more or less 'ready-made' from the educational system; that is, by reference to their formal qualifications, essentially in the manner that proponents of the IMS hypothesis would envisage. This, it would seem, is most often the case where academic education and vocational training have become highly coordinated and where it is important that employers, or clients, can be assured that at least certain minimum standards of performance will be met from the first.[15]

However, little basis can be found for the claim that this form of selection is that which must be typical, or at least prototypical, of modern societies because it is within schools, colleges, and universities that the 'primary' resource of human capital is now overwhelmingly generated (cf. Bell 1973: 116–19). On the contrary, such a complete reliance on the educational system would appear to be not all that extensive. Thus, it could be held that at least as common is the situation in which the educational attainments of prospective employees are viewed as relevant to assessing not their actual, but only their potential value to the organisation. Education may, for example, be treated primarily as an indicator of general knowledge and 'basic' skills or simply of mental flexibility and the capacity to learn (see e. g. Thurow 1972, 1984: ch. 7; Wilensky and Lawrence 1980; Cohen and Pfeffer 1986; Bills 1988); or again, as supporters of the thesis of credentialism would rather suggest, as an indicator of various socio–cultural characteristics that employers choose to consider as relevant, whether for performance-related or other reasons. Either way, though, educational level here serves as no more than a 'screening device' in recruitment, and is in no way regarded as being a substitute for more specific training or for other forms of socialization to be carried out 'in-house' or 'on-the-job'. And so far as subsequent promotion is concerned, educational qualifications are likely to be of yet smaller consequence. In Young's meritocracy, workplaces had 'ceased to be schools', all preparation for the level and type of employment that individuals would pursue being accomplished within the educational system before their entry into work (1958: 81–5). But this, one can safely say, is still far from being the case even in the economically most advanced societies of the present day.

Moreover, good evidence exists of a yet further range of circumstances in which merit in the eyes of management is conceived in terms of attitudinal and behavioural attributes to which education bears little relation at all, whether as determinant or indicator. Thus, for example, in recruiting to many subordinate jobs in both manufacturing industry and services, employers appear far less concerned with skills, actual or potential, than with worker characteristics such as 'discipline', 'steadiness', and 'responsibility' (Blackburn and Mann 1979: 102–9; Wood 1985). And in turn it is through displaying appropriate attitudes and behaviour, rather than acquiring new qualifications or skills, that workers are most likely to gain promotion: '*The internal labour market is fundamentally an apprenticeship in co-operation*. Demonstrate discipline on routine jobs and you may be rewarded! The essential point about jobs at the top of the hierarchy is not an unusual degree of skill but the costliness to management of error and the likelihood of error being made' (Blackburn and Mann, 1979: 108, emphasis in original).[16]

Finally, it is also relevant to note here that with the development of 'advanced personnel policies' or 'human resource management programmes'—themselves often regarded as characteristic features of post-industrial enterprises—selection for a wide range of positions, subordinate and managerial, is now increasingly guided by more or less elaborate techniques of personality and lifestyle assessment. These are typically aimed at identifying qualities such as 'loyalty', 'commitment', 'adaptability', and 'capacity for teamwork'; and what is of particular interest is the tendency for such assessments to be introduced as screening devices *prior to* that of educational attainment. Where this is the case, the clear implication, as one recent commentator (Townley 1989) has observed, is that 'attitude' is of greater concern to employers than formal qualifications; while training can, if necessary, be introduced to provide new skills, there is far less that can be done after recruitment by way of 'engineering' appropriate orientations to work.

In sum, while what is known about managerial selection procedures may not incline one to share in Hayek's confidence that individual freedom is thus well protected, it does none the less suggest that the essentials of his critique of meritocracy are in fact little affected by the existence of a predominantly 'employee society'. For most of the economically active population, the rewards they obtain from their work do indeed reflect judgements made about their merits by employers or their agents, rather than being determined directly and impersonally by the working of the market. But the variability of the criteria underlying these judgements is such that Hayek's claim that there can be no one objective—as distinct from politically imposed—standard of merit is more reinforced than undermined. Or, one could say, managerial practice serves to confirm that far from any conception of merit, or meritorious achievement, being 'societally given', as functionalists would wish to suppose, it must in fact be 'socially constructed' and that, within a market economy, it will be so constructed in a diversity of ways. In turn, then, Hayek's rejection of the possibility of a meritocratic legitimation of the inequalities that such an economy generates is also upheld. Managerial conceptions of what counts as merit need be little more stable than the market forces that shape the pattern of demand for labour of differing kinds, and can thus in large part be added to the latter as factors that will influence individuals' economic life-chances while remaining outside their capacity to control or even perhaps to predict.

From this standpoint, it may then be observed, the empirical results depicted in Figure 44.1 make rather better sense than from that of the IMS hypothesis. In the first place, while it is not of course surprising that an association should exist between E and D, there are no grounds for expecting that this association should itself overwhelmingly mediate that between O and D, nor that it should progressively strengthen over time. Rather, a connection of fluctuating strength could be anticipated, as the actual relevance of education to employers in implementing their selection criteria varies with the circumstances of particular periods, conjunctures, economic sectors, industries, and occupations (cf. Heath, Mills, and Roberts 1991; Jonsson 1992*b*).[17] And, one may add, it is in this context that one can perhaps best understand the recognition that has come to be given in studies of the kind represented in Figure 44.1 to the part that is played in occupational attainment by sheer luck (see e.g. Blau and Duncan 1967: ch. 5; Jencks 1972: 8–9, 227–8, 1979: 306–11). That is to say, such recognition should not be taken as denying that merit, in some sense, is involved—as Bell, for example, seeks to argue (1973: 432, n. 73). The point is rather that since what is seen as merit is so contingent and variable, much room for the play of chance exists in a person with attributes that might in some instances be regarded as meritorious being 'in the right place at the right time'.[18]

Secondly, there is no reason why any weakening should be looked for in the association between O and E. Since education does have value as an investment—and, indeed, for wider reasons than the IMS hypothesis would envisage—parents in more advantaged classes or strata may be expected to draw on their superior resources in order to preserve the competitive edge that they can give to their children in this respect. Furthermore, in so far as a steadily strengthening association between E and D is *not* an evident tendency, greater force is given to an account of why differentials in educational attainment persist that is attractive in going beyond the mere invocation of tastes and aspirations while still avoiding the 'over-explanation' that invalidates extreme structuralist or culturalist positions. Following Boudon (1973) and Gambetta (1987), it can be suggested that class or status differentials in education are maintained, despite expansion and institutional reform, essentially as a result of individuals' decisions on continuation within the educational system being made under differing degrees of constraint and with differing expectations of eventual succes; or, more specifically, because both the risks and the costs of failing in an attempt to achieve a higher level of education, relative to the potential benefits, tend to be greater for young people of less advantaged than for those of more advantaged backgrounds.[19] And if, then, uncertainty prevails, to a much greater degree than the IMS hypothesis would imply, over

the labour market returns that may be expected from investments in education, the idea that children of differing class origins are likely to arrive at different cost-benefit appraisals as regards their educational futures can only be made more plausible.

Conclusions

Young's sociological fantasy on the rise—and fall—of the meritocracy belongs to a long-standing English tradition of social satire that carries a serious critical intent. Young aimed to bring out, and to warn against, what appeared to him to be the ultimate implications of certain tendencies already well-established in the society in which he wrote: for example, the reliance on mental testing to allocate children within an rigidly tripartite system of education; the acceptance that different kinds of school should cater for children with different levels of ability, who were destined for correspondingly graded types of employment; the emphasis on education as primarily a *means*—whether of promoting economic growth or individual advancement. The logical extrapolation of these tendencies, Young sought to show, led to a form of society characterised by, at one extreme, an arrogant and patronising élite, upholding the one recognized measure of human worth—merit; and, at the other, a demoralized though resentful mass of those who had been found wanting in this respect and who were thus deprived of any excuse for their failure and likewise of any basis for radical protest. ('Since bottom agree with top that merit should reign, they can only cavil at the means by which the choice has been made, not at the standard which all alike espouse.')

However, it is notable that in the liberal—and especially the American liberal—reception of Young's work, its satirical and critical quality was in fact largely overlooked or, at all events, discounted. In envisaging his meritocracy, Young had taken over from American sociology the idea of achievement replacing ascription as the basis of social selection and in turn of reward, and this idea was then simply accepted back with little regard for what Young had endeavoured to reveal as its less attractive features. The rise of the 'achievement principle' was reaffirmed as a process inherent in industrial society, and as one that could, indeed, become only more manifest in the post-industrial era. Moreover, while for Young the very dominance of this principle was a cause for concern on account of its psychologically and politically debilitating effects on those who had failed to achieve and thus to gain the rewards of achievement, American enthusiasm for meritocracy appeared largely to derive from its legitimatory potential. It allowed an additional moral gloss to be given to arguments that sought to justify the prevailing form of social inequality (or something close to this) purely in terms of its functional efficiency.[20]

The possibility of meritocracy, one could then say, has engendered both fears and hopes. But what the foregoing discussion would chiefly suggest is that neither are likely to be realized to any substantial extent. Attempts to evaluate the hypothesis of increasing social selection by merit have led, it has been shown, to ambiguous and contested results, and primarily because various different understandings of what is to count as merit can be introduced into the interpretation of empirical findings. Furthermore, it has been argued that this is no way accidental. At least in the context of a society with a market economy and a pluralistic polity, no generally applicable answer to the question of what constitutes merit can in fact be given. No objective standard of merit is available, attempts to derive one from functionalist assumptions being quite uncompelling; and meritorious achievement could thus serve as the systematic basis of social selection and reward only if some comprehensive definition and scale of merit were to be politically established and maintained. Markets do not reward according to merit, but simply according to the economic value of goods and services that are offered, in the determination of which, factors beyond most individuals' control often play the decisive part. It is true that in a modern economy the economic life-chances of the majority of the workforce are shaped by judgements made on their merits as employees, or potential employees, by employing organizations. But these judgements would themselves appear to be informed by conceptions of merit that are sufficiently variable, by time and circumstance, for the outcomes for particular individuals often to appear as much under the influence of chance as those that result from the direct play of market forces.[21]

It cannot, therefore, be especially surprising to find that among the populations of present-day industrial, or post-industrial, societies there is little indication that a meritocratic ideology has become dominant. The relevant survey research does, to be sure, show a large consensus that the class or status positions which individuals hold are importantly determined by their own abilities, ambition and, above all, effort; there can be no doubt that notions of merit, and desert, are pervasive. However, frequent recognition is *also* given to the part that is played by a range of ascriptive attributes, especially class and status origins, and by various other, evidently 'non-meritocratic', factors such as social connections, subcultural characteristics, political affiliations, and so on. Again, while there is a wide acceptance of the principle of inequality in material rewards and indeed of reward in relation to achievement, the degree of inequality that actually prevails is still not, for the most part, seen as being morally justifiable on meritocratic (or indeed other) grounds. Desert is not the only criterion thought relevant to the distribution of resources—for example, needs and rights are also often invoked; and it would, moreover, appear that *even in terms of desert* a majority would still regard existing inequalities as too extreme.[22] In sum, one could say that, in popular perceptions, failure is not 'individualized' to the degree that a dominant meritocratic ideology would imply, nor is success taken to reflect so favourably on those who have attained it.

Confronted with the radical egalitarianism of the late 1960s, one American proponent of 'meritocracy', Irving Kristol, gave way to a revealing outburst against what he evidently regarded as the foolhardiness, if not perfidy, of Hayek's critique. Kristol complained that the opposition between a free society and a just one implied by Hayek's argument must, from the standpoint of a Samuel Smiles or a Horatio Alger, be regarded 'as slanderous to his fellow Christians, blasphemous of God, and ultimately subversive of the social order'. While declaring himself unsure about the first two of these accusations, Kristol was certainly ready to endorse the last: 'My reading of history is that, in the same way as men cannot for long tolerate a sense of spiritual meaninglessness in their individual lives, so they cannot for long accept a society in which power, privilege, and property are not distributed

according to some morally meaningful criteria.'
Hayek's rationale for modern capitalism was
not usable outside 'a small academic enclave'
and could probably not be believed 'except by
those whose minds have been shaped by over-
long exposure to scholasticism' (1970: 8–9).

Hayek's reply (1974: 73–4), however, is not
only that of a clearer thinker and more honest
apologist than Kristol; it also reveals an acute
appreciation of the realities of societies based
on market economies and of the way their
members are likely to respond to the vicissitudes to which they are exposed. Hayek agrees
that it is beneficial to the operation of such societies that individuals should *believe* that their
well-being depends primarily on their own
efforts and decisions and, for this reason, he
notes, such a belief is typically encouraged 'by
education and governing opinion'. But there
are at the same time dangers in 'an exaggerated
confidence' in its truth. For it must then
appear as 'a bitter irony and provocation' to
those who have failed but who regard themselves as being—and indeed perhaps *are*—as
able and deserving as those who have succeeded; while the latter are encouraged in their
self-esteem and self-righteousness, which
does not make them more popular. It is, Hayek
concludes, 'a real dilemma to what extent we
ought to encourage in the young the belief that
when they really try they will succeed or
should rather emphasize that inevitably some
unworthy will succeed and some worthy fail'.[23]

As Schaar (1967) has observed, the idea of
merit as the basis of selection and reward has a
wide appeal in the culture of modern societies;
to question its viability or desirability is thus
always likely to appear perverse. Apart from
anything else, such questioning would seem
to leave the way open for a return to ascriptive
criteria or, worse, to all manner of discriminatory practices in education and employment
alike. Meritocracy might thus be regarded as a
'necessary myth'. However, to seek to preserve such myths is not the responsibility of
the sociologist; and it has here been maintained that, on examination, the problems
attending the notion of meritocracy turn out
to be severe. The claim that modern societies
are, or are progressively becoming, meritocratic is difficult to sustain empirically, not so
much because it is clearly false as because it is
difficult to formulate, at least within a liberal
capitalist order, in a way that would allow
any conclusive empirical examination to be

made. This is so because what might count as
merit is in this context necessarily variable and
subjective. For essentially the same reasons, a
meritocratic legitimation of the social
inequality generated by a market economy is
unpersuasive and, furthermore, as Hayek so
clearly sees, could well prove dangerously
double-edged as the vision of 'post-industrialism' now becomes increasingly clouded.

Acknowledgements

In writing this paper I have benefited greatly from
the discussion of an earlier draft by participants at
the Gällivare seminar and from extensive written
comments received from Diego Gambetta, A. H.
Halsey, Patrick McGovern, and Adam Swift.
Valuable information and advice was also provided
by Geoffrey Evans, Gordon Marshall, David
Miller, and Wlodzimierz Wesolowski.

Notes

1. A close reading of Davis and Moore would
suggest that they see inequalities of reward as
being legitimated primarily, if not entirely, in
terms of 'objective' contributions; but in Parsons the idea of legitimation also in terms of
desert is explicitly introduced (see esp. 1954:
104–5). For Parsons, it would seem, it is itself a
prerequisite for the long-term stability of a
social system that in so far as performances
contribute to societal adaptiveness, their
claim to deserve superior rewards should be
widely recognized: in other words, instrumental requirements need to be underwritten
by prevailing values.
2. On the one hand, the 'Chelsea Manifesto'
rejected the subordination of the educational
system to the occupational structure and
the everlasting pursuit of economic expansion. Invoking Matthew Arnold's *Culture and
Anarchy*, it urged that the primary role of
education should be to encourage *all* human
talents, regardless of their economic significance, and to seek to do away with classes by
making 'the best that has been thought and
known in the world' current everywhere. On
the other hand, T. S. Eliot's *Notes towards the
Definition of Culture* became again widely read
as ideologically unsound groupings within the
élite sought to claim that their children were
not *just* children, but rulers born to a high destiny and fitted to it by their upbringing. The
despairing memorialist of the meritocracy can
only lament, 'Oh God, Oh Galton!'
3. While this problem has so far received rather

little sociological attention, the *dis*junction between talent and merit has often formed a crux in literary works. Here, though, attention has focused with perhaps most striking effect not on the sense of injustice felt by those whose talent is insufficiently recognized as meritorious, but rather on the anguish of those who are forced to realize that superior merit in no way guarantees superior talent. Peter Schaffer's *Amadeus* provides a recent example of great dramatic force in Salieri's outburst against his God after reading Mozart's scores: '*Capisco!* I know my fate. Now for first time I feel my emptiness as Adam felt his nakedness. Tonight at an inn somewhere in this city stands a giggling child who can put on paper, without actually setting down his billiard cue, casual notes which turn my most considered ones into lifeless scratches. *Grazie*, Signore! You gave me the desire to serve you—which most men do not have—then saw to it that the service was shameful in the ears of the server. *Grazie!* You gave me the desire to praise you—which most do not feel—then made me mute. *Grazie tante!* You put into me perception of the Incomparable—which most men never know!—then ensured that I would know myself forever mediocre *Why? . . . What is my fault?* Until this day I have pursued virtue with rigour. I have laboured long hours to relieve my fellow men. I have worked and worked the talent you allowed me. *You know how hard I've worked!*—solely that in the end, in the practice of the art which alone makes the world comprehensible to me, I might hear Your Voice! And now I do hear it—and it says only one name: MOZART! . . . Spiteful, sniggering, conceited, infantine Mozart!— who has never worked one minute to help another man!—shit-talking Mozart with his botty-smacking wife!—*him* you have chosen to be your sole conduct! And *my* only reward—my sublime privilege—is to be the sole man alive in this time who shall clearly recognize your Incarnation! *Grazie e grazie ancora!*'

4. In thus concentrating on sociology and on *Ideologiekritik*, the paper does not address in any direct way attempts made by social and political philosophers (e.g. Simon 1974; Daniels 1978; Fishkin 1983; Green 1988; Miller 1992*a*) to suggest how in some possible, rather than actually existing, society, meritocratic conceptions of social justice might be defined and implemented. It is, nevertheless, of interest to note that these attempts reveal a somewhat similar division to that indicated among functional theories of stratification in n. 1 above. That is, while some authors advance a purely 'consequentialist' case for meritocracy in terms of ensuring a maximum contribution to productivity, social welfare, etc., others would seek additionally, if not alternatively, to make a 'backward-looking' case in terms of desert. A further division is between those who argue for merit only as the criterion of selection and those who argue for it as the criterion of both selection and (unequal) reward. In so far as the present paper has relevance for such philosophical endeavours, it would be in raising questions about the realism of some of the empirical assumptions involved: for example, concerning the availability of appropriate ways of determining 'contributions', or the socio-political viability of establishing selection by merit but then denying its relevance to reward.

5. In the American literature similar arguments are presented, though without specific reference to 'meritocracy', in Blau and Duncan (1967) and Treiman (1970), while a more European-oriented treatment of tendencies towards meritocracy can be found in Husén (1974). For a fuller review of relevant literature, see Krauze and Slomczynski (1985).

6. Hope (1984: ch. 14) has argued, with, perhaps, Bell among others in mind, that the virtual identification of merit with desert is distinctively American, whereas in the British understanding merit is more a matter of entitlement to office. However, while it may be fair comment that 'Implicit in popular (and some neoconservative) American discussions of merit is the assumption that the purpose of holding an office is to draw its emoluments' (1984: 262), it has still to be recognized that dictionary definitions of merit, British as well as American, do consistently establish a connection with desert: e.g. 'the condition or fact of deserving', 'the quality of deserving well, or of being entitled to reward or gratitude' (*Shorter Oxford*): 'excellence that deserves honour or reward' (*Chambers*). It should, moreover, be observed that while it is, of course, open to sociologists or philosophers (cf. n. 4 above) to develop their own notions of merit that are not 'desert-based', the connection with desert that is established in common usage represents an obvious attraction of the idea of merit within the context of a legitimatory ideology.

7. That is to say, other ascriptive characteristics that could well be of relevance, such as those of gender, race, or ethnicity, are not for present purposes considered.

8. It should be added that few, if any, of the changes represented in Figure 44.1 could be regarded as *substantial*, even where statistically significant. One possible interpretation of the results reported would then be that the relative strengths of the relationships in question merely oscillate around some far more

stable basic pattern. It might also be noted here that studies aimed at investigating how closely actual processes of class or status attainment approximate to what might be regarded as an ideal state of meritocracy, based on education or qualifications, have concluded that a very wide gap remains. See, for example, Krauze and Slomczynski (1985), Jonsson (1988, 1992b).

9. Thurow's argument, it may be added, is advanced in the context of a generally sceptical discussion of the contribution of educational expansion to economic growth. 'Education becomes a good investment,' he maintains, 'not because it would raise people's incomes above what they would have been if no one had increased his education, but rather because it raises their income above what it will be if others acquire an education and they do not.'

10. This finding, it must be emphasized, is not to be seen as supporting the idea of the consistent 'reproduction' of class or status structures, as advanced in the work of authors such as Bourdieu and Passeron (1972) or Bowles and Gintis (1976), since it pertains to relative, not absolute, rates of social mobility. On the other hand, though, it forms the basis of an explicit challenge to the claim of Ganzeboom, Luijkx, and Treiman (1989) (cf. also Ganzeboom, Treiman, and Ultee 1991) that a 'world-wide secular trend towards increased societal openness' is in train.

11. It is relevant here to note that Bell's conception of the emerging social division of labour—on which his argument for advancing meritocracy is essentially dependent—appears in various respects distorted by an over-estimation of the force of 'post-industrial' tendencies. Thus, his 'venture in social forecasting' would seem clearly to exaggerate the growth in numbers of 'science-based' professional and higher technical positions within the services sector, *relative to* those in which skills of a more 'traditional' kind remain crucial, while at the same time failing to pick up the late-twentieth-century resurgence, rather than continued decline, of small-scale entrepreneurship. Again, it must be observed that Bell did not anticipate the return of another major feature of earlier industrialism, namely, mass unemployment, which has, of course, particularly damaging implications for the idea of a post-industrial meritocracy. Cf. n. 24 below.

12. However, even in a market economy, it should be added, Hayek still would not expect perfect efficiency to be obtained in the 'matching' of individuals to jobs. 'As society and its complexity extend', he writes (1960: 80) 'the rewards a man can hope to earn come to depend more and more, not on the skill and

capacity he may possess, but on their being put to the right use'; but, he goes on, 'There is perhaps no more poignant grief than that arising from a sense of how useful one might have been to one's fellow men and of one's gifts having been wasted. That in a free society nobody has a duty to see that a man's talents are properly used, that nobody has a claim to an opportunity to use his special gifts, and that, unless he himself finds such opportunity, they are likely to be wasted, is perhaps the gravest reproach directed against a free system, and the source of the bitterest resentment.' The point is thus underlined that, for Hayek, it is its contribution to freedom, rather than efficiency, that is the primary justification for a market economy. Even if a perfect meritocracy, more efficient than any market-based society, could be achieved, he would still reject it because of the curtailment of freedom that would be implied.

An interesting attempt can be found in Miller (1989: ch. 6) to argue, *contra* Hayek, that there are no fundamental reasons why markets should not allocate resources in accordance with personal deserts, and equilibrium prices serve as indicators of value when measuring deserts. However, Miller also makes it clear that, for this to be the case, a market economy would have to be subject to 'an appropriate regulatory framework,' and remarks, 'One can see why libertarians, who believe that social systems require only a simple set of ground rules to operate effectively, are wise to eschew the attempt to show that unfettered markets can be socially just.'

13. Viewing the question of increasing meritocracy in this light may have a particular relevance for the state socialist societies of postwar Central and Eastern Europe. In these societies the educational system was typically regarded by the dominant élites as an instrument of controlled social selection and manpower planning, and attempts were indeed made to develop, and to legitimate, reward structures in terms of 'contribution to society'. However, the use of the essentially political criteria that this notion implied led to increasingly evident 'dysfunctional' consequences for economic performance. See e.g. Wesolowski and Mach (1986).

14. At this point, one suspects, Hayek is sensitive to the most palpable weakness in the entire tradition of economic and political liberalism in which he stands: that is, the assumption that it is *only* the state that, on the basis of its monopoly of the means of physical violence, can be a source of arbitrary power. The tyranny that can also be exercised, on the basis of the private ownership of capital, by employers and their agents over their employ-

ees has thus to be disregarded or dismissed as being of little consequence. In this last respect, the standard argument is of course that dissatisfied employees are free to move— and the standard objection, that this freedom may often be far more apparent than real because of the risks and costs involved.

15. Thus, one supposes that even Jencks (cf. above, p. 669) would hesitate to undergo surgery in a hospital where those carrying out operations had been engaged without reference to qualifications—although being subject to deselection once incompetence had been clearly demonstrated.

16. Again, in the case of work that is repetitive and machine-paced or of an otherwise intrinsically unattractive kind and is usually taken only for the relatively high wages it offers, employers are likely to be concerned with worker characteristics indicative of 'stickability', with the aim of preventing quit rates becoming excessively high. Thus, in recruiting to the assembly-line and machine-shop jobs described in Goldthorpe *et al.* (1968), employers paid particular attention to two criteria: an applicant's previous record of job-changing and his current level of contractual debt.

17. One might of course also expect some amount of cross-national variation, dependent, for example, on differences in the institutional linkages between education (and training) and employment (see Erikson and Goldthorpe, 1992: 301–7) or, as Grusky (1983) has suggested, on the stage of development of national educational systems. With the case of Japan chiefly in mind, Grusky argues that the association between education and employment might be expected first to strengthen but then to weaken, once 'mass' higher education is established; for employers might at this stage quite rationally regard level of educational attainment as providing less information than before about workers' potential.

18. Thus, for example, the work Granovetter (1973, 1974) on 'getting a job' has pointed to the importance in providing information, contacts, etc., of what he calls 'weak ties': that is, relatively superficial social relations that are formed with persons outside an individual's usual circles of kin, neighbours, friends, workmates, etc., and often in ways in which a chance element is involved.

19. Cohen (1990) has pointed out that Murphy (1990) conspicuously neglects Boudon's work in claiming that class differentials in educational attainment may best be regarded as merely differences rather than as inequalities. In an earlier paper (1981) Murphy does in fact discuss Boudon's position at some length and

critically, and has responded (1992) to Cohen's observation. But in neither case does he engage effectively with the idea that inequality may inhere in the differing degrees of constraint and (justifiably) differing expectations of future returns under which educational choices are made. Murphy appears to be quite unaware of Gambetta's work.

20. Cf. n. 1 above. Acceptance of the principle that meritorious achievement brings deserved rewards could be seen as meeting the need for instrumental requirements to be underwritten by value consensus. Bell's résumé of Young (1973: 409 *et seq.*) is especially revealing in presenting the overthrow of the meritocracy by the Populists in a way far more sympathetic to the regret of the memorialist than to the satirical intent of the author. For Bell, 'populist reaction', emphasizing equality of condition rather than, or as well as, equality of opportunity, was clearly the major threat to what he wished to see as the emerging meritocracy of post-industrial America. Bell's response is thrown into relief by that of Rawls (1972: 100–7) whose concern is to show that the principle of 'fair opportunity' that he upholds does *not* lead to 'a callous meritocratic society'. One of the purposes of his celebrated 'difference principle' is to try to ensure that 'a confident sense of their own worth should be sought for the least favoured': for example, by allocating resources to education not 'solely or necessarily mainly according to their return as estimated in productive trained abilities, but also according to their worth in enriching the personal and social life of citizens, including here the less favoured'.

21. It might be contended that the market constraints under which most employing organizations operate must serve to narrow down quite significantly those managerial conceptions of merit that are in fact viable, and thus at the same time help to give employees a clearer idea of what they should do in order to be regarded as meritorious. But the empirical evidence would appear to go counter to this argument: that is, the constraints imposed by modern economies would seem often sufficiently loose, in this respect as in others, to allow for a wide margin of 'managerial discretion'.

22. A useful review of the research here alluded to is provided in Miller (1992*b*). New comparative data of major interest are, however, beginning to become available from the International Social Survey Programme (for preliminary results, see Smith, 1989; and for more extensive analyses Evans, forthcoming). Also awaited are results of evident relevance from the International Survey on Social Justice, recently completed.

23. Kristol, it seems, may now be more inclined to take Hayek's point. In a recent article he grapples with the problem of why the current American recession, though relatively mild according to economic indicators, should have been such a 'major trauma for the American people'. He notes, 'It has been a staple of conventional wisdom that, as we have moved to a "service" economy from an "industrial" economy, there would be a general improvement in the stability of employment.' Although automobile workers, for example, could expect to be laid off, employees in communications, computing, health services, legal services, insurance and banking, etc. were supposedly safe from such a demoralizing fate. However, this has proved to be a cruel illusion: 'while unemployment has not been all that high . . . an important segment of the middle class, the professional segment, suffered an unprecedently grievous wound. Suddenly our "post-industrial society" didn't look so post-industrial after all.' 'America's Mysterious Malaise', *Times Literary Supplement*, 22, May 1992.

References

Bell, D. (1972), 'On Meritocracy and Equality', *The Public Interest*, 29 (Fall).
—— (1973), *The Coming of Post-Industrial Society* (New York: Basic Books).
Berg, I. (1970), *Education and Jobs: The Great Training Robbery* (Harmondsworth: Penguin).
Bills, D. B. (1988), 'Credentials and Capacities: Employers' Perceptions of the Acquisition of Skills', *Sociological Quarterly*, 29.
Blackburn, R. M., and Mann, M. (1979), *The Working Class in the Labour Market* (London: Macmillan).
Blau, P. M., and Duncan, O. D. (1967), *The American Occupational Structure* (New York: Wiley).
Block, N., and Dworkin, G. (eds.) (1976), *The IQ Controversy* (London: Quartet Books).
Blossfeld, H. -P., and Shavit, Y. (eds.) (1993), *Persistent Inequality: Changing Educational Stratification in Thirteen Countries* (Boulder, Colo.: Westview Press).
Boudon, R. (1973), *L'Inégalité des chances* (Paris: Colin).
Bourdieu, P., and Passeron, J.-C. (1972), *La Reproduction* (Paris: Éditions de Minuit).
Bowles, S., and Gintis, H. (1976), *Schooling in Capitalist America* (New York: Basic Books).
Breen, R., and Whelan, C. T. (1993), 'From Ascription to Achievement? Origins, Education and Entry to the Labour Force in the Republic of Ireland During the Twentieth Century', *Acta Sociologica*, 36.

Cohen, P. (1990), 'Murphy, Boudon and a "Most Respectable Prejudice" ', *British Journal of Sociology*, 41.
Cohen, Y., and Pfeffer, J. (1986), 'Organizational Hiring Standards', *Administrative Science Quarterly*, 31.
Collins, R. (1971), 'Functional and Conflict Theories of Educational Stratification', *American Sociological Review*, 36.
—— (1979), *The Credential Society* (New York: Academic Press).
Daniels, N. (1978), 'Merit and Meritocracy', *Philosophy and Public Affairs*, 7.
Davis, K. (1942), 'A Conceptual Analysis of Stratification', *American Sociological Review*, 7.
——, and Moore, W. E. (1945), 'Some Principles of Stratification', *American Sociological Review*, 10.
Dore, R. (1976), *The Diploma Disease: Education, Qualification and Development* (London: Allen and Unwin).
Erikson, R., and Goldthorpe, J. H. (1992), *The Constant Flux: A Study of Class Mobility in Industrial Societies* (Oxford: Clarendon Press).
Evans, G. (forthcoming), *Class, Merit and Justice: Beliefs About Social Stratification and Opportunity in Britain* (Cambridge: Cambridge Univ. Press).
Featherman, D. L., and Hauser, R. M. (1978), *Opportunity and Change* (New York: Academic Press).
Fischer, C. S., Hout, M., and Arum, R. (1995), 'IQ Poverty and *The Bell Curve* Controversy', paper presented at the meeting of the ISA Research Committee on Social Stratification and Mobility, Zürich.
Fishkin, J. S. (1983), *Justice, Equal Opportunity and the Family* (New Haven: Yale Univ. Press).
Freidson, E. (1986), *Professional Powers* (Chicago: Univ. of Chicago Press).
Gambetta, D. (1987), *Were They Pushed or Did They Jump? Individual Decision Mechanisms in Education* (Cambridge: Cambridge Univ. Press).
Ganzeboom, H. B. G., Heath, A. F., and Roberts, J. (1992), 'Trends in Educational and Occupational Achievement in Britain' (Paper presented at the meeting of the ISA Research Committee on Social Stratification and Mobility, Trento).
——, Luijkx, R., and Treiman, D. J. (1989), 'Intergenerational Class Mobility in Comparative Perspective', *Research in Social Stratification and Mobility*, 8.
——, Treiman, D. J., and Ultee, W. (1991), 'Comparative Intergenerational Stratification Research: Three Generations and Beyond', *Annual Review of Sociology*, 17.
Goldthorpe, J. H. (1995a), 'Le "noyau dur": fluidité sociale en Angleterre et en France dans les années 70 et 80', *Revue française de sociologie*, 36.
—— (1995b), 'Class Analysis and the Reorientation of Class Theory: The Case of Persisting

Differentials in Educational Attainment', Manuscript, Nuffield College, Oxford.
— Lockwood, D., Bechhofer, F., and Platt, J. (1968), *The Affluent Worker: Industrial Attitudes and Behaviour* (Cambridge: Cambridge Univ. Press).
Gould, S. J. (1981), *The Mismeasure of Man* (New York: Norton).
Granovetter, M. (1973), 'The Strength of Weak Ties', *American Journal of Sociology*, 78, 360–80.
— (1974), *Getting a Job: A Study of Contacts and Careers* (Cambridge, Mass.: Harvard Univ. Press).
Green, J. D. (1988), 'Is Equality of Opportunity a False Ideal for Society?', *British Journal of Sociology*, 39.
Grusky, D. (1983), 'Industrialization and the Status-Attainment Process: The Thesis of Industrialism Reconsidered', *American Sociological Review*, 48, 494–506.
Halsey, A. H. (1977), 'Towards Meritocracy? The case of Britain', in J. Karabel and A. H. Halsey (eds.), *Power and Ideology in Education* (New York: Oxford Univ. Press).
—, Heath, A. F., and Ridge, J. M. (1980), *Origins and Destinations* (Oxford: Clarendon Press).
Hayek, F. (1960), *The Constitution of Liberty* (London: Routledge).
— (1976), *Law, Legislation and Liberty* (London: Routledge).
Heath, A. F., and Clifford, P. (1990), 'Class Inequalities in Education in the Twentieth Century', *Journal of the Royal Statistical Society*, series A, 153.
—, Mills, C., and Roberts, J. (1992), 'Towards Meritocracy? Recent Evidence on an Old Problem', in C. Crouch and A. F. Heath (eds.), *Social Research and Social Reform* (Oxford: Clarendon Press).
Herrnstein, R. J. (1971), 'IQ'. *Atlantic Monthly* (September).
— (1973), *IQ in the Meritocracy* (Boston: Atlantic Monthly Press).
Hochschild, A. R. (1983), *The Managed Heart: Commercialization of Human Feeling* (Berkeley: Univ. of California Press).
Hope, K. (1984), *As Others See Us: Schooling and Social Mobility in Scotland and the United States* (Cambridge: Cambridge Univ. Press).
Huaco, G. (1963), 'A Logical Analysis of the Davis-Moore Theory of Stratification', *American Sociological Review*, 28.
Husén, T. (1974): *Talent, Equality and Meritocracy* (The Hague: Nijhoff).
Jencks, C. (and associates) (1972), *Inequality: A Reassessment of the Effects of Family and Schooling in America* (New York: Basic Books).
— (1979), *Who Gets Ahead? The Determinants of Economic Success in America* (New York: Basic Books).
Jonsson, J. O. (1988), *Utbildning, social reproduk-tion och social skiktning* (Stockholm: Institutet för Social Forskning).
— (1992a), 'School Reforms, Educational Expansion and Educational Attainment: Trends towards Equality in Sweden', in Blossfeld and Shavit, eds. (1992).
— (1992b), 'Towards the Merit-Selective Society?' (Swedish Institute for Social Research, Univ. of Stockholm).
— (1993), 'Persisting Inequality in Sweden?' in Blossfeld and Shavit (eds.).
Kamin, L. J. (1974), *The Science and Politics of IQ* (New York: Wiley).
Krauze, T., and Slomczynski, K. M. (1985), 'How far to Meritocracy? Empirical Tests of a Controversial Theory'. *Social Forces*, 63.
Kristol, I. (1970), ' "When Virtue Loses All her Loveliness"—Some Reflections on Capitalism and "The Free Society" ', *The Public Interest*, 21 (Fall).
Marshall, G., and Swift, A. (1992), 'Social Class and Social Justice', *British Journal of Sociology*, 43.
Miller, D. (1989), *Market, State and Community: Theoretical Foundations of Market Socialism* (Oxford: Clarendon Press).
— (1992a), 'Deserving Jobs', *Philosophical Quarterly*, 42.
— (1992b), 'Distributive Justice: What the People Think', *Ethics*, 102.
Murphy, J. (1981), 'Class Inequality in Education: Two Justifications, One Evaluation but No Hard Evidence', *British Journal of Sociology*, 32.
— (1990), 'A Most Respectable Prejudice: Inequality in Educational Research and Policy', *British Journal of Sociology*, 41.
— (1992), 'A Most Respectable Prejudice—Boudon', *British Journal of Sociology*, 43.
Offe, C. (1970), *Leistungsprinzip und industrielle Arbeit* (Frankfurt: Europäische Verlagsanstalt).
Parkin, F. (1979), *Marxism and Class Theory: A Bourgeois Critique* (London: Tavistock).
Parsons, T. (1951), *The Social System* (New York: Free Press).
— (1954), 'A Revised Analytical Approach to the Theory of Social Stratification', in R. Bendix and S. M. Lipset (eds.), *Class, Status and Power* (New York: Free Press).
Payne, J., and Payne, C. (1994), 'Recent Trends in the Relationship Between Education and Occupation and in the Position of Women in Job Recruitment in Britain', manuscript, Policy Studies Institute and Nuffield College, Oxford.
Rawls, J. (1972), *A Theory of Justice* (Oxford: Clarendon Press).
Saunders, P. (1989), 'The Question of Equality', *Social Studies Review*, 5.
— (1990), *Social Class and Stratification* (London: Routledge).
Schaar, J. H. (1967), 'Equality of Opportunity, and Beyond', in J. R. Pennock and J. W.

Chapman (eds.), *Equality* (New York: Atherton Press).

Schiff, M., and R. Lewontin (1986), *Education and Class: The Irrelevance of IQ and Genetic Studies* (Oxford: Oxford Univ. Press).

Semmel, B. (1960), *Imperialism and Social Reform* (London: Allen and Unwin).

Simon, R. L. (1974), 'Equality, Merit and the Determination of our Gifts', *Social Research*, 41.

Smith, T. W. (1989), 'Inequality and Welfare', in R. Jowell, S. Witherspoon and L. Brook (eds.), *British Social Attitudes: Special International Report* (Aldershot: Gower).

Sutherland, G. (1984), *Ability, Merit and Measurement: Mental Testing and English Education, 1880–1940* (Oxford: Clarendon Press).

Thurow, L. C. (1984), *Dangerous Currents: The State of Economics* (New York: Vintage Books).

—— (1972), 'Education and Economic Inequality', *The Public Interest*, 28 (Summer).

Townley, B. (1989), 'Selection and Appraisal: Reconstituting "Social Relations"?', in J. Storey (ed.), *New Perspectives on Human Resource Management* (London: Routledge).

Treiman, D. J. (1970), 'Industrialization and Social Stratification', in E. O. Laumann (ed.), *Social Stratification: Research and Theory for the 1970s* (Indianapolis: Bobbs Merrill).

Tumin, M. M. (1953), 'Some Principles of Stratification: A Critical Analysis', *American Sociological Review*, 18.

Wesolowski, W. (1981), 'Stratification and Meritocratic Justice', *Research in Social Stratification and Mobility*, 1.

—— and B. Mach (1986), 'Unfulfilled Systemic Functions of Social Mobility', *International Sociology*, 1.

Wilensky, H. L., and Lawrence, A. T. (1980), 'Job Assignment in Modern Societies: A Re-examination of the Ascription-Achievement Hypothesis', in A. H. Hawley (ed.), *Societal Growth: Processes and Implications* (New York: Free Press).

Wood, S. (1985), 'Recruitment Systems and the Recession', *British Journal of Industrial Relations*, 23.

Young, M. (1958), *The Rise of the Meritocracy* (Harmondsworth: Penguin).

45

Equalization and Improvement: Some Effects of Comprehensive Reorganization in Scotland[1]

Andrew McPherson and J. Douglas Willms

Introduction

'[T]he 1944 Education Act brought England and Wales no nearer to the ideal of a meritocratic society . . . . Secondary education was made free in order to enable the poor to take more advantage of it, but the paradoxical consequence was to increase subsidies to the affluent'. This was one of the conclusions reached by Halsey, Heath and Ridge (1980: 210) in their study of men who entered post-primary schooling between the mid-1920s and the mid-1960s. Looking forward, however, they wrote: 'The tripartite secondary system . . . added educational to class rigidity. The future lies with the comprehensive schools where these rigidities may be eased' (*ibid*: 213).

Comprehensive reorganisation, however, has had a mixed press. The few British evaluations there have been at national level have not pointed to gains from reorganization that were socially or educationally significant. Indeed, for many commentators, of varying political, social and educational persuasions, the comprehensive school has come to symbolise the supposed 'failure' of the social-democratic ameliorism of British educational policy since 1944.[2] Much of the recent British debate over standards, accountability and the effectiveness of schooling can be read as a criticism of comprehensive schools and policies,[3] as can a number of recent policy initiatives in England and Wales culminating in the Education Bill that was in preparation in the summer of 1987. Equally, however, certain radical

alternatives to the present Government's own proposals for radical reform are also based on the assumption that comprehensive schools have failed (e.g. Hargreaves 1982: 68–9; Reynolds, Sullivan, and Murgatroyd 1987: ch. 6).

In one respect, however, conclusions on the potential and performance of comprehensive schooling in Britain are premature, for it was only in the 1970s that comprehensive schools became a majority of British secondary schools (Wright 1977: 73; Fig. 45.1 below), and in this sense began to constitute something approaching a comprehensive system. Our own study evaluates some of the effects of comprehensive reorganization between the early-to-mid 1970s and the early-to-mid 1980s. We look mainly at its impact on the social composition of secondary schools, and on the levels of examination attainment associated with pupils' gender and social class.

Our data come from Scotland, from three nationally representative and highly comparable cohorts of school leavers. The point at which each of the three cohorts entered secondary education is shown in Figure 45.1.[4] (The main definitions used in this figure and elsewhere in this paper are formally set out under 'Measures and Main Definitions'.) The 'early' cohort received its secondary education whilst comprehensive reorganization was proceeding apace. The 'late' cohort, however, only started at secondary school after the reorganisation of the maintained (non-private) sector was substantially completed. Thus we

From *Sociology*, 21 (1987), 509–39. Reprinted with permission.

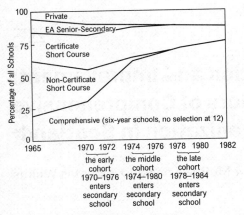

Fig. 45.1 Type of secondary school by year: percentages of all secondary schools

Note: 'Private' includes grant-aided schools; 'Comprehensive' here includes a subset of schools with non-selective entries at 12 years, but with intakes of pupils from short-course schools at 14 years or 16 years for certificate-course work (i.e., 'receiver-comprehensives'—see 'Measures and Main Definitions'). *Source:* see note 4.

have a quasi-experimental design spanning the later stages of the implementation of the reform, with repeated observations of schools derived from the pupils in the three cohorts.

The design has several unique features: it is the only British study of reorganization to incorporate a longitudinal analysis of the structure and effects of a national education system in the process of change; the only study to include data up to the mid-1980s and to describe the educational outcomes of pupils whose entire secondary education was received within a settled comprehensive system; and the only study to relate the experience of reorganisation at the local level to the changing national picture. These features provide a relatively good basis for causal inference, and also for generalisation. It is true that the institutional structure of Scottish education is distinctive (Gray, McPherson, and Raffe 1983). However, social-class relativities in attainment in Scotland between 1945 and the mid-1970s are known to have paralleled those in England (ibid. 226). Thus, it is not impossible that Scotland's experience *since* the mid-1970s can also be generalised to some degree, expecially if the causal processes are correctly identified.

Purposes of the Reform

The various purposes of comprehensive reform were, in some degree, conflicting, vague and contested. Some purposes were explicitly stated, but others must be inferred.[5] *First*, there was to be no selection of pupils when they transferred to secondary school (SED 1965a: para. 5). *Second*, as soon as possible, and in all but sparsely populated areas, there was to be only one type of secondary school: the 'all-through', fixed-catchment comprehensive school 'providing a full range of courses for all pupils from a particular district who would attend it throughout their secondary career' (ibid: para. 10).[6] A *third* purpose, one could argue, was that compulsory schooling should not terminate before the first stage of public certification. This was entailed by the raising of the school-leaving age to 16 years in 1972–73, known as ROSLA. The Labour Government of 1964–1970 regarded ROSLA as part of its policy for comprehensive reorganisation. We therefore treat it in this light, although a case for separate treatment could also be made.

These three purposes had largely been implemented in the public, maintained, sector by the mid-1970s, but others had not. A *fourth* purpose was to reduce between-school variation in pupils' backgrounds: the pupil intake to a school should 'represent a fuller cross-section of the community' (ibid: para. 5). But which 'community' was intended as the norm, the local or the national? Either way, did this purpose conflict with a fixed-catchment policy (purpose 2) that might restrict pupils to a school serving a socially homogeneous neighbourhood? A *fifth* and related purpose was to eliminate the 'creaming' of able pupils from one school catchment to another. Within the public sector this could largely be achieved by meeting purposes 1 and 2. Overall, however, it also required the elimination of the private sector, in which most schools selected pupils by ability, directly or indirectly. As Figure 45.1 indicates, this was not achieved.[7]

A *sixth* purpose of reorganization was to increase access to certification. To facilitate this a further institutional change, known as 'banding', was made in 1972–73 as part of ROSLA. Essentially, banding was a reform of certification that allowed pupils to receive an award even when they delivered what previously would have been regarded as a failing performance in the public examination at 16 years. More details are given under 'Measures and Main Definitions'. It should be noted that the banding arrangement, and the minimum leaving age of 16 years, applied to all members of our three cohorts. A *seventh* and important purpose was that the association of attainment with social class should fall. There was, however, no clear intention to reduce gender-related differentiation and inequalities. Indeed, some of the thinking on curriculum reform was marked by sexism.[8]

Methods

DATA

Our analysis employs data from the 1977, 1981 and 1985 Scottish School Leavers Surveys (SSLS). These surveyed random samples of pupils who left school respectively in 1976, 1980 and 1984. The sampling fractions were approximately 40 per cent in 1977 and 1981 and 10 per cent in 1985. The 1977 SSLS sample of 1976 leavers covered the entire leaver cohort only within the regions of Strathclyde, Tayside, Fife and Lothian, whereas the SSLS surveys of 1981 and 1985 had complete coverage for all of Scotland. Most of our analyses are based on pupils from the four regions. These regions comprise over 300 schools and nearly four-fifths of the Scottish population. Response rates were of the order of 80 per cent. In all analyses we employ a design weight to take account of biases arising from non-coverage. The last two rows of Table 45.1 show the achieved sample sizes of pupils and schools for the three surveys. Further details of the surveys, their sampling frames and coverage rates, are given by Burnhill, McPherson, Raffe, and Tomes (1987).

STRATEGY FOR ANALYSIS

A truly experimental examination of the impact of comprehensive reform would require that there were no 'selection biases': namely, that pupils were randomly allocated to schools, and that schools were randomly allocated to the various 'treatments' of reorganisation. Ideally also, the effects of other concurrent treatments, including period

Table 45.1. Sample characteristics and parameter estimates for regressions of SCE attainment on sex, SES, and an SES-by-sex interaction, by cohort (standard errors in brackets)

| | Four Regions | | | All of Scotland | |
	1970–1976	1974–1980	1978–1984	1974–1980	1978–1984
Percentage of Pupils in Selective Schools	36.6	8.7	8.0	9.6	8.9
Proportion of Variance in SES Between Schools	.293	.236	.258	.215	.231
Mean SCE Attainment	−.095	−.025	.093	.000	.130
	(.008)	(.007)	(.015)	(.007)	(.013)
Mean SES	−.115	−.029	.098	.000	.132
	(.008)	(.007)	(.015)	(.007)	(.013)
Regression Parameter Estimates					
Intercept (Expected Score of Nationally Average Male)	−.036	−.031	−.006	−.028	−.010
	(.009)	(.009)	(.018)	(.008)	(.016)
Sex (Difference Between Females and Males)	.001	.042	.111	.058	.123
	(.014)	(.013)	(.026)	(.012)	(.023)
SES (Attainment/SES Slope for Males)	.549	.480	.462	.472	.462
	(.009)	(.009)	(.018)	(.008)	(.015)
SES-by-Sex (Difference Between Female and Male Attainment/ SES Slope)	−.054	.003	.004	.001	−.018
	(.013)	(.013)	(.026)	(.012)	(.022)
Number of Schools	321	328	322	470	456
Number of Pupils	16307	18012	.4732	23151	6354

Note: In the first row 'selective' is defined to include EA senior-secondary schools, short-course feeder schools, and private schools (including grant-aided schools), but not modal-comprehensives, receiver-comprehensives, upgrading-comprehensives or new modal-comprehensives (see Measures and Main Definitions).

changes, would be controlled or excluded in some way. Reality, of course, meets none of these conditions. The question is how far a quasi-experiment can approximate them, and at what cost in assumptions made.

We use a measure of socioeconomic status (SES) to represent pupils' educational potential on entry to secondary school. But SES 'underspecifies' potential, and the design of the analysis must therefore attempt to minimise the extent to which 'selection effects' (the effects of selection bias arising from this underspecification) are confounded with the effects of reorganization itself. The design must also recognise that there have been many period changes over the years 1970 to 1985, and that these have almost certainly led to changes across the three cohorts in the incidence of factors that may influence educational attainment.[9]

To meet the requirements of the design, we employ three mutually supportive sets of analyses. The analyses in the first set are at the national level. They specify the distribution and attainment of different types of pupils across different types of schools, and the changes in these across time. These 'effects', however, may be due to period changes. The analyses in the second set therefore compare attainments across five subsectors of schools, each subsector having a different organizational history. We cannot assert that these histories were entirely uncorrelated with period changes and with unmeasured selection biases. Nevertheless, variations between subsectors in levels of attainment, and in the extent of change of those levels, allow us to distinguish some of the effects of school reorganisation from period effects.

The third set of analyses disaggregates the national-level analyses, and displays the experience of reorganisation within 20 communities served by more than one secondary school. These analyses are primarily intended to counter the possibility that the analysis by school subsectors may confound selection effects with the effects of reorganisation. Each community is defined in such a way that the large majority of pupils within the community, indeed in many cases virtually all pupils in the community, had no effective choice other than to attend a school in that community. This specification reduces selection bias arising from pupil movements when we use individual-pupil SES to estimate the educa-

tional potential of each community's pupils. Furthermore, within-community comparisons of the direction of change in levels and patterns of attainment following school reorganisation provide a more certain basis for causal inference than observations of covariation across communities at one point in time. This is because, without additional information, or a fuller theoretical specification, we have no means of knowing how far between-community variations in the relationships between SES and attainment are a function of concomitant variation in the validity of the SES measure as a proxy for educational potential. Whatever SES is within a local community, it is not something that changes overnight, classification changes apart. But the organisation of schooling may change rapidly, and, indeed, did so in many communities between our early and middle cohorts.[10]

MEASURES AND MAIN DEFINITIONS

The three cohorts. The '1970–1976 cohort' or the 'early cohort' consists of leavers from the sixth-year stage in 1976, all of whom had entered secondary school in 1970; leavers from the fifth-year stage in 1976, all of whom had entered in 1971; and leavers from the fourth-year stage in 1976, the largest group, all of whom had entered in 1972. (The approximate age of transfer to secondary school in Scotland is 12 years, not 11 years as in England). The two other leaver cohorts have similar structures, and all three are representative of virtually a complete cross-section of young people in terms of ability and attainment. The second cohort entered secondary school between 1974 and 1976, leaving in 1980. It is called the '1974–1980 cohort', or the 'middle cohort'. The third cohort, the '1978–1984' or 'late cohort', entered between 1978 and 1980, leaving in 1984.

Attainment. In all three sets of analyses we employ a single measure of attainment in the examinations for the Scottish Certificate of Education (SCE) at 16, 17 and 18 years. The measure therefore incorporates the effects of voluntary school enrolment after sixteen years. It has 14 categories describing the number of awards at the A–C level in examinations at the Ordinary Grade (O-grade) and the Higher Grade (Highers, or H-grade). Awards in the range A–C are officially recognised as passes in the Highers examination, but not in the examination for the O-grade since the introduction of 'banding' in 1972–73 (section 2). Unofficially, however, such awards are still widely regarded as passes. For pupils obtaining no A–C awards at the O-grade, account was taken of any SCE O-grade awards at the D or E grade. The attainment measure was scaled on a logit distribution, and was standardised using the data for the middle cohort; see Willms (1986) for details. The scaled values were then assigned to the corresponding attainment categories for the middle and late cohorts. One should bear in mind that all summaries of the attainment data are a function of this scaling. The advantage that the scaling has over a simple numbering of the categories is that the mean attainment score (and also the SES-adjusted attainment score) for any group is expressed as an 'effect size' (Glass, McGaw and Smith 1981). This is a measure of the attainment for that group relative to the national average for the middle cohort, expressed as a fraction of a standard deviation. At the centre of the attainment scale, an effect size of ten per cent of a standard deviation is roughly equivalent to one O-grade award at A–C. The scaling allows us to make readily interpretable comparisons both between subgroups within cohort, and across cohorts. But, like any summary statistic, the effect size summarises imperfectly because it throws information away.

Socioeconomic status (SES). Similarly, for all three cohorts we scaled and standardised a composite SES measure, again based on the middle cohort. The measure is the first principal component (Harman 1976) of three indicators of SES: father's occupation, mother's education, and number of siblings. All cohort members were scaled, including those who did not supply information on their fathers' occupations, or whose fathers had no occupation. We used the scaling for the middle cohort to scale the SES of members of the early and late cohorts.[11]

Social class. The occupations of pupils' fathers were classified into the Registrar General's seven social-class categories: professional, intermediate, skilled non-manual, skilled manual, partly skilled, unskilled and no occupation or unclassified (see note 11). The first three categories are referred to as 'middle class', and the fourth through sixth categories as 'working class'. The paper attaches no explanatory significance to the distinction between SES and social class.

Modal-comprehensive school.[12] This is the form of school recommended by the Labour Government in Scotland in 1965. It is defined as an all-through, six-year school accepting all pupils from its catchment area at the age of transfer, and only those pupils whether at 12 years or thereafter, for their entire secondary education to 16, 17 or 18 years.[13] (In Figure 45.1, which is derived from official statistics, the 'comprehensive' category includes both modal-comprehensives and receiver-comprehensives, defined below). Where a school had met our definition of modal-comprehensive by the year in which the oldest member of the cohort in question entered it, we use the term as it stands. Otherwise, we distinguish two sub-categories of schools that were building up to a modal-comprehensive status: namely *new modal-comprehensives* and *upgrading modal-comprehensives*.[14]

Selective school. This is defined as all types of school other than the modal-comprehensive school. It therefore includes not only the schools out of which less able, or lower SES, pupils were selected, but also the schools into which they were selected. The types of selective schools are sub-divided as follows:

Private school. This comprises all schools not wholly maintained by the state, and includes nearly all schools that were grant-aided by central government in 1965 (Highet 1969). (Following comprehensive reorganization, most grant-aided schools eventually became private, as, in effect, did one education-authority (EA) maintained school.)

EA senior-secondary school. This refers to all EA-maintained, six-year secondary schools having selective admission at 12 years, either based on evidence of high ability or high attainment, or as a consequence of preferential admission at 12 years for pupils from the school's primary department. Such schools were functionally equivalent to grammar schools in England. Nearly all of them had become either modal-comprehensives or receiver-comprehensives (see below) by the mid-1970s (Figure 45.1).

Short-course school. This covers all schools offering less than a six-year course. They are sub-divided as follows:

non-certificate, short-course school. This is a school with a selective intake at 12 years, that did not offer the early stages of certificate-course work, and that did not have structured arrangements for feeding certificate pupils to other schools. It corresponds, roughly, to the English secondary-modern school, and instances of it had almost entirely disappeared by the end of the 1970s (Figure 45.1).

certificate, short-course or *feeder school.* This describes a school that may or may not have had a selective intake at 12 years. It offered the early stages of certificate-course work, and it had structured arrangements for feeding SCE H-grade certificate pupils to other schools (all receivers—below), usually at age 14 years. Some offered SCE O-grade courses, but none offered Highers courses.

Receiver school. This describes schools with structured arrangements for receiving certificate pupils from certificate short-course, or feeder, schools. Such schools are of two types:

a subset of EA senior-secondary schools. Virtually all of these had disappeared by the late 1970s.

receiver-comprehensive school. This describes an EA-maintained school that would otherwise qualify as a modal-comprehensive were it not for its receiver status. We treat receiver-comprehensives as selective because they had intakes of pupils at 14 or 16 years who transferred from feeder schools in order to take SCE courses. Where our concern is simply to describe the incidence of selective entry to secondary school at 12 years, we make an exception to our definition of a 'selective' school, and treat receiver-comprehensives as non-selective. This occurs only in Figures 45.1 and 45.4 and in Table 45.1.

The classification of all schools was set to the year in which the oldest member of a leaver cohort entered first year; that is, to 1970 for the early cohort, to 1974 for the middle cohort, and to 1978 for the late cohort. We had no alternative but to set the school membership of the pupil to the last school he or she attended.

Community. This was defined in three stages. First, all schools, including private schools, were allocated to places as defined by the Registrar General, Scotland (RGS 1967). Second, all places served by more than one school were then identified. Third, if the schools in that place served all pupils in that place, and only those pupils, the place was defined as a multiple-school community. In setting this definition, only data on school location and catchment were used, and not details of individual pupil's home addresses. Where a school in one place served pupils living in another place, the places were concatenated until a set of places was identified such that it was the minimum set within which the schools served all pupils in that set, and only those pupils. This set was also then defined as a multiple-school community. We refer to multiple-school communities below simply as 'communities'.

Creamed/uncreamed modal-comprehensive school. All modal-comprehensive schools in a community were treated as 'creamed' if there was any selective school in that community.[15]

Between-school segregation. This is defined as the proportion of the total pupil-level variance in SES that lies between all schools. A zero value means that the SES of every school intake is typical of the population in question (e.g., Scotland, local community). Proportions above .3 represent considerable segregation; for example, see the discussion of Glasgow schools in Willms (1986).

Results

NATIONAL-LEVEL ANALYSES

Table 45.1 shows various national estimates for the three cohorts. Because the estimates for the early cohort are based on the four regions only, the table reports estimates for the middle and late cohorts both for the four regions and for all of Scotland. The first row shows the percentage of pupils in selective schools. Between the early and middle cohorts, the percentage declined from around 37 per cent to around nine per cent, and then remained steady.

Row two of Table 45.1 shows a decrease in between-school segregation between the first two cohorts. It fell from .29 in the early cohort to .24 in the middle cohort, but then rose to .26. The estimates for all of Scotland also show a small rise between the middle and late cohorts. However, analyses of between-school segregation at the community level are more telling (Figure 45.5).

Table 45.1 also shows the mean SCE attainment and the mean SES. In both an upward trend is apparent. The mean attainment for the four regions rose from 10 per cent of a standard deviation below the national average in the early cohort to three per cent below in the middle cohort, and then to nine per cent above in the late cohort. The average SES in the four regions increased by about nine per cent of a standard deviation between the first two cohorts, and then by a further 13 per cent. Clearly, account must be taken of these changes in SES when examining national trends in attainment.

This is done in the next four rows of Table 45.1. They show the parameter estimates and standard errors for the regressions of SCE attainment on sex and SES, and the SES-by-sex interaction. In these regressions, sex was coded zero for males, and one for females. Thus, the intercept is an estimate of the expected attainment for a male pseudo-pupil having an SES score that was nationally average in terms of the middle cohort (i.e., SES = 0). The expected attainment for the counterpart female pseudo-pupil is given by the intercept plus the coefficient for sex. Similarly, the parameter estimates for SES are estimates of the attainment/SES regression slope for males, while the total of the estimates for SES and the interaction term estimates the attainment/SES slope for females.

After adjusting for SES, the attainment score for males in the early cohort was about three per cent of a standard deviation below the national average for all pupils in the middle cohort. In the four regions it remained at that level in the middle cohort. Between the middle and late cohorts, however, there was a rise of two to three per cent. Female attainment also rose across the three cohorts, but by rather more than male attainment. It equalled that of males in the early cohort, but increased to four per cent of a standard deviation above males in the middle cohort, and to 11 per cent above in the late cohort. Separate analysis by social class also showed commensurate gains within each OPCS category for males and females alike, with the exception of males in social class V (unskilled) (no table shown—see Willms and Kerr 1987).

For both sexes, the relationship between attainment and SES decreased across the three cohorts. The decrease was greater for males, for whom the regression slope fell from .55 to .46. This change indicates an increase in the performance of low SES pupils relative to that of high SES pupils. The female slope also fell, but only from .50 to .47.

Figures 45.2A (males) and 45.2B (females) show cumulative attainment distributions across the three cohorts for middle- and work-

ing-class pupils.[16] The improvements in attainment summarised in Table 45.1 are apparent in the upward movement of the distributions across the three cohorts. One way to express the social-class difference is in terms of the gap in attainment between the middle-class and working-class groups at any cut-off point on the horizontal axis. For males the social-class difference at, for example, two or more O-grade passes declined over the eight years from 37.9 to 35.4, or by about seven per cent of the early-cohort difference. Among females it declined by 18 per cent of the early-cohort difference. However, there was no decline in social-class differences in attainment at the upper end of the attainment scale. Among males the social-class gap remained roughly constant. Among females it widened slightly at and above the cut-off of one or more Highers passes, a level attained by 28 per cent of all pupils in the middle cohort. This explains why the overall decline in social-class inequality among females has been less than among males (Table 45.1). There are other trends in Figures 45.2A and 45.2B on which we will not comment but, in general, they indicate that improvements in attainment among both males and females have not entirely worked through to the later stages of schooling and to the upper levels of attainment. It may therefore be that the contribution of the post-compulsory period to the social-selective functions of secondary schooling is of increasing importance, relative to the compulsory period.

HISTORIES OF REORGANIZATION

Figure 45.1 has shown that the *coup de grâce* to selection at 12 years in the maintained sector took effect between 1970 and 1974. How did the organisational history of the schools influence the attainments of their pupils? Figure 45.3 is confined to pupils from the three cohorts who entered schools that were modal-comprehensive schools by 1974, i.e., when the oldest pupils of the middle cohort began their secondary schooling. It shows expected attainment scores for the pseudo-pupil of nationally average SES for the middle cohort (males and females combined). The scores are shown separately for the three cohorts and for a creamed and an uncreamed sector, defined according to the position in 1974. (Thus some schools in the uncreamed sector were creamed when the early cohort entered, and

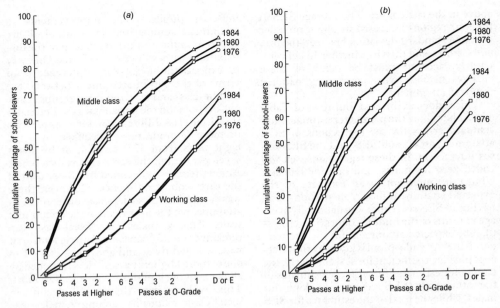

Fig. 45.2A. Cumulative attainment distribution by cohort and social class: males

Fig. 45.2B. Cumulative attainment distribution by cohort and social class: females

some schools in the creamed sector were uncreamed when the late cohort entered).

Both sectors are divided into the same five subsectors, defined by the schools' organisational history.[17] All five subsectors had non-selective intakes by 1974. However, three of the subsectors had selective intakes four years earlier, when the early cohort started secondary school. The selective intakes are indicated by the three small, solid symbols in the creamed and uncreamed sectors. Thus, in 1970 the 'downgraded senior-secondary' schools had selected able pupils in the early cohort at 12 years mainly on the basis of tests. The 'downgraded receiver-comprehensives' in 1970 were still admitting pupils from short-course schools at 14 or 16 years to prepare for certificate examinations. The 'upgrading comprehensives' in 1970 were short-course schools, certificate (O-grade only) and non-certificate alike, that 'lost' able pupils at 12, 14 or 16 years to receiver schools in the two subsectors just defined. The other two subsectors, which in one sense serve as a 'control', had non-selective intakes at 12 years in 1970. The 'steady comprehensives' had met our definition of modal-comprehensive by 1970. The 'upgraded comprehensives' had met it only in the following two years; that is, they

had developed SCE O- and H-grade courses after 1970, but had done so in time for the early cohort to present them for examination at the appropriate fourth- and fifth-year stages respectively. The early cohort had entered the upgraded comprehensives on a wholly non-selective basis. To repeat, by the time the oldest pupils in the middle cohort entered secondary school in 1974, all five subsectors consisted only of modal-comprehensive schools.

Several trends are apparent in Figure 45.3. The first is an homogenisation of attainment between the subsectors and between the creamed and uncreamed sectors. The effects on the early cohort of selective entry and differentiated provision are apparent in the wide dispersion of the attainment estimates for the nationally average pseudo-pupil. This dispersion is, indeed, a salutary reminder that pupil-level SES is not an adequate proxy for educational potential when applied in settings in which formal selection operates; hence the design of Figure 45.3. By the late cohort, 1978–1984, the range of the estimates for the ten types of school has fallen to little more than a tenth of a standard deviation, or roughly one O-grade award at A–C grade.

In two types of school, the uncreamed

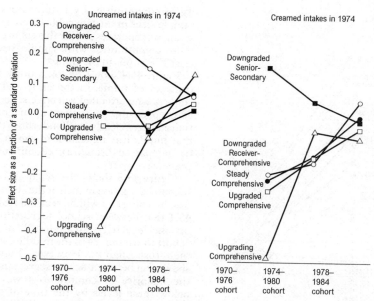

Fig 45.3. Expected attainment scores, adjusted for SES, by cohort, by the organizational history of the school subsectors, and by whether they were creamed in 1974

Note: School subsectors are defined in note 17.

steady comprehensives and the uncreamed upgraded comprehensives, attainment remained steady between the early and middle cohorts, and rose slightly in the late cohort. Elsewhere, however, all was change, but change with momentum and direction. In eight of the ten cases, the direction of change between the early and middle cohorts was continued through to the late cohort. The two exceptions were the uncreamed part of the downgraded senior-secondary subsector, and the creamed part of the upgrading comprehensive subsector. However, the changes in the direction of the trends in these two cases may reflect nothing more than sampling fluctuations.[18] In general, therefore, it seems that the organisational history of schools influences the attainment of their pupils. It is not enough simply to take account of a school's present status.

Further evidence that the history of schools affects attainment can be seen in the relative performance of the steady and the upgraded comprehensives. The steady comprehensives, remember, had been modal-comprehensives for longer. In both the uncreamed and creamed sectors, the steady comprehensives outperformed the upgraded in all three cohorts. (The one exception is the tie in the creamed sector of the middle cohort. A possible complication here is the superior performance of pupils in the late cohort in uncreamed upgrading schools, and of pupils in the middle cohort in creamed upgrading schools. Again, however, the first exception may arise from sampling error. But the second is statistically significant and we have no plausible explanation for it, other than chance).

The momentum of reform is also apparent in the changing levels of attainment of the five creamed subsectors as compared with their uncreamed counterparts. As the incidence of formal selection fell (Table 45.1) and Figure 45.4), so the incidence of creaming also declined. The percentage of all pupils in uncreamed comprehensives rose from 25 per cent to 42 per cent between the early and middle cohorts, and then remained roughly at that level (no diagram shown). In each of the three cohorts, each of the five creamed subsectors in Figure 45.3 did worse than its uncreamed counterpart; (the creamed upgrading comprehensives in the middle cohort are again the one exception, their attainment being very

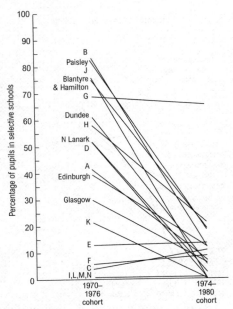

Fig. 45.4. Percentages of pupils in selective schools, in the early and middle cohorts, by community

Note: 'Selective' is defined here to include EA senior-secondary schools, short-course feeder schools, and private schools (including grant-aided schools) but not receiver-comprehensives or the three types of modal-comprehensive; see 'Measures and Main Definitions'.

slightly above their uncreamed counterparts). However, the size of these between-sector differences in attainment fell between the early and middle cohorts, and continued to fall between the middle and late cohorts. Most important here is the improving performance of the steady and upgraded subsectors that were creamed. These two types of school provided for a large part of the city population. By the late cohort, the levels of performance in these two types almost matched those of their uncreamed counterparts, which had themselves also risen.[19]

WITHIN–COMMUNITY ANALYSES
Our procedures for classifying schools into multiple-school communities (see 'Measures and Main Definitions' above) yielded 31 communities in the four regions. We excluded ten communities from the analysis where the sample size of either the early or the middle cohort was fewer than 175 pupils. We also excluded the 'community' of Argyll. For reasons of confidentiality we identify the major-

ity of communities by letter.[20] Because the sample sizes in the late cohort were relatively small, we report results for this cohort only for those communities with sample sizes of at least 175 pupils in the cohort.

Figure 45.4 shows, by community, the percentages of pupils in the early and middle cohorts who attended selective schools. The extent of change consequent upon reorganisation emerges clearly, and underlines the point that pupils leaving school in the mid-1970s had not passed through a predominantly comprehensive system.

Figure 45.5 shows the extent of between-school segregation in each of the 20 communities, by cohort. It will be recalled from Table 45.1 that between-school segregation at the national level fell from around .29 in the early cohort to around .24 in the middle cohort, but then rose slightly. However, Figure 45.5 shows that between-school segregation *within* the majority of communities was already below these levels by the time of the early cohort, and in many cases well below. In the early cohort, between-school segregation in fifteen of the twenty communities was at or

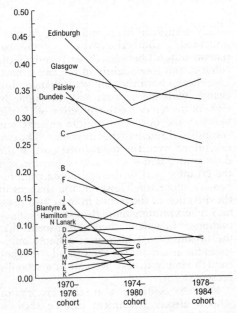

Fig. 45.5. Between-school SES segregation across the three cohorts, by community

Note: See 'Measurements and Main Definitions' for definitions. Estimates for the smaller communities in the late cohort are too unstable to show.

below .20, and in the majority of these it either remained steady, or declined slightly.[21] The six named areas contain almost a third of the population of Scotland. In all of them between-school segregation fell between the early and middle cohorts. Between the middle and late cohorts segregation continued to fall in Glasgow, Paisley, and Blantyre and Hamilton. It remained the same in Dundee and North Lanarkshire but increased slightly in Edinburgh (.32 to .37). Four of the communities in the figure can be publicly identified as New Towns (K, L, M, N)—see note 20. It is striking that there was virtually no between-school segregation in any of the four.

For each community, we also inspected the expected attainment scores for males and females, adjusted for SES (no table shown). Recall that each of these expresses the attainment of a pseudo-pupil whose SES is set at the national average for the middle cohort. In the six named communities, adjusted attainment levels varied between community and fluctuated between cohorts, especially among males. However, female attainment increased in all but one of the six. In the fourteen communities identified by letter there were even greater variations between communities and larger fluctuations across time. Some of this variation is random, but further comment on these issues must await a more powerful analysis.[22] Meanwhile, however, it is worth recording that the estimates for some communities (e.g., Edinburgh and Glasgow) show significant male and female gains in attainment that reflect the national picture described in Table 45.1. But other communities (e.g., Blantyre and Hamilton) do not. This indicates the need for caution in generalising to the national picture from an isolated study of one community.

Figure 45.6 displays evidence of a widespread change at the local level in the relationship between attainment and SES. In three of the named communities (Glasgow, Paisley and North Lanarkshire), the attainment/SES regression slopes decreased between the early and late cohorts by at least .10. In a fourth community, Edinburgh, the slope fell by almost .10, and in a fifth, Blantyre and Hamilton, it remained steady. In Dundee, however, there was a slight increase in SES inequalities in attainment. Amongst the 14 smaller communities, six showed decreases of at least .10 in their attainment/SES slopes between the

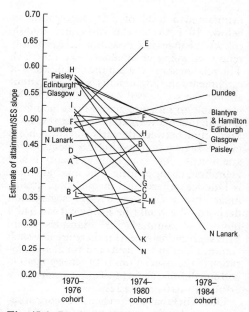

Fig. 45.6. Regression slope of SCE attainment on SES across the three cohorts, by community

Note: See 'Measurements and Main Definitions' for definitions. Estimates for the smaller communities in the late cohort are too unstable to show.

early and middle cohorts; six remained more or less stable; only two increased. A decrease of .10 in the attainment/SES slope indicates that the advantage that a nationally average pupil had over a pupil whose SES score was one standard deviation below the national average (in terms of the middle cohort) decreased by about one O-grade award at A–C. Over the country as a whole, as Table 45.1 has shown, the attainment/SES slope fell by about .10 for males (from around .55 to .46), but by less for females. Finally, it is worth observing that the lowest associations between attainment and SES were generally to be found in the four identified New Towns (K, L, M, N—the steep slope for K in the early cohort may have been caused by the selective arrangements then operative in K. Pupils in the middle cohort in K all entered modal-comprehensive schools).

There are some indications of a positive relationship between the equalisation of school catchments (Figure 45.5) and the equalisation of attainment between pupils of varying SES (Figure 45.6). (We discount here the 10 communities in Figure 45.5 that maintained a level of SES segregation of below .10 between the early and middle cohorts; changes in segregation here probably reflect sampling error alone—see note 21). The relationship between the equalisation of catchments and attainments is most apparent among the six named communities that we were able to measure across three points in time. In four of the six communities there was a reduction between the early and late cohorts in SES segregation and in SES inequality of attainment. One community, Blantyre and Hamilton, changed little. The main anomaly is Dundee, where SES inequality of attainment rose even though SES segregation declined. We would be happier if we had a number of counterfactual examples where SES segregation rose. But there are few such communities in the data, and further exploration of the associations between segregation and equalisation again must await a more powerful analysis (see note 22).

Our belief that comprehensive reorganisation caused an improvement at national level in the attainment of lower SES pupils, relative to higher SES pupils, also derives from the analysis summarised in Figure 45.3. Subject to our reservations over selection bias, the figure shows that reorganisation was associated with steep improvements in attainment among modal-comprehensives (steady comprehensives and upgraded comprehensives) in areas (mostly urban) where selection and creaming were being reduced. The figure does not show that lower SES groups shared disproportionately in this improvement. But the inference is almost irresistible given, first, that such groups were over-represented in urban schools and, second, that there was a decline in SES inequality in attainment in most urban areas. Furthermore, there is evidence from Scotland (McPherson and Willms 1986; Willms 1985, 1986) and elsewhere (e.g., Brookover *et al.* 1978; Shavit and Williams 1985), that the average characteristics of pupils in a school have a 'contextual' effect on individual attainment over and above individual-pupil characteristics: the higher the average SES or ability, the higher the attainment of otherwise comparable pupils. Thus one might expect a fall in segregation to lead to an equalisation of attainment between the social classes. Because the SES of the school population was rising over the period in which SES segregation between

schools was declining, the change in any contextual effect could be expected to be disproportionately beneficial to the attainment of lower SES groups. This accords with the observed trends, but we should add that the contextual effect is not well understood, and may sometimes be confounded with selection effects arising from the underspecification of educational potential at the pupil level (Hauser 1970; Willms 1986).

It is improbable that changes in examining standards or changes in patterns of examination presentations, if either have occurred at all, could adequately account for the variations in attainment summarised in the figures and table. But the effects of three other changes are not so easily discounted. First, ROSLA has almost certainly contributed to improving attainment, and possibly also to the reduction in SES differences in attainment (even though, to repeat, all our cohorts reached 16 years after ROSLA).[23] Second, levels of female attainment were rising before 1970 (Hutchison and McPherson 1976), and would probably have risen more than male levels whether or not schools had been reorganised. Third, declining employment prospects for young people have been associated with increases in voluntary school enrolment and in conformist behaviour, as indicated, for example, by a decline in 'serious' truancy (Raffe 1986). Because the rate of change in labour-market opportunities has itself varied locally, we cannot discount the possibility that it is associated with some of our predictors, including SES and the organisational history of the schools. But we do not think that the changing structure of labour-market opportunities can alone account for the changes we have observed.[24]

Summary and Discussion

SUMMARY

We have assessed the impact of comprehensive reorganisation in Scotland by examining the progress through secondary education of three, highly comparable and nationally representative, cohorts of pupils. The first cohort started in secondary education when twelve out of twenty pupils attended schools with non-selective intakes at 12 years. The last started after the completion of reorganisation in the maintained sector, when nineteen out of twenty attended such schools, the twentieth pupil being educated in a selective school in the private sector. This design enabled us to assess the effects on levels and patterns of attainment of a rapidly changing structure of public and private secondary-school provision. Our conclusions can be summarised in terms of two main trends: equalisation and improvement. By 'equalisation' we mean, not that equality of attainment between the social classes was achieved, but that inequality was reduced. By 'improvement' we mean a rise in average levels of certified school attainment.

Within the maintained sector, the reform eventually removed all selection at 12 years (purpose 1), and established the all-through school in almost all areas where the density of the population permitted (purpose 2). The raising of the school-leaving age (ROSLA) ensured that, for all but a small minority of pupils, the end of compulsory schooling would coincide with, or follow, the first stage of public certification (purpose 3). A selective, private sector of schools survived the reform. Nevertheless, the reform substantially equalised formal provision. It also had an equalising effect on the socioeconomic status (SES) of pupil catchments. The SES segregation between schools was largest in the cities but, in all of them, reorganization reduced it. City schools came to 'represent a fuller cross-section of the community' (purpose 4). Even so, reorganization did not reduce segregation in the cities to the lower levels it took in most burghs, partly because a private and selective sector survived in each of the cities, and partly, one presumes, because school-catchment boundaries in the cities were not redrawn in such a way as to reduce substantially the differentiating effect of residential segregation on catchments. Thus, even after reorganization, there remained considerable between-school variation in pupil SES at national level. This was a function partly of within-community variation in SES between schools, and partly of between-community variation in SES. Nevertheless, SES segregation declined at national level too, and the typical school became a little more representative of the national community. In the New Towns there was virtually no SES segregation.

Reorganization increased access to certification (purpose 6). This was done by providing a structure in which all schools could prepare pupils for public examinations that certified across a wider spectrum of difficulty than hitherto, and by implementing purpose 3 (ROSLA). Overall, there was an improvement in the attainment of the pupil of nationally average SES, but females improved more than males.

Both sexes experienced a trend towards SES equality in the levels of overall attainment (purpose 7), but the trend was stronger for males than for females. We may express its strength in terms of the attainment of a pseudo-pupil whose SES lies one standard deviation below the nationally average SES for the middle cohort, relative to the attainment of a pseudo-pupil with the nationally average SES for the middle cohort. Over the eight years separating the early and late cohorts, the reduction in inequality for males was from about five O-grade awards at A–C to about four. The decline for females was under half this size. Equalisation, however, was not evenly distributed across the attainment range. For both sexes, it resulted from the disproportionate improvement of lower SES pupils in the middle of the attainment range and towards its lower end. The attainment of lower SES pupils also improved at the top end of the attainment range. But, in the case of males, it improved no more than did the attainment of higher SES pupils, whilst for females it improved somewhat less. In other words, among females at the top end of the attainment range there was a slight increase in SES-related inequalities of attainment. This change is obscured by the average measure of attainment (the 'effect size') that we use. Our conclusions on attainment are also a function of our scaling of the attainment variable, but they are not seriously affected by it.

There is a second trend that runs counter to the main theme of equalisation. The mean level of attainment was identical for males and females in the early cohort, but, eight years later, the female of nationally average SES was gaining one O-grade award at A–C more than her male counterpart. The female advantage grew, it should be noted, in a system that was in the process of abandoning most of the little single-sex provision it made, that had no public educational programme of positive discrimination in favour of girls, and that was neglectful of gender equality in matters of curriculum.

We can identify several ways in which comprehensive reorganisation probably made a causal contribution to the trends of equalisation and improvement (there were probably also ways that our design does not identify). First, by abolishing selection at 12 years, reorganisation gave all pupils a formal opportunity of access to certificate courses. Second, ROSLA denied virtually all pupils the right to leave school before the first stage of public certification. Third, the abolition of selection at 12 years, the closure of many short-course schools, and the redefinition of school catchments led to a reduction in between-school segregation in many communities. This reduction, allied to the rise in the SES level of the school population, distributed the benefits of a favourable school context more widely, though it must be added that these benefits are not well understood. Fourth, our evidence allows us to infer that schools learned how to improve. At any one time, the longer that schools had been comprehensive the higher their levels of attainment tended to be.

In sum, since comprehensive reorganization was effected in the early 1970s there has been an equalisation of educational attainment between the social classes. This equalisation is apparent among males and females alike. Improvements in attainment have occurred across the full range of attainment, and for virtually all groups defined by gender and social class. However, the trend towards equality of attainment between the social classes has not fully worked through to the upper levels of attainment and to the later stages of secondary schooling. These are conclusions that we can state with a high degree of confidence. We do not think that comprehensive reorganisation alone caused these changes, but we think it played a part in each of them. No-one can ever be wholly confident in conclusions about causes, and our design is not free of assumptions and biases. Nevertheless, among the various explanations of equalisation and improvement that we have canvassed, comprehensive reorganization remains a highly probable one. We also assert that comprehensive reorganization was a precondition to the translation into educational gains of the potential for educational improvement of other changes, economic, social and educational, that have occurred since the mid-1960s.

SOME IMPLICATIONS

Current discussions of British schooling mostly assume that the comprehensive reforms that originated in the 1960s have failed, and perhaps could only have failed. The Scottish evidence indicates the opposite. It also provides some pointers to the achievement and potential of reorganization elsewhere in Britain. Under the system of universal, selective, secondary schooling introduced in 1945, Scotland's experience of social-class relativities in educational attainment was similar to that in England. Relativities only began to change in Scotland in the mid-1970s when the large majority of pupils were able to start their secondary education in schools that had already been reorganized into non-selective, uncreamed, all-through institutions with an established structure for post-compulsory provision. Arguably, it was only at this point that a comprehensive system of some integrity began to emerge.

The pessimistic interpretation of comprehensive reorganization in England and Wales may therefore be premature. The national research evidence on which the interpretation is based relates to an earlier period when the impact of reform had yet to show, indeed, when the reform itself had yet to be fully implemented. Moreover, in England in particular, reorganization has still not gone as far as it has in Scotland. England has more selection and creaming, proportionately fewer all-through schools, and proportionately fewer communities that are served by wholly comprehensive systems. The Scottish evidence shows that these features influence social-class differences in attainment. But it also shows that the legacy of history is not immutable: the lower the levels of selection, creaming and segregation, the lower tended to be the effect of social class on attainment; the longer established the comprehensive school, the higher tended to be the attainment. We would be surprised if a comparable study in England and Wales did not show comparable relationships.

Some writers have maintained that comprehensive schools have failed because they have not gone far enough in a second, and very different sense. For example Hargreaves (1982) argues that comprehensive schools have merely adopted the curriculum and standards of the grammar school, with two unfortunate consequences: public examinations dominate educational purposes, and many pupils continue to experience school as failure. The Scottish evidence gainsays neither of these consequences. A diluted academicism has been widespread in Scotland (Gray *et al.* 1983: Part 2), and all schools have pupils who feel that they have failed (Gow and McPherson 1980: *passim* especially Table 7).[25] Neither consequence is inconsistent with the equalisation and improvement that we have attributed to comprehensive reorganisation. What our analysis does indicate, however, is that there is a cost to be weighed when making the value judgement that a system of comprehensive schools should abandon the norm-referenced certification of academic subjects. The cost is that such a system can promote equalisation, and has certainly done so in Scotland. Comprehensive schools have probably done so in England too; nobody really knows. But, even if they have not, the Scottish evidence indicates that a comprehensive system probably could.[26]

To assess the significance of the extent of equalisation and improvement in Scotland, one must set the eight years in which these trends occurred against a preceding period of at least five or six decades during which there had operated a pattern of differential social access to selective post-primary schooling. The Scottish system that was finally ousted in the 1970s had been configured well before the First World War, and had changed little by 1965 (Anderson 1983; McPherson and Willms 1986). The secondary schools of the period up to 1945 constituted the greater part of the certificating sector of the system of selective secondary schooling that operated intact from 1945 to 1965. Thereafter, most of the pre-1945 secondary schools became modal-comprehensive schools, supplying about forty per cent of all Scotland's secondary schooling in the late 1970s. But advantage was not eliminated overnight. Attendance at these schools enhanced attainment; employment in these schools boosted teachers' careers and their access to positions of influence in the governance of education (McPherson 1983; McPherson and Raab, forthcoming, ch. 17). The benefits accrued disproportionately to pupils of higher SES because such pupils were over-represented in the schools of older foundation, both nationally and locally (McPherson and Willms 1986). Social-class differences in attainment

were spatially and politically structured, as well as culturally.

Modal-comprehensive schools formed after 1965 from other, less privileged, origins thus laboured under several disadvantages. Many were constructed from former short-course schools that had themselves been founded to serve predominantly working-class communities, often in the peripheral council-housing estates of urban areas. Hence there was a limit to the extent to which even the most ingenious reconstruction of school catchments could raise their average pupil SES, and perhaps thereby capture an improved contextual effect. Furthermore, before 1965 such schools typically had little, if any, experience of presenting pupils for public examinations. When they did acquire full certificating status, many in urban areas found themselves in competition with older-established secondary schools for the scarce resources of influential and experienced teachers, and of community esteem. The evidence indicates that such competition may have steepened social-class inequalities of attainment (*ibid.*). Thereafter, in 1981, competition between local schools was sanctioned by the introduction of a statutory parental right to choose a child's school. This confirmed the spatial patterning of social advantage (Adler, Petch and Tweedie 1987). We believe that these historical processes, with minor transformations, can also be discerned in England and Wales.

Only in later cohorts than those we have studied will one see the full effects of parental choice and of two other recent policies: the Assisted Places Scheme that now sustains the private sector throughout Britain; and the prospective secession of a number of maintained schools in England and Wales (but not Scotland) from local-authority control. Some of the evidence required for an evaluation of these developments will come from Scottish surveys in 1987, 1989 and 1991. We anticipate, however, that the policies will inhibit, or even reverse, the processes of equalisation and improvement. It may even be that a later historical perspective will have to acknowledge the early 1980s as the high point of egalitarian reform, both in Scotland and in England and Wales.

Nevertheless, the fact remains that, in a mere eight years, comprehensive reorganisation in Scotland significantly reduced social-class inequalities of attainment that had been established over at least six decades. Measured against this legacy, the achievements of social-democratic reform were not trivial, even though the falling levels of social-class inequality were still high. What the quasi-experimental design fails above all to capture is the sheer historical accumulation of interest and power that confronted the school reforms of the 1960s and 1970s, and the conflict and confusion that inevitably accompanied a first attempt to change matters.

That such an attempt could make progress against these odds might persuade some people that a renewed effort could achieve more. They could argue the practicality of their case from the fact that the initial attempt at reform eventually began to have the effects that were intended. And, as to the further potential of these effects, they could point towards communities like the New Towns where the levels of social-class inequality in attainment are dramatically lower than the levels that history bequeathed to the cities. In some the case against comprehensive schooling can no longer rest on grounds of practicality or standards, but only on grounds of values and cost.

Notes

1. This is an abridged version of a monograph presented at the Annual Meeting of the American Educational Research Association, Washington, DC, 20–24 April 1987. Pending acceptance of the manuscript by ERIC, copies of the unabridged monograph may be purchased from the CES. The research was supported by the Social Science and Humanities Research Council of Canada, grant 463-86-0017, and by the ESRC, grants C00220003 and C00280004. We are also grateful to the Scottish Education Department for financial and other support it has given to the three surveys analysed here. We thank colleagues at the CES for their extensive support and helpful criticism, and David Raffe for his contribution to the design. Mike Adler and Harvey Goldstein also commented helpfully on an earlier draft, but none of those who helped or financed us are necessarily in agreement with this version.
2. See, for example, CCCS (1981), Cox and Marks (1980), Hargreaves (1982) and Kogan (1983). The main national evaluation of examination outcomes in English schools is Steedman (1980, 1983). See also Aitkin and Longford (1986), Gray *et al.* (1983: ch. 14), Marks, Cox and Pomian-Srzednicki (1983), Marks and Pomian-Srzednicki (1985), Reynolds *et al.* (1987: ch. 2), Steedman, Fogelman and Hutchison (1980), Tibbenham, Essen and Fogelman (1978), and seven articles in *Oxford Review of Education* 1984, vol. 10, by Clifford and Heath; Fogelman; Gray, Jesson and Jones; Goldstein; Heath; Lacey; and Marks and Cox.
3. For reviews see Ball (1984: ch. 1), Stevens (1980: ch. 4) and Wright (1977: Part II).
4. Sources: SED (1966a: 33, Table A), supplemented by SED (1962); SED (1971b: 56, Table 4[4]), supplemented by USOMU (1970); GSS (1976: 14, Table 4[4]), supplemented by USOMU (1976); the 1978 SED School Index computer-listing, supplemented by USOMU (1978); the 1982 SED School Index computer-listing, supplemented by USOMU (1982). Note that Figure 45.1 describes schools, not pupils.
5. National policy sources include SED (1965a, 1966b, 1966c and 1971a). See also Gray *et al.* (1983: ch. 13) and McPherson and Raab (forthcoming: chs. 15 and 16).
6. By contrast, Circular 10/65 for England and Wales (DES 1965) endorsed six models for reorganisation (Benn and Simon 1972: ch. 3).
7. The political decision to reorganise was announced in October 1965. At that time, 93 per cent of all Scottish secondary pupils were educated in schools that were maintained by the education authorities. Four per cent were in grant-aided schools (similar to direct-grant schools in England and Wales), and three per cent were in private schools. Within the maintained sector, 34 per cent of Scottish pupils attended schools that were 'comprehensive' in that they had non-selective intakes to their first year. By 1970 this figure had risen to 63 per cent; and, by 1974, to 98 per cent. Ten years later, in 1984, the private sector, including by this time the majority of the former grant-aided schools, accounted for five per cent of all secondary pupils, the remaining 95 per cent being in the maintained sector. See for 1965, SED (1966a: Table A); for 1966, SED (1967: Table 5); for 1970, SED (1971b: Table 4[4]); for 1974, GSS (1976: Table 4[4]); and, for 1984, tables kindly supplied by the SED to the authors, and for the summary of which the authors alone are responsible.
8. See, for example, SED (1966b: para. 6).
9. Rising unemployment and changes in the occupational structure have affected the labour-market experiences of school leavers and parents CSO (1987), Kendrick (1983, 1986), Raffe (1984, 1987). There have also been changes in the family associated with the changing incidence of single parenthood,

divorce, fertility, and parental participation in the labour market (Kendrick 1983, 1986). Gender differences are changing (Burnhill and McPherson 1984), and the educational level of the adult population is rising. Overall staffing levels have improved since the mid-1970s (SED 1982: para. 2.3), and areal staffing disparities have declined. The upward trends in voluntary enrolments and in presentations for public examinations both began before 1965 (SED 1965*b*: ch. 4; SED 1986). Also, examining standards may have changed. For critiques of the validity of comparisons over time of examining standards, see Goldstein (1983) and Nuttall (1986). Nuttall concludes that 'the measurement of change in the level of performance of educational systems is not possible as there is no way of establishing an unchanging measuring instrument over any length of time' (*ibid.*: 164). This is true, but also unhelpful, because the logic that precludes comparisons over time can be extended to preclude all comparisons.

10. The strategy described in this paragraph does not dispose of the possibility that the validity of SES as a proxy for educational potential may vary by community, or, indeed, by other subgroups (see Gray *et al.* 1983: 263). However, this raises the wider question of the validity of the synchronic and atomistic assumptions of all the social classifications used here (McPherson and Willms 1986). Analyses of a subset of the middle cohort, for which information on one measure of ability was available, found that SES variables by themselves explained about 25 per cent of the variance in attainment, but that SES variables and ability together explained nearly 60 per cent of the variance. The correlation between SES and ability was .4 (Willms 1986). We do not presume that our measure of SES captures all of the educogenic factors affecting attainment, nor does our design require that such an assumption be met.

11. The occupations of fathers of members of the early cohort were classified by OPCS (1970), and those of the middle and late cohorts by OPCS (1980). Using the early cohort data, father's occupation was scaled for each individual using the Hope-Goldthorpe scale (Goldthorpe and Hope 1974). The average Hope-Goldthorpe value was then computed for all pupils within each of the OPCS categories. Those with no occupation or unclassified occupations were assigned a value between the partly-skilled and skilled manual groups. The occupational structure changed between our early and late cohorts, and the proportion of pupils not answering the occupation questions increased. These changes may have affected our measure of SES, but

only slightly because it is a composite (first principal component—see Harman 1976) of three indicators of SES: father's occupation, mother's education, and number of siblings (weights were .778, .728, and—.524 respectively). This composite accounts for 47 per cent of the variance in the set of three variables. See Willms (1986) for further details.

12. Sources for the classification of schools: USOMU (annual) and information from head teachers and local-authority administrators.

13. We abuse this definition when we apply it to the 1984 leavers, because we disregard section 1 of the 1981 Education (Scotland) Act. Because most successful secondary-school placing requests made by parents under the 1981 Act have occurred at the point of entry to secondary school (Adler, Petch and Tweedie 1987: 308), the consequences for our analysis are not serious. There were also some between-catchment movements in some education authorities before 1981.

14. *New modal-comprehensive school.* This describes a new school that, at the time to which the description refers, was building up to modal-comprehensive status in step with the progress of its first entry-cohort of pupils through the year-stages of secondary school; but it had no previous history as a 'short-course school' (section 3.3). *Upgrading modal-comprehensive school.* This is a school that was a short-course school when the cohort in question entered, but that subsequently offered SCE H- and O-grade courses in time for members of the cohort to present for public examination, and that otherwise met the definition of a modal-comprehensive school.

15. This operationalisation has probably failed to identify some non-city, modal-comprehensive schools that were creamed by private-sector city schools.

16. The gaps between attainment levels on the horizontal axes of Figures 2a and 2b are set so that the diagonal (45-degree) line describes the cumulative frequency distribution for all males and females in the middle cohort including those in the 'no occupation/missing data' group. The separate distributions by sex and year do not include pupils in the 'no occupation/missing data' group.

17. The following defines the five subsectors in Figure 45.3 in terms of the types of schools defined in Measures and Main Definitions. Downgraded senior-secondary: EA senior-secondary (in 1970), modal-comprehensive (1974, 1978). Downgraded receiver-comprehensive; receiver-comprehensive (1970), modal-comprehensive (1974, 1978). Upgrading comprehensive:

short-course school (1970), upgrading modal-comprehensive (1974), modal–comprehensive (1978). Steady comprehensive: modal-comprehensive (1970, 1974, 1978). Upgraded comprehensive: new or upgrading modal-comprehensive (1970), modal–comprehensive (1974, 1978). The figure relates only to schools in the four regions. The size of each symbol is proportional to the sample size for each type of school in the middle cohort. In each of the three cohorts, approximately three quarters of all pupils in the four regions are represented in the figure.

18. Some of the estimates of differences between the middle and the late cohorts are not statistically significant at the .05 level. The standard errors of the estimates for the late cohort range across the ten types from 3.1 to 8.2 per cent of a standard deviation; whereas the standard errors for the early and middle cohorts are about half that size.

19. The extent to which SES underspecifies educational potential in any one of the ten school types may itself change between cohorts. Some of the convergence between the attainment levels of otherwise comparable creamed and uncreamed school subsectors may thus be a function of a differential underspecification across cohorts arising mainly from reductions in selection and creaming.

20. The SSLS is conducted under a Code (CES 1979) which does not permit individual schools to be publicly identified, except in groups of five or more.

21. The small increases in communities A and C may reflect nothing more than sampling fluctuations. Willms and Cathy Garner of CES are currently examining alternative indices of between-school segregation and their sampling variability. See also Willms (1986).

22. The standard errors of the estimates of attainment in the 14 small communities range from .051 to .093 of a standard deviation. Also, some of the instability of the estimates may be owing to unmeasured, but locally variable factors. In addressing these and related problems we plan to draw on the work of researchers who have developed multilevel models that can simultaneously estimate the effects of variables at different levels of the schooling hierarchy (e.g., Aitkin and Longford 1986; Goldstein 1986; Mason, Wong and Entwisle 1984; Raudenbush and Bryk 1986).

23. For evidence that compulsory enrolment may enhance subsequent voluntary enrolment, see Burnhill (1984). Other CES evidence, as yet unpublished, shows that such compulsion has boosted individual attainment.

24. The main variation in rates of change in local labour-market opportunities lies between the regions within and outwith the central belt of Scotland. Yet, where we have tested them, the changes in attainment hold within the four regions, all of them in the central belt, as well as for Scotland as a whole. Also, the improvement in the attainment of females and of lower SES groups is apparent in measures based solely on attainment at sixteen years (Willms and Kerr 1987).

25. Unpublished analyses indicate that the proportion of such pupils has fallen since the early cohort.

26. In an article which appeared after our article was originally submitted for publication, Heath (1987) argues that comprehensive reorganisation had no discernible impact on social-class relativities in attainment up to the end of the 1970s. However, applied to our data, Heath's design would pool many of the members of our early and middle cohorts, and would therefore obscure effects that only began to show in the attainment of 16–18 year olds towards the end of the 1970s. More generally, the Scottish evidence cannot be reconciled with Heath's conclusion that 'in the face of this remarkable resilience of class inequalities, educational reforms seem powerless . . .' (*ibid.*: 15).

References

Adler, M. E., Petch, A. J., and Tweedie, J. W. (1987), 'The Origins and Impact of the Parents' Charter', in McCrone, D. (ed.), *The Scottish Government Yearbook 1987* (Edinburgh: University of Edinburgh. Unit for the Study of Government in Scotland).

Aitkin, M. A., and Longford, N. T. (1986), 'Statistical Modelling Issues in School Effectiveness Studies', *Journal of the Royal Statistical Society, Series A*, 149: 1–26.

Anderson, R. D. (1983), *Education and Opportunity in Victorian Scotland* (Oxford: Clarendon Press).

Ball, S. J. (1984), 'Introduction: Comprehensives in Crisis?' in Ball, S. J. (ed.), *Comprehensive Schooling: A Reader* (Lewes: Falmer).

Benn, C., and Simon, B. (1972), *Half Way There* (2nd edn., Harmondsworth: Penguin).

Brookover, W. B., Schweitzer, J., Schneider, M., Beady, C., Flood, P. K., and Wisenbaker, J. M. (1978), 'Elementary School Climate and School Achievement', *American Educational Research Journal*, 15: 301–18.

Burnhill, P. M. (1984), 'The Ragged Edge of Compulsory Schooling', in Raffe, D. (ed.), *Fourteen to Eighteen* (Aberdeen: Aberdeen Univ. Press).

—— and McPherson, A. F. (1984), 'Careers and Gender: The Expectations of Able Scottish School Leavers in 1971 and 1981', in Acker, S.

(ed.), *Is Higher Education Fair to Women?* (London: Society for Research in Higher Education).

——, Raffe, D., and Tomes, N. (1987), 'Constructing a Public Account of an Educational System', in Walford, G. (ed.), *Doing Sociology of Education* (Lewes: Falmer).

Central Statistical Office (CSO) (1987), *Social Trends No. 17—1987 Edition* (ed.) T. Griffin and J. Morris, London: HMSO).

Centre For Contemporary Cultural Studies (CCCS) (1981), *Unpopular Education* (London: Hutchinson).

Centre for Educational Sociology (CES) (1979), 'A Code of Practice for Collaborative Research', *Collaborative Research Newsletter*, 6 (Edinburgh: Univ. of Edinburgh, CES), 84–6.

Cox, C., and Marks, J. (1980), *Real Concern* (London: Centre for Policy Studies).

Department of Education and Science (DES) (1965), 'Organisation of Secondary Education' (London: HMSO, Circular 10/65).

Glass, C. V., McGaw, B., and Smith, M. L. (1981), *Meta-Analysis in Social Research* (Beverley Hills, Calif.: Sage).

Goldstein, H. (1983), 'Measuring Changes in Educational Attainment over Time: Problems and Possibilities', *Journal of Educational Measurement*, 20: 69–77.

—— (1986), 'Multilevel Mixed Linear Model Analysis using Iterative Generalized Least Squares', *Biometrika*, 73: 43–56.

Goldthorpe, J. H., and Hope, K. (1974), *The Social Grading of Occupations* (London: Oxford Univ. Press).

Government Statistical Service (GSS) (1976), *Scottish Educational Statistics 1974* (London: HMSO).

Gow, L., and McPherson, A. F. (1980), *Tell Them From Me* (Aberdeen: Aberdeen Univ. Press).

Gray, J. M., McPherson, A. F., and Raffe, D. (1983), *Reconstructions of Secondary Education* (London: Routledge and Kegan Paul).

Halsey, A. H., Heath, A. F., and Ridge, J. M. (1980), *Origins and Destinations* (Oxford: Clarendon).

Hargreaves, D. H. (1982), *The Challenge for the Comprehensive School* (London: Routledge and Kegan Paul).

Harman, H. H. (1976), *Modern Factor Analysis* (Chicago: Univ. of Chicago Press).

Hauser, R. M. (1970), 'Context and Consex: A Cautionary Tale', *American Journal of Sociology*, 75: 645–54.

Heath, A. (1987), 'Class in the Classroom', *New Society*, 17 July: 13–15.

Highet, J. (1969), *A School of One's Choice* (London: Blackie).

Hutchison, D., and McPherson, A. F. (1976), 'Competing Inequalities: The Sex and Social Class Structure of the First Year Scottish University Student Population', *Sociology*, 10: 111–16.

Kendrick, S. (1983), 'Social Change in Scotland', in Brown, G., and Cook, R. (eds.), *Scotland: The Real Divide* (Edinburgh: Mainstream).

—— (1986), 'Women's Economic Activity in Post-War Scotland: A Comparative Account'. (Edinburgh: Univ. of Edinburgh, Research Centre for the Social Sciences).

Kogan, M. (1983), 'The Case of Education', in Young, K. (ed.), *National Interests and Local Government* (London: Heinemann).

McPherson, A. F. (1983), 'An Angle on the Geist: Persistence and Change in the Scottish Educational Tradition', in Humes, W. M., and Paterson, H. M. (eds.), *Scottish Culture and Scottish Education 1800–1980* (Edinburgh: John Donald).

—— and Raab, C. D. (forthcoming), *Governing Education* (Edinburgh: Edinburgh Univ. Press).

—— and Willms, J. D. (1986), 'Certification, Class Conflict, Religion and Community: A Socio-Historical Explanation of the Effectiveness of Contemporary Schools', in Kerckhoff, A. C. (ed.), *Research in Sociology of Education and Socialization Volume 6* (Greenwich, Conn.: JAI Press).

Marks, J., Cox, C., and Pomian-Srzednicki, M. (1983), *Standards in English Schools* (London: National Council for Educational Standards).

—— and Pomian-Srzednicki, M. (1985), *Standards in English Schools: Second Report* (London: Sherwood Press).

Mason, W. M., Wong, G. Y., and Entwisle, B. (1984), 'Contextual Analysis Through the Multilevel Linear Model', in Leinhardt, S. (ed.), *Sociological Methodology 1983–1984* (San Francisco, Calif.: Jossey-Bass).

Nuttall, D. (1986), 'Problems in the Measurement of Change', in Nuttall, D. (ed.), *Assessing Educational Achievement* (Lewes: Falmer Press).

Office of Population Censuses and Surveys (OPCS) (1970), *Classification of Occupations 1970* (London: HMSO).

OPCS (1980), *Classification of Occupations 1980* (London: HMSO).

Raffe, D. (1984), 'The Transition from School to Work and the Recession: Evidence from the Scottish School Leavers Surveys 1977–1983', *British Journal of Sociology of Education*, 5: 247–65.

—— (1986), 'Unemployment and School Motivation: The Case of Truancy', *Educational Review*, 38: 11–19.

—— (1987), 'Youth Unemployment in the UK 1979–1984', Paper prepared for the International Youth Labour Office, Geneva, forthcoming in Brown, P., and Ashton, D. (eds.), *Education and Economic Life* (Lewes: Falmer Press).

Raudenbush, S. W., and Bryk, A. S. (1986), 'A

Hierarchical Model for Studying School Effects', *Sociology of Education*, 59/1: 1–7.

Registrar General, Scotland (RGS) (1967), *Annual Estimates of the Population of Scotland* (Edinburgh: HMSO).

Reynolds, D., Sullivan, M., and Murgatroyd, S. (1987), *The Comprehensive Experiment* (Lewes: Falmer Press).

Scottish Education Department (SED) (1962), 'List of Presenting Centres for the Scottish Leaving Certificate Examination' (Edinburgh: SED, unpublished mimeograph).

—— (1965*a*), 'Reorganisation of Secondary Education on Comprehensive Lines' (Edinburgh: HMSO (Circular 600)).

—— (1965*b*), *Education in Scotland in 1964* (Edinburgh: HMSO, Cmnd 2600).

—— (1966*a*), *Education in Scotland in 1965* (Edinburgh: HMSO, Cmnd 2914).

—— (1966*b*), *Raising the School Leaving Age: Suggestions for Courses* (Edinburgh: HMSO).

—— (1966*c*), 'Transfer of Pupils from Primary to Secondary Education' (Edinburgh: HMSO (Circular 614)).

—— (1967), *Scottish Educational Statistics 1966* (Edinburgh: HMSO).

—— (1971*a*), 'Raising the School Leaving Age' (Edinburgh: SED (Circular 813)).

—— (1971*b*), *Scottish Educational Statistics 1970* (Edinburgh: HMSO).

—— (1982), *Statistical Bulletin 3/A3/1982* (Edinburgh: SED).

—— (1986), *Statistical Bulletin 10/E2/1986* (Edinburgh: SED).

Shavit, Y., and Williams, R. A. (1985), 'Ability Grouping and Contextual Determinants of Educational Expectations in Israel', *American Sociological Review*, 50: 62–73.

Steedman, J. (1980), *Progress in Secondary Schools* (London: National Children's Bureau).

—— (1983), *Examination Results in Selective and Non-selective Schools* (London: National Children's Bureau).

——, Fogelman, K., and Hutchison, D. (1980), *Real Research* (London: National Children's Bureau).

Stevens, A. (1980), *Clever Children in Comprehensive Schools* (Harmondsworth: Penguin).

Tibbenham, A., Essen, J., and Fogelman, K. (1978), 'Ability Grouping and School Characteristics', *British Journal of Educational Studies*, 26: 8–23.

Universities of Scotland Organisation and Methods Unit (USOMU) (1970 and annually), *List of Presenting Centres for the Scottish Certificate of Education Examinations* (Edinburgh: Univ. of Edinburgh, USOMU).

Willms, J. D. (1985), 'The Balance Thesis: Contextual Effects of Ability on Pupils' O-grade Examination Results', *Oxford Review of Education*, 11: 33–41.

—— (1986), 'Social Class Segregation and its Relationship to Pupils' Examination Results in Scotland', *American Sociological Review*, 51: 224–41.

—— and Kerr, P. (1987), 'Changes in Sex Differences in Scottish Examination Results since 1975' (Edinburgh: Univ. of Edinburgh, CES) (published in *Journal of Early Adolescence*, June 1987, with an authors' correction in a subsequent issue).

Wright, N. (1977), *Progress in Education* (London: Croom Helm).

46

Social-Class Differences in Family–School Relationships: The Importance of Cultural Capital

Annette Lareau

The influence of family background on children's educational experiences has a curious place within the field of sociology of education. On the one hand, the issue has dominated the field. Wielding increasingly sophisticated methodological tools, social scientists have worked to document, elaborate, and replicate the influence of family background on educational life chances (Jencks *et al.* 1972; Marjoribanks 1979). On the other hand, until recently, research on this issue focused primarily on educational *outcomes*: very little attention was given to the *processes* through which these educational patterns are created and reproduced.

Over the past fifteen years, important strides have been made in our understanding of social processes inside the school. Ethnographic research has shown that classroom learning is reflexive and interactive and that language in the classroom draws unevenly from the sociolinguistic experiences of children at home (Bernstein 1975, 1982; Cook-Gumperez 1973; Heath 1982, 1983; Labov 1972; Diaz, Moll, and Mehan 1986; Mehan and Griffin 1980). Studies of the curriculum, the hidden curriculum, the social organization of the classroom, and the authority relationships between teachers and students have also suggested ways in which school processes contribute to social reproduction (Aggleton and Whitty 1985; Anyon 1981; Apple 1979; Erickson and Mohatt 1982; Gearing and Epstein 1982; Gaskell 1985; Taylor 1984; Valli 1985; Wilcox 1977, 1982).

Surprisingly, relatively little of this research has focused on parental involvement in schooling. Yet, quantitative studies suggest that parental behavior can be a crucial determinant of educational performance (Epstein 1984; Marjoribanks 1979). In addition, increasing parental participation in education has become a priority for educators, who believe it promotes educational achievement (Berger 1983; Seeley 1984; National Education Association 1985; Robinson 1985; Trelease 1982; Leichter 1979).

Those studies that have examined parental involvement in education generally take one of three major conceptual approaches to understanding variations in levels of parental participation. Some researchers subscribe to the culture-of-poverty thesis, which states that lower-class culture has distinct values and forms of social organization. Although their interpretations vary, most of these researchers suggest that lower-class and working-class families do not value education as highly as middle-class families (Deutsch 1967). Other analysts trace unequal levels of parental involvement in schooling back to the educational institutions themselves. Some accuse schools of institutional discrimination, claiming that they make middle-class families feel more welcome than working-class and lower-class families (Lightfoot 1978; Ogbu 1974). In an Australian study of home–school relationships, for example, Connell *et al.* (1982) argue that working-class parents are 'frozen out' of schools. Others maintain that

From *Sociology of Education*, 60 (1987), 73–85. Reprinted with permission.

institutional differentiation, particularly the role of teacher leadership, is a critical determinant of parental involvement in schooling (Epstein and Becker 1982; Becker and Epstein 1982).

A third perspective for understanding varying levels of parental involvement in schooling draws on the work of Bourdieu and the concept of cultural capital. Bourdieu (1977a, 1977b; Bourdieu and Passeron 1977) argues that schools draw unevenly on the social and cultural resources of members of the society. For example, schools utilize particular linguistic structures, authority patterns, and types of curricula; children from higher social locations enter schools already familiar with these social arrangements. Bourdieu maintains that the cultural experiences in the home facilitate children's adjustment to school and academic achievement, thereby transforming cultural resources into what he calls cultural capital (Bourdieu 1977a, 1977b).

This perspective points to the structure of schooling and to family life and the dispositions of individuals (what Bourdieu calls habitus [1977b, 1981]) to understand different levels of parental participation in schooling. The standards of schools are not neutral; their requests for parental involvement may be laden with the social and cultural experiences of intellectual and economic élites. Bourdieu does not examine the question of parental participation in schooling, but his analysis points to the importance of class and class cultures in facilitating or impeding children's (or parents') negotiation of the process of schooling (also see Baker and Stevenson 1986; Connell *et al.* 1982; Joffee 1977; Ogbu 1974; Rist 1978; McPherson 1972; Gracey 1972; Wilcox 1977, 1982).

In this paper I argue that class-related cultural factors shape parents' compliance with teachers' requests for parental participation in schooling. I pose two major questions. First, what do schools ask of parents in the educational experience of young children? Are there important variations in teachers' expectations of parental involvement in elementary schooling? Second, how do parents respond to schools' requests? In particular, how does social class influence the process through which parents participate in their children's schooling? The analysis and conclusions are based on an intensive study of home-school relationships of children in the first and second grades of a white working-class school and an upper-middle-class school.

I begin the discussion with a very brief review of historical variations in home-school relationships. Then, I describe the research sites and methodology. In the third section, I examine teachers' views of family involvement in schooling. This is followed by a description of family-school interactions in the working-class and middle-class communities. Finally, I analyze the factors contributing to social class variations in home-school relationships and review the implications for future research.

Historical Variations in Family–School Relationships

Families and schools are dynamic institutions; both have changed markedly in the last two centuries. Not surprisingly, family-school interactions have shifted as well. Over time, there has been a steady increase in the level of parental involvement in schooling. At least three major stages of family-school interaction can be identified. In the first period, parents in rural areas provided food and shelter for the teacher. Children's education and family life were intertwined, although parents evidently were not involved in the formal aspects of their children's cognitive development (Overstreet and Overstreet 1949). In the second period, marked by the rise of mass schooling, parents provided political and economic support for the selection and maintenance of school sites. Parents were involved in school activities and classroom activities, but again, they were not fundamentally involved in their children's cognitive development (Butterworth 1928; Hymes 1953; National Congress of Parents and Teachers 1944). In the third and current period, parents have increased their efforts to reinforce the curriculum and promote cognitive development at home. In addition, parents have played a growing role in monitoring their children's educational development, particularly in special education programs, and have moved into the classroom as volunteers (Berger 1983; Levy, Meltsner, and Wildavsky 1974; Mehan, Hertweck, and Meihls 1986).

These changes in family-school interactions do not represent a linear progression.

Nor is there only one form of relationship at any given time. Many factors—e.g., parents' educational attainment, the amount of non-work time parents can invest in their children's schooling—affect the kind and degree of parental involvement. Family-school relationships are socially constructed and are historically variable. Home-school partnerships, in which parents are involved in the cognitive development of their children, currently seem to be the dominant model, but there are many possible types of family-school relationships (Baker and Stevenson 1986). As in other social relationships, family-school interactions carry the imprint of the larger social context: Acceptance of a particular type of family-school relationship emerges as the result of social processes.

These aspects of family-school relationships are routinely neglected in social scientists' discussions of parental involvement (Epstein 1983, 1984; Seeley 1984). When home-school relationships are evaluated exclusively in terms of parental behavior, critical questions are neither asked nor answered. The standards of the schools must be viewed as problematic, and further, the researcher must ask what kinds of social resources are useful in complying with these standards.

Research Methodology

The research presented here involved participant-observation of two first-grade classrooms located in two different communities. Also, in-depth interviews of parents, teachers, and principals were conducted while the children were in first and second grade. Following other studies of social class differences in family life (Rubin 1976; Kohn 1977), I chose a white working-class community and a professional middle-class community. I sought a working-class community in which a majority of the parents were high school graduates or dropouts, employed in skilled or semiskilled occupations, paid an hourly wage, and periodically unemployed. For the professional middle-class school, I sought a community in which a majority of the parents were college graduates and professionals who had strong career opportunities and who were less vulnerable to changes in the economy. The two communities described here met these criteria.

Colton School (fictitious name) is located in a working-class community. Most of the parents of Colton students are employed in semiskilled or unskilled occupations (see Table 46.1). School personnel report that most of the parents have a high school education; many are high school dropouts. The school has about 450 students in kindergarten, first grade, and second grade. Slightly over one half of the children are white, one third are Hispanic, and the remainder are black or Asian, especially recent Vietnamese immigrants. About one half of the children qualify for free lunches under federal guidelines.

Prescott School (fictitious name) is in an upper-middle-class suburban community about 30 minutes from Colton. Most of the parents of Prescott students are professionals (Table 46.1). Both parents in the family are likely to be college graduates, and many of the children's fathers have advanced degrees. The school enrolls about 300 students from kindergarten to fifth grade. Virtually all the students are white, and the school does not offer a lunch program, although the Parents' Club sponsors a Hot Dog Day once a month.

Table 46.1. Percentage of parents in each occupational category, by school

Occupation	Colton	Prescott
Professionals, executives, managers	1	60
Semiprofessionals, sales, clerical workers, and technicians	11	30
Skilled and semiskilled workers	51	9
Unskilled workers (and welfare recipients)	23	1
Unknown	20	—

Note: The figures for Prescott school are based on the principal's estimation of the school population.
Source: California Department of Education 1983.

For a six-month period, January to June 1982, I visited one first-grade classroom at each school. My visits averaged once or twice a week per school and lasted around two hours. During this time, I observed the classroom and acted as a volunteer in the class, passing out paper and helping the children with math and spelling problems.

At the end of the school year, I selected six children in each class for further study. The children were selected on the basis of reading-group membership; a boy and a girl were selected from the high, medium, and low reading groups. To prevent the confounding effects of race, I chose only white children. I interviewed one single mother in each school; the remaining households had two parents. In both of the schools, three of the mothers worked full time or part time, and three were at home full time. All of the Colton mothers, however, had worked in recent years, when their children were younger. The Prescott mothers had worked prior to the birth of their children but had not been in the labor force since that time.

When the children finished first grade, I interviewed their mothers individually. When they finished second grade, I interviewed their mothers for a second time, and in separate sessions, I interviewed most of their fathers. I also interviewed the first- and second-grade teachers, the school principals, and a resource specialist at one of the schools. All the interviews were semistructured and lasted about two hours. The interviews were tape recorded, and all participants were promised confidentiality.

Teachers' Requests for Parental Involvement

The research examined the formal requests from the teachers and school administrators asking parents to participate in schooling, particularly surrounding the issue of achievement. It also studied the quality of interaction between teachers and parents on the school site. Although there were some variations among the teachers in their utilization of parents in the classrooms, all promoted parental involvement and all believed there was a strong relationship between parental involvement (particularly reading to children) and academic performance. At both schools, the definition of the ideal family–school relationship was the same: a partnership in which family life and school life are integrated.

In the course of the school year, teachers in both schools actively promoted parental involvement in schooling in several ways. For example, newsletters were used to notify families of school events and to invite them to attend. Teachers also reminded children verbally about school events to which parents had been invited and encouraged the children to bring their parents to classroom and school-wide events.

In their interactions with parents, educators urged parents to read to their children. The principal at Prescott school, for example, told the parents at Back to School Night that they should consider reading the child's homework. In every class at Colton school, there was a Read at Home Program, in which the teacher kept track of the number of hours a child read to an adult at home or was read to by a sibling or adult. A chart posted in the classroom marked hours of reading in 15-minute intervals. A child could choose a free book after eight hours of reading at home. This emphasis on reading also surfaced in the routine interactions between parents and teachers and between teachers and children. In the classroom, the teachers suggested that children check out library books, read to their parents, or have their parents read to them at home. At parent-teacher conferences, teachers suggested that parents read to their child at home. In one 20-minute parent-teacher conference, for example, the teacher mentioned five times the importance of reading to the child at home.

Other requests of parents were made as well. Teachers encouraged parents to communicate any concerns they had about their child. In their meetings with parents, teachers also expressed a desire for parents to review and reinforce the material learned in class (e.g., to help their children learn their spelling words). Generally, teachers at both schools believed that the relationship between parental involvement and academic performance was important, and they used a variety of approaches to encourage parents to participate in education.

Teachers and administrators spoke of being 'partners' with parents, and they stressed the need to maintain good communication, but it was clear that they desired parents to defer to their professional expertise. For example, a first-grade teacher at Prescott did not believe in assigning homework to the children and did not appreciate parents communicating their displeasure with the policy by complaining repeatedly to the principal. Nor did principals welcome parents' opinions that a teacher was a bad teacher and should be fired. Teachers wanted parents to support them, or as they put it, to 'back them up.'

Although generally persuaded that parental involvement was positive for educational growth, some teachers, particularly in the upper-middle-class school, were ambivalent about some types of parental involvement in schooling. The Prescott teachers were very concerned that some parents placed too much pressure on their children. Parental involvement could become counterproductive when it increased the child's anxiety level and produced negative learning experiences. As one Prescott teacher put it,

It depends on the parent. Sometimes it can be helpful, sometimes it creates too much pressure. Sometimes they learn things wrong. It is better for them to leave the basics alone . . . and take them to museums, do science, and other enrichment activities.

As Becker and Epstein (1982) have found, there was some variation among the teachers in the degree to which they took leadership roles in promoting parental involvement in schooling, particularly in the area of classroom volunteers. Although all the teachers in the study requested parents to volunteer and had parents in the classroom, there were other teachers in the school who used parents more extensively. Teachers also varied in how they judged parents. While the extreme cases were clear, the teachers sometimes disagreed about how supportive parents were or about how much pressure they were putting on their children. For example, the first-grade teacher at Prescott thought one boy's father placed too much pressure on him, but the second-grade teacher judged the family to be supportive and helpful. Thus, there were variations in teachers' styles as well as in the way they implemented the model of home-school partnerships.

This study does not, however, support the thesis that the different levels of parental involvement can be traced to institutional differentiation or institutional discrimination, i.e., to teachers' pursuit of different kinds of relationships with working-class and middle-class families (Connell et al. 1982; Epstein and Becker 1982). All of the first- and second-grade teachers in the study made similar requests to parents. In both schools, teachers made clear and repeated efforts to promote parental involvement in the educational process.

EDUCATIONAL CONSEQUENCES OF FAMILY–SCHOOL RELATIONSHIPS

Parents who agreed with the administrators'

and teachers' definition of partnership appeared to offer an educational advantage to their children; parents who turned over the responsibility of education to the professional could negatively affect their child's schooling.

Teachers' methods of presenting, teaching, and assessing subject matter were based on a structure that presumed parents would help children at home. At Colton, for example, spelling words were given out on Monday and students were repeatedly encouraged to practice the words at home with their parents before the test on Friday. Teachers noticed which children had practiced at home and which children had not and believed it influenced their performance.

This help at home was particularly important for low achievers. At Prescott, teachers encouraged parents of low achievers to work with them at home. In one case, a girl missed her spelling lessons because she had to meet with the reading resource teacher. Rather than fall behind in spelling, she and her mother did her spelling at home through most of the year. Colton teachers also tried to involve parents in the education of low achievers. One Colton teacher arranged a special conference at a student's home and requested that the parents urge the student to practice reading at home. The teacher complained that the girl didn't 'get that much help at home.' The teacher believed that if the parents had taken an active role in schooling, the child would have been promoted rather than retained.

In other instances, the initiative to help children at home came from parents. For example, at Prescott, one mother noticed while volunteering in the classroom that her son was somewhat behind in his spelling. At her request, she and her son worked on his spelling every day after school for about a month, until he had advanced to the lesson that most of the class was on. Prior to the mother's actions, the boy was in the bottom third of the class in spelling. He was not, however, failing spelling, and it was unlikely that the teacher would have requested the parent to take an active role. After the mother and son worked at home, he was in the top third of the class in his spelling work. The teacher was very impressed by these efforts and believed that the mother's active involvement in schooling had a positive effect on her son's performance:

She is very supportive, very committed. If she didn't work in the class [volunteering] her boys wouldn't do too well. They are not brilliant at all. But they are going to do well. She is just going to see that they are going to get a good foundation. A child like that would flounder if you let him.

Not all parental involvement in schooling was so positive, however. There is a dark side to the partnership, which is not usually addressed in the literature aimed at increasing parental participation in education (Epstein and Becker 1982; Seeley 1984). Particularly in the upper-middle-class school, teachers complained of the pressure parents placed on teachers and children for academic performance. One mother reported that her son had been stealing small objects early in first grade, a pattern the pediatrician and the mother attributed to the boy's 'frustration level' in schooling. A girl in the lowest reading group began developing stomach aches during the reading period in first grade. Teachers at Prescott mentioned numerous cases in which parental involvement was unhelpful. In these cases, parents had usually challenged the professional expertise of the teachers.

Generally, however, the teachers believed that the relationship between parental participation and school performance was positive. These results provide indications that teachers take *parental performance* in schooling very seriously. Teachers recall which parents participate and which parents fail to participate in schooling. They believe that their requests of parents are reasonable and that all parents, regardless of social position, can help their children in first and second grade.

Parents' Involvement in Schooling

Although teachers at both schools expressed a desire for parental participation in schooling, the amount of contact varied significantly between the sites. The response of parents to teachers' requests was much higher at the upper-middle-class school than at the working-class school.

ATTENDANCE AT SCHOOL EVENTS
As Table 46.2 shows, the level of attendance at formal school events was significantly higher at Prescott than at Colton. Virtually all Prescott parents attended the parent-teacher con-

ferences in the fall and spring, but only 60 per cent of Colton parents attended. Attendance at Open House was almost three times higher at Prescott than at Colton.

The difference between the two schools was apparent not only in the quantity of interaction but in the quality of interaction. Although teachers at both schools asked parents to communicate any concerns they had about their children, Colton parents rarely initiated contact with teachers. When Colton parents did contact the school, they frequently raised nonacademic issues, such as lunchboxes, bus schedules, and playground activities. One of the biggest complaints, for example, was that children had only 15 minutes to eat lunch and that slower eaters were often unable to finish.

Table 46.2. Percentage of parents participating in school activities, by school, first grade only, 1981–82

Activity	Colton (n=34)	Prescott (n=28)
Parent-teacher conferences	60	100
Open house	35	96
Volunteering in classroom	3	43

At Colton, the interactions between parents and teachers were stiff and awkward. The parents often showed signs of discomfort: nervous shifting, blushing, stuttering, sweating, and generally looking ill at ease. During the Open House, parents wandered around the room looking at the children's pictures. Many of the parents did not speak with the teacher during their visit. When they did, the interaction tended to be short, rather formal, and serious. The teacher asked the parents if they had seen all of their children's work, and she checked to see that all of the children had shown their desk and folder of papers to their parents. The classrooms at Colton often contained only about 10 adults at a time, and the rooms were noticeably quiet.

At Prescott, the interactions between parents and teachers were more frequent, more centered around academic matters, and much less formal. Parents often wrote notes to the teacher, telephoned the teacher at school, or dropped by during the day to discuss a problem. These interactions often centered around the child's academic progress; many

Prescott parents monitored their children's education and requested additional resources for them if there were problems. Parents, for example, asked that children be signed up to see the reading resource teacher, be tested by the school psychologist, or be enrolled in the gifted program. Parents also asked for homework for their children or for materials that they could complete at home with their children.

The ease with which Prescott parents contacted the school was also apparent at formal school events. At the Open House, almost all of the parents talked to the teacher or to the teacher's aide; these conversations were often long and were punctuated by jokes and questions. Also, many of the parents were friends with other parents in the class, so there was quite a bit of interaction between families. In inviting me to the Open House, the teacher described the event as a 'cocktail party without cocktails.' The room did indeed have the noisy, crowded, and animated atmosphere of a cocktail party.

In sum, Colton parents were reluctant to contact the school, tended to intervene over nonacademic matters, and were uncomfortable in their interactions in the school. In contrast, although Prescott parents varied in the level of supervision and scrutiny they gave their child's schooling, they frequently contacted teachers to discuss their child's academic progress.

Parents' attendance at school activities and their contact with teachers enabled the teachers to directly assess parents' compliance with requests for involvement. However, Prescott teachers had difficulty estimating the number of children whose parents read to them at home regularly. The teachers believed that a majority of children were read to several times per week and that many children spent time reading to themselves. Among the six families interviewed, all of the parents said that they read to their children almost every day, usually before bedtime. Colton teachers used the Read at Home Program to evaluate the amount of reading that took place at home. During the participant-observation period, only three or four children in the class of 34 brought back slips every day or every few days demonstrating that they had read at home for at least 15 minutes. Some children checked out books and brought back slips less frequently. The majority of the class earned only

two books in the program, indicating that they had read at home an average of 16 hours during the 180 days of school, or between two and four minutes a day.

The Read at Home Program was actively promoted by Colton teachers. Children were brought to the front of the class for applause every time they earned a book, and the teachers encouraged children to check out books and read at home. Nevertheless, in the interviews, only half of the parents said that they read to their children every day; the remainder read to their children much more irregularly. Colton parents clearly did not read to their children as often as the upper-middle-class parents at Prescott.

In addition, Prescott parents played a more active role in reinforcing and monitoring the school work of their children. Colton parents were asked by teachers to help review and reinforce the material at school, particularly spelling words. Though a few parents worked with their children, Colton teachers were disappointed in the response. Colton parents were also unfamiliar with the school's curriculum and with the specific educational problems of their children. Parents of children with learning disabilities, for example, knew only that their children's grades 'weren't up to par' or that their children 'didn't do too well' in school. Moreover these parents were unaware of the teacher's specific efforts to improve their child's performance.

Prescott parents, on the other hand, carefully followed their children's curriculum. They often showed children the practical applications of the knowledge they gained at school, made up games that strengthened and elaborated children's recently acquired knowledge, and reviewed the material presented in class with their children. Parents of low achievers and children with learning problems were particularly vigorous in these efforts and made daily efforts to work with children at home. Parents knew their child's specific problems and knew what the teacher was doing to strengthen their child's performance. Parents' efforts on behalf of their children were closely coordinated with the school program.

There were some variations in parents' response to teachers' requests in the two school communities. Notably, two of the Colton parents (who appeared to be upwardly mobile) actively read to their children at home, closely reviewed their children's school work, and emphasized the importance of educational success. The teachers were very impressed by the behavior of these parents and by the relatively high academic performance of their children. At Prescott, parents differed in how critically they assessed the school and in their propensity to intervene in their children's schooling. For example, some parents said that they 'felt sorry for teachers' and believed that other parents in the community were too demanding. The child's number of siblings, birth order, and temperament also shaped parental intervention in schooling. There was some variation in the role of fathers, although in both schools, mothers had the primary responsibility for schooling.

There were important differences, then, in the way in which Colton and Prescott parents responded to teachers' requests for participation. These patterns suggest that the relationship between families and schools was *independent* in the working–class school, and *interdependent* in the middle–class school.

Factors Structuring Parents' Participation

Interviews and observations of parents suggested that a variety of factors influenced parents' participation in schooling. Parents' educational capabilities, their view of the appropriate division of labor between teachers and parents, the information they had about their children's schooling, and the time, money, and other material resources available in the home all mediated parents' involvement in schooling.

EDUCATIONAL CAPABILITIES

Parents at Colton and Prescott had different levels of educational attainment. Most Colton parents were high school graduates or high school dropouts. Most were married and had their first child shortly after high school. They generally had difficulties in school as children; several of the fathers, for example, had been held back in elementary school. In interviews, they expressed doubts about their educational capabilities and indicated that they depended on the teacher to educate their children. As one mother stated,

I know that when she gets into the higher grades, I know I won't be able to help her, math especially, unless I take a refresher course myself. . . . So I feel that it is the teacher's job to help her as much as possible to understand it, because I know that I won't be able to.

Another mother, commenting on her overall lack of educational skills, remarked that reading preschool books to her young son had improved her reading skills:

I graduated from high school and could fill out [job] applications, but when I was nineteen and married my husband, I didn't know how to look up a word in the dictionary. When I started reading to Johnny, I found that *my* reading improved.

Observations of Colton parents at the school site and in interviews confirmed that parents' educational skills were often wanting. Prescott parents' educational skills, on the other hand, were strong. Most were college graduates and many had advanced degrees.

Parents in the two communities also divided up the responsibility between home and school in different ways. Colton parents regarded teachers as 'educated people.' They turned over the responsibility for education to the teacher, whom they viewed as a professional. As one mother put it,

My job is here at home. My job is to raise him, to teach him manners, get him dressed and get him to school, to make sure that he is happy. Now her [the teacher's] part, the school's part, is to teach him to learn. Hopefully, someday he'll be able to use all of that. That is what I think is their part, to teach him to read, the writing, any kind of schooling.

Education is seen as a discrete process that takes place on the school grounds, under the direction of a teacher. This mother's role is to get her son to school; once there, his teacher will 'teach him to learn.'

This mother was aware that her son's teacher wanted him to practice reading at home, but neither she nor her husband read to their son regularly. The mother's view of reading was analogous to her view of work. She sent her children to school to learn for six hours a day and expected that they could leave their schooling (i.e., their work) behind them at the school site, unless they had been given homework. She believed that her seven-year-old boy's afternoons and evenings were time for him to play. In this context, her son's reading at home was similar to riding his bike or to playing with his truck. The mother did not believe that her child's academic progress depended upon his activities at home. Instead, she saw a separation of spheres.

Other parents had a different conception of their role in schooling. They believed education was a shared responsibility: They were *partners* with teachers in promoting their children's academic progress. As one mother stated,

> I see the school as being a very strong instructional force, more so than we are here at home. I guess that I am comfortable with that, from what I have seen. It is a three-to-one ratio or something, where out of a possible four, he is getting three quarters of what he needs from the school, and then a quarter of it from here. Maybe it would be better if our influence was stronger, but I am afraid that in this day and age it is not possible to do any more than that even if you wanted to.

Prescott parents wanted to be involved in their child's educational process in an important way. In dividing up the responsibility for education, they described the relationship between parents and teachers as a relationship between equals, and they believed that they possessed similar or superior educational skills and prestige. One Prescott father discussed his relationship with teachers in this way:

> I don't think of teachers as more educated than me or in a higher position than me. I don't have any sense of hierarchy. I am not higher than them, and they are not higher than me. We are equals. We are reciprocals. So if I have a problem I will talk to them. I have a sense of decorum. I wouldn't go busting into a classroom and say something. . . . They are not working for me, but they also aren't doing something I couldn't do. It is more a question of a division of labor.

Prescott parents had not only better educational skills and higher occupational status than Colton parents but also more disposable income and more flexible work schedules. These material resources entered into the family-school relationships. Some Colton mothers, for example, had to make a series of complicated arrangements for transportation and child care to attend a school event held in the middle of the afternoon. Prescott parents, on the other hand, had two cars and sufficient resources to hire babysitters and housecleaners. In addition, Prescott parents generally had much greater flexibility in their work schedules than Colton parents. Material resources also influenced the educational pur-

chases parents made. Colton parents reported that most of the books they bought for their children came from the flea market. Prescott parents had the financial flexibility to purchase new books if they desired, and many of the parents of low achievers hired tutors for their children during the summer months.

INFORMATION ABOUT SCHOOLING

Colton parents had only limited information about most aspects of their children's experience at school: what they did know, they learned primarily from their children. For example, the Colton mothers knew the names of the child's teacher and the teacher's aide, the location of the classroom on the school grounds, and the name of the janitor, and they were familiar with the Read at Home Program. They did not know details of the school or of classroom interaction. The amount of information Colton parents had did not seem to vary by how much contact they had with the school.

In the middle-class community, parents had extensive information about classroom and school life. For example, in addition to knowing the names of their child's current classroom teacher and teacher's aide, the mothers knew the names and academic reputations of most of the other teachers in the school. The mothers also knew the academic rankings of children in the class (e.g., the best boy and girl in math, the best boy and girl in reading). Most of the mothers knew the composition of their child's reading group, the math and spelling packet the child was working on, and the specific academic problems to which the child was being exposed (e.g., adding single-digit numbers). Other details of classroom experience were also widely known, including the names of children receiving the services of the reading resource specialist, occupational therapist, and special education teacher. Although a few fathers had very specific information about the school, most depended on their wives to collect and store this information. The fathers were, however, generally apprised of the reputations of teachers and the dissatisfactions that some parents had with particular teachers.

Much of the observed difference between the schools in parents' information about schooling may be traced to differences in family life, particularly in social networks and childrearing patterns. Prescott families saw relatively little of their relatives; instead, many parents socialized with other parents in the school community. Colton parents generally had very close ties with relatives in the area, seeing siblings or parents three times per week or more. Colton parents had virtually no social contact with other parents in the school, even when the families lived on the same street. The social networks of the middle-class parents provided them with additional sources of information about their child's school experience; the networks of working-class parents did not (see Bott 1971; Litwack and Szeleny 1971).

The childrearing patterns of the two groups also differed, particularly in the leisure time activities they encouraged. At Colton, children's after-school activities were informal: bike riding, snake hunting, watching television, playing with neighbor children, and helping parents with younger siblings. Prescott children were enrolled in formal socialization activities, including swimming lessons, soccer, art and crafts lessons, karate lessons, and gymnastics. All the children in the classroom were enrolled in at least one after-school activity, and many were busy every afternoon with a lesson or structured experience. The parents took their children to and from these activities. Many stayed to watch the lesson, thus providing another opportunity to meet and interact with other Prescott parents. Discussions about schools, teachers' reputations, and academic progress were frequent. For many parents, these interactions were a major source of information about their children's schooling, and parents believed that the discussions had an important effect on the way in which they approached their children's schooling.

Discussion

Teachers in both schools interpreted parental involvement as a reflection of the value parents placed on their children's educational success (see Deutsch 1967; Strodbeck 1958). As the principal at Prescott commented,

This particular community is one with a very strong interest in its schools. It is a wonderful situation in which to work. Education is very important to the parents and they back that up with an interest in volunteering. This view that education is important helps kids as well. If parents value schooling and think it is important, then kids take it seriously.

The teachers and the principal at Colton placed a similar interpretation on the lack of parental participation at the school. Speaking of the parents, the principal remarked,

They don't value education because they don't have much of one themselves. [Since] they don't value education as much as they could, they don't put those values and expectations on their kids.

Interviews and observations of parents told a different story, however. Parents in both communities valued educational success; all wanted their children to do well in school, and all saw themselves as supporting and helping their children achieve success at school. Middle- and working-class parents' aspirations differed only in the level of achievement they hoped their children would attain. Several Colton parents were high school dropouts and bitterly regretted their failure to get a diploma. As one mother said, 'I desperately want her to graduate. If she can do that, that will satisfy me.' All of the Prescott parents hoped that their children would get a college diploma, and many spoke of the importance of an advanced degree.

Although the educational values of the two groups of parents did not differ, the ways in which they promoted educational success did. In the working-class community, parents turned over the responsibility for education to the teacher. Just as they depended on doctors to heal their children, they depended on teachers to educate them. In the middle-class community, however, parents saw education as a shared enterprise and scrutinized, monitored, and supplemented the school experience of their children. Prescott parents read to their children, initiated contact with teachers, and attended school events more often than Colton parents.

Generally, the evidence demonstrates that the level of parental involvement is linked to the class position of the parents and to the social and cultural resources that social class yields in American society. By definition, the educational status and material resources of parents increase with social class. These resources were observed to influence parental participation in schooling in the Prescott and Colton communities. The working-class parents had poor educational skills, relatively lower occupational prestige than teachers, and limited time and disposable income to supplement and intervene in their children's schooling. The middle-class parents, on the other hand, had educational skills and occupational prestige that matched or surpassed that of teachers; they also had the necessary economic resources to manage the child care, transportation, and time required to meet with teachers, to hire tutors, and to become intensely involved in their childrens' schooling.

These differences in social, cultural, and economic resources between the two sets of parents help explain differences in their responses to a variety of teacher requests to participate in schooling. For example, when asked to read to their children and to help them at home with school work, Colton parents were reluctant to comply because they felt that their educational skills were inadequate for these tasks. Prescott parents, with their superior educational skills, felt more comfortable helping their children in these areas. Parents at Colton and Prescott also differed in their perceptions of the appropriate relationship between parents and teachers. Prescott parents conceived of schooling as a partnership in which parents have the right and the responsibility to raise issues of their choosing and even to criticize teachers. Colton parents' inferior educational level and occupational prestige reinforced their trust in and dependence on the professional expertise of educators. The relatively high occupational position of Prescott parents contributed to their view of teachers as equals.[1] Prescott parents occasionally had more confidence in their right to monitor and to criticize teachers. Their occupational prestige levels may have helped both build this confidence and demystify the status of the teacher as a professional.

Finally, more straightforward economic differences between the middle- and working-class parents are evident in their different responses to requests to attend school events. Attendance at parent-teacher conferences, particularly those held in the afternoon, requires transportation, child care arrangements, and flexibility at the workplace—all more likely to be available to Prescott parents than to Colton parents.

The literature on family life indicates that social class is associated with differences in social networks, leisure time, and childrearing

activities (Bott 1971; Kohn 1977; Rubin 1976). The observations in this study confirm these associations and, in addition, indicate that social class differences in family life (or class cultures) have implications for family-school relationships. Middle-class culture provides parents with more information about schooling and promotes social ties among parents in the school community. This furthers the interdependence between home and school. Working-class culture, on the other hand, emphasizes kinship and promotes independence between the spheres of family life and schooling.

Because both schools promote a family-school relationship that solicits parental involvement in schooling and that promotes an interdependence between family and school, the class position and the class culture of middle-class families yield a social profit not available to working-class families. In particular, middle-class culture provides parents with more information about schooling and also builds social networks among parents in the school community. Parents use this information to build a family-school relationship congruent with the schools' definition of appropriate behavior. For example, they may request additional educational resources for their children, monitor the behavior of the teacher, share costs of a tutor with other interested parents, and consult with other parents and teachers about their children's educational experience.

It is important to stress that if the schools were to promote a different type of family-school relationship, the class culture of middle-class parents might not yield a social profit. The data do not reveal that the social relations of middle-class culture are intrinsically better than the social relations of working-class culture. Nor can it be said that the family-school relationships in the middle class are objectively better for children than those in the working class. Instead, the social profitability of middle-class arrangements is tied to the schools' definition of the proper family-school relationship.

Future research on parental participation in education should take as problematic the standards that schools establish for parental involvement in schooling and should focus on the role of class cultures in facilitating and impeding compliance with these standards. In addition, research might profitably examine the role of social class in structuring the conflict between the universalistic concerns of the teacher and the particularistic agenda of parents (Waller 1932; McPherson 1972). Parents and teachers may be 'natural enemies' (Waller 1932) and may face enduring problems of negotiating 'boundaries' between their 'territories' (Lightfoot 1978). Social class appears to influence the educational, status, monetary, and informational resources that each side brings to that conflict.

FAMILY–SCHOOL RELATIONSHIPS AND CULTURAL CAPITAL

These results suggest that social class position and class culture become a form of cultural capital in the school setting (Bourdieu 1977a; Bourdieu and Passeron 1977). Although working-class and middle-class parents share a desire for their children's educational success in first and second grade, social location leads them to construct different pathways for realizing that success. Working-class parents' method—dependence on the teacher to educate their child—may have been the dominant method of promoting school success in earlier periods within the middle class. Today, however, teachers actively solicit parents' participation in education. Middle-class parents, in supervising, monitoring, and overseeing the educational experience of their children, behave in ways that mirror the requests of schools. This appears to provide middle-class children with educational advantages over working-class children.

The behavior of parents in this regard is not fully determined by their social location. There are variations within as well as between social classes. Still, parents approach the family-school relationship with different sets of social resources. Schools ask for very specific types of behavior from all parents, regardless of their social class. Not all cultural resources are equally valuable, however, for complying with schools' requests. The resources tied directly to social class (e.g., education, prestige, income) and certain patterns of family life (e.g., kinship ties, socialization patterns, leisure activities) seem to play a large role in facilitating the participation of parents in schools. Other aspects of class and class cultures, including religion and taste in music, art, food, and furniture (Bourdieu 1984) appear to play a smaller role in structuring the behavior of parents, children, and teachers in the family-school relationship. (These aspects of class cultures might, of course, influence other dimensions of schooling.)

These findings underline the importance of studying the significance of cultural capital within a social context. In recent years, Bourdieu has been criticized for being overly deterministic in his analysis of the role of cultural capital in shaping outcomes (Giroux 1983; Connell et al. 1982). Connell et al., for example, argue that cultural capital

practically obliterates the person who is actually the main constructor of the home/school relationship. The student is treated mainly as a bearer of cultural capital, a bundle of abilities, knowledges and attitudes furnished by parents. (p. 188)

Moreover, Bourdieu has focused almost exclusively on the social profits stemming from high culture. Although he is quite clear about the arbitrary character of culture, his emphasis on the value of high culture could be misinterpreted. His research on the cultural capital of élites may be construed as suggesting that the culture of élites is intrinsically more valuable than that of the working class. In this regard, the concept of cultural capital is potentially vulnerable to the same criticisms that have been directed at the notion of the culture of poverty (Valentine 1968).

This study highlights the need for more extensive research in the area of cultural capital. It would be particularly useful for future research to take into account historical variations in definitions of cultural capital. Family-school relationships have changed over time; what constitutes cultural capital at one point in time may or may not persist in a future period. Historical studies help reveal the way in which cultural resources of social groups are unevenly valued in a society; these studies help illustrate the dynamic character of these value judgments. Historical work on definitions of cultural capital can also shed light on the arbitrariness of the current social standards.

In addition, research on cultural capital could fruitfully expand its focus to include more social groups. The research on high culture (Bourdieu 1977a, 1977b; DiMaggio and Useem 1982; Cookson and Persell 1985) has made a useful contribution to the field (see also Lamont and Lareau 1987). This study, however, suggests that middle-class families have cultural resources that become a form of cultural capital in specific settings. In moving beyond studies of élites, it might be useful to recognize that all social groups have cultural capital and that some forms of this capital are valued more highly by the dominant institutions at particular historical moments. As Samuel Kaplan (pers. comm. 1986) points out, members of the working class have cultural capital as well, but it is only rarely recognized by dominant social institutions. During World War II, for example, the dangerous and difficult task of the marksman was usually filled by working-class youths; only rarely was it assigned to a college boy. Marksman skills and, more generally, compliance with the expectations of supervising officers are important in the military. Here, the childrearing values of working-class parents (e.g., obedience, conformity) may advantage working-class youths; the values of middle-class families (e.g., self-direction, autonomy, and permissiveness) may disadvantage middle-class youth (Kohn 1977; Kohn and Schooler 1983).

Implications for Further Research

Educators and policymakers may seek to increase parental involvement in schooling by boosting the educational capabilities and information resources of parents. For sociologists interested in family, schools, and social stratification, a somewhat different task is in order. Families and schools, and family-school relationships, are critical links in the process of social reproduction. For most children (but not all), social class is a major predictor of educational and occupational achievement. Schools, particularly elementary and secondary schools, play a crucial role in this process of social reproduction; they sort students into social categories that award credentials and opportunities for mobility (Collins 1979, 1981c). We know relatively little about the stages of this social process.

The concept of cultural capital may help by turning our attention to the structure of opportunity and to the way in which individuals proceed through that structure (see also Collins 1981a, 1981b; Knorr-Cetina and Cicourel 1981). Moreover, the concept does not overlook the importance of the role of the individual in constructing a biography within a social structure. Class provides social and cultural resources, but these resources must be invested or activated to become a form of cultural capital. Analyzing the role of cultural capital in structuring family-school relationships, particularly parental participation in education, provides a rich setting for analyzing the linkages between micro and macro levels of analysis.

Note

1. Some Prescott parents, however, did report that they felt intimidated by a teacher on some occasions.

References

Aggleton, P. J., and Whitty, G. (1985), 'Rebels Without a Cause? Socialization and Subcultural Style Among the Children of the New Middle Classes', *Sociology of Education*, 58: 60–72.

Anyon, J. (1981), 'Social Class and School Knowledge', *Curriculum Inquiry*, 11: 1–42.

Apple, M. W. (1979), *Ideology and Curriculum* (London: Routledge and Kegan Paul).

Baker, D., and Stevenson, D. (1986), 'Mothers' Strategies for School Achievement: Managing the Transition to High School', *Sociology of Education*, 59: 156–66.

Becker, H. Jay, and Epstein, J. L. (1982), 'Parent Involvement: A Survey of Teacher Practices', *Elementary School Journal*, 83: 85–102.

Berger, E. H. (1983), *Beyond the Classroom: Parents as Partners in Education* (St. Louis: C. V. Mosby).

Bernstein, B. (1975), *Class, Codes and Control* iii (London: Routledge and Kegan Paul).

—— (1982), 'Codes, Modalities and the Process of Cultural Reproduction: A Model', in *Cultural and Economic Reproduction in Education*, (ed.) M. W. Apple (London: Routledge and Kegan Paul), 304–55.

Bott, E. (1971), *Family and Social Networks* (New York: Free Press).

Bourdieu, P. (1977a), 'Cultural Reproduction and Social Reproduction', in *Power and Ideology in Education*, (ed.) Karabel, J. and Halsey, A. H. (New York: Oxford Univ. Press), 487–511.

—— (1977b), *Outline of a Theory of Practice* (Cambridge: Cambridge University Press).

—— (1981), 'Men and Machines', pp. 304–17 in *Advances in Social Theory: Toward an Integration of Micro- and Macro-Sociologies*, (ed.) Knorr-Cetina, K., and Cicourel, A. V., (Boston: Routledge and Kegan Paul).

Bourdieu, P. (1984) *Distinction: A Social Critique of the Judgment of Taste*, transl. by Nice, R., (Cambridge, Ma: Harvard University Press).

——, and Passeron, J. C., (1977), *Reproduction in Education, Society and Culture*, transl. by Nice, R. (Beverly Hills: Sage).

Butterworth, J. E. (1928), *The Parent-Teacher Association and Its Work* (New York: Macmillan).

California Department of Education (1983), *California Assessment Program 1981–1982* (Sacramento, Ca.: California Department of Education).

Collins, R., (1979), *The Credential Society* (New York: Academic Press).

—— (1981*a*), 'Micro-Translation as a Theory-Building Strategy'. pp. 81–108 in *Advances in Social Theory: Toward an Integration of Micro- and Macro-Sociologies*, (ed.), Knorr-Cetina, K., and Cicourel, A. V., (Boston, Mass.: Routledge and Kegan Paul).

—— (1981*b*), 'On the Micro-Foundations of Macro-Sociology', *American Journal of Sociology* 86: 984–1014.

—— (1981*c*.), *Sociology Since Midcentury: Essays in Theory Cumulation* (New York: Academic Press).

Connell, R. W., Ashendon, D. J., Kessler, S., and Dowsett, G. W. (1982), *Making the Difference: Schools, Families and Social Division* (Sydney: George Allen and Unwin).

Cook-Gumperez, J. (1973), *Social Control and Socialization: A Study of Class Difference in the Language of Maternal Control* (Boston Mass.: Routledge and Kegan Paul).

Cookson, P. W., Jr., and Persell, Caroline H. (1985), *Preparing for Power: America's Elite Boarding Schools* (New York: Basic Books).

Deutsch, M. (1967), 'The Disadvantaged Child and the Learning Process' pp. 39–58 in *The Disadvantaged Child*, (ed.) Deutsch, M (New York: Basic Books).

Diaz, S., Moll, L. C., and Mehan, H. (1986), 'Sociocultural Resources in Instruction: A Context-Specific Approach' pp.187–230 in *Beyond Language: Social and Cultural Factors in Schooling Language Minority Students*, (ed.) Bilingual Education Office, Los Angeles: California State Univ., Evaluation, Dissemination, and Assessment Center.

DiMaggio, P., and Useem, M. (1982), 'The Arts in Cultural Reproduction' pp. 181–201 in *Cultural and Economic Reproduction in Education*, (ed.) Apple, M. W. (London: Routledge and Kegan Paul).

Epstein, J. (1983), 'Effect on Parents of Teacher Practices of Parent Involvement' Report No. 346, (Baltimore: Johns Hopkins University, Center for the Social Organization of Schools).

—— (1984), 'Effects of Teacher Practices and Parent Involvement on Student Achievement'

paper presented at the annual meetings of the American Educational Research Association, New Orleans.

——, and Becker, H. J. (1982), 'Teachers' Reported Practices of Parent Involvement: Problems and Possibilities' *Elementary School Journal* 83: 103–13.

Erickson, F., and Mohatt, G. (1982), 'Cultural Organization of Participation Structures in Two Classrooms of Indian Students' pp. 132–75 in *Doing the Ethnography of Schooling*, (ed.) Spindler, G. (New York: Holt, Rinehart and Winston).

Gaskell, J. (1985), 'Course Enrollment in the High School: The Perspective of Working-Class Females' *Sociology of Education* 58: 48–59.

Gearing, F., and Epstein, P. (1982), 'Learning to Wait: An Ethnographic Probe into the Operation of an Item of Hidden Curriculum' pp. 240–67 in *Doing the Ethnography of Schooling*, (ed.) Spindler, G. (New York: Holt, Rinehart and Winston).

Giroux, H. A. (1983), *Theory and Resistance in Education* (South Hadley, Ma: Bergin and Harvey).

Gracey, H. L. (1972), *Curriculum or Craftsmanship* (Chicago: Univ. of Chicago Press).

Heath, S. B. (1982), 'Questioning at Home and at School: A Comparative Study', in *Doing the Ethnography of Schooling*, (ed.) Spindler, G. (New York: Holt, Rinehart and Winston), 102–31.

—— (1983), *Ways with Words* (London: Cambridge Univ. Press).

Hymes, J. L., Jr. (1953), *Effective Home-School Relations* (New York: Prentice-Hall).

Jencks, C. *et al.* (1972), *Inequality* (New York: Basic Books).

Joffee, C. (1977), *Friendly Intruders* (Berkeley: Univ. of California Press).

Knorr-Cetina, K., and Cicourel, A. V. (1981), *Advances in Social Theory: Toward an Integration of Micro- and Macro-Sociologies* (Boston: Routledge and Kegan Paul).

Kohn, M. L. (1977), *Class and Conformity* (Chicago: Univ. of Chicago Press).

——, and Schooler, C. (1983), *Work and Personality: An Inquiry into the Impact of Social Stratification* (Norwood, NJ: Ablex).

Labov, W. (1972), *Sociolinguistic Patterns* (Philadelphia: Univ. of Pennsylvania Press).

Lamont, M., and Lareau, A. (1987), 'Cultural Capital in American Research: Problems and Possibilities', Working Paper No. 9 (Chicago: Center for Psychosocial Studies).

Leichter, H. J. (1979), 'Families and Communities as Educators: Some Concepts of Relationships', in *Families and Communities as Educators*, (ed.) Leichter, H. J. (New York: Teachers College Press), 3–94.

Levy, F., Meltsner, A. J., and Wildavsky, A. (1974),

Urban Outcomes (Berkeley: Univ. of California Press).

Lightfoot, S. L. (1978), *Worlds Apart* (New York: Basic Books).

Litwack, E., and Szeleny, I. (1971). 'Kinship and Other Primary Groups', in *Sociology of the Family*, (ed.) Anderson, M. (Middlesex: Penguin), 149–63.

Marjoribanks, K. (1979), *Families and Their Learning Environments: An Empirical Analysis* (London: Routledge and Kegan Paul).

McPherson, G. H. (1972), *Small Town Teacher* (Cambridge, Mass.: Harvard Univ. Press).

Mehan, H., and Griffin, P. (1980), 'Socialization: The View from Classroom Interactions', *Social Inquiry*, 50: 357–98.

—— Hertweck, A. L., and Meihls, J. L. (1986), *Handicapping the Handicapped* (Stanford: Stanford Univ. Press).

National Congress of Parents and Teachers (1944), *The Parent-Teacher Organization: Its Origins and Development* (Chicago: National Congress of Parents and Teachers).

National Education Association (1985), 'Teacher-Parent partnership Program, 1984–1985 Status Report', unpublished paper (Washington, DC: National Education Association).

Ogbu, J. (1974), *The Next Generation* (New York: Academic Press).

Overstreet, H., and Overstreet, B. (1949), *Where Children Come First* (Chicago: National Congress of Parents and Teachers).

Rist, R. C. (1978), *The Invisible Children* (Cambridge, Mass.: Harvard Univ. Press).

Robinson, S. (1985), 'Teacher-Parent Cooperation', paper presented at the annual meetings of the American Educational Research Association, Chicago.

Rubin, L. B. (1976), *Worlds of Pain* (New York: Basic Books).

Seeley, D. (1984), 'Home-School Partnership', *Phi Delta Kappan*, 65: 383–93.

Strodbeck, F. L. (1958), 'Family Interaction, Values, and Achievement', in *Talent and Society*, ed. D. D. McClelland (New York: Van Nostrand), 131–91.

Taylor, S. (1984), 'Reproduction and Contradiction in Schooling: The Case of Commercial Studies', *British Journal of Sociology of Education*, 5: 3–18.

Trelease, J. (1982), *The Read-Aloud Handbook* (New York: Penguin).

Valentine, C. A. (1968), *Culture and Poverty* (Chicago: Univ. of Chicago Press).

Valli, L. (1985), 'Office Education Students and the Meaning of Work', *Issues in Education*, 3: 31–44.

Waller, W. (1932), *The Sociology of Teaching* (New York: Wiley).

Wilcox, K. A. (1977), 'Schooling and Socialization for Work Roles', Ph.D. diss., Harvard Univ.

—— (1982), 'Differential Socialization in the Classroom: Implications for Equal Opportunity', in *Doing the Ethnography of Schooling*, (ed.) Spindler, G. (New York: Holt, Rinehart and Winston), 269–309.

47

The Politics of Culture: Understanding Local Political Resistance to Detracking in Racially Mixed Schools

Amy Stuart Wells and Irene Serna

Research on tracking, or grouping students into distinct classes for 'fast' and 'slow' learners, has demonstrated that this educational practice leads to racial and socioeconomic segregation within schools, with low-income, African American, and Latino students frequently placed in the lowest level classes, even when they have equal or higher test scores or grades (see Oakes 1985; Welner and Oakes 1995). Furthermore, being placed in the low track often has long-lasting negative effects on these students, as they fall further and further behind their peers and become increasingly bored in school. Partly in response to this research and partly in response to their own uneasiness with the separate and unequal classrooms created by tracking, educators across the country are beginning to respond by testing alternatives to tracking, a reform we call 'detracking.'

Over the last three years, our research team studied ten racially and socioeconomically mixed schools undergoing detracking reform, and attempted to capture the essence of the political struggles inherent in such efforts.[1] We believe that an important aspect of our qualitative, multiple case study is to help educators and policymakers understand the various manifestations of local political resistance to detracking—not only who instigates it, but also the ideology of opposition to such reforms and the political practices employed (see Oakes and Wells 1995).

This article focuses on how forces outside the school walls shaped the ability of educa-tors to implement 'detracking reform'—to question existing track structures and promote greater access to challenging classes for all students. More specifically, we look at those actors whom we refer to as the 'local élites'—those with a combination of economic, political, and cultural capital that is highly valued within their particular school community.[2] These élites are most likely to resist detracking reform because their children often enjoy privileged status in a tracked system. The capital of the élites enables them to engage in political practices that can circumvent detracking reform.

In order to understand the influence of local élites' political practices on detracking reform, we examine their ideology of entitle-ment, or how they make meaning of their privilege within the educational system and how others come to see such meanings as the way things 'ought to be.' According to Gramsci (cited in Boggs 1984), insofar as ruling ideas emanating from élites are internalized by a majority of individuals within a given community, they become a defining motif of everyday life and appear as 'common sense'—that is, as the 'traditional popular conception of the world' (p. 161).

Yet we realize that the high-status cultural capital—the valued tastes and consumption patterns—of local élites and the resultant ide-ologies are easily affected by provincial social contexts and the particular range of class, race, and culture at those sites (Bourdieu 1984). In a study of social reproduction in a postmodern

From *Harvard Educational Review*, 66 (1996), 93–118. Reprinted with permission.

society, Harrison (1993) notes that 'the task is not so much to look for the global correspondences between culture and class, but to reconstruct the peculiarly local and material micrologic of investments made in the intellectual field' (p. 40). Accordingly, in our study, we particularize the political struggles and examine the specific ideologies articulated at each school site. Because we were studying ten schools in ten different cities and towns, we needed to contextualize each political struggle over detracking reform within its local school community. These local contexts are significant because the relations of power and domination that affect people most directly are those shaping the social contexts within which they live out their everyday lives: the home, the workplace, the classroom, the peer group. As Thompson (1990) states, 'These are the contexts within which individuals spend the bulk of their time, acting and interacting, speaking and listening, pursuing their aims and following the aims of others' (p. 9).

Our research team used qualitative methods to examine technical aspects of detracking—school organization, grouping practices, and classroom pedagogy—as well as cultural norms and political practices that legitimize and support tracking as a 'common-sense' approach to educating students (Oakes and Wells 1995). Our research question was, What happens when someone with power in a racially mixed secondary school decides to reduce tracking? Guided by this question, we selected ten sites—six high schools and four middle schools—from a pool of schools that were undergoing detracking reform and volunteered to be studied. We chose these particular schools because of their diversity and demonstrated commitment to detracking. The schools we studied varied in size from more than three thousand to less than five hundred students. One school was in the Northeast, three were in the Midwest, one in the South, two in the Northwest, and three in various regions of California. Each school drew from a racially and socio-economically diverse community and served significant but varied mixes of White, African American, Latino, Native American/Alaska Native, and/or Asian students. We visited each school three times over a two-year period. Data collection during our site visits included in-depth, semi-structured tape-recorded interviews with administrators, teachers, students, parents, and community leaders, including school board members. In total, more than four hundred participants across all ten schools were interviewed at least once. We also observed classrooms, as well as faculty, PTA, and school board meetings. We reviewed documents and wrote field notes about our observations within the schools and the communities. Data were compiled extensively from each school to form the basis of cross-case analysis. Our study ran from the spring of 1992 through the spring of 1995.[3]

Descriptions of the 'Local Élites'

The struggles over tracking and detracking reforms are, to a large extent, concerned with whose culture and lifestyle is valued, and, thus, whose way of knowing is equated with 'intelligence.' Traditional hierarchical track structures in schools have been validated by the conflation of culture and intelligence. When culturally biased 'truths' about ability and merit confront efforts to 'detrack,' political practices are employed either to maintain the status quo or to push toward new conceptions of ability that would render a rigid and hierarchical track structure obsolete (see Oakes, Lipton, and Jones 1995).

While we acknowledge that many agents contribute to the maintenance of a rigid track structure, this article examines the political practices of local élites in the school communities we studied. The élites discussed here had children enrolled in the detracking schools and thus constitute the subgroup of local élites active in shaping school policies. Their practices were aimed at maintaining a track structure, with separate and unequal educational opportunities for 'deserving' élite students and 'undeserving' or non-élite students. Our analysis of élite parents' ideology of privilege and the resultant political practices therefore includes an examination of 'corresponding institutional mechanisms' (Bourdieu and Wacquant 1992: 188) employed to prevent structural change that would challenge their status and privilege.

Our intention is not to criticize these powerful parents in an unsympathetic manner. Yet, we believe that too often the cultural forces that shape such parents' agency as they try to do what is best for their children remain hidden from view and thus unquestioned. Our effort to unpack the 'knapsack' of élite privilege will expose the tight relationship between the 'objective' criteria of the schools and the cultural forces of the élite (McIntosh 1992).

Detracking, or the process of moving schools toward a less rigid system of assigning students to classes and academic programs, is a hotly contested educational reform. In racially mixed schools, the controversy surrounding detracking efforts is compounded by beliefs about the relationship among race, culture, and academic ability. In virtually all racially mixed secondary schools, tracking resegregates students, with mostly White and Asian students in the high academic tracks and mostly African American and Latino students in the low tracks (Oakes 1985; Oakes, Oraseth, Bell, and Camp 1990). To the extent that élite parents have internalized dominant, but often unspoken, beliefs about race and intelligence, they may resist 'desegregation' within racially mixed schools—here defined as detracking—because they do not want their children in classes with Black and Latino students.

Efforts to alter within-school racial segregation via detracking, then, are generally threatening to élites, in that they challenge their position at the top of the hierarchy. The perceived stakes, from an élite parent's perspective, are quite high. They argue, for instance, that their children will not be well served in detracked classes. And while these stakes are most frequently discussed in academic terms—for example, the dumbing down of the curriculum for smart students—the real stakes, we argue, are generally not academics at all, but, rather, status and power. For example, if a school does away with separate classes for students labeled 'gifted' but teachers continue to challenge these students with the same curriculum in a detracked setting, the only 'losses' the students will incur are their label and their separate and unequal status. Yet in a highly stratified society, such labels and privileged status confer power.

In looking at the ability of the upper strata of society to maintain power and control, Bourdieu (1977) argues that economic capital—that is, income, wealth, and property—is not the only form of capital necessary for social reproduction. He describes other forms of capital, including political, social, and cultural (Bourdieu and Wacquant 1992). In our analysis of resistance to detracking reforms, we focus on cultural capital and its relationship to dominant ideologies within our school communities because of the explicit connections between cultural capital and educational achievement within Bourdieu's work. According to Bourdieu (1984), cultural capital consists of culturally valued tastes and consumption patterns, which are rewarded within the educational system. Bourdieu discusses 'culture' not in its restricted, normative sense, but rather from a more anthropological perspective. Culture is elaborated in a 'taste' for refined objects, which is what distinguishes the culture of the dominant class or upper social strata from that of the rest of society. In order for élites to employ their cultural capital to maintain power, emphasis must be placed on subtleties of taste—for example, form over function, manner over matter. Within the educational system, Bourdieu argues, students are frequently rewarded for their taste, and for the cultural knowledge that informs it. For instance, élite students whose status offers them the opportunity to travel to other cities, states, and countries on family vacations are often perceived to be more 'intelligent' than other students, simply because the knowledge they have gained from these trips is reflected in what is valued in schools. When high-status, élite students' taste is seen as valued knowledge within the educational system, other students' taste and the knowledge that informs it is devalued (Bourdieu and Passeron 1979). In this way, high-status culture is socially constructed as 'intelligence'—a dubious relationship that élites must strive to conceal in order to legitimize their meritbased claim to privileged status. In other words, what is commonly referred to as 'objective' criteria of intelligence and achievement is actually extremely biased toward the subjective experience and ways of knowing of élite students. Similarly, Delpit (1995) describes the critical role that power plays in our society and educational system, as the worldviews of those in privileged positions are 'taken as the only reality, while the worldviews of those less powerful are dismissed as inconsequential' (p. xv). The education system is the primary field in which struggles over these cultural meanings take place and where, more often than not, high-status cultural capital is translated into high-status credentials, such as academic degrees from élite institutions (Bourdieu and Passeron 1977).

Thus, socially valuable cultural capital—form and manner—is the property many upper class and, to a lesser extent, middle-class families transmit to their offspring that substitutes for, or supplements, the transmission of economic capital as a means of maintaining class, status, and privilege across generations (Bourdieu 1973). Academic qualifications and high-status educational titles are to cultural capital what money and property titles are to economic capital. The form and manner of academic qualifications are critical. Students cannot simply graduate from high school; they must graduate with the proper high-status qualifications that allow them access to the most selective universities and to the credentials those institutions confer.

Through the educational system, élites use their economic, political, and cultural capital to acquire symbolic capital—the most highly valued capital in a given society or local community. Symbolic capital signifies culturally important attributes, such as status, authority, prestige, and, by extension, a sense of honor. The social construction of symbolic capital may vary from one locality to another, but race and social class consistently play a role, with White, wealthy, well-educated families most likely to be at the top of the social strata (Harrison 1993).

Because the cultural capital of the élite is that which is most valued and rewarded within the educational system, élite status plays a circular role in the process of detracking reform: parents with high economic, political, and cultural capital are most likely to have children in the highest track and most prestigious classes, which in turn gives them more symbolic capital in the community. The élite parents can then employ their symbolic capital in the educational decisionmaking arena to maintain advantages for their children. Educational reforms that, like detracking, challenge the advantages bestowed upon children of the élite are resisted not only by the élites themselves, but also by educators and even other parents and community members who may revere the cultural capital of élite families. The school and the community thus bestow élite parents with the symbolic capital,

or honor, that allows them political power.

The status of the local élites in the ten school communities we studied derived in part from the prestige they and their children endowed to public schools simply by their presence. The élite are the most valued citizens, those the public schools do not want to lose, because the socially constructed status of institutions such as schools is dependent upon the status of the individuals attending them. These are also the families most likely to flee public schools if they are denied what they want from them. For example, at Grant High School, an urban school in the Northwest, the White, upper-middle-class parents who sent their children to public schools held tremendous power over the district administration. Many of them were highly educated and possessed the economic means to send their children to private schools if they so chose.

While the élites at each of the schools we studied held economic, social, and political capital, the specific combination of these varied at each site in relation to the cultural capital valued there. Thus, who the élites were and their particular rationale for tracking varied among locations, based on the distinctive mix of race, class, and culture. For instance, at Liberty High School, located in a West Coast city, many of the White parents were professors at a nearby university. As 'professional intellectuals,' they strongly influenced the direction of Liberty High; although they were generally not as wealthy as business executives, they were nevertheless imbued with a great deal of high-status cultural capital. Meanwhile, educators and White parents at Liberty noted that most of the Black and Latino students enrolled in the school came from very low-income families. Many of the people we interviewed said there was a sizable number of middle-class Black families in this community, but that they did not send their children to public schools. This school's social class divide, which some educators and Black students argued was a caricature, allowed White parents to blame the school's resegregation through tracking on the 'family backgrounds' of the students, rather than on racial prejudice.

In the midwestern town of Plainview, the local White élites worked in private corporations rather than universities. Here, the high-status cultural capital was, in general, far more

conservative, pragmatic, and less 'intellectual' than at Liberty. Nonetheless, the élite
parents here and at each of the schools we
studied strove for the same advantages that
the élite parents at Liberty High demanded
for their children.

The African American students in Plainview comprised two groups—those who lived
in a small, working-class Black neighbourhood in the district and those who transferred
into Plainview from the 'inner city' through
an inter-district desegregation plan. At this
site, however, the social class distinctions
between the two groups of Black students
were blurred by many White respondents,
particularly in their explanations of why Black
students from both groups were consistently
found in the lowest track classes. For instance,
teachers could not tell us which Black students lived in Plainview and which rode the
bus in from the city. Some teachers also spoke
of Black students'—all Black students'—low
levels of achievement as the result of their
families' culture of poverty, and not the result
of what the school offered them. Despite the
relative economic advantages of many African
American students who lived in the Plainview
district as compared to those who lived in the
city, all Black students in this mostly White,
wealthy suburban school were doing quite
poorly. While African Americans constituted
25 per cent of the student population, less than
5 per cent of the students in the highest level
courses were Black. Furthermore, a district
task force on Black achievement found that
more than half of the Black students in the
high school had received at least one D or F
over the course of one school year.

In other schools, the interplay between race
and class was more complex, especially when
the local élite sought to distinguish themselves from other, lower income Whites. For
instance, in the small midwestern Bearfield
School District, which is partly rural and
partly suburban, wealthy, well-educated,
White suburban parents held the most power
over the educational system because they possessed more economic and highly valued cultural capital than rural Whites or African
Americans. When a desegregation plan was
instituted in the 1970s, it was Black and poor
rural White children who were bused. As the
Bearfield Middle School principal explained,
'As our business manager/superintendent
once told me, the power is neither Black nor

White; it's green—as in money. And that's
where the power is. Rich people have clout.
Poor people don't have clout.'

Still, the less wealthy and less educated
rural Whites in Bearfield, while not as politically powerful as the suburban Whites,
remained more influential than the African
American families. When the two middle
schools in the district were consolidated in
1987, Whites—both wealthy suburban and
poor rural—were able to convince the school
board to close down the newly built middle
school located in the African American community and keep open the older middle school
on the White side of the town.

Although the interplay between class and
culture within a racially mixed community is
generally defined along racial lines, we found
that was not always the case. For example,
King Middle School, a magnet school in a
large northeastern city, was designed to
attract students of many racial groups and varied socioeconomic status. A teacher explained
that the parents who are blue-collar workers
do not understand what's going on at the
school, but the professional and middle-class
parents frequently call to ask for materials to
help their children at home. Educators at
King insisted that middle-class and professional parents were not all White, and that
there was very little correlation between
income and race at the school, with its student
body composed of more than twenty
racial/ethnic groups, including Jamaican,
Chinese, Armenian, Puerto Rican, African
American, and various European ethnic
groups. While we found it difficult to believe
that there was no correlation between
race/ethnicity and income in this city with
relatively poor African American and Latino
communities, it is clear that not all of the local
élites at King were White.

Thus, the layers of stratification in some
schools were many, but the core of the power
élite in all ten communities consisted of a
group of parents who were more White,
wealthy, and well-educated relative to others
in their community. They were the members
of the school communities with the greatest
economic and/or high-status cultural capital,
which they have passed on to their children.
The schools, in turn, greatly rewarded the
children of these élite for their social distinctions, which were perceived to be distinctions
of merit (DiMaggio 1979).

The Political Ideology of Tracking and Detracking: 'Deserving' High-Track Students

Bourdieu's concepts of domination and social reproduction are particularly useful in understanding the education system, because education is the field in which the élite both 'records and conceals' its own privilege. Elites 'record' privilege through formal educational qualifications, which then serve to 'conceal' the inherited cultural capital needed to acquire them. According to Harrison (1993), 'What is usually referred to as equality of opportunity or meritocracy is, for Bourdieu, a 'sociodicy'; that is, a sacred story that legitimates the dominant class' own privilege' (p. 43).

The political resistance of the local élite to detracking reforms cannot, therefore, be understood separately from the 'sociodicy' or ideology employed to legitimize the privileged place élites and their children hold in the educational system. Ideology, in a Gramscian sense, represents ideas, beliefs, cultural preferences, and even myths and superstitions, which possess a certain 'material' reality of their own (Gramsci 1971). In education, societal ideas, beliefs, and cultural preferences of intelligence have found in tracking structures their own material reality. Meanwhile, tracking reinforces and sustains those ideas, beliefs, and cultural preferences.

According to Thompson (1990), ideology refers to the ways in which meaning serves, in particular circumstances, to establish and sustain relations of power that are systematically asymmetrical. Broadly speaking, ideology is *meaning in the service of power*. Thompson suggests that the study of ideology requires researchers to investigate the ways in which meaning is constructed and conveyed by symbolic forms of various kinds, 'from everyday linguistic utterances to complex images and texts; it requires us to investigate the social contexts within which symbolic forms are employed and deployed' (p. 7).

The ideology of the local élites in the schools we studied was often cloaked in the 'symbolic form' that Thompson describes. While the symbols used by politically powerful people to express their resistance to detracking differed from one site to the next, race consistently played a central, if not explicit, role. Although local élites rarely expressed their dissatisfaction with detracking reform in overtly racial terms, their resistance was couched in more subtle expressions of the politics of culture that have clear racial implications. For example, they said they liked the concept of a racially mixed school, as long as the African American or Latino students acted like White, middle-class children, and their parents were involved in the school and bought into the American Dream. At Central High, a predominantly Latino school on the West Coast with a 23 per cent White student body, the local élite consisted of a relatively small middle class of mostly White and a few Latino families. No real upper middle class existed, and most of the Latino students came from very low-income families; many were recent immigrants to the United States. A White parent whose sons were taking honors classes explained her opposition to detracking efforts at Central, exposing her sense of entitlement this way:

I think a lot of those Latinos come and they're still Mexicans at heart. They're not American. I don't care what color you are, we're in America here and we're going for this country. And I think their heart is in Mexico and they're with that culture still. It's one thing to come over and bring your culture and to use it, but it's another thing to get into that . . . and I'm calling it the American ethic. They're not into it and that's why they end up so far behind. They get in school, and they are behind.

This construct of the 'deserving minority' denies the value of non-White students' and parents' own culture or of their sometimes penetrating critique of the American creed (see Yonesawa, Williams, and Hirshberg, 1995), and implies that only those students with the cultural capital and underlying élite ideology deserve to be rewarded in the educational system. Yet because the political arguments put forth by powerful parents in the schools we studied sounded so benign, so 'American,' the cultural racism that guided their perspective was rarely exposed. Consequently, both the racial segregation within the schools and the actions of parents to maintain it were perceived as natural.

We found many instances in which élite parents attempted to distance their children from students they considered to be less deserving of special attention and services. For instance, at Rolling Hills Middle School, located in a southeastern metropolitan area with a large, county-wide desegregation plan, one wealthy White parent said she and her husband purchased a home in the nearby neighbourhood because Rolling Hills and its feeder high school are two of the handful of schools in the district that offer an 'advanced program.' She said several people had told her that in the advanced program the curriculum was better, fewer behaviour problems occurred in the classes, and students received more individualized attention from teachers. She also said that had her children not been accepted into the advanced program, she and her family would not have moved into this racially mixed school district, but would have purchased a home in one of the Whiter suburbs east of the county line. Interestingly enough, this parent did not know whether or not the White suburban schools offered an advanced program. Also of interest in this district is the creation of the advanced program in the same year as the implementation of the desegregation plan.

The White, well-educated parents at Grant High School often stated that the racial diversity of the student body was one characteristic they found most appealing about the school. They said that such a racially mixed environment better prepared their children for life in 'the real world.' One parent noted that 'the positive mixing of racial groups is important to learning to live in society.' But some teachers argued that while these parents found Grant's diversity acceptable—even advantageous—their approval was conditioned by their understanding that 'their children [would] only encounter Black students in the hallways and not in their classrooms.' Grant's assistant principal noted that 'many upper class, professional parents hold occupational positions in which they work toward equity and democracy, but expect their children to be given special treatment at Grant.'

This ideology of 'diversity at a distance' is often employed by White parents at strategic moments when the privileged status of their children appears to be threatened (Lareau 1989). In our study, the parents of honors students at Grant successfully protested the school's effort to eliminate the 'tennis shoe' registration process by which students and teachers jointly negotiated access to classes.[4] Some of the faculty had proposed that the school switch to a computer registration program that would guarantee Black and Latino students greater access to high-track classes.

The parents of the honors students stated that they were not protesting the registration change because they were opposed to having their children in racially mixed classes, but because 'they [felt] that their children [would] learn more in an environment where all students are as motivated to learn as they are—in a homogeneous ability classroom.'

Respondents at Grant said that parents assumed that if any student was allowed into an honors class, regardless of his or her prior track, it must not be a good class. The assumption here was that if there was no selectivity in placing students in particular classes, then the learning and instruction in those classes could not be good. Parents of the most advanced students 'assumed' that since the language arts department had made the honors and regular curriculum the same and allowed more students to enroll in honors, the rigor of these classes had probably diminished, despite the teachers' claims that standards had remained high.

At Liberty High School, where the intellectual élite were more 'liberal' than the élite in most of the other schools, parents also frequently cited the racial diversity of the school as an asset. For instance, one parent commented that it was the racial and cultural mix—'the real range of people here'—that attracted her to Liberty High. She liked the fact that her daughter was being exposed to people of different cultures and different socioeconomic backgrounds: 'We took her out of private school, where there's all these real upper middle-class White kids.' Yet, despite this espoused appreciation for diversity among White liberal parents at Liberty, they strongly resisted efforts to dismantle the racially segregated track system. According to another White parent of a high-track student at Liberty:

I think the one thing that really works at Liberty High is the upper track. It does. And to me, I guess my goal would be for us to find a way to make the rest of Liberty High work as well as the upper track. But it's crucial that we not destroy the upper track to do that, and that can happen . . . it really could . . . . I feel my daughter will get an excellent education if the program continues the way it is, if self-scheduling continues so that they aren't all smoothed together.

In all of the schools we studied, the most interesting aspect of élites' opposition to detracking is that they based their resistance on the symbolic mixing of high 'deserving' and low 'undeserving' students, rather than on information about what actually happens in detracked classrooms. For instance, an English teacher at Plainview High School who taught a heterogeneous American Studies course in which she academically challenged all her students said that the popularity of the Advanced Placement classes among the élite parents was in part based upon a 'myth' that 'they're the only classes that offer high standards, that they're the only courses that are interesting and challenging. And the myth is that that's where the best learning takes place. That's a myth.'

At Explorer Middle School, located in a mid-sized northwestern city, the identified gifted students—nearly all White, despite a school population that was 30 per cent American Indian—were no longer segregated into special classes or teams. Rather, 'gifted' students were offered extra 'challenge' courses, which other 'non-gifted' students could choose to take as well. The day after a grueling meeting with parents of the 'gifted' students, the designated gifted education teacher who works with these and other students in the challenge classes was upset by the way in which the parents had responded to her explanation of the new challenge program and the rich educational opportunities available in these classes:

And they didn't ask, 'well what are our kids learning in your classes?' Nobody asked that. I just found that real dismaying, and I was prepared to tell them what we do in class and here's an example. I had course outlines. I send objectives home with every class, and goals and work requirements, and nobody asked me anything about that . . . like they, it's . . . to me it's like I'm dealing with their egos, you know, more than what their kids really need educationally.

What this and other teachers in our study told us is that many élite parents are more concerned about the labels placed on their children than what actually goes on in the classroom. This is a powerful illustration of what Bourdieu (1984) calls 'form over function' and 'manner over matter.'

NOTIONS OF ENTITLEMENT

Symbols of the 'deserving,' high-track students must be juxtaposed with conceptions of the undeserving, low-track students in order for strong protests against detracking to make sense in a society that advocates equal opportunity. Bourdieu argues that 'impersonal domination'—the sociocultural form of domination found in free, industrial societies where more coercive methods of domination are not allowed—entails the rationalization of the symbolic. When symbols of domination are rationalized, the *entitlement* of the upper strata of society is legitimized, and thus this impersonal domination is seen as natural (Harrison 1993: 42).

In our study, we found that élite parents rationalized their children's entitlement to better educational opportunities based upon the resources that they themselves brought to the system. For instance, parents from the White, wealthy side of Bearfield Middle School's attendance zone perceived that the African American students who attended the school and lived on the 'other' side of town benefited from the large tax burden shouldered by the White families. One White parent noted, 'I don't feel that our school should have, you know, people from that far away coming to our school. I don't think it's right as far as the taxes we pay. . . . They don't pay the taxes that we pay, and they're at our schools also. Um, I just don't feel they belong here, no.' According to the superintendent of the school district, this statement reflects the widely held belief among Whites that they are being taxed to pay for schools for Black students, 'and therefore, the White community . . . should make the decisions about the schools . . . because they are paying the bill.' These perspectives explain in part why the consolidation of the district's two middle schools resulted in the closing of the mostly Black but much more recently built school, and favoured the old, dilapidated Bearfield building as the single middle school site.

At the same time, these parents balked at the suggestion that their own social privilege and much of their children's advantages had less to do with objective merit or intellectual ability than it had to do with their families' economic and cultural capital. Harrison (1993) expands upon Bourdieu's notion that culture functions to deny or disavow the economic origins of capital by gaining symbolic credit for the possessors of economic and political capital. Harrison argues that the seemingly legitimate and meritocratic basis upon which students 'earn' academic credentials is an important aspect of the dominant class' denial of entitlement as a process in which inherited economic and political power receives social consecration. In other words, the élite parents must convince themselves and others that the privileges their children are given in the educational system were earned in a fair and meritocratic way, and are not simply a consequence of the parents' own privileged place in society. 'The demonstration that the belief of merit is a part of the process of social consecration in which the dominant class's power is both acknowledged and misrecognized, is at the core of Bourdieu's analysis of culture' (Harrison 1993: 44).

There is strong evidence from the schools we studied that students frequently end up in particular tracks and classrooms more on the basis of their parents' privilege than of their own 'ability.' A school board member in the district in which Rolling Hills Middle School is located explained that students are placed in the advanced program depending on who their parents happen to know. Because the advanced program was implemented at the same time as the countywide desegregation plan, it has become a sophisticated form of resegregation within racially mixed schools supported by conceptions of 'deserving' advanced students. The school board member said that parents of the advanced students are very much invested in labels that their children acquire at school. When children are labeled 'advanced,' it means their parents are 'advanced' as well. In fact, said the board member, some of these parents refer to themselves as the 'advanced parents': 'There is still an elitist aspect as far as I am concerned. I also think it is an ego trip for parents. They love the double standard that their children are in Advanced Placement programs.'

Similarly, several élite parents of students in the advanced program at Grant High School expressed regret that the school had such a poor vocational education department for the 'other' students—those who were not advanced. Their lament for vocational education related to their way of understanding the purpose of the high school in serving different students. One of these parents, for example, stated that the role of the honors classes was to groom students to become 'managers and professionals' and that something else should be done for those kids who would grow up to be 'workers.'

According to Harrison (1993), the élite seek to deny the arbitrary nature of the social order that culture does much to conceal. This process, which he calls 'masking,' occurs when what is culturally arbitrary is 'essentialized, absolutized or universalized' (p. 45). Masking is generally accomplished via symbols—culturally specific as opposed to materially specific symbols (Bourdieu and Wacquant 1992). For example, standardized test scores become cultural symbols of intelligence that are used to legitimize the track structure in some instances while they are 'masked' in other instances.

An example of this 'masking' process was revealed to us at Grant High School, where élite parents of the most advanced students approved of using test scores as a measure of students' intelligence and worthiness to enroll in the highest track classes. But when children of the élite who were identified as 'highly able' in elementary school did not make the test score cutoffs for high school honors classes, the parents found ways to get their children placed in these classes anyway, as if the tests in that particular instance were not valid. The educators usually gave in to these parents' demands, and then cited such instances as evidence of a faulty system. The so-called faults within the system, however, did not lead to broad-based support among powerful parents or educators to dismantle the track structure.

Similarly, at Explorer Middle School, where the wealthy White 'gifted' students were all placed in regular classes and then offered separate challenge classes along with other students who chose to take such a class, the principal collected data on the achievement test scores for the identified gifted students and other students in the school. She found huge overlaps in the two sets of scores, with some identified 'non-gifted' students scoring in the 90th percentile and above, and some 'gifted' students ranking as low as the 58th percentile. Yet, when the mostly White parents of children identified by the district as 'gifted' were presented with these data, they attributed the large number of low test scores among the pool of gifted students to a handful of non-White students participating in that program, although the number of non-White 'gifted' students was far lower than the number of low test scores within the gifted program. The White parents simply would not admit that any of their children did not deserve a special label (and the extra resources that come with it). According to the teacher of the challenge classes, one of the most vocal and demanding 'gifted' parents was the mother of a boy who was not even near the top of his class: 'I still can't figure out how he got in the gifted program: he doesn't perform in any way at that high a level . . . She is carrying on and on and on . . .'

Despite evidence that the 'gifted' label may be more a form of symbolic capital than a true measure of innate student ability, the parents of students who had been identified as gifted by this school district maintained a strong sense of entitlement. For instance, a White, upper middle-class father of two so-called gifted boys told us he was outraged that the 'gifted and talented' teacher at Explorer spent her time teaching challenge classes that were not exclusively for gifted students. This father was adamant that the state's special funding for gifted and talented (G/T) programs should be spent exclusively on identified G/T students. He noted that at the other middle school in the district, the G/T teacher worked with a strictly G/T class, 'whereas at Explorer, the G/T teacher works with a class that is only 50 per cent G/T.' In other words, 'precious' state resources for gifted and talented students were being spent on 'non-deserving' students—many of whom had higher middle school achievement test scores than the students who had been identified by the school district as gifted many years earlier.

At Plainview High School, the English teacher who created the heterogeneous American Studies class began reading about the social science research on intelligence, and concluded that our society and education system do not really understand what intelligence is or how to measure it. When the principal asked her to present her research to parents at an open house, her message was not well received, particularly by those parents whose children were in the Advanced Placement classes. According to this teacher, 'If you were raised under the system that said you were very intelligent and high achieving, you don't want anyone questioning that system, OK? That's just the way it is.' She said that what some of the parents were most threatened by was how this research on intelligence was going to be used and whether the high school was going to do away with Advanced Placement classes. She recalled, 'I used the word "track" once and debated whether I

could weave that in because I knew the power of the word, and I didn't want to shut everyone down. It was very interesting.'

Political Practices: How the Local Élite Undermined Detracking

The ideology and related symbols that legitimate local élites' sense of entitlement are critical to educational policy and practice. As Harrison (1993) and Harker (1984) note, Bourdieu's work is ultimately focused on the strategic practices employed when conflicts emerge. In this way, Bourdieu identifies 'practices'—actions that maintain or change the social structures—within strategically oriented forms of conflict. These strategic actions must be rooted back into the logic or sense of entitlement that underlies these practices. In other words, we examined political practices that are intended to be consistent with an ideology of 'deserving' high-track students. These practices were employed by élite parents when educators posed a threat to the privileged status of their children by questioning the validity and objectivity of a rigid track structure (Useem 1990).

According to Bourdieu, when seemingly 'objective' structures, such as tracking systems, are faithfully reproduced in the dispositions or ways of knowing of actors, then the 'arbitrary' nature of the existing structure can go completely unrecognized (Bourdieu and Wacquant 1992). For instance, no one questions the existence of the separate and unequal 'gifted and talented' or 'highly advanced' program for children of the local élites, despite the fact that the supposedly 'objective' measures that legitimize these programs—standardized tests scores—do not always support the somewhat 'arbitrary' nature of student placement. This arbitrary placement system is more sensitive to cultural capital than academic 'ability.'

In the case of tracking, so-called objective and thus non-arbitrary standardized tests are problematic on two levels. First, the tests themselves are culturally biased in favor of wealthy White students, and therefore represent a poor measure of 'ability' or 'intelligence'. Second, scores on these exams tend to count more for some students than others. Elite students who have low achievement test scores are placed in high tracks, while non-White and non-wealthy students with high test scores are bound to the lower tracks (see Oakes *et al*. 1995; Welner and Oakes 1995). Still, test scores remain an undisclosed and undisputed 'objective' measure of student track placement and thus a rationale for maintaining the track structure in many schools.

When these undisclosed or undisputed parts of the universe are questioned, conflicts arise that call for strategic political practices on the part of élites. As Harrison (1993) states, 'Where the fit can no longer be maintained and where, therefore, the arbitrary nature of the objective structure becomes evident, the dominant class must put into circulation a discourse in which this arbitrary order is misrecognized as such' (p. 41). When the arbitrary nature of the 'objective' tracking structure becomes evident, detracking efforts are initiated, often by educators who have come to realize the cultural basis of the inequalities within our so-called meritocratic educational system.

Within each of our ten schools, when educators penetrated the ideology that legitimizes the track structure (and the advantages that high-track students have within it), élite parents felt that their privileges were threatened. We found that local élites employed four practices to undermine and co-opt meaningful detracking efforts in such a way that they and their children would continue to benefit disproportionately from educational policies. These four overlapping and intertwined practices were threatening flight, co-opting the institutional élites, soliciting buy-in from the 'not-quite élite', and accepting detracking bribes.

THREATENING FLIGHT

Perhaps nowhere in our study was the power of the local élite and their ideology of entitlement more evident than when the topic of 'élite flight' was broached, specifically when these parents threatened to leave the school. Educators in the ten schools we studied were acutely aware that their schools, like most institutions, gain their status, or symbolic capital, from the social status of the students who attend (Wells and Crain 1992). They know they must hold onto the local élites in order for their schools to remain politically viable institutions that garner broad public support. As a result, the direct or indirect

threat of élite flight can thwart detracking efforts when local élite parents have other viable public or private school options.

At Liberty High School, the liberal ideals and principles that are the corner-stone of this community were challenged when local élites were asked to embrace reforms that they perceived to be removing advantages held by their children. In fact, discussions and implementation of such reforms—for example, the creation of a heterogeneous ninth-grade English/social studies core—caused élite parents to 'put into circulation a discourse' that legitimized their claim to something better than what other students received. Without this special attention for high-track students, élite parents said, they had little reason to keep their children at Liberty. As one parent of a high-track student noted in discussing the local élite's limits and how much of the school's equity-centered detracking reforms they would tolerate before abandoning the school:

I think it happens to all of us; when you have children, you confront all your values in a totally different way. I mean, I did all this work in education, I knew all these things about it, and it's very different when it's your own child 'cause when it's your own child your real responsibility is to advocate for that child. I mean, I might make somewhat different decisions about Liberty High, though probably not terribly different, because as I say, I would always have in mind the danger of losing a big chunk of kids, and with them the community support that makes this school work well.

The power of the threat of élite flight is evident in the history of the creation of tracking structures in many of our schools, where advanced and gifted programs began to appear and proliferate at the same time that the schools in these districts were becoming more racially mixed, either through a desegregation plan or demographic shifts. This shift toward more tracking as schools became increasingly racially mixed follows the long history of tracking in the U.S. educational system. Tracking became more systematized at the turn of the century, as non-Anglo immigrant students enrolled in urban high schools (Oakes 1985). At Grant High School, which is located in a racially diverse urban school district surrounded by separate Whiter and more affluent districts, the highly advanced and 'regular' advanced programs were started shortly after desegregation at the insistence of local élite parents who wanted separate classes for their children. One teacher noted that the advanced programs were designed to respond to a segment of the White community that felt. 'Oh, we'll send our kids to public school, but only if there's a special program for them.'

At Grant, the chair of the language arts department, an instigator of detracking reform efforts, said that the parents of the 'advanced' students run the school district:

They scare those administrators the same way they scare us. They're the last vestiges of middle-class people in the public schools in some sense. And they know that. And they flaunt that sometimes. And they scare people with that. And the local media would spit [the deputy superintendent] up in pieces if she did something to drive these parents out of the school district. So, yeah, I'm sure she's nervous about anything we're doing.

Similarly, at Rolling Hills Middle School, where the Advanced Program began in the late 1970s, shortly after the county-wide desegregation plan was implemented, the mother of two White boys in the program noted. 'If I heard they were going to eliminate the Advanced Program, I would be very alarmed, and would seriously consider if I could afford a private school.' She indicated that she thought that most parents of students at Rolling Hills felt this way.

At Central High School, White flight consistently paralleled the influx of Latino immigrant students into the school. Administrators said they hoped that the relocation of the school to a new site in a more middle-class area of the district would allow Central to maintain its White population. But many educators said they felt that what keeps White students at Central is the honors program, which would have been scaled back under detracking reform. This reform effort has been almost completely derailed by political roadblocks from both inside the school and the surrounding community.

Suburban, midwestern Plainview High School was the school in which we perhaps noted the *perceived* threat of élite flight to be most powerful. There, the concept of 'community stability' was foremost on the minds of the educators. Many of the teachers and administrators in the Plainview district, particularly at the high school, came to Plainview from the nearby Hamilton School District, which experienced massive White flight two

decades earlier. Essentially, the population of the Hamilton district shifted from mostly White, upper middle class to all Black and poor in a matter of ten years—roughly between 1968 and 1978. According to these educators and many other respondents in Plainview, the status of the Hamilton district and its sole high school plummeted, as each incoming freshman class became significantly darker and poorer. Once regarded as the premier public high school in the metropolitan area, Hamilton suddenly served as a reminder of the consequences of White flight. The large numbers of White residents and educators who came to Plainview after fleeing Hamilton kept the memory of White flight alive, and used Hamilton as a symbol of this threat.

Of all the educators in the district, it was the Plainview High School principal, Mr. Fredrick, who appeared most fixated on issues of community 'stability' and the role of the schools in maintaining it:

Here's my problem, what I'm doing at Plainview High School is essentially trying to make it stable enough so that other people can integrate the neighborhood. Now if other people aren't integrating the neighborhood, I'm not doing it either. I'm not out there working on that, I don't have time to be out there working on that. I've got to be making sure that what we're doing in Plainview High School is strong, we're strong enough, and have the reputation of, so that as we integrate, which I'm hoping is happening, that Whites won't get up and flee. . .when they come in and say, I hope you're here in eight years, that is a commitment those White people are gonna be there in eight years.

Fredrick argues that an academically strong high school led by a principal who maintains a good relationship with the community will help stabilize the whole community. As he explains, 'I believe we can keep stability in Plainview while still being out in front of education. Now that's what I feel my job is.' Fredrick's goal of maintaining racial stability in the community is noble in many respects, but we learned during our visits to Plainview that his focus on White flight has resulted in intense efforts to please the élite White parents. These efforts to cater to élite parents have consistently worked against detracking reforms in the school. While some of the teachers and other administrators continued to push for more innovative grouping and instructional strategies. Fredrick has advocated more Advanced Placement courses and encouraged more students to take these classes. In this way, the threat of White élite flight has helped maintain the hierarchical track structure and an Advanced Placement curriculum that many teachers, students, and less élite parents argue is not creative or instructionally sound.

CO-OPTING THE INSTITUTIONAL ÉLITES

The threat of flight is one of the ways in which local élites provoke responses to their institutional demands. This threat, and the fear it creates in the hearts of educators, is related to the way in which the 'institutional élites'— that is educators with power and authority within the educational system—become co-opted by the ideology of the local élites. Both Domhoff (1983, 1990) and Mills (1956) write about institutional élites as 'high-level' employees in institutions (either private corporations or governmental agencies, such as the U.S. Treasury Department) who see their roles as serving the upper, capitalist-based class. At a more micro or local level, we find that the institutional élites are the educational administrators who see their roles as serving the needs and demands of the local élites. Indeed, in most situations, their professional success and even job security depend on their ability to play these roles.

For instance, in small-town Bearfield, the new superintendent, who is politically very popular with élite parents and community members, has developed a less than positive impression of detracking efforts at the middle school. Yet his view is based less on first-hand information about the reform through visits to the school or discussions with the teachers than on the input he has received from White parents who have placed their children in private schools. To him, the educators at Bearfield Middle School have 'let the academics slide just a little bit'. Because of the superintendent's sense of commitment to the powerful White, wealthy parents, the principal of Bearfield indicated that he feels intense pressure to raise standardized test scores and prove that academics are not sliding at the school. Thus, some degree of 'teaching to the test' has come at the expense of a more creative and innovative curriculum that facilitates detracking efforts by acknowledging, for example, different ways of knowing material. In a symbolic move, the teaching staff has rearranged the Black History Month curriculum to accommodate standardized test prepping in the month of February.

The relationship among the institutional élites at urban Grant High School, its school district office, and the local élite parents, however, demonstrates one of the most severe instances of 'co-optation' that we observed. At the district's main office and at the high school, many of the educational administrators are African American. Still, these administrators frequently have failed to push for the kinds of reforms that would benefit the mostly African American students in the lowest track classes. Several respondents noted that Black educators who have been advocates for democratic reform have not survived in this district, and that those who cater to the demands of powerful White parents have been promoted within the system.

At the end of the 1993–1994 school year, the African American principal of Grant, Mr. Phillips, rejected the language arts department's proposal to detrack ninth-grade English by putting 'honors' and 'regular' students together in the same classes and offering honors as an extra credit option for all students. The principal claimed that it was not fair to do away with separate honors classes when the proposal had not been discussed with parents. His decision, he explained, was based on frequent complaints he received from the mostly White parents of high-track students that changes were being made at the school, particularly in the language arts department, without their prior knowledge or consent. According to the language arts department chair, when her department detracked twelfth-grade electives, it 'really pissed people off.' Also, when these élite parents were not consulted about the proposal to change the school schedule to an alternative four-period schedule, they protested and were successful in postponing the change.

Furthermore, a recent attempt by Grant's history department to do away with separate honors classes at the request of some students was thwarted by the parents of honors students, who, according to one teacher, 'went through the roof.' Some of the teachers in other departments indicated that they suspected that the history department's move to eliminate honors classes was not sincere, but rather a political tactic designed to generate support among powerful élite parents for the honors program. In fact, the history department chair, who opposes detracking, noted that his only recourse to stop the detracking reform was to go to the parents and get them upset 'because they had the power to do things at school.'

At Grant, administrators at the district office have historically been very responsive to the concerns of White parents, and thus regularly implement policies designed to retain the White students. For instance, the district leadership convened an all-White 'highly capable parent task force' to examine issues surrounding the educational advanced programs for 'highly capable' students. The task force strongly recommended self-contained classrooms for advanced students, making detracking efforts across the district more problematic. According to one of the teachers at Grant, school board members would not talk about the élitism around this program because they were 'feeling under siege.'

At several schools in our study, educational administrators, especially principals, have lost their jobs since detracking efforts began, in part because they refused co-optation and advocated detracking. At Liberty High School, despite the principal's efforts to make detracking as politically acceptable to the élite parents as possible, in the end he was 'done in' by the institutional élites at the district office who would not give him the extra resources he needed to carry out detracking in a manner local élites would have considered acceptable.

BUY–IN OF THE NOT–QUITE ÉLITE

In an interesting article about the current political popularity of decentralized school governance and growth of school-site councils with broad decisionmaking power, Beare (1993) writes that the middle class is a very willing accomplice in the strategy to create such councils and 'empower' parents to make important decisions about how schools are run. He notes that it is the middle-class parents who put themselves forward for election to such governing bodies. Yet he argues that in spite of this new-found participatory role for middle-class parents, they actually have little control over the course of their children's schools, because such courses are chartered by a larger power structure. As Beare states, 'In one sense, then, participative decisionmaking is a politically diversionary tactic, a means of keeping activist people distracted by their own self-inflicted, busy work. The

middle class are willing accomplices, for they think they are gaining access to the decisionmaking of the power structures' (p. 202).

The ideology of the local élite's entitlement is so pervasive and powerful that the élites do not necessarily have to be directly involved in the decisionmaking processes at schools, although they often are. But between the local élites' threats to flee, co-optation of institutional élites, and ability to make their privilege appear as 'common sense,' such school-site councils will most likely simply reflect, as Beare (1993) points out, the broader power structure. In this way, the 'self-inflicted busy work' of the not-quite élites, which, depending on the context of the schools, tend to be the more middle- or working-class parents, is just that—busy work that helps the schools maintain the existing power relations and a highly tracked structure. This is what Gramsci (1971) would refer to as the 'consensual' basis of power, or the consensual side of politics in a civil society (see Boggs 1984: Gramsci 1971).

We saw a clear example of how this co-optation plays out at Plainview High School, where a group of about thirty predominantly White parents served on the advisory board for the most visible parent group, called the Parent-Teacher Organization, or PTO (even though there were no teachers in this organization). The PTO advisory board met with the principal once a month to act as his 'sounding board' on important school-site issues, particularly those regarding discipline. We found through in-depth interviews with many of the parents on the PTO board that these parents were not the most powerful or most élite parents in the one-high-school district. In fact, as the former president of the advisory board and the mother of a not-quite-high-track student explained, 'The Advanced Placement parents don't run the president of the PTO. As a matter of fact, I'm trying to think when the last time [was] we had a president of the PTO whose kids were on the fast track in Advanced Placement. I don't think we've had one in quite a few years.'

She did note, however, that there were 'a lot of parents on the [district-wide] school board whose kids are in the Advanced Placement classes'. Interestingly, in the Plainview school district, the school board and the central administration, and not the school-site councils such as the PTO advisory board, have the power to change curricular and instructional

programs—the areas most related to detracking reform—in the schools.

Furthermore, despite the past president's
assertion that the Advanced Placement parents do not run the PTO advisory board,
the board members we interviewed told us
they were unwilling to challenge the pro-
Advanced Placement stance of the principal.
Still, several of the PTO board members said
they believed there was too much emphasis on
Advanced Placement at Plainview, and that
they were at times uncomfortable with the
principal's constant bragging about the number of Advanced Placement classes the school
offers, the number of students taking
Advanced Placement exams, and the number
of students who receive 3's, 4's, or 5's on these
exams. Some of these parents said that, in
their opinion, a heavy load of Advanced Placement classes is too stressful for high school
students; others said the curriculum in the
Advanced Placement classes is boring rote
memorization. But none of these parents
had ever challenged the principal in his effort
to boost the number of Advanced Placement
classes offered and students enrolling in
them. According to one mother on the PTO
board:

I think parents have seen that there are so many
pressures in the world, they realize that this is high
school and they're fed up with all the competition.
At the same time they know you have to play the
game, you know. . .And again, it's hard to evaluate
with some of the top, top students, you know,
what's appropriate. . .I think a lot of this has to do
with Plainview as a community, too. Now, for
example, where I live right here is in Fillburn, and
that is a more upscale community [within the Plainview district]. Two houses from me is the Doner
school district, which is a community of wealthier
homes, wealthier people, many of whom have children in private schools.

During interviews, most of the not-quite-élite
parents at all of the schools in our study discussed their awareness of the demands that
families with high economic and cultural capital placed on the schools. They cited these
demands as reasons why they themselves did
not challenge the push for more Advanced
Placement or gifted classes and why they were
not supporters of detracking efforts—even
when they suspected that such changes might
be beneficial for their own children. For
instance, at Grant High School, the chair of
the language arts department formed a parent

support group to focus on issues of tracking
and detracking. This group consisted mostly
of parents of students in the regular and honors classes, with only a handful of parents of
very advanced students in the highest track.
The department chair said she purposefully
postponed 'the fight' with more of the
advanced parents. 'We thought if we could get
a group of parents who are just as knowledgeable. . .as we were, they should be the ones that
become the advocates with the other parents.
So that's probably our biggest accomplish-
ment this year is getting this group of parents
that we have together.' But one of the few parents of advanced students left the group
because she said her concerns were not being
addressed, and the advisory group disbanded
the following spring.

We saw other examples of 'not-quite-élite'
buy-in at schools where middle-class minority parents had become advocates of tracking
practices and opponents of detracking efforts,
despite their lament that their children were
often the only children of color in the high-
track classes. For instance, a Black professional parent at Rolling Hills Middle School,
whose two children were in the advanced program, noted that a growing number of African
American parents in the district were upset
with the racial composition of the nearly all-
White 'advanced' classes and the disproportionately Black 'comprehensive' tracks within
racially mixed schools. He said, 'So you have
segregation in a supposedly desegregated setting. So what it is, you have a growing amount
of dissatisfaction within the African American
community about these advanced programs
that are lily White.' Despite his dissatisfaction, this father explained that he is not against
tracking per se. 'I think tracking has its merits.
I just think they need to be less rigid in their
standards.'

Similarly, at Green Valley High School, a
rural West Coast school with a 43 per cent
White and 57 percent Latino student population, a professional, middle-class Latino couple who had sent their children to private
elementary and middle schools before
enrolling them in the public high school said
that the students at Green Valley should be
divided into three groups: those at the top,
those in the middle, and those at the bottom.
The father added that those students in
the middle should be given more of a tech
prep education, and that an alternative

school might be good for a lot of kids who won't go to college.

DETRACKING BRIBES

Another political practice employed by local élites in schools that are attempting detracking reforms is their use of symbolic capital to bribe the schools to give them some preferential treatment in return for their willingness to allow some small degree of detracking to take place. These detracking bribes tend to make detracking reforms very expensive and impossible to implement in a comprehensive fashion.

Bourdieu (in Harrison 1993) would consider such detracking bribes to be symbolic of the irreversible character of gift exchange. In exchange for their political buy-in to the detracking efforts, élite parents must be assured that their children are still getting something more than other children. In the process of gift exchange, according to Bourdieu, gifts must be returned, but this return represents neither an exchange of equivalents nor a case of cash on delivery:

What is returned must be both different in kind and deferred in time. It is within this space opened up by these two elements of non-identity [of the gifts] and temporality [deferred time] that strategic actions can be deployed through which either one actor or another tries to accumulate some kind of profit. The kind of profit accumulated is, of course, more likely to be either symbolic or social, rather than economic. (p. 39)

In the case of the detracking bribes, the élite parents tend to profit at the expense of broad-based reform and restructuring. Yet, detracking bribes take on a different shape and character in different schools, depending upon the bargaining power of the local élite parents and the school's resources. As Bourdieu notes, in the case of the gift exchange, it is the agent's sense of honor that regulates the moves that can be made in the game (Harrison 1993).

For instance, at King Middle School, located in a large northeastern city, the bribe is the school itself—a well-funded magnet program with formal ties to a nearby college and a rich art program that is integrated into the curriculum. Because King is a school of choice for parents who live in the surrounding area of the city, it is in many ways automatically perceived to be 'better than' regular neighborhood schools, where students end up by default. Still, an administrator noted that King must still work at getting élite parents to accept the heterogeneous grouping within the school: 'The thing is to convince the parents of the strong students that [heterogeneous grouping] is a good idea and not to have them pull children out to put them in a gifted program. It is necessary to really offer them a lot. You need parent education, along with offering a rich program for the parents so that they don't feel their children are being cheated.'

At Rolling Hills Middle School, where African American students are bused to this otherwise White, wealthy school, the detracking bribe comes in the form of the best sixth-grade teachers and a 'heterogeneous' team of students, which is skewed toward a disproportionate number of advanced program students. For instance, the heterogeneous team is comprised of 50 per cent 'advanced' students, 25 per cent 'honors' students, and 25 per cent 'regular' students, while the sixth grade as a whole is only about one-third 'advanced' students and about one-half 'regular' students. Thus, detracking at Rolling Hills is feasible when it affects only one of four sixth-grade teams, and that one team enrolls a disproportionate number of advanced students and is taught by the teachers whom the local élite consider to be the best. The generosity of the 'gifts' that the school gives the élite parents who agree to enroll their children in the heterogeneous team are such that this team has become high status itself. The 'parent network' of local élites at this school now promotes the heterogeneous team and advises élite mothers of incoming sixth-graders to choose that team. According to one wealthy White parent, 'the heterogeneous team is "hand-picked".' Another White parent whose daughter is on the heterogeneous team noted, 'It's also been good to know that it's kind of like a private school within a public school. And that's kind of fair, I hate to say that, but it's kind of a fair evaluation.'

Of course, Rolling Hills does not have enough of these 'gifts' to bribe all of the local élite parents to place their children on a heterogeneous team. In other words, Rolling Hills will never be able to detrack the entire school as long as the cost of the bribe remains so high and the élite parental profit is so great. By definition, the 'best' teachers at any given school are scarce; there are not enough of them to go around. In addition, the number of

Advanced Placement students in the school is too small to assure that more heterogeneous teams could be created with the same skewed proportion of advanced, honors, and comprehensive tracks.

At Grant High School, the bribe for detracking the marine science program consists of this unique science offering, coupled with the school's excellent science and math departments and one of the two best music programs in the city. These are commodities that élite parents cannot get in other schools— urban or suburban. As one teacher explained, 'So what options do these parents have? Lift their kids out of Grant, which they love? They can't get a science program like this anywhere else in the city.' Although the school itself is highly tracked, especially in the history department, the marine science classes enroll students from all different tracks. A marine science teacher noted that parents of the advanced students never request that their kids be placed in separate classes because curricula in this program are both advanced and unique.

Interestingly, the detracking bribe at Liberty High, as the school moved toward the ninth-grade English/social studies core classes, was to be smaller class sizes and ongoing staff development. Unfortunately, the district administration withheld much of the promised funding to allow the school to deliver these gifts to the parents of high-track students. Whether or not these parents were ever committed to this bribe—whether they thought the school was offering them enough in return—is not really clear. What we do know is that the principal who offered the gift was, as we mentioned, recently 'let go' by the district. His departure may have been the ultimate bribe with the local élites, because, as Bourdieu (in Harrison, 1993) argues, the kind of profit accumulated is, of course, more likely to be either symbolic or social, rather than economic.

Conclusions

When our research team began this study in 1992, we initially focused on what was happening *within* the racially mixed schools we were to study. Yet as we visited these schools, it became increasingly evident to us that the parents had a major impact on detracking reform efforts. Over the course of the last three years, we came to appreciate not only the power of this impact but its subtleties as well. In turning to the literature on élites and cultural capital, we gained a deeper understanding of the barriers educators face in their efforts to detrack schools.

As long as élite parents press the schools to perpetuate their status through the intergenerational transmission of privilege that is based more on cultural capital than 'merit,' educators will be forced to choose between equity-based reforms and the flight of élite parents from the public school system.

The intent of this article is not simply to point fingers at the powerful, élite parents or the educators who accommodate them at the ten schools we studied. We understand that these parents are in many ways victims of a social system in which the scarcity of symbolic capital creates an intense demand for it among those in their social strata. We also recognize the role that the educational system writ large—especially the higher education system—plays in shaping their actions and understanding of what they must do to help their children succeed.

Still, we hope that this study of ten racially mixed schools undertaking detracking reform is helpful to educators and policymakers who struggle to understand more clearly the political opposition to such reform efforts. Most importantly, we have learned that in a democratic society, the privilege, status, and advantage that élite students bring to school with them must be carefully deconstructed by educators, parents, and students alike before meaningful detracking reforms can take place.

Notes

1. Our three-year study of ten racially mixed secondary schools that are detracking was funded by the Lilly Endowment. Jeannie Oakes and Amy Stuart Wells were coprincipal investigators. Research associates were Robert Cooper, Amanda Datnow, Diane Hirshberg, Martin Lipton, Karen Ray, Irene Serna, Estella Williams, and Susie Yonezawa.
2. By 'school community', we mean the broad and diverse network of students, parents, educators, and other citizens who are connected to these schools as institutions.
3. For a full description of the study and its methodology, see Oakes and Wells (1995).
4. During the 'tennis shoe' registration, teachers

set up tables in the gymnasium with registration passes for each of the classes they will be offering. Students have an allocated time slot in which they are allowed into the gym to run from teacher to teacher and ask for passes for classes they want. Under this system, teachers are able to control who gets into their classes, and the children of the élite, who hold more political power in the school, are more likely to get the high-track classes that they want.

References

Beare, H. (1993), 'Different Ways of Viewing School–Site Councils: Whose Paradigm is in use Here?' in H. Beare and W. I. Boyd (eds.), *Restructuring Schools: An International Perspective on the Movement to Transform the Control and Performance of Schools* (Washington. DC: Falmer Press), 200–14.

Boggs, C. (1984), *The Two Revolutions: Gramsci and the Dilemmas of western Marxism*, (Boston: South End Press).

Bourdieu, P. (1973),'Cultural Reproduction and Social Reproduction', in R. Brown (ed.), *Knowledge, Education, and Cultural Change* (New York: Harper and Row), 487–501.

—— (1977), *Outline of a Theory of Practice*. (Cambridge: Cambridge Univ. Press).

—— (1984), *Distinction : A Social Critique of the Judgment of Taste*, (Cambridge, Mass.: Harvard Univ. Press).

—— (1979), *The Inheritors: French Students and their Relation to Culture*. (Chicago: Univ. of Chicago Press).

—— and Passeron, J.C. (1977), *Reproduction in Education, Society and Culture*, (Beverley Hills. Calif.: Sage).

—— and Wacquant, L. J.D. (1992), *An Invitation to Reflexive Sociology*, (Chicago, Ill.: Univ. of Chicago Press).

Delpit, I. (1995), *Other People's Children: Cultural Conflict in the Classroom*, (New York: New Press).

DiMaggio, P. (1979), 'Review Essay: On Pierre Bourdieu', *American Journal of Sociology*, 84: 1460–72.

Domhoff, W. G. (1983), *Who Rules America Now? A View for the 80s* (Englewood Cliffs, NJ: Prentice-Hall).

—— (1990), *The Power Elite and the State: How Policy is Made in America*, (New York: A. deGruyter).

Gramsci, A. (1971), *Selections from the Prison Notebooks*, (New York: International Publishers).

Harker, K. (1984), 'On Reproduction, *habitus* and Education', *British Journal of Sociology of Education*, 52: 117–27.

Harrison, P.R. (1993), 'Bourdieu and the Possibility of a Postmodern sociology', *Thesis Eleven*, 35: 36–50.

Lareau, A. (1989), *Home Advantage*, (London: Falmer Press).

McIntosh, P. (January/February, 1992), 'White Privilege: Unpacking the Invisible Knapsack', *Creation Spirituality*, 33–5.

Mills, C. W. (1956), *The Power Elite*, (London: Oxford Univ. Press).

Oakes, J. (1985), *Keeping Track: How Schools Restructure Inequalities*, (New Haven. Conn.: Yale Univ. Press).

——, Lipton, M., and Jones, M. (1995, April), *Changing minds: Deconstructing Intelligence in Detracking Schools*, (paper presented at the annual meeting of the American Educational Research Association, San Francisco).

——, Oraseth, T., Bell, R., and Camp, P. (1990), *Multiplying Inequalities: The effects of Race Social Class, and Tracking on Opportunities to Learn Mathematics and Science*, (Santa Monica, Calif.: Rand).

—— and Wells, A. S. (1995, April), *Beyond Sorting and Stratification: Creative Alternatives to Tracking in Racially Mixed Secondary Schools* (paper presented at the annual meeting of the American Educational Research Association, San Francisco), Calif.

Thompson, J. B. (1990), *Ideology and Modern Culture*, (Stanford.: Stanford Univ. Press).

Useem, B. (1990, April), *Social Class and Ability Group Placement in Mathematics in Transition to Seventh Grade: The Role of Parental Involvement*, (paper presented at the annual meeting of the American Educational Research Conference, Boston).

Wells, A. S., and Crain. R. L. (1992), 'Do Parents Choose School Quality or School Status?' A Sociological Theory of Free-Market Education, in P. W. Cookson (ed.), *The choice controversy* (Newbury Park, Calif.: Corwin Press), 65–82.

Welner. K., and Oakes, J. (1995, April), *Liability Grouping: The New Susceptibility of School Tracking Systems to Legal Challenges*, (paper presented at the annual meeting of the American Educational Research Association, San Francisco).

Yonesawa. S., Williams, E., and Hirshberg, D. (1995, April), *Seeking a New Standard: Minority Parent and Community Involvement in Detracking Schools*, (paper presented at the annual meeting of the American Educational Research Association, San Francisco).

48

Cultural Capital and Social Exclusion: Some Observations on Recent Trends in Education, Employment, and the Labour Market[1]

Phillip Brown

Education, Recruitment and the Occupational Structure

The relationship between education and occupational structure has been of long-standing interest to sociologists given that the nature of educational opportunities, job selection and rates of social mobility have been used as measures of social justice (Halsey 1980; Marshall and Swift 1993). Two of the most influential accounts of these issues can be contrasted in terms of 'technocratic' and 'social exclusion' theories. It will be shown that both theories have problems explaining recent changes in education, recruitment and the occupational structure, although 'social exclusion' theory does offer an important insight into the way middle-class families are attempting to 'shelter' from competitive pressures (Ashton 1986).

The *technocratic* explanation conforms closely to the 'liberal' theory of social mobility (Kerr *et al.* 1973; Erikson and Goldthorpe 1992). Here the level of technological development is taken to represent the defining feature of society. The more technologically advanced a society becomes, the greater the demand for technical, scientific and professional workers who require extensive periods of formal education and training, whilst the proportion of semi- and unskilled jobs declines over time (Clark 1962). Hence, the expansion of higher education during the sec-

ond half of the twentieth century is explained in terms of the exponential increase in scientific and technical knowledge, which has led to greater investment in tertiary education to supply the professional, managerial and technical workers required in a 'post-industrial' society (Bell 1973).

Kerr *et al.* (1973) also argue that industrialisation is characterised by high rates of social mobility because inequalities in the opportunity to advance within the educational system are inconsistent with the assignment of occupational roles: 'Industrialisation calls for flexibility and competition; it is against tradition and status based upon family, class, religion, race, or caste' (1973: 53). The political determination to generate equality of opportunity in order to achieve economic efficiency and social justice is reflected in what Parsons (1959) described as the 'axis of achievement' in industrial societies. The role of the labour market is to match the supply and demand for technical skills and competence, based on objective measures of future productive capacity. Technological progression will lead to a growing number of workers establishing technical, managerial and professional careers, which had previously been restricted to a small élite.

This account can be contrasted with the theory of 'social closure', founded upon neo-Weberian sociology and developed by Parkin (1979), Collins (1979), Murphy (1988) and

From *Work, Employment and Society*, 9 (1995), 29–51. Reprinted with permission.

Witz (1992). In Western capitalist societies it is recognised that there has been a fundamental shift in the nature of social exclusion, as Parkin (1979) suggests:

In modern capitalist society the two main exclusionary devices by which the bourgeoisie constructs and maintains itself as a class are, first, those surrounding the institutions of property; and, second, academic or professional qualifications and credentials. Each represents a set of legal arrangements for restricting access to rewards and privileges: property ownership is a form of closure designed to prevent general access to the means of production and its fruits; credentialism is a form of closure designed to control and monitor entry to key positions in the division of labour (47–8).

In Western capitalist societies the dominant form of social exclusion is 'individualist' rather than 'collectivist'. It is based upon formal equality before the law, where entry into élite groups is, at least in principle, attainable by all through an 'open' competition for credentials. Nevertheless, as Parkin (1974) also notes:

Individualist criteria of exclusion through the application of universal rules cannot guarantee the liberal conditions of justice as long as the state tolerates the intrusion of socially inherited handicaps and easements that directly affect the individual's capacity to perform (7–8).

In contrast, collectivist criteria of exclusion involve the direct transmission of advantage to other group members on the basis of 'proof of ancestry', caste, race, class or gender. The rules of exclusion are not based upon the specific attributes of individuals but the generalised attributes of social collectivities (that is, foreigners) (Crompton and Brown 1994).

Collins (1979) has specifically drawn upon social exclusion theory to address the question of education and the occupational structure. On theoretical grounds, he rejects the view that you can read-off the structure and organisation of the education system or the labour market simply in terms of a 'logic of industrialism'. On empirical grounds, he argues that there is little evidence to support the claim that skill levels have risen dramatically during the second half of the twentieth century. Indeed, some have suggested that, on balance, monopoly capitalism is characterised by a process of de-skilling rather than up-skilling or re-skilling (Braverman 1974; Wood 1982). He also found little evidence to support the

assertion that college-trained workers are more productive than those who have not had the benefits of higher education (Berg 1970). Moreover, it is suggested that the education system has little effect on learning, apart from the fact that it moulds those 'disciplined cultural styles already prominent among the higher social classes; grades simply reward and certify displays of middle-class self-discipline' (Collins 1979: 21).

For Collins, the changing relationship between education and occupational stratification should be understood in terms of group conflict over scarce resources (credentials, income, occupational status). This is because the middle classes have been increasingly dependent upon access to professional occupations as a means of reproducing social status and privileged life-styles between the generations, and given a bureaucratisation of the recruitment process where access to virtually all occupational careers has come to depend upon the acquisition of credentials through formal examination (Bourdieu and Boltanski 1978; Collins 1979). In such circumstances, educational credentials are used to provide the means to build specialised professional and technical enclaves, along with hierarchical staff divisions. Therefore, the growing numbers of students gaining tertiary level qualifications is a symptom of credential inflation, rather than a reflection of a burgeoning class of managerial, professional and technical workers (Dore 1976).

What is Wrong with these Theories?

The 'technocratic' assumption that there is a linear up-grading of the skills required in the workforce is clearly suspect, as is the view that this will lead to more middle class career opportunities. The empirical evidence in both Europe and North America reveals a complex process of de-skilling, re-skilling and up-skilling (Lane 1989; Block 1990). Technocratic theory is also flawed because it treats the acquisition of expert knowledge and occupational recruitment as a product of a meritocratic race, leading to a hierarchy of skills, matched with the technical requirements of specific occupational roles. But these processes do not take place in a social vacuum as they are dependent upon social differences in academic performance and employer definitions of 'acceptability' which, for instance, may mean that, even with the same qualifications and work experience, black or female job-seekers are disadvantaged in the competition for jobs (Jenkins 1985; Fevre 1992). Feminist researchers have also shown how the definition of 'skill' is a social fabrication which has served to favour male workers, managers and employers (Dex 1985).

A major weakness in Collins's argument is that he presents 'technocratic' and 'social exclusion' theories as *competing* explanations of the relationship between education and the occupational structure. In part, this is because they correspond to alternative representations of class formation. Technocratic theory has been associated with *'embourgeoisement'* and a shift to a 'professional' society, whereas social exclusion theorists have recognised the existence of enduring class divisions and power struggles between occupational groups (Parkin 1979; Collins 1979).

With the benefit of hindsight, Collins stands accused of failing to acknowledge that at least some of the increasing demand for higher educated labour may be a direct consequence of technological innovation. There have been a number of studies since the publication of *The Credential Society* which suggest that skill levels are increasing, although not in a linear fashion (Block 1990; Gallie 1991). Equally, to assume that the increasing demand for credentials has virtually nothing to do with the changing nature of work, fails to recognise that employers may modify their recruitment process and evaluation of academic credentials due to changes in the model of management and work organisation, as much as that which has resulted from the rapid pace of technological innovation.

A further problem with Collins's 'social exclusion' theory is that although he recognised a tenuous link between credentials and the occupational structure, he did not foresee (a problem he shares with technocratic theorists) that the dislocation between education, credentials and labour market opportunities may be the result of economic restructuring, recession and unemployment, as well as the more established practices of élite occupational groups fending off a growing number of well qualified people entering the labour market (Halsey 1993). Collins obscures the fact that there may be an increasing demand for

professional, managerial and technical workers as well as a more intensive struggle for competitive advantage in education and the labour market. Before examining how the middle classes have responded to this situation, further comment is required on the changing context of middle–class formations (Savage *et al.* 1992; Crompton 1993).

Cultural Capital and the Middle Classes

Cultural capital has long been recognised as vital to the reproduction of the middle classes. In Marshall's (1920) classic work on the *Principles of Economics* he recognised that 'The professional classes especially, while generally eager to save some capital for their children, are even more alert for opportunities of investing it in them' (562). More recently, Bourdieu and Passeron (1977) have suggested that the middle classes have increasingly capitalised on their cultural assets via the education system, given the need to acquire credentials from élite schools, colleges and universities as employers introduced bureaucratic entry and promotion procedures.

What I want to show here is that Bourdieu and others have exaggerated the inevitability of middle–class reproduction (Connell 1983). Although the odds in favour of the children from professional and managerial backgrounds gaining entry to higher education remain largely unchanged throughout the second half to the twentieth century, it is not a foregone conclusion (Goldthorpe 1987; Blackburn and Jarman 1993).[2] The perceived 'risks' associated with economic restructuring, unemployment and educational change since the mid-1970s have made parents more aware of the uncertainties of success and the consequences of failure (Ehrenreich 1989; Wilsher 1993).

Bourdieu's conceptualisation of cultural capital also underplays the contradictory nature of cultural capital in different institutional settings. It may, for instance, be deployed in the education system to facilitate academic success, but at the same time contradict changing models of managerial and professional competence (Atkinson 1985; Harvey 1989). Indeed, the increasing tendency for employers to adopt the discourse of the 'flexible' organisational paradigm[3] in their criteria for recruitment has important implications for the way cultural capital is deployed in the market for jobs. This, it can be argued, now poses a threat to the reproduction of large numbers of 'new' middle-class families who have relied on the bureaucratisation of education, recruitment and employment, given a relative lack of material capital.

The Threat to Bureaucratic Careers

A common feature of organisational restructuring over the last two decades has been the attempt to move to 'flexible', 'flatter' and 'leaner' corporate structures (Kanter 1991; Proctor et al. 1994). This has destabilised bureaucratic career structures enjoyed by a large proportion of managerial and professional staff. Fewer of those in middle-class occupations can now be guaranteed long tenure or career advancement, as organisations in the private sector 'down-size', 'merge', 'restructure' or are 'taken over' and those in the public sector are subject to 'market testing', 'competitive tendering', 'contracting out' or being 'sold off' (Newsweek 1993; duRivage 1992). Whether the process of economic restructuring will lead to an absolute decline in the number of jobs offering long-term career opportunities is an empirical question which cannot be answered conclusively because there is little to suggest that the process of restructuring is slowing. In Britain, W. H. Smith, Sainsbury, Tesco, BT, ICI, BP, British Gas, as well as the big clearing banks, are all in the process of 'down-sizing' their managerial and executive ranks as a way of reducing labour costs (Sunday Times 24 April 1994). Although the extent of such changes is difficult to gauge, there does seem to be an increase in the sense of 'risk' among employees at all levels of employing organisations, in both the private and public sector. The British Social Attitudes Survey recently reported that:

pessimism about the labour market has risen since 1989 among all income groups, but has increased almost fivefold among the highest earners (14 per cent of this group in 1989 expected unemployment to go up, compared with 71 per cent in 1991). After all, redundancies have risen by an unprecedented extent in the generally well-paid south east, in financial services and in the middle ranks of man-

agement. Indeed, responses to a number of questions reveal a faster increase in economic insecurity among the best-off than among other income groups (Cairncross 1992: 30).

A recent survey among members of the Institute of Management in Britain, who are likely to regard themselves as 'professional' managers and to be employed in large and medium-sized organisations, found that the horizontal or downwards movers had increased from 7 per cent in 1980 to nearly 15 per cent in 1992. The annual rate of job change among members also rose from 21 per cent to 29 per cent during the same time period. When managers were asked why they had changed jobs, 'reactive' reasons imposed by employers involving redundancies, transfers and dismissals, or due to merger or restructuring, increased from 21 per cent during the 1980–1982 recession to 41 per cent in 1992 (Inkson and Coe 1993).[4] In Britain in the early 1990s approximately 400,000 professional, managerial and technical workers were registered as unemployed (Wilsher 1993).

In the United States, even during a period of rapid employment growth between 1985 and 1989, 4.3 million employees who had been with their employers for at least three years were made redundant due to plant closure, business failure, or because they had been designated as 'surplus employees'. In total, over 1.5 million managerial and professional employees who had been with their employers for over three years lost their jobs between 1979 and 1989 (Herz 1991). Moreover, during the mid-1980s over two million Americans saw their jobs disappear or deteriorate as a result of an unprecedented level of mergers and acquisitions (Heckscher 1991). It has also been estimated that, during the 1980s, one in four of the American workforce were affected by some form of merger activity and similar trends have been registered in Western Europe (Hunt 1990; Gray and McDermott 1988). These statistics are likely to underestimate the extent of economic insecurity among managerial and professional workers. These employees prefer to 'resign' rather than be made redundant and to define themselves as consultants, self-employed or 'between jobs rather than be labelled 'unemployed'.

In contrast, projections of the future demand for managerial and professional workers suggest a significant increase. According to the Institute for Employment

Research in Britain, managerial and administrative occupations will increase by twelve per cent between 1990 and the year 2000. During the same period, professional occupations are predicted to increase by 21 per cent (*Financial Times* 1992). Figures published by the Department of Labour in the United States, likewise, predict that between 1990 and 2005 there will be a 76.6 per cent increase in the number of 'managerial' jobs. Such predictions are notoriously unreliable and need to be treated with extreme caution. In the US, for example, recent employment projections for the same period show a decline in the average annual number of vacancies in jobs requiring a degree, compared with opportunities available in the 1984–1990 period (Shelley 1992: 13).

Equally, the increase in the demand for managerial and professional workers does not mean that most of these jobs will offer organisational 'careers' (Hughes 1958; Wilensky 1960) because the underlying assumptions about employment contracts, conditions and relations in post-war Western capitalist societies no longer hold with the demise of bureaucratic work (Handy 1989). As a consequence, the 'work' and 'market' situations of those who have conventionally been grouped together under the label of the 'middle' or 'service' class are likely to become increasingly polarised. As Goldthorpe has acknowledged:

the basis of the expanding service class is an essentially bureaucratic one. Bureaucracies, through their very form, tend to establish 'career lines' for those who are employed within them, and success or failure for the latter is then largely defined in terms of how far along these lines they are able to progress. Thus, failure does not usually mean that the individual is actually relegated from the bureaucracy and forced to take up employment of a quite different class character, but only that he [or she] achieves relatively little advancement within the bureaucracy. A contrast may be drawn here with the consequences of failure in an entrepreneurial role, which would seem far more likely to lead to a decisive change in class position (1987: 333).

A common feature of 'flexible' organisational paradigms is the aim to incorporate elements of an 'enterprise' culture (Kanter 1991). This has not occurred simply as a result of technological innovation but due to changing organisational imperatives, which in most public

and private sector organisations has meant 'down-sizing' as a means to cost-cutting. The increasing tendency for employing organisations to distinguish between strategic 'core' employees and contract, peripheral and support workers (Harrison and Kelley 1993) also suggests that a hierarchy of 'occupations' and 'careers' cannot be juxtaposed as has been the convention. The de-layering of organisational bureaucracy serves in many instances to widen the division between the strategic core of senior managerial personnel and the remainder of the workforce (Heckscher 1991). Therefore, restricted career opportunities are likely to lead to status frustration, given that there are fewer opportunities for internal career progression in 'flatter' and 'leaner' organisations (Nicholson and West 1988; Scase and Goffee 1989).

As a result, 'flexible careers', rather than 'bureaucratic careers' (Whyte 1965; Brown and Scase 1994), can be expected to become more prevalent. Whereas bureaucratic careers are associated with a predictable linear progression within corporate hierarchies, flexible careers are invariably contingent and retrospective. They involve frequent job change irrespective of whether each move is voluntary or imposed. For the workers involved, the aim is to gain incremental progression with each move in terms of the employment package (seniority, salary, car and other fringe benefits).

An inevitable feature of 'flexible career' patterns is that they are inherently insecure. It is no longer simply a question of gaining access to a superior job, but of maintaining one's 'employability', of keeping fit in both the internal and external market for jobs through the acquisition of externally validated credentials, in-house training programmes, social contacts and networks.

The declining faith in the ability of employing organisations to offer secure long-term employment, or to meet their expectations of career advancement, will lead to an increasing emphasis on academic and professional credentials as an insurance policy in the same way that people insure themselves and their homes against adversity. This trend provides a plausible explanation of the increasing demand for post-compulsory education (Halsey 1993; Shelley 1992). It also reflects the anxiety among parents concerning the education of their children, given that the populist appeal of the enterprise culture and personal improvement through the acquisition of material property is correctly understood by the middle classes to be a 'risky business'. Social status and security is still seen to be more reliably secured through the acquisition of cultural capital, especially in the form of academic qualifications from prestigious institutions (Scott 1991; David 1992).

We can also predict that any de-coupling of bureaucratic career routes into the upper tiers of corporate hierarchies will place an even greater emphasis on access to initial 'fast track' training programmes in order to climb truncated corporate career ladders and to obtain a 'value added' *curriculum vitae*. Therefore, in the context of the 1990s the importance of credentials has increased, as the value of 'organisational' assets have declined (Savage *et al.* 1992).

Educational Expansion and Credential Inflation

If middle-class career patterns are being 'restructured', there is also considerable anxiety about recent changes in the education system. In an élite system of higher education the possession of a graduate qualification represents a passport into professional and managerial occupations. The recent move towards mass systems of higher education in a number of European countries, such as Britain, is removing the problem of access to higher education from middle-class families. It is also opening new opportunities to working-class, 'mature' and ethnic minority students for gaining graduate qualifications, and has been accompanied by increasing competition between the sexes. Despite marked differences in the academic programmes pursued by female and male students, with the former concentrated in the humanities and social sciences, the overall academic performance of female students has significantly improved. In Britain, the difference between the proportion of males and females under the age of 25 with qualifications above A-level (including degrees) narrowed in 1990 to within a single percentage point (11 per cent of males and 10 per cent of females) (*Employment Gazette* 1992). Moreover, in their study of gendered jobs and social change, Crompton and Sanderson (1990) conclude that:

The occupational order will always bear the imprint of gender, but in the present situation, some kind of convergence between male and female patterns is probably more likely in Western industrial societies than the restructuring of a highly segregated occupational matrix (183).

This increasing competition for credentials is occurring at a time when employers are finding it increasingly difficult to absorb the growing number of higher educated students. In 1987 recorded graduate unemployment in Britain stood at 6.9 per cent: in 1992 it had climbed to 14.5 per cent. This 'over-supply' of graduate labour has exacerbated the problem of 'credential inflation' (Dore 1976). This will lead employers to recruit graduates for jobs which previously did not require a university education. Hirsch (1977) has noted that:

the . . . excess of apparently qualified candidates induces an intensification of job screening that has the effect of lengthening the obstacle course of education and favouring those best able to sustain a longer or more costly race. These are the well off and the well connected (50).

Credential inflation is also intensifying the competition for credentials from élite universities because degree-holders stand 'relative' to one another in a hierarchy of academic and social worth. When market crowding occurs, employers become more discerning about the 'status' of credentials. A degree from Oxbridge or an Ivy League University is judged to have greater 'capital' value than one from a little-known university or college in the market for jobs.

The nature of credential inflation is well understood in the sociological literature, but less is known about the role of the credential in the context of recent economic and organisational restructuring. There is, for example, evidence to suggest that employers are intensifying their 'screening' of potential employees by recruiting students who have been on work experience programmes with the company in question; by preferring universities where courses have been tailored to the specific needs of employers; and by a greater use of 'assessment' centres in order to arrive at more informed 'gut feelings' about the acceptability of potential recruits (Brown and Scase 1994; Herriot 1984).

However, problems associated with the intermediary role played by credentials in the articulation between education and the occupational structure are not only a result of market crowding. In organisations which espouse a 'flexible' rather than 'bureaucratic' paradigm of organisational efficiency, credentials are seen to offer recruitment personnel less information about what they believe they need to know when attempting to judge the relative merits of different candidates, especially if they are being recruited to training programmes leading into middle or senior managerial positions. Changes in employer recruitment criteria, where personal and transferable skills assume greater significance, are related to changes in employer models of managerial and professional competence (Brown and Scase 1994).

Occupational Recruitment and Changing Codes of Symbolic Control

Within organisation theory a number of writers have drawn a distinction between what Burns and Stalker (1961) define as 'mechanistic' and 'organic' systems of management (see also McGregor 1960). Such 'ideal types' have much in common with the one used here which contrasts 'bureaucratic' and 'flexible' organisational paradigms (Brown and Scase 1994). In drawing this distinction it is important to caution against the exaggerated claims made by management gurus about the demise of the bureaucratic paradigm. Although 'flexible' organisations have the potential to release the creative and entrepreneurial energies of their employees, in reality this is the exception rather than the rule. The restructuring of IBM, which was held to be a model of human resource management in the 1980s, demonstrates that there is little contradiction between moving towards a more 'flexible' organisational structure and corporate indifference towards technical, managerial and professional staff (Hoerr 1994). We also should not be surprised to find a reluctance on the part of senior managers to abandon existing command and control systems, despite adopting the rhetoric of the 'flexible' organisation (Heckscher 1991; Ezzamel et al. 1993).

The use of the distinction between bureaucratic and flexible paradigms in this paper is intended to reflect the ways in which graduate employers are adopting the discourse of the flexible paradigm in their recruitment strategies. In particular, they express an increasing demand for candidates who exhibit 'charismatic' rather than 'bureaucratic' personality characteristics (Table 48.1).

Throughout the twentieth century the bureaucratic paradigm has represented the dominant discourse of corporate efficiency. Within this discourse, managerial work is based upon de-personalised relationships which involve clearly defined roles, rules and procedures (Bendix 1956). Weber described bureaucracy in terms of a 'form of

Table 48.1. Corporate recruitment, managerial qualities, and the changing code of symbolic control

	Code of Conduct	
	Bureaucratic Paradigm	Flexible Paradigm
Selection	De-personalized	Personalized
Socialization	Rule-following Inter-positional	Negotiated rule-making Inter-personal
Cognitive Style	Bureaucratic personality	Charismatic personality
Role Performance	Individual assignments	Team-work and project management
Mode of social control	Impersonal Explicit rules	Personalized Implicit rules
Hierarchy	Explicit and extended	Implicit and truncated
Leadership Style	Command and control	Facilitate and empower
Authority	Position and status	Leadership and contribution
Promotion	Explicit achievement criteria/ time-serving	Implicit achievement criteria/ contribution and personal compatibility
Corporate Culture	Weak	Strong

organisation that emphasises precision, speed, clarity, regularity, reliability, and efficiency, achieved through the creation of a fixed division of tasks, hierarchical supervision, and detailed rules and regulations' (Morgan 1986: 24–5).

The assignment of roles is based on technical expertise assessed through formal examination.[5] Organisational efficiency depends upon the development of the bureaucratic personality, which is characterised by a high degree of conformist and rule-following behaviour (Merton 1949). Moreover, in the same way that bureaucratic work involves extensive use of categorisation and compartmentalism based on the application of abstract principles, so there is a clear separation between the private social world of the individual and the public 'visible' role of the corporate official, at least during the exercise of official duties. The preservation of personal space and intimate relationships divorced from the impersonal and public performance of bureaucratic routine is a dominant feature of the bureaucratic personality (Merton 1949).[6]

Within the 'flexible' paradigm the bureaucratic personality is held to be a source of what Veblen described as 'trained incapacity' where what amounts to appropriate forms of socialisation and role performance in bureaucratic organisations is increasingly judged to be inappropriate (see Merton 1949: 198). In Max Weber's formulation of charismatic leadership, he applied it to a small number of extraordinary 'gifted' individuals among the religious prophets, military heroes, political leaders and social reformers. Weber noted that:

In contrast to any kind of bureaucratic organization of offices, the charismatic structure knows nothing of a form or of an ordered procedure of appointment or dismissal. It knows no regulated 'career', 'advancement', 'salary', or regulated and expert training of the holder of charisma or of his aids. It knows no agency of control or appeal, no local bailiwicks or exclusive functional jurisdictions; nor does it embrace permanent institutions like our bureaucratic 'departments', which are independent of persons and of purely personal charisma (in Gerth and Mills 1967: 246).

Edward Shils has questioned Weber's restricted use of charisma to refer to extraordinarily gifted individuals engaged in intense, concentrated and innovative action. Shils suggests that the 'normal' form of charisma is more attenuated and dispersed. Indeed, Weber clearly recognised that charisma invariably became 'routinised' into traditionalism or into bureaucratisation:

the routinization of charisma, in quite essential respects, is identical with adjustment to the conditions of the economy, that is, to the continuously effective routines of workaday life (in Gerth and Mills 1967: 54).

What is being suggested here is that many of the features which Weber associated with the charismatic personality are becoming part of a changing ideology of symbolic control, in an attempt to resolve command and control problems in 'flexible' organisations. The rhetoric of the charismatic personality can be characterised in terms of a demand for people who seek to undermine the structures of routine action and rule-following behaviour; where inner determination, drive and strength are given greater weight than conformity to external bureaucratic controls; where recognition, authority, legitimacy and rewards are achieved through 'proving one's worth' rather than derived on the basis of one's position in the organisational hierarchy. In essence, the charismatic personality is the opposite of the bureaucratic, in that it assumes 'personalised' relationships with colleagues and the need for mutual compatibility, as much as the acquisition of expert knowledge.

This increasing importance attached to the charismatic personality clearly sits comfortably with the 'great man, token woman' view of Western history and corporate success.[7] Its significance here is that the rhetoric of the characteristic personality has significant implications for the selection criteria adopted by graduate recruiters (Brown and Scase 1994).

As the definition of managerial qualities comes to assume elements of personal charisma, the 'rules of entry' and 'rules of the game' become increasingly 'personalised'. The distinction between the 'official' and the 'person' is weakened in the work situation, leading to an exposure of the 'whole' person in the assessment of adequate performance, which is reflected in the increasing use of student profiles, assessment centres and staff appraisal schemes (see also Foucault 1977; Cohen 1985). Moreover, the greater the emphasis upon normative control, the greater the demand for recruits to exhibit strong cultural affiliation to colleagues and the organisation (Burns and Stalker 1961; Handy 1989).

This is not to suggest that *social* qualifications were eliminated in recruitment to bureaucratic organisations. The selection of élites has traditionally been associated with a 'cultural code' consistent with images of masculine managerial authority; expert knowledge and the right school tie (Scott 1991; Scase 1992). Rather, if employers are rewarding the certified display of middle class self-discipline as Collins (1979) assumes, there has not only been a change in its form, but it has become an explicit element of employer recruitment practices. It is now the *whole* person who is on show and at stake in the market for managerial and professional work:

in order to have success it is not sufficient to have the skill and equipment for performing a given task but that one must be able to 'put across' one's personality in competition with many others shapes the attitude toward oneself . . . since success depends largely on how one sells one's personality, one experiences oneself as a commodity or rather simultaneously as the seller *and* the commodity to be sold (Fromm 1949: 70).

It is the 'personality package' based on a combination of credentials, technical skills and charismatic qualities which needs to be re-packaged and sold in the market for managerial and professional work. Without the appropriate 'social' education applicants will find it increasingly difficult to 'decode' the rules by which the selection process is being played (Bernstein 1975). Such a change in cultural 'code' will make the social background, gender and ethnic identity of applicants increasingly 'visible' and significant for entry to managerial and professional jobs, irrespective of one's academic credentials (Bernstein 1976).

So far it has been argued that changes within the labour market and higher education have intensified the competition for credentials in a bid to maintain or enhance 'positional' advantage in the market for managerial and professional careers. However, there is little to suggest that the importance of credentials will decline despite the expressed desire on the part of employers for graduate recruits who exhibit charismatic qualities. As more people enter the labour market with graduate qualifications, employers will intensify their screening process by only accepting

credentials from élite institutions; those with higher grades; or those with a post-graduate qualification such as an MBA. In this context the credential should be understood as the key which unlocks, but does not open, doors. The bureaucratic code of middle class self-discipline, which graduate credentials signify, is having to be repackaged.

Within the middle classes, the development of the 'charismatic' qualities of their children is becoming as important as arming them with the necessary credentials, contacts and networks. There is nothing new about this focus on the 'rounded' person, but whereas a range of broader interests and hobbies which offered time-out from academic study was seen as a form of cultural *consumption* which was to be enjoyed for its own sake, it has increasingly become a form of *investment* as part of the construction of a 'value added' *curriculum vitae*. This involves an increasing 'commodification' of the socio-emotional embodiment of culture, incorporating drive, ambition, social confidence, tastes and interpersonal skills (Bourdieu 1986).

The Changing Patterns of Exclusion

What this discussion suggests is that, even if there has been an increased proportion of jobs defined as managerial and professional, changes in the labour market and education system are heightening the 'competition for a livelihood' (Weber 1978). Given that few middle-class families can maintain their social position through direct inheritance, or through monopolistic control over the market for superior jobs, the key to occupational success is through access to market power: resources in the market place, rather than influence over markets (Hirsch 1977: 153). In the post-war period, the expansion of white collar occupations may not have created *'embourgeoisement'* but it has led to the spread of middle-class aspirations among a much larger section of the population. As long as the market for managerial and professional workers continued to expand, this did not pose a serious threat to the reproduction of middle-class households. However, over the last two decades the perceived threat to economic livelihood and social status has led the middle classes to seek shelter from competitive pressures through the exercise of market power.

This competition for 'positional' advantage is not only directed against the working class but between social groups which can be loosely described in terms of the 'old' and 'new' middle class (Savage *et al.* 1992; Crompton 1993). The 'old' has its power base in material property and the 'new', a large proportion of whom are employed in the public sector, have theirs in 'expert' knowledge systems which are wrapped in a professional ethos of service to the community (Perkin 1989). Historically, this has involved a conflict over property rights between the 'entrepreneurial' ideal of the 'old' middle class and the 'professional' ideal of the 'new'. In the context of the early 1990s, this conflict over property rights has been broadened into a more intensive distributional struggle over cultural capital in the reproduction of family status, life-style and property.

The attack on state professionals since the rise of neo-conservative governments in the late 1970s can be seen as part and parcel of this conflict, as Perkin (1989) has noted:

by far the most important division between the interest groups is between the public sector professions, those funded directly or indirectly by the state, and the private sector professions, chiefly the managers of private corporations. As the struggle between lord and peasant was the master conflict in feudal society and the struggle between capitalist and wage earner the master conflict in industrial society, so the struggle between the public and private sector professions is the master conflict of positional society (10).

Although Perkin over-states his case, the market reforms within education as well as in other areas of the welfare state can be interpreted as a form of 'professional' class conflict (Hirsch 1977).[8]

Given a commitment to the ideology of an open society, collectivist rather than individualist 'rules of exclusion' (involving a return to what Dewey described as the 'feudal dogma of social predestination') have not been pursued. Rather, there has been a change in the *rules of engagement* established to mediate the competition for credentials. Whereas in the post-war period the rules of engagement were based upon the ideology of meritocracy and the introduction of 'comprehensive' education, they are now based on 'market' principles and what has been called the 'ideology of

parentocracy' (Brown 1990).[9] As a consequence, educational selection is increasingly based on the *wealth* and *wishes* of parents rather than the individual *abilities* and *efforts* of pupils. Here, the equation 'ability + effort = merit' has been reformulated into 'resources + preference = choice'.[10]

The defining feature of the ideology of parentocracy, and the market policies it seeks to legitimate, is not the amount of education received but the social basis upon which educational selection is organised. Therefore, the expansion of higher education does not represent an equalising of opportunities because the recent increase in graduate numbers in Britain will simply mean that differences between institutions of higher learning will increase (rather like those found in the United States) as the labour market for graduates becomes polarised between the 'fast-track' leading to senior managerial positions and a mass of white-collar jobs which offer few prospects (Brown and Scase 1994).

In a political climate where the Right have claimed a moral legitimacy for a market system of education under the rhetorical slogans of 'choice', 'standards' and 'freedom', those parents who can exert their market power to gain a competitive advantage for their children are increasingly likely to do so, given an evaluation that educational success has become too important to leave to the chance outcome of a formally open competition (despite what the research evidence has taught us about social class and patterns of achievement—Brown 1990). The increased opportunity for the middle classes to exert the full weight of their market power in the competition for credentials will ensure that they will seek to dominate access to élite institutions at each stage of the education process—from the cradle to graduation and beyond.

This shift in the 'rules of engagement', from that based on 'merit' to 'the market', is associated with the increased importance of material capital required to meet the escalating costs involved in acquiring the appropriate forms of cultural capital. These costs are likely to increase further with the introduction of 'user pays' arrangements to fund higher education (Lauder 1991). We should also expect the 'old' middle class to use their superior material assets in the market for education, and other sources of cultural capital, in order to advance their interests against those of other classes (including the 'new' middle class) who have been largely dependent upon the rules of engagement based on 'merit' rather than 'the market'.

Moreover, as access to cultural capital in the form of scarce credentials and charismatic qualities come to depend upon market power, the education system can do little to improve the prospects of disadvantaged students. This is despite the fact that, in Britain, it is the less prestigious universities which have shown the greater willingness to modify their curricula and teaching programmes to meet the 'needs' of industry and commerce. For although employers are demanding that the educational system produces students with good personal, communication and transferable skills, the problem with incorporating non-academic 'qualities' into the educational assessment process is that the more students are judged on a 'subjective' basis, the less their credentials are likely to command credibility, given that the academic hierarchy remains tied to 'objective' performance in public examinations. When recruiting for 'fast track' training programmes, employers will justify the targeting of élite universities on the grounds that they need to recruit students of the highest calibre who, by definition, are believed to attend the élite universities because they have the highest academic entry requirements (Brown and Scase 1994).

Indeed, in the less prestigious universities catering for students from the 'new' middle class and a growing number of non-traditional students from working-class backgrounds, women and ethnic minorities, the introduction of social and personal skills teaching within the formal curriculum has striking parallels with the introduction of 'compensatory' education programmes for disadvantaged children in the 1960s and 1970s. The idea being that through such programmes it is possible to equalise competitive conditions between students irrespective of social background. Likewise, although social and personal skills appear to be open to all through formal programmes of learning, they ignore the social context in which the social qualities of tastes, manners, ways of knowing and personal compatibility are acquired and translated into cultural capital (Bourdieu 1986).

The growing demand for management 'potential' to exhibit 'charismatic' qualities has done little to alter the Darwinian view of most recruiters. Whereas in bureaucratic organisations the recruitment process was explicitly targeted on the search for 'raw' intellectual talent and technical expertise, it is now extended to include the 'gift' of charisma. This is clearly an example of *social* gifts being translated into *natural* gifts, legitimated through the educational system and occupational selection (Bourdieu and Passeron 1977).

Conclusion

In this paper it has been suggested that Western capitalist societies are experiencing class conflict in relation to education and the labour market. The intensification of global economic competition; high rates of unemployment; economic recession; attempts to subject the public sector to market forces; the challenge to the bureaucratic paradigm of organisational efficiency and the definition of managerial competence which it harbours; and the shift to mass systems of higher education: all have served to intensify a general sense of economic insecurity. In response, the middle classes (whilst not abandoning the individualist rules of exclusion) have undermined the meritocratic rules of engagement upon which the competition for a livelihood was legitimated in post-war Western capitalist societies. This has brought into sharp relief the tension between the need for the middle classes to legitimate themselves by preserving openness of access, and the desire to reproduce themselves socially by resort to closure on the basis of descent (Parkin 1979: 47). This change in the rules of engagement is giving the middle classes the opportunity to capitalise on their superior market power in the competition for credentials within a market-driven system of education. In this context, the role of the state has increasingly become one of manufacturing the conditions in which market forces can operate freely, rather than that of pursuing a liberal-democratic policy of 'equality of opportunity', where it is incumbent upon the state to constrain the powerful in the exercise of their market power.[11] However, although there can be little doubt that the middle classes remain in the ascendancy in the competition for a livelihood, some of the middle class are 'more equal than others' in their ability to exert market power.

These observations also raise questions about the way 'market' and 'work' situations have governed the location of occupations within class *schema* (Goldthorpe *et al.* 1987; Crompton 1993). There are, arguably, increasingly important differences in 'work' and 'market' situations in terms of job security, career opportunities, income and job satisfaction within the middle classes (Savage *et al.* 1992). It also seems likely that there will be an increasing polarisation in the fortunes of students from middle–class backgrounds. However, the extent and consequences of the trends identified in this paper must await detailed empirical investigation.

Notes

1. I would like to thank Pat Ainley, David Ashton, Sarah Cant, Rosemary Crompton, Nicola Kerry, Hugh Lauder, Ray Pahl, Frank Parkin and Mike Savage for their comments on an early draft of this paper, and Richard Scase for encouraging me to develop some of the ideas which we discussed during the writing of *Higher Education and Corporate Realities* (Brown and Scase 1994).
2. Bourdieu has noted that there is always a degree of risk involved in social reproduction, given that cultural capital cannot be directly transmitted or inherited (see Shilling 1993: 142–3; Connell 1983).
3. The use of the term 'flexible' organisations will be used throughout this paper to refer to post-bureaucratic organisational paradigms.
4. This research was based on a sample of 800 managers. It probably under-estimates the extent of managerial job change since only one third responded to the questionnaire.
5. 'The structure is one which approaches the complete elimination of personalised relationships and nonrational considerations (hostility, anxiety, affectual involvement, etc.)' (Merton 1949: 196).
6. However, in Whyte's (1965) account of the 'organisation man', it is suggested that the organisation not only consumed much of the time and energy of the official, but also placed considerable demands upon his (*sic*) family.
7. Gerth and Mills (1967) note that: 'Weber's conception of the charismatic leader is a continuation of a 'philosophy of history' which, after Carlyle's *Heroes and Hero Worship*, influenced a great deal of nineteenth-century his-

tory writing. In such an emphasis, the monumentalized individual becomes the sovereign of history' (53).
8. This conflict between public and private sector workers clearly has a gender dimension as Esping-Andersen has suggested: 'the Swedish employment-structure is evolving towards two economies: one, a heavily male private sector; the other, a female-dominated public sector . . . one might easily imagine a war between male workers in the private sector; and female workers in the welfare state' (in Crompton 1993: 206).
9. It is also important to note that the ideology of parentocracy has not emerged as a result of a groundswell of popular demand for radical educational reform among a majority of parents, and does not imply an increase in 'parent power' over the school curriculum or 'choice' of school. On the contrary, it is the state and not parents who have strengthened control over what is taught in schools, and it will be schools who choose pupils, rather than parents who choose schools, when it comes to gaining access to more popular educational establishments.
10. Paradoxically, despite the fact that the market rules of exclusion are based on the sovereignty of individual freedom, educational 'choice' is dependent upon parental wealth and preferences, whereas the 'ideology of meritocracy' is dedicated to the elimination of any impediment to individual competition apart from that based on ability and effort.
11. In Britain, no post-war government was prepared to abolish the élite private schools, although the number of students attending them declined in the 1960s and 1970s.

References

Ashton, D. (1986), *Unemployment under Capitalism* (Brighton: Wheatsheaf).

Atkinson, J. (1985), 'The Changing Corporation', in D. Clutterbuck (ed.), *New Patterns of Work* (Aldershot: Gower).

Bell, D. (1973), *The Coming of Post-Industrial Society* (New York: Basic Books).

Bendix, R. (1956), *Work and Authority in Industry* (New York: John Wiley).

Berg, I. (1970), *Education and Jobs: The Great Training Robbery* (New York: Praeger).

Bernstein, B. (1975), *Class, Codes and Control: Towards a Theory of Educational Transmission*, iii (2nd edn. London: Routledge).

—— (1976), 'Class and Pedagogies: Visible and Invisible', in J. Karabel and A. H. Halsey (eds.), *Power and Ideology in Education* (Oxford: Oxford Univ. Press).

Blackburn, R., and Jarman, J. (1993), 'Changing Inequalities in Access to British Universities', *Oxford Review of Education*, 19/2: 197–215.

Block, F. (1990), *Postindustrial Possibilities: A Critique of Economic Discourse* (Berkeley: Univ. of California).

Bourdieu, P. (1986), *Distinction: A Social Critique of the Judgement of Taste* (London: Routledge).

——, and Boltanski, L. (1978), 'Changes in Social Structure and Changes in the Demand for Education', in S. Giner and M. Archer (eds.), *Contemporary Europe: Social Structure and Cultural Change* (London: Routledge).

——, and Passeron, J. (1964), *The Inheritors: French Students and their Relation to Culture* (London: Univ. of Chicago).

—— (1977), *Reproduction in Education, Society and Culture* (London: Sage).

Braverman, H. (1974), *Labour and Monopoly Capitalism: The Degradation of Work in the Twentieth Century* (New York: Monthly Review Press).

Brown, P. (1987), *Schooling Ordinary Kids* (London: Tavistock).

—— (1990), 'The Third Wave: Education and the Ideology of Parentocracy', *British Journal of Sociology of Education*, 11/1: 65–85.

—— and Lauder, H. (1992), 'Education, Economy and Society: An Introduction to a New Agenda', in P. Brown and H. Lauder (eds.), *Education for Economic Survival: From Fordism to Post-Fordism?* (London: Routledge).

——, and Scase, R. (1994), *Higher Education and Corporate Realities: Class, Culture and the Decline of Graduate Careers* (London: UCL Press).

Burns, T., and Stalker, G. (1961), *The Management of Innovation* (London: Tavistock).

Cairncross, F. (1992), 'The Influence of the Recession', in R. Jowell *et al.* (eds.), *British Social Attitudes: The 9th Report* (Aldershot: Dartmouth).

Chitty, C. (1989), *Towards a New Education System: The Victory of the New Right?* (London: Falmer Press).

Clark, B. (1962), *Education and the Expert Society* (San Francisco: Chandler).

Cohen, S. (1985), *Visions of Social Control* (Oxford: Polity).

Collins, R. (1979), *The Credential Society: An Historical Sociology of Education and Stratification* (New York: Academic Press).

Connell, R. (1983), *Which Way is Up? Essays on Class, Sex and Culture* (London: George Allen and Unwin).

Crompton, R. (1993), *Class and Stratification: An Introduction to Current Debates* (Cambridge: Polity).

——, and Brown, P. (1994), 'Introduction', in P. Brown and R. Crompton (eds.), *A New Europe? Economic Restructuring and Social Exclusion* (London: UCL Press).

——, and Sanderson, K. (1990), *Gendered Jobs and Social Change* (London: Unwin Hyman).

David, M. (1993), *Parents, Gender and Education Reform* (Oxford: Polity).

Dex, S. (1985), *The Sexual Division of Work* (Brighton: Wheatsheaf).

Dore, R. (1976), *The Diploma Disease* (London: Allen and Unwin).

duRivage, V. (1992), 'Flexibility Trap: The Proliferation of Marginal Jobs', *The American Prospect*, 9 (Spring), 84–93.

Ehrenreich, B. (1989), *Fear of Falling: The Inner Life of the Middle Class* (New York: Pantheon).

Employment Gazette (1992), 'Economic Activity and Qualifications: Results from the Labour Force Study' (March), 101–33.

Erikson, R., and Goldthorpe, J. (1992), *The Constant Flux: A Study of Social Mobility in Industrial Societies* (Oxford: Clarendon).

Ezzamel, M., Lilley, S., and Wilmo, H. (1993), 'Be Wary of New Waves', *Management Today* (October), 100–2.

Fevre, R. (1992), *The Sociology of Labour Markets* (Hemel Hempstead: Harvester Wheatsheaf).

Financial Times (1992), 'Juggling Careers in the Jobs Circus' (13th November).

Foucault, M. (1977), *Discipline and Punish: The Birth of the Prison* (London: Tavistock).

Fromm, E. (1949), *Man for Himself: An Enquiry into the Psychology of Ethics* (London: Routledge).

Gallie, D. (1991), 'Patterns of Skill Change: Upskilling, Deskilling or the Polarization of Skills?', *Work, Employment and Society*, 5/3: 319–51.

Gerth, H., and Mills, C. W. (1967) (eds.), *From Max Weber* (London: Routledge).

Giddens, A. (1973), *The Class Structure of the Advanced Societies* (London: Hutchinson).

Goldthorpe, J. *et al.* (1987), *Social Mobility and Class Structure in Modern Britain* (2nd edn., Oxford: Clarendon).

Gray, S. J., and McDermott, M. C. (1988), 'International Mergers and Takeovers: A Review of Trends and Recent Developments', *European Management Journal*, 6: 1, 26–43.

Halsey, A. H. (1993), 'Trends in Access and Equality in Higher Education: Britain in International Perspective', *Oxford Review of Education*, 19/2: 129–40.

——, Heath, A., and Ridge, J. (1980), *Origins and Destinations* (Oxford: Clarendon).

Handy, C. (1989), *The Age of Unreason* (London: Business Books).

Harrison, B., and Kelley, R. (1983), 'Outsourcing and the Search for "Flexibility"', *Work, Employment and Society*, 7/2: 213–35.

Harvey, D. (1989), *The Conditions of Post-Modernity* (Oxford: Blackwell).

Heckscher, C. (1991), 'Can Business Beat Bureaucracy?', *The American Prospect* (Spring), 114–28.

Herriot, P. (1984), *Down From the Ivory Tower: Graduates and Their Jobs* (Chichester: John Wiley).

Herz, D. (1991), 'Worker Displacement Still Common in the Late 1980s', *Monthly Labor Review*, 114 (May), 3–9.

Hirsch, F. (1977), *Social Limits to Growth* (London: Routledge).

Hoerr, J. (1994), 'System Crash: How Workers at IBM Learned that Knowledge isn't Power', *The American Prospect* (Winter), 68–77.

Hughes, E. (1958), *Men and Their Work* (Glencoe: Free Press).

Hunt, J. W. (1990), 'Changing Patterns of Acquisition Behaviour in Takeovers and the Consequences for Acquisition Processes', *Strategic Management Journal*, 1/1: 69–77.

Inkson, K., and Coe, T. (1993), 'Are Career Ladders Disappearing?' (briefing paper, London: The Institute of Management).

Jenkins, R. (1985), 'Black Workers in the Labour Market: The Price of Recession', in B. Roberts, R. Finnegan, and D. Gallie (eds.), *New Approaches to Economic Life* (Manchester: Manchester Univ. Press).

Kanter, R. (1977), *Men and Women of the Corporation* (New York: Basic Books).

—— (1989), *When Giants Learn to Dance* (London: Simon and Schuster).

—— (1991), 'The Future of Bureaucracy and Hierarchy in Organisational Theory: A Report from the Field', in P. Bourdieu and J. Coleman (eds.), *Social Theory for a Changing Society* (Boulder, Colo.: Westview).

Kerr, C. *et al.* (1973), *Industrialism and Industrial Man* (Harmondsworth: Penguin).

Lane, C. (1989), *Management and Labour in Europe* (Aldershot: Edward Elgar).

Lauder, H. (1991), 'Education, Democracy and the Economy', *British Journal of Sociology of Education*, 12: 417–31.

Lipietz, A. (1987), *Mirages and Miracles: The Crisis of Global Fordism* (London: Verso).

Marshall, A. (1920), *Principles of Economics* (London: Macmillan).

Marshall, G., and Swift, A. (1993), 'Social Class and Social Justice', *British Journal of Sociology*, 44/2: 187–211.

McGregor, D. (1960), *The Human Side of Enterprise* (New York: McGraw-Hill).

Merton, R. (1949), *Social Theory and Social Structure* (New York: Free Press).

Morgan, G. (1986), *Images of Organisations* (London: Sage).

Murphy, R. (1988), *Social Closure: The Theory of Monopolization and Exclusion* (Oxford: Clarendon Press).

Newsweek (1993), *Jobs* (14 June), 10–25.

Nicholson, N., and West, M. (1988), *Managerial*

Job Change: Men and Women in Transition (Cambridge: Cambridge Univ. Press).

Parkin, F. (1974) (ed.), *The Social Analysis of Class Structure* (London: Tavistock).

—— (1979), *Marxism and Class Theory: A Bourgeois Critique* (London: Tavistock).

Parsons, T. (1959), 'The School Class as a Social System: Some of its Functions in American Society', *Harvard Educational Review*, 29: 297–318.

Perkin, H. (1989), *The Rise of Professional Society: England since 1880* (London: Routledge).

Proctor, S., Rowlinson, M., McArdle, L., Hassard, J., and Forrester, P. (1994), 'Flexibility, Politics and Strategy: In Defence of the Model of the Flexible Firm', *Work, Employment and Society*, 8/2: 221–42.

Reich, R. (1991), *The Work of Nations* (London: Simon and Schuster).

Sabel, C. (1982), *Work and Politics: The Division of Labour in Industry* (Cambridge: Cambridge Univ. Press).

Savage, M., Barlow, J., Dickens, P., and Fielding, T. (1992), *Property, Bureaucracy and Culture: Middle Class Formation in Contemporary Britain* (London: Routledge).

——, and Witz, A. (1992) (eds.), *Gender and Bureaucracy* (Oxford: Blackwell).

Scase, R. (1992), *Class* (Milton Keynes: Open Univ. Press).

——, and Goffee, R. (1989), *Reluctant Managers: Their Work and Lifestyles* (London: Routledge).

Schultz, T. (1960), 'Capital Formation by Education', *Journal of Political Economy*, 68: 571–83.

Shelley, K. (1992), 'The Future of Jobs for College Graduates', *Monthly Labour Review*, 115 (July), 13–21.

Shilling, C. (1993), *The Body and Social Theory* (London: Sage).

Shils, E. (1965), 'Charisma, Order and Status', *American Sociological Review*, 30: 199–213.

—— (1968), 'Charisma', *International Encyclopaedia of the Social Sciences*, 2: 286–90.

Scott, J. (1991), *Who Rules Britain?* (Cambridge: Polity).

Weber, M. (1978), *Economy and Society*, (ed.) G. Roth and C. Wittich (Berkeley: Univ. of California Press).

Whyte, W. (1965), *The Organisation Man* (Harmondsworth: Penguin).

Wilensky, H. (1960), 'Work, Careers, and Social Integration', *International Social Science Journal*, 12: 543–60.

Wilsher, P. (1993), 'The Mixed-up Manager', *Management Today* (October), 34–40.

Witz, A. (1992), *Professions and Patriarchy* (London: Routledge).

Wood, S. (1982) (ed.), *The Degradation of Work? Skill, Deskilling and the Labour Process* (London: Hutchinson).

49

Studying Inner-City Social Dislocations: The Challenge of Public Agenda Research

William Julius Wilson

Poverty, like other aspects of class inequality, is a consequence not only of differential distribution of economic and political privileges and resources, but of differential access to culture as well. In an industrial society groups are stratified in terms of the material assets or resources they control, the benefits and privileges they receive from these resources, the cultural experiences they have accumulated from historical and existing economic and political arrangements, and the influence they yield because of those arrangements. Accordingly, group variation in lifestyles, norms, and values is related to the variations in access to organizational channels of privilege and influence (Wilson 1987).

This fundamental argument links the structural and cultural aspects of life in poverty. Many current studies of poverty, however, fail to make this connection. Indeed, I believe that simplistic either/or notions of culture versus social structure have impeded the development of a broader theoretical context from which to examine questions raised by the continuing debate on the rise of inner-city social dislocations. In this presentation, I would like to address these questions using a framework that attempts to integrate social structural and cultural arguments. In the process I hope to move us beyond the narrow confines of this debate in two ways: (1) by outlining empirical and theoretical issues that guide further research, and (2) by suggesting variables that have to be taken into account to arrive at a satisfactory explanation of one of the most important domestic problems in the last quarter of the twentieth century—social

dislocation in the inner-city ghetto. Before I present this framework, however, I would like to place the growing problem of ghetto social dislocation in proper context and discuss the controversy concerning the interpretation of various dimensions of this problem, a controversy that poses a serious challenge to social scientists conducting research on the inner-city ghetto.

The Rise of Ghetto Poverty

Poverty in the United States has become more urban, more concentrated, and more firmly implanted in large metropolises, particularly in the older industrial cities with immense and highly segregated black and Hispanic residents. For example, in Chicago, the poverty rates in the inner-city neighborhoods increased by an average of 12 percentage points from 1970 to 1980. In eight of the ten neighborhoods that represent the historic core of Chicago's 'Black Belt,' more than four families in ten were living in poverty by 1980 (Wacquant and Wilson 1989).

In attempts to examine this problem empirically, social scientists have tended to treat census tracts as a proxy for neighborhoods. They define ghettos as those areas with poverty rates of at least 40 per cent. The ghetto poor are therefore designated as those among the poor who live in these extreme poverty areas.[1]

A recent study by Jargowsky and Bane (1990) shows that the proportion of the poor

From *American Sociological Review*, 56 (1991), 1–14. Reprinted with permission.

who live in ghettos also 'varies dramatically by race.' Whereas 21 per cent of black poor and 16 per cent of Hispanic poor lived in ghettos in 1980, only 2 per cent of the non-Hispanic white poor resided there. And nearly a third of all poor blacks within metropolitan areas lived in a ghetto in 1980. Of the 2.4 million ghetto poor in the United States, 65 per cent are black, 22 per cent are Hispanic, and 13 per cent are non-Hispanic and other races (Jargowsky and Bane 1990). Thus when one speaks of the ghetto poor in the United States, one is primarily referring to blacks and Hispanics. This is not only significant for descriptive purposes; as we shall soon see it also has theoretical significance.

It is also important to note that three-fourths (74 per cent) of the total increase in ghetto poverty during the 1970s was accounted for by only 10 cities. One-third of the increase was accounted for by New York City alone, and one-half by New York and Chicago combined. When Philadelphia, Newark, and Detroit are added these five cities account for two-thirds of the total increase in ghetto poverty in the 1970s. The other five cities among the top ten in the rise of ghetto poverty were Columbus (Ohio), Atlanta, Baltimore, Buffalo, and Paterson (New Jersey). So, when one speaks of the rise of ghetto poverty in the United States one is focusing mainly of the industrial metropolises of the Northeast and Midwest regions of the country.

Indeed Jargowsky and Bane (1990) found that of the 195 standard metropolitan areas that recorded ghetto poverty in 1970, 88 actually experience a decrease in the number of ghetto poor. Two types of cities account for the largest decreases in ghetto poverty in their study—Texas cities such as Brownsville, McAllen, Corpus Cristi, and San Antonio which experienced sharp drops in Hispanic ghetto poverty; and southern cities such as Shreveport, Charleston, Jackson (Mississippi), Memphis, New Orleans, and Columbus (Georgia) which recorded significant declines in ghetto poverty among blacks. These ten cities accounted for 46 per cent of the total decrease in ghetto poverty during the 1970s. Accordingly, 'the decreases were not nearly as localized in a few cities as the increases' (p. 40).

The focus of this presentation, however, is on the increase in ghetto poverty. The ques-

tions that concern me are why did this increase occur and why was most of it confined to the cities of the Northeast and Midwest.

We ought to be clear, however, about the nature of the problem. Because of the way poverty is defined by the United States Bureau of the Census, the official figures on concentrated poverty do not reflect the depth of the changes that have occurred. The poverty line represents arbitrary income thresholds established by the government. Anyone who lives in a family with an annual income below one of these thresholds is designated as poor. The thresholds vary with family size and are based on estimates of family needs. *These estimates were calculated in 1963 using family consumption data from a survey conducted in 1955.* Although the poverty thresholds are annually adjusted for inflation by the Census Bureau, the basic definition has never been updated to reflect changes in family need (Ruggles 1990).

There have been many changes in family consumption patterns since a family's basic needs were last defined 35 years ago. Whereas the average family spent roughly 34 per cent of its income on housing (including utilities) in 1955, today it spends 42 per cent. Whereas relatively few children lived with only one parent in 1955, today a large number of children live with a solo parent and therefore many more parents have to pay for child care. As Ruggles (1990) has pointed out, 'Increasing prices . . . are not the only source of changes in family needs. Family structures and resources, even the goods and services available, all change as well. All of these changes contribute to changes in minimum needs—especially over as much as 35 years' (p. A31).

The poverty threshold for a family of four was $12,092 in 1988. But, according to recent surveys, that threshold seems to be too low. In 1989, each month from July through October, the Gallup Poll presented the following question to a representative national sample of adult Americans: 'People who have income below a certain level can be considered poor. That level is called the "poverty line." What amount of weekly income would you use as a poverty line for a family of four (husband, wife, and two children in this community?' The average weekly income figure given by the respondents was converted to an annual amount and adjusted for inflation to make it comparable to the 1988 federal government poverty threshold for a family of four. The annual figure given by the Gallup Poll respondents was $15,017 or nearly $3000 (24 per cent) above the official poverty line. If the public's poverty threshold were used, 'The number of Americans considered poor would be close to 45 million, instead of the nearly 32 million considered poor under the government measure' (O'Hare, Mann, Porter, and Greenstein 1990: p. vi).[2]

Recent estimates by experts based on changes in housing and food expenditures would put the poverty threshold even higher than that indicated by the Gallup poll respondents. Such estimates 'imply that today's poverty line would have to be about 50 per cent higher to be comparable, in terms of minimum consumption needs, to the standard established in 1963' (Ruggles 1990, p. A31). In other words, a family of four would need an income of at least $18,138 (in 1988 dollars) to meet basic needs, over $6,000 above the current poverty line.

If the official measure of poverty does not capture the real dimensions of hardship and deprivation, it also does not reflect the changing depth or severity of poverty. In recent years, the Census Bureau established what might be called 'the poorest of the poor' category, that is, those individuals whose annual income falls at least 50 per cent below the officially designated poverty line. In 1975, 30 per cent of all the poor had incomes below 50 per cent of the poverty level, in 1988, 40 per cent did so. Among blacks, the increase was even sharper, from 32 per cent in 1975 to nearly half (48 per cent) in 1988 (U.S. Bureau of the Census 1988).

Accordingly, when we focus on changes in ghetto poverty, it is quite clear that the real depths of these changes are not captured by the standard definition of poverty. It is reasonable to conclude that not only has the number of ghetto poor increased, but the severity of economic deprivation among the ghetto poor has risen as well.

In sum, the 1970s witnessed a sharp growth in ghetto poverty areas, an increased concentration of the poor in these areas, a substantial rise in the severity of economic hardship among the ghetto poor, and sharply divergent patterns of poverty concentration between racial minorities and whites. It is clear, then; that one of the legacies of historic racial and class subjugation in America is a unique and growing concentration of minority residents in the most impoverished areas of large Northeastern and Midwestern central cities. This increase in poverty is associated with the rise of joblessness and other social dislocations that have received a good deal of attention in discussions that reflect the public agenda.

The Underclass Controversy

In the aftermath of the controversy over the Moynihan Report (1965) on the black family scholarly studies of the inner-city ghetto ground to halt. However, in recent years empirical research on ghetto poverty and other social dislocations has increased sharply. Coincidentally, this renewed research activity is occurring during a period of heightened public interest in the growing problems of the ghetto spurred in large measure by media reports and public discussion of life in the inner cities, including debates in academic circles. Similar to the previous discussion of the causes and consequences of urban poverty in the late 1960s that focused on the Moynihan Report and on Lewis's work on the culture of poverty (1959, 1961, 1966, 1968), much of this discussion is contentious and acrimonious.[3] A good deal of the debate has focused on the use or misuse of the concept 'underclass.'

A spate of studies highly critical of the use of the term 'underclass' has accompanied the increased research activity on the inner-city ghetto. The general view is that the term ought to be rejected because it has become a code word for inner-city blacks, has enabled journalists to focus on unflattering behavior in the ghetto, and has no scientific usefulness. Gans (1990) offers the most important, powerful, and representative critique of the use of the concept. He argues that while the term 'underclass' can be 'used as a graphic technical term for the growing number of persistently poor and jobless Americans, it is also a value-laden, increasingly pejorative term that seems to be becoming the newest buzzword for the *undeserving* poor' (p. 271).

Gans points out that when Myrdal coined the term 'underclass' in his 1962 book, *Challenge to Affluence*, it was used to describe those who had been driven to extreme economic marginality because of changes in what is now called postindustrial society. Myrdal's concern 'was with reforming the economy,' states Gans, 'not with changing or punishing the people who were its victims' (1990: 271). Myrdal's definition was used by other academics until the late 1970s when the focus tended to shift away from joblessness as the defining characteristic of the underclass to acute or persistent poverty.

However, another definition of the underclass surfaced at that time and has now, according to Gans, become the most widely used both inside and outside academia. This new definition, which Gans labels 'dangerous,' adds a number of behavioral patterns to the economic definition. It has been prominently used by certain researchers to estimate the size of the underclass with location-based measures. 'Underclass' neighborhoods are identified both by census tracts and by the degree of nonconforming behavior within those tracts. With these measures the researchers conclude that although the underclass is relatively small, it is growing (Ricketts and Sawhill 1986, Ricketts and Mincy 1986). In a critical reaction to these studies, Gans (1990) states that: 'The researchers tend to assume that the behavior patterns they report are caused by norm violations on the part of area residents and not by the conditions under which they are living, or the behavioral choices open to them as a result of these conditions' (p. 272).

The various definitions of the underclass, argues Gans (1990), have been the subject of vigorous debates between those on the right who maintain that 'the underclass is the product of the unwillingness of the black poor to adhere to the American work ethic, among other cultural deficiencies,' and those on the left who claim that 'the underclass is a consequence of the development of post-industrial economy, which no longer needs the unskilled poor' (p. 272). Efforts by scholars to resolve the debate have been largely unsuccessful, argues Gans. Meanwhile the behavioral definition of the underclass has increased

These debates have swirled around my book, *The Truly Disadvantaged* (Wilson 1987) in which, I assert, as Gans correctly observes, that 'this underclass exists mainly because of large-scale and harmful changes in the labor market, and its resulting spatial concentration as well as the isolation of such areas from the more affluent parts of the black community' (Gans 1990: 272). Efforts by scholars to resolve the debate have been largely unsuccessful, argues Gans. Meanwhile the behavioral definition of the underclass has increased

in the public discourse, especially among journalists.

For all these reasons Gans joins a growing number of social scientists who believe 'that the term underclass has taken on so many connotations of undeservingness and blameworthiness that it has become hopelessly polluted in meaning, ideological overtone and implications, and should be dropped—with the issues involved studied via other concepts' (Gans 1990: 272).

Gans comments are thoughtful and sobering and should be taken seriously by those conducting research on the urban poor. Any student of the social sciences who has read recent media reports on the behavior of the underclass is fully aware of the pejorative and value-laden use of the term by some journalists and a few highly visible conservative intellectuals (e.g. Hamill 1988; and Murray 1990).[4] But if there is a danger in the way the concept is now being used in many publications, there is also a potential danger for serious researchers from the fallout over the underclass debate. We only need to be reminded of what transpired following the controversy over the Moynihan Report on the black family in the late 1960s. The vitriolic attacks and acrimonious debate that characterized that controversy proved to be too intimidating to scholars, especially to liberal scholars. Indeed, in the aftermath of this controversy and in an effort to protect their work from the charge of racism or of 'blaming the victim,' liberal social scientists tended to avoid describing any behavior that could be construed as unflattering or stigmatizing to racial minorities. Accordingly, for a period of several years and well after this controversy had subsided the growing problems of poverty concentration, joblessness, and other social dislocations in the inner-city ghetto did not attract serious research attention. Until the mid-1980s, the void was partially filled by journalists, and therefore conclusions about the behavior of inner-city residents were reached without the benefit of systematic empirical research or thoughtful theoretical arguments.

However, in the last few years researchers have once again begun to study problems such as poverty and joblessness in the ghetto. A significant number of research projects on aspects of inner-city poverty and related problems have been launched. Several more have been organized by the Social Science Research Council which has established a major research program on the urban underclass involving scholars from the disciplines of sociology, psychology, political science, economics, anthropology, education, and history. What effect the current controversy will have on this research agenda is difficult to determine. In some quarters there is a tendency to be critical of any social scientist who analyzes cultural traits and behavior in the inner-city ghetto, even one who attempts to explain them in terms of macrostructural constraints.

Given the research momentum that has been generated, the first-rate scholars from multiple disciplines who are conducting the research, and the support of foundations and other funding agencies, it is unlikely that the controversy will result in the kind of scholarly boycott of research on the ghetto that followed the controversy over the Moynihan Report. Nonetheless, some social scientists may simply decide that it is not worth the hassle and therefore may focus their research on less sensitive issues.

However, articles such as those written by Gans could actually defuse the controversy. After all Gans is not calling for a boycott of research on the inner-city ghetto. Rather he wants the concept of underclass to be dropped 'with the issues involved studied via other concepts' (1990: 272). If researchers heed Gans's suggestion there could follow a more concentrated focus on research and theoretical issues and less fixation on disputed concepts or labels.

But heeding Gans's recommendation could lead to a negative consequence as well. To some extent the controversy over the underclass concept has been productive. The debate has led to more precise specifications of empirical issues and more careful elaboration of theoretical arguments concerning life in the inner-city ghetto, actually providing meaningful direction for empirical research and theory construction. Accordingly, any crusade to abandon the concept underclass, however defined, could result in premature closure of ideas just as important new studies on the inner-city ghetto, including policy-oriented studies, are being generated.

The merits of focusing exclusively on the issues of research may be more important for the research community in the long run.

Many of these issues have been obscured in the underclass debate. Gans points out that '[my] work has inspired a lot of new research not only about the underclass but about poverty in general' (1990: 272). I should therefore like, in the remainder of this presentation, to build on my previous work and put some of these issues in a broader theoretical context and move us away from the controversy over the concept underclass, including the simplistic either/or distinction between culture and social structure that has characterized so much of the debate. In order to keep us focused on research issues, I will substitute the term 'ghetto poor' for the term 'underclass' and hope that I will not lose any of the subtle theoretical meaning that the latter term has had in my writings.

A Framework for the Analysis of Ghetto Social Dislocations

I argue in *The Truly Disadvantaged* (Wilson 1987) that historic discrimination and a migration flow to large metropolitan areas that kept the minority population relatively young created a problem of weak labor-force attachment within this population, making it particularly vulnerable to the ongoing industrial and geographic changes in the economy since 1970. The shift from goods-producing to service-producing industries, increasing polarization of the labor market into low-wage and high-wage sectors, innovations in technology, relocation of manufacturing industries out of the central city, periodic recessions, and wage stagnation exacerbated the chronic problems of weak labor-force attachment among the urban minority poor. This resulted in accelerated increases in the rate of joblessness (unemployment and nonparticipation in the labor force) among urban blacks, despite the passing of antidiscrimination legislation and despite the creation of affirmative-action programs. The sharp climb in joblessness helped to trigger other problems such as the rise in concentrated urban poverty. However, what I did not make clear in my book is that the rise of ghetto poverty mainly occurred in only two regions of the country.

THE ECONOMY AND WEAK LABOR-FORCE ATTACHMENT IN THE INNER-CITY GHETTO

The ten cities that accounted for three-fourths of the increase in ghetto poverty in the United States during the 1970s have two things in common—they are all industrial centers and, except for Atlanta which recorded a relatively slight increase in the number of ghetto poor, they are all located in the Northeast and Midwest regions of the United States. Cities in the sunbelt regions of the country tended to experience job growth in all major sectors of the economy (manufacturing, retail/wholesale, white-collar and blue-collar services) between 1970 and 1986. However, as the recent research of John Kasarda so clearly shows (1989, 1990*a*, 1990*b*), the cities in the frostbelt experienced massive industrial restructuring and a loss of blue-collar jobs. These cities suffered overall employment decline because 'growth in their predominantly information-processing industries could not numerically compensate for substantial losses in their more traditional industrial sectors, especially manufacturing' (Kasarda 1990*a*: 241). One result of these changes for many urban blacks has been an increase in the problem of spatial mismatch between central-city residence and the location of employment.

Although studies using data collected up to 1970 failed to demonstrate convincingly that spatial mismatch affects employment for blacks (see, e.g., Ellwood 1986), data since 1970 shows clearly 'that the employment of central-city blacks relative to suburban ones has deteriorated' (Holzer 1990: 23). Recent research conducted mainly by labor and urban economists strongly support the notions that the decentralization of employment continues in the United States and that manufacturing employment, of which more than half is already suburbanized, has been declining in central-city areas, particularly in the Midwest and Northeast regions of the country; that central-city blacks have less access to employment in terms of the ratio of jobs to people and of average travel time to and from work than do central-city whites; that unlike most other groups of workers, less-educated blacks receive lower wages in the central city than their counterparts in the suburbs, and that the decline in earnings of central-city blacks is positively associated with the extent of job decentralization in the metropolitan area (Holzer 1990).

Are the differences in employment between suburban blacks and central-city blacks mainly a reflection of changes in the spatial location of jobs? It is possible, as Jencks and Mayer (1989*b*: 34) have pointed out, that in recent years black migration from the central city to the suburbs has become much more selective than it had been previously, so much so that the changes attributed to the spatial location of jobs are really due to selective black suburban migration. The pattern of black migration to the suburbs in the 1970s resembled the pattern of white migration to the suburbs during the 1950s and 1960s in the sense that it was concentrated among the younger and more educated residents of the central city (Frey 1985; Grier and Grier 1988). However, in the 1970s this was less true for whites than for blacks and therefore the education and income gaps between central-city and suburban blacks seemed to widen while gaps between central-city and suburban whites seemed to diminish (Holzer 1990). How much of the central-city/suburban employment gap would remain if one were able to control for personal and family characteristics?

This very question was addressed by Rosenbaum and Popkin (1989) in a recent study of the Gautreaux program in Chicago. This program, which began in 1976, is designed to help low-income public housing project black families move into private market housing in the Chicago metropolitan area. The program locates available apartments and arranges for participants to receive Section 8 federal housing subsidies. The design of the program permitted Rosenbaum and Popkin to compare systematically the employment experiences of a group of low-income blacks who were assigned private apartments in the suburbs to those of a control group with similar demographic characteristics and employment histories who were assigned private apartments in the city.[5] Their results support the spatial mismatch hypothesis. After controlling for personal characteristics (including pre-move human capital, family circumstances, family background, motivation, post-move education, and length of time since the respondent first moved on the Gautreaux program) those who moved to suburban apartments were significantly more likely than those who moved to city apartments to have a job following the move. When respondents were asked what made it easier to obtain employment in the suburbs, nearly all mentioned the availability of jobs.

There is also evidence suggesting that industrial restructuring has diminished the occupational advancement of the more disadvantaged urban minority members. Research by Kasarda (1989: 35) suggests that 'the bottom fell out in urban industrial demand for poorly educated blacks' in Northeastern and Midwestern cities, particularly in the goods-producing industries. Data collected from a survey in the Urban Poverty and Family Life Study (UPFLS) I directed in Chicago show that efforts by out-of-school inner-city black males to obtain blue-collar jobs in the industries that had previously employed their fathers have been impeded by industrial shifts as evident in the occupational changes of successive cohorts of young men. The most common occupation mentioned by the cohort of respondents at ages 19 to 28 shifted from assembler and operator jobs among the oldest cohorts to service jobs (janitors and waiters) among the youngest cohort (Testa and Krogh 1989).

Finally, a recent study reveals that whereas black employment in New York City declined by 84,000 in durable and nondurable manufacturing between 1970 and 1987 (industries with lower levels of education among workers), black employment increased by 104,000 in public administration and professional services (industries with more highly educated workers) (Bailey 1989). Thus, if industrial restructuring has diminished opportunities for the least educated blacks, it may have enhanced opportunities for more highly educated blacks.

Manufacturing industries, a major source of black employment in the twentieth century, are particularly sensitive to a slack economy and therefore a sizable number of job losses among blacks occurred during the recession-prone decade of the 1970s (Levy 1988). Freeman (1989) provided a unique test of the argument that many of the problems of joblessness among disadvantaged youth in 'the inner city are the direct result of the loss of jobs in local labor markets' (p. 2). He compared the employment situation of disadvantaged blacks youths from 1983 to 1987 in metropolitan areas that had the tightest labor markets in 1987. Based on annual merged data from two surveys, the Current Population Survey (CPS) and the National Longitudinal Survey (NLSY), Freeman showed that despite the social problems that 'plagued disadvantaged youths, particularly less educated black youths, and despite the 1980s twist in the American labor market against the less skilled, tight labor markets substantially improved the economic position of these workers' (1989: 2). Although jobless rates among disadvantaged young blacks remain high, dramatic progress occurred during the recent economic recovery period in the metropolitan areas with the tightest labor markets.

However, arguments demonstrating the impact of recent on-going geographic, industrial, and other shifts in the economy on poor urban blacks have been criticized in some quarters. Some think that the focus on impersonal economic forces overlooks willful acts of racial discrimination on the part of individuals, organizations, and institutions that effectively create employment problems for urban blacks (Bailey 1989). Although empirical studies on these issues are limited, research from the UPFLS's survey of employers in Chicago suggests that inner-city blacks, particularly black males, face a major problem of employer attitudes toward and perception of black workers. Indeed, interviews of a representative sample of Chicago-area businessmen indicate that many consider inner-city workers—especially young black males—to be uneducated, unstable, uncooperative, and dishonest. Furthermore, racial stereotyping is greater among those employers with lower proportions of blacks in their workforce, especially the blue-collar employers who tend to stress the importance of unobservable qualities such as work attitudes (Neckerman and Kirschenman 1990).

Accordingly, a number of employers practice what economists call 'statistical discrimination' whereby judgments about a job applicant's productivity, which is often too expensive or too difficult to measure, are based on his or her group membership (Kirshenman and Neckerman 1989; Neckerman and Kirschenman 1990). Although an overwhelming majority of the UPFLS's survey respondents did not express overt racist attitudes or a categorical dislike of blacks when explaining their hiring practices, the data strongly suggest that many did, in fact, practice statistical discrimination by screening out black applicants very early in the hiring process because of their inner-city residence, their class background, and their public school education. These factors were used as proxies for judgments about worker productivity. However, Freeman's research (1989) leads one to believe that the practice of statistical discrimination will vary depending on the tightness of the labor market and therefore ought not be analyzed without reference to the overall state of the local or national economy.

In a tight labor market, job vacancies are numerous, unemployment is of short duration, and wages are higher. Moreover, in a tight labor market the labor force expands because increased job opportunities not only reduce unemployment but also draw into the labor force those workers who, in periods when the labor market is slack, respond to fading job prospects by dropping out of the labor force altogether. Accordingly, in a tight labor market the status of disadvantaged minorities improves because unemployment is reduced, wages are higher, and better jobs are available. In contrast, in a slack labor market employers are—and indeed, can afford to be—more selective in recruiting and in granting promotions. They overemphasize job prerequisites and exaggerate experience. In such an economic climate, disadvantaged minorities suffer disproportionately and the level of employer discrimination rises (Tobin 1965).

In sum, basic economic shifts and transformations are important for understanding the changes in the life experiences of poor urban minorities. I have maintained that one of the major factors involved in the growth of ghetto poverty is industrial restructuring and labor-market swings in the Northeast and Midwest metropolitan areas. Another factor, argued in *The Truly Disadvantaged* (Wilson 1987), is the outmigration of higher income residents from certain parts of the inner city, resulting in a higher concentration of residents in extreme poverty or ghetto neighborhoods.

This thesis has been the subject of controversy. Research by Massey and Eggers (1990), for instance, found that although levels of interclass segregation among blacks increased during the 1970s, it was not sufficient to account for the rising concentration of urban black poverty. They argue that because of persisting segregation, higher income blacks 'are less able to separate themselves from the poor than the privileged of other groups' (Massey and Eggers 1990: 1186). Thus an increase in the poverty rate of a highly segregated group will automatically lead to an increase in the

concentration of poverty. However, analyzing a different data set, Jargowsky and Bane (1990) reject the hypothesis that 'poverty rate changes alone explain changes in ghetto poverty' (p. 48). The conflicting findings and conclusions are associated with the use of different measures of concentrated poverty.

Massey and Eggers (1990) use a segregation index to calculate the probability of intraclass contact among metropolitan groups. Although this measure allows for the description of the overall level of concentrated poverty in Standard Metropolitan Statistical Areas (SMSA), as Jargowsky and Bane (1990) appropriately point out, it does not 'identify specific neighborhoods that are ghettos and others that are not' (p. 6).

As indicated previously, Jargowsky and Bane (1990) identify ghetto and nonghetto neighborhoods. Focusing specifically on the cities of Philadelphia, Milwaukee, Cleveland, and Memphis, they found a significant geographical spreading of ghetto neighborhoods between 1970 and 1980. Areas that had become ghettos during that decade 'were mixed income tracts in 1970 that were contiguous to the 1970 ghetto areas' (p. 53). Their findings clearly support the hypothesis that a major factor in the increase of ghetto poverty since 1970 has been the outmigration of nonpoor from mixed income areas.[6] Jargowsky and Bane (1990) report that 'the poor were leaving as well, but the nonpoor left faster, leaving behind a group of people in 1980 that was poorer than in 1970' (p. 56). As the population spread out from mixed income areas in 1970 to other areas, the next 'ring' of areas that were mostly white and not poor became the home of a 'larger proportion of the black and poor population. The white nonpoor left these areas, which also lost population overall' (pp. 56–7). Thus, the black middle class exodus from inner-city areas that later became ghettos was not followed by a significant increase of interclass segregation among blacks in other neighborhoods. Unfortunately, the important process involving the geographical spread of ghetto poverty is not captured in studies that focus on the concentration of poverty in SMSAs using a segregation index (cf. Farley 1989). Although such studies are important for understanding the role of racial segregation in explaining changes in the level of metropolitan poverty concentration, the data they yield do not provide an appropriate test of the hypothesis that associates the increase of ghetto poverty with the higher-income black exodus from certain inner-city neighborhoods.

The significance of the higher-income black exodus, however, is not only that it was a factor in the growth of ghetto poverty, but also that the declining presence of working- and middle-class blacks deprives ghetto neighborhoods of key resources, including structural resources such as a social buffer to minimize the effects of growing joblessness and cultural resources such as conventional role models for neighborhood children. The economic marginality of the ghetto poor is strengthened, therefore, by conditions in the neighborhoods in which they live, a subject to which I now turn.

THE SOCIAL ENVIRONMENT IN THE INNER-CITY GHETTO AND WEAK LABOR-FORCE ATTACHMENT
In *The Truly Disadvantaged* (Wilson 1987), I focus on the growing concentration of urban poverty and argue that the central predicament of inner-city ghetto residents is jobless- ness reinforced by a growing social isolation in impoverished neighborhoods, as reflected, for example, in the rapidly decreasing access to job information network systems. In an important conceptual paper, Van Haitsma (1989) has more sharply delineated the con- nection between involvement in the labor market and the social environment by identi- fying those persons with weak attachment to the labor force and 'whose social context tends to maintain or further weaken this attach- ment' (p. 28). I would like to incorporate this more explicit notion into my framework by equating the 'social context' with the neigh- borhood.

'Weak labor-force attachment,' a concept that initially received systematic attention in the work of McLanahan and Garfinkel (1989), does not refer in this context to a willingness or desire to work (cf. Tienda and Stier 1989). Rather 'weak labor-force attachment' is used here as a structural concept embedded in a theoretical framework that explains why some groups are more vulnerable to joblessness than others. In other words, weak labor-force attachment refers to the marginal economic position of some people in the labor force because of structural constraints or limited opportunities, including constraints or opportunities in their immediate environ-

ment—for example, lack of access to informal job net-work systems. The key theoretical distinction I am trying to make here is that there are two major sources of weak labor- force attachment—one derives from macro- structural changes in the broader society, most notably the economy, the other from the individual's social milieu, I have discussed the former; now let me briefly discuss the latter.

In order to understand the unique position of inner-city ghetto residents it is important to emphasize the association between attach- ment to the labor force and the social environ- ment (neighborhood). A key hypothesis is that 'environments with low opportunity for stable and legitimate employment and high opportunity for alternative income- generating activities, particularly those which are incompatible with regular employment,' are those which perpetuate weak labor-force attachment over time (Van Haitsma 1989: 7).

Poor individuals who live in a social context that fosters or enhances strong labor-force attachment are less likely to experience persis- tent poverty than are those living in a social context that reinforces weak labor-force attachment. In other words, poor individuals with similar educational and occupational skills confront different risks of persistent poverty depending on the neighborhoods they reside in, as embodied in the formal and informal networks to which they have access, their prospects of marriage or remarriage to a stably employed mate, and the families or households to which they belong. Moreover, a social context that includes poor schools, inadequate job information networks, and a lack of legitimate employment opportunities not only gives rise to weak labor-force attach- ment, but increases the probability that indi- viduals will be constrained to seek income derived from illegal or deviant activities. This weakens their attachment to the legitimate labor market even further.

Furthermore, the social context has signif- icant implications for the socialization of youth with respect to their future attachment to the labor force. For example, a youngster who grows up in a family with a steady bread- winner and in a neighborhood in which most of the adults are employed will tend to develop some of the disciplined habits associated with stable or steady employment—habits that are reflected in the behavior of his or her parents and of other neighborhood adults. Accordingly, when this youngster enters the labor market, he or she has a distinct advantage over the youngsters who grow up in households without a steady breadwinner and in neighborhoods that are not organized around work—in other words, a milieu in which one is more exposed to the less disciplined habits associated with casual or infrequent work.

By observing the temporal organization of the life of the same individuals before and after they become jobless, Bourdieu (1965) pointed out in his study of work and workers in Algeria that work is not simply a means of making a living and supporting one's family.[7] It also constitutes the framework for daily behavior and patterns of interaction because of the disciplines and regularities it imposes. Thus in the absence of regular employment, what is lacking is not only a place in which to work and the receipt of regular income, but also a coherent organization of the present, that is, a system of concrete expectations and goals. Regular employment provides the anchor for the temporal and spatial aspects of daily life. In the absence of regular employment, life, including family life, becomes more incoherent. Unemployment and irregular employment, argues Bourdieu, preclude the elaboration of a rational planning of life, the necessary condition of adaptation to an industrial economy. This problem is most severe for jobless individuals and families in neighborhoods with low rates of employment. And the relative absence of rational planning in a jobless family is reinforced by the similar condition of other families in the neighborhood.

Indeed, I believe that there is a difference, on the one hand, between a jobless family whose mobility is impeded by the macrostructural constraints in the economy and the larger society but nonetheless lives in an area with a relatively low rate of poverty, and on the other hand, a jobless family that lives in an inner-city ghetto neighborhood that is not only influenced by these same constraints but also by the behavior of other jobless families in the neighborhood. The latter influence is one of culture—that is, the extent to which individuals follow their inclinations as they have been developed by learning or influence from other members of the community (Hannerz 1969). In other words, it is not sufficient to recognize the importance of macrostructural constraints; it is also imperative to see 'the

merits of a more subtle kind of cultural analysis of life in poverty' (p. 182).

Let me briefly elaborate this point with a different example of the kind of cultural analysis I am trying to convey. Joblessness, especially prolonged joblessness, is likely to be associated with or produce feelings of low perceived self-efficacy. In social cognitive theory (Bandura 1986), perceived self-efficacy refers to self-beliefs in one's ability to take the steps or courses of action necessary to achieve the goals required in a given situation. Such beliefs affect the level of challenge that is pursued, the amount of effort expended in a given venture, and the degree of perseverance when confronting difficulties. As Bandura (1982) has put it: 'Inability to influence events and social conditions that significantly affect one's life can give rise to feelings of futility and despondency as well as to anxiety' (p. 140). Two sources of perceived futility are distinguished in self-efficacy theory. People may seriously doubt that they can do or accomplish what is expected, or they may feel confident of their abilities but nonetheless give up trying because they believe that their efforts will ultimately be futile due to an environment that is unresponsive, discriminatory, or punitive. 'The type of outcomes people expect depend largely on their judgments of how well they will be able to perform in given situations' (p. 140).

Weak labor-force attachment, I would hypothesize, will tend to lower one's perceived self efficacy. I would therefore expect lower levels of perceived self-efficacy in ghetto neighborhoods—plagued by underemployment, unemployment and labor-force nonparticipation—than in less impoverished neighborhoods. Considering the importance of cultural learning and influence, I would also expect that perceived self-efficacy is higher among those who are weakly attached to the labor force in nonghetto neighborhoods than among their counterparts in ghetto neighborhoods.

In the more socially isolated ghetto neighborhoods, networks of kin, friends, and associates are more likely to include a higher proportion of individuals who, because of their experiences with extreme economic marginality, tend to doubt that they can achieve approved societal goals. The self-doubts may exist either because of questions concerning their own capabilities or preparedness, or because they perceive severe restrictions imposed by a hostile environment. The central hypothesis is that an individual's feelings of low self-efficacy grow out of weak labor-force attachment and they are reinforced or strengthened by the feelings and views of others in his or her neighborhood who are similarly situated and have similar self-beliefs. The end result, to use a term from Bandura's (1982) work, is lower collective efficacy in the inner-city ghetto. Research on the *transmission* of such views and feelings would represent a cultural analysis of life in poverty. The psychological self-efficacy theory is used here not in isolation but in relation to the *structural problem of weak labor-force attachment* and the *cultural problem of the transmission of self and collective beliefs in the neighborhood.*

The transmission of such beliefs are part of what I have called 'concentration effects,' that is the effects of living in a neighborhood that is overwhelmingly impoverished (Wilson 1987). I argue that these concentration effects, reflected in a range of outcomes from degree of labor force-attachment to social dispositions, are created by the constraints and opportunities that the residents of the inner-city neighborhoods face in terms of access to jobs and job networks, involvement in quality schools, availability of marriageable partners, and exposure to conventional role models.

Although earlier studies cast doubt on the importance of neighborhood residence on social outcomes (cf. Jencks and Mayer 1989a), several more recent studies present evidence that neighborhood effects do exist for teenage childbearing, school dropout rates, and welfare use (Crane 1989; Mayer 1989; Osterman 1990). These studies use a variety of different measures, including those that deal with the thorny problems of selection processes outlined in an important paper by Tienda (1989).[8] A number of new studies on concentration effects are currently being conducted.

Conclusion

I have presented a framework that links structural and cultural arguments on inner-city social dislocations without using the concept of 'underclass.' Hoping that I would not lose any of the subtle theoretical meaning that this concept has had in my writing, and to focus our attention less on controversy and more on research and theoretical issues, I have substituted the term 'ghetto poor.' There is a certain risk involved here because the concept 'underclass' derives its meaning from this framework, not from an isolated or arbitrary definition. The issue is not simply that the underclass or ghetto poor have a marginal position in the labor market similar to that of other disadvantaged groups, it is also that their economic position is uniquely reinforced by their social milieu. The concept 'underclass' or 'ghetto poor' can be theoretically applied to all racial and ethnic groups, and to different societies if the conditions specified in the theory are met. In studies in the United States, the concept will more often refer to minorities because the white poor seldom live in ghettos or extreme urban poverty areas.

However, if ghetto areas continue to be empirically defined on the basis of the current definition of poverty, empirical estimates of the size of the underclass or ghetto poor will invariably be too low. As I stated above, the official poverty line, although annually adjusted for inflation, has not been revised upward to reflect changes in family consumption patterns. Accordingly, to get a real idea of the dimensions of ghetto poverty, empirical definitions of the underclass or ghetto poor, based on the fundamental theoretical assumptions outlined here, will have to be applied to redefined areas—areas designated as ghettos on the basis of revised measures of poverty that reflect real changes in minimum family needs.

Fortunately, the underclass controversy has not diminished the enthusiasm for research on these issues. There exists now a climate for research in which many of the macrostructural and cultural issues discussed in this presentation are being pursued. With the reemergence of poverty on the nation's public agenda, researchers have to recognize that they have the political and social responsibility as social scientists to ensure that their findings and theories are interpreted accurately by those in the public who use their ideas. They also have the intellectual responsibility to do more than simply react to trends or currents of public thinking. They have to provide intellectual leadership with arguments based on systematic research and theoretical analyses that confront ideologically driven and short-sighted public views.

Notes

1. See Wacquant and Wilson (1990) and Jargowsky and Bane (1990). In discussing the extent to which extreme poverty census tracts correspond to ghetto neighborhoods in Chicago, Wacquant and Wilson (1990) state: 'Extreme-poverty neighborhoods comprise tracts with at least 40 per cent of their residents in poverty in 1980. These tracts make up the historic heart of Chicago's black ghetto: Over 82 per cent of the respondents in this category inhabit the West and South sides of the city, in areas most of which have been all black for half a century and more, and an additional 13 per cent live in immediately adjacent tracts. Thus when we counterpose extreme-poverty areas with low-poverty areas, we are in effect comparing ghetto neighborhoods with other black areas, most of which are moderately poor, that are not part of Chicago's traditional black belt' (p. 16). Using the same rationale on a national level, Jargowsky and Bane (1990) state: 'Based on visits to several cities, we found that the 40 per cent criterion came very close to identifying areas that looked like ghettos in terms of their housing conditions. Moreover, the areas selected by the 40 per cent criterion corresponded rather closely with the judgments of city officials and local census bureau officials about which neighborhoods were ghettos' (pp. 8–9).
Of course not all the residents who live in ghettos are poor. In the ten largest American cities (as determined by the 1970 census) the number of black residents residing in ghetto areas doubled between 1970 and 1980; the number of Hispanics tripled. In 1980, 16.5 per cent of Hispanics and 21 per cent of blacks in these ten cities lived in ghetto areas, in contrast to only 1.7 per cent of non-Hispanic whites (Wilson, Aponte, Kirschenman, and Wacquant 1988; Wacquant and Wilson 1989).

2. In their comprehensive analysis of the official measure of poverty, O'Hare, Mann, Porter, and Greenstein (1990) state that: 'The survey question used in the Gallup poll was designed to show people's perceptions of an appropriate poverty line varied according to where they lived. The question asked what level of income respondents would use as a poverty line *in their community*. The answers to the survey question varied according to which region of the country the respondents lived in. Those living in metropolitan areas would set the poverty line at a higher level than those living in non-metropolitan areas. Those in the Western portion of the United States would set the highest regional poverty line, and those in the South and the Midwest would set the lowest regional poverty lines. In every area of the country, however, the survey respondents set the poverty line for their community at a higher level than the government's poverty line.
'These poll results can be used to determine the number of people who would be considered poor if the public's poverty line were varied by geographic area. This is done by setting poverty lines for each area at the average levels that poll respondents from these areas said should be used to measure poverty in their communities. This approach provides a rough approximation of variations in the cost of living among different areas of the country. Using these geographically varied poverty lines, 44 million Americans would be considered poor. This is only slightly different from the 45 million said to be poor using the public's poverty line without any geographical variations. The total number of people considered poor does not change very much because, when the poverty line is varied by geographical area, decreases in some areas are offset by increases in others. Fewer people are counted as poor under the lower poverty lines used in non-metropolitan areas, in the Midwest, and in the South, but these reductions are offset by increases in the number of people considered poor under the higher poverty lines in metropolitan areas and in the West' (p. vii).
Some analysts believe that certain noncash government benefits such as housing subsidies and food stamps ought to be included as income in estimates of the number of families in poverty. O'Hare, Mann, Porter, and Greenstein pursued this point and found that 'even counting noncash benefits as income and using the public's poverty line, the number of people considered poor would still be substantially higher than under the government's poverty measure, which does not count noncash benefits. If food and housing benefits were counted as income, the number of Americans considered poor under the public's poverty line would be about 43 million, or 18 per cent of the American population. If medical benefits were also counted as income, the number of Americans considered poor would be 39 million, or 16 per cent of the population' (1990, p. viii).
See Jencks and Edin (1990) for another comprehensive study of family income and consumption among the poor.

3. For a comparative discussion of these two controversies see Wilson (1988). See Rainwater

and Yancey (1967) for a comprehensive discussion of the controversy over the Moynihan
Report.
4. For a critical discussion of these media reports
see Wilson (1988).
5 Rosenbaum and Popkin (1989) surveyed a random sample of 342 female heads of households
that included 224 in the suburbs and 108 in the
city. They pointed out that: 'Since participants
usually took the first apartment the program
offered, and unit availability often permitted
no choice of location, there should be few differences between city and suburban movers. In
fact, our analyses find no initial differences in
demographic characteristics or employment
between the experimental and control groups.
Therefore any differences in employment outcomes that we find are not likely to be the result
of dissimilarity between the city and suburban
movers' (pp. 6–7).
6. For a comprehensive study that presents similar findings, see Coulton, Chow, and Pandey
(1990).
7. I am indebted to Loic J. D. Wacquant for his
translation of a part of Bourdieu's (1965)
study. It is not yet available in English.
8. On this point, Tienda (1989) states: 'If systematic selection processes are the primary
mechanism bringing together individuals
with similar socioeconomic characteristics
and behavioral dispositions within spatially
bounded areas, then selection processes will be
confused with neighborhood effects unless one
can show that concentration itself accentuates
the manifestation and ramification of particular behaviors' (p. 21).

References

Anderson, E. (1989), 'Neighborhood Effects on
Teenage Pregnancy.' (Paper presented at a Con-
ference on *The Truly Disadvantaged*, Northwest-
ern University, Evanston, Il, October 19–21).
Bailey, T. (1989), 'Black Employment Opportuni-
ties', in *Setting Municipal Priorities, 1990*, ed.
Charles Brecher and Raymond D. Horton.
(New York: New York University Press),
80–111.
Bandura, A. (1982), 'Self-Efficacy Mechanism in
Human Agency', *American Psychologist*, 37
(February): 122–47.
—— (1986), *Social Foundations of Thought and
Action: A Social Cognitive Theory* (Englewood
Cliffs, NJ: Prentice Hall).
Bourdieu, P. (1965), *Travail et Travailleurs en
Algeria* (Paris: Éditions Mouton).
Coulton, C. J., Chow, J. and Pandey, S. (1990), *An
Analysis of Poverty and Related Conditions in
Cleveland Area Neighborhoods* (Cleveland, OH:

Center for Urban Poverty and Social Change,
Case Western Reserve University).
Crane, J. (1989), 'Neighborhood Effects on Drop-
ping Out and Teenage Childbearing', (Paper
presented at a Conference on *The Truly Disad-
vantaged*, Northwestern University, Evanston,
Il, October 19–21).
Ellwood, D. T. (1986), 'The Spatial Mismatch
Hypothesis: Are There Teenage Jobs Missing in
the Ghetto?' in *The Black Youth Employment
Crisis*, ed. R. B. Freeman and H. J. Holzer
(Chicago: University of Chicago Press), 147–8.
Farley, R. (1989), 'Trends in the Residential Seg-
regation of Social and Economic Groups Among
American Blacks: 1970 to 1980.' (Paper
presented at a Conference on *The Truly
Disadvantaged*, Northwestern University,
Evanston, Il, October 19–21).
Freeman, R. B. (1989), 'The Employment and
Earning of Disadvantaged Male Youths in a
Labor Shortage Economy.' (Paper presented at
the Conference on *The Truly Disadvantaged*,
Northwestern University, Evanston, Il, October
19–21).
Frey, W. (1985), 'Mover Destination Selectivity
and the Changing Suburbanization of Whites
and Blacks.' *Demography*, 22: 223–43.
Gans, H. J. (1990), 'Deconstructing the Under-
class: The Term's Danger as a Planning Con-
cept.' *Journal of the American Planning
Association*, 56 (Summer): 271–7.
Grier, E. S., and Grier, G. (1988), 'Minorities in
Suburbia: A Mid-1980s Update.' (Report to the
Urban Institute Project on Housing Mobility).
(March). (Washington, DC: The Urban Insti-
tute).
Hamill, P. (1988), 'Breaking the Silence', *Esquire*
(March), 91 ff.
Hannerz, U. (1969), *Soulside: Inquiries into Ghetto
Culture and Community* (New York: Columbia
University Press).
Holzer, H. J. (1990), 'The Spatial Mismatch
Hypothesis: What Has The Evidence Shown?'
(Paper presented at a conference on *The Truly
Disadvantaged*. Northwestern University, Evan-
ston, Il, October 19–21).
Jargowsky, P. A., and Bane, M. J. (1990), *Neighbor-
hood Poverty: Basic Questions* (Discussion Paper
Series, #H-90–3, Malcolm Wiener Center for
Social Policy, John F. Kennedy School of Gov-
ernment, Harvard University, Cambridge,
Mass).
Jencks, C., and Edin, K. (1990), 'The Real Welfare
Problem', *The American Prospect* (Spring, no. 1):
31–50.
—— and Mayer, S. E. (1989a), 'The Social Consequences of Growing Up in a Poor Neighborhood: A Review.' (Unpublished paper, Center
for Urban Affairs and Policy Research, Northwestern University).
—— and —— (1989b), *Residential Segregation*,

Job Proximity, and Black Job Opportunities: The Empirical Status of the Spatial Mismatch Hypothesis (Center for Urban Affairs Working Papers, North-western Univ.).

Kasarda, J. D. (1989), 'Urban Industrial Transition and the Underclass', *Annals of the American Academy of Political and Social Science*, 501 (January): 26–47.

—— (1990a), 'Structural Factors Affecting the Location and Timing of Urban Underclass Growth', *Urban Geography*, 11: 234–64.

—— (1990b), 'City Jobs and Residents on a Collision Course: The Urban Underclass Dilemma.' *Economic Development Quarterly*, 4 (November): 313–19.

Kirschenman, J., and Neckerman, K. (1989), 'We'd Love to Hire Them, But . . . ': The Meaning of Race for Employers.' (Paper presented at a conference on *The Truly Disadvantaged*. Northwestern University, Evanston, Il, October 19–21).

Levy, F. (1988), *Dollars and Dreams: The Changing American Income Distribution* (New York: Russell Sage Foundation).

Lewis, O. (1959), *Five Families: Mexican Case Studies in the Culture of Poverty* (New York: Basic Books).

—— (1961), *The Children of Sanchez* (New York: Random House).

—— (1966), *La Vida: A Puerto Rican Family in the Culture of Poverty—San Juan and New York*. (New York: Random House).

—— (1968), 'The Culture of Poverty', in *On Understanding Poverty: Perspectives from the Social Sciences*, ed. Daniel Patrick Moynihan (New York: Basic Books), 187–220.

Magnet, M. (1987), 'America's Underclass: What to Do?' *Fortune* (11 May) 130 ff.

Massey, D. S., and Eggers, M. L. (1990), 'The Ecology of Inequality: Minorities and the Concentration of Poverty, 1970–1980', *American Journal of Sociology* 95 (March): 1153–88.

Mayer, S. E. (1989), 'How Much Does a High School's Racial and Socioeconomic Mix Affect Graduation Rates and Teenage Fertility Rates.' (Paper presented at a Conference on *The Truly Disadvantaged*, Northwestern University, Evanston, Il, October 19–21).

McLanahan, S., and Garfinkel, I. (1989), 'Single Mothers, The Underclass, and Social Policy', *Annals of the American Academy of Political and Social Science*, 501 (January): 92–104.

Moynihan, D. P. (1965), *The Negro Family: The Case for National Action* (Washington, DC: Office of Policy Planning and Research, U.S. Department of Labor).

Murray, C. (1990), 'Here's the Bad News on the Underclass.' *The Wall Street Journal* (March 8), A14.

Neckerman, K. M., and Kirschenman, J. (1990), 'Statistical Discrimination and Inner-city

Workers: An Investigation of Employers' Hiring Decisions.' (Paper presented at the Annual Meeting of the American Sociological Association, Washington, DC, August 11–15).

O'Hare, W., Mann, T., Porter, K., and Greenstein, R. (1990), *Real Life Poverty in America: Where the American Public Would Set the Poverty Line* (A Center on Budget and Policy Priorities and Families USA Foundation Report, Washington, DC).

Osterman, P. (1990), 'Welfare Participation in a Full Employment Economy: The Impact of Family Structure and Neighborhood.' (Massachusetts Institute of Technology, Cambridge, MA. Unpublished manuscript).

Rainwater, L., and Yancey, W. L. (1967), *The Moynihan Report and the Politics of Controversy* (Cambridge, Mass.: Massachusetts Institute of Technology Press).

Ricketts, E. and Mincy, R. (1986), *Growth of the Underclass: 1970–1980* (Washington, DC: The Urban Institute).

——and Sawhill, I. (1986), *Defining and Measuring the Underclass* (Washington, DC: The Urban Institute).

Rosenbaum, J. E., and Popkin, S. J. (1989), 'Employment and Earnings of Low-Income Blacks Who Move to Middle-Class Suburbs.' (Paper presented at a Conference on *The Truly Disadvantaged*, Northwestern University: Evanston, Il, October 19–21).

Ruggles, P. (1990), 'The Poverty Line—Too Low for the 1990s.' *The New York Times* (Thursday, April 26), A31.

Testa, M., and Krogh, M. (1989), 'The Effect of Employment on Marriage Among Black Males in Inner-City Chicago.' (University of Chicago, Chicago, IL. Unpublished manuscript).

Tienda, M. (1989), 'Poor People and Poor Places: Deciphering Neighborhood Effects on Poverty Outcomes.' (Paper presented at the Annual Meeting of the American Sociological Association, San Francisco, CA, August 9–13).

—— and H. Stier, (1989), 'Joblessness or Shiftlessness: Labor Force Activity in Chicago's Inner-City.' (Paper presented at a Conference on *The Truly Disadvantaged*, Northwestern University, Evanston, Il, October 19–21).

Tobin, J. (1965), 'On Improving the Economic Status of the Negro', *Daedalus*, 94: 878–98.

U.S. Bureau of the Census (1988), 'Money Income and Poverty Status in the U.S.' (Table 2). In *Current Population Reports*. Series P–60 (Washington, D.C.: Government Printing Office).

Van Haitsma, M. (1989), 'A Contextual Definition of the Underclass.' *Focus*, 12 (Spring and Summer): 27–31.

Wacquant, L. J. D., and Wilson, W. J. (1989), 'Poverty, Joblessness and the Social Transformation of the Inner City', in *Welfare Policy for the 1990s*, (ed.) P. Cottingham and D. Ellwood.

(Cambridge, Mass.: Harvard Univ. Press), 70–102.

—— (1990), 'The Cost of Racial and Class Exclusion in the Inner City', *Annals of the American Academy of Political and Social Science*, 501 (January): 8–25.

Wilson, W. J. (1987), *The Truly Disadvantaged: The Inner City, The Underclass, and Public Policy* (Chicago: University of Chicago Press.).

—— (1988), 'The American Underclass: Inner-City Ghettos and the Norms of Citizenship, (Godkin Lecture, John F. Kennedy School of Government, Harvard University, Cambridge, MA. April 26).

—— Aponte, R., Kirschenman, J., and Wacquant, L. J. D. (1988), 'The Ghetto Underclass and the Changing Structure of American Poverty', in *Quiet Riots: Race and Poverty in the United States*, ed. Fred R. Harris and Roger W. Wilkins (New York: Pantheon), 123–54.

50

Racial Stratification and Education in the United States: Why Inequality Persists

John U. Ogbu

Introduction

I have heard both white and black Americans on several occasions ask (1) why racial inequality persists and (2) why black Americans continue to lag in school performance and educational attainment after all the improvements in race relations since 1960. They point to new employment opportunities in the private and public sectors for blacks who have a good education, and to the growing number of middle-class blacks. The belief that *things should be different now* because of improved opportunity structure can be seen in the number of black and white social scientists asserting that social class, rather than race, is now the important factor determining the life chances of black Americans (Katz 1993; Jencks and Peterson 1991; Joint Centre for Political Studies 1987; *Newsweek* 1991; *Policy Review* 1985; *Time* 1985; Wilson 1978, 1979: 159–76, 1987). They further argue that the emergence of an 'underclass' phenomenon is the reason for the current problems facing blacks in education, employment, housing, and the like.

The shift from race to class explanation of the economic, educational, and social problems is attractive to both white Americans and middle-class black Americans. For the whites it is compatible with their model of the United States as a society stratified by class. For middle-class blacks it gives a sense of achievement and reinforces their eagerness to distance themselves from those who have not made it or cannot make it. In the past the problem was 'racism' and was blamed on whites; today the

problem is 'poverty' and is blamed on the underclass. A closer examination of the situation indicates, however, that the changes in opportunity structure have not gone far enough or lasted long enough to undo instrumental barriers, let alone other untargeted barriers of racial stratification, and that class has not replaced race as the chief determinant of the life chances of black Americans.

In this article I will argue that the racial inequality persists because changes have occurred mainly in one aspect of racial stratification, in barriers in opportunity structure, but not in other domains; moreover, middle-class and college-educated blacks have been and continue to be the beneficiaries of 'a sponsored social mobility' in a labor-market and status mobility system that has not yet become color-blind. Another reason is that mainly white treatment of blacks has been targeted for change but not black responses to racial stratification. I also argue that the school-performance gap persists because the forces of racial stratification that created the gap in the first place continue to maintain it to some degree. Before taking up these two tasks I will define social stratification and distinguish racial stratification from stratification by social class.

Class Stratification versus Racial Stratification

WHAT IS SOCIAL STRATIFICATION?
When people talk about black–white inequality

From *Teachers College Record*, 96 (1994), 264–71 and 283–298. Reprinted with permission.

they often talk in terms of class inequality. But as I will argue, the inequality between blacks and whites is one not of class stratification but of racial stratification. A part of the reason for thinking that it is a class problem lies in the simplistic definition of social stratification and the tendency to confuse social stratification with social inequality and social ranking. Conventional definitions of social stratification with emphasis on the instrumental or economic aspect of stratification, coupled with the cult of quantification in some schools of thought, have resulted in the neglect of symbolic and relational aspects of social stratification.

It is not evident from the literature that social inequality is not the same thing as social stratification. For this reason, it is important to start with this distinction. Social inequality is a universal phenomenon; social stratification is not. The most common bases for social inequality are age and sex. Social ranking of individuals, which exists in stratified societies, should also be distinguished from social stratification. The ranking of individuals *as individuals* does not constitute or result in social stratification.

A society is stratified *when and only when* its individual members from different social groups are ranked on the basis of their membership in specific social groups that are also ranked, or when they are placed in such ranked social groups. It is always groups that are hierarchically ranked in social stratification, not individuals. Social stratification, then, is an arrangement of social groups or social categories in a hierarchical order of subordination and domination in which some groups so organized have unequal access to the fundamental resources of society (Berreman 1972; Fried 1960; Tuden and Plotnicov 1970).

A stratified society is a society in which there is a differential relationship between members of its constituent groups and the society's fundamental resources, so that *some people (e.g., white Americans), by virtue of their membership in particular social groups, have almost unimpaired access to the strategic resources*, while *some other people (e.g., black Americans), by virtue of their own membership in other social groups, have various impediments in their access to the same strategic or fundamental resources*. In addition, the different social groups in the hierarchy are separated by cul-

tural and invidious distinctions that serve to maintain social distance between them. In a stratified society there is usually an overarching ideology, a folk or/and scientific 'theory' embodying the dominant group's rationalizations or explanations of the hierarchical ordering of the groups (Tuden and Plotnicov 1970). Subordinate social groups do not necessarily accept the rationalizations of the system; however, they are not entirely free from its influence (Berreman 1967).

There are several types of social stratification that may coexist within the same society, such as American society. They include social class, ethnic, racial, caste, and gender stratifications. The bases for formation of the different types of stratification are economic status, cultural heritage, and social honor or esteem. Different systems of stratification may be compared with regard to the following features: basis or reasons for stratification (from the society or dominant group's point of view), presumed source of the factor on which stratification is based (such as whether it is extrinsic or intrinsic to the groups and their members), mode of recruitment of members, status summation, mobility across strata, symbols of identity, and degree of internal stratification (Berreman 1981). In this article I focus only on social class and racial stratifications.

Class Stratification

CONVENTIONAL PERSPECTIVES

There is no commonly accepted definition of class, although we can generally distinguish between two perspectives: Marxist and non-Marxist (Ogbu 1988: 163–82).

In the Marxist view, social class refers to a group's relation to the means of production and power struggle (Aronowitz 1981; Bowles and Gintis 1976; Cox 1948). The ideas of 'class conflict,' 'class struggle,' and 'economic exploitation' are important ingredients in the Marxist notion of class stratification. There are difficulties in using the Marxist class perspective to explain racial inequality in the United States.

One problem is that the Marxist framework is so dependent on relation to means of production and economic status that it ignores the existence of other types of social stratification. Some justify the lack of recognition of other forms of stratification by claiming that the ultimate source of inequality in U.S. society is corporate capitalism. The latter makes social class the fundamental form of stratification and inequality because it is based on economic differences and exploitation. They argue that racism, castism, and sexism are merely expressions of economic or class inequality (Cox 1948; Gordon and Yearkey 1980; Yearkey and Johnson 1980). The problem with this view is that anthropologists have documented the existence of caste and other forms of stratification in precapitalist societies and in societies without corporate capitalism (Hallpike 1968; Magnet 1961; Nadel 1954; Ogbu, in Berreman 1981; Richter 1980; and Todd 1977). Furthermore, class stratification based on economic status and stratification based on noneconomic factors can and do coexist in the United States, Britain, India, Japan, and elsewhere (Ogbu 1978, 1981).

Another problem is that the Marxist framework erroneously assumes that the labor market is color-blind, caste-blind, and gender-blind. On the contrary, there is ample evidence that 'the corporate economic market' has not historically treated blacks, other racial minorities, and females like their white male peers (Harrison 1972; Myrdal 1944; Norgren and Hill 1964; Ogbu 1973; and Wallace 1977). Nor do 'exploited' white workers treat black and other racial minority co-workers as co-sufferers and equal. This has been fully documented in the case of Chinese workers in California, and in the case of black workers nationwide (Chan 1991; Sandmeyer 1973; and Wallace 1977).

For non-Marxists, social classes are synonymous with socioeconomic status (SES) groups. A social class refers to a segment of society's population differentiated by education, occupation, and income, the interaction of which is believed to result in a particular life-style and a set of power relations. By defining social classes as SES groups, researchers usually assume that individuals who meet the criteria of their class index (namely, education, income, and jobs—instrumental criteria) belong to the same social class (e.g., upper class, middle class, working class, lower class, underclass, etc.) *and* that the individuals so included will manifest some assumed appropriate class behavior. The main research approach is

correlational because of the belief that members of the same SES group will manifest the same values and patterns of behavior (Herrnstein 1973; Jencks *et al.* 1972; Kohn 1969; and Tumin 1967).

One problem in applying class stratification to the analysis of racial inequality lies in the temporality of class membership in contrast to the permanence of racial group membership. Consider, for example, that on July 19, 1982, Dan Rather reported on CBS evening news that in one year, 1981, about 2 million Americans 'fell' into or joined the underclass because their income slipped below the official poverty line. No such sudden mass recruitment has ever been reported between racially stratified groups. Furthermore, note that some of the 2 million 'new recruits' of the underclass included retired middle-class people whose pension income fell below the poverty line because of inflation. I do not believe that these 'former' middle-class Americans would immediately assume under-class values and behaviors. The new recruits to the underclass also included temporarily unemployed skilled workers whose unemployment benefits ran out. They, too, would not suspend their own values and behaviors to take up those of the underclass 'temporarily' until they returned to their former life-style when the economy improved. So assigning people to different social classes, especially to the underclass, because of income and a few other instrumental criteria at a particular point in time may not be very meaningful.

We encounter more serious problems when people from different ethnic, racial, caste, and gender groups are lumped into the same SES groups because they have similar education, jobs, and wages. It is quite possible that the members of the different groups differ in some other ways that interfere with the influence the measured values and behaviors assumed to be determined by SES.

AN ALTERNATIVE PERSPECTIVE
Class stratification is but one type of stratification. Its distinguishing feature is that *it is based on economic status, an acquired characteristic* (Berreman 1981). Because the basis for membership in class groups can be acquired by an individual during a lifetime, social classes are open entities. Although they are more or less permanent, the entities have no clear boundaries; furthermore, their membership is not

permanent because people are continually moving in and out of them. Children can move up or down the different class strata and thereby can belong to different strata than their parents. Furthermore, children of an interclass mating can affiliate with the class of either parent. In a system of social class, occupational, social, and political positions are often based on training and ability rather than ascriptive criteria—at least this appears to be the case in the United States. Vertical mobility, upward or downward, from one ranked stratum to another is legitimated in a class system. Usually, there are built-in means of achieving such mobility.

Racial Stratification

Racial stratification is the hierarchical organization of *socially defined 'races' or groups* (as distinct from biologically defined 'races' or groups) on the basis of assumed inborn differences in *status honor* or *moral worth*, symbolized in the United States by skin color. The amount of the status honor that members of a given racial group are purported to have is usually determined by the value that members of the dominant group attach to skin color and is interpreted by them as an inherent or intrinsic part of the subordinate racial group and its individual members. The latter are believed to possess this lifelong attribute already at birth. This is in contrast to the extrinsic nature of the attributes of social classes and their members (e.g., economic status), which can be acquired or lost during a lifetime (Berreman 1981).

Recruitment into the racial strata, that is, the ranked racial groups, is by birth and descent. Racial groups are permanently organized hierarchically into more or less endogamous groups. In the past, marriage between blacks and whites was prohibited; even now that it is legally permitted the rule of descent has not changed. There is *a culturally sanctioned rule* that children of black and white mating, within or outside marriage, must affiliate with blacks. Throughout the history of the United States, all children of known black-white matings have been automatically defined as black by law and/or custom. In very rare cases do some blacks covertly become whites, through the painful and *nonlegitimated*

process of 'passing' (Berreman 1972). There have been some attempts in recent years by some individuals to have the U.S. courts reclassify them from black to white or vice-versa (Burma 1947; Eckard 1947. For an example of recent attempts by some people to be racially reclassified by the courts, see Dominguez 1986). Thus, it is not very meaningful to point to increasing interracial marriage as evidence that race no longer matters. In a system of racial stratification people are prohibited from changing their group membership. The prohibition is usually rationalized in the dominant group's ideology. In short, membership in racially stratified groups is permanent. The permanent racial groups are visible, recognized, and named. Social integration may occur, but assimilation is *not* an option, at least for black Americans.

In a racially stratified society, each racial stratum has its own social classes. The social classes of component strata are parallel but not equal. The reasons for the unequal social classes are that the origins of the classes may be different and that members of the racial groups do not have equal access to societal resources that enhance class development. For example, black Americans did not begin their social, occupational, and political differentiation because of differences in training, ability, or family background as did white Americans. Instead, blacks were initially collectively relegated to menial status as slaves without regard to individual differences. For almost a century after emancipation from slavery they also experienced a high degree of status summation. That is, their occupational and other roles depended more on their membership in a subordinate racial group than on individual education and ability. They were restricted from competing for desirable jobs and social positions. This is an important reason why black Americans are preoccupied with the civil rights 'struggle' for equal social, economic, and political opportunities. Here is an important difference between blacks as a subordinate racial stratum and lowerclass whites as a subordinate economic stratum. At least in the contemporary United States, there is no conscious feeling on the part of members of any social class in the general population that they belong to a corporate unity or that their common interests are different from those of other classes (Myrdal 1944). American lower-class people do not, for instance, share a collective perception of their social and economic difficulties as stemming from class subordination. Perhaps it is because of the absence of such perceptions and interpretations that I have not observed over the last thirty-two years white lower-class members engaged in a 'collective struggle' for better employment, credit rating, housing, political participation, and other opportunities (Myrdal 1944; Ogbu 1988). In contrast, most black Americans see racial barriers in employment, education, housing, and other areas as the primary causes of their menial positions and poverty.

Black Americans, like white Americans, are stratified by class but their social classes are not equal in development and they are qualitatively different. They are unequal in development because, as I have noted, blacks have had less access to jobs and training associated with class differentiation and mobility. As a result, until the 1960s, the people who made up the upper class among blacks were from a few professions, such as law, medicine, business, teaching, and preaching, with the last two comprising almost two-thirds of that class. These were professions that served primarily the needs of the black community. Blacks were largely excluded from other higher-paying professions such as architecture, civil engineering, accounting, chemistry, and management. Before 1960, the black upper class tended to overlap with the white middle-class segment and the black middle class overlapped with the white upper-lower class. The lower class among blacks was made up of an unstable working class, the unemployed, and the unemployable (Drake and Cayton 1970; Ogbu 1974).

The social classes among blacks are qualitatively different because the historical circumstances that created them and the structural forces that sustain them are different from those that created and sustained white social classes. I noted earlier the narrow base of black class differentiation during slavery. After slavery, racial barriers in employment—a job ceiling—continued for generations to limit their base of class differentiation and mobility (Higgs 1980; Ross and Hill 1967; Norgren and Hill 1964; Ogbu 1978). These collective experiences resulted in the evolution of shared perceptions among blacks of all social classes that they lack equal opportunity with whites and

that it is much more difficult for blacks to achieve economic and social self-betterment (Matusow 1989; Rowan 1975; Sochen 1971, 1972).

Another reason for the qualitative difference is that before the civil rights revolution of the 1960s blacks were forced to live in ghetto-like communities (Drake 1968; Ogbu 1978). Whites created and maintained the ghettos as clearly defined residential areas of the cities to which they restricted the black population. Blacks of all social classes were forced to share the ghetto life. This shared involuntary residential experience generated a shared feeling of oppression that transcended class boundaries (Drake 1968; Forman 1971).

Educational Consequences of Racial Stratification

CLASS ANALYSIS OF SCHOOL–PERFORMANCE GAP
As in the case of racial inequality in general, the preferred mode of analysis of the educational gap between blacks and whites is class (Bond 1981; Coleman *et al.* 1966; Ogbu 1972; Rist 1970; and Wilson 1980). While researchers may treat race as one 'variable', there is usually no reference to racial stratification. Indeed, this concept does not appear in the index of some of the most influential books on public policies and programs in minority education since the 1960s.

We can identify two forms of class analysis corresponding to the non-Marxist and Marxist concepts of class stratification respectively: correlational and cultural reproduction/resistance analyses. In correlational analysis social class is equated with socioeconomic status (SES). Correlational analysts appear to believe that children's school success depends on appropriate family background or attributes that can be correlated with school adjustment and performance. Because middle-class children are more successful in school, these researchers assume that middle-class attributes are more conducive to school success than lower-class or under-class attributes. And since they classify most black children as belonging to the lower class, they attribute the lower school performance of black children to their lower-class or underclass background (Bond 1981).

One major difficulty with correlational

studies is that they cannot explain why black and white children from similar social-class backgrounds perform differently in school. Correlational studies using black and white samples show two things: (1) within the black sample, as within the white sample, middle-class children do better in school and on standardized tests than do lower-class children; (2) however, when black children and white children from similar SES are compared, black children at every class level do less well than white children (Ogbu 1988: 163–82; Oliver et al. 1985; Slade 1982: 22E). That correlational studies cannot explain the gap in the school performance of blacks and whites of similar social class is illustrated by the following study.

This was a study of a southeastern suburban elementary school located in an area where black households had higher educational attainment, better job status, and higher income than white households; yet the school performance of black children lagged behind that of the whites. Specifically, in this suburban community about twice as many black adults as whites had college degrees and about one and one-half times as many blacks as whites held managerial and professional jobs; black unemployment was almost the same as white unemployment. The average annual income of a black household was about 39.1 per cent higher than the average annual income of a white household, a difference of about $10,000 per household in favor of blacks. In terms of class status, most black parents were of higher socioeconomic status than white parents. Still, black children lagged behind their white peers in the school district in academic achievement. Thus, in 1980–1981, the third-grade students at the elementary school (80 per cent black), scored at the 2.6 grade equivalent level, or about the tenth percentile nationally, while the county or school district average was 3.1 in grade-level-equivalent score. In the same year, the fifth-grade students at the elementary school scored at 4.7 grade equivalent level or about the thirty-eighth percentile nationally, whereas the school district average was 5.2 (Stern 1986).

The cultural reproduction/resistance school is usually associated with Marxist-oriented researchers. One version, which points to some resistance or opposition in the relationship between school culture and that of the students, suggests a more useful approach. As this theory is reformulated by Willis, working-class students fail in school because they consciously or unconsciously reject academic work as being effeminate (recognizing manual labor as masculine and ideal). These students repudiate school by forming a counterculture, which eventually impedes their school success and their chances of getting high-status jobs after leaving school. Working-class students are said to reject school knowledge because they do not believe that the kind of education they are receiving will solve their problem of subordination (Willis 1977). The Willis study introduced 'resistance' as a force of human agency in the process of the reproduction of class inequality through schooling. As Weis points out, this has helped researchers shift their attention to the day-to-day attitudes and behaviors or 'lived culture' of students (Weis 1985). It is precisely because of the introduction of students and school personnel as human agents actively involved in the process of cultural reproduction or resistance that this kind of study is relevant to the educational problems of racially stratified groups.

However, although resistance theory goes some way toward explaining the school failure of working-class youths, it too has some problems when applied to racial minorities. For example, in her study of black youths in Philadelphia, Weis found a paradox: Black youths accepted academic work and schooling, but behaved in ways that ensured that they would not, and did not, succeed. Weis recognized the difficulty of explaining black students' behavior within the framework of social class and repeatedly referred to 'racial struggle' in black American history. Nevertheless, she still ended up explaining the school failure of black youths within the framework of 'class struggle,' saying that the problem ultimately arises from 'the material conditions' of blacks (Weis 1985; Ogbu 1974; Johnson-Kuhn 1994).

There are two problems with the Marxist class analysis. One is that by and large Marxist researchers avoid explaining the discrepancies in the school performance of children from different racial/caste origins who belong to the same SES groups. Alternately, they erroneously treat the lower school performance of different types of subordinate groups as the result of resistance of an exploited working class. On the other hand, the cultural reproduction/resistance researchers are silent about the school success of Asian-American working-class students. On the whole, Marxist-oriented researchers do not have a satisfactory explanation for the paradox of both high educational aspirations and lower school performance among black students.

Cross-cultural comparisons suggest that class analyses do not shed much light on the educational experiences of racial and castelike minorities, not only in the United States but also in Britain, Japan, and elsewhere (Gibson and Ogbu 1991; Ogbu 1978, 1982: 269–89, 1991: 3–33; Shimahara 1991). A more satisfactory approach must take into account the unique features of the stratification systems that distinguish racial minorities from social classes.

SCHOOL PERFORMANCE GAP TRANSCENDS TIME AND CLASS BOUNDARIES

An enduring educational gap is one major consequence of the racial stratification between blacks and whites. However, in contemporary thinking the tendency is to discuss the academic problems of black children as if they are the product of black underclass status, or inner-city environment, or both. The assumption is also that these are 'new problems' that emerged when the 'better class' of blacks moved out of the ghetto (Wilson 1980). A closer look at the evidence suggests otherwise. The historical and persistent nature of the lower school performance of black children is well reflected in two school movements: *school desegregation* and *compensatory education*.

The school desegregation movement had as one of its goals the improvement of black school performance. Note, however, that a few years before *Brown* v. *Board of Education* several southern school districts began to publish the test scores of blacks and whites, and to use the lower test scores of blacks to oppose school desegregation (*Southern School News* 1952). In relatively affluent urban black communities, like Durham, North Carolina, and relatively poor ones like Memphis, Tennessee, black students lagged behind their white peers; and in both cities desegregation was intended to close the performance gap. It did not necessarily do so (Clement 1978; Collins and Noblitt 1978; Ogbu 1979, 1986).

In the North the situation was no better (Ferguson and Plant 1954; Ogbu 1978).

Compensatory education to improve the school performance of urban blacks began in St. Louis in 1956 and was operating in New York City by 1959. By 1961 this intervention strategy had spread to many other northern cities, even though there was no strong evidence that it was closing the gap between black and white children in school performance (Gordon and Wilkerson 1966; Ogbu 1978).

Another educational consequence of racial stratification is that even today the school-performance gap is not limited to poor blacks living in the inner cities. *And it never was.* As I pointed out earlier, it is true that among blacks, as among whites, middle-class children do better than those from the lower class. But even this type of *within-group comparison by social class* shows some racial difference. *The correlation between SES and academic performance is not as strong among blacks as it is among whites.* For example, a study of some 4,000 high school graduates in California in 1975 found that among blacks and Mexican-Americans, children from affluent and well-educated families were not benefiting from their parents' achievement. Like children from poorer families, the middle-class children had difficulty achieving academic qualification for college admission (Anton 1980). In their analysis of the 1987 California statewide test results, Haycock and Navarro found that eighth-grade black children whose parents had completed four or more years of college did less well than other black children whose parents had attended but not finished college (Haycock and Navarro 1988). Of particular note is that when blacks and whites come from similar SES background, at every level blacks consistently perform lower than their white counterparts (Slade 1982).

The performance of blacks on professional examinations such as teacher certification exams provides additional evidence that the problem is not confined to poor blacks (Bond 1994, 1993; Hartigan and Wigdor 1989; Rebell 1987). I was once attending a professional meeting where there was an extensive discussion of a state-mandated test for licensing. Many in attendance who had doctoral degrees said they failed the test several times and passed it only after the norm was lowered for minorities. But as would be expected, when we began to discuss black educational issues in general, my colleagues spoke as if the difficulty of passing academic and standardized tests were limited to the black underclass.

The problem of the school performance gap is found among blacks who live in affluent suburbs, including such places as Alexandria County, Virginia; Arlington County, Virginia; Fairfax County, Virginia; Montgomery County, Maryland; and Prince George's County, Maryland. In my current research in Oakland, California, black students attending the city's elite high school, Skyline, have an average GPA of 1.92 and an average GPA of 1.62 in the courses required to get into the University of California system. The comparable figures for Chinese and white students in the same school are 2.97/2.74 and 2.74/2.48 respectively (Alexandria County Public Schools 1993; Arlington County Public Schools 1991; Fairfax County Public Schools 1988; Montgomery County Public Schools 1993a and b; Prince George's County Public Schools 1993a and b; Ogbu 1991b). I need to add that many of the affluent school districts have an impressive array of remedial programs intended to close the gap in the school achievement.

There are three worrisome features of black school performance. First, while all minorities may start lower than their white peers in the early grades, Asian students improve and even surpass their white peers eventually; for black students, on the other hand, the progression is in the opposite direction: The gap widens between them and their white peers in subsequent years (Berkeley Unified School District 1985). Second, of all subgroups that I have studied, black males fare the worst. Third, not only are the average black GPA and other test scores lower than those of their white counterparts, but black students are often disproportionately underrepresented in courses that would enhance their chances of pursuing higher education (Prince George's County Public Schools 1990).

HOW RACIAL STRATIFICATION ENTERS INTO BLACK EDUCATION

The school-performance gap was created by forces of racial stratification: white treatment of blacks in the educational domain and black responses to schooling. The gap remains as long as these forces remain. How do these forces get into black education and maintain the gap?

There are three ways in which racial stratification enters into and adversely affects black education. One is through societal educational policies and practices. The societal channel includes denying blacks equal access to education through unequal resources, segregation, and the like—common phenomena in the past. This ensures that blacks do not receive equal education in terms of quantity and quality. If the U.S. society or one of her local communities provides blacks with less and inferior education, then blacks cannot perform as well or go as far as whites in school. This societal and community practice of unequal access was instrumental in the school desegregation movement (Bullock 1970; Ogbu 1968). The practice appears to be largely reversed, as the federal, state, and local school systems provide extra funds for special programs to improve minority educational achievement.

The other societal practice is denying blacks equal rewards with whites for their educational accomplishments through a job ceiling and related barriers, as discussed in the section on stratification and inequality. This probably historically discouraged blacks from developing 'effort optimism' in the pursuit of education. It may also have forced some to seek self-advancement through nonacademic routes.

The second way that racial stratification enters into black education lies in the way black students are perceived and treated in the specific schools they attend. These treatments include tracking, testing and misclassification, representation or nonrepresentation in textbooks and curriculum. Cultural, linguistic, and intellectual denigration is also part of the problem. I have described elsewhere the within-school treatment of black children in the schools I studied in Stockton, California, and how such treatment affected their adjustment and performance (Ogbu 1974, 1978; Payne 1987; Rist 1970). One incident will illustrate how the perception and treatment may result in an unequal educational outcome. In early 1969 I discovered with some neighborhood people that first-grade children in the neighborhood elementary school had not started to learn to read the book designated for that grade. On inquiry we were informed that the children's performance on the 'reading-readiness test' showed that they were not yet ready to read; they might be ready to read in March. On the other hand, first-grade children in the white middle-class schools in other parts of the city started on the same reader in September. In May of 1969 both groups of children would be given a state-mandated test based on the same reader. It does not take a great deal of imagination to see how poor black and Mexican-American children in my study school would perform on that test.

Racial stratification also enters into and adversely affects black education through *black people's own perceptions and responses* to their schooling in the context of their overall experience of racial subordination. The factors involved in this, third process is what I call *community forces*. I will elaborate on this mechanism because it is the least recognized, studied, or discussed.

Black Americans have not been helpless victims of racial subordination, as can be seen in the well-documented history of their 'collective struggle' (Lynch 1992; Morris 1984; Newman *et al.* 1978; Ogbu 1978). The way they have responded or adapted to their minority status, discussed in the earlier part of this article, has to some extent generated educational orientations and strategies that may not necessarily enhance school success, in spite of people's verbally expressed wish to succeed, namely, to get good grades in their schoolwork and obtain good school credentials for eventual good jobs and decent wages as adults (Johnson-Kuhn 1994; Luster 1992; Ogbu 1984, 1987, 1990; Weis 1985).

The community forces arise from three domains of black adaptation which I will call instrumental, symbolic and relational. *Instrumental adaptation* generates perceptions of opportunity structure that affect how blacks perceive and respond to schooling. For example, until the civil rights revolution of the 1960s, many black people did not see people around them who 'had made it' because of their education, contrary to the claims of 'underclass' theorists. In Stockton, California, hardly any of the adolescents I studied in the late 1960s knew anyone, except teachers, who had 'become somebody' or become successful because of their education. Yet there had been no 'exodus' of educated and professionally successful middle-class blacks from the city (Ogbu 1974). Many black parents in Stockton explained that they did not continue their education because 'education did not promise to pay.' One father said that he grew up in a town in Florida where college-educated blacks worked in the post office and at other low-prestige jobs; so he decided to go into the Navy. In my research both in Stockton and in Oakland, California, I have come across middle-class blacks who said that if they were white they 'would have been farther along' or more successful. Blacks compare themselves *unfavorably* with whites and usually conclude that, in spite of their education and ability, they are worse off than they should be because of racial barriers, rather than lack of education or qualification (Ogbu 1988; Johnson-Kuhn 1994; Luster 1992; Ogbu 1994, 1974).

One professional interviewed by Matusow in Washington, DC, illustrates this problem. He was a young lawyer who grew up in Alabama, believing that the civil rights revolution of the 1960s had indeed brought equal opportunities for blacks and whites. He took his education seriously, attended Princeton University, and eventually became a lawyer. But when he began to practice he began to feel that he could not be as successful as his white peers (Matusow 1989).

It is true that in spite of the historical experience of blacks in the opportunity structure, black folk theories for getting ahead stress the importance of education. But this verbal endorsement is not to be accepted at face value. It is often not accompanied by appropriate or necessary effort. I have previously mentioned the paradox of high educational aspiration and inappropriate academic behaviors discovered by Weis in her research in Philadelphia (Shack 1970-1). My students and I encounter the same phenomenon in various locations in California: The students verbally assert that making good grades and obtaining school credentials are important. They also say that in order to make good grades, one must pay attention in class, do what teacher says, answer questions in class, and do homework. However, from our observations in the classroom, in the family, and in the community I must conclude that many do not do these things (Weis 1985; Mitchell 1983; Luster 1992). I have suggested that the reason for this lack of adequate and persevering effort is probably that, historically, blacks were not adequately rewarded for their educational achievement. So they may not have developed a widespread effort optimism or a strong cultural ethic of hard work and perseverance in pursuit of academic work (Luster 1992). Furthermore, the folk theories stress other means of getting ahead under the circumstances that face black people. But these alternative or 'survival' strategies appear to detract from and conflict with their pursuit of formal education.

There are also factors arising from *symbolic adaptation* that do not particularly encourage striving for school success among lower-class as well as middle-class blacks. One such factor is how blacks perceive or interpret the cultural and language differences they encounter in school. I suggested earlier that black culture embodies a kind of oppositional cultural frame of reference vis-à-vis white American culture. Thus, for some blacks cultural and language differences between blacks and whites are consciously or unconsciously interpreted as symbols of group identity to be maintained, not barriers to be overcome. Moreover, they tend to equate the school culture (e.g., the curriculum and required behaviors) and standard English with white culture and language. They therefore perceive school learning not as an instrumental behavior to achieve the desired and verbalized goal of getting a good education for future employment, but rather as a kind of linear acculturation or assimilation, detrimental or threatening to collective identity. Some are afraid to behave according to what they see as the white cultural frame of reference for fear it may result in loss of minority cultural identity. The problem has been reported in studies of black students in high school, junior college, and graduate school and parents in adult school (Weis 1985; Mitchell 1983; Luster 1992). A black professor told Weis that 'a lot of Black students see [academic work] as a White world. (If I tell students, "you're going to be excellent—often times excellence means being—White—that kind of excellence is negative here" ' (Weis 1985). Based on his research findings in New York City, Labov explains that for some black youth accepting school values is equivalent to giving up self-respect because academic participation is equated with giving up black cultural identity (Labov 1972).

Apparently, some black educators and others agree with this interpretation that academic work is 'white' because they, too, complain that the school curriculum and language of instruction are 'white.' A careful study of the writings of some black scholars who are proposing changes in the education of black children indicates that their proposals are more or less based on the assumption that the school curriculum, standard practices, and standard English are white and detrimental to black children's cultural identity. Among them are advocates of Afrocentric curriculum and cultural infusion (Boykin 1986; Clark 1971; Hilliard 1991–2; Hilliard *et al.* 1991; Nobles 1991; Portland Public Schools 1990). I think that Claude Steele, a black psychologist at Stanford University, expresses the assumption of these black educators very well in a 1992 article in *The Atlantic Monthly*:

One factor is the basic assimilationist offer that schools make to Blacks: You can be valued and rewarded in school (and society), the schools say to these students, but you must first master the culture and ways of the American mainstream, and since that mainstream (as it is represented) is essentially White, this means you must give up many particulars of being Black—styles of speech and appearance, value priorities, preferences—at least in mainstream setting. This is asking a lot. (Steele 1992)

The equation of the school curriculum, the standard classroom behaviors and instructional language, the standard English, with white American culture and language results in conscious or unconscious opposition or ambivalence toward learning and using instrumental behaviors to make good grades and obtain the school credentials that the students say they need and want. This phenomenon, which has to do with identity choice, is a dilemma that cuts across class lines. It may partly explain the low school performance of some middle-class black students.

Racial stratification also affects black education through black *relational adaptation*. I will briefly point out two aspects of this. First, the deep distrust that blacks have developed for the public schools and those who control them—white Americans or their minority representatives—adversely affects communication between blacks and the schools and black interpretations of and responses to school requirements. Second, among blacks themselves, the practice of physical and social disaffiliation with the community by the academically and professionally successful middle class raises the question in the mind of community people about the real meaning of schooling.

Implications

From a comparative perspective, the persistence of black-white inequality in general and in education in particular is due to racial stratification, not class stratification. The barriers to equality caused by racial stratification go beyond those of jobs, income, housing and the like. These are the most obvious and are targets of public policies and efforts to achieve equality. There are other complex and subtle aspects of racial stratification in white treatment of blacks and black perceptions of and responses to their social reality, including their responses to schooling, that need to be better recognized, understood, and targeted for change.

Focusing on education, to promote a greater degree of academic success and good social adjustment, (1) it is essential to recognize, understand, and remove the obstacles from society and within the schools described earlier; and (2) it is equally necessary to recognize, understand, and attend to the community forces or the obstacles arising from black responses to racial stratification described above. At the moment, the role of community forces is the least known and the knowing is most resisted. Yet it is among the things that most distinguish immigrant minorities who are doing relatively well in school from non-immigrant minorities who are not doing as well. There are two parts to the problem of the school-performance gap. Community forces constitute one part.

References

Alexandria County Public Schools (1993), *1992–1993 ITBS/TAP Achievement Test Results, July 1993* (Alexandria, Va.: Alexandria County Public Schools, Monitoring and Evaluation Office).

Anton, K. P. (1980), *Eligibility and Enrollment in California Public Higher Education* (Ph.D. thesis, Univ. of California, Berkeley).

Arlington County Public Schools (1991), *Report on the Achievement and Participation of Black Students in the Arlington Public Schools, 1986–1990* (Arlington, Va.: Division of Instruction, Office of Minority Achievement).

Aronowitz, S. (1981), *The Crisis in Historical Materialism* (New York: Praeger).

Berkeley Unified School District (1985), *An Equal Education for All: The Challenge Ahead. A Report to the Berkeley Board of Education by the Task*

Force on School Achievement, June 12, 1985 (Berkeley: Board of Education).

Berreman, G. D. (1967), 'Caste in Cross-Cultural Perspective: Organizational Components', in *Japan's Invisible Race: Caste in Culture and Personality*, ed. G. DeVos and H. Wagatsuma (Berkeley: Univ. of California Press), 275–307.

—— (1972), 'Race, Caste, and Other Invidious Distinctions in Social Stratification', *Race*, 13: 385–414.

—— (1981), 'Social Inequality: A Cross-Cultural Analysis', in *Social Inequality: Comparative and Developmental Approaches*, ed. G. D. Berreman (New York: Academic Press), 3–40.

Bond, G. C. (1981), 'Social Economic Status and Educational Achievement: A Review Article', *Anthropology and Education Quarterly*, 12: 227–57.

Bond, L. (1993), 'Second Lawsuit Filed Against California Teacher Test', *FairiTest Examiner*, 7: 14.

—— (1994), personal communication, 15 April.

Bowles, S., and Gintis, H. (1976), *Schooling in Capitalist America: Educational Reform and the Contradictions of Economic Life* (New York: Basic Books).

Boykin, A. W. (1986), 'The Triple Quandary and the Schooling of Afro-American Children', in *The School Achievement of Minority Children: New Perspectives*, ed. U. Neisser (Hillsdale, NJ: Lawrence Erlbaum), 57–92.

Bullock, H. A. (1970), *A History of Negro Education in the South: From 1619 to the Present* (New York: Praeger).

Burma, J. H. (1947), 'The Measurement of Negro Passing', *American Journal of Sociology*, 52: 18–22.

Chan, S. (1991), *Asian Americans: An Interpretive History* (Boston: Twayne Publishers).

Clark, E. M. (1971), *A Syllabus for an Interdisciplinary Curriculum in African-American Studies* (Oakland, Calif.: Merritt College and Berkeley Unified School District).

Clement et al. (1978), *Moving Closer: An Ethnography of a Southern Desegregated School. Final Report* (Washington, DC: National Institute of Education).

Coleman, J. S., et al. (1966), *Equality of Educational Opportunity* (Washington, DC: Government Printing Office).

Collins, T. W., and Noblitt, G. W. (1978), *Stratification and Resegregation: The Case of Crossover High School. Final Report* (Washington, DC: National Institute of Education).

Cox, O. C. (1948: 1959 edn.), *Caste, Class and Race: A Study in Social Dynamics* (New York: Monthly Review Press).

Dominguez, V. R. (1986), *White by Definition: Social Classification in Creole Louisiana* (New Brunswick, NJ: Rutgers Univ. Press).

Drake, St Clair (1968), 'The Ghettoization of

Negro Life', in *Negroes and Jobs*, ed. L. A. Ferman, J. L. Kornbluh, and J. A. Miller (Ann Arbor: Univ. of Michigan Press), 112–28.

—— and Cayton, H. R. (1970), *Black Metropolis: A Study of Negro Life in a Northern City*, i and ii (New York: Harper).

Eckard, E. W. (1947), 'How Many Negroes "Pass"?' *American Journal of Sociology*, 52: 452–500.

Fairfax County Public Schools (1991), *Annual Report on the Achievement and Aspirations of Minority Students in the Fairfax County Public Schools, 1986–87* (Fairfax, Va.: Office of Research).

Ferguson, H. A., and Plant, R. L. (1954), 'Talent: To Develop or to Lose', *The Educational Record*, 35: 137–40.

Foner, P. S. (1974), *Organized Labor and the Black Worker, 1619–1973* (New York: International Publishers).

Forman, R. E. (1971), *Black Ghetto, White Ghetto, and Slums* (Englewood Cliffs, NJ: Prentice-Hall).

Fried, M. (1960), 'On the Evolution of Social Stratification and the State', in *Culture and History: Essays in Honour of Paul Radin*, ed. S. Diamond (New York: Columbia Univ. Press), 313–731.

Gibson, M. A., and Ogbu, J. U. (eds.) (1991), *Minority Status and Schooling: A Comparative Study of Immigrant and Involuntary Minorities* (New York: Garland).

Gordon, E. W., and Wilkerson, D. A. (1966), *Compensatory Education for the Disadvantaged: Programs and Practices: Preschool to College* (New York: College Examination Board).

—— and Yearkey, C. C. (1980), 'Review of Minority Education and Caste', *Teachers College Record*, 81 (Summer), 526–9.

Gould, W. B. (1977), *Black Workers in White Unions: Job Discrimination in the United States* (Ithaca: Cornell Univ. Press).

Hallpike, C. (1968), *The Konso of Ethiopia* (Oxford: Clarendon Press).

Harrison, B. (1972), *Education, Training, and the Urban Ghetto* (Baltimore: Johns Hopkins Univ. Press).

Hartigan, J. A., and Wigdor, A. K. (eds.) (1989), *Fairness in Employment Testing* (Washington, DC: National Academy Press).

Haycock, R., and Navarro, S. (1988), *Unfinished Business: Report from the Achievement Council* (Oakland, Calif.: Achievement Council).

Herrnstein, R. J. (1973), *IQ in the Meritocracy* (Boston: Little, Brown).

Higgs, R. (1980), *Competition and Coercion: Blacks in the American Economy, 1865–1914* (Chicago: Univ. of Chicago Press).

Hilliard, A. G. (1991–2), 'Why We Must Pluralize the Curriculum', *Educational Leadership*, 49 (Dec.-Jan.), 12–16.

——, Payton-Stewart, L., and Williams, L. O. (1991), *Infusion of African and African American Content in the School Curriculum: Proceedings of the First National Conference, October 1989* (Morristown, NJ: Aaron Press).

Jencks, C. et al. (1972), *Inequality: A Reassessment of the Effects of Family Schooling in America* (New York: Basic Books).

—— and Peterson, P. E. (eds.) (1991), *The Urban Underclass* (Washington DC: Brookings Institution).

Johnson-Kuhn, J. (1994), 'Working Hard/Hardly Working: Motivation and Perceptions of Success in a Fifth-Grade Classroom' (Honor thesis, Dept. of Anthropology, Univ. of California, Berkeley).

Joint Center for Political Studies (1987), 'Defining the Underclass: Researchers Ask Who is Included and What are the Policy Implications', *Focus* (June).

Katz, M. B. (ed.) (1993), *The 'Underclass' Debate: Views from History* (Princeton: Princeton Univ. Press).

Kohn, M. L. (1969), 'Social Class and Parent-Child Relationships: An Interpretation', in *Life Cycle and Achievement in America*, ed. R. L. Coser (New York: Harper), 21–48.

Labov, W. (1972), 'Rules for Ritual Insults', in *Rappin' and Stylin' Out: Communication in Urban Black America*, ed. T. Kochman (Urbana: Univ. of Illinois Press), 265–314.

Luster, L. (1992), 'Schooling, Survival, and Struggle: Black Women and the GED' (Ph.D. diss., Biola Univ.).

Lynch, A. (1992), *Nightmare Overhanging Darkly: Essays on Black Culture and Resistance* (Chicago: Third World Press).

Manquet, J. J. (1961), *The Premise of Inequality in Ruanda* (London: Oxford Univ. Press).

Matusow, B. (1989), 'Together Alone: What Do You Do When the Dream Hasn't Come True, When You're Black and Middle-Class and Still Shut Out of White Washington, When it Seems Time to Quit Trying?' *Washingtonian* (November), 153–9, 282–90.

Mitchell, J. (1983), 'Visible, Vulnerable, and Viable: Emerging Perspectives of a Minority Professor', in *Teaching Minority Students*, New Directions for Teaching and Learning, 16 (San Francisco: Jossey-Bass), 17–28.

Montgomery County Public Schools (1993*a*), *School Performance Program Report* (Rockville, Md.: Office of Evaluation).

—— (1993*b*), *Success for Every Student Plan: Second Annual Report on the Systemwide Outcomes* (Rockville, Md.: Office of Evaluation).

Morris, A. D. (1984), *The Origins of the Civil Rights Movement: Black Communities Organizing for Change* (New York: Free Press).

Mosteller, F., and Moynihan, D. P. (eds.) (1972), *On Equality of Educational Opportunity* (New York: Random House).

Myrdal, G. (1944), *An American Dilemma: The Negro Problem and Modern Democracy* (New York: Harper).

Nadel, N. S. (1954), 'Caste and Government in Primitive Society', *Journal of Anthropological Society of Bombay*, 8 (1954), 22.

Newman, D. K. *et al.* (1978), *Protest, Politics, and Prosperity: Black Americans and White Institutions, 1940–75* (New York: Pantheon).

Newsweek (1991), 'The Black Conservatives' (9 March), 29–33.

Nobles, A. W. (1991), 'The Infusion of African and African-American Content: A Question of Content and Intent', in Hilliard, A. G., Payton-Stewart, L., and Williams, L. O. (eds.), *Infusion of African and African American Content in the School Curriculum: Proceedings of the First National Conference, October 1989* (Morristown, NJ: Aaron Press), 4–26.

Norgren, P. H., and Hill, S. E. (1964), *Toward Fair Employment* (New York: Columbia Univ. Press).

Ogbu, J. U. (1974), *The Next Generation: An Ethnography of Education in an Urban Neighbourhood* (New York: Academic Press).

—— (1978), *Minority Education and Caste: The American System in Cross-Cultural Perspective* (New York: Academic Press).

—— (1979), 'Desegregation in Racially Stratified Communities: A Problem of Congruence', *Anthropology and Education Quarterly*, 9: 290–4.

—— (1981), 'Education, Clientage, and Social Mobility: Caste and Social Change in the United States and Nigeria', in *Social Inequality*, ed. Berreman, 277–306.

—— (1982), 'Equalization of Educational Opportunity and Racial/Ethnic Inequality', in *Comparative Education*, ed. P. G. Altbach, R. F. Arnove, and G. P. Kelly (New York: Macmillan), 269–89.

—— (1986), 'Structural Constraints in School Desegregation', in *School Desegregation Research: New Directions in Situational Analysis*, ed. J. Prager, D. Longshore, and M. Seeman (New York: Plenum Press), 21–36.

—— (1987a), *Understanding Community Forces Affecting Minority Students' Academic Efforts* (report prepared for the Achievement Council, Oakland, Calif.).

—— (1987b), 'Variability in Minority School Performance: A Problem in Search of an Explanation', *Anthropology and Education Quarterly*, 18: 312–34.

—— (1988), 'Class Stratification, Racial Stratification and Schooling', in *Class, Race and Gender in US Education*, ed. L. Weis (Buffalo: State Univ. of New York Press), 163–82.

—— (1990), 'Overcoming Racial Barriers to Equal Access', in *Access to Knowledge: An Agenda for Our Nation's Schools*, ed. J. I. Goodlad and P. Keating (New York: College Board), 59–89.

—— (1991a), 'Immigrant and Involuntary Minorities in Comparative Perspective', in Gibson, M. A., and Ogbu, J. U. (eds.), *Minority Status and Schooling: A Comparative Study of Immigrant and Involuntary Minorities* (New York: Garland).

—— (1991b), 'School Achievement of Urban Blacks' (paper prepared for the Committee on Research on the Urban Underclass, Social Science Council, San Francisco, Calif., 8–9 March).

—— (1994), 'Minority Education Project: A Preliminary Report, 1994' (unpubl. ms., Dept of Anthropology, Univ. of California, Berkeley).

Oliver, M. L., Rodriguez, C., and Mickelson, R. A. (1985), 'Brown and Black in White: The Social Adjustment and Academic Performance of Chicano and Black Students in a Predominantly White University', *The Urban Review*, 17: 3–24.

Payne, C. M. (1987), *Getting What We Asked For: The Ambiguity of Success and Failure in Urban Schools* (Westport, Conn.: Greenwood Press).

Policy Review (1985), 'What Black Conservatives Think of Reagan: A Symposium', 34 (Fall), 27–41.

Portland Public Schools (1990), *African-American Baseline Essays* (Portland, Oreg.: Portland Public Schools).

Prince George's County Public Schools (1990), *Black Male Achievement: From Peril to Promise. Report of the Superintendent's Advisory Committee on Black Male Achievement* (Upper Marlboro, Md.: Office of the Superintendent), 65.

—— (1993a), *Black Male Achievement: From Peril to Promise. Progress Report, December 1993* (Upper Marlboro, Md.: Office of Research and Evaluation).

—— (1993b), *1993 Maryland School Performance Program Report* (Upper Marlboro, Md.: Office of Research and Evaluation).

Rebell, M. A. (1987), 'Disparate Impact of Teacher Competency Testing on Minorities: Don't Blame the Test Takers—Or the Tests', in *What Should Teacher Certification Tests Measure?* ed. M. L. Chernoff, P. M. Nassif, and W. P. Gorth (Hillsdale, NJ: Lawrence Erlbaum).

Richter, D. (1977), 'Further Consideration of Caste in West Africa: The Senufo', *Africa*, 47: 37–44.

Rist, R. (1970), 'Student Social Class and Teacher Expectations: The Self-Fulfilling Prophecy in Ghetto Education', *Harvard Educational Review*, 40: 411–51.

Ross, A. M., and Hill, H. (1967), *Employment, Race, and Poverty: A Critical Study of the Disadvantaged Status of Negro Workers from 1865 to 1965* (New York: Harcourt).

Rowan, C. T. (1975), 'The Negro's Place in the American Dream', in *The American Dream: Vision and Reality*, ed. J. D. Harrison and A. B. Shaw (San Francisco: Canfield Press), 19–23.

Sandmeyer, E. C. (1973), *The Anti-Chinese Movement in California* (Urbana: Univ. of Illinois Press).

Shack, W. A. (1970–1), *On Black American Values in White America: Some Perspectives on the Cultural Aspect of Learning Behavior and Compensatory Education* (paper prepared for the Social Science Research Council, Sub-Committee on Values and Compensatory Education).

Shimahara, N. K. (1991), 'Social Mobility and Education: The Burakumin in Japan', in Gibson, M. A., and Ogbu, J. U. (eds.), *Minority Status and Schooling: A Comparative Study of Immigrant and Involuntary Minorities* (New York: Garland).

Slade, M. (1982), 'Aptitude, Intelligence or What?' *The New York Times* (October), 22E.

Sochen, J. (ed.) (1971), *The Black Man and the American Dream: Negro Aspirations in America, 1900–1930* (Chicago: Quadrangle Press).

—— (1972), *The Unbridgeable Gap: Blacks and their Quest for the American Dream, 1900–1930* (Chicago: Rand McNally).

Southern School News (1952), 'Under Survey', 3: 2.

Steele, C. M. (1992), 'Race and the Schooling of Black Americans', *Atlantic Monthly* (April), 68–75.

Stern, S. P. (1986), *School Imposed Limits on Black Family Participation: A View From Within and Below* (paper presented to the 85th annual meeting of the American Anthropological Association, Philadelphia, Dec. 4–7).

Thernstorm, S. (1973), *The Other Bostonians: Poverty and Progress in the American Metropolis, 1880–1970* (Cambridge, Mass.: Harvard Univ. Press).

Time (1985), 'Redefining the American Dilemma: Some Black Scholars Are Challenging Hallowed Assumptions' (11 November), 33–6.

Todd, D. M. (1977), 'Caste in Africa?', *Africa*, 47: 398–412.

Tuden, A., and Plotnicov, L. (eds). (1970), *Social Stratification in Africa* (New York: Free Press), 1–29.

Tumin, M. M. (ed.) (1967), *Readings in Social Stratification* (Englewood Cliffs, NJ: Prentice-Hall).

US Office of Civil Rights (1968), *Racial Isolation in the Public Schools: A Report* (i. Washington, DC: Government Printing Office).

Wallace, P. (ed.) (1977), *Equal Employment Opportunity: The AT&T Case* (Cambridge, Mass.: MIT Press).

Weis, L. (1985), *Between Two Worlds: Black Students in an Urban Community College* (Boston: Routledge and Kegan Paul).

Willis, P. (1977), *Learning to Labor: How Working-Class Kids Get Working-Class Jobs* (New York: Columbia Univ. Press).

Wilson, W. J. (1978), *The Declining Significance of Race* (Chicago: Univ. of Chicago Press).

—— (1979), 'The Declining of Race: Revisited But Not Revised', in *Caste and Class Debate*, ed. C. V. Willie (Bayside, NY: General Hall).

—— (1980), 'Race, Class and Public Policy in Education' (unpubl. lecture, for National Institute of Education, Vera Brown Memorial Seminar Series, Washington, DC).

—— (1987), *The Truly Disadvantaged: The Inner City, the Underclass, and Public Policy* (Chicago: Univ. of Chicago Press).

Yearkey, C. C., and Johnson, G. S. (1980), 'Review of *Minority Education and Caste*', *American Journal of Ortho-Psychiatry*, 49: 353–9.

51

Introduction to *The Bell Curve Wars*

Steven Fraser

Newsweek called it 'frightening stuff,' worrying that it 'may be a mirror for our morally exhausted times,' a book that 'plays to public anxieties over crime, illegitimacy, welfare dependency, and racial friction.' However, contributors to a symposium in *The National Review* described it as 'magisterial,' and noted that it 'confirms ordinary citizens' reasonable intuition that trying to engineer racial equality in the distribution of occupations and social positions runs against not racist prejudice but nature, which shows no such egalitarian distribution of talents.' *Time* magazine rejoined by characterizing the book as '845 pages of provocation-with-footnotes,' a work of 'dubious premises and toxic conclusions.' Rushing to the book's defense, the *Wall Street Journal* decried the liberal media for ganging up to excoriate the book, and in particular for engaging in 'a frantic race to denounce and destroy Charles Murray' (one of the book's two authors). While *Forbes* applauded the book, and Murray's Jeffersonian vision, *New York Magazine* saw it as 'grist for racism of every variety.' A columnist for *The New York Times* gloomily concluded: 'At least Rush Limbaugh has a sense of humor.' Meanwhile, the book was being featured on 'Nightline' and showing up on the shelves of K-Marts all over the country.

The Bell Curve: Intelligence and Class Structure in American Life by Richard J. Herrnstein and Charles Murray is clearly the most incendiary piece of social science to appear in the last decade or more. It's easy to understand why. *The Bell Curve* irritates every abraded nerve in our public consciousness about race and social class. In form it is practically a model of acad-emic etiquette, sober not inflammatory in style, dutifully acknowledging contrary views, encasing its own view-point in a thick statistical armature. But despite the hedgerows of caveats and equivocations with which the authors surround their most provocative claims, *The Bell Curve* is an explosive device. Its premises, its purported findings, its prescriptive advice for what ails American society are—whether or not the authors deliberately designed them to be so—shocking.

There is, for example, the book's hubris; the clear implication that it constitutes a kind of Rosetta stone with which to decipher in one fell swoop all of the country's social pathologies. Once we correctly understand the role of statistically measured intelligence, the inexorable logic of the social arithmetic that sorts us out into rich and poor, powerful and powerless, will become blindingly apparent. The authors assure us we will no longer 'grope with symptoms instead of causes' or 'stumble into supposed remedies that have no chance of working.'

It is hard to recall when there last appeared a work of such daunting omniscience, one offering such presumptuous singleminded wisdom. Many of the most painful dilemmas afflicting our society, when viewed through the prism of *The Bell Curve*, seem if not remediable then at least cleansed of their bewildering complexity. Low intelligence lurks in the shadows of 'irresponsible childrearing and parenting behavior.' It looms again as 'a cause of unemployment and poverty.' Indeed, not only poverty and unemployment but crime, unwed motherhood, school failure, workplace accidents, welfare dependency, and broken families emerge demonically out of the Pandora's box of sub-par IQ scores. This news about our social afflictions is terrible, but the simple elegance of the authors' diagnosis is nonetheless intellectually stunning.

From *The Bell Curve Wars* by Steven Fraser (Basic Books, 1995). Reprinted with permission.

Then there is the book's profound fatalism and austere elitism, both so extraordinary in a habitually optimistic and democratically inclined nation. If group differences in intelligence are to some large degree hereditary and therefore intractable, and if we have become a hierarchical society, polarized into an empowered 'cognitive elite' at the top and a sociopathic 'cognitive underclass' at the bottom—a hierarchy that merely replicates an ascending slope of IQ scores—then, the authors feel obligated to tell us, public policy stands helpless to do anything about it: thus, 'success and failure in the American economy, and all that goes with it, are increasingly a matter of the genes that people inherit,' and 'programs to expand opportunities for the disadvantaged are not going to make much difference.' Grim pronouncements indeed. Inequality, inequality of the most fundamental sort, is our inexorable fate however much the nation's democratic and egalitarian credo might groan in protest.

Yet alongside this air of fatalistic resignation, Murray and Herrnstein convey an equally astonishing sense of activism and missionary purpose, which also helps account for the book's remarkable notoriety. They worry about 'dysgenesis,' or what others have less elegantly characterized as the 'dumbing-down of America,' due to the higher fertility rates of the 'cognitive underclass.' Here the authors are more sanguine about the efficacy of public policy, suggesting, albeit with some tentativeness, given the extreme delicacy of the subject, that changes in immigration law and welfare and public health reforms targeted particularly at unwed mothers might arrest the genetic degradation of the national stock. Not since the eugenics craze of the 1920s has this line of thought occupied a serious place on the national agenda.

Numerous other claims and assertions have generated flash floods of letters to the editor in every major magazine and newspaper, not to mention over-the-air commentary on scores of radio and television shows. For example, the authors' insistence on the predominance of our genetic make-up over environmental factors in determining how well we do on an IQ test stirs controversy; so too, their presumption that 'intelligence,' or what some psychometricians call *g*, is a uniform, quantifiable power measurable across differences in history, culture, and environment. All of

these issues and more are examined in the essays that follow.

But above all, of course, it is what *The Bell Curve* says, or at least seems to say—notwithstanding disclaimers by the authors in and outside of the text—about race, intelligence, and social hierarchy that has ignited the media firestorm. In a country necessarily preoccupied throughout its whole history with race relations, the book's claim to offer scientific proof of the inferiority of black people was bound to eclipse all its other possible subjects in public debate. The authors demur, noting that there's hardly a word about race—or rather that the book is only about the 'white race'—until chapter 13, more than halfway through the main body of the text. More to the point, the subtitle of the book says it's about 'intelligence and class structure in American life,' not about intelligence and race. In some sense the authors are quite right. The book is indeed about class in America, a stark fact noteworthy in its own right. However, *The Bell Curve* colors the class structure in unmistakable shades of black and white, neutralizing simmering tensions over economic inequality with highly charged notions of race phobia and inferiority.

Words like 'class' and phrases like 'class structure' are rarely heard nowadays. To suddenly see them blazoned across the jacket of a best-selling book by two conservative social scientists is therefore especially striking. Yet for well over a century, from the age of Jackson through the age of FDR, such words were a common enough part of our national vocabulary. Usually they were deployed to signal serious maldistributions of power and wealth and often carried with them a moral opprobrium directed at landed, industrial, or financial elites. Then, sometime after World War II, questions of class inequalities lost their urgency, subsided, and even vanished from the public arena. To watch them resurface in the pages of *The Bell Curve* is a bracing reminder that the abrasions of social class remain an abiding reality for Americans, whether they are mirrored in popular rhetoric or not. More than that, however, the 'class struggle,' as retold in *The Bell Curve*, marks a seismic shift in the moral valence of the idea of class in American life.

If at one time, examining the nation's class structure implicitly called into question the moral legitimacy, democratic commitments, and economic fairness of the country's most powerful institutions and wealthiest individuals, *The Bell Curve* is telling us that the shoe is now very much on the other foot. While the authors lament the social isolation of the 'cognitive elite,' walled off from the rest of society in its privileged compounds, the brunt of the book is about the transgressions of the lower orders, cognitive or otherwise. At a time when most indices record expanding inequalities in American life—not only in income and wealth distribution, but in public and private schooling, in matters of health care, even in our varying capacities to rear the newborn—*The Bell Curve* naturalizes those phenomena, turns them into inescapable symptoms of a biological class fate. At the same time, by associating the 'cognitive underclass' with every grisly or disturbing form of social behavior, from crime to unwed teenage motherhood, the authors direct our gaze away from those institutional centers of power that in an earlier era might have had to shoulder the blame for our most grievous inequalities and social pathologies.

Once a way of interrogating the powerful, in the hands of Murray and Herrnstein, the study of 'class structure' has become instead an implicit indictment of the powerless, the 'scientific' rationale others may use to find them blameworthy and to prepare some condign punishment. This too helps account for the book's renown. It allows for discussion of the vexed issue of social inequality at a moment when the hierarchies of American life grow more distended and rigid; but it lets the anxieties and resentments naturally aroused by those developments flow downward toward a defenseless 'cognitive underclass.' The fact that that class turns out to be disproportionately black is undoubtedly an important political and psychological consolation for some—and it severely weakens the authors' contention that their book is not about race. Still, *The Bell Curve*'s distinctive class agenda is made unmistakably clear when the reader is reminded that 'the high rates of poverty that afflict certain segments of the white population are determined more by intelligence than by socioeconomic background.'

The Bell Curve Wars: Race, Intelligence, and the Future of America responds to these and other vital issues raised by the Murray and Herrnstein book. There is no neat way to pigeonhole the essays that follow. Some criticize *The Bell Curve*'s premises regarding genetics, the nature of human intelligence, and the very concept of race. Some dispute its statistical methods and findings or the credibility of its sources. Others question its depiction of America's 'class structure' or the book's policy recommendations. Several speculate about the remarkable public reaction to the book. A few do a bit of everything. Taken together they comprise a powerful antidote to a work of dubious premises and socially alarming predictions.

As Stephen Jay Gould once took on Herrnstein and Murray's predecessors in his book *The Mismeasure of Man*, so here he attacks *The Bell Curve*'s scientific pretensions as he dismantles its four most basic premises regarding intelligence and genetics: that intelligence can be described by a single number; that it is capable of ranking people in some linear order; that it is genetically based; and that it is immutable. Cognitive psychologist Howard Gardner questions the scientific underpinnings of *The Bell Curve* by noting that it ignores the past 100 years of biological, psychological, and anthropological research that challenges the notion of a single, uniform, and innate human intelligence, or *g*. He argues instead for the concept of 'multiple intelligences'—practical, social, musical, spatial, and so on—and for the enormously important but underrated role of training in the attainment of any kind of intelligence. The scientific assault is joined from yet another quarter by the eminent psychometrician Richard Nisbett. Based on his painstaking examination of all the existing serious scientific studies of intelligence, Nisbett finds that most point to a zero genetic contribution to the black–white differential in IQ. He concludes that Murray and Herrnstein's slipshod treatment of this and other vital statistical questions would prohibit their publication in any respectable peer-reviewed journal. *New Republic* editors Jeffrey Rosen and Charles Lane question the integrity of the book's scholarly infrastructure. Scrutinizing *The Bell Curve*'s footnotes and bibliography, Rosen and Lane conclude that the authors have in effect synthesized the work of 'disreputable race theorists and eccentric eugenicists' in mounting some of their key arguments. Dante Ramos of *The New Republic* similarly comments that there is 'too much counter-evidence relegated to endnotes, too much tendentious data interpretation, and too many not-quite-credible studies.'

A number of commentators have questioned the book's historical nearsightedness; for example, its conspicuous failure to explain the long-term decline in poverty during the reign of the welfare state (roughly from 1940 to 1970). In his essay here, Thomas Sowell, conservative intellectual and *Forbes* magazine columnist, challenges the authors' claims about the genetic basis for ethnic group differences in intelligence by appealing to the historical record. He points out that the relative performance of various ethnic groups on intelligence tests has changed greatly over time, and that these ethnic groups have dramatically shifted position on the IQ ladder even while their rates of intermarriage remained low and unchanged. This has been true not only of Ashkenazi Jews (the most favored 'race' within Murray and Herrnstein's 'cognitive elite'), but of Poles and Italians as well. Jacqueline Jones, historian of the working poor, both black and white, argues that *The Bell Curve* is only 'the most recent in a long line of efforts to prove the congenital inferiority of poor people in general . . . and black people in particular.' Her essay is an eye-opening comparison of *The Bell Curve* with those now long-forgotten justifications of slavery and segregation that rested on the alleged mental inferiority of African Americans. Henry Louis Gates, Jr., W. E. B. Du Bois Professor of the Humanities at Harvard, unearths an apposite observation by Frederick Douglass that reminds us of the creative labors of past master classes seeking some justification for their domination in the failings of those they dominated. Gates notes that *The Bell Curve* appears at a moment in our history when its behavioral explanation for the persisting misery of our inner cities sits well with an electorate, and especially a Congress, deeply reluctant to commit substantial resources toward the eradication of poverty.

Andrew Hacker, author of *Two Nations: Black and White, Separate, Hostile, Unequal*, and Alan Wolfe, author of several books on American intellectual life, challenge *The Bell Curve*'s version of today's class structure. Rejecting the book's thesis that the sort of verbal virtuosity or expertise at abstraction that tends to show up well on IQ tests is the equivalent of intelligence, Hacker denies that a caste of high test scorers or 'testocracy' dominates

our society. He furthermore asks why Murray and Herrnstein fail to analyze the criminal behavior of the white collar 'cognitive elite' (which after all entails a very substantial financial burden on the rest of us), speculating that the authors' social prejudice leads them to treat their crimes as less menacing 'because their commission calls for brains rather than brawn.' Alan Wolfe, who calls *The Bell Curve* a '*Communist Manifesto* for the mind,' shows that the book's attempt to prove there has been a revolution in the country's class structure falls apart upon close inspection. Wolfe maintains that there's no evidence of a relationship between test scores, even at the best colleges, and later career success, and no hard linkage between IQ and job performance; nor does IQ predict income disparities later in life. John Judis, who writes about American culture and intellectual history, notes that for a book ostensibly about the recent and alarming growth in disparities of income, wealth, and standard of living, *The Bell Curve* is remarkably silent about such clearly relevant considerations as the decline of trade unions, the out-sourcing of manufacturing, the growth of foreign competition, and so on.

Judis is even more upset, as are a number of other contributors, with the book's implications for public policy. He homes in on the authors' evasiveness, showing that despite public denials by Murray, *The Bell Curve* builds a brief on behalf of eugenics and the continued rule of the 'cognitive elite.' Mickey Kaus, author of *The End of Equality*, is disturbed by the harsh vision of America, appearing near the end of *The Bell Curve*, in which the 'cognitive underclass' ends up consigned to the stern ministrations of a 'custodial state.' Citing an avalanche of evidence suggesting the environmental basis of ethnic differences in intelligence, Kaus concludes that, in contrast to *The Bell Curve*'s relentless attack on most meliorative measures, there's every reason to believe improving the awful environment in which many black children grow up will markedly close *The Bell Curve* gap. So, too, the esteemed social scientist Nathan Glazer, while more agnostic about the underlying reasons for IQ differences, laments the book's 'quietism regarding our greatest social problem' when there's still so much that could be attempted to remedy the plight of African Americans.

A number of the contributions to *The Bell*

Curve Wars express the moral forebodings conjured up by a book so at odds with the nation's democratic and egalitarian faith. Martin Peretz, publisher of *The New Republic*, muses about the book's alarming reverberations in a country that sometimes seems all too much in a hurry to forsake its historic belief in equality. Leon Wieseltier, the literary editor of *The New Republic* (whose essay is a response to an article by Murray and Herrnstein appearing in that magazine) refuses to grant some privileged status to the authors' putative 'science' or to credit their portrait of themselves as heroic venturers into the intellectual unknown. Instead, he characterizes their views as 'old, dreary and indecent, philosophically shabby and politically ugly,' and argues that the determinism and materialism of the Murray and Herrnstein position are at odds with the American credo of individual freedom.

Wieseltier strikes a personal note, remarking on the significance of his own Jewish origins in the Herrnstein-Murray view of the world. Hugh Pearson, the biographer of Huey Newton, does something similar. While he deplores much about *The Bell Curve*, he doesn't want African Americans to use it as a psychological crutch, a justification 'to continue viewing ourselves as victims,' clinging to 'old standards' and 'old solutions.'

Public reaction to the book is very much on the minds of other contributors as well. Michael Lind, an editor at *Harper's* magazine, is particularly intrigued by the 'sudden and astonishing legitimation, by the leading intellectuals and journalists of the mainstream American right, of a body of racialist pseudo-science.' His essay explores the recent transformation of the conservative movement that now embraces an outlook that, even through the Reagan years, was repudiated by the intellectually responsible right wing.

Randall Kennedy of the Harvard Law School is deeply worried about the enormous hype surrounding the publication of *The Bell Curve* as well as its acceptance by important arbiters of public opinion as 'within the pale of respectable discussion,' despite its conspicuous deficiencies and its defamation of African Americans. Such a triumph lends great credence to a long tradition of pessimism

about the future of race relations in America. Kennedy probes the mores of the mass media to help explain how a book avowing a theory of black inferiority achieved such legitimacy.

Orlando Patterson, author of *Freedom*, concludes with an essay that ranges widely across much of the treacherous scientific and sociological terrain covered by *The Bell Curve*. Along the way, he asks a fundamental question raised by the book's success: 'Why is it that, in a land founded on the secular belief that 'all men are created equal,' we are so obsessed with the need to find a scientific basis for human inequality?'—an obsession that invariably seems directed at African Americans. Patterson notes, for example, that although there are clear regional variations between rural white Southerners and their Northern urban counterparts in measured IQ as well as in cultural and economic performance, no one has ever sounded a national alarm bell about these differences, except in the most sympathetic tones. While we do not neglect such discrepancies, we do not make them the occasion for 'wantonly insulting and dishonoring these people.' The reason is both obvious and chilling. If rural white people are considered members in good standing of the nation's social and moral community, black people are forever on probation. Professor Patterson's essay probes the reasons why.

The Bell Curve Wars does not pretend to offer a unified viewpoint. Its contributors have varying estimations of the book they were assembled to write about. But even the most conservative among them find themselves disturbed; either by one or several of its more suspect premises or conclusions, or by what the extraordinary reception accorded *The Bell Curve* might portend for our society. Inescapably, one must wonder whether its ubiquitous presence serves to validate—through its voluminous pages, its social scientese, its panoply of graphs, charts, and appendices—feelings deeply buried in our society about the inferiority of African Americans, feelings that have in recent years once again bubbled to the surface. What *The Bell Curve Wars* hopes to provide is a multifaceted challenge to a book whose prognosis for the future of America could hardly be grimmer.

52

The Family and Social Justice

A. H. Halsey and Michael Young

Last year we wrote a pamphlet for publication by the Institute for Public Policy Research (Young and Halsey 1995) urging a policy of child-centredness for the New Labour Party of Great Britain. To introduce it we asked Gallup to survey opinion among those aged 16 and over on the future prospects of children; 'Do you think that children today have a better future in front of them than you had when you were a child, a worse future, or about the same?' The overall result was: Better 8 per cent, Worse 63 per cent, Same 15 per cent, Don't Know 4 per cent.

The large majority for 'worse' showed up in all age groups, and regions, with parents of children under 16 being particularly pessimistic. The only exceptions were people of 65 and over, while people in the top class (socio-economic categories A/B) who replied 'worse' were in a much smaller majority than in other classes.

Our aim in the pamphlet was to persuade a party and a particular country. Here we want to put essentially the same argument into a wider historical and geographical context.

As a model and foundation of the just society, the family is not a property of the political right. It has been virtually forgotten that once upon a time the Labour Party socialist believed that a good factory or town or country should be one ruled by the principles governing a respectable working-class family. Of course, words are great deceivers in social discourse. Only in our own generation has the family come to mean the nuclear family. That is far too narrow a definition for the purposes of social policy. Declining fertility and accelerating geographical mobility have strained and weakened the extended family. Older political views of how to create a new commonwealth or a new Jerusalem or Socialism

presupposed a dense network of community relations, delivered by a technology and a productive organization which put great restraint on the movement of individuals. Even the great migrations tended to be the movement of tribes from one geographical point to another, maintaining their cultural, linguistic, and familial traditions (Schluter and Lee 1992). We now live in a world in which the labour market is virtually global; communication and transport technology develop with remorseless rapidity, and the possibilities of freedom seem to have no bounds. Some intellectuals, especially in the 1960s and 1970s, have seen freedom as possible only if we can all escape from the web of obligations created and maintained by family and community (Dennis 1993). In other words, we are talking about residential and relational patterns of life which, in effect, are still adapting themselves to shifts in the technological and economic base of production. Modern politics is a ceaseless attempt to optimize the values of liberty, equality, and community as our command over nature opens new possibilities, as kinship systems adapt to shifts between the domestic and the formal economy, and as the occupational profile of the economy is more or less rapidly transformed away from manual labour towards skilled middle-class jobs, and away from life-long, full-time long hours and low wages, towards mobile, part-time short hours and high wages.

The social sciences live under a handicap imposed by these circumstances. Yesterday's realities remain with us as today's concepts. There is a tired old joke used by lecturers to social-science beginners about the man who reduced the GNP by marrying his housekeeper. Measurement is fraught with conceptual difficulty. The Victorians, even Alfred

Marshall, judged that national wealth could be adequately measured without reference to the vast labour of women in the domestic economy. It was believed then that the proportion of all labour carried out in the home and in voluntary activity in the community was to become less and less determinant of national wealth. Economists knew perfectly well that the total of goods and services exchanged was thereby underestimated. But they thought that trends would make this phenomenon less important, and that in any case adding up the goods and services exchanged through markets and bureaucracies was valuable in its own right.

The sexual division of labour is now quite different, and women especially are typically in part-time employment, even in their (now shorter) period of childbearing. This has happened partly because more and more women have left behind the unpaid economy of the home and joined the paid economy of industry. The struggle for a rise in the all-round status of women has fired one of the great social movements of the century and, though there is still a long way to go before something like equality is achieved in home as well as in the workplace, great progress has been made. But the drawback is that attention has focused so much on the relations between adult men and women. For every ten thousand words about the rights and interests of women in relation to men, there have been a hundred about the rights and interests of children.

We hope that in the next stage of this great debate, the rights—and, we hope, the *duties* of women *and* of men—are related to the interests of children. There have been attempts by economists to produce extended or alternative accounts of national income and product, and there have been attempts to produce indicators of altruism which might well be developed to measure the extent to which a given generation allocates its energies as between its own satisfaction and the welfare of children. We seek measures of the moral as well as the material economy, for example of child attention and neglect.

The values which underpin the family when it is stable—duty, loyalty, love—have, we think, been in retreat for a long time now. In the family, seen as a small collective of a special kind, the emphasis is on co-operation rather than competition, and on long-term commitment rather than choice. In the family,

individuals are not valued so much for what they do—for their possessions or their success, their achievements or their accomplishments—as for what they are. As members of the family, they can have a commitment to other members which is more or less unlimited, or, if limited, then less so than in most other relationships. At any rate, in the ideal type of family, relationships are not based on a reciprocity of self-interest—'I'll do this for you if you'll do this for me'—but on a bond which goes beyond self-interest and rational calculation. The mother does not enquire whether she will be repaid before she does the washing for a sick daughter, the daughter whether she can afford the time to nurse her mother through a long illness.

Seen in this way, the family is at the heart of the moral economy. It teaches people the most precious ability of all, the ability to transcend self-interest and regard the interests of others as in some way their own: the kind of altruism which is at the heart of the collective conscience and which holds all societies together. When it is working well, the family is the seedbed of the virtue from which all the civic virtues stem, just as, when things go wrong, it can be the font of all the vices.

The moral economy is always in tension with the market economy. The market economy is bound to value people more for what they do than for what they are—for their efficiency, their productivity, their achievements—and to encourage people to compete against each other. The nepotism which is prized in the family is despised in the economy. The emphasis is on the choice which is beloved of economists and *Which?* magazine. Whatever it is they are doing, people are more aware of other places where they might choose to be, at other circumstances, in other offices, with other men or other women, on other moonlit nights. Modern society is bedevilled by the profusion of choice which can play havoc with the tranquillity even of the ordinary, relatively stable family, when all the members of it are hurrying down their own peculiar paths of individual fulfilment with hardly time to sit down together for a meal or just to be with each other. But the values of the market have become more dominant and, needless to say, we are not thinking just of the last 18 years.

It is not only that the measurements of economists are less than satisfactory. We are also deficient in sociology with respect to the measurement of the quality of life, perhaps especially for children and old people. We could, and indeed we do, take the view that the essential prerequisite for a civilized generation is the constant, enlightened, and supported attention to each child of two committed parents. Not quite true, some will say, and not quite possible, many others will add. Certainly many a good citizen has been reared by grandparents, and many lives have been saved by 'agents' such as health visitors or a sanitary inspector; and many a pathway of opportunity has been opened by an inspired or sympathetic schoolteacher. All this is true, and Heaven be praised; for politics cannot do everything. Bureaucrats do not work on August Bank Holiday Monday. Only mothers and fathers give unreasonable care, and every child at some time needs precisely that. We cannot precisely define committed parenting, especially in a society where men are being drawn back towards the domestic economy, where there is cohabitation, divorce, and separation as well as paid employment for mothers all on the increase. Being formally married or registering a birth from the same address are crude substitutes for adequate measurement of the quality of parenting. We do not even have estimates of the time spent by parents with children, though American studies suggest that this has halved in the past decade.

What governments can do is to foster the social conditions that maximize the chances of committed parenting. Governments, therefore, work indirectly through fiscal regimes that transfer money to or away from parents, through the provision of public services in health, education, and welfare, through relieving mothers of loneliness, anxiety, and ignorance, providing them with expert and protracted childcare services and with the income they must have if their children are to stay out of poverty. These are the dimensions of the moral order that we seek to measure.

What is necessary here is a review of the costs and benefits to society as a whole of the rapid movements in family structure which are daily taking place. We cannot, for example, be content with the recently fashionable view that children simply bounce back from divorce, and that new relationships simply add to a child's sum of reliable parents, grandparents, and siblings.

As socialists we are particularly concerned with the fact that such a high proportion of children are being brought up in poverty, and without absorbing the norms of responsibility and purposeful devotion to the creation or reformation of the next generation which, in the past, we have taken for granted. We note, for example, that in 1992 lone parents had an average gross income of £159 per week, less than half of the average for the country as a whole (£342.93 per week). The evidence from the Child Poverty Action Group (CPAG) is that children are increasingly slipping into poverty compared with adults. A new form of the lunatic nineteenth-century system, in which children were disproportionately born to the poor, has been recreated, even though the fertility rates of the better-off moved in the direction of sanity after the Second War. Moreover, punitive attacks on the allowances paid to lone parents which derive from ideological determination to reduce state spending seem peculiarly unlikely to raise the standards of upbringing vouchsafed to future generations. There is neither social justice nor social efficiency here.

Over the past two decades there have been sustained attempts to define an index of human development. The Human Development Reports 1990, 1991, 1992, and 1993 give details of progress in the movement towards comparable statistics. They refer mainly to industrial countries, though they tell us the numbers for the world as a whole and for categories and regions within it: they also indicate both current performances (1990) and trends (1960–1990) of life expectancy, real GNP per capita, and child welfare in various ways. Obviously they could be improved, and there is good technical discussion of roads to improvement in the 1993 volume. We could use them to indicate progress in terms of the major values sought by democratic socialists as follows:

1. Freedom or extent of individual choice.
2. Equality of access to essential capabilities.
3. Social solidarity or belonging to the country in question.

Point (1) can be measured by longevity and income, (2) by income distribution and (3) by the incidence of suicide, drug abuse, family break-up, and so forth. No doubt we could do better. But we can catch a glimpse of trends in the United Kingdom from these tables. The United Kingdom is placed tenth in the world's nations according to the HDI index. Between 1960 and 1990 the expectation of life at birth rose in the United Kingdom from 70.6 per cent to 75.7 per cent, whereas Japan began lower and ended higher at 78.6 per cent. In the industrial world as a whole, life expectation was 74.5 per cent, and in the world as a whole 64.7 per cent. The British real GDP per capita also rose, and was above average in both the European Community and among OECD countries. Britain's total health expenditure constituted 6.1 per cent of GDP by 1990, compared with 12.2 per cent in the United States, 8.6 per cent in Sweden and the Netherlands, 9.1 per cent among OECD countries, and 7.7 per cent in the European Community.

Looking at signs of weakening social fabric, it may be noted that Britain is high with respect to live births outside marriage. It had 25 per cent between 1985 and 1989, compared with 15 per cent in the European Community: and there were 41 per cent divorces compared with 27 per cent in the European Community. On the other hand, Britain records less murder and suicide by comparison with its European neighbours. Other indications of human distress suggest that the UK is not wildly different from Europe with respect to unemployment and inequality of income distribution: but the Nordic countries do better from both points of view.

While clarification of the measurement problems is incomplete, few can doubt that the family is in trouble. Parliament and people are now casting around for solutions to what is seen as a problem of endemic disorder— rising crime, intrusive squalor, spreading welfare dependency, collapsed community. Can we then conclude that what essentially has happened is that the past generation has failed to bring up its children to observe traditional civilities, and that the cure is political—to strengthen traditional families. It is important to get this right, i.e. to identify the causes, correlates, and consequences of changes in family structure (or more accurately, if pedantically, the circumstances of upbringing and the adolescent and adult behaviour that issues from them). If we get it wrong we can then only prescribe good and effective policy by accident.

The editor of The Sunday Times (28 February 1993) got it partly right and partly wrong. He was right to argue that 'the time has come to put the nuclear family at the centre of social policy. It needs to be preserved and nurtured'. He was, however, wrong to link the analysis to American theories of a burgeoning urban underclass. The mistake of taking seriously pronouncements from the American publicist Charles Murray presumably stems from a Sunday Times decision, 3 years before, to sponsor Murray's transportation of a version of underclass theory across the Atlantic. In fact it is wrong on both sides of that ocean. Professor William Julius Wilson has demolished it by careful empirical study in Chicago. David Smith has concluded from a sober review of the British evidence that 'it has not yet been shown that the underclass is a coherent explanatory idea in Britain' (Understanding the Underclass, PSI, 1992).

Unhappily, explanations of disorder and therefore remedial policies are bewilderingly complex. And to make matters worse, there are those, like Charles Murray or Roger Scruton, who insist that the fundamental causes are 'spiritual', beyond the reach of politics. First we need adequate description of the family in history. Thus we should face the fact that the crisis of control is not at all new. For example, as Peter Laslett has shown, nearly two-thirds of pregnancies in the early nineteenth century were outside wedlock, and public complaint about the neglect of old people by their families echoes down the centuries. Nor can anyone who reads Victorian or Edwardian accounts of London life, such as Arthur Morison's Child of the Jago, be in any doubt that the handing on of a moral tradition from parents to children has always been under threat. Contemporary social scientists are badly hampered by poor descriptive data: and that in itself is a scandal. If politicians want sound advice they must see to it that the funds for data collection and analysis are available, so that debate in a democracy is properly informed, whether conducted in the House of Commons, on television screens, or in the columns of newspapers. (How many people know, for example, that the whole of Western Europe is in incipient population decline in a world of exploding population numbers?)

The decline of the traditional family cannot be denied. Divorce, cohabitation, single-parenting, and births outside marriage have all risen sharply and recently. Moreover, the connection, on average, between the chances in life of children brought up by two committed parents and those of single or cohabiting parents is established even if not sufficiently detailed. Tricky problems of measurement impede social science here. How do you assess the stability or conviviality of a child's family environment, the degree of conflict between spouses, the significance of marriage as against birth registration by cohabitees at the same address? Readers may properly want to leave these tedious technicalities to the researchers. But the scope for sloppy substitution of prejudice for precision is all too large in matters of such high passion.

Nevertheless policy progress is possible, *pace* Roger Scruton and despite the accumulated anger of feminists, who rightly seek equality for women with men and are especially aware of the male tyranny so often embodied in the traditional working-class family: 'women's work', the double standard, no further education if she is 'only a girl', and so on. We find it ironic to remember that a working-class district in our own childhood had no locked doors. Mums were reliable police-officers. Parliament can do something towards realizing a better society. It can legislate a renewal of Eleanor Rathbone's family allowances and can, given the political will, link taxation to benefits so as to avoid poverty traps, the demeaning selectivity of means-tested allowances, and the present tilting of the fiscal system away from the family towards individual adults.

It can create what Beveridge assumed—a full-employment economy—which would strike mightily against the waste, hopelessness, and invitation to crime of enforced idleness for millions. (A fifth of our young people under 25 are out of work). The definition of full employment is, of course, much more complex now than it was 50 years ago when Beveridge wrote. In future it has to be a nice balance of home- with work-responsibilities, fully accepting part-time jobs, maternal periodicity, childcare provision, and fair-pension entitlements. Not least, there must be a realistic recognition that schools and other public services for health, education, and welfare must be drawn in to support the family, to make womens' occupational and domestic careers equal with men, to recruit 'third-age' people into the schooling of children every day up to 6 p.m. and throughout the year. There should be no latch-key children, and no schoolteachers who feel that their services to childrearing are underpaid or unappreciated.

There must be systematic education in the arts of committed parenting. Politics can take us some of the way.

Let us put causes and cures more abstractly. We need a renewed civic culture. The three great *dramatis personae* of Western politics in the modern age have been liberty, equality, and community: and all three have to be put in balance. In our own time liberty has had much the best of it (through economic growth and contraception). Equality has had limited gains through democracy and some diminution of status distinctions: but grotesque income inequalities remain—twenty, thirty, forty times at the top compared with the bottom. And community has worsened—roughly in inverse proportion to the sale of burglar alarms. We can and must turn this round if our children are to enjoy and to be part of a civilization.

The Voice of the Child

The National Children's Bureau thinks of itself as 'the powerful voice of the child'; it has been a characteristic institutional response to 'the century of the child'. It has also been a witness to the decline of the traditional family.

The thirty years of NCB's existence is a misleadingly short period for our purpose—scarcely more than a single generation. But as a social force, childhood is subjectively stretched in that it is carried as an evolving and more or less shared notion in the minds of children, parents, and grandparents. (Wadsworth 1991). Thus there were even a few people in Britain in 1960 who had had experience of the 1860s. They had been alive at a time before the State made its first serious incursion into the education of children, when married women were still legally the chattels of their husbands, when puberty was for the vast majority the end of formal schooling and the beginning of laborious life, when men worked and women waited, when a child's corpse was a domestic commonplace, Freud was unknown, health visitors and the germ theory unrecognized, and when fertility was both high and inversely correlated with family income.

Thus the corresponding and conflicting definitions of childhood coexist and contend in a period of rapid change: and the NCB can be aptly described as a public broker of the clash of ideas concerning upbringing between government and the governed, the churches and the laity, professionals and amateurs, parents and children, the classes, the genders, and most recently the ethnic groups. A conception of the changing scene in these terms must accordingly be one of great complexity. All we can offer here is a selective simplification.

In a summary of social trends Halsey (1988) described Britain as having emerged from the Second World War as a classical industrial economy, a centralized democratic polity, and a familistic social structure. The long historical roots of the country had been in a social order with minimal government, and with wealth and welfare principally determined by the relation between the family and the market for labour. In prototypic industrialism, as in the preceding agrarianism, the institutional division of labour consisted essentially of a triangle joining the family, the workplace, and the state. Families raised children; men worked in separate workplaces; women ran households. The economy produced; the family reproduced; and the state protected.

The NCB was an agent of transformation. A consensus was built during the war, expressed by Beveridge, Keynes, and Butler, that a prosperous and civilized future required a positive welfare state. It meant systematic 'interference' by government and its agents in the traditional exchanges between the family and the economy. That was the context defining the role of the NCB as the voice of the child. The rise of the welfare state entailed an elaboration of tax collection, to be used as redistributive resources for the education and health of children, the relief of men temporarily out of work, the maintenance of mothers without men to connect them to the economy, the sustenance of the old, and the protection of the health and safety of the population as a whole.

In the following generation, legislation and social practice ushered in a more elaborate division of labour between the members of the institutional triangle of traditional life. The family, it was recognized, produces as well as consumes. People live as well as work in factories, and work as well as live in houses. The family has fewer children, with an increasing minority conceived and born in cohabitation. The nuclear family re-forms on separation

and divorce as well as on death and departure. Women no longer merely wait, but have entered the formal economy, while men have been drawn into domesticity. Adults as well as children learn. The state provides parent substitutes as teachers, nurses, housing officers, and others in an unprecedented expansion of social services, supporting and even replacing the family. Altogether, in the past 30 years, there has been a renegotiation of the division of labour which has transformed the meaning and nature of childhood.

By no means all these changes were the expected outcome of deliberate political planning. In one sense the NCB emerged to take on the role of a monitoring agency for the unanticipated consequences of deliberate legal and administrative innovation. At all events the social statistics (meaning, historically, facts about the state) began to show intended trends such as the increase of women, especially married women, in employment and declining birthrates; but also the unintended increase in illegitimate births (now recorded as lone-parent births), cohabitation, divorces, remarriage, and single-person households. Between the end of the Second World War and 1990, the proportion of economically active women rose from just over a third to 52.8 per cent: and the proportion of economically inactive married women, which was 51 per cent in 1971, decreased sharply to 29 per cent in 1990, when the total female workforce was 12 million. Meanwhile between 1961 and 1989 the incidence of divorce rose from 2.1 to 12.7 per thousand married people. In 1972 16 per cent of women who were married had previously cohabited with their future husband, and this proportion climbed steeply to reach roughly half by 1987. Most women now have children, though families continue to get smaller. Rather less than a fifth of women born at the end of the 1950s are expected to remain childless. And, most significant, the percentage of births outside marriage, which was 4 or 5 per cent for the first half of the century, has risen from 5 per cent in 1960 to 11 per cent in 1979 and to 32 per cent in 1994.

The record also shows more men and women in adult education, as well as more children in extended schooling, and a rising level of qualification in the population at large. By 1990 72 per cent of men and 65 per cent of women of working age held a qualification.

Just as there had been a traditional inverse relation between family size and prosperity, so now there was an inverse correlation of educational qualification and age.

Meanwhile, and unplanned, there emerged a socially depressed tail (a so-called 'underclass') of children in poverty and with poorer educational and life chances, as the benefits of traditional two-parent families were withdrawn and were inadequately substituted by public services even in a burgeoning welfare state.

The Changing Family

We live now in a new demographic age, centred on Western Europe and those parts of the world which were once British colonial possessions. This new reproductive order has momentous potential implications for the twenty-first-century world as a whole. There are revolutionary comings in and goings out concerning ideas of birth, marriage, divorce, child-rearing, age, gender, and death which constitute the foundations of a new demographic era.

In essence the new regime is a balance of low fertility and low mortality. In other words, it is an historically unprecedented combination of fluctuating and small reproduction with steadily advancing longevity. An ageing population, along with proportionate reduction in the place of children, is a necessary demographic consequence. But economic affluence and increased geographical mobility add hitherto largely unrecognized implications and possibilities. The further social contingency of the decline of the traditional family as a reproductive unit (which some contend is cause rather than consequence) must also be included as a defining characteristic of the new regime. Finally, the new order is one of incipient population decline, if the now well-established trends of natural reproduction are not counteracted by reversal of traditional patterns of international mobility. There are, of course, already signs of such a reversal in the absorption of growing ethnic minorities in the metropolitan economies of Western Europe. Meanwhile low fertility, population ageing, and family frailty together bequeath a changing structure of production, reproduction, and distribution between age groups, ethnic groups, and the genders.

What, then, is new about the new order? It can be dismissed as a dramatized version of the industrial population-cycle as described by sociologists since Malthus. Agrarian societies had sparse populations balanced by high fertility and high mortality, yielding relatively young populations in which upbringing took place in strong families, small communities, and with well-defined skills, combined with relatively restricted information and social connections. Britain and early European industrialism led the way out of agrarianism. Reduced mortality and population explosion, with its menace to the rest of the world, followed in the late nineteenth and early twentieth centuries by accelerated reduction in fertility, leading after the Second World War to the new, low birth-death balance. None of that is particularly novel, but the associated features of unprecedented economic prosperity and the renegotiation of the division of labour between men and women portended a new society, smaller in numbers, older in years, and offering new egalitarian freedoms to women as well as a new political class of the 'Third Age'.

The fate of the family as the social unit of childrearing is thus brought into question. A first conventional indicator is marital breakdown. Divorce has risen rapidly over the past 30 years. When calculations are made as to the future proportions of marriages that will end in divorce, it turns out that four out of ten will collapse, even though one in every two couples will celebrate their silver and one in seven their golden wedding; the future of grandparenthood is buoyant.

A second indicator is that of births outside marriage. As we have noted, by 1994 the percentage had risen to 32. In Sweden the figure is 50 per cent, compared with 10 in Italy. Births outside marriage in Britain have trebled in a decade while births within marriage have actually fallen. Three-quarters of births to teenage mothers are outside marriage, which is roughly double the proportion of a decade ago. On the other hand, no single statistic can be taken as a sure index of the stability of childrearing circumstances. Thus, for example, the 'illegitimate' birth rate (now 'outside marriage') of earlier years took no account of the stability of the relationship between the parents. The recent records of birth registration suggest that at least half of the children born outside marriage have parents living together in a stable relation.

A third indicator of family instability is the record of one-parent families. The number of such families has grown from around 600,000 to over a million since the early 1970s, and the children number over one and a half million, i.e. about one in eight children now live in such families; and such reproductive circumstances are typically (though not exclusively) concentrated in the lower echelons of class and income, with higher rates of unemployment and poorer housing conditions. All in all, the evidence is of mounting multiple instability of marriage and increasingly tenuous support for mothers and children outside wedlock. To be sure, it is a situation of great complexity and heated dispute. There are pessimistic traditionalists who believe that the family is collapsing, with consequent chaos, crime, and crisis of civilization. There are also optimistic modernists who see a new dawn for opportunity and equality for women, the end of the stigma of illegitimate birth, and the demise of male tyranny.

Justice for Children and the Collectivist Ethic

Could it be that the gains for adults are at the expense of the interests of children? That is the central question of justice with which we are here concerned. From a democratic-socialist point of view it could end in disaster. Modern society has strange superstitions: and perhaps the central one is the belief that if ego maximizes his or her choices we are all better off (Dennis and Erdos 1992). Put more portentously, it is the fallacy that individual freedom is collective good. The family is the age-old disproof of this contemporary nonsense. The traditional family is the tested arrangement for safeguarding the welfare of children, and only a post-Christian country could believe otherwise. The individualist doctrine is a hallucination with two main sources. First is the spectacular advance of human power over nature, which has relieved so many of us so much from the life of toil that our grandparents had to take for granted. They invented the workplace, the career, the substitutes for human muscle and sweat; and we, with our microchips and washing machines, have both inherited and refined these escapes from the 'curse of Adam'. We call it the economy, or the productive system, and we employ economic statisticians and Treasury politicians to celebrate its continual growth. We use a language of productivity, employment, capital, and education which encourages us to imagine that the family has nothing to do with national prosperity.

Then, second, there is the developing assumption, so rampant in the 1980s, that the adult ego is self-sufficient. Children thereby become commodities—quality objects to be sure, but none the less things, just like cars or videos or holidays, which adults can choose to have in preference to other consumables. And if they do, that is their choice and their responsibility. Contraceptive control of our bodies enhances the illusion. So who needs a family or a community or, for that matter, a government other than to prevent ruin of the market for these good things by thieves and frauds? Surely technology has conquered nature and we can safely allow individuals to choose a consuming style, limited only by their willingness to work for money. Everybody is then free to buy the good life of their own definition. Marriage becomes a mere contract. The quality of life is measurable by calculation through methodological individualism rather than contained in organic conceptions of 'man' and 'nature'.

Our ancestors were poorer but wiser. They understood the notion of political economy. They knew what the modern fantasy forgets, that we are all dependent on one another. Atomized individuals calculate only for themselves and only for their own lives. Yet their very existence depends on calculation across generations. Few women and fewer men would rationally choose to have children in a world of exclusively short-term egotistical calculation: the costs and foregone satisfactions are too high. Hence rich countries which carry the modern ethos have declining or incipiently declining populations (for a stable population there must be a total period fertility rate of 2.1 children per woman; Britain has 1.8, West Germany 1.6, Italy and Spain 1.4 or even 1.2.) The individualized as distinct from socialized country eventually and literally destroys itself.

Nor is this the whole of the modern mirage. In reality the family is part of, not separate from, the economy. Parents are the main producers of tomorrow's wealth, and we all consume what they produce. That is why we need a just political economy to ensure that the beneficiaries pay their dues. Behind the fiscal and monetary façade, old-age pensions are dependent on the future work of today's children. Yet, paradoxically, our political economy, far from paying parents, actually punishes them for their folly in producing the producers of the future: our system of taxation and social security is systematically biased against the family in favour of the childless adult, and increasingly so since the 1960s.

How can all this be turned round? The first step is to get the facts right. We appreciate that 'facts' always appear in the context of assumptions about what is good or bad for human beings. We deal today with heated value discord in these matters. We share with our colleague Norman Dennis the value-position of the ethical socialist as set out in our *English Ethical Socialism*. Central to that position is the doctrine of personal responsibility under virtually all social circumstances. People act under favourable and unfavourable conditions, but remain responsible moral agents. History heavily conditions them and their own actions eventually become history, and therefore determine the future balance of favour and disfavour in the ceaseless effort to become good people in a good society. The whole question of the quality of life remains forever open. There are no ineluctable laws of history, only a continual reloading of the dice by millions of individual decisions. It follows that reproductive decisions are crucial to human destiny. Whatever the character of society or state, polity or economy, religion or culture, parents cannot escape responsibility for the quality of their children as citizens.

In the light of this political morality we see incontrovertible evidence of a weakening of the norms of the traditional family since the 1960s. It is not that we see a golden age of traditionalism. Material deprivation and inequality between the classes and the sexes were integral to British society in the first half of the century. There was no utopia. There was cruelty, a double standard of sexual morality, incest and child abuse, savage treatment of unmarried mothers, desertions, and separations. Nevertheless, the traditional family system was a coherent strategy for the ordering of relations in such a way as to

equip children for their own eventual adult responsibilities.

The much-needed reform of the system required comprehensive strengthening of supporting health, education, and security services if quality children were to be produced, women were to have freedom to combine motherhood with career, and men were to be encouraged to take a fuller part in the domestic rearing of their offspring. The Labour Party can be proud of its efforts to build up these elements of a modern welfare state. But the evidence of more recent change is that the supporting services have deteriorated, while the increment of economic growth has been transferred disproportionately to the individual pocket horizontally and to the rich vertically through the running down of family allowances, the raising of regressive national insurance contributions, the abandoning of joint taxation for spouses, the failure to fund adequate community care, and so on. In the 1980s the economic individual was exalted and the social community desecrated. Mrs Thatcher may well be seen by dispassionate future historians as a major architect of the demolition of the traditional family.

She was, to be sure, vigorously aided by other social and personal forces. Divorce, separation, birth outside marriage, and one-parent families as well as cohabitation and extramarital sexual intercourse have increased rapidly. Many applaud these freedoms. But what should be universally acknowledged is that the children of parents who do not follow the traditional norm (i.e. taking on personal, active, and long-term responsibility for the social upbringing of the children they generate) are thereby disadvantaged by their parents in many major aspects of their chances of living a successful life. Such children tend to die earlier, to have more illness, to do less well at school, to exist at a lower level of nutrition, comfort, and conviviality, to suffer more unemployment, be more prone to deviance and crime, and finally to repeat the cycle of unstable parenting from which they themselves have suffered (Elliot and Richards 1991; Bradshaw and Millar 1991; Kiernan 1992).

There has been a build-up of evidence about the effects of family disruption. Some of the best of it comes from the longitudinal studies which have followed the samples of children both in 1946 (the Douglas study), and later on, the 17,000 children born in 1958 (the National Child Development Study). The children in both studies have now grown up and are themselves having children, so that some of the long-term effects of disruption in one generation can be assessed. When the 1946 sample was looked at from this angle, the children who experienced their parents' divorce before they reached 15 had lower levels of attainment at school as well as more emotional disturbance and more delinquency, and were themselves more prone to divorce or separation, than those whose parents had remained married.

The 1958 sample has been examined in the same way and the outcome is, if anything, more dire. The people whose parents' marriages broke down are more likely to finish school at the minimum age and to leave home before they are 18; are much more likely to suffer from psychological problems; and the men are much more likely to be regular smokers. For children with a divorced parent and a stepfather or stepmother the differences from families with two natural parents are even more striking. Girls in step families run twice the risk of being fruitful and multiplying outside marriage while teenagers, and we know from other evidence that they run more risk of sexual abuse too, not infrequently from stepfathers. Girls and boys in stepfamilies are twice as likely to leave school at age 16.

It seems that children in families broken by divorce or separation suffer, in a sense, a fate worse than death. The death of a father or mother makes hardly any difference compared to the effect of losing a parent in another way. We are not, of course, saying that divorce and separation are the sole causes. They are also symptoms. Couples who stay together but only 'for the sake of the children' can provide just as harmful an early environment.

The evidence is formidable as well as tallying with commonsense (Burghes 1993). But we must be clear what the thesis does not say. The comparison is of averages. It is not maintained that traditionally reared children will all be healthy, intelligent, and good; nor that children from parentally deprived homes will all turn out to be sickly, stupid, and criminal. Like all social science, the relevant studies deal with multiple causes of multiple effects and give us estimates of statistical association for particular groups at particular moments in history. Nevertheless, it must be insisted that no contrary evidence is available to contradict the average differences postulated by the stated thesis. Accordingly, the conclusion must be drawn that committed and stable parenting must be a priority of social policy. If that view is accepted, it is no comfort either to the Right or the Left. Committed parenting cannot be the outcome of the market policies of economic liberals, nor of what Norman Dennis has dubbed the 'egotistic socialism' of irresponsible fathers. The challenge to social policy is to avoid both of these evils.

One clue is that there is a vast global correlate to this national trend. While the human species as a whole continues on its accelerating path towards astronomical numbers, the trends in the richer (that is, industrial) countries are in the opposite direction. Countries like Britain, America, and Japan are in the early stages of population decline (which means also an ageing of their people). There are 2 million less West Germans than there were 20 years ago. In southern, Catholic Europe, birth rates have plummeted. Even in Ireland, the classic case of the Malthusian law that reproduction expands to the limits of the food supply, births have now fallen below the threshold of 2.1 per woman which would ensure a stable population size. The British figure, as we have noted, is 1.8. So there is a pattern of hugely different contribution to the human population of the twenty-first century such that the industrialized West, including Japan and Taiwan, begin to subtract from future numbers while the developing (that is, poor) countries of Asia, Africa, and Latin America add to them.

What, then, is the explanation? Conventional wisdom offers two theories. One is economic—low fertility arises from economic growth. Rich countries can afford greater freedoms, including the freedom of sexual equality which permits women not to have children and to enter increasingly into the non-domestic world of men. The other theory is cultural (and indeed racist). Western cultures are nicer to women because they are more individualistic. They favour romantic love and women's careers, not arranged marriages, suttee, proscription of birth control, and so on. Either way, the consequence is that in the past the poor have reproduced themselves more than the rich, and that modernization liberates women to become more like men.

Neither theory works completely. Obviously Japan and Taiwan are oriental, not Western; and there are some poor countries, in the Indian sub-continent and in sub-Saharan Africa, where women are relatively more equal with men.

The 'cultural' theory is the weaker of the two. It is appreciation of the role of individualism that can rescue it and combine the two theories into more powerful explanation. Individualism is an ethic at the heart of human development. Individuals invent, produce, and choose. Individualism explains our leap forward in production and in control over nature and, finally, our entry into the modern demographic regime of low fertility. Ever since the Renaissance and the Reformation of the sixteenth century it has become increasingly clear that Christianity is the premier carrier of individualism, the cradle of freedom, the bearer of representative democracy, and the potential agent of escape from feudal and kingship tyranny in traditional peasant society. Western Christendom from Galileo onwards has fostered aggressive measurement, deserted fatalism, broken the bonds of superstition and helplessness, invented the steam engine, the telescope, and double-entry book-keeping. In short, individualism promised to bring heaven to earth.

So what is wrong with all that? The first answer is that free egotistical calculation apparently ensures the eventual disappearance of the species, for rational adults avoid parenthood. The second is that individualistic policy, despite its many benefits to industry and commerce, also spreads by its own logic into the family. Marriage becomes not a sacred long-run compact but merely a contract, to be broken at the will of either party; and children become consumables. If people choose to 'buy' them that is their right and their responsibility. Caveat Emptor. If only one parent is left (usually the mother) it is largely up to her to look after the interest of the child. Some libertarians deem this a reasonable price for freedom. Many turn their faces away from the evidence that *on average* the children of broken or one-parent families have impoverished life-chances—literally, impoverished chances of survival, of health, of educational attainment, of conviviality, of jobs, of avoidance of marital breakdown in their own lives, and so on.

The point about Mrs Thatcher in this context, as Norman Dennis insists, is that she tacitly assumed that the individualistic ethic, untrammelled, could not enter the family; but in fact it did, and was vigorously encouraged by 'egotistic socialists' as well as libertarian individualists. Meanwhile, and predating Thatcher, the state moved systematically to undermine support for the traditional family by the shifts in financial, fiscal, and social-services policies to which we have alluded. So, increasingly, we see a closer association of parenting with poverty and, most ominously, a new generation of males with little experience of or interest in responsible fatherhood. The organic solidarity between generations has been largely broken by reforms inspired by economic liberalism.

It could all be turned round by determined action. But not by mindless reaction. The old respectable working-class family system worked, but at high cost (the double standard of morality, the harsh treatment of 'fallen women' and 'bastards', the kitchen containment of mothers, the taboo on male participation in 'women's work'). Clearly those traditional conflicts and confinements are neither desirable nor any longer possible. Nevertheless, there are positive policy possibilities open to a richer country through serious reform of the schools, of working arrangements (Hewitt 1993), through 'third-age' grandparents, and properly provided family-friendly social services—a whole new programme of reform which dethrones the market mania of present government and turns instead to a wiser civilization.

Childhood is at a crucial moment in the history of post-industrial society. In Britain and all across Western Europe there are dramatic demographic developments, threatening both quantity and quality in the rising generation. Much of the rest of the world remains Malthusian, i.e. with rising populations based on high fertility and death-delaying technology. But Britain belongs to the sixteen or seventeen countries (including Western Europe, the 'Anglo-Saxon empire' and Japan) which have been labelled 'Third Age societies' (Laslett 1989). Their foremost characteristic is the rise of a new social and political class of people who are free from the obligations of paid employment and are possessed of sufficient health and wealth to dominate social policy, at least in political democracies. A democratized leisure class is historically unprecedented. The retired constitute a fifth of the British whole. A primary-school child can normally expect to join the third age, to live longer as a grandparent than as a parent or a child.

Children and the Welfare State

We are not for a moment suggesting that what remains of the welfare state should be scrapped and an entirely new start made, but that a large new strand of policy should be added to what is already there, beyond what was done by the last Children Act, which placed so many new duties on social-service departments, or anything else that has been done so far for the sake of children. The Beveridge scheme was, in the words of its originator, 'an attack upon Want'—Want being regarded as one of the five giants on the road to reconstruction, the others being Disease, Ignorance, Squalor, and Idleness. It was assumed that family allowances would be inaugurated, but otherwise there was barely any mention of the family, for the obvious reason that the durability of the institution was then taken for granted. The great problem of children in distress had not yet emerged on its present scale (or re-emerged: it was certainly evident in the nineteenth century); and certainly not shown up as what has become the biggest problem of all for social policy. To use Beveridge's term, it is the most towering giant of all. It is also a good deal more difficult to attack than perhaps any of the others; but that is no reason for inaction.

What, then, is to be done? In addition to continuing and adding to what is already established in the interests of children, there are two further vital steps which should be taken: extending child benefit, and reforming schools all over Britain.

On the first, Eleanor Rathbone, the pioneering campaigner for a family allowance, said in 1940, 'Children are not simply a private luxury; they are an asset to the community, and the community can no longer afford to leave the provision of this welfare solely to the accident of individual income.' Rathbone was making a case for a mother's wage which is even stronger today than it was then. The increasing fragility of the family and, consequently, of family income, puts even more

value on a reliable benefit which is tied unconditionally to the child. On these grounds, child benefit should be maintained and increased for all children.

We advocate the immediate introduction of a mother's wage (which signals a choice to be made for domestic employment rather than employment outside the home). In his forward to the CPAG's *The Cost of a Child: Living Standards for the 1990s*, Professor J. Bradshaw is unequivocal:

Between 1979 and 1991 average living standards increased by over 30 per cent . However, inequalities widened dramatically, families with children drifted down the income scale, and many more families found themselves dependants on income support and relatively worse off. This need not have happened. It was the result of this government's tax, benefit, and employment policies. If we are to begin to improve the living standards of children and avoid separating the very large number of them on income support from the normal patterns of life in Britain, then the child scale rates of income support must be increased now.

The findings of the CPAG show that income support does not allow families with children to reach even the low-cost standard of living (descending from Rowntree) used in the study. Income support, including the family premium, meets only 78 per cent of the low-cost budget for a child in a two-adult, two-child family; income support child allowances meets only 59 per cent, and child benefit only 35 per cent. Such a family would require a supplement of £5.74 per week, in addition to income-support child-rate plus family premium, to achieve the low-cost child standard.

But we do not think it follows that child benefit should be increased to the same extent for all children. The benefit could be used quite deliberately to support and encourage mothers (and sometimes fathers) to stay at home to look after their children, especially when the children are in their most formative years, that is, under 5. So we suggest a higher rate of child benefit for such children. In doing this we are, of course, taking sides, and intending to, in the debate on whether the needs of industry for women employees or the needs of their children should come first. Indeed, we can hardly see why there is a debate—it is so clear to us that, as far as public policy goes, the needs of children should come first. We are not saying that mothers should not go out to work if that is what they want to do; we are saying that the financial pressures on them to do so should not be as great as they are at present. The pressures are at their most harsh for lone parents. Nearly three-quarters of children in lone-parent families are living on the margins of poverty, compared with under a quarter of children in two-parent families. A higher rate of child benefit for the under-fives would target the benefit to where it is most needed without being subject to means-testing, with all the objections there are to that.

Single mothers, or indeed any mothers, should not have to work when their children are so young. After the age of 5 the choice about whether or not to work is less stark, since children are at school for part of the day. So the proposition is that there should be a two-tier system of child benefit, with the benefit being increased for every child, but increased a good deal more—say, doubled—for children under 5. Child benefit for the under-fives would then be, at present prices, about £15 per week, or £45 for three children under 5, instead of the level of £7.25 per child and £8.25 for an eldest child that it is at present. Also, mothers who had to go out to work even so would thereby get something extra with which they could pay, if they had to pay, those who were caring for their children.

Some mothers with children under 5 will have no choice but to do paid work, and they will need much more back-up than they have had from child-care services across the board, from day nurseries, childminders, playgroups, nursery schools and classes, in primary schools with provision for 'rising fives', and in the new and very promising family centres which have been pioneered by Barnardo's, the Children's Society, the NSPCC and other voluntary bodies. Such services are needed whether or not mothers are out at work; mothers need a break from their children even if they are not in paid jobs.

The primary school has to be seen against the background of these two demographic developments. The quality of childhood in the family is highly varied because, although the twentieth century is the single 'century of the child', it is still more the century of the individual, which also means a flight from parenthood. There is little prospect of reversing the natural and indeed the laudable aspiration of modern women to find ways of combining maternal domesticity with an independent career outside the home. In a serious sense

that is what the primary school was invented to provide. But all the research points to a melancholy outcome. The average two-parent child does better in health, personality, and educational attainment than the one-parent child.

The question therefore arises as to whether the Third Age can be brought in to help the First-Age, or primary-school child. We believe it can. The old concept must go much further. It must continue the old idea, and add to it the notion that, for an increasing minority, the teacher has to take on a much more direct parenting role (Young 1990). Of course, the immediate and justified response of many teachers is that they are already doing what the new world demands, or that the demand is impossible, being incompatible with limited professional time and responsibility. Such a demand is against the whole temper of modern individualistic times: it means extended hours of opening, operating in holidays as well as conventional schooldays, 'interfering' with family relations, and so on.

That is all true. But if the challenge of deterioration in the quality of childhood is to be realistically met, then the new concept must be nationally applied; one vital contribution to the solution can surely be sought from the new class of Third-Age people—the grandparents.

Third-Age people are, to be sure, often busy, if only with looking after their Fourth-Age elders. Yet they are a vast reservoir of potential social service, some of which can and must be recruited for the primary life as an auxiliary labour force for after-school supervision, clubs, and activities. Many schools have pioneered the necessary extended partnership; but these experiments must now become an integral part of the new system. It means a new professional leadership role for the primary teacher, new training arrangements for them and their Third-Age assistants, new attitudes to the whole life-experience of children, the end of the scandal of the 'latch-key' child. And, if it works, the status of the teacher will be enhanced, the stress on families, especially employed mothers, and most especially single mothers, will be reduced: and the quality of childhood will be restored to the high priority it requires if future civilization is to be safeguarded.

The problems of parents do not end when their children enter school; and these are partly the problems of time and timing caused by the practice of schools in closing down in mid-afternoon and for holidays which last weeks or months, not to speak of half-term holidays, which don't necessarily coincide if siblings are at different schools. The practices are a strange Victorian hangover from the period when state schools were influenced so much by the public schools which had long holidays and played games in the afternoons. The closure-times made some sense in state schools when most mothers were housewives instead of house-and-work-wives, so that they were at home anyway in the afternoons when their children got out of school and likewise in school holidays. Their children did not have to be latch-key children because the mothers could open the door. But all that has changed, and is continuing to change, as more and more mothers go out to work; and in the new conditions it no longer makes sense for schools to close their gates when increasing numbers of their pupils have nowhere to go except to an empty house.

The next step in education is to lay a duty upon Local Education Authorities and on schools to make provision for their pupils up to 6 o'clock on weekday evenings and during holidays, usually (but not necessarily) on their own premises. This would be done in the interests of parents as well as children. Schools would be open for any pupils who wanted to stay on in the afternoon to do their homework or, better, to play games and do other things—drawing, painting, photography, model-making, drama, dancing, pop music, computing—which there is not enough time for in school hours.

Clubs of this sort could make school seem attractive to children who are at present phobic about them. But for any such extension of the pastoral and, in a broad sense, educational functions of the school, new staff will be needed, auxiliaries on a large scale to supplement the ordinary teaching staff, organized in a new Educational Auxiliary Service.

Where are the new auxiliaries to come from? The conjunction of two similar figures—there are some 12 million children under the age of 16 living in Great Britain today, and some 10 million people over pensionable age—suggests a more plausible answer. Many retired people are as fit as ever

they were, possessing valuable skills and with many years of healthy life ahead of them. They have the indispensable asset of not being as busy as their adult children. In all societies grandparents, with their experience of having brought up children, have had a role as reserve parents, able to step in as replacements if the parents die or are absent. We do know that in Britain grandparents are often close at hand. A recent survey showed that in a national sample of adults in Britain, of those who had mothers alive, 53 per cent had one living within 5 miles, and of those who had grandmothers alive, 47 per cent had one living within the same 5-mile radius (Henley Centre for Forecasting, *Tabulations from Planning for Social Change*, London, 1990). Although there has not been any recent research on what grandparents—grandfathers as well as grandmothers—do for their grandchildren, it is clear that they do a great deal.

The Educational Auxiliary Service would provide more opportunity for children by giving a new opportunity for older people. After a short practical training, they would be paid an allowance for the work they did as auxiliaries in the classroom and to man and woman the after-school clubs and holiday clubs which are needed on a great scale for latch-key children and, indeed, for all children whom the cars have driven off the streets. Older people could not, of course, do the job all on their own, even for children of primary age. Some younger staff will also be needed. Older auxiliaries should not work only in the extended hours: they can also be very helpful in ordinary school-time as well. In Oxfordshire, older people already help in some schools with oral-history projects, by listening to children reading, taking children on trips, taking groups for football practice, teaching embroidery, painting, and cooking, reading stories, telling stories, reciting poetry; there is scope for a great multiplication of this kind of work.

If children can get the attention they need from others quite informally, from relatives or others, that is fine. But many do not have anyone they can turn to. This is where some of the older people in the new auxiliary service could be so helpful; but they should be seen as supplementing what teachers themselves can do. It is often to their teachers that distressed children turn, at any rate when they are of primary age. But teachers can only respond if they themselves are not too harassed and their ordinary classroom duties not as burdensome as they have become in an era when education at all levels has been subjected to such financial pressure. If there were more teachers they would have more time for such pastoral functions.

Quite apart from the extension of hours we are proposing, a new deal for education generally must have a central part in any social policy steered by the needs of children. Something radical needs to be done to reassert the values of collectivism for the sake of the nation's children, whose plight has been worsening in the past 25 years. We hope that such endeavours will again be possible in the 1990s; we even believe that, for the sake of a society of opportunity, there will be a swing back in this decade to forms of collectivism which will demonstrate fellow-feeling once again, even though the action taken will be very different from that taken after the Beveridge Report. But is this only wishful thinking, when our future is more often said to lie with our industry than with our children? Will the old attitude prevail—'why should I do anything for posterity, what has posterity ever done for me?' Taking heart from David Hume, we look forward to a more generous and far-sighted response than that. With so much at stake, we can say that Mr Major's 'open society' will not be achieved until children growing up in the Brixton of today have the same sort of chance as children growing up in Huntingdon. The way things are now, a lot of Britain's children won't be able to get a foot on any ladder unless their home background improves. More widely, we would assert or reassert that the quality of civilization largely turns on the quality of present childhood. Giant strides have been recently made in freeing mankind from 'the curse of Adam' and the grinding necessity of labour before an early death. Yet the sheer rapidity of change sets new challenges to liberate women, children, ethnic minorities, old people, and poor people from traditional tyrannies. It seems that education will be called upon to help solve these age-old problems to an unprecedented degree in the future.

References

Bradshaw, J., and Miller, J. (1991), 'Lone Parent Families in the UK', Department of Social Security Research Report 6 (HMSO).

Brown, J. (1989), 'Why Don't They Go to Work? Mothers on Benefit' (Social Security Advisory Committee).

Burghes, L. (1993) [Review of Research Literature for Family Policy Studies Centre].

Crellin, E., Kellmer Pringle, M. L., and West, P. (1971), 'Born Illegitimate' (a report by the National Children's Bureau, National Foundation for Educational Research in England and Wales).

Dennis, N. (1993), *Rising Crime and the Dismembered Family* (IEA).

—— and Erdos, G. (1992), *Families without Fatherhood* (Choice in Welfare No. 12, IEA Health and Welfare Unit).

—— and Halsey, A. H., *English Ethical Socialism*, (Oxford: 1988).

Elliot, J., and Richards, M. (1991), 'Children and Divorce: Educational Performance and Behaviour Before and After Parental Separation', *International Journal of Law and the Family*, 258–76.

Furstenberg, F. F., and Cherlin, A. J. (1991), *Divided Families: What Happens to Children when Parents Part* (Cambridge, Mass.: Harvard Univ. Press).

Halsey, A. H. (ed.) (1988), *British Social Trends Since 1900* (London: Macmillan).

Hewitt, P. (1993), 'About Time: The Revolution in Work and Family Life' (IPPR/Rivers).

Human Development Report (1993: Oxford University Press).

Kiernan, K. E. (1992), 'The Impact of Family Disruption in Childhood on Transitions Made in Young Adult Life', *Population Studies*, 46.

—— and Estaugh, V. (1993), 'Cohabitation: Extra-Marital Childbearing and Social Policy', Family Policy Studies Centre, Occasional Paper 17.

Kolvin, I., Miller, F. J. W., McI Scott, D., Gatzanis, S. R. M., and Fleeting, M. (1990), 'Continuities of Deprivation? The Newcastle 1000 Study' (ESRC DHSS Studies in Deprivation and Disadvantages: Avebury).

Laslett, P. (1989), *A Fresh Map of Life* (London: Macmillan).

Oldfield, N., and Yu, A. C. S. (1993), *The Cost of a Child: Living Standards for the 1990s* (CPAG).

Schluter, M., and Lee, D. (1992), *The R Factor* (Jubilee Centre, Cambridge).

Wadsworth, M. E. J. (1991), *The Imprint of Time: Childhood, History and Adult Life* (Oxford: Oxford University Press).

Young, M. (1990), *The Future of the Family* (Economic and Social Research Council).

—— and Halsey, A. H. (1995), *Family and Community Socialism* (IPPR).

Further Reading

Education, Culture, and Society

Acker, S. (1994), *Gendered Education* (Milton Keynes: Open University Press).

Apple, M. (1995), *Education and Power* (2nd edn., London: Routledge).

Arnot, M., and Weiner, G. (1989), *Gender and the Politics of Schooling* (Milton Keynes: Open University Press).

Ball, S. (ed.) (1990), *Foucault and Education: Discipline and Knowledge* (London: Routledge).

Bourdieu, P., and Passeron, J. C. (1977), *Reproduction in Education, Society and Culture* (Newbury Park, Ca.: Sage).

Dewey, J. (1916), *Democracy and Education* (New York: Free Press).

Dore, R. P. (1965), *Education in Tokugawa Japan* (Berkeley, Ca.: University of California Press).

Durkheim, E. (1956), *Education and Sociology* (New York: Free Press).

—— (1977), *The Evolution of Educational Thought* (London: Routledge and Kegan Paul).

Karabel, J., and Halsey, A. H. (eds.) (1977), *Power and Ideology in Education* (New York: Oxford University Press).

Peters, M., and Marshall, J. (1996), *Individualism and Community: Education and Social Policy in the Post Modern Condition* (London: Falmer Press).

Shilling, C. (1993), *The Body and Social Theory* (London: Sage).

Stone, L. (ed.) (1994), *The Education Feminism Reader* (New York: Routledge).

Usher, R., and Edwards, R. (1994), *Postmodernism and Education* (London: Routledge).

Weiner, G., and Arnot., M. (1987), *Gender Under Scrutiny: New Enquiries in Education* (Milton Keynes: Open University Press).

Education, the Global Economy, and the Labour Market

Ashton, D., and Green, F. (1996), *Education, Training and the Global Economy* (London: Edward Elgar).

Avis, J., Bloomer, M., Esland, G., Gleeson, D., and Hodkinson, P. (1996), *Knowledge and Nationhood: Education, Politics and Work* (London: Cassell).

Bash, L., and Green, A. (eds.) (1995), *Youth, Education and Work—World Yearbook of Education 1995* (London: Kogan Page).

Bowles, S., and Gintis, H. (1976), *Schooling in Capitalist America* (New York: Basic Books).

Brown, P., and Lauder, H. (eds.) (1992), *Education for Economic Survival: From Fordism to Post-Fordism?* (London: Routledge).

—— , and Scase, R. (1994), *Higher Education and Corporate Realities* (London: UCL Press).

Carnoy, M., and Levin, H. (1985), *Schooling and Work in the Democratic State* (Stanford: Stanford University Press).

Carnoy, M., Cardoso, F. H., Castells, M., and Cohen, S. (1993), *The New Global Economy in the Information Age* (Pennsylvania: Pennsylvania State University Press).

Collins, R. (1977), *The Credential Society: An Historical Sociology of Education and Stratification* (New York: Academic Press).

Drucker, P. (1993), *Post-Capitalist Society* (Oxford: Butterworth-Heinemann).

Gaskell, J. (1992), *Gender Matters: From School to Work* (Milton Keynes: Open University Press).

Green, A. (1997), *Education, Globalisation and the Nation State* (London: Macmillan)

Kenway, J. (ed.) (1994), *Economising Education: The Post Fordist Directions* (Geelong, Aus.: Deakin University).

Marginson, S. (1993), *Education and Public Policy in Australia* (Melbourne: Cambridge University Press).

Reich, R. (1991), *The Work of Nations* (New York: Simon and Schuster).

The State and the Restructuring of Teachers' Work

Archer, M. (1994), *The Social Origins of Educational Systems* (London: Sage).

Ball, S. (1990), *Politics and Policy Making in Education* (London: Routledge).

—— (1994), Education Reform: A Critical and Post Structuralist Approach (Milton Keynes: Open University Press).

Dale, R. (1989), *The State and Education Policy* (Milton Keynes: Open University Press).

Ginsburg, M., and Lindsay, B., (eds.) (1995), *The Political Dimension in Teacher Education: Comparative Perspectives in Policy Formation, Socialisation and Society* (London: Falmer Press).

Green, A. (1990), *Education and State Formation* (London: Macmillan).

Middleton, S. (1993), *Educating Feminists: Life History and Pedagogy* (New York: Teachers College Press).

Popkewitz, T. (1991), *A Political Sociology of Educational Reform: Power/Knowledge in Teaching, Teacher Education and Research* (New York: Teacher College Press).

Sarason, S. (1990), *The Predictable Failure of Educational Reform* (San Francisco: Jossey-Bass).

Politics, Markets, and School Effectiveness

Aronowitz, S., and Giroux, H. A. (1986), *Education Under Siege: The Conservative, Liberal and Radical Debate over Schooling* (London: Routledge and Kegan Paul).

Boyd, W. L., and Cibulka, J. G. (1989), *Private Schools and Public Policy: International Perspectives* (London: Falmer Press).

Chitty, C. (1989), *Towards a New Education System: The Victory of the New Right?* (London: Falmer Press).

Clune, W., and Witte, J. (1990), *Choice and Control in American Education, Vol 1: The Theory of Choice, Vol 2: The Practice of Choice* (London: Falmer Press).

Coleman, J. S., and Hobber, T. (1987), *Public and Private High Schools* (New York: Basic Books).

David, M. (1993), *Parents, Gender and Education Reform* (Cambridge: Polity Press).

Hannaway, J., and Carnoy, M. (1993), *Decentralisation and School Improvement: Can We Fulfil the Promise?* (San Francisco: Jossey-Bass).

Henig, J. (1994), *Rethinking School Choice: The Limits of the Market Metaphor* (Princeton: Princeton University Press).

Jones, K. (1989), *Right Turn: The Conservative Revolution in Education* (London: Hutchinson Radius).

Shor, I. (1986), *Culture Wars: School and Society in the Conservative Restoration 1969–1984* (New York: Methuen).

Whitty, G. (1996), 'Creating quasi-markets in education: a review of recent research on parental choice and school autonomy in three countries', *Review of Research in Education*, 22: 1–83.

Knowledge, Curriculum, and Cultural Politics

Apple, M. (1996), *Cultural Politics and Education* (New York: Teachers' College Press).

Aronowitz, S., and Giroux, H. (1991), *Postmodern Education: Politics, Culture and Social Criticism* (Minneapolis: University of Minnesota Press).

Blair, M., and Holland, J., with Sheldon, S. (eds.) (1995), *Identity and Diversity: Gender and the Experience of Education* (Milton Keynes: Open University Press).

Epstein, D. (ed.) (1994), *Challenging Lesbian and Gay Inequalities in Education* (Milton Keynes: Open University Press).

Giroux, H., and McLaren, P. (eds.) (1994), *Between Borders: Pedagogy and the Politics of Cultural Studies* (New York: Routledge).

Jordan, G., and Weedon, C. (1995), *Cultural Politics: Class, Gender and Race in the Post-Modern World* (Oxford: Blackwell).

Kanapol, B., and McLaren, P. (eds.) (1995), *Critical Multiculturalism* (New York: Bergin Garvey).

McCarthy, C., and Crichlow, W. (eds.) (1993), *Race, Identity and Representation in Education* (New York: Routledge).

Smith, R., and Wexler, P. (1995), *After Postmodernism: Education, Politics and Identity* (London: Falmer Press).

Troyna, B. (1993), *Racism and Education* (Milton Keynes: Open University Press).

Wexler, P. (1987), *Social Analysis of Education: After the New Sociology* (New York: Routledge).

Meritocracy and Social Exclusion

Coffield, F., and Williamson, B. (1997), *Transformation of Higher Education* (Milton Keynes: Open University Press).

Erikson, R., and Jonsson, J. (1996), *Can Education Be Equalised?* (Boulder: Westview Press).

Halsey, A. H. (1995), *Decline of Donnish Dominion: The British Academic Professions in the Twentieth Century* (2nd edn., Oxford: Clarendon Press).

——, Heath, A. F., and Ridge, J. M. (1980), *Origins and Destinations: Family, Class, and Education in Modern Britain* (Oxford: Clarendon Press).

Jencks, C. (1972), *Inequality: A Reassessement of the Effects of Family and Schooling in America* (New York: Basic Books).

—— (1979), *Who Gets Ahead? The Determinants of Economic Success in America* (New York: Basic Books).

Shavit, Y., and Blossfield, H.-P. (1993), *Persistent Inequality: Changing Educational Attainment in Thirteen Countries* (Boulder: Westview Press).

Wilson, W. J, (1987), *The Truly Disadvantaged* (Chicago: University of Chicago Press).

Young, M. (1958), *The Rise of the Meritocracy* (Harmondsworth: Penguin).

Index